Footprint Brazil

Alex Robinson
5th edition

*"If life throws you a bitter lemon
make it into a caipirinha"*

Brazilian proverb

Brazil Highlights

See colour maps at back of book

1. **Corcovado** The magnificent view of Rio from the Christ, statue, page 96.
2. **Tijuca National Park** A green oasis in the city with stunning views, page 103.
3. **Costa Verde** Chocolate-box villages and pristine islands, page 162.
4. **Diamantina** A pretty colonial town with wild surrounds, page 267.
5. **Iguaçu Falls** The world's largest, most magnificent waterfalls, page 300.
6. **Salvador** Brazil's pulsating African heart with lively nightlife, page 360.
7. **Chapada Diamantina** Excellent hiking and caving, page 431.
8. **Recife and Olinda** Pretty colonial streets and Brazil's best carnival, page 436.
9. **Fernando de Noronha** The best beaches and diving, page 452.
10. **Serra da Capivara** Bizarre beehive domes and ancient rock art, page 515.

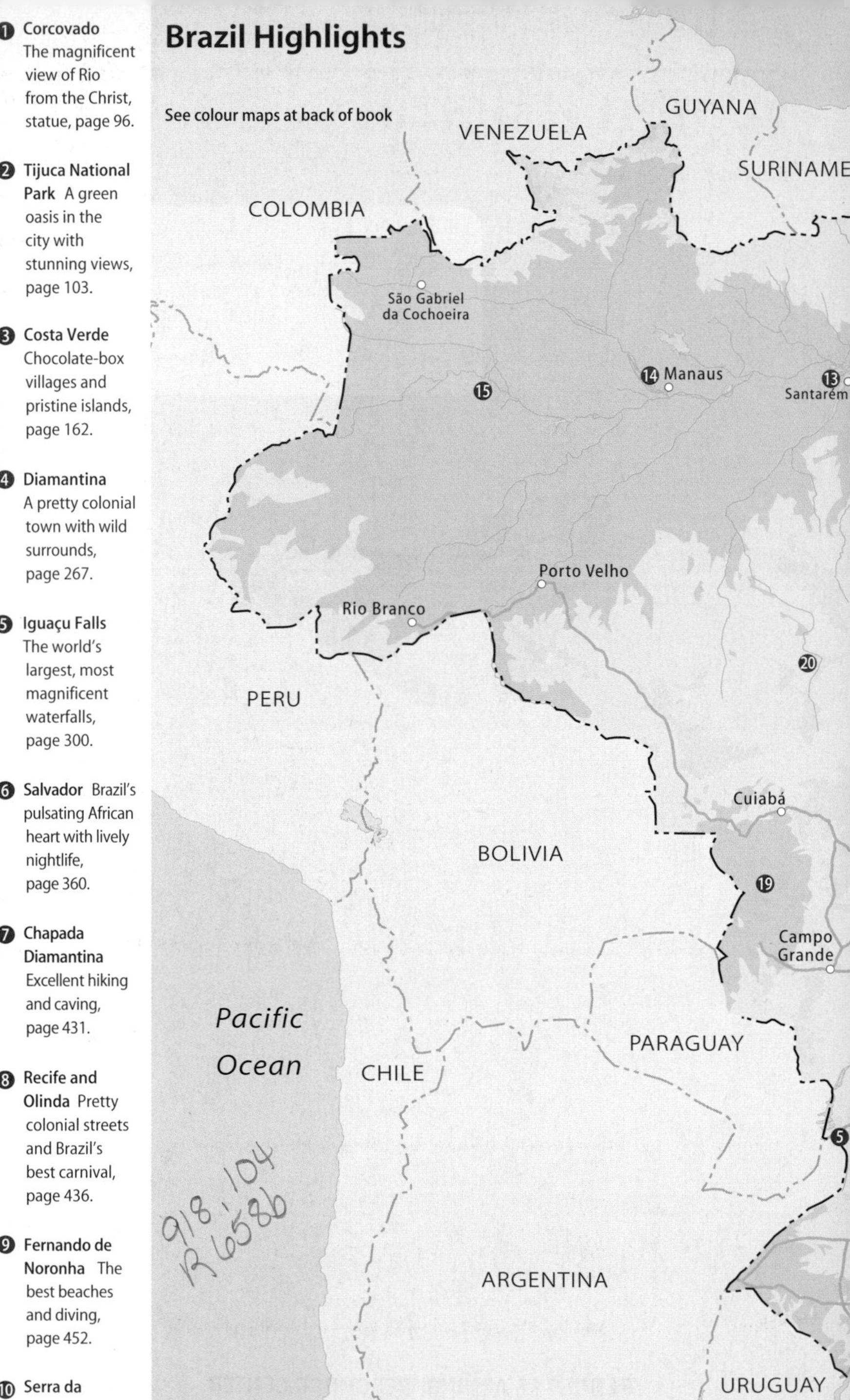

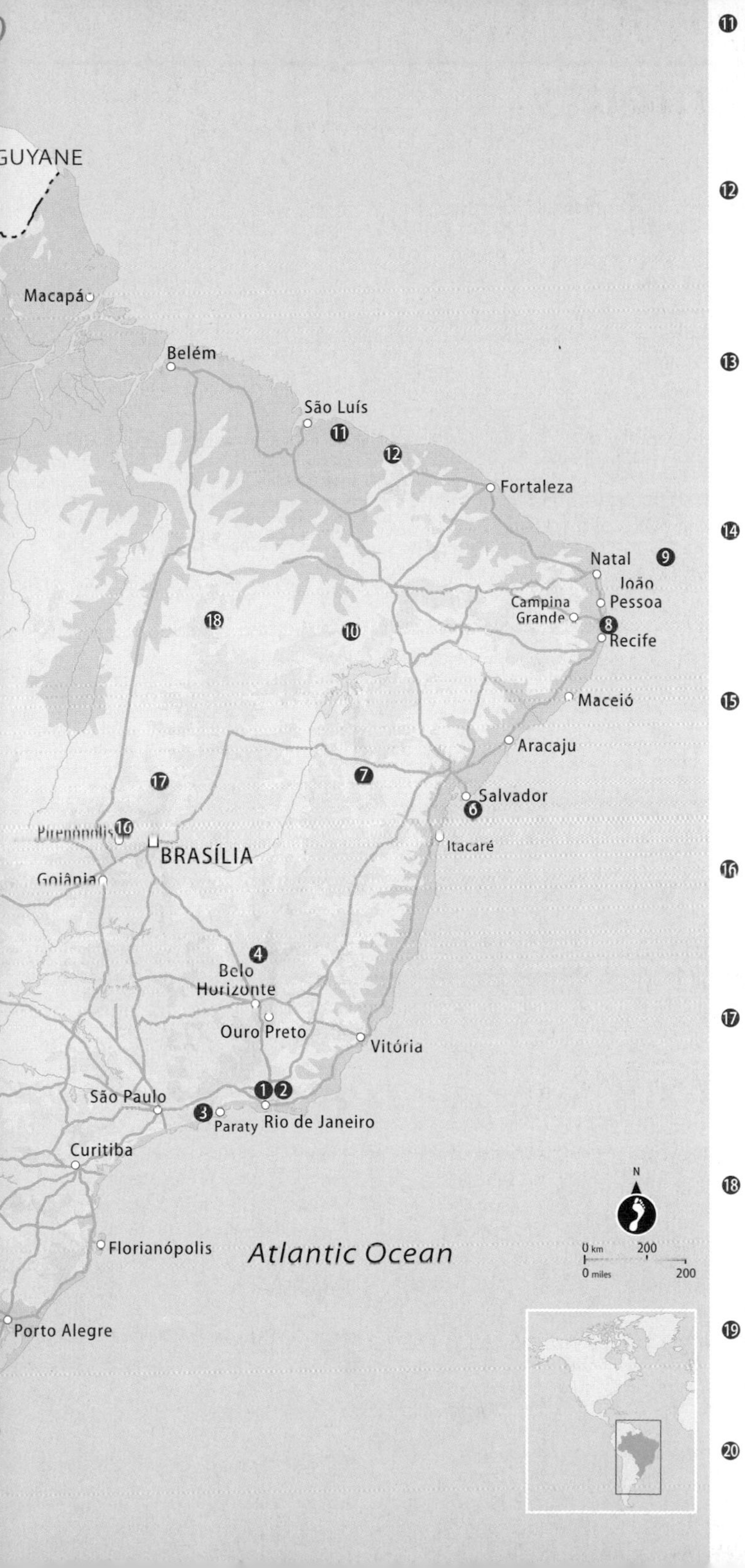

⓫ **Lençois Marahenses** Vast coastal dunes dotted with clear-water lakes, page 519.

⓬ **Delta do Parnaíba** Rich culture, thousands of islands and abundant wildlife, page 520.

⓭ **Alter do Chão** Blue rivers, pink dolphins and 10-km-long beaches, page 547.

⓮ **Analvilhanas Islands** The world's largest river archipelago, page 567.

⓯ **Mamirauá** One of the Amazon's most beautiful wilderness areas, page 569.

⓰ **Pirenópolis** A pretty colonial town surrounded by waterfall-filled forest, page 618.

⓱ **Chapada dos Veadeiros** Waterfalls, canyons, rock crystal and hiking, page 619.

⓲ **Jalapão** A vast wilderness of dunes and table-top mountains, page 628.

⓳ **Pantanal** The best place for wildlife in Brazil, page 631.

⓴ **Rio Cristalino** Abundant wildlife in the Amazon basin, page 663.

Contents

Minas Gerais & Espírito Santo

Iguaçu Falls & the south

Bahia

Recife & the northeast coast

Fortaleza

The Amazon

Brasília, Goias & Tocantins

Buriti palms follow the routes of underground rivers across the vast Chapada dos Veadeiros.

On the beach

During the week only fishing boats and terns sunbathe on Ilha Grande's beach in Rio de Janeiro state.

A foot in the door

There are few countries that can rival Brazil for sheer magnificence of landscape and diversity of culture. In the central Amazon, forest stretches unbroken in every direction for over 2000 km. The table-top mountains of the Goiás Cerrado, covered in medicinal plants and bushes laden with wild fruits, are drained by rivers which tumble through gorges and rush over spectacular waterfalls. Thousands of kilometres of pristine beaches line the Atlantic coast, some fringing mountainous islands in a warm, emerald sea, others backed by dunes the size of deserts. And then there are the marshlands of the Pantanal, where egrets fill the air like butterflies; the tiny cobble-and-whitewash gold mining towns of Minas Gerais; the 3-km-wide waterfalls at Iguaçu; the beaches and mountains of Rio and a continent's worth of sights which speckle a country big enough to swallow Australia and leave room for Germany and France combined.

Brazil's people are as diverse as its landscape. Bierfests, sushi bars, Bauhaus architecture, cowboys and capoeira are as Brazilian as Carnaval and World Cup football. Portugal, France, Ireland, Holland and Britain all laid claims here and left their cultures to mingle with the indigenous nations and the greatest numbers of Africans in the Americas. The south was a haven for US confederates, while São Paulo has the largest population of ethnic Japanese outside Japan. In short, Brazilians are from everywhere; a fevered mingling of the world, united by the lilting music of the Portuguese language, the rhythms of Africa and the spontaneity of a country bathed in perennial sunlight.

Brazil remains relatively undiscovered. There are still areas here where culture has not been re-packaged for the tourism market and where spontaneity is genuine. But things are changing – Brazil is becoming fashionable. Now is the time to visit.

Carnival

Carnival is poor Brazil's excuse to forget its problems and descend into a week of frenetic, unbounded Baccahanalia. The most famous is Rio's but there are Mardi Gras celebrations throughout the country – from street parties in Salvador and São Paulo to more traditional parades in Cidade de Goiás and Olinda, or middle-class hippy festivals on the beaches of Rio Grande de Norte and Bahia.

Sport

Sporting heroes are Homeric in Brazil. When Ayrton Senna died the country literally shut down and went into mourning. And when Brazil won the World Cup for the fifth time, millions of people flocked to the streets clad in yellow and green chanting 'Tudo o Mundo tenta mais so Brasil e Penta' (Everyone tried but only Brazil has won five times).

Religion

Brazil is nominally Catholic but in reality it is home to every kind of cult and creed. Fundamentalist Protestantism is growing rapidly among the urban poor, Rosicrucians advertise themselves with car bumper stickers, Brazilian voodoo is used to further careers, many of the São Paulo middle class are spiritists and members of Santo Daime get high on Amazonian hallucinogens.

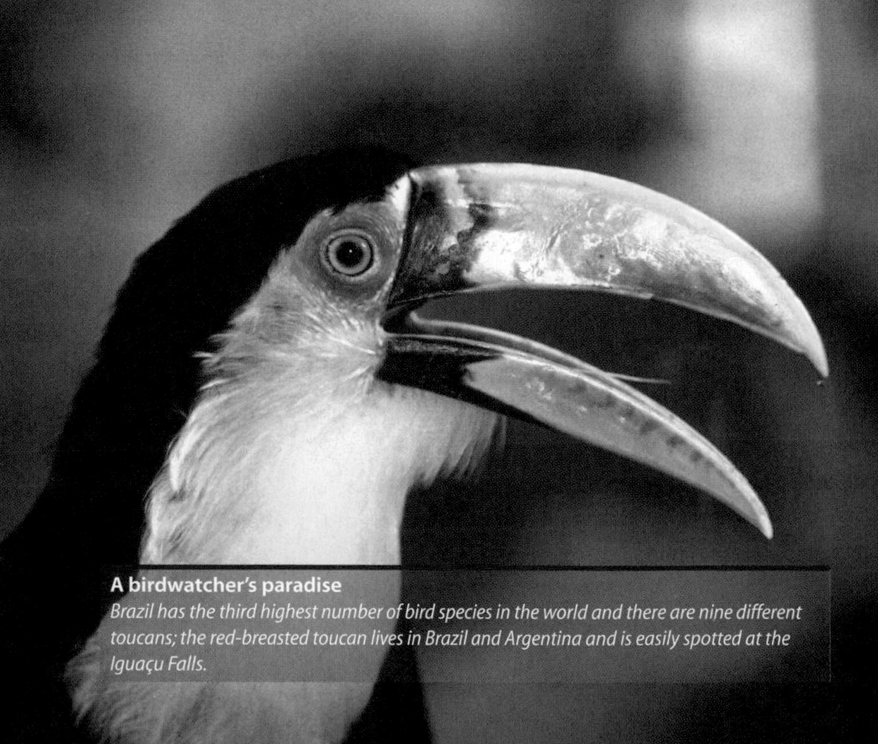

A birdwatcher's paradise
Brazil has the third highest number of bird species in the world and there are nine different toucans; the red-breasted toucan lives in Brazil and Argentina and is easily spotted at the Iguaçu Falls.

Music

The Girl from Ipanema is only played in gringo restaurants in Brazil. Music here has moved on. The centre of the club and hip hop scene is São Paulo. Rio uses real instruments and funksters like Jorge Ben play on the beaches and in clubs throughout the summer. Salvador vibrates to *axê* music and further north the *mangue-beat* scene fuses Brazilian rhythms with electronica. Beaches all-over pulse with a barefoot, bar-floor dance called *forró* and the forests of the Amazon gyrate to *guitarrada*, which sounds like Dick Dale on acid at 78 rpm.

Television

Brazilians are transfixed by their national television which pours out tacky studio chat shows, sensationalist news and melodramatic soap operas or *telenovelas* by the daily dozen. At the forefront is *TV Globo* – an archetypally Brazilian company, set up by a great patriarch, Roberto Marinho, who planned and organized everything presented on the station with an attention to detail and ideological bent to rival Rupert Murdoch. When Marinho died in 2003 *Globo* presenters wept openly on the news and the station broadcast hourly hagiographies.

Flower kissing

In Brazil hummingbirds are called beija-flores or 'flower kissers' and there are almost 100 different kinds – ranging in colour from brilliant emerald to midnight blue. The air in Itatiaia national park in Rio de Janiero is thick with them.

1

2

4

5

7

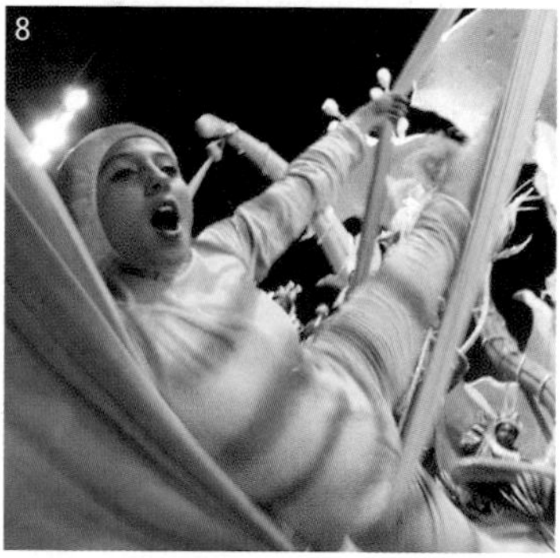

8

10

1 *Boats are the buses of the Amazon and journeys are long. A hammock and a good thick novel are travel essentials.* *›› See page 530.*

2 *Brazil's interior is dotted with little-visited colonial towns and villages with Portuguese buildings like these in Corumbá.* *›› See page 646.*

3 *The Festa do Divino in Pirenópolis is one of the most traditional in Brazil.* *›› See page 618.*

4 *Baroque artist Mestre Athayde asked his mulatta wife to pose as the Madonna for this church painting in Ouro Preto as a political statement against the racist Portuguese.* *›› See page 243.*

5 *Capoeira is one of the world's most graceful martial arts, fusing African dance and Brazilian fighting.* *›› See page 370.*

6 *The giant otter can measure up to 2m and is found along the tributaries of the Amazon.* *›› See page 713.*

7 *Camels watch the sunset from the dunes of Genipabu in Rio Grande do Norte.* *›› See page 477.*

8 *Rio's Carnaval involves two weeks of revelry and parades in the purpose-built Sambódromo arena.* *›› See page 122.*

9 *The rare capim dourado grass found in Jalapão is as brilliant as gold thread and is used to make jewellery by local craftsmen.* *›› See page 628.*

10 *Rio de Janeiro is a city of neighbourhoods; the suburbs of Botafogo and Urca nestle at the foot of the Sugar Loaf.* *›› See page 95.*

11 *Brazil has more primates than any other country; the brown capuchin can be seen in Itatiaia national park.* *›› See page 159.*

12 *Football is a way of life in Brazil and city beaches like these in Pelé's adopted home town of Santos become pitches for the city's poor after work and at weekends.* *›› See page 207.*

Amazon

This vast wilderness may be disappearing at a frightening rate, but is still one of the few places left on Earth where mankind can feel dwarfed by the immensity of Nature. Think of it not as a forest or a river but as a continent with as much diversity of scenery, people and culture as any other. A visit here is a must, preferably with some knowledge of the indigenous people who know it best. Visit from Tefe, Manaus or Tabatinga.

Cerrado

Brazil's great forests are not all rainforests. Between the Amazon and the coast is a broad band of dry forest replete with strangely scented flowers and medicinal plants, and interspersed with clear-water rivers, canyons and some of the continent's most beautiful waterfalls. Visit from the pretty colonial town of Pirenópolis or São Jorge in the dramatic Chapada dos Veadeiros mountains.

Pantanal

The world's largest wetland is, in wildlife terms, the Serengeti of the Americas. The sheer abundance of birds, mammals and reptiles here is staggering, from metre-long indigo parrots, to guinea pig-like rodents the size of a labrador. Storks, ibis and egrets flock by the hundred thousand, while huge cayman bask in the sun alongside 7-m-long anacondas. Visit from Cuiabá or Corumbá.

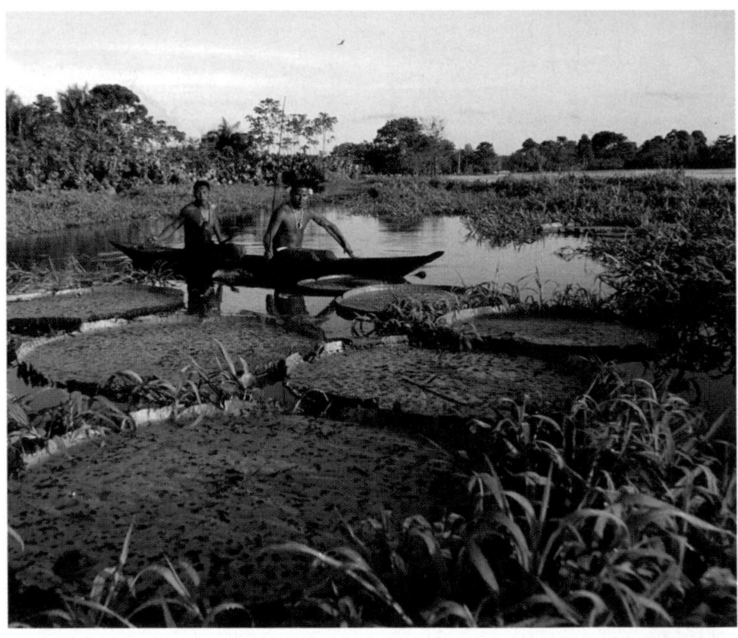

Many of Brazil's indigenous peoples, like the Tukanos, are well acquainted with the modern world but are nonetheless choosing to return to traditional ways of life.

Ilha Grande comprises mountainous jungle, historic ruins and some of the most beautiful beaches in the world – an unlikely location for what was once a notorious prison.

Beaches

Brazilians love their beaches and with good reason. There are stretches of sand to suit every taste – from little coves surrounded by lush forest in Rio de Janeiro state, to the sweeping surf beaches of Santa Catarina, and the endless expanse of sand along the coast of Maranhão, Ceará and Rio Grande de Norte.

Waterfalls

Iguaçu, the world's largest and most spectacular waterfall, lies on Brazil's border with Argentina. The falls stretch for almost 3 km and are surrounded on all sides by pristine rainforest filled with myriad bright butterflies and birds. You will need at least two days to see them.

Atlantic coastal forests

Brazil's most biodiverse forest is not the Amazon but the Mata Atlântica which extends for a tiny fraction of its original length but still shrouds the mountains which stretch along the country's southern coast. Views from Itatiaia National Park, the waterways around Cananeia and Superagui or the Serra da Graciosa are unforgettable. Visit from Rio, São Paulo or Curitiba.

Sertão

Northern Brazil's arid interior, often overlooked by tourists, holds countless treasures. From the rich wildlife of the Parque Nacional Grande Sertão Veredas, to the hulking escarpments of the Chapada Diamantina and the ancient rock art of the Serra de Capivara. Visit from Natal, Belo Horizonte or Salvador.

As far as the eye can see
A hiker looks out over the cerrado in Jalapão, Tocantins from the top of a table mountain.

Essentials

Footprint features

Planning your trip

Where to go

Rio de Janeiro was for a long time *the* image of Brazil, with its beautiful setting – the Sugar Loaf and Corcovado overlooking the bay and beaches, its world renowned carnival, the nightlife and its *favelas* (slums – which are now being incorporated into tourism). It is still a must on many itineraries, but Rio de Janeiro state has plenty of other beaches, national parks and colonial towns (especially **Paraty**) and the imperial city of Petrópolis. **São Paulo** is the country's industrial and financial powerhouse; with some fine museums and its cultural life and restaurants are very good. All the São Paulo coast is worth visiting and inland there are hill resorts and colonial towns. The state of **Minas Gerais** contains some of the best colonial architecture in South America in cities such as Ouro Preto, Mariana, São João del Rei and Diamantina. All are within easy reach of the state capital, Belo Horizonte. Other options in Minas include national parks with good hill scenery and bird-watching and hydrothermal resorts.

The atmosphere of the South is dominated by its German and Italian immigrants. The three states, Paraná, Santa Catarina and Rio Grande do Sul have their coastal resorts, especially near Florianópolis. **Rio Grande do Sul** is the land of Brazil's *gaúchos* (cowboys) and of its vineyards, but the main focus of the region is the magnificent **Iguaçu Falls** in the far west of Paraná, on the borders of Argentina and Paraguay.

The Northeast is famous for beaches and colonial history. Combining both these elements, with the addition of Brazil's liveliest African culture, is **Salvador de Bahia**, one of the country's most famous cities and a premier tourist destination. Huge sums of money have been lavished on the restoration of its colonial centre and its carnival is something special. Inland, Bahia is mostly arid sertão, in which a popular town is **Lençois**, a historical monument with a nearby national park. The highlight of the southern coast of Bahia is the beach and party zone around **Porto Seguro**, while in the north the beaches stretch up to the states of Sergipe and Alagoas and on into Pernambuco. **Recife**, capital of Pernambuco, and its neighbour, the colonial capital **Olinda**; also mix the sea, history and culture, while inland is the major handicraft centre of Caruaru. Travelling around to the north-facing coast, there are hundreds of beaches to choose from, some highly developed, others less so. You can swim, surf or ride the dunes in buggies. Last stop before the mouth of the Amazon is **São Luís**, in whose centre most of the old houses are covered in colonial tiles.

Through the North flows the **Amazon**, along which river boats ply between the cities of Belém, Santarém and Manaus. From **Manaus** particularly there are opportunities for exploring the jungle on adventurous expeditions or staying in lodges. North of Manaus is the overland route through Boa Vista to Venezuela. The forest stretches south to the central tableland which falls to the Pantanal in the far west. This seasonal wetland, the highlight of the Centre West, is one of the prime areas for seeing bird and animal life in the continent. At the eastern end of the Centre West is **Brasília**, built in the 1960s and now a World Heritage Site in recognition of its superb examples of modern architecture. Also in this region is one of the largest river islands in the world (Bananal – a mecca for fishing) and the delightful hill and river landscapes of **Bonito** in Mato Grosso do Sul.

One week

Rio, Beach and waterfall Rio de Janeiro city (over a weekend and including Friday and Monday), Búzios or Paraty (two nights), Foz de Iguaçu (arrive in the morning stay one night and leave the following late afternoon).

One week Carnaval Rio for the Sunday and Monday of Carnaval weekend, Salvador for Tuesday and Wednesday of Carnaval week, Recife/Olinda for the rest.

Two weeks

Rio, beaches and waterfalls Rio de Janeiro (as above) and either Ilha Grande, Paraty or Búzios and Foz de Iguaçu, or Porto Seguro-Itacare-Morro de São Paulo and Salvador.

Rio and the heartland of colonial Brazil Rio de Janeiro (as above), Ouro Preto and Congonhas, Diamantina, Brasília (half a day), Pirenópolis, Cidade de Goiás and then return to Rio. With more time, add Salvador and or Recife/Olinda at the end and a side trip to Paraty at the beginning.

Three weeks

Rio, wild Central Brazil and the Amazon Rio de Janeiro (as above), either Pantanal from Cuiabá, Chapada dos Guimarães and Cristalino Jungle Lodge; or Brasília, Jalapão and the Amazon from Manaus or Belém (Ilha do Marajó).

Salvador and the Northeast Salvador, Morro de São Paulo, Recife/Olinda, Praia da Pipa or Genipabu, Fortaleza, Jericoacoara, Lençóis Maranhenses, São Luis.

Four weeks

Rio and northern beaches Rio de Janeiro, Trancoso, Itacaré or Morro de São Paulo, Salvador, Praia da Pipa or Genipabu, Fortaleza, Jericoacoara, Delta do Parnaíba or Lençõis Maranhenses, São Luis. With more time add all or some of the following: Búzios, Itaúnas, Mangue Seco, Fernando de Noronha, Algodoal, Ilha do Marajó.

Rio, São Paulo, Iguacu and southern beaches Rio de Janeiro, Ilha Grande, Paraty and around, Ilhabela, São Paulo, Cananéia through to Ilha do Mel, Foz de Iguaçu, Florianopolis and the Ilha de Santa Catarina.

Wilderness Rio de Janeiro, Cananéia through to Ilha do Mel via Superagui, Foz de Iguaçu, Campo Grande for the Pantanal, and either Brasília, Chapada dos Veadeiros and Jalapão or Cuiabá, Chapada dos Guiamaraes and Alta Floresta.

When to go

The best time for a visit is from April to June, and August to October. Business visitors should avoid mid-December to the end of February, when it is hot and people are on holiday. In these months, hotels, beaches and transport tend to be very crowded. July is a school holiday month. If visiting tourist centres like Salvador, Rio and the colonial cities in Minas Gerais in the low season, be aware that some tourist sights may be closed for restoration.

Climate

In Rio de Janeiro conditions during the winter (May to September) are like those of a north European summer, including periods of rain and overcast skies, with temperatures from 14°C to the high 20s. It is more like a north European autumn in São Paulo and the southern states and it can get very cold in the far south; warmer clothing is required as temperature can change dramatically. It can get cold on high ground anywhere in Brazil; warm clothes are needed, particularly at night. The heaviest rain is from November to March in Rio and São Paulo, and from April to August around Recife (where irregular rainfall causes severe draughts). The rainy season in the north and Amazônia can begin in December and is heaviest from March to May, but it is getting steadily shorter, possibly as a result of deforestation. Few places get more than 2000 mm– the coast north of Belém, some of the Amazon basin, and a small area of the Serra do Mar between Santos and São Paulo, where the downpour has been harnessed to generate electricity. Summer conditions all over the country are tropical, although temperatures rarely reach 40°C.

The average annual temperature increases steadily from south to north, but even on the equator, in the Amazon basin, the average temperature is not more than 27°C. The highest recorded was 42°C, in the dry northeastern states. From the latitude of Recife south to Rio, the mean temperature is from 23° to 27°C along the coast, and from 18° to 21°C in the highlands. South of Rio, towards the boundary with Uruguay, the mean temperature is from 17° to 19°C. Humidity is relatively high in Brazil, particularly along the coast. The luminosity is also very high, and sunglasses are advisable.

Festivals

The most famous festival in Brazil is Carnaval, particularly that of Rio de Janeiro although there are other cities that have traditions just as interesting. Carnaval dates vary between February and early March. New Year's Eve is another popular party with beaches all over the country becoming packed with revellers. June is a busy month with São João festivities, especially in the Northeast, as well as the bull festival of Bumba-meu-Boi held in the North and Maranhão. Brazilians need little excuse to hold a party and there are always plenty of festivities year-round. » *See Festivals and events, page 54, for further information.*

Tour operators

UK

Austral Tours, 20 Upper Tachbrook St, London SW1V 1SH, T020-7233 5384, www.latinamerica.co.uk. Tours to Rio, the Amazon and the Northeast.

Condor Journeys and Adventures, 2 Ferry Bank, Colintraive, Argyll PA22 3AR, T01700-841318, www.condorjourneys-adventures.com. Tailor-made journeys to standard destinations.

Encounter Overland, 2001 Camp Green, Debenham, Stowmarket, Suffolk 1P14 6LA, T01728-862222, www.encounter.co.uk. Extended overland trips through the Amazon and throughout South America. Interesting routes.

Explore Worldwide, 1 Frederick St, Aldershot, Hants GU11 1LQ, T01252-760000, www.exploreworldwide.com. Standard small-group trips to the Northeast, Amazon and Rio.

Journey Latin America, 12-13 Heathfield Terr, Chiswick, London W4 4JE, T020-8747 8315, and 12 St Ann's Sq, 2nd floor, Manchester M2 7HW, T0161-832 1441, www.journeylatinamerica.co.uk. Long-established company with excellent escorted tours to some interesting areas like Goiás and the Chapada Diamantina. They also offer a wide range of good-value flight options.

Last Frontiers, Fleet Marston Farm, Aylesbury, Bucks HP18 0QT, T01296-653000, www.lastfrontiers.com. Imaginative tours to some interesting out-of-the-way locations including Fernando de Noronha.

Select Latin America, 79 Maltings Pl, 169 Tower Bridge Rd, London SE1 3LJ, T020-7407 1478, www.selectlatinamerica.co.uk. Quality tailor-made holidays and small group tours.

South American Experience, 47 Causton St, Pimlico, London SW1P 4AT, T020-7976 5511, www.southamericanexperience.co.uk. Standard itineraries with a few more unusual options like the Chapada Diamantina.

Steppes Latin America, 51 Castle St, Cirencester, Glos GL7 1QD, T01285-885333, www.steppeslatinamerica.co.uk. Tailor-made and group itineraries throughout Brazil and Latin America.

Sunvil Latin America, Sunvil House, Upper Square, Old Isleworth, Middlesex, TW7 7BJ, T020-8758 4774, www.sunvil.co.uk. A good range of options throughout Brazil, including some out-of-the-way destinations.

Trips Worldwide, 14 Frederick Place, Clifton, Bristol BS8 1AS, T0117-311 4400, www.tripsworldwide.co.uk. Tailor-made trips throughout South America.

Trivium, T062-212 6232, www.trivium.co.uk. Highly professional English-run company based in Goiás and offering an interesting range of general and specialist botanical tours throughout the state, especially to the Chapada dos Veadeiros and to the Atlantic coast rainforest. Much of the money goes back into local communities.

Veloso Tours, Ground Floor, 34 Warple Way, London W3 0RG, T020-87620616, www.veloso.com. An imaginative range of tours throughout Brazil and bespoke options on request.

Wildlife and birding specialists

Ornitholidays, 29 Straight Mile, Romsey, Hants, SO51 9BB, T01794 519445, www.ornitholidays.co.uk. Annual or biannual bird-watching trips throughout Brazil; usually to the Pantanal, Atlantic Coast rainforest and Iguaçu.

Reef and Rainforest Tours Ltd, 1 The Plains, Totnes, Devon, TQ9 5DR, T01803-866965, www.reefandrainforest.co.uk. Wildlife tours to the Pantanal.

Trivium (see above), Specialist botanical tours in conjunction with the Eden Project.

North America

4starSouth America, T1-800-8875686, www.4starSouthAmerica.com. Customized or scheduled tours throughout South America. Also has an office in Brazil at Av NS Copacabana 1066/907, Rio de Janeiro, T021-2267 6624.

Brazil For Less, 7201 Wood Hollow Dr, Austin, TX 78731, T1-877-269 0309 (US toll free) or T+44-203-002 0571 (UK), www.brazilforless.com. US-based travel firm with a focus solely on South America, with local offices and

operations, and a price guarantee. Good-value tours, run by travellers for travellers.
Ela Brasil Tours, 14 Burlington Dr, Norwalk, CT 06851, T203-840 9010, www.elabrasil.com. Excellent bespoke tours throughout Brasil to some very imaginative destinations. Uses only the best and most responsible local operators.
Ladatco Tours, 3006 Aviation Av 4C, Coconut Grove, Florida 33133, USA, T1800-327 6162, www.ladatco.com. Standard tours to Rio, Iguaçu and Manaus for the Amazon.
Mila Tours, 100 S Greenleaf Av, Gurnee, IL 60031-337, T847-248 2111, T800-387 7378 (USA and Canada), www.milatours.com. Itineraries to Rio, Iguaçu and the Northeast.
Tropical Nature Travel, PO Box 5276, Gainesville, Fl 326270 5276, USA, T352-376 3377, www.tropicalnaturetravel.com.

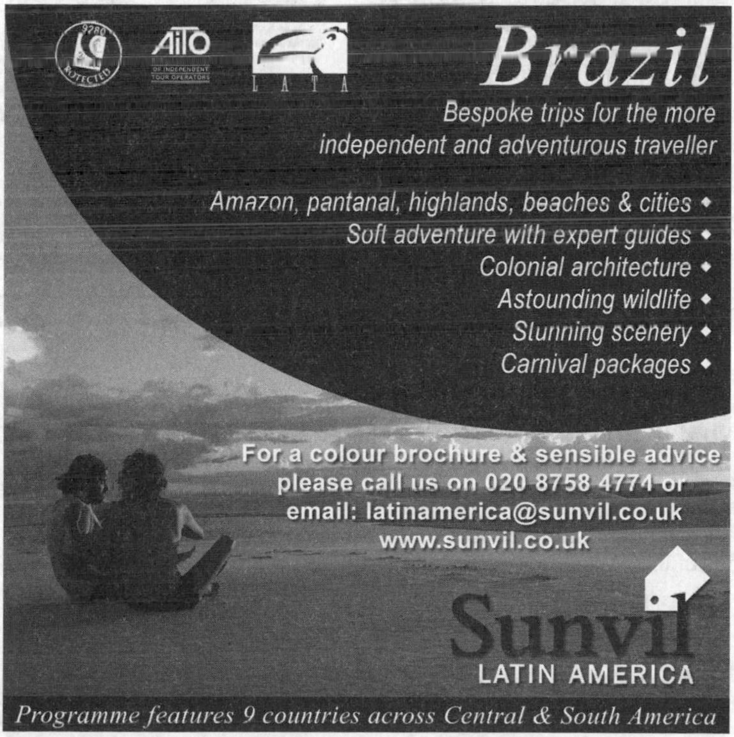

Wildlife and birding specialists
Field Guides, 9433 Bee Cave Rd, Building 1, Suite 150, Austin, Texas 78733, USA, T1-800-

7284953, www.fieldguides.com. Interesting birdwatching tours to all parts of Brazil.
Focus Tours, 103 Moya Rd, Santa Fe, NM87508, USA, T505-4664688, www.focustours.com. Specialists in birdwatching and environmentally responsible travel.

Brazil

Brazil Always Summer, SEPS EQ 714/914, Bloco E, Sala 409, Edificio Talento, Brasilia-DF, CEP 70390-145, T061-3345 4441, www.brazilalwayssummer.com. Tour operator specializing in holidays to Brazil. Services include hotel booking, Rio Carnaval tickets and excellent car rental rates.
Brazil Ventura, www.brazilventura.com. Carefully thought out, bespoke tours in Bahia from a team with first-rate insider knowledge. The best choice for the gay community.

Class Adventure Travel (**CAT**), Alameda Santos 1470, conj 502, São Paulo, www.cat-travel.com. Dutch-owned and run, set up in Peru 10 years ago, with offices in several Latin American countries. Tailor-made travel solutions throughout the continent.
Dehouche, T021-2512 3895, www.dehouche.com. Upmarket, carefully tailored trips throughout Brazil.
Manary Ecotours, R Francisco Gurgel, 9067, Ponta Negra Beach, Natal, T084-3204 2900, www.manary.com.br. If ecotourism means wildlife then Manary are not eco at all, but they do offer unusual, exciting tours to the northeastern *sertão*, including the spectacular Serra da Capivara (to see the rock paintings), Cariri and the fossilized dinosaur prints in Paraíba. Very professional service.
Open Door Tour Operator, R Barão do Rio Branco 314, Centro, Campo Grande/MS, T067-321 8303, www.opendoortur.com.br. Specialize in travel to the Pantanal and the Amazon.
Tatur Turismo, Av Tancredo Neves 274, Centro Empresarial Iguatemi, Sala 228, Bloco B, Salvador, 41820-020, Bahia, T071-450 7216, tatur@svn.com.br. Very helpful bespoke Bahia-based agency who can organize tours throughout Brazil, especially in Bahia, using many of the smaller hotels.

Finding out more

Tourist information

Tourist information can be obtained from Brazilian embassies and consulates. Other sources of information are:
Latin American Travel Advisor, PO Box 17-17-908, Quito, Ecuador, F593-2562566, USA and Canada toll free T1-800 3273573, www.amerispan.com/lata. A complete travel information service for South and Central America. Up-to-date information on public safety, health, weather, travel costs, economics and politics are highlighted for each nation. Also has a wide selection of Latin American maps. Individual travel planning assistance is available.
South American Explorers, formerly the South American Explorers Club, 126 Indina Creek Rd, Ithaca, NY 14850, T607-2770488, www.samexplo.org. A non-profit educational organization functioning primarily as an information network for South America. Useful for travellers to Brazil and the rest of the continent.

Business travellers

Brazil Report, published by Latin American Newsletters, has well-written articles on recent political and economic news. They can be contacted at 61 Old St, London EC1V 9HW, T020-72510012, www.latinnews.com.
American Chamber of Commerce in São Paulo. A good source of information on local markets, www.amcham.com.br.
Department of Trade and Industry's Brazil Desk, Bay 828, Kingsgate House, 66-74 Victoria St, London SW1E 6SW, T020-7215 4262, www.trasdepartners.gov.uk. Provides specific information for UK exporters.

Useful websites

For embassy websites, see page 31; newspaper and magazine websites, see page 68. The following are in English:
www.brazil.org.uk Provides a broad range of info on Brazilian history and culture from the UK Brazilian embassy.
www.brazil4you.com Comprehensive travel and tourism info on everything from sights to hotels and weather.
www.brazilmax.com Excellent information on culture and lifestyle.
www.braziltourism.org The official tourism website of Brazil, and the best.
www.gringos.com.br An excellent source of information on all things Brazilian for visitors and ex-pats.
www.ipanema.com A quirky, informative site on all things Rio de Janeiro.
www.maria-brazil.org A wonderfully personal introduction to Brazil, specifically Rio, featuring Maria's cookbook and little black book, features and reviews.
www.rainforestweb.org Excellent accurate information on rainforest related issues with detailed comprehensive information on Brazil and extensive links.

www.roteirosdecharme.com.br Complete listing of the hotels in this group – all selected for their style and personality very much in emulation of Spain's parador and Portugal's pousada network.

www.socioambiental.org Invaluable for up-to-the-minute, accurate information on environmental and indigenous issues.

www.survival-international.org The world's leading campaign organization for indigenous peoples with excellent info on various Brazilian indigenous groups.

www.worldtwitch.com Birding information and comprehensive listings of rainforest lodges.

Language

No quantity of dictionaries, phrase books or word lists will provide the same enjoyment of being able to converse directly with the people of Brazil. English is not widely spoken and it is definitely a good idea to learn some basic Portuguese before you go. As you travel you will pick up more of the language and the more you know, the more you will benefit from your stay. Efforts to speak Portuguese are greatly appreciated. Brazilians are very keen to communicate with foreigners and very patient generally. If you speak Spanish, you will probably be understood, but you will certainly have difficulty in understanding the answers. If you find yourself resorting to sign language, it might be useful to know that the 'ok' sign is actually an insult in Brazil and tugging your ear means 'delicious'. There are many differences between the Portuguese of Portugal and Brazil (particularly in the pronunciation) and, if learning Portuguese before you go to Brazil, you may want to get lessons with a Brazilian, or from a language course which teaches Brazilian Portuguese. There are Brazilian tutors in most cities (in London, see *Time Out* and *Leros*, the Brazilian magazine, for advertisements). For information on centres offering Portuguese courses in Brazil, see Directory text of the relevant towns and cities. ▸▸ *See Footnotes, page 724, for a list of useful words and phrases.*

Language schools

Amerispan, PO Box 58129, 117 South 17th St, 14th floor, Philadelphia, PA 19103, USA, T1-800-879 6640 or T1-215-751 1100, www.amerispan.com

Spanish Abroad, 5112 N, 40th St, Suite 103, Phoenix, AZ 85018, USA, T1-888-722-7623, worldwide, T602-778 6791, www.spanishabroad.com.

Specialist travel

Disabled travellers

As in most Latin American countries, facilities for disabled travellers are severely lacking. Wheelchair ramps are a rare luxury and getting a wheelchair into a bathroom or toilet is practically impossible, except for some of the more modern hotels. Pavements are often in a poor state of repair or crowded with street vendors requiring passers-by to brave the passing traffic. Disabled Brazilians obviously have to cope with these problems and mainly rely on the help of others to get on and off public transport and generally move around.

But of course only a minority of disabled people are wheelchair-bound and it is now widely acknowledged that disabilities do not stop you from enjoying a great holiday. It is well worth taking a valid European disabled sticker with you if you are planning to travel by car as all shopping centres and some public areas in Rio and Petrópolis have disabled spaces available if the sticker is displayed. Some travel companies are now specializing in exciting holidays, tailor-made for individuals depending on their level of disability. **A Global Access – Disabled Travel Network Site**, www.geocities.com/Paris/1502, provides travel information for 'disabled adventurers' and includes a number of reviews and tips from the public. You might also want to read *Nothing Ventured*, edited by Alison Walsh (Harper Collins), which gives personal accounts of worldwide journeys by disabled travellers, plus advice and listings.

Gay and lesbian travellers

Brazil is a good country for gay and lesbian travellers as attitudes are fairly liberal, especially in the big cities. Opinions in the interior and rural areas are far more conservative and it is wise to adapt to this. There is a well-developed scene in Rio de Janeiro and São Paulo while Salvador is also a popular destination. Local information can be obtained from the *Rio Gay Guide*, www.riogayguide.com, and in Salvador from the **Centro Cultura** ⓘ *R do Sodre 45*, close to the Museu de Arte Sacra da Bahia, which publishes a guide to the gay scene in the city for US$4.

Student travellers

If you are in full time education you will be entitled to an **ISIC** (International Student Identity Card), which is distributed by student travel offices and travel agencies in 77 countries. The ISIC card gives you special prices on all forms of transport (air, sea, rail etc), and access to a variety of other concessions and services. If you need to find the location of your nearest ISIC office contact: The **ISIC Association**, Box 15857, 1001 NJ Amsterdam, Holland, T+45-3393 9303. ISIC cards can be obtained in Brazil from **STB** agencies throughout the country such as Av Brig Faria Lima 1713, São Paulo, T011-870 0555. Remember to take photographs when having a card issued.

In practice, however, the ISIC card is rarely recognized or accepted for discounts outside of the South and Southeast of Brazil. It is nonetheless useful for obtaining half-price entry to the cinema. Youth hostels will often accept it in lieu of a IYHA card or at least give a discount, and some university accommodation (and subsidized canteens) will allow very cheap short-term stays to holders.

Travelling with children

Travel with children can bring you into closer contact with Brazilian families and, generally, presents no special problems. In fact the path is often smoother for family groups. Officials tend to be more amenable where children are concerned and they are pleased if your child knows a little Spanish or Portuguese. Moreover, even thieves and pickpockets seem to have some of the traditional respect for families, and may leave you alone because of it! People contemplating overland travel in Brazil with children should remember that a lot of time can be spent waiting for buses, trains, and especially for aeroplanes. On bus journeys, if the children are good at amusing themselves, or can readily sleep while travelling, the problems can be considerably lessened. If your child is of an early reading age, take reading material with you as it is difficult and expensive to find. The website, www.babygoes2.com, doesn't feature Brazil specifically and tends to focus on package holidays, but has good general advice for planning and packing, 'toy tips' and ideas for entertaining on journeys.

Food This can be a problem if the children are not adaptable. It is easier to take snacks and drinks with you on longer trips than to rely on meal stops where the food may not be to their taste. Avocados are safe, easy to eat and nutritious and can be fed to babies as young as six months. A small immersion heater and jug for hot drinks is invaluable, but remember that electric current varies. Try and get a dual-voltage one (110v and 220v).

Fares On all long distance buses you pay for each seat, and there are no half-fares if the children occupy a seat each. For shorter trips it is cheaper, if less comfortable, to seat small children on your knee. Often there are spare seats which children can occupy after tickets have been collected. In city and local excursion buses, small children generally do not pay a fare, but are not entitled to a seat when paying customers are standing. On sightseeing tours you should *always* bargain for a family rate – often children can go free. On trains, reductions for children are general, but not universal.

On internal flights, airlines charge half for children under 12 (less for children under two), but some military services don't have half-fares, or have younger age limits. Note that a child travelling free on a long excursion is not always covered by the operator's travel insurance; it is advisable to pay a small premium to arrange cover.

Hotels Try to negotiate family rates. If charges are per person, always insist that two children will occupy one bed only, therefore counting as one tariff. If rates are per bed, the same applies. In either case you can almost always get a reduced rate at cheaper hotels. Occasionally when travelling with a child you will be refused a room in a hotel that is 'unsuitable'. On river boat trips, unless you have very large hammocks, it may be more comfortable and cost effective to hire a two-berth cabin for two adults and a child. (In restaurants, you can normally buy children's helpings, or divide one full-size helping between two children.)

Volunteering in Brazil

Contact **RioVoluntário** ① *T021-2262 1110, ask for Isadora or Fábio, www.riovoluntario.org.br*, which supports 450 voluntary organizations, from environmental to healthcare. In the UK, **www.taskbrasil.org.uk**, T020-7394 1177, welcomes donations and volunteers (in the UK or Brazil) for its programme to help Brazilian street children. Similarly, **www.saomartinho.org.br**, T021-2242 2238, and its sister company in England (**Jubilee Action**, www.jubileecampaign.co.uk), seeks volunteers in both Brazil and abroad to assist in its project for street children.

Before you travel

Visas and immigration

Visas are not required for stays of up to 90 days by tourists from Andorra, Argentina, Austria, Bahamas, Barbados, Belgium, Bolivia, Chile, Colombia, Costa Rica, Denmark, Ecuador, Finland, France, Germany, Greece, Iceland, Ireland, Italy, Liechtenstein, Luxembourg, Malaysia, Monaco, Morocco, Namibia, the Netherlands, Norway, Paraguay, Peru, Philippines, Portugal, San Marino, South Africa, Spain, Suriname, Sweden, Switzerland, Thailand, Trinidad and Tobago, United Kingdom, Uruguay, the Vatican and Venezuela. For them, only the following documents are required at the port of disembarkation: a passport valid for at least six months (or *cédula de identidad* for nationals of Argentina, Chile, Paraguay and Uruguay); and a return or onward ticket, or adequate proof that you can purchase your return fare, subject to no remuneration being received in Brazil and no legally binding or contractual documents being signed. Venezuelan passport holders can stay for 60 days on filling in a form at the border.

Citizens of the United States, Canada, Australia, New Zealand and other countries not mentioned above, and anyone wanting to stay longer than 180 days, *must* get a visa before arrival, which may, if you ask, be granted for multiple entry. US citizens must be fingerprinted on entry to Brazil. Visa fees vary from country to country, so apply to the Brazilian consulate in your home country. The consular fee in the USA is US$55. Students planning to study in Brazil or employees of foreign companies can apply for a one- or two-year visa. Two copies of the application form, two photos, a letter from the sponsoring company or educational institution in Brazil, a police form showing no criminal convictions and a fee of around US$80 is required.

Extensions Foreign tourists may stay a maximum of 180 days in any one year. Ninety-day renewals are easily obtainable, but only at least 15 days before the expiry of your 90-day permit, from the Polícia Federal. The procedure varies, but generally you have to do the following: fill out three copies of the tax form at the Polícia Federal, take them to a branch of **Banco do Brasil**, pay US$15 and bring two copies back. You will then be given the extension form to fill in and be asked for your passport to stamp in the extension. According to regulations (which should be on display) you need to show a return ticket, cash, cheques or a credit card, a personal reference and proof of an address of a person living in the same city as the office (in practice you simply write this in the space on the form). Some offices will only give you an extension within 10 days of the expiry of your permit.

Some points of entry such as the Colombian border refuse entry for longer than 30 days, renewals are then for the same period, insist if you want 90 days. For longer stays you must leave the country and return (not the same day) to get a new 90-day permit. If your visa has expired, getting a new visa can be costly (US$35 for a consultation, US$30 for the visa itself) and may take anything up to 45 days, depending on where you apply. If you overstay your visa, or extension, you will be fined US$7 per day, with no upper limit. After paying the fine to Polícia Federal, you will be issued with an exit visa and must leave within eight days. If you cannot pay the fine you must pay when you next return to Brazil.

Officially, if you leave Brazil within the 90-day permission to stay and then re-enter the country, you should only be allowed to stay until the 90-day permit expires. If, however, you are given another 90-day permit, this may lead to charges of overstaying if you apply for an extension.

Identification You must always carry identification when in Brazil. Take a photocopy of the personal details in your passport, plus your Brazilian immigration stamp, and leave your passport in the hotel safe deposit. This photocopy, when authorized in a *cartório*, US$1, is a legitimate copy of your documents. Be prepared, however, to present the originals when travelling in sensitive areas such as near the borders. Always keep an independent record of your passport details. Also register with your consulate to expedite document replacement if yours gets lost or stolen.

Warning Do not lose the emigration permit they give you when you enter Brazil. Leaving the country without it, you may have to pay up to US$100 per person. It is suggested that you photocopy this form and have it authenticated at a *cartório*, US$1, in case of loss or theft.

Brazilian embassies and consulates

Argentina C Cerrito 1350, 1010 Buenos Aires, T005411-4515, F4515-2401, www.brasil.org.ar.

Australia 19 Forster Cres, Yarralumla, Canberra ACT 2600, T00612-62732372, www.brazil.org.au.

Austria Am Lugeck 1/5/15, A-1010 Wien, T00431-5120631, F5138374.

Belgium 350 Av Louise, 6ème Étage, Boîte 5-1050 Bruxelles, T00322-6402015, F6408134.

Bolivia C Capitán Ravelo 2334, Ed Metrobol, Sopocachi, La Paz, Casilla 429, T005912-8112233, F8112733.

Canada 450 Wilbrod St, Sandyhill, Ottawa, ON K1N 6M8, T001613-2371090, F2376144, www.brasembottawa.org.

Chile C Alonso Ovalle 1665, Santiago, T00562-6982486, F6715961, www.brasembsantiago.cl.

Colombia C 93, No 14-20, 8th floor, Aptdo Aéreo 90540, Bogotá 8, T00571-2180800, F2188393.

Denmark Ryvangs Alle, 24-2100 Kobenhavn Ø, T00453-9206478, F9273607.

France 34 Cours Albert I, 75008 Paris, T00331-45616300, F42890345, www.bresil.org.

Germany Kennedyallee 74-53175 Bonn, T0049228-959230, F373696.

Ireland Harcourt Centre, Europa House, 5th Floor, 41-54 Harcourt St, Dublin 2, T003531-4756000, F4751341.

Israel Beit Yachin, 2 Kaplin St, 8th floor, Tel Aviv, T009723-6963934, F6916060.

Israel Beit Yachin, 2 Kaplin St, 8th floor, Tel Aviv, T009723-6963934, F6916060.

Italy 14 Piazza Navona, 00186 Roma, T003906-683981, F6867858, www.ambasciatadelbrasile.it.

Japan 2-11-12 Kita-Aoyama, Minato-Ku, Tokyo 107-8633, T00813-34045211, F34055846, www.braemb.or.jp.

Netherlands Mauritskade 19-2514 HD, The Hague, T003170-3023959, F3023950.

New Zealand 19 Brandon St, level 9, Wellington 1, T00644-4733516, F4733517.

Norway Sigurd Syrs Gate 4, 1st floor, 0273 Oslo, T0047-22552029, F22443964.

Paraguay C Coronel Irrazábal esq , Av Mariscal López, 1521 Asunción, T0059521-214466, F212693, www.embajadabrasil.org.py

Peru Av José Pardo 850, Miraflores, Lima 100, T00511-4212759, F4452421

Portugal Estrada das Laranjeiras, 1649-021 Lisboa, T003511-217248510, www.emb brasil.pt.

South Africa Hadefields, Block c, 1st floor, 1267 Pretorius St, Hatfield 0083, Pretoria, T002712-4269400, F4289494, www.brazil.co.za.

Spain C Fernando El Santo, 6 DP 28010 Madrid, T00341-7004650, F7004660.

Sweden Sturgegatan 11, 2 Tr 114 36 Stockholm, T00468-234010, F234018.

Switzerland Monbijouster 68-3007 Berne, T004131-3718515, F3710525.

UK 32 Green St, London WIK 7AT, T020-749 0877, F73999100, www.brazil.org.uk.

USA 3006 Massachusetts Ave NW, Washington DC 20008-3699, T001202-2382700, F2382827, www.brasilemb.org.

Uruguay Blvd Artigas, 1328, Montevideo, Aptdo Postal 16022, T005982-7072119, F7072086, www.brasmont.org.uy.

Venezuela Centro Gerencial Mohedano, 6th floor, C Los Chaguaramos con Av Mohedano, La Castellana, 1060 Caracas, T00582-2616529, F2619601.

Customs

Duty-free allowance Clothing and personal articles are free of import duty. Articles such as cameras, camcorders, portable radios, tape recorders, typewriters and binoculars are also admitted free if there is not more than one of each. Tourists may also bring in, duty-free, 24 alcoholic drinks (no more than 12 of any one type), 400 cigarettes, 25 cigars, 280 g of perfume, up to 10 units of cosmetics, up to three each of any electronic item or watch, up to a total value of US$500 monthly. There is a limit of US$150 at land borders and a written declaration must be made to this effect. Duty-free goods may only be purchased in foreign currency.

Vaccinations

You should be immunized against typhoid, polio, tetanus and hepatitis A. Poliomyelitis vaccination is required for children from three months to six years. Proof of vaccination against **yellow fever** is necessary if you are visiting Amazônia and the centre west, or are coming from Bolivia, Colombia, Ecuador or Peru. It is strongly recommended that you have a yellow fever inoculation before visiting northern Brazil since anyone without a certificate will be inoculated on entering any of the northern and centre-western states. Although yellow fever vaccination is free it might be administered in unsanitary conditions. Yellow fever and some other vaccinations can be obtained from the **Ministério da Saúde**, R Cais de Pharoux, Rio de Janeiro. Less common vaccinations can be obtained at **Saúde de Portos**, Praça 15 de Novembro, Rio de Janeiro.

What to take

A **waterproof jacket** – it will probably rain several times on your trip. Light, natural fabrics are best in the heat, but bring a light sweater for chilly nights or air-conditioned buses. **Wax earplugs** (almost impossible to find outside large cities) and an airline-type **eye mask** can help you sleep in noisy hotels and on buses. **Sports sandals** are much cooler than sweat-inducing trainers and can be worn in showers to avoid athlete's foot. A **sarong** or **sheet sleeping bag** is invaluable for use as a towel, a bedsheet or beach towel. (Towels are provided at even the cheapest hotels, although not always at youth hostels.) A **hat** is necessary to protect against sunstroke.

Also useful are a **clothes line**, **nailbrush**, universal **plug**, **penknife**; **torch** (especially one that will clip on to a pocket or belt), a **padlock** (combination lock is best) and **chain** for securing luggage to bed or bus/train seat.

Take a small **first aid kit** including lip salve with sun protection, and pre-moistened wipes. Major cities have a wide selection of products for **contact lens** wearers.

Insurance

Insurance companies have tightened up considerably over recent years and it is now almost impossible to claim successfully if you have not followed procedures closely. The problem is that these often involve dealing with the country's red tape which can lead to some inconvenience at best and to some quite long delays at worst. There is no substitute for suitable precautions against petty crime.

The level of insurance is inevitably the highest if you go through the USA. Don't forget to obtain sports extensions if you are going to go diving, rafting, climbing, etc. Most policies do not cover very high levels of baggage/cash. Don't forget to check whether you can claim on your household insurance. They often have worldwide all-risks extensions. Most policies exclude manual work whilst away, although working in bars or restaurants is usually alright. **Direct Line** in the UK offer comprehensive travel insurance, T0845 2468744, www.directline.com.

Money

Currency

The unit of currency is the **real**, R$ (plural **reais**). In January 2007 the rate was US$1 = R$2.1; £1 = 4.2; €1 = 2.8. Any amount of foreign currency and 'a reasonable sum' in *reais* can be taken in, but sums over US$10,000 must be declared. Residents may only take out the equivalent of US$4000. Notes in circulation are: 100, 50, 10, 5 and 1 *real*; coins: 1 *real*, 50, 25, 10, 5 and 1 centavo. **Note** The exchange rate has been fairly volatile recently so check in advance.

ATMs

ATMs, or cash machines, are common in Brazil. As well as being the most convenient way of withdrawing money, they frequently offer the best available rates of exchange. They are usually closed after 2130 in large cities. There are two international ATM acceptance systems, **Plus** and **Cirrus**. Many issuers of debit and credit cards are linked to one, or both (eg Visa is Plus, MasterCard is Cirrus). **Banco do Brasil** and **HSBC** are the two main banks offering this service. **Red Banco 24 Horas** kiosks advertise that they take a long list of credit cards in their ATMs, including MasterCard and Amex, but international cards cannot always be used.

Find out before you leave what international 'functionality' your card has. Check if your bank or credit card company imposes handling charges. Internet banking is useful for monitoring your account or transferring funds. Do not rely on one card, in case of loss. If you do lose a card, immediately contact the 24-hour helpline of the issuer in your home country (keep this number in a safe place).

Exchange

Banks in major cities will change cash and traveller's cheques. If you keep the official exchange slips, you may convert back into foreign currency up to 50% of the amount you exchanged. The parallel market, found in travel agencies, exchange houses and among hotel staff, often offers marginally better rates than the banks. Many banks may only change US$300 minimum in cash, US$500 in traveller's cheques. Dollars cash (take US$5 or US$10 bills) are becoming more frequently used for tourist transactions and are useful for emergencies. Damaged dollar notes may be rejected. Parallel market and official rates are quoted in the papers and on TV news programmes.

Traveller's cheques

Rates for cheques are usually lower than for cash, they are harder to change and commission may be charged. Tourists cannot change US dollar traveller's cheques into dollar notes, but US dollar traveller's cheques can be obtained on an American Express card (against official policy). It is a good idea to take two kinds of cheque: if large numbers of one kind have recently been forged or stolen, making people suspicious, it is unlikely to have happened simultaneously with the other kind.

Credit cards

Credit cards are widely used. **Diners Club, MasterCard, Visa** and **American Express** are useful. MasterCard/Access is accepted by **Banco Real**. Overseas credit cards need authorization from São Paulo, which can occasionally take a while. MasterCard and Diners are equivalent to Credicard, and Eurocheques can be cashed at **Banco Alemão** (major cities only). Cash advances on credit cards will only be paid in *reais* at the tourist rate, incurring a 1.5% commission. Banks in small remote places may still refuse to give a cash advance: try asking for the manager (*gerente*).

Money transfers

Money sent to Brazil is normally paid out in Brazilian currency, so do not have more money sent out than you need for your stay. A recommended method is, before leaving, to find out which local bank is correspondent to your bank at home, then when you need funds, telex your own bank and ask them to telex the money to the local bank (confirming by fax). Give exact information to your bank of the routing number of the receiving bank. Funds can be received within 48 banking hours.

To open a bank account in Brazil, you need to have a visa valid for more than one year.

In most large cities **Citibank** will hold US personal cheques for collection, paying the day's tourist dollar rate in *reais* with no charge. **Banco do Brasil** offers the same service with a small charge. From the UK the quickest method of having money sent is **Swift Air**.

Cost of travelling

As a very rough guide, prices are about a third of those in Western Europe and the United States. The devaluation of the real in 1999 has greatly reduced costs, but Brazil is still more expensive than other countries in South America (including Argentina since the collapse of its economy).

Accommodation is good value in every price range. Budget hotels with few frills have rooms for as little as US$6, and you should have no difficulty finding a room costing US$10 wherever you are. Rooms are often pretty much the same price whether one or two people are staying. Eating is generally inexpensive, especially in *comida a kilo* (pay by weight) restaurants, which offer a wide range of food (salads, meat, pasta, vegetarian). Although bus travel is very reasonable, because of the long distances, costs can soon mount up. Internal flights prices have come down dramatically in the last couple of years and some routes work out cheaper than taking a bus.

Getting there

Air

International flights into Brazil generally land at either Rio de Janeiro or São Paulo. São Paulo has better domestic and international flight connections, although most tourists tend to choose Rio de Janeiro as their point of disembarkation. Prices are more competitive during the low season and cheap flights can be very difficult to find during the high season (generally between 15 December-15 January, the Thursday before Carnaval to the Saturday after Carnaval and 15 June-15 August).

If buying a ticket to another country but with a stopover in Brazil, check whether two tickets are cheaper than one. Airline tickets are expensive in Brazil, buy internal tickets with *reais* (you can pay by credit card). External tickets must be paid for in dollars. You cannot buy an air ticket in Brazil for use abroad unless you have a ticket out of Brazil.

Varig ① *T0845-603 7601, www.varig.co.uk*, also has an extensive 'Stopover' programme which gives reduced rates on transfers and hotel rooms in many cities in Brazil and throughout South America.

From Europe

Rio de Janeiro and São Paulo are connected to the principal European cities direct by **Aerolíneas Argentinas** (Amsterdam and Madrid), **Air France** (Paris), **Alitalia** (Rome), **British Airways** (London), **BRA** (Milan), **Gol** (Lisbon), **Iberia** (Barcelona and Madrid), **KLM** (Amsterdam), **LanChile** (Frankfurt and Madrid), **Lufthansa** (Frankfurt), **Swissair**

(Zurich), **TAM** (Paris), **TAP Air Portugal** (Lisbon) and **Varig** (Copenhagen, Frankfurt, London, Lisbon, Paris and Milan). **Varig** flies to Recife and Fortaleza from Milan and to Salvador from Rome. **TAP Air Portugal** flies to Fortaleza, Natal, Recife and Salvador from Lisbon.

From North America

Rio de Janeiro and São Paulo are connected to the USA direct by **American Airlines** (Chicago, Dallas, Miami), **Continental** (New York), **Delta** (Atlanta), **Gol** (Miami), **TAM** (Miami and New York), **United Airlines** (Chicago, Miami) and **Varig** (Los Angeles, Miami and New York). Other US gateways are Boston, Cincinnati, Denver, Detroit and San Francisco. The cheapest routes are probably from Miami.

American Airlines fly from Miami to Belo Horizonte. **Varig** fly from Miami to Belém, Fortaleza, Manaus and Recife. **Air Canada** flies direct to São Paulo from Toronto.

From Latin America

Most Latin American cities are connected by air to São Paulo and Rio de Janeiro. There are flights from Asunción with **American Airlines, TAM** and **Varig**; Bogotá with **Varig** and **Avianca**; Buenos Aires with **Aerolíneas Argentinas, TAM** and **Varig**; Caracas with **Varig**; Córdoba with **Varig**; Guayaquil with **Ecuatoriana** and **Vasp**; La Paz with **Varig**; Lima with **AeroMéxico, TAM** and **Varig**; Mexico City with **AeroMéxico** and **Varig**; Montevideo with **TAM, Pluna** and **Varig**; Santa Cruz with **LAB, TAM** and **Varig**; San José, Costa Rica with **Lacsa**; Santiago with **LanChile, TAM** and **Varig**; Quito with **Ecuatoriana** and **Vasp**.

Penta fly from Cayenne to Belém and Macapá. **Pluna** fly from Montevideo to Porto Alegre. **Surinam Airways** fly from Paramaribo to Belém. **Varig** fly from Asunción to Curitiba, Florianópolis and Foz do Iguaçu; Buenos Aires to Porto Alegre; Mexico City to Manaus; Montevideo to Porto Alegre; Santiago to Porto Alegre.

Air passes

Aerolíneas Argentinas, Austral, Lan Chile, Lapa, Líneas Aéreas Paraguayas, Pluna and **Varig** operate the **Mercosur Airpass**. Valid for a minimum of seven and a maximum of 30 days, the pass is for a maximum of eight flight coupons with no more than two stops allowed per country. At least two *Mercosur* member countries must be included; re-routing is not permitted. The airpass is available to all international return ticket holders travelling by air into the participating countries. Passes are price-banded according to mileage flown; fares range from US$225 to US$870. Children pay 67% whilst infants pay 10% of the adult fare and some of the carriers operate a blackout period between 17 December and 10 January.

LAB, Ecuatoriana and **Vasp** operate a **South American Airpass** valid for 90 days, available to non-residents of Brazil arriving in South America on long-haul flights. There is no child discount but infants pay 10% of the price, which varies between US$560 for up to four flights and US$1,100 for the maximum of nine flights. Up to two transfers of less than five hours are permitted and coverage is from northern Argentina, Chile, Bolivia, Peru, Ecuador and Brazil.

Baggage allowance

Airlines will only allow a certain weight of luggage without a surcharge; this is normally 30 kg for first class and 20 kg for business and economy classes, but these limits are often not strictly enforced when it is known that the plane is not going to be full. On some flights from the UK, special outbound concessions are offered (by Iberia, Air France) of a two-piece allowance up to 32 kg, but you may need to request this. Passengers seeking a larger baggage allowance can route via the USA, but with certain exceptions, the fares are slightly higher using this route. On the other hand, weight limits for internal flights are often lower; it is best to enquire beforehand.

Discount flight agents

Using the web to book flights, hotels and other services directly is becoming increasingly popular and you can get some good deals. Be aware, though, that cutting out the travel agents is denying yourself the knowledge and experience that they can give, not just in terms of the best flights to suit your itinerary, but also advice on documents, insurance, safety, routes and lodging. A reputable agent will also be bonded to give you some protection if arrangements collapse while you are travelling.

UK and Ireland

Journey Latin America, 12-13 Heathfield Terrace, Chiswick, London W4 4JE, T020-8747 8315, www.journeylatinamerica.co.uk.
STA Travel, 86 Old Brompton Rd, London, SW7 3LH, T020-74376262, www.sta travel.co.uk. Branches throughout the UK. Specialists in low-cost student/youth flights and tours. Good for student IDs and insurance.
Trailfinders, 194 Kensington High St, London, W8 7RG, T020-7938 3939, www.trail finders.com. 18 branches in London and throughout the UK. Also one in Dublin and 5 travel centres in Australia.

North America

Air Brokers International, 323 Geary St, Suite 411, San Francisco, CA94102, T01-800-883 3273, www.airbrokers.com. Consolidator and specialist on RTW and Circle Pacific tickets.
Discount Airfares Worldwide On-Line, www.etn.nl/discount.htm. A hub of consolidator and discount agent links.
International Travel Network/Airlines of the web, www.itn.net/airlines Online air travel information and reservations.
STA Travel, 5900 Wilshire Blvd, Suite 2110, Los Angeles, CA 90036, T1-800-777 0112, www.sta-travel.com. Also branches in New York, San Francisco, Boston, Miami, Chicago, Seattle and Washington DC.
Travel CUTS, 187 College St, Toronto, ON, M5T 1P7, T1-800-667 2887, www.travelcuts.com. Specialist in student discount fares, IDs and other travel services. Branches in other Canadian cities.
Travelocity, www.travelocity.com. Online consolidator.

Australia and New Zealand

Flight Centres, 82 Elizabeth St, Sydney, T13-1600; 205 Queen St, Auckland, T09-309 6171. Branches in other towns and cities.
STA Travel, T1300-360960, www.statravelaus.com.au 702 Harris St.
Travel.com.au, 80 Clarence St, Sydney, T02-929 01500, www.travel.com.au.
Ultimo, Sydney, and 256 Flinders St, Melbourne. In New Zealand: 10 High St, Auckland, T09-366 6673. Also in major towns and university campuses.

River

A popular entry point to the Amazon region is along the Rio Amazonas from Iquitos in Peru to Tabatinga in Brazil. Onward travel is then by river boat or air to Manaus. This border can also be crossed by land from Leticia in Colombia. Security is particularly tight on this triple border and there have been reports that Brazilian immigration often refuse to allow entry to Brazil for more than 30 days.

Road

Bus

There are good road connections between Argentina, Paraguay, Uruguay and the South of Brazil. Rio de Janeiro and São Paulo can easily be reached by international buses from Asunción, Buenos Aires, Santiago and Montevideo. Transport is not so easy in the north and west of the country, although a reasonable road now exists between Caracas and Manaus. Entry from Bolivia at Corumbá is fairly straightforward. Buses from here connect with the main Brazilian road system at

Campo Grande. Other border crossings from French Guiana at Oiapoque and from Guyana at Bonfim require some effort to actually get to the Brazilian border. Once there, bus services are frequent, although heavy rains may make for slow going and can cause cancellations.

Car → *See also Getting around, page 43.*

Foreign driving licences are acceptable in Brazil, although it may be worth taking an international licence as not all officials and rental companies recognize foreign licences. If requested, tourists driving in Brazil should be able to present their licence and a passport to the police. Road accidents should be reported to the department of transport, **Detran** ⓘ *Av Presidente Vargas 817, 2nd floor, Rio de Janeiro, T021-550 9744.*

There are agreements between Brazil and most South American countries whereby a car can be taken into Brazil (or a Brazilian car out of Brazil) for a period of 90 days without any special documents; an extension of up to 90 days is granted by the customs authorities on presentation of the paper received at the border, which must be retained. This may be done at customs posts and at the **Serviço de Controle Aduaneiro** ⓘ *Ministério da Fazenda, Av Presidente Antônio Carlos, Sala 1129, Rio de Janeiro.*

For cars registered in other countries, the requirements are proof of ownership and/or registration in the home country and valid driving licence. A 90-day permit is given by customs and procedure is very straightforward. Nevertheless, it is better to cross the border into Brazil when it is officially open because an official who knows all about the entry of cars is then present. You must specify which border station you intend to leave by, but application can be made to the customs to change this.

Sea

Travelling as a passenger on a cargo ship to South America is not a cheap way to go, but if you have the time and want a bit of luxury, it makes a great alternative to flying. The passage is often for round trips only.

The **Grimaldi Line** sails from Tilbury in the UK to Brazil (Vitória, Santos, Paranaguá, Rio) and Argentina (Buenos Aires) via Hamburg, Amsterdam and Antwerp, Le Havre, Southampton and Bilbao, round trip about 51 days, US$3040-5400, also from Genoa to Paranaguá, Santos and Rio for US$1100-1400 (round trip or southbound only, no northbound-only passages).

There is an 8% tax on international shipping line tickets bought in Brazil.

A number of German container ships sail the year round to the east coast of South America: Felixstowe, Hamburg, Antwerp, Bilbao or Algeciras, Santos, Buenos Aires, Montevideo, Rio Grande do Sul, Itajaí, Santos, Rio de Janeiro, Rotterdam, Felixstowe (about 45 days, £3100-3500 per person round trip). Four German vessels make a 49-day round trip: Tilbury, Hamburg, Antwerp, Le Havre, Suape, Rio de Janeiro, Santos, Buenos Aires, Montevideo, São Francisco do Sul, Paranaguá, Santos, Suape, Rotterdam, Tilbury. There are also German sailings from Genoa or Livorno (Italy), or Spain to the east coast of South America.

A cheaper option is **Polish Ocean Line**'s services to the east coast, Gdynia to Buenos Aires, Montevideo and Santos (2-2½ months).

From the USA, **Maritime Reederei** of Germany sails to Charleston, Miami, Puerto Cabello, Santos, Buenos Aires, Montevideo, Rio Grande do Sul, Santos, Puerto Cabello, Freeport, New York, from £3540 per person on a 42-day round trip. A German consortium has a 48-day round trip to New York, Savannah, Miami, Rio, Santos, Buenos Aires, Montevideo, Rio Grande do Sul, Santos, Salvador, Fortaleza, Norfolk, Philadelphia, New York, £4020 per person (one-way to Rio, 15 days £1395).

Shipping agents

UK

Cargo Ship Voyages Ltd, Hemley, Woodbridge, Suffolk IP12 4QF, T01473-736265, www.cargoshipvoyages.co.uk.
The Cruise People, 88 York St, London W1H 1QT, T020-7723 2450, www.members.aol.com/cruiseaz/freighters.htm.
Strand Voyages (Andy Whitehouse), 1 Adam St, London WC2N 6AB, T020-7766 8220, www.strandtravel.co.uk. Booking agents for all routes.

Europe

Wagner Frachtschiffreisen, Stadlerstrasse 48, CH-8404, Winterthur, Switzerland, T052-242 1442, F242 1487.

North America

Freighter World Cruises, 180 South Lake Av, Pasadena, CA 91101, T818-4493106.
Maris Freighter Travel Inc, 215 Main St, Westport, T06880-3210, T1-800-9962747.
Traveltips Cruise and Freighter Travel Association, 163-07 Depot Rd, PO Box 188, Flushing, NY 11358, T800-8728584.

Touching down

Airport information

For most visitors the point of arrival will either be **Tom Jobim international airport** (also known as **Galeão**) on the Ilha do Governador, 16 km from the centre of Rio de Janeiro, or **Cumbica International Airport** at Guarulhos in São Paulo. Details of other entry airports are given in their respective sections. Make sure you arrive two hours before international flights and it is wise to reconfirm your flight as departure times may have changed. ▸▸ *See pages 72 and 198 for detailed airport information in Rio de Janeiro and São Paulo respectively.*

Airport departure tax

The amount of tax depends on the class of airport. All airports charge R$69.50 (US$36) international departure tax. First class airports charge R$9.50 domestic tax; second class airports R$7; domestic rates are lower still in third and fourth class airports. Tax must be paid on checking in, in *reais* or US dollars. Tax is waived if you stay in Brazil less than 24 hours.

Tourist information

Embratur, the Brazilian Tourist Board, is at Setor Comercial Norte, Quadra 02, Bloco G, Brasília, DF, CEP 70710-500, Brazil, T061-328 9100, www.embratur.gov.br. Embratur also has an office in Rio de Janeiro at Rua Uruguaiana 174, 8 andar, Rio de Janeiro, RJ, CEP 20050-090, T021-5096017, rio@embratur.gov.br. See also tour operators page 20 for a list of specialist agencies operating from both inside and outside of Brazil.

Details of state and municipal tourist offices are given in the Essentials section of the respective towns and cities. They are not usually too helpful regarding information on cheap hotels. It is also difficult to get information on neighbouring states.

National parks are run by **Ibama**, the Instituto Brasileiro do Meio Ambiente e dos Recursos Naturais Renováveis (Brazilian Institute of Environmental Protection) ⓘ *SAIN, Avenida L-4, bloco B, Térreo, Edifiço Sede de Ibama, CEP 70800-200, Brasília, DF, T061-226 8221/9014, www.ibama.gov.br*. The Institute is under-funded, often under-staffed and visitors may find it difficult to obtain information. National parks are open to visitors, usually with a permit from Ibama. For further details, see individual parks in the text. ▸▸ *See page 66 for an explanation of phone codes in Brazil.*

Touching down

Business hours Generally 0900-1800 Monday-Friday; closed for lunch some time between 1130 and 1400. Shops are open on Saturday till 1230 or 1300. Government offices: 1100-1800 Monday-Friday. Banks: 1000-1600 or 1630, closed on Saturday.
In an emergency Ambulance T192. Directory enquiries T102. Police T190.
International phone code +55 Ringing: equal tones with long pauses. Engaged: equal tones, equal pauses.
Official time Brazil has four time zones: Brazilian standard time is three hours behind GMT; the Amazon time zone (Pará west of the Rio Xingu, Amazonas, Roraima, Rondônia, Mato Grosso and Mato Grosso do Sul) is four hours behind GMT, the State of Acre is five hours behind GMT; the Fernando de Noronha archipelago is two hours behind GMT. Clocks move forward one hour in summer for approximately five months (usually between October and February or March), but times of change vary. This does not apply to Acre.
Tipping Tipping is usual, but less costly than in most other countries, except for porters. Restaurants, 10% of bill if no service charge but small tip if there is; taxi drivers, none; cloakroom attendants, small tip; cinema usherettes, none; hairdressers, 10-15%; porters, fixed charges but tips as well; airport porters, about US$0.65 per item.
VAT Rate varies from 7-25% at state and federal level; average 17-20%.
Voltage Generally 110 V 60 cycles AC, but in some cities and areas 220 V 60 cycles AC is used.
Weights and measures Metric.

Local customs and laws

Clothing In general, clothing requirements in Brazil are less formal than in the Hispanic countries. It is, however, advisable for men visiting restaurants to wear long trousers (women in shorts may also be refused entry) and jackets or pullovers in São Paulo. As a general rule, it is better not to wear shorts in official buildings, cinemas, interstate buses and on flights.

Colour Racial discrimination is illegal in Brazil, however, there a complex class system which is informed both by heritage and by economic status. This effectively discriminates against the poor, who are chiefly (but by no means exclusively) black. There are very few black role models, television is dominated by white actors and there is no visible black political movement. Black visitors to the country may encounter racial prejudice. A surprising number of Brazilians are unaware that black Europeans exist, so you could become the focus of curiosity.

Conduct Men should avoid arguments or insults (care is needed even when overtaking on the road); pride may be defended with a gun. Gay men, while still enjoying greater freedom than in many countries, should exercise reasonable discretion. It is normal for men to stare and comment on a woman's appearance, and if you happen to look different or to be travelling alone, you will undoubtedly attract attention. Be aware that Brazilian men can be extremely persistent, and very easily encouraged; it is safest to err on the side of caution until you are accustomed.

Prohibitions Despite the wide distribution and use of **drugs** such as marijuana and cocaine, they are still illegal and you will face a heavy sentence if you are caught with

A hora brasileira

Peter Fleming, the author of one of the best travel books about Brazil, once said that 'a man in a hurry will be miserable in Brazil.' Remember this when you arrive ten minutes late to meet a friend in a bar and spend the next hour wondering if they've already gone after growing tired of waiting for you. They haven't. They've not yet left home. Unless you specify 'a hora britanica' then you will wait. And wait. And everyone will be mortified if you complain. Nobody does – it would be like getting upset about not being allowed to read the paper over someone's shoulder on London's Tube.

them. Be especially aware when crossing borders and on no account bring coca leaves from Bolivia. A campaign against the exploitation of minors for sexual purposes gained wide publicity in 1997 (in Brazilian law a minor is considered to be under the age of 18). Although the local bikinis leave little to the imagination you will be prosecuted for nude bathing except on an official nudist beach of which there are very few. Never carry firearms; their possession could land you in serious trouble.

Time-keeping Brazilians have a very 'relaxed' attitude towards time. It is quite normal for them to arrive an hour or so late even for business appointments. If you expect to meet someone more or less at an exact time, you can add *'em punto'* or *'a hora inglesa'* (English time) but be prepared to wait anyway.

Responsible tourism

Travel to the furthest corners of the globe is now commonplace and the mass movement of people for leisure and business is a major source of foreign exchange and economic development in many parts of South America. The benefits of international travel are self-evident for both hosts and travellers – employment, increased understanding of different cultures, business and leisure opportunities. At the same time there is clearly a downside to the industry. Where visitor pressure is high and/or poorly regulated, adverse impacts on society and the natural environment may be apparent. Paradoxically, this is as true in undeveloped and pristine areas (where culture and the natural environment are less 'prepared' for even small numbers of visitors) as it is in major resort destinations.

The travel industry is growing rapidly and increasingly the impacts of this supposedly 'smokeless' industry are becoming apparent. These impacts can seem remote and unrelated to an individual trip or holiday (eg air travel is clearly implicated in global warming and damage to the ozone layer, resort location and construction can destroy natural habitats and restrict traditional rights and activities), but individual choice and awareness can make a difference in many instances (see box, page 41), and collectively, travellers are having a significant effect in shaping a more responsible and sustainable industry.

In an attempt to promote awareness of and credibility for responsible tourism, organizations such as **Green Globe** ⓘ *T020-79308333, greenglobe@compuserve.com* and the **Centre for Environmentally Sustainable Tourism** (**CERT**) ⓘ *T01268-795772*, in the UK now offer advice on destinations and sites that have achieved certain commitments to conservation and sustainable development. Generally these are larger mainstream destinations and resorts, but they are still a useful guide and increasingly aim to provide information on smaller operations.

How big is your footprint?

- Where possible choose a destination, tour operator or hotel with a proven ethical and environmental commitment – if in doubt ask.
- Spend money on locally produced (rather than imported) goods and services and use common sense when bargaining – your few dollars saved may be a week's salary to others.
- Use water and electricity carefully – travellers may receive preferential supply while the needs of local communities are overlooked.
- Learn about local etiquette and culture – consider local norms and behaviour and dress appropriately for local cultures and situations.
- Protect wildlife and other natural resources – don't buy souvenirs or goods made from wildlife unless they are clearly sustainably produced and are not protected under CITES legislation (CITES controls trade in endangered species).
- Always ask before taking photographs or videos of people.
- Consider staying in local rather than foreign-owned accommodation – the economic benefits for host communities are far greater, as are the opportunities to learn about local culture.

Of course travel can also have beneficial impacts and this is something to which every traveller can contribute; many national parks are part funded by receipts from visitors. Similarly, travellers can promote patronage and protection of important archaeological sites and heritage through their interest and contributions via entrance fees. They can also support small-scale enterprises by staying in locally run hotels and hostels, eating in local restaurants and by purchasing local goods, supplies and arts and crafts.

Since the Responsible Travel section was first introduced in the *South American Handbook* in 1992 there has been a phenomenal growth in tourism that promotes and supports the conservation of natural environments and is also fair and equitable to local communities. This ecotourism segment is probably the fastest-growing sector of the travel industry and provides a vast and growing range of destinations and activities in South America. For example, the **Una Ecopark** ⓘ *T/F073-634 1118, vrisea@bitsnet.com.br*, in Bahia offers visits and experiences in Brazil's Atlantic forest (one of the most endangered ecosystems in the world). A visit to the park provides opportunities for walks in the forest canopy suspended high above the forest floor. Other initiatives can be found in São Paulo state (amazonadv@aol.com).

While the authenticity of some ecotourism operators' claims need to be interpreted with care, there is clearly both a huge demand for this type of activity and also significant opportunities to support worthwhile conservation and social development initiatives.

Organizations such as **Conservation International** ⓘ *T202-429 5660, www.ecotour.org*, the **Eco-Tourism Society** ⓘ *T802-447 2121, www.ecotourism.org*, **Planeta** ⓘ *www2.planeta.com/mader*, and the UK-based **Tourism Concern** ⓘ *T020- 7753 3330, www.gn.apc.org/tourismconcern*, have begun to develop and/or promote ecotourism projects and destinations and their websites are an excellent source of information and details for sites and initiatives throughout South America. Additionally, UK organizations such as **Earthwatch** ⓘ *T01865-311601, www.earthwatch.org*, and **Discovery International** ⓘ *T020-7229 9881, www.discoveryinitiatives.com*, offer opportunities to participate directly in scientific research and development projects throughout the region. » *See also Ecotourism, page 57.*

Safety

Although Brazil's big cities suffer high rates of violent crime, this is mostly confined to the *favelas* where poverty and drugs are the main cause. Visitors should not enter *favelas* except when accompanied by workers for NGOs, tour groups or other people who know the local residents well and are accepted by the community. Visitors may be targets of theft, but if you don't take anything you aren't prepared to lose and insure yourself adequately, it should not ruin your trip. If the worst does happen and you are threatened, don't panic, and hand over your valuables. Do not resist, but report the crime to the local tourist police later. It is extremely rare for a tourist to be hurt during a robbery in Brazil. Being aware of the dangers, acting confidently and using your common sense, will reduce many of the risks.

Certain parts of the country are areas of drug cultivation and should be avoided. These are mentioned where appropriate in the travelling text. All border areas should be regarded with some caution because of smuggling activities. Violence over land ownership in parts of the interior have resulted in a 'Wild West' atmosphere in some towns which should therefore be passed through quickly. Red-light districts should also be given a wide berth as there are reports of drinks being drugged with a substance popularly known as 'Good night Cinderella'. This leaves the victim easily amenable to having their possessions stolen, or worse.

Avoiding con tricks Never trust anyone telling sob stories or offering 'safe rooms', and when looking for a hotel, always choose the room yourself. Be wary of 'plain-clothes policemen'; insist on seeing identification and on going to the police station by main roads. Do not hand over your identification (or money) until you are at the station. On no account take them directly back to your hotel. Be even more suspicious if they seek confirmation of their status from a passer-by.

Hotel security Hotel safe deposits are generally, but not always, secure. If you cannot get a receipt for valuables in a hotel safe, you can seal the contents in a plastic bag and sign across the seal. Always keep an inventory of what you have deposited. If you don't trust the hotel, lock everything in your pack and secure it in your room when you go out. If you lose valuables, report to the police and note details of the report for insurance purposes.

Police There are several types of police: **Polícia Federal**, civilian dressed, who handle all federal law duties, including immigration. A subdivision is the **Polícia Federal Rodoviária**, uniformed, who are the traffic police on federal highways. **Polícia Militar** are the uniformed, street police force, under the control of the state governor, handling all state laws. They are not the same as the Armed Forces' internal police. **Polícia Civil**, also state-controlled, handle local laws and investigations. They are usually in civilian dress, unless in the traffic division. In cities, the **Prefeitura** controls the Guarda Municipal, who handle security. Tourist police operate in places with a strong tourist presence. In case of difficulty, visitors should seek them out in the first instance.

Protecting money and valuables Apart from the obvious precautions of not wearing jewellery (wear a cheap, plastic, digital watch), take local advice about safety and do not assume that daytime is safer than night. If walking after dark, walk in the road, not on the pavement/sidewalk and do not go on to the beach. Don't take valuables to the beach.

Photocopy your passport, air ticket and other documents, make a record of travellers' cheque and credit card numbers. Keep them separately from the originals and leave another set of records at home. Keep all documents secure; hide your main

Useful slang

Que legal that's great/cool
Jeito a way of getting around a problem
Cara literally 'face' meaning bloke/guy/geezer
Mano biker slang for bloke/guy
Brega cheesy/tacky
Mauricinho posh, spoilt boy with rich parents
Patricinha posh, spoilt girl with rich parents
Descolado in fashion/cool

cash supply in different places or under your clothes. Extra pockets sewn inside shirts and trousers, money belts (best worn below the waist), neck or leg pouches and elasticated support bandages for keeping money above the elbow or below the knee have been repeatedly recommended (the last by John Hatt in *The Tropical Traveller*).

Public transport When you have all your luggage with you at a bus or railway station, be especially careful and carry any shoulder bags in front of you. To be extra safe, take a taxi between airport/bus station/railway station and hotel, keep your bags with you and pay only when you and your luggage are outside; avoid night buses and arriving at your destination at night.

Rape This can happen anywhere in the world. If you are the victim of a sexual assault, you are advised firstly to contact a doctor (this can be your home doctor if you prefer). You will need tests to determine whether you have contracted any sexually transmitted diseases; you may also need advice on post-coital contraception. You should also contact your embassy, where consular staff are very willing to help in cases of assault.

Women travellers These additional hints have mainly been supplied by women, but most apply to any single traveller. When you set out, err on the side of caution until your instincts have adjusted to the customs of a new culture. Be prepared for the exceptional curiosity extended to visitors, especially women and try not to overreact. If, as a single woman, you can befriend a local woman, you will learn much more about the country you are visiting. There is a definite 'gringo trail' which you can follow which can be helpful when looking for safe accommodation, especially if arriving after dark (which is best avoided). Remember that for a single woman a taxi at night can be as dangerous as wandering around on your own. It is easier for men to take the friendliness of locals at face value; women may be subject to unwanted attention. Do not disclose to strangers where you are staying. By wearing a wedding ring and saying that your 'husband' is close at hand, you may dissuade an aspiring suitor. If politeness fails, do not feel bad about showing offence and departing. A good rule is always to act with confidence, as though you know where you are going, even if you do not. Someone who looks lost is more likely to attract unwanted attention.

Getting around

Public transport in Brazil is very efficient, especially compared to other South American countries. The main issue is the distances involved. Most visitors will find themselves travelling by buses and planes, except in the Amazon when a boat is often the only way to get around. Train routes are practically non-existent, car hire is expensive and hitchhiking not widely accepted. Taxis are very reasonable and easy to come by.

Air

Because of the size of the country, flying is often the most practical option and internal air services are highly developed. The larger cities are linked with each other several times a day and all national airlines offer excellent service. Internal flights used to be expensive, but recent deregulation of the airlines has reduced prices on some routes by about a third (although flights to and from the Amazon remain the most costly). In addition, no-frills airlines have been set up, offering fares that can be as cheap as travelling by bus. Gol is the main bargain airline; **BRA, Trip** and **ATA** are the three others. The largest airlines are **TAM, Varig** and **Vasp. Rio-Sul**and **Nordeste** (both allied to **Varig**), have extensive networks. Smaller airlines include **Penta,** who have recently built up a wide and cheap network throughout the Amazon region, and **Pantanal,** mainly operating flights between São Paulo state and Mato Grosso do Sul.

Double check all bookings and information given by ground staff. National toll-free numbers (except for **Gol,** which charges) for reservations and confirmations are detailed below. Most websites provide full information, including a booking service, although not all are in English. ▸▸ *For addresses and telephone numbers of airline offices, see directory of individual towns.*

Domestic airlines

BRA www.voebra.com.br.
Gol T0300 7892121 (US$0.10 per min), English-speaking operators, www.voegol.com.br, website in Portuguese only.
Nordeste T0800-992004, www.nordeste.com.
Ocean Air www.oceanair.com.br.
Pantanal T0800-125833, www.pantanal-airlines.com.br.
Rio-Sul T0800-992004, www.rio-sul.com.
TAM T0800-123100, www.tam.com.br.
Trip T0800-7018747; www.voetrip.com.br.
Varig T0800-997000, T0845-6037601 (UK), www.varig.com.br.
Webjet www.webjet.com.br.

Air passes

TAM and **Varig** offer 21-day air passes for people resident outside of Brazil, but since deregulation they are not as good value as they used to be. They also offer limited flexibility; you must buy your airpass outside of Brazil in conjunction with an international scheduled flight and decide your itinerary at the time of purchase. There are no discounts for children and infants pay 10% of the price.

The **Varig Airpass** is US$530 for five flights, with a maximum of four extra coupons available for US$100 each and valid for 21 days. Amendments may be made once prior to commencement of travel at US$30 per change. The **Varig** pass is only available to travellers arriving in Brazil with **Varig** or **British Airways.** The **TAM Airpass** allows you to arrive in Brazil on any airline. It costs US$530, is valid for 21 days and re-routing is permitted for US$50.

With airpasses, no journey may be repeated and none may be used on the Rio-São Paulo shuttle. Domestic airport tax has to be paid at each departure. Some hotels, such as the **Tropical** and **Othon** chains, offer discounts of 10% to **Varig** airpass travellers. Promotions on some destinations offer a free flight or hotel room; enquire when buying the airpass. Converting the voucher can take time, do not plan an onward flight immediately, check at terminals that the airpass is still registered, faulty cancellations have been reported. Cost and restrictions on the airpass are subject to change.

Small scheduled domestic airlines operate Brazilian-built *bandeirante*, 16-seater prop-jets, into virtually every city and town with any semblance of an airstrip. Internal flights often have many stops and are therefore quite slow. Most airports have left-luggage lockers (US$2 for 24 hours). Seats are often unallocated on internal flights; board in good time.

Rail

There are 30,379 km of railways which are not combined into a unified system. Brazil has two gauges and there is little transfer between them. Two more gauges exist for the isolated **Amapá** Railway and the tourist-only **São João del Rei** line. There are still passenger services in the state of São Paulo, but most passenger services have been withdrawn. Full details are given in the text.

River

The main areas where travel by boat is practical (and often necessary) are the Amazon region, along the São Francisco River and along the Atlantic coast. There are also some limited transport services through the Pantanal. ➡ *See also page 579 for details of river transport in the Amazon.*

Road

Though the best paved highways are heavily concentrated in the Southeast, those serving the interior are being improved to all-weather status and many are paved. Brazil has over 1,650,000 km of highways, of which 150,000 km are paved, and several thousand are all-weather. Most main roads between principal cities are paved. Some are narrow and therefore dangerous and many are in poor condition.

Bus

There are three standards of bus: *Comum*, or *Convencional* are quite slow, not very comfortable and fill up quickly; *Executivo* are more expensive, comfortable (many have reclining seats), and don't stop en route to pick up passengers so are safer. *Leito* (literally, bed) run at night between the main centres, offering reclining seats with leg rests, toilets, and sometimes refreshments, at double the normal fare. For journeys over 100 km, most buses have chemical toilets (bring toilet paper). Air conditioning can make buses cold at night, so take a jumper; on some services blankets are supplied.

Buses stop fairly frequently (every two to four hours) at *postos* for snacks. Bus stations for interstate services and other long distance routes are usually called *rodoviárias*. They are frequently outside the city centres and offer snack bars, lavatories, left-luggage stores (*guarda volume*), local bus services and information centres. Buy bus tickets at rodoviárias (most now take credit cards), not from travel agents who add on surcharges. Reliable bus information is hard to come by, other than from companies themselves. Buses usually arrive and depart in very good time. Many town buses have turnstiles which can be inconvenient if you are carrying a large pack. Urban buses normally serve local airports.

Car

Any foreigner with a passport can purchase a Brazilian car and travel outside Brazil. A letter in Spanish from your consul explaining your aims and that you will return the vehicle to Brazil can make life much easier at borders and check points. Foreigners do not need the CPF tax document (needed by Brazilians), and the official purchase receipt is accepted as proof of ownership. Don't buy an alcohol-driven car if you propose to drive outside Brazil. It is essential to have an external intake filter fitted, or dust can rapidly destroy an engine. VW kombi vans are cheapest in Brazil where they are made, they are equivalent to the pre-1979 model in Europe. If a lot of time is to be spent on dirt roads, the Ford Chevrolet pick-up is more robust.

Fuel It is virtually impossible to buy premium grades of petrol/gasoline anywhere. With alcohol fuel you need about 50% more alcohol than regular gasoline. Larger cars have a small extra tank for 'gasolina' to get the engine started; remember to keep this topped up. Fuel is only 85% octane (owing to high methanol content), so be prepared for bad consumption and poor performance and starting difficulties in non-Brazilian cars in winter. Diesel fuel is cheap and a diesel engine may provide fewer maintenance problems. Very few service stations open during Carnival week. Fuel prices vary from week to week and region to region: ordinary petrol, *gasolina comun*, is around US$1 per litre; *alcool comun* and diesel are cheaper. There is no unleaded fuel.

Preparation It's well worth installing extra heavy-duty shock-absorbers (such as Spax or Koni). Fit tubes on 'tubeless' tyres, since air plugs for tubeless tyres are hard to find, and if you bend the rim on a pothole, the tyre will not hold air. Take spare tubes, an extra spare tyre, spare plugs, fan-belts, radiator hoses and headlamp bulbs. Find out about your car's electrics and filters and what spares may be required. Similarly, know how to handle problems arising from dirty fuel. Take a 10-litre water container for self and vehicle. Note that in some areas gas stations are few and far between.

Security Spare no ingenuity in making your car secure. Try never to leave the car unattended except in a locked garage or guarded parking space. Remove all belongings and leave the empty glove compartment open. Also lock the clutch or accelerator to the steering wheel with a heavy, obvious chain or lock. Adult minders or street children will generally protect your car fiercely in exchange for a tip.

Documents Be very careful to keep *all* the papers you are given when you enter, to produce when you leave.

Insurance against accident and theft is very expensive. If the car is stolen or written off you will be required to pay very high import duty on its value. The legally required minimum cover for third party insurance is not expensive. If anyone is hurt, do not pick them up as you may become liable.

Car hire

Renting a car in Brazil is expensive – the cheapest rate for unlimited mileage for a small car is about US$50 per day. The minimum age is 21 and it is essential to have a credit card. Companies operate under the names *aluguel de automóveis* or *autolocadores*. Toll free numbers for nationwide firms are **Avis** ⓣ *T0800-558066* and **Localiza** ⓣ *T0800-992000, www.localiza.com.br*. Details of local companies are given in the text.

Car hire insurance Check exactly what the hirer's insurance policy covers. In many cases it will not apply to major accidents, or 'natural' damage (eg flooding). Ask if extra cover is available. Sometimes using a credit card automatically includes insurance. Beware of being billed for scratches which were on the vehicle before you hired it.

Cycling

A mountain bike is strongly recommended. The good quality ones (and the cast-iron rule is never to skimp on quality) are incredibly tough, with low gear ratios for difficult terrain, wide tyres with plenty of tread for good road-holding, cantilever brakes, and a low centre of gravity for improved stability. Although touring bikes – and to a lesser extent mountain bikes – and spares are available in the larger cities, most locally manufactured goods are shoddy and rarely last. Buy everything you possibly can before you leave home.

Equipment A small but comprehensive tool kit (to include chain rivet and crank removers, a spoke key and possibly a block remover), a spare tyre and inner tubes, a puncture repair kit with plenty of extra patches and glue, a set of brake blocks, brake and gear cables and all types of nuts and bolts, at least 12 spokes (best taped to the chain stay), a light oil for the chain (eg Finish-Line Teflon Dry-Lube), tube of waterproof grease, a pump secured by a pump lock, a Blackburn parking block (a most invaluable accessory, cheap and virtually weightless), a cyclometer, a loud bell, and a secure lock and chain. *Richard's Bicycle Book* makes useful reading for even the most mechanically minded.

Strong and waterproof front and back panniers are a must. When packed these are likely to be heavy and should be carried on the strongest racks available. Poor quality racks have ruined many a journey for they take incredible strain on unpaved roads. A top bag-cum-rucksack (eg Carradice) makes a good addition for use on and off the bike. A Cannondale front bag is good for maps, camera, compass, etc. (Other recommended panniers are Ortlieb – front and back – which is waterpoof and almost 'sandproof', Mac-Pac, Madden and Karimoor.) 'Gaffa' tape is excellent for protecting vulnerable parts of panniers and for carrying out all manner of repairs. Pack equipment and clothes in plastic bags to give extra protection against dust and rain.

Useful tips Wind, not hills, is the enemy of the cyclist. Avoid dehydration by drinking regularly and carry an ample supply of water. Give your bicycle a thorough daily check for loose nuts or bolts or bearings. See that all parts run smoothly. A good chain should last 3,200 km but keep it as clean as possible – an old toothbrush is good for this – and to oil it lightly from time to time. Traffic on main roads can be a nightmare; it is usually far more rewarding to keep to the smaller roads or to paths if they exist. A rearview mirror has been frequently recommended to forewarn you of vehicles which are too close behind. Also, watch out for oncoming, overtaking vehicles, unstable loads on trucks, protruding loads, etc. Make yourself conspicuous by wearing bright clothing and a helmet. Most towns have a bicycle shop of some description, but in an emergency it is amazing how one can improvise with wire, string, dental floss, nuts and bolts, odd pieces of tin or electrical 'Gaffa' tape!

The **Expedition Advisory Centre**, administered by the Royal Geographical Society, 1, Kensington Gore, London SW7 2AR, has published a useful monograph entitled *Bicycle Expeditions*, by Paul Vickers (March 1990), it is available direct from the Centre, price £6.50 (postage extra if outside the UK). In the UK there is also the **Cyclist's Touring Club** ⓘ *CTC, Cotterell House, 69 Meadrow, Godalming, Surrey GU7 3HS, T01483-417217, cycling@ctc.org.uk*, for touring and technical information.

Motorcycling

The machine you use should be off-road capable, eg the BMW R80/100/GS for its rugged and simple design and reliable shaft drive. A road bike can go most places an off-road bike can go, at the cost of greater effort. Japanese bikes are easiest to get serviced in Brazil.

Preparation Many roads are rough. Fit heavy-duty front fork springs, the best quality rebuildable shock absorber you can afford (Ohlins, White Power) and lockable luggage such as Krausers (reinforce luggage frames). A large capacity fuel tank (Acerbis), +300 mile/480 km range is essential if going off the beaten track. A washable air filter is a good idea (K&N), also fuel filters and fueltap rubber seals, a good set of trails-type tyres, as well as a high mudguard. Get to know the bike before you go, ask the dealers in your country what goes wrong with it and arrange a link whereby you can get parts flown out to you. If using a fully enclosed chaincase on a chain-driven bike, an automatic chain oiler is a good idea. The **Scott-Oiler** (106 Clober Road, Milngavie, Glasgow G62 7SS, Scotland) has been recommended. Fill it with Sae 90 oil. A hefty bash plate/sump guard is invaluable. A first-class tool kit is a must and if riding a bike with a chain then a spare set of sprockets and an 'o' ring chain should be carried. Parts are few and far between, but mechanics are skilled at making do and can usually repair things.

Security Try not to leave a fully laden bike on its own. An Abus D or chain will keep the bike secure. A cheap alarm can give you peace of mind. Look for hotels with a courtyard or secure parking and never leave luggage on the bike whilst unattended.

Documents Passport, International Driving Licence and bike registration document are necessary. Temporary import papers are given on entry, to be surrendered on leaving the country.

Taxi

Rates vary from city to city, but are consistent within each city. At the outset, make sure the meter is cleared and shows 'tariff 1', except (usually) from 2300-0600, Sunday, and in December when '2' is permitted. Check that the meter is working; if not, fix the price in advance. The **radio taxi** service costs about 50% more but cheating is less likely. Taxis outside larger hotels usually cost twice as much. If you are seriously cheated note the number of the taxi and insist on a signed bill; threatening to take it to the police can work. **Moto-taxis** are much more economical, but many are unlicensed and there have been a number of robberies of passengers.

Maps and guide books

A recommended series of general maps is published by **International Travel Maps** (ITM) ⓘ *345 West Broadway, Vancouver BC, V5Y 1P8, Canada, T604-8793621, F8794521*, compiled with historical notes, by the late Kevin Healey. Available are *South America South*, *North East* and *North West* (1:4M), *Rio de Janeiro* (1:20,000). Also available is *New World Edition*, Bertelsmann, Neumarkter Strasse 18, 81673 München, Germany, *Mittelamerika*, *Südamerika Nord*, *Südamerika Sud*, *Brasilien* (all 1:4M). London's **Stanfords** ⓘ *12-14 Long Acre, Covent Garden, WC2E 9LP, UK, T020-78361321, www.stanfords.co.uk*, also sells a wide variety of guides and maps.

Quatro Rodas, a motoring magazine, publishes an excellent series of maps and guides in Portuguese and English from about US$10. Its annual *Guia Brasil* is a type of Michelin Guide to hotels, restaurants (not the cheapest), sights, facilities and general information on hundreds of cities and towns in the country, including good country and street maps. These guides can be purchased from street newspaper vendors throughout the country and at Av das Nações Unidas 7221, 14 andar, Pinheiros, CEP 05425-902, T011-3037 6004, www.publiabril.com.br. *Quatro Rodas* guides may be bought in Europe from: 33, rue de Miromesnil, 75008 Paris, T00331-42663118, abrilparis@wanadoo.fr; and *Deltapress-Sociedade Distribuidora de Publicações*, Capa Rota, Tapada Nova, Linhó, 2710 Sintra, Portugal, T003511-9249940. In the USA: Lincoln Building, 60 East 42nd St, Suite 3403, New York, NY 10165/3403, T001212-5575990/3, abril@walrus.com.

Hotel price codes

LL	US$180 and over	C	US$26-40
L	US$120-179	D	US$15-25
AL	US$86-119	E	US$7-14
A	US$56-85	F	US$6 and under
B	US$41-55		

Prices include taxes and service charges, but are without meals unless otherwise stated. They are based on a double room, except in the E and F ranges where prices are almost always per person. For a quick reference price guide to our hotel categories, see inside the front cover.

Sleeping

Camping

Members of the Camping Clube do Brasil or those with an international campers' card pay only half the rate of a non-member, which is US$10-15 per person. The Clube has 43 sites in 13 states and 80,000 members. For enquiries, **Camping Clube do Brasil** ⓘ *Divisão de Campings, R Senador Dantas 75, 29th floor, Centro, Rio de Janeiro, CEP 20037-900, T021-210 3171*. It may be difficult to get into some Camping Clube campsites during the high season (January to February). Private campsites charge about US$8 per person. For those on a very low budget and in isolated areas where there is no campsite, service stations can be used as camping sites. They have shower facilities, watchmen and food; some have dormitories. There are also various municipal sites. Campsites often tend to be some distance from public transport routes and are better suited to those with their own transport. Never camp at the side of a road; wild camping is generally not possible.

Good camping equipment may be purchased in Brazil and there are several rental companies. Camping gas cartridges are easy to buy in sizeable towns in the South, eg in HM shops. *Guia de Camping* is produced by **Artpress** ⓘ *R Araçatuba 487, São Paulo 05058*; it lists most sites and is available in bookshops in most cities. **Quatro Rodas'** *Guia Brasil* also lists main campsites.

Homestays

Experiment in International Living Ltd ⓘ *287 Worcester Rd, Malvern, Worcestershire WR14 1AB, T01684-562577, F562212*, or **Friesdorferstrasse** ⓘ *194A, 53175 Bonn 9, T0228-957220, F358282*, can arrange stays with families from one to four weeks in Brazil; EIL has offices in 38 countries. This has been recommended as an excellent way to meet people and learn the language.

Hotels

Unless travelling in high season, always ask for a discount, especially if staying for more than one night. The best guide to hotels in Brazil is the *Guia Brasil Quatro Rodas*, with good maps of towns. Motels are specifically intended for very short-stay couples: there is no stigma attached and they usually offer good value (the rate for a full night is called the *pernoite*), though the decor can be a little unsettling. The type known as *hotel familiar*, to be found in the interior – large meals, communal washing, hammocks for children – is much cheaper, but only for the enterprising. Pousadas are the equivalent of bed-and-breakfast, often small and family run,

Brazil's best hotels

Luxury hotels

Fasano Ipanema, Rio de Janeiro city. Grand designer hotel, page 111.
Unique and **Unique Garden Spa**, São Paulo city. Designer hotel and spa, page 195 and page 196.
Angatu, Paraty. Luxury private beach home rental, page 170.
Toucan Cipó, Serra do Cipó. Luxury *fazenda*, page 271.
O Convento do Carmo, Salvador. In a grand converted colonial building, page 373.

Boutique hotels

Tijuco, Diamantina. Classic Niemeyer treasure, page 272.
Pousada do Boqueirão, Salvador. Small designer boutique, page 376.
Pousada Maravilha, Fernando de Noronha. Designer beach hotel, page 454.
Solar do Ponte, Tiradentes. Converted colonial mansion, page 454.
Pousada do Amparo, Olinda. Converted colonial town house, page 444.

Nature hotels

Amazon Clipper. Safari cruise boat, page 578.
Mamirauá Ecological Reserve. Floating lodge, page 569
Korubo, Jalapão. African-style safari camp in *cerrado* wilderness, page 630.
Fazenda Rio Negro, Nhecolândia. In the heart of the Pantanal, page 652.
Cristalino Jungle Lodge, Cristalino River. Jungle lodge, page 666.

although some are very sophisticated and correspondingly priced. Usually hotel prices include breakfast; there is no reduction if you don't eat it. In the better hotels (our category A and upwards), the breakfast is well worth eating: rolls, ham, eggs, cheese, cakes, fruit. Normally the *apartamento* is a room with a bath; a *quarto* is a room without a bath. Leave rooms in good time so frigobar bills can be checked.

The star rating system for hotels (five-star hotels are not price controlled) is not the standard used in North America or Europe.

Business visitors are strongly recommended to book accommodation in advance, and this can easily be done for Rio or São Paulo hotels with representation abroad. **Varig** has a good hotel reservation service, with discounts of up to 50% for its passengers.

It's a good idea to book accommodation in advance in small towns which are popular at weekends with city dwellers (eg near São Paulo and Rio de Janeiro).

Roteiros de Charme, in some 30 locations in the Southeast and Northeast, is an association of hotels and pousadas which aims to give a high standard of accommodation in establishments which represent the town they are in. It is a private initiative. If you are travelling in the appropriate budget range (our **A** price range upwards), you can plan an itinerary which takes in these high-class hotels, with a reputation for comfort and good food, and some fine places of historical and leisure interest. Roteiros de Charme hotels are listed in the text and any one of them can provide information on the group. Alternatively, contact the office in the **Caesar Park Hotel**ⓘ *Av Vieira Souto 460, Ipanema, Rio de Janeiro, www.roteirosdecharme.com.br*.

Also worth contacting are **Angatu**, www.angatu.com, which arranges luxurious private homes and bespoke trips along the Costa Verde; and the **Brazilian Beachouse Company,** www.brazilianbeachouse.com, for luxurious, tasteful properties in Bahia.

Youth hostels

For information about youth hostels contact **Federação Brasileira dos Albergues da Juventude** ⓘ *R dos Andradas 1137, conj 214, Porto Alegre, Rio Grande do Sul, CEP 90.020-007, www.albergues.com.br*; its annual book provides a full list of good value accommodation, with the addresses of the regional representatives. Also see the **Internet Guide to Hostelling** which has a list of Brazilian youth hostels, www.hostels.com/br.html. Several websites offer direct booking or reservation of hostel beds. See www.hostelworld.com or www.hostels.com for information.

Low-budget travellers with student cards (photograph needed) can often use the **Casa dos Estudantes** (CEU) network.

Advice and suggestions

1 The service stations (*postos*) and hostels (*dormitórios*) along main roads provide excellent value in room and food for those on a tight budget.
2 The electric showers used in many hotels should be checked for obvious flaws in the wiring; try not to touch the rose while it is producing hot water.
3 Some taxi drivers will try to take you to the expensive hotels, who pay them commission for bringing in custom. Beware!
4 Cockroaches are ubiquitous and unpleasant, but not dangerous. Take some insecticide powder if staying in cheap hotels; **Baygon** (Bayer) has been recommended. Stuff toilet paper in any holes in walls that you suspect of being parts of cockroach runs.
5 Away from the main commercial centres, many hotels, restaurants and bars have inadequate water supplies. Used toilet paper should not be flushed down the pan, but placed in the receptacle provided. Failing to do so will block the pan or drain.
6 Bring a mosquito net.

Eating and drinking

Cuisine → *For a glossary of food and drinks, see box page 53*

The most common dish is *bife* (*ou frango*) *com arroz e feijão*, steak (or chicken) with rice and the excellent Brazilian black beans. However, due to Brazil's rich cultural mix many other influences are found in the various regions. São Paulo is by far the best place for international and foreign cuisines.

Feijoada The most famous dish with beans is the *feijoada completa*: several meat ingredients (jerked beef, smoked sausage, smoked tongue, salt pork, along with spices, herbs and vegetables) are cooked with the beans. Manioc flour is sprinkled over it, and it is eaten with *kale* (*couve*) and slices of orange, and accompanied by glasses of *aguardente* (unmatured rum), usually known as *cachaça* (booze), though *pinga* (drop) is a politer term. Most restaurants serve the *feijoada completa* for Saturday lunch (up to about 1630).

Churrasco A mixed grill, including excellent steak, served with roasted manioc flour is available throughout Brazil. Originating from the cattlemen of Rio Grande do Sul, it is normally served in restaurants known as *churrascarias* or *rodízios* (or *espeto corrido*). In *rodízios*, waiters ask you in advance what types of meat you want and then bring them round to you until you tell them to stop. Each one has its own variation on the red light/green light system for communicating to the staff. *Churrascarias* usually have a self-service salad bar. Both are good places for large appetites.

Minas Gerais has two delicious special dishes with pork, black beans, *farofa* and *kale*: *tutu á mineira* and *feijão tropeiro*. A white hard cheese (*queijo prata*) or a slightly softer one (*queijo Minas*) is often served for dessert with bananas, or guava or *quince* paste. *Comida mineira* is quite distinctive and very wholesome and you can often find restaurants serving this type of food in other parts of Brazil.

Restaurant price codes

ΨΨΨ	US$15 and over
ΨΨ	US$8-14
Ψ	US$7 and under

Prices refer to the cost of a two-course meal, not including drinks.

Bahia has some excellent fish dishes (see the note on page); some restaurants in most of the big cities specialize in them. *Vatapá* is a good dish in the North; it contains shrimp or fish in a sauce of palm oil or coconut milk. *Empadinhas de camarão*, shrimp patties, with olives and heart of palm, are worth trying.

Desserts and fruits

There is fruit all the year round, ranging from banana and orange to mango, pawpaw, custard-apple (*fruta do conde*) and guava. Try *manga de Ubá*, a non-fibrous small mango. Also good are *amora*, a raspberry that looks like a strawberry, *jaboticaba*, a small black damson-like fruit, and *jaca* (jackfruit), a large yellow/green fruit. Don't miss the exotic flavours of Brazilian ice-creams.

Eating out

Portions are usually for two and come with two plates. If you are on your own, you could ask for an *embalagem* (doggy bag) or get a takeaway called a *marmita* or *quentinha* and offer it to a person with no food (many Brazilians do). Many restaurants now serve *comida por kilo* where you serve yourself and pay for the weight of food on your plate. This is good news if your Portuguese is not up to much, if you want a cheap meal, and also if you don't want to spend time waiting for your food to be served.

The main meal is usually taken in the middle of the day; cheap restaurants tend not to be open in the evening. Always ask the price of a dish before ordering and, if travelling on a tight budget, ask for the *prato feito* or *sortido*, an excellent value set menu. The *prato comercial* is similar but rather better and a bit more expensive. *Lanchonetes* are cheap eating places where you generally pay before eating. *Salgados* (savoury pastries), *coxinha* (a pyramid of manioc filled with meat or fish and deep fried), *esfiha* (spicy hamburger inside an onion bread envelope), *empadão* (a filling – eg chicken – in sauce in a pastry case), *empadas* and *empadinhas* (smaller fritters of the same type), are the usual fare. *Pão de queijo* is a hot roll made with cheese. A *bauru* is a toasted sandwich which, in Porto Alegre, is filled with steak, while further north has tomato, ham and cheese filling. *Cocada* is a coconut and sugar biscuit.

Warning Avoid mussels, marsh crabs and other shellfish caught near large cities: they are likely to have lived in a highly polluted environment.

Drinks

The local firewater, *aguardente* (known as *cachaça* or *pinga*), made from sugar-cane, is cheap and strong; São Francisco, Praianinha, Nega Fulô, '51' and Pitu are some recommended makes. Mixed with fruit juice, sugar and crushed ice, *cachaça* becomes the principal element in a *batida*, a delicious and powerful drink. The most popular is a lime batida or *batida de limão*; a variant of which is the *caipirinha*, a *cachaça* with several slices of lime; a *caipiroska* is made with vodka. *Cachaça* with Coca-Cola is a *cuba*, while rum with Coca-Cola is a *cuba libre*.

Some genuine Scotch whisky brands are bottled in Brazil, which are very popular because of the high price of Scotch imported in the bottle. Teacher's is the most highly regarded brand. Locally made gin, vermouth and campari are very good.

Food and drink

Brazilian dishes
Churrascaria restaurant with meat barbecue also known as *rodízio*.
Feijoada the national dish, a black bean and meat stew.
Pão do queijo brazilian cheesy bread

Bebidas Drinks
água mineral mineral water
água tónica tonic water
café coffee
cerveja beer
chá tea
chocolate quente hot chocolate
leite milk
refrigerante soft drink
suco fruit juice
uísque whisky
vinho wine

Frutas Fruit
abacaxi pineapple
banana banana
coco coconut
laranja orange
limão lime
maça apple
mamão papaya
manga mango
maracujá passion fruit
melancia watermelon
morango strawberry
uva grape

Carne Meat
bife beef
cabrito kid
cachorro quente hot dog
filé steak
frango chicken
misto quente toasted cheese and ham sandwich
peixe fish
peru turkey
porco pork
presunto ham
salsichas sausages

Legumes Vegetables
alface lettuce
arroz rice
batata potato
cebola onion
cenoura carrot
milho sweetcorn
salada salad
tomate tomato

Others
açúcar sugar
amendoim peanut
bolo cake
iogurte yoghurt
manteiga butter
mostarda mustard
ovo egg
pão bread
pastel pie
pimenta pepper
queijo cheese
sal salt
sanduiche sandwich
sorvete ice-cream

Imported drinks are expensive, but there are some fair local wines. Among the better ones are Château d'Argent, Château Duvalier, Almadén, Dreher, Preciosa and Bernard Taillan. The red Marjolet from Cabernet grapes, and the Moselle-type white Zahringer, have been well spoken of. A new *adega* tends to start off well, but the quality gradually deteriorates with time; many vintners have switched to American Concorde grapes, producing a rougher wine. Greville Brut champagne-type is inexpensive and very drinkable. A white wine sangria, containing tropical fruits such as pineapple and papaya, is worth looking out for. Chilean and Portuguese wines are sometimes available at little more than the cost of local wines.

The beers are good and there are plenty of brands: Antarctica, Brahma, Bohemia, Cerpa, Skol and Xingu black beer. Beer is cheaper by the bottle than on draught, which is known as *chope* or *chopp*, after the German Schoppen, and pronounced 'shoppi'.

There is an excellent range of non-alcoholic fruit juices, known as *sucos*. *Açai*, *acerola*, *caju* (cashew), *pitanga*, *goiaba* (guava), *genipapo*, *graviola* (*chirimoya*), *maracujá* (passion fruit), *sapoti* and *amarindo* are recommended. *Vitaminas* are thick fruit or vegetable drinks with milk. *Caldo de cana* is sugar-cane juice, sometimes mixed with ice. *Água de côco* or *côco verde* (coconut water from chilled, fresh green coconut) should not be missed. The best known of many local soft drinks is *Guaraná*, which is a very popular carbonated fruit drink, completely unrelated to the natural product from the Amazon. Coffee is ubiquitous and good tea is grown and sold.

Carnaval dates

- → **2007** 17-20 February
- → **2008** 2-5 February
- → **2009** 21-24 February
- → **2010** 13-16 February
- → **2011** 5-8 February

Bars

These can vary from basic neighbourhood bars open to the street, often known as *pésujos* or *botequins*, to sophisticated places with waiter service. Food and snacks are often served and there is usually some form of music for entertainment, whether a live band or the customers providing their own in an improvised samba session with guitars and drums.

Festivals and events

Festivals

The major festival is **Carnaval**, which is held three days up to, and including, Ash Wednesday and is celebrated all over Brazil. See boxes under Rio de Janeiro page 114, Salvador page 380 and Pernambuco page 448. **Semana Santa**, which ends on Easter Sunday, is celebrated with parades in many cities and towns. The **Festas Juninhas** throughout the country and **Bumba-meu-boi** in Maranhão are held throughout June, while the **Festa do Boi** is held in Parantins at the end of the month, see page 516.

Bahia has many festivals throughout the year but some of the most interesting are the **Lavagem do Bomfim** in January, the **Presente para Iemanjá** in February and the **Festa da Boa Morte** in August.

In the South the **Festa Nacional da Uva,** a grape and wine festival, is held in Caxias do Sul during February. São Paulo has the Brazilian Grand Prix at the end of March or beginning of April and the **Festa do Peão Boiadeiro in Barretos** during August.

In May the **Festa do Divino Espírito Santo** is celebrated throughout Brazil, but the parades in Pirenópolis are especially interesting.

Towards the end of the year in October the **Oktoberfest** is held in Blumenau, whilst the **Círio de Nazaré** festival takes place in Belém.

The festival year ends on 31 December with the hugely popular **Reveillon** festivities being held particularly on beaches.

National holidays

Aside from the festivals listed above, the main holidays are: 1 January, **New Year;** 21 April, **Tiradentes;** 1 May, **Labour Day;** June, **Corpus Christi;** 7 September, **Independence Day;** 12 October, **Nossa Senhora Aparecida;** 2 November, **All Souls' Day;** 15 November, **Proclamation of the Republic;** and 25 December, **Christmas.** The local holidays in the main cities are given in the text. Other religious or traditional holidays (including Good Friday and, usually, 1 November, **All Saints' Day** and 24 December, **Christmas Eve**) must be fixed by the municipalities. Other holidays are usually celebrated on the Monday prior to the date.

Shopping

What to buy

Gold, diamonds and gemstones are good buys throughout Brazil and there are innovative designs in jewellery. Buy at reputable dealers (the best value is in Minas Gerais), but cheap, fun pieces can be bought from street traders. There are interesting furnishings made with gemstones, and marble. Clay figurines from the Northeast, lace from Ceará, leatherwork, strange pottery from Amazônia, carvings in soapstone and in bone, tiles and other ceramic work, African-type pottery and basketwork from Bahia, are all worth seeking out. Brazilian cigars are excellent for those who like mild flavours. Recommended purchases are musical instruments, such as guitars, other stringed and percussion instruments. There are excellent textiles and good hammocks from the Northeast (ironmongers sell hooks – *ganchos pararede* – for hanging your hammock at home). Design in clothing is impressive, though unfortunately not equalled by manufacturing quality. Buy your beachwear in Brazil: it is matchless.

For those who know how to use them, medicinal herbs, barks and spices can be bought from street markets. Coconut oil and local skin and haircare products (fantastic conditioners) are better and cheaper than in Europe, but known brands of toiletries are exorbitant. Other bad buys are film (including processing), cameras and any electrical goods (including batteries). Sunscreen, sold in all department stores and large supermarkets, is expensive.

Prices and bargaining

As a rule, shopping is easier, quality more reliable and prices higher in the shopping centres (mostly excellent) and in the wealthier suburbs. Prices are often confusingly displayed as 3X (figure) which means that customers can pay in three monthly installments, even for items like bikinis. Better prices are posted at the small shops and street traders. Shopping is most entertaining at markets and on the beach. Bargaining (with good humour) is expected in the latter.

Sport and activities

Archaeology and palaeontology

There are many sites where remains can be found of the continent's original inhabitants, whether human or other species such as dinosaurs. The best areas are probably in the Central West and the Northeast. Cave paintings are to be found in Serra do Roncador in Mato Grosso, Serra da Capivara in Piauí and near Xique-Xique in Bahia. Dinosaur tracks can be seen at Souza in the interior of Paraíba, whilst eggs have been found at Peirópolis in western Minas Gerais.

Birdwatching

Brazil has more endemic species than any other country in South America, including the world's rarest bird, Spix's macaw. Habitats range from freshwater wetlands to lowland rainforest, dry *cerrado* and *caatinga*, Atlantic coastal forest, mangrove forest and wet pampa grassland. There are patches of *Araucaria* pine forest in the south. None is difficult to get to, but it would be impossible to visit every type of environment in one trip. The system of national parks and protected areas, including those offshore (Abrolhos, Fernando de Noronha), is designed to allow access to Brazil's areas of outstanding beauty. The best time for birding is from September to October as it is quiet relatively dry and flights are at their cheapest.

Top five birding spectaculars

Harpy eagle (*Gavião real/Harpia*) Huge monkey-eating eagle with a regal crest.
King vulture (*Urubu rey*) Magnificent white vulture with a multi-coloured face.
Guianan cock of the rock (*Galinha do Campo*) Brilliant orange and with a spectacular courtship dance.
Hyacinthine macaw (*Arara azul*). Deep indigo and the largest parrot in the world.
Jabiru stork (Tuiuiu) 1.5-m-tall stork with a bald head and red collar.

Pantanal Bird Club ⓘ *T065-3624 1930, www.pantanalbirdclub.org*, is the best for serious birding. Specialists, with a good reputation, **www.birdingbraziltours.com** operate out of Manaus and cover the whole country. **Focus Tours** ⓘ *111 Malaga Rd, Santa Fe, NM 87505, T505-989 7193, www.focustours.com*, specialize in birdwatching and responsible travel. The **Focus Conservation Fund** ⓘ *www.focusconservation.org*, is a non-profit organization concerned with projects in the Pantanal, the Amazon and the Caratinga region in Minas Gerais. **Ornitholidays** ⓘ *29 Straight Mile, Romsey, Hants, SO51 9BB, T01794-519445, www.ornitholidays.co.uk*, are the best company working in Brazil from Europe. **www.worldtwitch.com** and **www.camacdonald.com birding** are comprehensive. » *For more information on flora and fauna, see page 710.*

Canoeing

Canoeing is supervised by the **Confederação Brasileira de Canoagem** (R Fernando Abott 582/703, Estrela, CEP 95880-000, Rio Grande do Sul, T051-712 2600), founded in 1989. It covers all aspects of the sport, speed racing, slalom, downriver, surfing and ocean kayaking. For downriver canoeing, go to **Visconde de Mauá** (Rio de Janeiro state – see page 159 where the Rio Preto is famous for the sport); also the Rio Formoso at **Bonito** (Mato Grosso do Sul – see page 645). A recommended river for slalom is the Paranhana, **Três Coroas,** Rio Grande do Sul. For kayak surfing the best places are Rio, the Ilha de Santa Catarina and Ubatuba, while ocean kayaking is popular in Rio, Búzios and Santos (São Paulo).

Caving

→ *For cave diving, see Scuba diving, below.*

There are some wonderful cave systems in Brazil, and **Ibama** (see national parks, page 713) has a programme for the protection of the national speleological heritage. National parks such as **Ubajara** (see page 496) and **Chapada Diamantina** (page 410) and the state park of **PETAR** (page 220) have easy access for the casual visitor, but there are also many options for the keen potholer in the states of São Paulo, Paraná, Minas Gerais and the federal district of Brasília.

Climbing

As Brazil has no mountain ranges of Alpine or Andean proportions, the most popular form of climbing (*escalada*) is rock-face climbing. In the heart of Rio, you can see, or join, climbers scaling the rocks at the base of **Pão de Açúcar** and on the Sugar Loaf itself. Not too far away, the **Serra dos Órgãos** provides plenty of challenges, not least the **Dedo de Deus** (God's Finger – see page 151). In the state of São Paulo a good location for climbing is **Pedra do Báu** near São Bento do Sapucaí, and **Brotas** is popular for abseiling (*rappel*). **Pedra Branca** and the **Serra do Cipó** are recommended locations in Minas Gerais. Mato Grosso has the **Serra do Roncador** and there are other good areas in Paraná and Rio Grande do Sul.

Ecotourism

→ See also Responsible tourism, page 40.

Ecotourism, although less developed in Brazil than in Peru or Bolivia greatly contributes to a positive view of the value of forest among local people and visiting a lodge can greatly contribute to the preservation of the forest – tourist money keeps the lodge going, often ensures that private reserves are protected and offers employment to local people – sending out the message that ecotourism makes economic sense and changing attitudes. Ecotourism is very slowly becoming important as a form of sustainable development in the parts of Brazil most threatened by deforestation and as a way of alleviating local unemployment in a way that doesn't harm the environment. Many opportunities for visiting the rainforest are to be found in the North and efforts are being made to save what is left of the Atlantic forest cover in the Southeast.

Useful organizations include the **Instituo Brasileiro de Ecoturismo** (IEB) ⓘ *R Minerva 156, Perdizes, São Paulo, T011-3672 7571, www.ecoturismo.org.br*. In Minas Gerais, **Amo-Te** (Associação Mineira dos Organizadores do Turismo Ecológico) ⓘ *R Prof Morais 624, Apto 302, Savassi, Belo Horizonte, T031-3281 5094*, is helpful. **Terra Virgem** ⓘ *R Galeno de Almeida 179, CEP 05410-030, T/F011-883 7823, terravirgem@originet.com.br*, is a publishing house in São Paulo which publishes guides in Portuguese and English for adventure tourism, accompanied by books of photographs.

Fishing

There is enormous potential for angling given the number and variety of its rivers, lakes and reservoirs. Add to this the scope for sea-angling along the Atlantic Coast and it is not difficult to see why the sport is gaining in popularity. Officially, the country's fish stocks are under the control of **Ibama** (the national parks agency) and a licence is required for fishing in any waters. The states of Mato Grosso and Mato Grosso do Sul require people fishing in their rivers to get the states' own fishing permit, which is not the same as an Ibama licence. All details on prices, duration and regulations concerning catches can be obtained from Ibama; the paperwork can be found at Ibama offices, some branches of the Banco do Brasil and some agencies which specialize in fishing. In Mato Grosso and Mato Grosso do Sul information is provided by Sema, the Special Environment Secretariat, and documents may be obtained at fishing agencies or HSBC in Mato Grosso do Sul. Freshwater fishing can be practised in so many places that the best bet is to make local enquiries on arrival. You can then find out about the rivers, lakes and reservoirs, which fish you are likely to find and what types of angling are most suited to the conditions. Favoured rivers include tributaries of the Amazon, those in the Pantanal and the Rio Araguaia, but there are many others. Agencies can arrange fishing trips and there are local magazines on the subject.

Pura Pesca Tour operates in the Pantanal, Rio Araguaia and elsewhere, in São Paulo, T011-5355880/5435901, F55616447, or Cuiabá T065-6241660, F-6249966; **Eldorado Pantaneiro** operates tours in fishing boats with a/c apartments, bar and all equipment, T011-4340283, or Corumbá T067-2316369. **Fishing World**'s website, www.fishingworld.com.br, is not exclusively about Brazil and in Portuguese, but is informative and also includes diving.

Hang-gliding and paragliding

Hang gliding and paragliding are both covered by the **Associação Brasileira de Vôo Livre** (ABVL – Brazilian Hang-gliding Association) ⓘ *R Prefeito Mendes de Moraes s/n, São Conrado, Rio de Janeiro, T021-3322 0266, www.abvl.com.br*. There are state associations affiliated with ABVL and there are a number of operators offering tandem flights for those without experience. Launch sites (*rampas*) are growing in number. Among the best known is Pedra Bonita at Gávea in Rio de Janeiro, but there are others in the state. Popular *rampas* can also be found in São Paulo, Espírito Santo, Minas Gerais, Paraná, Santa Catarina, Rio Grande do Sul, Ceará, Mato Grosso do Sul and Brasília. A full list, and much else besides, can be found in the *Guia 4*

Wildlife spotting in Brazil

Mammals

Jaguar Fazenda San Francisco, Pantanal (page 651); Pousada Rio Vermelho, Pantanal (page 652); Fazenda Rio Negro, Mato Grosso do Sul (page 652); Pouso Alegre, Pantanal, Mato Grosso (page 665); Cristalino Jungle Lodge, Mato Grosso (page 666); Mamirauá Reserve, Amazonas (page 569).
Puma Parque Nacional das Emas, Goiás (page 620)
Ocelot Fazenda San Francisco, Mato Grosso do Sul (page 651); Fazenda Rio Negro, Mato Grosso do Sul (page 652).
Jaguarundi Parque Nacional das Emas, Goiás (page 620); Transpantaneira, Mato Grosso (page 662).
Maned wolf Parque Nacional Serra do Cipó, Minas Gerais (page 267); Parque Nacional das Emas, Goiás (page 620).
Bush dog Rio Sucuri, Bonito, Mato Grosso do Sul (page 651).
Giant otter Pousada Rio Vermelho, Pantanal, Mato Grosso do Sul (page 652); Fazenda Rio Negro, Mato Grosso do Sul (page 652).
Tapir Refugio Ecológico Caiman, Mato Grosso do Sul (page 651)
Uakari monkeys and spider monkeys Amazon Ecopark, Amazonas (page 574); Mamirauá Reserve, Amazonas (page 569)
Saki monkeys Cristalino Jungle Lodge, Mato Grosso (page 666).
Titi monkeys Fazenda Bela Vista, Pantanal, Mato Grosso do Sul (page 652).
Woolly spider monkey Parque Nacional Caparaó, Minas Gerais (page 274).

Reptiles

Black and spectacled caiman Rio Javari near Tabatginga, Rio Negro (page 569).
Pantanal caiman Anywhere near Miranda or the Estrada Parque, Mato Grosso do Sul (page 646) or the Transpantaneira, Mato Grosso (page 662).
Anaconda Transpantaneira, Pantanal, Mato Grosso (page 662); Estrada Parque, Pantanal, Mato Grosso do Sul (page 639).

Ventos Brasil, www.guia4ventos.com.br, which also contains information on launch sites in other South American countries.

Horse riding

Some of the best trails for horse riding are the routes that used to be taken by the mule trains that transported goods between the coast and the interior. A company like **Tropa Serrana**ⓣ *Belo Horizonte, T031-3344 8986, http://tropaserrana.zip.net*, is an excellent place to start because their tours, including overnight horse treks, explore many aspects of the Minas Gerais countryside that visitors do not normally see.

Mountain biking

Brazil is well-suited to cycling, both on and off-road. On main roads it is important to obey the general advice of being on the look out for motor vehicles as cyclists are very much second-class citizens. Also note that when cycling on the coast you may encounter strong winds which will hamper your progress. There are endless roads and tracks suitable for mountain biking, and there are many clubs in major cities which organize group rides, activities and competitions. **Serra da Canastra** in Minas Gerais is a popular area. **Tamanduá** in São Roque de Minas offer personalized tours and equipment hire. (See also Getting around, page 43.)

Mystical tourism

Brazil has a number of locations that have been claimed by seekers of hidden knowledge, or those interested in unusual sciences. Some of the best sites are to be found in the central west such as **Alto Paraíso de Goiás**, north of Brasília, and **Barra do Garças** in Mato Grosso. In these places 'new age' communities have formed dedicated to natural healing, alternative religions, or the search for UFOs and alien life-forms. In the south of Minas Gerais, a similar ambience is found at **São Tomé das Letras**, but there are many other examples across the country.

Rafting

Whitewater rafting started in Brazil in 1992. There are companies offering trips in São Paulo state (eg on the rios **Juquiá, Jaguarí, do Peixe, Paraibuna**), in Rio de Janeiro (also on the Paraibuna, at **Três Rios** in the Serra dos Órgãos), Paraná (**Rio Ribeira**), Santa Catarina (**Rio Itajaí**) and Rio Grande do Sul (**Três Coroas**). **Serra da Canastra** in Minas Gerais is also popular for the local sport of **Bóia-cross** (rafting with rubber tubes).

Scuba diving

The best diving in Brazil is the Atol das Rocas; only available through private charter through www.dehouche.com; very expensive but completely unspoilt, with visibility up to 40 m and with one of the highest levels of biodiversity in the tropical southern Atlantic. Fernando de Noronha has coral gardens, drop offs and wrecks which include a 50-m Brazilian navy destroyer with full armament. Visibility is up to 50 m, safe, current-free and drift diving. Amongst others, divers see at least two species of turtle, spinner dolphins, more than three species of shark, huge snapper and vast shoals of goatfish and jack. Arraial de Cabo is interesting because of the meeting of a southerly cold and northerly warm current and has the best marine life in southeast Brazil.

American/Brazilian Dive Club ⓘ *1645 SE 3 Road Court, Deerfield Bch, FL 33441, USA, T/F954-420 0009, can be accessed through www.cris.com/apavan*, which has links to dive sites in Brazil. There is a diving magazine called *Mergulho*. **Océan** is a dive shop and tour operator based in Rio de Janeiro state (Rio, Angra dos Reis, Ilha Grande, Arraial do Cabo) which has a **Diving in Brasil** website, www.ocean.com.br (Portuguese only).

In some areas in Brazil, diving includes underwater sport fishing; for details, contact a company which specializes in fishing.

Cave diving can be practised in many of the 200 underwater grottoes such as **Bonito, Mato Grosso do Sul, Lapa de São Jorge,** 280 km from Brasília, in Chapada Diamantina and **Vale do Ribeira** located between São Paulo and Paraná. **Gabriel Ganme,** Diving College, R Dr Mello Alves 700, São Paulo, T011-881 4723, and **Rafael de Nicola,** Divers University, are instructors in this specialized sport.

Spas and alternative therapies

Like many other places in the world Brazil has a growing spa and alternative therapy scene. And whilst there are few resort spas as wonderful as the best of Thailand or Mexico there are a number of freelance practitioners as good as any in the world. They often bring skills learnt from Brazilian indigenous traditions to their work and charge prices at a fraction of those in Europe or the USA. On top of this come a number of interesting Health and Well Being programmes, the foremost of which have won several international tourism awards.

Brazil's top 10 beaches

Ipanema and Leblon The most glorious stretches of urban sand in the world and the playground of Rio's beautiful people, page 99.
Mangue Seco Broad, tens of kilometres long, deserted and backed by impressive shifting dunes, page 408.
Ilhabela Myriad bays surrounded by rainforest covered hills and washed by an unfeasibly green sea, page 214.
Ilha de Santa Catarina, Santa Catarina; Brazil's favourite surf beaches in bays by the dozen, page 318.
Lençois Maranhenses The greatest concentration of perched dune lakes in the world along one of the continent's wildest stretches of coast, page 412.
Alter do Chão White sand, blue water, pink dolphins and a river so wide it looks like a sea, page 547.
São Gabriel da Cachoeira White sand, black tea coloured water set against rainforest studded with giant granite mountains. But bring insect repellent, page 572.
Pipa Relaxing little low key beach resort town surrounded by beautiful stretches of sand and backed by multi-coloured sandstone cliffs. Come outside the high season, page 475.
Tinharé, Bahia; archetypal Bounty island beaches of white sand, swaying coconuts and a gentle turquoise sea, page 387.
Fernando de Noronha Atlantic islands with the favourite beaches of Brazil's middle classes and the best snorkelling and diving in the country, page 452.

Resort spas

Casas Brancas, Alto do Humaitá 10, Búzios, Rio De Janeiro, T022-26231458. In one of the prettiest hotels in Búzios, with stunning views out over the ocean.
Costa Brasilis Resort, Av Beira Mar, 2000, Praia de Santo André, Santa Cruz Cabrália, T0800-7011413. A beach resort on a beautiful stretch of sand backed by coconut palms.
Kurotel Spa and Centre for Longevity, Nações Unidas, 533, Gramado, Rio Grande do Sul, T054-2862133. An old-fashioned, destination spa with dieting and medical consultation alongside various treatments.
Santa Clara, Boipeba, Bahia. Tiny little pousada with a great restaurant and a very special resident massage therapist, Norma Matos. Norma also works from Salvador and São Paulo and can be reached via T011-9154 7824, normalucia8@hotmail.com.
Txai, Ilhéus-Itacaré road, Km 48, Itacaré, Bahia T073-6346936. More a resort than a spa; in an idyllic beach location. Facilities and treatments include sauna, *ofuru* baths, *watsu* water therapy and various massages.

Heath and wellness programmes

Body and Soul Adventures, USA T086-63413180, UK T0800-9175506, www.bodysouladventures.com. Light activities preceded by yoga and followed by aromatherapy massages. The programmes take place on Ilha Grande and around Paraty in some of Brazil's most spellbinding scenery. Popular with celebs.
Lambent do Brasil – Lambent Life, T011-3040 1698, www.lambentdobrasil.com. Run by one of the world's leading experts on neuro-linguistic programming and life coaching. Spiritual disciplines include Adhyatma (Advaita yoga) to Vipassana Meditation. Stunning locations on the Atlantic Coast of Rio and São Paulo states, all of which provide real practical tools for change.

Individual therapists

See also Alto Paraíso in Goiás, page 620.
Silvia Luz, T011-32073983. One of Brazil's very best Shitasu and Ayurvedic practitioners. Very special treatments.

Surfing

This can be enjoyed in just about every coastal state. It does not require permits; all you need is a board and the right type of wave. Brazilians took up surfing in the 1930s and have been practising ever since. In this beach-obsessed country, with 8000 km of coastline, all shore and watersports are taken seriously. Surfers associations include: **Associação Brasileira de Surfe Profissional,** T048-223 1226; **Associação Brasileira de Bodyboard,** T021-259 0669. The best waves in the country are at Cacimba do Padre beach, Fernando de Noronha, the archipelago, 345 km out in the Atlantic. International surf championships are held here annually. Other good waves are found in the south, where long stretches of the Atlantic, often facing the swell head-on, give some excellent and varied breaks. Many Brazilian mainland surf spots are firmly on the international championship circuit, including Saquarema, in Rio de Janeiro state. One of the best states for surfing is Santa Catarina. For further information see the website www.brazilsurftravel.com and Footprint's *Surfing the World*.

Trekking

Trekking is very popular, especially in Rio de Janeiro, São Paulo, Minas Gerais, Paraná and Rio Grande do Sul. There are plenty of hiking shops and agencies which handle hiking tours. Trails are frequently graded according to difficulty; this is noticeably so in areas where *trilhas ecológicas* have been laid out in forests or other sites close to busy tourist areas. Many national parks and other protected areas provide good opportunities for trekking (eg the Chapada Diamantina in Bahia) and local information can easily be found to get you on the right track.

Health

The greatest disease risk in tropical Brazil is from the large number of insect disease carriers in the shape of mosquitoes and sandflies. The key **viral disease** is dengue fever, which is transmitted by a day biting mosquito. The disease is like a very nasty form of the flu with two to three days of illness, followed by a short period of recovery, then a second attack of illness. Westerners very rarely get the worst haemorrhagic form of the disease.

Bacterial diseases include tuberculosis (TB) and some causes of traveller's diarrhoea. The **parasitic diseases** are many, but the two key ones are malaria and South American trypanosomiasis (known as Chagas's Disease).

Risk areas for malaria are in states of Acre, Rondônia, Amapa, Amazonas, Roraima and Tocantins. Risk in parts of the states of Maranhão (western part), Mato Grosso (northern part), and Pará (except Belem city). There is also transmission in urban areas, including large cities such as Porto Velho, Boa Vista, Macapá, Manaus, Santarém and Marabá. The coastal states from the 'horn' south to the Uruguay border, including Iguaçu Falls, are not risk areas.

Before you go

Visit your GP/practice nurse or travel clinic at least six weeks before your departure for general advice on travel risks, malaria and recommended vaccinations. Your local pharmacist can also be a good source of readily accessible advice. Make sure you have travel insurance, get a dental check (especially if you are going to be away for more than a month), know your own blood group and if you suffer a long-term condition such as diabetes or epilepsy make sure someone knows or that you have a Medic Alert bracelet/necklace with this information on it. ▸▸ *For recommended vaccinations, see page 32.*

A-Z of health risks

Altitude sickness

Acute mountain sickness can strike from about 3000 m upwards and in general is more likely to affect those who ascend rapidly (for example by plane) and those who over-exert themselves. Acute mountain sickness takes a few hours or days to come on and presents with headache, lassitude, dizziness, loss of appetite, nausea and vomiting. Insomnia is common and often associated with a suffocating feeling when lying down in bed. You may notice that your breathing tends to wax and wane at night and your face is puffy in the mornings – this is all part of the syndrome. If the symptoms are mild, the treatment is rest and painkillers (preferably not aspirin-based) for the headaches. Should the symptoms be severe and prolonged it is best to descend to a lower altitude immediately and reascend, if necessary, slowly and in stages. The symptoms disappear very quickly - even after a few hundred metres of descent.

The best way of preventing acute mountain sickness is a relatively slow ascent. When trekking to high altitude, some time spent walking at medium altitude, getting fit and acclimatising is beneficial. When flying to places over 3000 m a few hours' rest and the avoidance of alcohol, cigarettes and heavy food will go a long way towards preventing acute mountain sickness.

Bites and stings

This is a very rare event indeed for travellers, but if you are unlucky (or careless) enough to be bitten by a venomous snake, spider, scorpion or sea creature, try to identify the culprit, without putting yourself in further danger (do not try to catch a live snake).

Snake bites in particular are very frightening, but in fact rarely poisonous – even venomous snakes bite without injecting venom. Victims should be taken to a hospital or a doctor without delay. It is not advised for travellers to carry snake bite antivenom as it can do more harm than good in inexperienced hands. Reassure and comfort the victim frequently. Immobilize the limb with a bandage or a splint and get the patient to lie still. Do not slash the bite area and try to suck out the poison. This also does more harm than good. You should apply a tourniquet in these circumstances, but only if you know how to. Do not attempt this if you are not experienced.

Certain tropical fish inject venom into bathers' feet when trodden on, which can be exceptionally painful. Wear plastic shoes if such creatures are reported. The pain can be relieved by immersing the foot in very hot water for as long as the pain persists.

Chagas's Disease

The disease occurs throughout Brazil and affects locals more than travellers. However, travellers can be exposed if sleeping in mud huts. The bug that carries the parasite bites and defecates on an exposed part of skin. You may notice nothing at all or a local swelling, with fever, tiredness and enlargement of lymph glands, spleen and liver. The seriousness of the infection is caused by the long-term effects which include gross enlargement of the heart and/or guts. Early treatment is required with toxic drugs. To prevent the disease, sleep under a permethrin treated bed net and use insect repellent.

Dengue fever

This is a viral disease spread by mosquitoes that tend to bite during the day. The symptoms are fever and often intense joint pains, also some people develop a rash. Symptoms last about a week but it can take a few weeks to recover fully. Dengue can be difficult to distinguish from malaria as both diseases tend to occur in the same countries. There are no effective vaccines or antiviral drugs though, fortunately, travellers rarely develop the more severe forms of the disease (these can prove fatal). Rest, plenty of fluids and paracetamol (not aspirin) is the recommended treatment

Diarrhoea and intestinal upset

Diarrhoea can refer either to loose stools or an increased frequency of bowel movement, both of which can be a nuisance. Symptoms should be relatively short-lived but if they persist beyond two weeks specialist medical attention should be sought. Also seek medical help if there is blood in the stools and/or fever.

Adults can use an antidiarrhoeal medication such as loperamide to control the symptoms but only for up to 24 hours. In addition keep well hydrated by drinking plenty of fluids and eat bland foods. Oral rehydration sachets taken after each loose stool are a useful way to keep well hydrated. These should always be used when treating children and the elderly.

Bacterial traveller's diarrhoea is the most common form. Ciproxin (Ciprofloxacin) is a useful antibiotic and can be obtained by private prescription in the UK. You need to take one 500 mg tablet when the diarrhoea starts. If there are so signs of improvement after 24 hours the diarrhoea is likely to be viral and not bacterial. If it is due to other organisms such as those causing giardia or amoebic dysentery, different antibiotics will be required.

The standard advice to prevent problems is to be careful with water and ice for drinking. Ask yourself where the water came from. If you have any doubts then boil it or filter and treat it. There are many filter/treatment devices now available on the market. Food can also transmit disease. Be wary of salads (what were they washed in, who handled them), re-heated foods or food that has been left out in the sun having been cooked earlier in the day. There is a simple adage that says wash it, peel it, boil it or forget it. Also be wary of unpasteurised dairy products as these can transmit a range of diseases.

Hepatitis

Hepatitis means inflammation of the liver. Viral causes of the disease can be acquired anywhere in the world. The most obvious symptom is a yellowing of your skin or the whites of your eyes. However, prior to this all that you may notice is itching and tiredness. Pre-travel hepatitis A vaccine is the best bet. Hepatitis B (for which there is a vaccine) is spread through blood and unprotected sexual intercourse, both of which can be avoided.

Leishmaniasis

A skin form of this disease occurs in Brazil. If infected, you may notice a raised lump, which leads to a purplish discolouration on white skin and a possible ulcer. The parasite is transmitted by the bite of a sandfly. Sandflies do not fly far and the greatest risk is at ground levels, if you can avoid sleeping on the jungle floor do so. Several weeks treatment is required under specialist supervision. The drugs themselves are toxic but if not taken in sufficient amounts recurrence of the disease is more likely. To prevent the disease, sleep above ground, under a permethrin treated net, use insect repellent and get a specialist opinion on any unusual skin lesions soon after return.

Malaria

Malaria can cause death within 24 hours and can start as something just resembling an attack of flu. You may feel tired, lethargic, headachy, feverish; or more seriously, develop fits, followed by coma and then death. Have a low index of suspicion because it is very easy to write off vague symptoms, which may actually be malaria. If you have a temperature, visit a doctor as soon as you can and ask for a malaria test. On your return home, if you suffer any of these symptoms, have a test as soon as possible. Even if a previous test proved negative, this could save your life.

Treatment is with drugs and may be oral or into a vein depending on the seriousness of the infection. Remember ABCD: Awareness (of whether the disease is present in the area you are travelling in), Bite avoidance, Chemoprohylaxis, Diagnosis.

To prevent mosquito bites wear clothes that cover arms and legs, use effective insect repellents in areas with known risks of insect-spread disease and use a mosquito net treated with an insecticide. Repellents containing 30-50% DEET (Di-ethyltoluamide) are recommended when visiting malaria endemic areas; lemon eucalyptus (Mosiguard) is a reasonable alternative. The key advice is to guard against contracting malaria by taking the correct anti-malarials and finishing the recommended course. If you are popular target for insect bites or develop lumps quite soon after being bitten use antihistamine tablets and apply a cream such as hydrocortisone.

Remember that it is risky to buy medicine, and in particular anti-malarials, in some developing countries. These may be sub-standard or part of a trade in counterfeit drugs.

Rabies

Rabies is endemic throughout certain parts of the world so be aware of the dangers of the bite from any animal. Rabies vaccination before travel can be considered but if bitten always seek urgent medical attention – whether or not you have been previously vaccinated – after first cleaning the wound and treating with an iodine base disinfectant or alcohol.

Sun

Take good heed of advice regarding protecting yourself against the sun. Overexposure can lead to sunburn and, in the longer term, skin cancers and premature skin aging. The best advice is simply to avoid exposure to the sun by covering exposed skin, wearing a hat and staying out of the sun if possible, particularly between late morning and early afternoon. Apply a high factor sunscreen (greater than SPF15) and also make sure it screens against UVB. A further danger in tropical climates is heat exhaustion

or more seriously heatstroke. This can be avoided by good hydration, which means drinking water past the point of simply quenching thirst. Also when first exposed to tropical heat take time to acclimatise by avoiding strenuous activity in the middle of the day. If you cannot avoid heavy exercise it is also a good idea to increase salt intake.

Typhoid fever

This a gut infection which can spread to the blood stream. You get it from someone else's muck getting into your mouth. A classic example would be the waiter who fails to wash his hands and then serves you a salad. The fever is an obvious feature, occasionally there is a mild red rash on the stomach and often you have a headache. Constipation or diarrhoea can occur. Gut pain and hearing problems may also feature. Antibiotics are required and you are probably best managed in hospital. The vaccine is very effective and is best boosted every three years. Watch what you eat and the hygiene of the place or those serving your food.

Underwater health

If you plan to dive make sure that you are fit do so. The British Sub-Aqua Club (BSAC), Telford's Quay, South Pier Road, Ellesmere Port, Cheshire CH65 4FL, UK, T01513-506200, F506215, www.bsac.com, can put you in touch with doctors who will carry out medical examinations. Check that any dive company you use are reputable and have appropriate certification from BSAC or Professional Association of Diving Instructors (PADI), Unit 7, St Philips Central, Albert Rd, St Philips, Bristol, BS2 OTD, T0117-3007234, www.padi.com.

Water

There are a number of ways of purifying water. Dirty water should first be strained through a filter bag and then boiled or treated. Bring water to a rolling boil for several minutes. There are sterilising methods that can be used and products generally contain chlorine (eg Puritabs) or iodine (eg Pota Aqua) compounds. There are a number of water sterilisers now on the market available in personal and expedition size. Make sure you take the spare parts or spare chemicals with you and do not believe everything the manufacturers say.

Other diseases and risks

There are a range of other insect borne diseases that are quite rare in travellers, but worth finding out about if going to particular destinations. Examples are sleeping sickness, river blindness and leishmaniasis. Fresh water can also be a source of diseases such as bilharzia and leptospirosis and it is worth investigating if these are a danger before bathing in lakes and streams. Also take heed of advice regarding protecting yourself against the sun (see above) and remember that unprotected sex always carries a risk and extra care is required when visiting some parts of the world.

Further information

Websites

Blood Care Foundation (UK), www.bloodcare.org.uk. A charity that will dispatch certified non-infected blood of the right type to the hospital/clinic where you are being treated.
British Travel Health Association (UK), www.btha.org. The official website of an organization of travel health professionals.
Communicable Disease Control (USA), www.cdc.gov. A US government site with excellent advice on travel health, has useful disease maps and details of disease outbreaks.
Department of Health Travel Advice, www.doh.gov.uk/traveladvice. An excellent site, also available as a free booklet, the *T6*, from UK post offices. It lists the vaccine advice requirements for each country.
Foreign and Commonwealth Office (FCO) (UK), www.fco.gov.uk. Useful reference.
Fit for Travel, www.fitfortravel.scot.nhs.uk This site from Scotland provides a quick A-Z of vaccine and travel health advice requirements.
Medic Alert (UK), www.medicalalert.co.uk The foundation that produces bracelets and necklaces for those with medical problems.
National Travel Health Network and Centre (NaTHNaC) www.nathnac.org.
NetDoctor (UK), www.netdoctor.co.uk. A general health advice site with a useful section on travel and an 'ask the expert' interactive chat forum.
Public Health Laboratory Service (UK), www.phls.org.uk. Advice on malaria and useful information for those who are pregnant, suffering from epilepsy or planning to travel with children.
Travel Screening Services (UK), www.travelscreening.co.uk. A private clinic that gives travel health advice, email and SMS text vaccine reminders and screens returned travellers for tropical diseases.
Tropical Medicine Bureau, www.tmb.ie. Good collection of general travel health information and disease risks.
World Health Organisation (WHO), www.who.int. Links to the WHO *Yellow Book* on travel advice. This lists the diseases in different regions of the world and makes clear which countries have Yellow Fever Vaccination certificate requirements.

Books and leaflets

Travellers' Health (3rd Ed Oxford. Oxford University Press, 2002), Dawood R, editor.
Expedition Medicine (The Royal Geographic Society) Editors David Warrell and Sarah Anderson ISBN 1 86197 040-4.
The Travellers Good Health Guide, Dr Ted Lankester (ISBN 0-85969-827-0).
Expedition Medicine (The Royal Geographic Society), Editors David Warrell and Sarah Anderson (ISBN 1 86197 040-4).
International Travel and Health, World Health Organisation Geneva (ISBN 92 4 158026 7).
The World's Most Dangerous Places, Robert Young Pelton, Coskun Aral and Wink Dulles (ISBN 1-566952-140-9).
The Travellers Guide to Health (T6) can be obtained by calling the Health Literature Line on T0800-555 777.
Advice for travellers on avoiding the risks of HIV and AIDS is available from Department of Health, PO Box 777, London SE1 6XH.
The Blood Care Foundation, order from PO Box 7, Sevenoaks, Kent TN13 2SZ, UK, T01732-742 427.

Keeping in touch

Communications

Internet

Brazil is said to be seventh in the world in terms of internet use. Public internet access is available in all towns and cities. There is usually an hourly charge of around US$3, but you can almost always use partial hours at a reduced rate. More and more hotels offer an internet service to their guests, while some government programmes even offer free use (notably in Manaus and Cuiaba). In some more remote locations, such as Lençois in Bahia, connections are so slow as to be almost pointless. For a regularly updated list of locations around the world, check www.netcafeguide.com. Internet cafés are listed in the Directory of individual towns.

Post

To send a **standard letter** or **postcard** to the USA costs US$0.75, to Europe US$0.85, to Australia or South Africa US$1. Air mail should take about seven days to or from Britain or the US. Franked and registered (insured) letters are normally secure, but check that the amount franked is what you have paid, or the item will not arrive. Aerogrammes are most reliable. To avoid queues and obtain higher denomination stamps go to the stamp desk at the main post office.

The post office sells cardboard boxes for sending **packages** internally and abroad. They must be submitted open; string and official tape are provided. You pay by the kilo and fill in a list of contents. Courier services such as **DHL**, **Federal Express** and **UPS** (recommended) are useful, but they may not necessarily operate under those names.

Postes Restantes usually only hold letters for 30 days. Identification is required and it's a good idea to write your name on a piece of paper to help the attendant find your letters. Charge is usually minimal but often involves queuing at another counter to buy stamps which are attached to your letter and franked before it is given to you. Poste Restante for Amex customers is dealt with by the Amex agents in most large towns.

Telephone

Important changes All ordinary phone numbers in Brazil are changing from seven-to eight-figure numbers. Enquire locally for the new numbers as in many cases whole numbers will change while others will simply add an extra digit. Where confirmed, eight-digit numbers have been included in the text. A trunk dialling system (DDD) links all parts of Brazil. Recent privatization of the telephone system has led to increased competition. The consumer must now choose a telephone company for all calls by inserting a two-digit code between the zero and the area code. Phone numbers are now printed in this way: 0XX21 (0 for a national call, XX for the code of the phone company chosen, 21 for Rio de Janeiro, for example), followed by the seven- or eight-digit number of the subscriber.

Nationwide and international telephone operators and their codes are: **Embratel**, 21 (nationwide); **Telefônica**, 15 (state of São Paulo); **Telemar**, 31 (Alagoas, Amazonas, Amapá, Bahia, Ceará, Espírito Santo, Maranhão, most of Minas Gerais, Pará, Paraíba, Pernambuco, Piauí, Rio de Janeiro, Rio Grande do Norte, Roraima, Sergipe); **Tele Centro-Sul**, 14 (Acre, Goiás, Mato Grosso, Mato Grosso do Sul, Paraná, Rondônia, Santa Catarina, Tocantins and the cities of Brasília and Pelotas); **CTBC-Telecom**, 12 (some parts of Minas Gerais, Goiás, Mato Grosso do Sul and São Paulo state); **Intelig**, 23.

National calls Telephone boxes are easy to come by in towns and cities. Major cities have telephone kiosks, for both local and international calls (with an international calling card), in the shape of large orange shells, for which *fichas* can be bought from bars, cafés and newsvendors; in Rio they are known as *orelhões* (big ears). Local phone calls and telegrams are quite cheap.

Telephone yellow pages in most cities (but not Rio) contain good street maps which, together with the Quatro Rodas maps, are a great help for getting around.

Phone cards are available from telephone offices, newsstands, post offices and some chemists. They cost US$1.50 for 30 units and up to US$3 for 90 units. Public boxes for intercity calls are blue. To use the telephone office, tell the operator which city or country you wish to call, go to the booth whose number you are given; make your call and you will be billed on exit. Not all offices accept credit cards. Collect calls within Brazil can be made from any telephone – dial 9, followed by the number, and announce your name and city. Local calls from a private phone are normally free.

For area codes see under individual towns, or look in the telephone directory.

If you need to find a telephone number, you can dial 102 in any city (*auxílio à lista*) and the **operator** will connect you to a pre-recorded voice which will give the number. To find the number in a different city, dial the DDD code, followed by 121 (so, if you are in Salvador and want to know a Rio number, dial 021 121). If your Portuguese is not up to deciphering spoken numbers, ask a hotel receptionist, for example, to assist you.

International calls Make sure you buy at least one 90-unit card or pay at the desk after making your call from a booth. The rate to Europe is US$1-2 per minute, to USA around US$1 depending on which operator you use. Between 2000 and 0600, and all day Sunday, rates are normally reduced by about a fifth, although again this depends on which operator you use. **Embratel** offer a good service, covering most of the world, with very helpful English-speaking operators and international calls at less than a dollar a minute. Embratel cards are available from newsagents in large towns and cities, and have English instructions.

Brazil is linked to North America, Japan and most of Europe by trunk dialling (DDI). Codes are listed in the telephone directories. **Home Country Direct** is available from hotels, private phones or blue public phones to the following countries (prefix all numbers with 00080); Argentina 54, Australia 61, Belgium 03211, Bolivia 13, Canada 14, Chile 56 (**Entel**), 36 (**Chile Sat**), 37 (**CTC Mundo**), Colombia 57, Costa Rica 50, Denmark 45, France 33, Germany 49, Holland 31, Hong Kong 85212, Israel 97, Italy 39, Japan 81 (**KDD**), 83 (**ITJ**), 89 (**Super Japan**), Norway 47, Paraguay 18, Peru 51, Portugal 35, Singapore 65, Spain 34, Sweden 46, Switzerland 04112, UK 44 (**BT Direct**), USA 10 (**AT&T**), 12 (**MCI**), 16 (**Sprint**), 11 (**Worldcom**), Uruguay 59, Venezuela 58. For collect calls (*a cobrar*) from phone boxes, dial 107 and ask for the *telefonista internacional*. No collect calls are available to New Zealand.

Mobile phones Mobiles have made a big impact in Brazil owing to past difficulties in getting fixed lines, especially outside the main towns. When using a cellular telephone you do not drop the zero from the area code as you now have to when dialling from a fixed line. In Rio de Janeiro and São Paulo, mobile phones, or even a line for your own phone, can be hired. Pay-as-you-go phones are now available, which is another option for travellers. The systems in Brazil are mainly AMPS analog or TDMA digital.

Fax services These operate in main post offices in major cities, at telephone offices, or from private lines. Rates are around US$1.50 per page within Brazil, US$5 to Europe and the USA. To receive a fax costs US$1.40.

Media

Newspapers and magazines

There is no national newspaper although the news magazines (see below) are distributed nationally. The main papers in **Rio de Janeiro** are *Jornal do Brasil* (www.jb.com.br), *O Globo* (www.oglobo.com.br), *O Dia* (www.uol.com.br/odia) and *Jornal do Commércio* (www.jornaldocommercio.com.br). In **São Paulo** Morning: *O Estado de São Paulo* (www.estado.com.br), *Folha de São Paulo* (www.uol.com.br/fsp), *Gazeta Mercantil* (www.gazeta.com.br/) and *Diário de São Paulo*. Evening: *Jornal da Tarde*, *A Gazeta*, *Diário da Noite* and *Ultima Hora*. Around the country, the major cities have their own local press. Of particular note are *A Tarde* in **Salvador** (www.atarde.com.br), the *Diário de Pernambuco* in **Recife** (www.dpnet.com.br) and the *Estado de Minas* in **Belo Horizonte** (www.estaminas.com.br).

Foreign-language newspapers include *The Brazilian Post* and *Sunday News* in English, and *Deutsche Zeitung* in German. In Europe, the *Euro-Brasil Press* is available in most capitals; it prints Brazilian and some international news in Portuguese. London office: 23 Kings Exchange, Tileyard Rd, London N7 9AH, T020-7700 4033, F7700 3540, eurobrasilpress@compuserve.com

There are a number of good, informative weekly news magazines which are widely read: *Veja* (www.uol.com.br/veja), *Istoé* (www.uol.com.br/istoe), *Epoca* and *Exame*.

Television

Nationwide TV channels are *Globo*, based in Rio de Janeiro, and *SBT*, *Record*, *Bandeirantes*, based in São Paulo. *Rede Amazônica* operates in the northern region. *TVE* is an educational channel showing documentaries and original-language films. Programming revolves around light entertainment, soap operas, foreign films dubbed in Portuguese and football.

Radio

South America has more local and community radio stations than practically anywhere else in the world; a shortwave (world band) radio offers a practical means to brush up on the language, sample popular culture and absorb some of the varied regional music. International broadcasters such as the *BBC World Service*, the *Voice of America* and Boston-based *Monitor Radio International* (operated by **Christian Science** Monitor) keep the traveller abreast of news and events, in English, Portuguese and Spanish.

There are English-language radio broadcasts daily at 15290 kHz, 19 m Short Wave (Rádio Bras, Caixa Postal 04/0340, DF-70 323 Brasília).

Compact or miniature portables are recommended, with digital tuning and a full range of shortwave bands, as well as FM, long and medium wave. Detailed advice on radio models and wavelengths can be found in the annual publication, *Passport to World Band Radio* (Box 300, Penn's Park, PA 18943, USA), £14.99. Details of local stations is listed in *World TV and Radio Handbook* (WTRH), PO Box 9027, 1006 AA Amsterdam, The Netherlands, £19.99. Both of these, free wavelength guides and selected radio sets are available from the *BBC World Service Bookshop*, Bush House Arcade, Bush House, Strand, London WC2B 4PH, UK, T020-75572576.

Rio de Janeiro

Footprint features

Introduction

Even those who know nothing else of Brazil will have heard of Rio, its Mardi Gras carnival and its spectacular beach and mountain scenery. What many do not realize is that Rio de Janeiro is a state as well as a city, and that this state hides beaches, forests and mountains just as beautiful as those in its capital. The southern coast, or Costa Verde, is fringed with emerald-green coves and bays that rise steeply to rainforest-covered hills pocked with national parks. Mountains swathed in coffee plantations lie behind Rio itself, with hill retreats once favoured by the imperial family dotted throughout their valleys and remnants of one of the world's most biodiverse forests covering parts of their slopes. And to the northeast of the city lies a string of surf beaches and little resorts, the most celebrated of which is Búzios, a fishing village put on the map by Brigitte Bardot in the late 1960s, which has now grown to become a chic little retreat for the state's middle classes.

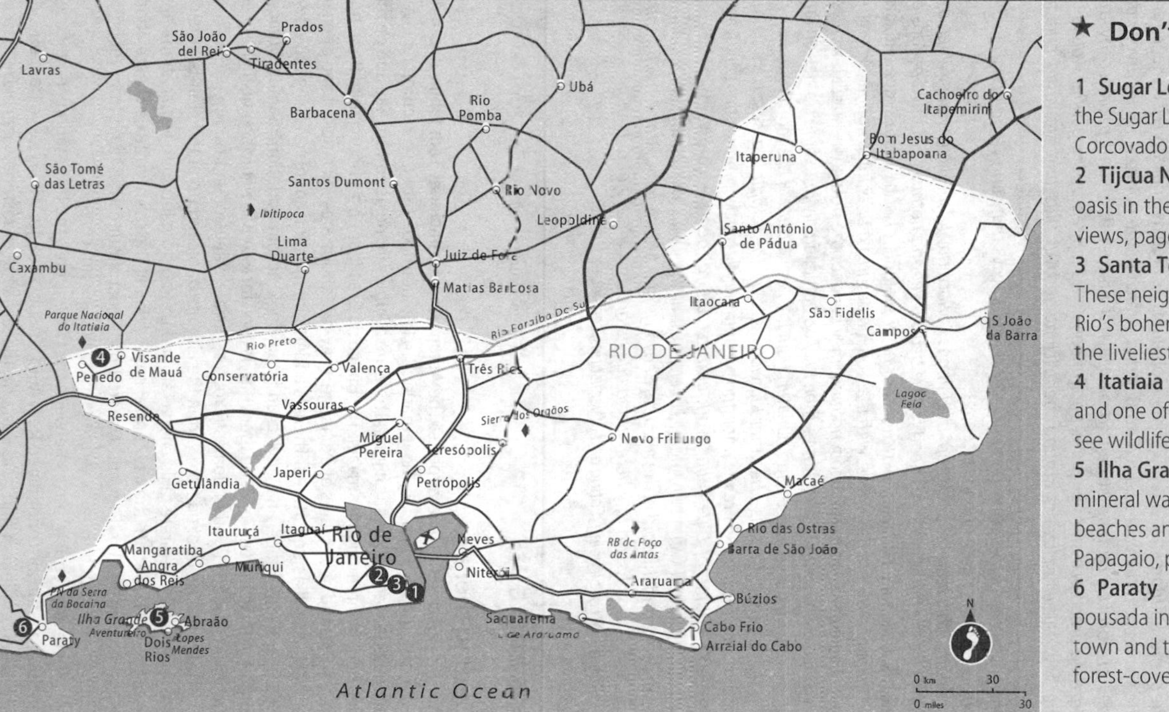

★ Don't miss...

1 Sugar Loaf and Corcovado Go up the Sugar Loaf in the early morning and Corcovado for sunset, pages 95 and 96.

2 Tijcua National Park A green oasis in the metropolis with stunning views, page 103.

3 Santa Teresa and Lapa at night These neighbouring boroughs form Rio's bohemian heart and are home to the liveliest samba clubs, page 118.

4 Itatiaia Brazil's oldest national park and one of the best places to hike and see wildlife in the southeast, page 159.

5 Ilha Grande Hike the trails past mineral waterfalls to pristine tropical beaches and climb the Pico do Papagaio, page 164.

6 Paraty Stay in a luxury house or pousada in the state's prettiest colonial town and take a boat trip round myriad forest-covered islands, page 165.

Rio de Janeiro city

➔ *Phone code: 021. Colour map 4, C3. Population: 8 million.*

According to Cariocas – the people of Rio de Janeiro – God made the world in six days and then spent the seventh lying on the beach in Ipanema. For in a city as beautiful as this, they say, only the philistine or the ungrateful would do anything else. Indeed, photographs cannot prepare you for Rio. There is far more to the city than Corcovado capped with Christ or the Sugar Loaf. These are overtures to the grand symphony of the scene. Rainforest-covered boulder mountains as high as Snowdon rise sheer from the sea around the vast Guanabara Bay and stretch to the horizon. Their curves and jags are broken by long sweeping beaches of powder-fine sand pounded by the dazzling green ocean, or by perfect half-moon coves lapped by the gentler waters of the bay. The city clusters around them, climbing over hills and crowding behind beaches and lakes. Its neighbourhoods are connected by tunnels bored through the ancient rock or across winding double-decker highways that cling vertiginously to the cliffs above the fierce Atlantic Ocean.

Against this magical backdrop, the famous Carioca day leisurely unwinds. When the sun is up the middle classes head for the beach, wearing nothing but tiny Speedos or bikinis. Here they surf, play beach volleyball or football, or soak up the rays between occasional dips into the waves, with the working day just a brief interruption. When the sun is down, still wearing almost nothing, they head for the botecos *– street bars – for an ice-cold draught beer or* chope. *Then they go home, finally put some clothes on and prepare to go out to* bater-papo *(chatter) until the early hours of the morning.*

From high on the hills, the other Rio watches over the middle classes. Here lie the favelas – slum cities where the poor and predominantly black communities live. These are Rio's engine of blue-collar work and its cultural heart – carnival, samba and Brazilian football were born here. Favelas are at the heart of the country's cinema resurgence and the soul of the music of Seu Jorge and Afro reggae. Brazil's joyful spirit can be felt mostly strongly here, alongside its greatest misery and its most shocking violence. ▸▸ *For Sleeping, Eating and other listings, see pages 106-136.*

Ins and outs

Getting there

Air Rio is served by two airports. The **Aeroporto Internacional Tom Jobim** (formerly Galaeão), on the Ilha do Governador, 15 km north of the city centre, receives international and domestic flights. There are *câmbios* in the departure hall and on the first floor of international arrivals. The **Banco do Brasil**, open 24 hours, third floor, has Visa ATMs and better rates of exchange. Duty-free shops are well stocked and open to arrivals as well as departures. There is a **Riotur** information counter, T021-3398 4073, which provides maps and advice and can book accommodation. **Santos Dumont airport**, right in the city on Guanabara Bay, is used for Rio–São Paulo shuttle flights (see Transport, page 131), other domestic routes, private planes or air taxis.

Taxis can be booked from within the airports or picked up at the stands outside the terminals. Fixed-rate taxis charge around US$20 from Jobim to Copacabana and Ipanema and US$15 to the city centre; buy a ticket at the counter. Taxis charge about half this from Santos Dumont. Metered taxis cost around US$12.50 from Jobim to Copacabana, but beware of pirate taxis, which are unlicensed.

There are frequent buses between the two airports, the bus station and the city; the best are the air-conditioned **Real Auto**, T0800-240850, which leave from outside arrivals at terminals 1 and 2, to Barra da Tijuca via the *rodoviária*, city centre, Santos

Dumont, Gloria, Flamengo, Botafogo, Copacabana, Ipanema and Gávea, every 30 minutes between 0530 and 2330 and until 2100 for Santos Dumont airport. Fares are collected during the journey; anywhere in Rio costs US$3.50. The bus can be flagged down along Leblon/Ipanema and Copacabana beaches and stops at all the large hotels on the seafront. Town buses M94 and M95, Bancários/Castelo, take a circular route passing through the centre and the interstate bus station; they leave from the second floor of Jobim airport. For more information visit www.infraero.gov.br and click on 'aeroportos'. » *See also Transport, page 131.*

Bus International and interstate buses arrive at the **Rodoviária Novo Rio** ⓘ *Av Rodrigues Alves, corner with Av Francisco Bicalho, just past the docks in the city centre, T021-2291 5151*. The *rodoviária* has a **Riotur** information centre, which can help with orientation and accommodation. Left luggage costs US$3. There are *câmbios* for cash only. It is best to take a taxi from here to your hotel or to the nearest metro station (Estácio). The metro runs south only as far as Copacabana (Siqueira Campos station). Take bus Metrô-Gávea or a taxi from Siqueira Campos for Ipanema and Leblon. Taxis can be booked at the booth on the ground floor of the *rodoviária* and bus 406A (Ônibus) runs from the *rodoviária* to Estácio metro.

The local bus terminal is just outside the *rodoviária*: turn right as you leave and run the gauntlet of taxi drivers. The bus station attracts thieves, so exercise caution. The air-conditioned **Real** bus (opposite the exit) goes along the beach to São Conrado and will secure luggage. If you need a taxi collect a ticket, which ensures against over-charging, from the office inside the entrance (to Flamengo US$6).

Getting around

Because the city is a series of separate districts connected by urban highways and tunnels heavy with traffic, you will need to take public transport or taxis to get around. An underground railway, the **Metrô** ⓘ *www.metrorio.com.br, Mon-Sat 0500-2400, Sun and holidays 0700-2300 and 24 hrs during Carnaval*, runs from the outer suburbs of the Zona Norte (not of tourist interest), through the city centre, Gloria, Flamengo, Botafogo and as far south as Copacabana. The Metrô Gávea bus connects

Rio de Janeiro orientation

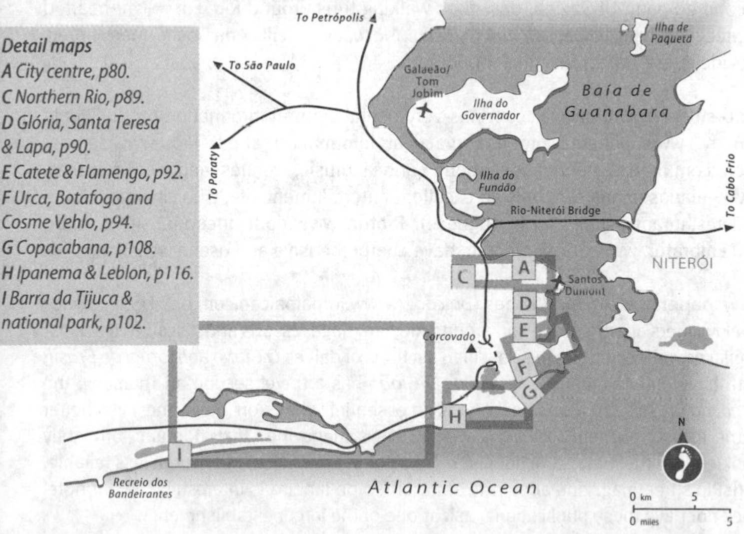

Detail maps
A City centre, p80.
C Northern Rio, p89.
D Glória, Santa Teresa & Lapa, p90.
E Catete & Flamengo, p92.
F Urca, Botafogo and Cosme Vehlo, p94.
G Copacabana, p108.
H Ipanema & Leblon, p116.
I Barra da Tijuca & national park, p102.

at the last station – Siquiera Campos – for Ipanema and Leblon. **Buses** run to all parts, but should be treated with caution at night, when taxis are a better bet. Buses are easy to catch: they are usually marked with the destination and any going south of the centre will call at Copacabana and generally Ipanema/Leblon. **Minivans** run from Avenida Rio Branco in the centre as far south as Barra da Tijuca and have the destination written on the window. **Taxis** should always be booked through a hostel or hotel, or caught from a designated taxi rank – the name of the rank will be inscribed on the side of the cab. Avoid freelance cabs hailed in the street or those without a taxi rank inscription. Santa Teresa is reached by **tram** which leaves from the Largo da Carioca near the Metrô station and the cathedral, passing over the Lapa viaduct and running along all the main streets in Santa Teresa and eventually reaching either Dois Irmãos or Paula Mattos at the far end of Santa Teresa.

Maps The *Guia Quatro Rodas – Rio* map book is the only completely comprehensive street map and is essential if you are driving. It can be bought at most news-stands.

Tourist information

Riotur ⓘ *R da Assembléia 10, 9th floor, Centro, T021-2217 7575, www.riode janeiro-turismo.com.br and www.rio.rj.gov.br/riotur*, is the city's government tourist office. They also have an office in Copacabana ⓘ *Av Princesa Isabel 183, T021-2541 7522, Mon-Fri 0900-1800*. The helpful staff speak English, French and German and can provide good city maps and a very useful free brochure. There are further information stands at the international airport (0600-2400), and at the Novo Rio bus station (0800-2000). The private sector **Rio Convention and Visitors Bureau** ⓘ *R Visconde de Pirajá 547, suite 610, Ipanema, T021-2259 6165, www.rioconventionbureau.com.br*, also offer information and assistance in English. **Alô Rio** ⓘ *T0800-707 1808, T021- 2542 8080, in English T021-2242 8000, daily 0900-1800*, is a telephone information service. **Turis Rio** ⓘ *R da Ajuda 5, 8th floor, T021-2215 0011, www.turisrio.rj.gov.br*, is very helpful and has information on Rio de Janeiro state. **Embratur** ⓘ *R Uruguaiana 174, 8th floor, Centro, T021-2509 6017, www.embratur.gov.br*, has information on the whole country. **Touring Clube do Brasil** ⓘ *Pres Antônio Carlos 130 and Av Brasil 4294 (out of town)*, publishes maps that are sold at news-stands and in some hotels.

Guidebooks *Trilhas do Rio*, by Pedro da Cunha e Meneses (Editora Salamandra, second edition), US$22.50, describes walking trips around Rio. For a light-hearted approach to living in Rio, see *How to be a Carioca*, by Priscilla Ann Goslin. Many hotels provide guests with a free tourist booklet.

Web sites www.brazilmax.com has very useful cultural information on the whole country. www.ipanema.com has practical information about Rio. www.samba-choro.com.br has information about carioca music, venues and new releases. www.guiadasemana.com.br is an excellent entertainment site, with cinema, theatre and restaurant listings (in Portuguese). **Riotur**, www.riodejaneiro-turismo.com.br, and **Embratur**, www.braziltour.com, have comprehensive and useful websites.

Newspapers and magazines *Balcão*, www.jornalbalcao.com.br, US$2, twice weekly, offers apartments in and around Rio, language lessons and discounted tickets; similar advertisements in the classified sections of dailies *O Globo* and *Jornal do Brasil*; both have entertainments pages too; *O Globo* has a travel section on Thursday; the *Jornal do Brasil's Programa* on Friday is an essential 'what's-on' magazine. Even better is the Rio supplement to *Veja*, a weekly news magazine. *They* (**Riotur**'s fortnightly booklet) lists the main attractions; *Rio This Month* is free from hotels, but less reliable. **TurisRio**'s free magazine about the state of Rio de Janeiro is interesting; if your hotel does not have these publications, ask at one of the larger establishments.

Climate

Rio has one of the healthiest climates in the tropics. Trade winds cool the air. June, July and August are the coolest months, with temperatures ranging from 22°C (18° in a cold spell) to 32°C on a sunny day at noon. December to March is hotter, from 32°C to 42°C. Humidity is high. October to March is the rainy season and the annual rainfall is about 1120 mm. Carnaval is a movable feast, running for five riotous days from the Friday afternoon before Shrove Tuesday to the morning hangover of Ash Wednesday.

Background

The coast of Rio de Janeiro was first settled about 5000 years ago. When the Europeans arrived, the indigenous inhabitants belonged to the Tupi or Tupi-Guarani, Puri, Botocudos and Maxacali linguistic groups. Tragically, no indigenous people in this region survived the European incursions.

The Portuguese navigator, Gonçalo Coelho, landed at what is now Rio de Janeiro on 1 January 1502. Thinking that the Baía de Guanabara (the name the local people used) was the mouth of a great river, they called the place the January River. But the bay wasn't settled until 1555 when the French, under the Huguenot Admiral Nicholas Durand de Villegagnon, occupied Lage Island. They later transferred to Seregipe Island (now Villegagnon), where they built the fort of Coligny. The fort has been demolished to make way for the Escola Naval (naval college), and the island itself, since the narrow channel was filled up, has become a part of the mainland. Villegagnon set up a colony as the starting point for what he called Antarctic France.

In 1559-1560, Mem de Sá, the third governor of Brazil, mounted an expedition from Salvador to attack the French, who were supported by Tamoio Indians. The Portuguese succeeded in capturing the French fort and putting an end to Antarctic France, but did not colonize the area until 1567 when they transferred their settlement to the Morro de São Januário. This is generally considered the date of the founding of the city of São Sebastião do Rio de Janeiro, so called in honour of the Portuguese prince who would soon assume the throne.

Though constantly attacked by local indigenous groups, the new city grew rapidly and when King Sebastião divided Brazil into two provinces, Rio was chosen as capital of the southern captaincies. Salvador became sole capital again in 1576, but Rio again became the southern capital in 1608 and the seat of a bishopric. There was a further French incursion in 1710-1711 as a result of the tension between France and Portugal during the war of Spanish Succession, and because of the flow of gold out of Minas Gerais through Rio. Rio de Janeiro was by now becoming the leading city in Brazil. Not only was it the port out of which gold was shipped, but it was also the focus of the export/import trade of the surrounding agricultural lands. On 27 January 1763, it became the seat of the Viceroy. After Independence, in 1834, it was declared capital of the empire and remained so for 125 years.

The shaping of a city

When the Portuguese royal family fled to Brazil in 1808, the ideas that were brought over from Europe started a major transformation of the city. True, works to beautify and clean up the place had been undertaken when the city acquired viceregal status, but the remodelling which occurred in the early 19th century was on a different scale (see Fine art and architecture on pages 701 and 704). The city also expanded, growing north into São Cristóvão and Tijuca and south through Glória, Catete, Flamengo and Botafogo. The prosperous coffee barons and business class built their mansions and the imperial court was the centre of the nation's attention. The decline of the coffee trade in Rio de Janeiro state and the proclamation of the Republic did not affect the city's dominance as political, economic and cultural heart of Brazil.

Growth continued into the 20th century and one of the most significant acts was the construction of a monumental new boulevard through the middle of the commercial district. The 33-m-wide Avenida Central, later renamed Avenida Rio Branco, was driven through the old city's narrow streets in 1904-1905 as the principal means of access in Rio. Meanwhile, the city continued to expand outwards: north into industrial zones; south around the coast; and inland, up the hills, mainly in the form of favelas (slums).

When, in 1960, the nation's capital was moved to Brasília, Rio went into decline, especially the commercial centre, and began to suffer badly from poor urban planning decisions and too many high-rise buildings. However, in the late 1990s, the mayor of the city, Luiz Paulo Conde, embarked on a massive programme of regenerating the centre through remodelling and attracting residents to neglected districts. As an architect and urbanist he brought a social vision which encompasses the improvement of favelas and a plan to clean up the south of the city as far as Leblon.

In December 1997 a new 25-km expressway, the Linha Amarela, was opened from the Ilha do Fundão, near the international airport, to Barra da Tijuca, cutting the journey time to Barra by more than half.

Sights

Central Rio and Lapa » pp106-136.

Hot and sweaty central Rio spreads back from Guanabara Bay in a jumbled grid of streets between Santos Dumont airport and the Jesuit Mosteiro São Bento. It dates from 1567, but much of its architectural heritage has been laid waste by successive waves of government intent on wiping out the past in favour of dubious and grandiose visions of Order and Progress. Nevertheless it remains the centre of Rio's history as well as the city, with some distinguished colonial buildings, Manueline follies and elaborate neoclassical facades huddled together under totalitarian blocks of flats and Le Corbusier-inspired concrete. All watch over a mass of cars and a bustle of people; business suits on lunch, beggars, skateboarders dressed in would-be New York oversized jeans and baseball caps, street performers, opportunists looking to snatch a purse. It can all feel a bit hectic and bewildering. But don't give up. There is plenty to explore here and a wealth of air-conditioned havens in which to escape for respite and a coffee.

The greatest concentration of historic buildings is in the south of the centre, near Santos Dumont airport and around **Praça 15 de Novembro**, from where Rio de Janeiro grew in its earliest days. Here you'll find most of the museums, some of the city's more beautiful little churches and colonial buildings such as the **Paço Imperial** and the **Palácio Tiradentes**. More colonial buildings lie at the centre's northern extremity around the Morro de São Bento. These include the finest baroque building in Rio, the **Mosteiro de São Bento**, and the city's most imposing church, **Nossa Senhora da Candelária**.

The city's main artery is the **Avenida Presidente Vargas**, 4½ km long and over 90 m wide, which divides these northern and southern sections. It begins at the waterfront, splits around the Candelária church, then crosses the Avenida Rio Branco in a magnificent straight stretch past the **Central do Brasil** railway station. Vargas is cut by two important arterial streets. **Avenida Rio Branco**, nearest to the sea, was once lined with splendid ornate buildings which were quite the equal of any in Buenos Aires. These have largely been razed to the ground but a few remain around **Cinelândia**. Avenida 31 de Março, further to the west beyond the railway station, leads to the **Sambódromo** and the Carnaval district. Some of the better modern architecture is to be found along Avenida República do Chile, including the conical 1960s **Metropolitan Cathedral of São Sebastião**.

Ins and outs

For Praça 15 de Novembro, Largo do Carioca, Cinelândia and Lapa take the Metro to Carioca in Cinelândia. For Candelária and São Bento take the Metrô to Uruguiana. For the Cidade Nova and Sambódromo take the Metrô to Praça Onze. Opening times for churches, museums and public buildings change frequently. All museums close during Carnaval.

Praça 15 de Novembro and the imperial palaces

Originally an open space at the foot of the Morro do Castelo – a hill which has now been flattened – the Praça 15 de Novembro (often called Praça Quinze) has always been one of the focal points in Rio de Janeiro. Today it has one of the greatest concentrations of historic buildings in the city. Having been through various phases of development, the area underwent major remodelling in the late 1990s. The last vestiges of the original harbour, at the seaward end of the praça, were restored. Avenida Alfredo Agache now goes through an underpass, creating an open space between the praça and the seafront and giving easy access to the ferry dock for Niterói. The area is well illuminated and clean and the municipality has started to stage shows, music and dancing in the praça. At weekends an antiques, crafts, stamp and coin fair (Feirarte II) is held from 0900-1900. The rather modest colonial former royal palace, **Paço Imperial** ⓣ *T021-2533 4407, Tue-Sun 1100-1830*, on the southeast corner of the Praça 15 de Novembro is one of the centre's landmarks. It was built in 1743 as the residence of the governor of the Capitania and was made into the royal palace when the Portuguese court moved to Brazil. After Independence it became the imperial palace. It fell into disuse in the mid-20th century to be resurrected as a temporary exhibition space and arts centre. There's often something interesting on here, and two decent air-conditioned café-restaurants – the **Bistro** and **Atrium** – provide respite from the heat. Just north of the palace is the **Chafariz do Mestre Valentim**, or Chafariz do Pirâmide; a fountain designed by the famous sculptor.

Beside the Paço Imperial, across Rua da Assembléia, is the grand neoclassical **Palácio Tiradentes** ⓘ *T021-2588 1000, Mon-Fri 1300-1900 by prior appointment*, named in honour of the former dentist (*tiradentes* means teeth puller), Joaquim José da Silva Xavier, who is often seen as the symbolic father of Brazilian independence, and who was held prisoner here and executed nearby. The building itself was constructed between 1922 and 1926 and is now the state legislative assembly. A **statue of Tiradentes** by Francisco de Andrade stands in front.

Largo da Misericórdia and the museums

There is a cluster of interesting little museums south of Praça XV on the way to Santos Dumont airport that can be reached by the Largo da Misericórdia, which runs immediately south of the Palácio Tiradentes. At the end of the largo is the **Ladeira da Misericórdia**; the oldest street in Rio and now just a severed stump on the side of the grand Santa Casa da Misericórdia hospital. This was once crowned by a magnificent monastery and fort that watched out over the bay. Next door to the hospital, in a series of handsome buildings, is the **Museu Histórico Nacional** ⓘ *Praça Marechal Âncora s/n, T021-2550 9224, Tue-Fri 1000-1730, Sat and Sun 1400-1800, US$2*. This is one of the city's more distinguished museums, with a collection of magnificent carriages, historical treasures, colonial sculpture and furniture, maps, paintings, arms and armour, silver and porcelain. It also retains a rampart from that first fort which crowned the former Morro do Castelo hill from the 1603 until the 20th century. The building was once the war arsenal of the empire, and was partly constructed in 1762 (this part is called the Casa do Trem). The **Museu da Imagem e do Som (MIS)** ⓘ *Praça Rui Barbosa 1, T021-2262 0309, Mon-Fri 1300-1800*, houses a collection of cinema images, photos of Rio and of Carioca musicians, and recordings of popular music including early *choro* by artists like Jacob do Bandolim. There are booths for listening to music and a small cinema for watching the 16 mm and 35 mm film archive.

Travessa do Comércio and the Carmelite churches

North of Praça XV, the **Travessa do Comércio** and its continuation to the left, the **Rua do Ouvidor**, are reached via the **Arco do Teles** directly across from the palace. The arch is all that remains of an 18th-century construction, now incorporated into a modern building, and the two streets give an idea of how most of Rio must have looked in the 19th century. Little bars and restaurants line the streets and are very lively after 1800. These include the **Arco Imperial**, where Carmen Miranda lived between 1925 and 1930 (her mother kept a boarding house). There are also some interesting bookshops and a pretty little baroque church, **Nossa Senhora da Lapa dos Mercadores** ⓘ *R do Ouvidor 35, Mon-Fri 0800-1400*. This began life as a street oratory erected in a blind alley by market vendors who traditionally petitioned Our Lady of Lapa for help in hard times; it became a church in 1750, was remodelled in 1869-1872 and has now been fully restored.

The busy thoroughfare of Rua 1 de Março cuts across the top of Praça XV and Rua Ouvidor and is littered with Carmelite churches; all of them worth a quick look. The most famous is at the northwestern corner of the praça: **Nossa Senhora do Carmo da Antiga Sé** ⓘ *R 1 de Março at R 7 de Setembro, Mon-Fri 0700-1700*, has one of the finest baroque interiors in Rio and occupies the site of the original founding convent chapel which stood here between 1590 and 1754. The building became the designated royal chapel with the arrival of the Portuguese royal family in 1808 and subsequently the city's first cathedral. The crypt allegedly holds the remains of Pedro Alvares Cabral, the European discoverer of Brazil; a claim disputed by the town of Santarém in Portugal. Just north of this church and right in front of the end of Rua Ouvidor is the **Igreja da Ordem Terceira do Monte do Carmo** ⓘ *R 1 de Março s/n, Mon-Fri 0800-1400, Sat 0800-1200*. This was built in 1754, consecrated in 1770 and rebuilt in the 19th century. It has strikingly beautiful portals by Mestre Valentim (see Fine Art and Sculpture, page 701), the son of a Portuguese nobleman and a slave girl. He also created the main altar of fine moulded silver, the throne and its chair and much else. At the rear of the old cathedral and the Igreja da Ordem Terceira do Monte do Carmo, on Rua do Carmo, is the **Oratório de Nossa Senhora do Cabo da Boa Esperança**; one of the few remaining public oratories from the colonial period in Rio.

Candelária and around

Rio's most imposing church lies on an island in a sea of traffic some 500 m north of Praça XV. The mock-Itallanate **Igreja de Nossa Senhora da Candelária** ⓘ *Praça Pio X s/n, Mon-Fri 0730-1200, 1300-1630, Sat 0800-1200, Sun 0900-1300*, has long been the church of Society Rio. Celebrities still gather here in the marble interior for the city's most prestigious weddings. The church is modelled on the Basilica da Estrela in Lisbon. The tiles in the dome are from that city, the marble inside is Veronan and the heavy bronze doors were commissioned from France. All were shipped across at vast expense in the late 18th century, during an era when even though such materials were readily available in Brazil at similar quality and far lower prices, snob value demanded that they be imported. The church was built on the site of a chapel founded in 1610 by the Spaniard Antônio Martins Palma who arrived in Rio after surviving a terrible storm at sea. He erected the chapel in homage to Nuestra Señora de Candelária, the patron saint of his home, La Palma island in the Canaries.

There are a number of cultural centres near the church. The **Espaço Cultural dos Correios** ⓘ *R Visconde de Itaboraí 20, T021-2503 8770, Tue-Sun 1200-2000*, in a smart Edwardian building with a little private park, is a great stop for an air-conditioned juice or coffee. It holds temporary exhibitions and cultural events, and a postage stamp fair on Saturdays. Just opposite, with entrances on Avenida Presidente Vargas and Rua 1 de Março 66, is the **Centro Cultural Banco do Brasil** (**CCBB**) ⓘ *R 1 de Março 66, T021-3808 2089, Tue-Sun 1230-1900*, in a fine turn-of- the-19th-century neoclassical building with a beautiful glass domed roof. The centre hosts many of the city's large and distinguished art shows, including some excellent photographic exhibitions. It also has an arts cinema, library, multimedia facilities and lunchtime concerts (around US$5). The restaurant is air-conditioned and the food respectable. At the corner of Rua Visconde de Itaboraí (No 253) and Avenida Presidente Vargas, just opposite Candelária, is the **Fundaçao Casa França-Brasil** ⓘ *R Visconde de Itaboraí 78, T021-2253 5366, Tue-Sun 1200-2000*, a Franco-Brazilian cultural centre that holds temporary exhibitions exploring the long relationship between the two countries. The newest of the cultural centres near Candelária is the **Espaço Cultural da Marinha** ⓘ *Av Alfredo Agache on the waterfront, T021-21046025, Tue-Sun, 1200-1700, US$2*. This former naval establishment, built on a jetty over the bay, now contains museums of underwater archaeology and navigation. *Galeota*, the boat used by the Portuguese royal family for sailing around the Baía de Guanabara is kept here and a Second World War submarine and warship, the *Bauru* (not to be confused with the sandwich of the same name), is moored outside. The museum is very popular with Brazilian children and is crowded at weekends.

Just offshore, but connected to the mainland by a causeway to Ilha das Cobras, is the **Ilha Fiscal** ⓘ *T021-3870 6879, boats leave Fri-Sun at 1300, 1430 and 1600, 30 minutes later Oct-Mar*. It was built as a customs house at the emperor's request, but he deemed it too beautiful, and said that it should be used only for official parties. Only one was ever held, five days before the Republic began. It is now a museum, linked with the Espaço Cultural da Marinha. The island is passed by the ferry to Niterói.

Mosteiro de São Bento

The Praça Mauá, which lies north of Avenida Presidente Vargas, marks the end of Centro and the beginning of the port zone. Many of the empty warehouses here are

A Rio de Janeiro centre

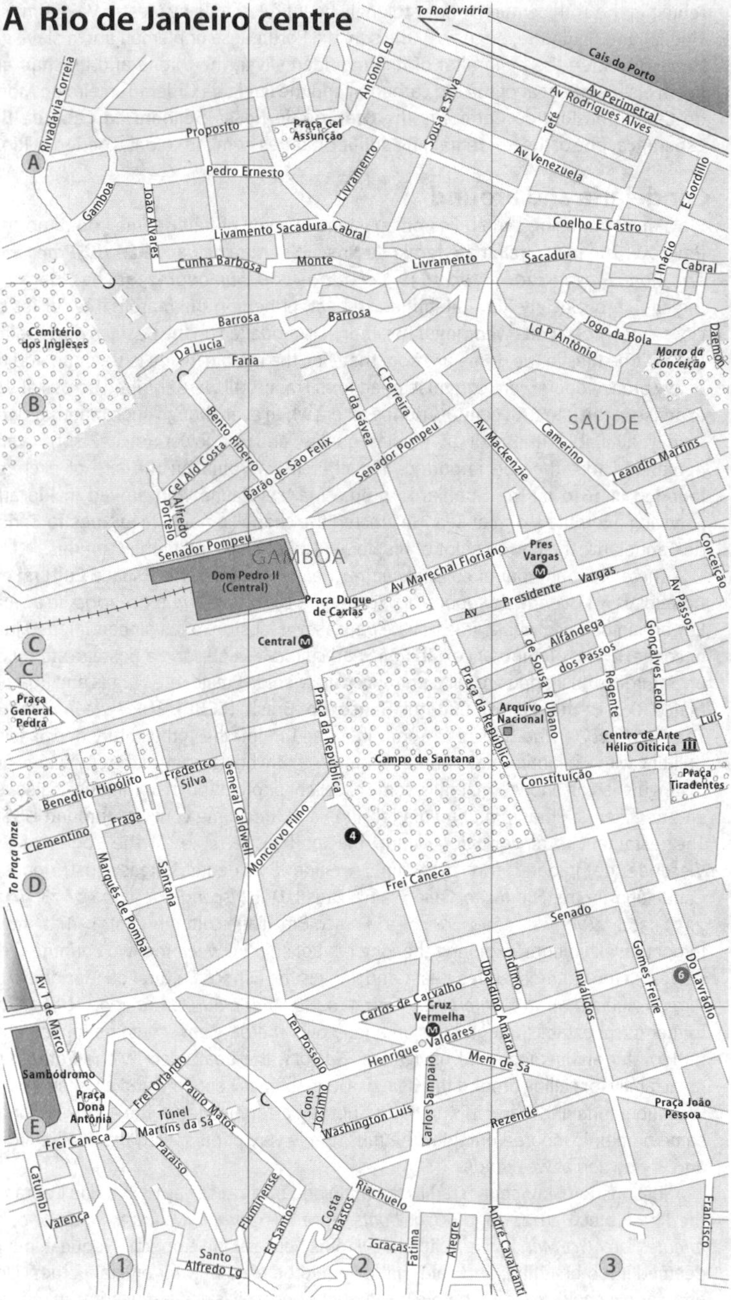

To Rodoviária
Cais do Porto
Av Perimetral
Av Rodrigues Alves
Av Venezuela
Rivadávia Correia
Proposito
Praça Cel Assunção
Antônio Lg
Sousa e Silva
Tefé
E Gordilho
Pedro Ernesto
Livramento
Gamboa
João Alvares
Livamento Sacadura Cabral
Coelho E Castro
Cunha Barbosa
Monte
Livramento
Sacadura
J Inácio
Cabral
Cemitério dos Ingleses
Barrosa
Barrosa
Da Lucia
Faria
Ld P Antônio
Jogo da Bola
Daemon
Morro da Conceição
V da Gávea
C Ferreira
Bento Ribeiro
Cel Ald Costa
Barão de Sao Felix
Senador Pompeu
Av Mackenzie
Camerino
SAÚDE
Leandro Martins
Alfredo Porteio
Senador Pompeu
GAMBOA
Dom Pedro II (Central)
Praça Duque de Caxias
Av Marechal Floriano
Pres Vargas
Av Presidente Vargas
Conceição
Av Passos
Central
Alfândega
dos Passos
T de Sousa
R Ubano
Gonçalves Ledo
Regente
Praça General Pedra
Praça da República
Praça da República
Arquivo Nacional
Luís
Centro de Arte Hélio Oiticica
Campo de Santana
Constituição
Praça Tiradentes
Benedito Hipólito
Frederico Silva
General Caldwell
Moncorvo Filho
Fraga
Clementino
To Praça Onze
Marquês de Pombal
Santana
Frei Caneca
Senado
Gomes Freire
Do Lavradio
Didimo
Ubaldino Amaral
Invalidos
Av 1 de Marco
Carlos de Carvalho
Cruz Vermelha
Henrique Valdares
Ten Possolo
Mem de Sá
Sambódromo
Praça Dona Antônia
Frei Orlando
Paulo Matos
Túnel Martins da Sá
Frei Caneca
Cons Josinho
Washington Luis
Carlos Sampaio
Rezende
Praça João Pessoa
Paraíso
Catumbi
Valença
Fluminense
Ed Santos
Costa Bastos
Riachuelo
Graças
Fatima
Alegre
André Cavalcanti
Francisco
Santo Alfredo Lg

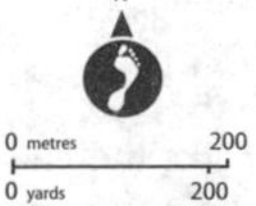

Eating
Adega Flor de Coimbra **3** *E4*
Café da Moda & Folic **2** *C4*
Confeitaria Colombo **8** *C4*
Republique **4** *D2*
Bar Luiz **1** *D4*
Sabor Saúde **7** *C5*

Bars & clubs
Rio Scenarium **6** *D3*

Ilha das Cobras
Mosteiro de São Bento
Morro de São Bento
Rangel
Praça Mauá
Lad J Home
Do Acre
Bento Cons Saraiva
Dom Gerardo
B do Bragança
Cais do Mineiros
Baía de Guanabara
To Ilha Fiscal
Visc de Inhaúma
M Nerja
Visc de Itaboraí
R Candelária
Santa Rita
Candelária
Teófilo Otoni
Antonio Largo Pharmacy Museum
Alfândega
1 de Março
Mercado
Buenos Aires
Do Rosário
Detail map B Praça 15 de Novembro, p77.
Ferry Dock
Uruguaiana
Miguel Couto
Ouvidor
Praça 15 de Novembro
Paço Imperial
Andradas
Quitanda
Carmo
Av Presidente Kubitschek
Real Gabinete Português de Leitura
Menezes Cortes Bus Terminal (Castelo-a/c Buses to Zona Sul)
Av Alfredo Agache
Da Assembleia
Rod Silva
Camões
São Francisco de Paula
São José
dom Manoel
Teatro
Gonçalves Dias
F Braga
Praça Rui Barbosa
Museu Histórico Nacional
Teatro João Caetano
7 de Setembro
Av Rio Branco
Av Nilo Peçanha
Museu da Imagem e do Som
Carioca
Av Presidente Antônio Carlos
Praça do Expedicionário
Largo da Misericórdia
Ordem Terceira de São Francisco da Penitência
Largo da Carioca
Carioca
Alm Barroso
Av General Justo
Convento de Santo Antônio
G Aranha
Debret
S Luzia
Av Mar Câmara
Av República do Chile
Av 13 de Maio
Museu Nacional de Belas-Artes
A Porto Alegre
Prof L Gama
Theatro Municipal
Palácio Capanema
Santa Luzia
Churchill
Catedral Metropolitana de São Sebastião
Praça Floriano
Biblioteca Nacional
Tram Terminus
Pedro Lessa
Roosevelt
Evaristo da Veiga
Alvin
Av México
S Luzia
To Santos Dumont Airport
Av República do Paraguai
Cinelândia
Sen Dantas
Av Pres Wilson
Arcos da Lapa
Marrecas
Praça Mahatma Gandhi
Av Infante D Henrique
Escola da Musica da Universidade Federal do Rio de Janeiro
Passeio Público
Av Beira Mar
Tex de Freitas
Av Augusto Severo
Museu de Arte Moderna
Sala Cecília Meirelles
Convento de Santa Teresa
Joaquim
Silvio Romero
Parque do Flamengo
LAPA
To Botafogo
D
B
1
2
3
4
5
6
7
8

used as workshops by the samba schools for the construction of their beautiful carnival floats. The area would be unremarkable were it not for the Benedictine **Mosteiro de São Bento**ⓘ *R Dom Gerardo 68, T021-2291 7122, daily 0800-1000 and 1430-1800, free, modest dress – no shorts, taxi from the city centre US$5*, whose sober Brazilian baroque façade sits on a promontory looking out over the bay. It is widely publicized as a World Heritage site, which it is not. But of all the city's colonial buildings this is the most worth visiting, both for its magnificent interior and for its significance as the most important Benedictine monument outside Europe. The church began life in 1586 with a group of monks who arrived in Rio from Salvador and it grew to become the most powerful monastery in the city. It preserves the most lavish gilt baroque interior in the city but is very poorly lit (the church charges an absurd US$5 to put on all of the electric lights). However, in the gloom it is possible to make out that not an inch remains unadorned. The three doors sculpted by Father Domingos da Conceição, which give access to the nave, and the sculptures of St Benedict, St Escolastica and Our Lady of Monserrat are particularly remarkable. The last, which is also by Domingos de Conceição, has painted birds' eggs for eyes. The painting is as wonderful as the carving; particularly the panels in the Blessed Sacrament chapel by Inácio Ferreira Pinto and *O Salvador*, the masterpiece of Brazil's first painter, Frei Ricardo do Pilar, which hangs in the sacristy. The enormous candelabra are attributed to Mestre Valentim, Rio's most celebrated church artisan, and are made from solid silver especially imported from Peru and the mines of Potosí in Bolivia at a price higher than Brazil's own gold. The monastery's library (open to men only) preserves a number of priceless religious manuscripts alongside 200,000 other books.

São Bento can be reached either by a narrow road from Rua Dom Gerardo 68, or by a lift whose entrance is at Rua Dom Gerardo 40. Both routes lead to a praça with tall trees, but arriving in the lift is more magical as you are whisked from the heat and bustle of the dock area to an oasis of calm which sets the mood beautifully for a wander around the monastery buildings. If you would rather walk, the monastery is a few minutes from Praça Mauá, turning left off Avenida Rio Branco; Rua Dom Gerardo 68 is behind the massive new RBI building. Every Sunday at 1000 there is a Latin Mass with plainsong. Arrive an hour early to get a seat. On other days, Mass is at 0715 and the monks often sing at vespers.

Largo da Carioca and around

This higgledy-piggledy street of colonial churches, modern buildings and street stalls sits between Rua da Carioca and the Carioca Metrô station about 1 km south of Praça XV along Rua da Assembléia. There is a variety of interesting sights here within a very small area. The **Convento de Santo Antônio**ⓘ *daily 0800-1800, free*, the second oldest in Rio, sits on a little hill off the Largo da Carioca. You will often see single women here gathered to pray: there are many more women than men in Brazil and St Anthony is traditionally a provider of husbands. The church interior is baroque around the chancel, main altars and two lateral altars, which are devoted to St Anthony, St Francis and the Immaculate Conception respectively. The beautiful sacristy is decorated with *azulejos* and adorned with paintings depicting scenes from St Anthony's life. Separated from this church only by a fence of iron railings is one of Rio's least-known baroque jewels; the little church of the **Ordem Terceira de São Francisco da Penitência** (closed for renovation in 2007). It was built 1653-1773 and has a splendid gilt interior with a fine panel painted by José de Oliveira. It houses an important collection of Franciscan relics and a small museum of sacred art.

Across Rua da Carioca and Rua 7 de Setembro, at the upper end of Rua do Ouvidor and dominating the square that bears its name, is the twin-towered church of **São Francisco de Paula**ⓘ *Largo São Francisco de Paula, Mon-Fri 0900-1300, free*, with some fine examples of Carioca art including carvings by Mestre Valentim, paintings by Vítor Meireles and murals by Manuel da Cunha. Across the Largo de São Francisco and on the corner of Rua Uruguiana and Ouvidor is the **Igreja de Nossa Senhora do Rosário e São Benedito dos Pretos**. Since the 17th century this church has been at the centre of African Christian culture in Rio. During the 19th century it was the site of an elaborate festival that recreated scenes from the courtly life of the King of Congo. A king and queen were crowned and they danced through the nearby streets followed by long parades of courtiers in fancy dress; a precursor perhaps for Carnaval. It was here that the announcements for the final abolition of slavery were prepared. The church once had a fabulous gilt interior but this was sadly destroyed in a fire in 1967. Next door to the church is a small museum devoted to slavery in Brazil, whose collection of instruments of subjugation speaks starkly of life for black people in the last Western country to abolish the slave trade. The **Real Gabinete Português de Leitura** ⓘ *R Luís Camões 30, T021-2221 3138, Tue-Fri 1000-1745, Sat and Sun 1400-1800, free*, sits just to the north of Largo São Francisco de Paula on Rua Luís de Camões. This is one of the city's hidden architectural treasures and one of the best pieces of mock-Manueline architecture in Brazil. Manueline architecture is usually described as Portuguese Gothic and takes its name from King Manuel I who ruled Portugal between 1495 and 1521. It is unlike any other European Gothic style, drawing strongly on Islamic and nautical themes – a lavish fusion of Islamic ornamentalism and sculpted seaweeds, anchors, ropes and corals, typified by the Cristo monastery in Tomar and the Mosteiro dos Jerônimos in Lisbon. The modest exterior of the Real Gabinete, which was designed by Portuguese architect Rafael da Silva e Castro in 1880, was inspired by the façade of Jerônimos. It is decorated with statues of Camões, Henry the Navigator, Vasco da Gama and Pedro Álvares Cabral, who claimed Brazil for Portugal. More interesting, however, is the magnificent reading hall built around the oldest central steel structure in Rio. Towering arches decorated with Islamic flourish ascend via coiled wooden ropes to an elaborate painted ceiling with skylights from which a massive iron chandelier is suspended. There are some 120,000 books in the library's collection, many of them very rare. The magnificent belle-époque coffee house, **Confeitaria Colombo**, is a short walk to the east, at Rua Gonçalves Dias 32 (see page 113).

Praça Tiradentes and the cathedral

One long block behind the Largo da Carioca and São Francisco de Paula is the Praça Tiradentes, old and shady, with a **statue to Dom Pedro I** carved in 1862 by Luís Rochet. The emperor sits on horseback shouting his famous 1822 declaration of Independence, the Grito de Ipiranga: 'Liberty or Death'. The **Teatro João Caetano** sits on the northeastern corner of the praça and is named after a famous 19th-century actor. Prince Dom Pedro first showed the green and yellow Brazilian flag in the original building, which was an important venue for meetings discussing Brazilian independence. The current theatre was constructed in 1920 after the original had fallen into disrepair. Two canvases by one of the city's most celebrated artists, Emiliano Di Cavalcanti, hang on the second floor. Just north of the praça, in a handsome salmon pink colonial building, is the **Centro de Arte Hélio Oiticica** ⓘ *R Luís de Camões 68, Mon-Fri 1000-1800*, named after another famous Carioca artist and now a smart contemporary art exhibition space with six galleries, a good art bookshop and an air-conditioned café. Important national and international artists exhibit here. Shops in nearby streets specialize in selling goods for umbanda, the Afro-Brazilian religion. The **Catedral Metropolitana de São Sebastião** ⓘ *Av República do Chile, T021-2240 2669, www.catedral.com.br, daily 0800-1800, Mass weekdays 1100, Sun 1000*, lies just south of the Praça Tiradentes and the Largo da Carioca; bordering Cinêlandia to the east and Lapa to the south. It is an oblate concrete cone fronted by a decorative ladder and replete with rich blue stained glass, which looks like a modernist Mayan temple. The design could be mistaken for a Niemeyer, but is in fact by another Brazilian Le Corbusier disciple, Edgar de Oliveira da Fonseca. It's best to visit in the late afternoon when the sunlight streams through the immense monotone stained-glass windows. There is a small sacred art museum in the crypt, which has a handful of relics including Dom Pedro II's throne and the fonts used for the baptizing of imperial Brazilian babies. The *bonde* (tram) to Santa Teresa leaves from behind the cathedral, the entrance is on Rua Senador Dantas (see page 90). Soon after leaving the station the tram traverses the Arcos da Lapa offering wonderful views.

One of the city's quirkier museums lies only a short walk from the cathedral. The **Antônio Largo Pharmacy Museum** ⓘ *R dos Andradas 96, room 1001, T021-2263 0791, Mon-Fri 1430-1700, US$1.50*, is a tiny reproduction of a 17th-century Brazilian apothecary's shop, complete with Dr Jeckyll cabinets and rows of dubious-looking herbal preparations in glass and porcelain vessels.

Cinelândia and Avenida Rio Branco

The area around Praça Floriano was the liveliest part of the city in the 1920s and 1930s when Hollywood hit Brazil. All of the best cinemas were situated here and their popularity became so great that the praça was named after them. Today Cinelândia remains lively, especially at the end of the week, owing to its proximity to the city's nightlife capital, Lapa (see Bars and clubs, page 118). The 30-m-wide Avenida Rio Branco, which bisects Cinelândia, is the financial heart of the city. Lined by an untidy mishmash of modernist and art deco skyscrapers it was built at the turn of 20th the century under the 'tear it down' regime of Mayor Pereira Passos. Rio once had long stately avenues that rivalled the best of Buenos Aires but only clusters have survived. Although it has seen better days, the **Theatro Municipal** ⓘ *Praça Floriano, T021-2299 1633, www.theatromunicipal.rj.gov.br, Mon-Fri 0900-1700, tours US$1.20, book in advance T021-2262 3501*, remains magnificent. The tour is worth it to see front of house and backstage, the decorations and the machine rooms in a luxuriously ornate temple to turn-of-the-20th-century Carioca high society. On either side of the lavish colonnaded façade are rotundas, surmounted by cupolas. The muses of poetry and music watch over all, alongside an imperial eagle, wings outstretched and poised for flight. The interior is a mock- European fantasy of Carrara-marble columns, crystal chandeliers and gilt ceilings fronted by a vast sweeping staircase. The stage is one of the largest in the world. The theatre was designed by Francisco de Oliveira Passos, son of the contemporaneous city mayor, who won an ostensibly open architectural competition together with French architect Albert Guilbert.

Opposite, on the other side of Avenida Rio Branco, is the **Museu Nacional de Belas-Artes** ⓘ *Av Rio Branco 199, T021-2240 0068, Tue-Fri 1000-1800, Sat and Sun 1400-1800, US$1*. Fine art in Rio and in Brazil was, as a whole, stimulated by the arrival in 1808 of the Portuguese royal family. In 1816 the Academia de Belas-Artes was founded by another Frenchman, Joaquim Lebreton. This building was constructed 1906-1908 to house the national gallery and contains the best collection of art in the country. This includes work by European visitors like Frans Post and Debret, and the best of 20th-century Brazilian art by important names such as Cândido Portinari, Emiliano Di Cavalcanti, Tarsila do Amaral and Victor Brecheret. Another gallery contains further works by foreign artists and the temporary exhibition hall houses many of Rio de Janeiro's most important international exhibitions.

Another of Cinelândia's stately buildings is the **Biblioteca Nacional** ⓘ *Av Rio Branco 219/239, T021-2262 8255, Mon-Fri 0900-2000, Sat 0900-1500, US$1*, another piece of eclectic Carioca neoclassical, this time with a touch of art nouveau. The building is fronted by a stately engaged portico supported by a Corinthian colonnade. Inside is a series of monumental staircases in Carrara marble. The stained glass in the windows is French. The first national library was brought to Brazil in 1808 by the Prince Regent, Dom João, from a collection in the Ajuda Palace in Lisbon. Today the library houses over nine million items, including a first edition of the *Lusiad of Camões*, a 15th-century Moguncia Bible and Book of Hours, paintings donated by Pedro II, scores by Mozart and etchings by Dürer.

The fall and rise of Lapa

In the belle époque, Lapa's colonial streets were the Bohemian heart of Rio and lined with bars and dance halls which were the haunt of artists and intellectuals like Di Cavalcanti. However, after the war they fell into decay and disrepute and only the dangerous walked here. For decades Lapa festered, until in the 1980s a series of performance artists in love with the memory of the area braved Lapa and the neighbourhood slowly began to revive. Others followed them and a small alternative community began to form. Art and antiques dealers moved in. Then came tango and samba clubs and a handful of restaurants. Today Lapa is once more the heart of Bohemian Rio and many of its decaying colonial houses are now renovated and freshly painted, but enough remain for Lapa to retain a slightly edgy, Havanesque feel. Come here for a great night out and a window on the panoply and polyphony of modern Rio. Arrive at around 2100 whilst it is still relatively quite, take a streetside table under the arches at anyone of the crumbling colonial cafes along Avenida Mem da Sa, order an absinthe and wait. Little by little characters from every walk of Rio life enter the living stage – down at heel favela couples drunk and stumbling, Patricinhas dressed in Zoomp's ultra expensive casual, capoeira artists, jugglers, old men in blazers with hula hoops round their necks, befuddled tourists, towering transvestites in lycra shorts the size of a glove. As their numbers increase to boiling point they become a throng, unable to keep apart from each other, moving in Brownian Motion past the doors of numerous gradually waking clubs; past the thump and thud of techno, the staccato whir of forró and the hip swing of Samba. Once the clubs have really got going, leave your table and join the throng – to dance to any music of your choice and become for a night... a Carioca.

Nearby is the **Palácio Capanema**, the former Ministry of Education and Health building and the first piece of modernist architecture in the Americas. It is on the Esplanada do Castelo, at the junction of Avenida Graça Aranha and Rua Araújo Porto Alegre, just off Avenida Rio Branco, and dates from 1937 1945. It was designed by a team of architects led by Lúcio Costa under the guidance of Le Corbusier and was the first project Oscar Niemeyer worked on. Inside are impressive murals by Cândido Portinari, one of Brazil's most famous artists, as well as works by other well-known names. The gardens were laid out by Roberto Burle Marx.

Lapa

Only a decade ago Lapa, which lies just south of the cathedral on the edge of Cinelândia, was a no-go area; tawdry and terrifying, walked only by prostitutes, thugs and drug addicts chasing the dragon in the crumbling porticoes of the colonial and art nouveau buildings. The area can still feel a little edgy, especially on weekdays after dark. But it has undergone an unimagined renaissance. This was once the Montmartre of Rio; the painter Di Cavalcanti wrote poetically of wandering its streets at night on his way home to Flamengo, past the little cafés and ballrooms and the rows of handsome town houses. Now the cafés are alive once more, spilling out onto the streets, and the ballrooms and town houses throb with samba and electronica. Opera is once more performed in the concert halls of the Escola de Música, and the area's once notorious thoroughfare, Rua do Lavradio, is now lined with smart little restaurants and clubs, playing host to one of the city's most interesting bric-a-brac and antiques markets on Saturdays (see Bars and clubs, page 118, and Markets, page 126). Although the area is

The story of Carnaval

Rio's story, and that of the world's most famous carnival is a tale of two cities: the European and the African. In the early 20th century the city was a prudish place, dominated by a stuffy elite, who enclosed themselves in mock-French palaces and mansions around the city's beautiful coves. The other Brazil was (and remains), poor and marginalized and clinging to the hills. Its people visited European Rio only to work at the quays where their African forefathers had been unloaded in crates a generation before.

The Mardi Gras carnival was a European affair. In homage to European balls, the Portuguese and their ancestors danced behind closed doors and masks to the fashionable rhythm of the time, polka. But black Brazil would not be excluded. Its people took the Portuguese instruments and polka dance steps out of Rio's ballrooms and into their *favela* shanty towns. Here they were fused with the West African rhythm of *maracatú*, frenetic with percussive hand-held *timpani* and resonating to the deep visceral throb of the *zabumba* drum. Over the top the Africans sung laments to their poverty and celebrations of the essential joys of life. These were echoed by a sung chorus. As the celebrations developed, the revellers began to dress in ever more elaborate costumes and dance and march in discrete *blocos* or individual parades. These were often themed according to the African tribal group from which the celebrants came and were led by a king and queen. In Pernambuco, whose carnival is the most traditional of all in Brazil, the *blocos* are still referred to as nations.

In the 20th century the celebrations had evolved into a fully-blown carnival which soon eclipsed the masked balls of the elite. And the Carnaval music became a particular style all its own – *samba*. By the end of the Second World War the *favela* carnivals had expanded into the streets of the city itself to become Rio's Carnaval. The *blocos* became *samba* schools, who spent an entire year preparing the carnival performance and making floats and costumes. Later even the middle and upper classes of Rio became involved and came to identify themselves with the African-Brazilian culture their ancestors had so despised.

Carnaval today is a multi-million dollar enterprise, sponsored by the gaming industry and featuring the stars of Brazil's equivalent of Bollywood – *TV Globo*. The top samba schools compete in front of crowds of hundreds of thousands and a board of judges, who mark them with Olympic precision according to a series of distinct categories. The 2006 winner was Vila Isabel.

best just for a cautious wander after 2000 at the end of the week, or for the Saturday market, there are a few interesting sights. The most photographed are the **Arcos da Lapa,** built in 1744 as an aqueduct to carry water from Santa Teresa to the Chafariz da Carioca, with its 16 drinking fountains, in the centre of the city. The aqueduct's use was changed at the end of the 19th century, with the introduction of electric trams in Rio. Tracks were laid on top of the arches and the inaugural run was on 1 September 1896. The tram is still in use today and is one of the city's most delightful journeys; it leaves from behind the Cathedral of São Sebastião. Bars huddle under their southern extremity on Avenida Mem de Sá, one of Rio's most popular nightlife streets. Street performers (and vagrants) often gather in the cobbled square between the Arcos and the cathedral. There are a number of moderately interesting buildings off this square.

The eclectic baroque/neoclassical **Escola da Musica da Universidade Federal do Rio de Janeiro** ⓘ *R do Passeio 98, open officially just for performances*, has one of the city's best concert halls. A stroll away is the bizarre baroque façade of another prestigious classical concert hall, the **Sala Cecília Mereilles** ⓘ *Largo da Lapa 47*. More picturesque are the mosaic-tiled **Ladeira do Santa Teresa** stairs which wind their way steeply from the square and from the back of Rua Teotônio to Santa Teresa. These are much beloved of music video directors and fashion photographers who use them as a backdrop to carefully produced gritty urban scenes. The steps are tiled in red, gold and green and bordered by little houses, many of which are dishevelled and disreputable but wonderfully picturesque. Be vigilant here. North of Avenida Mem de Sá is **Rua do Lavradio**. This was one of urban Rio's first residential streets and is lined with handsome 18th- and early 20th-century town houses. These are now filled by samba clubs, cafés, bars and antiques shops. Any day is good for a browse and a wander, and on Saturdays at the end of the month there is a busy antiques market, live street tango, no cars and throngs of people from all sections of Carioca society. Some of the houses here were once grand. Number 84 once belonged to the marquis who gave the street its name. Further along is what was once Brazil's foremost Masonic lodge, the imposing **Palácio Maçônico Grande Oriente do Brasil** which tellingly has had as its grand masters King Dom Pedro I and one of the country's most important Republican politicians, José Bonifácio Andrada e Silva.

Central do Brasil railway station

Central do Brasil or **Dom Pedro II** railway station, as it is also known, once served much of the country but now serves only Rio. This brutal 1930s art deco temple to progress was one of the city's first modernist buildings and was recently made famous by the Walter Salles film *Central Station*. The film's thronging crowd scenes were set here. For similar shots come with your camera in the morning or evening and watch hundreds of thousands of people bustle in and out of trains leaving for the northern and western parts of Rio.

Cidade Nova and the Sambódromo

The Cidade Nova is the centre of Carnaval Rio; for here lies the **Sambódromo** ⓘ *R Marquês de Sapucaí s/n, metro Central or Praça Onze, T021-2502 6996, Mon-Fri 0900-1700*, Oscar Niemeyer's 650-m-long stadium street purpose-built for the annual carnival parades. The area has long been important for black Carioca culture. **Praça Onze** near the Sambódromo is today the terminus of the city's main thoroughfare, Avenida Presidente Vargas. But it was once a square and an established meeting place for capoeristas whose acrobatic martial art to the rhythm of the *berimbau* and hand clap inspired much Carnaval choreography. A replica of the head of a Nigerian prince from the British Museum, erected in honour of **Zumbi dos Palmares**, sits on Avenida Presidente Vargas itself. Zumbi was a Bantu prince who became the most successful black slave emancipator in the history of the Americas, founding a kingdom within Brazil in the 19th century. For further details about Carnaval, see page 122.

Northern Rio

Cemitério dos Ingleses

Over the Morro da Providência, which is between the Estação Dom Pedro II and the bay, is the **Cemitério dos Ingleses** ⓘ *R da Gamboa 181*. The cemetery, the oldest in Rio, was granted to the British community by Dom João, Regent of Portugal, in 1810. Catholics who could afford a burial were laid to rest inside their churches (see the numbers on the church floors, marking the graves), but the British in Rio, being non-Catholic, were not allowed to be buried in the religious establishments.

Nossa Senhora da Penha

The church of **Nossa Senhora da Penha** ⓘ *Largo da Penha 19, T021-2290 0942, www.santuariodapenhario.com.br, Tue-Sun 1000-1600*, is one of the most important pilgrimage centres in the country, especially for black Brazilians. It sits on an enormous rock, into whose side 365 steps have been carved. Pilgrims ascend these on their knees during the festival month of October. The church in its present form dates from the early 20th century, but it was modelled on an early 18th-century chapel and a religious building has been on this site since the original hermitage was built in 1632. There are great views from the summit.

To get there take the Metrô to Del Castilho. Leave the station to the left, walk down the passageway and catch microbus (micro-ônibus) No 623 labelled 'Penha-Shopping Nova América 2' to the last stop. Get off at the shopping centre, in front of Rua dos Romeiros, and walk up that street to the Largo da Penha from where there are signposts to the church.

Maracanã stadium

ⓘ *T021-2568 9962, daily 0900-1700 (0800-1100 on match days); guided tour of the stadium (in Portuguese) from Gate 16 US$2, and of the museum US$0.50. Take the metro to Maracanã station on Linha 2, one stop beyond São Cristóvão. Bus Nos 238 and 239 from the centre, 434 and 464 from Glória, Flamengo and Botafogo, 455 from Copacabana, and 433 and 464 from Ipanema and Leblon all go to the stadium. Trips to football matches can be organized through www.bealocal.com.*

According to Brazilians, Maracanã is the largest sports stadium in the world. However Indianapolis in the USA and Strahov stadium in Prague, Czech Republic, are both larger and have seen bigger crowds. Nonetheless, the stadium is huge and was attended by the largest crowd ever to see a football match in 1950 when Brazil

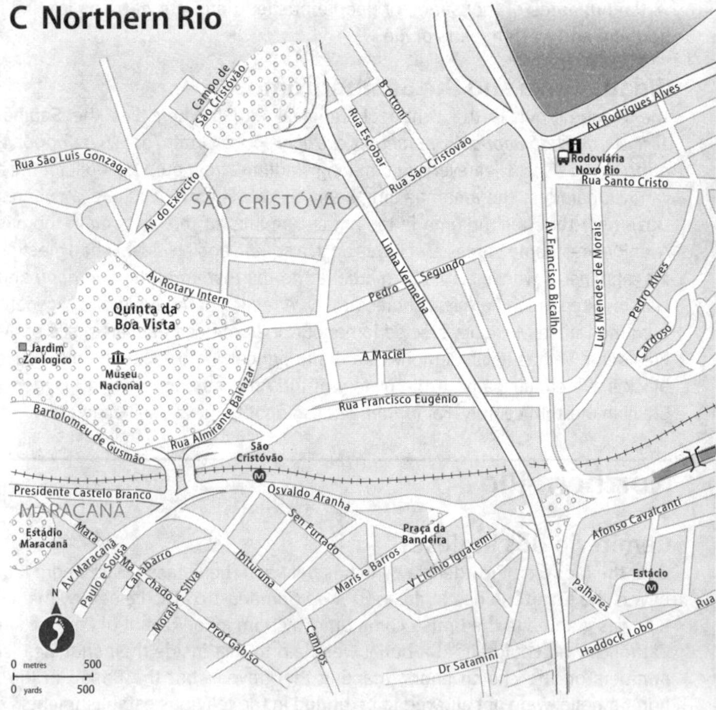

lost to Uruguay in front of more than 200,000 spectators. More importantly, it is the Mount Olympus of the country's football gods. This is where Pelé scored his 1000th goal in 1969. His feet, as well as those of Ronaldo and other Brazilian stars, are immortalized in concrete outside the stadium. Even if you're not a football fan, matches are worth going to for the spectators' samba bands and the adrenalin-charged atmosphere. There are three types of ticket: *cadeiras* (individual chairs), the most expensive; *arquibancadas* (terraces), good for watching the game but don't sit between rival groups of fans; *geral* (standing), the cheapest, not recommended, not safe. Prices vary according to the game, but it's more expensive to buy tickets from agencies than at the gate; it is cheaper to buy tickets from club sites on the day before the match. Maracanã is now used only for major games; Rio teams play most matches at their home grounds.

Don't take valuables or wear a watch; take special care when entering and leaving the stadium. The rivalry between the local clubs Flamengo and Vasco da Gama is intense, often leading to violence, so it is advisable to avoid their encounters. Don't be tempted to buy a club shirt or favour on match day: if you find yourself in the wrong place, you could be in trouble.

Quinta da Boa Vista

ⓘ *Take the metro to São Cristóvão and follow signs to Quinta da Boa Vista, a 5-min walk. Beware of muggings on weekdays.*

About 3 km west of Praça da República (beyond the Sambódromo) is the Quinta da Boa Vista, the emperor's private park from 1809 to 1889. The **Museu Nacional** ⓘ *Tue-Sun 1000-1600, US$2*, is housed in the former imperial palace. The building is crumbling and the collections dusty and poorly displayed. Only the unfurnished throne room and ambassadorial reception room on the second floor reflect past glories. In the entrance hall is the famous Bendegó meteorite, found in the state of Bahia in 1888; its original weight, before some of it was chipped, was 5360 kg. Besides several collections of foreign pieces (including Peruvian and Mexican archaeology, Graeco- Roman ceramics and Egyptian mummies), the museum contains collections of Brazilian indigenous weapons, costumes, utensils and historical documents. There are also frowsty collections of stuffed birds, beasts, fish and butterflies. Also in the park is the **Jardim Zoologico** (zoo) ⓘ *Av Dom Pedro II, T021-2569 2024, Tue-Sun 1000-1600, US$2*. The zoo is in the northeastern corner of the park. It has a collection of 2100 animals, most of which are kept in modern, spacious enclosures, and there is an important captive breeding programme for golden-headed and golden lion tamarins, spectacled bears and yellow-throated capuchin monkeys. The aviary is impressive and children can enjoy a ride in a little train through the park.

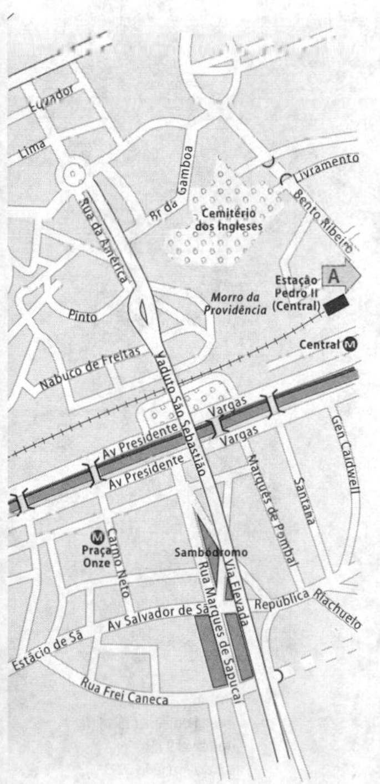

Santa Teresa » pp106-136.

A tram ride from the cathedral to Santa Teresa over the Arcos de Lapa viaduct is an unmissable Rio experience. The old yellow trams clatter up the winding, hilly streets lined with pretty colonial houses and lavish mansions towards the forested slopes of Tijuca national park, leaving in their wake sweeping views of Guanabara Bay and the Sugar Loaf. Along the way they pass the **Largo do Guimarães** and the **Largo das Neves**, little praças of shops and restaurants that feel as if they belong clustered around a village green rather than in a large city. For nowhere in this city of distinct neighbourhoods is more of a world unto itself than Santa Teresa. The neighbourhood has a strong community identity forged by one of the highest concentrations of artists, writers and

D Glória, Santa Teresa & Lapa

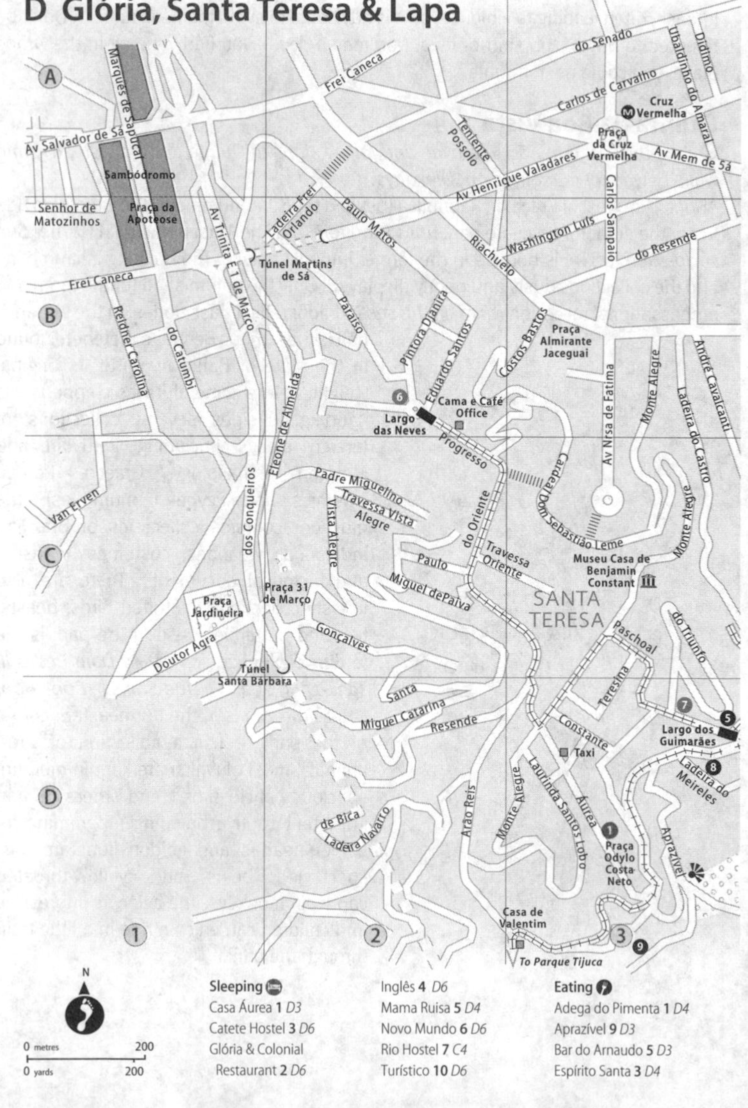

musicians in the city, who congregate in bars like **O Mineiro** on the Largo dos Guimarães or **Bar Porto das Neves** on the Largo das Neves. At weekends the lively nightlife spills over into clubs like **Espírito Santa** (see page 119) and then into neighbouring Lapa which is only a five-minute taxi ride away. Those who can bear to be far from the beach often find staying in Santa Teresa a far more culturally rewarding experience than the southern suburbs and there are many excellent options.

A sense of separation is reflected not only in the suburb's geography, but also its history. In 1624, Antônio Gomes do Desterro chose the area both for its proximity to Rio and its isolation, and erected a hermitage dedicated to Nossa Senhora do Desterro. The name was changed from Morro do Desterro to Santa Teresa after the construction in 1750 of a convent of that name dedicated to the patroness of the order. The convent exists to this day, but it can only be seen from the outside.

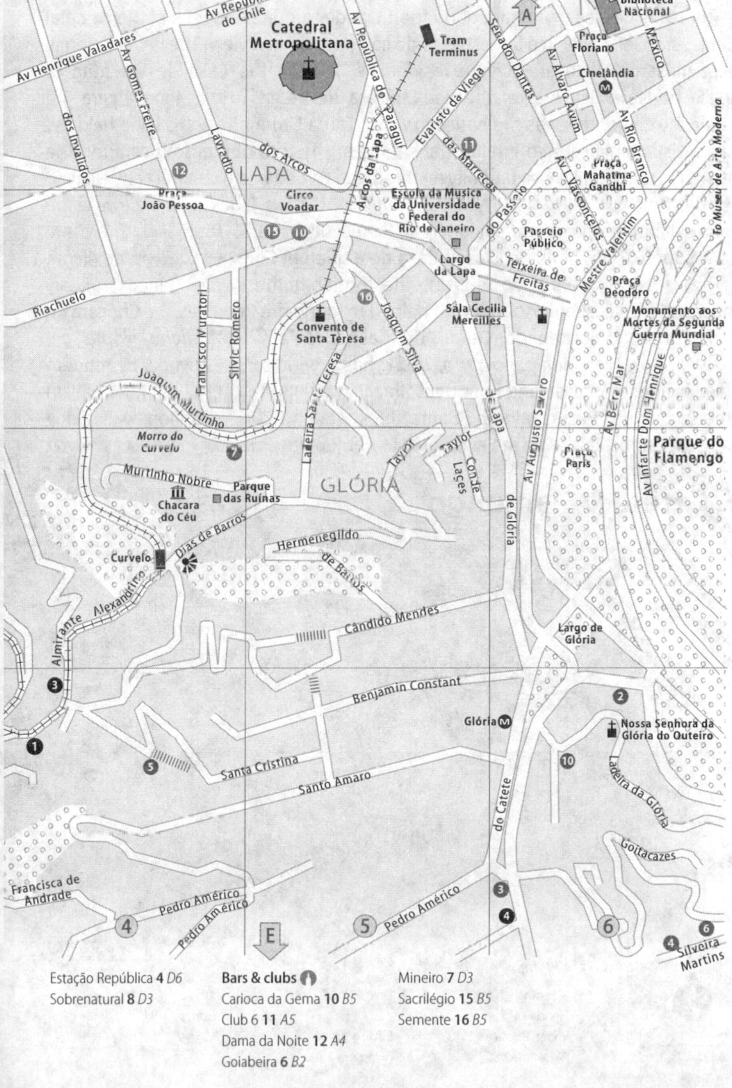

Estação República **4** *D6*
Sobrenatural **8** *D3*

Bars & clubs
Carioca da Gema **10** *B5*
Club 6 **11** *A5*
Dama da Noite **12** *A4*
Goiabeira **6** *B2*
Mineiro **7** *D3*
Sacrilégio **15** *B5*
Semente **16** *B5*

Ins and outs

Getting there and around Santa Teresa is best visited on the traditional open-sided tram, the *bondinho*. This can be caught from the terminus next to the Catedral Metropolitana or from Cinelândia: take the metro to Cinelândia station, go to Rua Senador Dantas then walk along to Rua Profesor Lélio Gama (look for Banco do Brasil on the corner); the station is up this street. Take the Paula Mattos line; the fare is US$0.40 one way. Bus Nos 206 and 214 run between Avenida Rio Branco in the centre and Santa Teresa. At night, take a taxi (about US$7 to the centre or Ipanema). In recent years, Santa Teresa has had a reputation for crime, however, the area is much more heavily policed nowadays. Be vigilant with your camera and be particularly wary after dark. Steer clear of any steps that lead down the hill and on Rua Almirante Alexandrino or at the Tijuca end of Largo dos Guimarães.

Sights

Santa Teresa is best seen by tram or on foot: wander around and look at the colonial buildings; stop for a beer in a little streetside café; admire the view. The better colonial houses, most of which are private residences, include the **Casa de Valentim** (a castle-like house in Vista Alegre), the tiled **Chácara dos Viegas** in Rua Monte Alegre and the **Chalé Murtinho**. This was the house in which Dona Laurinda Santos Lobo held her famous artistic, political and intellectual salons at the turn of the 20th century. The house was in ruins until it was partially restored and turned into a cultural centre called **Parque das Ruínas** ⓘ *R Murtinho Nobre 41, daily 1000-1700*. It has superb views of the city, an exhibition space and an open-air stage (live music Thursday). There are similarly superb views from the **Museu Casa de Benjamin Constant** ⓘ *R Monte Alegre 225, T021-2509 1248, daily 1000-1700*, the former home of the Carioca military engineer and positivist philosopher who helped to found the Republic. The **Chácara do Céu**, or Fundação Raymundo Ottoni de Castro Maia ⓘ *R Murtinho Nobre 93, T021-2285 0891, Wed-Mon 1200-1700, US$1*, has a wide range of works by modern painters, including Picasso and important Brazilian artists. To get to both the Chácara and the Parque das Ruínas take the Santa Teresa tram to Curvelo station, walk along Rua Dias de Barros, following the signposts to Parque das Ruínas.

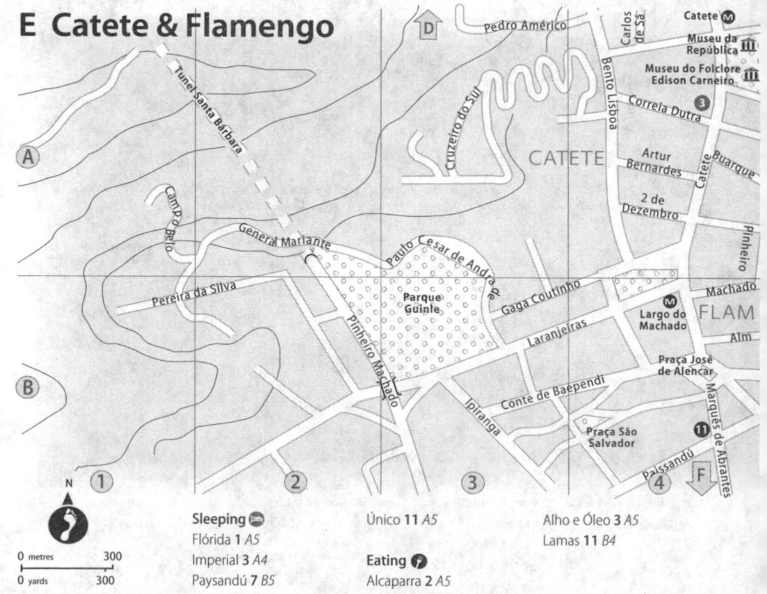

Glória, Catete and Flamengo

» pp106-136.

The city centre is separated from Copacabana and the other ocean beaches by a series of long white-sand coves that fringe Guanabara Bay and which are divided by towering rocks. The first of the coves is the Enseada da Glória, fronting the suburb of the same name and sitting next to the Santos Dumont airport. Avenida Infante Dom Henrique, a broad avenue lined with an eclectic mix of grand houses and squat office blocks, leads from here to what was once the city's finest beach, Flamengo, a long stretch of sand separated from the rest of southern Rio by the Morro da Viúva (widow's peak). The suburb of Catete lies just behind Flamengo. These three areas were once the heart of recreational Rio; the posing-spots of choice for the belle-époque middle and upper classes and perhaps the most coveted urban beaches in the world. These days the water is polluted and swimming ill-advised, but the suburbs are pleasant for a stroll.

Ins and outs

Bus No 119 from the centre or No 571 from Copacabana serve the neighbourhoods, as does the metro. The centrepiece of the three suburbs are the planned gardens of the Parque do Flamengo, on Avenida Infante Dom Henrique, reached from metro Glória, Catete, Largo de Machado or Flamengo. Closed to traffic on Sunday. Be careful after dark.

Sights

Before the pollution became too much, Burle Marx, Brazil's 20th-century Capability Brown, designed this handsome stretch of waterfront to separate Avenida Infante Dom Henrique from the city's most glorious beach, and gave it ample shade with a range of tropical trees and stands of stately royal palms. The gardens stretch from Glória through to the Morro da Viúva at the far end of Flamengo; they were built on reclaimed land and opened in 1965 to mark the 400th anniversary of the city's founding. The lawns and promenade are favourite spots for smooching lovers, especially at sundown. There are children's play areas too and a handful of monuments and museums. These include the impressive postmodern **Monumento aos Mortos da Segunda Guerra Mundial** ⓘ *Av Infante Dom Henrique, Tue-Sun 1000-1700 for the crypt museum; beach clothes and flip flops not permitted*, the national war memorial to Brazil's dead in the Second World War. The gently curved slab is supported by two slender columns, representing two palms uplifted to heaven and guarded by soldiers from the adjacent barracks. In the crypt are the remains of the Brazilian soldiers killed in Italy in 1944-1945. At the far northern end of the Parque do Flamengo is the **Museu de Arte Moderna** ⓘ *Av Infante Dom Henrique 85, T021-2240 4944, www.mamrio.com.br, Tue- Sun 1200-1700, last entry 1630, US$2*, another striking modernist building with the best collection of modern art in Brazil outside São Paulo. Works by many well-known Europeans sit alongside collections of Brazilian modern and contemporary art including drawings by Cândido Portinari and etchings of everyday work scenes by Gregório Gruber.

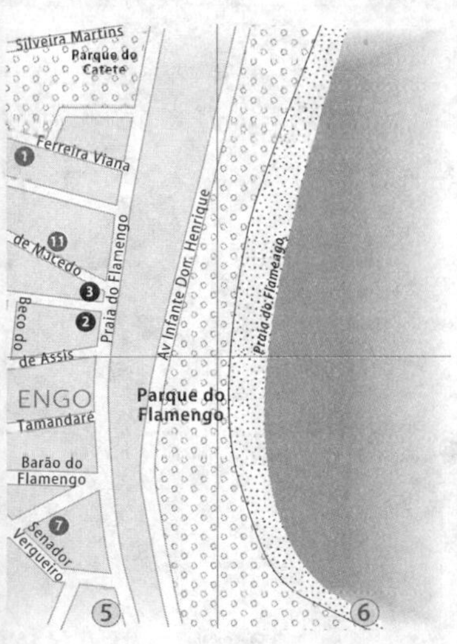

The beautiful little church on the Glória hill, overlooking the Parque do Flamengo, is **Nossa Senhora da Glória do Outeiro** ⓘ *Mon-Fri 1300-1700, Sat and Sun 0800-1200,* (1735-1791) It was the favourite church of the imperial family and Dom Pedro II was baptized here. The building is polygonal, with a single tower. It contains some excellent examples of the best *azulejos* in Rio and its main wooden altar was carved by Mestre Valentim. Next door there is a small **Museum of Religious Art** ⓘ *T021-25566434, same hours, but closed on Mon.* Behind Gloria and Flamengo is the rather down-at- heel suburb of Catete, which is dotted with museums. The best of these is the **Museu da República** ⓘ *R do Catete 153, T021-2557 3150, Sun-Tue 1200-1700, Wed 1400-1700, US$2.50, free Wed and Sun,* the former palace of a coffee baron, the Barão de Nova Friburgo. The palace was built in 1858-1866 and, in 1887, it was converted into the presidential seat, until the move to Brasília. The ground floor of this museum consists of the sumptuous rooms of the coffee baron's mansion. The first floor is devoted to the history of the Brazilian republic. You can also see the room where former president Getúlio Vargas shot himself. Behind the museum is the **Parque do Catete** which contains many birds and monkeys and is a popular place for practising Tai Chi.

The **Museu do Folclore Edison Carneiro** ⓘ *R do Catete 181, T021- 2285 0441, Tue-Fri 1100-1800, Sat and Sun 1500-1800, free,* houses a collection of amusing but poorly labelled small ceramic figures representing everyday life in Brazil, some of which are animated by electric motors. Many artists are represented and displays show the way of life in different parts of the country. There are also fine Candomblé and Umbanda costumes, religious objects, displays about Brazil's festivals and a small, but excellent library, with helpful staff who can help find books on Brazilian culture, history and anthropology. Flash photography is prohibited.

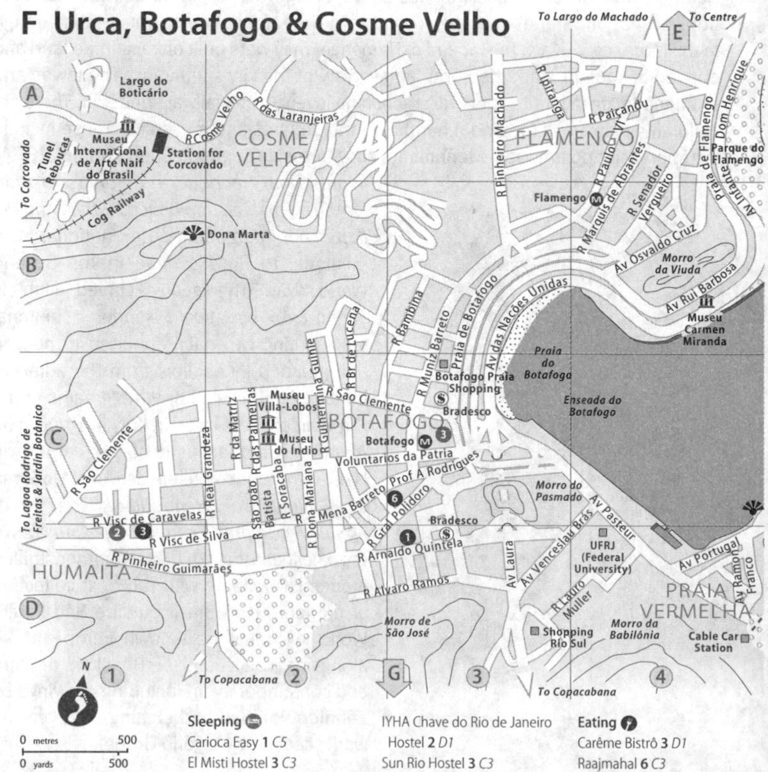

The **Museu Carmen Miranda** ⓘ *Parque Brigadeiro Eduardo Gomes (Parque do Flamengo), Flamengo, T021-2299 5586, Tue-Fri 1100-1700, Sat and Sun 1400-1700, US$1*, has over 3000 items related to the famous Portuguese singer forever associated with Rio, who emigrated to Brazil as a child and then to Hollywood. These include her famous gowns, fruit-covered hats, jewellery and recordings. There are occasional showings of her films.

Botafogo, Urca and the Sugar Loaf » pp106-136.

Pão de Açúcar, or the Sugar Loaf, looms over the perfect wine-glass bay of Botafogo, the next of the Guanabara Bay coves after Flamengo. Huddled around the boulder's flanks is the suburb of **Urca**, home to a military barracks and the safest middle-class houses in Rio. Remnant forest, still home to marmosets and rare birds, shrouds the boulder's sides and a cable car straddles the distance between its summit, the Morro de Urca hill and the houses below, making one of the continent's most breathtaking views easily accessible. Urca and Botafogo have a few sights of interest and make convenient bases for the centre with decent accommodation and restaurant options, particularly in the lower price ranges.

Ins and outs

Botafogo has a metro station. Buses that run between Copacabana and the centre stop in Botafogo, so take any bus marked 'Centro' from Copacabana or 'Copacabana' from the centre. Bus 107 (from the centre, Catete or Flamengo) and 511 from Copacabana (512 to return) take you to Urca and the cable-car station for the Sugar Loaf. Alternatively, walk 10 minutes northeast from behind the Rio Sul shopping centre to the cable-car station, which lies on Praça General Tiburcio, next to the Rio de Janeiro federal university. The rides themselves go up in two stages, the first to the summit of Morro da Urca, the smaller rock which sits in front of the Sugar Loaf, and the second from there to the top of the Sugar Loaf itself. Allow at least two hours for your visit.

Pão de Açúcar (Sugar Loaf)

The western hemisphere's most famous monolith rises almost sheer from the dark sea to just under 400 m, towering over Botafogo beach and separating Guanabara Bay from the open Atlantic Ocean. The views from the top, out over Copacabana, Ipanema and the mountains and forests of Corcovado and Tijuca are as unforgettable as the view from New York's Empire State Building or Victoria Peak in Hong Kong. The **cable car** ⓘ *Av Pasteur 520, Praia Vermelha, Urca, daily 0800-2200, US$15, every 30 mins*, runs to the top where there are extensive paths, plentiful shade and snack bars. Come early for the clearest air, best views and smallest crowds.

Paths up and around the Sugar Loaf There is more to Sugar Loaf than the views from the top. The surrounding rocks hide secluded little beaches, remnant forest and small colonial suburbs well worth seeing. The best place to begin is at Praia Vermelha, the beach to the south of the rock where there is a simple restaurant, the **Círculo Militar da Praia Vermelha** (no sign) with wonderful views. The walking track, **Pista Cláudio Coutinho** ⓘ *daily 0700-1800*, runs from here along the waterfront around the foot of the rock. You'll see plenty of wildlife at dawn, especially marmosets and colourful tanagers, along with various intrepid climbers scaling the granite. About 350 m from the beginning of the Pista Coutinho is a turning to the left for a path that winds its way up through the forest to the top of Morro de Urca, from where the cable car can be taken for US$10. You can save even more money by climbing the Caminho da Costa, a path to the summit of the Pão de Açúcar. Only one stretch of 10 m requires climbing gear; wait at the bottom of the path for a group going up. This way you can descend to Morro de Urca by cable car for free and walk down. There are 35 rock-climbing routes up the boulder. The best months for climbing are April to August. See page 130 for climbing clubs.

Botafogo

The Funai-run **Museu do Índio** ⓘ *R das Palmeiras 55, T021-2286 8899, Mon-Fri 1000-1730, Sat and Sun 1300-1700, US$1.75, 10-min walk from Botafogo metro or bus 571 from Catete*, preserves some 12,000 objects from over 180 Brazilian indigenous groups, including basketry, ceramics, masks and weapons as well as 500,000 documents and 50,000 photographs. Very few are on display and the museum's few rooms are mostly devoted to information panels and short film shows. The garden includes a Guaraní *maloca* and there is a small, well-displayed handicraft shop and a library of ethnology.

The **Museu Villa-Lobos** ⓘ *R Sorocaba 200, T021-2266 3845, www.museuvillalobos.org.br, Mon-Fri 1000-1700, free*, is a block east of the Museu do Índio. Such was the fame and respect afforded to Latin America's most celebrated composer (see page 138) that the museum ws founded only a year after his death in 1960. Inside the fine 19th-century building is a collection of his personal objects including instruments, scores, books and recordings. The museum has occasional concerts and temporary shows and supports a number of classical music projects throughout Brazil.

The **Dona Marta viewpoint**, which sits in the forest immediately above Botafogo and is connected by road to Corcovado, offers the best views of the Sugar Loaf in the city. Do not visit after 1730 as robbers from the nearby *favelas* frequent the roads.

Christ statue at Corcovado and Cosme Velho

Few famous sights in the world live up to the high expectations overexposure has placed on them. The view from **Corcovado mountain** is one of them. Come, if you can, for dusk. Almost a kilometre above the city and at the apex of one of the highest pinnacles in Tijuca forest stands **O Redentor** – Christ the Redeemer, lit in brilliant xenon and with arms open to embrace the urban world's most breathtaking view. At his feet to the west are a panoply of bays, fringed with white, and backed by twinkling skyscrapers and the neon of myriad street lights. To the east as far as the eye can see lie long stretches of sand washed by green and white surf. And in front and to the south , next to the vast ocean beaches, is the sparkle of Niterói watched over by low grey mountains and connected to Rio by a 10-km long sinuous bridge that threads its way across the 10-km expanse of Guanabara Bay. As the light fades, the tropical forest at Christ's back comes to life in a chorus of cicadas and evening birdsong loud enough to drown even the chatter of a thousand tourists.

At the base of the mountain is the sleepy suburb of **Cosme Velho,** leafy and dotted with grand houses, museums and a little artist's corner called the Largo do Boticario. The two are linked by a 3.8-km railway, opened in 1884 by Emperor Dom Pedro II.

Ins and outs

There are several ways to reach the top of Corcovado. A cog railway and a road connect the city to the mountain from the suburb of Cosme Velho. Both are on the northern side of the Rebouças tunnel, which runs to and from the Lagoa. From the upper terminus of the **cog railway** ⓘ *R Cosme Velho 513, T021-2558 1329, www.corcovado.com.br, daily 0830-1830 every 30 mins, takes 10 mins, US$8 one- way, US$15 return*, there is a climb of 220 steps to the top or you can take the newly installed escalator, near which there is a café. Mass is held on Sunday in a small chapel in the statue pedestal. There is a museum at the station with panels showing the history of the statue and the railway.

To get to the cog railway station take a taxi or bus to Cosme Velho and get off at the station. **Buses** are as follows: from the centre or Glória/Flamengo bus No 180; from Copacabana bus Nos 583 or 584; from Botafogo or Ipanema/Leblon bus Nos 583 or 584; from Santa Teresa take the micro-ônibus. **Taxis**, which wait in front of the station, also offer tours of Corcovado and Mirante Dona Marta and cost around US$25.

Do not walk back from Corcovado or visit the Mirante Dona Marta after dark; armed robbery is common. Take a taxi.

If going **on foot**, take bus No 206 from Praça Tiradentes (or No 407 from Largo do Machado) to Silvestre, where there is a station at which the train no longer stops. It is a steep 9-km walk from here to the top, along a shady road. Take the narrow street to the right of the station, go through the gate used by people who live beside the tracks and continue to the national park entrance. Walkers are not usually charged entrance fees. Allow a minimum of two hours (up to four hours depending on fitness).

By **car**, drive through Túnel Rebouças from the Lagoa and then look out for the Corcovado signs before the beginning of the second tunnel and off to your right. Ignore the clamour of the touts at the beginning of the Corcovado road. They will try to convince you that the road is closed in order to take you on an alternative route and charge a hefty fee. If going by car to Corcovado, the entrance fee is US$2.20 for the vehicle, plus US$2.20 for each passenger. If you are coming down after dark try to go in company or at weekends when more people are about.

Almost all the hotels, even the hostels, offer organized **coach trips** to Corcovado, which usually take in Sugar Loaf and Maracanã as well. These offer a fairly brief stop on the mountain and times of day are not always the best for light. **Helicopter tours** are available though these leave from the Sugar Loaf or the Lagoa.

Cosme Velho

The **Museu Internacional de Arte Naif do Brasil** (MIAN) ⓘ *R Cosme Velho 561, 300 m uphill on the same street as the station for Corcovado, T021-2205 8612, www.museu naif.com.br, Tue-Fri 1000-1800, weekends 1200-1800, US$3.20,* is one of the most comprehensive museums of naïf and folk paintings in the world with a permanent collection of 8000 works by naïf artists from 130 countries. The museum also hosts several thematic and temporary exhibitions through the year. Parts of its collection are often on loan around the world. There is a coffee shop and a souvenir shop where you can buy paintings, books, postcards and T-shirts. Courses and workshops on painting and related subjects are also available.

The **Largo do Boticário** ⓘ *R Cosme Velho 822*, is a pretty, shady little square close to the terminus for the Corcovado cog railway and surrounded by 19th- century buildings. It offers a glimpse of what the city looked like before all the concrete and highways. That the square exists at all is thanks to concerned residents who not only sought to preserve it but were also instrumental in rebuilding and refurbishing many of the buildings, using rubble from colonial buildings demolished in the city centre. Many of the doors once belonged to churches. The four houses that front the square are painted different colours (white, pale blue, caramel and pink), each with features picked out in decorative tiles, woodwork and stone. Many artists live here and can often be seen painting in the courtyard.

Copacabana and Leme » pp106-136.

➔ *See map page 108.*

Copacabana, which is called Leme at its northern end, epitomizes Rio both for better and for worse. Like the city as a whole, it is breathtakingly beautiful from afar and a little ugly close to. At first sight it looks magnificent. The beach is a splendid broad sweeping crescent of fine sand stretching for almost 8 km, washed by a bottle-green Atlantic and watched over by the **Morro do Leme** – another of Rio's beautiful forest- covered hills. Behind it is a wide neon- and argon-lit avenue lined with high-rises, the odd grand hotel and various bars, restaurants and clubs. The tanned and toned flock all around in little bikinis, *sungas* and colourful beach wraps, playing volleyball on the sand and jogging along the wavy black and white dragon's tooth pavements, while others busk, play capoeira and sell their wares. But, like much of Brazil, the devil is in the detail and up close Copacabana is a lot less appealing. The sand may be clean enough but those bottle-green waves are far from it. Many of the bars and hotels are tatty and tawdry, some of them frequented by a Pattaya-type crowd of young, thin Cariocas and fat older foreigners looking to buy more than a drink. And at night Copacabana can be dangerous. Soliciting is rife and muggings are not uncommon.

Ins and outs

Bus Nos 119, 154, 413, 415, 455 and 474 run between the city centre and Avenida Nossa Senhora de Copacabana, are plentiful and cost US$0.40. If you are going to the centre from Copacabana, look for 'Castelo', 'Praça XV', 'E Ferro' or 'Praça Mauá' on the sign by the front door. 'Aterro' means the expressway between Botafogo and downtown Rio (not open on Sunday). From the centre to Copacabana is easier as all buses in that direction are clearly marked. The 'Aterro' bus does the journey in 15 minutes. Numerous buses run between Copacabana and Ipanema; the two beaches are connected by Rua Francisco Otaviano or Rua Joaquim Nabuco, immediately west of the Forte de Copacabana. Copacabana has metro stations a few blocks inland from the beach at Cardeal Arcoverde and Siqueira Campos.

Sights

Copacabana has always been a beach and beyond it there are no sights here of any note. The area exploded in population after the construction of the Túnel Velho (Old Tunnel) in 1891 and the New Tunnel in the early 20th century and has been growing, mostly upward, ever since. Streets are lined with high-rise flats that huddle together even on the seafront, crowding around the stately neoclassical façade of the **Copacabana Palace** hotel, which was the tallest building in the suburb until the 1940s.

Apart from New Year's Eve, when the whole suburb becomes a huge party venue and bands play along the entire length of the beach, Copacabana is a place for little more than landscape and people-watching. It's possible to swim in the sea when the current is heading out from the shore, but otherwise not advisable. The best way to enjoy the area is to wander along the promenade from *posto* (lifeguard post) to *posto*, perhaps stopping to enjoy a coconut at one of the numerous beachfront snack bars, and noting the different crowd at each one. Everyone looks at everyone in Rio so don't be afraid to subtly stare.

At the far end of the beach is the **Museu Histórico do Exército e Forte de Copacabana** ⓘ *Av Atlântica at Francisco Otaviano, www.fortecopacabana.ensino.eb.br, Tue-Sun 1000-1600, US$2*, a museum charting the history of the army in Brazil through the colonial, imperial and republican periods, with cases of military artefacts and panels in Portuguese on campaigns such as the one fought at Canudos against Antônio Conselheiro. There are good views out over the beaches from the fort and a small restaurant.

Copacabana – what's in a name?

Copacabana is most famously a beach in Brazil. However, it is also a beach in New South Wales, a nightclub in New York, a small town in Bolivia and a song by Barry Manilow. All of these, one might think owe their name to Brazil's Copacabana. But it is not so. Copacabana is an Inca word meaning beholder of the blue horizon or beholder of the precious stone. The original Copacabana was a port for the islands of the Sun and the Moon on the shores of Lake Titicaca, endowed with spiritual significance for the Inca people. These islands were the mythical navel of the world and the birthplace of the Inca nation and the sun deities with which they are associated. As far as we know, the Incas never made it to Rio, and certainly were not responsible directly for naming Rio's Copacabana. For this we must thank the Virgin Mary . Sleight of hand from either the church or the Inca people themselves, who often used syncretism to preserve the heart of their spiritual practices led to the Bolivian Copacabana being transformed from an Inca shrine to a Christian one. In 1576, after surviving a storm on the lake, fishermen commissioned Francisco Yupanque, a direct descendant of the Inca nobility to carve a statue in homage to Our Lady whom they credited with having rescued them. The statue, which had strong Inca features was placed inside a purpose built church in the town of Copacabana, which was renamed Nuestra Señora de Copacabana. It quickly became a pilgrimage centre, especially for sailors and copies of the Inca Virgin were often carried on voyages between Spain and the New World. In the 17th century a boat sailing from Spain to South America came into great difficulties during a storm in the Atlantic. The sailors prayed to an image of Nuestra Señora de Copacabana that they had in their possession and, like those Inca fishermen, they were saved. Their captain promised to build a chapel to the Virgin when he reached land, and he did so in Rio de Janeiro. The Chapel, Nossa Senhora de Copacabana and the original image left their by the ship's captain stood at the far end of Copacabana on the Arpoador until 1914 when it was razed to the ground to make way for the Forte de Copacabana.

Ipanema and Leblon » pp106-136.

→ *See map page 116.*

Like Copacabana and Leme, Ipanema and Leblon are essentially one long curving beach enclosed by the monolithic Dois Irmãos rocks at the western end and the Arpoador rocks to the east. And like Copacabana and Leme, they have few sights beyond the sand, the landscape and the beautiful people. Comparisons, however, end there. Ipanema and Leblon are as fashionable and cool as Copacabana is grungy and frenetic. If Copacabana is samba, then Ipanema is bossa nova: wealthy, sealed off from the realities of Rio in a neat little fairy-tale strip of streets and watched over by twinkling lights high up on the flanks of the Morro Dois Irmãos. They look so romantic that it is easy to forget that they come from the world's largest favela.

Closeted and cosseted though it may be, these are the beach suburbs in which to base yourself whilst in Rio. Almost all of the city's best restaurants and bars are here (and in the suburbs of Gávea and Lagoa which lie behind). The streets are fairly clean and usually walked by nothing more dangerous than a small white poodle; there is plenty of reasonable accommodation, which doesn't rent by the hour at the lower end of the market; and the sea is good for swimming.

Rio's sun worshippers

Ipanema and Copacabana are the most famous beaches in the world and there can surely be no people more devoted to lazing in the sun than Cariocas. But it wasn't always so. In the 19th century Brazilians would only go near sea water if they had been ordered to do so by a doctor. Even then it would only be for a quick dip at the beginning or the end of the day when the sun was weak. A tan was regarded as unhealthy and a sign of being lower class; to actually sit in the sun was a serious breach of social propriety.

All this began to change when the famous French actress Sarah Bernhardt came to Rio in 1886 to star in *Frou Frou* and *The Lady of the Camelias* at the São Pedro theatre. During her time off she caused a scandal, appalling the great and the good by travelling to then distant Copacabana, throwing on a swimsuit, sunbathing and even swimming in the sea. By the turn of the 20th century others had begun to follow suit, and by 1917 going to the beach had become sufficiently fashionable that the city established strict rules and regulations to govern sun worship. People were permitted to bathe only between 0500-0800 and 1700-1900, had to wear appropriate dress and be quiet and discreet; failure to do so resulted in five years in prison. Official attitudes only began to change in the 1920s with the building of the Copacabana Palace and the arrival of more foreigners who ignored Rio's prudishness and convinced Cariocas to begin to enjoy the beach.

Ins and outs

There is no metro in Ipanema or Leblon. The destination for buses is clearly marked but, as a rule of thumb, any buses heading east along the seafront go to Copacabana or if going west to Barra da Tijuca, and those going inland will pass by the Lagoa or Gávea.

Sights

Like Copacabana, Ipanema and Leblon are places for people-watching. A half-day wandering around Ipanema/Leblon followed by a half-day wandering Copacabana/Leme can be most interesting. The crowds are quite different. While Copacabana attracts a real cross-section of Rio society, Ipanema and Leblon are predominantly haunts of the fashionable peacocks, who strut along the beachfront promenade, especially around Posto Nove. Beyond the people and the breathtaking landscape, there is little to see here but plenty to do, especially for avid consumers. Shopping is best on and around Garcia D'Avila and at the **Feira Hippy** (see Markets, page 126), where you will find everything from high-quality Brazilian designer swimwear to seed bracelets and T-shirts with pictures of Bob Marley. Those seeking culture but unwilling to leave the beach should head for the **Casa de Cultura Laura Alvim** ⓘ *Av Vieira Souto 176, T021-2247 6946*, comprising an arts cinema, art galleries (with temporary exhibitions), workshop spaces and a bookshop. If it is pouring with rain you could watch diamonds being cut and set at the **Museus H Stern** ⓘ *R Garcia D'Avila 113, T021-2106 0000*, or **Amsterdam Sauer** ⓘ *R Garcia D'Avila 105, T021-2512 1132*, or hang out in the **Garota de Ipanema**, the bar where the *Girl from Ipanema* was written in the late 1950s (see Bars and clubs page 119)

Gávea, Lagoa and Jardim Botânico » pp106-136.

Just inland from Ipanema and Leblon, nestled under the forested slopes of Corcovado and the Tijuca National Park and spread around the picturesque saltwater lagoon of Lagoa Rodrigo de Freitas, are these three mainly residential suburbs. There are a few sights of interest and all have lively top-end nightlife. Gávea tends to attract the young and wealthy, while the 30-somethings dine in the restaurants in Lagoa overlooking the lagoon and go out to clubs in Leblon or to the exclusive **Jockey Club** (see, page 120).

Ins and outs

Buses from the centre are marked Gávea or for the Jardim Botânico, Leblon, Gávea or São Conrado 'via Jóquei'. Bus Nos 571 and 170 from the centre go to the Jardim Botânico or bus No 172 from Flamengo or Botafogo. Bus No 584 runs between Jardim Botânico and Copacabana. Bus Nos 176 and 178 run from the centre and Flamengo and buses 591 and 592 from Copacabana go to the Planetarium.

Lagoa de Freitas

The Lagoa is another of Rio de Janeiro's unfeasibly beautiful natural sights and has long been admired. Darwin and German naturalists Spix and Martius mention it in their accounts. It is best seen in the early evening when thick golden sunlight bathes the rainforest-clad slopes of the **Serra da Carioca**, which rise high above it to reach their spectacular pinnacle with the distant xenon-white statue of Christ.

Like Copacabana and Guanabara Bay, it could be even more beautiful if only it were looked after a little better. The canal that links the lake to the sea is far too narrow to allow for sufficient exchange of water, pollution makes it unsafe for swimming and occasional summer algal blooms have led to mass fish deaths.

The lake is surrounded by a series of parks. Immediately next to it is the **Parque Tom Jobim** and contiguous are **Brigadeiro Faria Lima**, **Parque do Cantagalo** and **Parque das Taboas**. All have extensive leisure areas popular with roller skaters and volleyball players. There are live shows and *forró* dancing in the **Parque dos Patins** and kiosks serve a variety of food from Arabic to Japanese. Nearby is the **Parque Carlos Lacerda** ① *Av Epitacio Pessoa, daily 0800-1900*, an open-air art gallery with sculptures by local artists in a landscaped park shaded by ornamental trees.

Jardim Botânico (botanical gardens)

① *R Jardim Botânico 1008, T021-3874 1808, www.jbrj.gov.br, daily 0800-1700, US$2.*
These extensive 137-ha gardens protect 70,000 rare vascular plants and are home to 140 species of birds, and butterflies including the brilliant blue Morphos. There are stately stands of 40-m-high royal palms, large tropical ficus and ceiba trees and pau brasil, from which the country gets its name. Giant Amazonian victoria regia lilies cover many of the ponds and there are views up to Corcovado through the trees. The gardens were founded in 1808 by the king, Dom Joao VI, as a nursery for European plants and new specimens from throughout the world. When the electric tram line arrived in this part of the city, housing and industries soon followed, but the gardens, then as now, remained a haven of peace. There is a herbarium, an aquarium and a library as well as the **Museu Botânico**, housing exhibitions on the conservation of Brazilian flora, and the **Casa dos Pilões**, the first gunpowder factory in Brazil. A new pavilion contains sculptures by Mestre Valentim. Many improvements were carried out before the 1992 Earth Summit, including a new *orquidario*, an enlarged bookshop and a smart café. Birdwatchers can expect to see rarities including the social flycatcher, great and boat-billed kiskadees, cattle tyrants, sayaca, palm and seven- coloured (green-headed) tanagers as well as over 20 different kinds of hummingbird, roadside hawks, laughing falcons and various toucans and parakeets. There are marmosets in the trees.

Less than 1 km from the gardens is the little-visited **Parque Laje** ⓘ *R Jardim Botânico 414, daily 0900-1700, free*, which is more jungle-like than the Jardim Botânico and has a series of small grottoes, an old tower and lakes, as well as the **Escola de Artes Visuais** (visual arts school) housed in a large colonial house in the grounds.

The **Planetario** ⓘ *R Padre Leonel Franco 240, Gávea, www.rio.rj.gov.br/planetario, by appointment, free*, has a sculpture of the Earth and Moon by Mário Agostinelli. On Wednesday evenings at dusk, in clear weather, astronomers give guided observations of the stars. At weekends there are shows for children at 1630, 1800 and 1930. There are occasional *chorinho* concerts on Thursday or Friday.

The **Instituto Moreira Salles** ⓘ *R Marquês de São Vicente 476, Gávea, T021-3284 7400, www.ims.com.br, Tue-Fri 1300-2000, Sat and Sun 1300-1800, free*, is a cultural centre in a modernist mansion with gardens landscaped by Burle Marx. There are exhibition halls for photographic shows and an auditorium for concerts and films.

Rough paths lead to the summit of the flat-topped **Pedra da Gávea** and to magnificent views. Hang-gliders fly to the beach at São Conrado from the **Pedra Bonita** behind the Pedra da Gávea. See Activities and tours, page 127.

Barra da Tijuca and beyond » pp106-136.

This rapidly developing district modelled on Miami is one of the city's principal middle-class residential areas. It focuses on a 20-km sandy beach that is renowned for its surfing – especially at its far westernmost end – **Recreio dos Bandeirantes**. There are countless bars and restaurants, concentrated at both ends, as well as campsites (see page 112), motels and hotels. Budget accommodation tends to be self-catering.

Ins and outs

Buses from the city centre to Barra are Nos 175 and 176; from Botafogo, Glória or Flamengo take No 179; from Leme Nos 591 or 592; and from Copacabana via Leblon No 523 (45 minutes to one hour). A taxi from the centre costs US$25 (US$35 after 2400) or US$15 from Ipanema. A comfortable bus, **Pegasus**, goes along the coast from the Castelo bus terminal to Barra da Tijuca and continues to Campo Grande or Santa Cruz, or take the free 'Barra Shopping' bus. Bus 700 from Praça São Conrado goes the full length of the beach to Recreio dos Bandeirantes.

Sights

The **Bosque da Barra/Parque Arruda Câmara** ⓘ *daily 0700-1700*, at the junction of Avenida das Américas and Avenida Ayrton Senna, preserves the vegetation of the sandbanks which existed on this part of the coast before the city took over. The **Autódromo** (motor-racing track) is behind Barra and the Lagoa de Jacarepaguá, in the district of the same name. The Brazilian Grand Prix was held here during the 1980s before returning to Interlagos, São Paulo. **Terra Encantada** ⓘ *Av Ayrton Senna 2800, T021-2430 9800, www.terra-encantada.com.br, Thu-Sun 1000-2300*, is a 300,000-sq-m theme park in Barra whose attractions are based on the different cultural heritages of Brazil: indigenous, African and European. Among the attractions are roller coasters, river rapids, a cinema and shows. Rides close at 2200 and on the main street restaurants, bars and nightspots open. A bit further out is the **Museu Casa do Pontal** ⓘ *Estrada do Pontal 3295, Recreio dos Bandeirantes, Tue-Sun 0900-1930*. This is another collection of Brazilian folk art, put together by the French designer Jacques van de Beuque. Recommended.

Parque Nacional da Tijuca

Corcovado is situated within Tijuca National Park; one of the largest areas of urban rainforest in the world. It is a haven for city-weary Cariocas, as for some 200 species of birds, numerous small mammals and primates and hundreds of species of endangered Atlantic Coast rainforest plants. The forest has many natural springs, many of which have been diverted through bamboo channels to form natural showers – be sure to bring swimming gear. There is plenty of shade and the views from the various vantage points are almost as impressive as those from Corcovado.

The vegetation in the Parque Nacional da Tijuca is not primary. Most is natural regrowth and planned reforestation. It is a testament to what humans can do to regenerate lost forest. The first Europeans in the area cut down trees for use in construction and as firewood. The lower areas were cleared to make way for sugar plantations. When coffee was introduced to Rio de Janeiro in 1760 further swathes were cut down for *fazendas*. But the deforestation destroyed Rio's watershed and in 1861, in one of the world's first conservation projects, the imperial government decided that Tijuca should become a rainforest preserve. The enormous task of reforesting the entire area was given to an army major, Manuel Gomes Archer, who took saplings from other areas of Atlantic forest and replanted Tijuca with native trees and a selection of exotics in fewer than 13 years. The names of the six slaves who did the actual manual work is not known. Reforestation was continued by Tomas de Gama. In 1961 Tijuca was joined to several other patches of remnant forest to form a national park of 3300 ha.

Ins and outs

To get to the park entrance, take bus No 221 from Praça 15 de Novembro, No 233 ('Barra da Tijuca') or 234 from the *rodoviária* or No 454 from Copacabana to Alto da Boa Vista. The park is open daily 0600-2100. There is no public transport within the park and the best way to explore is by trail, tour, bicycle or car. If hiking in the park other than on the main paths, a guide may be useful if you do not want to get lost. Contact the **Sindicato de Guías**, T021-267 4582. For information on tours see page 131.

Sights

One of the best walks is to the **Pico da Tijuca** (1022 m). Views from the top are wonderful and the walk offers the chance to see plenty of animals. Allow two to three hours. To get to the trailhead enter the park at **Alto da Boa Vista** and follow the signposts (maps are displayed) to **Bom Retiro**, a good picnic place (1½ hours' walk). At Bom Retiro the road ends and there is another hour's walk up a fair footpath to the summit (take the path from the right of the Bom Retiro drinking fountain, not the more obvious steps from the left). The last part consists of steps carved out of the solid rock. There are several sheer drops at the summit which are masked by bushes – be wary. The route is shady for almost its entire length. The main path to Bom Retiro passes the **Cascatinha Taunay** (a 30-m waterfall) and the **Mayrink Chapel** (1860). Panels painted in the Chapel by **Cândido Portinari** have been replaced by copies and the originals will probably be installed in the Museu de Arte Moderna. Beyond the chapel is the wonderful little restaurant **Os Esquilos** which dates from 1945. Allow at least five hours for the walk.

Other viewpoints include the **Paulo e Virginia Grotto**, the **Vista do Almirante**, the **Mesa do Imperador** and the **Vista Chinesa** (420 m), a Chinese-style pavilion with a view of the Lagoa Rodrigo de Freitas, Ipanema and Leblon. **Museu Açude** ⓘ *Estrada do Açude 764, Alto da Boa Vista, T021-2492 2119, www.museuscastromaya.com.br, Thu-Sun 1100-1700, Sun brunch with live music 1230-1700*, is in the former home of tycoon Castro Maia with some impressive murals and *azulejos*.

Ilha de Paquetá

Paquetá Island, the second largest in Guanabara Bay, is noted for its gigantic pebble-shaped rocks, butterflies and orchids. Its name means 'many shells' in Tupi, but it has also been called the Ilha dos Amores. The only real reason to come here is for the wonderful views but there are a few historical buildings on the island including the **house of José Bonifácio**, a Cariocan anti-slavery campaigner, and the newly refurbished **Solar D'El Rei**, which houses a library. At the southwest tip is the interesting **Parque Darke de Mattos**, with beautiful trees, lots of birds and a lookout on the Morro da Cruz. The island has several beaches, but the water is none too clean. The only means of transport are bicycles and horse-drawn carriages (many have harnesses which cut into the horse's flesh). Neither is allowed into the Parque Darke de Mattos. A tour by *trenzinho*, a tractor pulling trailers, costs US$1.25, or just wander around on foot (quieter and free); bicycles can also be hired. The island is very crowded at weekends and on public holidays, but is usually quiet during the week.

The favelas

Brazil's reputation as a violent country comes almost exclusively from the gun fights against the police and the inter-gang wars which take place in the slums of Rio de Janeiro, São Paulo, Belo Horizonte, Salvador and other big cities. Such slums are known as *favelas* in Portuguese and although visits to are offered on organized tours, many are highly dangerous – closed communities where strangers enter in peril of their life; like the favela so shockingly portrayed in the multi award winning film, *Cidade de Deus* (City of God). The film was no exaggeration: Brazil's *favela*-driven crime statistics speak for themselves. A study undertaken in 2002 by British anthropologist, Luke Dowdney, in conjunction with Brazilian non-governmental organizations working in Rio's slums found that in the 14 years to that date almost 4000 under 18-year-olds were killed by firearms in Rio. Many died in inter-gang wars. Many were shot indiscriminately by the police. This compares with just under 500 children killed in the fighting between Palestinians and Israelis in the same period. The study also estimated that there were between 5000-6000 armed children in the city.

For some years now there has been a stand-off between the drug gangs and their child soldiers and the police and Rio's streets have been relatively safe for tourists. But in mid-2004, after three police officers were shot (one in front of his wife), the city police announced a knee jerk offensive called Operation Maximum Pressure, where 850 officers were sent to target drug gangs within the favelas themselves. Although many were arrested and large quantities of guns recovered the police as ever shot first and asked questions later. Rancour grew, and the operations targeted many favelas which until that point had been relatively peaceful. After the macho deputy state governor, Luiz Paulo Conde announced plans to build 10-ft-high concrete walls around Rocinha and Vidigal (which sit between Leblon and São Conrado), gang members took their fight to the streets of Copacabana, exchanging gunfire with the police on the Avenida Atlântica near Arpoador. Even after international condemnation from Amnesty International and complaints from the mayor, Conde refused to back down. The wall was not for social exclusion, he said, but to mark off territory and to protect Tijuca forest from the drug traffickers. Despite his remonstrations building has not yet begun. But all is not bad news. Even though the federal and state governments use little more than intimidation and brute force against the urban poor, more enlightened individuals, like the wife of the culture minister, Rosa Gil, and musicians like Grupo Afro Reggae in Rio and organizations like the Rudolph Steiner Monte Azul project in São Paulo are making a real difference by bringing education and the hope of work to the young urban poor. Crime statistics where they are working have shown a marked decrease. As yet government bodies have shown little interest in following their example, preferring the vote winning iron fist approach.

Ins and outs

Paquetá Island can be visited by ferry services that leave more or less every two hours from the boat terminal at Praça 15 de Novembro. **Boats**, T021-2533 7524, run 0515-2300 (from 0710 on Sunday and holidays), US$1, one hour. **Hydrofoils**, T021-3397 0656, run hourly 1000-1600, or 0800-1630 at weekends, US$4 (more expensive at weekends), 20 minutes.

Western Rio

Almost half of the municipal area of Rio de Janeiro is in what is referred to as the **Zona Oeste** (the West Zone). On the coast, this stretches from Barra da Tijuca past a whole succession of surf beaches such as **Prainha** and **Grumari** (very attractive, rustic beach bars), not accessible by public transport, but attracting heavy traffic at weekends. Further west still are the **Barra de Guaratiba** and **Pedra de Guaratiba** beaches and, finally, those at **Sepetiba**. This stunning coastal road (the start of the Costa Verde highway) is becoming obliterated by executive housing developments, so visit soon.

Sítio Roberto Burle Marx ⓘ *Estrada da Barra de Guaratiba 2019, Barra de Guaratiba, T021-2410 1171, daily 0930-1330, by prior appointment only*, was, from 1949 to 1994, the home of the great Roberto Burle Marx (1909-1994), world famous as a landscape designer and artist. His projects achieved a rare harmony between nature, architecture and man-made landscapes. He created many schemes in Brazil and abroad; in Rio alone his work includes the Parque do Flamengo, the pavements of the Avenida Atlântica in Copacabana, Praça Júlio de Noronha in Leme, the remodelling of the Largo da Carioca, the gardens of the Museu Nacional de Belas-Artes and of the Biblioteca Nacional and the complex at the Santa Teresa tram station near the Catedral Metropolitana.

Covering 350,000 sq m, the estate contains an estimated 3500 species of plants, mostly Brazilian. It is run now by the Instituto do Patrimônio Histórico e Artístico Nacional and one of its main aims is to produce seedlings of the plants in its collection. Also on view are Burle Marx's collection of paintings, ceramics, sculptures and other objets d'art, plus examples of his own designs and paintings. The library houses 2500 volumes on botany, architecture and landscape design.

Sleeping

The best places to stay in Rio are Santa Teresa, Ipanema and the Arpoador: the former for nightlife, culture and easy access to Lapa, the Sambódromo and carnival; the latter for the beach. Ipanema is probably the safest area of any in the city. Those looking for hotels with charm and personality will find Rio unremarkable. With a few notable exceptions those in the higher and mid-range bracket are a mix of anonymous business chain towers and fading leftovers from the 1970s, complete with period decor. Those at the lower end are almost invariably dubious hot-pillow establishments in equally dubious areas. Backpackers, however, are well catered for. Searches on sites like www.hostels.com or www.hostelworld.com will yield almost 50 and numbers are increasing every month. There are far too many for us to list them all here. We include our favourites.

All accommodation is considerably pricier over New Year and Carnaval. Reserve well in advance, especially budget accommodation.

Self-catering apartments This is a popular form of accommodation in Rio, available at all price levels. In Flamengo furnished apartments for short-term let, accommodating up to 6, cost US$300 per month. In Copacabana, Ipanema and Leblon prices range from about US$25 a day for a simple studio, starting at US$500-600 a month up to US$2000 a month for a luxurious residence sleeping 4-6. Heading south past Barra da Tijuca, virtually all the accommodation available is self-catering. Renting a small flat, or sharing a larger one, can be much better value than a hotel room.

Blocks consisting entirely of short-let apartments can attract thieves, so check the (usually excellent) security arrangements; residential buildings are called '*prédio familial*'. Higher floors ('*alto andar*') are quieter.

'Apart-Hotels' are listed in the *Guia 4 Rodas* and **Riotur**'s booklet. Agents and private owners advertise under '*Apartamentos – Temporada*' in publications like *Balcão* (twice weekly), *O Globo* or *Jornal do Brasil* (daily);

advertisements are classified by district and size of apartment: '*vagas e quartos*' means shared accommodation; '*conjugado*' (or '*conj*') is a studio with limited cooking facilities; '*3 quartos*' is a 3-bedroom flat. There should always be a written agreement when renting. A range of luxurious private homes throughout Rio and Rio state is offered by www.angatu.com and www.brazilianbeachhouse.com. **Cama e Café**, www.camaecafe.com.br, see below, offers homestays in Santa Teresa.

Santa Teresa *p90, map p90*

LL Mama Ruisa, R Santa Cristina 132, T021-2221 2117, www.mamaruisa.com. French-run boutique hotel with very carefully casual public spaces and 4 simply decorated, elegant hard wood and whitewash rooms decorated in a modern French colonial style and named in homage to French artistic icons. With a pool and sweeping views.

Al-E Cama e Café, T021-2224 5689, www.camaecafe.com.br. This company offers one of the most interesting options for a stay in Rio with a range of over 50 homestay deals in this most bohemian and artistic of neighbourhoods. Included in these are Mestre Valentim's mock neo-Gothic castle and Ronnie Biggs's former home. Homestays are very good value and provide the opportunity to get to know locals and see Rio from the inside. Mixing with your host is at guest's discretion. Rooms can be treated as impersonally as those in a hotel, or guests can fit in as part of the household. Stays range from the simple to the luxurious. **Cama e Café** work hard to match guests with hosts who share similar interests.

B-D Casa Áurea, R Áurea 80, T021-2242 5830, www.casaaurea.com.br. Tranquil, friendly, arty hostel and boutique hotel in a colonial house in a Santa Teresa backstreet. All rooms are different in shape, size and colour and they and the public spaces, which include a large garden patio, are decorated with tasteful art and craftwork. Attracts an interesting crowd. Close to the restaurant areas.

C-E Rio Hostel, R Joaquim Murtinho 361, T021-3852 0827, www.riohostel.com. Rio's best small hostel, clings to the side of a hill, has spectacular views of the centre and is on the doorstep of the city's best nightlife. Doubles and dorms are simple but well kept and overlook Rio or the little pool. Carina, the very friendly owner has an inexplicable love of Jamie Oliver as well as all things British and Australian. Excellent facilities and services include internet, kitchens, lockers, tours and a shuttle service.

Glória, Catete and Flamengo
p93, maps p90 and p92

Primarily residential areas between the centre and Copacabana. Catete and Glória to the north and Flamengo to the south lie next to a park landscaped by Burle Marx and a beautiful beach lapped by a filthy sea. They have good bus and Metrô connections.

LL Glória, R do Russel 632, Glória, T012-2555 7572, www.hotelgloriario.com.br. A stylish and elegant 1920s hotel. Not as grand as the **Copacabana Palace** but with far more charm than any others in Copacabana or Ipanema. Rooms have mock-Edwardian decor. The hotel has 2 pools, a spa and a theatre. Good for business travellers.

L-AL Flórida, Ferreira Viana 71/81, Catete, T021-2195 6800, www.windsorhoteis.com. Business-oriented hotel with a well-equipped business centre, one of the city's largest convention centres, bars (for private hire), a restaurant and modestly decorated no-nonsense modern rooms.

L-AL Novo Mundo, Praia Flamengo 20, Catete, T021-2105 7000, www.hotelnovo mundo-rio.com.br. Standard 4-star rooms in an art deco building with suites with balcony views of the Sugar Loaf.

A-B Paysandú, Paysandú, R Paissandú 23, Flamengo, T021-2558 7270, www.paysandu hotel.com.br. Old art deco tower next to the Palacio da República and Flamengo gardens, with spartan rooms but helpful staff, good location, organized tours available.

A-B Turístico, Ladeira da Glória 30, Glória, T021-2557 7698, F2558 5815. With breakfast, a/c, tourist information provided, mixed reports, some highly favourable.

For Sleeping and Eating price codes, see pages 49 and 52 or the inside front cover. For an explanation of phone codes, see page 66.

B Imperial, R do Catete 186, Catete, T021-2556 5212, www.imperialhotel.com.br. One of the city's very first grand hotels, built in the late 19th century. Rooms are divided between the grand old building and the new annexe whose modern US-style motel rooms are better equipped but overlook the car park.

B Inglês, R Silveira Martins 20, Glória, T021-2558 3052, www.hotelingles.com.br. Conveniently located next to the metro and in front of the Museu da República. The better rooms have been refurbished and have a/c.

C Único, R Buarque de Macedo 54, Catete, T021-2205 9932, F2205 8149. Plain rooms with TV, a/c and fridges. Recommended.

C-E Catete Hostel, R do Catete 92, casa 1, Catete, T021-3826 0522, www.catetehostel.com.br. Rooms and dorms all with en suites. Breakfast included in the price. 24-hr reception and check-in.

Camping

If travelling with a trailer, you can park at the Marina Glória car park, where there are showers and toilets, a small shop and snack bar. Pay the guards to look after your vehicle. See also www.camping-club.com.br.

Botafogo and Urca *p95, map p94*

C-E El Misti Hostel, Praia de Botafogo 462, casa 9, Botafogo, T021-2226 0991, www.elmistihostel.com. A converted colonial house with 6 dorms, shared bathrooms, kitchen and internet, capoeira classes and tour service.

C-E Sun Rio Hostel, R Praia de Botafogo 462, casa 5, Botafogo, T021-2226 0461, www.sunriohostel.com.br, next door to **El Misti**. A/c dorms, doubles and en suites, kitchen, internet, bike rental and tours organized.

G Copacabana

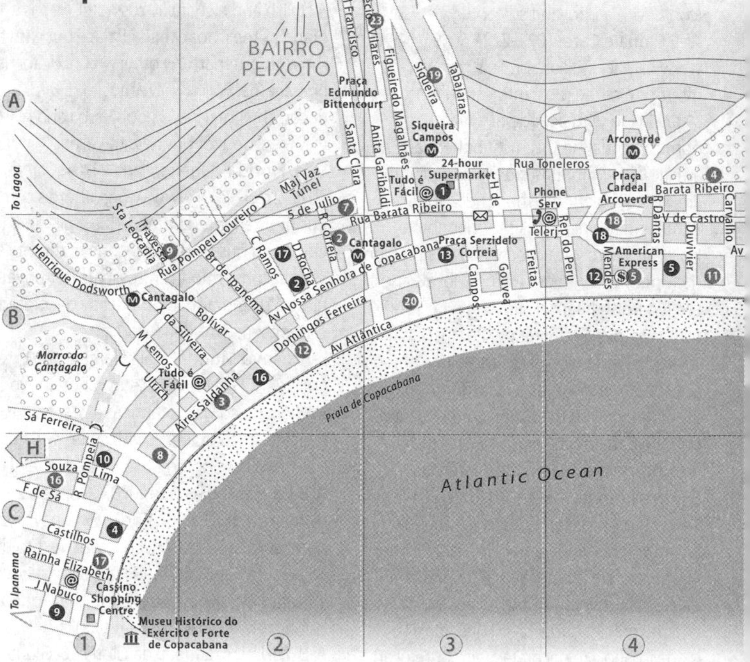

Sleeping
Angrense 3 *B2*
Benidorm Palace 2 *B2*
Copacabana Holiday 4 *A4*
Copacabana Palace & Cipriani Restaurant 5 *B4*
Copacabana Sol 7 *A2*
Copinha Hostel 6 *A5*
Debret 8 *C1*
Fantastic Rio 13 *B5*
Grandarrell Ouro Verde 11 *B4*
Holidays in Copacabana 17 *C1*
Le Meridien 10 *B5*
Marriott 20 *B3*
Mellow Yellow 18 *B4*
Newton's Rooftop 19 *A3*
Paulo de Tarso 21 *A5*
Pestano Rio Atlântica 12 *B2*
Rio Backpackers 9 *B1*
Rio Residences 22 *B5*
Santa Clara 23 *A3*
South American Copacabana 16 *C1*

D IYHA Chave do Rio de Janeiro Hostel, R Gen Dionísio 63, Botafogo, T021-2286 0303, www.riohostel.com.br. IYHA with 1 double and a range of small dorms, laundry and cooking facilities, decent breakfast, capoeira classes and the usual range of hostel tours. Cheaper for IYHA members. Very popular and sometimes noisy.

E Carioca Easy, R Marechal Cantuaria 168, Urca, T021-2295 7805, www.carioca hostel.com.br. Dorms and doubles in a colonial house with its own gardens situated on a quiet street at the base of Sugar Loaf in one of the safest and most spectacular neighbourhoods in Rio. Pool, kitchen, bike rental, boat trips and dorms and doubles.

Eating

Aipo & Aipim **2** *B2*
A Marisquera **1** *A3*
Casarão **10** *C1*
Cervantes **3** *A5*
Chon Kou **4** *C1*
Churrascaria Palace **5** *B4*
Copa Café **16** *B2*
La Tratoria **12** *B4*
Mala e Cuia **17** *B2*
Marakesh **13** *B3*
Siri Mole & Cia **9** *C1*
Taberna do Leme **14** *B5*
Traiteurs de France **18** *B4*

Copacabana *p98, map p108*

Once *the* place to stay in Rio but now increasingly sleazy. Ipanema is a better option. Many hotels charge about 30% more for a sea view, but some town-side upper rooms have good views of the mountains.

LL Copacabana Palace, Av Atlântica 1702, T021-2548 7070, www.copacabana palace.com.br. Rio's grande dame remains the city's only world-class large hotel, a mantle it has worn since first being made famous by Ginger Rogers and Fred Astaire, who filmed *Flying down to Rio* here. Pictures of them and hundreds of other famous faces adorn the upper gallery, in classy, understated black and white. Rooms are quiet, spacious and comfortable, with superb beds, effortless service, and conservative and rather European decor. The hotel restaurant, **Cipriani**, is of a similar high standard to its celebrated sister restaurants in Venice and New York.

LL Le Meridien, Av Atlântica 1020, T0800-111554, www.meridien br.com. An **Air France** hotel with pool, smallish rooms, and breakfasts with a wonderful view. Good for business travellers. Great restaurant.

LL Marriott, Av Atlântica 2600, T021-2545 6500, www.marriott.com. Rio's newest top-end business hotel with 245 guest rooms specifically designed for the business traveller, an executive floor, 12 meeting rooms and a whole gamut of other business services.

L Pestana Rio Atlântica, Av Atlântica 2964, T021 2548 6332, www.pestana.com. The best option in Copacabana after the **Palace**, with spacious bright rooms and a rooftop pool and terrace with sweeping views. Part of the well-managed Portuguese Pestana group. Very high standards. Highly recommended.

L-A South American Copacabana, R Francisco de Sá 90, T021-2522 0040, southamerican@uol.com.br. 2 blocks from the beach but in the Arpoador, which is safer than Copacabana. The front rooms are noisy, others are garishly decorated but well maintained. Helpful staff.

AL Grandarrell Ouro Verde, Av Atlântica 1456, T021-2542 1887, www.grandarrell.com.br. The best small hotel in Copacabana with spacious well-decorated rooms and a decent restaurant. Good for families – the hotel has a kids' club.

AL-A Benidorm Palace, R Barata Ribeiro 547, T021-2548 8880, www.benidorm.com.br.

Rather tacky though well-maintained hotel whose rooms look very B-grade *Saturday Night Fever*.

AL-A Copacabana Sol, R Santa Clara 141, T021-2549 4577, www.copacabanasolhotel.com.br. Newly refurbished, tiled, a/c rooms with cable TV, Wi-Fi, safes and en suites.

A Debret, Av Atlântica 3564, T021-2522 0132, www.debret.com. Bright, spacious, modern seafront rooms; others are a little dark.

A Hotel Angrense, Travessa Angrense 25, T021-2548 0509, www.angrensehotel.com.br. Well-kept basic a/c rooms in a little art deco block on a quiet street; 24-hr reception, English-speaking staff, reliable tour agency and good carnival rates.

A Santa Clara, R Décio Vilares 316, T021-2256 2650, www.hotelsantaclara.com.br. Bright, newly refurbished rooms a few blocks back from the beach. Well maintained, discreet and good value, at the lower end of this price range.

A-B Atlantis Copacabana, Av Bulhões de Carvalho 61, T021-25211142, atlantishotel@uol.com.br. Fading Arpoador hotel in a quiet, safe street very close to the beach. Small rooftop pool, sauna, and the best hotel rates in the area this close to the beach.

D-E Copinha Hostel, R Felipe de Oliveira 11, T021-22758520, www.copinhahostel.com.br. Clean, well-run little lemon-yellow hostel with a range of a/c dorms and doubles in white tile and with en suites. 24-hr reception, kitchen, cable TV and transport services.

D-E Mellow Yellow, R General Barbosa Lima 51, T021-25471993, www.mellowyellow.com.br. Enormous Australian-style party hostel with bars, tours, internet and impersonal service. Very popular and noisy.

D-E Newton's Rooftop, R Siqueira Campos 182, T021-2545 7499, www.newtonsrooftop.com.br. Dorms and doubles. Excellent value for longer stays. Good atmosphere – on Fri all guests are given a free *caiperinha*, and on Sat a free *feijoada* lunch. Helpful staff and tours, sun terrace, laundry, kitchen and internet.

D-E Rio Backpackers, Travessa Santa Leocadia 38, end of Av Pompeo Loureiro, T021-2236 3803, www.riobackpackers.com.br.

Self-catering apartments

Copacabana Holiday, R Barata Ribeiro 90A, T021-2542 1525, www.copacabanaholiday.com.br. Recommended, well-equipped small apartments from US$500 per month, minimum 30 days let.

Fantastic Rio, Av Atlântica 974, apt 501, Leme, beside **Hotel Meridien**, T021-2543 2667, http://fantasticrio.vilabol.uol.com.br. All types of furnished accommodation from US$20 per day. Good service, contact Peter Corr.

Holidays in Copacabana, Av Atlântica 4066, apt 605, T021-2513 0281. Rents apartments, all with phone, near beach, a/c, maid service; English, French, German spoken. All apartments owned by the agency, prices around US$50 per flat.

Paulo de Tarso, Av Princesa Isabel, 236, apt 102, T021-2542 5635, pauldetarso@ig.com.br. Apartments near the beach from US$25 per person. Several languages spoken, very helpful.

Rio Residences, Av Prado Júnior 44, apt 508, T021-2541 4568, F2541 6462. Swiss run, includes airport transfer.

Ipanema and Leblon

p99, map p116

LL Caesar Park, Av Vieira Souto 460, Ipanema, T021-2525 2525, www.caesar-park.com. Anonymous chain hotel with mock 19th-century flourishes in a beachfront tower. Some rooms have beach views. Decent service includes beach patrol and child-minding. Pool, sauna, restaurant and business facilities.

LL Fasano Rio, Av Vieira Souto 80, Ipanema, T021-3896 4000, www.fasano.com.br. This Philippe Starck-designed luxury hotel in the tasteful Paulistano hotel chain is by far the best in Ipanema and, aside from **La Suite** (see page 112), the best in Rio. The superior **Fasano Al Mare** restaurant serves delicious Italian seafood. There's a spectacular rooftop terrace, pool, fitness centre, sauna and massage, a good bar with live music, and limousine service for airport transfers.

L Best Western Sol Ipanema, Av Vieira Souto 320, Ipanema, T021-2625 2020, www.bestwestern.com. Part of the US group and world's largest chain, with the usual hotel catalogue rooms. Popular with agencies and business travellers.

L Marina Palace and Marina All Suites, Av Dolfim Moreira 630 and 696, Ipanema, T021-2294 1794, www.hotelmarina.com.br. 2 towers of 1980s vintage almost next door to each other. The former has smart, modern but standard 4-star rooms and a rooftop pool, the latter is a luxury boutique with designer suites and is favoured by the likes of Giselle Bundchen. By international standards it is shabby, but it has an excellent and fashionable sea view restaurant and bar which is great for breakfast and a light lunch or dinner.

AL-A Arpoador Inn, Francisco Otaviano 177, Ipanema, T021-2523 0060, F2511 5094. One of the best deals on the seafront. Well maintained, with off-season special offers. Recommended.

AL-A Mar Ipanema, R Visconde de Pirajá 539, Ipanema, T021-3875 9190, www.maripanema.com. Simple, smart, modern rooms a block from the beach. The front rooms on the lower floors are noisy.

A Ipanema Inn, Maria Quitéria 27, behind Caesar Park, Ipanema, T021-2523 3092, F2511 5094. Good value and location.

B San Marco, R Visconde de Pirajá 524, Ipanema, T021-2540 5032, www.sanmarcohotel.net. Newly renovated 2-star with simple rooms and a free *caipirinha* for every internet booking. Price includes breakfast. 2 blocks from beach. Recommended.

C-D Che Lagarto, R Barão de Jaguaripe 208, Ipanema, T021-2247 4582, www.chelagarto.com. Bright-red party hostel with young staff and a terrace with views of Corcovado. Dorms and doubles.

C-D Crab Hostel, R Prudente de Morais 903, Ipanema, T021-2267 7353, www.crabhostel.com.br. Party hostel a block from the beach with a pool, sauna, cable TV, dorms and rooms, some with en suites.

C-E Casa 6, R Barão da Torre 175, casa 6, Ipanema, T021-2247 1384, www.casa6ipanema.com. Charming, colourful simple French-owned B&B in a town house 3 blocks from the beach. Good long-stay rates.

C-E Harmonia, R Barão da Torre 175, casa 18, Ipanema, T021-2523 4905, www.hostelharmonia.com. 3 blocks from beach, doubles or dorms, kitchen facilities, English, Spanish, German and Swedish spoken, good internet, very welcoming and helpful.

C-E Hostel Ipanema, R Barão da Torre 177, Ipanema, T021-2247 7269, www.hostelipanema.com. Little residential house 3 blocks from the beach. English spoken, lockers, safes, internet and kitchen. 10% discount for *Footprint* readers on presentation of book at time of reservation. They also own the **Just Fly** hang-gliding company, see page 129.

C-E Ipanema Beach House, R Barão da Torre 485, Ipanema, T021-3203 3693, www.ipanemahouse.com. Great little hostel with very friendly staff, pool, internet, outdoor bar, continental breakfast, a range of dorms and doubles and 24-hr check-in.

Gávea *p101*

LL La Maison, R Sergio Porto 58, T021-7812 5836, www.lamaisonario.com. Rio's only other decent boutique hotel, also run by the French owners of **La Suite** (see page 112), sits in a period town house on a quiet backstreet in the residential suburb of Gávea. The bright spacious rooms are tastefully decorated in primary colours and there are wonderful views of Corcovado from the open-sided breakfast area and the little pool. The beach is a taxi ride away.

Barra da Tijuca and beyond *p102*

Spectacular settings, but isolated and far from centre.

LL La Suite, R Jackson de Figueiredo, 501, Joá, T021-2484 1962, fxdussol@hotmail.com. Rio's only boutique hotel of distinction opened in 2006 with 8 individually themed and exquisitely designed rooms perched like an eyrie over an exclusive beach in Rio's wealthiest small suburb. The rooms, the restaurant and the pool offer magical views. Pelé is a neighbour and the restaurant is run by Ludmila Soeiro, a former chef at one of Rio's best restaurants, **Zuka.**

LL Sheraton, Av Niemeyer 121, Vidigal (a suburb between Leblon and São Conrado), T021-2274 1122, www.sheraton-rio.com. One of the Sheraton's poorer hotels – a 1970s slab of concrete in painful need of restyling and refurbishing. Wonderful beach views though and a decent pool area.

Camping

Camping Clube do Brasil, reservations: Av Sen Dantas 75, 29th floor, Centro, CEP 20037-900, T021-2210 3171. There are 2 beach sites at Barra da Tijuca. The first is at Av Sernambetiba 3200, T021-2493 0628 (bus No 233 from centre, or 702/703 from the airport via the southern suburbs, US$5), a long way from the centre, with sauna, pool, bar, café, US$12 (half price for members). During Jan and Feb it is often full and may be restricted to members only.

There's a simpler site at Estrada do Pontal 5900, T021-2437 8400. Lighting, café, good surfing, US$6. Both have trailer plots.

Eating

There are many restaurants in Rio and very few good ones. With the arrival of decent food from São Paulo in the 1990s things have been improving, especially in Leblon. But it is important not to be taken in by appearances or hotel concierges. Expect to pay at least US$30 per person in the better restaurants. At the cheaper end of the spectrum, Rio lacks that almost ubiquitous Brazilian institution, the corner bakery. Cariocas generally wolf down their breakfast and snacks on foot at streetside bars so a decent sit-down breakfast that isn't mock-French in appearance (and price) can be hard to find. But there are plenty of stand-up juice booths serving fruit juices made from as many as 25 different fruits from orange to *açai* and carrot to *cupuaçu*, all of which are wonderful. You can eat a filling lunch for an average US$5 per person, less if you choose the *prato feito* (US$1.50-6), or eat in a place that serves food by weight (starting at about US$10 per kg).

Central Rio and Lapa

p76, maps p80 and p77

Many restaurants in the business district are open only for weekday lunch. Many *lanchonetes* in this area offer good cheap meals. The Travessa do Comércio has many extemporaneous street restaurants after 1800, especially on Fri, and is always buzzing with life. R Miguel Couto (opposite Santa Rita church) is called the 'Beco das Sardinhas' because on Wed and Fri in particular it is full of people eating sardines and drinking beer.

There are several Arab restaurants on Av Senhor dos Passos, which are also open Sat and Sun. In addition to those listed there are plenty of cafés, including a few chic new options on R Lavradio in Lapa, where the lively monthly Sat antiques market is held.

TTT Adega Flor de Coimbra, R Teotônio Regadas 34, Lapa, T021-2224 4582. *Chope* and reliable Portuguese food, including excellent *bacalhau* and sardines in olive oil. Served in a little restaurant bar founded in 1938, which was the home of the Carioca painter Cândido Portinari, this was once a haunt of Rio's left-wing intelligentsia who would gather here to discuss political theory over a glass of chilled French wine. Now the eclectic crowd is decidedly capitalist, mostly young after-workers and is particularly lively on Fri.

TTT Albamar, Praça Marechal Âncora, 184, Centro, T021-2240 8378. A long-established Rio seafood restaurant as popular with politicians and businessmen as it has been ever since its opening 70 years ago in the old Mercado Municipal. Getulio Vargas, Juscelino Kubitschek, Fernando Henrique Cardoso and

5 of the best restaurants in Rio

Aprazível (Santa Teresa) With a view, page 113.
Carême Bistrô (Botafogo) French, page 114.
Satyricon (Ipanema) Seafood, page 115.
Gero (Ipanema) and **Bar d'Hotel** (Leblon) People watching, page 115.
Espírito Santa (Santa Teresa) Brazilian, page 119.

almost all the other Brazilian presidents have dined here on dishes such as *bacalhau* with oysters and whiting fillet à la albamar, which have been on the menu for as long as anyone can remember. Great views out across Guanabara Bay.

Cais do Oriente, R Visconde de Itaboraí 8, Centro, T021-2233 2531, www.caisdo oriente.com.br. Wonderful restaurant with a range of different spaces, each with its own atmosphere; from a formal Portuguese-style belle-époque dining room to an informal palm-shaded open-air patio and a terrace with live music. The menu by French chef Alex Giraud is similarly varied with a broad selection of fusions and Mediterranean, Brazilian and oriental dishes.

Republique, Praça da República 63 (2nd floor), Centro, T021 2532 0000. A long established Rio favourite, now newly refurbished by the architect Chico Gouveia (whose decoration is based on the colours of the French flag), serving daring and ambitious South American fusion cooking by distinguished Rio chef Paulo Carvalho.

Bar Luiz, R da Carioca 39, Centro, T021-2262 6900. For 117 years this little bar in one of the few remaining colonial houses in the city centre has been at the heart of Rio life. Almost every Carioca you can name from Di Cavalcanti and Tom Jobim to Ronaldo and Chico Buarque has at one time or another formed part of the lively throng which gathers here on weekday evenings and most particularly on Fri and Sat to drink the famous *chope* and eat tapas. During the day it is a great place for a quiet snack and a respite from the heat and busyness of the city.

Café da Moda, Loja Folic, R Gonçalves Dias 49, 3rd floor, Centro, T021-2222 0610, www.folic.com.br. An a/c café devoted to the narrow waistline and located within the **Folic** shop. Salads are named after famous models - Gisele Bündchen, Kate Moss, Claudia Schiffer and so on, with more macho options for men, such as Zulu, which comprises buffalo mozzarella, maize, tomato, croûtons, lettuce and a garnish of marjoram. Light meals without fashionable names also available.

Bar das Artes, Paço Imperial, Praça XV de Novembro 48, Centro, T021-2215 5795. Neat, clean and peaceful café on the ground floor of the Paço Imperial (formerly the royal palace) in the busy centre of Rio. Salads, sandwiches, light meals and desserts like strawberry strudel.

Confeitaria Colombo , R Gonçalves Dias 32 (near Carioca Metrô station), Centro, T021-2232 2300, www.confeitaria colombo.com.br, afternoons only during the week. The only remaining belle- époque Portuguese coffee house in Rio, serving a range of café food, cakes, pastries and light lunches. The *feijoada colonial* on Sat is accompanied by live *choro*.

Sabor Saúde, R da Quitanda 21, Centro, T021-2252 6041, breakfast and lunch only. Vegetarian and wholefood including sandwiches (whose contents you can compile yourself), quiches, pastries, salads and light dishes such as grilled salmon with rosti.

Santa Teresa *p90, map p90*

Aprazível, R Aprazível 62, T021-3852 4935. Decent but unspectacular Brazilian dishes and seafood with one of the best restaurant views in the city: tables are outdoors in a tropical garden overlooking Guanabara Bay. This is a good Sun lunch spot when they have occasional *choro* and samba.

Adega do Pimenta, R Almte Alexandrino 296, Mon and Wed-Fri 1130-2200, Sun 1100-1800. A very small German restaurant in the Largo do Guimarães with excellent sausages, sauerkraut and cold beer.

Bar do Arnaudo, Largo do Guimarães, R Almte Alexandrino 316, T021-2252 7246. A modest-looking restaurant decorated with handicrafts but serving generous portions of wonderful northeast-Brazilian cooking. Try the *carne do sol* (sun-dried beef, or jerky) with *feijão de corda* (brown beans and herbs), or the *queijo coalho* (a country cheese, grilled).

Espírito Santa, R Almte Alexandrino 264, T021-2508 7095. Closed Mon. Lunch only Tue, Wed, Sun. Upstairs is a chic Mediterranean restaurant with a view. Downstairs is a funky weekend basement club. Great cocktails.

Sobrenatural, R Almte Alexandrino 432, T021-2224 1003. Simple, elegant seafood served by sexagenarian career waiters in bow ties. The huge dining room is always lively with chatter.

Glória, Catete and Flamengo *p93, map p90 and p92*

There are many cheap and mid-range eating places on R do Catete, all fairly similar.

Alcaparra, Praia do Flamengo 144, Flamengo, T021-2557 7236. Elegant traditional Italian/Portuguese restaurant overlooking the sea. A long-established favourite of senior politicians and business people who often ask for the *bacalhau*.

Colonial, **Hotel Glória**, R do Russel 632, T021-2555 7572. A formal open-plan dining room decorated with old prints and staffed by black-tie waiters. The broad international menu created by named Swiss chef Fredy Rothen is strong on seafood and pasta.

Alho e Óleo, R Buarque de Macedo 13, T021-2557 8541, Flamengo. Fashionable Italian with a strong emphasis on home-made pasta like the *picatina Al Capone* – tagliatelle with beef medallions in a cream sauce.

Lamas, R Marquês de Abrantes 18A, Flamengo, T021-2556 0799. This famous café brasserie with its conservative decor of white tablecloths and dark wood has been serving steaks, *bacalhau* and draught *chopp* to the Rio intelligentsia since 1874. It is still a wonderful place to see the city's movers and gives a real sense of how European the city once was.

Estação República, R do Catete 104, Catete, T021-2225 2650. A choice of more than 40 dishes – from soups and sushi to salads and stews, in this per kilo restaurant housed in the Palácio do Catete.

Botafogo and Urca *p95, map p94*

There are many cheap and mid-range options in the Botafogo Praia shopping centre.

Carême Bistrô, R Visconde de Caravelas, 113, Botafogo, T021-2537 5431. An elegant and intimate little restaurant serving some of the best French bistro food in Rio. The original chef Christophe Faivre, who created much of the menu, worked at Guy Savoy in Paris. He has since been replaced by his once-junior chef Flavia Quaresma who continues to produce house favourites like *coq au vin*, and by Argentinian executive chef Guillermo Martín Lusardi who has created a delicious new degustation menu. Respectable wine list.

Raajmahal, R General Polidoro 29, Baixo Botafogo, T021-2542 6242, www.raajmahal.com.br. One of the few restaurants in Brazil offering authentic Indian food with a huge menu including a range of vegetarian dishes such as *mater paneer*.

Yorubá, R Arnaldo Quintela 94, Botafogo, T021-2541 9387, evenings only except weekends; closed Mon, Tue. Rio's favourite Bahian restaurant, and several times voted the best in the city by *Veja* magazine. The menu comprises usual run of Bahian food from *acarajé* (beans fried in dendê palm oil) to *vatapá* (fish or chicken with coconut milk, shrimps, peanuts, dendê palm oil and chilli) alongside more unusual dishes such as chicken in ginger sauce with cashew nut rice.

Copacabana *p98, map p108*

There are stand-up bars selling snacks all around Copacabana and Ipanema. There are plenty of open-air restaurants along Av Atlântica, none of which can be recommended for anything but the view.

Cipriani, **Copacabana Palace** (see page 109). The best hotel restaurant for formal dining, with a chef from the Hotel Cipriani in Venice. Very good seafood and Italian fare.

Copa Café, Av Atlântica 3056, T021-2235 2947. A French bistro run by São Paulo chef Cássio Machado with light food and fabulous mini burgers with Dijon mustard. Very popular with Carioca celebrities like Caetano Veloso. DJ after dinner in the evenings at weekends.

Chon Kou, Av Atlântica 3880, T021-2287 3956. A traditional Chinese restaurant which bizarrely also offers an extensive sushi menu.

A/c with piped music; sit upstairs for good views over Copacabana beach. A welcome change from most other options in this area.

₸₸ Churrascaria Palace, R Rodolfo Dantas 16B. 20 different kinds of barbecued meat served on a spit at your table with buffet salads to accompany. Good value.

₸₸ Mala e Cuia, R Barata Ribeiro 638, T021-2545 7566. *Comida mineira* at another of the restaurants in this recommended chain.

₸₸ Siri Mole and Cia, R Francisco Otaviano 90, T021-2233 0107. Excellent Bahian seafood and Italian coffee in elegant a/c surroundings. At the upper end of this price bracket.

₸ Aipo and Aipim, Av Nossa Senhora de Copacabana 391b and 599 in Copacabana, and R Visconde de Pirajá 145 in Ipanema, T021-2267 8313. Plentiful tasty food sold by weight at this popular chain.

₸ A Marisquera, Barata Ribeiro 232, T021-2547 3920. Reasonable seafood dishes and Brazilian standard meals.

₸ Casarão, Souza Lima 37A. Cheap but decent café food and breakfasts.

₸ Cervantes, Barata Ribeiro 07-B at Prado Júnior 335B. Stand-up bar or sit-down a/c restaurant, open all night, queues after 2200. Said to serve the best sandwiches in town, a local institution.

₸ La Tratoria, Av Atlântica, opposite Hotel Excelsior. Italian. Good food and service very reasonable. Recommended.

₸ Marakesh, Av NS de Copacabana 599. Good-value pay-by-weight food.

₸ Taberna do Leme, corner of Princesa Isabel and Av NS de Copacabana. A simple, friendly bar/restaurant with helpful waiters and tables on pavement. Comprehensive menu all in English includes delicious crab pancakes. Recommended for eating as well as drinking.

₸ Traiteurs de France, Av NS de Copacabana 386. Delicious tarts and pastries.

Ipanema and Leblon *p99, map p108*

₸₸₸ Alessandro and Frederico, R Garcia D'Ávila 134, loja D, Ipanema, T021-2521 0828. Upmarket café with decent café latte and breakfasts. Great juice bar next door.

₸₸₸ Bar D'Hotel, Hotel Marina All Suites (see Sleeping, page 108). Light but very well-flavoured fish dishes served to people with tiny waists in casual designer cool surrounds. Very good cocktails. The best for breakfast or lunch with a beach view.

₸₸₸ Bistrô ZaZá, R Joana Angélica 40, Ipanema, T021-247 9101. Hippy chic pseudo-Moroccan/French restaurant that attracts a mix of tourist and bohemian Zona Sul Cariocas. Good fish dishes and cocktails and good fun. Evenings are best for intimate dining when the tables are lit by candles.

₸₸₸ Capricciosa, R Vinícius de Moraes 134, Ipanema, T021-2523 3394. The best pizzeria in town and a lynchpin in the TV and fashion scene – the famous and wealthy gather here to gossip and catch up. Queues can be long.

₸₸₸ Carlota, R Dias Ferreira 64, Leblon, T021-2540 6821. The best of many on a street lined with restaurants and bars. Great unpretentious Mediterranean food in an elegant, casual all-white dining room.

₸₸₸ Forneria, R Aníbal de Mendonça 112, Ipanema, T021-2540 8045. Paulistano restaurateur Rogerio Fasano's latest elegant eating space in Rio serves supreme burgers in pizza dough and cooked in a wood-fired oven, and other superior bar snacks. Full of an elegant after-beach crowd.

₸₸₸ Gero, R Aníbal de Mendonça 157, Ipanema, T021-2239 8158. Tasty Italian fare with excellent fish served to TV *Globo novella* stars and the like in a beautiful minimalist space.

₸₸₸ Manekineko, R Dias Ferreira 410, Leblon, T021-2540 7641. Rio's best Japanese with a large menu of superb traditional dishes and Japanese, European and South American fusion. The intimate dining area, comprising a corridor of low-lit booths, is always packed.

₸₸₸ Porcão, Barão de Torre 218, Ipanema, T021-2522 0999. One of the city's best *churrascarias* serving all manner of meat in unlimited quantities for a set price.

₸₸₸ Satyricon, R Barão da Torre 192, Ipanema, T021-2521 0627. The best seafood in Rio, especially the squid. Lively crowd in a large dining room which precludes intimacy. A favourite with businessmen, politicians and Ronaldo. Avoid Sat when there is a buffet.

₸₸₸ Zuka, R Dias Ferreira 233, Leblon, T021-3205 7154. One of the most fashionable restaurants in Rio with an exciting and eclectic fusion of everything – French and Japanese, American fast food and Italian – all presented on huge rectangular plates and in a carefully designed modern space.

Casa da Feijoada, Prudente de Morais 10, Ipanema, T021-2523 4994. Serves an excellent *feijoada* all week. Generous portions.

Celeiro, R Dias Ferreira 199, Leblon. Superior salads and buffet food which has been consistently voted the best in the city by the largest magazine *Veja*.

Fellini, R General Urquiza 104, Leblon, T021-2511 3600, www.fellini.com.br. The best per kilo in the city with a large range of delicious Brazilian and international dishes, salads and quiches. Plenty of options for vegetarians. Funky website.

Gergelim, R Vinícius de Moraes 121, Ipanema, T021-2523 7026. Veggie wholefood in an a/c café atmosphere. Good puddings.

Yemenjá, R Visconde de Pirajá 128, T021-2247 7004. Bahian cooking such as *moqueca*, *vatapa* and various other dishes cooked in déndê palm or coconut oil.

Amarelinho, R Farme de Amoedo 62, Ipanema. Great corner *lanchonete* with tables outside, fresh food, good value, friendly, open until 0300. Recommended.

Empório Saúde, R Visconde de Pirajá 414, Ipanema, T021-2522 1494, closed Sun and evenings. A large variety of vegetarian comfort-cooking from quiches to stews.

Gávea, Lagoa and Jardim Botânico *p101*

Gávea is the heartland of trendy 20-something Rio. The neighbourhoods of Jardim Botânico and Lagoa appear at first sight to offer unlimited exciting upmarket dining opportunities. But the restaurants are

H Ipanema & Leblon

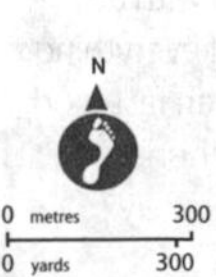

Sleeping
Arpoador Inn **12** *C5*
Atlantis Copacabana **13** *C5*
Best Western Sol Ipanema **11** *C4*
Caesar Park **1** *B3*
Casa 6 **15** *B4*
Che Lagarto **2** *B3*
Crab Hostel **3** *B4*
Fasano Rio **14** *C5*
Harmonia **15** *B4*
Hostel Ipanema **15** *B4*
Ipanema Beach House **18** *B3*
Ipanema Inn **6** *B3*
Marina All Suites **8** *B1*
Marina Palace **9** *B2*
Mar Ipanema **7** *B3*
San Marco **10** *B3*

Eating
Alessandro & Frederico **1** *B3*
Amarelinho **2** *B4*
Árabe da Gávea **3** *A1*
Bistrô ZaZá **15** *B4*
Capricciosa **4** *B4*
Carlota **5** *B1*
Casa de Feijoada **17** *B5*
Celeiro **6** *B1*
Empório Saúde **8** *B3*
Fellini **21** *B1*
Forneria **19** *B3*
Gergelim **9** *B4*
Gero **10** *B3*

mostly mutton dressed up as lamb. They look great, cost loads and serve dreadful food. Here are a very few exceptions:

𝆺 **Olympe**, R Custódio Serrão 62, Lagoa, T021-2539 4542. The Troisgros family were founders of nouvelle cuisine and run a 3-Michelin-star restaurant in Roanne. Claude Troisgros' cooking fuses tropical ingredients with French techniques, exemplified by the roasted quail filled with *farofa* and served with raisins, pearl onions and a sweet and sour *jabuticaba* sauce.

Roberta Sudbrack, Av Lineu de Paula Machado 916, Jardim Botânico, T021-3874 0139, www.robertasudbrack.com.br. Roberta was the private chef for President Henrique Cardoso and cooked for all the visiting international dignitaries who dined with him during his term of office. She is celebrated for her European-Brazilian fusion cooking and won *Veja*'s coveted chef-of-the- year award in 2006.

Árabe da Gávea, Gávea shopping mall, R Marquês de São Vicente 52, T021-2294 2439. By far the best Arabic restaurant in Rio.

Guimas, R José Roberto Macedo Soares, Baixo Gávea, T021-2259 7996. An old favourite for *Globo* actors and low-key celebrities, serving salt Portuguese food in a homely dining room or on the outside veranda on check tablecloths. Very crowded with fashionable under-30s after 2200 on Mon and towards the end of the week.

Mistura Fina, Av Borges de Medeiros 3207, Gávea, T021-2537 2844, www.misturafina.com.br. See Bars and clubs, page 120.

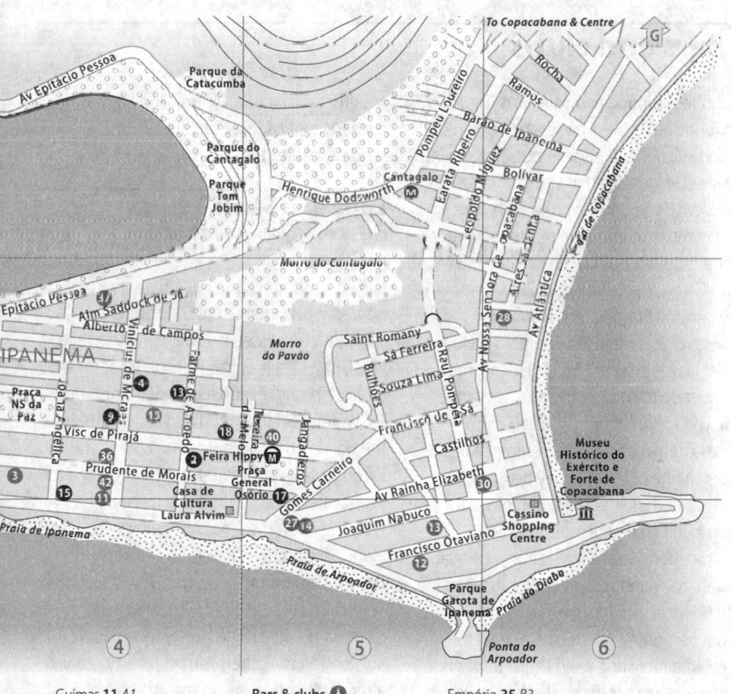

Guimas **11** *A1*
Manekineko **20** *B1*
Olympe **22** *A3*
Porcão **13** *B4*
Roberta Sudbrack **23** *A2*
Satyricon **13** *B4*
Yemenjá **18** *B4*
Zuka **16** *B1*

Bars & clubs
00 (Zero Zero) **24** *A1*
Academia da Cachaça **25** *B2*
Barril 1800 **27** *C5*
Bip Bip **28** *B6*
Bom Bar **29** *B1*
Bunker **30** *B6*
Caroline Café **31** *A2*
Cozumel **32** *A2*
Devassa **33** *B2*
El Turf **34** *A2*
Empório **35** *B3*
Garota de Ipanema **36** *B4*
Lagoa **37** *B4*
Melt **38** *C1*
Mistura Fina **39** *A2*
Shenanigans **40** *B5*
Sitio Lounge **41** *A1*
Vinícius **42** *B4*

What night where?

Monday Baixo Gávea, around Praça Santos Dumont with dancing pretty much limited to Cozumel, nearby in the Jardim Botânico. **Empório** in Ipanema has live music.
Tuesday **Devassa** in Leblon is busy on Tuesdays and **Bom Bar** down the road has an oriental night.
Wednesday **Clan Café** in Cosme Velho have live music. **Bunker** in Copacabana is good for dancing.
Thursday Pretty much anywhere is busy. The **Melt** club in Leblon has its busiest night, Lapa begins to get busy and all of the bars in Leblon have a decent crowd.
Friday Lively anywhere. **Mistura Fina** (Lagoa), **Clan Café** (Cosme Velho) usually have an interesting live jazz, MPB or bossa nova act. **Club Six** in Lapa has its busiest dance music night.
Saturday Much the same as Friday and the best night for Lapa and any of the samba clubs there, especially the **Rio Scenarium**, the **Bom Bar** and **Sítio Lounge**, all in Leblon. **Nuth** in Barra da Tijuca is always heaving.
Sunday Generally quiet, though Baixo Gávea is always busy and there are often live acts at **Melt** (Leblon); **00** (Gávea) has a gay night.

Bars and clubs

Rio nightlife is young and vivacious. Lapa is a current hotspot at weekends, once down-at-heel and still not entirely safe but undergoing a great renaissance, with a string of clubs along Mem de Sá and Lavradio with dance steps from samba and *forro* to techno and hip-hop. Similarly busy, even on Sun and Mon, is Baixa Gávea, where beautiful 20- somethings gather around Praça Santos Dumont.

Wherever you are in Rio, there's a bar near you. Beer costs around US$1.50 for a large bottle, but up to US$5 in the plusher venues, where you are often given a card which includes 2 drinks and a token entrance fee. A cover charge of US$3-7 may be made for live music, or there might be a minimum consumption charge of around US$3, sometimes both. Snack food is always available. Copacabana, Ipanema and Leblon have many beach *barracas*, several open all night. The seafront bars on Av Atlântica are great for people-watching; but avoid those towards Leme as some may offer more than beer.

Clubs on and around Rio's beaches are generally either fake Europe, eg **Melt** and **Bunker** (although decent DJs like Marky play here), or fake US, eg **Nuth** and **00**. Santa Teresa has the most interesting bohemian bars and is a good place to begin a weekend night before heading down the hill to Lapa, Rio's capital of nightlife (see box above), with a plethora of samba venues undergoing a steady renaissance. See also Samba schools, page 116.

Lapa and Santa Teresa

p85 and p90, maps p80 and p90

Lapa and Santa Teresa have Rio's most interesting, bohemian nightlife and shouldn't be missed if you are in Rio over a weekend. Ideally come early on a Sat for the afternoon market and live street tango on R Lavradio, eat in Santa Teresa and sample the bars on the Largo dos Guimarães and the Largo das Neves before returning to Lapa for live samba or funk. Although it is easy to walk between the 2 *bairros*, never walk alone. Always be wary of pickpockets.

Bar do Goiabeira, Largo das Neves 13, Santa Teresa, T021-2232 5751. One of several restaurant bars on this pretty little square. This and all the others attract an arty crowd after 2100, especially on the little streetside tables. Decent *petiscos* and a range of aromatic vintage *cachaças*.

Bar do Mineiro, R Paschoal Carlos Magno 99, Santa Teresa, T021-2221 9227, 100 m from Largo dos Guimarães. Rustic *boteco* opening right onto the street and with hundreds of black and white photos of Brazilian musicians hanging off its white-tiled walls. Always

attracts a busy, arty young crowd at weekends, downing Minas *petiscos* and bottled beer.
Carioca da Gema, Av Mem de Sá 79, Centro, T021-2221 0043. Great samba club café with live bands and sit-down tables; second only to the far larger **Rio Scenarium**.
Club Six, R das Marrecas 38, Lapa. Huge pounding European/NYC dance club with everything from hip-hop to ambient house.
Dama da Noite, R Gomes Freire 773, Lapa. Samba, *chorinho* and crêpes on the patio.
Espírito Santa, R Almte Alexandrino 264, Largo do Guimarães, Santa Teresa, T021-2508 7095, www.espiritosanta.com.br. Great little restaurant with a lively basement club where every Sat DJ Zod plays the best in Rio funk and West African dance. The bar manager, Adriana, makes superb cocktails.
Mercado, R do Mercado 32, Centro. A little bar with live *chorinho* every Thu from 2030.
Rio Scenarium, R do Lavradio 20, Lapa, T021-3852 5516, www.rioscenarium.com.br. 3-storey samba club in a colonial house used as a movie prop warehouse. Overflowing with Brazilian exuberance and joie de vivre, with people dancing furiously, to the bizarre backdrop of a 19th-century apothecary's shop or mannequins wearing 1920s outfits. This is Rio at its bohemian best. Buzzes with beautiful people of all ages on Fri. Come after 2300.
Sacrilégio, Av Mem de Sá 81, Lapa, next door to **Carioca da Gema**. T021-2507 3898. Samba, *chorinho*, *pagode* and occasional theatre. Close to many other bars.
Semente, R Joaquim Silva 138, Lapa, T021-2242 5165. Popular for samba, *choro* and salsa Mon-Sat from 2200, US$2.50 cover, minimum consumption US$2. Book at weekends. Great atmosphere inside and out. Recommended.

Glória, Catete and Flamengo
p93, maps p90 and p92.

Look out for the frequent free live music at the Marina da Glória and along Flamengo beach during the summer.

Botafogo and Urca *p95, map p94*

Casa de Matriz, R Enrique de Novais 107, Botafogo. Great grungy club with a bar, Atari room, small cinema and 2 dance floors. Full of Rio students.
Porão, under the Anglican church hall, R Real Grandeza 99, Botafogo. British ex-pats meet here on Fri nights.

Copacabana, Ipanema and Leblon *p98 and p99, maps p108 and p116*

There is frequent live music on the beaches of Copacabana and Ipanema, and along the Av Atlântica throughout the summer, especially around New Year.
Academia da Cachaça, R Conde de Bernadotte 26-G, Leblon, with another branch at Av Armando Lombardi 800, Barra da Tijuca. The best *cachacas*, great *caipirinhas* and traditional Brazilian dishes. Good on Fri.
Bar D'Hotel, **Hotel Marina All Suites**, Ipanema (see page 108). Models and media people drink the excellent house cocktails here at the cool long bar before dining on light Mediterranean fare. Beach views. Good for sunset in smart casual.
Barril 1800, Av Vieira Souto 110, Ipanema. Pleasant place to watch sunset. Highly recommended.
Bip Bip, R Almte Gonçalves 50. *Botequim* bar which attracts a crowd of jamming musicians every Tue.
Bom Bar, R General San Martin 1011, Leblon. A downstairs bar and an upstairs club. Packed after 2300, especially Sat.
Bunker, R Raul Pompéia 94. European-style dance club where the likes of DJs Marky and Patife play. Busy Wed-Sat. Gets going around 0200. The queues have become a party in themselves – at the bar next door.
Devassa, Av General San Martin 1241, Leblon. A 2-floor pub/restaurant/bar that is always heaving. Brews its own beer.
Empório, R Maria Quitéria 37, Ipanema. Street bar which attracts hordes. Mon is the busiest night.
Garota de Ipanema, R Vinícius de Moraes 49, Ipanema. Where the song *Girl from Ipanema* was written. Now packed with foreigners on the package Rio circuit listening to bossa. For the real thing head to **Toca do Vinícius** on a Sun afternoon (see page 121).
Melt, R Rita Ludolf 47, Leblon, T021- 2249 9309, www.melt-rio.com.br. Downstairs bar and upstairs sweaty club. Occasional performances by the cream of Rio's new samba funk scene – usually on a Sun. Always heaving on Thu.

Shenanigans, R Visconde de Pirajá 112, Ipanema. Obligatory mock-Irish bar with Guinness and Newcastle Brown. Not a place to meet the locals.
Vinícius, R Vinícius de Moraes 39, Ipanema, 2nd floor. Mirror image of the **Garota de Ipanema** with slightly better acts and food.

Gávea, Lagoa and Jardim Botânico *p101*

Bar Lagoa, Av Epitácio Pessoa 1674, Lagoa. Attracts a slightly older arty crowd on weekday evenings.
Caroline Café, R JJ Seabra 10, Jardim Botânico, T021-2540 0705, www.carolinecafe.com. Popular with Rio's young and good-looking middle classes. Kicks off after 2100. Food too.
Clan Café, R Cosme Velho 564 (in front of the Corcovado train station), T021-2558 2322, closed Sun, Mon. Great little sit-down *choro* and samba club almost unknown to tourists, with live music and decent bar food.
Cozumel, Av Lineu de Paula Machado 696, Jardim Botânico. The Rio equivalent of a Cairns foam disco – with free margaritas, tacky music and a tacky crowd, most of whom are looking not to go home alone.
El Turf (aka **Jockey Club**), opposite the Jardim Botânico, Praça Santos Dumont 31. Opens at 2200, gets going at 2300, you may have to wait to get in at the weekend if you arrive after 2400, no T-shirts allowed, very much a Rio rich-kid singles and birthday-party place; another in Rio Sul shopping centre.
Mistura Fina, Av Borges de Medeiros 3207, Gávea, T021-2537 2844, www.misturafina.com.br. Downstairs is a restaurant, upstairs is a jazz and bossa nova club. One of the few places not oriented solely to the young. Liza Minelli came here when she was in Rio.
Sitio Lounge, R Marques de São Vicente 10, Gávea. The nearest thing Rio has to a lounge bar. Good for a chilled out Sat night.
00 (Zero Zero), Av Padre Leonel Franca 240, Gávea. Mock-LA bar/restaurant/club with a small outdoor area. Currently the trendiest club in Rio for Brazil's equivalent of Sloanes or Valley Girls. Gay night on Sun.

Barra da Tijuca *p102*

Nuth, R Armando Lombardi 999, www.nuth.com.br. Barra's slickest club; very mock-Miami and frequented by a mixed crowd of rich-kid surfers, footballers (Romario comes here) and women with surgically enhanced beauty. The music is a mix of tacky Brazilian and Eurotrash with occasional samba funk live acts.
Pepe, Posto 2, Barra da Tijuca beach. One of a string of very popular beach bars frequented by toned, tanned surfers.

Entertainment

Cinema

There are cinemas serving subtitled Hollywood fare and major Brazilian releases on the top floor of almost all the malls. The normal seat price is around US$3. Discounts on Wed and Thu (students pay half price any day of the week). Alternative and art-house films are shown in the following theatres:
Centro Cultural do Banco do Brasil, R Primeiro de Março 66, Centro, T021- 808 2020. One of Rio's better arts centres with the best of the art films and exhibitions from fine art to photography (Metrô Uruguaiana).
Cinemateca do MAM, Infante Dom Henrique 85, Aterro do Flamengo, T021-2210 2188. Cinema classics, art films, roving art exhibitions and a good café with live music. Views of Guanabara Bay from the balconies.
Estaçao Ipanema, R Visconde de Pirajá 605, Ipanema. European art cinema, less-mainstream US and Brazilian releases.

Horse racing

Jockey Club Racecourse, by Jardim Botânico and Gávea, meetings on Mon and Thu evenings and Sat and Sun 1400, entrance US$1-2, long trousers required, a table may be booked. Take any bus marked 'via Jóquei'. Betting is by tote only.

SESC cultural centres

Little known to visitors but beloved of cultured Brazilians are the SESC centres. These are spaces devoted to arts in general, with fine art and photographic exhibitions, theatre, film and, in the **Espaço SESC** in Copacabana, live music. Many established high brow contemporary artists like Naná Vasconcelos and Egberto Gismonti have played here. There are several SESC centres in Rio and the excellent website www.sescrj.com.br (in Portuguese only but easy to follow) has information on forthcoming concerts.

Espaço SESC, Rua Domingos Ferreira 160, Copacabana, T021-2547 0156. **SESC Tijuca**, Rua Barão de Mesquita, 539, Barra da Tijuca, T021-3238 2100. **SESC Niterói**, Rua Padre Anchieta, 56, Niterói, T 021 2719 9119.

Music

Many young Cariocas congregate in Botafogo for live music. There are free concerts throughout the summer along the Copacabana and Ipanema beaches, in Botafogo and at the parks: mostly samba, reggae, rock and MPB (Brazilian pop): there is no advance schedule, information is given in the local press (see page 74). Rio's famous jazz, in all its forms, is performed in lots of enjoyable venues too, see www.samba-choro.com.br for more information.

Canecão, R Venceslau Brás 215, Botafogo, T021-2295 3044. A big, inexpensive venue for live concerts most nights, and a taste of some purely local entertainment on Mon.

Centro Cultural Carioca, R do Teatro 37, T021-2242 9642, www.centrocultural carioca.com, for advance information, 1830-late. This restored old house with wrap-around balconies and exposed brick walls is a dance school and music venue that attracts a lovely mix of people. Professional dancers perform with musicians; after a few tunes the audience joins in. Thu is impossibly crowded; Sat is calmer. Bar food available. US$3 cover charge. Highly recommended.

Praia do Vermelha, Urca. Residents bring musical instruments and chairs onto the beach for an informal night of samba from 2100-2400. Free. Bus No 511 from Copacabana.

Rhapsody, Av Epitácio Pessoa 1104, Lagoa, T021-2247 2104. Piano-bar restaurant with a mix of Brazilian and Diana Kraal-style crooning.

Toca do Vinícius, R Vinícius de Moraes 129C, Ipanema. Rio's leading bossa nova and *choro* record shop has concerts from some of the finest performers every Sun lunchtime.

See also **Clan Café**, **Melt**, **Nuth** and **Mistura Fina** in Bars and clubs, above.

Theatre

There are about 40 theatres in Rio, presenting a variety of classical and modern performances in Portuguese. Seat prices start at about US$15; some children's theatre is free. For information on particular performances, check in *Veja* at weekends, or ask at the tourist office.

Festivals and events

Carnaval → *See also box page 122.*

Tickets

The Sambódromo parades start at 1900 and last about 12 hrs. Gates open at 1800. There are *cadeiras* (seats) at ground level, *arquibancadas* (terraces) and *camarotes* (boxes). The best boxes are reserved for tourists and VIPs and are very expensive or by invitation only. Seats are closest to the parade, but you may have to fight your way to the front. Sectors 4, 7 and 11 are the best spots (they house the judging points); 6 and 13 are least favoured (being at the end when dancers might be tired) but have more space. The terraces, while uncomfortable, house the most fervent fans, tightly packed; this is the best place to soak up the atmosphere but it's

Carnaval

Carnival in Rio is as spectacular as its reputation suggests – a riot of colour, flamboyance and artistry unrivalled outside Brazil. On the Friday before Shrove Tuesday, the mayor of Rio hands the keys of the city to *Rei Momo*, the Lord of Misrule, signifying the start of a five-day party. Imagination runs riot, social barriers are broken and the main avenues, full of people and children wearing fancy dress, are colourfully lit. Areas throughout the city such as the Terreirão de Samba in Praça Onze are used for shows, music and dancing. And while things can be ghostly quiet in the southern beach zones, spectacularly dressed carnival groups throng around the the Sambódromo (Oscar Niemeyer's purpose built Caranval stadium, see page 87) strutting, drumming and singing in preparation for their parade, and there are *blocos* (parades) in neighbourhoods throughout the city, such as Santa Teresa and Ipanema.

Unlike Salvador which remains a wild street party, Rio's Carnaval is designated parade, taking place over a number of days and contained within the Sambódromo stadium. Alongside the parade are a number of *bailes* (parties) held within designated clubs, street shows like those held around Praça Onze.

There are numerous samba schools in Rio, which are divided into two leagues before they parade through the Sambódromo. The 14 schools of the Grupo Especial parade on Sunday and Monday while the Grupos de Acesso A and B parade on Saturday and Friday respectively. There is also a *mirins* parade (younger members of the established schools) on Tuesday. Judging takes place on Wednesday afternoon and the winners of the groups parade again on the following Saturday. Tickets to these winners' parades are always easy to get hold of even when all others are sold out.

Every school comprises 2500-6000 participants divided into *alas* (wings) each with a different costume and parading on or around five to nine *carros alegóricos* (beautifully designed floats). Each school chooses an *enredo* (theme) and composes a samba that is a poetic, rhythmic and catchy expression of the theme. The *enredo* is further developed through the design of the floats and costumes. A *bateria* (percussion wing) maintains a reverberating beat that must keep the entire school, and the audience, dancing throughout the parade. Each procession follows a set order with the first to appear being the

too crowded to take pictures. Tickets start at US$40 for *arquibancadas* and are sold at travel agencies as well as the Maracanã Stadium box office (see page 88). Tickets should be bought as far as possible in advance; they are usually sold out before Carnaval weekend but touts outside can often sell you tickets at inflated prices. Samba schools have an allocation of tickets which members sometimes sell, if you are offered one of these check its date. Tickets for the champions' parade on the Sat following Carnaval are much cheaper. Many tour companies offer Rio trips including carnival, but tickets are at inflated prices.

Sleeping and security
Be sure to reserve accommodation well in advance. Virtually all hotels raise their prices during Carnaval, although it is usually possible to find a reasonably priced room. Your property should be safe inside the Sambódromo, but the crowds outside can attract pickpockets; as ever, don't brandish your camera, and only take the money you need for fares and refreshments (food and drink are sold in the Sambódromo.) It gets hot, so wear shorts and a T-shirt.

Taking part
Most samba schools will accept a number of foreigners and you will be charged upwards

comissão de frente, a choreographed group that presents the school and the theme to the public. Next comes the *abre alas*, a magnificent float usually bearing the name or symbol of the school. The alas and other floats follow as well as *porta bandeiras* and *mestre salas*, couples dressed in 18th-century costumes bearing the school's flag, and *passistas*, groups traditionally of mulata dancers. An *ala of baianas*, elderly women with circular skirts that swirl as they dance is always included as is the *velha guarda*, distinguished members of the school who close the parade. Schools are given between 65 and 80 minutes and lose points for failing to keep within this time. Judges award points to each school for components of their procession, such as costume, music and design, and make deductions for lack of energy, enthusiasm or discipline. The winners of the Grupos de Acesso are promoted to the next higher group while the losers, including those of the Grupo Especial, are relegated to the next lowest group. Competition is intense and the winners gain a monetary prize funded by the entrance fees.

The Carnaval parades are the culmination of months of intense activity by community groups, mostly in the city's poorest districts. Rio´s bailes (fancy-dress balls) range from the sophisticated to the wild. The majority of clubs and hotels host at least one. The Copacabana Palace's is elegant and expensive whilst the Scala club has licentious parties. It is not necessary to wear fancy dress; just join in, although you will feel more comfortable if you wear a minimum of clothing to the clubs, which are crowded, hot and rowdy. The most famous are the Red & Black Ball (Friday) and the Gay Ball (Tuesday) which are both televised. Venues for these vary.

Bandas and blocos can be found in all neighbourhoods and some of the most popular and entertaining are Cordão do Bola Preta (meets at 0900 on Saturday in Rua 13 de Maio 13, Centro), Simpatia é Quase Amor (meets at 1600 Sunday in Praça General Osório, Ipanema) and the transvestite Banda da Ipanema (meets at 1600 on Saturday and Tuesday in Praça General Osorio, Ipanema). It is necessary to join a bloco in advance to receive their distinctive T-shirts, but anyone can join in with the bandas.

The expensive hotels offer special Carnival breakfasts from 0530. Caesar Park is highly recommended for a wonderful meal and a top-floor view of the sunrise over the beach.

of US$125 for your costume as your money helps to fund poorer members of the school. You should be in Rio for at least 2 weeks before Carnaval. It is essential to attend fittings and rehearsals on time, to show respect for your section leaders and to enter into the competitive spirit of the event. For those with the energy and the dedication, it will be an unforgettable experience.

Rehearsals

Ensaios are held at the schools' *quadras* from Oct onwards and are well worth seeing. It is wise to go by taxi, as most schools are based in poorer districts.

Carnaval shows

Tour agents sell tickets for glitzy samba shows, which are nothing like the real thing. When buying a Carnaval DVD, make sure the format is compatible (NTSC for USA or most of Europe, PAL for the UK, region 4).

Samba school addresses and parties

Samba schools hold parties through out the year, especially at the weekends. These are well worth visiting. There is information about these on the websites.

Acadêmicos de Salgueiro, R Silva Teles 104, Andaraí, T021-2238 5564, www.salgueiro.com.br.

Beija Flor de Nilópolis, Pracinha Wallace Paes Leme 1025, Nilópolis, T021-2791 2866, www.beija-flor.com.br.
Imperatriz Leopoldinense, R Prof Lacê 235, Ramos, T021-2270 8037, www.love-rio.com/imperatriz.
Mocidade Independente de Padre Miguel, R Coronel Tamarindo 38, Padre Miguel, T021-3332 5823, www.mocidade.com.
Portela, R Clara Nunes 81, Madureira, T021-3390 0471, www.gresportela.com.br.
Primeira Estação de Mangueira, R Visconde de Niterói 1072, Mangueira, T021-2567 4637, www.mangueira.com.br.
Unidos da Viradouro, Av do Contorno 16, Niterói, T021-2717 7540, www.databrasil.com/viradouro.
Vila Isabel, Boulevard 28 de Setembro, Vila Isabel, www.gresunidosdevilaisabel.com.br.

Useful information

Carnival week comprises an enormous range of official and unofficial contests and events which reach a peak on the Tue. Riotur's guide booklet and website gives concise information on these in English. The entertainment sections of newspapers and magazines such as O Globo, Jornal do Brasil, Manchete and Veja Rio are worth checking. Liga Independente das Escolas de Samba do Rio de Janeiro, www.liesa.com.br, Felipe Ferreira's Rio Carnival Guide has good explanations of the competition, rules, the schools, a map and other practical details.

Transport

Taxis to the Sambódromo are negotiable and will find your gate, the nearest Metrô is Praça Onze and this can be an enjoyable ride in the company of costumed samba school members. You can follow the participants to the concentração, the assembly and formation on Avenida Presidente Vargas, and mingle with them while they queue to enter the Sambódromo. Ask if you can take photos.

Other festivals

20 Jan The festival of **São Sebastião**, patron saint of Rio, is celebrated by an evening procession, leaving Capuchinhos church in Tijuca and arriving at the cathedral of São Sebastião. On the same evening, an *umbanda* festival is celebrated at the Caboclo monument in Santa Teresa.

Jun The **Festas Juninas** are celebrated throughout Brazil. In Rio they start with the festival of **Santo Antônio** on 13 Jun, when the main event is a Mass, followed by celebrations at the Convento do Santo Antônio and the Largo da Carioca. All over the state, the festival of **São João** is a major event, marked by huge bonfires on the night of 23-24 Jun. It is traditional to dance the *quadrilha* and drink *quentão*, *cachaça* and sugar, spiced with ginger and cinnamon, served hot. The Festas Juninas close with the festival of **São Pedro** on 29 Jun. Being the patron saint of fishermen, his feast is normally accompanied by processions of boats.

Oct This is the month of the feast of **Nossa Senhora da Penha** (see page 88).

Many people look for **umbanda** religious ceremonies. Those offered on the night tours sold at hotels are not genuine and are a disappointment. You need a local contact to see the real ones, which are usually held in *favelas* and are none too safe for unaccompanied tourists.

30 Dec Less hectic than Carnaval, but very atmospheric, is the festival of **Yemanjá** when devotees of the *orixá* of the sea dress in white and gather at night on Copacabana, Ipanema and Leblon beaches, singing and dancing around open fires and making offerings. The elected Queen of the Sea is rowed along the seashore. At midnight small boats are launched as offerings to Yemanjá. The religious event is dwarfed, however, by a massive New Year's Eve party, called **Reveillon** at Copacabana. The beach is packed as thousands of revellers enjoy free outdoor concerts by big-name pop stars, topped with a lavish midnight firework display. It is most crowded in front of the Copacabana Palace Hotel. Another good place to see the fireworks is in front of Le Meridien, famous for its fireworks waterfall at about 0010. Many followers of Yemanjá are now making their offerings on 29 or 30 Dec and at Barra da Tijuca or Recreio dos Bandeirantes to avoid the crowds and noise of Reveillon.

Shopping

Bookshops

Da Vinci, Av Rio Branco 185, lojas 2, 3 and 9. All types of foreign books, *Footprint* available.
Livraria da Travessa, R Visconde de Pirajá 572, Ipanema, T021-3205 9002. Classy little bookshop with broad selection of novels, magazines and guidebooks in English. Great café upstairs for a coffee while you read.
Saraiva, R do Ouvidor 98, T021-2507 9500. A massive (megastore) bookshop which also includes a music and video shop and a café; other branches in Shopping Iguatemi and Shopping Tijuca.

Camping equipment

On R 1 de Março, north of Av Pres Vargas, are military shops which sell jungle equipment such as hammocks, mosquito nets and clothing, eg **Casa do Militar**, No 145 and **London**, No 155; you can also buy the Brazilian flag in any size you want here.
Malamada, R da Carioca 13, is recommended for rucksacks.

Fashion

Fashion is one of the best buys in Brazil, with a wealth of Brazilian designers selling clothes of the same quality as European or US famous names at a fraction of the price. Rio is the best place in the world for buying high-fashion bikinis. The best shops in Ipanema are on Garcia D'Ávila and R Nascimento Silva, which runs off it. This is where some of the best Brazilian designers such as **Andrea Saletto** and **Rosana Bernardes**, together with international big-name stalwarts like **Louis Vuitton** and **Cartier**, and Brazil's classiest jeweller, **Antonio Bernardo**. Most of the international names, together with all the big Brazilian names like **Lenny** (Brazil's best bikinis), **Alberta**, **Salinas**, **Club Chocolate** and so on, are housed in the fashion mall in São Conrado.

In addition to those listed below, there are some little shops on Aires Saldanha, Copacabana (1 block back from beach), which are good for bikinis and cheaper than in the shopping centres.

Andrea Saletto, R Nascimento Silva 244, T021-2522 5858, and in the fashion mall, loja 211, T021-3225 4235. One of the most sophisticated labels in Rio – elegant and low-profile style, classical cuts and the use of light and tropical fabrics: cotton, linen and silk.
Blue Man, São Conrado fashion mall. Tiny bright bikinis beloved of those with perfect bodies.
Bum Bum, R Visconde de Pirajá 351, Ipanema, T021-2287 9951, www.bumbum.com.br. Together with **Rosa Cha**, one of the most internationally renowned bikini designers, tiny and beautifully cut.
Carlos Tufvesson, R Nascimento Silva 304, Ipanema, T021-2523 9200, www.carlostufvesson.com. Brazil's latest bright young star who received a standing ovation for his collection at the Barra fashion week in Rio. Sensual evening-wear in high-quality fabric.
Lenny, R Visconde de Pirajá, 351, Ipanema, T021-2287 9951, and in the Fashion Mall. Lenny Niemeyer is widely regarded as Brazil's most sophisticated bikini designer.
Maria Bonita, R Aníbal de Mendonça 135, Ipanema, T021-2540 5354. Impeccably cut, elegantly simple, sophisticated women's wear in high-quality fabrics. One of the oldest labels in Rio de Janeiro.
Saara is a multitude of little shops along R Alfândega and R Senhor dos Passos (between the city centre and Campo Santana), where clothing bargains can be found (especially jeans, kanga beach wraps and bikinis); it is known popularly as Shopping a Céu Aberto.
Salinas, R Visconde de Pirajá 547, Ipanema, T021-2274 0644, and fashion mall, T021-2422 0677. Very highly regarded Brazilian bikinis – small, exquisitely made with great attention to detail and using only the best fabrics, in a variety of contemporary styles from hand crochet and beading to reversibles in multiple colour combinations.

Jewellery

Only buy precious and semi-precious stones from reputable dealers. There are several good jewellery shops at the Leme end of Av NS de Copacabana.

The essential Rio beach kit

To get the best out of Rio dress as the locals do – become a *Carioca*. Leave your sense of shame and your board shorts, in the hotel and go out in search of the essential Carioca uniform. The first thing you will need is a *sunga*, a tiny piece of square lycra used barely to cover the essentials, or if you are a woman a bikini, which although even smaller is not, contrary to popular belief a 'dental floss' thong. The most fashionable places for these are in Ipanema or the fashion mall in São Conrado (see page 127). The next essential is a *canga* – a sarong of the kind ubiquitous in Asia; which is used as a wrap, towel and beach mat, easily found in boutiques on any main street in Rio; like Visconde de Pirajá in Ipanema. You will then need a *frescobol kit* – a wooden racket and a rubber ball to hit back and forth across the sand and a pair of *Havaianas* – Brazilian flip flops. Both are available for next to nothing in the supermarket. A tanned, perfect body and small white poodle (for women) and pair of cheap sunglasses (for men) complete the outfit.

Amsterdam Sauer, R Garcia D'Ávila 105. Have 10 shops in Rio and others throughout Brazil, plus St Thomas (US Virgin Islands) and New York; they offer free taxi rides to their main shop.

Antônio Bernado, R Garcia d'Ávila 121, Ipanema, T021-2512 7204, and in the fashion mall. Brazil's foremost jeweller who has been making beautifully understated pieces with contemporary designs for nearly 30 years. Internationally well known but available only in Brazil.

H Stern, R Visconde de Pirajá 490 and R Garcia d'Ávila 113, Ipanema. 10 outlets, plus branches in major hotels throughout the city (as well as elsewhere in Brazil and worldwide).

Mineraux, Av NS de Copacabana 195. For mineral specimens rather than cut stones. Belgian owner.

Markets

The **Northeastern market** takes place at Campo de São Cristóvão, with music and magic, on Sun 0800-2200 (bus No 472 or 474 from Copacabana or centre). There's a Sat **antiques market** on the waterfront near Praça 15 de Novembro, 1000-1700. Also on Praça 15 de Novembro is **Feirarte II**, Thu and Fri 0800-1800. **Feirarte I** is a Sun open-air handicrafts market (everyone calls it the **Feira Hippy**) at Praça Gen Osório, Ipanema, 0800-1800, touristy but fun: items from all over Brazil. **Babilônia Feira Hype** is held every other weekend at the Jockey Club 1400-2300. This lively and popular market has lots of stalls selling clothes and crafts, as well as massage and live music and dance performances. A **stamp and coin market** is held on Sun in the Passeio Público. There are **markets** on Wed 0700-1300 on R Domingos Ferreira and on Thu, same hours, on Praça do Lido, both Copacabana. Praça do Lido also has a **Feirarte** on Sat and Sun 0800-1800. There is an **artesania market** nightly by the Othon Hotel, near R Miguel Lemos: one part for paintings, one part for everything else. There's a **Sunday market** on R da Glória, colourful, cheap fruit, vegetables and flowers; and an early-morning food market, 0600-1100, R Min Viveiros de Castro, Ipanema. Excellent **food and household goods markets** take place at various places in the city and suburbs (see newspapers for times and places). **Feira do Livro** is a book market that moves around various locations (Largo do Machado, Cinelândia, Nossa Senhora da Paz – Ipanema), selling books at 20% discount.

Music

Modern Sound Música Equipamentos, R Barata Ribeiro 502D, Copacabana. For a large selection of Brazilian music, jazz and classical.

Toca do Vinícius, R Vinícius de Moraes 129C, Ipanema. Specializes in bossa nova books, CDs and souvenirs, doubles as a performance space (see also Music, page 121).

Photography

Flash Studio, R Visconde de Pirajá 156. For processing, expensive.
Honório, R Vinícius de Moraes 146E. Stocks lithium batteries.
Mecánica de Precisão, R da Conceição 31, shop 202. Good.
One Hour Foto, in the Rio Sul and Barra shopping centres. Recommended.
T Tanaka Cia Ltda, Av Franklin Roosevelt 39, office 516, T021-2220 1127. Nikon camera repairs.

Shopping centres

Rio Sul, at the Botafogo end of Túnel Novo, has almost everything the visitor may need. It has been refurbished and is convenient and very safe. Some of the services available are: **Telemar** (phone office) for international calls at A10-A, Mon-Sat 1000-2200, next door is **Belle Tours Câmbio**, A10. There is a post office at G2. A good branch of **Livraria Sodiler** is at A03. Entertainment includes the **Fun Club** nightclub on the 4th floor, open all night, very young crowd; live music at the **Terraço**; the Ibeas **Top Club** gym; and a cinema. Eating places include fast food restaurants, 2 branches of **Kotobuki** sushi bar (another branch on the road to Praia Vermelha, recommended) and **Chaika** for milkshakes, ice creams and sandwiches (4th floor, original branch on Praça NS da Paz, Ipanema). A US$5 bus service runs as far as the Sheraton passing the main hotels, every 2 hrs between 1000 and 1800, then 2130.
São Conrado Fashion Mall. The best designers and an excellent restaurant at the **Clube Chocolate** shop.

Other shopping centres, which have a wide variety of shops and services, include: **Cassino** (Copacabana), **Norte Shopping** (Todos os Santos), **Plaza Shopping** (Niterói), **Barra** in Barra da Tijuca.

Activities and tours

There are hundreds of excellent gyms and sports clubs; most will not grant temporary (less than 1 month) membership. Big hotels may allow use of their facilities for a small deposit.

Boat trips

Several companies offer trips to Ilha de Paquetá, and day cruises, including lunch, to Jaguanum Island, and a sundown cruise around Guanabara Bay.
Saveiros Tour, R Conde de Lages 44, Glória, T021-2224 6990, www.saveiros.com.br. Tours in sailing schooners around the bay and down the coast, also 'Baía da Guanabara Histórica' historical tours.

Cycling

Rio Bikers, R Domingos Ferreira 81, room 201, T021-2274 5872. Tours (hire available).

Diving

Squalo, Av Armando Lombardi 949-D, Barra da Tijuca, T/F021-2493 3022, squalo1@hotmail.com. Offers courses at all levels, NAUI and PDIC training facilities, also snorkelling and equipment rental.

Safety and favela tourism

Rio has a reputation for being violent and unsafe and though it can be so you are unlikely to encounter problems if you follow a few basic rules. These all boil down to common sense and not attracting attention to yourself. Enquire where is and where is not safe at your hotel or hostel – violence and thieves are almost always localized. Dress modestly and if possible like a local; flip-flops (not trekking sandals), locally bought shorts and a T-shirt or polo shirt. Keep expensive jewellery and watches out of sight. Carry a photocopy of your passport and leave the original and other valuables in the hotel safe box. Carry ready money in a pocket and a reserve in a money belt and wear your camera where it cannot be seen or keep it in a scruffy bag. Be especially careful after dark in the city centre and on quiet areas of Copacabana beach – never walk on the sand alone after dark. If you are mugged anywhere in Rio do not offer resistance and report the crime to the police or tourist police immediately. But bear in mind that Brazilians are generally the friendliest and most accommodating of people and although there is a great deal of violence in Rio, most of it is restricted to the *favelas* – which can be extremely dangerous.

There has been a growth in *favela* tourism in recent years and there are even pousadas opening in some of the favelas. *Favela* tours when conducted by reputable operators (see page 131) are pretty safe and illuminating and we strongly recommend them. The best companies have a relationship with the locals, permission to be there and visit only areas they know to be relatively safe. Beyond this, however, we are under no illusions about the dangers of *favelas*. Never enter a *favela* on your own or without someone you know very well and trust and bear in mind that a stay in a favela pousada will require that you do so. Violence in *favelas* is not a myth. To give some concrete examples: in the 14 years to 2003, when a UNESCO report was published on violence in Brazil; some 4000 under-18-year-olds were killed by firearms in Rio; almost all of them in the *favelas*. This compares with just under 500 killed in fighting between Palestinians and Israelis in the whole of Israel over the same period. And the numbers are not falling. According to the latest available statistics as of 2006, between 1979 and 2003 homicides in under 25 year olds in Brazil increased by 742.9% and more people died of gunfire in the country than in conflicts such as the Gulf War, the First and the Second Intifadas, the dispute between Israel and Palestine and the conflicts in Northern Ireland, both in terms of absolute figures and in annual averages.

Golf

Gávea Club, São Conrado, T021-3399 4141. 18 holes.
Itanhangá Golf Club, Jacarepaguá. 18-hole and 9-hole courses, visiting cards from Av Rio Branco 26, 16th floor.
Petrópolis Country Club, Nogueira. 9 holes.
Teresópolis Golf Club, Estr Imbuí (Várzea). 18 holes.

Hang-gliding

Delta Flight, T021-3322 5750, T021-9693 8800, www.deltaflight.com.br. Hang-gliding rides above Rio from Pedra Bonita mountain with instructors licensed by the Brazilian Hang-gliding Association. 19 years of experience and equipment is renewed every year. Contact Ricardo Hamond.

Just Fly, T/F021-2268 0565, T021-9985 7540 (mob), www.justfly.com.br. Tandem flights with Paulo Celani (licensed by the Brazilian Hang-gliding Association), pickup and drop-off at hotel included, flights all year, best time of day 1000-1500 (5% discount for *Footprint* readers on presentation of book at time of reservation).

Rejane Reis, Exotic Tours (see Tour operators, page 131) also arranges hang-gliding, as well as paragliding, microlight flights, walks and other activities.

Ultra Força Ltda, Av Sernambetiba 8100, Barra da Tijuca, T021-3399 3114; 15-min tandem hang-gliding flights.

Horse riding

Sociedade Hípico Brasileiro, Av Borges de Medeiros 2448, T021-2527 8090, Jardim Botânico.

Rio's best surf beaches

BB Beach Break; **PB** Point Break; **RB** Reef Break; **SB** Shore Break; **R** Right and **L** Left. Wave heights are given in feet. For further information see *Footprint Surfing the World*.

Arpoador Breaks next to the rocks, gets good, the beach is illuminated making night surfing possible, BB, L, 1-8 ft.

Barra da Guaratiba Rivermouth, perfect and powerful waves in the right conditions, B, L, 2-5 ft.

Barra da Tijuca 18-km beach with sand banks, closes out when big, BB, R&L.

Canto de Leblon On a big swell a wave breaks next to the rocks, gets good.

Copacabana Posto 5, needs a big swell and the water can be dirty, SB, R&L.

Forte BB, R&L, 1-4 ft.

Grumari BB, R&L, 1-7 ft.

Ipanema Hollow, not much shape, BB, R&L, 1-5 ft.

Leblon Hollow next to the breakwater, BB, R&L, 1-5 ft.

Macumba Small waves, BB, R&L, 1-4 ft.

Quebra Mar Next to the breakwater, hollow in the right conditions, BB, L, 1-7 ft.

Pepino Sometimes a good hollow left can break next to the rocks on the left side of the beach. Hang gliders land here, BB, R&L, 1-6 ft.

Prainha Wild and good, BB, R&L, 1-8 ft.

Recreio dos Bandeirantes Breaks by a rock a few metres from shore, on both sides and in different directions; can handle some size when other spots close out, BB, R&L, 2-8 ft.

São Conrado BB, R&L, 1-5 ft.

Parachuting and paragliding

Barra Jumping, Aeroporto de Jacarepaguá, Av Ayrton Senna 2541, T021-3325 2494, www.barrajumping.com.br. Tandem jumping (*Vôo duplo*).

Sr Ruy Marra, T021-3322 2286, or find him at the beach. Paragliding from Leblon beach with Brazilian paragliding champion (US$75). Several other people offer tandem jumping; check that they are accredited with the Associação Brasileira de Vôo Livre.

Private drivers

Dehouche (see Tour operators, page 131) can organize excellent private drivers with comfortable a/c cars and very good English.

José de Oliveira Lima Filho, T021-9243 1208. Ex-driver for the US Secret service in Rio. Has access to exclusive addresses and private parties. Expensive.

Personal Tour, T021-9216 2171, garcia clarissa@ig.com.br. Bilingual, great company and comfortable a/c cars. Ask for Clarissa.

Rock climbing and hillwalking

Clube Excursionista Carioca, R Hilário Gouveia 71, room 206, T021-2255 1348. Recommended for enthusiasts, meets Wed and Fri.

ECA, Av Erasmo Braga 217, room 305, T021-2242 6857. Personal guide US$100 per day, owner Ralph speaks English.

Sailing

Federação Brasileira de Vela e Motor, R Alcindo Guanabara 15, room 801, Centro, T021-2220 3738. For information.

Federação de Vela, Praça Mahatma Gandhi 2, 12th floor, T021-2220 8785. For information.

Clube do Rio de Janeiro, Av Pasteur, Urca, T021-2295 4482. Yachting.

Surfing

For the state of the waves on the beaches in and around Rio de Janeiro, see box above.

Associação Brasileira de Bodyboard, T021-2274 3614.

Federação de Bodyboard do Estado do Rio de Janeiro, T021-2256 5653.

Federação de Surf do Estado do Rio de Janeiro, T021-2287 2385.
Organização dos Surfistas Profissionais do Rio de Janeiro, T021-2493 2472.

Swimming

On all Rio's beaches you should take a towel or mat to protect you against sandflies. In the water stay near groups of other swimmers. There is a strong undertow. See also Tour operators, below.

Tour operators

Adrianotour, T021-2208 5103. For guided tours, reservations and commercial services. English, French, German and Spanish spoken.
Be A Local, T021-9643 0366, www.bealocal.com. The best of the favela tours with walking trips around Rocinha and money going towards community projects; trips to *baile funk* parties at weekends and to football matches.
Buggy Tour, T021-2220 2043, www.doloresbuggytour.com. Beach buggy tours of Rio with a real Carioca character, Dolores. Good English, Spanish, Italian and French.
Cultural Rio, R Santa Clara 110/904, Copacabana, T021-3322 4872 or T9911 3829 (mob), www.culturalrio.com.br. Tours escorted personally by Professor Carlos Roquette, English and French spoken, almost 200 options available.
Dehouche, T021-2512 3895, www.dehouche.com. Luxury, tailor-made tours throughout Brazil and Rio de Janeiro, including the best private flats, excursions to islands near Angra and driving a Ferrari around the Grand Prix circuit.
Fábio Sombra, T021-2295 9220, T9729 5455 (mob), fabiosombra@hotmail.com. Offers private and tailor-made guided tours focusing on the cultural aspects of Rio and Brazil.
Favela Tour, Estr das Canoas 722, bl 2, apt 125, São Conrado, T021-3322 2727, T021-9989 0074 (mob), www.favelatour.com.br. Safe, interesting guided tours of Rio's *favelas* in English, French, Spanish, Italian, German and Swedish. For the best attention and price call Marcelo Armstrong direct rather than through a hotel desk.
Guanatur Turismo, R Dias da Rocha 16A, Copacabana, T021-2548 3275. Sells long-distance bus tickets.
Helisight, R Visconde de Pirajá 580, loja 107, Térreo, Ipanema, T021-2511 2141, www.helisight.com.br. Helicopter sightseeing tours. Prices from US$50 per person for 6-7 mins from Morro de Urca or the Lagoa over Sugar Loaf and Corcovado, to US$150 per person for 30 mins over the city. Fly 7 days a week from 0900.
Marlin Tours, Av NS de Copacabana 605, of 1204, T021-2548 4433, bbm.robin@openlink.com.br. Recommended for hotels, flights and tours, English spoken.
Metropol, R São José 46, T021-2533 5010, www.metropolturismo.com.br. Cultural, eco, and adventure tours to all parts of Brazil.
Rejane Reis, Exotic Tours, T021-3322 6972, www.exotictours.com.br. Unusual trips throughout Rio such as Candomble, rafting, hikes up to the Pedra da Gávea. Cultural and favela tours. Good English spoken.
Rio by Jeep, T021-3322 5750, T021-9693 8800, www.riobyjeep.com. 5-hr tours in open or closed jeeps with local guides showing Rio from 3 perspectives: gorgeous beaches, historical downtown and Tijuca National Park. Contact Ricardo Hamond.
Turismo Clássico, Av NS de Copacabana 1059/805, T021-2523 3390, classico@infolink.com.br. Organized trips to samba shows cost US$50 including dinner; good, but it's cheaper to go independently. Recommended.

Transport

Air

See Ins and outs, page 72, for airport information. As well as international connections, Rio de Janeiro has flights to all the country's major airports, some via São Paulo, Brasilia or Salvador. The best deals on flights within Brazil are available through **Gol**, www.voegol.com.br; **Bra**, www.voebra.com.br; **Ocean Air**, www.oceanair.com.br; and TAM, www.tam.com.br.

There is a shuttle flight between Rio Santos Dumont Airport and **São Paulo**, (US$150 single, US$300 return). The shuttle services operate every 30 mins throughout the day from 0630-2230. Sit on the right-hand side for views to São Paulo, the other side coming back, book flights in advance.

Airline offices

Aerolíneas Argentinas, R São José 70, 8th floor, Centro, T021-2292 4131, airport T021-3398 3520. **Air France**, Av Pres Antônio Carlos 58, 9th floor, T021-2532 3642, airport T021-3398 3488. **Alitalia**, Av Pres Wilson 231, 21st floor, T021-2292 4424, airport T021-3398 3143. **American**, Av Pres Wilson 165, 5th floor, T0800-703 4000. **Avianca**, Av Pres Wilson 165, offices 801-03, T021-2240 4413, airport T021-3398 3778. **Bra**, www.voebra.com.br. **British Airways**, airport T021-3398 3889. **Iberia**, Av Pres Antônio Carlos 51, 8th and 9th floors, T021-2282 1336, airport T021-3398 3168. **Japan Airlines**, Av Rio Branco 156, office 2014, T021-2220 6414. **KLM**, Av Rio Branco 311A, T021-2542 7744, airport T021-3398 3700. **LAB**, Av Calógeras 30A, T021-2220 9548. **Lan Chile**, R da Assambléia 92, of 1301, T021-222 0972, T0800-554 9000, airport T021-3398 3797. **Lufthansa**, Av Rio Branco 156D, T021-2217 6111, airport T021-3398 5855. **Ocean Air**, www.oceanair.com.br, **RioSul/Nordeste**, Av Rio Branco 85, 10th floor, T021-2507 4488 (has an advance check-in desk in Rio Sul Shopping). **Swissair**, Av Rio Branco 108, 10th floor, T021-2297 5177, airport T021-3398 4330. **TAM**, www.tam.com.br, and **TAP**, Av Rio Branco 311-B, T021-2210 1287, airport, T021-3398 3455. **United**, Av Pres Antônio Carlos 51, 5th floor, T0800-245532. **Varig**, Av Rio Branco 277G, T021-2220 3821 information, T0800-997000 bookings; airport T021-3398 2122. Most staff speak English.

Bus

See Ins and outs, page 72, for bus station information. Travel agencies throughout the city sell tickets as do many hostels. Timetables are available on www.novorio.com.br; type your destination into the box provided.

Local

There are good services to all parts, but buses are very crowded and not for the aged and infirm during rush hours. Buses have turnstiles which are awkward if you are carrying luggage. Hang on tight, drivers live out Grand Prix fantasies. At busy times allow about 45 mins to get from Copacabana to the centre by bus. The fare on standard buses is US$0.40 and suburban bus fares are US$0.75. Bus stops are often not marked. The route is written on the side of the bus, which is hard to see until the bus has actually pulled up at the stop.

Private companies, including **Real**, **Pegaso** and **Anatur**, operate a/c *frescão* buses which can be flagged down practically anywhere. They run from all points in Rio Sul to the city centre, *rodoviária* and the airports. Fares are US$1.50 (US$1.80 to the international airport).

City Rio, T0800-258060, is an a/c tourist bus service with security guards which runs between all the major parts of the city. Bus stops, marked by grey poles, are found where there are concentrations of hotels. Good maps show what places of interest are close to each bus stop.

Long distance

Buses run from Rio to all parts of the country; it is advisable to book in advance. Some travel agents sell interstate tickets, or will direct you to a ticket office in the centre. Agencies include **Dantur Passagens e Turismo**, Av Rio Branco 156, subsolo loja 134, T021-2262 3424/3624; **Guanatur**, R Dias da Rocha 16A, Copacabana, T021-2235 3275; **Itapemirim Turismo**, R Uruguaiana 10, loja 24, T021-2509 8543, both in the centre; and an agency at R Visconde de Pirajá 303, loja 114, Ipanema. They charge about US$1 for bookings. Details of journey times and fares are given under destinations throughout the chapter.

To **Niteroi**, No 996 Gávea–Jurujuba, 998 Galeão–Charitas, 740-D and 741 Copacabana–Charitas, 730-D Castelo– Jurujuba, US$0.60-0.75 all run between Rio and Niterói.

To **Búzios**, 4 buses leave daily from Rio's *rodoviária* (US$8, 2½ hrs). Go to the **1001** counter, T022-2516 1001 for tickets. You can also take any bus from Rio to the town of **Cabo Frio** (these are more frequent), from where it's 30 mins to Búzios and vice versa. Buying the ticket in advance is only necessary on major holidays.

To **Petrópolis**, buses leave the *rodoviária* every 15 mins throughout the day (US$3) and every hour on Sun. A/c buses leave hourly (after 1100) from Av Nilo Peçanha. The journey takes 1½ hrs. Sit on the left-hand side for the best views.

To **Angra dos Reis**, buses run at least hourly from the *rodoviária* with **Costa Verde**, some direct; several go through Copacabana, Ipanema and Barra then take the *via litoral*, sit on the left, US$5.75, 2½ hrs. You can flag down the bus in Flamengo, Copacabana, Ipanema, Barra da Tijuca, but it may well be full at weekends. To link up with the ferry to Ilha Grande be sure to catch a bus before 1000.

To **Uruguaiana**, US$90, cheaper and quicker to get a through ticket.

International

The main bus station is reached by buses M94 and M95, Bancários–Castelo, from the centre and the airport; 136, 172, *rodoviária*–Glória–Flamengo–Botafogo; 127, 128, 136, *rodoviária*–Copacabana; 170, *rodoviária*–Gávea–São Conrado; 128, 172, *rodoviária* Ipanema–Leblon.

Asunción, 1511 km via Foz do Iguaçu, 30 hrs (**Pluma**), US$70; **Buenos Aires** (Pluma), via Porto Alegre and Santa Fe, 48 hrs, US$100 (book 2 days in advance); **Santiago de Chile**, (**Pluma** US$135, or **Gen Urquiza**), 70 hrs.

Car

Service stations are closed in many places on Sat and Sun. Road signs are notoriously misleading in Rio and you can end up in a favela (take special care if driving along the Estr da Gávea to São Conrado as it is possible to unwittingly enter Rocinha, Rio's biggest slum).

Car hire

There are many agencies on Av Princesa Isabel, Copacabana. A credit card is virtually essential for hiring a car. Recent reports suggest it is cheaper to hire outside Brazil; you may also obtain fuller insurance this way. **Avis**, Antônio Carlos Jobim

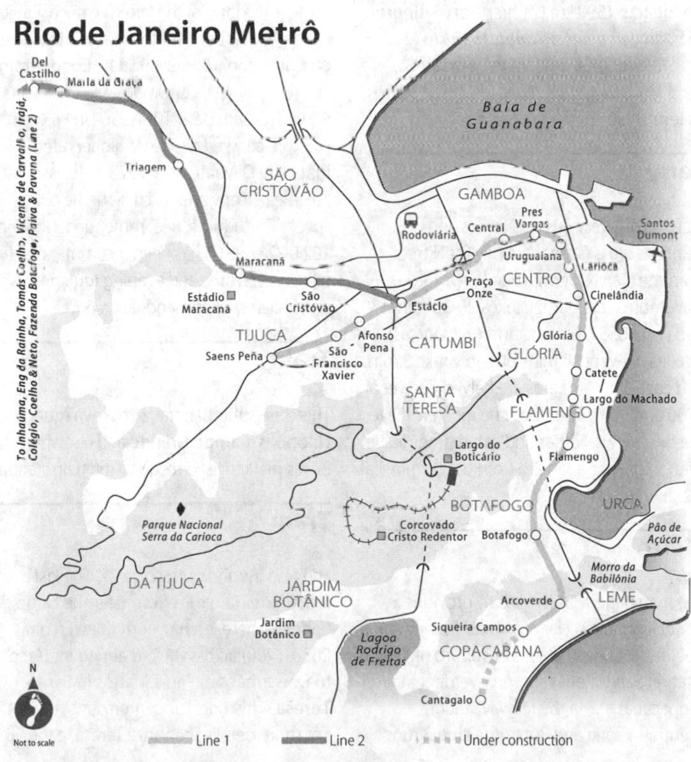

international airport, T021- 3398 5060, Santos Dumont airport, T021- 3814 7378, Av Princesa Isabel 150A and B, Copacabana, T021-2543 8481; **Hertz**, international airport, T021-398 4338, Av Princesa Isabel 273-A, Copacabana, T021-2275 7440; **Interlocadora**, international airport, T021-3398 3181; **Localiza**, international airport and Santos Dumont airport, T0800-992000, Av Princesa Isabel 150, Copacabana, T021-2275 3340; **Nobre**, Av Princesa Isabel 7, Copacabana, T021-2541 4646; **Telecar**, R Figueiredo Magalhães 701, Copacabana, T021-2235 6778.

Car repairs

Kyoso Team Mecânico Siqueira Campos, at the entrance to the old tunnel, T021-2255 0506. A good mechanic who enjoys the challenge of an unusual car. Recommended.

Distances and journey times

Juiz de Fora, 184 km (2¾ hrs); **Belo Horizonte**, 434 km (7 hrs); **São Paulo**, 429 km (6 hrs); **Vitória**, 521 km (8 hrs); **Curitiba**, 852 km (12 hrs); **Brasília**, 1148 km (20 hrs); **Florianópolis**, 1144 km (20 hrs); **Foz do Iguaçu**, 1500 km (21 hrs); **Porto Alegre**, 1553 km (26 hrs); **Salvador**, 1649 km (28 hrs); **Recife**, 2338 km (38 hrs); **Fortaleza**, 2805 km (48 hrs); **São Luís**, 3015 km (50 hrs); **Belém**, 3250 km (52 hrs).

Ferry

To **Niteroi**, every 10 mins ferries and launches cross Guanabara bay for Niterói from the 'Barcas' terminal at Praça 15 de Novembro. The journey takes 20-30 mins and costs US$1. Catamarans (*aerobarcas*) also leave every 10 mins but only take 3 mins and cost US$2.50. Fares are halved between 0700 and 1000. The slow, cheaper ferry gives the best views. Ferries and catamarans leave Niterói for Rio de Janeiro from the terminal at Praça Araribóia.

Metro

See map page 133. The Metrô provides a good service; it is clean, a/c and fast. **Line 1** operates between the inner suburb of Tijuca (station Saens Peña) and Arcoverde (Copacabana), via the railway station (Central), Glória and Botafogo. **Line 2** runs from Pavuna, passing Engenho da Rainha and the Maracanã stadium, to Estácio. It operates 0600-2300, Sun 1400-2000; closed holidays. The fare is US$0.50 single; multi-tickets and integrated bus/Metrô tickets are available.

Substantial changes in bus operations are taking place because of the extended Metrô system; buses connecting with the Metrô have a blue-and-white symbol in the windscreen.

Taxi

See also Ins and outs, page 72. The fare between Copacabana and the centre is US$7. Between 2300-0600 and on Sun and holidays, 'tariff 2' is used. Taxis have red number plates with white digits (yellow for private cars, with black digits) and have meters. Smaller ones (mostly Volkswagen) are marked TAXI on the windscreen or roof. Make sure meters are cleared and on 'tariff 1', except at those times mentioned above. Only use taxis with an official identification sticker on the windscreen. Don't hesitate to argue if the route is too long or the fare too much. Radio taxis are safer but almost twice as expensive, eg **Cootramo**, T021-2560 5442; **Coopertramo**, T021-2260 2022; **Centro de Táxi**, T021-2593 2598; **Transcoopass**, T021-2560 4888. Luxury cabs are allowed to charge higher rates; **Inácio de Oliveira**, T021-2225 4110, is a reliable taxi driver for excursions; he only speaks Portuguese. Recommended. **Grimalde**, T021-2267 9812, has been recommended for talkative daytime and evening tours, English and Italian spoken, negotiate a price.

Train

There are suburban trains to **Nova Iguaçu**, **Nilópolis**, **Campo Grande** and elsewhere. Buses marked 'E Ferro' go to the train station.

Tram

See also Ins and outs, page 72. The last remaining tram runs from near the Largo da Carioca (there is a museum open Fri only 0830-1700) across the old aqueduct (Arcos) to Dois Irmãos or Paula Mattos in **Santa Teresa** – historical and interesting, US$0.40. For more details see Santa Teresa, page 90.

Directory

Banks

Lloyds Bank, R da Alfândega 332, 7th floor; **Banco Internacional** (Bank of America and Royal Bank of Canada), R do Ouvidor 90; **Banco Holandês Unido**, R do Ouvidor 101; **Citibank**, R Assembléia 100, changes large US$ TCs Into smaller ones, no commission; **Banco do Brasil**, there are only 2 branches in Rio which will change US$ TCs, Praia de Botafogo, 384A, 3rd floor (minimum US$200) and the central branch at R Sen Dantas 105, 4th floor (minimum US$500 – good rates). The international airport is probably the only place to change TCs at weekends. Visa cash withdrawals at **Banco do Brasil** (many ATMs at the R Sen Dantas branch, no queues) and **Bradesco** (personal service or machines). MasterCard, Visa and Cirrus cash machines at **HSBC** branches throughout the city; **Itaú**, on Av Atlântica (next to Copacabana Palace), R Visconde de Pirajá, close to Praça Gen Osório (Ipanema) and other locations. Also at Santos Dumont airport.

Currency exchange Most large hotels and reputable travel agencies will change currency and TCs. Copacabana (where rates are generally worse than in the centre) is full of *câmbios* and there are also many on Av Rio Branco. **American Express**, Av Atlântica 1702, loja 1, T021-2548 2148, Mon-Fri 0900-1600, Av Pres Wilson 231, 18th floor, Centro, and at Antônio Carlos Jobim international airport, T021-3398 4251 (VIP room 1st floor), good rates (T0800 -785050 toll-free); **Câmbio Belle Tours**, Rio Sul Shopping, ground floor, loja 101, parte A-10, Mon-Fri 1000 1800, Sat 1000-1700, changes cash. In the gallery at Largo do Machado 29 are **Câmbio Nick** at loja 22 and, next door but one, **Casa Franca**.

Cultural centres

American Library, União Cultural Brasil-Estados Unidos, R Col Oscar Porto 208; **Centro Brasileiro Britânico**, R Ferriera de Araújo 741, Pinheiros, T021-3039 0567; **Centro Cultural Fiesp**, Av Paulista 1313, Tue-Sun 0900-1900, foreign newspapers and magazines. **Goethe- Instituto**, R Lisboa 974, Mon-Thu 1400-2030.

Dentist

Amílcar Werneck de Carvalho Vianna, Av Pres Wilson 165, suite 811, English-speaking; **Dr Mauro Suartz**, R Visconde de Pirajá 414, room 509, T021-2287 6745, speaks English and Hebrew, helpful.

Embassies and consulates

Argentina, Praia de Botafogo 228, T021-2553 1646. Very helpful over visas, 1130-1600; **Australia**, Av Presidente Wilson, T021-3824 4624. Mon-Fri 0900-1300, 1430-1800; **Austria**, Av Atlântica 3804, T021-2522 2286; **Canada**, R Lauro Müller 116, T021-2543 3004; **Denmark**, Praia do Flamengo 66, T021-2558 6050; **France**, Av Pres Antônio Carlos 58, T021-2210 1272; **Germany**, R Pres Carlos de Campos 417, T021 2553 6777; **Israel**, Av NS de Copacabana 680, T021-2548 5432; **Netherlands**, Praia de Botafogo 242, 10th floor, T021-2552 9028 (Dutch newspapers here and at KLM office on Av Rio Branco); **Paraguay**, same address, 2nd floor, T021-2553 2294, visas US$5; **Sweden, Finland** and **Norway**, Praia do Flamengo 344, 9th floor, T021-2553 5505; **Switzerland**, R Cândido Mendes 157, 11th floor, T021-2221 1867; **UK**, Praia do Flamengo 284, 2nd floor, T021-2553 3223 (consular section direct line), F2553 6850, consular section is open Mon-Fri 0900-1230 (consulate 0830-1700), Metrô Flamengo, or bus 170, the consulate issues a useful *Guidance for Tourists* pamphlet; **Uruguay**, Praia de Botafogo 242, 6th floor, T021-2553 6030; **USA**, Av Pres Wilson 147, T021-22927117, Mon-Fri 0800-1100, passports 1330-1500.

Immigration

Federal Police, Praça Mauá (passport section), entrance in Av Venezuela, T021-2291 2142. To renew a 90-day visa, US$12.50.

Internet

Internet cafés are easy to find throughout the city. There are several places in Rio Sul shopping centre, Botafogo; many on Av NS de Copacabana, and others on R Visconde de Pirajá, Ipanema. **Phone Serv**, Av NS de Copacabana 454, loja B, US$3 per hr internet, telephone service. **Tudo é Fácil**, 3 branches in Copacabana: R Xavier da Silveira 19, Av Prado Júnior 78 and R Barata Ribeiro 396. Well organized, with identification cards so once registered you can bypass the front desk, telephone booths and scanners, US$2 per hr, discounts for extended use.

Language courses

Instituto Brasil-Estados Unidos, Av Copacabana 690, 5th floor, 8-week course, 3 classes a week, US$150, 5-week intensive course US$260. Good English library at same address; **IVM Português Prático**, R do Catete 310, sala 302, US$18 per hr for individual lessons, cheaper for groups, helpful staff, recommended; **Cursos da UNE** (União Nacional de Estudantes), R Catete 243, include cultural studies and Portuguese classes for foreigners.

Laundry

Lavanderia, Visconde de Pirajá 631A, Ipanema, T021-2294 8142; **Fénix**, R do Catete 214, loja 20; **Laundromat** at Av NS de Copacabana 1216; **Lavlev Flamengo**, RC de Baependi 78, or R das Laranjeiras 43, L28. In Rio Sul there are self-service launderettes such as **Lavelev**, about US$7 for a machine, including detergent and drying, 1 hr. Also at R Buarque de Macedo 43B, Catete, R Voluntários da Patria 248, Botafogo, Av Prado Júnior 63B, Copacabana.

Medical services

Vaccinations at **Saúde de Portos**, Praça Mcal Âncora, T021-2240 8628/8678, Mon-Fri 1000-1100, 1500-1800 (vaccination book and ID required); **Policlínica**, Av Nilo Peçanha 38, for diagnosis and investigation; **Hospital Municipal Rocha Maia**, R Gen Severiano 91, Botafogo, T021-2295 2295/2121, near Rio Sul Shopping Centre, a good public hospital for minor injuries and ailments; free, but there may be queues; **Hospital Miguel Couto**, Mário Ribeiro 117, Gávea, T021-2274 6050, has a free casualty ward.

Post

The **Central Post Office** is on R 1 de Março 64, at the corner of R do Rosário. Also at Av NS de Copacabana 540 and many other locations. All handle international post. There is a post office at Antônio Carlos Jobim international airport; **Poste Restante** at Correios, Av NS de Copacabana 540 and all large post offices (letters held for a month, recommended, US$0.10 per letter); **Federal Express**, Av Calógeras 23 (near Santa Luzia church) T021-2262 8565, is reliable.

Students

Student Travel Bureau, Av Nilo Peçanha 50, SL 2417, Centro, T/F021-2544 2627, and R Visconde de Pirajá 550, loja 201, Ipanema, T021-2512 8577, www.stb.com.br, has details of travel, discounts and cultural exchanges for ISIC holders.

Telephone

International telephone booths are blue. International calls can be made at larger **Correios**, eg Av NS de Copacabana 540; larger **Embratel** offices also have telex and fax; at the **airports** and the **Novo Rio rodoviária**; at R Dias da Cruz 192, Méier-4, 24 hrs, 7 days a week; in **Urca**, near the Pão de Açúcar cable car; at **Praça Tiradentes 41**, a few mins' walk from Metrô Carioca; at **R Visconde de Pirajá 111**, Ipanema; and at **R do Ouvidor 60**, Centro.

Telephone numbers often change in Rio de Janeiro and other Brazilian cities. If in doubt, phone **Auxilio à Lista**, T102, which is the current daily updated directory of telephone numbers. This number can be used all over the country, but if you want to find out a Rio phone number from outside Rio, dial the city code 021, then 121. Note that these services are in Portuguese, so you may need to seek assistance from a hotel receptionist or similar.

Toilets

There are very few public toilets in Rio de Janeiro, but shopping centres, many bars and restaurants (eg McDonald's) offer facilities. Just ask for the *banheiro*.

East of Rio de Janeiro

Rio de Janeiro state is one of Brazil's smallest, but it is packed with great things to see. East of Rio the country gets drier and looks more Mediterranean. The coast, which is lined with fabulous beaches for hundreds of kilometres, is backed by a long series of saltwater lakes and drifting sand dunes. Most visitors ignore Niterói, the city immediately opposite Rio across Guanabara Bay, despite its having ocean beaches as good as or better than Rio's. Instead, they head straight for the surf towns around Cabo Frio or the fashionable little resort of Búzios, which has good beaches and lively summer nightlife. » *For Sleeping, Eating and other listings, see pages 142-148.*

Niterói » *pp142-148.*

Cariocas are rude about everywhere, but they are especially rude about their neighbour across Guanabara Bay. The only good thing about Niterói, they say, is the view it has of Rio de Janeiro. As a result few visitors make it here. However, its ocean beaches are less polluted and far less crowded than Rio's and the views from them across the bay, especially at sunset, are wonderful. Oscar Niemeyer's Museu de Arte Contemporânea, a flying-saucer-shaped building perched on a promontory in Niterói is one of his very best buildings. There is no reason to stay overnight in Niterói but the city is well worth visiting as a day trip or on the way to Búzios.

Ins and outs

Ferries and launches to Niterói leave from the 'Barcas' terminal at Praça 15 de Novembro. Boats run every 10 minutes and the journey takes 20-30 minutes, US$1. Catamarans (*aerobarcas*) take just three minutes and cost US$2.50. Fares are halved 0700-1000. Boats arrive at the Praça Araribóia terminal in Niterói.

Bus Nos 996 Gávea–Jurujuba, 998 Galeão–Charitas, 740-D and 741 Copacabana–Charitas, 730-D Castelo–Jurujuba, US$0.60-0.75, all run between Rio and Niterói. If you are driving the bridge across Guanabara Bay is well signposted. There is a toll of US$2. To get to the ocean beaches, take bus Nos 38 or 52 from Praça Gen Gomes Carneiro or a bus from the street directly ahead of the ferry entrance, at right angles to the coast road. For Jurujuba take bus No 33 from the boat dock; sit on the right-hand side, it's a beautiful ride.

For **tourist information** try contacting **Neltur** ⓘ *Estrada Leopoldo Fróes 773, São Francisco, T021-2710 2727, www.neltur.com.*

Sights

Surrounded by long curved walkways, the space-age building of the **Museu de Arte Contemporânea** ⓘ *Mirante da Praia da Boa Viagem, T021-2620 2400, www.macniteroi.com, Tue-Sun 1100-1800, US$1.50, free Wed,* is rapidly becoming the most famous work by Brazil's celebrated disciple of Le Corbusier, Oscar Niemeyer. It is in a fabulous location, sitting above a long bach with a sweeping view across Guanabara Bay to Rio as a backdrop. The building itself looks like a Gerry Anderson vision of the future; one can almost imagine *Thunderbird 1* taking off through its centre. The main gallery is a white circle of polished concrete perched on a low monopod and sitting in a reflection pool. It is reached by a coiling, serpentine ramp which meets the building on its second storey. The exhibitions comprise seasonal shows and a permanent collection of Brazilian contemporary art of all disciplines. The top level is devoted to temporary displays and the intermediate to the permanent collection. Niemeyer overcomes the problem of the unsuitability of a curved space for the exhibition of art

Villa-Lobos – Rio's greatest musical son

One of the many contradictory beauties of Brazil is that whilst the country as a whole is entrenchantly institutionalized and socially stratified, its best music has always burst forth spontaneously from the various roots of Brazil, and been loved by all. Gilberto Gil says in one song that it comes from 'beneath the soil at our feet'; the feet of Bahia. African feet. Marlui Miranda celebrates it as indigenous, Hermeto Pascoal and Egberto Gismonti as bursting from Nature. And none of these composers, revered though they are throughout Brazil move within set traditions – their music defies labels. This attitude to music within Brazil is as much a product of the vision of one man as it is a lucky fluke. Heitor Villa-Lobos, the country's most distinguished composer once famously stated: 'one foot in the academy and you are changed for the worst'. He went on to change the academy; founding a system of education, still used today which fused classical training with a love and appreciation for popular and traditional musical forms.

Like so many other great Brazilian musicians from Djavan to Tom Jobim, Villa-Lobos began his musical career in Rio's cafes. You could have seen him at the turn of the 19th century playing cello in places like **Bar Luiz** in the city centre. He then secured a place in the Rio Symphony Orchestra, where he played under the Strauss's baton, and where he began to compose. His early concerts enchanted Cariocas and by 1923, he had attracted enough official favour to win a government grant to study in Paris; a considerable amount of money at that time. Here he met and became friends with Milhaud, was strongly influenced by Satie and composed many of his most famous works – like the *Bachianas Brasileiras*, which re-invented and Brazilianized baroque music. On his return to Brazil Villa-Lobos founded the Conservatório Nacional de Canto Orfeónico and the Brazilian Academy of Music, where he invented and instilled his much revered system of musical education.

Villa-Lobos was a magnetic personality and a Carioca through and through. Julian Bream, the foremost European interpreter of his guitar music remembers him as 'larger than life, quite extraordinary. He didn't seem to be a composer. He wore loud checked shirts, smoked a cigar, and always kept the radio on, listening to the news or light music or whatever.' He was famous for his anecdotes which were told with a cigar in one hand a glass of brandy in the other. These were full of unlikely accounts of encounters with tribes of cannibalistic *indígena* and giant snakes, met on his numerous travels throughout the Amazon and North East, in search of Nature and traditional folk music.

His music too is idiosyncratic; anecdotal; visual and thoroughly Brazilian. *Bachianas Brasileiras* and *Little Caipira Train* are celebrations of daily Brazilian life. *Green Mansions* and *Saudades das Selvas Brasileiras* (*Longing for the Brazilian Forest*) are dedications to the beauty of the natural landscape. He even wrote a series of Choros; a musical style which fused Portugal and Africa and which would later produce Samba. He died, on November 17, 1959, in his beloved Rio de Janeiro.

His house is now a museum, see page 96.

by using an inner hexagonal core enclosed by flat screen walls. More difficult to overcome is that the glimpses of the stunning panorama of Rio through the gaps in the hexagon are far more captivating than most of the art. The building is worth seeing at dusk when it is lit; the sky above the streetlights of Rio is light peacock blue infused with lilac and the distant figure of the Corcovado Christ shines brilliant xenon-white over the dark mass of mountains.

Many buildings associated with the city's period as state capital are grouped around the **Praça da República**. None are open to the public. The city's main thoroughfare which runs from here, Avenida Ernâni do Amaral Peixoto, is lined with buildings similar to Avenida Presidente Vargas in Rio. At the end of the avenue is the dock for Rio, a statue of the Indian chief Araribóia and Bay Market shopping centre.

Perched on a rocky promontory at the mouth of Guanabara Bay, the 16th-century **Fortaleza Santa Cruz** ⓘ *Estrada General Eurico Gaspar Dutra, Guanabara Bay, T021-2710 7840, daily 0900-1600, US$1.50, tours have a compulsory guide, Portuguese only*, is still used by the Brazilian military and is the most important historical monument in Niterói. As well as the usual range of cannon, dungeons and bulwarks the tour includes a visit to gruesome execution sites and a little chapel dedicated to Saint Barbara. The statue of the saint inside was originally destined for Santa Cruz dos Militares in Rio. However, unlike most Cariocas, the saint obviously prefers Niterói: any attempts to move her image from here have allegedly been accompanied by violent storms.

Beaches

The beaches closest to the city centre are unsuitable for bathing (Gragoatá, Vermelha, Boa Viagem, das Flechas). The next ones, also in the city and with polluted water, have more in the way of restaurants, bars and nightlife and some of the best views in the whole country, especially at sunset and the break of day. **Icaraí** is the smartest district, with the best hotels and good nightlife. **São Francisco** and **Charitas** have the most fabulous views and lots of little beach bars for a sunset *caipirinha*. The road continues round the bay, past **Preventório** and **Samanguaiá** to **Jurujuba**, a fishing village at the end of the No 33 bus route. About 2 km from Jurujuba along a narrow road are the attractive twin beaches of **Adão** and **Eva** beneath the **Fortaleza Santa Cruz**, with more lovely views of Rio across the bay. These beaches are often used for *candomble* (Brazilian-African spirit religion) ceremonies.

Piratininga, Camboinhas, Itaipu and **Itacoatiara**, four fabulous stretches of sand, are the best in the area, about 40 minutes' ride from Niterói through picturesque countryside. Buses leave from the street directly ahead of the ferry entrance, at right angles to the coast road. The undertow at Itacoatiara is dangerous, but the waves are popular with surfers and the beach itself is safe. Itaipu is also used by surfers.

Costa do Sol » pp142-148.

To the east of Niterói lies a series of saltwater lagoons, the **Lagos Fluminenses.** Two small lakes lie behind the beaches of Piratininga, Itaipu and Itacoatiara, but they are polluted and ringed by mud. The next lakes, **Maricá** and **Saquarema**, are much larger; although they are still muddy, the waters are relatively unpolluted and wildlife abounds in the scrub and bush around the lagoons. This is a prime example of the *restinga* (coastal swamp and forest) environment. The RJ-106 road runs behind the lakes en route to Cabo Frio and Búzios, but an unmade road goes along the coast between Itacoatiara and Cabo Frio, giving access to the many long, open beaches of Brazil's Costa do Sol. The whole area is perfect for camping.

Maricá → *Phone code: 022. Population: 60,500.*

The 36-km Itaipu-Açu, with many wild, lonely stretches, leads to Maricá, a sleepy fishing village with sand streets, on its own lagoon. There is good walking in the **Serra do Silvado,** 14 km away on the road to Itaboraí. Between Maricá and Saquarema are **Ponta Negra** and **Jaconé**, both surfing beaches. Information is available from the **tourist office** ⓘ *Av Ver Francisco Sabino da Costa 477, www.marica.rj.gov.br.*

Saquarema → *Phone code: 022. Colour map 4, C3. Population: 44,000.*

Saquarema is a fishing and holiday village, known as the centre for surfing in Brazil. Its cold, open seas provide consistent, crashing waves of up to 3 m. Frequent national and international championships take place here, but beware of strong currents. The lovely white church of **Nossa Senhora de Nazaré** (1675) is on a green promontory jutting into the ocean. Local legend has it that on 8 September 1630, fishermen, saved from a terrible storm, found an image of the Virgem de Nazaré in the rocks. A chapel was founded on the spot and subsequent attempts to relocate the Virgin (as when the chapel was falling into disrepair) resulted in her miraculously returning to the original site. For **tourist information**, see www.saquarema.rj.gov.br.

Araruama → *Phone code: 022. Colour map 4, C3. Population: 66,500.*

The **Lagoa Araruama** (220 sq km), is one of the largest lakes in Brazil and is famous for its medicinal mud. The salinity is high, the waters calm and almost the entire lake is surrounded by sandy beaches, making it popular with families looking for unpolluted bathing. The constant breeze makes the lake perfect for windsurfing and sailing. The major industry of the area is salt, and all around are saltpans and wind pumps used to carry the water into the pans. The town itself is at the western end of the lake on the inland shore, 116 km from Rio.

At the eastern end of the lake, also inland, is **São Pedro de Aldeia**, which has a population of 55,500 and, despite intensive development, still retains much of its colonial charm. There is a lovely Jesuit church built in 1723, and a **tourist information office** ⓘ *Ton Av São Pedro, www.araruama.rj.gov.br.*

Arraial do Cabo → *Phone code: 022. Population: 21,500.*

This rather ugly little salt-industry town near Cabo Frio is considerably less busy than the resort at Cabo Frio a little to the north, and provides access to equally good beaches and dunes. The lake and the ocean here are divided by the Restinga de Massambaba, a long spit of sand mostly deserted except for the beaches of **Massambaba** and **Seca** at the western end and **Grande** in the east at Arraial do Cabo town itself. Arraial has lots of other small beaches on the bays and islands which form the cape, round which the line of the coast turns north, including the long, busy stretch at **Anjos, Praia do Forno** and **Prainha.** Excursions can be made by boat around the islets and by jeep or buggy over the sand dunes.

Ins and outs A very steep road connects the beaches of Itaipu and Itacoatiara with RJ-106 (and on to Bacaxá and Araruama) via the village of Itaipu-Açu. Most maps do not show a road beyond Itaipu-Açu; it is certainly too steep for buses. An alternative to the route from Niterói to Araruama through the lagoons is further inland than the RJ-106, via Manilha, Itaboraí and Rio Bonito on the BR-101 and RJ-124; this is a fruit-growing region.

Diving and adventure sports While Arraial is not a dive destination of international quality in its own right, it is one of the best in Brazil and there are a number of sites of varying difficulty with caverns and swim-throughs that are well worth exploring. Cold and warm currents meet here just off the coast and the marine life is more abundant than almost anywhere else on mainland southern Brazil. Expect to see schools of tropical and subtropical reef fish such as batfish and various tangs and butterfly fish, the occasional turtle, colonies of gorgonians and beautiful (though invasive) soft corals probably brought here on oil tankers from the Indo-Pacific. Dolphins are frequent visitors. The best visibility is between November and May. Water temperature is always below 20°C. The little town is also establishing itself as an adventure sports destination with activities like dune boarding, parachuting, kite surfing and kayaking available. ▸▸ *See Activities and tours, page 147.*

Excursions **Praia do Farol**, on Ilha do Cabo Frio, is one of Brazil's best beaches, with dunes and crystal-clear water. **Tourist information** ⓘ *T022-2620 5039, www.arraialdocabo-rj.com.br/zarony.html*, is at Praça da Bandeira. » *See Activities and tours, page 147.*

Cabo Frio » *pp142-148.*

→ *Phone code: 022. Colour map 4, C4. Population: 127,000.*

This busy tourist town, 168 km from Rio, is a popular middle-class Brazilian seaside resort, overflowing at the weekend with Cariocas. Although the town itself is very touristy, there are some attractive white-sand beaches, some with dunes and good surf and windsurfing, and accommodation nearby. Bring mosquito repellent.

Cabo Frio vies with Porto Seguro for the title of Brazil's first city. The navigator Amerigo Vespucci landed here in 1503 and returned to Portugal with a boatload of pau brasil. Since the wood in these parts was of better quality than that further north, the area subsequently became the target for loggers from France, the Netherlands and England. The Portuguese failed to capitalize on their colony here and it was the French who established the first defended settlement. Eventually the Portuguese took it by force but it was not until the second decade of the 17th century that they planned their own fortification, the **Forte São Mateus** ⓘ *daily 0800-1800*, which was started in 1618 on the foundations of the French fort. It is now a ruin at the mouth of the Canal de Itajuru, with rusting cannons propped up against its whitewashed ramparts. The canal connects Lagoa Araruama with the ocean.

The town beach, **Praia do Forte**, is highly developed and stretches south for about 7½ km to Arraial do Cabo, its name changing to **Praia das Dunas** (after the dunes) and **Praia do Foguete**. These waters are much more suited to surfing. North of the canal entrance and town is the small under-developed beach of **Praia Brava** (popular with surfers and naturists) and the wine glass bay of **Praia das Conchas**, which has a few shack restaurants. Next is **Praia do Peró**, 7 km of surf and sand on the open sea with a small town behind it and cheap accommodation. The best dunes are at Peró, Dama Branca (on the road to Arraial) and the Pontal dunes at Praia do Forte. There is a **tourist information office** ⓘ *Av Contorno 200, Praia do Forte, T022-2647 1689, www.cabofrio.tur.br*, a large orange building.

Búzios » *pp142-148.*

→ *Phone code: 022. Colour map 4, C4. Population: 18,000.*

Búzios is the principal resort of choice for Carioca and Mineira upper middle classes searching for their idea of St Tropez sophistication. When it was discovered by Brigitte Bardot in 1964 it was little more than a collection of colonial fishermen's huts and a series of pristine beaches hidden beneath steep hills covered in maquis-like vegetation. Now there are strings of hotels behind all of those beaches and the huts have become lost within a designated tourist village of bars, bikini boutiques and restaurants, most of which are strung along the pretty little main street – Rua das Pedras. Bardot sits here too – cheesily immortalized in brass and subsequently in tens of thousands of pictures taken by the troops of cruise line passengers who fill Búzios's streets in high season. St Tropez this is not, but it can be fun for twenty- somethings who are single and looking not to stay that way; the beaches are beautiful and there are a few romantic hotels with wonderful views.

Ins and outs

Getting there Four buses leave daily from Rio's *rodoviária* (US$8, 2½ hrs). Go to the **1001** counter, T022-2516 1001 for tickets. You can also take any bus from Rio to the town of Cabo Frio (these are more frequent), from where it's 30 minutes to Búzios. Buying the ticket in advance is only recommended on major holidays. The Búzios *rodoviária* is a few blocks' walk from the centre. Some *pousadas* are within 10 minutes' walk, eg **La Coloniale** and **Brigitta's**, while others need a local bus (US$0.50) or taxi. The buses from Cabo Frio run the length of the peninsula and pass several *pousadas*. The journey by car along the BR-106 takes about 2½ hours from Rio. Traffic back to Rio can be appalling on Sunday nights and during the peak holiday season.

Tourist information The main **tourist office** ⓘ *Manguinos, Pórtico de Búzios s/n, T022-2633 6200, T0800-249999, 24 hrs*, is at the entrance to town on the western edge of the peninsula. It has helpful staff, some of whom speak English. There's another office at ⓘ *Praça Santos Dumont, T022-2623 2099*, in the centre of Búzios town, which is more limited. For most of the hotels and services on the peninsula check www.buziosonline.com.br. Maps are available from hotels and tourist offices.

Beaches

During the daytime, the best option is to head for the beaches, of which there are 25. The most visited are **Geribá** (many bars and restaurants; popular with surfers), **Ferradura** (deep-blue sea and calm waters), **Ossos** (the most famous and close to the centre), **Tartaruga** and **João Fernandes**. The better surf beaches like **Praia de Manguinhos** and **Praia de Tucuns** are further from the town centre. To help you to decide which beach suits you best, you can join one of the local two- or three-hour schooner trips which pass many of the beaches, or hire a beach buggy (available from agencies on Rua das Pedras or through most hotels and hostels). These trips cost around US$10-15 and can be arranged through **Escuna Queen Lory**, T022-2623 1179.

Sleeping

Niterói *p137*

AL-A Tower Hotel, Av Almte Ari Parreiras 12, Icaraí, T021-2612 2121, www.towerhotel.com.br. Niterói's smartest hotel with ordinary 3-star hotel rooms, an indoor pool and reasonable business facilities.

A Icaraí Praia, R Belisário Augusto 21, T021-2710 2323, www.icaraipraiahotel.com.br. Plain rooms in a faded 1980s beachfront tower.

B Pousada Suba and Veja, R Mal Raul Albuquerque (Mirante de Piratininga), Km 18, T021-2619 0823. Wonderful views out over one of the most beautiful beaches on the Costa do Sol. Bar, restaurant, pool and sauna.

Camping

Piratininga, Estr Frei Orlando Km 2, T021-2609 4581.

Maricá *p139*

B Pousada Colonial, Ponta Negra, T/F022-2748 1707. Simple suites and bungalows, with breakfast.

B Solar Tabaúna, Ponta Negra, T022-2648 1626. Similar to the Colonial but with a pool.

Saquarema *p140*

B Pousada Pedra d'Água Maasai, Trav de Itaúna 17, T/F022-2651 1092, www.maasai.com.br. Good little beachfront hotel with 18 apartments, pool, sauna and a reasonable seafood restaurant.

C Pousada do Holandês, Av Vilamar 377, Itaúna beach. Many languages spoken by Dutch owner and his Brazilian wife. Good meals – follow the signs, or take a taxi, from Saquarema. Recommended.

C-D Pousada Canto da Vila, Av Min Salgado 52, T022-2651 1563, www.pousadacantodavila.com.br. 14 little rooms and 2 larger ones. Overlooking the beach. Pokey but well maintained.

D-E Garota de Itaúna, Av Oceânica 165, Itaúna, T022-2651 2321. Very simple

For Sleeping and Eating price codes, see pages 49 and 52 or the inside front cover. For an explanation of phone codes, see page 66.

rooms next to the beach and a good seafood restaurant.

D-E Ilhas Gregas, R do Prado 671, Itaúna, T022-2651 1008. Youth hostel with a pool, sauna, bar and restaurant.

Camping

Itaúna's, R dos Tatuís 999, access from Av Oceânica, T022-2651 1711.

Araruama *p140*

A Enseada das Garças, R José Costa 1088, Ponta da Areia, about 5 km from São Pedro de Aldeia, T022-2621 1924, www.roteirosdecharme.com.br. Beautiful little hotel overlooking the sea with access to good walking trails.

A Ver a Vista, R São Sebastião 400, São Pedro de Aldeia, T022-2665 4721, www.veravistahotel.com.br. Small apartment hotel with a sauna, bar and swimming pool.

C Pousada do Peu, RJ-132, Km 12, T022-2665 3614. Basic, popular with families.

E Praia do Sudoeste, R Pedro Américo, Lt 27, T022-2621 2763. Youth hostel with simple rooms, available in high season only.

Camping

Camping Clube do Brasil, RJ-106, Marica Km 81.5, Ponte dos Leites beach.

Camping da Colina , RJ-106, Km 108, Praia da Teresa, São Pedro de Aldeia, T022-2621 1919. Not much shade.

Arraial do Cabo *p140*

A Pousada Nautillu's, R Marcílio Dias 100, T022-2622 1611, www.pousadanautillus.com. Medium-sized pousada with a pool, sauna, bar and restaurant. Recommended.

B Pousada dos Atobás, R José Pinto Macedo 270, T022-2622 2461, www.pousadadosatobas.com.br. Small newly built hostel with a pool, sauna and bar.

C Orlamar, Av Beiramar 111, Recanto da Prainha, T/F022-2622 2410, www.pousadaorlamar.com. Literally on the beach – with car access only at low tide. Reasonable restaurant and bar.

Camping

Camping Clube do Brasil, Praia dos Anjos, T022-2622 1023. Crowded beach. Plenty of places to eat along the beach.

Cabo Frio *p141*

AL-B La Plage, R das Badejos 40, Peró, T022-2647 1746, www.redebela.com.br. Cheaper in low season. Newly refurbished with fully equipped suites; those upstairs have sea view, excellent for families. Right on the beach, services include pool and bar, à la carte restaurant, hydromassage, sauna, 24-hr cyber café, garage.

B Othon Sítio do Portinho, R Cnel Ferreira 281, T022-2644 9264, www.pousadasitiodoportinho.hpg.com.br. Cheaper in low season. A good *pousada* with very nice rooms set in gardens in this residential suburb, a/c and all usual facilities, pool and bar. You can get to Portinho district from Av Excelsior or along the canal (go under the bridge). For all **Othon** hotels see www.hoteis-othon.com.br.

B-C Pousada Água Marinha, R Rui Barbosa 996b, Centro, T022-2643 8447, p.aguamarinha@uol.com.br. Cheaper in low season. Plain white rooms with comfortable beds, a/c, fan, TV, frigobar, breakfast, pool and parking. Good choice in the centre, about 4 blocks from Praia do Forte.

C-E Pousada São Lucas, R Goiás 266, Jardim Excelsior, T022-2645 3037 (formerly a youth hostel). 3 mins from *rodoviária*. Price is for double room with TV. Also has dorms with hot shower, breakfast and fan (a little cheaper in low season).

E Albergue da Juventude São Lucas, R Goiás 266, Jardim Excelsior, 3 mins from the *rodoviária*, T022-2645 3037. IYHA youth hostel. Price per person.

E Albergue Internacional da Juventude de Muxarabi, R Leonor Santa Rosa, 13 – Jardim Flamboyant, T022-2643 0369. Youth hostel. Price per person.

E Albergue Peró, R Coutrin 13, Peró, T022-2644 3123, www.perohostel.com.br. IYHA youth hostel, a stroll from the Peró beach with bike rental, restaurant, dorms and doubles.

E Albergue Praia das Palmeiras, Praia das Palmeiras 1, T022-2643 2866. Youth hostel.

Camping

Camping Clube do Brasil, Estr dos Passageiros 700, 2 km from town, T022-2643 3124.

Camping da Estação, Estr dos Passageiros 370, T022-2643 1786.

Dunas do Peró, Estr do Guriri 1001, T022-2629 2323. Small *pousada* with a campsite on Praia do Peró.

The best rooms on the peninsula are not on the beaches but are those with a superb view, on the Morro do Humaitá hill, 10 mins' walk from the town centre; hire a beach buggy. Prior reservations are needed in summer, during holidays such as Carnaval and New Year's Eve, and at weekends. For cheaper options and better availability, try Cabo Frio.

Several private houses rent rooms, especially in summer and holidays. Look for the signs: '*Alugo quartos*'.

LL-L Casas Brancas, Alto do Humaitá 8, T022-2623 1458, www.casasbrancas.com.br. Far and away the best hotel in Búzios; a series of rooms perched on the hill in mock-Mykonos buildings with separate terraces for the pool and spa areas. Sweeping views over the bay. Wonderfully romantic at night when all is lit by candlelight. If you can't afford to stay, come for dinner. The **Abracadabra** next door is owned by Casas Brancas and is similar though cheaper and less stylish.

LL-L El Cazar, Alto do Humaitá 6, T022-2623 1620. Next door to **Casas Brancas** and almost as luxurious, though a little darker inside. Beautiful artwork on the walls and central-Asian kelims on the ipe wood floors. Tasteful and relaxing.

L-AL Pousada Byblos, Alto do Humaitá 14, T022-2623 1162, www.byblos.com.br. Wonderful views out over the bay and bright, light rooms with tiled floors and balconies.

AL Pousada Pedra da Laguna, R 6, lote 6, praia da ferradura, T/F022-2623 1965, www.pedradalaguna.com.br. Spacious rooms, the best with a view, 150 m from the beach. Part of the **Roteiros do Charme** (see page 50).

A Pousada Hibiscus Beach, R 1 No 22, quadra C, Praia de João Fernandes, T022-2623 6221, www.hibiscusbeach.com. A peaceful spot, run by its British owners, overlooking Praia de João Fernandes, 15 pleasant bungalows, a/c, satellite TV, garden, pool, light meals available, help with car/buggy rentals and local excursions. One of the best beach hotels.

A-B Brigitta's Guest House, R das Pedras 131, T/F022-2623 6157, www.búzios online.com.br/brigitta. Beautifully decorated little *pousada* where Bardot once stayed, with just 4 rooms on the main street. Its delightful restaurant, bar and tea house overlooking the water are worth a visit.

A-B Casa da Ruth, R dos Gravatás, Geribá, T022-2623 2242, www.búziosturismo.com/casadaruth. Simple mock-Greek rooms in lilac overlooking the beach and pool.

C-E Praia dos Amores, Av José Bento Ribeiro Dantas 92, T022-2623 2422, www.buziosturismo.com/auberge. IYHA, not far from the bus station, next to Praia da Tartaruga and just under 1 km from the centre. About the best value in Búzios.

C-E Ville Blanche, R Manoel T de Farias, 222, T022-2623 1840. A hostel and hotel right in the centre in the street parallel to R da Pedras with a/c dorms for up to 10, and light-blue tiled doubles with fridges, en suites and a balcony. Can be noisy.

Camping and Chalets

E Country Camping Park, R Maria Joaquina Justiniano 895, (off Praça da Rasa), Praia Rasa, Km 12, T022-2629 1155, www.búzios camping.com.br. Chalets and a well-run shady campsite 1 km from the beach.

Eating

Niterói *p137*

ŦŦŦ Marius, Pref Sílvio Picanço 479, Charitas, T021-2610 1111. Excellent *churrascaria* (grilled meat barbecue), seafood, European and Brazilian cooking in a restaurant overlooking the sea. Decent wine list.

ŦŦ Da Carmine, R Matriz de Barros 305, Icaraí, T021-3602 4988. Decent Italian seafood and pasta and a respectable wine list.

ŦŦ La Sagrada Familia, R Domingues de Sá 325, Icaraí, T021-2610 3556, www.lasagradafamilia.com.br. The best restaurant in Niterói, varied menu and reasonable wine list and housed in a beautiful colonial building.

Saquarema *p140*

ŦŦŦ Le Bistrô, Av São Rafael 1134, Itaúna. The best restaurant in the area with good seafood.

ŦŦ Tem Uma Né Chama Teré, on the main square. Decent Brazilian standards and fish.

Araruama *p140*

ŦŦ Don Roberto, Av Getúlio Vargas 272, São Pedro de Aldeia, T022-2621 3913. Wood-fired pizzas.

ŦŦ-Ŧ O Pirata, RJ-106 Amaral Peixoto 16, São Pedro de Aldeia. A varied menu including reasonable seafood.

Arraial do Cabo *p140*

Ŧ Todos os Prazeres, R José Pinto Macedo, T022-2622 2365. A decent varied menu of Franco-Brazilian fusion; closed on Mon and Wed off season.

Cabo Frio *p141*

The neat row of restaurants on Av dos Pescadores are worth a browse for good-value seafood and pasta. They have French-style seating on the pavement under awnings.

ŦŦŦ-ŦŦ Picolino, R Mcal F Peixoto 319, T022-2643 2436. In a nice old building, very smart, mixed menu of seafood and a few international dishes.

ŦŦ Gaijin, R José Bonifácio 28, T022-2643 4922. Reasonable Japanese food in generous portions.

ŦŦ Hippocampo, R Mcal F Peixoto 283, next door but one, T022-2645 5757. One of the better seafood restaurants with good *robalo* (bass) and *badejo* (whiting).

ŦŦ-Ŧ Chico's, Av Teixeira e Souza 30, upstairs in Centro Comercial Víctor Nunes da Rocha, town centre, T022-2645 7454. Clean, smart, does breakfast, self-service, some more expensive dishes. On the ground floor is the **Coffee Shop.** More a stand than a shop, cheap; but better coffee in **Branca**.

ŦŦ-Ŧ "In" Sônia, Av dos Pescadores 140, loja 04. Good service and tasty fish, many dishes offered for 2 people.

ŦŦ-Ŧ Tonto, Av dos Pescadores, next door to "In" Sônia, T022-2645 1886 for delivery. Also serves pizza and has a bar, too.

Ŧ Branca, Praça Porto Rocha, in the centre of town. Lunch by the kilo 1100-1700, also fast food, pizza after 1800, coffee, pastries and cakes, good; a big, popular place.

Ŧ Chez Michou, Av dos Pescadores. For crêpes (as in Rio Sul shopping centre in Rio de Janeiro – closed Mon). Upstairs are a number of bars and nightclubs, eg **Eleven**, above San Francisco restaurant, and others.

Búzios *p141*

See also **Casas Brancas** page 144 (fine views and romantic dining) and **Brigitta's** page 144 (funky seafood bistro). There are many restaurants on and around R das Pedras and one of the charms of Búzios is browsing here. The cheaper options tend to be off the main drag. There are plenty of beachside *barracas* (palapas) all over the peninsula serving the usual beans, rice and chips combinations outside of the low season.

ŦŦŦ Acquerello, R das Pedras 130, T022-2623 2817. Smart a/c seafood and Italian restaurant with a reasonable wine list. The best on the street.

ŦŦŦ Satyricon, Av José Bento Ribeiro Dantas 500, Praia da Armação (in front of Morro da Humaitá), T022-2623 1595. Búzios's most illustrious restaurant specializing in Italian seafood. Decent wine list.

ŦŦ Moqueca Capixaba, R Manoel de Carvalho 116, Centro, T022-2623 1155. Bahian seafood, with dishes cooked in coconut or déndê oil.

Ŧ Banana Land, R Manoel Turíbio de Farias 50, T022-2623 0855. Cheap and cheerful per kilo buffet.

Ŧ Chez Michou, R das Pedras, 90, Centro, T022-2623 2169. An open-air bar with videos, music and dozens of choices of pancakes accompanied by ice-cold beer. Always busy.

La Prima, Av Manuel Turibo de Farias. Homely, sandwiches and self-service food; doubles as a bakery.

There are a few other very cheap places on Praça Santos Dumont, off R das Pedras, and a small supermarket a couple of doors away from La Prima.

Bars and clubs

Búzios *p141*

In season Búzios nightlife is young, beautiful and buzzing. Out of season it is non-existent. Most of the bars and the handful of clubs are on R das Pedras. These include **Guapo Loco**, a bizarrely shaped Mexican theme-bar and restaurant with dancing. **Privilege**, Av José Bento Ribeiro Dantas 550, R Orla Bardot, Búzios's main club and one of Brazil's best European-style dance clubs with pumping techno, house and hip-hop, and 5 rooms, including a cavernous dance floor, sushi bar and lounge. **Ta-ka-ta ka-ta**, R das Pedras 256, is strewn with motorbike parts and has its walls covered completely with graffiti. The Dutch owner obstinately refuses to say where he comes from. There are plenty of others including lively options like **Bar do Zé**, R das Pedras 382, T022-2623 4986 and **Alexo**, next door.

Shopping

Búzios *p141*

Many of Brazil's fashionable and beautiful come here for their holidays and Búzios is therefore a good place to pick up the kind of beach clothes and tropical cuts which they would wear. Although seemingly expensive these clothes are a fraction of what you would pay for labels of this quality in Europe, the US or Australia. Shopping is best on R das Pedras. Aside from the boutiques, there is little else of interest beyond the expected range of tourist tack shops. Of the boutiques the best are as follows:

Allegra, R das Pedras. Sexy light dresses, skirts, T-shirts and tops.

Bum Bum Ipanema, R das Pedras 321, T022-2623 4139. Bright young bikinis in gorgeous cuts.

Farm, R das Pedras 233, T022-2623 7477. Elegant and cool beachwear and light clothes for women.

Lenny, R das Pedras 233, T022-2623 3745. The most à la mode bikinis – from the point of view of Brazilians.

Salinas, R das Pedras. Beautifully crafted bikinis and beachwear. Together with **Rosa Chá**, the most á la mode – from the point of view of foreigners.

Tenda, R das Pedras. A little boutique with the pick of Brazilian designers including the supermodels' bikini choice – **Rosa Chá**.

Tepo, R Manoel Turíbio de Farias 202D (parallel to R das Pedras), T022-2623 7140. Upmarket indigenous arts and crafts, jewellery and fashion.

Festivals and events

Niterói *p137*

Mar-May Festa do Divino, a festival which traditionally begins on Easter Sun and continues for the next 40 days, in which the *bandeira* (banner) *do Divino* is taken around the local municipalities. The festival ends at Pentecost with sacred and secular celebrations.

24 Jun São João, lots of parades, *forró* dancing and barn-dance costumes.

22 Nov Founding of the town. Parades, concerts and dancing.

Saquarema *p140*

Mar-May Festa do Divino, see Niterói, above.

8 May Founding of the town. Dancing, concerts and plenty of drinking.

29 Jun Festival of São Pedro, at the end of the Festas Juninas.

7 Sep Nossa Senhora de Nazaré, the town's patron saint's day.

Araruama *p140*

16 May Founding of the town.

29 Jun São Pedro, patron saint day of São Pedro de Aldeia.

Arraial do Cabo *p140*

13 May Founding of the town.

May/Jun Corpus Christi.

Activities and tours

Niterói *p137*
Rio Cricket Associação Atlética (RCA), R Fagundes Varela 637, T021-2717 5333. Bus No 57 from the ferry.
Rio Sailing Club (late Clube de Niterói), Estr Leopoldo Fróes 418, lote 338, T021-2610 5810. Bus No 33 marked 'via Fróes'.

Arraial do Cabo *p140*
Deep Trip, Av Getulio Vargas 93, Praia Grande, Arraial do Cabo, T022-2622 1800, www.deeptrip.com.br. The only PADI-affiliated dive operator in Arraial, with a range of courses and dive trips.
Gas, Av Litoranea 80, Praia Grande, T022-9956 1222, www.arraialdocabo-rj.com.br/gas. Various adventure sports including dune boarding, parachuting and kayak surfing. Runs dive trips but is not PADI accredited.
K-Kite School, R da Alegria 15, T022-2662 9465, www.kkite.hpg.ig.com.br. Windsurfing and kitesurfing, and lessons.

Trips to Ilha do Cabo Frio
Barco Lindo Olhar, T022-2647 4493, ask for Vadinho or Eraldo in the town's main marina.
Zarony tours, Marina dos Pescadores, 2nd pier on Praia dos Anjos, T022-2622 5837, www.arraialdocabo-rj.com.br/zarony.html.

Cabo Frio *p141*
Planeta Costa Azul, Square Shopping, loja 21, T022 2645 2023, www.planetacostado sol.com.br. For flights and local packages.

Búzios *p141*
Malizia, R das Pedras, T022-2623 2022. Money exchange, car hire and other services.
Mister Tours, R Germiniano J Luis 3, Centro, T022-2623 2100.

Transport

Niterói *p137*
Boat Ferries and launches run between the terminal at Praça Araribóia in Niterói and the 'Barcas' terminal at Praça 15 de Novembro in **Rio de Janeiro** every 10 mins (15-20 mins, US$1). There are also catamarans (*aerobarcas*) every 10 mins (3 mins, US$2.50; US$1.25 0700-1000. The slow, cheaper ferry gives the best views.

Bus Buses running between Niterói and **Rio de Janeiro** include No 996 Gávea–Jurujuba, No 998 Antônio Carlos Jobim international airport–Charitas, No 740-D and No 741 Copacabana–Charitas, No 730-D Castelo–Jurujuba, US$0.60-0.75.

Saquarema *p140*
Bus To **Rio de Janeiro** (Mil e Um, 1001), every 2 hrs 0730-1800, 2 hrs, US$3.40.

Arraial do Cabo *p140*
Bus To **Rio de Janeiro**, US$6.

Cabo Frio *p141*
Air A new airport has opened linking the area with **Belo Horizonte**, **Brasília**, **Rio de Janeiro** and **São Paulo**.

Bus
Local Salineira and Montes Brancos lines run the local services. US$0.75 to places such as **Búzios**, **São Pedro da Aldeia**, **Saquarema**, **Araruama**, **Arraial do Cabo**; US$0.50 for closer destinations. The urban bus terminal is near Largo de Santo Antônio, opposite the BR petrol station.

Long distance The *rodoviária* is 2 km from the centre. Buses to **Rio de Janeiro** every 30 mins, 2½ hrs, US$8.To **Búzios**, from the local bus terminal in the town centre, every hr, US$1. Útil to **Belo Horizonte** US$20. Unifac to **Belo Horizonte**, **Juiz da Fora**, **Petrópolis**. Macaense runs frequent services to **Macaé**. To **São Paulo**, at 2100, US$22.60.

For the route from Cabo Frio to **Vitória** either take Macaense bus to **Macaé** (about 5¼ hrs), or take **1001** to **Campos**, 3½ hrs, US$5.60, and change. **1001** stops in Campos first at the Shopping Estrada *rodoviária*, which is the one where the bus connection is made, but it's outside town (US$3 taxi to the centre, or local bus US$0.35). The **1001** then goes on to the local *rodoviária*, closer to the centre, but there are no long-distance services from that terminal. Shopping Estrada *rodoviária* has a tourist office, but no cheap hotels nearby. Aguia Branca buses to **Vitória** at 0900 and 1900, US$8.10, 3 hrs 40 mins.

Búzios *p141*
Beach buggies A popular way to get around the cobbled streets of Búzios. Buggy

rental available at **Malízia**, T022-2623 2022 or **Rent Buggy**, T022-2623 6421.

Bus The Búzios *rodoviária* is a few blocks' walk from the centre. **1001**, T021-2516 1001, to **Rio de Janeiro** US$8, 2½ hrs (be at the bus terminal 20 mins before departure), 4 departures daily. Buses running between the *rodoviária* Novo Rio in **Rio de Janeiro** and **Cabo Frio** stop at Búzios and are more frequent. Cabo Frio is a 30-min journey from Búzios. Buying the ticket in advance is only recommended on major holidays.

Car By car via BR-106 takes about 2½ hrs to **Rio de Janeiro** and can take far longer on Sun nights and on Brazilian public holidays.

Directory

Niterói *p137*
Banks Banco 24 Horas, Niterói Shopping, R da Conceição 188; **Bradesco**, R Gavião Peixoto 108. **Internet** O Lido Cyber C@fé, Av Rui Barbosa 29, loja 124, São Francisco. **Laundry** Lavlev, R Pres Backer 138. **Medical services** Universitário Antônio Pedro, Av Marques do Paraná, T021-2620 2828.

Saquarema *p140*
Banks Bradesco, Rod Amaral Peixoto 83.

Araruama *p140*
Banks Bradesco, Av São Pedro 120, São Pedro de Aldeia.

Arraial do Cabo *p140*
Banks Bradesco, R Sen Macedo Soares 44, Ponta Negra. **Unibanco**, R Dom Pedro, will not change cheques and has no ATM.

Cabo Frio *p141*
Banks Banco do Brasil, Praça Porto Rocha 44, the only bank with exchange, *câmbio* 1100-1430; **Bradesco**, Av Assunção 904, has Visa ATM; **HSBC**, Av Assunção 793, has ATM for AmEx, Visa/Plus, MasterCard/Cirrus. **Internet** Aç@i, Av João Pessoa, near R Casemiro de Abreu, US$0.75 per 30 mins, older machines, not always open; **Cyber Mar**, Nunes da Rocha, Av Teixeira e Souza 30, new, a/c, minimum US$1.50 for 30 mins, US$2.20 per hr, daily 0800-2000; **Cyber Tel**, Praça Porta Rocha 56, T022-2649 7575, in gallery next to Banco do Brasil. Only 3 machines, but good and fast, US$2 per hr.

Búzios *p141*
Banks There are banks and money exchanges on R das Pedras; **Banco do Brasil**, R Manuel de Carvalho 70, Centro, T022-2523 2302. **Internet** Búzios@internet, Av J B Ribeiro Dantas 97, close to Shopping One, US$1.20 per 30 mins.

Inland resorts and coffee towns

The mountain resorts of Petrópolis, Teresópolis and Nova Friburgo are set high in the scenic Serra do Mar behind Rio. All three are lovely mountain retreats with accommodation in charming fazendas. *The imperial city of Petrópolis retains many of its original buildings and boasts what is perhaps Brazil's finest museum. This is a beautiful area that is becoming increasingly popular for walking, as well as horse riding and other activities. The resorts were originally established because the cool mountain air offered a respite from the heat of Rio and from yellow fever and other diseases that festered in the unhealthy port in the 19th century. They also provided the routes that brought first gold, then coffee from the interior to the coast.* *» For Sleeping, Eating and other listings, see pages 155-158.*

Petrópolis *» pp155-158.*

→ Phone code: 024. Colour map 4, C3. Population: 290,000.

Emperor Pedro I, who tired of the sticky summer heat in Rio, longed for a summer palace in the cool of the Atlantic Coast mountains but abdicated before he could realize his dream. When the new emperor, Pedro II, took the throne, he soon approved plans presented by the German architect Julius Friedrich Köler for a palace and a new city, to be settled by immigrants. The result was Petrópolis. The city was founded in 1843 and in little over a decade had become a bustling Germanic town and an important imperial summer retreat. The emperor and his family would spend as much as six months of each year here and, as he had his court in tow, Köler was able to construct numerous grand houses and administrative buildings. Many of these still stand – bizarre Rhineland anomalies in a neotropical landscape.

Ins and outs

There are buses from the *rodoviária* in Rio every 15 minutes throughout the day and every hour on Sundays. Air-conditioned buses leave hourly from Avenida Nilo Peçanha. The journey takes about 1½ hours. Sit on the left-hand side for best views and bring travel sickness pills if you are prone to nausea on winding roads. Return tickets are not available, so buy tickets for the return journey on arrival in Petrópolis. The main **tourist office** ⓘ *Praça da Liberdade, Mon-Sat 0900-1800, Sun 0900-1700*, is at the far southwestern end of Avenida Koeler. It has a list of tourist sights and hotels, and a good, free, colour map of the city, also a very useful pamphlet in various languages. Some staff are multilingual; all are helpful.

Sights

Three rivers dominate the layout of Petrópolis: the **Piabanha**, **Quitandinha** and the **Palatino**. In the historic centre, where most of the sites of tourist interest are to be found, the rivers have been channelled to run down the middle of the main avenues. Their banks are planted with flowering trees and the overall aspect is unusual in Brazil; you quickly get a sense that this was a city built with a specific purpose and at a specific time in Brazil's history.

Petrópolis's main attraction is its imperial palace. The **Museu Imperial** ⓘ *R da Imperatriz 220, T024-2237 8000, Tue-Sun 1100-1730, last entry 1700, US$4, under 6s free, expect long queues on Sun during Easter and high season*, is Brazil's most visited museum and is so well kept you might think the imperial family had left the day before,

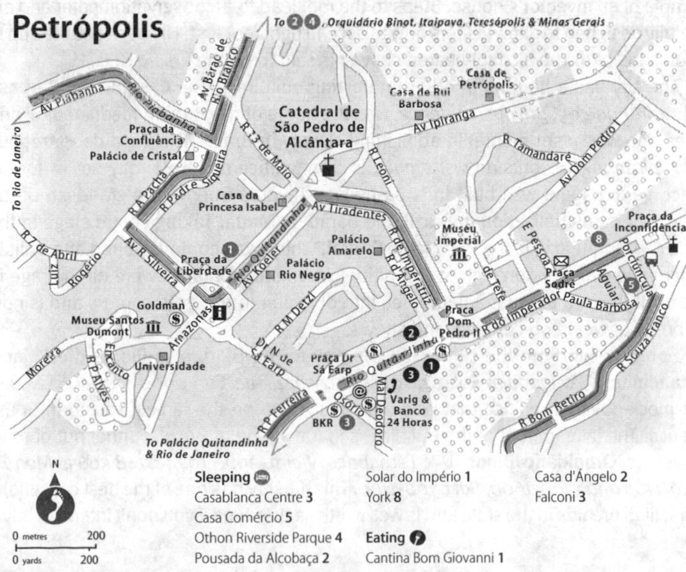

rather than in 1889. It's modest for an emperor, neoclassical in style and fully furnished, and is worth a visit if just to see the Crown jewels of both Pedro I and Pedro II. The palace gardens in front are filled with little fountains, statues and shady benches. Descendants of the original family live in a house behind the palace. Horse-drawn carriages wait to be hired outside the gate; not all the horses are in good shape.

Opposite the Museu Imperial is the handsome **Palácio Amarelo** ⓘ *Praça Visconde de Mauá 89, T024-2291 9200, Tue-Sun 0900-1800, US$1*, built in 1850 as the palace of another Brazilian baron and now the Câmara Municipal (town hall). The twin shady praças **dos Expedicionários** and **Dom Pedro II** (which has a pigeon-covered statue of the emperor) lie opposite each other at the junction of Rua do Imperador and Rua da Imperatriz, 100 m south of the Museu Imperial (left as you leave the museum). A small market is held here on Sundays and there is a handful of cafés and restaurants.

At the northern end of Rua da Imperatriz (right out of the museum and following the river as it curves left along Avenida Tiradentes) is the Gothic revival **Catedral de São Pedro de Alcântara** ⓘ *R São Pedro de Alcântara 60, T024-2242 4300, Tue-Sun 0800-1200 and 1400-1800, free*, where Emperor Pedro II, his wife Princesa Teresa, Princesa Isabel and Count D'Eu are entombed in mock-European regal marble. This lies at the end of the city's most impressive avenue, **Avenida Koeler**, which is lined with mansions built by the imperial and republican aristocracy. Among them are the neoclassical **Palácio Rio Negro** ⓘ *Av Koeler 255, T024-2246 9380, Mon 1200-1700, Wed-Sun 0930-1700, US$1.50, under-6s free, multilingual guides*, built in 1889 by the Barão do Rio Negro as the summer retreat of Brazilian presidents, and the **Casa da Princesa Isabel** ⓘ *Av Koeler 42, outside visits only*, the former residence of Dom Pedro II's daughter and her husband the Count D'Eu.

Avenida Koeler ends at the Praça da Liberdade (formerly known as Praça Rui Barbosa) where there are cafés, goat-drawn carts for children and very photogenic views of the cathedral. A further 100 m west of the praça (away from Avenida Koeler) is the **Museu Santos Dumont** ⓘ *R do Encanto 22, T024-2247 3158, Tue-Sun 0930-1700, US$1.50, free for under 6s*. The summer home of Alberto Santos Dumont, who Brazilians claim was the first man to fly an aeroplane, was designed in 1918 as a mock-Alpine chalet. Santos Dumont called it 'the enchanted one', and it is a delightful example of an inventor's house. Steps to the roof lead to an observation point and are carefully designed to allow visitors only to ascend right foot first. His desk doubled up to become his bed. The alcohol-heated shower is said to be the first in Brazil.

The city has a handful of other interesting buildings. The **Casa de Rui Barbosa** ⓘ *Av Ipiranga 405, private residence*, was the home of the Bahian media mogul and writer who was instrumental in abolishing slavery in Brazil. The **Casa de Petrópolis** ⓘ *Av Ipiranga 716, outside visits only*, is a magnificent Gothic folly set in formal French gardens and was built in 1884 by Jose Tavares Guerra, the grandson of the founder of industrialization in Brazil, the Barão de Mauá. Taking centre stage in the Praça da Confluência is the **Palácio de Cristal**, which was commissioned and built in France following London's great exhibition, when such palaces were all the rage in Europe. It opened to great aplomb, fell into disrepair in the 20th century and is now the home of weekend concerts and shows.

Some 10 km from the centre, on the way to the BR-040 to Rio, is the **Palácio Quitandinha** ⓘ *Av Joaquim Rolla 2, T024-2237 1012, Tue-Sun 0900-1700, US$2.50*, a vast mock-Bavarian edifice that was built in 1944 to be the largest casino in South America. The lake in front of the building is in the shape of Brazil. Further out of town still is the **Orquidário Binot** ⓘ *R Fernandes Vieira 390, T024-2248 5665, Mon-Fri 0800-1100 and 1300-1600, Sat 0700-1100*. This nursery has one of the best collections of Brazilian orchids in the state and is well worth seeing even if you don't intend to buy.

Teresópolis » pp155-158.

➔ *Phone code: 021. Colour map 4, C3. Population: 140,000.*

At 910 m this is the highest city in the state of Rio de Janeiro. It was the favourite summer retreat of Empress Teresa Cristina and is named after her. Development in recent years has destroyed some of the city's character, but most visitors use the town as a base for visiting the Serra dos Órgãos, which lie nearby.

Because of its altitude and the relatively low temperatures, the area was not exploited by the early colonists since they could not grow the tropical crops which were in demand in Europe. The existence of *fazendas* in the region was first documented in the early 19th century, the best-known being that of George March, an Englishman. In order to accommodate a constant stream of visitors, March added lodgings to his farm and, not long after, other landowners followed suit. Before taking the name of the empress, the parish was called Santo Antônio de Paquequer.

Ins and outs

Information is available from the **Secretaria de Turismo** ⓘ *Praça Olímpica, T021-2742 3352, ext 2082*, and **Terminal Turístico Tancredo Neves** ⓘ *Av Rotariana, T021-2642 2094, www.teresopolis.rj.gov.br*, at the entrance to town from Rio. There are very good views of the serra from here. Eight buses a day run between Teresópolis and Petrópolis.

Sights

The **Colina dos Mirantes** is a 30-minute steep climb from Rua Jaguaribe (2 km from the centre; an inexpensive taxi ride), and offers sweeping views of the city and surroundings. Around the town are various attractions, such as the Sloper and Iaci lakes, the Imbui and Amores waterfalls and the **Fonte Judith**, which has mineral-rich water, and is accessed from Avenida Oliveira Botelho, 4 km southwest. Just off the road to Petrópolis is the **Orquidário Aranda** ⓘ *Alameda Francisco Smolka, T021 2742 0628*, 5 km from the centre.

The road to Nova Friburgo (see page 153) is known as the **Vale das Hortaliças** because it passes through a zone where vegetables and flowers are cultivated. There is a rock formation called **A Mulher de Pedra**, 12 km out of Teresópolis on this road.

Serra dos Órgãos » pp155-158.

These mountains near Teresópolis, named after their strange rock formations which are said to look like organ pipes, preserve some of the most diverse stretches of Atlantic Coast forest in the state of Rio de Janeiro. The wildlife, plant and birdwatching here are excellent, as are the walks and rock climbs. The best way to see the park is on foot. A number of trails cut through the forest and head up into the alpine slopes, including the ascent of the **Dedo de Deus**, or God's finger; a precipitous peak which requires some climbing skills. Other trails lead to the highest point in the park, the **Pedra do Sino** (Bell Rock), 2263 m, a three- to four-hour climb up a 14-km path. The west face of this mountain is one of the hardest climbing pitches in Brazil. Other popular walks include the **Pedra do Açu trail** and walks to a variety of anatomically named peaks and outcrops: O Escalavrado (The Scarred One), O Dedo de Nossa Senhora (Our Lady's Finger), A Cabeça de Peixe (Fish Head), A Agulha do Diabo (The Devil's Needle) and A Verruga do Frade (The Friar's Wart).

Ins and outs

If you have a car, a good way to see the park is to do the Rio–Teresópolis–Petrópolis–Rio road circuit, stopping off for walks in the forest. This can be done in a day. The park has two ranger stations, both accessible from the BR-116: the Sede (headquarters, T/F021-2642 1070) is closer to Teresópolis (from town take Avenida Rotariana), while the Sub-Sede is just outside the park proper, off the BR-116. By the Sede entrance is the Mirante do Soberbo, with views to the Baía de Guanabara. Both the Sede station and the Mirante can be reached on the bus marked 'Mirante do Soberbo', which leaves every half an hour from the Teresópolis *rodoviária* and city centre. Anyone can enter the park and hike the trails from the Teresópolis gate, but if you intend to climb the Pedra do Sino, you must sign a register (those under 18 must be accompanied by an adult and have permission from the park authorities). Entrance to the park is US$2, with an extra charge for the path to the top of the Pedra do Sino. For information from **Ibama** for the state of Rio de Janeiro, T021-2231 1772.

Flora and fauna

The park belongs to the threatened Mata Atlântica coastal rainforest, designated by **Conservation International** as a global biodiversity hot spot and the preserve of what are probably the richest habitats in South America outside the Amazonian cloudforests. There are 20- to 30-m-high trees, such as *paineiras* (floss-silk tree), *ipês* and *cedros*, rising above palms, bamboos and other smaller trees. Flowers include begonias, bromeliads, orchids and *quaresmeiras* (glorybushes). The park is home to numerous rare and endemic birds including cotingas, the rarest of which is the grey-winged cotinga, guans, tanagers, berryeaters and trogons. Mammals include titi and capuchin monkeys, all of the neotropical rainforest cats including jaguar and oceleot, tapir and white collared peccary. Reptiles include the sapo-pulga (flea-toad), which at 10 mm long vies with the Cuban pygmy frog as the smallest amphibian in the world.

Nova Friburgo » pp155-158.

→ *Phone code: 024. Colour map 4, C3. Population: 175,000.*

This town, standing at 846 m in a beautiful valley with excellent walking and riding, is a popular resort during the summer months. It was founded by Swiss settlers from Fribourg, the first families arriving in 1820. Apart from tourism, Nova Friburgo has an important textile industry, specializing in lingerie, and also produces cheeses, preserves, sweets and liqueurs. Information is available from the **Centro de Turismo** ⓘ *Praça Demerval Barbosa Moreira, T024-2523 8000, ext 236.*

A cable car, US$5, from Praça dos Suspiros goes 650 m up the **Morro da Cruz**, for a magnificent view of the rugged country. Most of the interesting sites are in the surrounding countryside, so a car may be necessary to see everything. About 10 km northeast are the **Furnas do Catete**, an area of forest, caves, waterfalls and rock formations, one of which is called the Pedra do Cão Sentado (The Seated Dog); there is a small entry fee. Other natural attractions are the Pico da Caledônia (2310 m) 15 km southwest, and the Véu de Noiva waterfall, 9 km north. The district of **Lumiar**, 34 km southeast, has beautiful scenery, waterfalls, natural swimming pools and good canoeing in the Rios Macaé and Bonito. These two rivers meet at a point called Poço do Alemão, or Poço Verde, 4½ km south of Lumiar.

Towns in the coffee zone

Although coffee no longer dominates this part of Brazil as it did in the 19th century, there are still many reminders of the wealth of this trade. It can be seen in the towns of Vassouras and Valença, and especially in the *fazendas*, which were the homes and production headquarters of the coffee barons. Today many of these plantations have been incorporated into a rural, cultural and historic tourist circuit. The train journey from Miguel Pereira has spectacular views of this mountainous terrain.

The coffee zone covered the valley of the Rio Paraíba do Sul and neighbouring hills and valleys. Before the coming of the railways in the second half of the 19th century, mule trains carried the coffee from the interior to the coast on roads such as the Estrada do Comércio from Minas Gerais, through Valença and Vassouras, to the town of Iguaçu on the river of the same name. At the end of the 19th century, the abolition of slavery, the exhaustion of the land and lower international prices for coffee caused the collapse of the coffee trade. The towns had to adapt to new economic activities or die, but many of the *fazendas* remain and, although not easy to get to, are worth the effort to visit. (*Fazendas: As Casas Grandes Rurais do Brasil*, by Fernando Tasso Frajoso Pires, Abbeville Press, is a beautiful book showing these magnificent houses.)

Miguel Pereira → *Phone code: 024. Colour map 4, C3. Population: 24,000.*

This town, 113 km north of Rio de Janeiro, has an excellent mountain climate. In the mid-19th century the area was entirely given over to coffee; other industries were introduced when a railway branch line reached here in the late 19th century. The town was named after a doctor, who, in the 1930s, promoted the region for holidays away from the coast. About 3 km from town on the road to Rio is the **Javari lake**, a popular recreational spot. Mountain roads through the Serra do Mar head east to Petrópolis (see page 148) and Vassouras (see page 154), but ask about their condition before using either of them. For tourist information, go to **Setur** ⓘ *Av Manuel Guilherme Barbosa 375, T024-2484 1616.* There are a few cheap hotels in town and a number of mid- range options stretched along the main road and in the countryside on the outskirts.

Vassouras and around » pp155-158.

→ *Phone code: 024. Colour map 4, C3. Population: 32,000.*

It is hard to believe that the small town of Vassouras was once one of the most important cities of the Brazilian empire. During the coffee boom in the 19th century, it was surrounded by coffee farms whose owners became immensely rich. These coffee barons acquired noble titles and, as their power increased, they built enormous, opulent town houses in Vassouras. The majority of these buildings are still there, surrounding the beautiful main Praça Barão de Campo Belo. The Emperor Pedro II visited the city several times.

In 1875 the railway station was opened in Vassouras, allowing the local farmers to send their produce directly to Rio de Janeiro. But the town went into decline when the coffee boom ended. For many years it had almost no economic activity, except for some cattle ranching and small-scale agriculture. Now it has a university and is being rediscovered by the tourist industry. It still retains its small-town calm, but the reminders of its golden past mix with the student nightlife in the bars along a street called, unofficially, 'The Broadway'.

Sights

The best way to explore Vassouras is on foot. Starting at the *rodoviária*, walk as far as the **Estação Ferroviária**, the former railway station. Recently restored, it is now the headquarters of the Universidade de Vassouras. Continue straight on to the **Praça Barão de Campo Belo**, where you will find the most important old houses and public buildings, all dating from the 19th century. Note the neoclassical influence. One of these old 'baronial' houses, at Rua Custódio Guimarães 65, on the left-hand side of the square, houses the **Casa da Cultura**, a municipal cultural centre that has tourist information and temporary exhibitions of local art and folklore. Ask if you can go upstairs and, on the second floor at the top of some of the internal walls, look for where the paint has peeled. You can see the 19th-century method of house construction, using clay over a frame of interwoven wood and bamboo.

At the top end of the praça is the church of **Nossa Senhora da Conceição**, the most important in the city, completed in 1853 in neoclassical style. Behind the church is the small **Praça Sebastião Lacerda**, surrounded by huge fig trees. Allegedly there is one fig tree for each of the rich coffee barons who lived in Vassouras in the last century. Keep on walking until you come to the cemetery. A visit is recommended; most of the wealthiest men of Brazil's second empire are buried here. Rich mausolea decorated with Italian and Portuguese marble sculptures show the competition among the families. Two of the most important clans are represented: the Teixeira Leite family and the Correa e Castro family. On the grave of Monsenhor Rios, a Catholic priest who died in 1866, a strange purple flower blooms every year in November on the Day of the Dead. Its intense smell is reminiscent of rotting flesh. Scientists have studied it, but have reached no conclusion as to what it is. The flower vanishes after a few days and the small bush lives on until January or February. It is now protected by a small iron fence and a number of miracles are reported to have occurred there.

Back at Praça Barão de Campo Belo, on Rua Barão de Vassouras, is the **Palacete do Barão do Ribeirão**, the former residence of a coffee baron, later converted into the town's court. It is currently closed for restoration as it has been badly attacked by termites. Turn right and at the end of Rua Dr Fernandes Junior (No 160) you will find the fascinating **Casa da Hera museum** ⓘ *T024-2471 2342, Wed-Sun 1100-1700*, an old country house covered with ivy, which belonged in the 19th century to one of the richest men in the town, Joaquim Teixeira Leite. After his death the house was inherited by his daughter, Eufrásia Teixeira Leite, who lost interest in the coffee business. She went to Paris, living a life of parties and luxury for many years. After she died in 1930 the house was made into a museum, in accordance with her will. All the furniture, decoration and architecture is original, from the golden years of coffee. The wide variety of imported tapestries, pianos and porcelain contrasts with the very rough building materials: a fantastic portrait of life in the 1850s. On some Sundays, depending on the number of visitors, tea is served in a re-creation of the atmosphere of the old coffee *fazendas*.

Because Vassouras is a university centre, it has more variety than other towns of a similar size. The action is concentrated in Rua Expedicionário Oswaldo de Almeida Ramos, but you won't need to pronounce that: simply ask for the Broadway and everybody will direct you to the right place. Here there are enough bars and open-air restaurants to suit all tastes and budgets.

Another possibility is a guided visit to the food technology centre at the **Senai**, close to the main praça. Here students learn how to process fruit, vegetables, meat and also how to work in a brewery. Most of the hotels can arrange a weekend guided visit.

Excursions from Vassouras

As yet, Vassouras lacks a well-developed tourist infrastructure. There is a lot to see around the city, especially the old *fazendas*, but they are only just starting to open to the public. The majority of them are privately owned and can only be visited with a prior appointment. The bigger hotels can arrange guided tours with transport at weekends. During the week, the only option is to go by car, as some of the *fazendas* are a long way away, down dirt roads. The best *fazendas* in the vicinity are: **Santa Mônica, São Fernando, Paraíso** and **Oriente**. More information can be obtained from the Casa da Cultura or from the **Tourism Secretary** ⓘ *Municipalidade, Praça Barão de Campo Belo, T024-2471 1367*.

Valença and Conservatória

Like Vassouras, **Valença** is a historical monument and its history follows much the same pattern, with wealth from the coffee trade followed by some small-scale industry and agriculture. There are a number of *fazendas* nearby and, in the town, a faculty of medicine. Information is available from the **Secretaria de Turismo** ⓘ *T024-2442 0102*.

About 35 km from Valença is **Conservatória**, another town in the coffee zone. Although it did not become as wealthy as Vassouras or Valença, it still has some fine 19th-century houses and is much more peaceful. In Conservatória, local farm produce can be bought, as well as blankets, macramé and crochet work. A local custom is the serenade through the streets; serenaders meet at the **Museu da Seresta** ⓘ *R Osvaldo Fonseca*, on Friday and Saturday. This region can also be reached via the Japeri turning on the BR-116, a beautiful mountain drive. The **Secretaria de Turismo** ⓘ *T024-3438 1188*, is in the centre of town. There are a few moderate and cheap hotels in town and the Secretaria can advise on stays in *fazendas*.

Sleeping

Petrópolis *p148, map p149*

Good budget accommodation is hard to find, but bargaining is possible Mon-Fri.

LL Locanda della Mimosa, Alameda das Mimosas, Vale Florido, T024-2233 5405, www.locanda.com.br. A 6-room pousada in a terracotta Palladian villa in the serra near town, overlooking a little pool. The owner is one of the finest chefs in Brazil, see page 157.

LL Solar do Império, Av Koeler 276, T024-2103 3000, www.solarimperio.com.br. A luxury boutique hotel with period furniture in a converted mansion opposite the Palácio Rio Negro. Excellent spa and restaurant.

L Pousada da Alcobaça, R Agostinho Goulão 298, Correas, T024-2221 1240, www.pousadadaalcobaca.com.br. In the **Roteiros de Charme** group (see page 50). Delightful, family-run large country house set in flower- filled gardens leading down to a river, with pool and sauna. Worth stopping by for tea on the terrace, or for dinner at the restaurant. Recommended.

A Othon Riverside Parque, R Hermogéneo Silva 522, Retiro, 5 mins from the centre, T0800-248011, T024-2231 0730, www.hoteis-riverside.com.br. Mock-colonial hotel with a nice outdoor pool set in attractive gardens with views of the surrounding countryside. The helpful owner can arrange tours.
B Casablanca Centre, R General Osório 28, T024-2242 2612, www.casablanca hotel.com.br. Old 1960s block, reasonable rooms and restaurant. Somewhat faded.
B York, R do Imperador 78, near the *rodoviária*, T024-2243 2662, www.hotel york.com.br. Convenient package-tour hotel with faded 1980s rooms, decent breakfast.
C Casa Comércio, R Dr Porciúncula 56, opposite *rodoviária*, T024-2242 3500. One of the cheapest options. Clean but simple with shared baths or en suites. Is linked to a tour agency, www.rioserra.com.br/trekking, which offers trips in the surrounding mountains.

Camping

Associação Brasileira de Camping and YMCA, Araras district. Space can be reserved through Rio YMCA, T024-231 9860.

Teresópolis *p134*

There are many cheap hotels in R Delfim Moreira, near the praça.
L Fazenda Rosa dos Ventos, Km 22 on the road to Nova Friburgo, T021-2742 8833, www.hotelrosadosventos.com.br. In the **Roteiros de Charme** and the **Relais et Chateaux** groups (see page 50). One of the best hotels in inland Rio with a range of chalets in 1 million sq m of private forest and with wonderful views. Excellent restaurant.
C Várzea Palace, R Sebastião Teixeira 41, T021-2742 0878. Simple hotel with very friendly staff. Highly recommended.
D-E Recanto do Lord Hostel, R Luiza Pereira Soares 109, Centro-Artistas, T021-2742 5586, www.teresopolishostel.com.br. Family-oriented hostel with rooms and dorms, kitchen, cable TV and barbecue area. Breakfast included. Tours, treks and climbing in the serra can be organized from here. Book in advance for Jan and Feb. Camping is permitted beside the hostel.

Camping

Quinta de Barra, R Antônio Maria 100, Km 3 on Petrópolis Rd, T021-2643 1050.

Serra dos Órgãos *p151*

Ibama has some hostels, US$5 full board, or US$3 first night, US$2 thereafter, a bit rough.
Reserva Ecológica de Guapi Assu (REGUA), caixa postal 98112, Cachoeiras de Macacu-RJ, T021-2745 3998, www.regua.co.uk. A British-run conservation NGO and ecotourism project focused on a large main house with several rooms, set in primary rainforest. Expert guided walks into the reserve in the Serra dos Órgãos, in one of the richest areas in the state for birds, mammals and orchids.
Serra dos Tucanos, Caixa Postal 98125, Cachoeiras do Macacu, T021-2649 1557, www.serradostucanos.com.br. One of the best wildlife and birdwatching lodges in Brazil with excellent guiding, equipment and accommodation in a comfortable lodge set in the Atlantic coastal rainforest.

Camping

Two sites in the Sub-Sede part, one close to the museum, the other not far from the natural swimming pool at Poço da Ponte Velha; one site in the Sede part. The Sede has a restaurant and the Sub-Sede a *lanchonete*.

Nova Friburgo *p153*

AL Bucsky, 5 km out on the Niterói Rd, T021-2522 5052. With meals, tours and guided walks available.
AL Pousada do Riacho, Estr Nova Friburgo Km 8, Cardinot, T021-2522 2823, www.pousadadoriacho.com. A **Roteiros de Charme** hotel (see page 50). Charming upmarket hotel with extensive gardens and surrounded by gentle mountains.
A Fazenda São João, 11 km from **Garlipp** (same ownership) up a side road, T021-2542 1304. Riding, swimming, sauna, tennis, hummingbirds and orchids. The owner will meet guests in Nova Friburgo or even in Rio.
A Garlipp, Muri, 8 km south, Km 70 from Rio, T/F021-2542 1173. German-run chalets.
B Fabris, Av Alberto Browne 148, T021-2522 2852. Central, with plain en suite rooms with TVs hot showers. Large breakfast buffet.
C-D Maringá, R Monsenhor Miranda 110, T021-2522 2309. Standard but with a very good breakfast. Recommended.

Camping

Camping Clube do Brasil has sites on the Niterói Rd, at Caledônia (7 km out, T021-

2522 0169) and Muri (10 km out, T021- 2542 2275).

Fazenda Sanandu, 20 km out on the same road. Private campsite.

Vassouras *p154*

AL Santa Amália, Av Sebastião Manoel Furtado 526, T/F024-2471 1897, close to the *rodoviária*. Located in a very pleasant and quiet park, swimming pool, sauna, volleyball and soccer pitches, one of the best in town, try to negotiate in the low season (Mar-Jun and Aug-Nov) and during the week.

B Gramado da Serra, R Aldo Cavalcanti 7, T/F024-2471 2314. With bar, restaurant, pool, sauna.

B Mara Palace, R Chanceler Dr Raul Fernandes 121, T024-2471 1993. In a house built in 1870, fully and tastefully preserved, swimming pool, bar, sauna, sports, nice atmosphere and good service, owner (Gerson) can arrange visits to *fazendas*.

C-D Pousada Bougainville, T024-2471 2451. Modest little guesthouse with breakfast included in the price.

D Pousada Veredas, T024-2471 2728. Basic but with helpful staff and breakfast included.

Eating

Petrópolis *p148, map p149*

There are many bakeries and cheap eateries around the *rodoviária*.

TTT Locanda della Mimosa, Alameda das Mimosas, Vale Florido, T024-2233 5405, www.locanda.com.br. One of the best restaurants in Brazil with European-Brazilian fusion cooking with a strong focus on game, by Danio Braga, 4 times *Quatro Rodas* chef of the year. The 3000 bottle wine cellar includes heavyweights like 1990 Château Haut-Brion.

T Cantina Bom Giovanni, R do Imperador 729, T024-2242 5588. A 1st-floor simple, canteen-style Italian restaurant. Justifiably popular for self-service lunch and dinner.

T Casa d'Ângelo, R do Imperador 700, by Praça Dom Pedro II. A traditional, long-established teahouse with self-service food. Doubles as a bar at night.

T Falconi, R do Imperador 757, T024 2242 1252. Traditional restaurant with rustic elegance that has been serving Italian food since 1914. Good value, with pasta and pizza for US$3. Recommended.

Teresópolis *p151*

TTT Da Irene, R Tte Luís Meireles 1800, T021-2742 2901. Very popular upmarket Russian restaurant. Reservations necessary.

TT Bar Gota d'Água, Praça Baltasar da Silveira 16. A little bar, simple fish dishes and *feijoada*.

TT Taberna Alpina, Duque de Caxias 131. Excellent German cuisine.

There are cheap eats and a good café in the ABC supermarket.

Nova Friburgo *p153*

There are many options to choose from, several in European styles, which reflect the background of the people who settled in the area. You can also find Brazilian food, pizzas and *confeitarias*.

TTT Chez Gigi, Av Euterpe Friburguense 21, T024-2523 0107. Excellent Brazilian-French fusion cooking with dishes like duck's breast in *jabuticaba*, pear and damson sauce.

TT Auberge Suisse, R 10 de Outubro, T024-2541 1270. Fondue, *roschti* and other Swiss options alongside very good steak.

Vassouras *p154*

The best and best-value restaurants are located in the centre, on R Expedicionário Oswaldo de Almeida Ramos, The Broadway.

Festivals and events

Petrópolis *p148, map p149*

16 Mar Foundation day.

29 Jun **São Pedro de Alcântara**, the patron saint of Petrópolis.

Jun **Bohemia Beer Festival**. Brazil's earliest beer dates from 1853; it was originally brewed in the city and, although production has now been moved to Rio, the festival is still celebrated in Petrópolis.

Teresópolis *p151*

May Festa das Colônias.

13 Jun Santo Antônio, the patron saint of Teresópolis.

29 Jun São Pedro, celebrated with fireworks.

7 Jul Foundation day.

15 Oct Santa Terezinha.

Nova Friburgo *p153*

May Maifest festival throughout the month.

16 May Founding of Nova Friburgo.

24 Jun São João Batista, patron saint's day.

Vassouras *p154*

Feb/Mar Carnaval is one of the best in the region, with its own samba schools and balls.

Jun Santo Antônio, São Pedro and São João are celebrated with traditional parties.

8 Dec Feast of Nossa Senhora da Conceição, the city's patron saint, with a Mass and procession.

Shopping

Petrópolis *p148, map p149*

Rua Teresa, southeast of the centre, is where the textile industry exhibits its wares. In common with **Itaipava**, it draws buyers from all over the country and is a good place to find high-quality knitwear and bargain clothes. Closed Mon morning and Sun.

Activities and tours

Petrópolis *p148, map p149*

Tour operators

Rio Serra, T024-2235 7607, www.rioserra.com.br/trekking. Horse riding, trekking , white-water rafting and a range of trips into the scenic mountain area, multi-lingual guides.

Verticalia, T024-9387 2572, www.alaya.com.br. Tree-based adventures with zip lines, canopy obstacle courses and the like for adults and children over 5.

Serra dos Órgãos *p151*

Tour operators

Tours are available through the tourist office or the **IYHA Recanto do Lord** in Teresópolis.

Focus Tours, (see page 24), www.focustours.com. Birdwatching trips.

Lazer Tours, T024-2742 7616. Tours of the park are offered by Francisco (find him at the grocery shop on R Sloper 1). Recommended.

Transport

Petrópolis *p148, map p149*

Bus Buses run to **Rio de Janeiro** every 15 mins throughout the day (US$3) with **Única Fácil**, Sun every hr, 1½ hrs. Sit on the right-hand side for best views. Ordinary buses arrive in Rio at the *rodoviária*; a/c buses run hourly and arrive at Av Nilo Peçanha, US$4. Book your onward journey as soon as you arrive in Petrópolis. Bus to **Niterói**, US$4.50; to **Cabo Frio**, US$10. To **Teresópolis**, Viação Teresópolis, 8 a day, US$3. Salutário to **São Paulo** daily at 2330.

Teresópolis *p151*

Bus Buses run to **Rio de Janeiro** every 30 mins and arrive at the Novo Rio *rodoviária*. Book your onward journey as soon as you arrive in Teresópolis; the *rodoviária* is at R 1 de Maio 100. Fare US$3.60. From Teresópolis to **Petrópolis**, 8 a day, US$3.

Nova Friburgo *p153*

Bus Bus station, Ponte da Suadade, T024-2522 0400. To **Rio**, every hr, 2 hrs, US$4.

Vassouras *p154*

Bus Several daily to **Rio**'s Novo Rio *rodoviária* with **Normandy**. Around 1½ hrs between departures 0615-2030, 2 hrs, US$6.50. More buses during summer and holidays.

Directory

Petrópolis *p148, map p149*

Banks Banco do Brasil, R Paulo Barbosa 81; Banco 24 Horas ATM is located by the Varig office at R Mcal Deodoro 98. Travel agencies with exchange; BKR, R Gen Osório 12; Goldman, R Barão de Amazonas 46 (between Praça da Liberdade and the university); Vert Tur, R 16 de Março 244, 1000-1630. **Internet** Compuland, R do Imperador opposite Praça Dr Sá Earo, US$1.50 per hr. **Post office** R do Imperador 350 in the Palácio dos Correios. **Telephone** R Mcal Deodoro, just above Praça Dr Nelson de Sá Earp, no fax.

Teresópolis *p151*

Banks Cash or TCs at **Teretur**, Trav Portugal 46. English spoken. **Internet** Cott@ge Cybercafe, R Alfredo Rebello Filho 996, 2nd floor, US$3 per hr.

Nova Friburgo *p153*

Banks Bradesco, Praça Demerval Barbosa Moreira.

Vassouras *p154*

Banks Banco do Brasil, R Caetano Furquim, in the centre, has an ATM but does not change money.

West of Rio de Janeiro

Towns to the west of Rio are mostly spread along the ugly Rio–São Paulo motorway known as the Dutra. None are appealing. But the mountains which watch over them preserve important tracts of Atlantic Coast rainforest, particularly around Itatiaia. This is one of the best places close to Rio for seeing wild animals and virgin rainforest and is the country's oldest protected area. The little mock-Alpine resort of Visconde de Mauá sits in the same mountain chain a little further towards São Paulo, although the forest here is less well preserved. ▸▸ *For Sleeping, Eating and other listings, see pages 161-162.*

Penedo → *Phone code: 024. Altitude: 600 m. Colour map 4, C3. Population: 8000.*

In the same region, 175 km from Rio, is the small town of Penedo which in the 1930s attracted Finnish settlers who brought the first saunas to Brazil. There is a Finnish museum, a cultural centre and Finnish dancing on Saturdays. This popular weekend resort also provides horse riding and swimming in the Portinho River.

There are five buses a day from Resende. **Tourist information** ⓘ *Av Casa das Pedras, T024-3351 1876*, and there are plenty of mid-range and cheap hotels in town.

Visconde de Mauá → *Phone code: 024. Altitude: 1200 m. Colour map 4, C3.*

About 33 km beyond Penedo (part of the road is unpaved) is the charming small village of Visconde de Mauá in the **Serra da Mantiqueira**. In the early 20th century Swiss and German immigrants settled in the town, which is popular with tourists today. The surrounding scenery is lovely, with green valleys, clear rivers, wild flowers and opportunities for good walks and other outdoor activities. Many places offer acupuncture, shiatsu massage and macrobiotic food and there is a hippy feel to the crafts on sale. Horses can be hired in **Visconde de Mauá** from Berto (almost opposite Vendinha da Serra), or Pedro (Lote 10) and many places in Maringá arrange riding. The Rio Preto is good for canoeing and there is an annual national event (dates change, check in advance). The **tourist office** ⓘ *T024-3387 1283*, is closed out of season.

Three other small hill towns are nearby: **Mirantão**, at 1700 m, with semi-tropical vegetation; **Maringá**, just across the state border in Minas Gerais and a delightful two-hour walk; and **Maromba**. On the way to Maromba is the **Mirante do Posto da Montanha**, a lookout with a view of the Rio Preto, which runs through the region and is the border between Rio de Janeiro and Minas Gerais states. Also in Minas Gerais, 6 km upriver from Maringá but on a different road, are the **Santa Clara falls** (turn off before Maromba). Between Visconde de Mauá and Maringá is a natural pool in the river (turn left before crossing the bridge). After Maromba follow the signs to **Cachoeira e Escorrega**, a small waterfall and waterslide with a cold natural swimming pool, a 2-km walk. A turning off this road leads to another waterfall, the **Cachoeira Véu da Noiva**.

Although served by buses from both São Paulo and Rio, *pousadas* are spread out and the area is best visited with a car. For **tourist information**, the website www.guiamaua.com.br lists many of the hotels and restaurants and gives a good overview of the area (in Portuguese but with pictures).

Parque Nacional de Itatiaia ▸▸ *pp161-162.*

→ *Colour map 4, C3.*

Deep valleys shrouded in pristine rainforest hiding rocky clear-water rivers and icy waterfalls; one-hour, four-hour, one-day and two-day walks are possible on little winding trails watched over by some of world's rarest birds and mammals; there's a whole swathe of different ecosystems (and hotels and guesthouses to suit all budgets from which to explore them); and all is within easy reach of Rio or São Paulo. Itatiaia is a must for those who wish to see Brazilian forest and animals and have a restricted itinerary or limited time. This 30,000-ha mountainous park is Brazil's oldest. It was founded in 1937 to protect Atlantic Coast rainforest in the Serra de Mantiqueira mountains, and important species still find a haven here, including jaguars and pumas, brown capuchin and black-faced titi monkeys. This is good hiking country with walks through subtropical and temperate forests, grasslands and *paramo* to a few peaks just under 3000 m. The best trails head for Pedra de Taruga, Pedra de Maçã and the Poranga and Véu de Noiva waterfalls. The Pico das Agulhas Negras and Serra das Prateleiras (up to 2540 m) offer good rock climbing. There is a **Museu de História Natural** ⓘ *Tue-Sun 1000-1600*, near the park headquarters with a depressing display of stuffed animals from the 1940s.

Ins and outs

Getting there and around Itatiaia lies just off the main São Paulo–Rio motorway, the Dutra. The best way to see the park is to hire a car; however, there are bus connections to Itatiaia town or nearby Resende from both Rio and São Paulo. There is only one way into the park from Itatiaia town and one main road within it – which forks off to the various hotels, all of which are signposted. Four times a day (variable hours), a bus marked '504 Circular' leaves Itatiaia town for the park, calling at the hotels and stopping at **Hotel Simon.** Coming from Resende this may be caught at the crossroads before Itatiaia. Through tickets to São Paulo are sold at a booth in the large bar in the middle of Itatiaia main street.

Tourist information Entry per day is US$10 per car. Basic accommodation in cabins and dormitories is available in the village strung along the road leading to the park. There are some delightful options inside the park but they are more expensive. Avoid weekends and Brazilian holidays if you want to see wildlife. Information and maps can be obtained at the park office. The **Administração do Parque Nacional de Itatiaia** operates a refuge in the park which acts as a starting point for climbs and treks. Information can be obtained from **Ibama,** T024-33521461 for the local headquarters, or T021-3224 6463 for the Rio de Janeiro state department. Information on treks can be obtained from **Clube Excursionista Brasileira** ⓘ *Av Almirante Barroso 2, 8th floor, Rio de Janeiro, T021-2220 3695*.

Flora and fauna

The park is particularly good for birds. It has a list of over 350 species with scores of spectacular tanagers, hummingbirds (including the ultra-rare Brazilian ruby, with emerald wings and a dazzling red chest), cotingas (included the black and gold cotinga, which as far as we are aware has never been photographed) and manakins. Guans squawk and flap right next to the park roads. The vegetation is stratified by altitude so that the plateau at 800-1100 m is covered by forest, ferns and flowering plants (such as orchids, bromeliads, begonias), giving way on the higher escarpments to pines and bushes. Higher still, over 1900 m, the distinctive rocky landscape has low bushes and grasses, isolated trees and unique plants adapted to high winds and strong sun. There is also a great variety of lichens.

Engenheiro Passos → *Phone code: 024. Population: 3500.*

Further along the Dutra highway (186 km from Rio) is the small town of Engenheiro Passos, from which a road (BR-354) leads to São Lourenço and Caxambu in Minas Gerais (see page 278). By turning off this road at the Registro pass (1670 m) on the Rio-Minas border, you can reach the **Pico das Agulhas Negras**. The mountain can be climbed from this side from the **Abrigo Rebouças** refuge at 2350 m which is manned all year round. Take your own food, US$2.50 to stay.

Sleeping

Visconde de Mauá *p159*

There are many *fazendas*, pousadas and chalets in the vicinity, but very little budget accommodation.

LL Fronteira, Estr Visconde de Mauá-Campo Lindo, Km 4, T024-3387 1219. A **Roteiros de Charme** hotel (see page 50). Huge cabins with tiny private gardens set in a forested garden with wonderful views. Sauna, pool and a good restaurant and bar.

C-D Encanto, on the road to Maringa, Km 7, T024-3387 1155, www.guiamaua.com.br/encanto. 7 chalets in woodland and a sauna. Popular with 20- and 30-somethings.

C-D Fazenda Boa Vista, Vale das Flores, on the road to Maringa, Km 15, T024-9998 3614, www.fazendaboavista.com.br. Great views, a pool and a range of organized activities. The simple chalets sit in a private rainforest reserve. Minimum 2-day stay.

C-D Sitio Portal da Travessia, on the road to Maringa, Km 7, T024-3387 1154, www.portaldatravessia.com.br. 6 chalets next to a mountain stream and with a spring-water natural pool. The range of activities include hikes and horse riding.

Camping

Barragen's, Marinqá, T024-3387 1354. One of several campsites in the area.

Parque Nacional de Itatiaia *p159*

A Hotel Donati, T024-3352 1110, www.hoteldonati.com.br. One of the most delightful hotels in the country – mock-Swiss chalets and rooms, set in tropical gardens visited by animals every night and early morning. A series of trails leads off from the main building and the hotel can organize professional birding guides. Decent restaurant and 2 pools. Highly recommended.

A Simon, Km 13 on the road in the park, T024-3352 1122, www.hotelsimon.com.br. A 1970s concrete block with *Hawaii Five 0* decor at the top of the park by the trailhead for the higher walks to Agulhas Negras and Três Picos. Great views from the fading rooms.

B Pousada do Elefante, Km 12, 15 mins' walk back downhill from **Hotel Simon**. Good food, swimming pool, lovely views, may allow camping.

B-C Hotel Cabanas de Itatiaia, T024-3352 1252. Magical views from these comfortable but ridiculously Swiss chalets on a hillside. Pool and good restaurant too.

C-D Cabanas da Itatiaia, T024-33521152, www.hotelcabanasitatiaia.com.br. Price per person in these simple chalets in secondary forest overlooking a stream in the lower reaches of the park. The sister hotel (**Aldeia dos Passaros**) opposite has a pool. Both share facilities and are very friendly and helpful. Great breakfasts, good off-season rates and a riverside sauna.

D Hotel Alsene, at 2100 m, 2 km from the side entrance to the park, take a bus to São Lourenço and Caxambu, get off at Registro, walk or hitch from there (12 km). Very popular with climbing and trekking clubs, dormitories or camping, chalets available, hot showers, fireplace, evening meal after everyone returns, drinks but no snacks.

E Ipê Amarelo, R João Maurício Macedo Costa 352, Campo Alegre, T/F024-3352 1232. IYHA youth hostel.

Camping

Camping Clube do Brasil site is entered at Km 148 on the Via Dutra.

Engenheiro Passos *p160*

Around Engenheiro Passos there are many *fazenda* hotels.

L Fazenda Villa Forte, 1 km from town, T/F024-3357 1122. With meals, bar, sauna, massage, gym and other sports facilities.

A Fazenda Palmital, Km 11 BR-354 towards Caxambu, T/F024-3357 1108. Chalets on the edge of the national park, arranged around a lake in a garden and with a waterfall nearby. Facilities include a pool, sauna, horse riding and a play area for kids.

Eating

Visconde de Mauá *p159*

Everywhere in town shuts at about 2200.

Gosto com Gosto, R Wenceslau Brás, Mineiro. Self-service Minas Gerais dishes that are heavy on meat and flavour.

Bar do Jorge. Café.

Parque Nacional de Itatiaia *p159*
The hotels in the park all have restaurants. Hotel Donati and Cabanas de Itatiaia, the latter with a view, have the best (see Sleeping, above).

¶¶-¶ **Via Park**, 1441 Estr Parque, Itaitia town, 4 km before the park entrance, T024- 9268 7934. Delicious trout with Brazilian accompaniments, in super-generous portions.

Bars and clubs

Visconde de Mauá *p159*
Adega Bar, open till 2400, live music and dancing (Sat only).
Forró da Marieta for *forró* dancing.

Activities and tours

Parque Nacional de Itatiaia *p159*
Wildlife guides
Ralph Salgueiro, T024- 33511823, www.ecoralph.com; and **Edson Endrigo**, T024-37428374, www.avesfoto.com.br, offer birdwatching trips in Itatiaia and throughout Brazil, English spoken.

Transport

Visconde de Mauá *p159*
Bus From Visconde de Mauá to **Resende**, 2 hrs, at 0830 and 0900, returning from Resende at 1500 and 1630, US$5. Direct bus to/from **Rio de Janeiro**, Cidade de Aço, 2 daily, 3½ hrs, US$7.

Costa Verde

The Rio de Janeiro–Santos section of the BR-101 is one of the world's most beautiful highways, hugging the forested and hilly Costa Verde southwest of Rio. The Serra do Mar mountains plunge down to the sea in a series of spurs that disappear into the Atlantic to reappear as a cluster of islands offshore. The most beautiful of these is Ilha Grande: an 80,000-ha mountain ridge covered in rainforest and fringed with wonderful beaches. Beyond Ilha Grande, further down the coast towards São Paulo, is one of Brazil's prettiest colonial towns, Paraty, which sits surrounded by long white beaches in front of a glorious bay of islands. Seen from the harbour in the morning light, this is one of Brazil's most photographed sights. » *For Sleeping, Eating and other listings, see pages 169-174.*

Ins and outs

The BR-101 is paved all the way to Santos (see page 207), which has good links with São Paulo. Buses run from Rio to Angra dos Reis, Paraty, Ubatuba, Caraguatatuba and São Sebastião, where it may be necessary to change for Santos or São Paulo. Hotels and pousadas have sprung up all along the road, as have expensive housing developments, though these have not spoiled the views. The drive from Rio to Paraty should take four hours, but it would be better to break the journey and enjoy some of the attractions. The coast road has lots of twists and turns so, if prone to motion sickness, get a seat at the front of the bus to make the most of the views.

Mangaratiba → *Phone code: 021. Population: 25,000.*

About 22 km down the coast, this fishing village is halfway between Rio and Angra dos Reis. It stands on a little bay within the Baia de Sepetiba and in the 18th century was a port for the export first of gold, later coffee, and for the import of slaves. During the coffee era, it was the terminus for the Estrada São João Marcos from the Rio Paraíba do Sul. Mangaratiba's beaches are muddy, but the surroundings are pleasant and better beaches can be found outside town, for example **Ibicuí** (2 km) and **Brava** (between Ibicuí and Saí) to the east, at the head of the bay **Saco**, **Guiti** and **Cação**, and further west **São Brás**. There are numerous hotels in town. Boats run to Ilha Grande several times a day. Times vary according to the season but the last usually departs around 1400. For details see Ilha Grande transport, page 164.

The Caiçaras

Brazilians of mixed Indian, African and Portuguese race living on the coast and leading traditional lives fishing and hunting are known as *caiçaras*. Until the 1970s almost all the beaches and islands between Rio de Janeiro and Santos were home to *caiçara* communities. But then the Rio to Santos main highway was constructed and floods of visitors began to pour in. With them came developments for luxury private houses, hotels and condominiums, like Laranjeiras – which is home to members of Brazil's wealthy and allegedly highly corrupt elite. *Caiçara* communities were bought off for pittance or forced from their land with threats of violence or even death. And an entire way of life and knowledge of the Atlantic Coast forest, strongly rooted in indigenous traditions is in danger of being entirely lost. All the *favelas* in Angra dos Reis bear the name of a different beach on Ilha Grande or the beaches and islands around the bay. Nowadays there are *caiçara* communities only on a few isolated stretches between Rio and Santos – like the Ponta da Joatinga peninsula south of Paraty and Aventureiros beach in Ilha Grande. Many think that carefully managed, sensitive ecotourism will help protect them and spread the story of their plight is little known even within Brazil.

Angra dos Reis and around

» pp169-174.

→ *Phone code: 024. Colour map 4, C3. Population: 120,000.*

The vast bay of Angra dos Reis is studded with more lush islands than there are days in the year. Some are the private playgrounds of Carioca playboys. Others are media islands, owned by magazines devoted to the cult of the Brazilian celebrity, and permanently twinkling with camera flashes. A few are thronged with bikinis and board shorts in high season and pulsate to *forró* and samba beats. And many are as wild and unspoilt as they were when the Portuguese arrived 500 years ago. Yachts and speedboats flit across the bay, ferrying their bronzed and smiling cargo between the islands and beaches. In between, they dock at floating bars and restaurants for an icy *caipirinha* or catch of the day, and at night to dance or be lulled by the gentle sound of bossa nova. Angra town itself is scruffy and down at heel – little more than a jumping-off point to the private islands and to Ilha Grande, an increasingly popular destination for international travellers. This is a result of the migration of the wealthy out of Rio and their acquisition of beaches and property from the local fishermen (whose families now live in the favelas that encrust the surrounding hills, see box – the Caiçaras page 163).

Angra was once as pretty a colonial town as Paraty further along the coast. Several buildings remain from its heyday. Of particular note are the church and convent of **Nossa Senhora do Carmo**, built in 1593 (Praça General Osório), the **Igreja Matriz de Nossa Senhora da Conceição** (1626) in the centre of town and the church and convent of **São Bernardino de Sena** (1758-1763) on the Morro do Santo Antônio. On the Largo da Lapa is the church of **Nossa Senhora da Lapa da Boa Morte** (1752) and a **Museum of Sacred Art** ⓘ *Thu-Sun 1000-1200, 1400-1800*.

On the Península de Angra, west of the town, is the **Praia do Bonfim**, a popular beach; offshore is the island of the same name, on which is the **hermitage of Senhor do Bonfim** (1780). Some 15 km east are the ruins of the **Jacuecanga seminary** (1797).

The **tourist office** ⓘ *Av Julio Maria, T024-3365 2041, www.angra-dos-reis.com, and www.angra.rj.gov.br*, is just behind the Cais de Santa Luiza quay. The websites have more information than the office. Angra is connected to Rio and Paraty by regular buses, to Ilha Grande by ferry and fishing boat, and to Ilha do Gipóia by fishing boat.

Ilha Grande

pp169-174.

→ *Phone code: 021. Colour map 4, C3.*

Ilha Grande is a mountain ridge covered in tropical forest protruding from the emerald sea and fringed by some of the world's most beautiful beaches. As there are no cars and no roads, just trails through the forest, the island is still relatively undeveloped. And with luck it will remain so, as much of Ilha Grande forms part of a state park and biological reserve, and cannot even be visited. That the island has so much forest is largely a fluke of history. The island was a notorious pirate lair in the 16th and 17th centuries and then a landing port for slaves. By the 20th century it was the site of an infamous prison for the country's most notorious criminals, including the writer Graciliano Ramos (see Literature, page 697), whose *Memórias do cárcere* relate his experiences. The prison closed in 1994 and is now overgrown; since then Ilha Grande has been a well-kept Brazilian secret, and is gradually becoming part of the international backpacker circuit.

Ins and outs

Fishing boats and ferries with **Barcas SA**, T021-2533 7524, leave from Angra dos Reis and Mangaratiba taking two hours or so to reach Vila do Abraão, the island's only real village. From Angra they only leave in the morning and early afternoon and must be chartered (US$60-100 per boat; it is usually possible to get a group together in high season). The weather is best from March to June and the island is overrun during the Christmas, New Year and Carnaval periods. There is a helpful **tourist office** on the jetty at Abraão. Further information and pictures can be found at www.ilhagrande.com. Be wary of undercover police searching for backpackers smoking cannabis on Ilha Grande's beaches.

Beaches and walks

The beach at **Abraão** may look beautiful to new arrivals but those further afield are far more spectacular. The two most famous are **Lopes Mendes** – a long stretch of sand on the eastern, ocean side, backed by flatlands and patchy forest – and **Aventureiro** – fringed by coconut palms and tropical forest, and whose powder-fine sand is pocked with boulders and washed by a transparent aquamarine sea. Lopes Mendes is two hours' walk from Abraão. Aventureiro is over six hours, but it can be reached by boat. A few fishermen's huts and *barracas* provide food and accommodation here but there is no camping. Good beaches closer to Abraão include the half-moon bay at **Abraãoozinho** (15 minutes' walk) and **Grande das Palmas**, which has a delightful tiny

Ferry times to Ilha Grande

	Mon-Fri	Sat, Sun and holidays
Mangaratiba–Abraão	0800	0800
Abraão–Angra	1000	1000
Angra–Abraão	1530	1330
Abraão–Mangaratiba	1730	1730

An extra ferry runs between Mangaratiba and Abraão on Fridays at 2200. Telebarcas, T021-4004 3113, 24hrs, for changes see www.ilhagrande.com.br.

whitewashed chapel (one hour 20 minutes' walk). Both lie east of the town past **Hotel Sagu**. There are boat trips to **Lagoa Azul**, with crystal-clear water and reasonable snorkelling, **Freguesia de Santana** and **Saco do Céu**.

There are a couple of good treks over the mountains to **Dois Rios**, where the old jail was situated. There is still a settlement of former prison guards here who have nowhere to go. The walk is about 13 km each way, takes about three hours and affords beautiful scenery and superb views. Another three-hour hike is to **Pico do Papagaio** (980 m) through forest; it's a steep climb for which a guide is essential, however, the view from the top is breathtaking. **Pico da Pedra d'Água** (1031 m) can also be climbed.

Paraty » pp169-174.

→ Phone code: 024. Colour map 4, C2. Population: 30,000.

Paraty is one of Brazil's prettiest colonial towns and one of Rio de Janeiro's most popular tourist destinations. It is at its most captivating at dawn, when all but the dogs and chickens are sleeping. As the sun peeps over the horizon the little rectilinear streets are infused with a rich golden light which warms the whitewash and brilliant blue and yellow window frames of the colonial town houses and the façades of the Manueline churches. Brightly coloured fishing boats bob up and down in the water in the foreground and behind the town the deep green of the rainforest-covered mountains of the Serra da Bocaina sit shrouded in their self-generated wispy cloud. The town was founded in the 17th century as a gold port and most of its historic buildings date from this period.

At the weekend Paraty buzzes with tourists who browse in the little boutiques and art galleries or buy souvenirs from the indigenous Guarani who proffer their wares on the cobbles. At night they fill the numerous little bars and restaurants, many of which, like the pousadas, are owned by the bevy of expat Europeans who have found their haven in Paraty and who are determined to preserve its charm. During the week, especially off season, the town is quiet and intimate, its atmosphere as yet unspoilt by the increasing numbers of independent travellers.

The town's environs are as beautiful as Paraty itself. Just a few kilometres away lie the forests of the **Ponta do Juatinga Peninsula**, fringed by wonderful beaches, washed by little waterfalls and still home to communities of Caiçara fishermen who live much as they have done for centuries. Islands pepper the bay, some of them home to ultra-rare animals such as the tiny golden lion tamarin monkey which is found nowhere else. The best way to visit these destinations is on a boat trip, operated by the town's fishermen from the quay.

Paraty is at its most captivating at dawn, when all but the dogs and chickens are sleeping.

Ins and outs

The *rodoviária* is at the corner of Rua Jango Padua and Rua da Floresta. There are direct bus connections with Rio and São Paulo several times daily, and with a number of destinations along the coast. Taxis charge a set rate of US$4 from the bus station to the historic centre, which is pedestrianized and easily negotiable on foot. Staff at the **Centro de Informações Turísticas** ⓘ *Av Roberto Silveira, near the entrance to the historic centre, T024-3371 1266*, are friendly and helpful and some speak English. There is a good town map in the *Welcome to Paraty* brochure, www.eco- paraty.com. More information is available at www.paraty.com.br. The wettest months are January, February, June and July. In spring, the streets in the colonial centre may flood, but the houses remain above the waterline. » *See Transport, page 173.*

Sights

In keeping with all Brazilian colonial towns, Paraty's churches were built according to social status and race. There are four churches in the town, one for the 'freed coloured men', one for the blacks and two for the whites. **Santa Rita** (1722), built by the 'freed coloured men' in elegant Brazilian baroque, faces the bay and the port. It is probably the most famous picture postcard image of Paraty and houses a small

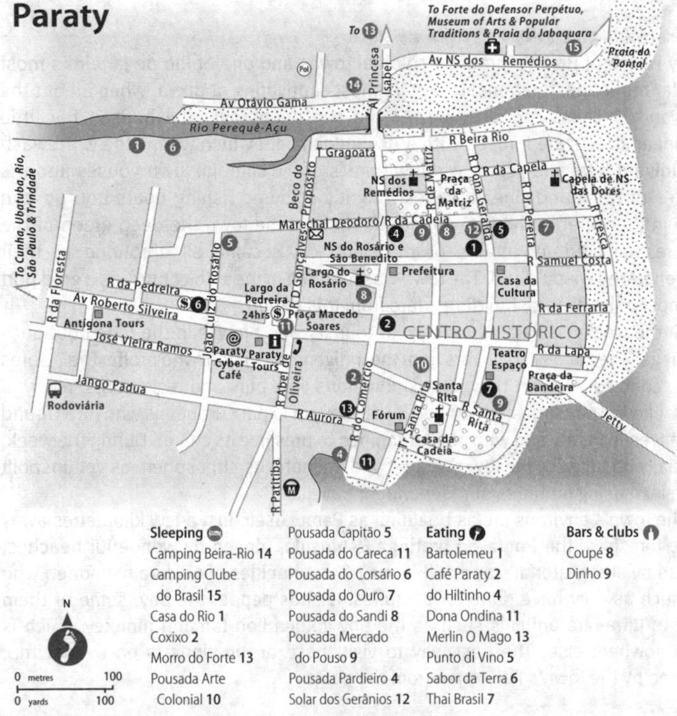

Museum of Sacred Artⓘ *Wed-Sun 0900-1200, 1300-1800, US$1.* **Nossa Senhora do Rosário e São Benedito**ⓘ *R do Comércio, Tue 0900-1200*, (1725, rebuilt 1757) built by black slaves, is small and simple; the slaves were unable to raise the funds to construct an elaborate building. **Nossa Senhora dos Remédios**ⓘ *Mon, Wed, Fri, Sat 0900-1200, Sun 0900-1500*, is the town's parish church, the biggest in Paraty. It was started in 1787 but construction ended only in 1873. The church was never completely finished as it was built on unstable ground; the architects decided not to add weight to the structure by putting up the towers. The façade is leaning to the left, which is clear from the three doors (only the one on the right has a step). Built with donations from the whites, it is rumoured that Dona Geralda Maria da Silva contributed gold from a pirate's hoard found buried on the beach. **Capela de Nossa Senhora das Dores** ⓘ *Thu 0900-1200* (1800), is a chapel facing the sea. It was used mainly by wealthy 19th-century whites.

There is a great deal of distinguished Portuguese colonial architecture in delightful settings. **Rua do Comércio** is the main street in the historic centre. It was here that the prominent traders lived, the two-storey houses having the commercial establishments on the ground floor and the residences above. Today the houses are occupied by restaurants, pousadas and tourist shops.

The **Casa da Cadeia**, close to Santa Rita Church, is the former jail, complete with iron grilles in the windows and doors. It is now a public library and art gallery.

On the northern headland is a small fort, **Forte do Defensor Perpétuo**, built in 1822, whose cannon and thick ruined walls can be seen. From the fort there are good views of the sea and the roofs of the town. It's about 15 minutes' walk from the centre. To get there, cross the Rio Perequê Açu by the bridge at the end of the Rua do Comércio; climb the small hill, which has some attractive pousadas and a cemetery, and follow the signs. Also here is the **Museum of Arts and Popular Traditions** ⓘ *Wed-Sun*, in a colonial-style building. It contains carved wooden canoes, musical instruments, fishing gear and other items from local communities. On the headland is the gunpowder store and enormous hemispherical iron pans which were used for extracting whale oil, which was used for lamps and to mix with sand and cement for building.

Boat trips and beaches

The most popular trip, and highly recommended, is a five-hour **schooner tour** around the bay for swimming, US$15, lunch (optional) extra. Smaller boats are available for US$10 an hour or US$20 for three hours. Many beautiful beaches are visited.

Praia do Pontal is the town beach, five minutes' walk from the historic centre – cross the bridge and turn right along the river. The water and sand are not very clean but its handful of *barracas* under the trees is a nice place to hang out. **Praia do Jabaquara** is about 20 minutes away on foot – cross the bridge and continue straight up the hill. There are a few *barracas* here and the sand is cleaner, but the water tends to be muddy.

There are other beaches further from town, many of which make worthwhile excursions. Scruffy **Boa Vista** is just south of town and beyond this (reachable only by boat) are, in order, the long, broad and clean stretches of **Praia da Conçeicao, Praia Vermelha** and **Praia da Lula**, all of which have simple restaurants and are backed by forest and washed by gentle waves. The **Saco da Velha**, further south still, is small and intimate, protected by an island and surrounded by rainforested slopes.

The small town of **Paraty Mirím**, is 17 km away and has a vast sweeping beach with a Manueline church built on the sand and some ruined colonial buildings. It is reached by boat or by four buses a day (three on Sunday) and has simple restaurants and spots to camp. Fishing boats leave from here for other islands and beaches including the **Praia do Pouso da Cajaíba,** which has lodgings of the same name, and the spectacular sweep at **Martim do Sá**. The **Saco do Mamanguá** is a long sleeve of water which separates the Ponta da Juatinga and Paraty Mirím, which has good snorkelling.

Caminho do Ouro (Gold Trail) → *www.caminhodoouro.com.br*

This partly cobbled trail through the mountains was built by slaves in the 18th century to bring gold down from Ouro Preto before transporting it to Portugal. Recently restored, it can be visited, along with the ruins of a toll house, on foot or horseback as a day trip. Tours leave from the **Teatro Espaço** ⓘ *R Dona Geralda 327, T024-3371 1575*, at 1000.

There are several *cachoeiras* (waterfalls) in the area, such as the **Cachoeira da Penha**, near the church of the same name. It is 10 km from town on the road to Cunha; take a local bus from the *rodoviária*, US$1, there are good mountain views on the way. The tourist office and travel agencies have details on the waterfalls and hikes.

A recommended excursion is to **Fazenda Murycana** ⓘ *T024-3371 3930 for tours and information*, an old sugar estate and 17th-century *cachaça* distillery with original house and waterwheel. You can taste and buy the different types of *cachaça*; some are aged in oak barrels for 12 years (try the *cachaça com cravo e canela*, with clove and cinnamon). There is an excellent restaurant and horse riding is available but English is not spoken by the employees. Mosquitoes can be a problem at the *fazenda*, take repellent and don't wear shorts. Take a Penha/Ponte Branca bus from the *rodoviária*, four a day; alight where it crosses a small white bridge and then walk 10 minutes along a signed, unpaved road. There is a good chance of hitching a lift back to Paraty.

Trindade » pp169-174.

Ramshackle little Trindade may not be as beautiful in its own right as Paraty but its setting, sandwiched between rainforested slopes and emerald sea, is equally spectacular. And unlike Paraty it has a long, broad beach. The town has long been a favourite hang-out for young middle-class surf hippies from São Paulo and Rio, who still come here in droves over Christmas and New Year. Now it is gradually finding its place on the international backpacker circuit and it's easy to see why. The beach is spectacular, the pousadas and restaurants cheap and cheerful, and there are a number of campsites. Sadly there is no sewage treatment and when the town is full, foul black water flows onto the sand. There are plenty of unprepossessing restaurants along the town's main drag, **Avenida Principal.** All serve the usual 'beans and rice and chips' combinations. Avoid coming here during Christmas, New Year, Carnaval and Easter.

Ins and outs Trindade is 30 km south of Paraty. It is reached by a steep, winding 7-km road lying off the Rio–Santos road (BR-101). Paraty–Ubatuba-bound buses all pass the turning to Trindade and will drop you or pick you up here. Ask for 'Patrimonio' or 'Estrada para Trindade' (pronounced *Tringdajee*). In high season there are vans from here to Trindade (US$2). In low season you'll have to hitch or walk; cars pass regularly. Be wary of carrying any drugs – the police at the turn-off post are very vigilant and searches are frequent. Trindade has no banks. Tourist information is available at the booth at the entrance to town (no English spoken) or through the Paraty website, www.paraty.com.br and tourist office. There are plenty of simple restaurants.

Around Trindade

Beyond Trindade and the upmarket condominium at Laranjeiras there is a series of beaches. **Sono** is a long, sweeping stretch of sand backed by *barracas*, some of which have accommodation to rent. Sanitation is a problem however. **Ponta Negra** is a little *caiçara* village, beautifully situated in a cove between rocky headlands. It has its own beach, simple but elegant homestay accommodation, fishing-boat trips and organized treks into the surrounding forest, which is rich in birdlife and full of waterfalls. It is possible to climb to the highest peak on the peninsula for views out over the Paraty area. The community is traditional and conservative; visits should be arranged in advance through village leaders, see Sleeping page 171.

Sono and Ponta Negra are reached from the Sono trailhead which lies at the end of the bus route to Trindade/Laranjeiras. The path is easy to find and follow. Allow 1½ hours for Sono and three hours for Ponta Negra. There are several buses a day to Trindade and the trailhead from Paraty, see Transport, page 174.

Sleeping

Angra dos Reis and around *p163*

Only stay in Angra town if you miss your bus or boat. There are a few cheap hotels near the port and main praça.

L do Frade, on the road to Ubatuba, Km 123 BR-101, 33 km from Angra, T024-3369 2244. Luxury hotel on the Praia do Frade with restaurants, bar, sauna, sports facilities on land and sea.

AL Pestana, Estr Do Contorno 3700, Km 13, T024-3367 2754, www.pestanahotels.com.br. A range of bungalows on a forested hillside overlooking an emerald-green sea. Very pretty, peaceful and secluded with a decent open-sided restaurant and bar overlooking the water and excellent service.

B Caribe, R de Conceição 255, T024 3365 0033. Central and well kept, a good option.

E-C IYHA Angra Hostel, Praça da Matriz 152 at R do Comércio, T024-3364 4759. A block back from the boat dock for Ilha Grande and next to the Igreja Matriz. Clean, well run, with internet, lockers, dorms and doubles. The cheapest option for the early boat. Maps of Angra provided.

Ilha Grande *p164*

Accommodation on the island is in pousadas at Vila do Abraão or camping elsewhere. It is possible to hire a fisherman's cottage on Aventureiro Beach, which can be reached on the *Maria Isabel* or *Mestre Ernani* boats (T021-3361 9895 or T021-9269 5877) that leave from the quay in front of the BR petrol station in Angra dos Reis; alternatively boats can be chartered direct from Angra dos Reis (2-3 hrs). There is a handful of upmarket options in isolated locations reachable only by boat.

Vilo do Abraão

Reservations are only necessary in peak season or on holiday weekends.

B Ancoradouro, R da Praia 121, T024 3361 5153, www.ancoradouro.ilha grande.com. Clean, simple rooms with en suite in a beach-front building, 10 mins' walk east of the jetty.

B-C Farol dos Borbas, Praia do Abraão, T024-3361 5866, www.ilhagrande tour.com.br. 1 min from the jetty. Simple, well-maintained, fan-cooled rooms with tiled floors and breakfast tables and chairs. The best have balconies. The worst have no windows. Boat trips organized.

C Porto Girassol, R do Praia 65, T024-3261 5277, portogirasol@ilhagrande.com. Simple rooms in a mock-colonial beach house 5 mins east of the jetty.

C-E Aqua Rio Hostel, Town Beach, Abraão, T024-3361 5405, www.aquario.ilha grande.com. Party hostel on a peninsula overlooking the beach; with dorms, scruffy rooms, a large, relaxing bar area, seawater pool and great ocean views.

C-E Che Lagarto Ilha Grande Hostel, Town Beach, Abraão, Book through the website - www.chelagarto.com. Large beachside party hostel with well-kept dorms, doubles, bar and tours including trail walking and kayaking

C-E IYHA Albergue Holdandes, R Assembleia de Deus, T024-3361 5034, www.holandes.com.br. Book ahead. Dorms, doubles and 4 little chalets in the forest on the edge of town. Breakfast included, laundry and advice on boats and tours. Good atmosphere.

C-E Pousada Cachoeira, 12-min walk from centre, T024-3361 5083, www.cachoeira.com. Price per person. Great little pousada full of character, with small rooms in chalets in a forest garden. Run by a German-Brazilian couple; English spoken. Good breakfasts.

D Colibri, R da Assembléia 70, T024- 3361 5033, www.colibriresort.com. Smart little Swedish-owned resort with rooms decorated with a personal touch and an outdoor breakfast area. Tours around the island offered.

D Estalagem Costa Verde, R Amâncio Felicio de Souza 239a, ½ a block behind the church, T024-3104 7490, www.estalagem costaverde.com.br. Bright hostel with light, well-maintained rooms decorated with a little thought. Great value.

Camping

Emilia Ecocamping, R Amâncio F de Souza 18, T024-3361 5094, www.ecocamping.com.br. Hot showers, lockers, fridges, communal living area with table tennis, a campsite with lots of shade and cabins (**E** per person).

Outside Vila do Abraão

LL **Angatu**, T011-3872 0945, www.angatu.com. The very best private houses and private islands in Ilha Grande bay, with exclusive entry to the private jet-set parties frequented by the likes of Naomi Campbell. Bookings come with your own yacht or motor cruiser, full complement of staff and, if you choose, guides and tours around the bay and to Paraty.

LL-L **Sitio do Lobo**, T024-2227 4138, www.sitiodolobo.com.br. An architect-commissioned house converted into a small boutique hotel and sitting on an isolated peninsula with its own little dock. The views are marvellous: emerald sea, rainforest, mountains in the distance, fiery red sunsets. The best rooms are the suites; the others which overlook the pool are boxy. Access to the rest of the island is only by boat. The restaurant serves the best food on the island.

AL-A **Sankay**, Enseada do Bananal (1 hr by boat from Angra or Abraão), T024-3365 1090, www.pousadasankay.com.br. A beautiful little pousada perched on a peninsula with wonderful views. Simple rooms with brick or stone walls. The best is the Cavalo Marinho (Seahorse) suite. Sauna and bar. Dinner included. Used for much of the year by **Body and Soul Adventures** (see page 60).

Paraty *p165, map p166*

There are many options in Paraty and 2 beautiful places in the hills nearby. Also browse www.paraty.com.br/frame.htm.

LL **Angatu**, T011-3872 0945, www.angatu.com. The very best private houses in the region, including Prince João de Orleans e Braganza's waterfront home and luxury villas on the surrounding islands. All come with your own yacht and, if you choose, guides and tours around the bay and to Ilha Grande.

L **Bromelias Pousada and Spa**, Rodovia Rio–Santos, Km 562, Graúna, T/F024-3371 2791, www.pousadabromelias.com.br. An Asian-inspired spa pousada with its own aromatherapy products and a range of massage treatments. Accommodation is in tastefully decorated chalets perched on a hillside forest garden overlooking the sea and islands. Pool, sauna and restaurant.

L **Pousada do Ouro**, R Dr Pereira (or da Praia) 145, T/F024-3371 1311, www.pousadaouro.com.br. Near Paraty's eastern waterfront and built as a private home with a fortune made on the gold route. Plain rooms in an annexe and suites in the main building. The tropical garden houses an open-air poolside pavilion. Pictures of previous guests such as Mick Jagger, Tom Cruise and Linda Evangelista adorn the lobby.

L **Pousada do Sandi**, Largo do Rosário 1, T024-3371 2100, www.pousadadosandi.com.br. The most comfortable in town set in an 18th-century building with a grand lobby, comfortable mock-colonial rooms and a very good adjoining restaurant and pool area. Superior breakfast, parking and excellent tours organized through www.angatu.com.

L **Pousada Pardieiro**, R do Comércio 74, T024-3371 1370, www.pousadapardieiro.com.br. Tucked away in a quiet corner, with a calm, sophisticated atmosphere. Attractive colonial building with lovely gardens, delightful rooms facing internal patios and a little swimming pool. Always full at weekends. Does not take children under 15.

AL **Hotel Coxixo**, R do Comércio 362, T024-3371 1460, www.hotelcoxixo.com.br. A converted colonial building in the heart of the 17th-century town, which has been turned into a temple to its Brazilian movie-star owner, Maria Della Costa. Black and white pictures of her from the 1950s adorn every corner. Rooms are decked out in Catholic kitsch. The best rooms in the hotel and in Paraty are the plush colonial suites.

A-B **Le Gite d'Indaitiba**, Rodovia Rio–Santos (BR-101) Km 562, Graúna, T024-3371 7174, www.legitedindaiatiba.com.br. French-owned pousada with one of the best restaurants in southeastern Brazil. Carefully designed stylish chalets set in gardens on a hillside overlooking a mountain stream. Sweeping views of the sea and bay of islands and a 2-m-wide spring water swimming pool.

A-B Morro do Forte, R Orlando Carpinelli, T/F024-3371 1211, www.pousadamorrodo forte.com.br. Lovely garden, good breakfast, pool, German owner Peter Kallert offers trips on his yacht. Out of the centre. Recommended.

B Pousada Capitão, R Luiz do Rosário 18, T024-3371 1815, www.paraty.com.br/ capitao. Converted colonial building, close to the historic centre, swimming pool, English and Japanese spoken.

B Pousada do Corsário, Beco do Lapeiro 26, T024-3371 1866, www.pousadadocorsario. com.br. New building with a pool and its own gardens, next to the river and 2 blocks from the centre. Simple, stylish rooms, most with hammocks outside. Highly recommended.

B Pousada Mercado do Pouso, Largo de Santa Rita 43, T/F024-3371 1114, www.paraty com.br/mercadodepouso. Historic building close to waterfront decked out in lush wood, good sea views. Family atmosphere, no pool.

B-C Pousada Arte Colonial, R da Matriz 292, T024-3371 7231, www.paraty.com.br/ artecolonial. One of the best deals in Paraty. A colonial building in the centre decorated with style and a personal touch by its French owner, with artefacts and antiques from all over the world. Friendly, helpful, beautiful and with breakfast. Highly recommended.

C-D Solar dos Gerânios, Praça da Matriz, T/F024-3371 1550, www.paraty.com.br/ geranio. Beautiful colonial family house on main square in traditional rustic style that is a welcome antidote to the more polished pousadas. Rooms have lovely wooden lattice balconies – ask for the corner one which has 2. Very reasonably priced, English spoken. Warmly recommended.

D-E Casa do Rio, R Antônio Vidal 120, T024-3371 2223, www.paraty.com.br/casadorio. Youth hostel in a little house with riverside courtyard and hammocks. There's a kitchen and price includes breakfast. Trips by jeep or on horseback to waterfalls, mountains and beaches. Dorms a little crowded.

D-E Pousada do Careca, Praça Macedo Soares, T024-3371 1291. Simple rooms. Those without street windows are musty.

Camping

Camping Beira-Rio, just across the bridge, before the road to the fort.

Camping Clube do Brasil, Av Orlando Carpinelli, Praia do Pontal, T024-3371 1877. Small, good, very crowded in Jan and Feb, US$8 per person.

Praia Jabaquara, T024-3371 2180.

Trindade *p168*

Expect no frills in Trindade.

D Chalé e Pousada Magia do Mar, T024 3371 5130. Thatched hut with space for 4. Views out over beach.

D Pousada Marimbá, R Principal, T024-3371 5147. Simple colourful rooms and a breakfast area.

D-F Ponta da Trindade Pousada and Camping, T024-3371 5113. Simple fan-cooled rooms and a sand-floored campsite with cold showers and no electricity.

Ponta Negra *p168*

C-D Ponta Negra homestays, contact Teteco T024-3371 2673, teteco@ paratyweb.com.br, or Cauê, francocvc@hotmail.com.

Eating

Ilha Grande *p164*

Aside from **Sito do Lobo** (guests only, see Sleeping, above), food on the island is fairly basic: fish, chicken or meat with beans, rice and chips. There are plenty of restaurants serving these exciting combinations in Abraão. We list the very few better options.

Lua e Mar, Abraão, on the waterfront, T024-3361 5113. A few more adventurous fish-based options than the other restaurants.

Corsário Negro, R da Vila, T024-3361 5321. The best in Abraão with good seafood, vegetarian food and excellent *caipirinhas*. The owner is a mine of information about the island and is fascinating to chat to.

Paraty *p165, map p166*

The best restaurants in Paraty are in the historic part of town and are almost as good as any you will find in Rio or São Paulo. Watch out for surreptitious cover charges for live music, which are often very discreetly displayed. The less expensive restaurants, those offering *comida a quilo* (pay by weight) and the fast-food outlets are outside the historic centre, mainly on Av Roberto Silveira.

Paraty's regional specialities include *peixe à Parati* – local fish cooked with herbs and green bananas and served with *pirão*, a mixture of manioc flour and the sauce that the fish was cooked in. Also popular is the *filé de peixe ao molho de camarão* – fried fish fillet with a shrimp and tomato sauce. There is plenty of choice in Paraty so have a browse. Also see **Le Gite d'Indaitiba**, page 170.

TTT Bartolomeu, R Samuel Costa 179, T024-3371 5032. Argentinian steaks, fish (including good ceviche) and great cocktails from ex-*Elite* fashion model turned gourmet cook, Deborah Cortes.

TTT do Hiltinho, R Mcal Deodoro 233, historical centre, T024-3371 1432. Decent seafood, including local dishes.

TTT Merlin O Mago, (next to **Hotel Coxixo**), R do Comercio 376, historic centre, T024-3371 2157, www.paraty.com.br/merlin.htm. Franco-Brazilian cooking in an intimate dining room/bar, by a German cordon bleu chef and illustrious photojournalist. Decent wine list. Highly recommended.

TTT Punto Di Vino, R Mcal Deodoro 129, historical centre, T024-3371 1348. The best for seafood in town; owned and run by a Neapolitan who catches his own catch of the day. Great wood-fired pizza, live music and an excellent selection of wine.

TTT Thai Brasil, R Dona Geralda 345, historic centre, T024-3371 0127, www.thaibrasil.com.br. Beautiful restaurant decorated with handicrafts and furnished with hand-painted chairs and tables. The cooking comprises well-executed Thai standards without spices (Brazilians yelp in pain at the sight of a chilli).

TT Café Paraty, R da Lapa and Comércio, historic centre. Sandwiches, appetizers, light meals, also bar with live music nightly (cover charge). A local landmark. Open 0900-2400.

TT Catimbau, Baía de Paraty, T024-33711847. A restaurant and bar sitting between 2 giant boulders on a tiny island in the bay. It is run by ex-Hollywood line producer and local fisherman Caca and his Dutch wife Mimi and serves simple but very fresh seafood accompanied by ice-cold beer or *caipirinhas*. Can be visited by request on any bay tour.

TT Dona Ondina, R do Comércio 2, by the river, historic centre. Family restaurant with well-prepared simple food (closed on Mon, Mar and Nov). Good value.

TT Vila Verde, Estrada Paraty–Cunha, Km 7, T024-3371 7808, www.vilaverdeparaty.com.br. It's worth a stop off here on the way to or from the waterfalls, the Caminho Douro or Cunha. The restaurant serves light Italian and its open sides overlook a tropical garden which attracts numerous Morpho butterflies, humming birds and tanagers.

T Kontiki, Ilha Duas Irmãs, T024-999 9599, www.paraty.com.br/kontiki.htm. A tiny island, 5 mins from the pier where a small speed boat runs a (free) shuttle service. Wonderful island setting; ordinary food. Daily 1000-1500 and Fri and Sat for dinner, reservations recommended.

T Sabor da Terra, Av Roberto Silveira, next to Banco do Brasil. Reliable, if not bargain-priced self-service food. Closes 2200.

Bars and clubs

Paraty *p165, map p166*

The best way to sample Paraty's nightlife is to wander its handful of streets.

Bar Coupé, Praça da Matriz. A popular hang-out with outside seating. Good bar snacks and breakfast.

Bar Dinho, Praça da Matriz at R da Matriz. Good bar with live music at weekends, sometimes mid-week.

Umoya, R Comendador José Luiz. Video bar and café, live music at weekends.

Entertainment

Paraty *p165, map p165*

Teatro Espaço, R Dona Geralda 327, T024-3371 1575, ecparati@ax.apc.org. Wed, Sat 2100, US$12. This world-famous puppet show should not be missed. The puppets tell stories, without words, which are funny, sad, even shocking, with incredible realism. The short pieces (lasting 1 hr) are works of pure imagination and emotion and a moving commentary on the human condition.

Festivals and events

Angra dos Reis and around *p163*

New Year Festa do Mar, boat processions.

5 Jan Folia dos Reis, the Three Kings, culmination of a religious festival that begins at Christmas.

6 Jan Founding of Angra dos Reis.
May Festa do Divino and, on the 2nd Sun, the Senhor do Bonfim maritime procession.
Jun As elsewhere in the state, the Festas Juninas are celebrated.
8 Dec Festival of Nossa Senhora da Conceição.

Paraty *p165, map p166*
Feb/Mar Carnaval, hundreds of people cover their bodies in black mud and run through the streets yelling like prehistoric creatures (anyone can join in).
Mar/Apr Semana Santa (Easter Week) with religious processions and folk songs.
Mid-Jul Semana de Santa Rita, traditional foods, shows, exhibitions and dances.
Aug Festival da Pinga, the *cachaça* fair at which local distilleries display their products and there are plenty of opportunities to over-indulge.
Sep (around the 8th) **Semana da Nossa Senhora dos Remédios**, processions and religious events.
Sep/Oct Spring Festival of Music, concerts in front of Santa Rita Church.
31 Dec New Year's Eve, a huge party with open-air concerts and fireworks (reserve accommodation in advance).

As well as the Dança dos Velhos (see Music and dance, page 689), another common dance in these parts is the *ciranda*, in which everyone, young and old, dances in a circle to songs accompanied by guitars.

Shopping

Paraty *p165, map p166*
Shopping here is by and large a disappointment. There are many shops but most sell the kind of tack you'd find in any tourist town in the world; key rings, fridge magnets, cheesy T-shirts and so on. The best items are fine art (which tends to be overpriced), and artisan ware – fish trays, small wooden canoes and boats. The Guarani people sell their arts and crafts on the R da Matriz. Paraty *cachaça* is some of the best in the state, although it can't compare with bottles from Minas.

Activities and tours

Angra dos Reis and around *p163*
Angatu, T011-3872 0945, www.angatu.com. The best private tours and diving around the bay in luxurious yachts and motor cruisers, with private entries to the exclusive island parties. Book well ahead.

Ilha Grande *p164*
Boat trips
These are easy to organize on the quay in Abraão on Ilha Grande.

Scuba diving
Ilha Grande Dive, R da Praia , s/n, Vila do Abraão, T021-3361 5512, igdive@bol.com.br (next to the *farmacia* on the seafront). Offers trips around the entire bay.

Paraty *p165, map p166*
Tour operators
Angatu, T011-3872 0945, www.angatu.com. The best luxury tours, cruises and private villa rental in and around Paraty. Highly recommended.
Antígona, Praça da Bandeira 2, Centro Histórico, T/F024-3371 1165, www.antigona.com.br. Daily schooner tours, 5 hrs, bar and lunch on board. Recommended.
Paraty Tours, Av Roberto Silveira 11, T/F024-3371 1327, www.paratytours.com.br. Good range of trips. English and Spanish spoken.
Soberana da Costa, R Dona Geraldo 43, in Pousada Mercado do Pouso, T/F024- 3371 1114. Schooner trips. Recommended.

Transport

Angra dos Reis and around *p163*
Bus Costa Verde buses run at least hourly to the *rodoviária* in **Rio de Janeiro**, some are direct, others take the *via litoral* and go through Barra, Ipanema and Copacabana, US$5.75, 2½ hrs. Sit on the right for the best views. Busy at weekends. There are also regular buses to and from **São Paulo**, **Paraty**, **Ubatuba** and the São Paulo coast.

Ferry Ferries run to **Ilha Grande**, see the timetable on page 165. Fishing boats will also take passengers for around $5 per person before 1300 or when full. Boat charter costs around US$60-100.

Ilha Grande *p164*
Bicycles Can be hired and tours arranged; ask at pousadas.

Ferry For boats to Ilha Grande, see under Angra dos Reis and the on page 165.

Paraty *p165, map p166*
Bus On public holidays and in high season, the frequency of bus services usually increases. Costa Verde runs 9 buses a day to **Rio de Janeiro** (241 km, 3¾ hrs, US$8.10). To **Angra dos Reis** (98 km, 1½ hrs, every 1 hr 40 mins, US$4); 3 a day to **Ubatuba** (75 km, just over 1 hr, São José company, US$4), **Taubaté** (170 km) and **Guaratinguetá** (210 km); 2 a day to **São Paulo**, 1100 and 2335 (304 km via **São José dos Campos**, 5½ hrs, US$8.50 (Reunidas book up quickly and are very busy at weekends), and **São Sebastião**.

Taxi Set rate of US$4 for historic centre.

Trindade and around *p168*
Paraty–Ubatuba buses all pass the turning to Trindade and will pick you up from here. In high season there are vans from Trindade to the turning (US$2). In low season you'll have to hitch or walk. Frequent cars pass and hitching here is normal. There are 4 or 5 direct buses a day which also call in on **Laranjeiras** for the trailhead to **Sono** and **Ponta Negra**.

Directory

Angra dos Reis and around *p163*
Banks There are several banks in town, with ATMs and money-changing facilities. These include Banco 24 Horas, R do Comércio 250 and Bradesco, R do Comércio 196.

Ilha Grande *p164*
Banks Only open at weekends.

Paraty *p165, map p166*
Banks Banco do Brasil, Av Roberto Silveira, just outside historic centre. ATM. Exchange 1100-1430, ask for the manager. **Internet** Connections are plentiful, but neither fast nor cheap. Paraty Cyber Café, Av Roberto Silveira 17. Friendly, 0900-2300, coffee and snacks served. US$3, 30 mins. **Laundry** Paraty Wash Shopping Martins, loja 15, opposite bus station. **Medical services** Hospital Municipal São Pedro de Alcântara (Santa Casa), Av Dom Pedro de Alcântara, T024-3371 1623. **Post office** R da Cadeia and Beco do Propósito, Mon-Sat 0800-1700, Sun 0800-1200. **Telephone** International calls, Praça Macedo Soares, opposite the tourist office. Local and long-distance calls can be made from public phones; buy phone cards from newspaper stands in the centre.

São Paulo

Footprint features

Introduction

São Paulo is as famous for its ugliness as Rio is for its beauty. But while Rio looks marvellous from a distance and less than perfect close to, São Paulo is the opposite. Restaurants, shops, hotels and nightlife here are infinitely better than in Rio. And while wandering and browsing in plush neighbourhoods like Jardins, it is even possible to forget that few cities in the world have quite so much relentless concrete punctuated with quite so few green spaces; or have rivers quite so disgracefully polluted as the Tietê. Marlene Dietrich perhaps summed it up when she said – "Rio is a beauty – but São Paulo; ah... São Paulo is a city."

Indeed, São Paulo is more than a city. It is also a state a little larger than the UK; and whilst most of its interior is dull agricultural hinterland, its coast is magnificent; just as beautiful as Rio de Janeiro's but far less visited by international tourists. The northern beaches are long and glorious and pounded by some of South America's finest surf. Brazil's largest island, which is every bit as pristine and romantic as Ilha Grande, lies a short boat ride off shore. Beaches further south are less beautiful but far wilder and behind them and stretching into the neighbouring state of Paraná are the largest expanses of primary forest on Brazil's Atlantic coast.

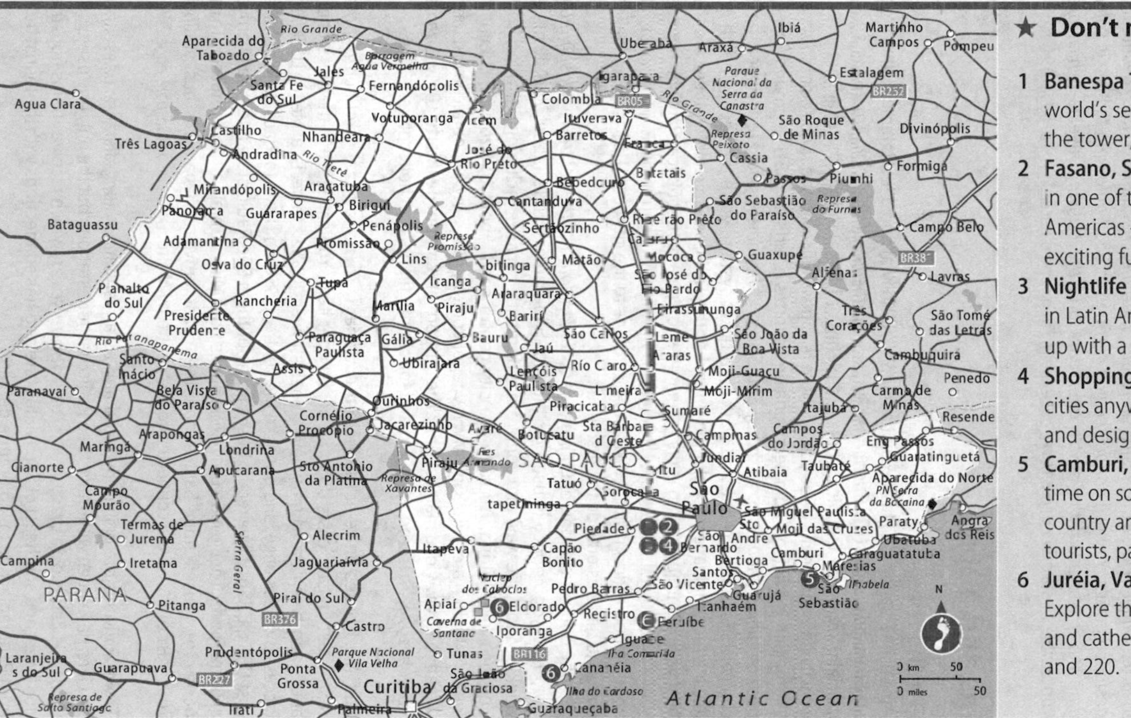

★ Don't miss...

1 **Banespa Tower** Admire the view of the world's second largest city from the top of the tower, page 187.

2 **Fasano, Sakamoto or 348** Enjoy a meal in one of the best restaurants in the Americas – for French, Italian, Japanese or exciting fusion cuisine, page 196-197.

3 **Nightlife** Take in a concert in the best city in Latin America for live music and follow it up with a state-of-the-art club, page 198.

4 **Shopping** Stock up at one of the best cities anywhere for quality clothes, shoes and designer goods, page 200.

5 **Camburi, Maresias and Ilhabela** Spend time on some of the best beaches in the country and the least visited by international tourists, pages 212 and 214.

6 **Juréia, Vale do Ribeiro and Cananéia** Explore the virgin forests, deserted beaches and cathedral-sized caves, pages 219 and 220.

São Paulo city

→ *Phone code: 011. Colour map 5, A5. Altitude: 850 m. Population: 18-20 million.*

São Paulo is vast and can feel intimidating on first arrival. But this is a city of separate neighbourhoods, only a few of which are interesting for visitors and once you have your base it is easy to negotiate. São Paulo is the intellectual capital of Brazil. Those who don't flinch at the city's size and leave, who are instead prepared to spend time (and money) here, and who get to know Paulistanos, are seldom disappointed and often end up preferring the city to Rio. Nowhere in Brazil is better for concerts, clubs, theatre, ballet, classical music, all-round nightlife, restaurants and beautifully designed hotels. You will not be seen as a gringo *in São Paulo, and the city is safer than Rio if you avoid the centre after dark and the outlying* favelas *(which are impossible to stumble across).* » *For Sleeping, Eating and other listings, see pages 194-206.*

Ins and outs

Getting there

Air All international flights (except a handful to Bolivia) and a few internal flights stop at **Guarulhos airport** ⓘ *Guarulhos, 30 km northeast of the city, T011-6445 2945*, officially known as **Cumbica**. There are plenty of banks and money changers in the arrivals hall open daily 0800-2200. There is a post office on the third floor of Asa A. Information is available from **Secretaria de Esportes e Turismo (SET)** ⓘ *ground floor of both terminals, Mon-Fri 0730-2200, Sat, Sun and holidays 0900-2100*. Airport taxis charge US$25 to the centre and work on a ticket system: go to the second booth on leaving the terminal and book a Co-op taxi at the Taxi Comum counter; these are the best value. **Emtu** buses run every 30 minutes to Praça da República, Paulista, the bus station and Congonhas airport, US$6.50, 30-45 minutes, 0500-0200. Buy a ticket at the booth in domestic arrivals. A taxi from Guarulhos to the city costs US$35-40 and takes about 30 minutes outside the rush hour.

The domestic airport of **Congonhas** ⓘ *14 km south of the centre, Av Washington Luiz, T011-5090 9000*, is used for the Rio–São Paulo shuttle (about 400 flights a week US$100 one-way) and some other domestic services including Salvador, Belo Horizonte and Vitória. A taxi to the city centre costs about US$20. The cheapest internal flights are with **Gol**, www.voegol.com.br, **Bra**, www.voebra.com.br, and **Ocean Air**, www.oceanair.com.br. The airport at **Campo de Marte** ⓘ *Av Santos Dumont 1979, T011-290 2699*, is used for charter flights and helicopters.

Bus Most buses arrive at the **Tietê rodoviária** ⓘ *T011-235 0322, 5 km north of the centre*. Left luggage costs US$0.80 per day per item. You can sleep in the bus station after 2200 when the guards have gone; showers US$2. There is a Metrô, US$0.60 (access by stairs only), and buses to the centre, US$0.80. Taxis to Praça da República cost US$5, US$9 at weekends. Buses from southern São Paulo state and Paraná arrive at **Barra Funda,** T011-3666 4682, while buses from Minas Gerais arrive at **Bresser,** T011-6692 5191. Buses from Santos and the coast arrive at **Jabaquara** bus station, T011-5581 0856. All are connected to the centre by Metrô. » *See also Transport, page 204.*

Train Railways are being privatized and as a result many long-distance passenger services have been withdrawn. São Paulo has four stations but the only one useful for tourists is **Estação da Luz** ⓘ *Metrô Luz, T0800-550121*, which receives trains from the northwest and southeast of São Paulo state and has connections with the tourist train from Paranapiacaba to Rio Grande de Serra.

Arriving late at night

São Paulo's airport has 24-hour facilities (for food, banking and, of course, taxis) if you arrive late at night or in the early hours of the morning. It is a long drive from the airport to the city and the air-conditioned bus to Praça da República does not operate between 0200 and 0500 and the service to Avenida Paulista does not run from 2315 to 0645. A taxi to the centre of the city will cost around US$35. Congonhas airport – which is connected to most of Brazil's major cities – is in the city centre. Although there are no 24 hour services there are hotels across the road from the terminal (via the pedestrian footbridge) and most areas in and around the centre are a maximum of US$10 taxi ride away.

Getting around

The best and cheapest way to get around São Paulo is on the excellent Metrô system, which is clean, safe, cheap and efficient; though rather limited in its coverage. The first Metrô in Brazil, it began operating in 1975 and has two main lines intersecting at Praça de Sé: north–south from **Tucuruvi** to **Jabaquara**; and east–west from **Corinthians Itaquera** to **Barra Funda**, both operate 0500-2400. A third line runs west–south from **Vila Madalena** to **Imigrantes** via Avenida Paulista, and operates 0600-2200. Stations are well-policed and safe. Fare US$0.75, US$6 for a book of 10 tickets; backpacks are allowed. Combined bus and Metrô ticket are available, US$1, eg to Congonhas airport.

Bus routes can be confusing for visitors and slow due to frequent traffic jams. However, buses are safe, clean and only crowded at peak hours. Maps of the bus and Metrô system are available at depots, eg Anhangabaú. All the *rodoviárias* (bus stations) are on the Metrô, but if travelling with luggage, take a taxi.

Taxis display their tariffs in the window (starting at US$3) and have meters. Ordinary taxis are hailed on the street or at taxi stations such as Praça da República. Radio taxis are more expensive but less hassle, see page 205 for a list of companies.

Best time to visit

São Paulo sits on a plateau at around 800 m and the weather is temperamental, influenced by the city's altitude and by the sea, whose cold or warm air is pushed up by the coastal mountains. Rainfall is ample and temperatures fluctuate greatly. Summer temperatures vary between 20° and 30°C, occasionally peaking into the high 30s or even 40s. The winter fluctuates between 15° and 25°C, occasionally dropping to below 10° when a cold front comes up from the Atlantic. The winter months (April-October) are also the driest, with minimal precipitation in June and July. Christmas and New Year are wet. When there are thermal inversions, air pollution can be troublesome.

Tourist information

There are tourist information booths with English-speaking staff in international and domestic arrivals (ground floor) at **Cumbica airport** (Guarulhos); and tourist information booths in the bus station and in the following locations throughout the city: **Praça da República** ⓘ *T011-231 2922, daily 0900-1800,* very helpful; **Praça Dom José Gaspar** ⓘ *corner of Av São Luís, T011-257 3422, Mon-Fri 0900-1800*; **Avenida Paulista** ⓘ *Parque Trianon, T011-251 0970, Sun-Fri 0900-1800*; and on **Avenida Brig Faria Lima** ⓘ *opposite the Iguatemi shopping centre, T011-211 1277, Mon-Fri 0900- 1800*. An excellent map is available free at these offices. **Editora Abril** also publishes maps: their excellent *Guide to São Paulo – Sampa*, and a guide to cheap travel, *Viajar Bem e Barato*, are available at news-stands and bookshops throughout the city.

Orientation

São Paulo is a city of many neighbourhoods. These cluster around the **Centro Histórico**, which is pedestrianized at its heart. There are a number of sights here, including the Pátio de Colégio, Mosteiro São Bento and the Edifício Banespa and Edifício Itália, but this is an area to visit during the day and not to stay in at night. The Centro Histórico is served by Metrô Sé, São Bento, Anhangabaú and República.

Just north of the Centro Histórico is the neighbourhood of **Luz**, which centres around the 19th-century Estação de Luz and the state art gallery, the Pinacoteca. There are several other interesting museums here and the area is served by Metrôs Luz and Tiradentes. Immediately south of the Centro Histórico **Liberdade** remains the centre of São Paulo's large Japanese community. There is an interesting Museu da Imigração Japonesa and many good Japanese restaurants. The area is served by Metrô Liberdade.

Immediately southwest of the Centro Histórico is the city's grandest and most photographed skyscraper-lined street, **Avenida Paulista**. The Museo de Arte de São Paulo (MASP), the best art gallery in the southern hemisphere is found here. South of Avenida Paulista is the neighbourhood of **Jardins**. This is the city's most affluent inner neighbourhood with elegant little streets hiding Latin America's best restaurants and designer clothing boutiques. There are plenty of luxurious hotels and some budget options, and you are safe here at night. Avenida Paulista and the Jardins are served by Metrô Consolação, Trianon MASP, Brigadeiro and Paraíso.

The **Parque do Ibirapuera**, 5 km south of the centre and next to Jardins, is the inner city's largest green space. It is home to many interesting museums, including the Museu Afro-Brasil, Museum of Modern Art (MAM), the planetarium, the Pavilhão Japonês and the Oca. There is also a lake and a sculpture garden and frequent free live concerts on Sundays. The adjoining neighbourhood of **Vila Mariana** has a few hotel options and good live music at SESC Vila Mariana. There are no direct Metrô stations for Ibirapuera but Metrô Ana Rosa is a 15-minute walk east of the park (turn right out of the station and walk due west along Avenida Conselheiro Rodrigo Alves and Avenida Dante Pazzanese); and any bus to DETRAN stops opposite Ibirapuera.

Sao Paulo metrô

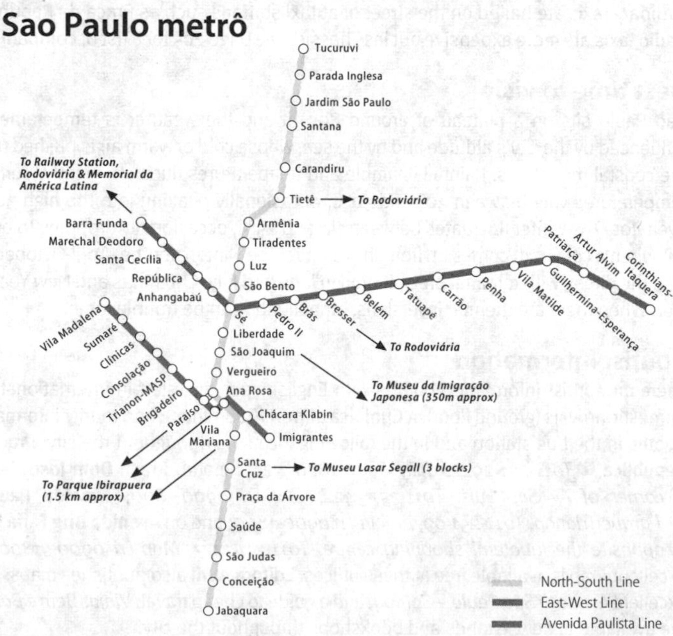

Situated between Ibirapuera and the river, **Itaim, Moema** and **Vila Olímpia** are (along with Vila Madalena) the nightlife centres of São Paulo with a wealth of streetside bars, ultra-chic designer restaurants and European-style dance clubs. Hotels tend to be expensive as these areas border the new business centre on Avenida Brigadeiro Faria Lima and Avenida Luis Carlos Berrini, in the suburb of **Brooklin**.

Pinheiros and **Vila Madalena**, to the west of the centre, are more hippy and studenty than Itaim and Vila Olímpia but equally lively at night and have the funkiest shops. Vila Madalena is served by Metrô Vila Madalena.

Background

The history of São Paulo state and São Paulo city were much the same from the arrival of the Europeans until the coffee boom transformed the region's economic and political landscape. According to John Hemming (*Red Gold*, see page 685), there were approximately 196,000 indigenous inhabitants living in what is now São Paulo state. Today their numbers have been vastly diminished and of the few who survived, some live in villages within São Paulo itself and can be seen selling handicrafts in the centre.

The first official settlement in the state was at São Vicente on the coast, near today's port of Santos. It was founded in 1532 by Martim Afonso de Sousa, who had been sent by King João III to drive the French from Brazilian waters, explore the coast and lay claim to all the lands apportioned to Portugal under the Treaty of Tordesillas.

In 1554, two Jesuit priests from São Vicente founded São Paulo as a *colégio* (a combined mission and school) on the site of the present Pátio de Colégio in the Centro Histórico. The Jesuits chose to settle inland because they wanted to distance themselves from the civil authority, which was based in Bahia and along the coast. Moreover, the plateau provided better access to the indigenous population who they hoped to convert to Catholicism. Pioneers seeking to found farms followed in the Jesuits' wake and as the need for workers on these farms grew, expeditions were sent into the interior of the country to capture and enslave the indigenous people. These marauders were known as *bandeirantes* after the flag wielder who ostensibly walked at their head to claim territory. Their ignominious expeditions were responsible for the opening up of the country's interior and supplying the indigenous slave trade. One of Victor Brecheret's statues sits on the edge of Ibirapuera in homage to the *bandeirantes* (see box, page 210).

In a sense, the *bandeirantes*' success in discovering gold led to a demise of São Paulo in the 18th century. The inhabitants rushed to the gold fields in the *sertão*, leaving São Paulo to fall to ruin and fall under the influence of Rio de Janeiro. The relative backwardness of the region lasted until the late 19th century when coffee spread west from Rio de Janeiro. Landowners became immensely rich. São Paulo changed from a small town into a financial and residential centre. Exports and imports flowed through Santos and the industrial powerhouse of the country was born. As the city boomed, industries and agriculture fanned outwards to the far reaches of the state.

Between 1885 and the end of the century the boom in coffee and the arrival of large numbers of Europeans transformed the state beyond recognition. By the end of the 1930s more than a million Italians, 500,000 Portuguese, nearly 400,000 Spaniards and 200,000 Japanese had arrived in São Paulo state. It is the world's largest Japanese community outside Japan and their main contribution to the economy of São Paulo has been in horticulture, raising poultry and cotton farming, especially around cities such as Marília. Significant numbers of Syrian-Lebanese arrived too, adding an extra dimension to the cultural diversity of the city.

Much of the immigrant labour that flooded in during the early years of the 20th century was destined for the coffee *fazendas* and farms. Others went to work in the industries that were opening up in the city. By 1941 there were 14,000 factories and today the city covers more than 1500 sq km – three times the size of Paris.

São Paulo

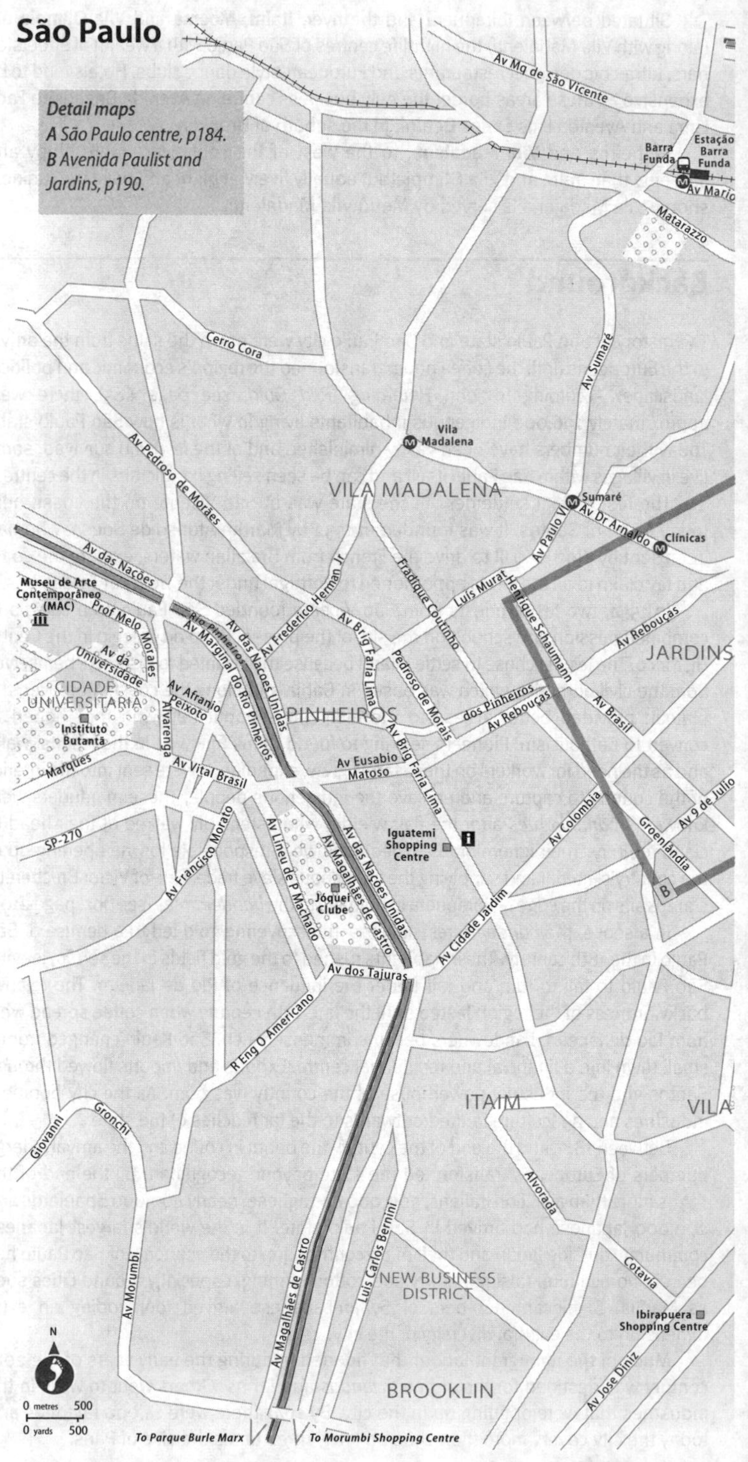

Detail maps
A São Paulo centre, p184.
B Avenida Paulist and Jardins, p190.
Av Mq de São Vicente
Barra Funda
Estação Barra Funda
Av Mario
Matarazzo
Cerro Cora
Av Sumaré
Vila Madalena
VILA MADALENA
Av Pedroso de Morães
Sumaré
Av Dr Arnaldo
Clínicas
Av Paulo VI
Av das Nações
Museu de Arte Contemporâneo (MAC)
Prof Melo Morales
Av da Universidade
CIDADE UNIVERSITARIA
Instituto Butantã
Alvarenga
Marques
Av Afranio Peixoto
Rio Pinheiros
Av Marginal do Rio Pinheiros
Av das Nacoes Unidas
Av Frederico Herman Jr
Fradique Coutinho
Luís Murat
Henrique Schaumann
Av Rebouças
JARDINS
Av Brig Faria Lima
Pedroso de Morais
dos Pinheiros
Av Brasil
PINHEIROS
Av Vital Brasil
Av Eusabio Matoso
SP-270
Av Francisco Morato
Av Lineu de P Machado
Av Magalhães de Castro
Av das Nacões Unidas
Iguatemi Shopping Centre
Jóquei Clube
Av Colombia
Groenlandia
Av 9 de Julho
B
Av Cidade Jardim
Av dos Tajuras
R Eng O Americano
ITAIM
VILA
Giovanni
Gronchi
Alvorada
Cotavia
Av Morumbi
Av Magalhães de Castro
Luis Carlos Bernini
NEW BUSINESS DISTRICT
Ibirapuera Shopping Centre
Av Jose Diniz
BROOKLIN
N
0 metres 500
0 yards 500
To Parque Burle Marx
To Morumbi Shopping Centre

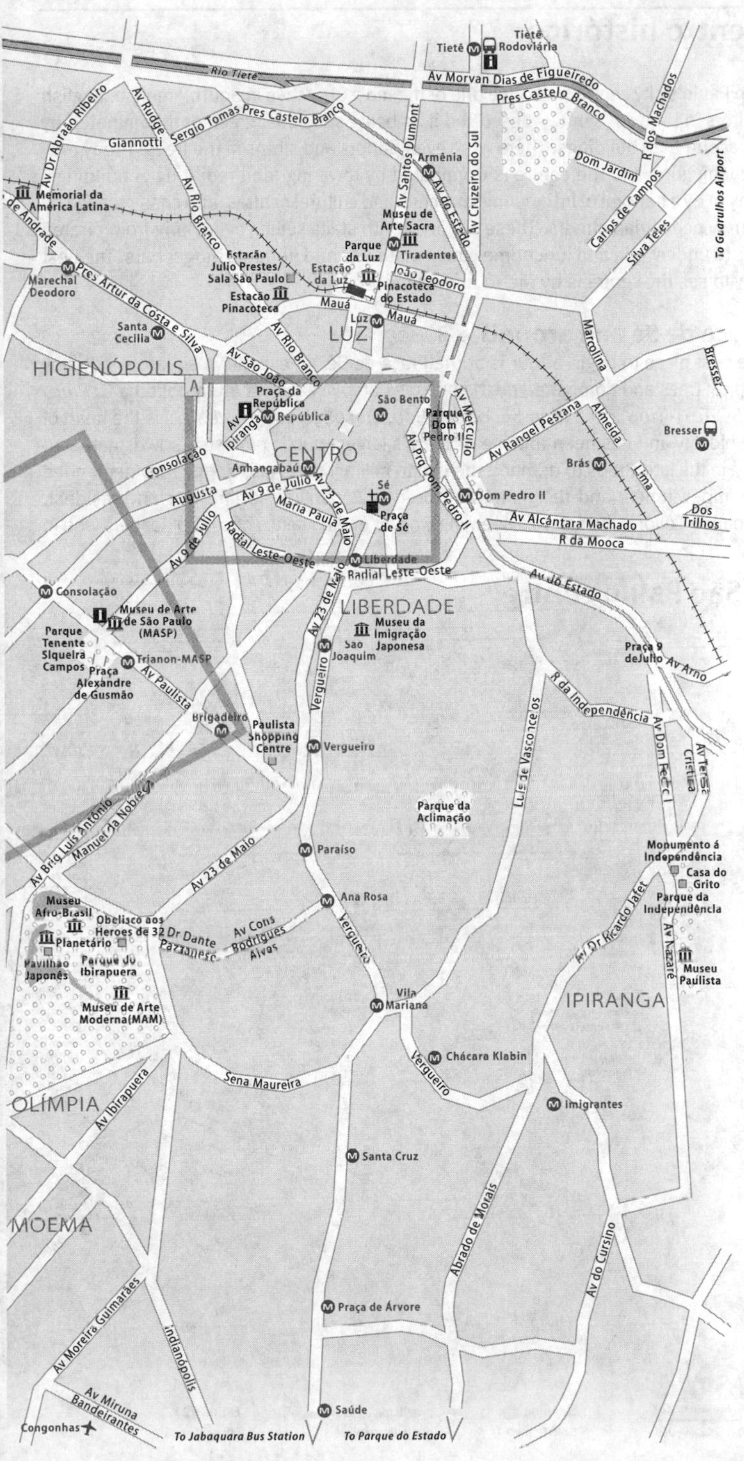
Tietê
Tietê
Rodoviária
Rio Tietê
Av Morvan Dias de Figueiredo
Pres Castelo Branco
R dos Machados
Av Dr Abraão Ribeiro
Av Rudge
Sergio Tomas
Pres Castelo Branco
Av Santos Dumont
Giannotti
Armênia
Av Cruzeiro do Sul
Dom Jardim
Av do Estado
Carlos de Campos
To Guarulhos Airport
Memorial da
América Latina
Av Rio Branco
Museu de
Arte Sacra
Silva Teles
de Andrade
Parque
da Luz
Tiradentes
Estação
Julio Prestes/
Sala São Paulo
Estação
da Luz
João Teodoro
Marechal
Deodoro
Pres Artur da Costa e Silva
Estação
Pinacoteca
Pinacoteca
do Estado
Mauá
Luz
Mauá
Santa
Cecilia
LUZ
Marcolina
Av Rio Branco
Bresser
HIGIENÓPOLIS
Av São João
A
Praça da
República
São Bento
Av Mercurio
Av
Ipiranga
República
Parque
Dom
Pedro II
Av Rangel Pestana
Almeida
Bresser
Consolação
CENTRO
Av Prq Dom Pedro II
Anhangabaú
Brás
Augusta
Av 9 de Julio
Av 23 de Maio
Sé
Lima
Maria Paula
Dom Pedro II
Praça
de Sé
Dos
Trilhos
Av Alcântara Machado
Av 9 de Julio
R da Mooca
Radial Leste-Oeste
Liberdade
Radial Leste Oeste
Av do Estado
Consolação
LIBERDADE
Museu de Arte
de São Paulo
(MASP)
Museu da
Imigração
Japonesa
Parque
Tenente
Siqueira
Campos
São
Joaquim
Praça 9
deJulio
Av Arno
Trianon-MASP
Praça
Alexandre
de Gusmão
Av Paulista
Vergueiro
R da Independência
Av Dom Pedro I
Brigadeiro
Paulista
Shopping
Centre
Vergueiro
Cristina
Parque da
Aclimação
Manuel da Nobrega
Av Brig Luís Antônio
Monumento á
Independência
Casa do
Grito
Paraíso
Av 23 de Maio
Parque da
Independência
Ana Rosa
Museu
Afro-Brasil
Obelisco aos
Heroes de 32
Dr Dante
Pazzanese
Av Cons
Rodrigues
Alves
Planetário
Av Dr Ricardo Jafet
Av Nazaré
Museu
Paulista
Pavilhão
Japonês
Parque do
Ibirapuera
Vergueiro
Museu de Arte
Moderna(MAM)
Vila
Mariana
IPIRANGA
Chácara Klabin
Vergueiro
Sena Maureira
Imigrantes
OLÍMPIA
Av Ibirapuera
Santa Cruz
MOEMA
Abrado de Morais
Av do Cursino
Praça de Árvore
Av Moreira Guimarães
Indianópolis
Av Miruna
Bandeirantes
Saúde
Congonhas
To Jabaquara Bus Station
To Parque do Estado

Centro histórico

São Paulo's city centre was once one of the most attractive in South America. English visitors in the 19th century described it as being spacious, green and dominated by terracotta-tiled buildings. There were even parrots and sloths in the trees. Today they are long gone and the centre is dominated by towering (and rather ugly) buildings, broken by a handful of interesting churches and cultural centres, and criss-crossed by narrow pedestrian streets. These are lined with stalls selling everything from pirated CDs to underwear, and lunchtime café restaurants and portable burger bars. The best way to see the centre is by Metrô and on foot.

Praça de Sé and around → *Metrô Sé*

The best place to begin a tour is at the **Praça de Sé**, an expansive square shaded by tropical trees and dominated by the hulking Catholic **Catedral Metropolitana** ⓘ *Praça de Sé, T011-3106 2709, Mon-Sat 0800-1800, Sun 0830-1800, free*. This is the heart of the old city and has been the site of Brazil's largest public protests. Crowds gathered here in the late 1980s to demand the end to military rule. And in 1992 they demanded the impeachment and resignation of the new Republic's second elected president, Fernando Collor – the first in a seemingly never-ending series of corrupt leaders who in

São Paulo centre

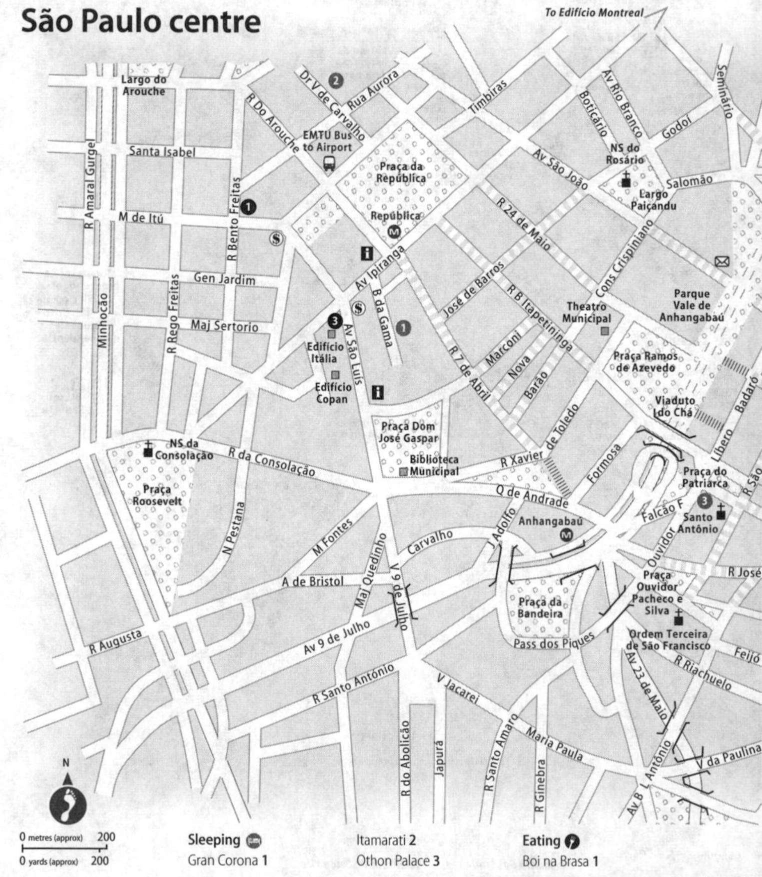

1990 had frozen the country's savings accounts and personally pocketed millions. The praça is always busy with hawkers, beggars, shoeshiners and business men rushing between meetings. Evangelists with megaphones proselytize on the steps of the cathedral – a symbol of the war between Christians for the souls of the poor which dominates contemporary urban Brazil. The praça is a great spot for street photography though be discreet with your camera and careful you aren't followed after taking your shots. Like the São Paulo itself, the cathedral is more remarkable for its size than its beauty and is an unconvincing mish-mash of neo-Gothic and Renaissance. A narrow nave is squeezed uncomfortably between two monstrous 97-m-high spires beneath a bulbous copper cupola. It was designed in 1912 by the inappropriately named engineer Maximiliano Hell, inaugurated in the 1950s and fitted with its full complement of 14 towers only in 2002. The interior is as bare but for a few stained glass windows designed in Germany and Brazil and capitals decorated with Brazilian floral motifs.

There are a few other sights of interest around the praça. Next door to the cathedral itself and housed in a 1930s art deco building is the **Conjunto Cultural da Caixa** ⓘ *Praça de Sé 111, T011-3107 0498, Tue-Sun 0900-2100, US$2*, a gallery that hosts art and photography exhibitions and has a small banking museum with colonial furniture, on one of its upper floors. Two minutes' walk immediately to the west of the cathedral, squeezed between ugly modern buildings at the end of Rua Senador Feijó, is the **Igreja da Ordem Terceiro de São Francisco** ⓘ *Largo de São Francisco 133, T011-3106 0081, daily 0730-2000, free*. This is one of the city's oldest churches, preserving a modest baroque interior (parts of which date to the 17th century) painted in celestial blue. It is quiet and meditative inside. The exterior is largely an 18th-century excrescence. The church is often referred to as *O Convento de São Francisco* after a beautiful baroque convent that stood here until the 1930s. It was demolished along with vast swathes of the old colonial centre.

Pátio do Colégio and around → *Metró Sé*

The site of the founding of São Paulo can be reached by walking north from the bottom of the Praça de Sé (farthest from the cathedral) along Rua Santa Teresa and to the Praça Pátio do Colégio. Here lies the **Pátio de Colégio and Museu de Anchieta** ⓘ *Praça Pátio do Colégio, T011-3105 6899, www.pateodocollegio.com.br, Mon-Fri 0800-1700, US$3, free on the last Sun of the month*. Jesuit priests, led by 18-year-old Padre José de Anchieta arrived here in 1554, when the area was a tiny clearing on a hill in the midst of a vast forest.

They made camp and instructed their domicile indigenous Guarani to construct a simple wattle and daub hut. They inaugurated the building with a celebration of Mass on 25 January 1554, the feast of the conversion of São Paulo. Their simple hut took the saint's name, the *Colégio de São Paulo de Piratinga*. The hut became a school for converted *indígena* seduced from the forests around. The school became a church and the church gave its name to a settlement for *bandeirante* slaving raids into the Brazilian interior; São Paulo. In 1760, the Jesuits were expelled from the city they founded, for opposing the *bandeirantes* and their indigenous slave trade. But the Pátio do Colégio (as the complex of buildings came to be known) remained, becoming the palace of the fledgling province's Portuguese colonial Captains General, and then of its Brazilian imperial governors. But the church's tower fell down in 1886 and shortly after, the whole building, but for one piece of wattle and daub wall was demolished. The Jesuits didn't return to São Paulo until 1954 but they had long memories and immediately set about building an exact replica of their original church and college, which is what stands today. Most of the buildings are occupied by the Museu Padre Anchieta. This preserves, amongst other items, a modernist and not altogether sympathetic painting of the priest, by Italian Albino Menghini, bits of his corpse (which is now that of a saint after Anchieta was canonized by Pope John Paul II), a 17th-century font used to baptize the *indígena* and a collection of Guaraní art and artefacts from the colonial era.

The exhibition spaces, cultural centres and concert halls of the **Centro Cultural Banco do Brasil** ⓘ *R Álvares Penteado 112, T011-3113 3651, www.bb.com.br/appbb/portal/bb/ctr/sp/index.jsp, Mon-Fri 0900-1800, free except for exhibitions*, can be reached by turning immediately west from the front of the Pátio do Colégio along Rua do Tesouro and then right for a block along Rua Álvares Penteado. These are housed in an attractive art deco building with a pretty glass ceiling. Many of the galleries are contained within the banks original vaults, some of which retain their massive iron doors.

Mosteiro do São Bento and around → *Metrô São Bento*

The most beautiful of all the churches in São Paulo is the Benedictine Basilica de Nossa Senhora de Assunção, known as the **Mosteiro São Bento** ⓘ *Largo São Bento s/n, T011-3228 3633, www.mosteiro.org.br, Mon-Fri 0600-1800, Sat and Sun 0600-1200 and 1600-1800, Latin Mass with Gregorian chant Sun 1000; Latin vespers Mon-Fri 1725, Sat 1700, free*. Benedictines arrived on this site in 1598, shortly after the Jesuits and, like them, proceeded to proselytize the indigenous people. Despite their long history in the city the monastery is a modern church dating from the 1920s. It was designed by Munich-based architect Richard Bernal in homage to the English Norman style. Its façade is strikingly similar to Southwell cathedral in Nottinghamshire, though with added Rhineland roofs and baroque revival flourishes. But few visit São Bento for the exterior. The church preserves a striking Beuronese interior painted by Dom Adelbert Gresnicht, a Dutch monk of the Order. The style is named after techniques developed by Benedictines in the monastery of Beuron in southwest Germany in the late 19th and early 20th centuries. It finds much inspiration in Byzantine art and is characterized by compressed perspective and iconic, almost exaggerated colours. São Bento is one of the finest Beuronese churches in the world. The stained glass (and much of the statuary) are also by Dom Adelbert. Most of the windows show scenes from the life of St Benedict with the most beautiful, at the far end of the nave, showing Our Lady ascending to heaven guided by the Holy Spirit in the form of a dove. The church has Brazil's finest organ which is given its own festival in November and December every year. And with this being a Benedictine monastery, there is of course a temple to commerce: the shop sells delicious sweets home-made by the monks in their bakery.

In 1928 Mario de Andrade described São Paulo as "most beautiful", its seven hills are... "kissed by the slender and restless lymph of the river Tietê", its streets "intersected with roads... adorned with the most graceful statuary and finely wrought lamp posts...".

Black and white photography

One of the legacies of Brazil's love affair with France is an enduring tradition of beautifully observed and masterfully printed black and white documentary photography. Its most famous exponent, Sebastião Salgado has won numerous international awards including the prestigious World Press Photo prize. But he is the tip of a large iceberg whose bulk is made-up of photographers little published outside of Brazil. José Bassit and Thiago Santana have both documented the rich tapestry of religious life that has changed little in centuries in the country's poor and arid interior. Claudia Andujar focuses on the Amazon and has produced remarkable, intimate and deeply touching images of the lives of the indigenous people and rural poor who live there, including series of double or triple exposed dream-like images portraits where faces and bodies mix with the landscape like an Australian Aboriginal wall painting. The best places to see Brazilian photographic art are on the ground floor of the **Pinacoteca**, Praça da Luz 2, T011-3229 9844; the **Galeria Vermelho**, R Minas Gerais 350, Higienópolis, T011-3257 2033, www.galeriavermelho.com.br; and the **Íma Foto Galería**, R Fradique Coutinho 1239, Vila Madalena T011-3816 1290, www.imafotogaleria.com.br.

Immediately in front of the monastery, at the corner of Avenida São João and Rua Libero Badaró, is the **Edifício Martinelli (Martinelli Building)** ⓘ *Av São João 35, not open to the public*. This was the city's first skyscraper and, when it was built, looked out over a sea of terracotta roofs and handsome tree-lined avenues. The building is reminiscent of New York's upper east side but is by no means as distinguished: while colonial São Paulo was unique and beautiful, the buildings that replaced it looked tawdry and crowded next to the New York it longed to imitate.

Around the corner is another architectural pastiche, the **Edifício Banespa (Banespa Tower)** ⓘ *R João Bricola 24, T011-3249 7180, 1000-1700, US$4*, looking like a wan Empire State Building small enough to collapse under the weight of a King Kong. The view from the observatory is best experienced at dusk when the chaos of multi-storey concrete is set against a smog-filled purple sky and the vast highways are lit by a thousand paralysed cars. The city stretches far and wide, over the polluted black gutter of the Tietê and to every distant horizon. On its fringes are the vast favelas and new neighbourhoods with infant skyscraper flats.

Praça da República and around → *Metrô República*

There are a few interesting sites here. Most notable is the **Edifício and Terraço Itália** ⓘ *Av Ipiranga 344, T011-3257 6566, www.traccoitalia.com.br, US$5*, an unremarkable restaurant housed in the city's tallest building with a truly remarkable view from the observation deck. Arrive half an hour before sunset for the best balance of natural and artificial light, and bring a tripod. The skyscraper immediately in front of the *terraço* is Oscar Niemeyer's **Edifício Copan** ⓘ *Av Ipiranga 200, not open to the public though some visitors are allowed to go to the terraço at discretion of security*; built in 1951 in a spate of design by the architect which also included the nearby **Edifício Montreal** ⓘ *Av Ipiranga at Cásper Líbero*, and the **Edifício Califórnia** ⓘ *R Barão de Itapetininga*.

A 10-minute walk east of Praça da República along Rua 24 de Maio (at the north east extreme of the Praça da República), brings you back into the main part of the city centre and Metrô Anhangabaú, via the ugly, wedding-cake **Teatro Municipal Opera House** and the **Viaduto do Chá** steel bridge riding over the small, dirty Vale de Anhangabaú park and the Avenida 23 de Maio and 9 de Julho highways.

Luz and north of the centre

Luz → *Metrô Luz & Tiradentes*

Some of São Paulo's finest museums are to be found a few kilometres north of the city centre in the neighbourhood of Luz. The area is dominated by two striking 19th and early 20th-century railway stations, the **Estação da Luz** ⓘ *Praça da Luz 1, T0800- 550121 for information on suburban trains,* and **Estação Julio Prestes** ⓘ *Praça Julio Prestes 51*. The former marked the realisation of a dream for O Ireneu Evangelista de Sousa, the Visconde de Mauá, who was Brazil's first industrialist. A visit to London in the 1840s convinced de Sousa that Brazil's future lay in rapid industrialization – a path he followed with the founding of an ironworks employing some 300 workers from England and Scotland. It made him a millionaire and in 1854 he opened his first railway – designed and run by the British. It linked Jundiaí in the heart of the São Paulo coffee region with Santos on the coast via what was then the relatively small city of São Paulo. The grandness of the Estação de Luz station, which was completed in 1900, attests to the fact that the city quickly grew wealthy by exploiting its position at the railway junction. By the time the Estação Julio Prestes was built, Britannia no longer ruled the railways. This station was modelled on Grand Central and Penn in New York. In 1999 the enormous 1000-sq-m grand hall was converted into the **Sala São Paulo** ⓘ *Praça Julio Prestes 51, T011-3337 5414, for details of shows see www.guiasp.com.br or look in a copy of Veja*, the city's premier classical music venues and home to Brazil's best orchestra, the Orquestra Sinfônica do Estado de São Paulo.

The city's finest collection of Brazilian art collection lies 100 m from the Estação da Luz in the **Pinacoteca do Estado** ⓘ *Praça da Luz 2, T011-3229 9844, Tue-Sun 1000- 1800, US$3, excellent museum shop and café*. Here you will find works by Brazilian artists from the colonial and imperial eras, together with paintings by the founders of Brazilian modernism, such as Lasar Segall, Tarsila do Amaral, Candido Portinari and Alfredo Volpi. The gallery also contains sculpture by Rodin, Victor Brecheret and contemporary works by artists such as the Nipo-Brazilian painter Tomie Ohtake. The excellent photography gallery in the basement displays some of the world's greatest black and white photographers, many of whom are from Brazil. The museum overlooks the Parque da Luz, a green space dotted with modernist sculpture. Take care here after dark.

The Pinacoteca's sister gallery, the **Estação Pinacoteca** ⓘ *Largo General Osório 66, T011-3337 0185, daily 1000-1730, US$2, free on Sat,* is just over 500 m west of the Pinacoteca along Rua Mauá, next to the Estação Julio Prestes. It houses 200 of the country's finest modernist paintings from the archive of the Fundação José e Paulina Nemirovsky, including further key pieces by Tarsila do Amaral, Emiliano Di Cavalcanti, Portinari Anita Malfatti, Victor Brecheret and Lasar Segall. International art includes Chagall, Picasso and Braque. There is an excellent air-conditioned café.

Luz's other excellent museum is the **Museu de Arte Sacra** ⓘ *Av Tiradentes 676, 400 m north of the Pinacoteca, next to Tiradentes Metrô, T011-3227 7687, http://artesacra.sarasa.com.br, Mon-Fri 1000-1700, Sat and Sun 1000-1900, US$2*. Housed in a functioning Conceptionist monastery, parts of which date from 16th century, it is a haven of peace. Displays include works by many of Brazil's masters, including Francisco Xavier de Brito who brought baroque to Brazil, his pupil, Aleijadinho, who carved Minas Gerais's most exquisite churches, Mestre Valentim, who was responsible for some of the finest work in Rio's churches, and paintings by Mestre (Manoel da Costa) Athayde, one of the country's most important 19th-century artists. There is also a haunting Afro-Brazilian São Bento (with blue eyes) and an extraordinarily detailed 18th-century Neapolitan nativity crib comprising almost 2000 pieces; it is the most important of its kind outside Italy.

The Revolution will not be bossa nova

Forget bossa electronica, MPB, samba funk and the rest. The most exciting musical movement in Brazil by far is Brazilian rap. Don't for a minute think it is imitation USA. This is genuine protest music poured out in a range of Brazilian styles and infused not only with anger and outrage but also with hope and the possibility of real change. It is irresistibly funky, thick with the rhythms of samba, maracatú, capoeira, and samba rock. And unlike the cosy middle class tropicalismo of Caetano Veloso it comes from the heart of the country – from the innumerable, innumerate majority, the marginalized of the urban shantytowns or *favelas*.

Rappers from Brazil's vast poor underclass use music to declaim their country's great social divide, its racial injustice and corrupt politicians. They sing of living conditions that make Detroit's 8 Mile look like Rodeo Drive. In the words of Racionais MCs: '60% of youth in the poor suburbs without criminal records have already suffered police violence; three of every four people killed by the police are black; in Brazilian Universities only 2% of students are black; every four hours, a young black person dies violently in São Paulo'.

Solidarity born out of this increased awareness has led to the formation of community organizations or crews who dedicate themselves to various art forms from MC poetry to graffiti and dance and increasingly to community service work. Community projects like Grupo Afro Reggae in Rio and A Casa do Hip-Hop in São Paulo now function in most *favelas* and peripheral poor areas in Brazil's big cities offering educational workshops, classes, free concerts, and libraries. They are succeeding where government has failed – bringing many young people out of the drug trade into music.

For a taste of Brazilian rap buy a CD by Racionais MCs, Rappin' Hood, Afro Reggae or Marcelo D2.

Further afield, the **Memorial da América Latina** ⓘ *Av Mário de Andrade 664, next to Barra Funda Metrô station, T011-3823 9611, www.memorial.org.br, Tue-Fri 0900-2100, Sat 0900-1800, Sun 1000-1800, free*, was designed by Oscar Niemeyer and built in March 1989. Inside, under a glass floor, is a relief map of Central and South America. As well as a permanent exhibition of handicrafts from all over Latin America, there is a photo library, books, magazines, newspapers and films shown on video.

A few blocks west is **SESC Pompeia** ⓘ *R Clélia 93*, a sports and arts complex with a library designed by Lina Bo Bardi 1982-1986. It is a vibrant place, with a theatre, exhibitions, workshops, restaurant and café, as well as areas for sunbathing and watching television.

Avenida Paulista, Liberdade and Jardins

Liberdade → *Metrô Liberdade*

Liberdade was the first centre for the Japanese community in São Paulo; a city with more ethnic Japanese than any outside Japan. It lies directly south of the Praça da Sé but can easily be reached on foot. There are all manner of Asian shops selling everything from woks to manga and the streets are illuminated by lights designed like Japanese lanterns. A market selling Asian produce and food is held every Sunday in the Praça da Liberdade and there are many excellent Japanese restaurants (see Eating, page 196).

The **Museu da Imigração Japonesa** ⓘ *R São Joaquim 381, 3rd floor, T011-279 5465, Tue-Sun 1330-1730, US$3,* in the Japanese-Brazilian cultural centre is a modern, well-kept little museum with exhibitions telling the story of the Japanese migration to Brazil, including reconstructions of early Japanese Brazilian houses, artefacts and information panels. All are in Portuguese.

Avenida Paulista

➔ *Metrô Vergueiro or Paraíso for the southeastern end of Paulista. Trianon-MASP for MASP. Consolação for Jardins.*

Immediately southwest of the Centro Histórico, **Avenida Paulista,** is lined by skyscrapers and thick with six lanes of cars. It is one of São Paulo's classic postcard shots and locals like to compare it to Fifth Avenue in New York. In truth, it's more commercial and lined with functional buildings, most of which are unremarkable individually and awe-inspiring as a whole.

The avenue was founded in 1891 by the Uruguayan engineer Joaquim Eugênio de Lima, who wanted to build a Paulistano Champs D'Elysee. After he built a mansion on Avenida Paulista, many coffee barons followed suit and by the early 20th century,

Paulista had become the city's most fashionable promenade. The mansions and the rows of stately trees that sat in front of them were almost all demolished in the 1940s and 1950s to make way for ugly offices and in the 1980s these were in turn demolished as banks and multinationals established their headquarters here.

The highlight of Avenida Paulista is **Museu de Arte de São Paulo (MASP)** ⓘ *Av Paulista 1578, T011-3251 5644, www.masp.uol.com.br, Tue-Sun 1100-1800, US$5*. This is the most important and extraordinary gallery in the southern hemisphere, preserving some of Europe's greatest paintings. If it were in the US or Europe it would be as busy as the Prado or the Guggenheim, but here, aside from the occasional noisy group of schoolchildren, the gallery is invariably deserted. Even at weekends, visitors can stop and stare at a Rembrandt or a Velazquez at their leisure. France gets star-billing, with 11 Renoirs, 70 Degas, and a stream of works by Monet, Manet, Cezanne, Toulouse- Lautrec and Gauguin. Renaissance Italy is represented by a Raphael Resurrection, an impeccable Bellini and a whole series of exquisite late-15th-century icons. The remaining walls are adorned with paintings by Bosche, Goya, Van Dyck, Turner, Constable and many others, cherry-picked from post-War Europe.

On Sunday, an antiques fair is held in the open space beneath the museum, see Shopping page 200. Opposite MASP is the **Parque Tenente Siqueira Campos** ⓘ *R Peixoto Gomide 949 and Av Paulista, daily 0700-1830*, also known as Parque Trianon, covering two blocks on either side of Alameda Santos. It is a welcome, luxuriant, green area located in what is now the busiest part of the city. The vegetation includes native plants typical of the Mata Atlântica. Next to the park is the smaller Praça Alexandre de Gusmão.

Jardins

Immediately west of Paulista, an easy 10-minute walk from Consolação Metro along Rua Haddock Lobo, is the plush neighbourhood of Jardins. There are no sights of note but this is by far the most pleasant area to stay in São Paulo. It is also the best place for shopping (see page 200) and has excellent casual and fine dining (see page 196).

Parque do Ibirapuera

The **Parque do Ibirapuera** ⓘ *entrance on Av Pedro Álvares Cabral, daily 0600-1730*, was designed by architect Oscar Niemeyer and landscape artist Roberto Burle Marx for the city's fourth centenary in 1954. It is the largest of the very few green spaces in central São Paulo and its shady woodlands, lawns and lakes offer a breath of fresher air in a city that has only 4.6 sq m of vegetation per inhabitant.

The park is also home to a number of museums and monuments and some striking Oscar Niemeyer buildings that were designed in the 1950s but are still being built today. These include the **Oca** ⓘ *Portão 3, open for exhibitions*, a brilliant white polished concrete dome, built in homage to an indigenous Brazilian roundhouse. It stages major international art exhibitions and has an auditorium shaped like a giant wedge. The **Bienal buildings** ⓘ *Portão 3, open for exhibitions*, are also by Niemeyer and house the city's flagship fashion and art events: **São Paulo fashion week** and the **Art Bienal**, the most important events of their kind in the southern hemisphere. A **sculpture garden** separates the Bienal from the Oca. And this garden is watched over by **O Museu de Arte Moderna (MAM)** ⓘ *Portão 3, T011-5549 9688, www.mam.org.br, Tue, Wed, Fri 1200-1800, Thu 1200-2200, Sat and Sun 1000-1800, US$2*. This small museum showcases the best Brazilian contemporary art in temporary exhibitions. There is always something worth seeing here and the gallery has an excellent restaurant. MAM is linked by a covered walkway to the **Museu Afro-Brasil** ⓘ *Portão 10, T011-5579 0593, Wed-Sun 1000-1800, free*, which lies inside Niemeyer's spectacular, stilted **Pavilhão Manoel de Nobrega** building and devotes more than 12,000 sq m to a celebration and exploration of black Brazilian culture. As well as exhibitions, the museum has regular film showings and musical, dance, and theatrical events.

A few hundred metres to the west of here, on the shores of the artificial lake, the **Planetário e Museu de Astronomia (Planetarium)** ⓘ *Portão 10, T011-5575 5206, Sat and Sun 1200-1800, US$5,* was restored in 2006 and is now one of the most impressive in Latin America. Shows are in Portuguese.

Less than 100 m to the south, is the **Pavilhão Japonês** ⓘ *Portão 10, T011-5573 6453, Sat-Sun 1000-1700, free except for exhibitions.* The building and gardens were designed in strict adherence to Japanese aesthetic principles, and materials were imported from Japan. The pavilion on the lower floor has an exhibition space devoted to Japanese-Brazilian and Japanese culture and a traditional Japanese tearoom upstairs.

The park also has a running track, football pitches and hosts regular concerts on Sundays. Those seeking something quieter on a Sunday can borrow a book from the portable library and read it in the shade of the Bosque da Leitura or 'reading wood'. Bicycles can be hired in the park (US$3 per hour).

Ibirapuera also has a few monuments of note. **O Monumento as Bandeiras**, which sits on the northern edge of the park, is a brutalist tribute to the marauding and bloodthirsty slave traders or *bandeirantes* who opened up the interior of Brazil. It was created by Brazil's foremost 20th-century sculptor, Victor Brecheret. The **Obelisco aos Héroes de 32**, on the eastern edge of the park, is a monumental Cleopatra's needle built in honour of the Paulistano rebels who died in 1932 when the dictator Getúlio Vargas crushed resistance to his Estado Novo regime.

Further afield

Cidade Universitária

Instituto Butantã/Butantã Snake Farm and Museum ⓘ *Av Dr Vital Brasil 1500, T011-813 7222, Tue-Sun 0900-1700, US$1,* on the university campus is one of the most popular tourist attractions in São Paulo. The snakes are milked for their poison six times a day and the antidotes made from the venom have greatly reduced deaths from snakebite in Brazil. The centre also deals with spider and scorpion venom, has a small hospital and is a biomedical research institute. Visitors are not likely to see the venom being milked, but there is a museum of poisonous animals, which is well organized and educational, with explanations in Portuguese and English. To get there from Praça da República take the bus marked 'Butantã' or 'Cidade Universitária' (Nos 701U or 792U) along Avenida Paulista, and ask to be let out at Instituto Butantã.

In the Prédio Novo da Reitoria, the **Museu de Arte Contemporâneo (MAC)** ⓘ *T011-3818 3039, Tue-Sat 1200- 1800, Sun 1000-1800, free,* has an important and beautifully presented collection of Brazilian and European modern art, with pieces by Braque, Picasso, Modigliani, Matisse and Tarsila do Amaral. Also in the university is the **Museu de Arqueologia e Etnologia (MAE)** ⓘ *R Reitoria 1466, T011-3812 4001,* with a collection of Amazonian and ancient Mediterranean material.

On the west bank of the Rio Pinheiros, just southeast of the campus, is the palatial **Jóquei Clube (Jockey Club)** ⓘ *Av Lineu de Paula Machado 1263, T011-816 4011,* a racecourse in the Cidade Jardim area. Race meetings are held on Monday and Thursday at 1930 and on weekends at 1430. The racecourse is easily accessible by bus (Butantã from República, among others). It has a **Museu do Turfe** ⓘ *Av Lineu de Paula Machado 1263, T011-816 4011, Tue-Sun, closed Sat and Sun mornings.*

Parque da Independência

In the suburb of Ipiranga (a Tupi-Guarani word meaning 'red clay'), 5½ km southeast of the city centre, the **Parque da Independência** contains the famous **Monumento à Independência** to commemorate the declaration of Brazilian Independence. Beneath the monument is the **imperial chapel** ⓘ *Tue-Sun 1300-1700,* containing the tomb of the first emperor, Dom Pedro I, and Empress

Leopoldina. The monument was the second to be built to commemorate the centenary of Independence in 1922. The little house of **Casa do Grito** ⓘ *Tue-Sun 0930-1700*, is a replica of the house where Dom Pedro I spent the night before his famous Cry of Ipiranga, 'Independence or Death', which declared Brazil's separation from Brazil (see Background, page 677). At the time when Independence was declared, Ipiranga was outside the city's boundaries, in an area where bricks were made, on the main trade route between Santos and São Paulo.

The **Museu Paulista** ⓘ *Tue-Sun 0900-1645, www.mp.usp.br. US$1*, is housed in a huge palace at the top of the park. The original building, later altered, was the first monument to Independence. The museum contains old maps, traditional furniture, collections of old coins, religious art and rare documents, and has a department of indigenous ethnology. Behind the museum is the **Horto Botânico/Ipiranga Botanical Garden** ⓘ *Tue-Sun 0900-1700*, and the **Jardim Francês**, designed as a garden for plant study, now a recreational area. There is a light and sound show on Brazilian history in the park on Wednesday, Friday and Saturday at 2030. To get there, take either bus No 478P (Ipiranga–Pompéia for return) from Ana Rosa, or take bus No 4612 from the Praça da República.

Parque do Estado (Jardim Botânico)

This large park housing the botanical and zoological gardens is 15 km south of the centre at **Água Funda** ⓘ *Av Miguel Estefano, T011-3031 3687*. The **Jardim Botânico** ⓘ *T011-5584 6300, Wed-Sun 0900-1700*, has a vast garden esplanade surrounded by magnificent stone porches, with lakes and trees and places for picnics, and a very fine orchid farm worth seeing during the flowering season (November to December). Over 19,000 different kinds of orchids are cultivated. There are orchid exhibitions in April and November. The astronomical observatory nearby is open to the public on Thursday afternoons. Howler monkeys, guans and toco toucans can be seen here towards the end of the day. To get there take the Metrô to São Judas on the Jabaquara line, then take a bus.

Burle Marx Park ⓘ *Av Dona Helena Pereira de Moraes 200, daily 0700-1900*, was designed by the famous landscape designer Burle Marx. It is the only place in the city where you can walk along trails in the mata Atlântica (Atlantic rainforest).

Excursions from São Paulo

Santo Amaro Dam (Old Lake) and Interlagos

The **Brazilian Grand Prix** is staged at Interlagos, www.fasp-net.com.br, overlooking a vast artificial lake set in remnant forest. Information on races is available from the tourist office or visit www.guiasp.com.br. ▸▸ *See box, page 203, for more on the Brazilian Grand Prix.*

Paranapiacaba

This tiny 19th-century town, nestled in the cloudforest of the Serra do Mar about 50 km southeast of São Paulo, was built by English railway workers who constructed the São Paulo–Santos railway. Almost all of the houses are made of wood and many look like they belong in suburban Surrey. There is a small railway museum and a handful of little pousadas and restaurants. ▸▸ *See Transport, page 204.*

Embu

This colonial town, 28 km southwest of São Paulo, has become a centre for artists and craftsmen. The town itself is on a hill, which is surrounded by industry and modern developments; the colonial centre is quite small. Many of the old houses are brightly coloured and most contain arts, furniture, souvenir or antiques shops. To get to Embu take a São Paulo–Pinheiros bus from Clínicas, which takes the main highway to Embu (40 minutes, US$0.80). Alight at Largo 21 de Abril in Embu. To return to São Paulo, walk up Rua da Matriz from 21 de Abril, turn left down Avenida Junior, then left again on Rua Solano Trindade to a junction where the buses stop.

Campos do Jordão → *Phone code: 012. Colour map 5, A6. Population: 38,000.*

This tacky mountain resort between Rio de Janeiro and São Paulo, 1628 m high in the Serra da Mantiqueira, is full of very ugly mock-Alpine hotels set in denuded hills. Although it is popular with Paulistanos there is little reason to come here except perhaps for the classical music and dance festivals in June and July. Walking is far better in Itatiaia or Visconde de Mauá.

The **tourist office** ⓘ *T011-262 2755, F262 4100*, is in the alpine-looking gateway to the city, the **Portal da Cidade**. There are plenty of hotels and restaurants on and around the main street and banks with ATMs and money-changing services. Regular buses run to and from São Paulo.

Sleeping

São Paulo has the best hotels in Latin America and by far the best in Brazil. There are designer hotels that Ian Shrager would be proud of and business towers that combine all the requisite facilities with an almost personal touch. However, rooms are expensive and while there are some reasonable budget options they are not in the best locations. Sampa (as São Paulo is affectionately known) is a place where you have to spend money to enjoy yourself. The best places to stay are Jardins (the most affluent area) and Paulista (close to one of the business centres). Business travellers will find good hotels on Faria Lima and Av Luis Carlos Berrini (in the new centre in the south of the city). Some of the better hostels are in seemingly random locations or are in the seedy centre, which is an undesirable place to be at night.

The youth hostel association, **Associação Paulista de Albergues da Juventude**, is at R 7 de Abril 386, Conj 22, T/F011-258 0388, www.alberguesp.com.br.

Centro histórico *p184, map p184*

AL Othon Palace, R Líbero Badaró 190, T011-3291 5000, www.othon.com.br. The only business hotel of quality in the Triângulo; in a 1950s heritage building.

A Gran Corona, Basílio da Gama 101, T011-214 0043, F214 4503, in a small street. Comfortable, good services and restaurant. Warmly recommended.

B Itamarati, Av Dr Vieira de Carvalho 150, T011-222 4133, F222 1878. Good location, safe. Highly recommended and very popular.

Liberdade *p189*

B Banri, R Galvão Bueno 209, T011-270 8877, F278 9225. Good. Chinese owners. Recommended.

E Ikeda, R dos Estudantes. With breakfast, shared bath, quiet. Both near Metrô station.

Av Paulista and Jardins *p191, map p190*

LL Emiliano, R Oscar Freire 384, T011-3069 4369, www.emiliano.com.br. The best suites in the city – bright, light and beautifully designed with attention to every detail. No pool but a relaxing small spa. Excellent Italian restaurant, location and service.

LL Fasano, R Vittorio Fasano 88, T011-3896 4077, www.fasano.com.br. One of the world's great hotels, which looks like a modernist gentleman's club designed by Armani. There's a fabulous pool and the best formal haute-cuisine restaurant in Brazil. The lobby bar is a wonderful place to arrange a meeting. Excellent position in Jardins.

LL L'Hotel, Av Campinas 266, T/F011-283 0500. Part of the **Roteiros de Charme** group, see page 50. Suites decorated in mock-French style, convenient for Paulista.

LL Renaissance, Alameda Santos 2233 (at Haddock Lobo), T011-3069 2233, www.marriott.com/property/propertypage/Sãobr. The best business hotel off Av Paulista with standard business rooms, a good spa, gym, pool and 2 squash courts. There are excellent business and conference facilities including a full business centre, secretarial services and airline booking.

LL Unique, Av Brigadeiro Luis Antonio 4700, Jardim Paulista, T011-3055 4700, www.hotelunique.com. The most ostentatiously designed hotel in the country: an enormous half moon on concrete uprights with curving floors, circular windows and beautiful use of space and light. The bar on the top floor is São Paulo's answer to the LA Sky Bar and is filled with the beautiful and famous after 2130. Coldplay stayed here on their last world tour.

LL-AL George V, R Jose Maria Lisboa 1000, T011-3088 9822, www.george-v.com.br. Proper apartments of 60-180 sq m, with living rooms, fully equipped kitchens (with dishwashers and washing machines), huge bathrooms, closets and comprehensive business services. Shared facilities include sauna, indoor pool and modern gym. Special deals through the website.

A Golden Tulip Park Plaza, Alameda Lorena 360, T011-3058 4055, www.parkplaza.com.br. Modern tower with apartments of 30 sq m, spa and well-equipped gym. Good value.

A Transamérica Ópera, Alameda Lorena 1748, T011-3062 2666, www.transamericaflats.com.br. Conservatively decorated but elegant and well-maintained modern flats of 42 sq m in a tower between the heart of Jardins and Av Paulista. At the bottom end of this price range.

B Landmark Residence, Alameda Jaú 1607, T011-3082 8677, www.landmarkresidence.com.br. Spacious apartments with hotel catalogue furnishings and a shared gym, gardens and modest business centre. Good location.

B-C Ibis São Paulo Paulista, Av Paulista 2355, T011-3523 3000, www.accorhotels.com.br. Great value. Modern, business-standard rooms with a/c in a tower right on Av Paulista. Cheaper at weekends. Online reservations.

C Formule 1, R Vergueiro 1571, T011-5085 5699, www.accorhotels.com.br. Another great value business-style hotel, with apartments big enough for 3 (making this an **E** option for those in a group). Right next to Paraíso Metrô in a safe area. Rooms have a/c.

C Paulista Garden, Alameda Lorena 21, T/F011-3885 8498, www.paulistagardenhotel.com.br. Small, simple rooms with a/c, cable TV and fridges. Close to Ibirapuera Park.

C Pousada Dona Zilah, Alameda Franca 1621, Jardim Paulista, T011-3062 1444, www.zilah.com. Little pousada in a renovated colonial house with plain but well-maintained rooms and common areas decorated with thought and a personal touch. Excellent location, bike rental and generous breakfast included. Triple rooms available (**D**).

D-F Pousada dos Franceses, R dos Franceses 100, Bela Vista, T011-3262 4026, www.pousadadosfranceses.com.br. Price per person. A plain little pousada 10 mins' walk from Brigadeiro Metrô, with dorms, doubles and singles. Free internet, TV room and breakfast included.

Further afield *p192, map p182*

Brooklin and the New Centre

This is São Paulo's new business capital. Most hotels are to be found on Av Br Faria Lima and Av Luis Carlos Berrini.

LL-L Grand Hyatt São Paulo, Av das Nações Unidas 13301, T011-6838 1234, www.saopaulo.hyatt.com. A superb business hotel close to Av Luis Carlos Berrini, which successfully fuses corporate efficiency and requisite services with designer cool. Spa, pool, state-of-the-art business centre and marvellous views from the upper-floor suites.

AL-L Blue Tree Towers, Av Brigadeiro Faria Lima 3989, Vila Olímpia, T011-3896 7544, www.bluetree.com.br. Modern business hotel with discreetly designed rooms and excellent service. Ideally positioned for Faria Lima's business district and the restaurants and nightlife of Vila Olímpia and Itaim. Pool, massage, gym, sauna and well-equipped business centre.

Cogonhas and around

D ACE Hostel, R Gastão da Cunha 253, Congonhas airport, T011-5034 2472, www.bedandbreakfast.com.br. Friendly pocket-sized hostel in a brightly painted residential house. Services include TV, DVD and movies, broadband internet, kitchen, laundry book exchange and pick-up. Tours of São Paulo available.

E Primavera, R Mariz e Barros 346, Vila Santa Eulália (bus No 4491 from Parque Dom Pedro in the centre), T011-215 3144. Hostel with cooking and laundry facilities, friendly staff.

E-F Praça da Árvore IYHA, R Pageú 266, Saúde, T011-5071 5148, www.spal

bergue.com.br. Well-kept pousada in a quiet back street. Friendly and helpful. 2 mins from Praça do Arvore Metrô. kitchen, laundry and internet service. Overpriced.

Beyond the city

LL Unique Garden Spa, Estrada 3500, Serra da Cantareira, T011-4486-8724, www.uniquegarden.com.br. The über-cool style of hotel **Unique** (see above) transposed into a natural setting of the Serra da Cantareira subtropical forest, 40 mins north of São Paulo. The buildings are equally impressive, with Ruy Ohtake's iron-grey post-industrial half-moon replaced with a series of Frank Lloyd Wright inspired post-modernist bungalows. The spa treatments are wonderful. Shuttles can be organized through hotel **Unique**.

Eating

Those on a budget can eat to their stomach's content in per kilo places or, if looking for cheaper still, in bakeries (*padarias*). There is one of these on almost every corner. They all serve sandwiches like *Misto Quentes*, *Beirute's* and *Americanos* – delicious Brazilian burgers made from decent meat and served with ham, egg, cheese or salad. They always have good coffee, juices, cakes and set lunches (*almoços*) for a very economical price. Most have a designated seating area, either at the *padaria* bar or in an adjacent room; you aren't expected to eat on your feet as you are in Rio. Restaurants in São Paulo are safe on the stomach. Juices are made with mineral or filtered water.

Centro histórico *p184, map p184*

Restaurants in the old centre tend to be lunchtime only; there are many per kilo options and *padarias*.

TTT Boi na Brasa, R Bento Freitas by Praça da República. Very good meat dishes and *feijoada* at a reasonable price.

TTT Terraço Italia, Av Ipiranga 344, T011-3257 6566. Average and overpriced Italian with the best views in the city. Come for a coffee, although there's a minimum charge of US$10 (for the view).

TT-T Café da Pinacoteca, Pinacoteca Museum, Praça da Luz 2, T011-3326 0350. Portuguese-style café with marble floors and mahogany balconies. Great coffee and cakes.

Liberdade *p189*

TT Gombe, R Tomas Gonzaga 22, T011-3209 8499. Renowned for grilled tuna and various noodle dishes.

TT Sushi Yassu, R Tomas Gonzaga 98, T011-3209 6622. The best of Liberdade's traditional Japanese restaurants. Excellent sushi/sashimi combinations.

Av Paulista and Jardins *p191, map p190*

TTT Charlô Bistro, R Barão de Capanema 440 (next to **DOM**), Jardins, T011-3088 6790, with another branch at the high-society set **Jockey Club**, Av Lineu de Paula Machado 1263, Cidade Jardim, T011-3034 3682. One of the premier VIP and old family haunts in the city. Run by a scion of one of the city's establishment families. Decked out in tribute to a Paris brasserie and with food to imitate.

TTT DOM, R Barão de Capanema 549, Jardins, T011-3088 0761. São Paulo's evening restaurant of the moment. Alex Attala has won the coveted *Veja* best chef of the year award twice. Contemporary food, fusing Brazilian ingredients with French and Italian styles and served in a large open modernist dining room to the sharply dressed.

TTT East, Al Jaú, 1303, Jardins, T011-3081 1160, www.eastrestaurante.com.br. Asian-Brazilian fusion cooking by Helen Assunção, formerly of **E&O** in Notting Hill. Superior cocktails, including vodka Martinis made with the best vodka in the city, and a carefully designed, intimate atmosphere.

TTT Fasano, **Hotel Fasano** (see Sleeping), R Fasano, T011- 3896 4077, www.fasano.com.br. Long regarded as the best restaurant for gourmets in São Paulo. A huge choice of modern Italian and French cooking, modelled on the best of Milan from chef Salvatore Loi. An intimate space in a magnificent room where diners have their own low-lit booths and are served by flocks of black-tie waiters. Exemplary wine list. Formal dress.

TTT Figueira Rubaiyat, R Haddock Lobo 1738, T011-3063 3888. The most interesting of the **Rubaiyat** restaurant group, with steaks prepared by Argentinian chef, Francis Mallman. Very lively for lunch on a Sun and remarkable principally for the space: open walled, light and airy and under a huge tropical fig tree.

TTT Gero, R Haddock Lobo 1629, T011-3064 0005. Fasano's version of a French bistro, but serving pasta and light Italian food. Ever-so-casual design by architect Aurelio Martinez Flores and an evening clientele that includes some of the best-known faces in São Paulo high society. Be prepared for a long wait at the bar alongside people who are there to be seen. No reservations.

₸₸₸ **Jun Sakamoto**, R Lisboa 55, Jardins, T011-3088 6019. Japanese with a touch of French. Superb fresh ingredients, some of it flown in especially from Asia and the USA. The dishes of choice are the dégustation menu and the duck breast teppaniyaki.

₸₸₸ **La Tambouille**, Av 9 de Julho 5925, Jardim Europa, T011-3079 6276. The favourite Franco-Italian restaurant of the city's old money society. Chef Andre Fernandes's signature dishes are the saffron linguini with fresh mussels and prawn sauce and the brie ravioli with rocket and pinoli infused with white truffles. Excellent wine list.

₸₸₸ **Mani**, R Joaquim Antunes 210, Pinheiros, T011-3085 4148. Superior light Mediterranean menu, which utilizes Brazilian ingredients and perfectly complements the waistlines of the celebrity crowd. Daniel Redondo and partner Helena Rizzo have worked in Michelin-starred restaurants in Europe.

₸₸₸ **Massimo**, Alameda Santos 1826, Cerqueira Cesar, Jardins, T011-3284 0311. One of São Paulo's longest-established Italian restaurants serving northern Italian food to the city's politicians and business executives. Credit cards are not accepted, despite the costly price.

₸₸ **A Mineira**, Alameda Joaquim Eugenio de Lima 697, Jardins, T011-3283 2349. Self-service Minas food by the kilo. Lots of choice. *Cachaca* and pudding included in the price.

₸₸ **Baalbeck**, Alameda Lorena 1330, Jardins, T011-3088 4820. Lebanese cooking vastly superior to its setting. Great falafel.

₸₸ **Fran's Café**, open 24 hrs, Av Paulista 358, and all over the city. The Brazilian equivalent of Starbuck's, with a menu of light eats.

₸₸ **Kayomix**, R da Consolação 3215, Jardins, T011-3082 2769. Brazilian-oriental fusions like salmon taratare with shimeji and shitake.

₸₸ **Namesa**, R da Consolação 2967, Jardins, T011-3088 7498. Great little gourmet snacks such as wild boar pâté with pistachio pesto, created by the chef from DOM.

₸₸ **Restaurante do MASP**, Av Paulista 1578, T011-3253 2829. In the basement of the museum, reasonably priced standards like lasagne and stroganoff, often accompanied by live music.

₸₸ **Sattva**, R da Consolação 2904, Jardins, T011-3083 6237. Light vegetarian curries, stir fries, salads and pastas.

₸₸ **Sujinho**, R da Consolação 2068, Consolação, T011-3256 8026. South American beef in large portions. Other carnivorous options available.

₸ **Cheiro Verde**, R Peixoto Gomide 1413, Jardins, T011-289 6853 (lunchtimes only). Hearty vegetarian food, such as vegetable crumble in gorgonzola sauce and wholewheat pasta with buffalo mozzarella and sundried tomato.

Further afield *p192, map p182*

Vila Olímpia, Moema and Itaim

These areas, south of the centre, have ultra-trendy restaurants with beautiful people posing in beautiful surroundings. We include only a handful of the best.

₸₸₸ **348 Parrilla Porteña**, R Comendador Miguel Calfat, 348, Vila Olímpia, T011-3849 2889. An Argentinian restaurant with the best steak in the country from the choicest cuts available only on export from Buenos Aires. The *ojo del bife* cuts like brie and collapses in the mouth like watered chocolate. The accompanying wines are equally superb, especially the 2002 Cheval dos Andes. Great, unpretentious atmosphere.

₸₸₸ **Boo**, R Viradouro 132, Itaim Bibi, T011-3078 7477. Opposite **Kosushi**, with a carbon-copy crowd, Luso-Asian cooking and a beautiful garden setting.

₸₸₸ **Kosushi**, R Viradouro 139, Itaim Bibi, T011-3167 7272. The first of São Paulo's chic Japanese restaurants which began life in Liberdade and is now housed in a beautifully designed Asian modernist space. Full of the famous sitting to be seen. Great sushi combinations.

₸₸₸ **Parigi**, R Amauri 275, Itaim, T011-3167 1575. One of the premier places to be seen; celebrity couples come here for intimate public-view Franco-Italian dining. The menu also has classical French dishes like *coq au vin*. Attractive dining room, beautifully lit, and decked out in lush dark wood.

Bars and clubs

São Paulo has more nocturnal panache than Rio. There is great live music on most nights of the week. Large concert venues such as **Pacaembu stadium** host the likes of U2 or Ivete Sangalo. Medium-sized venues such as **Credicard Hall**, are played by acts like Caetano Veloso, Gilberto Gil and Chico Buarque. Smaller venues include SESC's (cultural centres with excellent concert halls), and are found in Vila Mariana and Pompéia. They host smaller, classy artists like Otto, Naná Vasconcelos, João Bosco and Seu Jorge. It is also worth checking out **Bourbon Street**, **Urbano** and **Grazie a Dio** for emerging acts such as Tutti Baê and Mombojó.

DJs like Marky and the sadly deceased Suba have made the São Paulo club scene world famous. Marky is resident DJ at the **Lov.E Club** (see below). Fri's biggest party is **Vapour at the Prime Club** (see below). Other fashionable spots include **30Hz at Jive**, Alameda Barros, 376, Higienópolis on Sat, T011-3824 0097, and **The Bass**, R Vitória 810, City Centre, T011-3337 1915, on Sun.

The city is dotted with bars serving cold lager beer or *chope* (pronounced 'chopee'). Almost all serve food and many have live music. You won't have too much difficulty finding one, especially if you head to Vila Madalena, Itaim or Vila Olimpía. Beer and snacks are also available at the bar in any *padaria* (bakery).

Av Paulista and Jardins *p191, map p190*

Jardins has a few bars, the most famous of which are in the better hotels.

Apollinari, R Oscar Freire 1206, T011-3061 9965. Smart restaurant-bar frequented by the city's glitterati.

Bar Balcão, R Doutor Melo Alves 150, T011-3063 6091. After-work meeting place, very popular with young professionals and media types who gather on either side of the long low wooden bar, which winds its way around the room like a giant snake.

Barretto, in the **Fasano Hotel** (see Sleeping). Feels rather conservative with its heavy dark wood, mirrors and cool live bossa jazz. The crowd is mostly the Cuban cigar type with a sprinkling of the tanned and toned, in figure-enhancing designer labels.

Emiliano Bar, Hotel Emiliano (see Sleeping). Similar crowd to **Skye** (see below) but despite its popularity, it can feel like a sterile corridor rather than an intimate space. DJs play on Fri nights.

Finnegan's Pub, R Cristiano Viana 358, Pinheiros, T011-3062 3232, www.finnegan.com.br. One of São Paulo's Irish bars; every city has one. This one is actually run and owned by an Irishman and is very popular with ex-pats.

Skye, the rooftop bar at the hotel **Unique**. Another fashionable spot with a definite door policy. The views of glistening skyscrapers pocked by patches of green and red tile are wonderful.

Further afield *p192, map p182*

Vila Madalena/Pinheiros

Vila Madalena and adjacent Pinheiros lie just northeast of Jardins. A taxi from Jardins is about US$7; there is also a Metrô station, but this closes by the time the bars get going. These suburbs are the favourite haunts of São Paulo 20-somethings, more hippy chic than Itaim, less stuffy than Jardins. This is the best part of town for live Brazilian music and uniquely Brazilian close dances such as *forró*; as opposed to international club sounds. It can feel grungy and informal but is buzzing. The liveliest streets are Aspicuelta and Girassol and the current bars of choice are **Grazie A Dio!** and **A Marcenaria**.

A Marcenaria, R Fradique Coutinho 1378, T011-3032 9006, www.amarcenaria.com.br. This is the bar of choice for the young, single and hippy chic who gather here from around 2130, until the dancefloor fills up at und 2300.

Bourbon Street, R dos Chanés 127, Moema, T011-5095 6100, www.bournbon street.com.br. Great little club with acts like funkster Tutti Bae and international acts like BB KIng.

AMP Galaxy, R Fradique Coutinho 352, T011-3085 7867, www.ampgalaxy.com.br. A fusion of a retro 1950s bar and café, clothing boutique and, after 2300, packed dancefloor with alternate live music and DJs. The crowd is 20-something and bohemian.

Grazie a Dio, R Girassol, 67, T011-3031 6568, www.grazieadio.com.br. The best bar in Vila Madalena to hear live music – there's a different band every night with samba on Sun. Great for dancing. Always packed.

Five of the best Brazilian cocktails

Agua de coco (coconut milk), good for rehydration, perfect for hangovers.
Caipirinha, the national cocktail made from sugar cane rum, lots of sugar cane firewater (*cachaça*) and fresh limes, strawberries or passion fruit. It tastes as alcoholic as a Bacardi breezer, but packs a punch like a triple whisky. Less mind-blowing are *Caipiroska* and *Caipisakes/Sakirinhas* which are the same but made with vodka or sake.
Suco, fresh juice such as *acerola*, an Amazonian cherry. *Vitaminas* (see below) also contain guarana.
Batida, comprises vodka or *cachaça* with fresh juice and/or condensed milk. *Batidas* with acerola, *maracujá* (passion fruit) or *umbú*, are particularly delicious. A non-alcoholic *batida* is called a *vitamina*.
Açai (pronounced assayear), a fashionable Amazonian fruit drink.

Mood, R Teodoro Sampaio 1109, T011-3060 9010. European-style club with the latest sounds and DJs like Mau Mau and Felipe Venancio.
Posto 6, R Aspicuelta 644, Vila Madalena, T011-3812 7831. An imitation Rio de Janeiro *boteco* with attractive crowds and backdrop of bossa nova and MPB. Busy from 2100.
Urbano R Cardeal Arcoverde 614, Pinheiros, T011-3085 1001, www.urbano.com.br. São Paulo's premiere dance club, modelled on a London club with a lounge bar area, huge dancefloor and a combination of live bands and DJs. Popular with musicians and creative industry 20- and 30-somethings.
Vapour at the Prime Club, R dos Pinheiros 783, Pinheiros, T011-308 7466. Big party on Fri.

Vila Olímpia Moema and Itaim

This area, just south of Ibirapuera and north of the new centre, is about US$10 by taxi from Jardins and US$15 from the Centre, but well worth the expense of getting here. It is packed with street-corner bars, which are great for a browse. The bars here, although informal, have a style of their own, lively and varied crowds and decent service. The busiest streets for a bar wander are R Atilio Inocenti near the junction of Av Juscelino Kubitschek and Av Brigadeiro Faria Lima, Av Hélio Pellegrino and R Araguari, which runs behind it.
Columbia, upstairs, R Estados Unidos 1570. Lively. **Hell's Club** downstairs. Opens 0400, techno, wild.
Liquid Lounge, Av Hélio Pellegrino 801, Vila Olímpia, T011-3849 5014, www.liquid lounge.com.br. Pulsing European-style dance club with a smart bar area. Always busy.
Lov.E Club and Lounge, R Pequetita 189, Vila Olímpia, T011-3044 1613. Trance, house, drum 'n' bass; big-name DJs. The most famous night is Thu's **Vibe**, which is played by the top local and international Djs. This year Marcus Intalex, Calibre, Bryan Gee and E-Z Rollers played there.
Na Mata Café, R da Mata 70, Itaim, T011- 3079 0300, www.namata.com.br. Popular flirting and pick-up spot for 20- and 30-something rich kids who gyrate in the dark dance room to a variety of Brazilian and European dance tunes and select live bands.

Entertainment

São Paulo *p178, maps 182, p184 and p190*
For listings of concerts, theatre, museums, galleries, cinema, bars and restaurants visit www.guiasp.com.br, or look in the *Guia da Folha* section of *Folha de São Paulo*, and the *Veja São Paulo* section of the weekly news magazine *Veja*.

Art galleries

Casa da Fazenda, Morumbi, exhibits in 19th-century house. **Espaço Cultural Ena Beçak**, R Oscar Freire 440. **Galeria São Paulo**, R Estados Unidos 1456.

Cinema

Entrance is usually half price on Wed; normal seat price is US$3 in the centre, US$5-6 in R Augusta, Av Paulista and Jardins. There is no shortage of multi-screen cinemas in the city showing the latest releases, eg **Belas Artes**, R da Consolação 2423. There are also cine clubs, eg **Cine SESC**, R Augusta 2075; **Espaço Unibanco**, R Augusta 1470/1475, and cinemas at the **Museu da Imagem e do Som**, **Centro Cultural Itaú** and **Centro Cultural São Paulo**.

Theatre

The **Teatro Municipal**, see Sights, page 187, is used by visiting theatrical and operatic groups, as well as the City Ballet Company and the Municipal Symphony Orchestra who give regular performances. There are several first-class theatres: **Aliança Francesa**, R Gen Jardim 182, Vila Buarque, T011-259 0086. **Itália**, Av Ipiranga 344, T011-257 9092. **Paiol**, R Amaral Gurgel 164, Santa Cecília, T011-221 2462. Free concerts at **Teatro Popular do Sesi**, Av Paulista 1313, T011-284 9787, at midday, under MASP (Mon-Sat).

Festivals and events

São Paulo *p178, maps 182, p184 and p190*

Throughout the year there are countless anniversaries, religious feasts, fairs and exhibitions. To see what's on while you're in town, look in the press or the monthly tourist magazines.

25 Jan Foundation of the city.

Feb Carnaval. *Escolas de samba* parade in the Anhembi Sambódromo. Note that during Carnaval most museums and attractions are closed.

Jun Festas Juninas and the Festa de São Vito, the patron saint of the Italian immigrants.

Sep Festa da Primavera.

Dec Christmas and New Year festivities.

Shopping

São Paulo *p178, maps 182, p184 and p190*

Bookshops

Livrarias Saraiva and Laselva are found in various shopping malls and at airports, sell books in English.

Book Centre, R Gabus Mendes 29, between Basílio da Gama and 7 de Abril (Praça da Republica). Books in English and German.

Cinema Elétrico, R Augusta 973, Centro. Postcards and books on cinema and art.

Duas Cidades, R Bento Freitas 158, near República. Good selection of Brazilian and Spanish-American literature.

Gusto, Gôsto, Gusta, R Augusta 2161. Art books and CDs.

Letraviva, Av Rebouças 1986. Mon-Fri 0900-1830, Sat 0900-1400. Specializes in books and music in Spanish.

Librairie Française, R Barão de Itapetininga 275, ground floor. Wide selection, also at R Prof Atilio Innocenti 920, Jardins.

Livraria Cultura, Av Paulista 2073, loja 153, Conjunto Nacional. New books in English.

Livraria Freebook, R da Consolação 1924. Ring bell for entry, wide collection of art books and imported books in English.

Livraria Kosmos, Av São Luís 258, loja 6. International stock.

Livraria Triângulo, R Barão de Itapetininga 255, loja 23, Centro. Sells books in English.

Sodiler, Shopping Market Place, Av Nações Unidas 13947, Brooklin, loja 121A, floor T.

Sola Cinemateca, R Fradique Coutinho 361. Sell postcards and books on cinema and art.

Fashion stores and boutiques

São Paulo is one of the new hot spots on the global fashion circuit and the designers based here have collections as chic as any in Europe or North America, but at a fraction of the price. Best buys include smart casual day wear, bikinis, shoes, jeans and leather jackets. *Havaiana* flip flops, made famous by Gisele Bundchen and Fernanda Tavares, are around a tenth the price of Europe. The best areas for fashion shopping are Jardins (around R Oscar Freire) and the **Iguatemi shopping centre** (Av Faria Lima). The city's most exclusive shopping emporium is **Daslu**, see below.

Adriana Barra, R Peixoto Gomide, 1801, casa 5, Jardins, T011-3064 3691. Elegantly whimsical clothing in beautiful fabrics displayed in an artsy little boutique.

Ale Ribeiro, R Tupi 564, T011-3667 2323. One of the newest of São Paulo's emerging group of exciting women designers with lush jersey wrap dresses and tops. Has worked for Carlos Miele and Daslu's amongst others.

Alexandre Herchcowitz, R Haddock Lobo 1151, T011-3063 2889. The most famous Brazilian designer, using brightly coloured materials to create avant garde designs strongly influenced by European trends.

Andre Lima, R Dr Cardoso de Mello 474, Vila Olímpia, T011-3849 3444. Another bright new star on the São Paulo fashion scene. André grew up in the Amazon and his collections are light, tropical and sensual.

Daslu, Av Chedid Jafat 131, T011-3841 3000, www.daslu.com.br. This temple to snobbery is worth visiting if only for anthropological reasons. It is the fashion store of choice for South America's high society and it's not uncommon for customers to fly in from Argentina or Mato Grosso on private planes and spend up to US$50,000 in a single shopping spree. Collections include that of **Daslu** itself, alongside Brazilian names like **Ricardo Almeida** and international designers. These sit alongside boutiques selling everything from high-class wines to beautiful coffee-table books.

Fause Haten, Alameda Lorena 1731, Jardins, T011-3081 8685. One of Brazil's most internationally renowned designers who works in laminate plastic, lace, leather, mohair and denim with laminate appliqués, selling through, amongst others, Giorgio Beverly Hills.

Forum, R Oscar Freire 916, Jardins T011-3085 6269, www.forum.com.br. A huge white space attended by beautiful shop assistants helping impossibly thin 20-something Brazilians squeeze into tight, but beautifully cut jeans and other fashion items.

Hotel Lycra, R Oscar Freire 1055, Jardins, T011-3897 4401, www.hotellycra.com. A favourite shopping spot for the Jardins teenybopper set who park their expensive open-top 18th birthday presents outside and pop in to browse the collection from a rotating selection of young, new Brazilian designers.

Iodice, R Oscar Freire 940, T011-3085 9310, and **Shopping Iguatemi**, T011-3813 2622, www.iodice.com.br. Sophisticated and innovative knitwear designs sold abroad in boutiques like **Barney's NYC**.

Lenny, **Shopping Iguatemi**, T011-3032 2663, and R Escobar Ortiz 480, Vila Nova Conceicao, T011-3846 6594, www.lenny.com.br. Rio de Janeiro's premiere swimwear designer and Brazil's current favourite.

Mario Queiroz, R Alameda Franca 1166, T011-3062 3982, www.marioqueiroz.com.br. Casual and elegant clothes with a strong gay element, for 20-something men.

Ocimar Versolato Luxo, Bela Cintra 2190, Jardins and in Shopping Iguatemi. Brazil's foremost and most famous fashion figure made his name in Paris as the creative director of **Lanvin**, and is still based there. He is famous for his uninhibited haute couture evening gowns ('my dresses bear the mark of a country where people are not ashamed of their bodies'), which sell in Paris for around US$15,000. His São Paulo shop sells his range of sexy, flirty, luxury, ready-to-wear clothes and jeans.

Ricardo Almeida, Daslu and Shopping Iguatemi, T011-3812 6947. One of the few Brazilian designers who styles for men. His clothes are a range of dark suits and slick leather jackets aimed at would-be bit-part actors from *The Matrix*.

Rosa Chá, R Oscar Freire 977, T1130812793, and Shop X76, Shopping Iguatemi, T011-3032 3078. The world's best fashion label in designer swimwear. Beautifully cut bikinis in top quality materials.

Shopping Iguatemi, Av Brigadeiro Faria Lima 2232. The leading shopping mall in the city with a healthy representation of most of Brazil's foremost labels.

Victor Hugo, R Oscar Freire 816, T011-3082 1303. Brazil's most fashionable handbag designer.

Walter Rodrigues, R Natingui 690/696, Vila Madalena, T011-3031 8562. Haute couture for women, renowned for evening gowns which are fluid, sensual and very much inspired by the belle époque.

Zoomp, R Oscar Freire 995, T011-3064 1556, Shopping Iguatemi, T011-3032 5372, www.zoomp.com.br. **Zoomp** have been famous for their figure-hugging jeans for nearly 3 decades and have grown to become a nationwide and now international brand.

Handicrafts

São Paulo has no handicrafts tradition but some items from the rest of Brazil can be bought at **Parque Tte Siqueira Campos/Trianon** on Sun from 0900-1700.

Casa dos Amazonas, Av Jurupis 460.
Ceará Meu Amor, R Pamplona 1551, loja 7. Good-quality lace from the northeast.
Galeria Arte Brasileira, Av Lorena 2163, galeria@dialdata.com.br. Good value.
Sutaco, República Metrô station. Handicrafts shop promoting items from the state of São Paulo, Tue-Fri 1000-1900, Sat 1000-1500; there is a showroom at R Augusta 435.

Jewellery

Many shops sell precious stones.
Amsterdam Sauer, has outlets at Av São Luís 29, hotels **Maksoud Plaza** and **Sheraton**, shopping centres Iguatemi, Morumbi, and at the international airport.
H Stern, Praça da República 242, R Augusta 2340, R Oscar Freire 652 and at Iguatemi, Ibirapuera, Morumbi, Paulista and other shopping centres, hotels **Hilton**, **Sheraton** and **Maksoud Plaza**, and at the international airport.

Markets

The '**Hippy Fair**' that used to take place in Praça da República was moved to Tiradentes Metrô station but is not nearly as lively or colourful. **Oriental Fair**, Praça de Liberdade Sun 1000-1900, good for Japanese snacks, plants and some handicrafts, very picturesque, with remedies on sale, tightrope walking, gypsy fortune tellers, etc. Below the Museu de Arte de São Paulo, an **antiques market** takes place Sun 1000-1700. **Av Lorena**, which is one of the upmarket shopping streets off R Augusta in Jardins, has an open-air market on Sun selling fruits and juices. There are flea markets Sun in **Praça Don Orione** (main square of the Bixiga district) and in **Praça Benedito Calixto** (Pinheiros). São Paulo is relatively cheap for film and clothes (especially shoes). The **Ceasa flower market**, Av Doutor Gastão Vidigal 1946, Jaguaré, Tue and Fri 0700-1200, should not be missed.

Photography

Cine Camera Service, R Conselheiro Crispiniano 97, 2nd floor. For repairs to Canon and other makes.

Supermarkets and malls

Typical of modern development are the huge **Iguatemi**, **Ibirapuera** and **Morumbi** shopping centres. They include luxurious cinemas, snack bars and most of the best shops in São Paulo. Other malls include **Paulista** and **Butantã**. On a more humble level are the big supermarkets of **El Dorado** (Av Pamplona 1704) and **Pão de Açúcar** (Praça Roosevelt, near the **Hilton**); the latter is open 24 hrs a day (except Sun).

Activities and tours

São Paulo

Football

The most popular local teams are Corinthians, Palmeiras and São Paulo who generally play in the Morumbi and Pacaembu stadiums.

Golf courses

The following courses are within half an hour's drive from the centre.
Anglo Sports Center, Barretos. 9 holes.
Clube de Campo São Paulo, Reprêsa Guarapiranga, Estr Paralheiros, Km 34. 18 holes.
Clube de Golf de Campinas, Via Anhangüera, Km 108, Campinas. 18 holes.
Guarapiranga Golf e Country, Reprêsa Guarapiranga, Estr Paralheiros, Km 34. 18 holes.
International Golf Club, Via Dutra Km 232, Guaratinguetá. 9 holes.
São Fernando Golf Club, Estr de Cotia, Km 29. There is a lakeside club at Km 50 on the Santos road with 18 holes.
São Francisco Club, Estr de Osasco, Km 15. 9 holes.
São Paulo Golf Club, Praça Dom Francisco Souza 635, Santo Amaro. 18 holes in beautiful surroundings.

Tour operators

São Paulo has several large agencies offering tours around the country.
Ambiental Viagens e Expedições, Av Prudente Morais 344, conj 5, T011-814 8809. Recommended for trips to less well known places. English and Spanish spoken, helpful.
AmEx office in **Hotel Sheraton Mofarrej**, Av Santos 1437, T011-284 3515.
Kontik-Franstur (AmEx representative), R Marconi 71, T011-259 7566.
STB, Av Brig Faria Lima 1713, T011-870 0555. ISIC cards and student discounts.

The Brazilian Grand Prix

Motor racing has had a long and distinguished history in Brazil and the first race day for cars and motorcycles at Interlagos was held on 12 May 1940. The first Brazilian Grand Prix was held there in 1972 and Emerson Fittipaldi won in 1973 driving a Lotus in a time of one hour 43 minutes at an average speed of 183 kmph. He repeated this with an even faster time of one hour 24 minutes the following year in a McLaren and in 1975 another Brazilian, José Carlos Pace (after whom the track is named), won in a Brabham. During the 1980s the race was held at the Jacarepaguá racetrack in Rio de Janeiro where the outspoken Nelson Piquet won twice in 1983 and 1986 with some of the fastest lap times seen on this track.

The race returned to the reformed Interlagos during the 1990s and the legendary Ayrton Senna won here in 1991 and 1993. After his tragic death, owing to a mechanical failure in 1994, Brazilian viewing figures for motor racing fell drastically. Today, however, Formula One is enjoying a resurgence in popularity. Rubens Barrichello, who partnered Michael Schumacher from 2000-2005, is now the most experienced driver on the grid and hopes to continue his considerable success alongisde teammate Jenson Button at Honda. His replacement at Ferrari, Felipe Massa, put himself on top of the podium at Interlagos in 2006 and received a huge reaction from the home crowd.

The Brazilian Grand Prix in 2007 will be the last in the season, on 21 October. The race consists of 72 laps of the 4.292-km circuit for a total distance of 309.024 km. Approximately 55,000 people attend the race in addition to the millions watching around the world. The training session takes place on Friday morning; the time trial on Saturday morning and the race itself on Sunday afternoon with warm ups and the drivers' parade in the morning. Tickets can be bought from the racetrack during the whole week or by contacting ABN Amro Bank on T011-5507 2500 from abroad and T0800-170200 inside Brazil. Minimum ticket price is US$75 rising to US$350 depending on the viewing sector. Sectors A and G are uncovered and the cheapest, whilst sector D (S do Senna) is covered, provides a better view and is more expensive. Tickets for the training sessions are cheaper and can be bought from 0700 on the day from the box office at the circuit. VIP hospitality is readily available but at a high price.

Private cars are banned from the racetrack but park-and-ride facilities (US$5) are available on Saturday from Shopping SP Market, Avenida das Nações Unidas 22540, and on Sunday from Hipermercado, Avenida das Nações Unidas 4403 and Shopping Interlagos, Avenida Interlagos 2255. There are also buses (Saturday-Sunday) from Praça da República, between Rua do Arouche and Rua Marquês de Itu (295), from Praça Com Linneu Gomes at Congonhas airport and from Rua dos Jequitibás in front of the Jabaquara bus station (189). All buses have different coloured stickers to indicate which drop-off point they serve. Further general information about the Grand Prix in English can be obtained from www.gpbrasil.org.

Walking

Free Way, R Leôncio de Carvalho 267, Paraíso, T011-285 4767. For nature trails.

Yachting, sailing and rowing

See Santo Amaro reservoir (see page 193).

São Paulo *p178, maps 182, p184 and p190*
See also Ins and outs, page 178.

Air

Cumbica international airport (also known as **Guarulhos**, operates services to all parts of the world and much of Brazil. To get to the airport, **Emtu** buses run every 30 mins from Praça da República 343 (northwest side, corner of R Arouche) 0530-2300, and from Tietê *rodoviária*, US$6.50, 30-45 mins. Buses also run from Bresser bus station and there are buses from Jabaquara bus terminal, without luggage space, usually crowded. Taxi fares from the city to the airport are between US$35-40 and vary from cab to cab. Rush-hour traffic can easily turn this 30-min journey into an hour. **Varig** has its own terminal for international flights, adjoining the old terminal and shared with only a handful of other airlines. The cheapest internal flights are with **Gol**, **Bra** and **Ocean Air**.

To get to the domestic **Congonhas** airport, take an **Emtu** bus the centre or a taxi, US$20.

Airline offices Aerolíneas Argentinas, Araújo 216, 6th floor, T011-259 0319 (Guarulhos T011-64453806). **Alitalia**, Av São Luís 50, cj 291, T011-257 1922 (Guarulhos T011-6445 3791). **American Airlines**, Araújo 216, 1st floor, T011-568010. **Avianca**, R da Consolação 293, 10th floor T011-257 6511 (Guarulhos T011-6445 3798). **Bra**, throughout the city, eg in Shopping Ibirapuera, www.voebra.com.br. **British Airways**, Av São Luís 50, 32nd floor, T011-259 6144 (Guarulhos T011-6445 2462). **Continental**, R da Consolação 247, 13th floor, T0800-554777 (Guarulhos T011-6445 4187). **Delta**, R Marquês de Itu 61, T011-258 5866. **GOL**, at Congonhas, www.voe gol.com.br. **Iberia**, Araújo 216, 3rd floor, T011-250 76711 (Guarulhos T011-6445 2060). **JAL**, Av Paulista 542, 2nd floor, T011-251 5222 (Guarulhos T011-6445 2040). **KLM**, Av São Luís 86, T011-257 1363 (Guarulhos T011-6445 2011). **LanChile**, R da Consolação 247, 12th floor, T011-259 2900 (Guarulhos T011-6445 2824). **Lufthansa**, R Gomes de Carvalho 1356, 2nd floor, T011-3048 5868 (Guarulhos T011-6445 2220). **Ocean Air**, Congonhas and through agencies, www.oceanair.com.br. **Rio-Sul**, R Bráulio Gomes 151, T011-5561 2161. **TAM**, R da Consolação 247, 3rd floor, T011-5582 8631 (Guarulhos T011-6445 2220). **TAP**, Av São Luís 187, T011-255 5366 (Guarulhos T011-6445 2400). **United**, Av Paulista 777, 9-10th floor, T011-253 2323 (Guarulhos T011-6445 3283). **Varig**, R da Consolação 362/372, Av Paulista 1765, T011-5091 7000 (Guarulhos T011-6445 2825, Congonhas T011-535 0216).

Bus

There is a convenient Metrô connection to the main *rodoviária*, **Tietê**, but the only way to the platforms is by stairs. This is very difficult for people with heavy luggage and, for the disabled, almost impossible. Tietê handles buses to the interior of São Paulo state, to all state capitals and international destinations. Buses to **Rio**, 6 hrs, every 30 mins, US$12.50 (*leito* US$25), special section for this route in the *rodoviária*, request the coastal route via Santos (*via litoral*) unless you wish to go the direct route. To **Florianópolis**, 11 hrs (US$23.75, *leito* US$36.25). To **Porto Alegre**, 18 hrs, US$36.50 (*leito* US$60). To **Curitiba**, 6 hrs, US$10.25-12.50. To **Salvador**, 30 hrs, US$51 (*leito* US$64). To **Recife**, 40 hrs, US$60-70. To **Campo Grande**, 14 hrs, US$33. To **Cuiabá**, 24 hrs, US$42. To **Porto Velho**, 60 hrs (or more), US$75. To **Brasília**, 16 hrs, US$30 (*leito* US$60). To **Foz do Iguaçu**, 16 hrs, US$30. To **São Sebastião**, 4 hrs, US$8.85 (say 'via Bertioga' if you want to go by the coast road, beautiful journey but few buses take this route).

There are 3 other bus terminals: **Barra Funda**, to cities in southern **São Paulo state** and many destinations in Paraná, including **Foz do Iguaçu** (check for special prices on buses to **Ciudad del Este**, which can be cheaper than buses to Foz).

Bresser (Metrô Bresser), for **Cometa** (T011-6967 7255) or **Transul** (T011-6693 8061) serving destinations in Minas Gerais. **Belo Horizonte**, 10 hrs, US$15.60, 11 a day (*leito* US$31.20), 9 a day with **Gontijo**. **Translavras** and **Util** also operate out of this station. Prices are given under destinations.

Buses from **Jabaquara**, at the southern end of the Metrô line for **Santos**, US$3.60, leave every 15 mins, taking about 50 mins, last bus at 0100. Also serves destinations on the southern coast of São Paulo state.

International buses From the main *rodoviária* at Tietê. Buses to Uruguay include: **Montevideo**, via Porto Alegre, with TTL, departs Mon, Thu, Sat 2200, 31 hrs, US$100, cold a/c at night, plenty of meal stops, bus stops for border formalities, passengers disembark only to collect passport and tourist card on the Uruguayan side. To **Chuy** with EGA, US$67, Tue, Fri, Sun.

Buses to Paraguay include: **Asunción** (1044 km), 18 hrs with Pluma (US$57, *leito* US$112), Brújula (US$64) or RYSA (US$110), all stop at **Ciudad del Este** (US$43, US$50 and US$84 respectively, Pluma *leito* US$84). Cometa del Amambay runs to **Pedro Juan Caballero** and **Concepción**.

To **Buenos Aires** (Argentina), Pluma, 36 hrs, US$145. To **Santiago** (Chile), Pluma or Chilebus, 56 hrs, US$130, Chilebus, poor meals, but otherwise good, beware over-booking.

Car hire

Avis, Araújo 232 and at the airports, T0800-118 066; Budget, R da Consolação 328, loja 1, and at Guarulhos, T011-256 4355; Hertz, Araújo 216, 1st floor, and at the airports, T011-883 7300 or T0800-147300; Interlocadora, several branches, São Luís T011-2555 604, M Fontes T011-257 3544, Guarulhos T011-6445 3838, Congonhas T011-240 9287; Localiza, T0800-992000, or www.localiza.com.br, for all reservations, 8 branches in the city.

Hitchhiking

To hitch to Rio, take the Metrô to Armênia, then a bus to Guarulhos, alighting where the bus turns off the Rio road for Guarulhos.

Taxi

Radio taxis include: Central de Táxi, T011-974 0182; Central Rádio Táxi, T011-6914 6630; TeleTáxi, T011-233 1977; Vermelho e Branco, T011-251 1733; or check the phone book for others. Public phone calls not accepted.

Trains

From **Estação da Luz**, a train runs 8 times a day to connect with the tourist train from **Paranapiaçaba** to **Rio Grande da Serra**, US$0.50.

From **Barra Funda** station, services go to **São José do Rio Preto** (overnight), **Barretos**, **Ourinhos**, **Londrina**, **Maringá**, **Sorocaba** and **Ponta Grossa**.

Directory

São Paulo *p178, maps 182, p184 and p190*

Banks

Banking hours are generally 1000-1600, although times differ for foreign exchange transactions (check at individual branches). Banco do Brasil will change cash and TCs and will advance cash against Visa. All transactions are done in the foreign exchange department of any main branch (eg Av São João 32, Centro), but queues are long. Banespa, R Duque de Caxias 200, Centro, or Praça da República 295, accepts Visa, TCs and cash. Citibank, Av Ipiranga 855, or Av Paulista 1111, open 1100-1500. MasterCard, R Campo Verde 61, 4th floor, Jardim Paulistano, cash against card.

Money changers There are many *câmbios* on or near Praça da República. Most travel agents on Av São Luís change TCs and cash at good rates, but very few are open on Sat. Amoretur, Praça da República 203, will change TCs. Avencatur, Av Nações Unidas 1394, Morumbi, changes TCs, euro, good rates. Coraltur, Praça da República 95. Interpax, Praça da República 177, loja 13, changes cash (many currencies) and TCs, Mon-Fri 0930-1800, Sat 0930-1300.

Cultural centres

If you are interested in cultural articles related to São Paulo and Brazil in general, check out the website of the Instituto Cultural Itaú, www.ici.org.br.

Alliance Française Theatre, see under Theatre, page 200. American Library, União Cultural Brasil-Estados Unidos, R Col Oscar Porto 208. Centro Brasileiro Britânico, R Ferriera de Araújo 741, Pinheiros, T011-3039 0567. Centro Cultural Fiesp, Av Paulista 1313, Tue-Sun 0900-1900, has foreign newspapers and magazines. Goethe-Instituto, R Lisboa 974, Mon-Thu 1400-2030.

Embassies and consulates

Argentina, Av Paulista 1106, T011-284 1355, 0900-1300, very easy to get a visa here. **Australia**, R Tenente Negrão 140, T011-3849 6281. **Austria**, R Augusta 2516, 10th floor, T011-282 6223, Mon-Thu 0930-1130. **Bolivia**, R Honduras 1447, T011-3081 1688, 0900-1300. **Canada**, Av Nações Unidas 12901, T011-5509 4343, 0900-1200, 1400-1700. **Denmark**, R Oscar Freire 379, T011-3061 3625, (Mon-Thu 0900-1700, Fri 0900-1400). **France**, Av Paulista 1842, 14th floor, T011-287 9522, 0830-1200. **Germany**, Av Brigadeiro Faria Lima 2092, T011-3814 6644, 0800-1130. **Ireland**, Av Paulista 2006, 5th floor, T011-287 6362, 1400-1700. **Israel**, Av Brig Faria Lima 1713, T011-3815 7788. **Netherlands**, Av Brigadeiro Faria Lima 1779, T011-3813 0522, 0900-1200. **New Zealand**, Av Campinas 579, T011-288 0700. **Norway**, R Oscar Freire 379, 3rd floor, T011-883 3322, 0900-1300. **Paraguay**, R Bandeira Paulista 600, 15th floor, T011-3849 0455, 0830-1600. **Peru**, R Votuverava 350, T011-3819 1793, 0900-1300. **South Africa**, Av Paulista 1754, T011-285 0433. **Sweden**, R Oscar Freire 379, 3rd floor, T011- 3061 1700, 0900-1300. **Switzerland**, Av Paulista 1754, 4th floor, Caixa Postal 30588, T011-253 4951. **UK**, Av Paulista 37, 17th floor, T011-287 7722, consulad@uol.com.br. **Uruguay**, Av Santos 905, T011-284 0998, 1000-1600. **US**, R Padre João Manuel 933, T011-3081 6511, 0800-1700. **Venezuela**, R Veneza 878, T011-3887 4583, 0900-1130.

Immigration

Federal Police, Marginal Tietê, open 1000-1600 for visa extensions.

Internet

Av Paulista 1499, conj 1001 (Metrô Trianon), 1100-2200, English spoken, second-hand books. **Kiosknet**, Shopping Light, 4th floor, R Cel Xavier de Toledo 23, opposite Teatro Municipal, T011-3151 3645, US$2.50 per hr. **O Porão**, R Tamandaré 1066, near Vergueiro metro station. **Saraiva Megastore**, Shopping El Dorado, US$3.

Language courses

The official **Universidade de São Paulo (USP)** is situated in the Cidade Universitária (buses from main bus station), beyond Pinheiros. They have courses available to foreigners, including a popular Portuguese course. Registry is through the **Comissão de Cooperação Internacional**, R do Anfiteatro 181, Bloco das Colméias 05508, Cidade Universitária, São Paulo.

Other universities include the **Pontifical Catholic University (PUC)**, and the **Mackenzie University**. Both these are more central than the USP, Mackenzie in Higienopolis, just west of the centre, and PUC in Perdizes. Take a taxi to either. Both have noticeboards where you can leave a request for Portuguese teachers or language exchange, which is easy to arrange for free. Any of the *gringo* pubs are good places to organize similar exchanges.

Laundry

Chuá Self Service, R Augusta 728, T2584953, limited self-service, not cheap. **Di-Lelles**, R Atenas 409, T011-7298 3928, pricey.

Medical services

Hospital das Clínicas, Av Dr Enéias de Carvalho Aguiar 255, Jardins, T011-3069 6000. **Hospital Samaritano**, R Cons Brotero 1468, Higenópolis, T011-824 0022. Recommended. Both have *pronto-socorro* (emergency services). Contact your consulate for names of doctors and dentists who speak your language. **Emergency and ambulance:** T192. **Fire:** T193.

Post office

Correio Central, Praça do Correio, corner of Av São João and Prestes Máia, T011-831 5222. Booth adjoining tourist office on Praça da República, Mon-Fri 1000-1200, 1300-1600, for letters and small packages only.

Telephone

Embratel, Av São Luís 50, and Av Ipiranga 344. For the international operator dial T000111, for international collect calls dial T000107. Red phone boxes are for national calls, blue ones for international phone calls.

The coast of São Paulo

São Paulo's coast is packed at the weekend (when the city dwellers leaves for the beach) and deserted during the week. There are many beautiful beaches to choose from: some backed by rainforest-covered mountains and all washed by a bottle-green warm Atlantic. The best are along the northernmost part of the state coast, the Litoral Norte, around Ubatuba, and along the Litoral Sul near Cananéia. There are beautiful islands too including Brazil's largest, Ilhabela, and her wildest, Ilha do Cardoso. The dividing point between the Litoral Norte and Litoral Sul is the historic city of Santos; made most famous by Pelé (and with a museum devoted to him), and dotted with a few interesting buildings and museums in a spruced-up, attractive colonial city centre. » *For Sleeping, Eating and other listings, see pages 221-228.*

Santos and São Vicente » *pp221-228.*

→ *Phone code: 013. Colour map 5, A6. Population: 418,000.*

The Portuguese knew how to choose a location for a new settlement. **Santos** stands on an island in a bay surrounded by towering mountains and extensive areas of lowland mangrove forest – a setting equally as beautiful as that of Salvador or Rio. When it was dominated by colonial houses, churches and clean white sand beaches Santos itself must have been one of Brazil's most enchanting cities. But in the 20th century an evil reputation for yellow fever and industrial pollution from nearby Cubatão left the city to decay and it lost much of its architecture along with its charm. Contemporary Santos, however, is getting its act together. The old colonial centre has been tidied up and Scottish trams ferry tourists past the city's sights. These include a series of colonial churches and the Bolsa do Café – a superb little museum whose cafe-restaurant serves the most delicious espresso in Brazil. Santos is also Pelé's home and the city he played for almost all his career. Santos FC has a museum devoted to the club and to Pelé and it is easy to attend a game.

On the mainland, **São Vicente** is, to all intents and purposes, a suburb of Santos, having been absorbed into the conurbation. It was the first town founded in Brazil, in 1532, but nowadays it is scruffy and with very few sights of interest but for the rather dilapidated colonial church, the Matriz São Vicente Mártir (1542, rebuilt in 1757) in the Praça do Mercado. The Litoral Sul (see page 218) begins after São Vicente.

Background

Santos is one of Brazil's oldest cities and has long been its most important port. The coast around the city is broken by sambaqui shell mounds that show the area has been inhabited by humans since at least 5000 BC (see page 673). When the Portuguese arrived, the Tupinikin people dominated the region. However, the first settlements at neighbouring São Vicente (1532) were constantly under attack by the Tamoio who were allies of the French. The French were defeated at Rio in 1560 and the Tamoio massacred soon after.

By the 1580s Santos was a burgeoning port with some 400 houses. The first export was sugar, grown as cane at the foot of the mountains and on the plateau. By the late 19th century this had been replaced by coffee, which rapidly became Brazil's main source of income. The city was connected to São Paulo and the coffee region by the British under the guidance of Barão Visconde de Mauá, and the city grew wealthy. The seafront was lined with opulent coffee mansions and the centre was home to Brazil's most important stock exchange, the Bolsa do Café.

In the 1980s, the hinterland between the sea and mountains became the site of one of South America's most unpleasant industrial zones. The petrochemical plants of Cubatão were so notorious that they were referred to in the press as the 'The Valley of Death'. Santos and around was said to be the most contaminated corner of the planet, with so much toxic waste undermining the hills that the whole lot threatened to slip down into the sea. In the late 1980s, a spate of mutant births in Cubatão eventually prompted a clean-up operation, which is said to have been largely successful.

Ins and outs

Getting there Santos is served by regular buses from São Paulo as well as towns along the Litoral Norte and Litoral Sul such as Curitibia, Rio de Janeiro and Florianópolis. Buses arrive at the **rodoviária** ⓘ *Praça dos Andrades, T013-3219 2194*, close to the colonial centre. Those from São Paulo also stop at Ponta da Praia and José Menino, which are nearer to the main hotel district in Gonzaga. A taxi to Gonzaga from the bus station is about US$5; all taxis have meters.

Getting around The best way to get around the centre of Santos is by the newly restored Victorian trams, which leave on guided tours (daily except Monday 1100-1700) from in front of the Prefeitura Municipal on Praça Visconde de Mauá. The tram passes most of the interesting sights, including the *azulejo*-covered houses on Rua do Comércio, the Bolsa do Café and some of the oldest churches. Local buses run from the colonial centre and *rodoviária* to the seafront – look for Gonzaga or Praia on their destination plaque. Bus fares within Santos are US$0.60; to São Vicente US$0.90.

Orientation The centre of the city is on the north side of the island. Due south, on the Baía de Santos, is **Gonzaga**, São Paulo's favourite beach resort where much of the city's entertainment takes place. Between these two areas, the eastern end of the island curves round within the Santos Channel. At the eastern tip, a ferry crosses the estuary to give access to the busy beaches of Guarujá and Praia Grande. The city has impressive modern buildings, wide, tree-lined avenues, and wealthy suburbs.

Tourist information There are **SETUR** offices at the *rodoviária*, at Praía do Gonzaga on the seafront (in a disused tram, very helpful, lots of leaflets), and next to the British railway station on Largo Monte Alegre. The **Orquidário Municipal** ⓘ *T0800-173887, www.santos.sp.gov.br*, has limited opening hours. Although poverty is apparent the city is generally safe but it is wise to exercise caution at night and near the port.

Sights

The heart of the colonial centre is **Praça Mauá**. The surrounding streets are very lively in the daytime, with plenty of cheap shops and restaurants. The most interesting buildings are to be found here and all can be visited by tram. The most impressive is the **Museu do Café** ⓘ *R 15 de Novembro 95, T013-3219 5585, www.museudocafe.com.br, Tue-Sat 0900-1700, Sun 1000-1700, US$2*, housed in the old Bolsa Oficial de Café. Its plain exterior hides a grand marble-floored art deco stock exchange and museum, with a café serving some of the best coffee and cakes in South America. The building was once open only to wealthy (and exclusively male) coffee barons who haggled beneath a magnificent stained-glass skylight, depicting a bare-breasted Brazil – the *Mãe Douro* – crowned with a star in a tropical landscape populated with tropical animals and perplexed Indians. The skylight and the beautiful neo-Renaissance painting of Santos that decorates the walls of the exchange are by Brazil's most respected 19th-century artist, Benedito Calixto, who was born in Santos. One of the few remaining coffee baron mansions the, **Fundação Pinacoteca** ⓘ *Av Bartolomeu de Gusmão 15, T013-3288 2260, www.pinacoteca.unisanta.br, Tue-Sun 1400-1900, free*, on the seafront, is now a gallery housing some of his paintings, most of them landscapes, which give some idea of the city's original beauty.

Santos has a few interesting and ancient colonial churches. Only the **Santuário Santo Antônio do Valongo** ⓘ *Marquez de Monte Alegre s/n, Tue-Sun 0800-1700, guided tours most days after 1000 in Portuguese only*, is regularly open to the public. Its twee mock-baroque interior is from the 1930s, but the far more impressive original

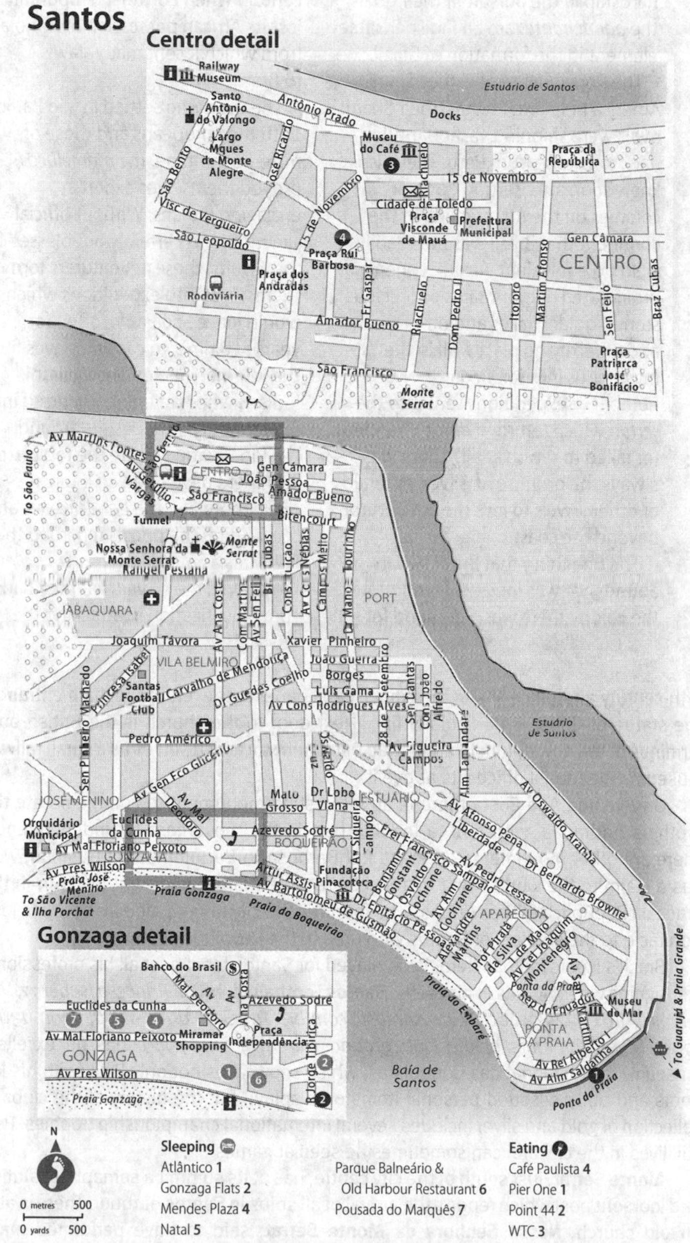

The Bandeirantes

Reviled in some quarters for their appalling treatment of Indians, revered in others for their determination and willingness to withstand extreme hardship in the pursuit of their goals, the *bandeirantes* are an indispensable element in the formation of Brazil.

The Portuguese knew that South America held great riches; their Spanish rivals were shipping vast quantities back to Europe from Peru. They also knew soon after setting up their colonies on the Atlantic side of the continent that Brazil was not readily yielding equivalent wealth. Legends proliferated of mountains of precious stones, golden lakes and other marvels, also of terrifying places, all in the mysterious interior. Regardless of the number of expeditions sent into the *sertão* which returned empty-handed (or failed to return at all), there was always the promise of silver, emeralds or other jewels to lure the adventurous beyond the coast.

The one thing that Brazil had in abundance was Indians. Throughout the colony there was a demand for slaves to work the plantations and farms and the indigenous population satisfied the need for labour. This was especially true in the early 17th century when Portugal temporarily lost its African possession of Angola, from which it sent many slaves to Brazil.

The men who settled in São Paulo, both the Europeans and those of mixed parentage, the *mamelucos*, proved themselves expert at enslaving Indians. Without official sanction, and certainly not blessed by the Jesuits, these adventurers formed themselves into expeditions which would leave São Paulo, often for years at a time, to capture slaves for the internal market. The Guaraní Indians who had been organized into *reducciones* by the Jesuits around the Río Paraguay were the top prize and there developed an intense rivalry between the *bandeirantes* and the Jesuits. The priests regarded the Paulistas as murderous and inhumane; the slavers felt they had some justification in attacking the

17th-century altarpiece sits in the Franciscan chapel to the left of the main entrance. The statue of Christ is particularly fine. Next door to the church is the British-built terminus of the now defunct Santos-São Paulo railway which serves as a small railway museum. The tourist office sits above it.

On Avenida Ana Costa there is an interesting monument to commemorate the brothers Andradas, who took a leading part in the movement for Independence. There are other monuments on Praça Rui Barbosa to Bartolomeu de Gusmão, who has a claim to the world's first historically recorded airborne ascent in 1709; in the Praça da República to Brás Cubas, who founded the city in 1534; and in the Praça José Bonifácio to the soldiers of Santos who died in the Revolution of 1932.

Brazil's iconic football hero, Pelé, played for Santos for almost all his professional life, signing when he was in his teens. **Santos Football Club**ⓘ *R Princesa Isabel 77, Vila Belmiro, T013-3257 4000, www.santosfc.com.br, Tue-Sun 0900-1900, Mon 1300-1900, US$3, for tours of the club ground call T013-3225 7989*, has an excellent museum, the Memorial das Conquistas, which showcases not only Pelé (with his kit, boots and other assorted personal items on display), but the history of the club. Its collection of gold and silver includes several international championship trophies. Pelé still lives in the city and can sometimes be seen at games.

Monte Serrat, just south of the city centre, has at its summit a semaphore station and look-out post which reports the arrival of all ships in Santos harbour. There is also an old church, **Nossa Senhora da Monte Serrat**, said to have performed many

missions because they were in Spanish territory and, in the 17th century, the entire western boundary of Brazil was in dispute.

This was one side of the coin. The other was that the bandeirantes were incredibly resourceful, trekking for thousands of kilometres, withstanding great hardships, travelling light, inspired not just by the desire to get rich, but also by a fierce patriotism. They certainly did show barbaric treatment to the Indians, but the enthusiasm that inspired the slave drives combined well with the desire to demystify the sertão, to uncover its riches. It was this which fuelled the prospecting expeditions after Angola had been recaptured in 1648. The *bandeirantes* trekked into Minas Gerais, Goiás and Mato Grosso looking for precious metals. Through their efforts, the Minas Gerais gold rush began. They were also enlisted by governors in the northeast to wage war on Indians and they were involved in the destruction of the *quilombo* at Palmares).

The principal effect of the expansionist spirit of the bandeira movement was that the interior of Brazil was explored. In the *bandeirantes'* footsteps came settlers and cattle herders who took over the lands that had been emptied of their Indian population. Although Indians were exploited as labour and became a source of income for the Paulistas, they also intermarried with the Europeans. The mixed-race *mamelucos* and even Indians themselves took part in the *bandeiras*, hastening the miscegenation process which became so evident throughout Brazil. Portuguese control of territory was extended by the bandeirantes' journeys. In their later phase, these journeys also filled Portugal's coffers because much of the wealth derived from the discovery of gold was sent back to Europe.

To find out more, read John Hemming, *Red Gold* (chapters 12 and 13); and Richard M Morse (editor), *The Bandeirantes*.

miracles. The top can be reached on foot or by **funicular**, which leaves every 30 minutes (US$6). Seven shrines have been built on the way up and annual pilgrimages are made by the local people. There are fine views.

In the western district of José Menino is the **Orquidário Municipal** ⓘ *Praça Washington, orchid garden Tue-Sun 0900-1700, bird enclosure 0800-1100, 1400-1700, US$0.50*. The flowers bloom from October to February and there is an orchid show in November. Visitors can wander among giant subtropical and tropical trees, amazing orchids and, when the aviary is open, meet macaws, toucans and parrots. The open-air cage contains hummingbirds of 20 different species and the park is a sanctuary for other birds.

Beaches

Santo has 8 km of beaches stretching round the Baía de Santos to those of São Vicente at the western end. From east to west they are **Ponta da Praia**, below the sea wall and on the estuary, no good for bathing, but fine for watching the movements of the ships. Next are **Aparecida, Embaré, Boqueirão, Gonzaga** and **José Menino** (the original seaside resort for the merchants of Santos). São Vicente's beaches of **Itararé** and **Ilha Porchat** are on the island, while **Gonzaguinha** is on the mainland. The last beach is **Itaquitanduva**, which is in a military area but may be visited with authorization. In all cases, check the cleanliness of the water before venturing in (a red flag means it is too polluted for bathing).

The small island of **Ilha Porchat** is reached by a bridge at the far end of Santos/São Vicente bay. It has beautiful views over rocky precipices, of the high seas on one side and of the city and bay on the other. At the summit is **Terraço Chopp** ⓘ *Av Ary Barroso 274*, a restaurant with live music most evenings and wonderful views. On summer evenings the queues to get in can last up to four hours, but in winter, even if it may be a little chilly at night, you won't have to wait.

Litoral Norte

» pp221-228.

The resorts immediately north of Santos – Guarujá, Praia Grande and Bertioga – are built-up and none too clean. Things become more beautiful at Camburi, the southernmost beach of São Sebastião province, named after the historical town that sits in front of Ilhabela, an island fringed with glorious beaches. Further north, Ubatuba, borders the state of Rio de Janeiro and has dozens of beautiful stretches of golden sand backed by forest-covered mountains.

Camburi and Maresias → *Phone code: 012.*

Beyond Boracéia are a number of beaches, including Barra do Una, Praia da Baleia and **Camburi**. The latter is the first beach in São Sebastião province and is surrounded by the *mata atlântica* forest. It has a long stretch of sand with some surf, many pousadas and two of the best restaurants in São Paulo state. The best place for swimming is at **Camburizinho** (though you should avoid swimming in the river which is not clean). You can walk on the Estrada do Piavu into the Mata Atlântica to see vegetation and wildlife; bathing in the streams is permitted, but use of shampoo and other chemicals is forbidden. About 5 km from Camburi is **Praia Brava**, 45 minutes' walk through the forest, camping is possible. The surf here is very heavy, hence the name.

The road continues from Camburi, past beaches such as **Boiçucanga** (family-orientated with many pousadas) to **Maresias**, which is beloved of well-to-do Paulistas who come here mostly to surf. It has some chic pousadas and restaurants and tends to be younger and less family orientated than Camburi.

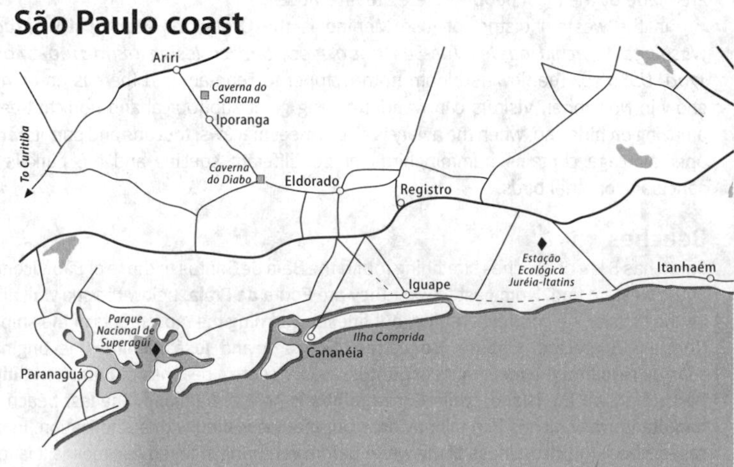

São Sebastião → *Phone code: 012. Colour map 5, A6. Population: 59,000.*

From Maresias it is 21 km to São Sebastião, which was once as attractive as Paraty and still retains a pretty colonial centre. Ferries leave from here for the 15-minute crossing to **Ilhabela** (see page 214), the largest offshore island in Brazil, which is shrouded in forest on its ocean side and fringed with some of the São Paulo's best beaches.

The city was founded at the time when Brazil's rainforest stretched all the way from the coast to the Pantanal, and all the land north to Rio de Janeiro was ruled by the indigenous Tamoio and their French allies. The settlement was initially created as an outpost of the indigenous slave trade and a port from which to dispatch armies to fight the French and claim Rio for the Portuguese crown. After this was achieved and the Tamoio had been massacred, São Sebastião grew to become one of Brazil's first sugar-exporting ports and the hinterland was covered in vast fields of cane tilled by the enslaved *indígena*. When the number of local slaves became depleted by the lash and disease, the city became one of the first ports of the African slave trade.

Ins and outs São Sebastião is served by regular buses from Ubatuba and Santos and is also connected to São Paulo. Ferries (for cars as well as passengers), US$2 from Ilhabela run 24 hours (for times see page 227) and take 15 minutes. The **tourist office** ⓘ *daily 1000-1700, www.prefeituradesaosebastiao.com.br*, lies on the waterfront one block towards the sea from Praça Major João Fernandes. Staff are very helpful and can provide maps and information on ferries to Ilhabela and beaches in the entire São Sebatstião province. The city is far cheaper for accommodation than Ilhabela.

Sights São Sebastião's remaining colonial streets are in the few blocks between the shoreline and the Praça Major João Fernandes, which is dominated by the **Igreja Matriz** ⓘ *daily 0900-1800*. Although this retains remnants of its original 17th-century design, this is predominantly a 19th-century reconstruction devoid of much of its original church art. However, the newly refurbished **Museu de Arte Sacra** ⓘ *a block south of the praça, R Sebastião Neves 90, T012-3892 4286, daily 1300-1700, free*, in the 17th-century chapel of São Gonçalo, preserves a number of 16th-century statues found in cavities in the wall of the Igreja Matriz during its restoration in 2003.

The city has a few sleepy streets of Portuguese houses, fanning out from the square, and a handful of civic buildings worth a quick look before the ferry leaves for Ilhabela. The most impressive is the **Casa Esperança** ⓘ *Av Altino Arantes 154, not open to the public although they often let visitors in on request*, on the waterfront. It was built from stone and wattle and daub glued together with whale oil, and then whitewashed with lime from thousands of crushed shells collected on the beaches of Ilhabela. The interior has some peeling 17th-century ceiling paintings.

Ilhabela (Ilha de São Sebastião)

➔ *Phone code: 012. Colour map 5, A6. Population: 21,000 (100,000 high season).*

Ilhabela is Brazil's largest oceanic island and one of its prettiest. It is wild enough to be home to ocelots, especially in the lush forests if its ocean side, 80% of which is protected by a state park, which drips with waterfalls and is fringed with glorious beaches. Its centre is crowned with craggy peaks, often obscured by mist: **Morro de São Sebastião**, 1379 m above sea-level, **Morro do Papagaio**, 1309 m, **Ramalho**, 1285 m and **Pico Baepi**, 1025 m. Rainfall on the island is heavy, about 3000 mm a year, and there are many small biting flies known locally as *borrachudos*.

The island is considered the *Capital da Vela* (capital of sailing) because its 150 km of coastline offers all types of conditions. The sheltered waters of the strait are where many sailors learn their skills and the bays around the coast provide safe anchorages. There are, however, numerous tales of shipwrecks because of the unpredictable winds, sudden mists and strange forces playing havoc with compasses, but these provide plenty of adventure for divers. There are over 30 wrecks that can be dived, the most notable being the *Príncipe de Asturias*, a trans-Atlantic liner that went down off the Ponta de Pirabura in 1916.

Ins and outs There are good transport connections with the mainland. **Litorânea** buses from São Paulo connect with a service right through to Ilhabela town. **Ferries** run day and night and leave regularly from the São Sebastião waterfront, taking about 20 minutes; free for pedestrians, cars US$1 weekdays, US$10 at weekends. It is very difficult to find space for a car on the ferry during summer weekends. A bus meets the ferry and runs to Ilhabela town and along the west coast. Try to visit during the week when the island feels deserted and avoid high season (December to February) at all costs. Hotels and pousadas are expensive; many people choose to stay in São Sebastião instead. For information contact the **Secretaria de Turismo** ⓘ *R Bartolomeu de Gusmão 140, Pequeá, T012-472 1091, www.ilhabela.sp.gov.br.* ▸▸ *See Transport, page 227.*

Sights Most of the island's residents live on the sheltered shore facing the mainland, along which are a number of upmarket pousadas. Swimming is not recommended on this side of the island within 4 km of São Sebastião because of pollution. Watch out for oil, sandflies and jellyfish on the sand and in the water.

About 20 minutes north of the ferry terminal is the main population centre, **Vila Ilhabela**. The village has some pretty colonial buildings and the parish church, **Nossa Senhora da Ajuda e Bom Sucesso**, dates from the 17th century and has been restored. There are restaurants, cafés and shops. Four kilometres north of Ihlabela, **Pedras do Sino** (Bell Rocks) are curious seashore boulders which, when struck with a piece of iron or stone, emit a loud bell-like note. There is a beach here and a campsite nearby.

From Vila Ihlabela, the road hugs the coast, sometimes high above the sea, towards the south of the island. An old *fazenda*, **Engenho d'Água**, a few kilometres from town in a grand 18th-century mansion, gives its name to one of the busiest beaches. About 10 km further, you can visit the old **Feiticeira** plantation. The *fazenda* has underground dungeons, and can be reached by bus, taxi, or horse and buggy. A trail leads down from the *fazenda* to the beautiful beach of the same name.

On the south coast is the fishing village of **Bonete**, which has 500 m of beach and can be reached either by boat (1½ hours), or by driving to Borrifos at the end of the road, then walking along a trail for three hours.

Much of the Atlantic side of the island is protected by the **Parque Estadual de Ilhabela**. There is a dirt road across to the east of the island, but it requires a 4WD. A few kilometres along this road is a turning to the terraced waterfall of **Cachoeira da Toca** (US$4). Set in dense jungle close to the foot of the Baepi peak, the cool freshwater pools are good for bathing and attract lots of butterflies. The locals claim that there are over 300 waterfalls on the island, but only a few of them can be reached on foot; those that can are worth the effort. There is a 50-km return trek from Vila Ilhabela over the hump of the island down towards the Atlantic. The route follows part of the old slave trail and requires a local guide as it negotiates dense tropical forest.

São Sebastião & Ilhabela

Beaches ○
Armação **2**
Arrastão **48**
Arrozal **6**
Barraqueçaba **57**
Cabras **17**
Castelhanos **33**
Caveira **37**
Centro **52**
Cigarras **46**
Curral **23**
Deserta **50**
Enchovas **27**
Engenho d'Água **13**
Enseada **45**
Eustáquio **35**
Feiticeira **20**
Figueira **32**
Fome **42**
Grande (Ilhabela) **22**
Grande (São Sebastião) **54**
Guaecá **58**
Guànxuma **36**
Itaguaçu **14**
Itaquanduba **15**
Jabaquara **43**
Julião **21**
Mercedes **9**
Olaria **47**
Pacuíba **44**
Pedra do Sino **5**
Pedra Miúda **18**
Pequeá **12**
Perequê **16**
Pinto **3**
Pitangueiras **55**
Poço **40**
Ponta Azeda **4**
Ponta da Cabeçuda **34**
Ponta da Pirabura **30**
Ponta das Canas **1**
Ponta da Sela **25**
Ponta da Sepetiba **26**
Ponta do Boi **29**
Ponta do Diogo **28**
Ponta do Lobo **41**
Ponta Grossa **39**
Pontal da Cruz **49**
Portinho **19**
Porto Grande **51**
Preta **53**
Saco do Indaiá **10**
Saco Grande **31**
Serraria **38**
Siriúba **7**
Timbó **56**
Veloso **24**
Viana **8**

Some of the island's best beaches are on the Atlantic side of the island and can only be reached by boat. **Praia dos Castelhanos** is recommended. At the cove of **Saco do Sombrio** English, Dutch and French pirates sheltered in the 16th and 17th centuries. Needless to say, this has led to legends of hidden treasure, but the most potent story about the place is that of the Englishman, Thomas Cavendish. In 1592 he sacked Santos and set it on fire. He then sailed to Saco do Sombrio where his crew mutinied, hanged Cavendish, sank their boats and settled on the island.

Ubatuba » pp221-228.

➔ Phone code: 012. Colour map 5, A6. Population: 67,000.

This is one of the most beautiful stretches of the São Paulo coast and has been recognized as such by the local tourist industry for many years. In all, there are 72 beaches of varying sizes, some in coves, some on islands. Surfing is the main pastime, of which it is said to be capital, but there is a whole range of watersports on offer, including sailing to and around the offshore islands. The **Tropic of Capricorn** runs through the beach of Itaguá, just south of the town.

The beaches are spread out over a wide area, so if you are staying in Ubatuba town and don't have a car, you will need to take one of the frequent buses. The area gets very crowded at carnival time as Cariocas come to escape the crowds in Rio.

The commercial centre of Ubatuba is at the northern end of the bay by the estuary, by which the fishing boats enter and leave. A bridge crosses the estuary, giving access to the coast north of town. A small jetty with a lighthouse at the end protects the river mouth and this is a pleasant place to watch the boats come and go. The seafront, stretching south from the jetty, is built up along its length, but there are hardly any high-rise blocks. In the commercial centre are shops, banks, services, lots of restaurants (most serving pizza and fish), but few hotels. These are mainly found on the beaches north and south and can be reached from the Costamar bus terminal. The **tourist office** ① *Av Iperoig opposite R Prof Thomaz Galhardo*, is on the seafront.

Ins and outs

The road from São Sebastião is paved, so a journey from São Paulo along the coast is possible. Ubatuba is 70 km from Paraty (see page 165). There are regular buses from São Paulo, São José dos Campos, Paraibuna, Caraguatatuba, Paraty and Rio de Janeiro. Taxis in town can be very expensive. » *See Transport, page 227.*

Background

This part of the coast was hotly contested between the local indigenous population and the Portuguese. The Jesuits José Anchieta and Manuel Nóbrega came to the village of Iperoig, as it was called in 1563, to put a stop to the fighting; the former was even taken hostage by the locals during the negotiations. A cross on the Praia do Cruzeiro (or Iperoig) in the centre commemorates what the town proudly claims to have been the first peace treaty on the American continent. The colonists eventually prevailed and the town of Vila Nova da Exaltação da Santa Cruz do Salvador de Ubatuba became an important port until Santos overtook it in the late 18th century. In the 20th century its development as a holiday resort was rapid, especially after 1948 when it became an Estância Balneária. The shortened name of Ubatuba derives from the Tupi-Guarani, meaning 'place of ubas', a type of tree used for making bows and canoes. Cariocas disparagingly refer to it as Uba 'chuva' – as it can rain heavily here at any time.

Sights

Ubatuba has a few historic buildings, such as the **Igreja da Matriz** on Praça da Matriz, dating back to the 18th century. It has only one tower, the old 19th-century prison, which now houses the small historical museum. Other interesting buildings include: **Cadeia Velha** on Praça Nóbrega; the 18th-century **Câmara Municipal** on Avenida Iperoig; and the **Sobrado do Porto**, the 19th-century customs house at Praça Anchieta 38, which contains **Fundart** (the Art and Culture Foundation). Mostly, though, it is a modern, functional town. In the surrounding countryside there are *fazendas* which are often incorporated into the *trilhas ecológicas* (nature trails) along the coast.

The **Projeto Tamar** ⓘ *R Antonio Athanasio da Silva 273, Itaguá, T012-432 6202*, is a branch of the national project which studies and preserves marine turtles. The **Aquário de Ubatuba** ⓘ *R Guarani 859, T012-432 1382, Fri-Wed 1000-2200*, has well-displayed Amazon and Pantanal species including caimans and piranhas.

There is a small airport from which stunt fliers take off to wheel and dive over the bay. In summer 10-minute panoramic flights and helicopter rides over Ubatuba are offered from US$15.

Beaches

The only place where swimming is definitely not recommended is near the town's outflow between Praia do Cruzeiro and Praia Itaguá. The sand and water close to the jetty don't look too inviting either. The most popular beaches are **Praia Tenório, Praia Grande** and **Praia Toninhas** (4½ km, 6 km and 8 km south respectively). Condominiums, apartments, hotels and pousadas line these beaches on both sides of the coast road. Of the municipality's 72 beaches, those to the south are the more developed although the further you go from town in either direction, the less built-up they are. Boogie boards can be rented at many of the beaches, or you can buy your own in town for around US$5.

Saco da Ribeira, 13 km south, is a natural harbour that has been made into a yacht marina. Schooners leave from here for excursions to **Ilha Anchieta** (or dos Porcos), a popular four-hour trip (see Activities and tours, page 227). On the island are beaches, trails and a prison, which was in commission from 1908 to 1952. The **Costamar** bus from Ubatuba to Saco da Ribeira runs every half an hour (US$0.85) and will drop you at

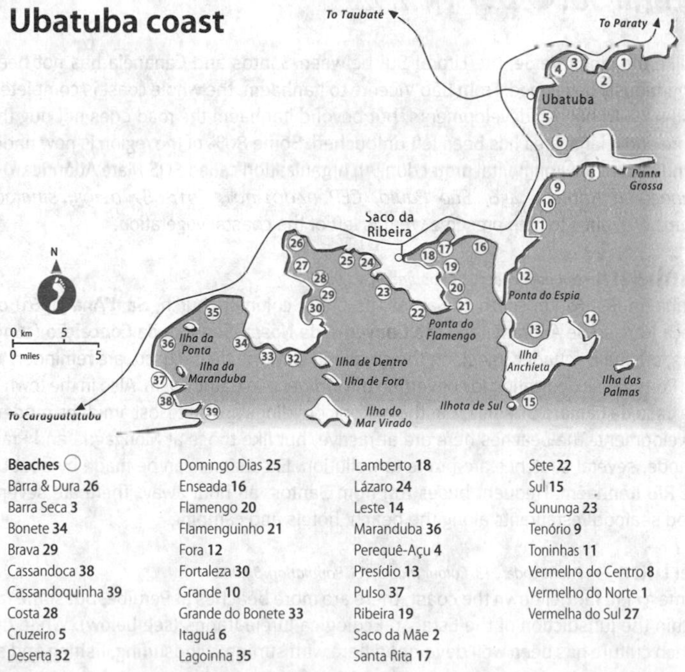

the turning by the **Restaurante Pizzeria Malibu**. It's a short walk to the docks and boatyards where an unsealed road leads to the right, through the boatyards, to a track along the shore. It ends at the **Praia da Ribeira** from where you can follow the track round a headland to the beaches of **Flamengo**, **Flamenguinho** and **Sete Fontes**. It's a pleasant stroll (about one hour to Flamengo), but there is no shade and you need to take water. Note the sign before Flamengo on one of the private properties: "*Propriedade particular. Cuidado c/o elefante!*".

Parque Nacional Serra da Bocaina

ⓘ *Permission to visit must be obtained in advance from Ibama in São José do Barreiro, the nearest town, T012-3117 2183/88. There are hotels and trekking agencies here, including Vale dos Veados, Estr da Bocaina, Km 42, T012-577 1194, F577 1303, part of the Roteiros de Charme hotel group, see page 50.*

Straddling the border of São Paulo and Rio de Janeiro states, the Parque Nacional Serra da Bocaina rises from the coast to its highest point at **Pico do Tira** (or Chapéu) at 2200 m, encompassing three strata of vegetation. Up to 1000 m the forest is mainly made up of large trees such as *maçaranduba* (milk, or cow trees), *jatobá* (courbaril), cedar and *angelim* (angely). Between 1000 and 2000 m the predominant varieties are pines and myrtles. Higher than this, the landscape is more grassy and open, with bromeliads, orchids and lichens. The main river flowing through it is the **Mambucaba**, which cascades down the mountainsides in a series of waterfalls. Trails lead to some of the falls and an old gold trail leads through the park (a three or four-day hike).

All the remaining patches of Mata Atlântica along the Linha Verde provide habitat for some of Brazil's rarer endemic birds. A book such as Nigel Wheatley's *Where to Watch Birds in South America* has more details for those interested in rare birds. Otherwise, contact specialists locally and, where necessary, ask permission to birdwatch on private land.

Litoral Sul

» *pp221-228.*

Unlike the Linha Verde, the Litoral Sul between Santos and Cananéia has not been continuously developed. From São Vicente to Itanhaém, the whole coast is completely built-up with holiday developments, but beyond Itanhaém the road does not hug the shore and a large area has been left untouched. Some 80% of the region is now under some form of environmental protection. An organization called **SOS Mata Atlântica** ⓘ *R Manoel da Nóbrega 456, São Paulo, CEP 04001-001, T011-887 01195, smata@ax.apc.org*, aims to help preserve what is left of the coastal vegetation.

Itanhaém → *Phone code: 013. Population: 72,000.*

Itanhaém lies 61 km south of Santos. Its pretty colonial church, **Sant'Ana** (1761) on Praça Narciso de Andrade, and the **Convento da Nossa Senhora da Conceição** (1699-1713, originally founded 1554), on the small hill of Morro de Itaguaçu, are reminders of the Portuguese dedication to converting the *indígena* to Catholicism. Also in the town is the **Casa de Câmara e Cadeia**, but the historic buildings are quite lost amid the modern development. The beaches here are attractive, but like those at Mongaguá and Praia Grande, several stretches are prone to pollution. Excursions can be made by boat up the **Rio Itanhaém**. Frequent buses run from Santos, an hour away. There are several good seafood restaurants along the beach, hotels and camping.

Peruíbe → *Phone code: 013. Colour map 5, A5. Population: 52,000.*

Some 31 km further down the coast, there are more beaches at Peruíbe, but some fall within the jurisdiction of the Estação Ecológica Juréia-Itatins (see below). While the beach culture has been well developed here with surfing, windsurfing, fishing and so on, a number of 'alternative' options have recently flourished. The climate is said to be unusually healthy owing to a high concentration of ozone, which helps to filter out harmful ultraviolet rays from the sun. UFO watchers and other esoterics claim that it is a very mystical place. Local rivers have water and black mud proven to contain medicinal properties. And the neighbouring ecological station is a major draw now that ecotourism has become big business in São Paulo state. Peruíbe's history dates back to 1530 when the village of Abarebebê was founded; about 9 km northeast of here, the ruins can be visited, with its church built of stone and shells. There is a **Feira do Artesanato** ⓘ *Av São João, Sat and Sun 1400-0100 (1400-2300 in winter).*

Buses connect the town with Santos, for São Paulo. For tourist information, contact the **Secretaria de Turismo** ⓘ *R Nilo Soares Ferreira 50, T013-455 2070*. You may have to ask permission in the **Departamento da Cultura** ⓘ *Centro de Convenções, Av Sã João 545, T013-455 2232*, to visit Abarebebê and other sites. Also at this address is the **Secretaria Estadual do Meio Ambiente** ⓘ *T013-457 9243*, for information on the **Estação Ecológico Juréia-Itatins**.

Estação Ecológico Juréia-Itatins

ⓘ *For permission to visit the ecological station, contact the Secretaria Estadual do Meio Ambiente, address above, or the Instituto Florestal (DRPE), R do Horto 931, CEP 02377, São Paulo, T011-9528555.*

Peruíbe marks the northernmost point of the Estação Ecológico Juréia-Itatins, 820 sq km of protected Mata Atlântica. The four main ecosystems are *restinga*, mangrove forest, Mata Atlântica and the vegetation at about 900 m on the Juréia mountains. Its wildlife includes many endangered species including rare flowers and other plants. There are deer, jaguar, monkeys, dolphins, alligators and birds, including the yellow-headed woodpecker and toucans. Human occupation of the area has included sambaqui, builders, *fazendeiros* and present-day fishing communities who preserve an isolated way of life.

The ecological station was founded in 1986. Tourism is very carefully monitored and only certain areas are open to the public. These are: the **Núcleo Itinguçu**, 18 km from Peruíbe, which contains the Cachoeira do Paraíso (Paradise Falls) and other

pools and waterfalls; **Vila Barra do Una**, a fishing village with a 2-km beach, camping and places to eat, 25 km from Peruíbe; and **Canto da Praia da Juréia** at the extreme southern end, 38 km from Iguape, with 7 km of beach and all the coastal ecosystems.

Hikers can walk the 4-km **Trilha do Arpoador** and the 5-km **Trilha do Imperador**, but both need prior reservation and numbers are limited; similarly for the Despraiado mountain bike trail. Trips can be made, with authorization, up the **Rio Guaraú** (8 km from Peruíbe) and the **Rio Una do Prelado** (25 km from Peruíbe). Other places of interest are **Vila do Prelado**, which was a stop on the Imperial São Vicente-Iguape post route (electric light was only installed in 1995), and the **Casa da Farinha**, where manioc flour is made, 28 km from Iguape.

Iguape and Ilha Comprida → *Phone code: 013. Colour map 5, A5. Population: 28,000.*

At the southern end of the ecological station is the town of Iguape, founded in 1538. In the early days of its existence, ownership of the town was disputed between Spain and Portugal because it was close to the line drawn by the Pope marking their respective territories in the 'New World'. Typical of Portuguese architecture, the small **Museu Histórico e Arqueológico** ⓘ *R das Neves 45, Tue-Sun 0900-1730*, is housed in the 17th-century Casa da Oficina Real de Fundição. There is also a **Museu de Arte Sacra** ⓘ *Praça Rotary, Sat and Sun 0900-1200, 1330-1700*, in the former Igreja do Rosário. The main church, the **Basílica de Bom Jesus**, is a mid-19th-century construction. Information is available from **Prefeitura Municipal** ⓘ *R 15 de Novembro 272, T013-841 1626.*

The main attractions for tourists are yachting, fishing and half a dozen beaches. Excursions include the ruined *fazenda* of **Itaguá**. Handicrafts include items made from wood and clay, basketware and musical instruments.

Opposite Iguape is the northern end of the **Ilha Comprida** with 86 km of beaches, some of which are disappointing. This **Área de Proteção Ambiental** is not much higher than sea level and is divided from the mainland by the Canal do Mar Pequeno. The northern end is the busiest and on the island there are hotels, a supermarket and some good restaurants; the fresh fish is excellent.

Caverns of the Vale do Ribeiro (Caverna do Santana)

→ *Colour map 5, A5.*

ⓘ *Buses to Apiaí run from the Barra Funda rodoviária in São Paulo. If coming to Iporanga from Curitiba, change buses at Jacupiranga on the BR-116 for Eldorado Paulista.*

This cave system, 40 km from Eldorado, west of the BR-116, forms one of the largest concentrations of caverns in the world. Among the best known is the 8-km **Caverna do Diabo** (Devil's Cave) or **Gruta da Tapagem** ⓘ *Mon-Fri 0800-1100, 1200-1700, Sat, Sun and holidays 0800-1700, US$2*. It as huge as a cathedral with well-lit formations in the 600 m that are open to the public.

Some 43 km from Caverna do Diabo is **PETAR**, the Parque Estadual Turístico do Alto Ribeira, with three groups of caves. The **Núcleo Santana**, contains the Cavernas de Santana (5.6 km of subterranean passages and three levels of galleries), Morro Preto and Água Suja, plus a 3.6-km ecological trail to the waterfalls in the Rio Bethary, and the **Núcleo Ouro Grosso**. This section of the park is 4 km from the town of **Iporanga**. Iporanga is the most convenient town for visiting all the caves; it is 64 km west of Eldorado Paulista, 42 km east of Apiaí, on the SP-165, 257 km southwest of São Paulo. The third group, **Núcleo is Caboclos**, near the town of Apiaí. Guided tours of PETAR cost US$50 a day from the **Associação Serrana Ambientalista**, T015-556 1188.

Registro → *Phone code: 013. Population: 49,000.*

A suitable stopping place for visiting the caves area is Registro on the BR-116, in the heart of the tea-growing region, populated mainly by Japanese-Brazilians. There are a number of cheap hotels around the corner from the *rodoviária* (including **Brasília** D on Rua Brasília) and banks with ATMs.

Cananéia → *Phone code: 013. Colour map 5, A5.*

The 18th-century façades of the little port town of **Cananéia** stand, gradually decaying, at the heart of the wildest region in southeastern Brazil. Extensive mangrove wetlands, lowland forests and porpoise-filled estuaries surround the town on all sides. Rising up behind them are the rugged, rainforest-covered mountains of the Serra do Mar, which stretch all the way into neighbouring Paraná. The white sands of **Ihla do Cordoso** are accessible by boat, and the long broad beaches of **Boqueirão Sul**, southern Ilha Comprida, are just five minutes by ferry across the little brackish river that fronts the town.

Although this is one of the country's oldest cities (it was one of Martim Afonso de Souza's landfalls), Cananéia lacks the twee charm and tourist facilities of its cousins, Morretes to the south and Paraty to the north. The 17th-century **church of São João Batista** has plants growing out of its belltower and the façades of its colonial buildings are crumbling in the humidity. The only time of year that sees many visitors is Carnaval and New Year. This is a town with an *Under the Volcano* atmosphere; it feels like the end of the line. Pousadas have doors that open at whim. Restaurants are limited to fish, beans and rice served on plastic tables by friendly waiters. However, for those seeking out-of-the-way places, herein lies its appeal.

Ins and outs Cananéia can be easily visited on the way from São Paulo or Santos to Curitiba. At least two buses a day run to those destinations from the little *rodoviária*, a block west of the central Praça Martim Afonso de Souza.

Car and passenger ferries leave every 30 minutes from in front of the praça for the beach at Boqueirão Sul in southern Ilha Comprida. It takes about an hour to walk from the ferry dock to the beach. A few simple pousadas line the way. It is also possible to take boats all the way to Ilha do Mel in Paraná (see page 298).

Ilha do Cardoso

The densely wooded Ilha do Cardoso is a Reserva Florestal e Biológica. Marujá, the only village on the island, is tiny and has no electricity. There are some very rustic pousadas and restaurants and camping is allowed at designated places, but the island is otherwise uninhabited. There are lots of idyllic beaches, where spectacled caiman can be spotted lazing on the virtually untouched white sand; the best for surfing is Moretinho.

There are three daily ferry services from Cananéia, the journey takes four hours (the ticket office as it Rua Princesa Isabel, T013-841 1122). Boats run tours from the docks for around US$7 per person in high season and at weekends. Launches can be hired for about US$70 for a full day at other times. Alternatively, drive 70 km along an unpaved road, impassable when wet, to **Ariri**, from where the island is 10 minutes by boat.

Sleeping

Santos *p207, map p209*

Discounts of up to 50% are available during low season. There are many cheap hotels near the Orquidário Municipal a few blocks from the beach.

A Mendes Plaza, Av Floriano Peixoto 42, a block from the beach in the main shopping area, T013- 3208 6400, www.mendesplaza.com.br. A large, newly refurbished 1970s business-orientated hotel with 2 restaurants and a rooftop pool.

A Parque Balneário Hotel, Av Ana Costa 555, Gonzaga, T013-3289 5700, www.parquebalneario.com.br. The city's 5-star hotel, with full business facilities and a rooftop pool overlooking the beach. Close to the shops and restaurants. Refurbished in 2006.

A-B Atlântico, Av Pres Wilson 1, T013-3289 5961, www.atlantico-hotel.com.br. A/c rooms in a newly renovated, well-kept 1930s hotel on the seafront. All rooms have TV; the best are in the upper floors with sea views.

There's a decent business centre, sauna, bar and restaurant.

A-B Gonzaga Flats, R Jorge Tibiriça 41, Gonzaga, T013-3289 5800, www.gonzaga flat.tur.br. Apartments in a 1990s block, all with kitchenettes and small sitting rooms with sofa beds. Space for up to 4 people.

C-D Hotel Natal, Av Mal Floriano Peixoto 104, Gonzaga T013-3284 2732, www.hotel natal.com.br. Fan-cooled or a/c apartments with or without bathrooms. Cable TV.

C-D Pousada do Marquês, Av Floriano Peixoto 202, Gonzaga, T013-3237 1951, www.pousadadomarques.com.br. Very simple en suite rooms with fan and cable TV.

Camburi and Maresias *p212*

A Camburyzinho, Estr Camburi 200, Km 41, Camburizinho, T012-38652625, www.pousadacamburizinho.com.br. Approximately 30 smart rooms around a pool with a bar and beach service.

B Piccolo Albergo, R Nova Iguaçu 1979, Maresias, T012-3465 6227, www.piccolo albergo.com.br. 5 smart chalets in a forest setting near a waterfall. With sauna and a natural swimming pool.

B Pousada das Praias, R Piauí 70, Camburizinho, T012-3865 1474, www.pousadadaspraias.com.br. Pleasant little beachside pousada with a pool and sauna.

São Sebastião *p213*

The city itself is not particularly desirable – head for Ilhabela and stay in São Sebastião only if you have to. There are a few cheap places near the main praça and *rodoviária*.

C-E Roma, Praça João Fernandes 174, T012-3892 1016, www.hotelroma.tur.br. Simple but well-maintained rooms around a fig tree filled courtyard. The simplest are a little scruffy. Includes breakfast.

Camping

Camping do Barraqueçaba Bar de Mar de Lucas, near the beach about 6 km south of São Sebastião. Hot showers, English spoken, cabins available. Recommended.

Ilhabela *p214, map p*

There are a number of moderate and cheap hotels on the road to the left of the ferry.

LL-L Maison Joly, R Antonio Lisboa Alves 278, Morro do Cantagalo, T012-3896 1201, www.maisonjoly.com.br. Exquisite little pousada perfect for couples. Each cabin is tastefully decorated in its own style and has a wonderful view out over the bay. Great restaurant and pool. Private, intimate and quiet. No children allowed.

L-AL Barulho d'Agua, R Manoel Pombo 250, Curral, Km 14, T012-3894 1406, www.barulho dagua.com.br. Intimate little cabins set in rainforest next to a clear river. Very romantic.

A Ilhabela, Av Pedro Paulo de Morais 151, Saco da Capela. T012-3896 1083, www.hotel ilhabela.com.br. One of the larger pousadas, orientated to families and with a well-equipped but small gym, pool, restaurant and bar and good breakfast. Recommended.

A Porto Pousada Saco da Capela, R Itapema 167, T012-3896 2255, www.sacodacapela.com.br. 18 carefully decorated cabins set in a rocky forest garden on a steep hill. Good pool and breakfast.

B Pousada dos Hibiscos, Av Pedro Paulo de Morais 714, T012-3896 1375, www.pousada doshibiscos.com.br. Little group of cabins set around a pool with a sauna, gym and bar. Nice atmosphere. Recommended.

B Vila das Pedra, R Antenor Custodio da Silva 46, Cocaia, T012-3896 2433, www.viladas pedras.com.br. 11 chalets in a forest garden. Tastefully decorated and a very nice pool.

C Canto Bravo, Praia do Bonete, T012-9766 0478. Set on a secluded beach 1½ hrs' walk (or 20-min boat ride) from Ponta de Sepituba. Modest and elegantly decorated cabins and excellent simple breakfast and lunch (included in the price).

C-D Tamara, R Jacob Eduardo Toedtli 163, Itaquanduba, T012-3896 2543, www.pousada-tamara.com.br. 17 cabañas with a/c around a small pool.

E Ilhabela, Av Col José Vicente Faria Lima 1243, Perequê, T012-472 8468, hostelling@ iconet.com.br. IYHA youth hostel. Price per person.

Camping

In addition to **Pedra do Sino**, there are campsites at **Perequê**, near the ferry dock, and at **Praia Grande**, a further 11 km south.

Ubatuba *p216, map p223*

Very cheap accommodation is hard to come by and at all holiday times no hotel charges less than US$20.

Beach hotels

L Recanto das Toninhas, Praia das Toninhas, T012-3842 1410, www.toninhas.com.br. Part of **Roteiros de Charme** group (see page 50). Elegant cabañas with sea views set around a very pretty pool with a full range of services and activities, including a sauna, restaurant, bar, tennis court and excursions.

AL Refúgio do Corsário, Baia Fortaleza, 25 km south of Ubatuba, T012-443 9148, F443 9158. A clean quiet hotel on the waterfront with full board and a range of activities including sailing and swimming. Very relaxing.

AL Saveiros, R Laranjeira 227, Praia do Lázaro, 14 km from town, T012-3842 0172, www.hotelsaveiros.com.br. Pretty little pousada with a pool and a decent restaurant. English spoken.

A Solar das Águas Cantantes, Estr Saco da Ribeira 253, Praia do Lázaro, Km 14, T012-442 0178, www.ubatuba2000.com.br/solar. A mock-Portuguese colonial house replete with *azulejos* and set in a shady tropical garden. The restaurant is one of the best on the São Paulo coast and serves excellent seafood and Bahian dishes.

B-C Rosa Penteado, Av Beira-Mar 183, Praia de Picinguaba, T012-3833 8998, www.ubatubasite.com.br/atelierrosapenteado. 4 pretty beachside *cabañas* all decorated with paintings and objects made by the artist owner. The price includes a very good breakfast and dinner.

E Maurício, Av Abreu Sodré 607, north of town, near Praia do Perequê-Açu. Cheap rooms in a private house. Laundry service.

Ubatuba town

B São Charbel, Praça Nóbrega 280, T012-432 1090, F432 1080. Very helpful and comfortable, on the busy main square. The advertised rooftop 'pool' is, in reality, a tiny plunge pool.

C São Nicolau, R Conceição 213, T012-432 5007, F432 3310. A 3-min walk from the bus station, convenient for the town beach restaurants and services. A/c rooms have a

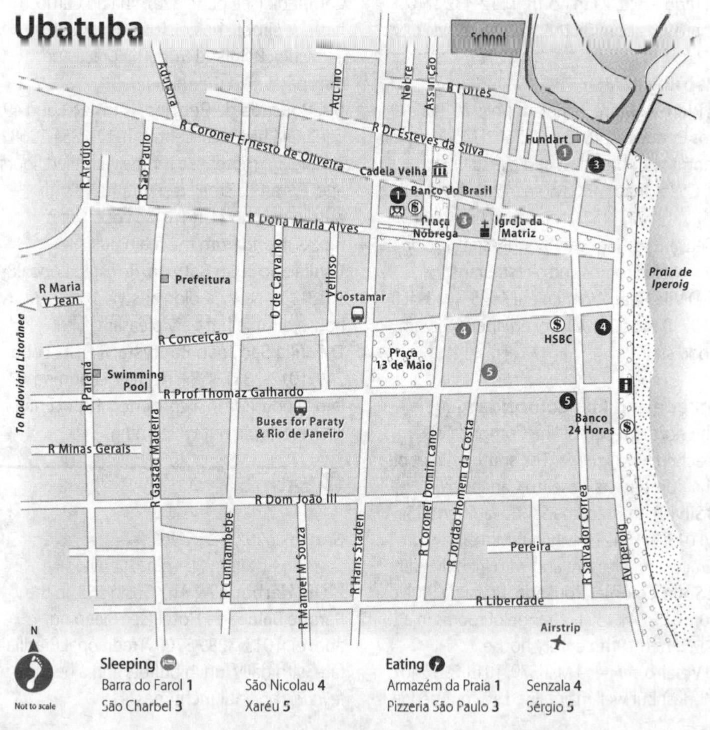

TV and fridge. Well run and looked after, with a good breakfast.

C Xaréu, R Jordão Homem da Costa 413, T012-432 1525, F432 3060. 3-min walk from the bus station, convenient for the town beach restaurants and services. Pretty rooms with wrought-iron balconies in a pleasant garden area. Good value, excellent breakfast. Recommended.

D Barra do Farol, R Dr Félix Guizard Filho 6, T012-432 2019. Homely, motel-style rooms close to seafront.

E Cora Coralina, Rod Oswaldo Cruz Km 89, near the Horto Florestal, T011-2580388. Price per person. IYHA youth hostel, 0800-2300. Simple dorms and doubles. Friendly and helpful.

E JS Brandão, R Nestor Fonseca 173, Jardim Sumaré, near the Tropic of Capricorn sign south of town, T012-432 2337. Price per person. IYHA youth hostel, 0700-2300. Pleasant staff, modest accommodation but clean and well kept.

Camping

Camping Clube do Brasil sites at Lagoinha (25 km from town), T012-443 1536, and Praia Perequê-Açu, 2 km north, T012-432 1682. There are about 8 other sites in the vicinity.

Peruíbe *p218*

A Piero Al Mare, R Indianópolis 20, Praia Orla dos Coqueiros, T013-458 2603. Modest, plain rooms with breakfast and a restaurant.

B-C Waldhaus, R Gaviotas 1201, Praia do Guaraú, T013-457 9170. Small hotel in a pleasant setting with friendly staff, a/c or fan-cooled rooms and a restaurant.

C-D Vila Real, Av Anchieta 6625, T013-458 2797. Basic but well looked after and with good staff.

Iguape and Ilha Comprida *p220*

The northern part of Ilha Comprida is reached from Iguape. The southern part of Ilha Comprida is closer to Cananéia.

B Silvi, R Ana Cândida Sandoval Trigo 515, T/F013-841 1421, silvihotel@virtualway.com.br. Simple, but pleasant and with friendly staff.

C Solar Colonial Pousada, Praça da Basilica 30, T013-841 1591. A range of rooms in a converted 19th-century house.

D Veleiro, Av Beira Mar 579, T013-895 2407. Modest but well maintained. Recommended.

Camping

There is a campsite at **Praia da Barra da Ribeira**, 20 km north, and wild camping is possible at **Praia de Juréia**, the gateway to the ecological station.

Caverns of the Vale do Ribeiro *p220*

C Pousada das Cavernas, Iporanga, T015-556 1168 (or T011-543 3082). Pleasant, simple with breakfast.

D Pousada Rancho da Serra, Iporanga, T015-556 1168 or T011-588 2011. Friendly staff who give advice about caving.

E Youth hostel, near the Caverna do Diabo, Província de Tokushima, Parque Estadual da Caverna do Diabo, Km 43, SP-165, Eldorado Paulista.

Camping

Camping in **PETAR** costs US$3 per person, 3 sites.

Cananéia and Ilha do Cardoso *p221*

There are a few cheap hotels in Cananéia town and other more expensive options across the water (2 mins on ferry and about 30-min walk) on the southern end of Ilha Comprida (see page 220). Ilha do Cardoso has one simple hostel. R Tristã Lobo lies a few blocks inland from the praça and runs parallel to the shoreline.

B-C Pousada de Pedrino, R Tristão Lobo 49, Cananéia historical centre, T013-3851 1368. Simple a/c motel-like rooms with tiled floors and TVs and a small restaurant. No sign outside the hotel. R Tristão Lobo lies 2 blocks inland from the main praça.

C Villa São João Batysta, R Tristão Lobo 289, T013-3851 1587. Colonial-style 18th-century house, simple but very pleasant.

D-E Villa São João Baptysta, R Tristã Lobo 289, T013-3851 1587. A small, charming family pousada in a converted 18th-century house. Simple but welcoming.

Eating

Santos *p207, map p209*

See also hotels in Sleeping, above.

Old Harbour, Av Ana Costa 555, in the **Parque Balneário Hotel** (see Sleeping, above), T013-3289 5700. Traditional Brazilian fare with daily lunch buffets and a hearty *feijoada* on Sat lunchtimes.

TT Pier One, Av Almirante Saldanha da Gama, Ponta da Praia. Good evening option in a restaurant perched over the water next to the Ponte Edgard Perdigao bridge. Very good *meca santista* – a local fish speciality served with banana, manioc flour and bacon – and live music at weekends.

TT WTC, R 15 de Novembro 111/113, Centro Histórico, T013-3219 7175. A business man's club housed in a handsome 19th century building. Popular with local bigwigs. One of the best restaurants in the city with a Mediterranean-influenced menu.

TT-T Point 44, R Jorge Tibiriçá 44. Great lunchtime buffet with enormous choice of *churrascaria*, in a large bustling dining room. Bar snack menu, live music Tue-Sat evening and dancing on Tue, Thu and Sat.

T Café Paulista, Praça Rui Barbosa 8 at R do Comércio, Centro Histórico, T013-3219 5550. A Santos institution. This café was founded in 1911 by Italians and has been serving great Portuguese standards such as *bacalhau*, and good bar snacks (the *empada camarão* is a local legend), and coffee.

Camburi and Maresias *p212*

There are numerous cheap and mid-range restaurants with bars and nightclubs in Camburi, Camburizinho and Maresias.

TTT Manacá, R do Manacá, T012-3865 1566, closed Mon and Wed in Nov and Mar. The best restaurant on the São Paulo coast and one of the best in the state, with French cooking techniques with Brazilian, Asian and seafood ingredients. Specialities include sole in orange and ginger sauce with puréed potato and wasabi. Very romantic setting – in a little tropical rainforest garden reached by a candlelit boardwalk. Come for dinner. Well worth a special trip.

São Sebastião *p213, map p215*

T São Sebastião bar and restaurant, Praça Major João Fernades 278, diagonally opposite the Igreja Matriz, T012-3892 4100. Generous *pratos feitos*, fish and chicken and great juices. Very good value.

Ilhabela *p214, map p215*

There are cheaper places in the main town, including a decent *padaria* (bakery) and some snack bars.

TTT Pizzabela, Hotel Ilha Deck, Av Alm Tamandaré 805, Itaguassu, T012-3896 1489. Paulistanos consider their pizza the best in the world. This is one of the few restaurants outside the city serving pizza, São Paulo-style. Expect lots of cheese. Nice surrounds.

TTT Viana, Av Leonardo Reale 1560, Praia do Viana, T012-3896 1089. The best and most expensive restaurant on the island, with excellent seafood and light Italian dishes. Good wine list. Book ahead.

Ubatuba *p216, map p223*

There is a string of mid-range restaurants along the seafront on Av Iperoig, as far as the roundabout by the airport.

TTT Giorgio, Av Leovigildo Dias Vieira 248, Itaguá. Sophisticated Italian restaurant and bar.

TTT Solar das Águas Cantantes, (see Sleeping, above). Very good seafood and Bahian restaurant in elegant surrounds.

TT Arabí, R Guarani 610, Itaguá. Popular, brightly lit, serving hot and cold Arabic food and desserts.

TT Pizzeria São Paulo, Praça da Paz de Iperoig 26. Undeniably chic gourmet pizzeria in beautifully restored building. Owned by a young lawyer who brings the authentic Italian ingredients for the gorgeous pizzas from São Paulo every weekend.

TT Senzala, Av Iperoig. Established 30 years ago, this Italian has a lovely atmosphere. Don't miss the seafood spaghetti. Recommended.

T Armazém da Praia, R Cel Ernesto de Oliveira 149, opposite the post office. Pretty, family-run self-service, open for lunch only.

T Sérgio, R Prof Thomaz Galhardo 404. Serving ice-cream, pizza and, at weekends, *feijoada*. Open for dinner, weekends only.

Bars and clubs

Santos *p207, map p209*

Bar do Três, Av Washington Luiz 422, Gonzaga. Bar with live music.

Disco Friday, Mendes Convention Center, Av Francisco Gilcério 206, T013-3228 7575. A/c complex with 6 bars and dancefloors. House and pop music. US$2 entry.

Internetbar, Av Mcal Floriano Peixoto 302, Pompéia. Popular, cheap internet access when eating or drinking.

Torto, Av Siqueira Campos 800, Boqueirão. Reggae and MPB. Rock nights Thu-Sun.

The biggest rodeo in the world

The world's biggest annual rodeo, the Festa do Peão Boiadeiro, is held during the third week in August in Barretos, some 115 km northwest of Ribeirão Preto. The town is completely taken over as up to a million fans come to watch the horsemanship, enjoy the concerts, eat, drink and shop in what has become the epitome of Brazilian cowboy culture. There are over 1000 rodeos a year in Brazil, but this is the ultimate. The stadium, which has a capacity for 35,000 people, was designed by Oscar Niemeyer so that the wind funnels through the middle, cooling the competitors and the spectators. Since the 1950s, when Barretos' rodeo began, the event grew slowly until the mid-1980s when it really took off. Tours from the UK are run by **Last Frontiers**, Fleet Marston Farm, Aylesbury, Bucks HP18 0PZ, T01296-658650, F658651, www.lastfrontiers.co.uk

Entertainment

Santos *p207, map p209*

Art galleries Galeria de Arte Nélson Penteado de Andrade, Praça dos Expedicionários 10, Gonzaga, T013-3235 4245.

Cinemas Av Ana Costa, Gonzaga. Mainstream films. **Cine Arte**, Posto 4, Av Vicente de Carvalho. Brazilian and foreign films.

Theatre Teatro Municipal Brás Cubas, Av Sen Pinheiro Machado 48, Vila Mathias, T013-3233 6086.

Festivals and events

Santos *p207, map p209*

26 Jan Foundation of Santos.
Mar/Apr Good Fri.
Jun Corpus Christi; Festejos Juninos. Throughout the summer there are many cultural, educational and sporting events.
8 Sep Nossa Senhora de Monte Serrat.

São Sebastião *p213*

20 Jan Festival of the Patron Saint, featuring *congadas*, a song and dance derived from slaves from the Congo.

Ilhabela *p214*

Feb Carnaval.
May Ilhabela is rich in folklore and legends. Its version of the *congada* (see above and Music, page 689) is famous, particularly at the Festival of São Benedito.
28 Jun São Pedro, with a maritime procession.
1st week of Jul Santa Verônica in Bonete.
Sep The town's anniversary.

There are sailing weeks and fishing tournaments throughout the year; dates change annually.

Ubatuba *p216, map p223*

Feb Carnaval.
End Jun São Pedro.
Jul Festa do Divino Espírito Santo.
Sep Ubatuba is known for its handicrafts (carved wood, basketware) and it holds an annual Festa da Cultura Popular.
28 Oct Ubatuba's anniversary. Surfing championships are also held.

Peruíbe *p218,*

18 Feb Founding of Peruíbe.
Jun Festival do Inverno.
Oct Mês das Missões.

Iguape and Ilha Comprida *p220*

Throughout the year there are various sporting and cultural events.
Jan/Feb Summer festival in Iguape.
Feb Carnaval on Ilha Comprida.
Mar/Apr Semana Santa.
Jun Corpus Christi.
Aug The month of the pilgrimage of Senhor Bom Jesus de Iguape.
3 Dec Iguape's anniversary.

Activities and tours

Santos *p207, map p209*

Golf Santos Golf Club, Av Pérsio de Queiroz Filho, São Vicente. 9-hole course.

Ubatuba *p216, map p223*

Tour operators

Agencies that run schooner trips to Ilha Anchieta and elsewhere include: **Central de Passeios de Escuna**, Saco da Ribeira, T012-441 1338; **Mykonos**, Av Leovigildo Dias Vieira 1052, Itaguá, T012-432 2042, office also in Saco da Riberia; **Oceano Azul**, R Flamenguinho 277, Saco da Ribeira, T012-442 0564.

Trekking

The **Guide Association**, T012-9141 3692, www.ubatuba.com.br/ecoturismo, can provide information. **Guaynumby**, T012-432 2832, and **Terra Brasil**, T012-435 1275, can provide guides. Trails are graded according to difficulty and last from 2 hrs to 2 days (to Pico do Corcovado).

Transport

Santos *p207, map p209*

Bus To **São Vicente**, US$0.90. For most suburbs buses leave from Praça Maua, in the centre of the city.

There are buses to **São Paulo** (50 mins, US$3.60) approximately every 15 mins, from the *rodoviária* near the city centre, José Menino or Ponta da Praia (opposite the ferry to Guarujá). Note that the 2 highways between São Paulo and Santos are sometimes very crowded, especially at rush hours and weekends. To **Guarulhos/ Cumbica airport**, **Expresso Brasileiro** at 0600, 1330, 1830, return 0550, 0930, 1240, 1810, US$5, allow plenty of time as the bus goes through Guarulhos, 3 hrs. **TransLitoral** from Santos to **Congonhas airport** then to Guarulhos/Cumbica, 4 daily, US$7.25, 2 hrs. To **Rio de Janeiro**, **Normandy**, several daily, 7½ hrs, US$22.50. To Rio along the coast road is via **São Sebastião** (US$7.25, change buses if necessary), **Caraguatatuba** and **Ubatuba**.

Taxi All taxis have meters. The fare from Gonzaga to the bus station is about US$5. **Cooper Rádio táxi**, T013-3232 7177.

São Sebastião *p213*

Bus 2 buses a day to **Rio de Janeiro** with **Normandy**, 0830 and 2300 (plus 1630 on Fri and Sun), can be heavily booked in advance, US$30 (US$10 from Paraty) 6½ hrs; 12 a day to **Santos**, via Guarujá, 4 hrs, US$7.60; 11 buses a day also to **São Paulo**, US$12, which run inland via **São José dos Campos**, unless you ask for the service via **Bertioga**, only 2 a day. Other buses run along the coast via **Maresias**, **Camburi** or north through **Ubatuba**. Last bus leaves at 2200.

Ferry Free ferry to **Ilhabela** for foot passengers, see below.

Ilhabela *p214, map p215*

Bus A bus runs along the coastal strip facing the mainland. **Litorânea** runs buses from Ilhabela town through to **São Paulo** (office at R Dr Carvalho 136).

Ferry The 15- to 20-min ferry to **São Sebastião** runs non-stop day and night. Free for foot passengers; cars cost US$1 weekdays, US$10 at weekends.

Ubatuba *p216, map p223*

Bus There are 3 bus terminals. Rodoviária Costamar, R Hans Staden and R Conceição, serves all local destinations.

The *rodoviária* at R Prof Thomaz Galhardo 513, for **São José** buses to **Paraty**, US$2.25, some **Normandy** services to **Rio de Janeiro**, US$9 and some **Itapemirim** buses.

Rodoviária Litorânea is the main bus station. To get there, go up Conceição for 8 blocks from Praça 13 de Maio, turn right on R Rio Grande do Sul, then left into R Dra Maria V Jean. Buses go to **São Paulo**, 3½ hrs, frequent, US$8, **São José dos Campos**, US$6, **Paraibuna**, US$5, **Caraguatatuba**, US$2.

Iguape and Ilha Comprida *p220*

Bus Buses run from Iguape to **São Paulo**, **Santos** or **Curitiba**, changing at Registro.

Ferry A continuous ferry service runs from Iguape to Ilha Comprida (free but small charge for cars); buses run until 1900 from the ferry stop to the beaches. From Iguape it is possible to take a boat trip down the coast to **Cananéia** and **Ariri**. Tickets and information from **Dpto Hidroviário do**

Estado, R Major Moutinho 198, Iguape, T013-841 1122. It is a beautiful trip, passing between the island and the mainland.

Caverns of the Vale do Ribeiro *p220*
Bus Buses from Apiaí run to the Barra Funda *rodoviária* in **São Paulo**, US$22. If heading to **Curitiba**, take the bus from Iporanga to Jacupiranga on the BR-116 and change.

Directory

Santos *p207, map p209*
Banks 1000-1730. ATMs in Santos are very unreliable and often out of order. Visa ATMs at Banco do Brasil, R 15 de Novembro 195, Centro and Av Ana Costa, Gonzaga. Many others. **Embassies and consulates** Denmark, R Frei Gaspar 22, 10th floor, 106, T013-3219 6455, 1000-1100, 1500-1700. France, R General Câmara 12, sala 51, T013-3219 5161. Germany, R Frei Gaspar 22, 10th floor, 104, T013-3219 5092. UK, R Tuiuti 58, 2nd floor, T013-3219 6622. **Immigration** Polícia Federal, Praça da República. F hop, Shopping Parque Balneário. US$3 per hr. **Laundry** Av Mcal Floriano Peixoto 120, Gonzaga, self-service, wash and dry US$5. **Medical services** Ana Costa, R Pedro Américo 42, Campo Grande, T013-222 9000; Santa Casa de Misericórdia, Av Dr Cláudio Luiz da Costa 50, Jabaquara, T013-234 7575. **Post office** R Cidade de Toledo 41, Centro and at R Tolentino Filgueiras 70, Gonzaga. **Telephone** R Galeão Carvalhal 45, Gonzaga.

Ilhabela *p214, map p215*
Banks Bradesco, Praça Col Julião M Negrão 29 in Vila Ilhabela.

Ubatuba *p216, map p223*
Banks There is a Banco 24 Horas next to the tourist office and an HSBC ATM at 85 R Conceição. The branch of Banco do Brasil in Praça Nóbrega does not have ATMs. **Internet** Chat and Bar, upper floor of Ubatuba Shopping. US$3 per hr, Mon-Sat 1100-2000. **Post office** R Dona Maria Alves between Hans Staden and R Col Dominicano. **Telephone** On Galhardo, close to Sérgio restaurant.

Minas Gerais and Espírito Santo

Footprint features

Introduction

The inland state of Minas Gerais, or General Mines, was once described as having a heart of gold and a breast of iron. The state was founded solely to provide precious metals for the imperial coffers. As the gold-mining camps grew and prospered they became towns of little cobbled streets crowned with opulent Manueline churches. Many of the towns are well preserved and these and the rugged forested hills around them are the principal reasons to visit.

Espírito Santo, immediately to the east of Minas, is less visited. But although its coastline is not as pretty as that of Bahia, to its north, it is far less developed. Beaches here can be almost deserted but for the visiting turtles. The state's interior is rugged, swathed in coffee and eucalyptus and dotted with giant granite rocks even larger than those to the south in Rio de Janeiro. The most famous and striking is Pedra Azul, which is on the main highway between Espírito Santo and Minas.

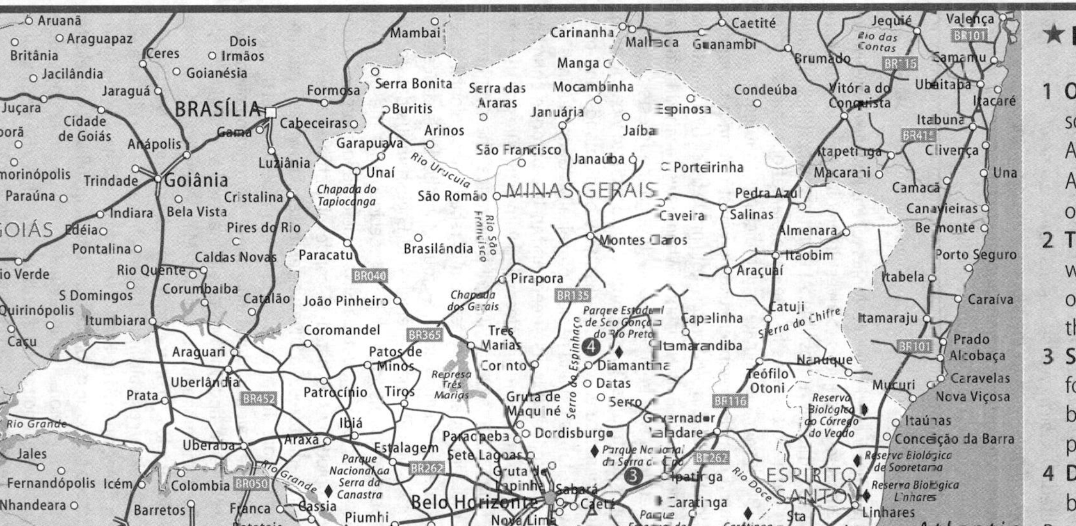

★ Don't miss...

1 **Ouro Preto and Congonhas** Admire some of the finest baroque art in the Americas, carved by the famous Aleijadinho – a cripple without the use of his hands or feet, pages 243 and 252.

2 **Tiradentes** Little cobbled streets, whitewash colonial town houses, ornate baroque churches and some of the best restaurants in Minas, page 255.

3 **Serra do Cipo** Waterfalls, *cerrado* forest, maned wolves and some of the best birdwatching in the country, page 267.

4 **Diamantina** One of the prettiest and best-preserved colonial mining towns in Brazil set in the heart of pristine *cerrado* forest, page 267.

5 **Pedra Azul** Enjoy watching the giant smooth-sided monolith change colour, from slate blue to fiery orange, as the day progresses, page 283.

Minas Gerais

The state of Minas Gerais is a little larger than France and almost as mountainous. In the south the land rises to over 2700 m on the border of Itatiaia National Park in Rio, and in the east, to 2890 m at the Pico da Bandeira in the Caparaó National Park. Both these areas of highland are part of the continuous chain of forest-clad mountains that forms the escarpment, which cuts Minas Gerais off from the coastal lowlands of the states of Rio de Janeiro and Espírito Santo. The foremost of the colonial towns are Tiradentes, Ouro Preto and Diamantina. Many of these have churches decorated with carvings by the country's most celebrated sculptor, Aleijadinho. The north of Minas is a dry and desolate region known as the sertão, *protected by the large national park, Grande Sertão Veredas, which contains significant areas of* cerrado *forest and the groves of* buriti *palms (known as* veredas*), which give the park its name. Some of the country's rarest and most intriguing animals, such as the maned wolf and giant anteater, live here. The state capital, Belo Horizonte, has few real attractions but good transport links.*

Background

Like the Spanish, the Portuguese looked to their colonies for easy money. Outside the Jesuit reduction cities, there were never plans to invest in empire, only to exploit the land and the local people as ruthlessly as possible. At first it was wood that attracted the Portuguese, and then indigenous slaves for the cane plantations that stretched along the northern coast. But it was the ultimate in rich pickings that led to colonial Brazil becoming more than a coastline empire. In 1693, whilst out on a marauding expedition, a Paulista bandeirante found *ouro preto* – gold made black by a coat of iron oxide – in a stream south of modern Belo Horizonte. When news reached home, an influx of adventurers trekked their way from São Paulo through the forests to set up makeshift camps along the gold streams. These camps developed into wealthy towns such as Ouro Preto and Mariana. Later, with the discovery of diamonds and other gemstones, a captaincy was established and named, prosaically, 'General Mines'.

The wealth of Minas was reflected in its streets and in the baroque churches, whose interiors were covered in gold plate and decorated with sculptures by the best artisans in Brazil. And with the wealth came growing self-importance. The Inconfidencia (see box, page 250), the most important manifestation of rebellion in colonial Brazil, began in Ouro Preto in the late 18th century under a group of intellectuals educated in Portugal who were in contact with Thomas Jefferson and English industrialists. The Inconfidencia never got beyond discussion but it was decided that the only non-aristocratic member of the group, José Joaquim da Silva, would be in charge of taking the governor's palace, occupied by the hated Visconde of Barbacena, who was responsible for levying the imperial taxes. Da Silva was derisively known as Tiradentes (the tooth puller) by his compatriots. Today he is the only Inconfidente rebel that most Brazilians can name and he is celebrated as a folk hero – one of the common people who dared to challenge the powerful elite, and who was cruelly martyred as a result.

After Brazil changed from an empire into a republic, Minas Gerais vied for power with the coffee barons of São Paulo and, in the 20th century, produced two Brazilian presidents. Juscelino Kubitschek, an establishment figure chosen by the electorate as the best alternative to the military, opened up Brazil to foreign investment in the 1960s, and founded Brasília. Tancredo Neves also opposed the Brazilian military, was elected to power in 1985. A few days before his inauguration he died in mysterious circumstances. His last words were reportedly "I did not deserve this". He was replaced by José Sarney, a leading figure in the Brazilian landowning oligarchy.

Belo Horizonte

➔ *Phone code: 031. Colour map 4, B3. Population: 5 million.*

The capital of Minas Gerais is the third largest city in Brazil. Although moderately attractive it offers little in the way of sights, beyond a handful of museums and parks. Most travellers who come here for more than a change of bus on the way to Ouro Preto or Tiradentes do so to find work as English language teachers. The bustling modern skyscraper-filled centre sits in a bowl circled by dramatic mountains which regularly trap pollution as the city strains under ever-increasing tides of rural migration. The city is pocked with hills that rise and fall in waves of red-tiled houses, tall apartment blocks and jacaranda- and ipe-lined streets. These are clogged with cars, particularly during the rush hour, a situation which has led the municipal government to introduce an efficient integrated public transport system linking the bus and metro networks, in imitation of Curitiba, in Paraná. ⏩ *For Sleeping, Eating and other listings, see pages 238-242.*

Belo Horizonte orientation & Pampulha

Sleeping
Ouro Minas Palace **3**

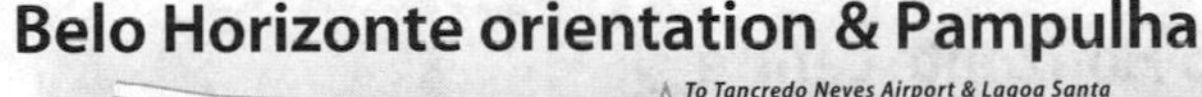

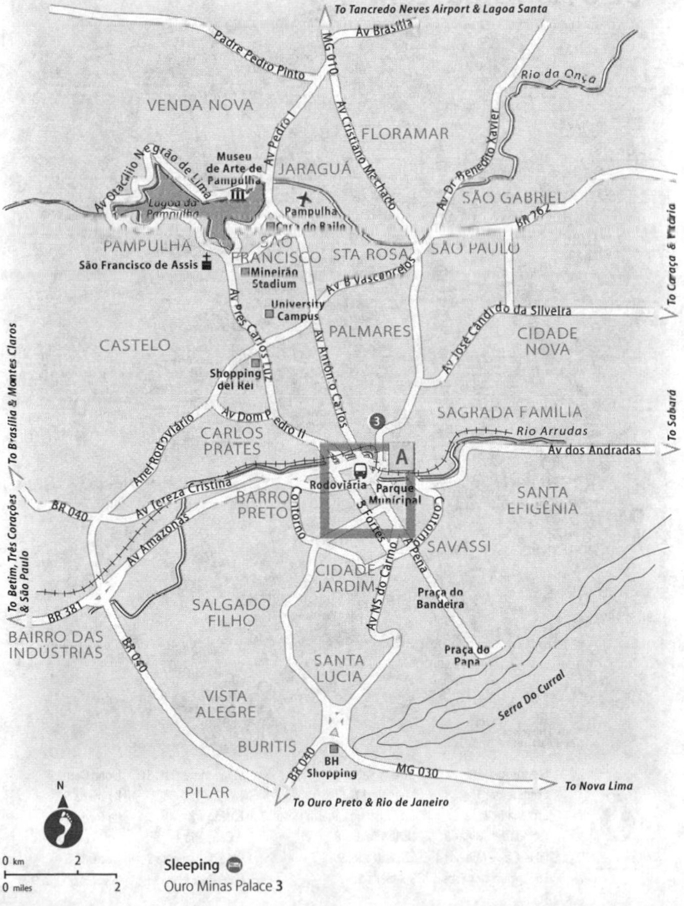

Ins and outs

Getting there International flights land at **Tancredo Neves International Airport**, T031-3689 2130, at Confins, 39 km north of Belo Horizonte. A taxi to the centre costs US$40. Buses from the airport, either *executivo* from the exit (US$11), or the comfortable normal bus, **Unir**, from the far end of the car park (hourly, US$2), go to the *rodoviária*. Closer to the city, the domestic airport at **Pampulha**, T031-490 2000, has air shuttle services to several cities including Rio, Salvador and São Paulo. **TAM, GOL, BRA, Varig** and **Webjet** all fly here. Blue bus No 1202 to the city centre leaves across the street from the airport (25 minutes, US$0.65), passing the *rodoviária* and the cheaper hotel district. Interstate buses arrive at the *rodoviária* next to Praça Rio Branco at the northwest end of Avenida Afonso Pena. The bus station is clean and well organized with toilets, a post office, telephones, left-luggage lockers (US$2, attended service 0700-2200) and shops. ▸▸ *See also Transport, page 241.*

Getting around The focus is on the large Parque Municipal in the heart of downtown Belo Horizonte and on the broad main avenue of Afonso Pena. This is constantly full of

pedestrians and traffic, except on Sunday morning when cars are banned and part of it becomes a huge open-air market. Daytime activity is concentrated on the main commercial district on Avenida Afonso Pena and around – the best area to eat in at lunchtime. At night, activity shifts to Savassi, southwest of the centre, which has a wealth of restaurants, bars and clubs. The city has a good public transport system and some buses integrate with the regional, overground Metrô.

Best time to visit Central Minas enjoys an excellent climate (16-30°C) except for the rainy season (December to March); the average temperature in Belo Horizonte is 21°C.

Tourist information The municipal information office, **Belotur** ① *R Pernambuco 284, Funcionários, T031-3277 9797, www.pbh.gov.br/belotur*, is very helpful, with lots of useful information and maps. The monthly *Guía Turística* for events, opening times and information, is freely available. **Belotur** also has offices at the southwest corner of Parque Municipal, at Confins and Pampulha airports, and at the *rodoviária*. The tourism authority for Minas Gerais, **Turminas** ① *Praça Rio Branco 56, T031-3272 8573, www.turminas.mg.gov.br/intminas.html*, is also very helpful; its *Gerais Common Ways* booklet has a useful facts section. **Ibama** ① *Av do Contorno 8121, Cidade Jardim, T031-3337 2624, F3335 9955*, can offer information on national parks. A useful website is www.picfish.com, which has pictures of journeys undertaken in Brazil with links to tour operators, hotels and other services.

Safety As in any large city, watch out for sneak thieves in the centre and at the bus station. The Parque Municipal is not safe after dark, so it is best not to enter alone.

Sights

Although dotted with green spaces like the **Parque Municipal** ① *Tue-Sun 0600-1800*, and a few handsome buildings such as the arts complex at the **Palácio das Artes** ① *Afonso Pena 156*, central Belo Horizonte has few sights of interest beyond a handful of small museums. The **Museu Mineiro** ① *Av João Pinheiro 342, T031-3269 1168, Tue-Fri 1000-1700, Sat and Sun 1000-1600*, houses religious and other art in the old senate building, close to the centre. There is a section dedicated specifically to religious art, with six pictures attributed to Mestre Athayde (see Ouro Preto, page 246), exhibitions of modern art, photographs and works by *naïf* painters. Also of interest are the woodcarvings by Geraldo Teles de Oliveira (GTO). The **Museu Histórico Abílio Carreto** ① *Av Prudente de Morais 202, Cidade Jardim, T031-3277 8861, Tue, Wed, Fri, Sun 1000-1700, Thu 1000-1200*, is in an old *fazenda* which has been here since 1883, when Belo Horizonte was a village called Arraial do Curral d'el Rey. The *fazenda* now houses antique furniture and historical exhibits. To get there, take bus 2902 from Avenida Afonso Pena.

Pampulha

The city's most interesting attraction by far is the suburb of Pampulha; a complex of Oscar Niemeyer buildings set around a lake in formal gardens landscaped by Roberto Burle Marx. The project was commissioned by Juscelino Kubitschek in the 1940s, when he was governor of Minas Gerais and a decade before he became president. Some see it as a proto-Brasília, for this was the first time that Niemeyer had designed a series of buildings that work together in geometric harmony. It was in Pampulha that he first experimented with the plasticity of concrete; the highlight of the complex is the **Igreja São Francisco de Assis** ① *Av Otacílio Negrão de Lima, Km 12, T031-3441 9325, daily 0800-1800*. This was one of Niemeyer's first departures from the orthodox rectilinear forms of modernism and one of the first buildings in the world to

O Aleijadinho

Brazil's greatest sculptor, Antônio Francisco Lisboa (1738-1814) was the son of a Portuguese architect and a black slave woman and was known as O Aleijadinho (the little cripple). A debilitating disease – probably leprosy – left him so badly maimed that he was forced to work on his knees and later on his back with his chisels strapped to his useless hands. Like Mestre Athayde and many other Mineira baroque artists his art was political. He was strongly sympathetic with the Inconfidentes movement and was probably a friend of Tiradentes. Many of his sculptures contain subtle references to Tiradentes's martyrdom and veiled criticisms of the Portuguese. His most remarkable work, are the haunting, vivid statues of the prophets in Congonhas, which are so lifelike that they almost seem to move, and the church decoration in Ouro Preto.

mould concrete, with its series of parabolic waves running together to form arches. Light pierces the interior through a series of louvres and the curves are offset by a simple free-standing bell tower. The outside walls are covered in *azulejo* tiles by Candido Portinari, Brazil's most respected modernist artist. These were painted in a different style from his previous social realism, as exemplified by pictures such as *O Mestiço*. The building provoked a great deal of outrage because of its modernist design. One mayor proposed its demolition and replacement by a copy of the church of Saint Francis in Ouro Preto.

There are a number of other interesting Niemeyer buildings on the other side of the lake from the church. With its snaking canopy leading up to the main dance hall, the **Casa do Baile** ⓘ *Av Octacílio Negrão de Lima 751, T031-3277 7433, Tue-Sun 0900-1900, free*, is another example of his fascination with the curved line. There are wonderful views out over the lake from its windows. People would dance here and then take a boat to the glass and marble **Museu de Arte de Pampulha** (MAP) ⓘ *Av Octacílio Negrão de Lima 16585, T031-3443 4533, www.comartevirtual.com.br, Tue-Sun 0900-1900, free*, which was then a casino set up by Kubitschek. Today it houses a fine collection of Mineira modern art and more than 900 works by national artists.

Just 700 m south of the lake are the twin stadia of **Mineirão** and **Mineirinho**, clear precursors to the Centro de Convenções Ulysses Guimarães in Brasília, which was designed by Niemeyer's office though not the architect himself. Mineirão is the second largest stadium in Brazil after the Maracanã in Rio, seating 92,000.

Around Belo Horizonte » pp238-242.

Caves

The hilly countryside around Belo Horizonte is honeycombed with some of Brazil's most beautiful caves. The best and most famous is the **Gruta de Maquiné** ⓘ *off the BR040/MG231, 120 km from Belo Horizonte, daily 0800-1700, US$5*, near the town of **Cordisburgo**. The cave has six chambers open to visitors; these are well lit and encrusted with beautiful speleological formations. It's best to come at the beginning or end of the day, and avoid the weekend when there are crowds. Cordisburgo has a handful of hotels and was the home of Brazil's most celebrated modern writer, João Guimarães Rosa, the author of the great Minas Gerais epic *Grande Sertão: veredas*. The **Casa Museu de Guimarães Rosa** ⓘ *Av Padre João 744, Tue-Sun 0800-1700*, is dedicated to the writer and housed in his former home. It preserves many of Guimarães Rosa's original manuscripts.

Less than 40 km to the south (and some 80 km northwest of Belo Horizonte) is the town of **Sete Lagoas**, near the **Gruta Rei do Mato** ⓘ *T031-773 0888, 0800-1700*, where prehistoric inscriptions and cave paintings have been found. The **Gruta de Lapinha** ⓘ *Tue-Sun 0900-1700, US$2 entry to caves and small archaeological museum*, is only 36 km north of the city.

Ins and outs

Cordisburgo and the Gruta Maquiné are served by three buses daily from Belo Horizonte (2½ hours). Sete Lagoas, which has accommodation, is served by three buses daily (1½ hours) and Gruta Lapinha by four buses (one hour).

Parque Natural de Caraça

ⓘ *The park is open 0700-2100; if staying overnight you cannot leave after 2100; park entrance US$5 per vehicle.*

This remarkable reserve sits in the heart of the Serra do Espinhaço mountains about 120 km east of Belo Horizonte and is perhaps the best place in South America for seeing maned wolf. It covers a range in altitude of 720-2070 m. The lower areas are rich in Atlantic forest while the higher areas support *cerrado*, grassland and other mountain habitats. There are lakes, waterfalls and rivers. Since the early 1980s, the monks have been leaving food for maned wolves on the seminary steps, and at least four can usually be seen every evening. Other endangered mammals in the park include southern masked titi monkeys, which can often be spotted in family groups, tufted-eared marmosets and brown capuchin monkeys. Birdlife includes various toucans, guans and hummingbirds (such as the Brazilian ruby and the white-throated hummingbird), various tanagers, cotingas, antbirds, woodpeckers and the long-trained and scissor- tailed nightjars. Some of the bird species are endemic, others are rare and endangered.

The trails for viewing the different landscapes and the wildlife are marked at the beginning and are quite easy to follow, although a guide (available through the seminary) is recommended.

The **seminary buildings** and the church are beautifully set in a shallow valley 1220 m above sea level and surrounded on three sides by rugged mountains that rise to 2070 m at the Pico do Sol. The name Caraça means 'big face', so called because of a hill that is said to resemble the face of a giant who is looking at the sky. This can be best appreciated by climbing up to the cross just above the church. The church itself has a painting of the Last Supper attributed to Mestre Athayde (see page 246) with a trompe l'oeil effect. The eyes of Judas Iscariot (the figure holding the purse) seem to follow you as you move. Part of the seminary has been converted into a hotel, which is the only place to stay in the park (see Sleeping, page 238). It is also possible to stay in **Santa Bárbara**, 25 km away on the road to Mariana, which has a few cheap hotels, and hitchhike to Caraça.

Ins and outs

Santa Bárbara is served by 11 buses a day from Belo Horizonte (fewer on Saturday and Sunday). There is also a bus service to Mariana, a beautiful route, via Catas Altas, which has an interesting church and a pousada belonging to the municipality of Santa Bárbara. To get to the park, turn off the BR-262 (towards Vitória) at Km 73 and go via Barão de Cocais to Caraça (120 km). There is no public transport to the seminary. Buses go as far as Barão de Cocais, from where a taxi is US$12. Book the taxi to return for you, or hitch (which may not be easy). The park entrance is 10 km before the seminary. The alternative is to hire a guide from Belo Horizonte, about US$75, including guiding, transport and meals.

Belo Horizonte *p233, maps p233 and p234*

There are cheap options near the *rodoviária* and on R Curitiba, but many of these hotels are hot-pillow establishments; you will have a more comfortable stay in one of the youth hostels. You can spend the night in the *rodoviária*, but only if you have an onward ticket (police check at 2400).

L **Ouro Minas Palace**, Av Cristiano Machado 4001, T031-3429 4001 (toll free T0800-314000), www.ourominas.com.br. The most luxurious hotel in the city with palatial suites, including several for women only on the top floors. Excellent service, a pool, sauna, gym with personal trainers and good business facilities. Not central but within easy reach of the centre and airports.

AL **Grandarrell Minas**, R Espírito Santo 901, T031-3248 0000, www.grandarrell.com.br. One of the best and most central business hotels, with a very large convention centre and full business facilities, fax and email modems in the rooms. Rooftop pool. Not much English spoken.

AL **Liberty Palace Hotel**, R Paraíba 1465, Savassi, T031-2121 0900, www.liberty palace.com.br. Recently opened business hotel right in the heart of the Savassi restaurant district with standard 1990s business rooms with spacious marble bathrooms. 24-hr room service, IDSL in all rooms and a well-appointed business centre.

AL **Othon Palace**, Av Afonso Pena 1050, T031-3247 0000, www.hoteis-othon.com.br. A 1980s chain hotel with a rooftop pool, good service and an excellent location in the centre opposite the Parque Municipal. Rooms on lower floors can be noisy.

A **Sol Meliá**, R da Bahia 1040, T031-3274 1344, www.solmeliabh.com.br. Well-renovated 1990s business hotel in the centre with a pool, sauna and respectable service.

B **Le Flamboyant flats**, R Rio Grande do Norte 1007, Savassi, T031-3261 7370, www.clan.com.br. Well-maintained 1980s flats with a pool. Separate sitting rooms with TVs, and kitchens with cookers. Some have 2 bedrooms.

B **Mercure**, Av Do Contorno 7315 (Santo Antonio), T031-3298 4100, www.accorhotels. com.br. The newest of the city's business hotels with a good pool, sauna, gym and rooms decked out in standard business attire. A few kilometres from the centre.

C **Esplanada**, Av Santos Dumont 304, T031-3273 5311. An upmarket cheapie with bright en suite rooms with soap and towels provided and generous breakfasts. Triples available for little more than doubles; prices are negotiable.

C **Villa Emma flats**, R Arturo Toscanini 41, Savassi, T031-3282 3388, www.clan.com.br. The cheapest option in Savassi. Spacious flats in need of a lick of paint, with 2 bedrooms, separate living areas and a kitchen. Internet access in some rooms.

D **Continental**, Av Paraná 241, T031-3201 7944. Central, quiet, with small interior rooms newly renovated with modern fittings. Recommended.

D **São Salvador**, R Espírito Santo 227, T031-3222 7731. Small well-kept rooms, the best of which are the triples with en suites. Reasonable breakfast and a public telephone. One of many similar cheapies in the area.

D-E **O Sorriso do Lagarto hostel**, R Padre Severino 285, Savassi, T031-3283 9325, www.osorrisodolagarto.com.br. Simple little hostel in a converted town house with kitchen, internet and fax service, breakfast, lockers, washing machines and a living area with DVD player.

E-F **IYHA Chalé Mineiro**, R Santa Luzia 288, Santa Efigênia, T031-3467 1576, www.chale mineirohostel.com.br. Attractive and well maintained, with dorms and doubles, a small pool and shared kitchen, TV lounge and telephones. Towels and bed linen are extra. To get here take bus 980 from the *rodoviária*.

Parque Natural de Caraça *p237*

AL-B **Santuário do Caraça**, reservations: Caixa Postal 12, T031-3596 0000, Santa Bárbara. This on-site hotel has reasonable rooms, the restaurant serves good food from farms within the seminary's lands, lunch 1200-1330. No camping is permitted.

Eating

Belo Horizonte *p233, maps p233 and p234*

Mineiros love their food and drink and Belo Horizonte has a lively café dining and bar scene. Savassi overflows with bohemian streetside cafés, bars and restaurants and is the best place in the city for a food browse. There is a lively, cheap street food market on R Tomé de Souza, between Pernambuco and Alagoas in Savassi every night around 1900-2300: think Bangkok with Minas food and buzzing bars. Pampulha, on the outskirts, has the best of the fine-dining restaurants, which are well worth the taxi ride. There are plenty of cheap per kilo restaurants and *padarias* near the budget hotels in the centre.

🍴🍴🍴 **Aurora**, R Expedicionário Mário Alves de Oliveira 421, São Luís, T031-3498 7567. One of the best restaurants in the city, in a garden setting next to the Lago da Pampulha. Imaginative menu with dishes fusing Mineira and Italian techniques and making use of unusual Brazilian fruits. Respectable wine list. Closed Mon and Tue.

🍴🍴🍴 **Taste Vin**, R Curitiba 2105, Lourdes, T031-3292 5423. French food. Excellent soufflés and provençale seafood. The respectable wine list includes decent Brazilian options. Recommended.

🍴🍴🍴 **Vecchio Sogno**, R Martim de Carvalho 75 and R Dias Adorno, Santo Agostinho, under the Assembléia Legislativo, T031-3292 5251. The best Italian in the city with an inventive menu fusing Italian and French cuisine with Brazilian ingredients. Excellent fish. Good wine list. Lunch only on Sun.

🍴🍴🍴 **Xapuri**, R Mandacaru 260, Pampulha, T031-3496 6198. *Comida mineira*, great atmosphere, live music, very good food, expensive and a bit out of the way but recommended. Closed on Mon.

🍴🍴🍴-🍴🍴 **Dona Derna** , R Tomé de Souza, Savassi, T031-3223 6954. A range of restaurants in one. Upstairs is Italian fine dining with excellent dishes and a respectable wine list. Downstairs on weekdays is traditional Italian home cooking and by night a chic pizzeria called **Memmo.**

🍴🍴 **La Traviata**, Av Cristovão Colombo 282, Savassi, T031-3261 6392. An atmospheric little Italian with a terrace overlooking the dragon's tooth pavements of Cristovão Colombo. The menu is strong on meat and fish with reasonable pasta and pizzas. Modest wine list, good-value house bottles.

🍴🍴-🍴 **Kauhana**, R Tomé de Souza, Savassi, T031-3284 8714. Tasty wood-fired pizzas, both savoury and sweet, in an array of flavours. Pleasant open-air dining area.

🍴🍴-🍴 **Sushi Beer**, R Tomé de Souza, Savassi, T031-3221 1116. A large open-air dining area overlooked by a long bar and with a lively crowd and good atmosphere. Food ranges from superior per kilo Minas and Japanese food to meats and pizzas. Respectable range of beers and whiskies.

🍴 **A Cafeteria**, Av Cristovão Colombo 152, Savassi, T031-3223 9901. Salads, great sandwiches in pitta bread and a range of mock-Italian standards served to a lively young crowd and accompanied by live music most nights. One of several café-bars on the corner of Colombo and Albuquerque.

🍴 **Café da Travessa**, Av Getúlio Vargas 1405 at Praça Savassi, T031-3223 8092. Great little café-bookshop. Dishes range from rosti to Brazilian tapas, pasta and wraps. Pizza upstairs. Good coffee and a tasteful choice of books and Brazilian CDs. Breakfast till late.

🍴 **Café Tina**, Av Cristovão Colombo 336, Savassi, T031-3261 5068. Bohemian café in a 19th-century town house serving soups, risottos and delicious puddings to an arty young crowd. Closed Mon.

Seriously cheap *comida mineira* is served in the restaurants around the *rodoviária*, *prato feito* US$1.50.

Bars and clubs

Belo Horizonte *p233, maps p233 and p234*

Bars

There are plenty of bars around Tomé de Souza in Savassi, where a young and arty crowd spills out onto the street, and the beer and *caipirinhas* are cheap and plentiful. Always lively are **Bar do James**, Vargas at Tomé de Souza and **Koyote**, R Tomé de Souza 1012.

Clubs

Recommended are **Ao Bar**, R Cláudio Manoel 572, Funcionários, T031-3261 7443; **L'Apogée**, R Antônio de Albuquerque 729, T031 3227 5133; **Máscaras,** R Santa Rita Durão 667, T031-3261 6050; and **Partenon,** Rio Grande do Norte 1470, T031-3221 9856.

Entertainment

Belo Horizonte *p233, maps p233 and p234*

Cinema

Belo Horizonte is a good place to watch high-quality Brazilian and foreign films. There are many art cinemas and cineclubs in the centre such as the **Espaço Unibanco**, R Guajajaras 37.

Theatre

Belo Horizonte has at least a dozen theatres, including **Teatro da Cidade**, R da Bahia 1341, T031-3273 1050; **Teatro Alterosa**, Av Assis Chateaubriand 499, Floresta, T031-3237 6610; and **Teatro Marília**, Av Alfredo Balena 586, Centro, T031-3222 4445. The city prides itself on its theatre and dance companies (look out for the *Grupo Galpão*); don't expect to find many shows in any language other than Portuguese. The local press and tourist literature give details of shows and events.

Festivals and events

Belo Horizonte *p233, maps p233 and p234*

Maundy Thu Corpus Christi.
15 Aug Assunção (Assumption).
8 Dec Conceição (Immaculate Conception).

Shopping

Belo Horizonte *p233, maps p233 and p234*

Bookshops

Acaiaca, R Tamóios 72. Good for dictionaries.
Daniel Vaitsman, R Espírito Santo 466, 17th floor, T031-2229071. English-language books.
Livraria Alfarrábio, R Tamóios 320, T031-3271 3603. Used foreign-language books.
Livraria Van Damme, R das Guajajaras 505, T031-3226 6492. National, Portuguese and local titles.

Gems and jewellery

Manoel Bernardes, Av Contorno 5417, Savassi, T031-3225 4200. Attractive jewellery. Very reasonable prices.

Markets

Mercado Central, Av Augusto de Lima 744. Large and clean, open every day until 1800 selling arts, crafts and bric-a-brac. There is a Sun handicraft fair on **Av Afonso Pena**. Hippies still sell their wares on **R Rio de Janeiro**, 600 block, each evening.
A **flower market** is held at Av Bernardo Monteiro, near Av Brasil, every Fri 1200-2000. Also here on Sat is a **food and drinks market**.

Music

Cogumelo, Av Augusto de Lima 399, T031-274 9915.

Activities and tours

Belo Horizonte *p233, maps p233 and p234*

Caving

Grupo Speleo, at the Universidade Federal de Minas Gerais, has the most experience in visiting out-of-the-way caves.

Ecotourism and adventure sports

Amo-Te, Associação Mineira dos Organizadores do Turismo Ecológico, R Monte Verde 125, Lípio de Melo, T031-3477 5430, oversees ecotourism in the state of Minas Gerais. This includes trekking, riding, cycling, rafting, jeep tours, canyoning, national parks and *fazendas*. For companies which arrange these special-interest tours, speak to Amo-Te first.

Horse riding

Tropa Serrana, T031-3344 8986, T031-9983 2356 (mob), tropaserrana@hotmail.com. Recommended.

Tour operators

Ametur, R Alvarengo Peixoto 295, loja 102, Lourdes, T/F031-3292 1976. Information on *fazendas* that welcome visitors and overnight guests.
Master Turismo (American Express representative), R da Bahia 2140, T031-3330 3655, www.masterturismo.com.br, at Sala VIP, Aeroporto de Confins and Av Afonso Pena 1967, T031-3330 3603. Very helpful.
Ouro Preto Turismo, Av Afonso Pena 4133, grupo 109, Serra, T031-3221 5005. Recommended.
Revetur, R Espírito Santo 1892, 1st floor, Lourdes, T031-3337 2500. Recommended.

Transport

Belo Horizonte *p233, maps p233 and p234*

Air

Belo Horizonte has connections with **São Paulo** and **Rio de Janeiro**. For airport information, see Ins and outs, page 234. Buses for **Confins airport** leave from the *rodoviária*, US$11 (*executivo*). To get to **Pampulha airport**, take the blue bus No 1202 from the *rodoviária*, 25 mins, US$0.65.

Airline offices American, R Guajajaras 557, T031-3273 3622, Confins airport, T031-3689 2670. **BRA**, T031-3263 0000, www.voebra.com.br. **GOL**, T0300-7892121, www.voegol.com.br. **TAM**, Pampulha Airport, T031-3443 5500. **United**, R Paraíba 1000, 10th floor, Funcionários, T031-3261 7777, Confins airport, T031-3689 2736. **Varig/RioSul/Nordeste**, Av Olegário Maciel 2251, Lourdes, T031-3291 6444, Confins airport, T031-3689 2305, Pampulha airport, T031-3491 2466. **Webjet**, T0300-210 1234, www.webjet.com.br.

Bus

Local Red buses run on express routes and charge US$0.75; **yellow buses** have circular routes around the Contorno, US$0.50; **blue buses** run on diagonal routes charging US$0.65. Some buses link up with the regional overground Metrô.

Long distance For information on the bus station, see Ins and outs, page 234. To **Rio** with **Cometa**, T031-3201 5611 and **Util**, T031-3201 7744, 6½ hrs, US$12.75 and *leito* US$25.50. To **Vitória** with São Geraldo, T031-271 1911, US$14.50 and *leito* US$29. To **Brasília** with **Itapemirim**, T031-2919991, and Penha, T031-3271 1027, 10 hrs, 6 a day including 2 *leitos*, only 1 leaves in daylight (0800), US$19.25, *leito* US$38.50. To **São Paulo** with Cometa and Gontijo, T031-3201 6130, 10 hrs, US$15.60. To **Foz do Iguaçu**, 22 hrs, US$42. To **Salvador** with Gontijo, 24 hrs, at 1900 daily, US$40, and São Geraldo at 1800. São Geraldo also goes to **Porto Seguro**, 17 hrs, direct, via Nanuque and Eunápolis, US$33. To **Recife** with Gontijo, 2000, US$41; to **Fortaleza**, US$63; to **Natal**, US$66. To **Belém** with Itapemirim at 2030, US$72. To **Campo Grande** with Gontijo (at 1930) and Motta, 3 a day, T031-3464 0480, US$31-36, a good route to Bolivia, avoiding São Paulo. All major destinations served. For buses within Minas Gerais, see under each destination.

Car hire

Interlocadora, R dos Timbiras 2229, T031-275 4090; **Localiza**, Av Bernardo Monteiro 1567, Pampulha and Confins airports, T031-247 7957, or T0800-992000.

Taxi

Taxis are plentiful but hard to find at peak hours. **BH Táxi**, T031-3215 8081, **Coopertáxi**, T031-3421 2424.

Train

To **Vitória**, daily 0700, tickets sold at 0530, US$17.50 *executivo*, US$11.50 1st class, US$7.80 2nd class, 14 hrs.

Around Belo Horizonte *p236*

Lakes and grottoes

Buses (Útil) to the **Gruta de Lapinha** leave Belo Horizonte daily at 1015 and 1130, returning 1600, also Mon at 1830, 1¼ hrs, US$3.25 one way. Half-hourly bus service Belo Horizonte–**Lagoa Santa**, US$2. Bus Lagoa Santa–**Lapinha** every 30 mins. The local bus stop for Lagoa Santa is 2 km downhill from the Lapinha caves. To **Gruta de Maquiné**, several buses daily (**Irmãos Teixeira**), 2¼ hrs, US$8.

Directory

Belo Horizonte *p233, maps p233 and p234*

Banks Banco do Brasil, R Rio de Janeiro 750, Av Amazonas 303. Cash is given against credit cards at **Banco Itaú**, Av João Pinheiro 195. Visa ATM at **Bradesco**, R da Bahia 947. **Citibank**, R Espírito Santo 871. **Master Turismo**, Av Afonso Pena 1967, T031-3330 3603, Amex representative. **Nascente Turismo**, Rio de Janeiro 1314, no commission. Changing TCs is difficult, but hotels will change them for guests at a poor rate. **Embassies and consulates** Austria, R José Américo Cançado Bahia 199, T031-3333 5363. **Denmark**, R Paraíba 1122, 5th floor, T031-3286 8626. **France**, R Pernambuco 712A, T031-3261 7805. **Germany**, R Timbiras 1200, 5th floor, T031-3213 1568. **Italy**, Av Afonso Pena 3130, 12th floor, T031-3281 4211. **Netherlands**, R Sergipe 1167, loja 5, T031-3227 5275. **UK**, R dos Inconfidentes 1075, sala 1302, Savassi, T031-3261 2072, britcon.bhe@terra.com.br. **USA**, R Timbiras 1200, 7th floor, T031-213 1571. **Immigration** Polícia Federal, R Nascimento Gurgel 30, T031-291 0005. For visa extensions. To get there take bus 7902 from the corner of R Curitiba and Av Amazonas and get off at the Hospital Madre Teresa. **Internet** Internet Café Club, R Fernandes Tourinho 385, Plaza Savassi, US$5 per hr. There are numerous others throughout the city. **Medical services** **Mater Dei**, R Gonçalves Dias 2700, T031-339 9000. Recommended. **Post office** Av Afonso Pena 1270. Poste restante is behind the main office at R de Goiás 77. The branch on R da Bahia is less slow. **Telephone** Av Afonso Pena 1180, by the *correios*, daily 0700-2200.

Colonial cities near Belo Horizonte

Streets of whitewashed 18th-century houses with deep-blue or yellow window frames line steep and winding streets leading to lavishly decorated churches with Manueline façades and rich gilt interiors. Behind lies a backdrop of grey granite hills and green forests, still filled with tiny marmoset monkeys and flocks of canary-winged parakeets. The colonial gold-mining towns of southern Minas are the highlights of any visit to the state – islands of history and remnant forest in an otherwise dull agricultural landscape. Most lie south of Belo Horizonte and many people choose to visit them on the way to or from Rio. However, they make a far more charming and restful base than Belo Horizonte and we would recommend spending time here and stopping either for a bus change or a quick night in the state capital on the way north or south. » *For Sleeping, Eating and other listings, see pages 260-266.*

Ins and outs

The cities fall into three groups: south of Belo Horizonte (Ouro Preto, Mariana, Congonhas do Campo, São João del Rei and Tiradentes); east (Sabará and Caeté); and north (Diamantina and Serro). All of the southern towns are on the main Rio highway (Ouro Preto being the closest to the state capital and São João del Rei the furthest from it). The towns to the east are on the main highway to Espírito Santo. Those to the north are a longer journey from Belo Horizonte, off the inland route to Bahia.

The most famous of the towns is **Ouro Preto**. It can be visited in a day trip from Belo Horizonte, but a day is nothing like enough and Ouro Preto makes a more interesting and pleasant place to stay than the capital. **Mariana** is easy to see in a day trip from Ouro Preto. The spectacular Aleijadinho church in **Congonhas do Campo**, further south, requires only a few hours to visit and is now reachable by a new highway. There is no need to stay overnight. **Tiradentes**, further south still, is the prettiest, best-preserved and most visited of all the cities but feels somewhat tourist twee. Nearby **São João del Rei** is more decrepit but more of a real city. They are linked at weekends by a 30-minute steam train ride and daily by frequent buses. **Sabará** and **Caeté**, to the east of the capital, can be visited as an easy day trip from Belo Horizonte or on the way to Espírito Santo. **Diamantina** and **Serro** are far to the north, on one of the routes to Bahia from Belo Horizonte, and are easiest to see as a stopover en route to Bahia.

Milton Nascimento – the voice of Minas

Milton Nascimento is the most influential Brazilian singer and composer not to have come out of Bahia or Rio. He has produced some of Brazil's most haunting music, been nominated for a Grammy and had songs covered by almost as many artists as Paul McCartney.

Milton grew up in rural Minas in a town like many others – lost in a landscape of lush green hills and cattle pasture and where life focused on the praça and local church. He was raised by his stepmother who'd once sung in a choir conducted by Villa Lobos, and who exposed him to religious music from an early age. Catholicism came to underlie both his musical style and lyrical themes, which were expressed most memorably on a string of ground breaking 1970s albums. The music on these is unique - with rich choral harmonies, jazz interludes and sweetly melancholic melodies interplaying with Afro-Brazilian rhythms and sound effects. Lyrics poetically exalt the day to day life of the oppressed. And Milton's golden voice soars over the top.

You'll hear Milton's songs throughout Ouro Preto. If you are tempted to buy one of his records, opt for **Clube de Esquina**, his 1972 classic.

Ouro Preto » *pp260-266.*

→ *Phone code: 031. Altitude: 1000 m. Colour map 4, C3. Population: 67,000.*

Ouro Preto, named after the black iron oxide-coated gold that was discovered here by the adventurer Antônio Dias, was one of the first of the Minas gold towns to be founded. As a former state capital, it became the wealthiest and most important town in the region. Although it now has a hinterland of ugly blocks of flats and crumbling *favelas* it preserves some of the most significant colonial architecture in Brazil and remains, at heart, an 18th-century city of steep church-crowned hills, cobbled streets, *azulejos*, plazas and fountains. In homage to its historical importance Ouro Preto becomes the capital of Minas Gerais once again every year for one day only, on 24 June. The modern city bustles with young Brazilians studying and partying at the various local universities and has a thriving café and nightlife scene. Sadly the historic centre, once closed to traffic, is now thick with buses and cars, which is taking its toll on some of the beautiful buildings.

Ins and outs

Getting there Ouro Preto's **rodoviária** ⓘ *R Padre Rolim 661, T031-3559 3225*, is 1 km north of Praça Tiradentes. A 'circular' bus runs from the *rodoviária* to Praça Tiradentes, US$0.40; it is a long walk to the centre. Taxis charge exorbitant rates. There are frequent connections to Belo Horizonte (three hours) and daily buses to Rio (eight hours) and São Paulo (nine hours) as well as other cities throughout Minas, including Congonhas, with buses passing through Conselheiro Lafaiette. » *For Transport information, see page 265.*

Tourist information The **tourist office** ⓘ *Praça Tiradentes 41, T031-3559 3269, 0800-1800, www.ouropreto.org.br*, has details of accommodation in *casas de família*, *repúblicas* and other places. It also has leaflets showing the opening times of sights, which change frequently, and can organize a local guide from the **Associação de Guias de Turismo (AGTOP)** ⓘ *R Padre Rolim, s/n, T031-3551 2655, Mon-Fri 0800-1800, Sat and Sun 0800-1700, little English spoken*, which has its own office opposite the bus station. Cássio Antunes is recommended.

Praça Tiradentes and around

The city has a number of churches and chapels as well as some excellent examples of public fountains (*chafariz*), oratories (*passos*) and stone bridges. The best place to start exploring the city is the central **Praça Tiradentes**, where you'll see a **statue of Tiradentes**, the leader of the Inconfidentes (see box page 250). Another Inconfidente, the poet Tomás Antônio Gonzaga, lived at Rua Cláudio Manoel 61 near the São Francisco de Assis church, and was exiled to Africa. Most Brazilians know his poem based on his forbidden love affair with the girl he called *Marília de Dirceu*. Visitors are shown the bridge and decorative fountain where the lovers held their trysts. The house where she lived, on the Largo Marília de Dirceu, is now a school.

On the north side of Praça Tiradentes is a famous **Escola de Minas** (School of Mining). It was founded in 1876, is housed in the fortress-like Palácio dos Governadores (1741-1748) and includes the **Museu de Mineralogia e das Pedras** ⓘ *No 20, Mon, Wed-Fri 1200-1645, Sat and Sun 0900-1300, US$1.50,* which has displays of rocks, minerals, semi-precious and precious stones from all over the world. Just north of the praça, towards the *rodoviária*, is the church of **Nossa Senhora das Mercês e Misericórdia** (1773-1793).

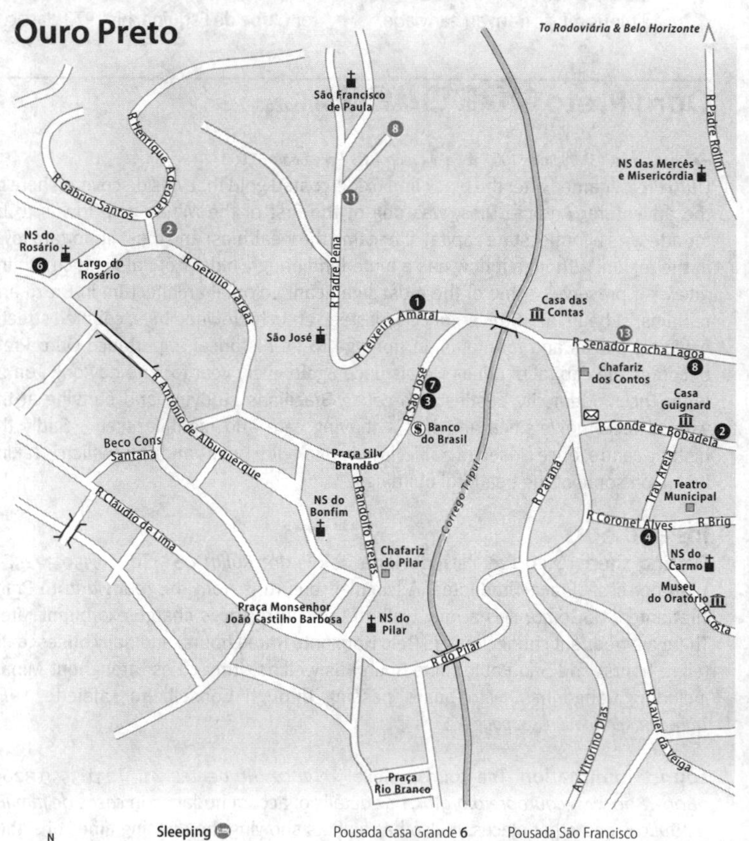

On the south side of the praça, next to Carmo church, is the **Museu da Inconfidência** ⓘ *No 139, T031-3551 1121, Mon-Fri 0800-1800, US$1.50*, a fine historical and art museum in the former Casa de Câmara e Cadeia, containing drawings by Aleijadinho and the Sala Manoel da Costa Athayde.

West of Praça Tiradentes

The church of **Nossa Senhora do Carmo** ⓘ *R Brigadeiro Mosqueira, Tue-Sun 1300-1700, entry is shared with Nossa Senhora do Pilar*, built 1766-1772, was planned by Manoel Francisco Lisboa, and both his son and Mestre Athayde worked on the project. It was a favourite church of the aristocracy. The best of the city's museums is housed in an annexe of the church, the modern and well-appointed **Museu do Oratório** ⓘ *T031- 3551 5369, daily 0930-1200, 1330-1730*. Inside is a selection of exquisitely crafted 18th- and 19th-century prayer icons and oratories, many of them with strong indigenous design and some disguised as bullet cases. On the opposite side of the road, the **Teatro Municipal** ⓘ *R Brigadeiro Musqueiro, daily 1230-1800*, is the oldest functioning theatre in Latin America, built in 1769.

A block north of the theatre, **Casa Guignard** ⓘ *R Conde de Bobadela 110, T031-3551 5155, Tue-Fri 1200-1800, Sat, Sun and holidays 0900-1500, free*, displays the

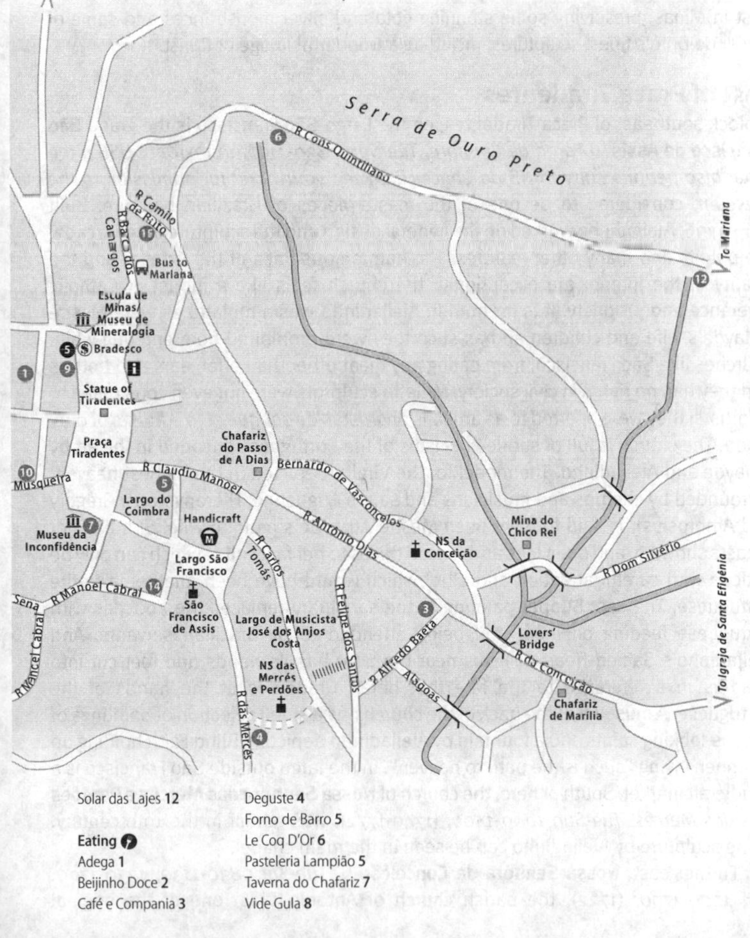

paintings of Alberto da Veiga Guignard. Further west, just before the river, the **Casa das Contas** ⓘ *R São José 12, T031-355 1444, Tue-Sat 1230-1730, Sun and holidays 0900- 1500, US$0.50*, built 1782-1784, houses a museum of money and finance on its upper storeys. Far more interesting is the damp, dark basement where slaves were formerly housed. In colonial Preto a slave's life was literally worth less than a chicken: swapping an African Brazilian for poultry was considered a good deal.

Following Rua Teixeira Amaral across the river, the church of **São José** was begun in 1752, but not completed until 1811; some of the carving is by Aleijadinho. Up on the hill, **São Francisco de Paula** ⓘ *0900-1700*, was started in 1804, making it the last colonial church in Ouro Preto. Further west, on the Largo do Rosário, the church of **Nossa Senhora do Rosário** dates from 1785, when the present church replaced a chapel on the site. It has a curved façade, which is rare in Brazilian baroque. The interior is simpler than the exterior, but there are interesting side altars.

One of the city's grandest churches, **Nossa Senhora do Pilar** ⓘ *just north of R do Pilar, Tue-Sun 0900-1100 and 1200-1700,* was attended by the Portuguese upper classes. The ceiling painting by João de Carvalhães features a trompe l'oeil effect – as you walk to the front of the church the lamb appears to move from one side of the crucifix to the other – a symbol of the resurrection. Manoel Lisboa, Aleijadinho's father, was responsible for all the carving except the heavily gilded work around the altar, which is by Francisco Xavier de Brito. The **museum** in the church vaults is one of the best in Minas, preserving some stunning gold and silver monstrances and some of Xavier de Brito's finest sculptures, including a wonderful image of Christ.

East of Praça Tiradentes

A block southeast of Praça Tiradentes, on the Largo São Francisco is the grand **São Francisco de Assis** ⓘ *Largo de Coimbra, Tue-Sun 0830-1150, 1330-1640, US$2; the ticket also permits entry to NS da Conceição, keep your ticket for admission to the museum*, considered to be one of the masterpieces of Brazilian baroque. Built 1766-1796, Aleijadinho worked on the general design and the sculpture of the façade, the pulpits and many other features. The harmonious lines of the exterior and the beauty of the interior are exceptional; the church feels like a model of Catholic reverence and propriety. It is far from it. Aleijadinho was a mulatto as were Mestre Athayde's wife and children and as such they were prohibited from entering white churches like São Francisco, from eating any meat other than offal, ears and trotters and they had no rights in civil society. Mulatto sculptors were not even considered to be artists; they were referred to as artisans or *artistas de sangue sujo* – artists of dirty blood. The church is full of subtle criticisms of the Portuguese encoded in the art by Athayde and Aleijadinho. The model for the Virgin (depicted in the highest heaven, surrounded by cherubs and musicians and saints Augustine, Hieronymous, Gregory and Ambrosius), is said to have been Mestre Athayde's mulatto wife. She has her breasts showing, and open legs and African traces to her face; all of which can only be noticed with careful attention and all of which would have been anathema to the Portuguese. The Last Supper painting in the sanctuary replaces the apostles with Portuguese feeding on meat and being attended to by Brazilian servants. And Aleijadinho's Sacred Heart of Jesus near the altar has its hands and feet cut into quarters in a reference to the fate that befell Tiradentes at the hands of the Portuguese. A **museum** at the back of the church has a small selection of paintings of serious-looking saints and a fountain by Aleijadinho depicting Blind Faith holding up a banner saying "such is the path to heaven". In the largo outside São Francisco is a handicraft market. South of here, the church of **Nossa Senhora das Mercês e Perdões** ⓘ *R das Mercês, Tue-Sun 1000-1400,* (1740-1772), was rebuilt in the 19th century. Some sculpture by Aleijadinho can be seen in the main chapel.

Further east, **Nossa Senhora da Conceição** ⓘ *Tue-Sat 0830-1130, 1330-1700, Sun 1200-1700,* (1722), the parish church of Antônio Dias (one of the original

Racism under the Portuguese

To Brazilians under the shackles of Portuguese colonial rule, Tiradentes was far more than a failed revolutionary. He was a hero who had risen from the oppressed classes to dare to stand up against the tyrannical Portuguese rule and was revered as a saint and martyr after his death. Under the Portuguese the black, indigenous and mixed race majority were regarded as lower than animals. Little of the wealth from the mines ever reached Brazilian hands and whilst the Portuguese and their religious and lay brotherhoods lived in luxurious opulence, the Brazilians who tore the gold from the hills were poor and oppressed. Slaves were forced to sleep in dark, damp dungeon-like quarters under the houses of their masters – like those in the **Casa dos Contos** museum in Ouro Preto – and there value was literally less than a chicken, for which they were readily exchanged. They were prohibited from eating meat or poultry and were allowed only offal and scraps – thrown together with beans into *feijoada* stews. Anyone with a noticeable trace of African or indigenous blood was forbidden from mixing with Portuguese. Not only were they required to attend separate churches; they were forbidden from passing in front of the spire of the white church as it would cause offence to God. The mulatto artists and their sympathisers, like Aleijadinho and Mestre Athayde (whose wife was a black Brazilian) also experienced prejudice and were known as 'artistas de sangue sujo' or artists with dirty blood, relegated to the level of craftsmen rather than true fine artists. They in turn used their ecclesiastical art as a form of disguised political and social protest. Many of the paintings and sculptures replace prophets, saints or Christ himself with Tiradentes. Aleijadinho's Christ crucified is symbolized by a medal showing severed hands and feet around a gold heart on the tabernacle of the church of **São Francisco de Assis** in Ouro Preto and the medal of the church of the same name in São João del Rey – a reference to Tiradentes who was hung drawn and quartered by the Portuguese. Mestre Athayde's last supper painting in São Francisco de Assis, Ouro Preto depicts drunken and decadent Portuguese feasting on meat and wine with a servant in attendance, and his masterpiece – the painting on the ceiling of the same church – replaces the normally white virgin Mary with a mixed race Brazilian woman, thought to have been modelled on his wife.

settlements that became Vila Rica de Albuquerque), is heavily gilded and contains Aleijadinho's tomb. It has a **museum** devoted to him but with very few of his pieces. Be sure to see the exquisite miniature crucifixion on the basement floor. Across the river, the **Mina do Chico Rei** ⓘ *R Dom Silvério, 0800-1700, US$1.50*, is not as impressive as some other mines in the area, but is fun to crawl about in and has a restaurant attached. The Chico Rei was supposedly an African king called Francisco, who was enslaved but bought his freedom working in the mine.

On the eastern edge of town, **Santa Efigênia** ⓘ *Ladeira Santa Efigênia and Padre Faria, Tue-Sun 0800-1200* (1720-1785), has wonderful panoramic views of the city. This was a church used by black Brazilians only and the gilt that lines the interior is said to have been made from gold dust washed out of slaves' hair. Manuel Francisco Lisboa (Aleijadinho's father) oversaw the construction and much of the carving is by Francisco Xavier de Brito (Aleijadinho's mentor).

Around Ouro Preto

The **Cachoeira das Andorinhas**, a waterfall north of town, is reached by taking a bus to Morro de Santana and then walking 25 minutes. To walk all the way takes 1½ hours. Near the waterfall it is possible to visit the **Zen Buddhist monastery** ⓘ *apply in advance to Mosteiro Zen Pico de Rajos, Morro de São Sebastião, Caixa Postal 101, 35400-000, Ouro Preto, T031-9612484*. Excursions of 2½ hours are arranged at 0830 and 1430 visiting many cultural and ecological sites of interest.

The town is dominated by a huge cross, easily reached from the road to Mariana, which affords lovely views of the sunset; but don't go alone as it's in a poor district.

Parque Estadual de Itacolomi and the **Estação Ecológica do Tripuí** are protected areas close to the city. The former (a three-hour walk from the centre, cars prohibited) includes the peak of Itacolomi, which the first gold prospectors used as a landmark, the source of the Rio Doce as well as endangered wildlife and splendid views. Tripuí is in the valley where the first gold was found; it protects a rare flatworm, *Peripatus acacioi*. It can also be reached on foot, or the bus to Belo Horizonte will drop you near the entrance.

Minas de Passagem

ⓘ *Ouro Preto T031-551 1068, Mariana T031-557 1340, 0900-1800, US$7.50, 30 mins' walk from the bus stop to the mine.*

Between Ouro Preto and Mariana is the Minas de Passagem gold mine, dating from 1719. A 20-minute guided tour visits the old mine workings and underground lake (take bathing suit). There is a waterfall, **Cachoeira Serrinha**, where swimming is possible; walk 100 m towards Mariana then ask for directions. Note that some signs say 'Mina de Ouro', omitting 'da Passagem'.

The nearest town to the mine is **Passagem de Mariana**. The bus stops at the edge of town by the **Pousada Solar dos Dois Sinos**, which has a church behind it.

Mariana

» *pp260-266.*

→ *Phone code: 031. Altitude: 697 m. Colour map 4, C3. Population: 47,000.*

Mariana, another colonial mining city, is the oldest in Minas Gerais, founded by *bandeirantes* a few years before Ouro Preto, on 16 July 1696. At first, when it was little more than a collection of huts, it was called Arraial de Nossa Senhora do Carmo. But by 1711 it had become the town of Vila de Nossa Senhora do Carmo, and by the mid-18th century it had grown to be the most important administrative centre in the newly created Capitania de São Paulo e Minas do Ouro. Its name was changed to Mariana in honour of the wife of Dom João V, Dona Maria Ana of Austria. It retains many fine colonial buildings, most of them constructed in the second half of the 18th century. The artist Mestre Athayde was born here, as was the Inconfidente Cláudio Manuel da Costa. The town was declared a national monument in 1945.

Unlike its more famous neighbour, Ouro Preto, in whose shadow the town tends to sit, Mariana has remained a working mining centre. For many years the **Companhia do Vale do Rio Doce** (**CVRD**), the state mining company, had major operations here and provided a great deal of assistance for the restoration of the colonial heritage. Since CVRD's concentration on its new investments at Carajás, and its subsequent privatization, there have been doubts about its commitment to mining in Mariana and consequently to the town itself.

Ins and outs

Getting there Buses from Ouro Preto and Belo Horizonte stop at the new *rodoviária*, out of town on the main road, then at the **Posto Mariana**, before heading back to the centre at Praça Tancredo Neves. Many buses seem to go only to the *posto* (petrol station) above the town, but it's a long walk from the centre. A bus from the *rodoviária* to the centre via the *posto* and Minas de Passagem costs US$0.40.

Tourist information The **tourist office** ⓘ *Praça Tancredo Neves, T031-3557 9044, www.mariana.mg.gov.br*, will help organize guides and tours and has a map and free monthly booklet, *Mariana Agenda Cultural*, packed with local information. **Mariana Turismo** ⓘ *R Direita 31*, also has information. » *For Transport information, see page 266.*

Sights

The historic centre of the town slopes gently uphill from the river and the **Praça Tancredo Neves**, where buses from Ouro Preto stop. The first street parallel with the

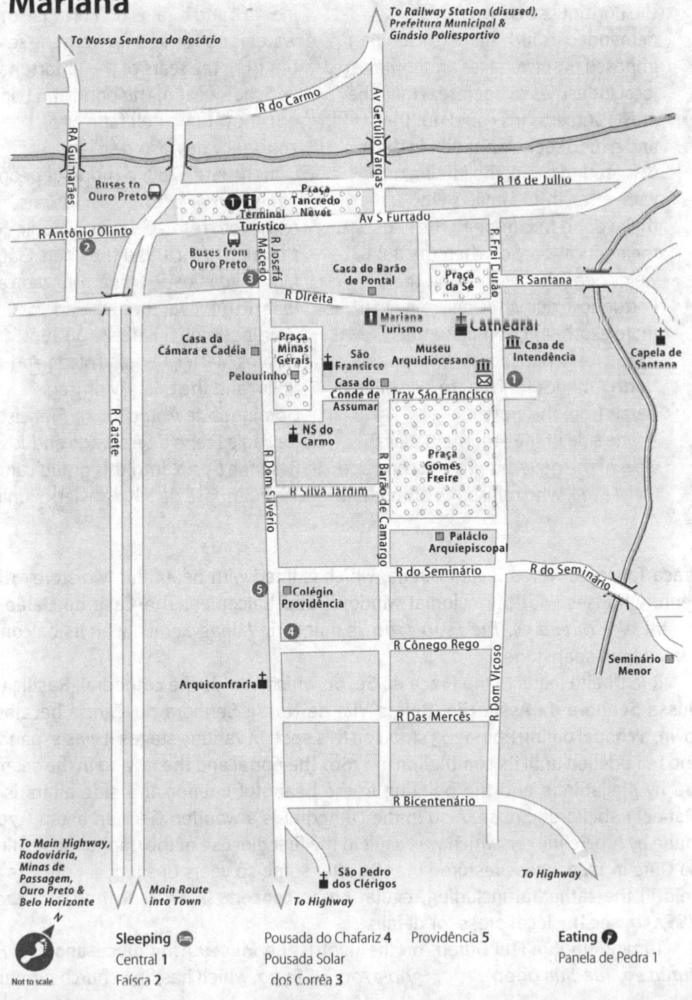

Tiradentes and the Inconfidência Mineira

In the last quarter of the 18th century, Vila Rica de Nossa Senhora do Pilar do Ouro Preto was a dynamic place. Gold had brought great wealth to the city and this was translated into fine religious and secular buildings. Much of the artistry that went into these constructions and their decoration was home-grown, such as the genius of O Aleijadinho (see page 236). In conjunction with this flowering of the arts an intellectual society developed. And yet all this went on under the heavy hand of the Portuguese crown, which demanded its fifth share (the *quinto*), imposed punitive taxes and forbade local industries to operate. While the artists and artisans could not travel and had to seek inspiration in what was around them, the intellectuals were often from families who sent their young to Europe to further their education. So, when the gold yields began to decline and the Portuguese demands became even more exorbitant, some members of society began to look to Europe and North America for ways to free Minas Gerais from the crown.

One side of the argument was the view of the governor, the Visconde de Barbacena, who refused to admit that the mines were exhausted and that poverty was beginning to affect the community. As far as he was concerned, there was no gold because it was being smuggled out of the captaincy and there was no economic problem, just a large unpaid debt to the Portuguese crown. On the other side was the idea, as expressed by the French poet Parny, that Brazil was a paradise on earth, with everything except liberty. The Jesuit Antônio Vieira, who lived in the previous century, put it thus: 'the cloud swells in Brazil and it rains on Portugal; the water is not picked up from the sea, but from the tears of the unfortunate and the sweat of the poor, and I do not know how their faith and constancy has lasted so long.'

In the late 1780s a group of people began to have secret discussions on how to resolve the intolerable situation. It included the poets Cláudio Manuel da Costa, Tomás Gonzaga and Ignacio de Alvarenga, the doctors Domingos Vidal Barbosa and José Alvares Maciel, Padres Toledo and Rolim and the military officers Domingos de Abreu Vieira, Francisco de Paula Freire de Andrade and José de Resende Costa. Into this group came Joaquim José da Silva Xavier, a junior

Praça Tancredo Neves is Rua Direita, which is lined with beautiful, two-storey 18th-century houses with tall colonial windows and balconies. The **Casa do Barão de Pontal** ⓘ *R Direita 54, Tue 1400-1700*, is unique in Minas Gerais, with its balconies carved from soapstone.

Rua Direita leads to the Praça da Sé, on which stands the cathedral, **Basílica de Nossa Senhora da Assunção.** Before Vila de Nossa Senhora do Carmo became a town, a chapel dating from 1703 stood on this spot. In various stages it was expanded and remodelled until its completion in 1760. The portal and the lavabo in the sacristy are by Aleijadinho and the painting in the beautiful interior and side altars is by Manoel Rabello de Sousa. Also in the cathedral is a wooden German organ (1701), made by Arp Schnitger, which was a gift to the first diocese of the Capitania de Minas do Ouro in 1747. It was restored in 1984 after some 50 years of silence. Concerts are held in the cathedral including regular **organ concerts** ⓘ *Fri 1100 and Sun 1200, US$7.50*, see the local press for details.

Turning up Rua Frei Durão, on the right is the **Museu Arquidiocesano** ⓘ *R Frei Durão 49, Tue-Sun 0900-1200, 1300-1700, US$1.50*, which has fine church furniture,

officer (*alferes*), who was born at the Fazenda de Pombal near São João del Rei in about 1748. He was also a dentist and became known by the nickname Tiradentes – tooth-puller. Already dissatisfied with the way the army had treated him, by failing to promote him among other things, in 1788 he was suspended from active duty because of illness. The subsequent loss of pay roused him further. In trying to get reinstated he met Freire de Andrade and Alvares Maciel and later conversations prompted him to tell them of his idea of an uprising against the Portuguese. The Inconfidência grew out of these types of meeting, some planning action, others the future political and economic organization of a new, independent state.

The conspirators worked to gain support for their cause, but one soldier they approached, Coronel Joaquim Silverio dos Reis, used the information he had been given to betray the cause. The governor received reports from other sources and began to build up a picture of what was going on. Tiradentes was the first to be arrested, at the beginning of May 1789, in Rio de Janeiro. It seems that the plotters at this time still had no clear idea of what their ultimate aim was, nor of the importance of their attitudes. They never got the chance anyway because all were arrested soon after Tiradentes. They were imprisoned and kept incommunicado for two years while the case against them was prepared. Tiradentes was singled out as the most important member of the group and, under questioning, he did not disabuse his captors, taking full responsibility for everything. A defence for the Inconfidentes was prepared, but it almost totally ignored Tiradentes, as if he were being made a scapegoat. It made no difference, though, because the defence lost; 11 Inconfidentes were sentenced to death in November 1791. Soon afterwards the authorities in Brazil read out a surprising letter from the queen, Dona Maria I, commuting the death sentence for 10 of the conspirators to exile in Portugal or Africa. The 11th, Tiradentes, was not spared. On 21 April 1792 he was hanged and his body was quartered and his head cut off, the parts to de displayed as a warning against any similar attempts to undermine the crown. Even though Tiradentes would never have been freed, one of the astonishing things about the queen's letter was that it was dated 18 months before it was brought to light.

a gold and silver collection, Aleijadinho statues and an ivory cross. On the opposite side of the street is the **Casa da Intendência/Casa de Cultura** ⓘ *R Frei Durão 84, 0800-1130, 1330-1700*, which holds exhibitions and has a museum of music. The ceilings in the exhibition rooms are very fine; in other rooms there are *esteiro* (flattened bamboo) ceilings.

The large **Praça Gomes Freire** was where horses would be tied up (there is an old drinking trough on one side) and where festivals were held. Now it has pleasant gardens. On the south side is the **Palácio Arquiepiscopal**, while on the north side is the **Casa do Conde de Assumar**, home of the governor of the capitania from 1717 to 1720; it later became the bishop's palace.

Praça Minas Gerais has one of the finest groups of colonial buildings in Brazil. In the middle is the **Pelourinho**, the stone monument to justice at which slaves used to be beaten. The fine **São Francisco church** ⓘ *daily 0800-1700*, (1762-1794), has pulpits, a fine sacristy and an altar designed by Aleijadinho, and paintings by Mestre Athayde, who is buried in tomb No 94. The statue of São Roque is most important as he is the patron saint of the city (his day is 16 August). Among Athayde's paintings are the panels showing the life of St Francis, on the ceiling of the right-hand chapel. The church is one of the most simple in Mariana but, in terms of art, one of the richest. There is a small exhibition of the restoration work funded by CVRD.

At right angles to São Francisco is **Nossa Senhora do Carmo** ⓘ *daily 1400-1700*, (1784), with steatite carvings, Athayde paintings, and chinoiserie panelling. Its exterior is considered the most beautiful in Mariana by some. Unfortunately this church was damaged by fire in 1999. Across Rua Dom Silvério is the **Casa da Cámara e Cadéia** (1768), once the Prefeitura Municipal. It is a superb example of civic colonial construction.

On Rua Dom Silvério the **Colégio Providência** at No 61 was the first college for boarding students in Minas Gerais. Also on this street is the **Igreja da Arquiconfraria** and, nearing the top of the hill, the **Chafariz de São Pedro**. On the Largo de São Pedro is the church of **São Pedro dos Clérigos**, founded by Manuel da Cruz, first bishop of the town (1764), one of the few elliptical churches in Minas Gerais. It is unadorned, although there is a painting by Athayde, *A Entrega do Menino Jesus a Santo Antônio*. The cedar altar was made by José Pedro Aroca. Look for the cockerel, carved in memory of the biblical verses about St Peter betraying Christ before the cock has crowed three times. Ask to see the view from the bell tower.

The **Capela de Santo Antônio**, wonderfully simple and the oldest in town, is some distance from the centre on Rua Rosário Velho. Overlooking the city from the north, with a good viewpoint, is the church of **Nossa Senhora do Rosário** ⓘ *R do Rosário*, (1752), with work by Athayde and showing Moorish influence.

Outside the centre to the west, but within easy walking distance, is the **Seminário Menor**, now the Instituto de Ciencias Históricas e Sociais of the federal university.

South of the river, Avenida Getúlio Vargas leads to the new **Prefeitura Municipal**. It passes the **Ginásio Poliesportivo** and, across the avenue, the **railway station**. This is a romantic building with a clock tower, but it is rapidly falling into disrepair. No trains run on the line any more.

Around Mariana

The small village of **Antônio Pereira**, 24 km north of Mariana, is where imperial topaz is mined. Tours can be made of an interesting cave with stalactites: pay local children a small fee to show you round. » *For Transport information, see page 266.*

Congonhas do Campo » *pp260-266.*

→ *Phone code: 031. Altitude: 866 m. Colour map 4, C3. Population: 42,000.*

In the 18th century, Congonhas was a mining town. Today, in addition to the business brought by the tourists and pilgrims who come to the sanctuary, it is known for its handicrafts. There is little need to stay in Congonhas as the town's main sight – Aleijadinho's beautiful church and chapel-lined stairway – can be seen in a few hours between bus changes. Leave your bags at the information desk in the bus station.

Ins and outs

The *rodoviária* is 1½ km outside town; a bus to the centre costs US$0.40. In town, the bus stops in Praça JK from where you can walk up Praça Dr Mário Rodrigues Pereira, cross the little bridge, then go up Rua Bom Jesus and Rua Aleijadinho to the Praça da Basílica. A bus marked 'Basílica' runs every 30 minutes from the *rodoviária* to Bom Jesus, 5 km, US$0.45. A taxi from the *rodoviária* will cost US$5 one-way, US$10 return including the wait while you visit the sanctuary. **Fumcult** ⓘ *in the Romarias, T031-3731 1300 ext 114*, acts as the tourist office and is very helpful.

On the hill are a **tourist kiosk**, souvenir shops, the **Colonial Hotel** and **Cova do Daniel** restaurant. There are public toilets on the Alameda das Palmeiras.

O Santuário de Bom Jesus de Matosinhos

ⓘ No direct bus from Congonhas do Campo or Rio to the sanctuary; change at the town of Conselheiro Lafaiete, from where there is a frequent service, US$1. Tue-Sun 0700-1900.

The great pilgrimage church and its Via Sacra dominate the town. The idea of building a sanctuary belonged to a prospector, Feliciano Mendes, who promised to erect a cross and chapel in thanks to Bom Jesus after he had been cured of a serious illness. The inspiration for his devotion came from two sources in Portugal, the cult of Bom Jesus at Braga (near where Mendes was born) and the church of Bom Jesus de Matosinhos, near Porto. Work began in 1757, funded by Mendes' own money and alms he raised. The church was finished in 1771, six years after Mendes' death, and the fame that the sanctuary had acquired led to its development by the most famous architects, artists and sculptors of the time as a Sacro Monte. This involved the construction of six linked chapels, or *pasos* (1802-1818), which lead up to a terrace and courtyard before the church.

There is a wide view of the country from the church terrace, below which are six small chapels set in an attractive sloping area with grass, cobblestones and palms. Each chapel shows scenes with life-size Passion figures carved by Aleijadinho and his pupils in cedar wood. In order of ascent they are: the chapel of the Last Supper; the chapel of the Mount of Olives; the chapel of the betrayal of Christ; the chapel of the flagellation and the crowning with thorns; the chapel of Jesus carrying the Cross; and the chapel of Christ being nailed to the Cross.

On the terrace stand the 12 prophets sculpted by Aleijadinho 1800-1805; these are thought of as his masterpieces. Carved in soapstone with a dramatic sense of movement, they constitute one of the finest works of art of their period in the world. Note how Aleijadinho adapted the biblical characters to his own cultural references. The prophets are sculpted wearing leather boots, as all important men in his time would have done. Daniel, who entered the lion's den, is represented with the artist's own conception of a lion, never having seen one himself: a large, maned cat with a face rather like a Brazilian monkey. Similarly, the whale that accompanies Jonah is an idiosyncratic interpretation. Each statue has a prophetic text carved with it. The statues "combine in a kind of

Santuário de Bom Jesus de Matosinhos

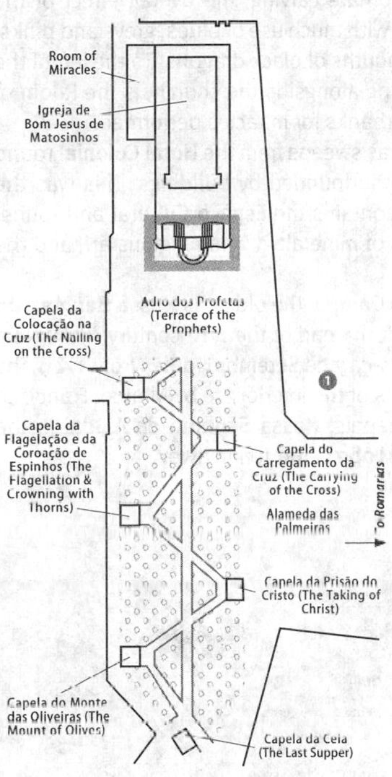

Adro dos Profetas detail

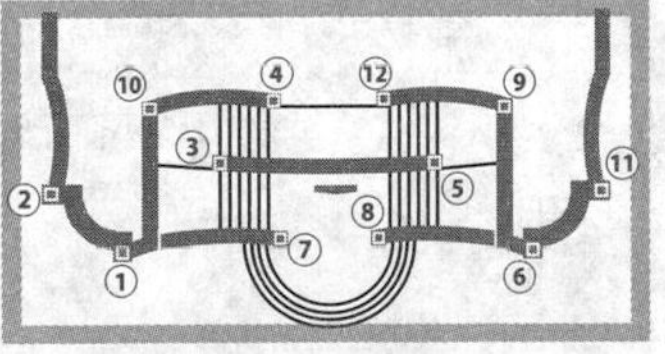

N

Not to scale

Sleeping ⊖
Colonial & Cova do Daniel Restaurant **1**

Prophets ◯
Abdias **1**
Amós **2**
Baruc **3**
Daniel **4**
Ezquiel **5**
Habacuc **6**
Isaías **7**
Jeremias **8**
Joel **9**
Jonas **10**
Naum **11**
Oséias **12**

sacred ballet whose movements only seem uncoordinated; once these sculptures cease to be considered as isolated units, they take on full significance as part of a huge composition brought to life by an inspired genius." (*Iberian-American Baroque*, edited by Henri Stierlin, page 178.) The beauty of the whole is enhanced by the combination of church, Via Sacra and landscape over which the prophets preside.

Inside the church, there are paintings by Athayde and the heads of four sainted popes (Gregory, Jerome, Ambrose and Augustine) sculpted by Aleijadinho for the reliquaries on the high altar. Other artists involved were João Nepomuceno Correia e Castro, who painted the scenes of the life and passion of Christ in the nave and around the high altar, João Antunes de Carvalho, who carved the high altar, and Jerônimo Félix and Manuel Coelho, who carved the crossing altars of Santo Antônio and São Francisco de Paula. Despite the ornate carving, the overall effect of the paintwork is almost muted and naturalistic, with much use of blues, greys and pinks. Lamps are suspended on chains from the mouths of black dragons. To the left of the church, through the third door in the building alongside the church, is the Room of Miracles, which contains photographs and thanks for miracles performed.

Up on the hill, the Alameda das Palmeiras sweeps from the **Hotel Colonial** round to the **Romarias**, a large, almost oval area surrounded by buildings. This was the lodging where the pilgrims stayed. It now contains the **Espaço Cultural** and tourist office, as well as workshops, the museums of mineralogy and religious art, and the **Memória da Cidade.**

Of the other churches in Congonhas do Campo, the oldest is **Nossa Senhora do Rosário**, Praça do Rosário, built by slaves at the end of the 17th century. The **Igreja Matriz de Nossa Senhora da Conceição**, in Praça 7 de Setembro, dates from 1749; the portal is attributed to Aleijadinho, while parts of the interior are by Manuel Francisco Lisboa. There are also two 18th-century chapels, **Nossa Senhora da Ajuda**, in the district of Alto Maranhão, and the church at **Lobo Leite**, 10 km away.

Tiradentes

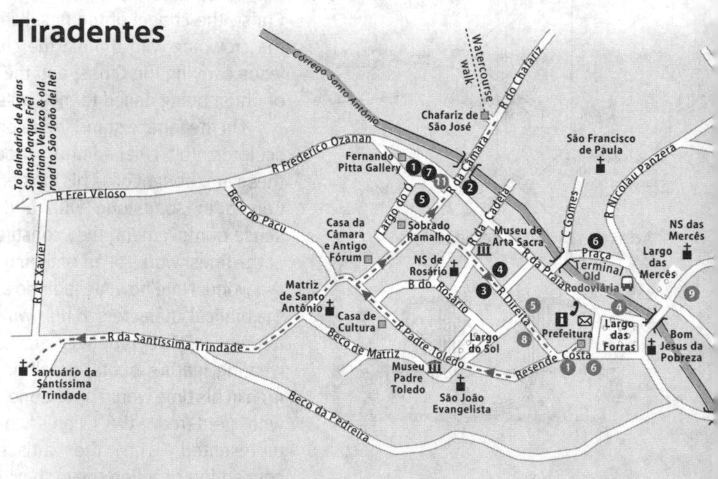

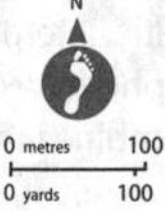

Sleeping
Ponto do Morro 1
Porão Colonial 2
Pousada do Alferes 3
Pousada do Arco Iris 11
Pousada do Largo 4
Pousada do Laurito 5
Pousada Mãe d'Água 6
Pousada Maria Bonita 7
Pousada Três Portas 8
Pouso das Gerais 10
Solar da Ponte 9

Eating
Aluarte 1

Tiradentes » pp260-266.

→ *Phone code: 032. Colour map 4, C3. Population: 6000.*

Aside from Ouro Preto, Tiradentes is the most visited of the Minas colonial towns. Its winding, hilly streets lined with carefully restored baroque Portuguese churches and neat whitewashed cottages huddle around the Santo Antonio river, beneath the rugged hills of the Serra de São José. Inside are art galleries, restaurants, souvenir shops and pousadas, all busy with tourists even during the week. Horse-drawn carriages clatter along the cobbles and at weekends a steam train puffs its way slowly below the mountains to **São João del Rei** towing Pullmans full of delighted children.

Ins and outs

Tiradentes and São João del Rei lie within less than 30 minutes of each other and buses leave every 30 to 40 minutes. Tiradentes is the more twee; São João is uglier but more of a real town. Tiradentes has a far greater choice of accommodation. São João has better bus connections – to Rio, São Paulo, Belo Horizonte, Mariana and Ouro Preto. The **tourist office** ⓘ *R Resende Costa 71*, is in the *prefeitura*.

Sights

A suggested walking tour is as follows. From the main praça, **Largo das Forras**, take Rua Resende Costa up to the Largo do Sol, a lovely open space where you'll find the simple church of **São João Evangelista** ⓘ *Wed-Mon 0900-1700*. Built by the *Irmandade dos Homens Pardos* (mulattos), it has paintings of the four Evangelists and a cornice painted in an elaborate pattern in pink, blue and beige. Beside the church is the **Museu Padre Toledo**, the house of this leader of the Inconfidência Mineira, which is now a museum protecting some handsome colonial furniture and a painted roof depicting the Five Senses. The **Casa de Cultura** in the row of 18th-century houses on Rua Padre Toledo, which leads from Largo do Sol to the Igreja Matriz de Santo Antônio, is protected by the same organization.

The **Igreja Matriz de Santo Antônio** ⓘ *daily 0900-1700, US$1, no photography*, first built in 1710 and enlarged in 1736, contains some of the finest gilded woodcarvings in the country. The main church is predominantly white and gold. Lamps hang from the beaks of golden eagles. The symbols on the panels painted on the ceiling of the nave are a mixture of Old Testament and medieval Christian symbolism (for instance the phoenix, and the pelican). A carved wooden balustrade separates the seating in the nave from richly carved side chapels and altars. The principal altar is also ornately decorated, as are the walls and ceiling around it. The church has a small but fine organ brought from Porto in the 1790s. The upper part of the reconstructed façade is said to follow a design by Aleijadinho. In front of the church, on the balustrade which overlooks the main street and the town, are also a cross and a sundial by him.

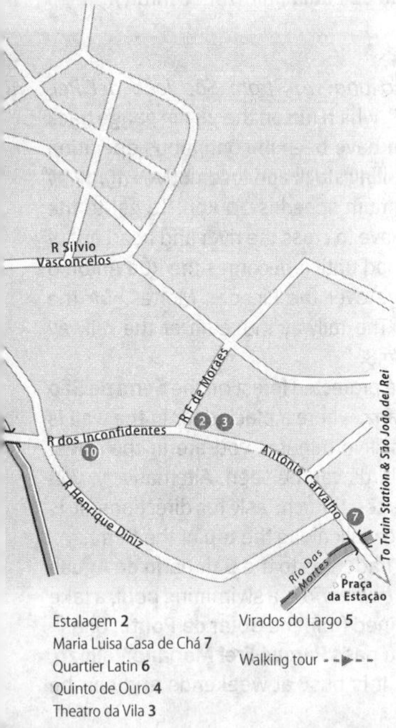

From Santo Antônio, it is well worth taking a detour up to the **Santuário da Santíssima Trindade**. The chapel itself is 18th century while the Room of Miracles associated with the annual Trinity Sunday pilgrimage is modern.

Heading back down past Santo Antônio along Rua da Câmara, you come to the **Casa da Câmara e Antigo Fórum**. Here the road divides, the left-hand street, Jogo de Bola, leads to the Largo do Ó (which rejoins the main street), while Rua da Câmara goes to the crossroads with Rua Direita. At this junction is the **Sobrado Ramalho**, said to be the oldest building in Tiradentes. It is believed to be where the gold was melted down, and contains many soapstone carvings. It has been beautifully restored as a cultural centre.

Before taking Rua Direita back to Largo das Forras, carry straight on towards the river and cross the bridge to the magnificent **Chafariz de São José** (public fountain), installed in 1749. The water is brought by a stone aqueduct from springs in the forest at the foot of Serra São José. It is still used for drinking, washing and watering animals.

Rua Direita has some interesting old buildings. The charming **Nossa Senhora do Rosário** ⓘ *Praça Padre Lourival, Wed-Mon 1200-1600, US$0.50*, has fine statuary and ornate gilded altars. On its painted ceiling colonnades rise to heaven; two monks stand on a hill and the Virgin and Child are in the sky. Other ceiling panels depicting the life of Christ are in poor shape. The church contains statues of black saints, including São Benedito, patron saint of cooks; in one of the statues he is holding a squash. The church dates from 1727, but building by the *Irmandade dos Pretos Cativos* (black slave brotherhood) began as early as 1708.

Opposite Praça Padre Lourival, is the **Antiga Cadeia** (18th-19th century) which now contains the **Museu de Arta Sacra**. Rua Direita meets the Largo das Forras at the **Prefeitura Municipal**, a two-storey building with an extra room under the roof. It now houses the tourist, post and phone offices.

If you have any energy left, there are other churches and chapels in the town, including the **Igreja de Bom Jesus da Pobreza**, on the Largo das Forras. Across the river, the 18th-century **Nossa Senhora das Mercês** ⓘ *Largo das Mercês, Sun 0900-1700*, has an interesting painted ceiling and a notable statue of the Virgin. On the grassy Morro de São Francisco is the small chapel of **São Francisco de Paula** (mid-18th century).

Excursions from Tiradentes

The **steam trains** ⓘ *Fri-Sun and holidays, 1000 and 1415 from São João del Rei, returning from Tiradentes at 1300 and 1700, US$8*, which run on the 76-cm gauge track between São João del Rei and Tiradentes (13 km) have been in continuous operation since 1881 – a testament to the durability of the rolling stock and locomotives made by the Baldwin Company of Philadelphia. The maximum speed is 20 kph. To get to the railway station from the centre of the village you have to cross the river and head out of town on the Rua dos Inconfidentes. Follow this road until it becomes the Rua Antônio Teixeira Carvalho, which carries on to the bridge over the Rio das Mortes. On the opposite bank is a small park and the station. The railway museum at the railway station in São João del Rei is described on page 258.

A recommended walk from Tiradentes is to the protected forest on the **Serra de São José**. The easiest access is from behind the Chafariz, where a black door in the wall is opened at 0730 (Wednesday to Sunday). In just five minutes you are in the forest following the watercourse, where monkeys and birds can be seen. Alternatively, you can walk up into the **Serra** from behind the Mercês Church; ask for directions. It is recommended that you take a guide if you wish to walk along the top of the Serra.

There is a good one- or two-hour walk from Tiradentes to the **Balneário de Águas Santas**, which involves crossing the Serra. At the *balneário* is a swimming pool, a lake and a *churrascaria*, **Senzala**. A map can be obtained from the **Solar da Ponte**, or ask locally for directions (taxi US$15). On the way you pass **Parque Frei Mariano Vellozo**, which contains the Cachoeira do Mangue falls. It is busy at weekends and can be reached by car on the old road to São João.

São João del Rei

» pp260-266.

➔ *Phone code: 032. Colour map 4, C3. Population: 79,000.*

São João del Rei lies at the foot of the Serra do Lenheiro, astride what once must have been a winding little stream. This has now sadly been transformed into a concrete gutter with grass verges. Eighteenth-century bridges cross the stream leading to streets lined with colonial buildings and plazas with crumbling churches, the most interesting and best preserved of which is the church of **São Francisco**. The town feels far less of a tourist museum piece than nearby Tiradentes. There is a lively music scene here – with two renowned orchestras and an annual arts festival in July, and the bars are filled with locals rather than tourists waiting for their coach. There is a good view of the town and surroundings from **Alto da Boa Vista**, where there is a **Senhor dos Montes** (Statue of Christ).

São João del Rei is famous as the home of Tiradentes and of Tancredo Neves. The former was born in the **Fazenda de Pombal**, about 15 km downstream from Tiradentes on the Rio das Mortes. After his execution, the *fazenda* was confiscated. It is now an experimental station owned by **Ibama**. Tancredo Neves, to whom there is a memorial in the town, was the man who would have become the first civilian president of Brazil after the military dictatorships of the mid-20th century, had he not mysteriously died before taking office.

São João del Rei

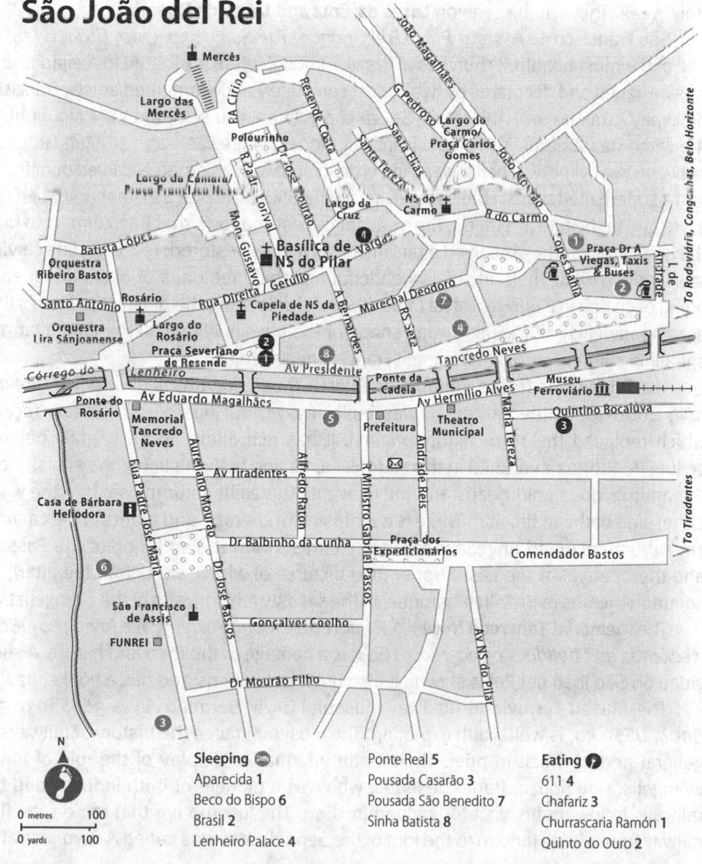

Ins and outs

São João is a good base for visiting Tiradentes (or vice versa); less than 30 minutes away by bus or an hour away at weekends via one of Brazil's most memorable steam train rides. The **Secretaria de Turismo** ⓘ *in the house of Bárbara Heliodora, T032-3372 7338, 0900-1700*, provides a free map. The *rodoviária*, 2 km west of the centre, has a telephone office, toilets, luggage store, *lanchonetes* and a tourist office.

Many streets and squares seem to have more than one name, which can be a little confusing, but as the town centre is not large, it is hard to get lost. One such street crosses the Ponte da Cadeia from Rua Passos; it has three names: Rua da Intendência, Manoel Anselmo and Artur Bernardes.

Sights

The Córrego do Lenheiro, a stream with steep grassy banks, runs through the centre of town. Across it are two fine, stone bridges, **A Ponte da Cadeia** (1798) and **A Ponte do Rosário** (1800), as well as several other modern bridges. Both sides of the river have colonial monuments, which are interspersed with modern buildings. On the north side are many streets with pleasant houses, but in various states of repair. **Rua Santo Antônio** has many single-storey eclectic houses from the imperial period, which have been restored and painted. **Rua Santo Elias** has several buildings all in the same style. Behind the church of Nossa Senhora do Pilar (see below), the **Largo da Câmara** leads up to **Mercês church**, which has quite a good view. Throughout the city you will see locked portals with colonial porticos. These are *passinhos*, shrines that are opened in Holy Week. They can be seen on **Largo da Cruz** and **Largo do Rosário**.

São Francisco de Assis ⓘ *Praça Frei Orlando, Tue-Sun 0830-1700, US$1*, (1774), is one of the most beautiful churches in Brazil. Although often attributed to Aleijadinho, it was designed and decorated by two almost completely undocumented artists, Francisco de Lima Cerqueira and Aniceto de Souza Lopes (who also sculpted the Pelourinho in the Largo da Câmara). The magnificent but modest whitewash and stone façade sits between two cylindrical bell towers and is decorated with an ornately carved door frame and a superb medal of St Francis receiving illumination. The praça in front is shaped like a lyre and in the late afternoon, the royal palms cast shadows that interconnect to form the lyre's strings. The six carved altars inside have been restored; revealing fine carving in sucupira wood. Their artistry is wonderful and the three pairs of altars mirror each other, each pair in a different style (note the use of pillars and the different paintings that accompany each altar). The overall shape of the nave is elliptical, the gold altar has spiralling columns and an adoring St Francis kneels atop.

The **Basílica de Nossa Senhora do Pilar** ⓘ *R Getúlio Vargas (formerly R Direita), daily 1000-1600*, the cathedral, was built in 1721, but has a 19th-century façade which replaced the 18th-century original. It has rich altars and a brightly painted ceiling (Madonna and Child in the middle, saints and bishops lining the sides). Note the androgynous gold heads and torsos within the eight columns set into the walls either side of the main altar. There is a profusion of cherubs and plants in the carving. This abundance and angelic innocence contrasts with the suffering of the Passion and the betrayal of the Last Supper (two pictures of which are before the altar), all common themes in Brazilian baroque. In the sacristy are portraits of the Evangelists.

The **Memorial Tancredo Neves** ⓘ *R Padre José Maria Xavier 7, Wed-Fri 1300- 1800, weekends and holidays 0900-1700, US$1*, is a homage to the man and his life. A short video on São João del Rei is shown. It also holds exhibitions and has a bookshop.

The **Museu Ferroviário** (Railway Museum) ⓘ *Av Hermílio Alves 366, T032-371 8004, US$0.50*, is well worth exploring. The museum traces the history of railways in general and in Brazil in brief. There is an informative display of the role of Irineu Evangelista de Souza, Barão de Mauá, who was a pioneer of both industry and the railways following his visit to England in 1840. The locomotive that ran on the first railway from Rio de Janeiro to the foot of the Serra do Mar was called *A Baronesa* after his wife. The railway to São João, the *Estrada de Ferro Oeste de Minas*, was not a success, but it was instrumental in the development of the region. In the museum is an 1880 Baldwin 4-4-0 locomotive from Philadelphia (No 5055) and a 1912-1913 VIP carriage, both still used on the steam journey to Tiradentes. Outside, at the end of the platforms are carriages and a small Orenstein and Koppel (Berlin) engine. You can walk along the tracks to the round house, where there are several working engines in superb condition, an engine shed and a steam-operated machine shop, still working. It is here that the engines get up steam before going to couple with the coaches for the run to Tiradentes. On days when the trains are running, you can get a good, close-up view of operations even if not taking the trip. Highly recommended. » *See page 256 for the train to Tiradentes.*

Sabará

» *pp260-266.*

→ *Phone code: 031. Colour map 4, B3. Population: 116,000.*

Some 23 km east of Belo Horizonte is the colonial gold-mining (and steel-making) town of Sabará. The town is strung along the narrow steep valleys of the Rio das Velhas and Rio Sabará. Since the late 17th century, the Rio das Velhas was known as a gold-bearing river and a community soon grew up there. By 1702 it was the most populous in Minas Gerais. In 1711, the name Villa Real de Nossa Senhora da Conceição de Sabará was given to the parish and in 1838 it became the city of Sabará.

Ins and outs

There are regular buses from Belo Horizonte, US$0.75, 30 minutes. If travelling by car, there is a road, mostly unpaved, that runs to Sabará from Ravena on the BR-381 Belo Horizonte-Vitória highway, which crosses the hills and is a pleasant drive. Tourist information is available from the **Secretaria de Turismo** ⓘ *R Pedro II 200, T031-671 1522*. *Passeio a Sabará*, by Lúcia Machado de Almeida, with splendid illustrations by Guignard, is an excellent guide to the town.

Sights

There are a number of old churches, fountains, rambling cobbled streets and simple houses with carved doors of great interest. From the bus terminus, walk up Rua Clemente Faria to Praça Santa Rita, where there's a large *chafariz* (fountain). The square adjoins Rua Dom Pedro II, which is lined with beautiful 18th-century buildings. They include the **Solar do Padre Correa** ⓘ *R Dom Pedro II 200*, (1773) now the Prefeitura, a mansion with a rococo chapel and main reception room (*salão nobre*); the **Casa Azul** ⓘ *R Dom Pedro II 215*, (also 1773), now the INSS building, with a chapel and a fine portal; and the **Teatro Municipal**, former opera house, built in 1770 and the second oldest in Brazil. It has a superb interior, with three balconies, a carved wooden rail before the orchestra pit, wooden floors and *esteiro* (flattened, woven bamboo) ceilings.

At the top of Rua Dom Pedro II is the Praça Melo Viana, in the middle of which is **Nossa Senhora do Rosário dos Pretos** ⓘ *Tue-Sun 0800-1100, 1300-1700*, left unfinished at the time of the slaves' emancipation. Behind the façade of the unfinished building are the chancel, sacristy (both 1780) and the first chapel (1713). There is a museum of religious art in the church. To the right of the church is the **Chafariz do Rosário**. Also on the praça are the ornate Fórum Ministro Orozimbo Nonato and two schools. From Praça Melo Viana, take Rua São Pedro to the church of **São Francisco** (1781); beyond the church is the **Chafariz Kaquende**.

In Rua da Intendência is the museum of 18th-century gold mining, the **Museu do Ouro** ⓘ *Tue-Sun 1200-1730, US$1*. It contains exhibits of gold extraction, as well as religious items and colonial furniture. The building itself is a fine example of colonial architecture. Sources disagree as to its date of construction, but the general view is that it was before 1730. Originally the foundry, it became the Casa da Intendência in 1735. For most of the 19th century it was abandoned and became the gold museum in 1945.

Another fine example of civil colonial architecture is the **Casa Borba Gato** ⓘ *R Borba Gato 71*, so called because tradition has it that it belonged to the famous *bandeirante*, Manoel de Borba Gato, one of the first to settle on the Rio das Velhas, but exiled from the region after the murder of the king's representative, Rodrigo de Castel Blanco in 1682. The building currently belongs to the Museu do Ouro.

On Rua do Carmo is the church of **Nossa Senhora do Carmo** ⓘ *US$1, a leaflet about the town is given out*, (1763-1774), with doorway, pulpits and choir loft by Aleijadinho and paintings by Athayde. From the ceilings, painted blue and grey and gold, religious figures look down surrounding the Virgin and Child and the Chariot of Fire. In the chancel, the Ten Commandments in blue work have a distinctly Moorish air, what with the tents and the night-time scenes.

Similar in style externally is the **Capela de Nossa Senhora do Pilar**, which is beside the municipal cemetery and in front of a large building with blue gates and doors.

Nossa Senhora da Conceição ⓘ *Praça Getúlio Vargas, free*, (1720), has a lot of visible woodwork and a beautiful floor. The carvings have a great deal of gilding, there are painted panels, and paintings by 23 Chinese artists brought from Macau. The clearest Chinese work is on the two red doors to the right and left of the chancel.

Nossa Senhora do Ó, built in 1717 and showing unmistakable Chinese influence (paintings in need of restoration), is 2 km from the centre of the town at the Largo Nossa Senhora do Ó. To get there, take the local bus marked 'Esplanada' or 'Boca Grande'.

If you walk up the **Morro da Cruz** hill from the **Hotel do Ouro** to a small chapel, the **Capela da Cruz**, or Senhor Bom Jesus, you can get a wonderful view of the whole region. Look for beautiful quartz crystals while you are up there.

Excursions from Sabará

Some 25 km from Sabará and 60 km from Belo Horizonte is **Caeté**. The town, originally called Vila Nova da Rainha, has several historical buildings and churches. On the Praça João Pinheiro are the **Prefeitura** and **Pelourinho** (both 1722), the **Igreja Matriz Nossa Senhora do Com Sucesso** ⓘ *daily 1300-1800*, (1756, rebuilt 1790) and the **Chafariz da Matriz**. Also on the praça is the **tourist information office** ⓘ *in the Casa da Cultura, T031-651 1855*. Other churches are **Nossa Senhora do Rosário** (1750-1768), with a ceiling attributed to Mestre Athayde, and **São Francisco de Assis**. The **Museu Regional** ⓘ *R Israel Pinheiro 176, Tue-Sun 1200-1700*, in the house of the Barão de Catas Altas, or Casa Setecentista, contains 18th- and 19th-century religious art and furniture. The house itself is a fine example of 18th-century civic architecture, with two floors and an interior patio. From Caeté you can go to the **Serra da Piedade** mountains.

Sleeping

Ouro Preto *p243, map p244*
Many hotels will negotiate lower prices off season. Ask at the tourist office for reasonably priced accommodation in *casas de família*. Avoid touts who greet you off buses and charge higher prices than those advertised in hotels; it is difficult to get hotel rooms at weekends and holiday periods. Accommodation can be booked through www.ouropretotour.com or www.ouropreto.com.

AL Grande Hotel, R das Flores 164, Centro T031-3551 1488, www.hotelouropreto.com.br. One of a handful of gorgeous Niemeyer hotels dotted throughout Minas, newly restored and with views over the city.

A Pousada do Mondego, Largo de Coimbra 38, T031-3551 2040, F551 3094. Beautifully kept colonial house in a fine location by São

Francisco Church, room rates vary according to view, small restaurant, Scotch bar, popular with groups. Recommended (a **Roteiros de Charme** hotel, see page 50), the hotel runs a *jardineira* bus tour of the city, 2 hrs, minimum 10 passengers, US$10 for non-guests.

A Pousada Solar de NS do Rosário, Av Getúlio Vargas 270, T031-3551 5200, www.hotelsolardorosario.com.br. Fully restored historic building with a highly recommended restaurant, bar, sauna, pool; all facilities in rooms.

B Luxor Pousada, R Dr Alfredo Baeta 16, Praça Antônio Dias, T031-3551 2244, www.luxorhoteis.com.br. Converted colonial mansion, no twin beds, comfortable and clean but spartan, good views, restaurant good but service slow.

C Pousada Casa Grande, R Conselheiro Quintiliano, 96, T/F031-3551 4314, www.hotelpousadacasagrande.com.br. A large colonial town house with 21 smart, but simply appointed rooms with polished wooden floors, en suites and some with views out over the city.

D Colonial, Trav Padre Camilo Veloso 26, close to Praça Tiradentes, T031-3551 3133, www.hotelcolonial.com.br. A little colonial house with 14 rooms. All are well maintained. Some are distinctly smaller than others so it is worth looking at a few. Decor is modest, with furniture sitting on a polished wooden floor.

D Pousada Itacolomi, R Antônio Pereira 167, T031-3551 2891. Small but well kept with good rates for the 3-room apartments. Recommended. Next door to the Museu da Inconfidência.

D Pousada Nello Nuno, R Camilo de Brito 59, T031-3551 3375. The cheaper rooms have no bath. The friendly owner, Annamélia, speaks some French. Highly recommended.

D Pousada Tiradentes, Praça Tiradentes 70, T031-3551 2619. The rooms are spartan but well kept and moderately comfortable. Each has a TV, fridge. Conveniently located.

D Pouso Chico Rey, R Brig Musqueira 90, T031-3551 1274. A fascinating old house with Portuguese colonial furnishings, very small and utterly delightful, book in advance (room No 6 has been described as a 'dream').

D Solar das Lajes, R Conselheiro Quintiliano 604, T/F031-3551 3388, www.solardaslajes.com.br. A little way from the centre but with an excellent view and a pool. Well run.

E Hostel Ouro Preto, R Costa Sena, 30 Largo de Coimbra, T031-3551 6705, www.hostel.org.br. A colonial building next to the São Francisco de Assis church right in the centre. Well-kept rooms with polished wooden floors and space for 12. Towels are extra.

E Pousada dos Bandeirantes, R das Mercês 167, T031-3551 1996. Behind the São Francisco de Assis Church and offering beautiful views.

E Pousada São Francisco de Paula, R Pe José Marcos Pena 202, next to the São Francisco de Paula church, T031-3551 3456. One of the best views of any in the city; from the rooms or from a hammock in the garden. Services and facilities include the free use of a kitchen, multilingual staff, excursions. The hostel has 8 rustic rooms including a dormitory, which come with or without a simple breakfast, private or communal bathrooms. Full breakfasts and snacks are available, 100 m from the *rodoviária*. Recommended.

F Brumas, R Pe José Marcos Pena 68, T031-3551 2944, www.brumasonline.hpg.com.br. 150 m downhill from *rodoviária*, just below São Francisco de Paula church, T031-3335 7809. Dormitory, kitchen and laundry and superb views. Don't walk down from the bus station after dark.

Student hostels

During holidays and weekends students may be able to stay at the self-governing hostels, known as *repúblicas* (described as very welcoming, 'best if you like heavy metal music' and 'are prepared to enter into the spirit of the place'). The Prefeitura has a list of over 50 *repúblicas* with phone numbers, available at the **Secretaria de Turismo**. Many are closed between Christmas and Carnaval.

Camping

Camping Clube do Brasil, Rodovia dos Inconfidentes, Km 91, 2 km north, T031-3551 1799. Quite expensive but very nice.

Mariana *p248, map p249,*

Most of these hotels are housed in colonial buildings. Further details can be found on www.mariana.mg.gov.br.

C Faísca, R Antônio Olinto 48, T031-3557 1206. Up the street from the tourist office. Suites and rooms, breakfast included.

C Pousada Solar dos Corrêa, R Josefá Macedo 70 and R Direita, T/F031-3557 2080. A restored 18th-century townhouse with spacious a/c rooms.

D Pousada do Chafariz, R Cônego Rego 149, T031-3557 1492, www.pousadado chafariz.hpg.com.br. A converted colonial building with parking, breakfast and a family atmosphere. Recommended.

D Providência, R Dom Silvério 233, T031-3557 1444. Has use of the neighbouring school's pool when classes finish at noon.

D-E Central, R Frei Durão 8, T/F031- 3557 1630. A charming but run-down colonial building on the Praça Gomes Freire. Recommended but avoid the downstairs rooms.

Congonhas do Campo *p252, map p253*

E Colonial, Praça da Basílica 76, opposite Bom Jesus, T031-3731 1834. Good and comfortable but noisy, breakfast extra, cheaper without bath. Fascinating restaurant, **Cova do Daniel**, downstairs is full of colonial handicrafts and good local food.

E Freitas, R Marechal Floriano 69, T031-3731 1543. Basic, with breakfast, cheaper without bath.

Tiradentes *p255, map p254*

Prices drop in the more expensive hotels Sun-Thu. www.tiradentesturismo.com.br has details and pictures of many of the pousadas.

AL Solar da Ponte, Praça das Mercês, T032-3355 1255, www.roteirosdecharme/sol.htm. The atmosphere of a country house, run by John and Anna Maria Parsons, the price includes breakfast and afternoon tea, only 12 rooms, fresh flowers, bar, sauna, lovely gardens, swimming pool, light meals for residents only. Highly recommended (it is in the **Roteiros de Charme** group, see page 50).

B Pousada Mãe D'Água, Largo das Forras 50, T032-3355 1206. One of the larger pousadas, with an outdoor pool set in a small garden, sauna, pool room and a/c rooms. Price includes breakfast.

B Pousada Três Portas, R Direita 280A, T032-3355 1444. Charming central hotel in a restored town house with 8 rooms and a suite. Facilities include a heated indoor pool, sauna and room service. Great for couples.

B-C Pouso das Gerais, R dos Inconfidentes 109, T032-3355 1234, www.pousodasgerais.hpg.com.br. Spotless, fresh fan-cooled rooms with parquet flooring, desk, TV and marble basins in the bathrooms. Central, quiet, pool and breakfast included. Recommended.

C Hotel Ponto do Morro, Largo das Forras 2, T032-3355 1342. A central motel, just off the main square. Avoid the darker, lower rooms.

C Porão Colonial, R dos Inconfidentes 447, T032-3551251. Pleasant, though a little out of town. With a pool, sauna and parking.

C Pousada Maria Bonita, R Antônio Teixeira Carvalho 134, T/F032-3355 1227, www.idas brasil.com.br. A motel with a pool and a garden full of gnomes leading down to the river. About 10 mins out of town, near the station. At the weekend the price includes breakfast, lunch and an evening snack.

C-D Pousada do Arco Iris, R Frederico Ozanan 340, T032-3355 1167. The best of a string of pousadas in houses on this stretch of road just out of town. Swimming pool, popular, family run, 5 rooms only. Price includes breakfast. Book ahead.

D Pousada do Alferes, R dos Inconfidentes 479, T032-3355 1303. Simple but central on the main shopping street close to the square.

D Pousada do Largo, Largo das Forras 48, T/F032-3355 1219. With a pool, sauna and rooms with Brazilian TV.

D Pousada do Laurito, R Direita 187, T032-3355 1268. Central, cheap and good value. Very popular with international backpackers.

São João del Rei *p257, map p257*

B Lenheiro Palace, Av Pres Tancredo Neves 257, T/F032-3371 8155. Modern hotel with good facilities, parking, cheaper in low season, teahouse, breakfast.

C Ponte Real, Av Eduardo Magalhães 254, T/F032-3371 7000. Modern, comfortable, sizeable rooms, good restaurant.

C-D Beco do Bispo, Beco do Bispo 93, 2 mins west of the São Francisco church, T032-3371 8844, www.becodobispo.com.br. The best in town. Well-kept, bright a/c rooms with firm sprung mattresses, hot showers, cable TV, a pool, convenient location and a very helpful English-speaking staff. Organizes tours. Highly recommended.

D Aparecida, Praça Dr Antônio Viegas 13, T032-3371 2540. Unillustrious but centrally located by the bus and taxi stop, with a restaurant and *lanchonete*.

D **Pousada Casarão**, Ribeiro Bastos 94, opposite São Francisco church, T032-3337 17447. Housed in a delightful converted mansion. The decent-sized rooms have firm beds. Also a games room with a pool table.

E **Brasil**, Av Pres Tancredo Neves 395, T032-3371 2804. In an old house full of character, on the opposite side of the river from the railway station, cheap. Recommended but basic, no breakfast.

E **Pousada São Benedito**, R Mcal Deodoro 254, T032-3371 7381. Price per person. Basic, with shared rooms and bathrooms.

E **Sinha Batista**, R Manock Anselmo 22, T032-3371 5550. The best of the cheaper options. With largish rooms in a colonial building conveniently located by the central canal.

Sabará *p259*

B **Del Rio**, R Sao Francisco 345, T031-671 3040. Standard 3-star rooms. Reasonable service.

C **Solar das Sepúlvedas**, R da Intendência 371, behind the Museu do Ouro, T031-671 2708. Grandiose, popular with Brazilian families and with a pool.

E **Hotel do Ouro**, R Santa Cruz 237, Morro da Cruz, T031-671 5622. Rooms with en suite bathrooms, hot water, breakfast and a marvellous view, great value.

Eating

Ouro Preto *p243, map p244*

Try the local *licor de jaboticaba*.

TTT **Le Coq D'Or**, R Getúlio Vargas 270 (next to the Rosário church), T031-3551 5200. Brazilian-French fusion cooking in a smart dining room with live music. One of the city's best.

TT **Adega**, R Teixeira Amaral 24, 1130-1530, T031-3551 4171. Vegetarian smorgasbord, US$5, all you can eat. Highly recommended.

TT **Beijinho Doce**, R Direita 134A, Café Gerais, 124 R Direita. Decent *bacalhau* and steaks, delicious pastries and cakes but lousy coffee. Try the truffles.

TT **Café e companhia**, R São José 187, T031-3551 0711, closes 2300. Very popular, *comida por kilo* at lunchtime, good salads and juices.

TT **Deguste**, R Coronel Alves 15, T031-3551 6363. Large portions, good value.

TT **Pasteleria Lampião**, Praça Tiradentes. Good views at the back (better at lunchtime than in the evening).

TT **Taverna do Chafariz**, R São José 167, T031-35512828. Good local food. Recommended.

T **Forno de Barro**, Praça Tiradentes 54. Decent Mineira buffet with varied plates and sweet puddings. Generous portions.

T **Vide Gula**, R Sen Rocha Lagoa 79a, T031-3551 4493. Food by weight, good, friendly atmosphere. Recommended.

Mariana *p248, map p249*

TT **Engenho Nôvo**, Praça da Sé 26. Bar at night, English spoken by the owners and clients. Recommended.

TT **Mangiare della Mamma**, D Viçoso 27. Italian. Recommended.

TT **Tambaú**, R João Pinheiro 26. Regional food.

T **Panela de Pedra**, in the Terminal Turístico. Serves food by weight at lunchtime.

Congonhas do Campo *p252, map p253*

T **Estalagem Romaria**, 2 mins from Hotel Colonial in the Romarias. Good restaurant and pizzeria, reasonable prices.

Tiradentes *p255, map p254*

There are many other restaurants, snack bars and *lanchonetes* in town and it is a small enough place to wander around and see what takes your fancy.

TTT **Estalagem**, R Min Gabriel Passos 280, T032-33551144. Excellent and generous traditional Mineira meat dishes.

TTT **Quartier Latin**, R São Francisco de Paula 46, Praça da Rodoviária, T032-3355 1552. French-trained cordon bleu chef with a menu of French-inspired, Italian and good seafood. Salads are made from their own organic vegetables. Respectable wine list. Good and expensive.

TTT **Quinto de Ouro**, R Direita 159. Mineira and international dishes. Recommended.

TTT **Theatro da Vila**, R Padre Toledo 157, T032-3355 1275. A gourmet restaurant with Italian, French and Brazilian fusion cooking and an excellent wine list. Good views out over the little garden and performances in summer in the restaurant's garden theatre.

TTT **Virados do Largo**, Largo do Ó, T032-3355 1111. The best Mineira restaurant in town together with **Estalagem**.

Let them eat queca

In the 18th and 19th century many British railway workers and miners came and settled in Minas and their legacy can still be seen today. Indeed many of the habits thought to be quintessentially Minas Gerais by other Brazilians are obviously English to European eyes. Mineiras are famous throughout Brazil for saying 'Why so?' when perplexed. Mock Tunbridge-ware inlaid boxes and desks can be found in many traditional Minas homes. And at tea time, near Christmas many older Mineiras eat 'Queca'.... Identical to British fruit cake: rich, sweet and inlaid with crystallised fruit and introduced to Minas by the bored wives of English miners who settled in Nova Lima. It is traditionally accompanied by cups of weak, milky tea.

Aluarte, Largo do Ó 1, T032-3355 1608. Bar with live music in the evening, nice atmosphere, US$4 cover charge, garden, sells handicrafts. Recommended.

Maria Luisa Casa de Chá, Largo do Ó 1, diagonally opposite **Aluarte**, T032-3355 1502. Tea, cakes and sandwiches in an arty Bohemian atmosphere. Great for breakfast.

São João del Rei *p257, map p257*

Churrascaria Ramón, Praça Severiano de Resende 52. One of the town's better *churrascarias* with generous portions and plenty of side dishes.

Quinto do Ouro, Praça Severiano de Resende 04, T032-3371 7577. Tasty and well-prepared regional food at reasonable prices. Said to be the best Mineira cooking in town.

Chafariz, R Quintino Bocaiuva 100, T032-3371 8955. The best per-kilo restaurant in town with an enormous choice of dishes and plenty of options for vegetarians.

Restaurant 611, R Getúlio Vargas 145, T032-3371 8793. Very cheap but excellent Mineira cooking. Eat as much as you like for less than US$2. Plenty of choice. A local favourite.

Sabará *p259*

Cê Que Sabe, R Mestre Caetano 56. Mineira and other Brazilian fare. Recommended.

Entertainment

São João del Rei *p257, map p257*

Music

São João del Rei has 2 famous orchestras which play baroque music. In colonial days, the music master not only had to provide the music for Mass, but also had to compose new pieces for every festival. All the music has been kept and the **Ribeiro Bastos** and **Lira Sanjoanense** orchestras preserve the tradition. Both have their headquarters, rehearsing rooms and archives on R Santo Antônio (Nos 54 and 45 respectively). The Orquestra Ribeiro Bastos plays at Mass every Sun in São Francisco de Assis at 0915 and Fri 1900 at the Matriz do Pilar, as well as at many religious ceremonies throughout the year (eg Holy Week). The Orquestra Lira Sanjoanense – which is said to be the oldest in the Americas (founded in 1776) - plays at Mass in Nossa Senhora do Pilar at 1900 every Thu and on Sun in Nossa Senhora do Rosário at 0830 and Nossa Senhora das Mercês at 1000, as well as on other occasions. It is best to check at their offices for full details.

There are similar orchestras in Prados and Tiradentes, but the latter is not as well supported as those in São João.

Festivals and events

Ouro Preto *p243, map p244*

Many shops close during Holy Week and on winter weekends.

Feb Carnival Attracts many people.

Mar/Apr Ouro Preto is famous for its **Holy Week** processions, which actually begin on the Thu before Palm Sun and continue (but not every day) until Easter Sun. The most famous is that commemorating Christ's removal from the Cross, late on Good Fri.

Jun Corpus Christi and Festas Juninas.

Jul The city holds the **Festival do Inverno da Universidade Federal de Minas Gerais**

(UFMG), the 'Winter Festival', about 3 weeks of arts, courses, concerts and exhibitions.
8 Jul Anniversary of the city.
15 Aug Nossa Senhora do Pilar, patron saint of Ouro Preto.
12-18 Nov Semana de Aleijadinho, a week-long arts festival.

Mariana *p248, map p249*
Feb Carnival
Mar/Apr Holy Week are celebrated in traditional style in the town.
29 Jun São Pedro.
Jul Mariana shares some events of **Festival do Inverno da UFMG** with Ouro Preto.

São João del Rei *p257, map p257*
Feb **Carnaval** is lively and popular here and going through a bit of a renaissance.
Apr Semana Santa
15-21 Apr Semana da Inconfidência.
May/Jun **Festival do Inverno,** with many cultural events.
Jul FUNREI, the university (on R Padre José Maria Xavier), holds **Inverno Cultural**.
Aug First 2 weeks, **Nossa Senhora da Boa Morte**, with baroque music (*novena barroca*).
12 Oct Nossa Senhora do Pilar, patron saint of the city.
8 Dec Founding of the city.

Sabará *p259*
25 Dec-6 Jan Folia de Reis.
Jun Festas Juninas and **Festival da Cachaça**
Oct 2nd Sun. Festival of **Nossa Senhora do Rosário**, the patron saint.

Shopping

Ouro Preto *p243, map p244*
Buy soapstone carvings at roadside stalls rather than in the cities; they are much cheaper. Many artisans sell soapstone carvings, jewellery and semi-precious stones in the Largo de Coimbra in front of São Francisco de Assis Church. Also worth buying is traditional cookware in stone, copper or enamelled metal.

Gems and jewellery
Gems are not much cheaper from freelance sellers in Praça Tiradentes than from the shops. If buying gems on the street, ask for the seller's credentials.
Gemas de Minas, Conde de Bobadela 63. One of the city's better jewellers.
Videmaju, R Conselheiro Santana 175. The home of Vincente Júlio de Paula, a professor at the School of Mines who sells stones at very good prices.

Tiradentes *p255, map p254*
Art galleries
Fernando Pitta, Beco da Chácara, T/F032-355 1475. Produces fascinating painting, mixed media and sculpture, worth a visit.
Oscar Araripe, R da Câmara. Paintings of Tiradentes and other local scenes in bright colours, popular and commercial.

São João del Rei *p257, map p257*
The pewter factory, Av Leite de Castro 1150, T032-3371 8000, 10 mins' walk from the rodoviária, 0900-1800. Run by Englishman John Somers and his son Gregory, is worth a visit for both its exhibitions and its shop. The nearby town of **Resende Costa** (30 km north) is known for its textile handicrafts.

Activities and tours

Ouro Preto *p243, map p244*
Yoga centre, down an alley between Nos 31 and 47 (Cine Teatro Vila Rica), Praça Alves de Brito, T031-3551 3337. Offers shiatsu and Kerala massage.

Tiradentes *p255, map p254*
For horse-riding treks, contact John Parsons at the **Solar da Ponte**, see page 262.

Transport

Ouro Preto *p243, map p244*
Bus There are 11 buses a day to/from **Belo Horizonte**, 2 hrs, **Pássaro Verde**, US$3.75 (taxi US$30). Day trips are possible; book your return journey to Belo Horizonte early if returning in the evening; buses get crowded. To **Mariana**, buses run from the Escola de Minas near Praça Tiradentes every 30 mins, US$0.60, all passing **Minas de Passagem** (buses also leave from Ouro Preto *rodoviária*).

For Sleeping and Eating price codes, see pages 49 and 52 or the inside front cover. For an explanation of phone codes, see page 66.

There is a bus to **Rio**, **Útil** at 0705, 1715 and 2000 (US$15, 12 hrs); to **Brasília** at 1830 (12 hrs); to **Vítoria** at 2100 (8 hrs). There are also **Útil** buses to **Conselheiro Lafaiete**, 3-4 a day via Itabirito and direct services to **Congonhas do Campo** via the new Caminho de Ouro highway. Other **Útil** services to **Rio**, **Barbacena**, **Conselheiro Lafaiete** and **Congonhas** go via Belo Horizonte. Direct buses to **São Paulo**, 3 a day with Cristo Rei, 11 hrs, US$19.25. **Gontijo** go to Salvador via Belo Horizonte.

Mariana *p248, map p249*
Bus Buses to **Ouro Preto** can be caught by the bridge at the end of R do Catete, every 30 mins, US$0.60, all passing **Minas de Passagem**. There is a bus to **Belo Horizonte** (via Ouro Preto), US$4.50, 2¼ hrs. Buses for **Santa Bárbara** (near Caraça) leave from the *rodoviária*.

Around Mariana *p252*
Bus There are 3 buses a day from Mariana to **Antônio Pereira**, Mon-Fri, 0800, 1200, 1445, plus 1100, 1750 and 2100 on Sat.

Congonhas do Campo *p252, map p253*
Bus A bus marked 'Basílica' runs every 30 minutes from the *rodoviária* to **Bom Jesus**, 5 km, US$0.45. A taxi from the *rodoviária* will cost US$5 one way, US$10 return including the wait while you visit the sanctuary.

Buses run to **Belo Horizonte**, 1½ hrs, US$3, 8 times a day. To **São João del Rei**, 2 hrs, US$3.60, tickets are not sold until the bus comes in. To **Ouro Preto** or **Rio**, buses go via Belo Horizonte, Murtinho or Conselheiro Lafaiete. There is a frequent bus service to **Conselheiro Lafaiete**, US$1.

Tiradentes *p255, map p254*
Bus Last bus back to **São João del Rei** is 1815, 2230 on Sun.
Taxi Around town there are pony-drawn taxis; ponies can be hired for US$5. A taxi to **São João del Rei** costs US$10. See

Train See page 256 for the train between Tiradentes and **São João del Rei**.

São João del Rei *p257, map p257*
Bus Buses to **Rio**, 5 daily with **Paraibuna** (3 on Sat and Sun), 5 hrs, US$10-12. **Cristo Rei** to **São Paulo**, 8 hrs, 5 a day (also to Santos), and **Translavras**, 4 a day (also to Campinas), US$12.50. **Belo Horizonte**, 3½ hrs, US$6.60. To **Juiz de Fora**, US$5.40, at least 8 a day with **Transur**. Frequent service to **Tiradentes** with **Meier**, 8 a day, 7 on Sat, Sun and holidays, US$0.65; on the return journey to São João, the bus stops outside the railway station before proceeding to the *rodoviária*.

Sabará *p259*
Bus To/from **Belo Horizonte** with **Viação Cisne**, US$0.75, 30 mins, from separate part of Belo Horizonte *rodoviária* from main departure hall.

Directory

Ouro Preto *p243, map p244*
Banks **Banco 24 Horas**, Praça Alves de Brito, next to Correios; **Banco do Brasil**, R São José 189, good rates, also for TCs; **Bradesco**, corner of Sen Rocha Lagoa and Padre Rolim, opposite the Escola de Minas. **Internet Point**, R Xavier da Veiga 501A, language school and cultural centre. **Post office** Praça Alves de Brito.

Tiradentes *p255, map p254*
Post office and telephone Combined office on Largo das Forras in the Prefeitura Municipal, R Resende Costa 71. It closes at 1200 for lunch.

São João del Rei *p257, map p257*
Banks Bradesco, Av Hermílio Alves 200, next to the Theatro Municipal, has an exchange, 1000-1600 and a Visa cashpoint.

Northern and western Minas Gerais

The population thins out in Northern Minas and as it stretches into the sertão backlands and the state of Bahia, the landscape gets ever more arid. Water mostly comes from the river São Francisco, a blue streak cutting through the beiges and browns of the semi-desert. Few tourists, however, get further than the colonial mining town of Diamantina, recently declared a World Heritage site and every bit as pretty as its more famous contemporaries to the south. There are extensive tracts of beautiful cerrado *forest towards the border with Goiás, parts of it protected by the Serra do Cipó and Grande Sertão Veredas national parks. Western Minas is less visited still, yet there are some beautiful stretches of forest in the Serra da Canastra, which can be visited on the way to or from Mato Grosso or Goiás.* » *For Sleeping, Eating and other listings, see pages 271-273.*

Parque Nacional da Serra do Cipó » *pp271-273.*

① *Information from Ibama in Belo Horizonte. T031-3291 6588, www.ibama.gov.br.* The Serra do Cipó, 120 km northeast of Belo Horizonte, protects 33,400 sq km of important *cerrado* and gallery forest, which provide a home for ultra-rare bird species like *cipo canastero* and grey-backed tachuri. Endangered mammals are also found here, including one of the more wimpy carnivores, the maned wolf, looking like a giant fox with overly long legs, which hunts small grassland rodents with its feet. There are also masked titi and brown capuchin monkeys and a number of endemic carnivorous plants. The walks that cut through the park pass through some of the most beautiful rugged grassland country in the state, leading to waterfalls and strands of tropical forest.

The national park can be reached via road MG-010. This road continues unpaved to Serro (see Colonial cities, page 242); buses run on this route. Agencies offer excursions from the city to the park. It is recommended to take a guide because the trails are unmarked; ask locally. The nearest accommodation is in the municipalities of Santana do Riacho, a town northwest of the park, or in Jaboticatubas.

Diamantina » *pp271-273.*

→ *Phone code: 038. Altitude: 1120 m. Colour map 4, B3. Population: 48,000.*

Diamantina, a UNESCO World Heritage site and northern Minas's prettiest colonial town sits nestled in rugged hills 300 km north of Belo Horizonte. The town's churches are less spectacular than those in Ouro Preto or São João del Rey, but the city has a wonderful architectural unity and is better preserved and less touristy.

The *cerrado* forests that swathe the countryside around the town are home to some of the rarest birds and mammals on the continent. The recently opened São Gonçalo do Rio Preto state park, 45 km from Diamantina is the best base from which to explore them. Regular flights from Belo Horizonte to Diamantina have made visiting far easier than it used to be; it is now possible to continue overland from the town to Bahia.

Ins and outs

Diamantina can be reached by plane with **Total** twice a week, and by regular buses from Belo Horizonte and the Serra do Cipó. It is connected to Brasília through Curvelo, and Araçuaí and Itaubim from Porto Seguro in Bahia. The **tourist office** ⓘ *Casa de Cultura, Praça Antônio Eulálio 53, 3rd floor, T038-3531 1636*, is friendly and helpful and provides pamphlets and a reliable map, as well as information about church opening times, buses and local guides. Taxis are expensive in Diamantina. Excursions in the area can be organized through **Real Receptivo** (see Activities and tours, page 273).

Background

Like Minas's other colonial towns Diamantina owes its existence and colonial finery to mining wealth; in this case diamonds, which were first found here in 1728 at the then settlement of Arraial do Tijuco. The settlement soon became a city, grew rapidly in wealth and equally as rapidly in discontent at the Portuguese tyranny. The majority black and mixed-race population were treated as they were in the other colonial towns in Minas – as subhuman. They were considered of such low birth that they were banned from walking in front of façades of the white churches as it would be an affront to God. They remained largely in poverty, leading many of the citizens to sympathise with the Inconfidentes (see page 250). One local priest, José da Silva de Oliveira Rolim (Padre Rolim), joined the movement.

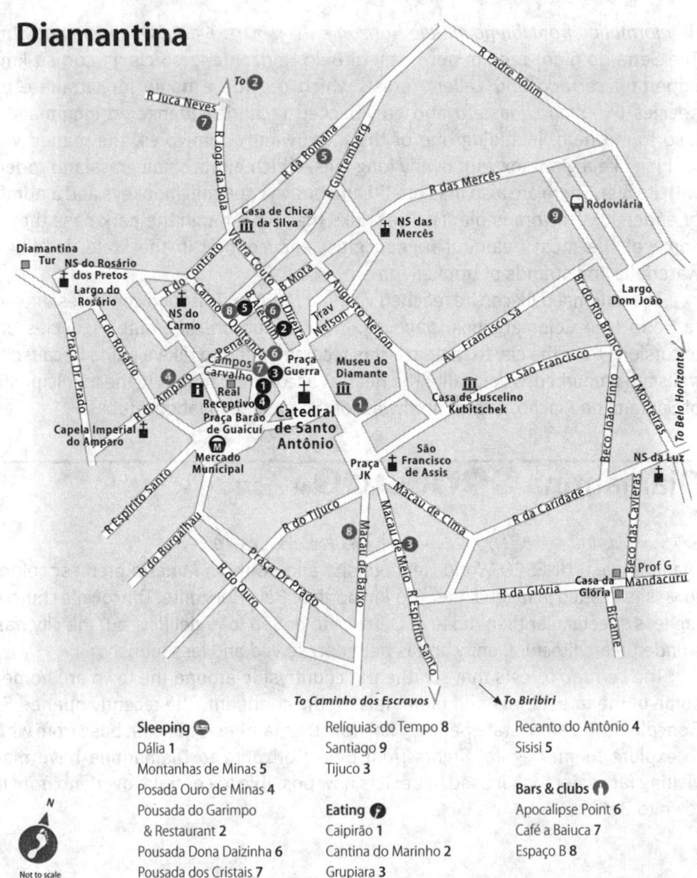

Sights

Diamantina is easily manageable on foot – the city centre is compact and there are plenty of little street-side cafés and bars. The best place to start exploring is the **Praça Guerra** (Praça do Sé) which is dominated by the towering 1930s cathedral. The most interesting church, **Nossa Senhora do Carmo** ⓘ *R do Carmo, Tue-Sat 0800-1200, 1400-1800, Sun 0800-1200*, is a short walk from here, west along Rua Carmo Quitanda. It is most remarkable for its beautiful interior paintings, carried out by José Soares de Araujo a former bodyguard from Braga in Portugal. Many of the city's churches are painted by him, but this is by far his finest work. The Carmelites are said to have been founded before the time of Christ by the prophet Elijah, who is depicted on the magnificent ceiling, ascending to heaven in a chariot of fire, and brandishing a sword on one of the side altars. Another ceiling painting shows the patron saint and founder of the Third Order of Mount Carmel, the 12th-century English saint, St Simon Stock, receiving a scapular from the Virgin. The placing of the church tower at the back of the building was ostensibly to please Chica Silva; the black slave of Padre Rolim. In an era when black Brazilians were valued less than chickens she achieved liberty, married the wealthy diamond merchant João Fernandes de Oliveira, and became the most influential woman in the city, living in luxury with him and their 14 children in a house overlooking the Praça Lobo de Mesquita. The house is now a museum, the **Casa de Chica da Silva** ⓘ *Praça Lobo Mesquita 266, free.*

Just south of Nossa Senhora do Carmo is the church of **Nossa Senhora do Rosário dos Pretos** ⓘ *Largo Dom Joaquim, Tue-Sat 0800-1200 and 1400-1800, Sun 0800-1200*, designated for the black underclass who were not permitted to attend mass at Nossa Senhora do Carmo. Its simple interior has a magical meditative silence. Outside is an original 18th-century public fountain, the Chafariz do Rosário where water pours from the mouths of distinctly African faces.

Diamantina has a number of other interesting small museums worth exploring. The **Museu do Diamante** ⓘ *R Direita 14, Tue-Sat 1200-1730, Sun 0900-1200, US$1*, in the house of Padre Rolim houses an important collection of the materials used in the diamond industry, together with some beautiful 18th- and 19th-century oratories and icons and the iron collars that were once fitted to the slaves that worked the mines.

The **Biblioteca Antônio Torres** ⓘ *R Quitanda 48, Mon-Fri 1400-1700*, is a smart 18th-century townhouse, which is also known as the **Casa Muxarabie** after the enclosed Moorish balcony on one of the windows.

Behind the 18th-century building that now houses the **Prefeitura Municipal** (originally the diamonds administration building) at Praça Conselheiro Matta 11, is the **Mercado Municipal** or **dos Tropeiros** (muleteers) ⓘ *Praça Barão de Guaicuí*. It was built in 1835 as a residence and trading house before being expanded and has wooden arches. The **Casa da Glória** ⓘ *R da Glória 297*, is the city's most photographed building. Two houses on either side of the street are connected by a covered corridor-bridge. This was once part of a convent school and the girls would laugh and flirt through the small windows. It is now part of a university.

President Juscelino Kubitschek, the founder of Brasília, was from Diamantina and his house lies on the outskirts of town. It has been converted into a **museum** ⓘ *R São Francisco 241, Tue-Sun 1000-1200 and 1400-1800, US$2.*

Excursions from Diamantina

» pp271-273.

There is a good walk along the **Caminho dos Escravos**, the old road built by slaves between the mining area on Rio Jequitinhonha and Diamantina. A guide is essential and not expensive; ask at the Casa de Cultura. Beware of snakes and thunderstorms.

About 9 km from town is the **Gruta de Salitre**, a big cave with a strange rock formation. There are no buses, but it is a good walk and you can find some interesting minerals along the way. Ask the tourist office for directions, or take a taxi. Closer to the town is the **Cachoeira da Toca**, a 15-m waterfall, which is good for swimming.

Along the riverbank it is 12 km on a dirt road to **Biribiri**, a pretty village with a well-preserved church and an abandoned textile factory. It also has a few bars and is popular and noisy at weekends. About halfway there are swimming pools in the river; opposite them, on a cliff face, are red animal paintings of unknown age and origin. There is some interesting plant life along the river and beautiful mountain views.

The sleepy little town of **São Gonçalo do Rio Preto**, which sits next to a beautiful mountain river, is famous for its traditional festivals. It lies some 60 km from Diamantina on the edge of the **Parque Estadual de São Gonçalo do Rio Preto** – an area of stunning, pristine *cerrado* filled with flowering trees and particularly rich in birdlife. There are pousadas in São Gonçalo and *cabañas* in the park (reachable by taxi). Guides are also available.

Serro → *Phone code: 038. Colour map 4, B3. Population: 22,000.*

This unspoiled colonial town on the Rio Jequitinhonha has six fine baroque churches, a museum and many beautiful squares. It makes *queijo serrano*, one of Brazil's best cheeses and is in the centre of a prosperous cattle region. The most conspicuous church is **Santa Rita**, on a hill in the centre of town, reached by a long line of steps. On the main Praça João Pinheiro, by the bottom of the steps, is **Nossa Senhora do Carmo**, arcaded, with original paintings on the ceiling and in the choir. The town has two large mansions: **Barão de Diamantina** ⓘ *Praça Presidente Vargas*, is in ruins, but **Barão do Serro** ⓘ *R da Fundição, Tue-Sat 1200-1700, Sun 0900-1200*, across the river, is beautifully restored and used as the town hall and Casa de Cultura. There are old mine entrances in the hillside behind the courtyard. The **Museu Regional Casa dos Ottoni** ⓘ *Praça Cristiano Ottoni 72*, is an 18th-century house now containing furniture and everyday objects from the region. The Ottoni brothers, who were born here, were prominent naval officers turned politicians in the 19th century. For information contact **Secretaria de Turismo** ⓘ *Chácara do Barão do Serro, T038-3541 1368 ext 234*.

Just by the Serro turn-off is the town of **Datas**, whose spacious church (1832) decorated in red and blue, contains a wooden image of Christ with the crown of thorns.

Rio São Francisco

Passenger services on the river have been discontinued but masters of cargo boats in the port may permit passage. The regular stops are at **Januária** (famous for Brazil's reputed best *cachaça*) and **Bom Jesus da Lapa** in Bahia. The latter is a pilgrimage centre with a church built in a grotto inside a mountain, but it's a very poor town. There are hotels and a choice of bars on the river beach.

Pirapora → *Phone code: 038. Colour map 4, B3. Population: 50,000.*

North of Três Marias is this terminus for boat journeys on the Rio São Francisco. The cutting down of trees, in part as fuel for the boats, and the low rainfall in recent years, has reduced the river's flow. The town itself is a tourist attraction because of the falls in the river which make for excellent fishing. The fishermen use punt-like canoes. The sandy river beaches are used for swimming. The riverboats' grotesque figureheads, *carrancas*, are made in the workshops of **Lourdes Barroso** ⓘ *R Abaeté 390*.

São Francisco → *Phone code: 038. Colour map 4, A3. Population: 50,000.*

Between Pirapora and Januária is the colonial fishing town of São Francisco, with many attractive houses and a good handicraft market in the town hall. Of the two remaining wood-burning stern-wheel boats (allegedly built for Mississippi services in the 1860s and imported from the USA in 1922 to work on the Amazon) one, the *Gaiola*, was restored for services on the Rio São Francisco. The town is popular during Semana Santa, Festas Juninas and a carnival in July.

Western Minas Gerais and the Serra da Canastra

» pp271-273.

Parque Nacional da Serra da Canastra

Information from Ibama, Av do Contorno 8121, Cidade Jardim, Belo Horizonte, T031-3291 6588 ext 119/122; or from Caixa Postal 01, São Roque de Minas, T031-3433 1195. Gates close at 1800.

South of Araxá is the Serra da Canastra national park, in which the Rio São Francisco rises. It is a cool region (May and June average 18°C), comprising two ranges of hills, the Serra da Canastra and the Serra das Sete Voltas, with the Vale dos Cândidos between. The altitude ranges from 900 m to 1496 m and the vegetation is mostly grassland, rising to high-altitude plants on the uplands. Animals include the maned wolf, the great anteater, armadillos and deer. Birds that can be seen include rheas, owls, seriema, king vulture and the diving duck. There are also other birds of prey, partridges and tinamous. Besides the source of the Rio São Francisco (6½ km from the São Roque park entrance), visitors can see the two parts of the **Dasca d'Anta waterfall**.

The park has a **visitor centre** just inside the park, at the São Roque de Minas entrance. There are three other entrances: Casca d'Anta, São João Batista and Sacramento. The park is best reached from Piumhi, on the MG-050, 267 km southwest of Belo Horizonte (this road heads for Ribeirão Preto in São Paulo). From Piumhi you go to São Roque de Minas (60 km).

Uberaba and around → *Phone code: 034. Colour map 4, B1. Population: 240,500.*

From Araxá, the BR-262 heads 120 km west to Uberaba, also in the Minas Triangle on the Rio da Prata, and 485 km from São Paulo. It is an important road junction on the direct highway between São Paulo and Brasília and serves a large cattle-raising district. At the beginning of April each year, the Rural Society of the Minas Triangle holds a famous cattle and agricultural exhibition at Uberaba.

Between Uberaba and Ponte Alta (31 km east on the BR-262) is **Peirópolis**, which is an incredibly important palaeontological site, with dinosaur remains and eggs. The **Centro de Pesquisas Paleontológicas – Museu do Einossauro** *T034-9720023, weekdays 0800-1800, Sat and Sun 1100-1700*, is 23 km east of Uberaba, at Km 784.5.

Uberlândia → *Phone code: 034. Population: 439,000.*

About 100 km north of Uberaba is Uberlândia, founded in 1888 as São Pedro do Uberabinha. It is a fast-growing city with good communications by air and road. Several major bus routes (eg Campo Grande-Brasília) pass through here. There is a helpful tourist information kiosk in the *rodoviária*.

Sleeping

Parque Nacional da Serra do Cipó *p267*

LL Toucan Cipó, exclusively through www.dehouche.com as part of a tour. A British-owned luxury *fazenda* in pristine cerrado forest cut by clear-water streams. Very rich in bird and mammal life.

AL-A Cipó Veraneio, Rodovia MG-10, Km 95, Jaboticatubas, www.cipoveraneiohotel.com.br. Comfortable a/c rooms with cable TV, fridges and en suites in terraces of stone cabins next to the road that cuts through the park. The hotel has a pool, sauna, very good tour operator and a *cachaça* distillery just up the road, which produces some of Minas's finest.

Camping

Camping Véu da Noiva, Km 101, Santana do Riacho, T031-3201 1166, www.guiaserradocipo.com.br/acm. Pretty little campsite in a forest grove near a waterfall and Swiss-style chalets (from **D** per person).

Diamantina *p267, map p268*

Rooms are usually half price for those travelling alone. Unless otherwise stated, all are within 10 mins' walk of the centre.

AL Tijuco, R Macau do Melo 211, T038-3531 1022, www.hoteltijuco.com.br. A wonderful Niemeyer design that looks like a building from Thunderbird island. The large rooms have been refurbished whilst staying true to the original 1960s kitsch. The best rooms are at the front with balconies and glorious views.

A Pousada do Garimpo, Av da Saudade 265, T/F038-3531 2523, pgarimpo@diamantina.uemg.br. Plain, well-kept rooms in a smart hotel on the outskirts of town - a taxi ride from the centre. There's a pool, sauna and a restaurant serving some of the city's best Minas cooking from celebrated chef, Vandeka.

A Relíquias do Tempo, R Macau de Baixo 104, T038-3531 1627, www.diamantinanet.com.br/pousadareliquiasdotempo. Cosy wood-floored rooms with en suites in a pretty 19th-century house just off Praça JK. Public areas are decorated like a colonial family home. Breakfasts are generous.

B-C Hotel Montanhas de Minas, R da Roman 264, T038-3531 3240, www.montanhasdeminas.com.br. Spacious rooms with stone floors and en suites, some with balconies. Decent breakfasts.

C Dália, Praça JK (Jota-Ka) 25, T038-3531 1477, www.hoteldalia.com.br. Well-kept rooms with solid beds, parquet floors and large bathrooms. Ask to see several rooms as some are musty.

C-D Hotel Santiago, Largo Dom João 133, T038-3431 3407, hotelsantiago@jk.net. Plain, small but spruce rooms with en suites. Reasonable breakfast.

C-D Pousada dos Cristais, R Joga da Bola 53, T038-3531 3923, www.diamantinanet.com.br/pousadadoscristais. A range of simple, large rooms in white, with wooden floors. Situated on the edge of town with views out across the mountains.

C-D Pousada Ouro de Minas, R do Amparo 90A, T038-3531 2306. Simple well-kept rooms with stone floor rooms with tiny bathrooms in a converted colonial house.

C-E Pousada Dona Daizinha, R Direita 131, T038-3531 1351. Simple wood-floor rooms in a colonial house; some with space for up to 5. Very good breakfast and friendly service.

Camping

Wild camping is possible near the waterfall just outside town.

Serro *p270*

B Pousada Vila do Príncipe, R Antônio Honório Pires 38, T/F038-3541 1485. Very clean, in an old mansion containing its own museum, the artist Mestre Valentim is said to have been born in the slave quarters. There are other cheaper hotels.

Pirapora *p270*

C Canoeiras, Av Salmeron 3, T038-741 1933. Used by river-tour parties.

C Pirapora Palace, Praça Melo Viana 61, 7 blocks west and 1 block south of the *rodoviária*, T038-741 3851. Ask for a room on the garden, safe.

E Daila, Praça JK 13. With breakfast, no bath.

E Grande, R da Quitanda 70. With bath, but without breakfast.

São Francisco *p270*

B Hotel Green Fish, R Min Hermenegildo de Barros 560, T/F6311106.

Uberaba *p271*

B Novotel, Av Filomena Cartafina 150, 5 km from town, T034-3336 4288. Pool, restaurant.

B Pousada São Francisco, BR-330, 7 km from town, T034-3314 5553. Offers horse riding.

C Karajá, Av Fernando Costa 146, T034-3336 1000.

D Porto Bello, Av Barão do Rio Branco 1000, T/F034-3336 6701.

Uberlândia *p271*

A Plaza Inn Master, R da Bandeira 400, T034-3239 8000, F239 8100. With restaurant.

B Estância das Flores, Km 166 BR-050, T034-3234 0120. Horse riding and fishing available.

E Hotel Nacional, Higino Guerra 273, opposite the *rodoviária*, T034-3235 4983. With view (cheaper without), shower and breakfast.

Eating

Diamantina *p267, map p268*

TTT Cantina do Marinho, R Direita 113, T038-3531 1686. This formal restaurant decorated with bottles of wine and attended by black-tie waiters is celebrated for its *salmão provençale* and *bacalhau*.

₸₸₸ Grupiara, R Campos Carvalho 12, T038-3531 3887. Decent regional cooking, a convivial atmosphere and good-value per-kilo options at lunch.

₸₸ Caipirão, R Campos Carvalho 15, T038-3531 1526. Minas cooking with a lunchtime buffet cooked over a traditional wood-fired clay oven and evening à la carte.

₸₸ Recanto do Antônio, Beco da Tecla 39, T038-3531 1147. Minas food and decent steak served in a chic rustic dining room in a colonial house.

₸ Sisisi, Beco da Mota 89, T038-3531 3071. Pasta, Minas cooking and a very good value *prato feito* at lunchtime.

Bars and clubs

Diamantina *p267, map p268*

Apocalipse Point, Praça Barão de Guaicuí 78, T038- 3531 9296. *Sertaneja* music, *axe* and live music upstairs. Lively at weekends with a 20- and 30-something crowd.

Café a Baiuca, Rua da Quitanda. Coffee bar by day with old men reading the paper, and by night a funky little bar with music DVDs and a crowd spilling out onto the street.

Espaço B, R Beco da Tecla. A bookshop-cafe serving crêpes and draught beer to an arty crowd until the small hours.

Festivals and events

Diamantina *p267, map p268*

During the famous **Vesperatas**, musicians and singers serenade from balconies along the colonial streets and drum troupes and bands parade along them. Twice a month always on a Sat.

Feb Carnival is said to be very good here and the town is trying to establish another out of season festival in Sep, **Semana Santa**.

May-Jun Corpus Christi.

13 Jun Santo Antônio.

Jul Held 50 days after Pentecost, **O Divino Espírito Santo**, is a major 5-day feast.

12 Sep O Dia das Serestas, the Day of the Serenades, for which the town is famous; this is the birthday of President Juscelino Kubitschek, who was born here.

Oct First half of the month, Festa do Rosário.

Activities and tours

Diamantina *p267, map p268*

Diamantina Tur, Praça do Garimpeiros 616, T038-8801 1802. City tours, adventure activities (rappel and trekking) and trips to nearby natural attractions and Biri Biri. From US$8 per person per day.

Real Receptivo, R Campos Carvalho 19, loja 12, T038-3531 1636, www.realreceptivo.com.br. City tours and trips to nearby natural attractions. From $8 per person per day for groups of 4 or more.

Transport

Diamantina *p267, map p268*

Bus There are 6 buses a day to **Belo Horizonte** (5 hrs) US$20, via Curvelo (for connections to Brasília, 10 hrs), with Pássaro Verde. There are daily buses to **Montes Claros**, with daily connections here for **Brasília** and **Parque Nacional Grande Sertão Veredas**. For the **Serra do Cipó** take the bus to Serro (2 daily) and change for Santa Ana do Riacho and the Serra do Cipó. There is one bus per day to **São Gonçalo do Rio Preto**.

If en route to Bahia, there are 2 daily buses to **Araçuaí** (4 hrs) from here kombis and buses run to **Itaubim** ($4, 2 hrs) from where there are connections to **Vitória da Conquista** (US$5.50, 4 hrs) and on to **Porto Seguro** and other destinations in Bahia. (At Araçuaí is **E** Pousada Tropical, opposite the *rodoviária*, T038-3731 1765. With bath, clean and friendly.) The BR-116 passes interesting rock formations at Pedra Azul (see page 283) before crossing the border with Bahia.

Uberaba *p271*

Bus To **Belo Horizonte**, US$15 (*leito* US$30), 7 hrs.

Uberlândia *p271*

Air Airport 8 km from town, T034-2125192.

Airline offices Rio-Sul, T034-3236 1414. TAM, T034-3253 1000.

Bus To **Brasília**, 6 hrs, US$9; to **Belo Horizonte**, 9 hrs, US$15; to **São Paulo**, US$18.

Directory

Diamantina *p267, map p268*

Banks Banco do Brasil, Praça Cons Mata 23.

Eastern and southern Minas Gerais

The border area between Minas and Espírito Santo is the most rugged in the state. Marked by the ridges and remnant forests of the Serra do Caparaó, which are home to some of the country's highest peaks, it remains an important centre for semi-precious stone processing and crystal carving. The two principal towns, Governador Valadares and Teófilo Otôni, are on the BR-116 inland Rio-Salvador road, and both have good connections with Belo Horizonte. ▸▸ *For Sleeping, Eating and other listings, see pages 278-280*

Caratinga Biological Station

ⓘ *US$15 per person per day, payable only in reais. Tours can be arranged through Focus Tours, www.focustours.com, see page 24.*

The privately owned Caratinga Biological Station, set in 880 ha of mountainous, inland Atlantic forest, is protected by a conscientious family and **Conservation International.** The reserve is home to four rare primates: half of the world's northern muriquis (*Brachyteles hypoxanthus*), a sub-species of woolly spider monkeys, which are the largest primates in the Americas and one of the most critically endangered; the brown (or black-capped) capuchin; the brown howler monkey and a sub-species of tufted eared marmoset (the buffy-headed marmoset). Also at the station are brown-throated three-toed sloths and one of the largest inventories of birds outside the Andean regions of the Amazon – 217 species at last count. The primates and many of the birds are easily seen.

Parque Estadual do Rio Doce

ⓘ *T031-822 3006, or phone the Instituto Estadual de Florestas T031-330 7013. Access is by the BR-262 or 381, from which you have to turn off onto dirt roads to get to the park.*

The Parque Estadual do Rio Eoce is 248 km east of Belo Horizonte in the municipalities of Dionísio, Timóteo and Marliéria. Between 230 m and 515 m above sea level and covering almost 36,000 ha, this is one of the largest tracts of Mata Atlântica in southeast Brazil. As well as forest there are a number of lakes, on which boat trips are possible, besides swimming and fishing. The park is home to a great many birds and animals. There is an information centre, a campsite 6 km into the park and trails that have been marked out for hiking.

Parque Nacional Caparaó ▸▸ *pp278-280.*

This is one of the most popular parks in Minas, with good walking through strands of Atlantic rainforest, *paramo* and to the summits of three of Brazil's highest peaks, **Pico da Bandeira** (2890 m), **Pico do Cruzeiro** (2861 m) and the **Pico do Cristal** (2798 m). Wildlife is not as plentiful as it is in Caratinga as the park has lost much of its forest and its floral biodiversity. However, there are still a number of Atlantic Coast primates here, like the brown capuchins, together with a recovering bird population. From the park entrance (where a small fee has to be paid) it is 6 km on a poorly maintained road to the car park at the base of the waterfall. From the hotel (see Sleeping, page 278) jeeps (US$20 per jeep) run to the car park at 1970 m (2½ hours' walk), then it's a three- to four-hour walk to the summit of the Pico da Bandeira, marked by yellow arrows; there are plenty of camping possibilities all the way up, the highest being at **Terreirão** (2370 m). It is best to visit during the dry season (April to October), although it can be quite crowded in July and during Carnaval.

Ins and outs

Getting there The park is 49 km by paved road from Manhuaçu on the Belo Horizonte-Vitória road (BR-262). If you have your own transport, drive from the BR-262, go through Manhumirim, Presidente Soares and Caparaó village, then 1 km further to the **Hotel Caparaó Parque**. There are bus services from Belo Horizonte (twice a day), Ouro Preto or Vitória, to Manhumirim, 15 km south of Manhuaçu. From Manhumirim, take a bus direct to Caparaó, or to Presidente Soares (7 km), then hitch 11 km to Caparaó. ▸▸ *See Transport, page 280.*

Tourist information Contact via Caixa Postal 17, Alto Jequitibá, T255, via operator on 101-PS 1, Alto do Caparaó. **Ibama,** T031-291 6588 ext 119/122, also has information.

Towards southern Bahia → *Phone code: 033. Population: 127,500.*

Situated 138 km from Governador Valadares, **Teófilo Otoni** is popular with dealers of crystals and gemstones, and has the best prices in the state. There are various hotels (see Sleeping page 278). Regular buses arrive from Belo Horizonte and travel on to Porto Seguro via **Nanuque**, where it is possible to break the Belo Horizonte-Salvador journey, with accommodation near the *rodoviária*.

Parque Florestal de Ibitipoca

→ *Altitude: 1760 m.*

ⓘ *Daily 0800-1600, US$2. By unpaved road it is 27 km from Lima Duarte to Conceição de Ibitipoca. The road is rough and difficult in the wet, but in the dry season especially, ordinary cars can make it. From Conceição it is a 3-km walk (or hitchhike) to the park. Take a bus from Juiz da Fora to Lima Duarte and from there to Ibitipoca.*

This park is 85 km from Juiz de Fora, the largest city in southwestern Minas (with plenty of hotels and good transport). It contains quartzite caves, interesting rock formations, waterfalls, rivers, many different types of vegetation, orchids, bromeliads, cacti and lots of lichens and flowers, such as purple *quaresmeiras*. Evidence suggests that it was under the sea at one time; more recently it was on the *bandeirantes*' trails (see box page 210). A little gold was found, but it was mostly mica that was extracted; there is quartzite everywhere you look.

Ibitipoca preserves birds and animals, including monkeys, which you are likely to hear rather than see. The French botanist Auguste St-Hilaire visited the area in 1822. To see all that the park has to offer takes about four days. There are a number of trails of varying length; on the longest be prepared for stretches of up to eight hours (take water and protection against the sun). You can stay overnight (see Sleeping page 278).

The nearest village, **Conceição de Ibitipoca**, is one of the oldest in Minas Gerais. Its church was built in 1768 and has original paintings on the ceiling. There is a statue of São Sebastião and a separate bell tower. The key for the church is at **Ibiti-Bike**. Mass is held once a month. Modern buildings in the village give it a messy look, but the park is definitely worth visiting. There are various eating places in the village and the local speciality is *pão de canela*. Hand-dyed and woven bedspreads and handicrafts in wood are also made in the village.

São Tomé das Letras ▸▸ *pp278-280.*

→ *Phone code: 035. Colour map 4, C2. Population: 6,750.*

São Tomé das Letras, 35 km from Três Corações, is a beautiful hilltop town which is very popular at weekends. The streets were once lined with houses made of local stone, giving the town a distinctive architectural identity, but its popularity as a tourist destination has seen many of these replaced or overshadowed by ugly concrete buildings and São Tomé is sadly beginning to lose its charm. At 1291 m it is one of the five highest places in Brazil. The average maximum temperature is 26°C and the minimum is 14°C. The rainy season is October to March.

Rock paintings found in caves nearby have been dated to about 2000 BC. The inscriptions have lent the town a mystical reputation, attracting 'new age' visitors. Many believe it is a good vantage point for seeing UFOs (some claim the inscriptions are extraterrestrial in origin) and that there are places with special energies. The **Carimbado cave** is rich in myths and legends, such as that its passages lead to an underground civilization and that its powers form an energy source linked to Machu Picchu in Peru. The Shangri-lá rapid, which is a beautiful spot, is also called the **Vale do Maytréia.** The shops reflect this atmosphere and the hotels are classified by UFOs instead of stars. Whatever you think of it, São Tomé is certainly an unusual place.

Ins and outs

There are three daily buses (two on Sunday) from Três Corações, 1½ hours (the first 30 minutes on a paved road); take the one that leaves Três Corações at dawn to see the mist in the valleys. If driving to the town, take care at the unsigned road junctions. After the pavement ends, at the next main junction, turn right. There is a **tourist office** ⓘ *R José Cristiano Alves 4*, for information.

Background

A quarry town since the beginning of the 20th century, there is evidence of the industry everywhere you look. Settlement in colonial times dates from the mid- to late-18th century when the *bandeirantes* from São Paulo moved into this area, displacing the indigenous inhabitants. Even before the 20th-century 'alternative' arrivals, the hill acquired a legend: at the end of the 18th century, an escaped slave hid in a cave for a long time. A finely dressed man appeared, asking him why he was living there. On hearing the slave's story, the man gave him a message on a piece of paper which, on presentation to his master, would earn the slave forgiveness. The slave duly did as the man said and the master, impressed by the writing and the paper, went to the cave to seek the mysterious man for himself. He found no one, but instead a statue of São Thomé (St Thomas). The master therefore built a chapel at the site, which was replaced by the Igreja Matriz in 1784, now standing beside the cave. The inscriptions, in red, can just about be seen in the cave; they are the 'Letras' of the town's name.

Sights

The town is almost at the top of the hill. Behind it are rocky outcrops on which are the **Pyramid House**, the **Cruzeiro** (cross) at 1430 m, with good 360-degree views, the **Pedra da Bruxa** and paths for walking or, in some parts, scrambling.

The bus stops at the main praça, where there is the frescoed 18th-century **Igreja Matriz** beside the fenced cave. A second church, the 18th-century **Igreja das Pedras** (Nossa Senhora do Rosário) is on a praça to the left as you enter town (Rua Ernestina Maria de Jesus Peixoto). It is constructed in the same style as many of the charming old-style buildings, with slabs of the local stone laid on top of each other without mortar.

Tours from São Tomé das Letras

In the surrounding hills are many caves: **Sobradinho**, 12 km; **Carimbado**, 5 km; **Gruta do Feijão**, a short walk from town; **Gruta da Bruxa**, 6 km. Seven waterfalls are also close by, including: **Cachoeira de Eubiose**, 4 km; **Véu de Noiva**, 12 km; **Paraíso**, near Véu de Noiva; **Vale das Borboletas da Lua**, 8 km; and **do Flávio**, 6 km. There are also rapids such as **Shangri-lá**, 17 km, and **Vale dos Gnomos**, near the Vale das Borboletas. Some of these places make a good hike from the town, but you can also visit several in a day on an organized tour, see Activities and tours, page 280.

Towns and spas of southwestern Minas » pp278-280.

A group of popular spas are easily reached by road from Rio de Janeiro and São Paulo. Most of the hydro resorts lie south of the Dutra Highway (BR-381, Belo Horizonte-São Paulo). These are Cambuquirá, Lambari, São Lourenço and Caxambu, south of the town of Três Corações, which also gives access to the centre of São Tomé das Letras. Further west and north, on the Minas/São Paulo border is the much larger resort of Poços de Caldas. Some 240 km southwest of Belo is the huge lake formed by the Furnas Dam. It can be seen from the BR-381 road to São Paulo.

Tres Corações → *Phone code: 035. Colour map 4, C2. Population: 64,000.*

The modern city of Tres Corações is a convenient place for making connections to the spas but is desperately uninteresting. It is, however, the birthplace of Pelé, the legendary football star, to whom there is a statue in Praça Coronel José Martins.

The *rodoviária* is beside the old railway station where a steam engine is on show (the railway is used but there is no passenger traffic). At Avenida Getúlio Vargas 154 is the **Casa de Cultura Godofredo Rangel** (Departamento de Turismo e Cultura and Library). **Praça Odilon**, on Rua de Andrade, has a post office and **Banco do Brasil** (but no exchange facilities). From Praça Martins, Avenida Julião Arbex leads steeply uphill to a statue of Christ on top of a chapel on Praça Monsehnor Fonseca.

Hydro resorts » pp278-280.

Cambuquirá → *Phone code: 035. Altitude: 946 m. Population: 13,000.*

Some 20 km south of Três Corações by paved road, Cambuquirá's **Parque das Águas** is a hilly town with a pleasant atmosphere. Horse-drawn taxis ferry visitors around. Nearby *fazendas* sell *cachaça*.

Lambari → *Phone code: 035. Altitude: 900 m. Population: 19,000.*

This is another hilly town, 27 km south of Cambuquirá. The **Parque das Águas** ⓘ *daily 0600-1800*, has seven mineral springs and mineral water swimming pools on Praça Conselheiro João Lisboa. There are boat trips on the **Lago Guanabara** and to **Ilha dos Amores**. The resort has a casino.

The spas of Minas Gerais & São Paulo

São Lourenço ➔ *Phone code: 035. Altitude: 850 m. Population: 35,000.*

São Lourenço, 60 km southeast of Lambari, is easily accessible from Rio de Janeiro (five or six hours by bus) or São Paulo (six or seven hours by bus), and is useful as a junction but is fairly dull in its own right. There is a splendid park with tennis, boating, swimming, a flying field and fishing. Its rich mineral waters are used in the treatment of various medical complaints. The famous carbo-gaseous baths are unique in South America and can be found at **Parque das Águas** ⓘ *Praça Brasil, daily 0800-1700.*

Caxambu ➔ *Phone code: 035. Altitude: 900 m. Population: 21,000.*

The waters at Caxambu, 31 km northeast of São Lourenço, are used for treating stomach, kidney and bladder diseases, and are said to restore fertility (the Parque das Águas is closed on Monday). The waters seemed to work for Princess Isabel, daughter of Dom Pedro II, who produced three sons after a visit. The little church of **Santa Isabel da Hungária** (1868) stands on a hill as a thanks offering. The surrounding mountains and forests are very beautiful and there is a view over the city from **Morro Caxambu**, 1010 m.

Poços de Caldas » *pp278-280.*

➔ *Phone code: 035. Colour map 4, C2. Population: 124,000.*

The city is right on the São Paulo state border, some 150 km north of the hydro resorts around Lindóia. It is 272 km from São Paulo, 507 km from Rio and 510 km from Belo Horizonte. Sited at 1180 m on the crater of an extinct volcano in a mountainous area, it has an excellent climate. The resort, a traditional honeymoon centre, has thermal establishments for the treatment of rheumatic, skin and intestinal diseases (you need a local doctor's certificate to use these facilities). Venetians from Murano settled here and established a crystal-glass industry.

The *rodoviária* is 3 km from the centre and receives buses from Rio de Janeiro and São Paulo. A monorail runs down main avenue, Avenida Francisco Sales, to the cable car station.

Excursions from Poços de Caldas

From Poços de Caldas it is possible to visit the **Véu das Noivas** with its three waterfalls illuminated at night; the tall statue of **Cristo Redentor** at 1678 m, which can be reached by cable car and is popular with hang-gliders; **Pedra Batão**, an 80-m granite rock; and the Japanese teahouse at the **Recanto Japonês**.

Sleeping

Parque Nacional Caparaó *p274*

C Caparaó Parque, 2 km from the park entrance, 15 mins' walk from the town of Caparaó, T032-741 2559. Pleasant.

E São Luiz, Manhumirim. Good value, but the bar next door has better food.

Camping

Ask locally where camping is permitted in the park.

Towards Southern Bahia *p275*

There are several hotels (**C**) in Teófilo Otoni.

D Pousada Tio Miro, R Dr Manoel Esteves 389, T033-3521 4343. Relaxed atmosphere. Recommended.

Parque Florestal de Ibitipoca *p275*

D Estrela da Serra, Conceição de Ibitipoca. Price per person, more expensive with TV and fridge, price includes breakfast and dinner; lunch costs US$10.

Camping

Ibiti-Lua, in the park itself, is a campsite for 50 tents, with toilets, showers, restaurant/bar and car park.

Tres Corações *p277*

C Cantina Calabreza, R Joaquim Bento de Carvalho 65, T/F035-3231 1183. Pool, sauna, has a reasonable restaurant (Italo-Brasileira), and a takeaway service.

E Avenida, Av Getúlio Vargas 55. Very basic, older and more decrepit than the **Capri**.

E Capri, Av Getúlio Vargas 111, not far from the bridge across the river, T035-3231 1427. With or without bath, simple but okay, TVs in the more expensive rooms.

There are other, more basic hotels near the *rodoviária*.

São Tomé das Letras *p275*

There are lots of pousadas and rooms to let all over town. Streets are hard to follow because their names can change from one block to the next; numbering is also chaotic.

C-E Rancho Paraíso, 8 km on the road to Sobradinho, T035-3237 1342. Basic lodging, campsite, restaurant, garden and trekking.

D Pousada Arco-Iris, R João Batista Neves 19, T/F035-3237 1212. Rooms and chalets, sauna, swimming pool.

E Fundação Harmonia, on the road to Sobradinho (4 km), Bairro do Canta Galo, São Tomé das Letras, T035-3237 1280, or T011-3204 3766 in São Paulo. Cheap and cheerful accommodation, price per person. The community emphasizes several disciplines and principles for a healthy lifestyle, for mind and body, 'new age', workshops, massage, excursions, vegetarian food (their shop is on the main praça).

E Hospedaria dos Sonhos I, R Gabriel Luiz Alves. Price per person. Clean, with bath, no TV, restaurant, shop, groups accommodated.

E Mahã Mantra, R Plínio Pedro Martins 48, T035-3989 5563. IYHA Youth hostel.

E Pousada Baraunas, R João Cristiano Alves 19, T035-3346 1330. Basic youth hostel with dorms and double. Price per person.

E Pousada Novo Horizonte, R João Cristiano Alves 10. Price per person. Simple rooms, friendly staff, information on local attractions.

E Sonhos II (do Gê), Trav Nhá Chica 8, T035-3237 1235. Price per person. Very nice, restaurant, swimming pool, sauna, television in rooms. Recommended.

Hydro resorts *p277*

As well as those listed there are many others in all price ranges.

B Emboabas, Av Jorge Amado 350, São Lourenço, T035-3332 4600. Standard plain town hotel with a restaurant.

B Parque Hotel, R Américo Werneck 46, Lambari, T035-3271 2000. Central, standard town hotel with plain rooms.

C Itaici, R Dr Jos dos Santos 320, Lambari, T/F035-3271 1366. Simple, anonymous but centrally located.

C Pousada Canto do Sabiá, about 3 km out of Caxambu, BR-354 towards Itamonte, T035-3341 3499. This charming pousada has chalets and serves excellent breakfast.

D Santos Dumont, Av Virgílio de Melo Franco 400, Cambuquirá.

Camping

Fazenda Recanto das Carvalhos, BR-460 towards Pouso Alto, 10 km from Lambari, T035-3332 2098.

Poços de Caldas *p278*

There are many others in the **B** range, but very few under US$50 a night.

B Novo Hotel Virgínia, R Minas Gerais 506, T035-3722 2664. Simple standard town hotel with a/c and fan-cooled rooms.

B Palace, Praça Pedro Sanches, T035-3722 3636. Old-fashioned but well run, with sulphur baths. Good.

Eating

Tres Corações *p277*

ŦŦ Xodó Quinta da Bock, Av Getúlio Vargas, opposite the Cantina Calabreza, just up from Hotel Capri, open-air restaurant serving beer.

ŦŦ-Ŧ Pizzeria Jardins, 1st floor, Av Getúlio Vargas 363, beyond the praça. Cheap, good *executivo* menu and other dishes, popular.

São Tomé das Letras *p275*

There are many other restaurants and bars.

ŦŦŦ O Alquimista, R Capt Pedro Martins 7. The best in town, with a decent menu of Minas dishes. Closed Mar-Jun and Aug-Nov.

ŦŦ das Magas, R Camilo Rosa. A varied menu of Minas and pasta dishes. Good lasagne.

For Sleeping and Eating price codes, see pages 49 and 52 or the inside front cover. For an explanation of phone codes, see page 66.

Padarias Bom Dia, opposite the bus stop on the main praça. Pleasant bakery with a range of cheap lunches and sandwiches.
Veranda Pôr-do-Sol, R Plínio Pedro Martins, *comida caseira*. Pizza. Brazilian home-cooking including a range of Minas dishes and pizzas.
Ximama, Martins at the corner of G L Alves. Simple pizza restaurant with generous lashings of cheese on the toppings.

Poços de Caldas *p278*
There are plenty of restaurants and all the good hotels have dining rooms. Local specialities are smoked cheese, sausages, sweets and jams (try squash-and-coconut).

Festivals and events

Poços de Caldas *p278*
Feb Carnival
1-13 May São Benedito.
Aug 2nd half of the month. The **Festa UAI** of popular *mineira* music and dance, foods and handicrafts.

Activities and tours

Parque Florestal de Ibitipoca *p275*
Serra do Ibitipoca, R Braz Bernardino 105, loja 212, Braz Shopping, Juiz de Fora. Organized tours to the park.

São Tomé das Letras *p275*
Tours to the caves, waterfalls and rapids surrounding the town can be arranged. To the waterfalls Flávio, Eubiose, Paraíso and Véu de Noiva, US$50; Shangri-lá, US$70; Vale das Borboletas, Gruta do Carimbado and Ladeira do Amendoim (a slope on which cars appear to run uphill when in neutral – like the one in Belo Horizonte), US$50, T035-3237 1283 or enquire at the **Néctar** shop on R José Cristiano Alves. Tours also run on weekends and holidays from the praça at 1000 and 1400 to waterfalls and caves, T035-3237 1353 and ask for Jaime or Iraci.

Transport

Parque Nacional Caparaó *p274*
Bus There are direct services to **Manhumirim**, 15 km south of Manhuaçu, US$1, from where there are connections to **Belo Horizonte** (twice a day with Pássaro Verde), **Ouro Preto** or **Vitória**. Or hitch the 11 km to **Presidente Soares** and take a bus to Manhumirim from there (several, 7 km).

Parque Florestal de Ibitipoca *p275*
Bus From Ibitipoca, take a bus to **Lima Duarte**, 2 daily; then from there to **Juiz da Fora** with Frota Nobre, 8 a day, US$2.10.

São Tomé das Letras *p275*
Bus To **Três Corações**, 3 daily buses (2 on Sun), US$1.65, 1½ hrs.

Tres Corações *p277*
Bus There are 3 daily buses (2 on Sun) to **São Tomé das Letras**, US$1.65, 1½ hrs (the first 30 mins is on a paved road); take the one that leaves Três Corações at dawn to see the mist in the valleys.
To **Belo Horizonte**, **Gardénia**, 4 a day (3 on Sun), US$10.50, 5½ hrs, roadworks permitting. To **São Paulo**, **Transul**, 7 a day, US$8.10. **Beltour** runs buses to **Rio de Janeiro**; **Cristo Rei** to **Santos**.

Hydro resorts *p277*
Bus São Lourenço and Caxambu have frequent, numerous buses to **São Paulo**, **Rio** and **Belo Horizonte**. São Paulo-**Três Corações** bus (**Gardênia**) passes through Cambuquira, US$8.10. 4 buses a day from Bresser station in São Paulo to **Lambari**, US$8.10.

Poços de Caldas *p278*
Bus To **Rio**, 8 hrs, US$13.25; to **São Paulo**, 4½ hrs, US$7.25.

Directory

São Tomé das Letras *p275*
Bank Bemge in the main praça. **Post office** In the group of buildings at the top right of the praça, facing the Gruta São Tomé.

Espírito Santo

Sandwiched between Rio de Janeiro, Minas Gerais and Bahia, the coastal state of Espírito Santo is relatively unknown, except by Mineiros heading for the coast for their holidays. It has many beaches, but they are overshadowed by those of its northern and southern neighbours. There are a number of nature reserves and turtle breeding grounds in Espírito Santo, and European immigration has given the towns a distinctive atmosphere. The state capital, Vitória, is also the main industrial and commercial centre. People here are known as Capixabas, after a former tribe.

The state has a hot, damp seaboard with a more-or-less straight, low coastline and long beaches open to the Atlantic. The south is mountainous and dotted with vast granite boulders even larger than Sugar Loaf. The most spectacular is Pedra Azul. The slopes are covered with pine plantations and remnants of Mata Atlântica rainforest. The coast is covered with restinga scrub and grassland. The north of the state is flat and dominated by vast eucalyptus plantations which run down to the long coastal sand dunes. ▸▸ *For Sleeping, Eating and other listings, see pages 285-288.*

Background

Espírito Santo was one of the original captaincies created by the Portuguese in the 16th century, but their colony was very precarious in its early days. During the struggle for supremacy, the son of Mem de Sá (the governor in Bahia) was killed, but, as elsewhere, the invaders eventually prevailed, though not as successfully as in many of the other captaincies, as the Portuguese were only able to gain a foothold on the coastal plains. When the focus of attention moved to the mines in Minas Gerais in the 18th centuries, the state became strategically important. Initially it was not on the gold exporting route, but after iron mining began a trail from Belo Horizonte to Vitória was created. This remains one of the major economic corridors in the country.

Vitória ▸▸ *pp285-288.*

→ *Phone code: 027. Colour map 4, C5. Population: 266,000.*

The town of Vitória is beautifully set on an island, its entrance second only to Rio's. The beaches are just as attractive, but smaller, and the climate is less humid. Five bridges connect the island with the mainland. Vitória dates from 1551 and takes its name from a battle won by the Portuguese over the local indigenous people. There are a few colonial remnants, but it is largely a modern city and port. The upper, older part of town, reached by steep streets and steps, is much less hectic than the lower harbour area which suffers dreadful traffic problems. A rail connection westwards to Minas Gerais provides transport for export of iron ore, coffee and timber. Port installations at Vitória and nearby Ponta do Tubarão have led to some beach and air pollution.

Ins and outs

Getting there Eurico Salles airport ⓘ *Goiaberas, 11 km from the city, T027-327 0811*, and has connections with Belém Belo Horizonte, Brasília, Rio de Janeiro, Salvador and São Paulo. The *rodoviária* is 15 minutes' walk west of the centre. There is a daily train service from Belo Horizonte, 14 hours.

Tourist information Cetur ⓘ *Av Princesa Isabel 54, T027-322 8888, at the airport T027-327 8855 and at the rodoviária*, has friendly staff and a good free map. **Instituto Jones dos Santos Neves** ⓘ *Av Marechal Campos 310, 3rd floor, Edif Vitória Center, CEP 29040-090, T027-322 2033 ext 2215*, also provides information.

Sights

On Avenida República is the huge **Parque Moscoso**, an oasis of quiet, with a lake, playground and tiny zoo. Other parks are the **Morro da Fonte Grande**, a state park with good views from the 312-m summit, and the **Parque dos Namorados**, 6 km from the centre at Praia do Canto. Two islands reached by bridge from Praia do Canto are **Ilha do Frade** and **Ilha do Boi**.

Colonial buildings still to be seen in the city are the **Capela de Santa Luzia**, Rua José Marcelino in the upper city (1551), now an art gallery; the church of **São Gonçalo**, Rua Francisco Araújo (1766) and the ruins of the **Convento São Francisco** (1591), also in the upper city. In the **Palácio do Governo**, or **Anchieta**, on Praça João Climaco (upper city), is the tomb of Padre Anchieta, the 16th-century Jesuit missionary and one of the founders of São Paulo. The **Catedral Metropolitana** was built in 1918 and stands in Praça Dom Luís Scortegagna. The **Teatro Carlos Gomes**, on Praça Costa Pereira, often presents plays as well as holding jazz and folk festivals.

Vila Velha, reached by a bridge across the bay, has an excellent beach, but is built up and noisy: take a bus from Vitória marked Vilha Velha. Visit the ruined, fortified monastery of **Nossa Senhora da Penha**, on a hill above Vila Velha; the views are superb. The Dutch attacked it in 1625 and 1640. There is also a pleasant ferry service to Vila Velha.

Beaches

Urban beaches such as **Camburi** can be affected by pollution (some parts of it are closed to bathers), but it is quite pleasant, with fair surf. South of the city is Vila Velha (see above), but for bigger waves go to **Barra do Jucu**, which is 10 km further south.

There is a hummingbird sanctuary at the **Museu Mello Leitão** ⓘ *Av José Ruschi 4, T027-259 1182, Tue-Fri 0800-1200, 1300-1700*, a library including the works of the

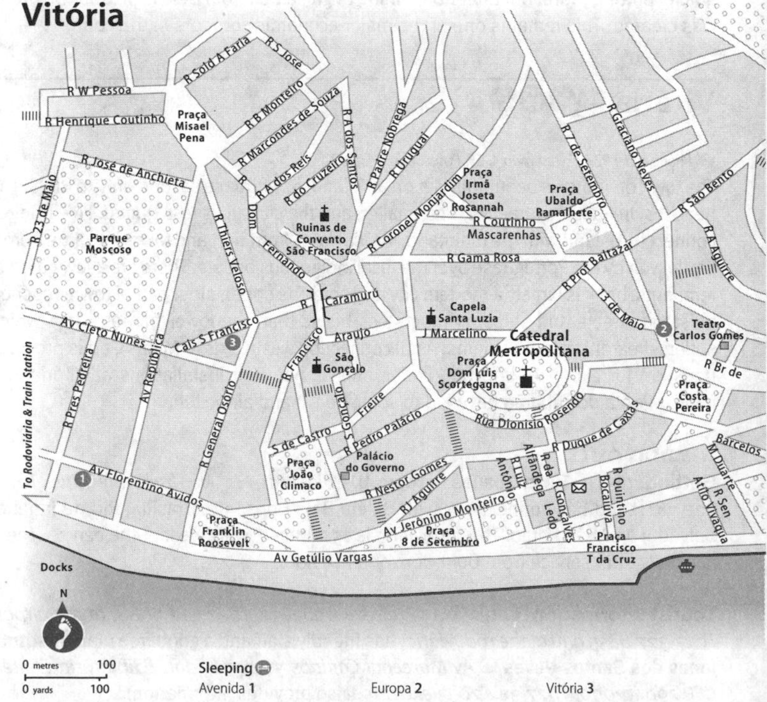

hummingbird and orchid scientist, Augusto Ruschi. Hummingbird feeders are hung outside the library. Also in the municipality is the **Dr Augusto Ruschi Biological Reserve** (formerly the Nova Lombardia National Biological Reserve), a forest rich in endemic bird species, including several endangered hummingbirds, Salvadori's antwren, cinnamon-vented Piha, russet-winged spadebill, Oustalet's tyrannulet, rufous-brown solitaire and hooded berryeater. Before visiting, permission must be obtained from **Ibama** ⓘ *Av Marechal Mascarenhas de Moraes 2487, Caixa Postal 762, Vitória ES, CEP 29000.*

Coastal mountains » *pp285-288.*

Mountains separate Vitoría from Minas. These were once covered in lush Atlantic coastal rainforest, which now survives only in isolated patches and has been replaced by pine and coffee plantations. The road to Minas is nonetheless picturesque, climbing steeply off the coastal plain and winding its way around the hills and through steep valleys. Many of the towns here were settled by Germans and Swiss and their alpine heritage lives on in a curiously kitsch way: it never freezes here but the tourist chalets are built with long sloping roofs that look like they could fend off a ton of snow. Some customs brought over in the 1840s by the first German and Swiss settlers, are loosely preserved in the villages of **Santa Leopoldina** and **Domingos Martins,** both around 45 km from Vitória, less than an hour by bus (two companies run to the former, approximately every three hours). Domingos Martins (also known as Campinho) has a Casa de Cultura with some items of German settlement. Santa Leopoldina has an interesting **museum** ⓘ *Tue-Sun 0900-1100, 1300-1800*, covering the settlers' first years in the area. **Santa Teresa,** which lies beyond them, is a favourite weekend retreat for people from Vitoría. It is linked to Santa Leopoldina by a dirt road.

Whilst these towns are moderately interesting, the only real reason to break the journey between Vitoría and Minas is to see **Pedra Azul** ⓘ *www.pedraazul.com.br*, a giant granite mountain that juts out of the nearby hills and changes colour from slate blue to deep orange as the day passes. Although surrounded by pine plantations it preserves a little indigenous forest around its flanks, and the state park in which it sits is good for a day's light walking.

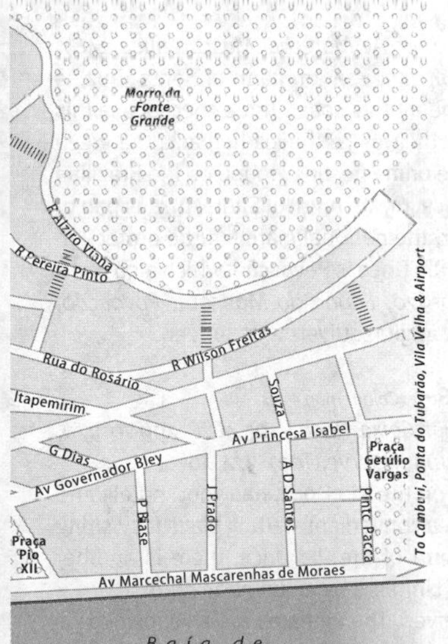

South of Vitória

» *pp285-288.*

Cachoeiro do Itapemirim is a busy city on both banks of the fast-flowing Rio Itapemirim. **Cachoeira Alta,** with a natural swimming pool, is 38 km away on the road to Castelo. The countryside south of Vitoría is flat and uninteresting, broken only by fields of sugar cane and the occasional granite mountain looming over the plain. The beaches that dot the coast are less beautiful than those in the north of the state and considerably less beautiful than those in neighbouring Rio. The most popular are those at **Guarapari**, some 50 km south of Vitória on the coast road. The town gets very crowded at holiday times, especially mid-December to the end of February when Mineiros flood down from Belo Horizonte. The sand here is mildly radioactive but if the Casa de Cultura in town is to be believed, the radiation is good for the health. Plenty of Capixabas and Cariocas seem to agree, as they come here to cure everything from rheumatism to backache. There are many hotels and plenty of cheap seafood restaurants in town and by the beach. A little further south still is the far quieter village of **Ubu** and, 8 km beyond, **Anchieta**, which has a small estuarine river much beloved of water birds. Boatmen from the Colônia da Pesca charge about US$20 for a short trip along the river. Close by is **Iriri**, a small village in a beautiful setting with two beaches, Santa Helena and Inhaúma. There are a few hotels. Five kilometres beyond is **Piúma**, a calm, little-visited place, renowned for its craftwork in shells, a skill that has been passed down through generations of craftsmen and women. The name derives from the indigenous word *pium*, meaning mosquito. The resort town of Marataízes is the last before the border with Rio de Janeiro state.

North of Vitória » pp285-288.

Santa Cruz

The ES-010 road follows the coast from Vitória north to the mouth of the Rio Doce. It passes beaches such as Manguinhos and Jacaraípe, and the town of Nova Almeida before reaching Santa Cruz, 60 km north of the state capital. The town, at the mouth of the Rio Piraquê-Açu, depends economically on cellulose factories, which have been the subject of an international outcry over child labour. It is a simple place, with few facilities. The coast around Santa Cruz, called **Aracruz**, has several good beaches, mostly undeveloped, which are tranquil and uncrowded.

Turtle beaches

The **Reserva Biológica Comboios** ⓘ *contact Ibama, Av Marechal Mascarenhas 2487, Caixa Postal 762, CEP 29000, Vitória, T027-264 1452*, 44 km north of Santa Cruz, is designed to protect the marine turtles that frequent this coast. Three species use this long stretch of sand backed by *restinga* to lay their eggs: the leatherback, the green (*arauanã*) and the *cabeçuda*, for which this is the prime nesting ground on the Brazilian seaboard. **Regência**, at the mouth of the Rio Doce, 65 km north of Santa Cruz, is part of the reserve and has a regional base for **Tamar**, the national marine turtle protection project. On the north shore of the mouth of the Rio Doce is **Povoação**, which also has a **Tamar office** ⓘ *Caixa Postal 105, CEP 29900-970, Lagoa do Monsorá, Povoação, Linhares, ES*. Regência is popular with sailors, anglers, divers and surfers.

Linhares and Sooretama reserves → Colour map 4, B5.

ⓘ *For information on turtles, contact Tamar at Caixa Postal 105, CEP 29900-970, Linhares. For authorization to visit the Sooretama Reserve, T027-374 0016.*

The town of **Linhares**, 143 km north of Vitória on the Rio Doce, has good hotels and restaurants but is otherwise dull. However, it is a convenient starting place for visiting the turtle beaches. Besides those at the mouth of the Rio Doce, there is another Tamar site at **Ipiranga**, which is 40 km east of Linhares by an unmade road.

Linhares is close to two other nature reserves. The **Linhares Reserve**, owned by **CVRD** (the former state-owned mining company, now privatized), is possibly the largest remaining lowland tract of Atlantic forest; permission from the reserve's director must be obtained to visit. There is very good birdwatching in the reserve and specialities include red-billed curassow, minute hermit, rufous-sided crake, blue-throated (ochre-cheeked) parakeet, black-billed scythebill and black-headed berryeater.

The **Sooretama Biological Reserve**, some 45 km north of Linhares and 65 km south of Conceição da Barra, on the BR-101, protects tropical Atlantic rainforest and fauna. It contains several bird species not found in the Linhares Reserve, and much of the wildlife is rare and endangered. Both Sooretama and Linhares have orchids apparently not found anywhere else. Sooretama has been protected since 1969. With year-round tropical humidity, vegetation here is dense with ancient trees reaching over 40 m in height. Two rivers, the Barra Seca and the Cupido, cross the reserve and, together with Lagoa Macuco, provide marshlands which attract migratory birds as well as numerous resident flocks. The reserve is strictly monitored by **Ibama** and is not open to the public, but drivers and cyclists can cut across it by road.

São Mateus, 88 km north of Linhares, is another unillustrious but inoffensive inland town. It is 13 km from good beaches at Guriri, which is another base for **Tamar** ① *Caixa Postal 130.153, CEP 29930-000 São Mateus, T027-761 1267*.

Conceição da Barra → *Phone code: 027. Colour map 4, B5. Population: 25,500.*

The most attractive beaches in Espírito Santo are around Conceição da Barra, 261 km north of Vitória. It is an organized town that welcomes visitors. Many people come in summer and for Carnaval, otherwise it is quiet. Viewed from its small port, the sunsets are always spectacular. Corpus Christi (early June) is celebrated with an evening procession for which the road is decorated with coloured wood chips.

Itaúnas

Itaúnas, 27 km north of Conceição, is an interesting excursion (it has some pousadas and a small campsite). The small town has been swamped by sand, and has been moved to the opposite riverbank. There is now a fantastic landscape of 30-m-high dunes, coastal swamp land (with numerous capybara) and deserted beaches. From time to time, winds shift the sand dunes enough to reveal the buried church tower. The theory is that the sudden encroachment of the sands in the 1970s was caused by massive deforestation of the surrounding area. The coast here, too, is a protected turtle breeding ground; for information contact **Tamar** ① *Caixa Postal 53, Conceição da Barra, T027-762 1124*. Buses run here three to four times a day from Conceição da Barra. The town is very popular in high season with middle-class Mineiros and Paulistanos who regard it as less spoilt than Trancoso and the other once laid-back resort towns of southern Bahia.

The beach of **Meleiras**, 3 km south, is accessible only on foot or by boat and is one of a number of pleasant trips. It is 12 km long and offers fabulous diving and fishing. **Guaxindiba**, 3 km north, is partially developed, with hotels and restaurants, but the natural vegetation is still intact. It is possible to drive all the way along dirt roads into southern Bahia if you have a 4WD.

Sleeping

Vitória *p281, map p282*

There are a string of adequate but scruffy hotels opposite the *rodoviária* and plenty of others in the beach areas: **Camburi** to the north, **Vila Velha** to the south, both about 15 mins from city centre. Accommodation is very easy to find here except in the high season.

AL Senac Ilha do Boi, R Bráulio Macedo 417, Ilha do Boi, T027-3450111, www.hotelilhadoboi.com.br. The most luxurious in town with its own marina, bay views and restaurant and pool.

A Best Western Porto do Sol, Av Dante Michelini 3957, Praia de Camburi, 7 km from the centre, T027-3337 2244. A beachside hotel built in the 1980s, with a restaurant, pool, sauna and bar.

B Pousada da Praia, Av Saturnino de Brito 1500, Praia do Canto, T/F027-225 0233. Ordinary little hotel near the beach. Pool.

C Avenida, Av Florentino Avidos 350, T027-223 4317. Adequate but undistinguished rooms with a/c and a decent breakfast. Recommended.

C Vitória, Cais de São Francisco 85, near Parque Moscoso. Basic hotel with a good restaurant, changes money. Recommended.
D Europa, 7 de Setembro, corner of Praça Costa Pereira. Hotel and restaurant, noisy but cheap. Advice on nearby veggie restaurants.
E Jardim da Penha, R Hugo Viola 135, take Universitário bus, get off at the first University stop, T027-324 0738. Youth hostel.
E Praia da Costa, R São Paulo 1163, Praia da Costa, Vila Velha, T027-329 3227. IYHA youth hostel.
E Príncipe Hotel, Av Dario Lourenço de Souza 120, Ilha do Príncipe, T027-322 2799, F223 3392. IYHA youth hostel.

The coastal mountains *p283*

C Pousada Peterle, Estrada Pedra Azul, Domingos Martins, T027-3248 1171. Spacious mock-Swiss chalets set in a little garden with good views of the rock and a generous breakfast. No restaurant.

South of Vitória *p283*

There are plenty of hotels and pousadas near the various beaches. The most popular beach is **Castelhanos** and its extension **Guanabara**, which separate Anchieta from Ubu. Castelhanos has more beachside palapa restaurants. Gunanbara is quieter. Both have calm waters.
AL Flamboyant, Km 38, Rod do Sol, Guarapari, T/F027-2290066, www.hotelflamboyant.com.br. *Fazenda* hotel with fishing and horse riding. 5 days minimum stay.
A Best Western Porto do Sol, Av Beira Mar 1, Praia do Morro, Guarapari, T027-361 1100, www.geocities.com/portadosol. Mediterranean-style village on a rocky point overlooking a calm beach, pool, sauna.
A Thanharu Praia, R Jovina Serafim dos Anjos, Praia de Castelhanos, between Anchieta and Ubu, T/F027-536 1246, www.thanaru.com.br. Beachside hotel with a pool and sauna. Popular with families and on one of the livelier beaches.
A-B Praia Costa Azul, Iriri. Lodging in private houses is possible. A regular bus runs from Guarapari.
B Pontal de Ubu, R Gen Oziel 1, Praia de Ubu, T027-261 3111, www.hotelpontaldeubu.com.br. Popular family hotel with a pool, saunas, bike rental and organized activities.
B-C Pousada da Meméia, R Manuel Alves Abrantes, Iriri, T027-3534 1534, www.pousadamemeia.com.br. A range of rooms in a medium-sized pousada with a bar and sauna.
B-C Pousada Haras Monte Agha, R das Castanheiras, Piúma, T027-3520 1363. *Fazenda* hotel with horse riding.
C Costa Sul, R Getúlio Vargas 101, Guarapari. Basic, friendly, clean and good breakfast. Much beloved of Brazilians and mosquitoes.
C-D Alto da Praia, Av Estr Dos Cancelas 111, Alto da Praia, Marataízes, T027-3532 3630, www.altodapraia.com.br. Small *pousada* with a/c rooms and a pool.
C-D Coqueiros Praia, Av D Helvécio 1020, Praia dos Namorados, Iriri, T027-3534 1592. Small beachside pousada with a/c rooms and a play area for kids.
C-D Dona Judith, Av Lacerda de Aguiar 353, Marataízes, T027-532 1436, F532 1305. Basic but friendly.
C-D Pousada do Sol, Av das Ostras, Praia da Guanabara, between Anchieta and Ubu, T027-3536 1643, www.pousadadosol.com. Small pousada with a/c rooms and a pool near the beach. Good value.
E Youth hostel Simple IYHA hostel at Guarapari popular with students from Vitória.

Camping

Marataízes, Praia do Siri, 9 km south of Marataízes centre, T027-325 2202. Municipal site.
Praia de Itapessu, R Antônio Guimarães s/n, quadra 40, Guarapari, T027-261 0475, F261 0448. Turn left out of the *rodoviária*, then right and right again, past **Pousada Lisboa**, 2 blocks, across a dual carriageway (Av Jones de Santos Neves), 1 block to the campground, US$10 with good breakfast. Recommended.

Santa Cruz *p284*

There are pousadas at Praia Formosa, 3 km south of town, and campsites at Barra do Sahy, Praia do Putiry and Formosa beaches.
B Pousada dos Cocais, Praia de Sauê, T/F027-250 1515. With a restaurant and a pool.
C Coqueiral Praia Park, Praia do Coqueiral, 6 km along the road to Barra do Riacho, T027-250 1214. A/c rooms with TVs and a restaurant, pool, pretty location.
D Pousada das Pedras, Praia dos Padres, T027-250 1716. Basic but friendly with plain rooms.

Linhares and Sooretama reserves *p284*
B-D Reserva Natural da Vale do Rio Doce, BR-101, Km 120, T027-3371 9797, www.cvrd.com.br/linhares. Beautiful location within the reserve. Great for birds and wildlife. With a bar, sauna and simple but pleasant rooms.
B-D Virgínia, Av Gov Santos Neves 919, Linhares, T/F027-2641699. Modern building with a range of rooms at different prices. Good if you get stuck in town.

Conceição da Barra *p285*
There are plenty of beach hotels to choose from here and you will have no problem finding one after a short browse – as long as it is not high season.
C Pousada Gandia, Av Atlântica 1054, (Praia de Guaxindiba), T/F027-7621248. Small pousada with simple rooms, a pool, baby sitting services and helpful staff.
C Praia da Barra, Av Atlântica 350, T/F027-762 1100, www.hotelpraiadabarra.com.br. Simple and friendly 50-room pousada with a/c or fan, a pool and sauna.
D Caravelas, Av Dr Mário Vello Silvares 83, a block from the beach, T027-762 1188. Basic with shared bathrooms and a light breakfast. Recommended.
E Pousada Pirámide, next to the *rodoviária*, T027-762 1970. The owner, Lisete Soares, speaks English, good value, 100 m from beach. Recommended.

Camping
Camping Clube do Brasil, Rod Adolfo Serra, Km 16, T027 762 1346. Site with full facilities.

Itaúnas *p285*
There are numerous attractive little pousadas on and around the town's grassy main square.
C Pousada Bem Te Vi, R Adolpho Pereira Duarte 41, T027-3762 5012, www.pousadabemtevi.com. One of the few pousadas in town with a pool, with a range of modern rooms organized around a courtyard; all with a/c or fans, TVs, fridges and breakfast.
C Pousada Cambucá, just off the Praça Principal, T027-3762 5004, www.portonet.com.br/cambuca. Wooden-floored rooms, some with balconies and a decent seafood restaurant.
C -D Casa da Praia, R Dercílio Fonseca, T027-3762 5028, www.casadapraiaitaunas.com.br. Simple pousada close to the beach.

Eating

Vitória *p281, map p282*
Moqueca capixaba, a seafood dish served in an earthenware pot, is the local speciality. It is a variant of the *moqueca*, which is typical of Bahia.
TTT Lareira Portuguesa, Av Saturnino de Brito 260, Praia do Canto, T027-345 0329. Portuguese, expensive.
TT Mar e Terra, opposite the rodoviária. Good food, live music at night.
TT Pirão, R Joaquim Lírio 753, Praia do Canto. Regional food.
T Lavacar, Praia Camburi. One of many similar on this beach that serves food and has live music.

South of Vitória *p283*
T Peixada do Garcia, Av Magno Ribeiro Muqui, Guarapari. Respectable seafood.
T Peixada do Menelau Garcia, Av Mário Neves, Guarapari. More respectable seafood.

Conceição da Barra *p285*
There are plenty of simple seafood restaurants town and some basic palapas on the beach.
T Tia Teresa, R Dr Mário Vello Silvares 135. Brazilian food, self-service, good value.

Transport

Vitória *p281, map p282*
Air There are flights to **Belém**, **Belo Horizonte**, **Brasília**, **Guarapari**, **Maceió**, **Porto Alegre**, **Recife**, **Rio de Janeiro**, **Salvador** and **São Paulo**.
Airline offices Rio Sul/Nordeste, Av NS dos Navegantes 2091, conj 102, T027-227 1588. **TAM**, Av Fernando Ferrari 3055, Goiaberas, T027-327 0868. **Varig**, Av Jerônimo Monteiro 1000, loja 3, at airport T027-327 0304. **Vasp**, R Desembargador Sampaio 40, T027-324 1499, at airport, T027-327 0236.

Bus To **Rio**, 8 hrs, US$15 (*leito* 25). To **Belo Horizonte**, US$14.50 (*leito* 29). To **Salvador**, 18 hrs, US$27; to **Porto Seguro** direct 11 hrs with lots of stops, US$18 (also *leito* service); alternatively, take a bus to Eunápolis, then change to buses which run every hour.

Car hire Localiza, Praça do Aeroporto, T027-327 0211; at the airport T0800-992000; **Vila Velha**, Av Carlos Lindemberg 2707, T027-200 4466.

Hitchhiking To hitch to **Salvador**, take a bus to Serra, which is 13 km beyond Carapina, itself 20 km north of Vitória; alight where the bus turns off to Serra.

Train Daily passenger service to **Belo Horizonte**, 14 hrs, US$17.50 *executivo* (very comfortable), US$11.50 1st class, US$7.80 2nd class.

South of Vitória *p283*

Bus There are regular buses to **Gurarpari** from Vitoría and onward from here to the other resorts down the coast. The **Alvorada** bus company has a separate *rodoviária* from **Itapemirim/Penha, Sudeste, São Gerardo** and others. They are close together, 15 mins' walk from the city centre or US$5 by taxi. **Penha** tickets are sold at **R-Tur Turismo**, in the centre at R Manoel Severo Simões and R Joaquim da Silva Lima, where air tickets, free brochures, maps, and hotel addresses can also be obtained. To **Vitória**, 1 hr with **Sudeste**, US$2. To **Rio** with **Itapemirim**, 2 a day, US$12.

Linhares and Sooretama reserves *p284*

Bus Frequent buses from Vitoría. Most Bahia-bound buses stop at Linhares.

Itaúnas *p285*

Bus Bus from the *padaria* in Conceição da Barra at 0700, returns 1700.

Directory

Vitória *p281, map p282*

Banks American Express: Saytur, Av Des Santos Neves 1425, T027-325 1899, F325 1391. **Embassies and consulates** **Denmark**, R do Sol 141, Sala 210, T027-222 4075, 0900-1300, 1500-1900. **Spain**, R Aristides Freire 22, Centro, T027-223 2846. **Medical services** Santa Casa, R Dr Jones de Santos Neves 143, T027-322 0074. **Post office** Av Jerônimo Monteiro, between R Gonçalves Ledo and R Quintino Bocaiúva. **Telephone** Palácio do Café, Praça Costa Pereira 52.

South of Vitória *p283*

Banks **Banco 24 Horas**, Praça do Coronado, Praia da Areia, Guarapari; **Banco do Brasil**, R Joaquim da Silva Lima 550, Guarapari; **Bradesco**, R Henrique Coutinho 901, Guarapari; **Banco do Brasil**, Av Lacerda de Aguiar 356, Marataízes.

Iguaçu Falls and the south

Footprint features

Introduction

Southern Brazil is famous first and foremost for one sight – Iguaçu. These are the world's mightiest and grandest waterfalls, surrounded on all sides by lush subtropical forest, stretching for almost 3 km, and falling in a thunderous two-tier curtain from a height almost twice that of Niagara. But although Iguaçu is undoubtedly the highlight, it would be a shame to rush in and out of southern Brazil without seeing anything else. There are many other spectacularly beautiful natural sights: toy trains winding their way through jagged, verdant mountain ranges to some of the largest stretches of lowland coastal forest in South America; bays studded with islands, each of which is home to different and often unique fauna; the crumbling ruins of Jesuit monasteries and, of course, miles of glorious beaches.

The feel of the south is very different to the rest of Brazil; towns are more European and made up of settlers from the Ukraine, Germany and Italy. In Joinville and Blumenau an archaic Bavarian dialect is still widely spoken and there is an annual bierfest. Buses run on time, streets are relatively clean and many of the people don't talk much. Things change again in the border country with Argentina and Uruguay, which retains an insular and macho gaúcho culture that seems to have more in common with the Pampas than Brazil.

★ Don't miss...

1 **Serra da Graciosa** Cross Brazil's prettiest mountains on one of the most attractive railway lines in South America, page 295.
2 **Ilha do Mel and the Parque Nacional de Superagüi** Hang out at the laid-back beach in the midst of Brazil's largest stretch of coastal forest, pages 298 and 299.
3 **Iguaçu Falls** Join the sightseers and stand in awe at the largest waterfalls on the planet, page 300.
4 **Florianópolis** Take time out at this relaxed little city on an island fringed with the country's best surf beaches, page 318.
5 **Praia da Rosa** Watch the humpback and sperm whales during the calving season (June to November) at Brazil's best whale-watching spot, page 328.
6 **São Miguel das Missões** Visit the hulking ruins of the Guaraní mission camps whose story inspired *The Mission*, page 345.

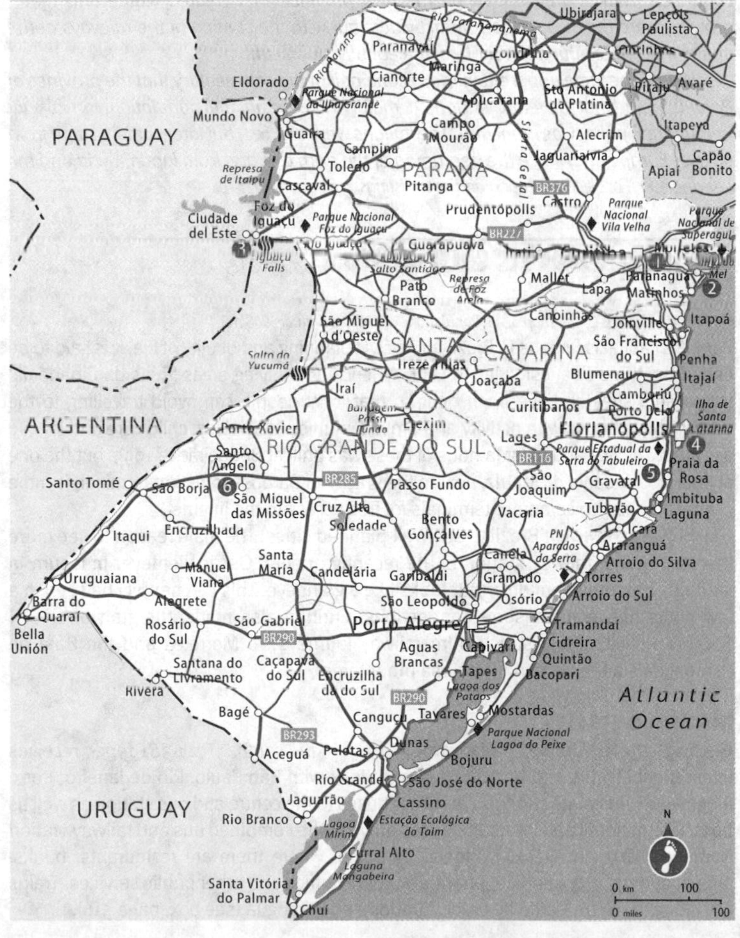

Paraná

→ *Population: 9.5 million.*

Paraná is most famous for the Iguaçu falls, the largest and most magnificent waterfalls in the Americas. No guidebook can do justice to the spectacle and they are a must on any itinerary to Brazil. Besides Iguaçu, Paraná has a great deal to offer those in search of pristine nature: the largest area of coastal rainforest in Brazil swathes the mountains of the northern coast; little beach-fringed islands, like Ilha do Mel, sit a short way offshore. Both are easily reached from the neat and tidy capital, Curitiba, on one of the continent's most impressive railway journeys. The interior of the state is pocked with villages and towns founded by the European settlers that flocked here at the end of the 19th century.

The area of what is now Paraná was neglected by the Portuguese until the beginning of the 17th century when gold was discovered. The region fell under the control of São Paulo, but there was no great success in the extraction of gold, partly because of a lack of indigenous labour (they had all been sent elsewhere or had died of disease). As soon as the metal was discovered in Minas Gerais, the mines shut down in Paraná. Instead, the colonists turned to agriculture and cattle-raising and, in the 18th and 19th centuries, the state was dominated by fazendeiros *and drovers. Until 1853, the area was controlled from São Paulo. When the new province was created, cattle and* maté*-growing were the most important activities, but with the coming of the railways at the end of the 19th century, timber became equally significant.*

When it became apparent in the second half of the 19th century that the province of Paraná would not develop without a major increase in the population, an official immigration policy was launched. The Italians were the first, but later settlers came from all over Europe and, since the beginning of the 20th century, from Japan, Syria and the Lebanon. » *For Sleeping, Eating and other listings, see pages 307-318.*

Curitiba

» *pp307-318.*

→ *Phone code: 041. Colour map 5, A4. Population: 1.6 million. Altitude: 908 m.*

Paraná's capital is famous in Brazil for its civic planning and quality of life. It is said to be one of the three cleanest cities in Latin America. In outlying areas 'Ruas da Cidadania' (citizenship streets), have been built so that local people can avoid travelling to the centre. These throng with activity and provide municipal services, child care and leisure activities. The first and most famous of these was built at Boqueirão in 1995, but the one at Rua da Cidadania da Matriz, next to the Praça Rui Barbosa transport terminal, is more central and has 20 computer terminals for free access to the internet.

However, few visit Brazil to see well-planned cities. The main reason to see more than the bus or railway station is the recently opened Oscar Niemeyer museum: a stunning modernist building that looks like a giant eye. This can happily be seen in a few hours between transport connections. Curitiba also marks the start of one of South America's most spectacular railway journeys: to Morretes and the Baía de Paranaguá via the Serra da Graciosa mountains.

Ins and outs

Getting there Afonso Pena airport ⓘ *21 km south, T041-381 1515,* receives international flights and has direct connections with São Paulo, Rio de Janeiro, Porto Alegre and other state capitals. There are buses to the centre and bus station as well as taxis. International and interstate buses arrive at the combined bus and railway station **Rodoferroviária** on Avenida Alfonso Camargo, where there are restaurants, banks, shops, phones, a post office, pharmacy, tourist office and other public services. Trains run along the Serra Verde between Curitiba and Parangua (see box, page 316).

Sete Quedas waterfall

In the far northwest of the state, also on the Rio Paraná, were the tremendous waterfalls known in Brazil as Sete Quedas (the Seven Falls), and in Spanish Latin America as the Salto de Guaíra. They were drowned by the filling of the lake behind the Itaipu Dam in 1982. The 1978 *South American Handbook* described Sete Quedas thus: "The great river, nearly 5 km wide, hurls itself through the rocky gorges of the falls with a tremendous roar. Rocky islands between the falls are connected by wooden suspension bridges; the whole area can warrant a whole day. Many of the falls are from 30 to 40 m high. This is the most enormous volume of falling water in the world; it is double Niagara's."

Within the city there is an integrated transport system with several types of bus route; pick up a map in one of the tourist booths for details. The Transport–City Circular–Linha Turismo circles the major transport terminals and points of interest in the city centre and costs US$7 for five stops. » *See also Transport, page 315.*

Tourist information The main office is in the **Instituto Municipal de Turismo/ Curitiba Turismo** ⓘ *R da Glória 362 , 1st floor, T041-3250 7729, Mon-Fri 0800-1200 and 1400-1800.* There is also an office at the **rodoferroviária** ⓘ *Av Presidente Afonso Camargo 330, T041-3320 3121, Mon-Fri, 0800-1800, Sat 0800-1400*, and a tourist booth on the 24-hour street, **Rua 24 Horas** ⓘ *T041-3324 7036, daily 1000-1800.*

Background

The city was founded on 19 March 1693 as Vila Nossa Senhora da Luz dos Pinhais on the spot that is now Praça Tiradentes. For many years it was little more than a pit stop for cattle herders on their way between Rio Grande do Sul and the cities to the north. But in 1842 it was elevated to the rank of city and given the name of Curitiba and, in 1853, it was made the state capital. It received waves of Italian, German and eastern-European immigrants in the late 19th and 20th centuries, which led to the state's distinctive European identity, and rapid deforestation.

Sights

The city has extensive open spaces and some attractive modern architecture. There is a good panoramic view from the glass observation deck of the telecommunications tower, **Torre Mercês**, built by Telepar and so is also known as the **Telepar Tower** ⓘ *R Jacarezinho, corner of R Professor Lycio Veloso 191, T041-322 8080, Tue-Fri 1230-2030, weekends 1030-2030, US$1.50*. The 110-m tower stands at an elevation of 95 m above sea level. There is a map of the city on the floor so that you can locate key sites.

The commercial centre is the busy Rua 15 de Novembro, part of which is a pedestrian area called **Rua das Flores**. Since urban planning first began in 1720, the Rua das Flores has been a focus for street life and street entertainment and is now perennially decorated with flowers and trees, and lined with benches, cafés, restaurants, cinemas and shops. At its southern end, the **Boca Maldita** is a particularly lively and a popular meeting place.

On Praça Tiradentes is the **cathedral** ⓘ *R Barão do Serro Azul 31, T041-3324 5136*, built in neo-Gothic style and inaugurated in 1893 (restored in 1993). Behind the cathedral, near Largo da Ordem, is a pedestrian area with a flower clock and old buildings. It is very atmospheric in the evening when it is illuminated by old gas lamps. City centre bar and nightlife is concentrated here. There is an art market on Sunday morning in **Praça Garibáldi**, beside the attractive Rosário church.

Museums worth visiting include the **Museu Paranaense** ⓘ *Praça Generoso Marques, Palácio São Francisco, R Kellers 289, T041-3304 3300, www.pr.gov.br/museupr, Tue-Fri 0930-1730, Sat and Sun 1100-1500*, which has temporary shows and concerts in the garden on Sunday, alongside a collection of ethnological and historical material, and the **Museu de Arte Contemporânea** ⓘ *R Desembargador Westphalen 16, Praça Zacarias, T041-222 5172, Tue-Fri 0900-1900, Sat and Sun 1400-1900*, which showcases Brazilian contemporary works, with an emphasis on artists from Paraná.

Unlike most Brazilian cities, Curitiba has plenty of green spaces. The most popular is the **Passeio Público** ⓘ *closed Mon*, in the heart of the city, with three lakes, each with an island, and a playground.

About 4 km east of the *rodoferroviário*, the **Jardim Botânico Fanchette Rischbieter**. This has a fine glass house, again with domes, curves and lots of steel, inspired by the Crystal Palace in London. The gardens are in French style and there is also a **Museu Botánico** ⓘ *R Ostoja Roguski (Primeira Perimetral dos Bairros), T041-321 8646*. It can be reached by the orange Expreso buses from Praça Rui Barbosa.

Near the shores of Lagoa Bacacheri, on the northern edge of the city, is one of Brazil's many hidden quirks: an **Egyptian temple** ⓘ *R Nicarágua 2453*. The temple is devoted to the Rosicrucian cult – a 19th-century offshoot of Theosophical occultism which has taken hold in Brazil alongside many other arcane religions. This is surely the only country on Earth where Rosicrucians advertise themselves with car bumper stickers. Visits can also be arranged to the Brazilian centre of the Rosicrucians; take the Santa Cândida bus to Estação Boa Vista, then walk.

Museu Oscar Niemeyer

The **Museu Oscar Niemeyer (MON)** ⓘ *3 km north of the centre, R Marechal, Hermes 999, T041-350 4400, www.museuoscarniemeyer.org.br, Tue-Sun 1000-1830, US$2,* opened in late 2002 and was designed by and is devoted to the famous Brazilian modernist architect who designed Brasília and was a disciple of Le Corbusier, alongside other Paranense artists. The stunning principal building is shaped like a giant eye and the whole museum serves as a gallery for diverse shows, which in the past have ranged from Picasso drawings to modern Japanese art. An underground passage, also lined with a range of (always high quality) exhibits and photographs links the eye to a sculpture garden.

Curitiba to Paranaguá ▸▸ *pp307-318.*

When the first European ships arrived at Paraná in the mid-16th century, they would have been daunted by the prospect of conquering the lands of southern Brazil. From the sea, the thickly forested and steep crags of the **Serra da Graciosa** must have seemed an insurmountable wall fortifying the continent from the coast. But in a cruel twist of fate, it was native trails cutting through the mountains that led to inland Paraná being colonized. After the paths were discovered, the Portuguese forced African slaves to pave them with river stones. Miners and traders were soon dragging mules laden with gold, silver, textiles and *herva maté* up and down the mountains. As trade grew, the port at Paranaguá became the most important south of Santos and little towns of white-washed churches and smart Portuguese buildings like Morretes and Antonina grew up along the trails. In 1885 the routes were busy enough to merit the construction of a railway, which wound its way around the slopes, across rushing rivers and through the forest to the sea. This remains the most spectacular railway journey in Brazil, cutting through numerous tunnels, crossing dizzy viaducts (especially imported from Belgium), offering sudden views of deep gorges and high peaks and waterfalls before arriving at the sea in Paranaguá. Near Banhado station (Km 66) is the waterfall of **Véu da Noiva,** and from the station at Km 59 you can reach the Marumbi mountain range. The principal trail between Curitiba and Paranaguá is now a spectacular cobbled road that runs for 15 km through the mountains and the Marumbi National Park. There are fire grills, shelters and camping at the various rest stops. You can also hike the original trail which follows the road and passes the rest stops; trails leave from just outside Morretes railway station and are well signposted. Take food, water and plenty of insect repellent. ▸▸ *For information on the Curitiba to Paranaguá train, see Transport, page 315.*

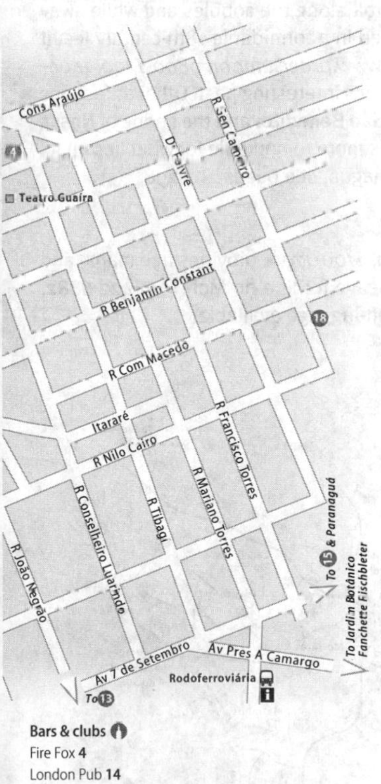

Bars & clubs
Fire Fox **4**
London Pub **14**
The Farm **13**
Tuba's **12**

Morretes ➔ *Colour map 5, A5.*

Morretes, which was founded in 1721, is one of the prettiest colonial towns in southern Brazil. A parade of whitewashed Portuguese colonial buildings with painted window frames straddle the pebbly river, and church spires stick up from a sea of red-tiled roofs against the backdrop of the deep-green forest-swathed hills. The Estrada da Graciosa road passes through Morretes and the train stops here too, for a lunch break. There are a handful of pousadas and numerous restaurants serve the local speciality, *barreado* (meat stew cooked in a clay pot), which was originally served a day in advance of Carnaval in order to allow women to escape from their domestic cooking chores and enjoy the party. The town itself is tiny and easily managed on foot. There is a tourist office by the river and a series of walks lead from the town into the mountains.

Antonina, just 14 km from Morretes, is almost as picturesque and sits on the Bahia do Paranaguá. It can be reached by local bus from Morretes.

Paranaguá and around » *pp307-318.*

➔ *Phone code: 041. Colour map 5, A5. Population: 128,000.*

After the endless lorry parks and the messy dual carriageway leading into the town, the centre of Paranaguá, 268 km south of Santos, comes as a pleasant surprise, especially around the waterfront. Colonial buildings decay quietly in the heat and humidity, some are just façades encrusted with bromeliads; and fishermen get quietly drunk in little *botiquines*.

There's not much to do in the town but stroll along the cobbles and while away the time in the interesting city museum, housed in a formidable 18th-century **Jesuit convent** ⓘ *R 15 Novembro 575, T041-423 2511, www.proec.ufpr.br, 0800-1200, 1400-1800, US$1*, which showcases aspects of the city's interesting past. Other attractions include a 17th-century fountain, the church of **São Benedito**, and the shrine of **Nossa Senhora do Rocio**, 2 km from town. The town is more remarkable for what lies on its doorstep – the Ilha do Mel and Bahia do Paranaguá, see pages 297-298.

Ins and outs

The **tourist office** ⓘ *outside the railway station, 1100-1700*, provides free maps, and at the docks in front of the pier where boats leave for Ilha do Mel (T041-422 6882, 0800-1900), with boat schedules, toilet and left-luggage available.

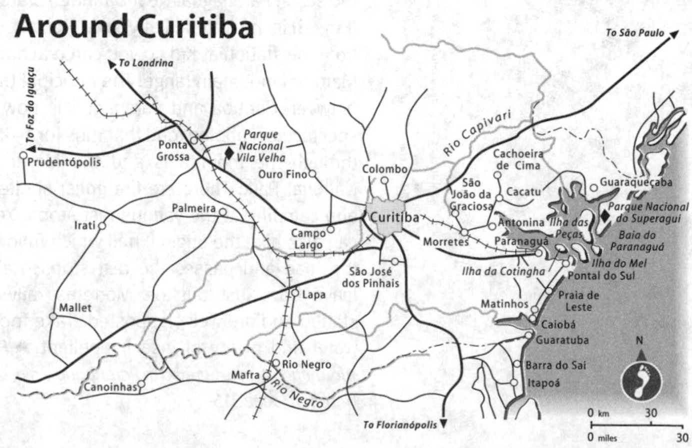

Background

Before it became Paranaguá, the region was an important centre of indigenous life. Colossal shell middens, called *sambaquis* (see the Museu Arqueológico do Sambaqui in Joinville, page 327) have been found on the surrounding estuaries, protecting regally adorned corpses. The mounds can be as high as a two-storey building and date from between 7000 and 2000 years ago. They were built by the ancestors of the *tupinguin* and *carijo* people who were here when the first Europeans arrived. The bay's outer islands were initially claimed and occupied by the Spanish (who thought they had reached the coast near Potosí in Bolivia, thousands of miles inland, when they first saw the Serra da Graciosa). But in the late 16th century a *bandeira* expedition under Heiliodoro Eobano found gold in Paranaguá. When the Portuguese realized the importance of the area, they beat the Spanish off the land and fortified the southern end of Ilha do Mel, establishing a port at Paranaguá.

Excursions from Paranaguá

Matinhos, 40 km south, is a medium-sized Mediterranean-style resort, invaded by surfers in October for the Paraná surf competition. About 8 km further south is **Caiobá**, at the mouth of a bay, the other side of which is **Guaratuba**, which is less built up than Caiobá. The ferry between the two towns is frequent and is a beautiful crossing (free for pedestrians, US$1.50 for cars). Each of these towns has a few hotels but most close in winter; there is camping at Matinhos and Guaratuba.

Parque Nacional Vila Velha

On the road to Ponta Grossa is Vila Velha, now a state park, 97 km from Curitiba, 10 km from Ponta Grossa. The sandstone rocks have been weathered into fantastic shapes, although many have been defaced by thoughtless tourists. Nearby are the **Lagoa Dourada**, surrounded by forests, and the **Furnas**: three waterholes, the deepest of which has a lift (US$1, not always working) that descends almost to the level of the lake. The park office is 300 m from the highway and the park a further 1½ km. You can camp in the church grounds or put your tent up in a disused campground, which is now overgrown and has no facilities. Allow all day if visiting all three sites (unless you hitch, or can time the buses well; it's a lot of walking).

Ins and outs The park is open from 0800-1900. Tickets cost US$3.50 for the stones and US$2 for the crater lakes and Lake Dourada; tickets also include entrance to the Furnas. To get there, purchase tickets from the **Princesa dos Campos** bus company in Curitiba on a bus heading towards Ponta Grossa and ask the driver to let you out at Parque Estadual de Vila Velha. It's about 1½-hour journey. The last bus back is at 1600 and stops outside the park along the main road, purchase return tickets on board bus (US$5). » *See Transport page 316.*

Bahia do Paranaguá

The Bahia do Paranaguá is one of Latin America's biodiversity hotspots and the best place on the Brazilian coast to see rare rainforest flora and fauna. Mangrove and lowland subtropical forests, islands, rivers and rivulets combine to form the largest stretch of Atlantic coast rainforest in the country. The area protects critically endangered species like the black-faced lion tamarin, which was only discovered in 1990, and the red-tailed Amazon parrot (which despite its name is only found here), alongside a full gamut of South American spectaculars including jaguars. Most of the bay is protected by a series of national and state parks (see Superagüi, page 299), but it is possible to visit on an organized tour from Paranaguá (or with more difficulty from Guraquecaba on the northern side of the bay). The **BARCOPAR boatman's cooperative** ⓘ *T041-422 8159*, reached through the tourist office on the waterfront, offers a range of excellent trips in large and small vessels ranging from two hours to two days and US$10 per person to US$100.

Ilha do Mel → *Colour map 5, A5.*

Ilha do Mel is a weekend escape and holiday island popular with Paraná and Paulista surfers, twenty-something hippies and day-tripping families. There are no roads, no vehicles and limited electricity. Outside of Carnaval and New Year it is a laid-back little place. Bars pump out Bob Marley and *maranhão* reggae; spaced-out surfers lounge around in hammocks; and barefooted couples dance *forró* on the wooden floors of simple beachside shacks. Much of the island is forested, its coastline is fringed with broad beaches and, in the south, broken by rocky headlands. Its location in the mouth of the Bahía de Paranaguá made it strategically important to the Portuguese in the 18th century. The lighthouse, **Farol das Conchas**, was built in 1872 to guide shipping into the bay. The cave of **Gruta das Encantadas** is surrounded with myths and legends about mermaids, enchanting all who came near.

The island divides into two sections connected by a spit of sand at the **Nova Brasília** jetty, the principal port of arrival. The rugged eastern half, where most of the facilities are to be found, is fringed with curving beaches and capped with a lighthouse. The flat, scrub forest-covered and balloon-shaped western half is predominantly an ecological protection area. Its northern side is watched over by the **Fortaleza Nossa Senhora dos Prazeres**, a fort built in 1767 on the orders of King José I of Portugal, to defend what was one of the principal ports in the country. In 1850, a

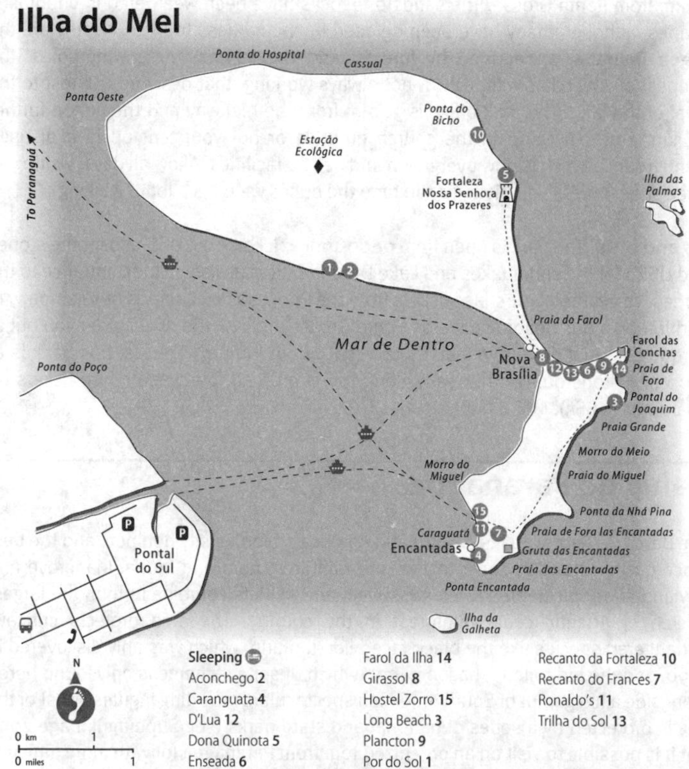

British warship captured three illegal slave trading ships, giving rise to a battle known as **Combate Cormorant**. The view from the 20th-century gun emplacements on the hill above the fort is the best on the island.

The best surf beaches are **Praia Grande** and **Praia de Fora**. Both are about 20 minutes' walk from the Nova Brasília jetty. **Fortaleza** and **Ponta do Bicho** on the north shore are more tranquil and are safe for swimming. They are about 45 minutes' walk from the jetty or five minutes by boat. **Farol** and **Encantadas** are the liveliest and have the most accommodation, restaurants and nightlife. However, Encantadas has become somewhat polluted, with the cesspits overflowing into open sewers in the wet.

Walking on Ilha do Mel A series of well-signposted trails lead throughout Ilha do Mel and its coast. The most walked are as follows: the **lighthouse trail from Farol beach** (20 minutes), which is paved but steep; the views are wonderful. The **Nova Brasília to Encantadas trail** (three hours) offers a series of beautiful views, paths through the forest and stretches of semi-deserted beach. However, once you reach the end of the trail, you will either have to return the same way or take a boat taxi around the rocks back to Nova Brasília. This involves clambering over rocks at the end of Praia Grande; take appropriate footwear. The **Nova Brasília to Fortaleza trail** takes 1½ hours. It is also possible to take a long day walking around the entire island (apart from the stretch between Encantadas and Nova Brasília, which requires a boat taxi).

Ins and outs There are two main routes. From Paranaguá, large ferries leave from Rua General Carneiro (Rua da Praia) in front of the tourist information kiosk and run to Encantadas and Nova Brasília (twice daily, one hour 40 minutes, US$4). There are no shops on the island so stock up before you go. Alternatively, there are regular buses from Paranaguá to Pontal do Sul, from where a small boat runs to the island, daily 0800-1800, US$2.50 (every hour at weekends, less frequently during the week). There are souvenir and handicraft stalls at the ferry point. The last bus back to Paranaguá leaves at 2200. » *See Transport, page 316*

Parque Nacional de Superagüi

The island of **Superagüi** and its neighbour, **Ilha das Peças** lie at the heart of the largest single stretch of Atlantic Coast rainforest in the country and are the focus for the Guaraqueçaba Environmental Protection Area, which is part of the **Nature Conservancy's Parks in Peril Programme** ⓘ *http://parksinperil.org*. They also form a national park and UNESCO World Heritage site. Access to the park and accommodation can be arranged through the village on Superagüi beach, just north of Ilha do Mel. Many endangered endemic plants and animals live in the park, including hundreds of orchids, Atlantic rainforest specific animals like brown howler monkeys and large colonies of red-tailed Amazons (a parrot on the Red list of critically endangered species and which can be seen nowhere else but here). There are also rare neotropical animals here like jaguarundi, puma and jaguar. There are several Guarani villages in the area; other inhabitants are mostly of European descent, making a living from fishing. There is superb swimming from deserted beaches, but watch out for stinging jellyfish.

Ins and outs Boats run from Paranaguá on Saturday at 1000 (arriving 1400) and return on Sunday at 1530 (two stops en route), US$6 one way. Private boats from Praia da Fortaleza on Ilha do Mel run if the weather is good. Contact **Ibama** ⓘ *on the island, 2 km out of the village T041-252 0180*, for information and commercially organized tours.

Iguaçu Falls » pp307-318.

→ *Colour map 5, A2. Phone code 045, www.fozdoiguaçu.pr.gov.br.*

Foz do Iguaçu, or Las Cataratas del Iguazú as they are known in Spanish, are the most overwhelming and spectacular waterfalls in the world. Situated on the Rio Iguaçu (meaning 'big water' in Guaraní), which forms the border between Argentina and Brazil, they are made up of no less than 275 separate waterfalls. The Paraguayan city of Ciudad del Este is just a few kilometres away but Paraguay does not share territory on the falls themselves.

The Caiagangue people originally inhabited the region, but the first European visitor to the falls was the Spaniard Alvaro Núñez Cabeza de Vaca in 1541. He nearly fell off one of the waterfalls on his search for a connection between the Brazilian coast and the Río de la Plata, and named them the Saltos de Santa María (Santa Maria waterfalls). Though the falls were well known to the Jesuit missionaries, they were largely forgotten until the area was explored by a Brazilian expedition sent out by the Paraguayan president, Solano López, in 1863.

The most spectacular part is the **Garganta do Diabo** (Devil's Throat), the mouth of a 28-km-long gorge which stretches downstream to the Alto Río Paraná. It is best visited from the Argentine side (see Ins and outs, below).

Viewed from below, the water tumbles and roars over the craggy brown cliffs, framed by verdant rainforest encrusted with bromeliads, orchids, begonias and dripping ferns. A seemingly perpetual rainbow hovers over the scene and toco toucans, flocks of parakeets, caciques and great dusky swifts dodge in and out of the vapour whilst a vast number of butterflies dance over the forest walkways and lookouts.

Iguaçu Falls orientation

Ins and outs

Around 80% of the falls lie in Argentina, which offers the most spectacular views and the best infrastructure. There are national parks protecting extensive rainforest on both sides. Transport between the two parks is via the **Ponte Tancredo Neves,** as there is no crossing at the falls themselves.

The **Brazilian park** offers a superb panoramic view of the whole falls and is best visited in the morning (four hours is enough for the highlights) when the light is better for photography. The **Argentine park** (which requires at least half a day) is great value and includes a railway trip in the entrance fee as well as offering closer views of the individual falls. To fully appreciate the forest, with its wildlife and butterflies, you need to spend a full day and get well away from the visitor areas. Both parks can, if necessary, be visited in a day, starting at about 0700. However, in the heat, the brisk pace needed for a rapid tour is exhausting. Sunset is best from the Brazilian side.

The busiest times are holiday periods and on Sunday, when helicopter tours are particularly popular. Both parks have visitor centres, though the information provided by the Argentine centre is far superior to that in the Brazilian centre. Tourist facilities on both sides are constantly being improved.

There are many advantages to staying in Foz and commuting to the Argentine side (a bigger choice of hotels and restaurants, for example). Whichever side you decide to stay on, most establishments will accept reais, pesos or dollars. Cross-border transport usually accepts guaraníes as well.

A useful guidebook is *Iguazú, The Laws of the Jungle* (in Spanish, *Iguazú, Las Leyes de la Selva*), by Santiago G de la Vega, Contacto Silvestre Ediciones (1999), available from the visitor centre.

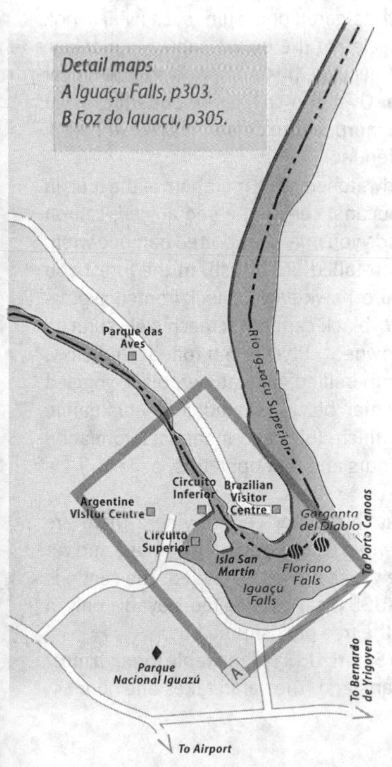

Getting there from Brazil Buses leave Foz do Iguaçu from the Terminal Urbana on Avenida Juscelino Kubitschek, one block from the infantry barracks. The grey or red **Transbalan** service goes to the falls every 30 minutes, 0530-2330, past the airport and **Hotel das Cataratas,** 40 minutes, US$0.80 one way, payable in reais only. Return buses 0800-1900. The bus terminates at the visitor centre, where you must pay the entrance fee and transfer to the free park shuttle bus, which leaves every five minutes or so from 0830-1900. If driving, cars must be left in the visitor centre car park. Taxis from Foz do Iguaçu charge US$7 one way or US$30 for return trip, including waiting (negotiate in advance). Many hotels organize tours to the falls, which have been recommended in preference to taxi rides.

Getting there from Argentina Transportes El Práctico buses run every hour from the Puerto Iguazú bus terminal, stopping at the park entrance to buy entry tickets and continuing to Puerto Canoas. Fares US$5 return to the visitor centre (cars US$3), a further US$0.50 to Puerto Canoas, payable in pesos, dollars, guaraníes or reais.

The first bus leaves at 0740, the last is at 1940, and the last return is at 2000, journey time 30 minutes. Buses are erratic, especially when wet, even though the times are clearly indicated. There are fixed rates for taxis, US$15 one-way, up to five people. A tour from the bus terminal, taking in both sides of the falls, costs US$40.

Clothing In the rainy season when water levels are high, waterproof coats or swimming costumes are advisable for some of the lower catwalks and for boat trips. Cameras should be carried in a plastic bag. Wear shoes with good soles, as the rocks can be very slippery in places.

Parque Nacional Foz do Iguaçu (Brazil)

The Brazilian national park was founded in 1939 and designated a World Heritage site by UNESCO in 1986. The park covers 185,262 ha on the Brazilian side and 67,000 ha on the Argentinian side, extending along the north bank of the Rio Iguaçu, then sweeping northwards to Santa Tereza do Oeste on the BR-277. The subtropical rainforest benefits from the added humidity in the proximity of the falls, creating an environment rich in vegetation and fauna. Given the massive popularity of the falls, the national parks on either side of the frontier are surprisingly little visited.

Fauna The parks on both sides of the falls are replete with wildlife and are a haven for birders. The most common mammals seen are coatis, which look like long-nosed racoons and squeakily demand food from visitors; do not be tempted as these small animals can be aggressive. There are other mammals here too, including jaguar, puma, ocelot and margay, which can occasionally be seen along the park roads just before and after dawn. They are wary of humans, although in 2003 a jaguar broke into the Parque das Aves (see page 305) and ate the zoo's prize caiman. Most frequently encountered are little and red brocket deer, white-eared opossum, *paca* (which look like large dappled guinea pigs) and a subspecies of the brown capuchin monkey. Other mammals present include white-lipped peccary, bush dog and southern river otter. The endangered tegu lizard is common. Over 100 species of butterflies have been identified, among them the electric blue morpho, the poisonous red and black heliconius and species of papilionidae and pieridae.

The birdlife is especially rewarding for birdwatchers. Five members of the toucan family can be seen: toco and red-breasted toucans, chestnut-eared araçari, saffron and spot-billed toucanets. In the bamboo stands you may see spotted bamboo wren, grey-bellied spinetail, several antshrikes, short-tailed ant-thrush. In the forest you might see rufous-thighed kite, black-and-white hawk-eagle, black-fronted piping-guan, blue ground dove, dark-billed cuckoo, black-capped screech-owl, surucua trogon, rufous-winged antwren, black-crowned tityra, red-ruffed fruitcrow, white-winged swallow, plush-crested jay, cream-bellied gnatcatcher, black-goggled and magpie tanagers, green-chinned euphonia, black-throated and utlramarine grosbeaks, yellow-billed cardinal, red-crested finch. (Bird and mammal information supplied by Douglas Trent, **Focus Tours**; see Tours and tour operators, page 20.)

The falls All cars and public buses stop at the visitor centre, where there are souvenir shops, a **Banco do Brasil** ATM and *câmbio* (1300-1700), a small café and car park. If possible, visit on a weekday when the walks are less crowded. The centre is open daily 0800-1700 and there is a 10 reais (US$3) car-parking fee, payable only in Brazilian currency. This includes a transfer to the free park shuttle bus.

The first stop on the shuttle bus is **Macuco Safari**, US$33 (bookable through most agencies, which may charge a premium for transfers). The safari takes one hour 45 minutes, leaving every 15 minutes, and visits the forest near the falls, with an option to take a boat to the edge of the falls themselves.

The second stop is the **Cataratas Trail** (starting from the hotel of the same name, non-residents can eat at the hotel, midday and evening buffets). This 1½-km paved

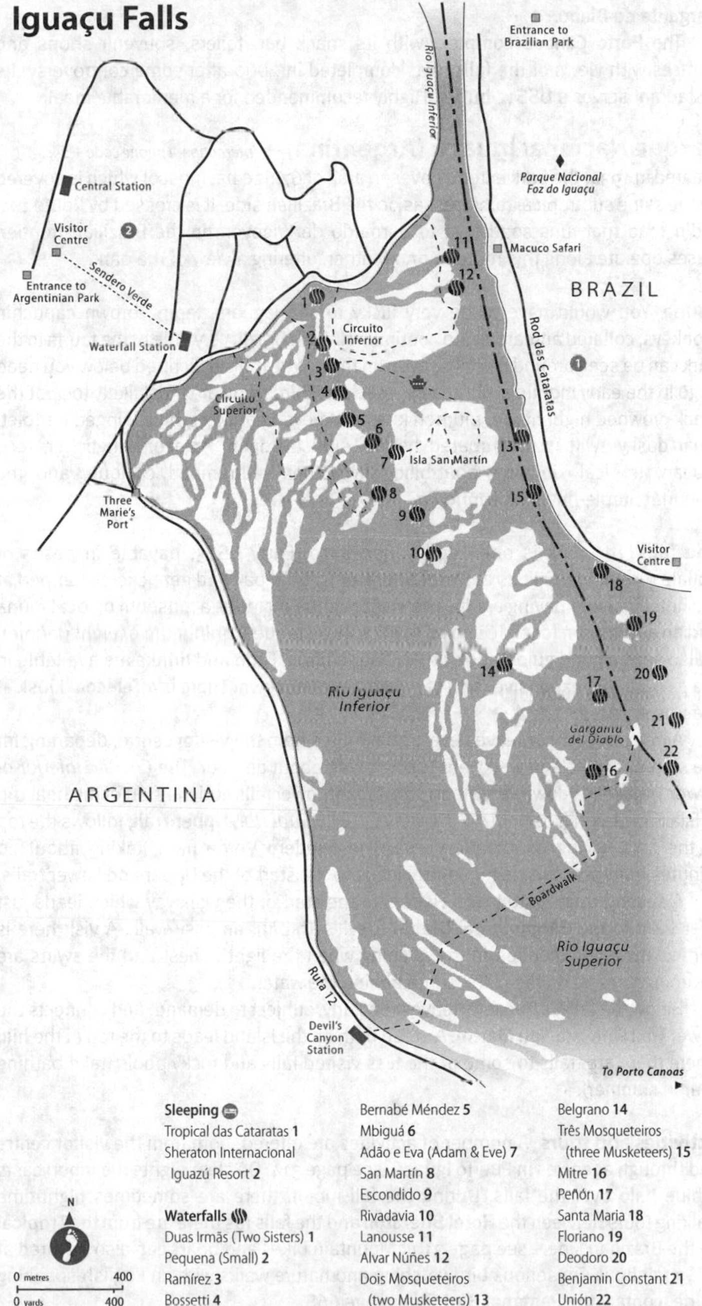

walk runs part of the way down the cliff near the rim of the falls, giving a stupendous view of the whole Argentine side of the falls. It ends up almost under the powerful **Floriano Falls**; from here an elevator used to carry visitors to the top of the Floriano Falls but has not been functioning recently; a path adjacent to the elevator leads to Porto Canoa. A catwalk at the foot of the Floriano Falls gives a good view of the **Garganta do Diabo**.

The **Porto Canoas** complex, with its snack bar, toilets, souvenir shops and terraces with views of the falls, was completed in 2000 after some controversy. Its restaurant serves a US$12 buffet. Highly recommended for a memorable meal.

Parque Nacional Iguazú (Argentina) → *International phone code + 54.*

Created in 1934, the park extends over an area of 67,620 ha, most of which is covered by the same subtropical rainforest as on the Brazilian side. It is crossed by Route 101, a dirt road that runs southeast to Bernardo de Yrigoyen on the Brazilian frontier. Buses operate along this route in dry weather, offering a view of the park.

Fauna You would have to be very lucky to see jaguars, tapirs, brown capuchin monkeys, collared anteaters and coatimundi. As in Brazil, very little of the fauna in the park can be seen around the falls; even on the nature trails described below you need to go in the early morning. Of the 400 species of birds, you are most likely to spot the black-crowned night heron, plumed kite, white-eyed parakeet, blue-winged parrolet, great dusky swift, scale-throated hermit, suruca trogon, Amazon kingfisher, toco toucan, tropical kingbird, boat-billed flycatcher, red-rumped cacique, and the colourful purple-throated euphonia.

The falls The park is open daily 0800-1900. Entry US$5, payable in pesos or dollars (not reais). Guests at **Hotel Sheraton** should pay and get tickets stamped at the hotel to avoid paying again. The visitor centre includes a museum of local fauna and an auditorium for slide shows (available on request, minimum of eight people). It also sells a good guide book on Argentine birds. Food and drinks are available in the park but are expensive, so it is best to take your own. There is a Telecom kiosk at the bus stop.

A free train service leaves every 20 minutes from the visitor centre, departing for the start of two sets of walkways, both taking about an hour. The *Circuito Inferior* or **Lower Trail**, leads down very steep steps to the lower falls and the start of the boat trip to Isla San Martin (see below). The easy *Circuito Superior*, **Upper Trail**, follows the top of the falls, giving panoramic views. The **Sendero Verde** path, taking about 20 minutes from near the visitor centre, leads to the start of the Upper and Lower trails.

A second train route takes visitors to the start of the walkway which leads just over 1 km to the **Garganta del Diablo** (Devil's Throat), an easy walk. A visit here is particularly recommended in the evening when the light is best and the swifts are returning to roost on the cliffs, some behind the water.

Below the falls, a free ferry leaves regularly, subject to demand, and connects the Lower Trail with **Isla San Martín**. A steep path on the island leads to the top of the hill, where there are trails to some of the less-visited falls and rocky pools (take bathing gear in summer).

Activities and tours A number of activities are offered, both from the visitor centre and through agencies in Puerto Iguazú, see page 314. On clear nights the moon casts a blue halo over the falls. During the full moon, there are sometimes night-time walking tours between the **Hotel Sheraton** and the falls (as there are from the **Tropical** on the Brazilian side – see page 310). Mountain bikes and boats can also be hired at US$3 per hour. For serious birdwatching and nature walks with an English-speaking guide, contact the **Pantanal Bird Club**, page 668.

Foz do Iguaçu and around

» pp307-318.

→ Phone code: 045. Colour map 5, A2. Population: 260,000.

The proximity of the falls have made Foz the third most visited city in Brazil. The town has no attractions of its own but is only 28 km from the falls and although there are some upmarket hotel options, the town has a greater range of cheap accommodation and restaurants. It is linked by air and road to the main cities of southern Brazil and Asunción in Paraguay.

The closest artificial beaches on **Lake Itaipu** (see Itaipu Dam, page 306) are at **Bairro de Três Lagoas**, at Km 723 on BR-277, and in the municipality of **Santa Terezinha do Itaipu** ⓘ *US$2.50*, 34 km from Foz. The leisure parks have grassy areas with kiosks, barbecue sites and offer fishing as well as bathing. It is also possible to take boat trips on the lake.

The **Parque das Aves** ⓘ *Rodovia das Cataratas Km 16, US$10* (bird park), is well worth visiting. It contains rare South American (and foreign) birds including various currasows, guans, parrots, macaws and toucans. These are housed in large aviaries through which you can walk, with the birds flying and hopping around you. There is

Foz do Iguaçu

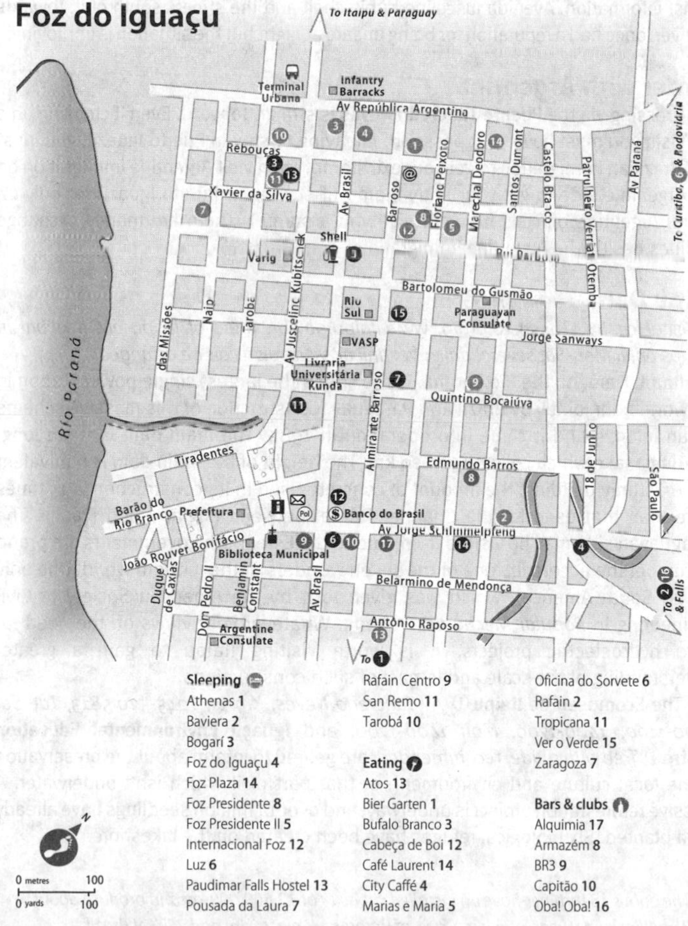

also a butterfly house. The bird park is within walking distance of the **Hotel San Martin**. The **Paudimar Falls Hostel** (see Sleeping, page 311) offers a discount for its guests. The national park bus stops here, 100 m before the entrance to the falls.

Ins and outs

Getting there **Iguaçu international airport**, 18 km south of town near the falls, has a **Banco do Brasil** and *câmbio*, car rental offices, a tourist office and an official taxi stand. Taxis cost US$8 to the town centre (US$11 from town to airport). **Transbalan** (Parque Nacional) buses run to town, US$0.50 but don't permit large amounts of luggage (backpacks okay). Many hotels run minibus services for a small charge.

The **rodoviária** ⓘ *Av Costa e Silva, 4 km from centre on road to Curitiba, T045-522 3633*, receives long-distance buses. There is a tourist office, **Cetreme** desk for tourists who have lost their documents, *guarda municipal* (police) and luggage store. Buses run to the centre, US$0.65. Book onwards departures as soon as possible.

Tourist information The **Secretaria Municipal de Turismo** ⓘ *Praça Getulio Vargas, 0700-2300*, is very helpful, as is 24-hour tourist helpline ⓘ *T045-521 1125*. Information is also available at the *rodoviária* and airport, open for all arriving flights, with a free map and bus information. *Triplice Fronteira* is a local newspaper with street plans and tourist information. Avenida Juscelino Kubitschek and the streets south of it, towards the river, once had a reputation for being unsafe at night but the situation is improving.

Border with Argentina

This crossing via the **Puente Tancredo Neves** is straightforward. Even if crossing on a day visit, you must have your passport. If leaving to stay in Puerto Iguazú, you must visit Brazilian immigration to get your exit stamp. Then visit Argentine immigration on the Argentine side to get your entry stamp (if staying in Puerto Iguazú for only 24 hours, Argentine officials may not give you a stamp). There are money exchange facilities beside the Argentine immigration.

Itaipu Dam → *Colour map 5, A2.*

ⓘ *Visitor centre, T045-520 6999, www.itaipu.gov.br, tours of Itaipu are free but in groups only, Mon-Sat several daily; 'technical' visits also can be arranged.*

The Itaipu Dam, on the Río Paraná, is the site of the largest single power station in the world built jointly by Brazil and Paraguay. Construction of this massive scheme began in 1975 and it came into operation in 1984. The main dam is 8 km long, creating a lake which covers 1400 sq km. The height of the main dam is equivalent to a 65-storey building, the amount of concrete used in its construction is 15 times more than that used for the Channel Tunnel between England and France. The Paraguayan side may be visited from Ciudad del Este. Both governments are proud to trumpet the accolade, 'one of the seven wonders of the modern world' (the only one in South America), which was given to it by the American Society of Civil Engineering in *Popular Mechanics* in 1995. Whatever your views on the need for huge hydroelectric projects, it is worth visiting Itaipu to gain a greater understanding of the scale and impact of such constructions.

The **Ecomuseu de Itaipu** ⓘ *Av Tancredo Neves, Km 11, T045-520 5813, Tue-Sat 0900-1100, 1400-1700, Mon 1400-1700*, and **Iguaçu Environmental Education Centre** ⓘ *free with guide, recommended*, are geared to inform about the preservation of the local culture and environment, or that part of it which isn't underwater. A massive reforestation project is underway, and over 14 million seedlings have already been planted. Six biological refuges have been created on the lakeshore.

The dam's 18 turbines have an installed capacity of 12,600,000 kw and produce about 75 billion kwh a year, providing 80% of Paraguay's electricity and 25% of Brazil's.

If it's sunny go in the morning as the sun is behind the dam in the afternoon and you will get poor photographs. The visitor centre has a short video presentation (ask for the English version) with stunning photography and amazing technical information. The spillways are capable of discharging the equivalent of 40 times the average flow of the Iguaçu Falls. If you are lucky, the spillways will be open. After the film and a brief visit to the souvenir shop where an English guidebook is available, a coach will take you to the dam itself. As it crosses the top, you get a stomach-churning view of the spillways and really begin to appreciate the scale of the project.

To get to Itaipu, the 'executive' bus and agency tours are an unnecessary expense. Buses No 110 or 120 from Terminal Urbana (stand 50 Batalhão) go every 13 minutes to the Public Relations office at the main entrance (US$0.40).

Ciudad del Este (Paraguay) » pp307-318.

→ Phone code: 061. International phone code + 595. Population: 140,000.

Described as the biggest shopping centre in Latin America, Ciudad del Este attracts Brazilian and Argentine visitors in search of bargain prices for electrical goods, watches, perfumes, etc. Founded as Ciudad Presidente Stroessner in 1957, the city grew rapidly during the construction of the Itaipú hydroelectric project. Dirty, noisy, unfriendly and brashly commercial, it is worth a visit just for the people watching, but be careful with valuables and be particularly cautious after dark.

The Paraguayan side of the **Itaipú Hydroelectric Project** ⓘ *Mon-Sat 0730-1200, 1330-1700, Sun and holidays 0800-1200, 1330-1630, free guided tours include a film show (in several languages) 45 mins before bus tours, check times in advance and take your passport*, can be visited. Buses run from Rodríguez y García, outside the terminal, to the visitor centre. On the way to Itaipú is **Flora y Fauna Itaipú Binacional** ⓘ *0830-1030, 1330-1630*, with animals and plants rescued from the area when the dam was built. It is about 2 km from the visitor centre on the road back to Ciudad del Este.

Cascada de Monday (Monday Falls), where the Río Monday drops into the Paraná Gorge 10 km south of Ciudad del Este, is a worthwhile trip; there is good fishing below the falls. Return fare by taxi US$20.

Border with Paraguay

Immigration and transport There is an hourly passenger ferry service from Porto de Lanchas and Porto Guaíra to Salto del Guayra on the Paraguayan side, US$0.50, and an hourly car ferry from Porto Guaíra (US$4 for car with two people). The car ferry runs until 1830 (Brazilian time). Customs and immigration for documentation close at 1700. There is a time change when you cross the Paraná (Paraguay is one hour behind Brazil). The area is intensively patrolled for contraband and stolen cars; ensure that all documentation is in order.

Sleeping

Curitiba *p292, map p294*

General information: www.ondehospedar.com.br/pr/curitiba.php and www.cmoraes.com.br/webhotelshtml/curitiba.shtml. There are good hotels southeast of the centre in the vicinity of the *rodoferroviária*, but the cheaper ones are seedy and close to the wholesale market, which operates noisily throughout the night.

AL Bourbon & Tower, R Cândido Lopes 102, T041-3322 4001, www.bourbon.com.br. One of the better modern hotels in the centre with a mock old-fashioned charm engendered by wood panelling and fake period furniture. Rooms have jacuzzis. Business facilities.

AL Grand Hotel Rayon, R Visconde de Nacar, T041-3027 6006, www.rayon.com.br. Centrally located, staidly decorated, but much the best option for business travellers. All the expected services alongside a pool, saunas, well- equipped gym and travel agency.

AL Slaviero Palace, R Sen Alencar Guimarães, T041-3017 1000, T0800-7043311, www.hotelslaviero.com.br. The best of the second-grade business hotels in the centre. Anonymously decorated but with a business centre and airport transfer.

A Mercure, R Emiliano Perneta 747, T041-3234 1212, www.accorhotels.com.br. Standard 2nd-grade business hotel in the centre with a pool and business centre.

B Del Rey, R Ermelino de Leão 18, T/F041-3322 3242, www.hoteldelrey.com.br. Central, upmarket yet relaxed, large rooms, good restaurant, gym. Good value. Recommended.

B Deville Express, R Amintas de Barros 73, T041-3322 8558, www.deville.com.br. In the city centre with a bar, small modest restaurant. All rooms a/c with fridge.

B Slaviero Braz, Av Luis Xavier 67, T/F041-3017 1000, T0800-704 3311, www.hotelslaviero.com.br. Refurbished hotel in a 1940s building preserved as '*Patrimonio Histórico*'. Business facilities.

C Kings, Av Silva Jardim 264, T041-3022 8444, www.kingshotel.com.br. Modern, secure and well-maintained apartment hotel.

C Lumini, R Gen. Carneiro, T041-3264 5244, www.hotellumini.com.br. Good apartment hotel in a quiet street. All rooms have a/c.

C Nova Lisboa, Av 7 de Setembro 1948, T041- 3264 1944. With breakfast, bargain for cheaper rates without breakfast. Recommended.

C Tourist Universo, Praça Gen Osório 63, T041-322 0099, F223 5420. On one of the city's most attractive squares, in centre. Very smart for price, with sauna and pool. Intimate and excellent value. Recommended.

D Parati, R Riachuelo 30, T041-3223 1355 , www.hotelparati.com.br. An anonymous 1980s block next to the Federal University of Paraná and near the centre with well-kept apartments with kitchen. Breakfast included.

D-E Hostel Roma, R Barao do Rio Branco 805, T041-3322 2838, www.hostelroma.com.br. Smart hostel with 110 beds in single-sex dorms. All have private bathrooms. TV room, fax, internet and a member's kitchen. Breakfast included.

D-E Curitiba Eco-hostel, R Luiz Tramontin 1693, Campo Comprido, T041-3029 1693, www.curitibaecohostel.com.br. A new hostel with all services. Situated in the Tramontina borough and set in attractive gardens with their own sports facilities.

Camping

Camping Clube do Brasil, BR-116, Km 84, 16 km in the direction of São Paulo, T041-3358 6634.

Morretes *p296*

For information see www.morretes.com.br.

B Pousada Graciosa, Estrada da Graciosa Km 8 (Porto da Cima village), T041-3462 1807, www.morretes.com.br/pousadagraciosa. Much the best in the area; some 10 km north of Morretes with simple but comfortable wooden chalets set in rainforest. No children under 12.

C Pousada Cidreira, R Romulo Pereira 61, T041-3462 1604. Centrally located with characterless but clean rooms, most with balconies and all with TV and en suites. Some rooms have space for 3. Breakfast included.

D Hotel Nhundiaquara, R General Carneiro 13, T041-3462 1228, F3462 1267. A smart whitewashed building beautifully set on the river whose exterior appearance belies the hotel's poor service, gloomy public areas and very ordinary rooms. With breakfast.

Paranaguá *p296*

For information see www.paranagua.pr.gov.br.

AL Hotel Camboa, R João Estevão (Ponta do Caju), T041-3423 2121, www.hotelcamboa.com.br. Family resort with tennis courts, large pool, saunas, trampolines, restaurant and a/c rooms. Out of town near the port. Book ahead.

AL São Rafael, R Julia Costa 185, T041-3423 2123, www.sanrafaelhotel.com.br. Business hotel with plain tiled rooms, a business centre, restaurants, pool and jacuzzis in the en suites.

D Hotel Ponderosa, R Pricilenco Corea 68 at 15 Novembro, a block east and north of the boat dock, T041-3423 2464. Tiled rooms with en suites, some rooms have a sea view.

D Pousada Itibere, R Princesa Isabel 24, 3 blocks east of the boat dock. T041-3423 2485. Very smart spartan rooms with polished wood floors, some with sea views. Friendly service from the Portuguese owner.

Camping

Arco Iris, Praia de Leste, on the beach, 29 km south of Paranaguá, T041-458 2001.

Excursions from Paranaguá *p297*

There are 4 campsites and a few other cheap pousadas in Matinhos.

B Praia e Sol, R União 35, Matinhos, T041-452 1922. Recommended.

Ilha do Mel *p298, map p298*

For information see www.ilhadomel online.com or www.pousadasilhadomel.com.br. All rooms are fan-cooled unless otherwise stated.

You can rent a fisherman's house on Encantadas – ask for **Valentim's Bar**, or for Luchiano. Behind the bar is **Cabanas Dona Maria**, shared showers, cold water; food available if you ask in advance. Many pousadas and houses with rooms to rent (shared kitchen and living room). Shop around, prices from about US$10 double, low season, mid-week.

B Long Beach, Praia Grande, T041-9906 4040, www.lbeach.cjb.net. The best on this beach with comfortable chalets for up to 6 with en suites. Very popular with surfers. Book in advance.

C Caranguata, Encantadas, T041-3426 9097 or T041-9998 7770, http://martinetas.sites.uol.com.br. A/c en suites in wood with fridge and Monet prints on walls. Very close to jetty.

C Dona Quinota, Fortaleza, T041-3423 6176. Little blue-and-cream cottages with polished wood floors and en suites. Right on the beach. 3 km from Nova Brasília. Price includes breakfast and supper. **Dona Clara** next door is very similar in yellow instead of blue.

C Enseada, Farol, T/F041-3426 8040. 4 rooms with en suites, TVs and fridges. Charmingly decorated. Lots of rescued cats.

C Por do Sol, Nova Brasília, T041-3426 8009, www.pousadapordosol.com.br. Simple but elegant en suite rooms in grey tile and wood around a garden shaded by sombrero trees. A large deck with hammock-strewn cabanas sits next to the beach. Includes breakfast.

C Recanto do Frances, Encantadas, T041-3354 3904. French-owned and full of character, with each chalet built in a different style to represent a different French city. 5 mins from Prainha or Encantadas. Good crêpe restaurant.

D Aconchego, Nova Brasília, T041-3426 8030, http://clubmatrix.com.br/aconchego. 10 scrupulously clean rooms in a house behind an expansive beachside deck strewn with hammocks. Public TV and breakfast areas. Charming. Includes breakfast.

D Girassol, T041-3426 8006, heliosilva@onda.com.br. Wooden rooms with en suites in a little bougainvillea and fruit tree garden. Very close to jetty. Includes breakfast.

D Plancton, Farol at Fora, T/F041-3426 8061. A range of wooden buildings in a humming-bird filled garden. Rooms for 5 split over 2 levels. Wood and slate-tiled en suites. Clean, fresh. Italian food available in high season.

D Recanto da Fortaleza, Ponta do Bicho, T041-3275 4455, www.ilhadomel pousada.com.br. The best of the 2 next to the fort. Basic cabins with en suites and tiled floors. Free pick-up by boat from Nova Brasília (ring ahead), bike rental. Price includes breakfast and dinner.

D Ronaldo's, Encantadas, T041-3426 9019. Simple rooms with private bathrooms. Friendly owner.

D-E D'Lua, Farol, T041-3426 8031. Basic and hippy with a very friendly new-age owner, Jo.

D-E Farol da Ilha, Nova Brasília, T041-3426 8017. Plain wood and terracotta tiled dorms and double rooms in a garden. Surfboards for rent. Price includes generous breakfast.

D-E Hostel Zorro, Encantadas, T041-3426 9052, www.hostelzorro.com.br. A party hostel overlooking the beach. Small but clean wooden rooms and dorms, and all the usual facilities.

D-E Trilha do Sol, Farol, T041-3426 8025. Simple wooden rooms with en suites.

Camping

There are mini campsites with facilities at **Encantadas, Farol** and **Brasília**. Camping is possible on the more deserted beaches (good for surfing). If camping, watch out for the tide, watch possessions and beware of the *bicho de pé* which burrows into feet (remove with a needle and alcohol) and the *borrachudos* (discourage with **Autan** repellent).

Iguaçu Falls *p300, map p305*

Brazil

The best hotels with the most modern facilities and the easiest access to Iguaçu are all near the falls. There is little here for budget travellers.

L Hotel Tropical das Cataratas, directly overlooking the falls, 28 km from Foz, T045-3521 7000, www.tropicalhotel.com.br. The only hotel within the park on the Brazilian side is a mock-belle époque building with slightly frayed rooms, grand public areas and a poolside garden visited by numerous birds, butterflies and, at dawn, small mammals. The hotel is right next to the falls offering by far the easiest access and the best chance to beat the crowds. The food is adequate, as good as any in town, but hardly dazzling. Non-resident evening diners will be in the park after it closes and must take a taxi back to town.

D-E Paudimar Campestre, Rodovia das Cataratas Km 12.5, Remanso Grande, near airport, T045-3529 6061, www.paudimar.com.br. Youth hostel with spotless single-sex dorms , pool, communal kitchen, football pitch, IYHA camping and gardens visited by birds and small mammals. From the airport or town take the Parque Nacional bus (0525-0040) and get out at the Remanso Grande bus stop, by **Hotel San Juan**, then take the free shuttle bus (0700-1900) to the hostel, or walk the 1200 m from the main road. Breakfast included. Tours arranged. There's a **Paudimar** desk at the *rodoviária*. Only IYHA members in high season when the hostel gets very busy.

Camping

Sleeping in your car inside the park is prohibited. You can camp at the **Paudimar IYHA**, but it's pretty cold and damp in winter.

Argentina

AL Sheraton Internacional Iguazú Resort, Parque Nacional Iguazú, Argentina, www.starwood.com. A 1970s wedge of concrete built on the opposite side of the falls from the **Hotel das Cataratas**. Views are spectacular, especially out over the pool from the room balconies on the upper storey. But the falls are a 20-min walk from the hotel. Well maintained, well run. Baby-sitting service available.

Camping

Camping Puerto Canoas, 600 m from Puerto Canoas, with tables, but no other facilities, the nearest drinking water is at the park entrance.

Foz do Iguaçu *p305, map p305*

Many hotels offer excursions to the falls. In a bid to get their commission, touts may tell you the hotel of your choice no longer exists, or offer you room rates below what is actually charged. In high season (eg Christmas-New Year) you will not find a room under US$15, but in low season there are many good deals.

L Internacional Foz, R Alm Barroso 2006, T045-3521 4100, www.internacionalfoz.com.br. The only 5-star hotel in the region with excellent business and conference facilities. Spacious but very standard upmarket hotel rooms and services.

A Rafain Centro, Mcal Deodoro 984, T/F045-3523 1213, www.rafaincentro.com.br. The smart and upmarket communal areas and attractive pool area belie the rather well-worn rooms.

B Baviera, Av Jorge Schimmelpfeng 697, T045-3523 5995, www.hotelbavieraiguassu.com.br. A mock-Bavarian folly with a chalet-style exterior. On the main road, central for bars and restaurants. The rooms look as if they haven't been renovated since the 1980s.

B Suiça, Av Felipe Wandscheer 3580, T045-3525 3232, www.hotelsuica.com.br. Old 1970s hotel with dark tiled rooms and a pool. Helpful Swiss manager.

C Bogarí, Av Brasil 106, T/F045-3523 2243, www.bogarihotel.com.br. Restful atmosphere, large pool with pleasant walled terrace, central, in shopping street.

C Foz do Iguaçu, Av Brasil 97, T045-3523 4455, hotelfoz@purenet.com.br. Another gloomy 1970s monstrosity with faded rooms. But good value, and with large breakfasts included in the price.

C Foz Plaza Hotel, R Marechal Deodoro 1819, T/F045-3523 1448, www.challengerhoteis.com.br. Serene and well-refurbished 1980s hotel with a restaurant and a bar, swimming pool, fitness centre, sauna and a games room.

C Foz Presidente, R Xavier da Silva 1000, T/F045-3572 4450, www.fozpresidentehoteis.com.br. Restaurant, pool, with breakfast, convenient for buses. Brighter and more modern than most of Foz's offerings. Recommended.

C Foz Presidente II, R Mcal Floriano Peixoto 1851, T045-3523 2318, www.fozpresidentehoteis.com.br. Smaller and a little more expensive than its sister hotel (with whom it shares leisure areas), but also with pool, bar and restaurant.

D Luz, Av Costa e Silva Km 5, near *rodoviária*, T045-3522 3535, www.luzhotel.com.br. Well-kept but bog standard small 1980s hotel with a buffet restaurant. Rooms have a/c and Brazilian TV. Recommended.

D Tarobá, R Tarobá 1048, T045-523 9722, www.hoteltaroba.com.br. Good value. Clean with plain tiled a/c rooms, a tiny indoor pool and helpful staff. Recommended.

D-E Paudimar Falls Hostel, R Antônio Raposo 820, T045-3028 5503, www.paudimarfalls.com.br. Despite its name, the companion hostel to the **Paudimar** near the falls, is in the centre of town. It has similar facilities, with doubles, cramped dorms, pool and the usual hostel services.

D-E Pousada da Laura, R Naipi 671, T045-3572 3374. Secure and run by the enthusiastic Laura who speaks some Spanish, English, Italian and French. The hostel has a kitchen, laundry facilities and en suites and is a good place to meet other travellers. Good breakfast.

D-E Pousada Evelina Navarrete, R Irlan Kalichewski 171, Vila Yolanda, T/F045-3574 3817, pousada.evelina@foznet.com.br. Lots of tourist information, internet, well-maintained dorms, doubles and singles (some with a/c) and good breakfast. English, French, Italian, Polish and Spanish spoken. Helpful staff with lots of useful tourist information and organized walks. Near Av Cataratas on the way to the falls – take a bus to Parque Nacional from the bus station and ask to be let off after 3.5 km, near the Chemin supermarket. R Irlan Kalichewski is down the hill, 3 blocks towards the city on the left. Warmly recommended.

E Athenas, R Almte Barroso 2215 on corner of Rebouças, T045-574 2563. Good value, special rates for backpackers, some rooms with shared bath, fan, breakfast extra, beers sold.

E San Remo, R Xavier da Silva 563 at Taroba, T045-3523 1619, roberto_171@hotmail.com. Scrupulously clean though small rooms with TVs and writing desks. All-you-can-eat breakfast. English, Spanish and Hebrew spoken. In house travel agency.

Camping

E Pousada Internacional, R Manêncio Martins 21, 1.5 km from Foz town, T045-3523 3053, www.campinginternacional.com.br. US$10 per person (half price with International Camping Card), pool, clean basic cabins. Park vehicle or put tent away from trees in winter in case of heavy rainstorms. The food here is poor and the refectory closes at 2300.

Ciudad del Este (Paraguay) *p307*

The international dialling code for Paraguay is +595. Accommodation is generally expensive.

A Convair, Adrián Jara y García, T061-500342. Comfortable business-style hotel with cheaper rooms without bath.

B Panorama Inn, Pampliega at Eusebio Alaya, T061-500110. A modern, corporate hotel with anonymous hotel catalogue rooms, breakfast and reasonable service.

C Munich, Fernández y Miranda, T061-500347. Standard town block with a/c rooms, parking and breakfast.

D Austria (also known as **Viena**), Fernández 165, above restaurant, T061-500883. With good breakfast and a/c, Austrian family, views from upper floors. Warmly recommended.

E Caribe, Emiliano Fernández, facing **Austria**. A/c rooms with hot-water showers set in a nice garden, helpful owner. Recommended.

Eating

Curitiba *p292, map p294*

Hot sweet wine is sold on the streets in winter to help keep out the cold.

Boulevard, R Vol da Pátria 539 (centre), T041-3224 8244. The city's most celebrated restaurant serving a mix of French, Italian and Brazilian cooking to a smart crowd. Reasonable wine list. Closed on Sun.

Baviera, Alameda Augusto Stellfeld, Av Dr Murici (centre), T041-3232 1995. A Curitiba institution, established over 30 years and serving pizza in an intimate beer cellar setting. Open 1830-0100. Delivery service.

Durski, R Jaime Reis, 254 (centre), T041-3225 7893. Good Eastern European food, including a locally celebrated and lavish banquet of pâtés, borcht, *platzki*, filled pasties and a variety of meat dishes.

Green Life, R Carlos de Carvalho 271 (centre), T041-3223 8490. Vegetarian buffet restaurant, open for lunch only.

Happy Rango, Av Visconde de Nacar 1350, near R 24 Horas. Brightly lit, basic corner joint selling fast food and pizzas, open 24 hrs.
Mister Sheik, Av Vicente Machado 534. Arabic fast food in pitta with salad, popular for deliveries. Recommended.
Saccy, R São Franscisco 350, at Mateus Leme. Pizza, tapas and a popular bar with live music, see Bars and clubs, page 313.
Salmão, R Emiliano Perneta 924, T041-3225 2244. Restaurant in historic house, delicious fish and pizza, often special promotions, live music every night, open until 0100. Short taxi ride from centre.

There are a couple of *lanchonetes* in the market which is close to the *rodoferroviária*. Also good meals in the bus station.

Morretes *p296*

Armazém Romanus, R Visc do Rio Branco 141, T041-3462 1500. Family-run restaurant with the best menu and wine list in the region. Dishes made from home-grown ingredients include excellent *barreado* and flambéed desserts.
Madalozo, R Alm Frederico de Oliveira 16, overlooking the river, T041-3462 1410. Good *barreado* and generous salads.
Terra Nossa, R XV Novembro 109, T041-3462 2174. *Barreado*, pasta pizzas and fish. Middle of the road but generous portions and a small wine list. From R$25 for a 2-person *prato da casa*.

Paranaguá *p296*

The choice here is poor.
Danúbio Azul, R XV Novembro 95, T041-3423 3255, www.restaurantedaxcnubioazul.com.br. The best in town with a range of fish and chicken dishes, pastas and pizzas; all in enormous quantities. 1 block back from the sea at the east end of town.
Divina Gula, R XV Novembro 165, T041-3422 2788 (until 1400 only). Seafood buffet and *feijoada* at weekends. 3 blocks east of the Ilha do Mel dock.
Restaurant Rosa, R Praia 16, T041-3423 2162. Cheap but decent seafood, good risotto. A block west of the Ilha do Mel dock.

Ilha do Mel *p298, map p298*

Many pousadas also serve food – some only in season (Christmas to Carnaval). Many have live music or dancing (especially in high season). Things kick off after 2200.
Fim da trilha, Prainha (Fora de Encantadas), T041-3426 9017. Spanish seafood restaurant. One of the best on the island.
Colmeia, Farol, T041-3426 8029. Snacks, crêpes, good cakes and puddings.
Mar e Sol, Farol, T041-3426 8021, www.restaurantemaresol.com. Huge portions of fish and chicken, all with chips and rice. Also a small selection of more adventurous dishes like bass in shrimp sauce.
Recanto do Frances, Encantadas. French crêpes and Moroccan cous cous.
Toca do Abutre, Farol. Live music and the usual huge portions of fish or chicken with rice, beans and chips.
Zorro, Encantadas. One of several cheap fish, beans and rice restaurants on the seafront, shaded by palapas. *Forró* dancing in the evenings.

Foz do Iguaçu *p305, map p305*

Bufalo Branco, R Rebouças 530, T045-3523 9744, superb all-you-can-eat *churrasco*, includes *filet mignon*, salad bar and dessert. Sophisticated surroundings and attentive service. Highly recommended.
Cabeça de Boi, Av Brasil 1325, T045-3523 2100. *Churrascaria* with live music and a buffet, coffee and pastries also.
Rafain, Av das Cataratas, Km 6.5, T045-3523 1177, closed Sun. Set price for excellent buffet with folkloric music and dancing (2100-2300); touristy but very entertaining. Out of town, take a taxi or arrange with travel agency. Recommended.
Tropical das Cataratas, the nearest dining to the falls themselves (see page 310).
Zaragoza, R Quintino Bocaiúva 882, T045-3574 3084. Large and upmarket, for Spanish dishes and seafood. Respectable wine list. Recommended.
Atos, Av Juscelino Kubitschek 865, T045-3572 2785. Per kilo buffet with various meats, salads, sushi and puddings. Lunch only.
Bier Garten, Almirante Barroso 550, a bustling pizzeria and *choperia*.
Tropicana, Av Juscelino Kubitschek 228. All-you-can-eat pizza or *churrascaria* with a salad bar, good value.
Café Laurent, Av Jorge Schimmelpfeng 550, T045-3574 6666. Smart student café serving decent tea, coffee, cakes and pies.

City Caffé, Av Jorge Schimmelpfeng 898. Stylish café open daily 0800-2330 for sandwiches, Arabic snacks and pastries.
Marias e Maria, Av Brasil 50. Good *confeitaria*.
Oficina do Sorvete, Av Jorge Schimmelpfeng, 244 daily 1100-0100. Excellent ice creams, a popular local hang-out.
Ver o Verde, R. Almirante Barroso 1713, T045-3574 5647. Buffet vegetarian food with some white meat and fish. Great value. Lunch only.

Ciudad del Este *p307*
Most restaurants close on Sun. Cheaper restaurants can be found along García and in the market.
Coreio, San Blas 125. Good Korean food.
Hotel Austria/Viena (see Sleeping, above). Good Austrian food in large portions.
Mi Ranchero, Adrián Jara. Good food, service and prices, well known.

Bars and clubs

Curitiba *p292, map p294*
A cluster of bars at the square of Largo da Ordem have tables and chairs on the pavement, music which tends to be rock, and bar food: **Fire Fox**, Av Jaime Reis 46, flanked by **Tuba's** and **The Farm**. **London Pub**, São Francisco 350, São Francisco. Recommended.

R 24 Horas is an indoor street with very similar, functional bars and cafés, open 24 hrs. **Saccy**, R São Franscisco, 350, corner with Mateus Leme, 12. Pizza, tapas and lively bar with live music.

Foz do Iguaçu *p305, map p305*
Most bars double as restaurants and are concentrated on Av Jorge Schimmelpfeng for 2 blocks from Av Brasil to R Mal Floriano Peixoto. Wed-Sun are best nights; the crowd tends to be young.
Alquimia, Av Jorge Schimmelpfeng 334, T045-572 3154. Popular nightclub, attached, 2400-0500, US$3.
Armazém, R Edmundo de Barros 446, intimate and sophisticated, attracts discerning locals, good atmosphere, mellow live music, US$1 cover. Recommended.
BR3, Av Jorge Schimmelpfeng corner with Av Brasil. Modern, open until 2400.
Capitão Bar, Av Jorge Schimmelpfeng 288 and Almte Barroso, T045-572 1512. Large, loud and popular, nightclub attached.
Oba! Oba!, Av das Cataratas 3700, T045-574 2255 (Antigo Castelinho). Live samba show Mon-Sat 2315-0015, very popular, US$9 for show and 1 drink.
Rafain, Av das Cataratas Km 6.5. With floor show and food, see page 312.

Entertainment

Curitiba *p292, map p294*
Best to look in the newspaper for music and what's on in the bars, clubs and theatres. *Gazeta do Povo* has an arts and what's on section called *Caderno G*.

Cinema
Tickets are usually US$4-5 Mon-Thu, US$6-8 at weekends.
Shopping Center Água Verde, T041-242 8741.
Shopping Crystal, R Comendador Araújo 731, T041-323 3061.
Shopping Curitiba, Praça Oswaldo Cruz 2698, T041-326 1412.
Shopping Novo Batel, T041-222 2107.

Foz do Iguaçu *p305, map p305*
Casinos
Organized tours to casinos (illegal in Brazil) over the border in Paraguay and Argentina take 3 hrs.
Casino Iguazú, Ruta 12 Km, 1640, Puerto Iguazú, Argentina, T3757-498000. Weekdays 1800-0500, 24 hrs weekends, restaurant.

Cinema
Boulevard, Av das Cataratas 1118, T045-523 4245. Large complex open from 1700 and all day Sun. Also bowling, games rooms and bingo.

Festivals

Curitiba *p292, map p292*
Feb Ash Wed (half-day).
Mar/Apr Maundy Thu (half-day).
8 Sep Our Lady of Light.

Shopping

Curitiba *p292*

Curitiba is good for clothes and shoes.

Bookshop O Livro Técnico, Shopping Itália, R João Negrão and Mcal Deodoro.

Jewellers H Stern jewellers at Mueller Shopping Centre.

Souvenirs and handicrafts Feira de Arte e Artesanato, Praça Garibáldi, Sun 0900-1400. **Lojas de Artesanato,** Casa de Artesanato Centro, R Mateus Leme 22, T041-352 4021. **Lojas de Artesanato 'Feito Aquí'**, Dr Muricy 950, international airport and Shopping Mueller. Try **Lojas Leve Curitiba**, at several locations, R 24 Horas, Afonso Pena airport, Ópera de Arame, Jardim Botánico, Memorial de Curitiba. There is also an art market at **Praça Rui Barbosa.**

Foz do Iguaçu *p292, map p305*

Av Brasil is the main shopping street.

Bookshop Kunda Livraria Universitária, R Almte Barroso 1473, T045-523 4606. Guides and maps of the area, books on the local wildlife, novels, etc in several languages, including French and English.

Souvenirs and handicrafts Tres Fronteiras, Rodovia das Cataratas, Km 11. Large shop on road to falls, frequent stop on tours. Chocolates, and huge selection of crafts and jewellery, some of it overpriced.

Ciudad del Este *p307*

Prices are decidedly high for North American and European visitors. The **leather market** is well worth a visit, be sure to bargain. Don't buy perfume at tempting prices on the street, it's only coloured water. Make sure that shops that package your goods pack what you actually bought. Also watch the exchange rates if you're a short-term visitor from Argentina or Brazil.

Activities and tours

Curitiba *p292, map p294*

Tour operators BMP Turismo (American Express), R Brig Franco 1845, T041-224 7560.

Foz do Iguaçu *p305, map p305*

Helicopter tours

Helicopter tours over the falls leave from the **Hotel das Cataratas**, US$60 per person, 10 mins. Booked through any travel agency or direct with **Helisul**, T045-523 1190. Apart from disturbing visitors, the helicopters are also reported to present a threat to some bird species which are laying thinner-shelled eggs: the altitude has been increased, making the flight less attractive.

Tour operators

Beware of touts at the bus terminal who often overcharge for tours (they have been known to charge double the bus station price) and airport and be sure that the park entrance fees of around US$15 and all the transfer fees are included in the price. There are many travel agents on Av Brasil and in larger hotels. Most do not accept credit cards.

Acquatur, Av das Cataratas 3175, T045-3523 9554, www.acquaturturismo.com.br. Offer full range of tours in executive cars with bilingual guides and airport transfers.

Jaha Iguassu , Av Republica Argentina 926, T045-3572 4158 www.jahaiguassu.bio.br. Backpacker-orientated tours, hotel bookings and connections through to Rio, the Pantanal and the Amazon.

Macuco Safari, T045-3523 6475, www.macucosafari.com.br. Boat and forest tours suitable for all ages. Make sure you bring a waterproof bag for your camera.

Recommended guides

Chiderly Batismo Pequeno, R Almte Barroso 505, Foz, T045-3574 3367.

Ruth Campo Silva, STTC Turismo, **Hotel Bourbon**, Rodovia das Cataratas, T045-3574 3849, F574 3557 (American Express).

Wilson Engel, T045-3574 1367. Friendly, flexible.

Parque Nacional Iguazu *p304*

Puerto Iguazú

Aventura Náutica is a journey by launch along the lower Río Iguazú, US$15. **Safari Náutico**, a 4-km journey by boat above the falls, US$15. **Gran Aventura**, an 8-km ride through the jungle, with commentary on the flora and fauna in English and Spanish, followed by a boat trip on the rapids to the Devil's Throat, US$33. This trip is longer and better value than the Macuco Safari on the Brazilian side. The full day combines Safari Náutico with Aventura Náutica, US$30 (5 hrs), or US$45 with Gran Aventura (7 hrs).

Transport

Curitiba *p292, map p294*

Air

Bus no 208 goes to Afonso Pena airport every 25 mins, US$0.60, 30 mins from hotels Presidente and Araucária with a stop near the bus terminal. Flights to **Campinas**, **Cascavel**, **Foz do Iguaçu**, **Joinville**, **Londrina**, **Maringá**, **Porto Alegre**, **Rio de Janeiro** and **São Paulo**.

Airlines offices Bra, T011-6445 4310, www.voebra.com.br. **Gol**, T0300-789 2121, www.voegol.com.br. **Ocean Air**, T0300-789 8160, www.oceanair.com.br. **TAM**, at airport, T041-323 61812, www.tam.com.br. **Web Jet**, T0300-210 1234, www.webjet.com.br.

Bus

See also Ins and outs, page 292.

Local There are several route types on the integrated transport system; pick up a map for full details. There are 25 transfer terminals along the exclusive busways and trunk routes, allowing integration between all the different routes. **Express** are red, often articulated, and connect the transfer terminals to the city centre, pre-paid access, they use the 'tubo' bus stops. **Feeder** are orange conventional buses that connect the terminals to the surrounding neighbourhoods. **Interdistrict** green conventional or articulated buses run on circular routes, connecting transfer terminals and city districts without passing through the centre. **Direct** or **speedy** silver grey buses use the 'tubo' stations (3 km apart on average), to link the main districts and connect the surrounding municipalities with Curitiba. **Conventional** yellow buses operate on the normal road network between the surrounding municipalities, the Integration Terminals and the city centre. **City circular** white minibuses, **Linha Turismo**, circle the major transport terminals and points of interest in the traditional city centre area. US$3.50 (multi-ticket booklets available), every 30 mins from 0900-1700, except on Mon. First leaves from R das Flores, narrow street in front of McDonald's. 3 stops allowed.

Long distance Frequent buses to **São Paulo** (6 hrs, US$10.25-12.50) and **Rio de Janeiro** (12 hrs, US$25). To **Foz do Iguaçu**, 10 a day, 10 hrs, US$15, **Porto Alegre**, 10 hrs; **Florianópolis**, every 2 hrs, 4½ hrs, US$12; **Blumenau**, 4 hrs, US$6.50, 7 daily with Penha/Catarinense; good service to most destinations in Brazil. Pluma bus to **Buenos Aires** and to **Asunción**. TTL runs to **Montevideo**, 26 hrs, 0340 departure (*semi-cama*).

Car hire

Interlocadora, at the airport, T041-381 1370, F332 4648. **Localiza**, at the airport and Av Cândido de Abreu 336, T041-253 0330.

Ferry

Ferries from R Gen Carneiro (R da Praia) in front of the tourist information kiosk run to **Ilha do Mel**, at 0930 and 1500 (1 hr 40 mins, US$4). Alternatively, go to the small harbour in Paranaguá and ask for a boat to Ilha do Mel, US$15 one-way (no shade). Make sure the ferry goes to your chosen destination (Nova Brasília or Encantadas are the most developed areas).

Train

Passenger trains to **Paranaguá**, see below.

Curitiba to Paranaguá *p295*

Train There are 2 trains running from Curitiba to **Paranaguá**. The *Litorina* is a modern a/c railcar with on-board service and bilingual staff, which stops at the viewpoint at the Santuário da Nossa Senhora do Cadeado and Morretes. Hand-luggage only. Tickets can be bought 2 days in advance and cost US$50 one-way to Morretes and US$35 for the return leg to Curitiba. The ticket includes a drink and a sandwich. The windows don't open and are scratched, making pictures difficult. The *Trem* stops at Marumby and Morretes, buy tickets 2 days in advance they cost US$25 outward to Morretes and US$17 return, on tourist class; and US$32 and US$23 on executive class. The journey takes 4 hrs. Schedules change frequently; check times in advance with **Serra Verde Express**, T041-3323 4007, www.serraverdeexpress.com.br. Tickets are sold at the *rodoferroviária*, Portão 8, Curitiba, 0800-1800. Sit on the left-hand side on the journey from Curitiba. On cloudy days there's little to see on the higher parts. The train is usually crowded on Sat and Sun. Many travellers recommend returning by bus

Serra Verde train timetable

Curitiba–Paranaguá From Curitiba the train leaves daily at 0815, stopping at Marumby at 1035, Morretes at 1115 and arriving at Paranaguá at 1215. A litorina servcie runs at weekends, leaving Curitiba at 0915.
Paranaguá–Curitiba Monday to Friday from Morretes at 1500, stopping at Marumby at 1540 and Curitiba at 1800. At weekends the train runs from Paranaguá at 1400, stopping at Morretes at 1600, Marumby at 1640 and reaching Curitiba at 1900.

(1½ hrs, buy ticket immediately on arrival, US$6.50), if you do not want to stay 4½ hrs. A tour bus meets the train and offers a tour of town and return to Curitiba. For current train times see the table above.

Morretes *p296*
Bus The Paranaguá–Antonina bus stops at Morretes, 11 daily: to **Paranaguá**, US$1, to **Antonina** US$1.50. 12 buses daily to **Curitiba** US$2.

Paranaguá *p296*
Bus All operated by Graciosa. To **Curitiba**, US$3, many 1½ hrs (only the 1500 to Curitiba takes the old Graciosa road); direct to **Rio** at 1915, 15 hrs, US$23. 8 buses a day to **Guaratuba** (US$1, 2 hrs), **Caiobá** and **Matinhos**. The buses to Guaratuba go on the ferry, as do direct buses to Joinville, 0740, 1545.

Car hire Interlocadora, T041-423 4425, F332 4648.

Parque Nacional Vila Velha *p297*
Bus Take a bus from Curitiba to the national park, not to the town 20 km away. Ask the bus driver where you should get off. **Princesa dos Campos** bus from Curitiba at 0730 and 0930, 1½ hrs, US$5.65 (return bus passes park entrance at 1600); it may be advisable to go to **Ponta Grossa** and return to Curitiba from there. Last bus from Vila Velha car park to Ponta Grossa at 1800. Bus from Vila Velha at 1310, 1610 and 1800, US$1, 4½ km to turn-off to Furnas (another 15-min walk) and Lagoa Dourada (it's not worth walking from Vila Velha to Furnas because it's mostly uphill along the main road).

Ilha do Mel *p298, map p298*
Ferry See Ins and outs, page 299. Boats run from Encatadas and Nova Brasília to **Paranaguá** and **Pontal do Paraná** (Pontal do Sul). The last bus from Pontal do Paraná to Paranaguá leaves at 2200.

Foz do Iguaçu *p305, map p305*
Air Daily flights to **Rio**, **São Paulo**, **Curitiba** and other Brazilian cities.

Airline offices Rio Sul, R Jorge Sanways 779, T045-574 1680, freephone T0800-992994. **TAM**, R Rio Branco 640, T045-523 8500 (offers free transport to Ciudad del Este for its flights, all cross-border documentation dealt with). **Varig**, Av Juscelino Kubitschek 463, T045-523 2111. **Vasp**, Av Brasil 845, T045-523 2212.

Bus For transport to the falls, see page 301. To get to the bus station take any bus that says '*rodoviária*'. To **Curitiba**, Pluma, Sulamericana, 9-10 hrs, 3 daily, paved road, US$15; to **Guaíra** via Cascavel only, 5 hrs, US$10; to **Florianópolis**, Catarinense and Reunidas, US$28, 14 hrs; Reunidas to **Porto Alegre**, US$30; to **São Paulo**, 16 hrs, Pluma US$30, *executivo* 6 a day, plus 1 *leito*; to **Rio** 22 hrs, several daily, US$38. To **Asunción**, Pluma, RYSA (direct at 1430), US$11.

Car hire Avis, airport, T045-523 1510. **Localiza** at airport, T045-529 6300, and Av Juscelino Kubitschek 2878, T045-522 1608. **Unidas**, Av Santos Dumont, 1515, near airport, T/F045-339 0880.

Taxi Only good value for short distances when you are carrying all your luggage.

Border with Argentina *p306*

Bus Buses to **Puerto Iguazú** run every 20 mins from the Terminal Urbana in Foz, crossing the frontier bridge; 30 mins' journey, **Três Fronteiras**, US$1.50, or 2 reais. If you have to get out of the bus to get your passport stamped at immigration, the bus waits. To get to the Argentine side of the falls without going into Puerto Iguazú, get off the bus from the frontier bridge at the first traffic lights and cross the road for the bus to the falls. To **Buenos Aires**, Pluma daily 1200, US$46. It is cheaper to go to **Posadas** via Paraguay.

Taxi From Foz do Iguaçu to the border, waiting for Brazilian immigration, US$10; Foz-Argentina US$35, US$45 to **Hotel Sheraton Iguazú**.

Ciudad del Este *p307*

Air To **Asunción**, Arpa, 3 flights Mon-Sat, 1 on Sun. Also TAM daily en route to São Paulo.

Airline offices TAM, Edif SABA, Monseñor Rodríguez.

Bus The terminal is on the southern outskirts. No 4 bus from the centre goes there, US$0.50 (taxi US$3.50). Many buses (US$17.50 *rápido*, 4½ hrs, at night only; US$10 *común*, 6 hrs) to and from **Asunción**. Nuestra Señora and Rysa recommended. To **Encarnación** (for Posadas and Argentina), along a fully paved road, frequent, 3 hrs, US$7.50 (cheaper than via Foz do Iguaçu).

To Brazil International bus from outside the terminal to the new long-distance terminal (*rodoviária*) outside Foz. Local buses from the terminal run along Av Adrián Jara and go to the city terminal (*terminal urbana*) in **Foz** every 15 mins, 0600-2000, US$0.65. Most buses do not wait at immigration, so disembark to get your exit stamp, walk across the bridge (10 mins) and obtain your entry stamp; keep your ticket and continue to Foz on the next bus free. Paraguayan taxis cross freely to Brazil (US$20), but it is cheaper to walk across the bridge and then take a taxi, bargain hard. You can pay in either currency.

To Argentina Direct buses to **Puerto Iguazú**, frequent service by several companies from outside the terminal, US$2, you need to get Argentine and Paraguayan stamps (not Brazilian); the bus does not wait so keep your ticket for the next bus.

Directory

Curitiba *p292, map p294*

Banks Bradesco, R 15 de Novembro, Visa ATM. Plus or Cirrus-associated credit cards can be used at **Citibank**, R Mcal Deodoro 711, or at Buenos Aires 305 near Shopping Curitiba. **Credicard**, R Saldanha Marinho 1439, Bigorrillo. Cash with MasterCard. **Diplomata**, R Pres Faria 145 in the arcade. **Transoceânica**, R Mcal Deodoro 532, English and German spoken. **Triangle Turismo Travel**, Praça Gen Osório 213. Cash and TCs.

Morretes *p296*

Banks Banco do Brasil, does not officially change money, but friendly staff will sometimes do so. It has an ATM.

Paranaguá *p296*

Banks Banco do Brasil, Largo C Alcindino 27. **Bradesco**, R Faria Sobrinho 188. **Câmbio**, R Faria Sobrinho. For cash.

Foz do Iguaçu *p305, map p305*

Banks There are plenty of banks and travel agents on Av Brasil. **Banco do Brasil**, Av Brasil 1377 has ATM. High commission for TCs. **Bradesco**, Av Brasil 1202. Cash advance on Visa. **Banco 24 Horas** at Oklahoma petrol station. **HSBC**, Av Brasil 1151, ATM. **Embassies and consulates** Argentina, Travessa Eduardo Bianchi 26, T045-574 2969 (Mon-Fri 1000-1430). **France**, R Federico Engels 48, Villa Yolanda T045-574 3693. **Paraguay**, Bartolomeu de Gusmão 480, T045-523 2898. **Internet** Boulevard, Av das Cataratas 1118, T045-523 4245. **Café Internet**, R Rebouças 950, T/F045-523 2122, US$1.50 per hr; also phone, fax and photocopying. Ask for fastest machine, Mon-Sat 0900-2300 and Sun afternoon. **Café Pizzanet**, R Rio Branco, 412, corner with Av Juscelino Kubitschek, US$2 per hr. Pizzeria, fax, phone, photocopier. **Zipfoz.com**, R Barão do Rio Branco 412, corner with Av Juscelino Kubitschek. Smart, a/c, US$1.50 per hr. **Laundry** Londres Lavanderia, R Reboucas, 711, only US$1.50 per kg, open Sat. **Medical services** There is a free 24-hr clinic on Av Paraná, 1525, opposite Lions Club, T045-573 1134. Few buses so take taxi or walk (about 25 mins). **Post office** Praça Getúlio Vargas 72. **Telephone** Telepar on Edmundo de Barros.

Banks Local banks open Mon-Fri 0730-1100. Dollars can be changed into reais in town. **Banco Holandés Unido**, cash on MasterCard, 5% commission. Several exchange houses: **Cambio Guaraní**, Monseñor Rodríguez, changes TCs for US$0.50. Branch on Friendship Bridge has good rates for many currencies, including dollars and reais. **Tupi Cambios**, Adrián Jara 351. **Cambios Chaco**, Adrián Jara y Curupayty. **Casa de cambio** rates are better than street rates. Money changers (not recommended) operate at the bus terminal, but not at the Brazilian end of the Friendship Bridge. **Embassies and consulates** Brazil, C Pampliega 337, corner of Pai Perez, T061-5615 0984, F5616 3283.
Telecommunications Antelco, Alejo García and Pai Pérez, near the centre on the road to the bus terminal.

Santa Catarina

→ *Population: 5.5 million*

Santa Catarina is famous above all for its beaches, especially those around the cities of Florianópolis and Laguna. These are among the most beautiful in southern Brazil, and have the best surf in the country. The state is also famous for its beautiful people – supermodel Gisele Bundchen is from Santa Catarina. Like many Santa Catarenses she defies the stereotype and is tall, blonde and blue eyed. For this was an area that saw much northern-European immigration in the 20th century. Immigrant communities still give a unique personality to a number of the state's towns and districts where German and Ukrainian are spoken as much as Portuguese. Every year one million people visit the Oktoberfest in Blumenau. The highlands, just in from the coast, are among the coldest in Brazil and are covered in remnant Aracauria pine forest, a tree related to the Chilean monkey puzzle. Except for the summer months of January and February, Santa Catarina's beaches are pleasant and uncrowded. The best months to visit are March, April and May before the water gets too cold for swimming.

As well as each region having its own climate and scenery, Santa Catarina also has a distinctive culture depending on its immigrants. The Portuguese from the Azores settled along the coast, the Germans moved along the Itajaí Valley, the Italians headed for the south and into Rio Grande do Sul, while in the north there are Ukrainians, Japanese, Africans, Hispanics and Indians. Each group maintains its traditions and festivals, its architecture, food and language or accent. The vast majority of people today can trace their family to these ethnic origins. » *For Sleeping, Eating and other listings, see pages 329-336.*

Florianópolis » pp329-336.

→ *Phone code: 048. Colour map 5, B5. Population: 345,000.*

Halfway along the coast of Santa Catarina is the state capital Florianópolis, founded in 1726 as the gateway to Ilha de Santa Catarina. The natural beauty of the island, beaches and bays make Florianópolis a magnet for holidaymakers in summer. The southern beaches are good for swimming, the eastern ones for surfing, but be careful of the undertow. 'Floripa' is accepted as a shortened version of Florianópolis, with the people known as 'Floripans', although they like to call themselves 'Ilhéus', or islanders.

Ins and outs

Getting there International and domestic flights arrive at **Hercílio Luz airport** ⓘ *Av Deomício Freitas, 12 km from town, T048-236 0879.* There are car hire booths, shops, cafes and a small tourist information office in the airport. Aeroporto/Corredor Sudoeste buses run between the airport terminal and the **local rodoviária** ⓘ *R Antônio Luz 260,*

Forte de Santa Bárbara, T048-3324 1415, in the city centre, every 20 minutes until midnight. A taxi to the city costs around US$20.

The main *rodoviária*, **Rita Maria** ⓘ *15 mins' walk from the centre, Av Paulo Fontes 1101, T048-3212 3100*, is served by buses from all major cities in the south and southeast, with frequent connections to Curitiba, Porto Alegre, São Paulo, Rio and Santos. There are also buses between the city and Joinville, Blumenau, Gramado, Foz do Iguaçu and connections to Uruguay and Argentina. » *See Transport, page 335.*

Getting around The city is fairly small and compact, quite hilly, but easy and safe to walk around. Standard buses, and more expensive yellow microbuses, run to nearly every important point on the island. There are buses to the eastern and southern

Florianópolis

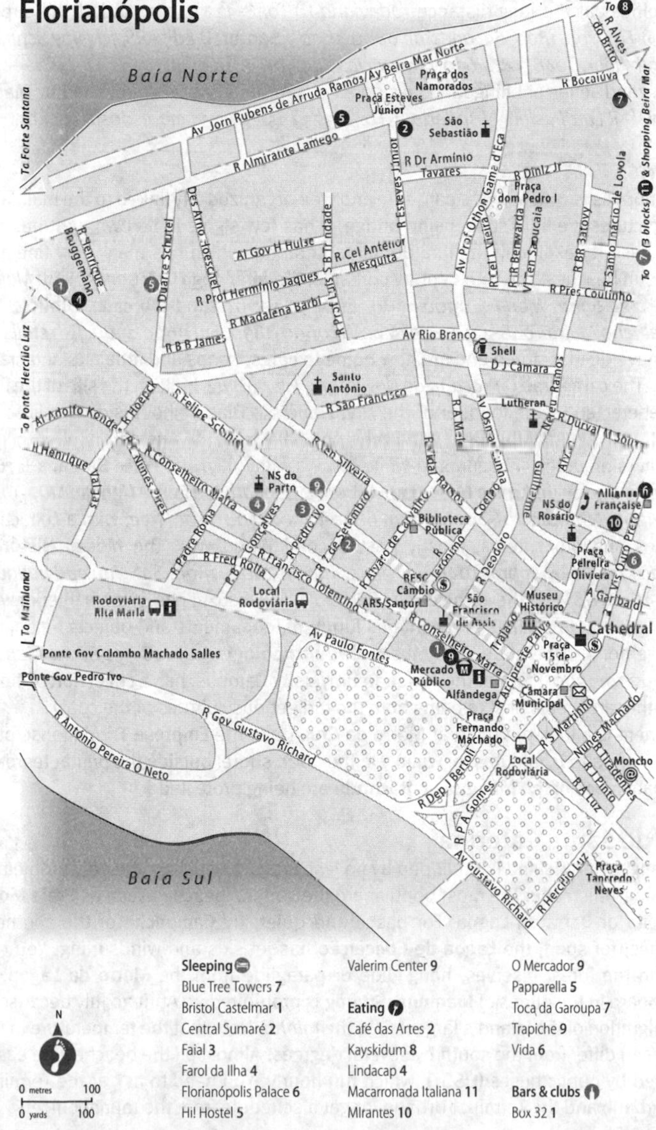

beaches (beaches and sights like Joaquina, Lagoa, Lagoa do Peri and Pantano do Sul) from the local *rodoviária* on Rua Antônio Luz 260. Buses to the north of the island leave from another local *rodoviária* on Rua Francisco Tolentino immediately in front of the long-distance *rodoviária*. There are also combis to the beaches leaving from Praça 15 de Novembro in the city centre.

Tourist information The main **tourist office** ⓘ *Mercado Público, 3rd booth along from R Arcipreste Paiva, T048-3244 5822, Mon-Fri 0800-1200, 1330-1800, Sat and Sun 0800-1200, www.florianopolisturismo.sc.gov.br*, has maps and some information in English. **Setur** ⓘ *Portal Turístico de Florianópolis, mainland end of the bridge, Av Eng Max de Souza 236, Coqueiros, T048-3244 5822, Mon-Fri 0800-2000, Sat and Sun 0800-1800*, maps available, free (www.guiafloripa.com.br). There are also offices at the long-distance *rodoviária* ⓘ *T048-3223 2777*, and at the airport ⓘ *Mon-Fri 0700-1800, Sat and Sun 0800-1800*. **Santur** ⓘ *Edif ARS, R Felipe Schmidt 249, 9th floor, T048-3224 6300, www.ciasc.gov.br*, is helpful.

A good series of bilingual books on all of southern Brazil is published by **Mares do Sul** ⓘ *R Luiz Pasteur, Trindade, T/F048-3333 1544, www.maresdosul.com.br.*

Sights

Florianópolis is a pleasant, clean, safe and well-organized city linked to the mainland by a picturesque little suspension bridge. It has few sights in its own right but is a good base for exploring the Ilha de Santa Catarina, which has many very fine and lively surf beaches. The 19th-century port area, the **Alfândega** ⓘ *R Conselheiro Mafra, T048-3224 6082, Mon-Fri 0900-1900, Sat 0900-1200*, and **Mercado Público** ⓘ *R Conselheiro Mafra T048-225 3200, Mon-Fri 0600-1830, Sat 0600-1300, fish stalls on Sun*, have been restored and are now home to cafés, shops and little arts and crafts stalls. The **cathedral** ⓘ *Praça 15 de Novembro,* (1773), was built on the site of the first chapel erected by the founder of the city, Francisco Dias Velho. Inside is a life-size sculpture in wood of the flight into Egypt, originally from the Austrian Tyrol.

There are a few museums to while away a rainy day. The **Forte Santana** (1763) houses a **Museu de Armas Major Lara Ribas** ⓘ *beneath the Ponte Hercílio Luz, T048-229 6263, Mon 1400-1800, Tue-Sun 0830-1200, 1400-1800, free*, with a collection of guns and other items, mostly post Second World War. The **Museu Histórico** ⓘ *Praça 15 de Novembro, T048-221 3504, Tue-Fri 1000- 1800, Sat, Sun and holidays 1000-1600, US$1*, in the 18th-century Palácio Cruz e Souza, has a lavish interior with highly decorated ceilings and contains furniture, documents and objects belonging to governors of the state. The **Museu de Antropólogia** ⓘ *T048-331 8821, Mon-Fri 0900-1200, 1300-1700*, at the Trindade University Campus, has a collection of stone and other archaeological remains from the indigenous cultures of the coast.

There is a look-out point at **Morro da Cruz** (take the **Empresa Trindadense** bus, US$0.60, waits 15 minutes, or walk). On the north shore, outside the perimeter road, the mangroves of the **Mangue do Itacorubi** are being protected.

Ilha de Santa Catarina

The long, skinny island is scalloped by no less than 42 beaches; the only problem is choosing which one. The most popular are the surfers' beaches such as **Praia Mole, Joaquina** or **Barra da Lagoa**. For peace and quiet, try **Campeche** or the southern beaches; for sport, the **Lagoa de Conceição** has jet skis and windsurfing. You can walk in the forest reserves, hang-glide or paraglide from the **Morro da Lagoa**, or sandboard in the dunes of **Joaquina**. Surfing is prohibited 30 April-30 July because of the migration of the island's largest fish, the *tainha*. Note that the temperature in the north can differ from the south by several degrees. Almost all the beaches are easily reached by public buses (US$1), which run hourly. You need to ask at the Terminal Interurbano and the Terminal Urbano, or get a schedule from the tourist office.

Lagoa da Conceição is worth visiting for its beaches, sand dunes, fishing and the church of Nossa Senhora da Conceição (1730). It also has a market every Wednesday and Saturday. For tandem hang-gliding, contact **Lift Sul Vôo Livre** (T048-232 0543). From the Centro da Lagoa on the bridge there are daily boat trips to Costa da Lagoa which run until about 1830, check when you buy your ticket, US$4 return. The service is used mostly by the local people who live around the lake and have no other form of public transport. The ride is spectacular and there is a charming restaurant to greet you at the end of a thirsty journey. A recommended meal is the local fish, *tainha*, with salad, chips and an abundance of rice.

On the east of the island at **Barra da Lagoa** is a pleasant fishing village and beach, lively in the summer season, with plenty of good restaurants. You can walk across the wooden suspension bridge to one overlooking the bay, a spectacular setting for a meal. It is reached by **Transol** bus No 403 (every 15 minutes from Terminal Urbano, 55 minutes, US$0.75). The same bus goes to beaches at **Mole**, which is a soft-sand beach, good for walking. South of Mole is **Joaquina**, where surfing championships are held in January.

In the north of the island, there is a pleasant fishing village at **Ponta das Canas**, and a good beach at **Canasvieiras** with many watersports on offer (bus US$0.75). Praia Brava, a 1-km walk to the east, is good for surfing. Just south of here, is **Praia dos Ingleses** (bus 602), which gets its name from an English ship that sank in 1700. Dunes separate it from **Praia Santinho**, where Carijó inscriptions can be seen on the cliffs. Both are surfing beaches. Other northern beaches are **Jureré**, **Daniela** and **Forte**. Overlooking the latter, **Forte São José da Ponta Grossa** ⓘ *US$1.50*, is beautifully restored and has a small museum about its history.

On the west side of the island, north of Florianópolis, you can visit the 'city of bees' and **Museo da Apicultura** (a apiary museum), and the **church of Santo Antonio Lisboa**. Take Trindadense bus No 331 or any bus going north to the turn-off on the way to Sambaqui beach and fishing village (fare US$0.65).

In the south of the island is **Praia do Campeche**, 30 minutes by bus (Pantano do Sul or Costa de Dentro) from Florianópolis. Offshore is an island with a beach that is good for diving. Just inland from **Praia da Armação** is **Lagoa do Peri**, a protected area. After Armação look for a bar by the roadside called **Lanchonette e Bar Surf**. Just before the bar there is a road to the left. Walk up a red clay path and after about 200 m you should see a path (unsignposted) on the left, leading up into the hills. A steady walk of up to two hours will lead you over two *montes* with a fabulous view from the top, down to **Praia da Lagoinha de Leste**. This is a beach rarely visited by the hoards and you can get away from the crowds even in the summer months. Camping is permitted. Further south is **Pantano do Sul**, an unspoilt and relaxed

Ilha de Santa Catarina

Sights
Forte Nossa Senhora da Conceição 1
Forte São José da Ponta Grossa 2

fishing village with a long, curved beach and lovely views across to the Três Irmãs islands. There are several pousadas, bars and restaurants, though not much nightlife. For **Praia dos Naufragados**, take a bus to Caieira da Barra do Sul and walk for an hour through fine forests. **Forte Nossa Senhora da Conceição** is on a small island just offshore. It can be seen from the lighthouse near Praia dos Naufragados or take a boat trip with **Scuna Sul** (see Activities and tours, page 334) from Florianópolis.

Around Florianópolis

The BR-282 heads west from the capital to Lages (see page 329). About 12 km along are the hot springs at **Caldas da Imperatriz** (41°C) and **Águas Mornas** (39°C). The latter are open to the public Monday to Friday morning only. Both have good spa hotels (see page 324).

The **Parque Estadual da Serra do Tabuleiro**, just south of the BR-282, is the largest protected area in Santa Catarina, covering 87,405 ha, or nearly 1% of the state. Apart from its varied and luxuriant flora, which is home to many birds and animals, it is also important to Florianópolis for its water supply. There is a small **reserve**ⓘ *daily 0800-1700*, near the park headquarters (near Paulo Lopes, Km 252, BR-101), where animals and birds previously in captivity are rehabilitated before returning to the wild.

North of Florianópolis

» *pp329-336.*

Porto Belo and around

→ *Phone code: 047. Colour map 5, B5. www.portobelo.com.br.*

The coast north of Florianópolis is dotted with resorts. They include **Porto Belo**, a fishing village on the north side of a peninsula settled in 1750 by Azores islanders, with a calm beach and a number of hotels and restaurants. Around the peninsula are wilder beaches reached by rough roads: **Bombas**, **Bombinhas** (both with the same sort of accommodation as Porto Belo), **Quatro Ilhas** (quieter, good surfing, 15 minutes' walk from Bombinhas), **Mariscal** and, on the southern side, **Zimbros** (or Cantinho). Many of the stunning beaches around Bombinhas are untouched, accessible only on foot or by boat. Its clear waters are marvellous for diving.

Southwest of Porto Belo, reached by turning off the BR-101 at Tijucas and going west for 30 km, is **Nova Trento**, a small town in a valley first colonized by Italians and still showing heavy Italian influence. The local cuisine includes cheese, salami and wine such as you might find in Italy; there are several Italian restaurants and wine producers where you can buy *vinho artesanal*. There is a good view of the Tijucas valley and as far as the sea (on a clear day) from the **Morro da Cruz**, at 525 m. West of Porto Belo is **Praia de Perequê**, with a handful of hotels on the long beautiful beach.

Itapema, 60 km from Florianópolis, is another former fishing village on a wide sweep of sandy beach now dominated by tourism. In high season the town accommodates around 300,000 visitors. The **Plaza Itapema Resert e Spa**, T047-368 2222, is all-inclusive and the best such establishment on this part of the coast. Around the headland there are several smaller and quieter beaches, **Praia Grossa** being one of the best, with good surf.

Camboriú

→ *Phone code: 047. Colour map 5, B5. Population: 42,000.*

Some 80 km north of Florianópolis is Camboriú, once beautiful, but now the most concentrated urban development on Brazil's southern coast. From 15 December to late February it is very crowded and expensive, and in low season it is popular with retired people. A few kilometres south, at **Lojas Apple**, there is **Parque Cyro Gevaerd**, a museum (archaeology, oceanography, fishing, local arts and crafts), zoo and aquarium; and **Meia Praia**, which is quieter and cleaner than Camboriú. A *teleférico* (cable car) has been built to **Praia Laranjeiras**, previously deserted (US$5 return from Barra Sul shopping centre to Laranjeiras via Mata Atlântica station). Between Itajaí and Camboriú is the beautiful, deserted and rough beach of **Praia Brava**. Note that from mid-July to mid-August it can be chilly.

The resort is served by direct buses from Florianópolis, Joinville and Blumenau. International buses from Uruguay to São Paulo pass through here. There are a huge number of modern hotels, four-star and downwards, and aparthotels. From March to November it is easy to rent furnished apartments by the day or week. Turning up and finding a room is very straightforward.

Itajaí and around → *Phone code: 047. Colour map 5, B5. Population: 135,000.*

At the mouth of the Rio Itajaí-Açu, some 94 km up the coast from Florianópolis, is the most important port in Santa Catarina. It has thriving fishing and shipbuilding industries and is the centre of a district largely colonized by Germans and Italians, although the town itself was founded by immigrants from the Azores.

Despite the port, tourism is heavily promoted and in summer the population triples. Itajaí celebrates a **Marejada Festival** in October in honour of Portugal and the sea. It is held in the Centro de Promoções Itajaí Tur, where there are musical and folkloric festivities, a pavilion for dancing and shows, and a pavilion for food (with lots of different ways of preparing *bacalhau* and masses of seafood). For **tourist information**, contact the **Centro de Promoções Itajaí Tur** ⓘ *T047-348 1080*.

The local beaches are **Atalaia, Geremias** and **Cabeçudas** (within walking distance, quiet and small), but within the municipality there is also **Praia do Morcego** which is considered a health resort because of the high mineral content of the water. There is also a cave here, the **Caverna do Morcego**, about which there are many myths and legends.

About 50 km southwest of Itajaí is the **Caverna de Botuverá**, which you enter through a dripping tunnel, which can flood in the wet season. The first gallery is like a cathedral, with stalactites and rock formations, one of which is called 'the organ', and the guide will play a sort of tune for you. Not all the galleries are fully explored. Pillars of 20 m have been found; each metre of rock taking 10,000 years to form. To get to Botuverá, take the road to Brusque off the BR-101, where there is tourist information and they can give you directions and other details.

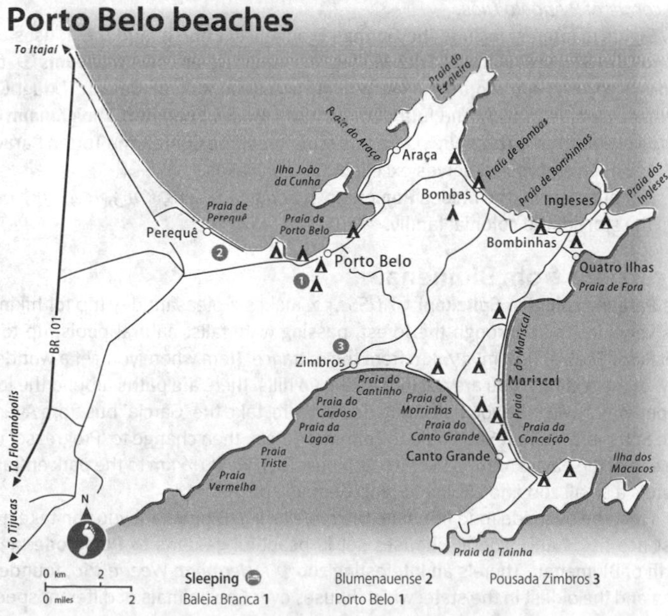

Penha

→ *Population: 15,000.*

About 20 km north of Itajaí is Penha, another resort along the BR-101, with a broad, curved, sandy beach with rocky headlands at either end, offering smaller coves for swimming, surfing and fishing. The town was founded by Portuguese fishermen in the 18th century and fishing is still important as anywhere else along the coast. Tourism took off in the 1970s and during the high season the population rises to 100,000. Its major claim to fame is the **Beto Carrero World**, one of the largest theme parks in the world, which opened in 1991 on Praia de Armação. Penha even offers themed shopping, at the **Shopping Temático** on Avenida Eugênio Krause, where you can visit different countries in different ages. There are several festivals and events in Penha (see page 334) as well as hotels, pousadas and camping.

Other resorts north of Itajaí include **Piçarras**, with sandy beaches interspersed with rocky headlands (ideal for fishing, several hotels), and **Barra Velha**, with a good, cheap hotel, **Hotel Mirante**, which has a restaurant, and two more expensive hotels.

Blumenau

» *pp329-336.*

→ *Phone code: 047. Colour map 5, B4. Population: 262,000.*

Blumenau is in a prosperous district settled mostly by Germans. A clean, orderly city with almost caricatured Germanic architecture, the German *enxaimel* design (exposed beams and brickwork) typifies some of the more famous buildings such as the **Mayor's** Residence, the **Molemann Shopping Centre**, which resembles a medieval German castle, and the **Museum of the Colonial Family** ⓘ *Av Duque de Caxias 78, Mon-Fri 0800-1130, 1330-1730, Sat morning only, US$0.15*, (1868), the German immigrant museum. Blumenau offers a charming alternative to the less-organized Brazilian way of life.

The first Germans to arrive were the philosopher Herman Bruno Otto Blumenau and 16 other German explorers, who sailed up the river in 1850. Work began to build schools, houses and the first plantations, and the city soon became a notable textile centre. Today, high-tech and electronics industries are replacing textiles as the town's economic mainstay. There is a helpful **tourist office** ⓘ *R 15 de Novembro, on the corner of R Ângelo Dias.*

Sights of interest include the **German Evangelical Church**, and the houses of **Dr Bruno Otto Blumenau** and of **Fritz Müller**. The latter two are now **museums** ⓘ *both 0800-1800*, and are worth a visit. Müller, a collaborator of Darwin, bought the Blumenau estate in 1897 and founded the town. **Museu Ervin Kurt Theichmann** ⓘ *R 15 de Novembro 791, T047-387 0282*, has sculptures. The **Confeitaria Torten Paradies** ⓘ *R 15 de Novembro 211*, serves excellent German cakes.

Just out of town, the **Museu Pomerano** ⓘ *Rodovia SC 418, Km 3, T047-387 0477*, tells the story of the colonial family.

Excursions from Blumenau

The **Parque Ecológico Spitzkopf** ⓘ *US$1.50*, makes a pleasant day trip for hiking. It has very nice trails through the forest, passing waterfalls, natural pools, up to the Spitzkopf Peak at 936 m, 5½ km from the entrance, from where you get a wonderful view of the region. If you are not into hiking up hills, there are paths around the lower slopes which will take you half a day. To get there, take the 'Garcia' bus from Avenida 7 de Setembro via Rua São Paulo to Terminal Garcia, then change to 'Progresso' until the end of the paved road, US$0.60 each bus. Then walk 1½ km to the park entrance, There's a small zoo and cabins to rent (German spoken).

From the riverside road opposite the *prefeitura* in Blumenau, you can take a bus past rice fields and wooden houses set in beautiful gardens to **Pomerode**, 33 km north of Blumenau. There's an interesting **zoo** ⓘ *R Hermann Weege 160*, founded in 1932 and the oldest in the state, which houses over 600 animals of different species.

Blumenau's Oktoberfest

In 1983, Blumenau suffered a great flood. After its destructive impact, the idea was born to introduce a German-style 'traditional' Oktoberfest beer-festival to motivate people to reconstruct the city. The festival celebrating German music, beer and the German way of life was started in 1984 here, and was expected to become the second largest in the world after Munich's (bands come from Germany for the event). It is the second largest street party in Brazil, after Carnaval. It is set next to the São Francisco de Assis National Park and usually held in the first half of October. During the day the narrow streets are packed around the Molemann Shopping Centre, which is where many locals like to begin their festivities before the Oktoberfest Pavilion opens. The centre contains a mixture of bars, live music and, of course, *chopp*.

At 1900 the doors open and you will find four decorated pavilions, each holding different events from drinking competitions to the 'sausage Olympics', all accompanied by non-stop traditional German music. The cultural pavilion holds traditional dress and cake-making competitions, as well as getting the audience involved in the singing, which grows steadily worse as the evening rolls on. There is also a fun fair and folk dancing shows. Food around the stalls is German and half a litre of *chopp* will cost you around US$2. Brazilian popular bands are slowly being introduced, much to the disapproval of the older inhabitants. Visitors report it is worth attending on weekday evenings but weekends are too crowded. It is repeated, but called a 'summer festival', in the three weeks preceding Carnaval.

The tourist office can be contacted on T047-387 2627. Next door to the Prefeitura Municipal is the **Associação dos Artistas e Artesãos de Pomerode**, where you can find exhibitions of local arts and crafts and a shop. The north German dialect of Plattdeutsch is still spoken here and there are several folkloric groups keeping alive the music and dance of their ancestors: *Alpino Germânico, Pomerano, Edelweiss* and *Belgard*. Shooting and hunting is also traditional in the area and there are 16 **Clubes de Caça e Tiro** which are active at all festivities. The men compete for the title of **Rei do Tiro Municipal** in July and the women compete for the **Rainha do Tiro Municipal** in November. See also Activities and tours, page 334.

A half-day excursion to **Gaspar** (15 km) allows you to visit the cathedral, **Igreja Matriz São Pedro Apóstolo**, set high above the river. To get here take a **Verde Vale** bus from the stop outside the huge supermarket on Rua 7 de Setembro in the centre of Blumenau (for tickets, see Transport page 335). There are two water parks in Gaspar with water slides and other amusements: **Parque Aquático Cascanéia** ⓘ *R José Patrocínio dos Santos, T047-339 0690*, with chalets, parking, restaurants, and **Cascata Carolina** ⓘ *Estrada Geral da Carolina-Belchior Alto, T047-339 0779*, with water coming straight from the rocks.

Further west along the Rio Itajaí–Açu, around Ibirama, the river is good for whitewater rafting. You can take a break between rapids to bathe in the waterfalls.

Blumenau to Iguaçu

An alternative to taking a direct bus from Florianópolis or Blumenau to Iguaçu, is to travel through rich and interesting farming country in Santa Catarina and Rio Grande do Sul, stopping at the following places: **Joaçaba**, a town of German immigrants, in the centre of the Vale do Contestado (for information, T047-522 3000); **Erexim**, which has a strong *gaúcho* influence; **Iraí**, a town with thermal springs, situated in an Italian immigrant area. The latter is good for semi-precious stones. From any of these places you can go to Pato Branco and Cascavel and thence to Foz do Iguaçu.

Two hours from Joaçaba is **Treze Tílias**, a village where 19th-century Tyrolean dialect is still spoken and the immigrant culture is perfectly preserved. It was settled in 1933 by a group led by Andreas Thaler, who had been the Austrian Minister of Agriculture. Dairy farming is the main economic activity and children are taught German and Portuguese in school. The style of architecture has been lifted straight from the Alps and the city prides itself on being in the mountains, with all the associated romanticizing of European mountain life found in such resorts throughout Brazil. It may get a bit chilly but it never snows. The major festivity of the year is the four-day **Tirolerfest** in October, celebrating the customs of the Tirol, with food, sculpture and art. There's **tourist information** ⓘ *Praça Andreas Thaler 25, T/F047-537 0176*, and buses run to and from Joaçaba and Blumenau.

São Francisco do Sul → *Phone code: 047. Population: 27,000.*

At the mouth of the Baia de Babitonga, São Francisco do Sul is the port for the town of **Joinville** (see below), 45 km inland at the head of the Rio Cachoeira. It is the country's third oldest city (Binot Paulmier de Gonneville landed here in 1504), after Porto Seguro in Bahia and São Vicente in Rio de Janeiro. The colonial centre has over 150 historical sites and has been protected since 1987. An interesting **Museu Nacional do Mare** ⓘ *R Manual Lourenço de Andrade, T047-444 1868, Tue-Fri 0900-1800, Sat and Sun 1100-1800, US$1*, reflects Brazil's seafaring history. The **cathedral**, Nossa Senhora da Graça (1719), still has its original walls made with sand, shells and whale oil. The **Museu Histórico de São Francisco do Sul** ⓘ *R Coronel Carvalho*, is in the 18th-century Cadeia Pública. There is a **tourist information** desk in the cinema behind the Prefeitura. Not far from the historical centre is the modern port. Petrobrás has an oil refinery here.

There are about 13 excellent **beaches** nearby, such as **Ubatuba**, **Enseada**, which has good nightlife, hotels, pensions and three campsites, **Prainha** (surf championships are held here) and **Cápri**. Quieter waters can be found at **Ingleses**, **Figueiras**, **Paulas** and **Calixtos** but, being in the bay, the sea is polluted. A ferry crosses the Baia de Babitonga from Bairro Laranjeiras, 8 km from the centre, to Estaleiro, 30 minutes. The historic town of **Vila da Glória** (6 km from Estaleiro) can be visited. For schooner trips contact T047-974 7266. Take mosquito repellent.

Joinville » pp329-336.

→ *Phone code: 047. Colour map 5, B5. Population: 430,000.*

The state's largest city lies 2 km from the main coastal highway (BR-101), within a two-hour drive of Curitiba and Florianópolis. Joinville is known as the 'city of the princes' for its historical connections with royalty. It is also nicknamed the 'city of flowers', and even 'Manchester Catarinense'. The large German population gives it a distinctly European feel, however there is not much reason for visitors to stop here. **Tourist information** ⓘ *corner of Praça Nereu Ramos with R do Príncipe, T047-433 1511*, and at **Promotur** ⓘ *Centreventos, Av José Vieira 315, sala 20, T047-423 2633, www.promotur.com.br and www.joinville.sc.gov.br.*

Sights

The **Museu Nacional da Imigração e Colonização** ⓘ *R Rio Branco 229, Tue-Fri 0900-1800*, in the Palácio dos Príncipes, has a collection of objects and tools from the original German settlement and other items of historical interest. **Arquivo Histórico de Joinville** ⓘ *Av Hermann August Lepper 65, T047-422 2154, Mon-Fri 0830-1200, 1330-2000*, houses a collection of documents dating from the town's foundation.

The **Museu Arqueológico do Sambaqui** ⓘ *R Dona Francisca 600, T047-433 0114, Tue-Sun 0900-1200, 1400-1800*, has a collection dating back to 5000 BC, with an exhibition devoted to the life of the indigenous people who built the sambaqui shell mounds along the south coast of Brazil (see page 297). There are also two archaeological reserves: **Sambaqui do Rio Comprido**, carbon dated to BC 2865, and **Sambaqui Morro do Ouro.**

The **Alameda Brustlein**, better known as the **Rua das Palmeiras**, is an impressive avenue of palm trees, leading to the **Palácio dos Príncipes.** The trees were planted in 1873 by Frederico Brustlein with seeds brought in 1867 by Louis Niemeyer. The **railway station** ⓘ *R Leite Ribeiro, T047-422 2550*, dates from 1906 and is a fine example of the German style of architecture, and the **Mercado Municipal** ⓘ *Praça Hercílio Luz*, is in the *enxaimel* style. At the other end of the spectrum, the **cathedral**, on Avenida Juscelino Kubitscheck with Rua do Príncipe, is futuristic with spectacular windows recounting the story of man. The **Cemitério dos Imigrantes** ⓘ *R 15 de Novembro 978, Mon-Fri 1400-*

Joinville

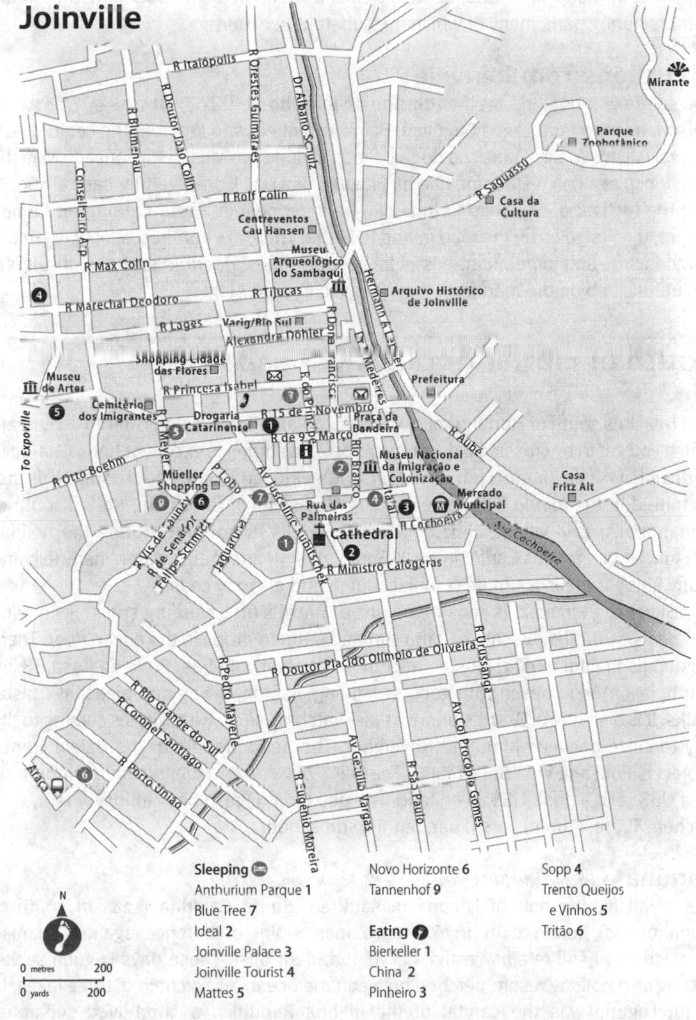

 1730, is interesting; the attached **Casa da Memória do Imigrante** has information on the town's history, with audiovisual and documentary displays.

The **Parque Zoobotânico** ⓘ *R Pastor Guilherme Rau 462, T047-433 1230, Tue-Sun 0900-1800, 15 mins' walk in the direction of Mirante*, is a good zoo and park, with many local species of birds and animals and a children's park. From here it is 25 minutes' walk to the **Mirante** for a beautiful view of the town and the bay. The tower on the top is at an altitude of 250 m and you can walk up a spiral staircase on the outside for a panoramic view. An **orchid farm** ⓘ *R Helmuth Fallgatter 2547, opposite the Terminal de Integração Tupy, Boa Vista, 0800-1200, 1330-1800*, is open to the public for sales or just to look around.

At **Expoville,** 4 km from the centre on BR-101 (continuation of 15 de Novembro), is an exhibition of Joinville's industry, although it is used for many other exhibitions and festivals as well. The new, multi-functional **Centreventos Cau Hansen** has been built to house sporting activities, shows, festivals, conferences and other events. It is home to the first Bolshoi Ballet School outside of Moscow. The tiled mural around the entrance, by Juarez Machado, depicts a circus. There are some 600 industries in the manufacturing park, many of which are substantial exporters.

Excursions from Joinville

You can take a boat trip on the **Príncipe de Joinville III** ⓘ *T047-455 0824, US$10 per person*, at 1000 from Lagoa Saguaçú, Bairro Espinheiros (9 km from the centre), past several islands to São Francisco do Sul. Stops include the Museu Nacional do Mar, the port, lunch at a fish restaurant, Ilha da Rita and Ilha das Flores, getting back at 1600.

The **festival of São João** in June can be seen best in Santa Catarina at **Campo Alegre**, the first town on the road inland to Mafra. There are bonfires, a lot of (German) folk dancing, and large quantities of local specialities, *quentão* and *pinhões*. It is a beautiful climb on the road from the BR-101 to Campo Alegre.

South of Florianópolis » *pp329-336.*

Two beaches south of Florianópolis worth a stop are **Pinheira** and **Guarda do Embaú**, which you get to by crossing a river in a canoe. The surfing is excellent here; Guarda in particular is a favourite spot of surfers from Rio and São Paulo (surfing is not permitted in the *tainha* fishing season, 15 May-15 July). **Garopaba**, 89 km south of Florianópolis, is a village of 11,000, which swells to 100,000 during the holiday season. Its indigenous Carijó name 'Y-Gara-Paba' means 'much water, many fish and many hills'. There is a simple colonial church and a sandy coast.

Silveira, 3 km east, is considered one of Brazil's finest surfing spots. Swimming can be risky, though, because of the surf and sudden drops in the ocean floor. There is good fishing for *tainha*, lobster, anchovy and other varieties. **Praia da Rosa**, 18 km south, is a 3½-km beach with good swimming, fishing, diving and pleasant coastal walks. It is also one of Brazil's prime whale-watching sites, with whales coming to the bay to calve between June and November. The headquarters of the Baleia Franca project is **Pousada Vida Sol e Mar** ⓘ *T048-354 0041, www.vidasolemar.com.br*, trips cost US$42 in a boat, US$20 on land. The pousada (L) also has cabins for rent, with kitchen, TV, restaurant, sushi bar, tennis, surf school.

Laguna → *Phone code: 048. Colour map 5, B4. Population: 48,000.*

The small fishing port of Laguna in southern Santa Catarina (124 km south of Florianópolis), founded in 1676, was a focal point of defence against Spanish invasions and still retains vestiges of its turbulent past. These days Laguna serves mainly as a holiday resort, perched between the ocean and a chain of three lakes. In 1839, Laguna was the capital of the Juliana Republic, a short-lived separatist movement led by Italian idealist Guiseppe Garibáldi. At that time he met a devoted lover, Ana Maria de Jesus Ribeiro, who followed him into battle, was taken prisoner, escaped and rejoined Garibáldi at Vacaria. Their first son, Menotti, was born in Rio Grande do Sul, but the family moved to Montevideo in 1841, where they lived in poverty. They later moved to Argentina and then to Italy, where they fought for the unification of the peninsula. Ana Maria (or Anita) died near Ravenna in 1849 while they were fleeing to Switzerland from the Austrian army. She became a heroine in both Brazil and Italy and there are monuments to her in Rome, Ravenna, Porto Alegre, Belo Horizonte, Florianópolis, Juiz da Fora, Tubarão and Laguna. At Laguna is the **Anita Garibáldi Museum**, containing documents, furniture and her personal effects.

Laguna's beach, 2 km from the centre, is not very good, but 16 km away (by ferry and road) are beaches and dunes at **Cavo de Santa Marta**. Also from Laguna, take a **Lagunatur** or **Auto Viação São José** bus to **Farol** (four buses a day Monday to Friday, one on Saturday, US$1.50, a beautiful ride). You have to cross the mouth of the Lagoa Santo Antônio by ferry (10 minutes) to get to Farol; look out for fishermen aided by dolphins (*botos*). Here is a fishing village with a lighthouse, the **Farol de Santa Marta**, the largest lighthouse in South America with the third largest view in the world. It was built by the French in 1890 of stone, sand and whale oil. Guided tours available (taxi, US$10, not including ferry toll). It may be possible to bargain with fishermen for a bed, or there are campsites at Santa Marta Pequena by the lighthouse, popular with surfers.

Lages and around

→ *Phone code: 049. Colour map 5, B4. Population: 160,000.*

West of Florianópolis, the area around Lages is particularly good for 'rural tourism', with lots of opportunities for hiking, horse riding, river bathing and working on a farm. The weather can get really cold in winter and even the waterfalls have been known to freeze. Many of the local *fazendas* are open for visitors and offer accommodation. This is *gaúcho* country and you will get *gaúcho* hospitality, culture and food.

Sleeping

Florianópolis *p318, map p319*

L Blue Tree Towers, R Bocaiúva 2304, next to Shopping Beiramar, T048-3251 5555, www.bluetree.com.br. Very smart, well-equipped modern business hotel. Good restaurant, pool, gym and sauna.

AL-A Pousada Pau de Canela, Rio Taveres 606, T048-3338 3584, www.pousada paudecanela.com.br. Well located pousada with 10 personalized rooms, restaurant, bar and swimming pool.

B Bristol Castelmar, R Felipe Schmidt 1260, T048-3225 3228, www.bristolhoteis.com.br. Standard 1980s B-grade business hotel with a restaurant, pool and sauna. There are great views from the upper-floor rooms.

B Faial, R Felipe Schmidt 603, T048-3225 2766, www.hotelfaial.com.br. Comfortable and traditional with simple rooms and a good restaurant.

B **Florianópolis Palace**, R Artista Bittencourt 14, T048-3224 9633, www.floph.com.br. Once the best hotel in town; now a 1970s throwback but with a decent pool, sauna and large a/c rooms. Recommended.

C **Farol da Ilha**, R Bento Gonçalves 163, T048-3225 2766, www.hotelfaial.com.br. Well-kept 1990s hotel with 35 a/c rooms, owned by the hotel **Faial**. Convenient for the bus station.

C **Valerim Center**, R Felipe Schmidt 554, T048-3225 1100. Functional 2-star with large rooms, hot water and hard beds.

C-D **Central Sumaré**, R Felipe Schmidt 423, T048-3222 5359. Clean and friendly, good value but some rooms are significantly better than others so look at several. Breakfast included. More expensive with bath.

E **Hi! Hostel**, R Duarte Schutel 227, T048-3225 3781, www.floripahostel.com.br. Price per person, IYHA youth hostel, breakfast included, cooking facilities, clean, some traffic noise, very friendly, will store luggage. Recommended. Prices rise in Dec-Feb; more expensive for non-members. They also have a branch in Canasvieiras, see page 330.

Camping

Camping Clube do Brasil, São João do Rio Vermelho, north of Lagoa da Conceição, 21 km out of town; also at Lagoa da Conceição, Praia da Armação; Praia dos Ingleses and Praia Canasvieiras.

'Wild' camping allowed at Ponta de Sambaqui and Praias Brava, Aranhas, Galheta, Mole, Campeche, Campanhas and Naufragados; 4 km south of Florianópolis, camping site with bar at Praia do Sonho on thew mainland, beautiful, deserted beach with an island fort nearby.

'Camping Gaz' cartridges from **Riachuelo Supermercado**, on R Alvim and R São Jorge.

Ilha de Santa Catarina *p320, map p321*

L **Aguas Mornas Palace Hotel**, Águas Mornas, T048-245 1315, at the springs. Well-maintained luxury spa with a range of treatments.

L **Lexus-Hotel**, RHG Pereira 745, Canasvieiras, T048-266 0909, F266 0919. Studio flats on the beach, with breakfast. Friendly.

L-A **Porto Ingleses**, R das Gaivotas 610, Praia dos Ingleses, T048-269 1414, www.portoingleses.com.br. Small resort with a pool, play area for kids, restaurant and beach service. All accommodation has a/c and is spacious.

AL **Plaza Caldas da Imperatriz**, Caldas da Imperatriz, T048-245 1333. Very well appointed with baths, swimming pools and a range of treatments.

A **Caldas da Imperatriz**, Caldas da Imperatriz, T048-245 1388. A grand, old-fashioned European spa built in 1850 under the auspices of Empress Teresa Cristina, originally with public baths. All meals are included in the price.

A **Hotel Cris**, Joaquina, T048-232 5380. Very comfortable cabins and friendly staff. Recommended.

A **Hotel São Sebastião da Praia**, Av Campeche 1373, Praia de Campeche, T/F048-237 4247, www.hotelsaosebastiao.com.br. Resort hotel on a splendid beach. Offers special monthly rate Apr-Oct, excellent value.

A **Pousada 32**, on beach, Barra da Lagoa, T/F048-232 3665. Comfortable apartments with kitchens and helpful staff.

B **Pousada dos Tucanos**, Estr Geral da Costa de Dentro 2776, near Pântano do Sul, T048-237 5084, Caixa Postal 5016. English, French, Spanish spoken, spacious bungalows in garden setting. Excellent organic food. Very highly recommended. Take bus to Pântano do Sul, walk 6 km or telephone and arrange to be picked up by German owner.

B-C **Vila Tamarindo**, Av Campeche 1836, Praia do Campeche, T048-3237 3464, www.tamarindo.com.br. Very well-run, friendly beachside hotels with a range of rooms from simple tile-floor suites to doubles with a jacuzzi. The best have sea views.

C **Pousada Floripaz**, Estrada Geral (across hanging bridge at bus station), Barra da Lagoa, T048-232 3193. Safe, family-run and with helpful owners. Boat and car tours. Highly recommended. Book in advance.

C-D **Barratur**, R Felipa Benta Ramos 18, Barra da Lagoa, T048-3232 3000. A range of brightly painted beach chalets, the largest of which have room for up to 6, good value.

D **Compania Inglesa**, R Dr João Becker 276, Praia dos Ingleses, T048-269 1350, www.hotelciainglesa.com.br. Little beach hotel with a pool and friendly staff. Good for families.

D **Pousada Zilma**, R Geral da Praia da Joaquina 279, Lagoa da Conceição, T048-

232 0161. Quiet, safe and simple with helpful staff. Recommended.

D-E Hi Hostel Canasvieiras, R Dr João de Oliveira 517, esq Av das Nações, Canasvieiras, T048-3266 2036, www.floripahostel.com.br. IYHA youth hostel, 2 blocks from sea with well-kept dorms and doubles. Only open 15 Dec-15 Mar.

E-F Albergue do Pirata, Päntano do Sul, www.alberguedopirata.com.br. Doubles and dorms with breakfast in natural surroundings with lots of trails.

Camping

Camping da Barra, Barra da Lagoa, T048-232 3199. Beautiful clean site, helpful owner.

Porto Belo and around *p322, map p323*

B Baleia Branca, Av Nena Trevisan 98, Porto Belo, T047-369 4011, www.hotelbaleia branca.com.br. 12 chalets in a garden with a pool, sauna and camping area.

B Porto Belo, R José Amâncio 246, Porto Belo T047-369 4483, F243 1057. IYHA. Lots of apartments, most sleep 4-6, good value for a group.

B Pousada Zimbros, R da Praia 527, Zimbros, T047-369 3225. Cheaper off-season, on beach, sumptuous breakfast, restaurant. Highly recommended.

C-D Blumenauense, Av Sen Atílio Fontana, Praia do Perequê, T047-369 4208. Simple rooms with en suites and breakfast; on the beach.

Camping

There are lots of campsites around the peninsula.

Itajaí and around *p323*

B-C Marambaia Cabeçudas, Praça Marcos Konder 46, Praia de Cabeçudas, 6 km out of town, www.maramabaiahotel.com.br. Modern resort hotel with a pool and gym. Comfortable though anonymous rooms.

C Grande, R Felipe Schmidt 198, T047-348 0968, www.iai.matrix.com.br/grandehotel. Classic 1940s hotel now looking a bit frayed.

Blumenau *p324*

C Schroeder, R 15 de Novembro 514, T047-387 0933. A/c, TV, phone, fridge, pool.

D Pousada Max, R 15 de Novembro 257, T047-387 0598. Apartment with satellite TV, fridge, a/c, parking.

Excursions from Blumenau *p324*

AL Fazenda Park Hotel, Estrada Geral do Gasparinho 2499, Gaspar, T047-326 5696. Swimming pool, fishing, walking and riding.

D Pousada Ecológoca Spitzkopf, R Bruno Schreiber 3777, T047-336 5422. Beautiful, clean and extremely quiet, with pool, heating and a bar, but no restaurant,

Joinville *p326, map p327*

A Anthurium Parque, R São José 226, T/F047-433 6299, www.anthurium.com.br. In a colonial building, once home to a bishop, good value, English spoken, pool, sauna, part of the **Roteiros de Charme** hotel group, see page 50.

A Blue Tree, Av Juscelino Kubitschek 300, T047-461 8000, www.bluetree.com.br. Excellent business hotel with very good service and facilities. Spick and span modern rooms. Sauna, gym and an excellent restaurant and bar.

A Tannenhof, R Visc de Taunay 340, T/F047-433 8011, www.tannenhoff.com.br. 4-star, pool, gym, traffic noise, excellent breakfast, restaurant on 14th floor.

B Joinville Tourist, R 7 de Setembro 40, T047-433 1288, www.touristhotel.com.br. Smart though anonymous 3-star with a pool, bar and restaurant.

B-C Joinville Palace, R do Príncipe 142, T047-433 6111, www.joinvillepalacehotel.com.br. Simple a/c rooms with heating and TV. Visa accepted.

D Ideal, R Jerônimo Coelho 98, T047-422 3660. Simple, well kept and convenient for the *rodoviária* municipal.

D-E Mattes, 15 de Novembro 801, T047-433 9886. Simple but with good service and facilities and a big breakfast.

E Novo Horizonte, at the bus station. Very basic fan-cooled rooms but clean.

South of Florianópolis *p328*

LL Ponta dos Ganchos, Governador Celso Ramos, T048-3262 5000, www.ponta dosganchos.com.br. One of the most luxurious resorts in Brazil; isolated on its own steep peninsula with bungalows tucked away on the higher slopes. The best are almost 100 sq m with sweeping (private) views out over the Atlantic. Good restaurant and excellent service. Pick-up service from Florianópolis airport.

A **Morada do Bouganvilles**, Estr Geral do Morro, Praia da Rosa, T048-355 6100, www.pousadabougainville.com.br. Chalets in a bougainvillea-filled garden with a small pool and a bar.

A **Quinta do Bucanero**, Estr Gerald a Rosa, Praia da Rosa, T048-355 6056, www.bucanero.com.br. Tastefully decorated luxury resort with private access to the beach. Set in lush vegetation in a protected area with a range of activities from horse riding to boat trips available. Closed Jun-Jul. No children.

B **Pousada da Lagoa**, R Rosalina de Aguiar Lentz 325, Garopaba, T/F048-254 3201, www.pousadadalagoa.com.br. Comfortable countryside pousada with an outdoor pool, reasonable restaurant and bar and a series of trails running into the environs.

C **The Rosebud**, Estr Geral do Morro, Praia da Rosa, T048-355 6101. Simple little pousada with breakfast.

E **Praia do Ferrugem**, Estr Gerals do Capão, Garopaba, T048-254 0035. IYHA youth hostel. Price per person.

Laguna *p328*

L-A **Laguna Tourist**, Av Castelo Branco, Praia do Gi, 4 km, T048-647 0022, www.lagunatourist.com.br. 1970s resort with a view out over the bay from its hilltop setting. Popular with families, with many activities on offer.

C **Turismar**, Av Rio Grande do Sul 207, T048-647 0024, F647 0279. A simple 2-star with a view out over Mar Grosso beach.

D **Beiramar**, 100 m from **Recanto**, opposite Angeloni Supermarket, T048-644 0260. Clean, TV, rooms with view over lagoon.

D **Recanto**, Av Colombo 17, close to bus terminal. With breakfast. Modern but basic.

Lages and around *p329*

A **Grande**, R João de Castro 23, T/F049-222 3522. Standard 3-star town hotel.

D **Rodeio**, T049-223 2011. One of 3 similar hotels near the *rodoviária* with rooms with or without bath and a good breakfast. In the same building there is a good *churrascaria*, open in the evening, US$7.50.

Fazendas near Lages

All on working farms. On average, prices include all meals.

A **Fazenda Aza Verde**, Antiga BR-2, Soroptimista 13, T049-222 0277. Horses, fishing, boats, games room, heating, pool.

A **Fazenda Ciclone**, BR-116, Km 276, localidade Vigia, T049-222 3382. Horses, fishing, table tennis, billiards, river beach.

A **Fazenda do Barreiro**, Rod SC 438, Km 43, T049-222 3031. Games room, library, horses, pool, fishing, boats, TV.

A **Fazenda Dourado Turismo Rural**, Estr Lages-Morrinhos Km 14, T049-222 2066/ T049-9982 2094. Simple but comfortable a/c chalets surrounding a grassy lawn and in the edge of Araucária pine forest. With restaurant, pool and live music at weekends.

A **Fazenda Nossa Senhora de Lourdes**, R Aristiliano Ramos 565, T049-222 0798. Pool, games room, library, horses, fishing, good walking.

A **Fazenda Rancho do Boqueirão**, BR-282, Km 4, Saída São José do Cerrito, T049-226 0354, F226 0354. Heating, TV, library, games room, pool, horses, bicycles, good walking, fishing.

A **Fazenda Refúgio do Lago**, Rod SC 438, Km 10, Pedras Brancas, T049-222 1416. Pool, games room, library, horses, shooting, fishing, boats, river beach.

Eating

Florianópolis *p318, map p319*

Take a walk along R Bocaiúva, east of R Almte Lamego, to find the whole street filled with Italian restaurants, barbecue places.

TTT **Toca da Garoupa** R Alves de Brito 178, just off R Bocaiúva. The city's best seafood restaurant housed in a rustic-chic wood slat house.

TT **Lindacap**, R Felipe Schmidt 1162 (closed Mon, Sun lunch only), T048-3222 4002. Fish, chicken and meat *pratos* as well as seafood, smart, good buffet.

TT **Macarronada Italiana**, Av Beiramar Norte 2458. Good, comfortable, upmarket Italian, with a decent pizzeria next door. In front of the **Blue Tree Towers** hotel.

TT **O Mercador**, Box 33/4 Mercado Público. Excellent self-service specializing in fish and seafood, tables outside on cobbled street. Recommended.

ŸŸ **Papparella**, Almte Lamego 1416. Excellent and enormous pizzas thick with cheese.
ŸŸ **Trapiche**, Box 31, Mercado Público. Self-service fish and seafood, tables on pavement.
ŸŸ **Vida**, R Visc de Ouro Preto 298, next to Alliance Française. Decent vegetarian set-meals and pay by weight.
Ÿ **Café das Artes**, at north end of R Esteves Junior 734. Nice café, excellent cakes.
Ÿ **Cía Lanches**, Ten Silveira e R Trajano, downstairs, and, in Edif Dias Velho, Av R Felipe Schmidt 303. A wide selection of juices and snacks.
Ÿ **Kayskidum**, Av Beiramar Norte 2566. *Lanchonete* and crêperie, very popular.
Ÿ **Mirantes**, R Alvaro de Carvalho 246, Centro, with other branches on R Branco and a *churrascaria* on R 7 de Setembro. Buffet self-service, good value food with a set menu for less than US$5 per kilo.

Ilha de Santa Catarina *p320, map p321*
ŸŸ-Ÿ **Oliveira**, R Henrique Veras, Lagoa da Conceiçao. Excellent simple seafood in pleasant surrounds.
Ÿ **Meu Cantinha**, R Orlando Shaplin 89, Barra da Lagoa. Very good, simple seafood dishes.

Joinville *p326, map 327*
ŸŸŸ **Pinheiro**, R Rio Branco 299, T047-455 1254. Well worth a visit for excellent fish and shrimp dishes.
ŸŸŸ **Tritão**, R Visc de Taunay 902, T047-433 4816. Very good seafood and a handful of other national dishes.
ŸŸ **Bierkeller**, R 15 de Novembro 497, T047-422 1360. Respectable German cooking.
ŸŸ **China**, R Abdon Batista 131, opposite the cathedral, T047-422 3323. Eat in or home-delivery service for oriental food.
ŸŸ **Sopp**, R Mcal Deodoro 640, on corner with R Jaraguá, T047-422 3637. German cooking with a sausage-heavy menu.
ŸŸ **Trento Queijos e Vinhos**, R 15 de Novembro 2973, T047-453 1796. Traditional Italian with reasonable pastas and pizza.

The **Müeller Shopping** has a good food hall.

Bars and clubs

Florianópolis *p318, map p319*
To find out about events and theme nights check the Beiramar Shopping Centre for notices in shop windows, ask in surf shops or take a trip to the University of Santa Catarina in Trindade and check out the noticeboards. The newspaper *Diário Catarinense* gives details of bigger events, eg **Oktoberfest**.

The **Mercado Público** in the centre, which is alive with fish sellers and stalls, has a different atmosphere at the end of the day when hard-working locals turn up to unwind. However, this area is not particularly safe at night and most bars and restaurants are closed by 2200. The stall, **Box 32**, is good for seafood and has a bar specializing in *cachaça*. **Restaurant Pirão** overlooks the market square with a quieter view and live Brazilian music on Tue, Thu and Fri. **Empórium**, Bocaiúva 79, is a shop by day and popular bar at night.

You may need a car to get to other clubs and bars such as **Café Matisse**, Av Irineu Bornhausen 5000, inside the Centro Integrade de Cultura, or the hot spots at the beaches. **Ilhéu**, Av Prof Gama d'Eça e R Jaime Câmara, US$5. Bar open until early hours, tables spill outside, very popular with locals, fills up quickly, venue for live music rather than a disco (tiny dancefloor). **Café Cancun**, Av Beiramar Norte, T048-225 1029. Wed-Sun from 2000, US$5, bars, restaurant, dancing, sophisticated.

Ilha de Santa Catarina *p320, map p321*
Throughout the summer, the beaches open their bars day and night; during the rest of the year the beginning of the week is very quiet. The beach huts of **Praia Mole** invite people to party all night (bring a blanket), while the **Club Seven** (in the Boulevard) and **L'Equinox** bar (Joaquina) are more for clubbers who don't mind 'sand in their shoes'. **Seven** offers theme nights and is very popular with surfers. Any bars are worth visiting in the Lagoon area (around the Boulevard and Barra da Lagoa) where the great Brazilian phrase '*qualquer lugar é lugar*' fits perfectly. This means 'whichever place is the place to be', reflecting the laid-back Brazilian mood at the beach. Other clubs and bars generally require a car: **Latitude 27**, near Praia Mole, Ilhéus bar (Canasvieras) and the popular **Ibiza** nightclub in Jureré.

Entertainment

Florianópolis *p318, map p319*

Cinema The 3-screen cinema at **Shopping Centre Beiramar** has international films with subtitles.

Music Free live music every Sat morning at the marketplace near the bus terminal.

Festivals

Florianópolis *p318, map p319*

Easter **Farra de Boi** (Festival of the Bull). It is only in the south that the bull is actually killed on Easter Sun. Despite being controversial, the festival arouses fierce local pride and there is much celebration around this time.

Dec and Jan The whole island dances to the sound of the **Boi-de-Mamão**, a type of dance that incorporates the puppets of Bernunça, Maricota (the Goddess of Love, a puppet with long arms to embrace everyone) and Tião, the monkey. The Portuguese brought the tradition of the bull, which has great significance in Brazilian celebrations.

Penha *p324*

Feb Seafood festival and **Carnaval**

May/Jun **Festa do Divino**. A procession and crowning of the Emperor.

24-29 Jun **Festa de São João e São Pedro**. A tradition from the Azores.

Joinville *p326, map p327*

Nov **Annual flower festival**, mostly orchids, disappointing, US$1.50 entry.

Oct **Fenachopp**, beer festival.

May **Fenatiro**, the annual festival for the 2000 members of the local shooting clubs.

Jul Joinville hosts one of the largest **dance festivals** in the world; around 4000 dancers stay for 12 days and put on shows and displays, ranging from jazz and folklore to classical ballet, seen by some 30,000 spectators in a variety of locations.

Shopping

Florianópolis *p318, map p319*

Shopping Centre Beiramar is the largest mall with the usual range of fashion (with plenty of surfwear), music and assorted shops. There are many smaller shopping malls dotted around the resorts. However, bargain hunters are better off bartering in the family-run businesses at the **Mercado Público**. Here, **Casa da Alfândega**, has a good selection of crafts and souvenirs.

Activities and tours

Florianópolis *p318, map p319*

Brazil Ecojourneys, Servidão Ilha Paraíso 113, Campeche, T048-3232 9270, www.brazilecojourneys.com.

Ilhatur Turismo e Cambio, R Jerónimo Coelho 185, T048-224 6333, F223 6921.

Scuna Sul, T048-222 1806, www.scunasul.com.br. Very popular boat trips from US$7.50.

Excursions from Blumenau *p324*

Activities on offer include parapenting, T047-387 0803, a jeep club, T047-387 2328, horse riding, T047-387 2290 and swimming pools with water slides. Ask at the tourist office for details.

Transport

Florianópolis *p318, map p319*

Air
Flights to **São Paulo** (Congonhas), **Rio de Janeiro**, **Porto Alegre** and **Curitiba**. To get to the airport take a **Ribeiroense** bus 'Corredor Sudoeste' from Terminal Urbano.

Airline offices Aerolíneas Argentinas, R Tte Silveira 200, 8th floor, T048-3224 7835, F222 7267. **Bra**, T011-6445 4310, www.voebra.com.br **Gol**, T0300-789 2121, www.voegol.com.br. **Nordeste/Rio Sul**, Jerônimo Coelho 185, sala 601, T048-3224 7008, airport T048-3236 1779. **Ocean Air**, T0300- 789 8160, www.ocean air.com.br. **TAM**, at airport, T048-3236 1812, www.tam.com.br. **Varig**, Av R Branco 796, T048-3224 7266, F222 2725.

Bus
Local There are 3 bus stations for routes on the island, or close by on the mainland: **Terminal de Ônibus Interurbano** between Av Paulo Fontes and R Francisco Tolentino, west of the Mercado Público; **Terminal Urbano** between Av Paulo Fontes and R Antônio Luz, east of Praça Fernando Machado; a terminal at R Silva Jardim and R José da Costa. Yellow microbuses (**Transporte Ejecutivo**), starting from the south end of Praça 15 de Novembro and other stops, charge US$0.75-1.45 depending on the destination. Similarly, normal bus fares cost from US$0.65, according to the destination.

Long distance International buses and those to other Brazilian cities leave from the *rodoviária* **Rita Maria** on the island, at the east (island) end of the Ponte Colombo Machado Salles.

Regular daily buses to **Porto Alegre** (US$16, 7 hrs), **São Paulo**, 9 hrs (US$23.75, *leito* US$36.25), **Rio de Janeiro**, 20 hrs (US$31 *convencional*, US$42 executive, US$55 *leito*); to **Foz do Iguaçu** (US$22, continuing to **Asunción** US$30). To **São Joaquim** at 1145, 1945 with **Reunidos**, 1815 with **Nevatur**, 5-6 hrs, US$9.30; to **Laguna** US$5.25. No direct bus to Corumbá, change at Campo Grande.

To **Montevideo** (Uruguay), US$52, daily, by TTL. **Buenos Aires** (Argentina), US$55, Pluma, buses very full in summer, book one week in advance.

Car hire
Auto Locadora Coelho, Felipe Schmidt 81, vehicles in good condition. **Interlocadora**, T048-236 0179 at the airport, F236 1370, rates from US$40 a day before supplements. **Localiza** at the airport, T048-236 1244, and at Av Paulo Fontes 730, T048-225 5558.

Porto Belo and around *p322*

Bus To **Florianópolis**, several daily with Rainha, US$3, fewer at weekends, more frequent buses to **Tijucas**, **Itapema** and **Itajaí**, all on the BR-101 with connections. Buses run from Porto Belo to the beaches on the peninsula.

Blumenau *p324*

Bus Coletivos Volkmann (T047-387 1321), to **Pomerode**, daily US$0.75, 1 hr, check schedule at tourist office. **Verde Vale** office at R Angêlo Dias 220, sala 207, T047-326 6179, www.braznet.com.br/~verdetur/ index.html.

Excursions from Blumenau *p324*

There are buses from Pomerode to **Jaraguá do Sul**, **Joinville**, **São Bento do Sul**, **Florianópolis**, **São Paulo**, **Curitiba** and other local places with **Rex** (T047-387 0387), **União**, **Reunidas** and **Penha/Itapemirim** (T047-387 0387).

São Francisco do Sul *p326*

Bus The bus terminal is 1½ km from centre. Direct bus (**Penha**) daily to **Curitiba** at 0730, US$6, 3½ hrs.

Joinville *p326, map p327*

Air Airport 5 km from city, T047-467 1000.

Airline offices TAM, T047-433 2033. Varig/Rio Sul, R Alexandre Dohler 277, T047-433 2800.

Bus To **Blumenau**, US$3, 2¼ hrs. The *rodoviária* is 2½ km outside the town, south exit, T047-433 2991 (regular bus service).

Car hire Interlocadora, R do Príncipe 839, T047-422 7888. **Localiza**, R Blumenau 1728, T047-433 9393, or at the airport T047-467 1020. **Olímpia**, R 9 de Março 734, T047-433 1755.

Laguna *p328*
Bus To **Porto Alegre**, 5½ hrs, with Santo Anjo Da Guarda; same company goes to **Florianópolis**, 2 hrs, US$5.25, 6 daily; to **Tubarão**, every hr with **Alvorada**, US$2.75, 50 mins.

Lages *p329*
Bus The bus station is 30 mins' walk southeast of the centre. Bus to the centre (Terminal Municipal), 'Rodoviária' runs Mon-Fri only, or 'Dom Pedro II' every 40 mins at weekends. To **Florianópolis**, 6-8 buses daily on the direct road (BR-282), 5 hrs, US$10; to **Caxias do Sul**, 3¾ hrs, US$5.60.

Directory

Florianópolis *p318, map p319*
Banks Açoriano Turismo, Jaime Câmara 106, T048-224 3939, takes Amex. Money changers on R Felipe Schmidt outside BESC. Banco do Brasil, Praça 15 de Novembro, exchange upstairs, 1000-1500, huge commission on cash or TCs. Lots of ATMs downstairs. **Banco Estado de Santa Catarina** (BESC), *câmbio*, R Felip, Schmidt e Jerônimo Coelho, 1000-1600, no commission on TCs. ATM for MasterCard/ Cirrus at **Banco Itaú**, Shopping Centre Beiramar (not in the centre, bus Expresso). **HSBC**, ATM, R Felipe Schmidt 376, corner with R Álvaro de Carvalho. **Lovetur**, Av Osmar Cunha 15, Ed Ceisa and **Centauro Turismo**, same address. **Embassies and consulates** Austria, R Luiz Delfino 66, Apto 501, T048-222 5952 (Mon-Fri 1500-1700), phone in advance. **Chile**, R Alvaro de Carvalho 267, 6th floor, Edif Mapil, T048-223 3383. **France**, Alliance Française, T048-222 7589 (Fri 0900- 1200). **Spain**, R Almte Alvim 24, Casa 9, T048-222 1821, F224 1018. **Uruguay**, R Prof Walter de Bona Castela 26, T048-234 4645 (0800-1200, 1400-1800). **Internet** Moncho, Tiradentes 181. **Language schools** Step 1 Idiomas, R Joe Collaço 99, Córrego Grande, T048-3233 6605, www.step1.com.br. Portuguese classes for foreigners with short and longer-term courses. **Laundry** Lav e Lev, R Felipe Schmidt 706, opposite Valerim Plaza. **Post office** Praça 15 de Novembro 5. **Telephone** Praça Pereira Oliveira 20.

Joinville *p326, map p327*
Internet Biernet Bar, R Visconde de Taunay 456. **Medical services** 24-hr pharmacies: **Drogaria Catarinense**, Filial Boa Vista, in front of the Hospital Regional, T047-437 2355, or Filial São João, Av Getúlio Vargas 1343, T047-422 7691. **Farmacia Catarinense**, R 15 de Novembro 503, T047-422 2318.

Rio Grande do Sul

Brazil's southernmost state regards itself as different from the rest of the country and has long been lobbying for independence. Its people identify more with Uruguay and Argentina and, like their counterparts on the Pampas, refer to themselves as gauchos.

The scenery is different too. An escarpment, in places over 1000 m high, runs down the coastal area as far as Porto Alegre providing escape from the summer swelter. The state capital is the most industrialized and cosmopolitan city in the south and tops the country's urban quality of life rankings. All along the coast, the green hills of Rio Grande do Sul are fringed by sand bars and lagoons, making one of the world's longest beaches. On the border with Santa Catarina in the north is the remarkable Aparados da Serra National Park where it can snow.

In southern Rio Grande do Sul, the grasslands stretch as far as Uruguay to the south and over 800 km westwards to Argentina, and are scattered with the remains of Jesuit missions. This is the distinctive land of the gaúcho (cowboy) and the herders are regularly seen in traditional garb. In restaurants, steaks the size of Texas are order of the day. In the far west are the remains of Jesuit missions. Look out for local specialities such as comida campeira, te colonial and quentão. » *For Sleeping, Eating and other listings, see pages 348-356.*

Background

The first people to settle in the area were pioneer farmers, and the traditional dress of the *gaúcho* (pronounced ga-oo-shoo in Brazil) can still be seen: the flat black hat, *bombachas* (baggy trousers) and poncho. The indispensable drink of the southern cattlemen is *ximarão* (*mate* without sugar, also spelt *chimarrão*). The *gaúcho* culture has developed a sense of distance from the African-influenced society further north. Many people will tell you they have more in common with Uruguayans or Argentines than Brazilians – apart from when it comes to football. Today, there are many millions of cattle, sheep and pigs, and the production of rice is on the increase with the state providing some 75% of all Brazilian wine.

Since 1999, the state government has implemented a radical consultative scheme whereby people in all 497 municipalities jointly decide school, road and other infrastructure spending. The Participatory Budget, pioneered for over a dozen years in Porto Alegre, is widely supported and has attracted international acclaim. For more info log onto www.estado.rs.gov.br. The state tourism website is: www.turismo.rs.gov.br.

Porto Alegre

» *pp348-356.*

→ *Phone code: 051. Colour map 5, B3. Population: 1,361,000.*

Sited at the meeting of five rivers and freshened by over a million trees, Porto Alegre is one of Brazil's more pleasant cities. Culturally rich, ethnically diverse and progressive, it is the capital of the southern frontier and the hub of trade with Argentina and Uruguay. It is a good base for exploring the rest of Rio Grande do Sul's natural beauty and historical sites.

The capital of Rio Grande do Sul is where cowboy culture meets the bright lights. Though it is the biggest commercial centre south of São Paulo, it is friendly and manageable on foot. Get a map out in downtown Porto Alegre and someone will try to help you (get a map out in downtown São Paulo and they will probably try to rob you).

Ins and outs

Getting there International and domestic flights arrive at **Salgado Filho airport** ⓘ *Av dos Estados, 8 km from the city, T051-3342 1082*. There are regular buses to the bus station and a Metrô service to the city centre. International and interstate buses arrive at the **rodoviária** ⓘ *Largo Vespasiano Júlio Veppo, Av Mauá with Garibáldi, T051-3286 8230, www.rodoviaria-poa.com.br*, an easy walk from the city centre. There are good facilities, including a post office and long-distance telephone service until 2100. » *See also Transport, page 353.*

Getting around First-class minibuses (*lotação*), painted in a distinctive orange, blue and white pattern, stop on request. They are safer and more pleasant than normal buses and cost about US$0.60. The Trensurb Metrô runs from the southern terminal at the Mercado Público (station beside the market), going as far north as Sapucaia do Sul. The second station serves the *rodoviária*, and the fifth station serves the airport (10 minutes), 0500-2300, single journey US$0.40.

Tourist information For general information contact the **Secretaria do Turismo** ⓘ *T0800-517686, www.portoalegre.rs.gov.br/turismo*. Also helpful are the **Central de Informações Turísticas** ⓘ *R Vasco da Gama 253, Bom Fim, T051-311 5289, daily 0900-2100*, and **Setur** ⓘ *Borges de Medeiros 1501, 10th floor, T051-3228 5400, also at the airport and rodoviária*, who provide free city maps. There are free guided walks on Sunday from Praça da Alfândega or on Saturday from Praça da Matriz, T0800-517686, 1500 or 1600. Contact the tourist office, or ask in the Mercado Público.

Maps Army maps (1:50,000) of Rio Grande's trekking regions (Canela, Parque Nacional de Aparados da Serra) are available at **Junta Servicio Militar** ⓘ *Prefeitura Municipal, R Prof E Castro 850, T051-3223 3611*. These maps are not available in rural areas.

Climate Standing on a series of hills and valleys on the banks of Lake Guaíba, Porto Alegre has a temperate climate through most of the year, though the temperature at the height of summer can often exceed 40°C and drop below 10°C in winter.

Safety Avoid the market area in Praça 15 de Novembro and the bus terminal at night; thefts have been reported in Voluntários da Pátria and Praça Parcão.

Porto Alegre

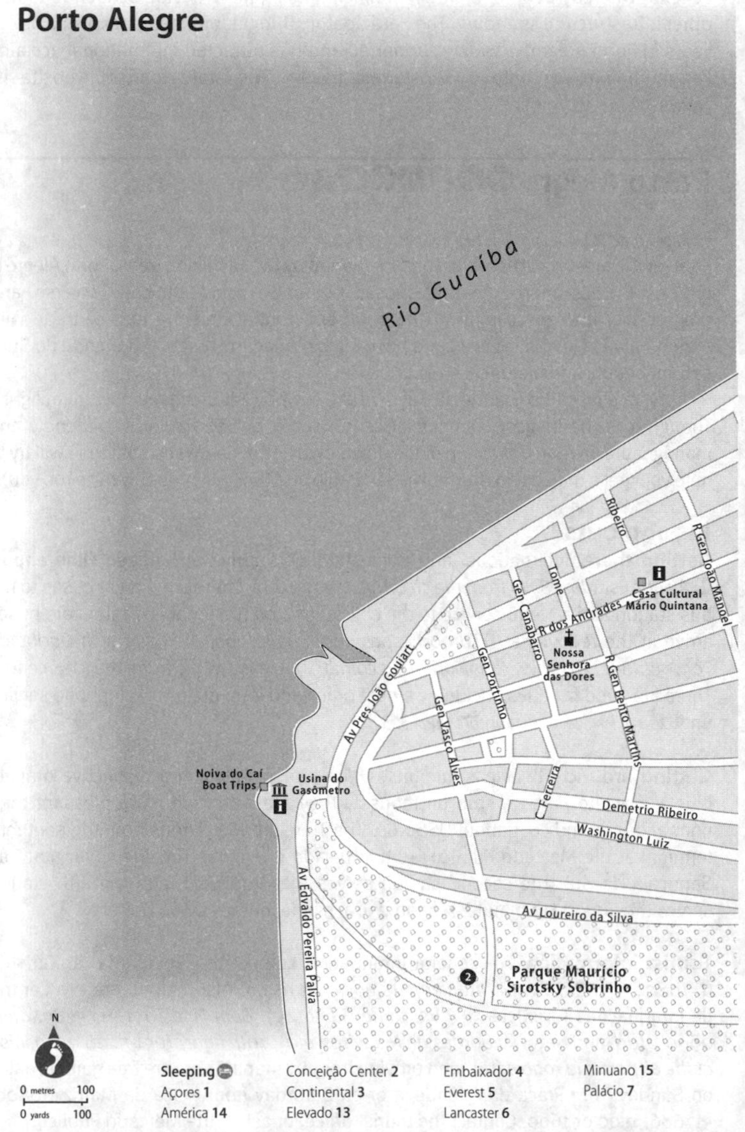

Sleeping
Açores 1
América 14
Conceição Center 2
Continental 3
Elevado 13
Embaixador 4
Everest 5
Lancaster 6
Minuano 15
Palácio 7

Sights

The older residential part of the town is on a promontory, dominated previously by the **Palácio Piratini** (governor's palace) and the imposing 1920s metropolitan **cathedral** on the **Praça Marechal Deodoro** (or da Matriz). Also on, or near, this square are the neoclassical **Theatro São Pedro** (1858), the **Solar dos Câmara** (1818, now a historical and cultural centre) and the **Biblioteca Pública**, but all are dwarfed by the skyscraper of the **Assembléia Legislativa**. Down Rua General Câmara from Praça Marechal Deodoro is the **Praça da Alfândega**, with the old customs house, the **Museu de Arte de Rio Grande do Sul**, the old post office and the Banco Meridional. A short walk east from here, up Rua 7 de Setembro, is the busy Praça 15 de Novembro,

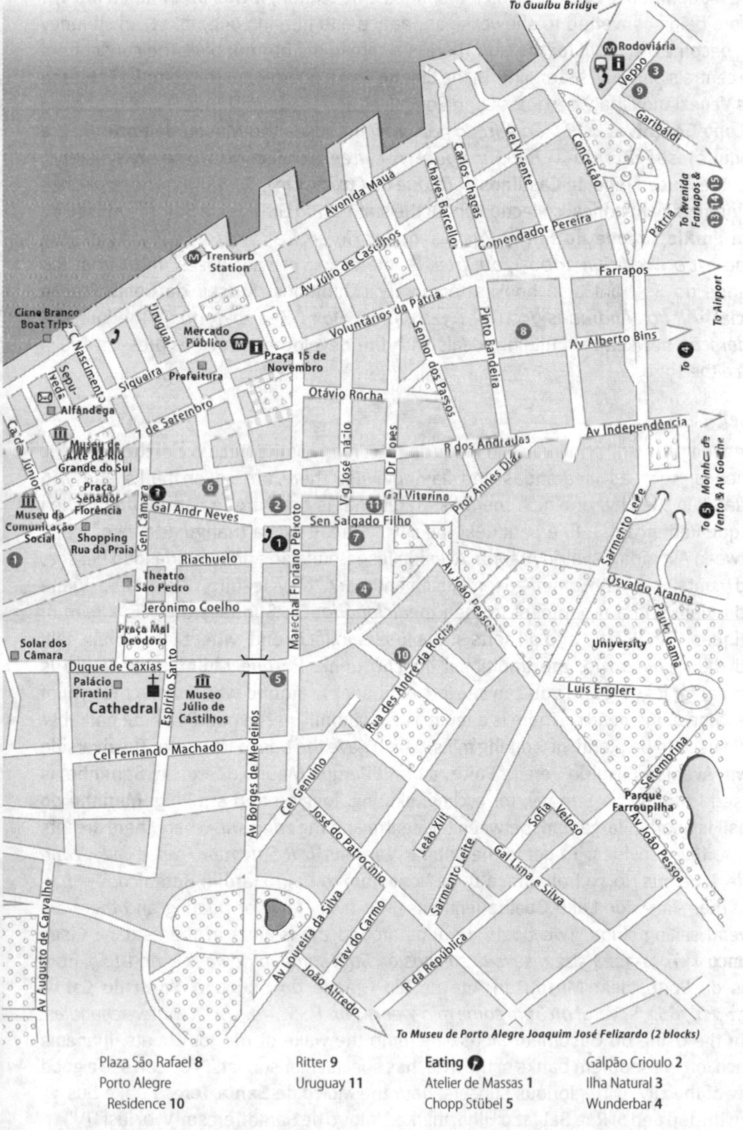

Plaza São Rafael 8
Porto Alegre Residence 10
Ritter 9
Uruguay 11

Eating
Atelier de Massas 1
Chopp Stübel 5
Galpão Crioulo 2
Ilha Natural 3
Wunderbar 4

 where the neoclassical **Mercado Público** sells everything from religious artefacts to spice and meat.

Do not miss the pedestrianized part of **Rua dos Andradas** (Rua da Praia). It is the city's principal outdoor meeting place, the main shopping area, and by around 1600 it is jammed full of people. Going west along Rua dos Andradas, you pass the pink **Casa de Cultura Mário Quintana** in the converted **Hotel Majestic** (see Entertainment, page 345). A little further along is a wide stairway leading up to the two high white towers of the church of **Nossa Senhora das Dores,** the only National Heritage graded church in the city. Many tall buildings in this part of the city rise above the fine, sometimes dilapidated, old houses and the streets are famous for their steep gradients. On the banks of Lake Guaíba, the **Usina do Gasômetro** is Porto Alegre's answer to London's Tate Modern. Built 1926-1928 as a thermoelectric station, it was abandoned in 1974 before being converted to showcase art, dance and film in 1992. Its 117-m chimney has become a symbol for the city. There is a café in the bottom of it. The sunset from the centre's balcony is stunning. In the **Cidade Baixa** quarter are the colonial **Travessa dos Venezianos** (between Ruas Lopo Gonçalves and Joaquim Nabuco) and the **house of Lopo Gonçalves** ⓘ *R João Alfredo 582*, which houses the **Museu de Porto Alegre Joaquim José Felizardo** ⓘ *Tue-Sun 0900-1700, free*, a collection on the city's history.

The **Museu Júlio de Castilhos** ⓘ *Duque de Caxias 1231, Tue-Sun 0900-1700*, has an interesting historical collection about the state of Rio Grande do Sul. The **Museu de Arte do Rio Grande do Sul** ⓘ *Praça Senador Florêncio (Praça da Alfândega), Tue 1000-2100, Wed-Sun 1000-1700, free*, is interesting. It specializes in art from Rio Grande do Sul, but also houses temporary exhibitions. **Museu de Comunicação Social** ⓘ *R dos Andradas 959, T051-322 44252, Mon-Fri 1200-1900*, in the former *A Federação* newspaper building, deals with the development of the press in Brazil since the 1920s.

Parks

Porto Alegre is well endowed with open spaces. Many of the trees are of the flowering varieties, such as jacarandas and flamboyants. There are seven parks and 700 squares in the city, of which the most traditional is the **Parque Farroupilha** (called Parque Redenção), a fine park near the city centre. It has a triangular area of 33 ha between Avenida Osvaldo Aranha, Avenida José Bonifácio and Avenida João Pessoa, and contains a lake, mini-zoo, amusement park, bicycle hire, the Araújo Viana auditorium and a monument to the *Expedicionário*. On Sundays there is a *feira* of antiques, handicrafts and all sorts at the José Bonifácio end, where locals walk, talk and drink *chimarrão*, the traditional *gaúcho* drink. **Parque Moinhos de Vento** is popular for jogging and you can see lots of fit people around who train in the gym of the same name nearby. There is a replica of a windmill in the middle of the park, but there used to be plenty of working mills, which gave the *bairro* its name. The riverside drive, Avenida Edvaldo Pereira Paiva, around Parque Maurício Sirotsky Sobrinho, is closed to traffic on Sunday, for cycling, skating, jogging and strolling. **Marinho do Brasil** is another large park between the centre and the *zona sul*, where there are lots of sporting activities. To get to the **botanic gardens** ⓘ *R Salvador França 1427, zona leste*, take bus No 40 from Praça 15 de Novembro to Bairro Jardim Botânico.

The 5-km-wide **Lake Guaíba** lends itself to every form of boating and there are several sailing clubs. Two boats run trips around the islands in the estuary: **Cisne Branco** ⓘ *T051-3224 5222, several sailings on Sun, some mid- week, 1 hr, US$5*, from Cais do Porto, near Museu de Arte de Rio Grande do Sul; and **Noiva do Caí** ⓘ *T051-211 7662, several on Sun, some mid-week, 1 hr, US$1.90, check winter schedules*, from the Usina do Gasômetro. Jet-skiers jump the wake of the tour boats. **Ipanema beach,** on the southern banks of the river, has spectacular sunsets. You can see a good view of the city, with glorious sunsets, from the **Morro de Santa Teresa** (take bus 95 from the top end of Rua Salgado Filho, marked 'Morro de Santa Teresa TV' or just 'TV').

Beaches around Porto Alegre » pp348-356.

Tramandaí to Torres → *Phone code: 051. Population: 31,000.*

The main beach resorts of the area are to the east and north of the city. Heading east along the BR-290, 112 km from Porto Alegre is **Osório**, a pleasant lakeside town with a few hotels. From here it is 18 km southeast to the rather polluted beach resort of **Tramandaí**. The beaches here are very popular, with lots of hotels, restaurants and seaside amenities. Extensive dunes and lakes in the region provide an interesting variety of wildlife and sporting opportunities. The beach resorts become less polluted the further north you travel, and the water is clean by the time you reach **Torres**.

The BR-101 heads north, just inland of the coast from Osório to Florianópolis and beyond. A series of lakes separates the road from the coastal belt, but there is another road running all along the coast from Tramandaí to Torres and the border with Santa Catarina. Between the two towns are the resorts (heading south to north) of **Atlântida do Sul, Capão da Canoa, Arroio Teixeira** and **Arroio do Sal** (**Casa da Sogra** serves good food). At **Capão da Canoa** there is surfing at Atlântida beach, while the **Lagoa dos Quadros**, inland, is used for windsurfing, sailing, waterskiing and jet-skiing.

Porto Alegre coast

Torres → *Phone code: 051. Colour map 5, B4. Population: 30,900.*

Torres is a well developed resort, with a number of beaches, high-class hotels and restaurants as well as professional surfing competitions and entertainment. There is a lively club scene during the holidays. There is no lack of cheap places to stay, but from Christmas to Carnaval rooms are hard to find. Torres holds a ballooning festival in April. There is an annual independence day celebration, when a cavalcade of horses arrives in town on 16 September from Uruguay.

Torres gets its name from the three huge rocks, or towers, on the town beach, **Praia Grande**. Some 2 km long, the beach is safe for swimming and there is surf near the breakwater. Fishing boats can be hired for a trip to **Ilha dos Lobos**, a rocky island 2 km out to sea, where sea lions spend the winter months. Dolphins visit Praia dos Molhes, north of the town, year round, and whales en route to Santa Catarina can occasionally be seen in July. On the edge of Rio Mampituba, which marks the state boundary, the beach is good for net fishing and has restaurants. About 2 km south of Torres, past rocky little Prainha, is **Cal** (camping is possible at **Paradise Dunas**, December to February only), popular with surfers. A further 2 km south, passing the Praia da Guarita leisure development, is **Itapeva**, with a campsite open year round. The water here is calm, okay for swimming and there is good dune trekking in the **Parque da Guarita**. There are bars and cafés and a **tourist information office** ⓘ *R Rio Branco 315, Torres, T051-664 1219/ T051-626 1937.*

Tramandaí to São José do Norte → *Phone code 051.*

A paved road runs south from Tramandaí (mostly prohibited to trucks) along the coast to **Quintão**, giving access to many beaches. One such beach is **Cidreira**, 26 km south of Tramandaí. It is not very crowded and has **Hotel Farol** on the main street. A bus from Porte Alegre costs US$3.40. A track continues to charming **Mostardas**, thence along the peninsula on the seaward side of the Lagoa dos Patos to São José do Norte, opposite Rio Grande (see Excursions from Rio Grande, page 345). There is accommodation in **Palmares do Sul** (across the peninsula from Quintão) and Mostardas. The latter also has a Banco do Brasil and good pizzeria (Rua Luís Araújo 941, closed Monday). About 30 km south of Mostardas is **Tavares**, with a barely passable hotel (F) in the praça.

Mostardas makes a good base for visiting the **Lagoa do Peixe National Park** ⓘ *information at Praça Luís Martins 30, Mostardas, T051-673 1464*, one of South America's top spots for migrating birds. Flamingos and albatrosses are among the visitors. There is free access to the park, which has no infrastructure. From Mostardas you can hop off the bus (daily at 1045) that passes through the northern end of the park on its way to the beach, where there are basic hotels and restaurants. The main lake, which has the highest bird concentration, is about 20 km from both Mostardas and Tavares.

Serra Gaúcha » *pp348-356.*

Some of the Serra Gaúcha's most stunningly beautiful scenery is around the towns of Gramado and Canela, 130 km north of Porto Alegre. There is a distinctly Swiss/ Bavarian flavour to many of the buildings in both towns. In spring and summer the flowers are a delight, and in winter there are frequent snow showers.

This is excellent walking and climbing country among hills, woods, lakes and waterfalls. The Rio Paranhana at Três Coroas is well known for canoeing, especially for slalom. It is 25 km south of Gramado. In both towns it is difficult to get rooms in high season. Local crafts include knitted woollens, leather, wickerwork and chocolate.

Gramado → *Phone code: 054. Colour map 5, B4. Population: 28,600.*

At 850 m above sea level, Gramado provides a summer escape from the 40°C heat of the plains. The town lies on the edge of a plateau with fantastic views. It is clean and full of Alpine-style buildings making it feel like a Swiss Disneyworld. Gramado lives almost entirely by tourism. Its main street, Avenida Borges de Medeiros, is full of kitsch artisan shops and fashion boutiques. In the summer, thousands of hydrangeas (*hortênsias*) bloom. Among its parks are **Parque Knorr** and **Lago Negro**, and **Minimundo** ⓘ *T054-286 1334, Tue-Sun 1300-1700*, a collection of miniature models such as European castles. About 1½ km along Avenida das Hortênsias heading towards Canela is the **Prawer chocolate factory** ⓘ *Av das Hortênsias 4100, T054-286 1580, www.prawer.com.br, Mon-Fri 0830-1130 and 1330-1700*, which offers free tours of the truffle-making process and free tasting. Opposite is the incongruous but good **Hollywood Dream Car Automobile Museum** ⓘ *Av das Hortênsias 4151, T054-286 4515, 0900-1900, US$2.10*, which has an excellent collection of American gas-guzzlers dating back to a 1929 Ford Model A and Harley-Davidson motorbikes from 1926. For a good walk or bike ride into the valley, take the dirt road Turismo Rural 28, *Um Mergulho no Vale* (A Dive into the Valley), which starts at Avenida das Hortênsias immediately before the chocolate factory. Each August, Gramado holds a festival of Latin American cinema. There are two **tourist information offices** ⓘ *Av das Hortênsias (Pórtico), T054-286 1418*, and ⓘ *Praça Maj Nicoletti/Av Borges de Medeiros 1674, T054-286 1475, www.gramadosite.com.br.*

Canela and around → *Phone code: 054. Colour map 5, B4. Population: 33,600.*

A few kilometres along the plateau rim, Canela has been spared the plastic makeover of its neighbour. The painted wooden buildings provide a certain downtown charm. Canela is surrounded by good parks and is developing as a centre of adventure tourism, with rafting, abseiling and trekking on offer. There's a **tourist office** ⓘ *Laga da Fama 227, T054-282 2200, www.canela.com.br*.

About 7 km from Canela is the **Parque Estadual do Caracol** ⓘ *T054-278 3035, 0830-1800, US$1.75*, which has a spectacular 130-m high waterfall. Emerging from thick forest, Rio Caracol tumbles like dry ice from an overhanging elliptical escarpment. The falls are east-facing, so photography is best before noon. A 927-step metal staircase leads to the plunge pool. If cycling, there is an 18-km circular route continuing on to Park Ferradura (along a 4-km spur), where there is a good view into the canyon of the Rio Cai. From the Ferradura junction, turn right to continue to the national forest **Floresta Nacional** ⓘ *T054-282 2608, 0800-1700, free*, run by Ibama (the Brazilian Environment Ministry) with woodland walks. From here, the dirt road continues round to Canela. Another good hike or bike option is the 4-km dirt track southeast of Canela past Parque das Sequóias to Morro Pelado. At over 600 m, there are spectacular views from the rim edge.

Army maps exist at a scale of 1:50,000 but are only available from military posts in Caxias do Sul and Porto Alegre. The urban department in Canela's Prefeitura Municipal, Rua Dona Carlinda, and the environmental lodge in Parque Estadual do Caracol have copies available for viewing only.

Parque Nacional de Aparados da Serra

ⓘ *Aparados da Serra, Wed-Sun 0900-1700, US$2.10 plus US$1.75 for a car, T054-251 1262; Serra Geral is open all year, daily, free. It has no infrastructure but there is a campground. The best time to visit is May-Aug; rain is heaviest in Sep. For information contact Ibama, R Miguel Teixeira 126, Cidade Baixa, Caixa Postal 280, Porto Alegre, T051 3225 2144, www.ibama.gov.br, or the the Centro Cultural Cambará do Sul, R Adail Valim 39, T051-251 1320, daily 0800-1200, 1330-1800. For guides in Cambará do Sul visit the Centro Cultural, R Adail Valim 39, T054-251 1320 (which has a 1:50,000 scale trekking map on view), and in Praia Grande T048-532 0330. Some of the hotels in Cambará run trips into the park (see page 349).*

Some 88 km from São Francisco de Paula (138 km east of Canela, 117 km north of Porto Alegre) are the spectacular Aparados da Serra and Serra Geral. Formed 115-130 million years ago when the American and African plates were separating, the parks lie in a 250-km mountain range. **Parque Nacional Aparados da Serra**'s major attraction is the Itaimbezinho canyon, which is 7.8 km long and 720 m deep. Here, two waterfalls cascade 350 m into a stone circle at the bottom. For experienced hikers (with a guide) there is a difficult path to the bottom of Itaimbezinho. Other easier hikes follow the upper rim of the canyon. You can then hike 20 km to Praia Grande in Santa Catarina. **Parque Nacional da Serra Geral** was opened in 1992. Its main attractions are the Malacara and Fortaleza canyons; the latter is 1170 m deep. From the top there are spectacular views to the coast. As well as the canyons, the parks and surrounding regions have several bird specialities. The red-legged seriema, a large conspicuous bird, can be seen on the way to the park, and there are two fox species.

The nearest town to the park is **Cambará do Sul** (bus from São Francisco de Paula at 0945 and 1700, 1¼ hours, US$2 and one direct bus per day from Porto Alegre). The park entrance is at Guarita Gralha Azul, 18 km along an unpaved road. There's a bus from Cambará do Sul or it's possible to hitchhike. There is also a 20-km unpaved road from Praia Grande. There is a snack bar but no accommodation and camping is banned. From Cambará do Sul to the Fortaleza canyon is 23 km on an unpaved road.

South of Porto Alegre

» pp348-356.

Pelotas → *Phone code: 053. Colour map 5, C3. Population: 323,200.*

Pelotas, Rio Grande do Sul's second largest city, was founded in the early 19th century and grew rich on the *charque* (dried beef) trade. On the BR-116, 271 km south of Porto Alegre, it lies on the banks of Rio São Gonçalo, which connects the Lagoa dos Patos with the Lagoa Mirim. The heyday was 1860-1890 and its early colonial architecture enhances the city's air of being stuck in a time warp. It is sleepy yet prosperous, with much typically Brazilian charm. It has an array of shops in the pedestrianized town centre, and pleasant parks with lots of green spaces. There is a 19th-century cathedral, **São Francisco de Paula**, and, as testament to British settlers of the time, the Anglican church **Igreja Episcopal do Redentor**, a couple of blocks from the main square on Rua XV de Novembro. The tree-lined Avenida Bento Gonçalves offers a pleasant escape from the summer heat. Pelotas is famous for its cakes and sweets; try some of the preserved fruits from the many small confectioners.

Ins and outs The *rodoviária* is out of town, with a bus every 15 minutes to the centre. There's no official tourist information centre but **Terrasul** ⓘ *R Gen Neto 627, T053-227 9973*, has local maps and can organize good value city and regional tours. Recommended. Also try **Cispella Viagens** ⓘ *R Andrade Neves 1991, T053-225 5944*.

Excursions from Pelotas

Within a radius of 60 km (about an hour's drive), there are numerous excursions to the farms of settlers of German descent in the hilly countryside (for example Cerrito Alegre and Quilombo), where you can find simple and clean accommodation, with cheap, good and plentiful food.

West of town, the **Lagoa dos Patos** is very shallow; at low tide it is possible to walk 1 km out from the shore. During heavy rain, saltwater entering the lake brings with it large numbers of crabs which are a local delicacy. Fishermen are generally happy to take tourists out on sightseeing or fishing trips for a small fee (it's best to go in a group). **Praia do Laranjal** is full of local beach houses and there are several friendly bars. **Barro Douro** is very green with a campsite but no beach. It's the site of a big local festival for *Iemanjá* on 1-2 February; well worth visiting. From Pelotas, take a **Ze3** bus (or taxi US$30).

South of Pelotas, on the BR-471, is the **Taim Water Reserve** ⓘ *information from Ibama in Porto Alegre, T051-226 7211, www.ibama.gov.br*, on the Lagoa Mirim. The road cuts the reserve in two and capibaras, killed by passing traffic, are sadly a common sight along the route. Many protected species, including black-necked swans and the quero-quero bird, migrate to the Taim for the breeding season. There are no facilities. About 5 km from Taim there is an **ecological station** with a small museum of regional animals; there is some accommodation for scientists or other interested visitors. However, most visitors stay in Rio Grande, 80 km away, or in Pelotas.

Rio Grande → *Phone code: 053. Colour map 5, C3. Population: 186,500.*

At the entrance to the Lagoa dos Patos, 274 km south of Porto Alegre, is Rio Grande, founded in 1737. The city lies on a low, sandy peninsula, 16 km from the Atlantic Ocean. Today it is the distribution centre for the southern part of Rio Grande do Sul, with significant cattle and meat industries.

During the latter half of the 19th century, Rio Grande was an important centre. It has lost much of its importance but is still notable for the charm of its old buildings. The **Catedral de São Pedro** dates from 1755-1775. The **Museu Oceanográfico** ⓘ *2 km from the centre on Av Perimetral, T053-231 3496, daily 0900-1100, 1400-1700*, has an interesting collection of 125,000 molluscs. To get there take bus 59 or walk along the waterfront. At Praça Tamandaré is a small zoo. There is a **tourist office** at the junction of Rua Duque de Caxias and Rua Gen Becaler.

Excursions from Rio Grande

Cassino is a popular seaside town with hotels and shops, 24 km from Rio Grande via a good road. There are several beaches within easy reach of Cassino, but they have no facilities. A wrecked ship remains on the shore where it was thrown by a storm in 1975. Travelling south, the beaches are, in order: **Querência** (5 km), **Stela Maris** (9 km), **Netuno** (10 km), all with surf.

The *barra* (breakwater), 5 km south of Cassino, through which all vessels entering and leaving Rio Grande must pass, is a tourist attraction. Barra–Rio Grande buses, from the east side of Praça Ferreira, pass the *superporto* where there is very good fishing. The coastline here is low and straight, lacking the bays found to the north of Porto Alegre. One attraction is railway flat-cars powered by sail (agree the price in advance); the railway was built for the construction of the breakwater.

Across the inlet from Rio Grande, the little-visited settlement of **São José do Norte** makes a pleasant trip (see Tramandaí to São José do Norte, page 342). Founded in 1725 and still mostly intact, the village depends on agriculture and crab fishing. There are only three hotels and a good campsite, **Caturritas**, T053-238 1476, in pine forests 5 km from the town. There are also several long beaches. Ferries (departing every half-hour, 30 minutes) link São José with Rio Grande; there are also three car ferries daily, T053-232 1500. **Tourist information** ⓘ *R General Osório 127*.

Western Rio Grande do Sul » *pp348-356.*

Passo Fundo → *Phone code: 054. Colour map 5, B3. Population: 168,500.*

Northwest of Porto Alegre by 328 km is Passo Fundo, regarded as 'the most *gaúcho* city in Rio Grande do Sul', so much so that the town's square boasts a statue of a *maté* gourd and bombilla. There is an international *rodeio* in December. The town has several hotels in the A-B category.

Santo Ângelo and the Jesuit Missions → *Phone code: 055. Colour map 5, B2.*

West of Passo Fundo are the **Sete Povos das Missões Orientais**. **Santo Ângelo** is a pleasant town with the best infrastructure for visiting the missions. It has a missionary museum in the main square where there is a **cathedral** with a hideous fresco of missionaries indoctrinating the indigenous population. The only considerable Jesuit remains in Brazilian territory are the very dramatic ones at **São Miguel das Missões**, some 50 km from Santo Ângelo. At São Miguel, now a World Heritage site, there is a church, 1735-45, and small **museum** ⓘ *0900-1800*. A *son et lumière* show in Portuguese is held daily, in winter at 2000, and later in summer, although all times rather depend on how many people there are. The show ends too late to return to Santo Ângelo and there are one or two options for accommodation (see Sleeping, page 342). It is difficult to find a good place to eat in the evening; you could try a snack bar for hamburgers. *Gaúcho* festivals are often held on Sunday afternoons, in a field near the Mission (follow the music).

Porto Xavier and the Argentine missions

You can continue into Argentina to see the mission ruins at San Ignacio Miní and Posadas by getting a bus from Santo Ângelo (0615, 1300 or 1930) to the quiet border town of **Porto Xavier** (four hours, US$4), on the Rio Uruguay. Buses also run to Porto Xavier from Porto Alegre (one daily), and Santa Maria.

 Border crossing The Policia Federal post for the entry and exit stamps is about 100 m north of the ferry in a white building. Take the **ferry** ⓘ *Mon-Fri 0800-1145, 1400-1745, Sat 0900-0945, 1500-1545, closed Sun, US$1*, to Puerto Javier, on the Argentine side of Rio Uruguay. From there, there are frequent buses to Posadas and, via connections at Alem and Santa Ana, to Iguaçu Falls.

Salto do Yucumâ

Between November and April, the Rio Uruguay overflows along its east bank for over 1800 m, creating the world's longest waterfall. The 12-m-high Salto do Yucumâ is in the 17,000-ha Parque do Turvo. Its isolation (530 km northwest of Porto Alegre on the Argentine border) means few tourists visit. Accordingly it is a wildlife haven with over 220 bird species and 34 mammal species (12 threatened). The nearest town, **Derrumbadas**, 4 km from the park and has an **information point** ⓘ *T054-3551 1558, ext 228*. Lemon extract production is an important local industry.

Uruguaiana and the border with Argentina

➔ *Phone code: 055. Colour map 5, B1. Population: 127,000.*

It is also possible to cross the border through Uruguaiana, a cattle centre 772 km from Porto Alegre, and its twin Argentine town of Paso de los Libres in the extreme west. A 1400-m bridge over the Rio Uruguai links the two cities.

Border crossing Brazilian immigration and customs are at the end of the bridge, five blocks from the main praça. Buses connect the bus stations and centres of each city every 30 minutes. If you have to disembark for visa formalities, the next bus will pick you up without extra charge. There are bus services to Porto Alegre. **Planalto** buses run from Uruguaiana via Barra do Quaraí/Bella Unión (US$4.50) to Salto and Paysandú in Uruguay. Exchange and information is available in the same building. Exchange rates are better in the town than at the border. There are a number of cheap and mid-range hotels in town. A taxi or bus across the bridge is about US$3.50.

The crossing furthest west is **Barra do Quaraí** to **Bella Unión**, via the Barra del Cuaraim bridge. This is near the confluence of the Uruguai and Quaraí rivers. Bella Unión has three hotels and a campsite in the Parque Fructuoso Rivera. **Brazilian Consulate** ⓘ *C Lirio Moraes 62, T/F055-739 2054*; buses to Salto and Montevideo.

Some 30 km east is another crossing from **Quaraí** to **Artigas**, in a cattle-raising and agricultural area. **Brazilian Consulate** ⓘ *C Lecueder 432, T055-8642 2504, F8642 4504*. Artigas has hotels, a hostel and campsites. Buses run to Salto and Montevideo.

There are two further crossings at **Aceguá**, 60 km south of Bagé, 59 km north of the Uruguayan town of Melo, and further east, **Jaguarão/Rio Branco**. The 1½-km-long Mauá bridge across the Rio Jaguarão joins these two towns. The police post for passport checks is 3 km before the bridge; customs are at the bridge.

Santana do Livramento and the border with Uruguay

➔ *Phone code: 055. Colour map 5, C2. Population: 91,100.*

The southern interior of the state is the region of the real *gaúcho*. Principal towns of this area include Santana do Livramento. Its twin Uruguayan city is Rivera. All you need to do is cross the main street, but by public transport this is not a straightforward route between Brazil and Uruguay. For motorists there are three customs offices in Santana do Livramento; about 30 minutes is needed for formalities. For road traffic, Chuy is better than Río Branco or Aceguá.

Border crossing Before crossing into Uruguay, you must visit Brazilian Polícia Federal to get an exit stamp; if not, the Uruguayan authorities will send you back. **Brazilian consulates** are at ⓘ *R Del Pilar 786, Melo, T0462-2136*, and at ⓘ *Río Branco, Lavalleja and Palomeque*. Exchange rates are usually better at Melo than at the border.

Uruguayan immigration ⓘ *Sarandí y Viera, 14 blocks, 2 km, from the border; take bus along Agraciada*, is in the new Complejo Turístico. There is also a tourist office. Note that you must have a Brazilian exit stamp to enter Uruguay and a Uruguayan exit stamp to enter Brazil. Luggage is inspected when boarding buses out of Rivera; there are also three checkpoints on the road out of town.

Chuí and the border with Uruguay → *Phone code: 053. Colour map 5, C2.*

On the Brazilian side of the border is Chuí, a tranquil town; on the Uruguayan side is the town of Chuy. The BR-471 from Porto Alegre and Pelotas skirts the town and carries straight through to Uruguay, where it becomes Ruta 9. Each country's immigration is outside the town (see below); if you are staying in town you can walk anywhere as long as you do not go beyond the immigration posts. The main street is Avenida Internacional: on the Brazilian side it is called Avenida Uruguaí and on the Uruguayan side Avenida Brasil. Each side carries two-way traffic. On the Brazilian side the shops are mainly clothes, shoes and household goods, while the Uruguayan side has duty-free shops and a casino. **São Miguel fort**, built by the Portuguese in 1737, now reconstructed with period artefacts, is worth a visit. A lighthouse 10 km west marks the Barro do Chuí inlet, which has uncrowded beaches and is visited by sea lions.

The Uruguayan town of **Chuy** is 340 km from Montevideo. On the Uruguayan side, on a promontory overlooking Laguna Merín and the *gaúcho* landscape of southern Brazil, stands the restored fortress of **San Miguel** ⓘ *closed Mon, US$0.20, bus from Chuy US$0.45*, dating from 1752 and surrounded by a moat. It is set in a park in which many plants and animals are kept. Tours (US$10 from Chuy) end for the season after 31 March. **Parador San Miguel**, nearby, is excellent, beautiful rooms, fine food and service.

Brazilian immigration Immigration is about 2½ km from the border, on BR-471, the road to Pelotas. All buses, except those originating in Pelotas, stop at customs on both sides of the border; if coming from Pelotas, you must ask the bus to stop for exit formalities. International buses, for example TTL from Porto Alegre, make the crossing straightforward. The company holds passports – hand over your visitor card on leaving Brazil and get a Uruguayan one on entry. Have luggage available for inspection. Make sure you get your stamp or you will have trouble leaving Brazil.

Uruguayan immigration Uruguayan passport control is 2½ km before the border on the road into Chuy, US$2.50 by taxi, officials are friendly and co-operative. If travelling by bus, make sure the driver knows you want to stop at Uruguayan immigration, it will not do so automatically. If you stay overnight in Chuy you cannot get your exit stamp in advance. You may only do so immediately prior to leaving the country.

Entering Brazil From Uruguay, on the Uruguayan side, the bus will stop if asked, and wait while you get your exit stamp (with bus conductor's help); on the Brazilian side, the appropriate form is completed by the *rodoviária* staff when you purchase your ticket into Brazil. The bus stops at Polícia Federal (BR-471) and the conductor completes formalities while you sit on the bus. Customs officials may ask you to open your luggage for inspection. Also, if entering by car, fill up with petrol in Brazil, where fuel is cheaper.

Entering Uruguay To enter Uruguay, you must have a Brazilian exit stamp and a Uruguayan entry stamp, otherwise you will not be permitted to proceed. Those requiring a visa must have a medical examination before a visa can be issued in Chuí, cost about US$20 and US$10 respectively.

Porto Alegre *p337, map p338*
Hotels in the area around R Garibáldi and Voluntários da Patria between Av Farrapos and *rodoviária* are overpriced and used many times a day.

L **Plaza São Rafael**, Av Alberto Bins 514, T051-3222 7000, www.plazahoteis.com.br. Newly refurbished 1970s luxury hotel with excellent service and business facilities including laptop computer rental and 2 free internet lines in each room. Gym and sauna. Less anonymous than the city's US chain hotels (there is a Sheraton in town).

AL **Continental**, Lg Vespasiano Júlio Veppo 77, T051-3211 2344, www.hoteiscontinental.com.br. Reasonable business hotel with a pool, gym and with good weekend discount rates. Recommended.

AL **Everest**, R Duque de Caxias 1357, T051-3215 9500, www.everest.com.br. Modest 4-star with a business centre and good views.

A **Porto Alegre Residence**, R Des André da Rocha 131, T051-3225 8644, F3224 0366. Large rooms. Recommended.

B **Açores**, R dos Andradas 885, T051-3221 7588, F3225 1007. Centrally located but with cramped rooms. Friendly staff and weekend discounts.

B **Embaixador**, R Jerônimo Coelho 354, T051-3215 6600, www.embaixador.com.br. Comfortable 4-star with gym, sauna and an unexciting restaurant. Weekend discounts.

B **Ritter**, Lg Vespasiano Júlio Veppo 55, opposite *rodoviária*, T051-3228 4044, www.ritterhoteis.com.br. 4-star and 3-star wings, English, French, German spoken, bar, small pool, sauna. Fine restaurant, good service. Recommended.

C **Conceição Center**, Av Sen Salgado Filho 201, T051-3225 7774, www.hoteisconceicao.com.br. Simple but respectable town hotel with plain but well-kept a/c rooms with fridges. Has a cheaper (**D**) sister hotel, see website for details.

C **Lancaster**, Trav Acelino de Carvalho 67, T051-3224 4737, F3224 4630. Centrally located, quiet, a/c rooms and a restaurant.

D **Elevado**, Av Farrapos 65, T/F051-3224 5250, www.hotelelevado.com.br. Big rooms, noisy at the front, microwave and coffee, good value.

D **Palácio**, Av Vigário José Inácio 644, T051-3225 3467. Centrally located and with hot water, family and a safe. Recommended.

E **América**, Av Farrapos 119, T/F051-3226 0062, www.hotelamerica.com.br. Bright, friendly, large rooms with sofas, quiet rooms at back, garage. Highly recommended.

E **Minuano**, Av Farrapos 31, T/F051-3226 3062. Small immaculate rooms, and parking.

E **Uruguay**, Dr Flores 371. Simple fan-cooled rooms. Recommended.

Camping

Praia do Guarujá, 16 km out on Av Guaíba.

Beaches around Porto Alegre
p341, map p341

A **Solar da Barra**, R Plínio Kroeff 465, Mampituba, near Torres, T051-664 1811, F664 1090. Low-season discounts. 2 pools, one of which is thermal, sauna, children's playground.

B **Beira-Mar**, Av Emancipação 521, Tramandaí beach, T051-661 1234, F661 1133. Pleasant but simple hotel with a thermal pool and sports facilities.

B **Napoli**, Av Paraguassu 3159, Capão da Canoa, T/F051-665 2231. Simple beach pousada (**C** low season).

B-C **Pousada Brisa do Mar**, R Júlio de Castilhos and R Borges de Medeiros, Torres, T051-664 2019. With a good breakfast. Recommended.

C **Alvorada**, Arroio Teixeira on the beach, T051-622 1242. Good facilities, café, only open Dec-Mar.

C **Ibiama**, R Dr Mário Santo Dani 1161, Osório beach, T/F051-663 2822. Simple rooms and breakfast.

C **Kolman**, R Sepé 1800, Capão da Canoa, T051-625 2022, T051-625 2021. Standard family beach hotel with a pool.

D **Hotel Costa Azul**, Av José Bonifácio 382, Torres, T/F051-664 3291. Friendly and close to *rodoviária*, with breakfast.

D **São Jorge**, F Amaral 19, Tramandaí beach, T051-661 1154. Quiet, simple and recommended.

E **São Domingos**, R Júlio de Castilhos 875, Torres, T051-664 1865, F664 1022. IYHA youth hostel, clean, closed out of season. Price per person.

E Tramandaí, R Belém 701, Tramandaí beach, T051-228 3802, F226 5380. IYHA youth hostel with dorms and doubles. Price per person.

Camping

Marina Park, RS-389, 7 km, Capão da Canoa, T051-301 6150.
Pinguela Parque, BR-101, 22 km, Osório beach, T051-628 8080.
Praia de Itapeva, 5 km, Torres, T051-605 5112.

Tramandaí to São José do Norte *p342*

D Hotel Farol, on the main street, Cidreira. With bath.
E Hotel Mostardense, R Bento Conçalves 200, Mostardas, T051-673 1368. Good.

Gramado *p342*

AL Serra Azul, R Garibáldi 152, T051-286 1082, F286 3374. Sauna, massage, tennis and 2 pools, one of which is thermal.
A Estalagem St Hubertus, R da Carriere 974, Lago Negro, T/F051-286 1273. Part of the Roteiros de Charme group, see page 50.
A Gramado Parque, R Leopoldo Rosenfeldt 818, T/F051-286 2588. Bungalows, good breakfast, reasonable laundry service.
A Ritta Höppner, R Pedro Candiago 305, T051-286 1334, F286 3129. Cabins with TV and fridge. Very good value, friendly, good breakfasts. German owners, pool and miniature trains in grounds, closed in May.
B Chalets do Vale, R Arthur Reinheimer 161 (off Av das Hortênsias at about 4700), T051-286 4151, chaletsdovale@via-rs.net. 3 high-quality chalets in lovely wood setting, 2 double beds, kitchen, TV. Good deal for groups of 4 or families. Recommended.
B Pequeno Bosque, R Piratini 486, located in wood close to Véu da Noiva waterfall, T051-286 1527, F286 1771. Simple but pleasant and with a good breakfast.
B Pousada Zermatt, R da Fé 187, Bavária, T/F051-286 2426. Simple and plain accommodation but recommended.
C Luiz, Sen Salgado Filho 432, T051-286 1026. Pleasant rooms, friendly service and a good breakfast.
C Pousada Pertuti, Av Borges de Medeiros 3571, T051-286 2513. Good breakfast, use of kitchen, friendly. Recommended.
D Brisa Pousada, R Tristão de Oliveira 252, T051-286 6788. Another good cheap option.
D Dinda, R Augusto Zatti 160, T051-286 1588. Basic but one of the cheapest in town.
E Albergue Internacional de Gramado, Av das Hortênsias 3880, T051-295 1020. 50 dormitory beds in new, cosy hostel.

Canela and around *p343*

AL Laje de Pedra, Av Pres Kennedy Km 3, T054-2824300, F282 4400. Restaurant, pool, thermal pool, sauna, tennis.
A Vila Suzana Parque, R Col Theobaldo Fleck 15, T054-282 2020, F282 1793. Chalets, heated pool, attractive.
C Canela, Av Osvaldo Aranha, 223, T054-282 2774. Breakfast, English-speaking staff. Recommended.
C Pousada das Sequóias, R Godofre de Raymundo 1747, T054-282 1373, www.sequoias.cjb.net. Pretty forest cabins and decent service and breakfast.
D Central, Av Júlio de Castilhos 146. Safe, simple fan-cooled rooms. Recommended.
D Pousada Schermer, Travessa Romeu 30, T054-282 1746. Basic backpacker accommodation but very friendly, well kept and highly recommended.
E Pousada do Viajante, R Ernesto Urbani 132, behind *rodoviária*, T054-282 2017. Youth hostel offering dorms and doubles with kitchen facilities. Recommended.

Camping

Camping Clube do Brasil, 1 km from waterfall in Parque do Caracol, 1 km off main road (signposted), take bus for Parque Estadual do Caracol, 8 km from Canela. Excellent honey and chocolate for sale. Highly recommended.
Sesi, R Francisco Bertolucci 504, 2½ km outside Canela, T/F054-282 1311. Cabins also available, restaurant, clean. Recommended.

Parque Nacional de Aparados da Serra *p343*

L Parador Casa da Montanha, Estrada Parque Nacional, T054-504 5302, reservations T054-9973 9320, www.paradorcasadamontanha.com.br. 7 cabins up a precarious dirt road, all with stunning views. Very beautiful. Full board included in the price and optional excursions into the park on horseback or foot. Minimum stay 2 days.
D Itaimbeleza, next to the *rodoviária*. Very simple fan-cooled rooms and advice on getting into the park.

Pelotas *p344*

A Manta, R Gen Neto 1131, T053-225 2411, www.hoteismanta.com.br. Blocky 1970s hotel with a pool, restaurant and bar. The best in town though somewhat frayed.

D Aleppo Hotel, R Gen Osório 708, T/F053-225 3950. Bright, clean and big rooms and breakfast. Recommended.

D Motel Mediterâneo, Av Presidente João Goulont 5473, T053-271 4746. About 150 m from the *rodoviária*. Recommended if arriving late.

Rio Grande *p344*

A Atlântico Rio Grande, R Duque de Caxias 55, T/F053-231 3833. Standard town hotel with a/c rooms. Good value. Recommended.

B Europa, R Gen Neto 165, main square, T/F053-231 3933. Conveniently located in the centre of town with a range of a/c rooms.

D Paris, R Mcal Floriano Peixoto 112. An old colonial building. Charming. Recommended.

Excursions from Rio Grande *p345*

A Atlântico, Av Rio Grande 387, Cassino, T053-236 1350. Clean, refurbished and with special rates for students.

B Marysol, Av Atlântica 700, Cassino, T053-236 1240. Friendly, simple pousada near the beach.

Santo Ângelo and the Jesuit Missions *p345*

A Maerkli, Av Brasil 1000, Santo Ângelo, T/F055-312 2127. Pleasant but basic 1980s hotel.

C Hotel Barichello, Av Borges do Canto 1567, São Miguel das Missões, T055-3381 1272. Nice, clean and quiet. It also has a restaurant, **Churrasco**, for lunch.

D-E Hotel Nova Esperança, Trav Centenario 463, Santo Ângelo, T055-3312 1173, behind the bus station. Simple, reasonably well maintained but with no breakfast.

E Comércio, Av Brasil 1178, Santo Ângelo, T055-3312 2542. A bit run down but good for the price, clean, friendly.

E Pousada das Missões, next to the ruins, São Miguel das Missões, T055-3381 1030, pousada.missoes@terra.com.br. Very good youth hostel.

Porto Xavier and the Argentine missions *p345*

D Rotta, Av Mal Fl Peixoto 757, near the praça. Plain rooms with or without a/c, and/or TV, bath, breakfast, good restaurant closed Sat and Sun evening; good cheap, pizzeria on the terrace on the main square. Recommended. The hotel is about 5 mins' walk from the ferry at the end of the main street.

Salto do Yucumâ *p346*

There are several cheap hotels in the area.

C-D Hotel Imperial, Av Jn Castilhos 544, Três Passos, 28 km from the park, T055-3522 2135. Standard small town hotel with breakfast included.

In Tenente, 16 km from the park are:

F Hotel Avenida, beside the petrol station, T055-3551 1859; and **F Hotel Iucuma**, R Tapulas 271, T055-3551 1120.

Chuí and the border with Uruguay *p347*

Brazil

B Turis Firper, Av Samuel Prilliac 629, Chuí, T053-265 1398, F265 1068. Basic with a/c rooms, TV and bar.

E Bianca, Chile 1620, Chuí, T053-265 1500. Very simple but adequate for short stays. All rooms have a bath.

E San Francisco, Av Colômbia and R Chile. Very simple rooms with a bath and an equally simple restaurant.

Uruguay

The international phone code for Uruguay is +598.

B Nuevo Hotel Plaza, Gral Artigas y Arachanes, Chuy, T/F0474-2309. On the plaza, central, helpful and with breakfast, TV and a restaurant, **El Mesón de la Plaza.**

B-C Alerces, Laguna de Castillos 578, Chuy, T0474-2260. Simple rooms with heaters, bath, TV, breakfast.

D Madrugada, C S Priliac y India Muerta, Chuy, T0474-2346. Very simple but well looked-after and quiet.

Camping

Barra del Chuy campsite, Ruta 9, Km 331, turn right 13 km, T2425. Good bathing, many birds. *Cabañas* for up to 4 cost up to US$20 daily, depending on amenities. From Chuy, buses run here every 2 hrs.

Eating

Porto Alegre *p337, map p338*

Gaúcho cooking features large quantities of meat, while German cuisine is also a strong influence. Regional farm (*campeiro*) food, now a dying art, uses plenty of rice, vegetables, and interesting sauces. Vegetarians might try some of the *campeiro* soups and casseroles and growing number of alternative or natural restaurants, otherwise stick to Italian restaurants or *churrascaria* salad bars.

Apart from the many good restaurants, much of the tastiest food can be found in street stalls and cheap *lancherias*; the central market along the praça is lined with them.

TTT **Galpão Crioulo**, Av Loureiro da Silva (Parque da Harmonia aka Maurício Sirotsky Sobrinho, Cidade Baixa), T051-3226 8194. Good *churrascaria* with a show and dancing, 1130-1600, 1900-0100.

TTT **Portoalgrense**, Av Pará 913, São Geraldo, T051-3343 2767, closed Sun. The best carnivore restaurant in the city with excellent beef steak and a respectable wine list.

TT **Atelier de Massas**, R Riachuelo 1482, T051-3225 1125. Lunch and dinner, closed Sun. Fantastic pastas and 8 cm thick steaks, excellent value. Highly recommended.

TT **Chopp Stübel**, R Quintino Bocaiúva 940, Moinhos de Vento, T051-3332 8895. Open 1800-0030, closed Sun. One of the best in the city for reasonably priced German food. Recommended.

TT **Le Bon Gourmet**, Av Alberto Bins 514 (in **Plaza São Rafael** hotel), 1900-2300, closed Sun. Steaks, pasta and fine fish dishes. The 24-hr **514 Bar** is at the back of hotel lobby.

TT **Wunderbar**, R Marquês do Herval 598, Moinhos de Vento, T051-3222 4967. Popular and very friendly German restaurant and bar which is always very busy. Open 1830 until the last diner leaves. Recommended.

T **Coqueiros**, R João Alfredo 208, T051-3227 1833. 1130-1430, 1930-2400, closed Sun and Mon evenings. Cheap and cheerful *churrrascaria*. The meat tends to be salty and a bit overdone.

T **Ilha Natural**, R Gen Câmara 60, T051-3224 4738. Self-service, cheap, lunch only Mon-Fri.

T **Nova Vida Restaurant Alternativo**, Av Borges de Medeiros 1010, 1100-1500, closed Sun. Good lasagne and salads. Also at Demetrio Ribeiro 1182.

T **Restaurant Majestic and Café Dos Cataventos**, Casa de Cultura Mário Quintana, R dos Andrades 736. 2 snack and *almoco* restaurants – the latter in the courtyard and the other on the roof. Both serve good drinks, snacks and meals. Fantastic rooftop sunsets.

Gramado *p342*

There's no lack of choice with plenty of decent, if pricey, restaurants along Av Borges de Medeiros.

TT **Churrascaria Patrão Velho**, Av das Hortênsias 4759, T054-286 0823. Very good meat and side dishes. Recommended.

TT **Gasthof Edelweiss**, R da Carriere 1119, T054-286 1861. Some of the best German food in town.

T **Lancheria Tissot**, Av Borges de Medeiros 3283. Tasty, inexpensive snacks and meals in family-run snack bar.

Canela *p343*

TT **Bifão & Cia**, Av Osvaldo Aranha 301, T054-282 9156. Reasonable *churrascaria* with huge slabs of meat and side dishes.

T **Café Canela**, Praça Joa Correa 7, T054-282 3304. Good meat and cheese dishes.

T **Parati Lanches**, Praça Joã Correa 97. Traditional watering hole with pool tables, 0800-2400.

Pelotas *p344*

TTT **El Paisano**, R Mcal Deodoro 1093, T053-227 1507. Legendary Uruguayan steak. Closed Mon, opening hours vary seasonally.

TT **Lobão**, Av Bento Gonçalves 3460, T053-225 6197. Standard barbecue *churrascaria*, plenty of side dishes.

T **Mama Pizza**, R Gen Osório 720. Good affordable pizza run by **Hotel Manta**.

Rio Grande *p344*

TT **Blue Café**, R Luís Loréa 314. Expresso machine and good cake, 0830-1930 (2300 Fri, jazz/blues music).

T **Barrillada Don Lauro**, R Luís Loréa 369, T053-233 2037. Uruguayan steak in pleasant restaurant.

T **Rio's**, R Val Porto 393, T053-231 1180. Vast but good *churrascaria*.

Chuí and the border with Uruguay *p347*
Most restaurants are on Av Brasil.
Los Leños, Av Gral Artigas, Chuí. For meat and pizzas.
Parrillada Jesús, at the corner of L Olivera, Chuí. A good bet.
Parrillada/Pizzería Javier, Arachanes 589, Chuí. Reasonable food.

Bars and clubs

Porto Alegre *p337, map p338*
There are many classy bars, cafés and bistros in the pleasant **Moinhos de Vento**, the city's richest suburb. Try the roads (like R Padre Chagas) around Moinhos de Vento shopping centre (a US$2 taxi ride from downtown).

On weekend nights, thousands spill out of the huge beer bars and clubs along Av Goethe between R Vasco de Gama and R Dona Laura in Rio Branco (a US$2 taxi ride from the centre).

Bar do Beto, Av Venâncio Aires 876, Cidade Baixa, T051-3332 0063. Open 1700-0300, serves food too.
Bar do Goethe, R 24 de Outubro 112, Moinhos de Vento, T051-222 2043, www.compuserve.com.br/bardogoethe. Bar hosting a gathering each Tue 2030 for foreign-language speakers.
Bar do Nito, Av Cel Lucas de Oliveira 105, Moinhos de Vento, T051-3333 4600. Popular music bar.
Cía Sandwiches, Getúlio Vargas 1430, T051-3233 7414. Open 1800-0200, beer, sandwiches and music.
Cult, R Gen Lima e Silva 806, Cidade Baixa, T051-3221 6299. Open 1900-late, restaurant too.
Doce Vício, R Vieira de Castro 32. 3 floors with games room, bar and restaurant, Tue-Sun 1830-0230.
Dr Jekyll, Travessa do Carmo 76, Cidade Baixa, T051-3226 9404. Nightclubs open from 2200, closed Sun.
Fly, R Gonçalvo de Carvalho 189. Wed-Mon 2100-0200. Predominantly male, attractive gay bar with art exhibition, sophisticated.
João de Barro, R da República 546, Cidade Baixa. Good jazz.
Kripton, R Mariante 606, Rio Branco, T051-3331 6651. Bar with popular music.
Ossip, Av Republica 677 (corner with João Afredo). Pleasant wine bar.
Restaurant Majestic, R dos Andradas 736. Don't miss a sunset drink here, on the roof of Casa de Cultura Mário Quintana.
Sargeant Peppers, Dona Laura 329, T051-3331 3258. Bar with live music Thu-Sat, closed Mon.
Teatro de Elis, Av Protásio Alves 1670, Petrópolis, T051-3286 3475. Nightclub.
Trivial, R Dona Laura 78, Rio Branco, T051-3346 7046, www.trivialbar.com.br. Bar open from 2100.
Wanda Bar, R Comendador Coruja 169, Floresta, T051-3224 4755. Gay nightclub, open from 2030.

Entertainment

Porto Alegre *p337, map p338*
Casa de Cultura Mário Quintana, R dos Andradas 736, T051-3221 7147. A centre for the arts, exhibitions and theatre. Mon-Fri 0900-2100, Sat-Sun 1200-2100.
São Pedro, Praça Mcal Deodoro, T051-3227 5100. Theatre with free noon and late afternoon concerts Sat, Sun, art gallery, café.
Usina do Gasômetro, Av Pres João Goulart 551, T051-3227 1387. Tue-Sun 1000-2200. Art gallery with displays by young artists.

Festivals

Porto Alegre *p337, map p338*
2 Feb The main event is the festival of Nossa Senhora dos Navegantes (*Iemanjá*), whose image is taken by boat from the central quay in the port to the industrial district of Navegantes.
Sep Semana Farroupilha celebrates *gaúcho* traditions with parades in traditional style, its main day being 20 Sep. The Carnaval parade takes place in Av A do Carvalho, renamed Av Carlos Alberto Barcelos (or Roxo) for these 3 days only, after a famous carnival designer.

Shopping

Porto Alegre *p337, map p338*
Bookshops
Idiomas, Galeria Central Park, R Mostardeiro 333, Mon-Fri 0900-1200, 1400-1830, Sat 0930-1230, closed Sun.
Livraria Londres, Av Osvaldo Aranha 1182. Used books in English, French and Spanish and old *Life* magazines.

Prosa i Verso, Galeria Av Center, R Mostardeiro 120, T051-3222 2409. 0930-1800, closed Sun.
Saraiva Megastore, Shopping Praia de Belas.
Siciliano, R dos Andradas 1273 and other branches. Each year a **Feira do Livro** is held in Praça da Alfândega, Oct-Nov.

Jewellers

H Stern, jewellers at the shopping centre Iguatemi and international airport.

Markets

There is a street market (leather goods, basketware) in the streets around the central post office. Good leather goods are sold on the streets. Sun morning handicraft and bric-a-brac market (plus sideshows) Av José Bonifácio (next to Parque Farroupilha). There is a very good food market.

Shopping centre

The **Praia de Belas** shopping centre, is among the largest in Latin America. US$1.50 taxi ride from town.

Activities and tours

Porto Alegre *p337, map p338*

Golf Porto Alegre Country Club, Av Libero Badaró 524, Bela Vista, 18 holes, closed to non-members.

Swimming Forbidden from the beaches near or in the city because of pollution – except for **Praia do Lami**, in the south of the city, which has been cleaned up. Beaches in Belém Novo and Ipanema are okay too.

Tour operators Klift Tur, R Mcal Floriano 270, T051-3211 3255, F228 7959. American Express. One of several tour companies offering trips to Foz do Iguaçu and Ciudad del Este, overnight journey each way (12 hrs in Paraguay) 3-day trips with 1 night's hotel accommodation, US$30 including sightseeing (time at the falls may be limited).

See also the 'Turismo' section in *Zero Hora* classifieds (Tue) for tour company' adverts.

Beaches around Porto Alegre *p341, map p341*

Marcelo and Saraia Müller, Blue Beach Tur, Av Silva Jardim 257, Torres T/F051-664 3096, bluebeach@terra.com.br. Boat trips up Rio Mampitumba, abseiling, trekking, and visits to Parque Nacional Aparados da Serra/Geral. Recommended.

Canela and around *p343*

Atitude, Av Osvaldo Aranha 391, T054-282 6305, www.atitude.tur.br. Rafting, waterfall abseiling, and trips to Aparados da Serra National Park. Recommended.
JM Turismo, Av Osvaldo Aranha 1038, T054-282 1542, www.jmrafting.com.br. Class 3 and 4 rapids.

Santo Ângelo and the Jesuit Missions *p345*

Caminho das Missões, R Marguês do Herval 1061, T055-331 29632, www.caminhodas missoes.com.br. 3- to 7-day 'pilgrimages' (80- 180 km) between the various ruins. US$77-150. Open to all beliefs.

Transport

Porto Alegre *p337, map p338*

See also Ins and outs, page 337.

Air

There are international flights to Uruguay and Argentina as well as internal connections with **Curitiba**, **São Paulo**, **Rio de Janeiro** and **Florianópolis**.

Bus

There are 2 sections to the *rodoviária*; the ticket offices for interstate and international destinations are together in 1 block, beside the municipal tourist office (very helpful). The intermunicipal (state) ticket offices are in another block; for travel information within the state, ask at the very helpful booth on the station concourse.

To **Rio**, US$60, 24 hrs (Itapemirim www.itapemirim.com.br); **São Paulo** (Itapemirim), US$29.80 (*leito* 51), 18 hrs; **Brasília** (Itapemirim), US$60, 34 hrs; **Uruguaiana** (Pluma, www.pluma.com.br), US$17.50, 8 hrs; **Florianópolis**, US$16, 7 hrs with Santo Anjo (take an *executivo* rather than a *convencional*, which is a much slower service); **Curitiba** (Itapemirim), from US$21 *convencional* to US$17.50 (*leito* 28.50), coastal and *serra* routes, 12 hrs; **Rio Grande**, US$9, every 2 hrs from 0600, 4 hrs. **Foz do**

Iguaçu, *convencional* US$26, 15 hrs, *executivo* US$30, 13 hrs (*leito* once a week 41). Many other destinations. To **Cascavel** (Paraná) for connections to Campo Grande, Cuiabá and Porto Velho: 4 daily with **Unesul**, US$27, 12 hrs. To **Jaguarão** on Uruguayan border at 2400, US$10, 6 hrs.

International buses Take your passport and tourist card when purchasing international bus tickets. To **Montevideo** (Uruguay), with TTL *executivo* daily 2030 US$43; *leito* Fri only at 2100, US$43, alternatively take bus to border town of Chuí at 1200 and 2330 daily, US$12.60, 7 hrs, then bus to Montevideo (US$13). To **Asunción** (Paraguay) with **Unesul** at 1900, Tue, Fri, 18 hrs via **Foz do Iguaçu**, US$18. To **Santiago** (Chile), with **Pluma** 0705, Tue and Fri, US$79.

There are bus services to **Buenos Aires** (Argentina) with **Pluma**, US$54, 19 hrs depending on the border, 1805 daily, the route is via Uruguaiana, Paso de los Libres, Entre Ríos and Zárate. For **Misiones** (Argentina), take the 2100 bus (not Sat) to Porto Xavier on the Río Uruguay, 11 hrs, US$15, get exit stamp at police station, take a boat across to San Javier, US$2, go to Argentine immigration at the port, then take a bus to Posadas (may have to change in Leandro N Além).

Car
Good roads radiate from Porto Alegre, and Highway BR-116 is paved to Curitiba (746 km). To the south it is paved (mostly in good condition), to Chuí on the Uruguayan frontier, 512 km. In summer, visibility can be very poor at night owing to mist, unfenced cows are a further hazard. The paved coastal road to Curitiba via Itajaí (BR-101), of which the first 100 km is the 4-lane Estrada General Osório highway, is much better than the BR-116 via Caxias and Lajes. The road to Uruguaiana is entirely paved but bumpy.

Car hire Allocar, R 25 de Julho 102, T051-3337 1717, www.allocar.com.br. **Bazzoni**, T051-3325 2913, www.bazzoni.com.br. **Hello Rent a Car**, T051-3342 2422, www.hellocar.com.br. At airport and delivers to hotels. **Milhas**, R Pereira Franco 400, T051-3337 2223. **Pontual**, Av Pernanbuco 1700, São Geraldo, T051-3342 2282.

Beaches around Porto Alegre *p341, map p341*
Bus Porto Alegre-**Tramandaí**, 5 a day, US$3.50. **Osório–Mostardas/Tavares**, 1600 daily, US$4.40. Porto Alegre-**Torres**, 9 a day, US$6; **Tramandaí** 1300, 1700 daily, **Osório** 0630, 1100, 1300, 1830.

Tramandaí to São José do Norte *p342*
Bus There are 3 buses a week from Mostardas and Tavares to **São José do Norte** (130 km) via Bojuru (leaving Mostardas 0630 and Tavares 0700 Sun, Wed, Fri, 5 hrs, US$4.50). If travelling northwards from São José do Norte, the bus leaves 0800, Tue, Thu, Sat. There is also a daily bus from both Tavares and São José do Norte to **Bojuru**, where there is a basic hotel. The road south of Tavares is called the **Estrada do Inferno**. Car drivers should carry a shovel and rope. 4WD only after rains.

Taxi For local transport from Mostardas, try **José Carlos Martins Cassola**, T051-673 1186, or **Itamar Velho Sessin**, T051-673 1431.

Gramado *p342*
Bus Buses to **Canela**, 10 mins, run every 20 mins. Several daily buses to **Porto Alegre** US$3.85.

Canela and around *p343*
Bus To **Parque Estadual do Caracol**, from outside **Parati Lanches**, Praça Joã Correa, 0800, 1200, 1730, US$0.30 (returning at 1220, 1800). Several daily to **Caxias do Sul**, 2 hrs, US$2. Every 2 hrs to **São Francisco de Paula**, US$1.10. (Take 0800 for connection to Cambará for Parque Nacional de Aparados da Serra.) To **Florianópolis**, it is quickest to go via Porto Alegre (US$4.15).

Bike hire From **Pousada das Sequóias** or **Pousada Casa Rosa**, R Gov Flores da Cunha 150, T054-282 2400.

Pelotas *p344*
Air Mon-Fri flight to **Porto Alegre** (1530, US$60).

Bus Frequent daily buses to **Porto Alegre**, 244 km (US$7.50, 3-4 hrs, paved road); **Rio Grande** (US$1.80, 1 hr); **Chuí** (5 daily, US$6.15). TTL bus services (Montevideo-

Porto Alegre) depart at 2400 daily, US$35. Bus service to **Buenos Aires** via Uruguaiana (0710, 2030, US$18). From Bagé, where there is a police post, the Uruguayan company Núñez runs buses 3 times a week to **Melo**, via Aceguá. Good direct road northwest to Iguaçu via **São Sepé**, **Santa Maria** and **São Miguel** mission ruins. **Santa Maria** (5 daily, US$8.80, 4 hrs) and **Santa Ângelo** (0805 daily, US$16, 8 hrs).

Taxi Radio Taxi Princesa, T053-225 8466. Recommended.

Rio Grande *p344*
Boat There's a boat trip across mouth of Lagoa dos Patos, to the pleasant village of **São José do Norte**, every hour from Porto Velho.
Bus To **Pelotas**, every 30 mins (1 hr, 56 km, US$1.75); to **Bagé**, 280 km, 0700 and 1400; to **Santa Vitória**, 220 km; to **Porto Alegre**, 5 a day, US$10, 4 hrs; to **Itajaí**, 14 hrs, US$15. All buses to these destinations go through Pelotas. The road to the Uruguayan border at **Chuí** is paved, but the surface is poor (5 hrs by bus, at 0700 and 1430). Bus tickets to **Punta del Este** or **Montevideo** (daily 2330) at *rodoviária* or **Benfica Turismo**, Av Silva Paes 373, T054-232 1807.

Santo Ângelo and the Jesuit Missions *p345*
Bus To **Porto Alegre**, 5 *convencional* daily, 6 hrs, US$15, and *executivo* at 1830, US$19.50. To **São Miguel**, 0715, 1100, 1530, 1700 (Sat 1000, 1330, Sun 0930, 1830), 1 hr, US$2. To **Foz do Iguaçu**, via Cascavel, 1930, 13 hrs, US$21.

Salto do Yucumâ *p346*
Bus There are 4 buses daily from **Três Passos** to Santo Ângelo. 2 daily **Tenente Portela**–Santo Ângelo.

Santana do Livramento and the border with Uruguay *p346*
Bus The *rodoviária* is at Gen Salgado Filho and Gen Vasco Alves. To **Porto Alegre**, 2 daily, 7 hrs, US$20; 3 daily to **Urugaiana** (4 hrs, US$10), services also to **São Paulo** and other destinations.

Chuí *p347*
The *rodoviária* is on R Venezuela. Buses run to **Pelotas** (6-7 daily, US$6.60, 4 hrs), **Rio Grande** (0700, 1400, 5 hrs, US$6.10) and **Porto Alegre** (1200, 2400, 7¾ hrs, US$13); also from Chuí to **Santa Vitória do Palmar** nearby, US$0.60, where there are a few hotels and rather quicker bus services to the main cities.

To Uruguay To **Montevideo** (COT, Cynsa, both on Av Brasil between Olivera and Artigas, or **Rutas del Sol**, on L Oliveria), US$13, 5 hrs.

Directory

Porto Alegre *p337, map p338*
Banks Banco do Brasil, Uruguai 185, 9th floor. Open 1000-1500, good rates for TCs. **Bradesco**, Praça Sen Florência. Visa machine. **Citibank**, R7 de Setembro 722, T051-3220 8619. Exchange on Av Borges de Medeiros, good rate, cash only. **Lloyds Bank**, R Gen Câmara 249. Open 1000-1630. **Platino Turismo**, R dos Andrades and Av Borges de Medeiros (only one to change TCs, Amex, but 6 less than cash). **Exprinter**, Sen Salgado Filho 247 (best for cash). **MasterCard**, cash against card, R 7 de Setembro 722, 8th floor, Centro. For other addresses consult tourist bureau brochure. **Cultural centres** Sociedade Brasileira da Cultura Inglesa, Praça Mauricio Cardoso 49, Moinhos de Vento. **Instituto Goethe**, 24 de Outubro 122. Mon-Fri 0930-1230, 1430-2100, occasional concerts, bar recommended for German *Apfelkuchen*. See also Casa de Cultura Mário Quintana and Usina do Gasômetro, see page 352. **Embassies and consulates** **Argentina**, R Coronel Bordini 1033, Moinhos de Vento, T/F051-3321 1360 (0900-1600). **Germany**, R Prof Annes Dias 112, 11th floor, T051-3224 9255, F3226 4909 (0830-1130). **Italy**, Praça Marechal Deodoro 134, T051-3228 2055 (0900-1200). **Japan**, Av João Obino 467, Alto Petrópolis, T051-3334 1299, F3334 1742 (0900-1230, 1500- 1700). **Portugal**, R Prof Annes Dias 112, 10th floor, T/F051- 3224 5767 (0900-1500). **Spain**, R Eng Ildefonso Simões Lopez 85, Três Figueiras, T051-3338 1300, F3338 1444 (0830- 1330). **Sweden**, Av Viena 279, São Geraldo, T051-3222 2322, F3222 2463 (1400- 1745). **UK**, R Itapeva 110, Sala 505, Edif Montreal,

Bairro Passo D'Areia, T/F051- 3341 0720 (0900-1200, 1430-1800). **USA**, R Riachuelo 1257, 2nd floor, T051-3226 3344 (1400-1700). **Uruguay**, Av Cristóvão Colombo 2999, Higienópolis, T051-3325 6200, F3325 6200 (0900-1500).
Internet **Ciber Café**, Câncio Gomes e C Colombo 778, T051-3346 3098. 0900-2300. **.Com Cyber Café**, R da Praia Shopping, S17, R dos Andradas 1001, T051-3286 4244, www.com-cybercafe.co.br. US$3 per hr. **Livraria Saraiva Megastore**, Shopping Praia de Belas, T051-3231 6868, www.livraria saraiva.com.br. Mon-Sat 1000-2200. **PC2 Publicidad Café**, Duque de Caxias 1464, T051-3227 6853, pc2.com@terra.com.br. US$2 per hr. **Portonet**, R Maracheal Floriano 185, T051-3227 4696. 0900-2100, US$2.50 per hr. **Language courses** Portuguese and Spanish, **Matilde Dias**, R Pedro Chaves Barcelos 37, Apdo 104, T051-3331 8235, malilde@estadao.com.br. US$9 per hr. **Laundry** Several along Av Andre da Rocha including **Lavandería Lav-Dem**, No 225. US$1.50 per kg wash and dry. **Post office** R Siqueria Campos 1100, Centro. Mon-Fri 0800-1700, Sat 0800-1200. **UPS**, T051-343 4972 (Alvaro). **Telephone** R Siqueira de Campos 1245 and upstairs at the *rodoviária*.

Beaches around Porto Alegre *p341, map p341*
Banks **Banco do Brasil**, 15 de Novembro 236, Torres and at the Torres *rodoviária*.

Gramado *p342*
Banks **Banco do Brasil**, R Garibáldi corner Madre Verónica. **Internet** **Cyber**, Av Borges de Medeiros 2016, T054-286 9559. 1300-2300, US$2.80 per hr.

Canela *p343*
Banks **Banco do Brasil**, Av Julio de Castilhos 465. **Internet** **Posto Telefônico**, Av Júlio de Castilhos 349, Sala 5, T054-282 3305, 0800-2100, Sat 0900-2000, Sun 1000-1200, 1400-1800.

Pelotas *p344*
Banks **Banco do Brasil**, corner R Gen Osório and R Lobo da Costa. Also at R Anchieta 2122. Will change TCs. It is difficult to change money at weekends.

Rio Grande *p344*
Embassies and consulates **Denmark**, R Mcal Floriano 122, T053-233 7600 (0800-1200, 1330-1800). **UK**, R Riachuelo 201, T053-233 7700, F321 1530 (0800-1200, 1330-1730). **Telephone** R Gen Neto 227.

Santo Ângelo and the Jesuit Missions *p345*
Banks **Banco do Brasil** charges a commission of US$15 for TCs. Good rates for cash at the garage with red doors opposite Hotel Maerkli on Av Brasil.

Santana do Livramento and the border with Uruguay *p346*
Banks **Banco do Brasil**, Av Sarandí. Best rates for Amex TCs at Val de Marne.

Chuí and the border with Uruguay *p347*
Brazil
Banks Cambios on the Uruguayan side, see below. **Banco do Brasil**, Av Uruguaí, 3 blocks west of post office. Change all remaining Uruguayan pesos into reais before leaving Uruguay, not even black marketeers in Brazil want them. **Post office** Av Uruguaí, Colômbia y Argentina. **Telephone** Corner of R Chile and Av Argentina.

Uruguay
Banks Several *cambios* on Av Brasil, eg **Cambio Gales**, Gral Artigas y Brasil, Mon-Fri 0830-1200, 1330-1800, Sat 0830-1200; in World Trade Center 1000-2200. Also **Los Aces and Val**, either side of Gales. All change TCs at US$1 per cheque and US$1 commission and give similar rates, without commission, for cash (pesos, dollars and reais). On Sun, try the casino, or look for someone on the street outside the *cambios*. Brazilian currency can be bought here. **Banco de la República Oriental Uruguay**, Gral Artigas, changes TCs. **Embassies and consulates** Brazil, A Fossati, T0474-2049. **Telephone** **Antel**, S Priliac, between C L Olivera and C Gen Artigas, 0700-2300.

Bahia

Footprint features

Introduction

White-sand beaches backed by coconut palms, steep winding streets lined with pastel-coloured houses, ornate baroque churches, Afro-Brazilian ceremonies, gymnastic martial art ballet, the rhythm of the *berimbau*, the aroma of coconut milk and spices... Bahia conjures up as many exotic images, sounds and smells as Rio de Janeiro but has an even stronger claim to be the heart of Brazil. The state capital, Salvador, was the country's first city for far longer than any other, and is considered by many to be the country's cultural centre.

Brazil's most famous novelist, Jorge Amado, was a Bahian, as were many of its greatest musicians – it was Bahia that gave the world samba, capoeira, Carnaval and *candomblé*. The state has by far the best cuisine in the country, along with many of its best beaches. Bahia's beautiful coast stretches far to the north and south of Salvador and is dotted with resorts along its length – laid-back little places like Itacaré, Morro de São Paulo and Trancoso, and larger more hedonistic party-towns like Porto Seguro and Arraial de Ajuda. Inland, in the wild semi-desert of the *sertão*, is one of Brazil's best hiking destinations, the Chapada Diamantina, whose towering escarpments are cut by clearwater rivers and dotted with plunging waterfalls.

★ Don't miss...

1 **Salvador** Brace yourself for Brazil's most vibrant city, with its riotous Carnaval celebrations and beautiful historic city centre, page 360.

2 **Morro de São Paulo** Wind down on this tropical island with coconut palm beaches, a relaxed atmosphere and a young crowd, page 387.

3 **Itacaré** Enjoy southern Bahia's up-and-coming beach destination, with great restaurants, chic little hotels, Atlantic Coast rainforest and tens of kilometres of white sand and coconut palms, page 389.

4 **Porto Seguro** Let your hair down at Bahia's nightlife capital, or head south to Arraial de Ajuda, a little quieter and cheaper, but with the same intense beach bar and nightlife scene, page 392.

5 **Trancoso** Lie back and enjoy the endless stretches of beautiful sand and a smattering of cool little bars and restaurants on the pretty colonial square, page 395.

6 **Praia do Forte** Discover pristine turtle-nesting beaches near Salvador's sophisticated little beach resort getaway with lively nightlife, page 407.

7 **Chapada Diamantina** Hike over table-top mountains, through canyons and along gorges, page 410.

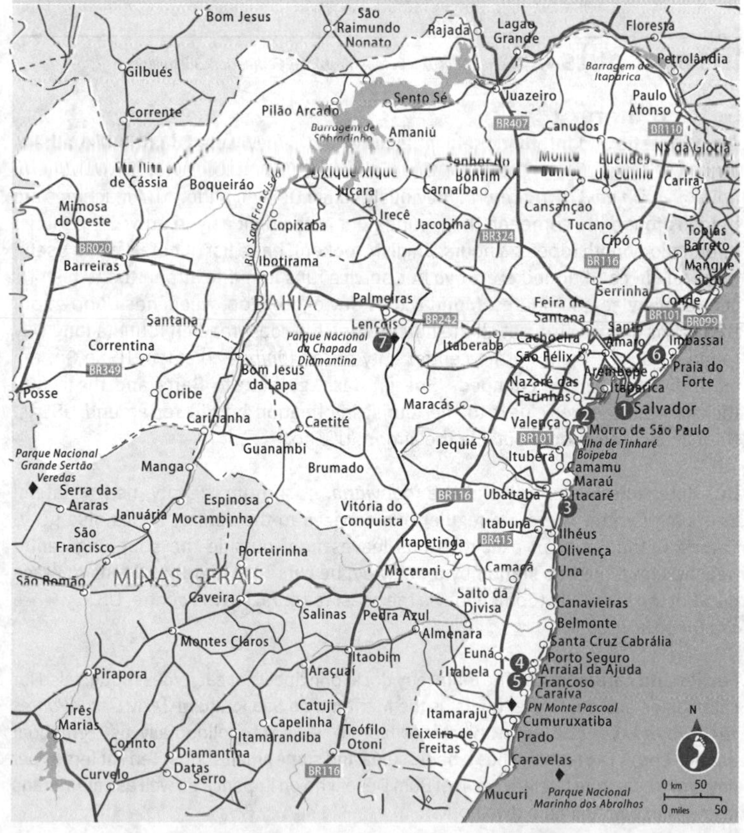

Salvador and the Recôncavo

Salvador is the capital not just of Bahia but of African Brazil. The country's African heritage is at its strongest here – in the carnival rhythms of the drum troupe orchestras of Ilê Aiyê and Olodum, the rich, spicy cooking, the rituals of candomblé *– Brazil's equivalent of* santeria *and in the martial art ballet of capoeira. You will see this being played on Salvador's beaches and in the squares and cobbled streets of the city's historical centre, the Pelourinho. The Pelourinho is also home to one of the most impressive collections of colonial architecture in South America. There are myriad baroque churches here. Some, like the Convento do São Francisco, have interiors covered with tons of gold plate. Others, like Nossa Senhora do Rosário, are decorated with statues of black saints and art that celebrates African Brazilian culture. The city is famous for its frenetic carnival which, unlike Rio's, takes place in the streets to the pounding rhythms of* axé *music. The crowds are overwhelming.*

The Recôncavo is Brazil's largest bay and is dotted with islands, many of them private and home to some of the Northeast's wealthy, others weekend resorts for people from Salvador. The best known is Itaparica, a long thin island lined with palms, with a pretty colonial capital and some reasonable beaches. Many buses run from here to the south and taking the ferry across from Salvador and then road transport from Itaparica is the quickest way of getting to southern Bahia. *» For Sleeping, Eating and other listings, see pages 373-386.*

Ins and outs → *Phone code: 071. Colour map 4, A6. Population: 3.2 million.*

Getting there

Air Domestic and international flights arrive at the new **Luís Eduardo Magalhães airport** ⓘ *Praça Gago Coutinho, São Cristóvão, T071-3204 1010, www.infraero.gov.br, 32 km east of the centre*, previously called Dois de Julho. ATM machines are hidden around the corner on the ground floor to the right as you arrive. The tourist information booth (open 24 hours, English spoken), has a list of hotels and a useful map. An air- conditioned *executivo* bus service runs from the airport to the historic centre, every 30-40 minutes, Monday to Friday 0500-2200, weekends 0600-2200, US$3. This service stops at all the hotels along the coast road en route (a long way round if you are going to the centre). City buses (*ônibus coletivo*), US$0.80, are more direct but more cramped. 'Special' taxis go both to Barra and the centre (tickets from the desk next to the tourist information booth) for around US$35. Normal taxis leave from outside the airport, US$30.

Bus Interstate buses arrive at the *rodoviária*, 5 km from the city, near Iguatemi Shopping Centre. There are regular bus services to the centre; buses also go to Campo Grande and an executive bus leaves from outside the shopping centre (reached from the bus station by a walkway; be careful at night) and runs to Praça da Sé or the lower city (Comércio) via the coast road. Taxi to the centre, US$15. *» See also Transport, page 384.*

Ferries and catamarans The main ferry dock, principally for car ferries though also for catamarans and passenger boats, is the **Marítimo de São Joaquim** ⓘ *Av Oscar Pontes 1051, T071-3254 1020, www.twbmar.com.br*. It is known colloquially as 'Ferry-boat (fairhee bort)'. The terminal has a bank, cafés and some small shops. Ten car ferries per day arrive here from the little town of Bom Despacho on Itaparica as well as catamarans from Morro de São Paulo (two hours).

Salvador's other boat terminal is smaller and serves only passengers. It lies opposite the Mercado Modelo, about five minutes' walk from the historic centre, and is known as the **Terminal Marítimo de Mercado Modelo** or Terminal Marítimo Turistico. Ferries and catamarans arrive here from the Baía de Todos os Santos, including the village of Mar Grande on Itaparica (every 30 minutes) and there are catamarans from Morro de São Paulo (five a day). There are a couple of cafés and news-stands.

Getting around

The city is built on a broad peninsula and is at the mouth of the Baía de Todos os Santos. On the opposite side of the bay's entrance is the Ilha de Itaparica (see page 371). The commercial district of the city and its port are on the sheltered, western side of the peninsula; residential districts and beaches are on the open, Atlantic side. Barra lies at the point of the peninsula.

The centre of the city is divided into two levels, the **Cidade Alta** (Upper City) where the historic centre lies, and the **Cidade Baixa** (Lower City), which is the commercial and docks district. The two levels are connected by a series of steep hills called *ladeiras*. The easiest way to go from one level to the other is by the *Lacerda* lift, which connects Praça Municipal (Tomé de Sousa) in the Upper City with Praça Cairu and the famous Mercado Modelo. There is also the Plano Inclinado Gonçalves, a funicular railway that leaves from behind the cathedral going down to Comércio, the commercial district.

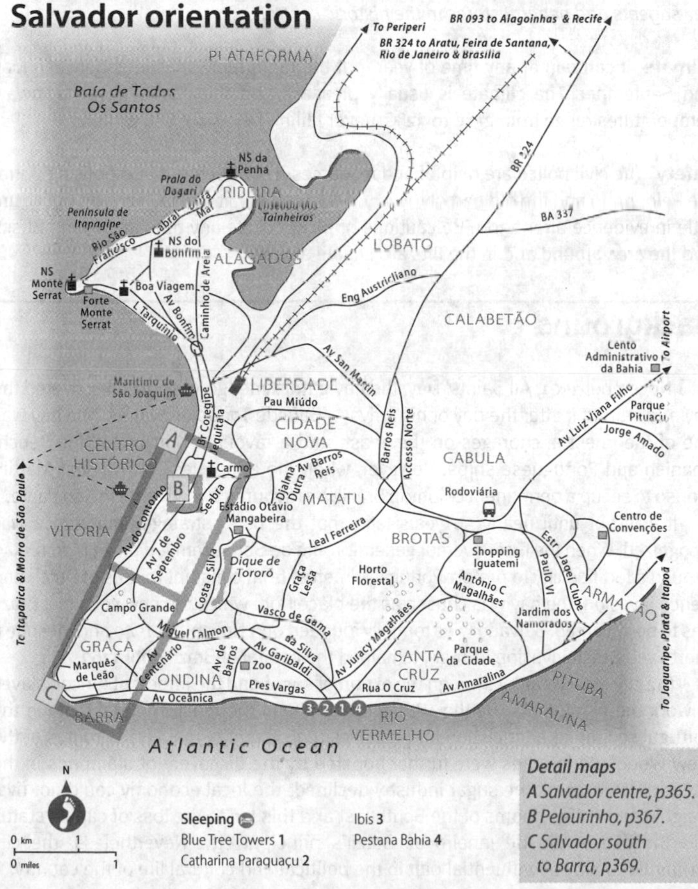

Most visitors limit themselves to the centre, Barra, the Atlantic suburbs and the Itapagipe peninsula, which is north of the centre. The roads and avenues between these areas are straightforward to follow and are well served by public transport. Other parts of the city are not as easy to get around, but are of less interest to most visitors. If going to these areas, a taxi may be advisable until you know your way around. ⏩ *For local bus information, see Transport, page 384.*

Tourist information The main office of **Bahiatursa** ⓘ *Av Simon Bolivar s/n, Centro de Convenções da Bahia, 1st floor, T071-3117 3000, www.bahiatursa.ba.gov.br*, has lists of hotels and accommodation in private homes, can advise on travel throughout the state of Bahia, and has noticeboards for messages. There are also branches at the following locations: **airport** ⓘ *T071-3204 1244, daily 0730-2300*; **Mercado Modelo** ⓘ *Praça Visconde de Cayru 250 T071-3241 0242, Mon-Sat 0900-1800, Sun 0900-1330*; **Pelourinho** ⓘ *R das Laranjeiras 12, Pelourinho, T071-3321 2133/2463, daily 0830-2100*; **Rodoviária** ⓘ *T071-3450 3871, daily 0730-2100*; **SAC Shopping Barra** ⓘ *Av Centenário 2992, T071-3264 4566, Mon-Fri 0900-1900, Sat 0900-1400*. The useful website www.bahia-online.net lists cultural events and news.

Maps Available from **Departamento de Geografia e Estadística** ⓘ *Av Estados Unidos (opposite Banco do Brasil, Cidade Baixa; also from news-stands including the airport bookshop, US$1.50. Illustrated maps of the Pelourinho and around are available from newsagents and general stores in the historic centre.*

Climate It can rain at any time of year, but the main rainy season is between May and September. The climate is usually pleasant and the sun is never far away. Temperatures range from 25°C to 32°C, never falling below 19°C in winter.

Safety The civil police are helpful and resources have been put into policing Barra, the Pelourinho and the old part of the city. All are well lit at night. However, police are little in evidence after 2300. Be cautious of pickpockets any time after dark. Buses and the area around and in the lifts are unsafe at night.

Background

On 1 November 1501, All Saints' Day, the navigator Amérigo Vespucci discovered the bay and named it after the day of his arrival – Baía de Todos os Santos. The bay was one of the finest anchorages on the coast, and a favourite port of call for French, Spanish and Portuguese ships. However, when the Portuguese crown sent Martim Afonso to set up a permanent colony in Brazil, he favoured São Vicente in São Paulo.

It was not until nearly 50 years later that the bay's strategic importance was recognized. When the first governor general, Tomé de Sousa, arrived on 23 March 1549 to build a fortified city to protect Portugal's interest from constant threats of Dutch and French invasion, the bay was chosen as the place from which the new colony of Brazil was to be governed. Salvador was formally founded on 1 November 1549 and, despite a short-lived Dutch invasion in 1624, remained the capital of Brazil until 1763.

The city grew wealthy through the export of sugar and the import of African slaves to work the plantations. By the 18th century, it was the most important city in the Portuguese Empire after Lisbon and ideally situated on the main trade routes of the 'New World'. Its fortunes were further boosted by the discovery of diamonds in the interior. However, as the sugar industry declined, the local economy could not rival the gold and coffee booms of the Southeast and this led to the loss of capital status and the rise of Rio de Janeiro as Brazil's principal city. Nevertheless, the city continued to play an influential part in the political and cultural life of the country.

Candomblé

Candomblé is a spiritual tradition that developed from religions brought over by Yoruba slaves from West Africa. It is focused on relationships with primordial spirits or *orixás* who are linked with natural phenomena and the calendar. The *orixas* are invoked in temples (*terreiros*). These can be elaborate, decorated halls, or simply someone's front room with tiny altars. Ceremonies are divided into two distinct parts. The first is when the *orixás* are invoked through different rhythms, songs and dances. Once the dancers have been possessed by the *orixá*, they are led off in a trance-like state to be changed into sacred, often very elaborate costumes, and come back to the ceremonial area in a triumphant procession in which each one dances separately for their deity. Overseeing the proceedings are *mães* or *pães de santo*, priestesses or priests.

Candomblé ceremonies may be seen by tourists, usually on Sundays and religious holidays – although many are just for show and not the real thing. The ceremonies can be very repetitive and usually last several hours, although you are not under pressure to remain for the duration. Appropriate and modest attire should be worn; visitors should not wear shorts, sleeveless vests or T-shirts. White clothing is preferred, black should not be worn especially if it is combined with red. Men and women are separated during the ceremonies, women always on the left, men on the right. No photography or sound recording is allowed. Most temples are closed during Lent, although each one has its own calendar. *Bahiatursa* often has information about forthcoming ceremonies, but accurate information on authentic festivals is not always easy to come by.

African presence

For three centuries, Salvador was the site of a thriving slave trade, with much of the workforce for the sugar cane and tobacco plantations coming from the west coast of Africa. Even today, Salvador is described as the most African city in the Western hemisphere, and the University of Bahia boasts the only choir in the Americas to sing in the Yoruba language. The influence permeates the city: food sold on the street is the same as in Senegal and Nigeria, the music is fused with pulsating African polyrhythms, men and women nonchalantly carry enormous loads on their heads, fishermen paddle dug-out canoes in the bay, and the pace of life is more relaxed than in other parts of the country.

Modern Salvador

Salvador today is a fascinating mixture of old and modern, rich and poor, African and European, religious and profane. The city has 15 forts, 166 Catholic churches and 1000 *candomblé* temples. It remains a major port, exporting tropical fruit, cocoa, sisal, soya beans and petrochemical products. However, its most important industry is tourism, and it is the second largest tourist attraction in the country, after Rio. Local government has done much to improve the fortunes of this once run-down, poor and dirty city.

Major investments are being made in its infrastructure and public health areas. A new comprehensive sewage system has been installed throughout the city, with a view to improving living conditions and dealing with pollution.

The once-forgotten Lower City, Ribeira and the Itapagipe Peninsula districts have received major facelifts. Bahia has become more industrialized, with major investments being made by multinational firms in the automotive and petrochemical industries, principally in the Camaçari complex, 40 km from the city. The Bahian economy is currently the fastest growing in the country.

Centro Histórico

Most of the interesting sights are concentrated in the Cidade Alta (Upper City), particularly the Centro Histórico. From Praça Municipal to the Carmo area, 2 km north along the cliff, the Centro Histórico is a national monument and protected by UNESCO. It was in this area that the Portuguese built their fortified city, and it is here that some of the most important examples of colonial architecture in the Americas can be found today. The historic centre has undergone a massive restoration programme. The colonial houses have been painted in pastel colours. Many of the bars have live music which spills out onto the street on every corner. Patios have been created in the open areas behind the houses, with open-air cafés and bars. Artist ateliers, antique and handicraft stores have brought new artistic blood to what was once the bohemian part of the city. Many popular traditional restaurants and bars from other parts of Salvador have opened new branches in the area.

Praça Municipal and Praça da Sé

Dominating the Praça Municipal is the old Casa de Câmara e Cadeia or **Paço Municipal** (Council Chamber, 1660), while alongside is the **Palácio Rio Branco** (1918), once the governor's palace and now the headquarters of **Bahiatursa**, the state tourist board. Heading north from the praça, Rua Misericôrdia runs past the church of **Santa Casa Misericôrdia** ⓘ *T071-3227 666, open by arrangement 0800-1700*, (1695), with its high altar and painted tiles, to **Praça da Sé**. This praça, with its mimosa and flamboyant trees, has a statue of Salvador's founder, Thomé da Souza, and good views of the bay. On the platform is the Cruz Caido, by the sculptor Mario Cravo. It is dedicated to the old Igreja da Sé, which was pulled down in 1933 and whose remaining foundations have been uncovered. One of the viewing pits displays the remains of slaves and mariners who were buried in the church's grounds in the 16th century.

Terreiro de Jesus

Terreiro de Jesus is a picturesque praça named after the church that dominates it. Built in 1692, the 'Church of the Jesuits' became the property of the Holy See in 1759 when the Jesuits were expelled from all Portuguese territories. The façade is one of the earliest examples of baroque in Brazil – an architectural style that was to dominate the churches built in the 17th and 18th centuries. Inside, the vast vaulted ceiling and 12 side altars, in baroque and rococo, frame the main altar, completely leafed in gold. The tiles in blue, white and yellow in a tapestry pattern are also from Portugal. It houses the tomb of Mem de Sá (see Background, page 675). The church is now the **Catedral Basílica** ⓘ *daily 0900-1100, 1400-1700*. Across the square is the church of **São Pedro dos Clérigos** ⓘ *Sun 0800-0930*, which is beautifully renovated. Alongside is the church of the **Ordem Terceira de São Domingos** ⓘ *Mon-Fri 0800-1200, 1400- 1700, US$0.25*, which has a beautiful painted wooden ceiling.

Also on the Terreiro de Jesus, the **Museu Afro-Brasileiro** ⓘ *Mon-Fri 0900-1700, US$1*, is in the former faculty of medicine building. Its interesting displays (all in Portuguese) compare African and Bahian *orixás* (deities) celebrations; there are some beautiful murals and carvings. In the basement of the same building, the **Museu Arqueológico e Etnográfico** ⓘ *Mon-Fri 0900-1700, US$0.40*, houses archaeological discoveries from Bahia, such as stone tools, clay urns, an exhibition on the *indígena* of the Alto Rio Xingu area, including artefacts, tools, photos. It is highly recommended. The **Memorial de Medicina** (museum of medicine) is in the same complex.

São Francisco

Facing Terreiro de Jesus is Praça Anchieta and the church of **São Francisco** ⓘ *0830-1700, cloisters US$0.20, church free*. Its simple façade belies the treasure inside. The

A Salvador centre

0 metres 200
0 yards 200

Sleeping
O Convento do Carmo 7
Portas Velhas 8
Pousada das Flores 2
Pousada do Boqueirão 3
Pousada Redfish 1
Pousada Villa Carmo 4
Villa Santo Antônio 6

Eating
Solar do Unhão 3

The Sand Captains

In his earlier works, Bahia's most famous son, the internationally renowned author Jorge Amado (see page 391), campaigned for the oppressed. One of his own favourites is the novel *Capitães de areia* (Sand Captains), which is about the daily life of a group of abandoned street children in Salvador. The problem of street children still exists in Salvador and their treatment at the hands of the authorities and vigilante groups sometimes makes international headlines.

Projeto Axé (pronounced *ash-ay*, Yoruba for 'life source') was begun by Cesare Florio de la Rocca and an Italian NGO, Terra Nuova, to reach out to children and adolescents living on their wits in the streets of Salvador.

Using a team of highly professional educators and sociologists, the project won the trust of the children who had hitherto seen any approach from adults as being potentially threatening. Once initial contact had been made, the children would gain confidence and seek further contact with the project where they would be offered the opportunity to take part in activities such as capoeira, dance, percussion and circus skills. A number of local companies offer them work experience and training programmes monitored by the project. There is a paper recycling unit and a clothes manufacturing unit, where all stages, from design to the final finished product, are taught. Goods such as T-shirts and paper products can be purchased in the project's store in Rua Francisco Muniz Barreto das Laranjeiras. All proceeds go to the project. There is a visitor centre in Rua Professor Lemos Brito in Barra, where there is more information in English.

The Projeto Axé is a shining example of a major social problem being dealt with in a non-patronizing way, laying real foundations in the future instead of the sands of the past.

entrance leads to a sanctuary with a spectacular painting on the wooden ceiling by local artist José Joaquim da Rocha (1777). The main body of the church is the most exuberant example of baroque in the country. The cedar woodcarving with gold leaf was completed after 28 years, in 1748. The cloisters of the monastery are surrounded by a series of blue and white tiles from Portugal. Next door is the church of the **Ordem Terceira de São Francisco** ⓘ *0800-1200 and 1300-1700, US$0.20*, (Franciscan Third Order, 1703), with its façade intricately carved in sandstone. Inside is a quite remarkable chapterhouse, with striking images of the Order's most celebrated saints.

Largo do Pelourinho

Rua Alfredo Brito, a charming, narrow cobbled street lined with fine colonial houses painted in different pastel shades, leads to the Largo do Pelourinho (Praça José Alencar). Considered the finest complex of colonial architecture in Latin America, it was once the site of a slave market and a pillory where slaves were publicly punished and ridiculed. After complete renovation in 1993, new galleries, boutiques and restaurants have opened, and at night the Largo is lively, especially on Tuesdays (see Bars and clubs, page 379). **Nosso Senhor Do Rosário Dos Pretos** ⓘ *small entrance fee*, the 'Slave Church', dominates the square. It was built by former slaves over a period of 100 years, with what little financial resources they had. The side altars honour black saints and the painted ceiling is very impressive. The overall effect is of tranquility, in contrast to the complexity of the cathedral and the São Francisco church.

At the corner of Alfredo Brito and Largo do Pelourinho is a small museum dedicated to the work of local author Jorge Amado, **Casa da Cultura Jorge Amado**

ⓘ *Mon-Sat 0900-1900, free.* Information is in Portuguese only, but the café walls are covered with colourful copies of his book jackets. A good way to get a feel of the city and its people is to read Jorge Amado's *Dona Flor e seus dois Maridos* (*Dona Flor and Her Two Husbands*, 1966). The Carmo Hill is at the top of the street leading out of Largo do Pelourinho. The **Carmo church** ⓘ *Mon-Sat 0800-1130, 1400-1730, Sun 1000-1200, US$0.30*, (Carmelite Third Order, 1709) houses one of the sacred art treasures of the city, a sculpture of Christ made in 1730 by a slave who had no formal training, Francisco Xavier das Chagas, known as *O Cabra*. The drops of blood are made from whale oil, ox blood, banana resin and 2000 rubies. **Museu do Carmo** ⓘ *Mon-Sat 0800-1200, 1400-1800, Sun 0800-1200, US$0.10*, in the Convento do Carmo, has a collection of icons and colonial furniture.

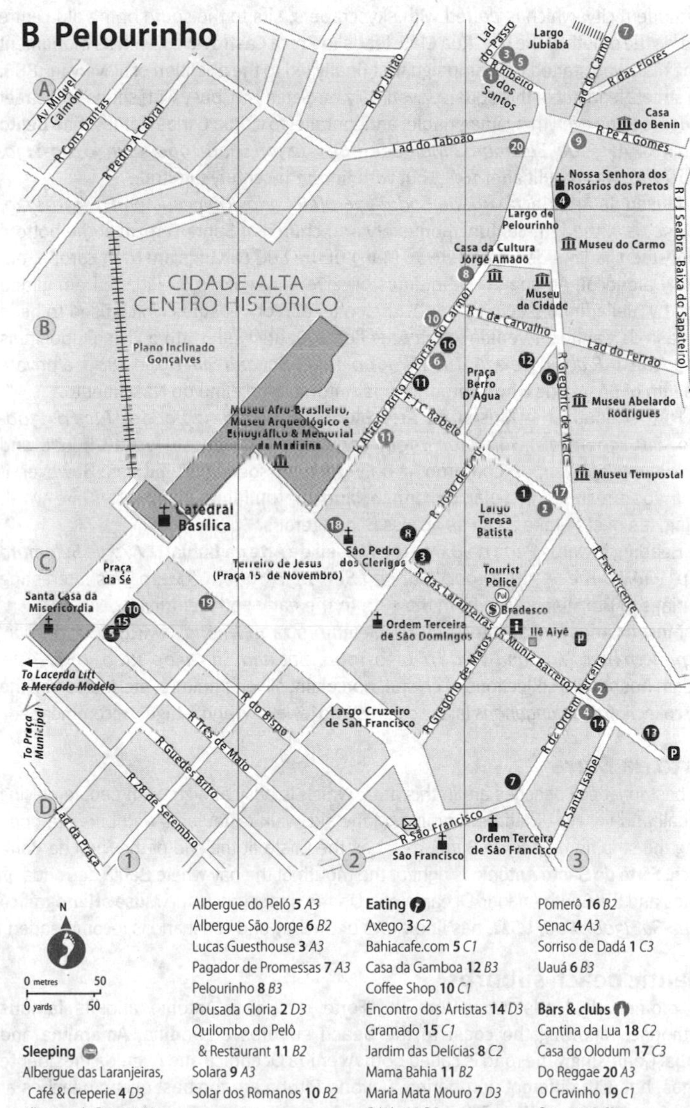

Sleeping
Albergue das Laranjeiras, Café & Creperie 4 *D3*
Albergue do Passo 1 *A3*
Albergue do Peló 5 *A3*
Albergue São Jorge 6 *B2*
Lucas Guesthouse 3 *A3*
Pagador de Promessas 7 *A3*
Pelourinho 8 *B3*
Pousada Gloria 2 *D3*
Quilombo do Pelô & Restaurant 11 *B2*
Solara 9 *A3*
Solar dos Romanos 10 *B2*

Eating
Axego 3 *C2*
Bahiacafe.com 5 *C1*
Casa da Gamboa 12 *B3*
Coffee Shop 10 *C1*
Encontro dos Artistas 14 *D3*
Gramado 15 *C1*
Jardim das Delícias 8 *C2*
Mama Bahia 11 *B2*
Maria Mata Mouro 7 *D3*
O Nilo 13 *D3*
Pomerô 16 *B2*
Senac 4 *A3*
Sorriso de Dadá 1 *C3*
Uauá 6 *B3*

Bars & clubs
Cantina da Lua 18 *C2*
Casa do Olodum 17 *C3*
Do Reggae 20 *A3*
O Cravinho 19 *C1*
Quereres 2 *C3*

The **Museu Abelardo Rodrigues** ⓘ *Solar Ferrão, Pelourinho, Tue-Sun 1300-1900, US$0.40*, is a religious art museum, with objects from the 17th, 18th and 19th centuries, mainly from Bahia, Pernambuco and Maranhão.

The **Museu da Cidade** ⓘ *Largo do Pelourinho, Tue-Fri 0930-1830, Sat 1300-1700, Sun 0930-1300, free*, has exhibitions of arts and crafts and old photographs. From the higher floors of the museum there is a good view of the Pelourinho.

Below Nossa Senhora do Rosario dos Pretos, **Casa do Benin** ⓘ *Mon-Fri 1000-1800*, shows African crafts, photos and a video show on Benin and Angola.

South of the centre

The modern city, which is dotted with skyscrapers, sits to the south of the old centre towards the mouth of the bay. Rua Chile leads to **Praça Castro Alves**, with its monument to the man who started the campaign that finally led to the abolition of slavery in 1888. Two streets lead out of this square, Avenida 7 de Setembro, busy with shops and street vendors selling everything imaginable, and, parallel to it, Rua Carlos Gomes. **São Bento church** ⓘ *Av 7 de Setembro, Mon-Sat 0630-1230, 1600-1900, Sun 0700-1130, 1700-1900*, was rebuilt after 1624, but with fine 17th-century furniture.

Museu de Arte Sacra ⓘ *R do Sodré 276 off R Carlos Gomes, Mon-Fri 1130-1730, US$1.50*, is in the 17th-century monastery and church of Santa Tereza, at the bottom of the steep Ladeira de Santa Tereza. Many of the 400 carvings are from Europe, but several are local. Among the reliquaries of silver and gold is one made from gilded wood by Aleijadinho (see page 236). The collection of treasures which used to be in the Casa de Calmon, Avenida Joana Angêlica 198, are well worth a visit. Opposite is **Tempostal** ⓘ *R do Sodré 276, Tue-Fri 0900-1830, Sat and Sun 0900-1800*, a private museum of postcards whose proprietor is Antônio Marcelino do Nascimento.

Further south, the **Museu de Arte Moderna** ⓘ *T071-329 0660, Tue-Fri 1300-2100, Sat 1500-2100, Sun 1400-1900*, converted from an old estate house and outbuildings off Avenida Contorno, is only open for special exhibitions. However, it has a good restaurant, **Solar do Unhão**, and the buildings themselves are worth seeing. It's best to take a taxi as access is dangerous.

Heading towards Porta da Barra, the **Museu de Arte da Bahia** ⓘ *Av 7 de Setembro 2340, Vitória, Tue-Fri 1400-1900, Sat and Sun 1430-1900, US$1.20*, has interesting paintings of Brazilian artists from the 18th to the early 20th century.

Museu Carlos Costa Pinto ⓘ *Av 7 de Setembro 2490, Vitória, www.guasar.com.br/mccp/mccp.htm, Mon and Wed-Fri 1430-1900, Sat and Sun 1500-1800, US$2*, is a modern house with collections of crystal, porcelain, silver, furniture, etc. It also has the only collection of *balangandãs* (slave charms and jewellery) and is highly recommended.

Porto da Barra

The best inner-city beaches are in this area, which is busy at night with people playing football and volleyball, and swimming. Many sidewalk restaurants and bars are open along the strip from Porto da Barra, as far as the Cristo at the end of the Farol da Barra beach. **Forte de Santo Antônio** is right at the mouth of the bay where Bahia de Todos os Santos and the South Atlantic Ocean meet. On the upper floors, the **Museu Hidrográfico** ⓘ *Tue-Sat 1300-1800, US$1*, has fine views of the bay and coast and is recommended.

Atlantic beach suburbs

The promenade leads away from the Forte de Santo Antônio and its famous lighthouse, following the coast to the beach suburbs of **Ondina**, **Amaralina** and **Pituba**. Confusingly the road is called both Avenida Oceânica and Avenida Presidente Vargas, but with different numbering. Beyond Pituba are the best ocean beaches at **Jaguaripe**, **Piatã** and **Itapoã** (take any bus from Praça da Sé marked Aeroporto or

C Salvador south to Barra

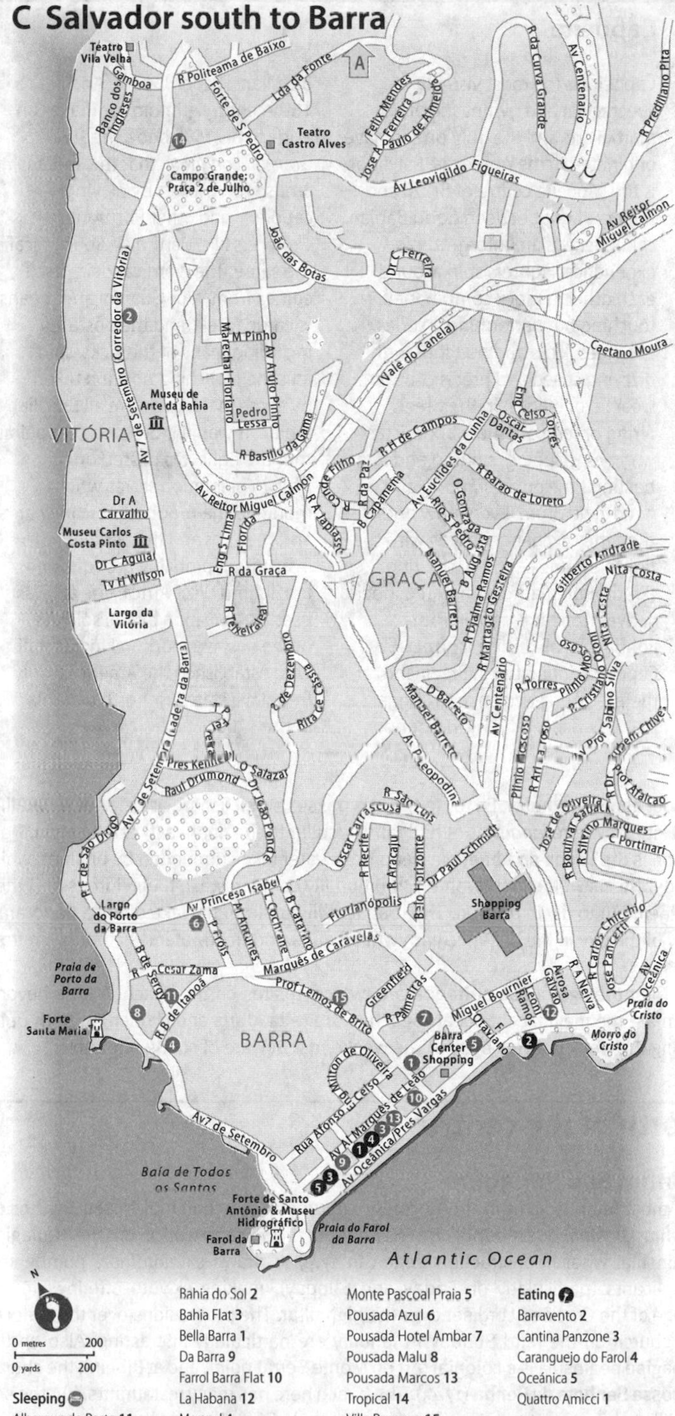

Sleeping
Albergue do Porto 11
Bahia do Sol 2
Bahia Flat 3
Bella Barra 1
Da Barra 9
Farrol Barra Flat 10
La Habana 12
Marazul 4
Monte Pascoal Praia 5
Pousada Azul 6
Pousada Hotel Ambar 7
Pousada Malu 8
Pousada Marcos 13
Tropical 14
Villa Romana 15

Eating
Barravento 2
Cantina Panzone 3
Caranguejo do Farol 4
Oceánica 5
Quattro Amicci 1

Capoeira

Capoeira is the most visually spectacular and gymnastic of all martial arts and the only one to have originated in the Americas. Salvador is the capoeira centre of Brazil and seeing a fight between good Bahian capoeristas is an unforgettable experience. Fighters spin around each other in mock combat, never touching but performing a series of lunges, kicks and punches with dizzying speed and precision. Some wear razor blades on their feet. A ring or *roda* of other capoeristas watches, clapping, singing and beating time on a *berimbau* and hand-held drum. Every now and then they exchange places with the fighters in the centre of the ring.

Although many claim that capoeira derives from an Angolan foot-fighting ritual, this is incorrect. Capoeira originated in Brazil and there is strong evidence to suggest that it was invented by indigenous Brazilians. Padre Jose de Anchieta a 16th-century ethnologist makes an aside in his 1595 book *The Tupi Guarani Language* that the 'Indians amuse themselves by playing capoiera' and other Portuguese explorers like Martim de Souza recall the same. The word capoeira itself comes from Tupi-Guarani and means 'cleared forest' and the postures, including many of the kicks, spins and the crouching position taken by those in the circle are all Brazilian-Indian. It was in indigenous capoeiras that the fight was passed on to African plantation slaves who modified them, added African chants and rhythms and the *berimbau*; an instrument probably brought to Brazil from West Africa. The art was used as a weapon by the soldiers of the enslaved African king Zumbi who established the Americas' only free slave state just north of Bahia in the 1700s.

Itapoã, about one hour). En route the bus passes small fishing colonies at Amaralina and Pituba, where *jangadas* (small rafts peculiar to the northeast) can be seen. Near Itapoã is the **Lagoa do Abaeté**, a deep freshwater lake surrounded by brilliant, white sands. This is where local women traditionally come to wash their clothes and then lay them out to dry in the sun. The road leading up from the lake offers a panoramic view of the city in the distance with white sands and freshwater less than 1 km from the sea.

Near the lighthouse at **Itapoã** are two campsites on the beach. A little beyond them are the magnificent ocean beaches of **Stella Maris** and **Flamengo**, both quiet during the week but very busy at the weekends. Beware of strong undertow.

North of the centre

Bonfim and Itapagipe

The most famous sight in the northern suburbs is the church of **Nosso Senhor do Bonfim** ⓘ *Mon 0630-0800, Tue-Sun 0600-1200, 1400-2000*, on the Itapagipe peninsula, whose construction began in 1745. It draws extraordinary numbers of supplicants (particularly on Friday and Sunday), making ex-voto offerings to the image of the Crucified Lord set over the high altar. The processions over the water to the church on the third Sunday in January are particularly interesting. Also on the Itapagipe peninsula is a colonial fort on Monte Serrat point, and at Ribeira, the church of **Nossa Senhora da Penha** (1743). The beach here has many restaurants, but the sea is polluted. To get here, take a bus from Praça da Sé or Avenida França.

Excursions from Salvador » pp373-386.

From the Cidade Baixa, the *Trem do Leste* (train) leaves Calçada for a 40-minute journey through the bayside suburbs of **Lobato**, **Plataforma** (canoes and motor boats for Ribeira on the Itapagipe peninsula), **Escada** (17th-century church), **Praia Grande**, **Periperi** and **Paripe** (take a bus for the 17th-century church at São Tomé de Paripe). The train runs Monday to Friday only; the same trip can be made by bus – a more comfortable journey but less picturesque.

About 36 km from the city is the **Museu do Recôncavo** (Museu do Vanderlei do Pinho) ⓘ *near the town of São Francisco do Conde, 7 km from the main highway, Tue, Thu and Sun 0900-1700*, in the old Freguesia Mill (1552), where you can find artefacts and pictures of the economic and social life of this region, going back three centuries. The Casa Grande e Senzala (the home of the landowner and the combined dwelling and working area of the slaves) is still intact. It is a peaceful way to spend an afternoon, but difficult to get to by public transport.

Ilha de Itaparica → *Phone code: 071. Colour map 4, A6.*

Across the bay from Salvador lies the island of Itaparica, 29 km long and 12 km wide. The town of **Itaparica** is very picturesque and well worth a visit, with a decent beach and many fine residential buildings from the 19th century. The church of São Lourenço is one of the oldest in Brazil, and a stroll through the old town is delightful. During the summer the streets are ablaze with the blossoms of the beautiful flamboyant trees.

From Itaparica town, take a bus or kombi by the coast road (Beira Mar) which passes through the villages of **Manguinhos**, **Amoureiras** and **Ponta de Areia**. The beach at Ponta de Areia is one of the best on the island and is always very popular. There are many *barracas* on the beach, the most lively is **Barraca Pai Xango**.

There are many pousadas in **Mar Grande** and at the nearby beaches of **Ilhota** and **Gamboa** (both to the left as you disembark from the ferry). The beaches at Mar Grande are fair but can be dirty at times.

Ins and outs The island is connected to the mainland by bridge or boat. The main passenger ferry runs from the São Joaquim terminal in Salvador (see page 360) to **Bom Despacho**, every 45 minutes 0540-2230. A one-way ticket for foot passengers during the week costs US$1, US$1.20 at weekends. A catamaran service for Bom Despacho departs twice daily, US$3. **Mar Grande** can be reached by a small ferry (*lancha*) from the Terminal Marítimo, in front of the Mercado Modelo in Salvador. The ferries leave every 45 minutes and takes 50 minutes, US$1.80 return.

The bridge is on the southwest side of the island. Buses from mainland towns such as Nazaré das Farinhas, Valença and Jaguaribe (a small, picturesque colonial port), arrive at Bom Despacho.

From Bom Despacho there are many buses, kombis and taxis to all parts of the island. Kombis and taxis can be rented, but be prepared to bargain, US$30 for a half-day tour. » *See Transport, page 385, for details.*

Nazaré das Farinhas → *Phone code: 075 Population: 25,000*

On the mainland some 60 km inland from Itaparica, Nazaré das Farinhas is reached over a bridge by bus from Bom Despacho. This 18th-century town is celebrated for its market, which specializes in the local ceramic figures, or *caxixis*. There is a large market in Holy Week, particularly on Holy Thursday and Good Friday. From here buses run to southern Bahia. About 12 km from Nazaré (taxi from Salvador US$4.25, bus at 1530) is the village of **Maragojipinha**, which specializes in making the ceramic figures.

Recôncavo Baiano » pp373-386.

The area around the bay and immediately south of Salvador is known as the Recôncavo Baiano. This was one of the chief centres of sugar and tobacco cultivation in the 16th century and there is some fine colonial architecture here. The most impressive town is **Cachoeira**, which is also famous for its numerous festivals. There are other small fishing villages on the bay that are worth exploring, such as **Bom Jesus dos Pobres**. Dotted throughout the countryside are the decaying ruins of once-productive sugar refineries (*engenhos*), some of which can be visited.

Leaving Salvador on the Feira road, fork left at Km 33 on the BR-324 to visit the **Museu do Recôncavo Vanderlei de Pinho**. Further west, round the bay, is **São Francisco do Conde**, 54 km from Salvador, with a church and convent of 1636 and the ruins of Don Pedro II's agricultural school, said to be the first in Latin America.

Santo Amaro da Purificação and around → *Phone code: 075. Colour map 4, A6.*

Some 73 km from Salvador, Santo Amaro da Purificação is an old and sadly decaying sugar centre. It is noted for its churches (which are often closed because of robberies), the municipal palace (1769), fine main praça and ruined mansions including **Araújo Pinto**, former residence of the Barão de Cotegipe. It is also the birthplace of the singers Caetano Veloso and his sister Maria Bethânia. Other attractions include the splendid beaches of the bay, the falls of Vitória and the grotto of Bom Jesus dos Pobres. There are also a number of interesting festivals, see page 382. Craftwork is sold on the town's main bridge. There are no good hotels or restaurants.

About 3 km beyond Santo Amaro on BR-420, turn right onto the BA-878 for **Bom Jesus dos Pobres**, a small, traditional fishing village with a 300-year history. There is one good hotel (see Sleeping, page 377). To get there, take a bus from Salvador's *rodoviária* (four a day, **Camurjipe**, US$3).

Cachoeira → *Phone code: 075. Colour map 4, A6.*

At 116 km from Salvador, and only 4 km from the BR-101 coastal road, are the towns of Cachoeira (Bahia's 'Ouro Preto') and **São Félix**, on either side of the Rio Paraguaçu below the Cachoeira dam. In Cachoeira there's a **tourist office** ⓘ *Casa de Ana Néri*.

Set deep in the heart of some of the oldest farmland in Brazil, **Cachoeira** was once a thriving riverport that provided a vital supply link with the farming hinterland and Salvador to the east. The region was the centre of the sugar and tobacco booms, which played such an important role in the early wealth of the colony. The majestic *saveiro*, a gaff-rigged boat, traditionally transported this produce down the Rio Paraguaçu to Salvador across the bay. These boats can still be seen on the river at Cachoeira. The town was twice capital of Bahia: once in 1624-1625 during the Dutch invasion, and once in 1822-1823 while Salvador was still held by the Portuguese.

With the introduction of roads and the decline of river transport and steam, the town stopped in its tracks in the early 20th century and thus maintains its special charm. As in Salvador, *candomblé* plays a very important part in town life (see box page 363). Easy access by river from Salvador allowed the more traditional *candomblé* temples to move in times of religious repression. Cachoeira was the birthplace of Ana Néri, known as 'Mother of the Brazilians', who organized nursing services during the Paraguayan War (1865-1870).

The town's main buildings are the **Casa da Câmara e Cadeia** (1698-1712), the **Santa Casa de Misericórdia** (1734, the hospital; someone may let you see the church), the 16th-century **Ajuda** chapel (now containing a fine collection of vestments) and the convent of the **Ordem Terceira do Carmo**, whose church has a heavily gilded interior. Other churches are the **Matriz**, with 5-m high *azulejos*, and **Nossa Senhora da Conceição do Monte.** There are beautiful lace cloths on the church altars. All churches are either restored or in the process of restoration. The **Museu Hansen Bahia** ⓘ *R Ana Néri*, houses fine engravings by the German artist who made the Recôncavo his home in the 1950s. Recommended.

There is a great woodcarving tradition in Cachoeira and many of its artists can be seen at work in their studios. Best are **Louco Filho, Fory,** both in Rua Ana Néri, **Doidão** in front of the Igreja Matriz, and **J Gonçalves** on the main praça. A 300-m **railway bridge** built by the British in the 19th century spans the Rio Paraguaçu to São Felix, where the **Danneman cigar factory** can be visited to see hand-rolling in progress. A trail starting near the **Pousada do Convento** leads to some freshwater bathing pools above Cachoeira. There are beautiful views from above São Félix.

Excursions from Cachoeira

About 6 km from Cachoeira, on the higher ground of the Planalto Baiano, is the small town of **Belém** (the turning is at Km 2.5 on the road to Santo Amaro), which has a healthy climate and is a popular place for summer homes. **Maragojipe**, a tobacco exporting port with a population of 39,000, is 22 km southeast of Cachoeira along a dirt road (BA-123); it can also be reached by boat from Salvador. If you visit, look out for the old houses and the church of São Bartolomeu, with its museum. The main festival is **São Bartolomeu,** in August. Good ceramic craftwork is sold in the town. The tobacco centre of **Cruz das Almas** can also be visited, although transport is poor.

Sleeping

Salvador *p360, maps p361, 365 and 367*
The **Centro Histórico** is the ideal place to stay; the **Pelourinho** if you're on a tight budget and **Santo Antônio** if you are looking for reasonably priced hotels with real charm and character. The best hotel in the city, O Convento do Carmo lies between the 2. **Barra** also has some reasonable options; especially for apartments with kitchens and it lies on the seafront. Business visitors will find good hotels in **Rio Vermelho**, overlooking the ocean and a 10-min taxi ride from both the centre and the airport. There are plenty of other services in this neighbourhood too.

Accommodation in the city tends to get very full over Carnaval and New Year, when prices go up. At Carnaval it is a good idea to rent a flat or stay in a shared room in a private house (*pensionatao*), as other accommodation can be hard to come by and hotels and hostels are heaving. *Pensionatos* usually charge between US$5 and US$35 per person. Be careful with your belongings as not all householders are honest.

The tourist office has a list of estate agents for flat rental (eg José Mendez, T071-3237 1394/6) or you can find flats through **Bahia Online**, www.bahia-online.net.

Houses or rooms can be rented from **Pierre Marbacher**, R Carlos Coqueijo 68A, Itapoã, T071-3249 5754 (Caixa Postal 7458, 41600 Salvador), who is Swiss, owns a beach bar at Rua K and speaks English.

Centro Histórico
LL O Convento do Carmo, R do Carmo 1, Pelourinho, T071-3327 8400, www.pousadas.pt. Far and away the best hotel in the city and the best historical hotel in Brazil; with a range of suites in a beautifully converted baroque convent. Facilities include an excellent restaurant and spa, a small swimming pool and business services.
LL Portas Velhas, Largo da Palma 6, Santana, T071-3324 8400, www.acasadasportas

velhas.com.br. Over-priced New York-owned themed boutique hotel in the square made famous by Jorge Amado's *Dona Flor and Her Two Husbands*. Small but tastefully decorated a/c rooms, 1 larger suite and a good restaurant. The streets running from here to the centre are unsafe at any time of day. Take a cab.

B Hotel Pelourinho, R Alfredo Brito 20, T071-3243 2324, www.hotelpelourinho.com. A newly refurbished 1960s hotel with bright tiled and white-walled a/c en suites. The bathrooms have marble basins and glass shower cubicles. Some rooms have great views out over the Baía de Todos os Santos.

B-D Hotel Quilombo do Pelô, R Alfredo Brito 13, T071-3322 4371. A range of rooms from simple dorms and doubles to the top floor 'Rei Zumbi' suite with its own jacuzzi and views out over the city. All are themed and the restaurant serves Jamaican food.

C Hotel Solar dos Romanos, R Alfredo Brito 14a, T071-3322 6158. A range of basic cavernous rooms in a colonial house; some of which are gloomy and without windows and the best of which are a/c with sea views.

C Lucas Guesthouse, R do Passo 7, T071-3327 5746. A spacious upper suite with a little terrace and space for up to 4 people. Also 4 very simple fan-cooled rooms partitioned with chipboard.

C Solara, Praça José de Alencar 25, T071-3326 4583. A cavernous building with very basic rooms, all en suite, with lino floors and mattresses covered in uncomfortable plastic. Some have TVs and fridges. The best have good views out over the Pelourinho. Recently painted but still in need of refurbishment.

C-E Albergue das Laranjeiras, R Inácio Acciolli 13, T/F071-3321 1366, www.laranjeirashostel.com.br. IYHA hostel with a range of dorms, doubles and family rooms housed in a colonial building in the heart of the historic centre. Can be noisy. Café and crêperie downstairs, English spoken and a full range of hostel services. Good for meeting other travellers.

C-E Albergue do Passo, R Ladeira do Passo 3, T071-3326 1951 Clean, safe and friendly, with breakfast, and a range of standard hostel services.

C-E Albergue do Peló, R Ribeiro dos Santos 5, T071-3242 8061, www.alberguedo pelo.com.br. A bright reception area leads to simple, but freshly-painted and slate-floored dorms for 4-12 people. All are single sex. Breakfast included.

C-E Albergue São Jorge, R Alfredo de Brito, T071-3266 7092. Brightly-painted but cramped single-sex dorms, and a few doubles. Internet access and breakfast.

C-E Pousada Gloria, R das Laranjeiras 34, T071-3321 8249. Clean and well-kept rooms some of which have en suites and views out over the historical centre. No breakfast.

D-E Pagador de Promessas, Ladeira do Carmo 19, T071-3243 5716, www.opagador depromessas.com.br. Much the best option for backpackers in the Pelourinho, with a series of fan-cooled dorms and doubles in a converted colonial house; all immaculately clean, with hardwood floors and in cool, high-ceilinged rooms. Tours organized. No breakfast.

South of the centre

Campo Grande/Vitória is a quiet, upmarket residential area, between Barra and the city centre, convenient for museums.

L Tropical, Av Sete de Setembro 1537, Campo Grande, T071-2105 2000, www.tropical hotel.com.br. A recently renovated 1950s business hotel. Good service, pool, sauna, business facilities and a discount for **Varig** customers. Convenient city centre location.

A Bahia do Sol, Av 7 de Setembro 2009, T071-3338 8800, www.bahiadosol.com.br. Comfortable and safe family-run hotel in a 1970s tower. Good breakfast and restaurant, bureau de change, but no pool. Rooms have a/c, fridges, safes and en suites. The best are on the upper floors and have recently been refurbished. Ask to see at least a couple.

Porto da Barra

Barra is the best beach neighbourhood in the historic centre. The sea is none too clean but the neighbourhood has plenty of restaurants, beach bars and nightlife.

A Bahia Flat, Av Oceânica 235, Barra, T071-3339 4140, www.bahiaflat.com.br. A range of flats. The best are tastefully decorated and newly refurbished with Miró prints on the walls, patent leather sofas, glass coffee tables, large fridges, hi-fis and expansive mirror-fronted wardrobes. The best have sea views. The hotel has a pool and sauna.

AL Marazul, Av 7 de Setembro 3937, Barra, T071-3264 8151, www.marazulhotel.com.br. Blocky 1970s tower on the seafront with standard 3-star rooms with anonymous catalogue furniture. The best are at the top of the building and have magnificent views. The restaurant has a pool, conference facilities and business services.

A Monte Pascoal Praia, Av Oceânica 176, Farol beach, T071-3203 4000, www.monte pascoal.com.br. Newly renovated 1970s hotel decorated in garish colours but well-kept and well-run. With pool, sauna, gym, restaurant and decent service.

B Farol Barra Flat, Av. Oceanica 409, T071-3339 0000, www.farolbarraflat.com.br. Over 100 faded, simple yet well-kept apartments with kitchenettes; all with microwaves, TVs and the best with sweeping ocean views.

B La Habana, Av Oceânica 84, T071-3237 5105, www.hospederiadelahabana.com.br. Newly renovated brilliant yellow seafront hotel with 13 a/c rooms; all with polished brick floors and en suites. Quiet during the week but popular at the weekends. With a lively bar and restaurant.

B Pousada Azul, R Praguer Fróis. A quiet pousada in a semi-residential street. Spartan rooms furnished with solid hardwood beds and commodes.

C Pousada Hotel Ambar, R Afonso Celso 485, T071-3264 3791, www.ambar pousada.com.br. A French-owned pousada with very simple, small fan-cooled rooms gathered around a colourful little courtyard. Internet and decent breakfast.

B-C Villa Romana, R Lemos Brito 14, T071-3264 6522, www.villaromana.com.br. Simple a/c rooms with wooden floors, desks, wardrobes and en suites.

D-C Pousada Malu, 7 de Setembro 3801, T071-3264 4461. Small, somewhat boxy rooms lying along an external corridor in a hotel overlooking the sea. Some rooms are musty. With breakfast, cooking and laundry facilities.

D Bella Barra, R Afonso Celso 439, T071-3264 3260, www.hotelbella barra.com.br. Very simple a/c whitewash and brown-tiled rooms with foamy mattresses and en suites. In need of a lick of paint.

D Hotel da Barra, Av. Almirante Marques de Leão 138, T071-3264 2481. Clean, bright but very simple fan-cooled or a/c rooms all with en suites (with no shower curtains). The best are on the upper floors.

E-F Albergue do Porto, R Barão de Sergy 197, Barra, T071-3264 6600, www.albergue doporto.com.br. IYHA hostel in a turn-of-the-20th-century house. Spacious, high ceilinged fan-cooled rooms with wooden floors; a comfortable communal area and good breakfast, English spoken and double a/c rooms with baths available alongside dorms. Other facilities include, kitchen, laundry, safe, TV lounge, games room and internet. Very popular.

E-F Pousada Marcos, Av Oceânica 281, Barra, T071-3264 5117, www.pousada marcos.com.br. A very simple hostel-style guesthouse. In a good location near the lighthouse. Always busy.

North of the centre

Santo Antônio is a quiet district just 5 mins' walk northeast of Pelourinho and Carmo. In recent years it has been a popular place for Europeans to open up carefully designed *pousadas* in beautifully restored buildings. A number have magnificent views of the bay. Most are mid-range, but there are cheaper options too.

AL Villa Santo Antônio, R Direita de Santo Antônio 130, Santo Antônio, T071-3326 1270, www.hotel-santoantonio.com. Very stylish, bright and comfortable converted colonial town house, the best rooms have magnificent views out over the bay from your bed. All the a/c rooms have en suites and little balconies; all are different. Good service and breakfast.

A-AL Pousada Redfish, Ladeira do Boqueirão 1, T071-3243 8473, www.hotel redfish.com. English-owned, stylish little boutique with plain, large rooms; some with terraces and open-air showers.

A-AL Pousada das Flores, R Direita de Santo Antônio 442, T071-3243 1836, www.pflores. com.br. A beautiful, tranquil old house decorated in colonial style and owned by a Brazilian/French couple. Great breakfast. Full of character.

For Sleeping and Eating price codes, see pages 49 and 52 or the inside front cover. For an explanation of phone codes, see page 66.

A-AL Pousada do Boqueirão, R Direita do Santo Antônio 48, T071-3241 2262, www.pousadaboqueirao.com.br. The most stylish of all the pousadas in Salvador; lovingly renovated by the Italian interior-designer owner and with a variety of different themed rooms. Wonderful views, good service and excellent food. Several languages spoken.

B Pousada Villa Carmo, R do Carmo 58, T/F071-3241 3924, www.pousadavilla carmo.com.br. Very comfortable, rooms with fan or a/c in an Italian/Brazilian-owned colonial house. Several languages spoken.

Rio Vermelho

This modern suburban area on the coast between the city centre and the airport, has long been the home of Salvador's well-to-do artists and musicians (Carlinhos Brown lives here). It has a handful of decent restaurants, some good bars and a far safer feel than the Pelourinho, which is a 10-min taxi or 20-min bus ride away. It is particularly suited to business visitors and families.

LL Pestana Bahia, R Fonte de Boi 216, T071-3453 8000, www.pestanahotels.com.br. Newly revamped tower with wonderful views out over the ocean, a pool, gym, restaurant, sauna and very good business facilities. Online discounts available. With restaurant and bar.

LL-L Blue Tree Towers, R Monte Conselho 505, T071-3330 2233, www.bluetree.com.br. Smart new business hotel in this excellent Brazilian chain. Very good service and decent facilities including pool, tennis courts and a respectable restaurant.

A-B Catharina Paraguaçu, R João Gomes 128, Rio Vermelho, T071-3247 1488, www.hotelcatharinaparaguacu.com.br. Small colonial-style hotel with attractive courtyards and a range of decent rooms, some of which, however, are distinctly better than others. Very good service. Recommended.

C Ibis, R Fonte do Boi 215, T071-3330 8300, www.accorhotels.com.br. Blocky new hotel in this budget business chain. Safe, a/c and great seaviews from the upper floors. Very good value.

Camping

Swimming in the sea is dangerous in the areas near the campsites.

Camping Clube do Brasil, R Visconde do Rosario 409, Rosario, T071-3242 0482.

Camping de Pituaçu, Av Prof Pinto de Aguiar, Jardim Pituaçu, T071-3231 7143.

Ecológica, R Alameida da Praia, near the lighthouse at Itapoã, take bus from Praça da Sé direct to Itapoã, or to Campo Grande or Barra, change there for Itapoã, 1 hr, then 30 mins' walk, T071-3374 3506. Bar, restaurant, hot showers. Highly recommended.

Igloo Inn, Terminal Turistico de Buraquinho, Praia Lauro de Freitas, T071-3379 2854.

Ihla de Itaparica *p371, map p371*

A Pousada Arco Iris, Estrada da Gamboa 102, Mar Grande beach, T071-3833 1130. Magnificent, though dishevelled 19th-century building romantically set in a garden of mango trees. Decent restaurant with slow service, a pool and unkempt but shady camping facilities available in the owners' adjacent property.

B Quinta Pitanga, Itaparica town, T071-3831 1554. Beautifully decorated beachfront property lovingly run by owner, Jim Valkus. 3 suites, 2 singles and an excellent restaurant open to non-guests.

C-B Galeria Hotel, Praia do Sol, Barra Grande, T071-3636 8441, www.galeria-hotel.com. German and Brazilian owned pousada with simple tile-floored a/c en suites around a large pool. Good restaurant.

C Pousada Canto do Mar, Av Beira Mar s/n, Praia de Aratuba, T071-3638 2244, www.pousadaumcantodomar.com.br. Brightly coloured, simple *cabañas* over-looking what is a lively beach in summer and a quiet beach the rest of the year. Friendly staff, decent breakfast.

D Pousada Casarão da Ilha, near the church in the main praça, Mar Grande beach, T071-3833 1106. Spacious a/c rooms, pool and a great view of Salvador across the bay.

D Pousada Estrela do Mar, Av NS das Candeias 170, Mar Grande beach, T071-3833 1108. Modest but well-kept a/c or fan-cooled rooms.

D Pousada Scórpio, R Aquárius, Mar Grande beach, T071-3823 1036. Simple rooms set around a little swimming pool. Reasonable breakfast and a weekend restaurant.

D Pousada Sonho do Verão, R São Bento 2, Mar Grande beach. Chalets and apartments with cooking facilities, French and English spoken. Bike and horse rental (US$3/5 per hr).

D Pousada Zimbo Tropical, Aratuba beach, Estrada de Cacha Pregos, Km 3, R Yemanjá, T/F071-3838 1148. Pretty little bungalows in a tropical garden. Good breakfast, optional evening meals.

E Hotel Village Sonho Nosso, Estrada Praia Cacha Pregos, Km 9 Cacha Pregos, T071-3837 1040. Very clean huts on one of the island's cleanest beaches. The good service includes pick-up from anywhere on the island. Bom Despacho Kombis stop a 5-min walk from the front door.

Santo Amaro da Purificação *p372*

A Água Viva, T075-699 1178, reservations T071-3359 1132, on one of the region's oldest farms, on the beachfront. Chalets or apartments, a/c or fan, good breakfast and restaurant. Good beach. Recommended.

Cachoeira *p372*

B Pousada do Convento de Cachoeira, R Inocência Boaventura, T075-3725 1716. 26 rooms in a newly restored 18th-century convent. Decent restaurant.

D Pousada Paraquaçu, Av Salvador Pinto 1, São Félix, T075-3725 2550. A pretty riverside pousada, with spartan rooms and breakfast

D Santo Antônio, near the *rodoviária*, T075-3725 1402. Basic but safe, with laundry facilities. Recommended.

E-F Pousada Tia Rosa, near Casa Ana Neri, T075 3725 1692. Very basic and simple but with a reasonable breakfast.

Eating

Salvador *p360, maps p361, 365 and 367*

Centro Histórico

TTT Mama Bahia, R Alfredo Brito 21, T071-3322 4397, www.mamabahia.com.br. Steaks and northeastern meat dishes like *carne do sol* accompanied by a respectable, if modest, list of Argentinian, Brazilian and Chilean wines.

TTT Maria Mata Mouro, R da Ordem Terceira 8, T071-3321 3929. International menu, excellent service, relaxing atmosphere, a quiet corner in bustling Pelourinho.

TTT O Nilo, R das Laranjeiras 44, T071-9159 0937. Superior Lebanese food in an intimate little restaurant decorated with black-and-white prints. Great tagines and a vegetarian degustation.

TTT Sorriso de Dadá, R Frei Vicente 5, T071-3321 9642, www.dada.com.br. Bahia's most famous chef has cooked for, amongst others, Jorge Amado, Gilberto Gil and Hillary Clinton. Her *moqueca de camarão* and her *vatapas* are signature dishes.

TTT Uauá , R Gregorio de Matos, 36, T071 3321 3089. Elegant, colonial restaurant and bar serving northeastern cooking and seafood, including some Bahian specialities. The restaurant's name means 'firefly' in Tupi.

TTT-TT Axego, R João de Deus 1, T071-3242 7481. An established restaurant celebrated for its seafood. The *moquecas* are among the best in the Centro Histórico and there is excellent *feijoada* on Sun lunchtime.

TTT TT Encontro dos Artistas, R das Laranjeiras 15, T071-3321 1721. Excellent seafood and *moquecas* served in a little streetside restaurant decorated with a mock-Da Vinci *Last Supper*, set in Salvador.

TTT-TT Jardim das Delícias, R Joao de Deus, 12, T071-3321 1449. An award-winning, elegant restaurant and antiques shop set in a pretty tropical garden serving Bahian and international food accompanied by live classical or acoustic music. Very good value for its quality.

TT Quilombo do Pelô, R Alfredo Brito 13, T071-3322 4371. Rustic Jamaican restaurant, daily 1100-2400, good food with relaxed, if not erratic service. One of the few places offering vegetarian options.

TT Senac, Praça José Alencar 13-15, Largo do Pelourinho, T071-3324 4557. A catering school with 2 restaurants. Upstairs is typical Bahian cooking; downstairs per kilo and open only for lunch; both are a/c. Dishes are better upstairs but there is plenty of choice in the buffet and options for vegetarians.

TT-T Pomerô, R Alfredo Brito 33, T071-3321 5556, www.pomero.com.br. Good value, simple and barely garnished grilled meats, fish steaks, bar snacks and lightly spiced *moquecas* in a popular restaurant housed in a colonial house. Closed on Mon.

T Bahiacafe.com, Praça da Sé, 20, T071-3322 1266. Smart, Belgian-run internet café with good coffee, a European-style breakfast menu and decent snacks.

T Coffee Shop, Praça da Sé 5, T071-3322 7817. Cuban-style café serving sandwiches.

Bahian cuisine

Bahian cooking is spiced and peppery. The main dish is *moqueca* – seafood cooked in a sauce made from coconut milk, tomatoes, red and green peppers, fresh coriander and *dendê* (palm oil). It is traditionally cooked in a wok-like earthenware dish and served piping hot at the table. Served with *moqueca* is *farofa* (manioc flour) and a hot pepper sauce which you add at your discretion, it's usually extremely hot so try a few drops before venturing further. The *dendê* is somewhat heavy and those with delicate stomachs are advised to try the *ensopado*, a sauce with the same ingredients as the *moqueca*, but without the palm oil.

Nearly every street corner has a *Bahiana* selling a wide variety of local snacks, the most famous of which is the *acarajé*, a kidney bean dumpling fried in palm oil, which has its origins in West Africa. To this the Bahiana adds *vatapá*, a dried shrimp and coconut milk paté (also delicious on its own), fresh salad and hot sauce (*pimenta*). For those who prefer not to eat the palm oil, the *abará* is a good substitute. *Abará* is steamed and wrapped in banana leaves. Seek local advice on which are the most hygienic stalls to eat from.

Recommended *Bahianas* are **Chica**, at Ondina beach (in the street behind the Bahia Praia Hotel), **Dinha**, in Rio Vermelho (serves *acarajé* until midnight, extremely popular), **Regina** at Largo da Santana (very lively in the late afternoon), and **Cira** in Largo da Mariquita. Bahians usually eat *acarajé* or *abará* with a chilled beer on the way home from work or the beach at sunset. Another popular dish with African origins is *xin-xin de galinha*, chicken on the bone cooked in *dendê*, with dried shrimp, garlic and squash.

Excellent coffee and tea served in china cups. Doubles as cigar shop.
Ɏ **Gramado**, Praça da Sé 16, T071-3322 1727. The best of the few per kilo restaurants in the area. Scrupulously clean and with a reasonable choice. Lunch only.

Barra
There are many a/c restaurants from cheap to medium-priced in **Shopping Barra** and **Barra Center Shopping**.
ɎɎɎ **Barravento**, Av Oceanica 814, T071-3247 2577. Very popular upmarket beach bar restaurant with a marquee roof. Decent cocktails, *chope* and a menu of seafood, *moquecas* and steaks.
ɎɎ **Cantina Panzone**, Av Oceánica 114, T071-3264 3644. Reasonable pizza and pasta. Lively crowd in high season.
ɎɎ **Oceánica**, Presidente Vargas 1, T071-3264 3561. A long-established popular Bahian seafood restaurant. Open until late, especially on weekends.
ɎɎ **Quatro Amicci**, R Dom Marcos Teixeira 35. Excellent wood-fired oven pizzas served in a bright modern space in a converted 19th- century house. Lively weekend crowd.
Ɏ **Caranguejo do Farol**, Av Oceánica 235, T071-3264 7061. A buzzing bar and seafood restaurant serving great Bahian food in *refeição* portions large enough for 2. Cheap bottled beer. Strong *caipirinhas*.

Elsewhere
ɎɎ **Casa da Dinha**, R João Gomes 25, just west of the **Catharina Paraguaçu Hotel** and a few yards from the Largo de Santana, T071-3333 0525. One of the best mid-range Bahian restaurants in the city with a varied menu peppered with Bahian specialities, steaks, fish and standard international options like pasta.
ɎɎɎ **Solar Do Unhão**, Av Contorno, Campo Grande, T071-3329 5551, www.solardo unhao.com.br. African slaves arriving into Brazil were processed in this former sugar mill on the edge of the bay. The building has now been gutted and turned into a Bahian restaurant where waiters in traditional

costume serve lunch and dinner. Some of the best live *capoeira* in the city can be seen here.

Ihla Itaparica*p371, map p371*

There are many Bahianas selling *acarajé* in the late afternoon and early evening, in the main praça and by the pier at Mar Grande.

ΨΨΨ Philippe's Bar and Restaurant, Largo de São Bento, Mar Grande, Itaparica. The best restaurant on the island with delicious fish dishes cooked by the French owner.

Ψ Rafael, in the main praça, Mar Grande, Itaparica. Basic with pizzas and snacks.

Cachoeira *p372*

ΨΨ Do Nair, R 13 de Maio. Delicious food and occasional live music.

Ψ Cabana do Pai Thomaz, 25 de Junho 12. Excellent Bahian food, good value, also a hotel, **C**, with private bath and breakfast.

Ψ Xang-hai, São Félix, good, cheap food, try the local dish, *maniçoba* (meat, manioc and peppers). Warmly recommended.

Bars and clubs

Salvador *p360, maps p361, 365 and 367*

Centro Histórico

Nightlife is concentrated on and around the **Pelourinho**, where there is always a free live street band on Tue and at weekends. The Pelourinho area is also good for a bar browse, but be wary after 2300. There are many bars on the **Largo de Quincas Berro d'Água**, especially along **R Alfredo do Brito**. **R João de Deus** and its environs are dotted with simple pavement bars with plastic tables.

The most famous music from Salvador are the *maracatú* drum orchestras like **Olodum** and **Ilê Aiyê**, whose 40-piece drum orchestras can be heard frequently around the Pelourinho (Olodum played on Paul Simon's *Rhythm of the Saints* album). Both groups have their own venues and play in the individual parades or *blocos* at Carnaval. See box, page 380, for times and venues of the *bloco* rehearsals. There is live music all year round but the best time to hear the most frenetic performers – particularly the *axê* stars – is during Carnaval.

Bar do Reggae and Praça do Reggae, Ladeiro do Pelourinho, by the Nossa Senhora dos Rosarios dos Pretos church. Live reggae bands every Tue and more frequently closer to carnival.

Cantina da Lua, Praça Quinze de Novembro 2, Terreiro De Jesus, T071-3322 4041. Open daily, popular and a good spot on the square with outdoor seating, but gets crowded and the food isn't great.

Casa do Olodum, R das Laranjeiras, T071-3321 5010, www2.uol.com.br/olodum. Olodum's headquarters where they perform live every Tue and Sun at 1930 to packed crowds.

O Cravinho, Praça 15 de Novembro 3, T071-3322 6759. Dark little bar with occasional live music. Always busy. Greasy bar food is served at tree-trunk tables, usually accompanied by plentiful *cachaça*, which is made here and stored in barrels behind the bar. Be careful in this area after 2300.

Quereres, R Frei Vicente 7, T071-3321 1616. Lively little club in a colonial house playing Brazilian samba funk, hip hop and *axë*. Busy on Tue and Fri.

Porto da Barra

Barra nightlifeis concentrated around the **Farol da Barra** (lighthouse) and **R Marquês de Leão**, which is busy with pavement bars. Like the Pelourinho the whole area is good for a browse, but be wary of pickpockets.

Habeas Copos, R Marquês de Leão 172. A popular and traditional street-side bar – a Salvador institution.

Elsewhere/Rio Vermelho

The district of **Rio Vermelho** was once the bohemian section of town and it still has good live music and exciting bar nightlife. There are a number of lively bars around the **Largo de Santana**, a block west of Hotel Catharina Paraguaçu.

Café Calypso, Travessa Prudente Moraes 59, Rio Vermelho, T071-3334 6446. Live Brazilian rock music on Tue and Fri.

Café Cancun, Otavia Mangabeira 6000, Aeroclube Plaza, Boca do Rio, T071-3461 0603. The city's premier dance club for Bahian 20- to 40-something middle classes. Kicks off after 2300. Busiest on Wed, *forró* night.

Fashion Club, Av Octávio Mangabeira, 2471, Jd dos Namorados, T071-3346 0012. Similar to **Café Cancun** but with a predominantly 20-something crowd. Busy on Thu.

Carnaval in Bahia

Carnival in Bahia is the largest in the world and encourages active participation. It is said that there are 1½ million people dancing on the streets at any one time.

The **pre-carnival festive season** begins with São Nicodemo de Cachimbo (penultimate Sunday of November), followed by Santa Bárbara (4 December), then the Festa da Conceição da Praia, centred on the church of that name (open 0700-1130) at the base of the Lacerda lift. The last night is 8 December (not for those who don't like crowds!). The Festa da Boa Viagem takes place in the last week of December, in the lower city; the beach will be packed all night on 31 December. The new year kicks off on 1 January with a beautiful boat procession of Nosso Senhor dos Navegantes from Conceição da Praia to the church of Boa Viagem, on the beach of that name in the lower city. The leading boat, which carries the image of Christ and the archbishop, was built in 1892. You can follow in a sailing boat for about US$1; go early (0900) to the dock by the Mercado Modelo. A later festival is São Lázaro on the last Sunday in January.

Carnaval itself officially starts on Thursday night at 2000 when the keys of the city are given to the Carnaval King '*Rei Momo*'. The unofficial opening though is on Wednesday with the Lavagem do Porto da Barra, when throngs of people dance on the beach. Later on in the evening is the Baile dos Atrizes, starting at around 2300 and going on until dawn, very bohemian, good fun. Check with Bahiatursa for details on venue and time (also see under Rio for Carnaval dates).

There are two distinct musical formats. The **afro blocos** are large drum-based troupes (some with up to 200 drummers) who play on the streets, accompanied by singers atop mobile sound trucks. The first of these groups was the Filhos de Gandhi (founded in 1949), whose participation is one of the highlights of Carnaval. Their 6000 members dance through the streets on the Sunday and Tuesday of Carnaval dressed in their traditional costumes, a river of white and blue in an ocean of multi-coloured carnival revellers. The best known of the recent *afro blocos* are Ilê Aiye, Olodum, Muzenza and Malê Debalê. They all operate throughout the year in cultural, social and political areas. Not all of them are receptive to foreigners among their numbers for Carnaval. The basis of the rhythm is the enormous *surdo* (deaf) drum with its *bumbum bumbum bum* anchorbeat, while the smaller *repique*, played with light twigs, provides a crack-like overlay. Ilê Aiye take to the streets around 2100 on Saturday night and their departure from their headquarters at Ladeira do Curuzu in the Liberdade district is not to be missed. The best way to get there is to take a taxi to Curuzu via Largo do Tanque, thereby avoiding traffic jams. The ride is a little longer but much

Havana Music Bar, R Cardeal da Silva 117, Rio Vermelho, T071-3237 5107. Live bands (mostly rock) Wed-Sat. Best after 2230.
Korunn, R Ceará 1240, Pituba, T071-3248 4208. Lively dance club with a bohemian crowd. Very popular Thu-Sat.
Pimentinha, Boca do Rio. One of the few clubs to be lively on a Mon.
Rock In Rio Café, Aeroclube Plaza Show, Boca do Rio, T071-3461 0300. Dance club with a young crowd and an emphasis on rock and MPB. Busiest at the weekends.
Teatro Sesi Rio Vermelho, R Borges dos Reis 9, Rio Vermelho, T071-3334 0668. The best place in the city to see contemporary Salvador bands live.

Cachoeira *p372*
Casa do Licor, R 13 Maio 25. Interesting bohemian bar with a range of bizarre drinks. Try the banana-flavoured spirit.

quicker. A good landmark is the Paes Mendonça supermarket on the corner of the street, from where the *bloco* leaves. From there it's a short walk to the departure point.

The enormous **trios eléctricos**, 12-m sound trucks with powerful sound systems that defy most decibel counters, are the second format. These trucks, each with its town band of up to 10 musicians, play songs influenced by the *afro blocos* and move at a snail's pace through the streets, drawing huge crowds. Each *afro bloco* and *bloco de trio* has its own costume and its own security personnel, who cordon off the area around the sound truck. The *bloco* members can thus dance in comfort and safety.

The traditional Carnaval route is from Campo Grande (by the Tropical Hotel da Bahia) to Praça Castro Alves near the old town. The *blocos* go along Avenida 7 de Setembro and return to Campo Grande via the parallel Rua Carlos Gomes. Many of the *trios* no longer go through the Praça Castro Alves, once the epicentre of Carnaval. The best night at Praça Castro Alves is Tuesday (the last night of Carnaval), when the famous '*Encontro dos Trios*' (Meeting of the Trios) takes place. *Trios* jostle for position in the square and play in rotation until the dawn on Ash Wednesday. It is not uncommon for major stars from the Bahian (and Brazilian) music world to make surprise appearances.

There are grandstand seats at Campo Grande throughout the event. Day tickets for these are available the week leading up to Carnaval. Check with Bahiatursa for information on where the tickets are sold. Tickets are US$10 (or up to US$30 on the black market on the day). The *blocos* are judged as they pass the grandstand and are at their most frenetic at this point. There is little or no shade from the sun so bring a hat and lots of water. Best days are Sunday to Tuesday. For those wishing to go it alone, just find a friendly *barraca* in the shade and watch the *blocos* go by. Avoid the Largo da Piedade and Relógio de São Pedro on Avenida 7 de Setembro: the street narrows here, creating human traffic jams.

The other major centre for Carnaval is Barra to Ondina. The **blocos alternativos** ply this route. These are nearly always *trios eléctricos*, connected with the more traditional *blocos* who have expanded to this now very popular district. Not to be missed here is Timbalada, the drumming group formed by the internationally renowned percussionist Carlinhos Brown.

Ticket prices range from US$180 to US$450. The quality of the *bloco* often depends on the act that plays on the *trio*. For more information see the official Carnaval site, www.carnaval. salvador.ba.gov.br.

Entertainment

Salvador *p360, maps p361, 365 and 367*

The **Fundação Cultural do Estado da Bahia** edits *Bahia Cultural*, a monthly brochure listing the main cultural events for the month. These can be found in most hotels and **Bahiatursa** information centres. Local newspapers *A Tarde* and *Correio da Bahia* have good cultural sections listing all events in the city.

Cinema

The main shopping malls at Barra, Iguatemi, Itaigara and Brotas, and **Cineart** in Politeama (Centro), run more mainstream movies. The impressive Casa do Comércio building near Iguatemi houses the **Teatro do SESC** with a mixed programme of theatre, cinema and music Wed-Sun.

Theatre and classical music

Associação Cultural Brasil Estados Unidos (ACBEU), Corredor de Vitória. US cultural shows and cinema.
Teatro Gregorio de Matos, Praça Castro Alves, T071-3322 2646. Programmes dedicated to showcasing new productions and writers.
Teatro Vila Velha, Passeio Publico, T071-3336 1384. Márcio Meirelles, the theatre's director, works extensively with **Grupo Teatro Olodum**; although performed in Portuguese, productions here are very visual and well worth investigating.
Teatro XVIII, R Frei Vicente, T071-3332 0018. Experimental theatre in Portuguese.
Theatro Castro Alves, Largo 2 de Julho, bairro de Campo Grande, T071-3339 8000. The city's most distinguished performance space and the home of the **Bahian Symphony Orchestra** and the **Castro Alves Ballet Company**. The theatre also hosts occasional performances by more cerebral MPB artists and contemporary performers like Hermeto Pascoal or Egberto Gismonti.

Festivals and events

Salvador *p360, maps p361, 365 and 367*
6 Jan Epiphany. Public holiday with many free concerts and events. Beautiful masses in many of the historic churches.
Jan Festa do Nosso Senhor do Bonfim. On the 2nd Sun after Epiphany. On the preceding Thu there is a colourful parade at the church with many penitents and a ceremonial washing of the church itself. Great for pictures.
Feb Carnival, see box page 380.
2 Feb Pescadores do Rio Vermelho. Boat processions with gifts for Yemanjá, Goddess of the Sea, accompanied by African Brazilian music.
Mar/Apr Holy Week. The week before Easter sees many colourful processions around the old churches in the upper city.

Santo Amaro da Purificação *p372*
24 Jan-2 Feb Festival of Santo Amaro.
2 Feb Nossa Senhora da Purificação.
13 May Bembé do Mercado.

Cachoeira *p372*
24 Jun São João, 'Carnival of the Interior'. Celebrations include dangerous games with fireworks, well attended by tourists.
Mid-Aug Nossa Sehora da Boa Morte.
4 Dec A famous **candomblé ceremony** at the Fonte de Santa Bárbara.

Shopping

Salvador *p360, maps p361, 365 and 367*

Arts, crafts and cigars

Artesanato Santa Bárbara, R Alfredo Brito 7, Pelourinho. Excellent handmade lace.
Atelier Portal da Cor, Ladeira do Carmo 31, Pelourinho, T071-3242 9466. A gallery run by a co-operative of artists, Totonho, Calixto, Raimundo Santos, Jô, good prices. Recommended.
FIEB-SESI, Av Tiradentes 299, Bonfim; Av Borges dos Reis 9, Rio Vermelho; and Av 7 de Setembro 261, Mercês. Some of the best artisan products in the city ranging from textiles and ceramics to musical instruments.
Ilê Aiyê, R das Laranjeiras 16. Souvenirs and music.
Instituto Mauá, R Gregorio de Matos 27, Pelourinho, open Tue-Sat 0900-1800, Sun 1000-1600. Good-quality items, better value and quality than the Mercado Modelo.
Loja de Artesanato do SESC, Largo Pelourinho, T071-3321 5502, Mon-Fri 0900-1800 (closed for lunch), Sat 0900-1300.
Oficina de Investigação Musical, Alfredo Brito 24, T071-3322 2386, Mon-Fri 0800-1200 and 1300-1600. Handmade traditional percussion instruments (and percussion lessons for US$15 per hr).
Rosa do Prado, R Inacio Aciolly 5, Pelourinho. Cigar shop packed with every kind of Brazilian '*charuto*' imaginable.

Bookshops

Graúna, Av 7 de Setembro 1448, and R Barão de Itapoã 175, Porto da Barra. Many English titles.
Livraria Brandão, R Ruy Barbosa 104, Centre, T071-3243 5383. Second-hand English, French, Spanish and German books.
Livraria Planeta, Carlos Gomes 42, loja 1. Sells used English books.

Jewellery

Casa Moreira, Ladeira da Praça, just south of Praça da Sé. Exquisite jewellery and antiques. Most are expensive, but there are some affordable charms.

Scala, Praça da Sé, T/F071-3321 8891. Handmade jewellery using locally mined gems (eg aquamarine, amethyst and emerald), workshop at back.

Markets

Feira de Artesanjato, Santa Maria Fort, Wed 1700-2100. Arts and crafts in the fort at the far end of Porto da Barra beach.

Feira de São Joaquim, 5 km from Mercado Modelo along the seafront, daily 0800-1900, Sun 0800-1200. The largest and least touristy market in the city selling mainly foodstuffs and a few artisan products. Very smelly.

Mercado Modelo, Praça Cairu, Cidade Baixa, Sat 0800-1900, Sun 0800-1200. Live music and dancing, especially Sat. Expect to be asked for money if you take photos. Many tourist items such as woodcarvings, silver-plated fruit, leather goods, local musical instruments. Lace items for sale are often not handmade (despite labels), are heavily marked up, and are much better bought at their place of origin (eg Ilha de Maré, Pontal da Barra and Marechal Deodoro).

Music and carnival souvenirs

Boutique Olodum, Praça José Alencar, Pelourinho. Olodum CDs, music, T-shirts and musical instruments.

Cana Brava records, R João de Deus 22, T071-3321 0536, www.bahia-online.net. Great little CD shop with a friendly and knowledgeable American owner. Stocks a whole range of classy Brazilian artists, less internationally famous names and back catalogue artists.

Flashpoint, Shopping Iguatemi. One of the best general music and CD shops in the city.

Ilê Aiyê, R das Laranjeiras 16, T071-3321 4193, www.ileaiye.com.br. Bags, clothes, books, music and other such items from this famous Carnaval drum orchestra and *bloco*.

Shopping centres

These are the most comfortable places to shop in Salvador – havens of a/c cool in the heat of the Bahian summer offering a chance to rest over an ice cold beer, to lunch and to shop for essentials like Havaianas, bikinis, CDs and beach wraps along with comestibles like batteries, supermarket food and suntan cream. **Barra** and **Iguatemi** are the largest and best stocked.

Activities and tours

Salvador *p360, maps p361, 365 and 367*

Football

Otávio Mangabeira Stadium, Trav Joaquim Maurício, Nazaré, T/F071-3242 3322. 90,000-seat stadium which is home to the **Esporte Clube Bahia** and **Vitória** football clubs. 10 mins away from the Pelourinho, and the Barroquinha terminal.

Tours and tour operators

Bus tours are available from several companies, including **LR Turismo**, T071-3264 0999, who also offer boat trips, **Itaparica Turismo**, T071-248 3433, **Tours Bahia**, T071-3322 3676, and **Alameda Turismo**, T071-3248 2977, who run a city tour for US$15 per person.

Tatur Turismo, Av Tancredo Neves 274, Centro Empresarial Iguatemi, Bloco B, Sala 228, Iguatemi, Salvador, T071-3450 7216, www.tatur.com.br. Excellent private tours of the city and the state as well as general travel agency services including flight booking and accommodation. Can organize entire packages prior to arrival, in Bahia or Brazil as a whole. Good English, reliable. Owned by Conor O'Sullivan from Cork.

Itaparica and other bay islands *p371, map p371*

Tour operators

Small boats for trips around the bay can be hired privately at the small port by the Mercado Modelo in Salvador. A pleasant trip out to the mouth of the bay should take 1½ hrs as you sail along the bottom of the cliff. When arranging to hire any boat, check that the boat is licensed by the Port Authority (Capitânia dos Portos) and that there are lifejackets are on board.

Companhia de Navegação Bahiana, T071-3321 7100. Sails 5 times a week to Maragojipe on the Rio Paraguaçu to the west (see page 373). The trip across the bay and up the valley of the river takes 3 hrs. There are some very beautiful views along the way with 2 stops. A good trip would be to continue to Cachoeira by bus from Maragojipe and return to Salvador the following day. Departures from Salvador from the Terminal Turístico in front of the Mercado Modelo, Mon-Thu 1430 (1530 in summer). Fri departure is at 1130. Departures from Maragojipe Mon-Thu 0500 and Fri 0830, US$4.50.

Steve Lafferty, R do Sodré 45, apt 301, T071-3241 0994. A US yachtsman, highly recommended for enjoyable sailing trips around Salvador, for up to 4 people.

Recôncavo Baiano *p372*

Guides Claudio, T075-3982 6080. Local tour guide, doesn't speak much English, but is friendly and knowledgeable.

Transport

Salvador *p360, maps p361, 365 and 367*

See also Ins and outs, page 360.

Air

To get to the airport: a/c buses leave from Praça da Sé via the coast road between 0630 and 2100, US$4, 1¼ hrs (1 hr from Barra). Ordinary buses 'Aeroporto' from same stop US$0.80.

International flights to **Amsterdam**, **London**, **Lisbon** and **Rome**. Charter flights from London can be one of the cheapest ways of reaching Brazil – usually the best deals are with **Airtours** (BA). There are domestic flights to all of Brazil's major cities, some with connections through **Recife**, **Belo Horizonte** or **São Paulo**; the best prices are usually to **Rio de Janeiro** and **São Paulo**.

BRA, www.voebra.com.br. **Gol**, www.voegol.com.br. **Ocean Air**, www.ocean air.com.br. **TAM**, www.tam.com.br. **TAP**, www.tap-airportugal.com.br. **Varig**, www.vag.com.br. **Webjet**, www.webjet.com.br.

Bus

Local US$0.70, a/c *executivos* US$1.40, US$1.5 or US$3 depending on the route. On buses and at the ticket sellers' booths, watch your change and beware pickpockets (one scam used by thieves is to descend from bus while you are climbing aboard). Take a 'Barra' bus from Praça da Sé for the nearest ocean beaches. The Aeroporto *frescão* (last 2130) leaves from R Chile, passing **Barra, Ondina, Rio Vermelho, Amaralina, Pituba, Costa Azul, Armação, Boca do Rio, Jaguaripe, Patamares, Piatã** and **Itapoã**, before turning inland to the airport. The glass-sided Jardineira bus goes to **Flamengo** beach (30 km from the city), following the coastal route; it passes all the best beaches; sit on the right-hand side for best views. It leaves from the Praça da Sé daily 0730-1930, every 40 mins, US$1.50. For beaches beyond Itapoã, take the *frescão* to **Stella Maris** and **Flamengo** beaches. These follow the same route as the Jardineira.

Long distance To get to the *rodoviária* take bus RI or RII, 'Centro-Rodoviária-Circular', US$0.70. Get on in the lower city at the foot of the Lacerda Lift (the journey can take up to 1 hr especially at peak periods). A quicker executive bus from Praça da Sé or Praça da Inglaterra (in front of McDonalds), Comércio, runs to **Iguatemi Shopping Centre**, US$1.50, weekdays only, from where there is a walkway to the *rodoviária* (take care in the dark, or a taxi, US$10). There are frequent services to the majority of destinations; a large panel in the main hall of the bus terminal lists destinations and the relevant ticket office.

To **Belém**, US$48 *comercial* with Itapemirim. To **Recife**, US$18-25, 13 hrs, 2 a day and 1 *leito*, **Itapemerim**, T071-3358 0037. To **Rio de Janeiro**, 28 hrs, US$45.50, *leito* US$91, **Itapemirim**, good stops, clean toilets, recommended. To **São Paulo,** 30 hrs, US$51, *leito* US$64 (0815 with **Viação Nacional**, 2 in afternoon with **São Geraldo**, T071-358 0188). To **Fortaleza**, 19 hrs, US$33 at 0900 with **Itapemerim**. To **Ilhéus**, 7 hrs, **Aguia Branca**, T071-3358 7044, *comercial* US$14.50, *leito* US$29, several. To **Lençóis** at 2200, 8 hrs, US$12 with **Real Expresso**, T071-3358 1591. To **Belo Horizonte**, **Gontijo**, T071-3358 7448, at 1700, US$40 *comercial*, US$50 *executivo*, **São Geraldo** at 1800. There are daily bus services to **Brasília** along the fully paved BR-242, via Barreiras, 3 daily, 23 hrs, **Paraíso**, T071-3358 1591, US$27.

For the shortest route to **Valença**, take the ferry from São Joaquim to Bom Despacho on Itaparica island, from where it is 130 km to Valença via Nazaré das Farinhas (see page 372).

Car hire
There are various car hire booths in the airport and cars in Salvador can be booked through **Hertz**, www.hertz.com.br, **Interlocadora**, www.interlocadora.com.br, and **Localiza**, www.localiza.com.

Taxis
Meters start at US$0.50 for the 'flagdown' and around US$0.15 per 100 m. They charge US$15 per hr within city limits, and 'agreed' rates outside. **Taxi Barra-Centro,** US$5 daytime; US$6 at night. Watch the meter, especially at night; the night-time charge should be 30% higher than daytime charges. **Teletaxi** (24-hr service), T071-3321 9988.

Ferries and boats
See also Ins and outs, page 360, and Ilha de Itaparica, page 371. Boats and catamarans to the **Ilha de Itaparica**, other islands in the Baía de Todos os Santos and to **Morro de São Paulo** leave from one of 2 ferry docks in Salvador's Cidade Baixa:

From the main ferry dock, **Marítimo de São Joaquim**, Av Oscar Pontes 1051, T071-3254 1020, www.twbmar.com.br, there are 10 car ferries per day to **Itaparica** as well as catamarans to **Morro de São Paulo** (2 hrs).

From Salvador's other boat terminal, the **Terminal Marítimo de Mercado Modelo** (or Terminal Marítimo Turistico), ferries and catamarans run to the **Baía de Todos os Santos**, including **Itaparica** around every 30 mins. Catamarans also run to **Morro de São Paulo**, 5 a day. See www.morrodesao paulo.com.br for the latest ferry timetable .

Itaparica and other bay islands *p371, map p371*
Ferry
There are regular ferry services to **Salvador**. The main passenger ferry leaves from Bom Despacho and runs to the **Marítimo de São Joaquim** ferry dock. The first ferry to Salvador is at 0515 and the last one at 2300, running at intervals of 45 mins. During the summer months the ferries are much more frequent. (Buses for Calçada, Ribeira stop across the road from the ferry terminal; the 'Sabino Silva-Ribeira' bus passes in front of the Shopping Barra). Enquiries at the **Companhia de Navegação Bahiana** (CNB), T071-3321 7100 from 0800 to 1700.

A one-way ticket for foot passengers on Mon-Fri is US$1, Sat and Sun US$1.20. There is also a catamaran service which departs from Bom Despacho twice daily, US$3.

From Mar Grande a smaller ferry (*lancha*) runs to the **Terminal Marítimo**, in front of the Mercado Modelo in Salvador. The ferries leave every 45 mins and the crossing takes 50 mins, US$1.80 return.

Road
From **Bom Despacho** there are many buses, kombis and taxis to all parts of the island. The best beaches are at Ponta de Areia, Mar Grande (US$1 by kombi), Berlinque, Aratuba and Cacha Pregos. Kombis and taxis can be rented for trips around the island but be prepared to bargain, US$30 for a half-day tour.

Recôncavo Baiano *p372*
Bus
To **Salvador** (Camurjipe) every hour from 0530. To **Feira Santana**, 2 hrs, US$3.

Directory

Salvador *p360, maps p361, 365 and 367*
Banks Selected branches of major banks have ATMs (which accept Visa and Cirrus cards) and exchange facilities. Don't change money on the street, especially in the Upper City where higher rates are usually offered. Changing at banks (open 1000-1600) can be bureaucratic and time consuming. **Citibank**, R Miguel Calmon 555, Comércio, centre, changes TCs. Branch at R Almte Marquês de Leão 71, Barra, has ATM. **Banco Econômico**, R Miguel Calmon 285, Comércio is the American Express representative (also in Ondina, under Ondina Apart Hotel). Visa ATM at **Banco do Brasil**, Av Estados Unidos 561, Comércio, in the shopping centre opposite the rodoviária (also a *câmbio* here), very high commission on TCs, at the airport on the 1st floor (Mon-Fri 0830-1530, 1600- 2100 and Sat, Sun and holidays 0900-1600); branches in Barra, R Miguel Bournier 4, in Shopping Barra and in Ondina. MasterCard at **Credicard**, 1st floor, Citibank building, R Miguel Calmon 555, Comércio. **Figueiredo**, opposite Grande Hotel da Barra on Ladeira da Barra, will exchange cash at good rates. **Shopping Tour** in Barra Shopping centre changes US dollars, as will other tour agencies. If stuck, all the big hotels

will exchange, but at poor rates. **Cultural centres** Associação Cultural Brasil-Estados Unidos, Av 7 de Setembro 1883, has a library and reading room with recent US magazines, open to all, free use of internet for 30 mins. **Cultura Inglesa**, R Plínio Moscoso 357, Jardim Apipema. **German Goethe Institut**, Av 7 de Setembro 1809, also with a library and reading room. **Embassies and consulates** Austria, R Jardim Armacao, T071-3371 4611. **Belgium**, Av Trancredo Neves 274A, sala 301, Iguatemi, T071-3623 2454. **Denmark**, Av 7 de Setembro 3959, Barra, T071-3336 9861 (Mon-Fri 0900-1200, 1400-1700). **France**, R Francisco Gonçalves 1, sala 805, Comércio, T071-3241 0168 (Mon, Tue, Thu 1430-1700). **Germany**, R Lucaia 281, floor 2, Rio Vermelho, T071-3334 7106 (Mon-Fri 0900-1200). **Holland**, Av Santa Luzia, 1136 Edif, Porto Empresarial Sala 302, T071-3341 0410 (Mon-Fri 0800-1200). **Italy**, Av 7 de Setembro 1238, Centro, T071-3329 5338 (Mon, Wed, Fri 1500-1800). **Norway**, Av Estados Unidos, 14, floor 8, T071-3326 8500 (Mon-Fri 0900-1200, 1400-1600). **Portugal**, Largo Carmo, 4, Sto Antonio, T071-3241 1633. **Spain**, R Mcal Floriano 21, Canela, T071-3336 1937 (Mon-Fri 0900-1400). **Sweden**, Av EUA 357, Edif Joaquim Barreto, sala 501, Comércio, T071-3242 4833. **Switzerland**, Av Tancredo Neves 3343, 5th floor, sala 506b, T071-3341 5827. **UK**, Av Estados Unidos 4, 18B, Comércio, T071-3243 7399 (Mon-Thu, 0900-1100, 1400-1600, Fri 0900-1100). **USA**, R Pernam buco, 51 Pituba, T071-3345 1545 (Mon-Fri), 0900-1130, 1430-1630. **Immigration** Polícia Federal, Av O Pontes 339, Aterro de Água de Meninos, Lower City, T071-3319 6082. Open 1000-1600. For extensions of entry permits show an outward ticket or sufficient funds for your stay, visa extension US$15. **Internet** There are numerous internet cafés throughout the touristy parts of the city. **Language courses** Casa do Brasil, R Milton de Oliveira 231, Barra, T071-3264 5866, www.casadobrazil.com.br. Portuguese for foreigners. **Diálogo**, R Dr João Pondé 240, Barra, T071-3264 0007, www.dialogo-brazilstudy.com, with optional dance, *capoeira* and cooking classes and accommodation arranged with host families. **Superlearning Idiomas**, Av 7 de Setembro 3402, Ladeira da Barra, T071-3337 2824, www.allways.com.br/spl. **Laundry** Kit Lavaderia, Av Amaralina 829, Amaralina. **Laundromat**, R Oswaldo Cruz, Rio Vermelho. **Lav e Lev**, Av Manoel Dantas da Silva 2364, loja 7. **Unilave**, Av Magalhães Neto 18, Pituba. **Medical services** Clinic, Barão de Loreto 21, Graça. **Delegação Federal de Saúde**, R Padre Feijó, Canela. Free yellow fever vaccinations.

Cachoeira *p372*

Banks Bradesco, in the main square, ATM accepts Visa credit but not debit cards, Mon-Fri 0830-1700. **Post office** in the main square, Mon-Fri 0900-1700.

Southern coast of Bahia

The seemingly endless coast of Bahia has one magnificent beach after another. Heading south from Salvador, the main resort town is Porto Seguro, which has a notoriously hedonistic party scene. Things are a little quieter in Arraial de Ajuda just next door, and more upmarket in Trancoso, further to the south, where Leonardo Di Caprio has bought up property in one of the super luxurious condominiums. Morro de São Paulo, on the island of Tinharé, offers beautiful beaches and lively nightlife. Those seeking seclusion should head for Itacaré, the latest discovery on the Bahian coast, where the coconut-shaded white sand is relatively peaceful... for the time being.
▸▸ *For Sleeping, Eating and other listings, see pages 396-406.*

Valença ▸▸ *pp396-406.*

→ *Phone code: 075. Colour map 4, A5.*

Although Valença has a few colonial buildings and two moderately interesting churches, it is essentiallly an ugly town. The best reason to come here is to take a boat to or from Tinharé, taking an hour or two perhaps to stroll around the dirty market and visit the church of **Nossa Senhora do Amparo**, from where there are good views out over the town, the estuary and the surrounding mangroves. Valença is in the middle of an area producing black pepper, cloves and *piaçava* (used in making brushes and mats) but it markets itself as the prawn capital of Brazil and smells the part. Other industries include the building and repair of fishing boats (*saveiros*).

Ins and outs

The city has a little **airport** ⓘ *15 km from the centre at Praia Guaibim, T075 353 9227*, which receives flights from Salvador, and is a 20-minute taxi ride from town. Long-distance buses arrive at the new **rodoviária** ⓘ *Av Maçônica, T075-741 1280*, while the old *rodoviária* is for local buses. There are frequent buses between Valença and Salvador. The fastest go via the island of Itaparica (two to three hours including the ferry). Avoid touts at the *rodoviária*; it's better to visit the friendly **tourist office** ⓘ *at the port, T075-641 3311, www.valencabahia.com.br*, which has maps and transport information. Boats arrive from Tinharé at least once a day.

Tinharé and Morro de São Paulo ▸▸ *pp396-406.*

→ *Phone code: 075. Colour map 4, A5.*

Depending on whom you ask, Tinharé is either a single large island separated from the mainland by the estuary of the Rio Una and mangrove swamps, or a mini archipelago divided by estuaries, mangroves and an impossibly turquoise sea. The beaches here are some of the best within easy access of Salvador.

The main town here, **Morro de São Paulo**, is one of the tourist hotspots of southern Bahia. It is fringed with beaches, all of them backed by swaying coconut palms, and busy with little pousadas and hotels. The town is situated on the headland at the northernmost tip of Tinharé, which is lush with patches of fern-filled forest and coconut palms. The town is dominated by a lighthouse and the ruins of a colonial fort (1630), built as a defence against European raiders. However, this did not stop the Dutch and French using the waters around the island as hiding places for attacks on the Portuguese.

Morro de São Paulo has a landing place on the sheltered landward side, dominated by the old gateway of the fortress. From the lighthouse a path leads to a ruined lookout with cannon, which has panoramic views. Dolphins can be seen in August. The **Fonte de Ceu** waterfall is reached by walking along the beach to **Gamboa**, then inland. Make sure you check the tide times; it is best to take a guide. Alternatively, take a boat back to Morro (US$0.50-1). All roads are unmade and no motor vehicles are allowed on the island. The beaches are good and you can swim or watch fish in the saltwater pools that appear at low tide. Fish can be bought from the fishermen in summer, or borrow a pole and catch your own at sunset. On 7 September there is a big fiesta with live music on the beach. There are four beaches – named prosaically, Primeira (1st), Segunda (2nd), Terceira (3rd), Quarta (4th) and Quinta Praia (beach). Quinta is the furthest from town and is the quietest; pretty much all the pousadas are on the first four beaches.

Ins and outs

Getting there There are direct 20-minute flights from Salvador's airport to the third beach at Morro de São Paulo with **Addey Taxi Aereo** ⓘ *T075-3652 1242, www.addey.com.br*, and **Aerostar Taxi Aereo** ⓘ *T075-3652 1312*. Both fly three times daily and cost around US$90 return. Catamarans run from both of Salvador's ferry terminals (see page 360), taking around two hours. Times vary according to the weather but there are usually several a day from 0800 to 1400; check with the tourist office or **Catamarã Gamboa do Morro,** T075-9975 6395. Part of the trip is on the open sea, which can be rough. There are also numerous water taxis. Boats also run from Salvador via Valença (which is connected to southern Bahia) and Itaparica. The website www.morrodesaopaulo.com.br has the latest timetables for all transport options. ▸▸ *See Transport, page 405.*

Getting around Morro is tiny and easily negotiable on foot. A walk from the town to Quarta Praia takes around 30 minutes. Boat trips around the island are bookable through hotels or agencies in the village; a full day costs around US$20. Some of these visit Ilha de Boipeba (see below).

Tourist Information There is a tourist booth, **Centro de Informações ao Turista (CIT)** ⓘ *Praça Aureliano Lima s/n T075-3652 1083, www.morrosp.com.br*. The website is poor but www.morrodesaopaulo.com.br has lists of agencies and hotels as well as other useful information, in several languages. There is a port tax of US$1 payable at the *prefeitura* on leaving the island, which is resented by many.

Best time to visit Morro is expensive between December and March and gets very crowded during public holidays. This influx of tourists means it is not the paradise it once was; beware of drugs and theft at the busiest times.

Ilha de Boipeba → *Colour map 4, A5.*

Ilha de Boipeba, a few hours from Morro, is a similar but far quieter island and with less infrastructure. Accommodation is split between the little town where the riverboat ferry arrives, the adjacent beach, **Boca da Barra**, which is more idyllic and the fishing village of **Moreré** half an hour's boat ride to the south (high tide only). With just a few simple restaurants and a football field on the beach overlooking a beautiful turquoise bay, life here is tranquil even by Bahian standards. Expect to pay at least US$20 for a boat to Moreré. Walking along the beaches will take about two hours. Have your camera at the ready, bring sunscreen and go at low tide as there is a river to ford.

Ins and outs Boat trips leave daily from Morro de São Paulo at 0900 in front of the Fazenda Caiera and visit much of the island. They can leave you on Boipeba but you must pay the full tour fare (around US$15). Tractors and 4WDs leave from Morro's second beach every morning at around 0800 (one hour, US$12), and return at midday. Contact **Zé Balacha,** T075-9148 0343 or book through your pousada.

South to Itacaré » pp396-406.

Ituberá and Camamu → Phone code: 073. Colour map 4, A5.

These two towns, which have yet to be overrun by seasonal visitors, are the first stops south on the bus route from Valença. Neither have good beaches but both have access to decent ones by boat. Ituberá is a tiny town sitting on a deep inlet – the most beautiful beach in the area, **Barra do Carvalho**, is two hours away by boat; Camamu sits in a maze of mangroves some 30 km further south. It is the jumping-off point for the peninsula of Maraú; the next stretch of the Bahian coast in line for beach resort development. The town has a handful of pretty colonial buildings, including the 17th-century church of **Nossa Senhora da Assunção**.

Barra Grande and the Peninsula de Maraú → Phone code: 073.

This long thin peninsula stretches north from the town of Maraú, near Itacaré, towards the southern extremity of the island of Tinharé and is fringed with beautiful beaches along its entire ocean length. Access is difficult to many of these beaches if you don't have a car (and it's only possible without a 4WD in dry weather) but some can be reached on foot from the little fishing village of **Barra Grande** at the tip of the peninsula. Tractors run from the village to the more remote beaches further south.

Ins and outs Boats run from Camamu several times a day between October and March and once a day in the morning all year round (two to three hours, US$4). There are plenty of pousadas in Barra; see www.barragrande.net, and Sleeping, page 398.

Itacaré → Phone code: 073.

Itacaré is the latest discovery on the Brazilian tourist circuit. The picturesque fishing village sits in the midst of remnant Atlantic Coast rainforest at the mouth of the Rio de Contas, and is rapidly becoming a sophisticated resort town for the discerning São Paulo middle classes. Much of the accommodation here is tasteful, blending in with the natural landscape. There are many excellent restaurants and lively, if still low-key, nightlife. Some of Bahia's best beaches stretch north and south. A few are calm and crystal clear, the majority are washed by moderately powerful waves which are great for surfing. There are plenty of beaches within walking distance of town.

Pousadas are concentrated on and around Praia da Concha, the first beach south of the town centre. More deserted beaches lie along dirt roads to the south and north. To explore the area to the full you will need a car. If you speak some Portuguese, it's worth taking the time to find your way to one of the smaller places. Itacaré is very busy with Brazilian tourists in high season but receives relatively few international visitors.

Ins and outs The *rodovíaria* is a few minutes' walk from town. Porters are on hand with barrows to help with luggage. The **Secretaria de Turismo de Itacaré** ⓘ *T073-251 2134, www.itacare.com.br*, provides information.

Ilhéus and around » pp396-406.

→ Phone code: 073. Colour map 4, A5. Population: 242,500.

Everyone is happy to point out that Ilhéus is the birthplace of Jorge Amado (1912) and the setting of one of his most famous novels, *Gabriela, cravo e canela* (*Gabriela, Clove and Cinnamon*, 1958). Amado also chronicled life on the region's cocoa plantations in two novels, *Cacau*, (1933) and the much better-known *Terras do Sem Fim* (*The Violent Lands*, 1942). A later novel, *São Jorge dos Ilhéus* (1944), continues the story.

Ilhéus's history stretches back to the earliest days of Portuguese colonization, when it was one of the captaincies created by King João III in 1534. Today the port, which sits at the mouth of the Rio Cachoeira, serves a district that produces 65% of all Brazilian cocoa. Shipping lines call regularly. There are good views of the city from the Convento de Nossa Senhora da Piedade. Most tourists stay a day or so before heading north towards Itacaré or south towards Porto Seguro.

The church of **São Jorge** ⓘ *Praça Rui Barbosa*, (1556), is the city's oldest and has a small museum. The cathedral of **São Sebastião** ⓘ *Praça Dom Eduardo, near the seashore*, is a huge, early 20th-century building. In Alto da Vitória is the 17th-century **Nossa Senhora da Vitória**, built to celebrate a victory over the Dutch. The house where Jorge Amado grew up and wrote his first novel is now a small **museum** ⓘ *R Jorge Amado 21, 0900-1600, US$0.50.*

Ins and outs The airport is located in Pontal on the south bank of the river, linked to Ilhéus by bridge. The *rodoviária* is 4 km from the centre on Rua Itabuna, but the Itabuna–Olivença bus goes through the centre of Ilhéus. The **tourist office** ⓘ *on the beach opposite Praça Castro Alves*, is a few minutes' walk from the cathedral, friendly, maps US$2, recommended.

Around Ilhéus

The city beach itself is polluted but the beaches around the town are splendid and increasingly deserted the further you go. North of Ilhéus, two good beaches are **Marciano**, with reefs offshore and good surfing, and **Barra**, 1 km further north at the mouth of the Rio Almada. South of the river, the beaches at **Pontal** can be reached by 'Barreira' bus; alight just after the **Hotel Jardim Atlântico**. Between Ilhéus and Olivença are a number of fine beaches, for example **Cururupe, Batuba** (good surfing) and Cai n'Água in **Olivença** itself (also a surfers' beach). The **Balneário de Tororomba**, on the Rio Batuba, 19 km from Ilhéus, has hot mineral baths. São Jorge or Canavieiras buses stop there and frequent buses also run to Olivença.

Buses run every 30 minutes to **Itabuna** (32 km), the trading centre of the rich cocoa zone; there are also many lumber mills. **Ceplac installations** ⓘ *Km 8, on the Itabuna–Ilhéus road, T073-214 3000, Mon-Fri 0830-1230*, demonstrates the processing of cocoa. Tours of cocoa plantations can be arranged through the **Ilhéus Praia** hotel (see Sleeping, page 399).

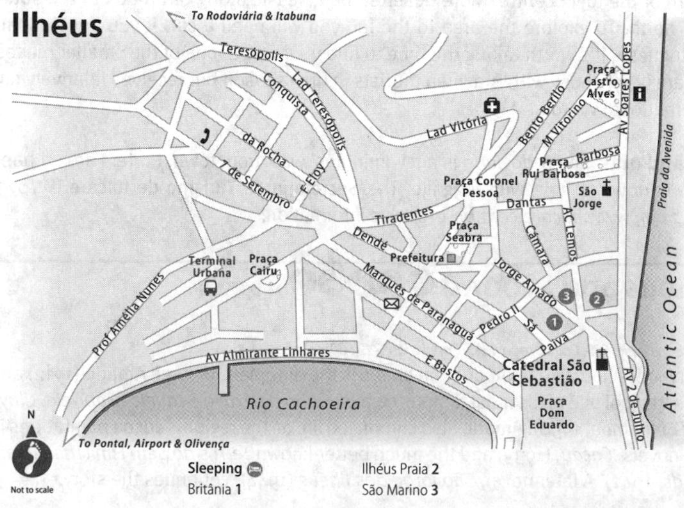

Jorge Amado

Amado is by far the most popular Brazilian writer of the 20th century. Born in 1912 on a cocoa plantation near Ilhéus, he had a very adventurous youth, and had direct experience of the endemic violence surrounding land claims, which he later dramatized in novels such as *Terras do sem-fim* (*The Violent Land*, 1943). His political commitment was always to the Left, though his position has softened in later years, accompanying changes in his fiction. In his early works (1931-1952), his views were manifested in an interest in the rural and urban poor. In novels such as *Jubiabá* (1935), about the self- education of a black man, and *Capitães da areia* (1937), one of his best, centred on a gang of street children, he began to show interest in the power of *candomblé* (Afro-Brazilian religion) as a way of raising political consciousness.

In 1946 he became a federal deputy for the Communist Party. However, two years later the party was banned and he went into exile in Europe wehre he was something of a propagandist for Soviet Communism, receiving the Stalin Peace Prize in 1951. The fiction he wrote at this time, including *Seara vermelha* (*Red Harvest*), is considered to be his worst.

In 1953 he returned to Brazil and abandoned politics for comedy and myth. His career was given a new lease of life in 1958, with the publication of *Gabriela, cravo e canela* (*Gabriela, Clove and Cinnamon*). The novel, set in Ilhéus in the 1920s when the harbour is about to open, is presented to us through a colourful array of characters, at the centre of whom are Nacib, an Arab immigrant and shopkeeper, and spicy Gabriela, a girl from the interior whose cooking and sexual prowess keep him in her thrall. It is a modern, optimistic version of Alencar's *Iracema* (see Background, page 698): immigrant meets native girl, and has to adjust to her culture, while in the background, the economy (exporting cocoa) is opening up. *Gabriela* was a phenomenal success, selling 100,000 copies in just over a year. In part, Amado had tuned into the optimism created in the years of the Kubitschek presidency, which led to the foundation of Brasília.

Sex, comedy and cookery proved a potent combination. Other novels since *Gabriela* have been equally successful, including *Dona Flor e seus dois maridos* (*Dona Flor and her Two Husbands*, 1966), about a cookery teacher whose respectable second marriage is haunted by the ghost of her bohemian first husband (it actually provides the reader with recipes); and *Tenda dos milagres* (*The Tent of Miracles*, 1969) about racial discrimination. Many of them are set in the city of Salvador (Bahia). Amado has been attacked by critics as being unconsciously anti-feminist and even racist (his black characters tend to be stereotypically good-hearted, with a perpetual smile on their face). However, perhaps this is missing the point, for Amado is essentially a popular novelist in the tradition of Scott, Dumas and others, who were, in effect, predecessors of television soap operas. His work has often been successfully adapted to that medium.

Also at Km 8, the Projeto Mico-Leão Baiano at the **Reserva Biológica del Una** ⓘ *T073-633 1121, US$15, book in advance, buses from Salvador 6½ hrs, US$12*, was founded to protect the *mico-leão da cara dourada* (golden-faced tamarin). This is the wettest part of Bahia (most notably in October). Jeeps leave from the *rodovíaria*.

Beyond Ilhéus, the paved coastal road continues south through Olivença and Una, ending at **Canavieiras**, a picturesque town which benefited from the cocoa boom. It has several fine beaches. A rough road continues from there to Port Seguro.

Porto Seguro and around

» pp396-406.

→ *Phone code: 073. Colour map 4, B5. Population: 96,000.*

Pedro Álvares Cabral is credited with being the first European to lay eyes on Brazil, sighting land at Monte Pascoal south of Porto Seguro in 1500. The sea here was too open to offer a safe harbour, so Cabral sailed his fleet north, entering the mouth of the Rio Burnahém to find the harbour he later called 'Porto Seguro' (safe port). On the road between Porto Seguro and Santa Cruz Cabrália a cross marks the spot where the first mass was celebrated. A tourist village, **Coroa Vermelha**, has sprouted at the site

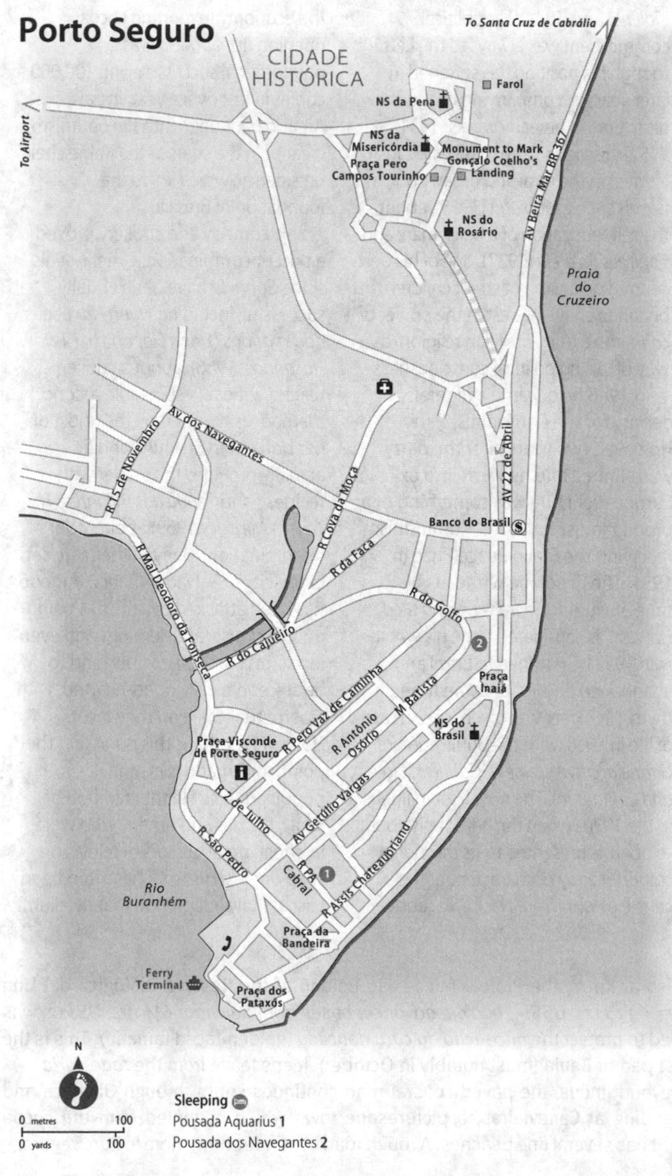

The festival of Nossa Senhora da Pena

The cult of Nossa Senhora da Pena began in Leiria, Portugal, a century after the reconquest of the country from the Moors. The tradition began in Porto Seguro in 1535 when a Portuguese noble, Donatário Pero do Campo Tourinho (a recipient of one of Brazil's 16th-century *capitanias*), brought with him a small image of Nossa Senhora da Pena (Our Lady of Suffering). He named his captaincy 'Villa de Nossa Senhora da Pena de Porto Seguro' and built a small church to house his favourite saint. The church was rebuilt in the 18th century.

Nossa Senhora da Pena is the patron saint of art and literature. She is celebrated on 8 September in the historic city on the cliff, overlooking the beach hotels of the modern resort of Porto Seguro. Devotees of the cult, called *romeiros,* travel great distances to her shrine and the surrounding area becomes a huge campsite of tents, caravans and tour buses.

The festival resembles a cross between a Brazilian street party and a market, with cheap clothes, household goods, ice-cold beer and barbecued meat on sale. Throughout the weekend there are displays of capoeira and nightly dances of *pagôde* and *forró*. After prayers on the afternoon of the 8th, the festival is officially closed with a religious procession through the streets of this beautiful colonial town.

of Cabral's first landfall, 20 minutes by bus to the north of Porto Seguro. It has a rather uncoordinated array of beach bars, hotels, rental houses and souvenir shops selling indigenous Pataxó-Tupi items

Today, the old town of Porto Seguro is a popular holiday resort and Bahia's second most popular tourist destination. While many visit Bahia's beaches to escape the hustle and bustle, those who come to Port Seguro are in search of it. Don't expect peace and quiet, unspoilt coastline or pretty colonial buildings here.

From the roundabout at the entrance to Porto Seguro, a wide, steep, unmarked path leads uphill to the **Cidade Histórica** (historical city), a small peaceful place with lovely gardens and panoramic views. Here you will find three churches: **Nossa Senhora da Misericórdia** (1530), **Nossa Senhora do Rosário** (1534) and **Nossa Senhora da Pena** (1718). The former jail is also here, with a stone monument marking the landfall of Gonçalo Coelho.

The best beaches are north of the town along the road to Santa Cruz de Cabrália (known as Avenida Beira Mar – BR-367). The most popular are **Itacimirim**, **Curuípe**, **Mundaí** and **Taperapuã**. There are many *barracas* on these lively beaches. The biggest (and busiest) are **Barra Point, Toá Toa, Axé Moi, Vira Sol** and **Barramares.** Most of these have jet-ski and other watersports facilities for hire. Some cater mainly for coach groups from the larger charter companies, so expect crowds. Regular buses run along the seafront from Praça dos Pataxós in Porto Seguro, or take a bus to Porto Belo or Santa Cruz Cabrália from the port. For beaches south of the Rio Buranhém, see Arraial d'Ajuda (below) and points further south.

Ins and outs

There are many charter companies flying directly from Rio de Janeiro and São Paulo. The **airport** ⓘ 3 km north of town, T073-288 1877. A taxi to the centre costs US$6. The **rodoviária** ⓘ *on the road to Eunápolis, 2 km from the centre*, has a reliable luggage store and lounge on third floor. Buses run through the city to the old *rodoviária* near the port every 30 minutes, $0.30. Taxis charge US$5 from the *rodoviária* to the town or ferry (negotiate at quiet times). The **tourist office** ⓘ *T073-288 4124, turismo@portonet.com.br*, has information on tours. » *See also Activities and tours, page 404.*

Santa Cruz Cabrália → *Phone code: 073. Colour map 4, B5.*

About 10 minutes north of Coroa Vermelha, Santa Cruz Cabrália is a delightful small town at the mouth of the Rio João de Tiba, with a lovely beach, river port, and a 450-year-old church with a fine view. It is believed to be the site of the first landing in Brazil by the Portuguese explorer Pedro Álvares Cabral in 1500. A good trip from here is to **Coroa Alta**, a reef 50 minutes away by boat. It passes along the tranquil river to the reef with crystal waters and good snorkelling. There is a daily departure at 1000. A recommended boatman is **Zezé** (T/F073-282 1152) on the square by the river's edge; he is helpful and knowledgeable. The trip costs around US$15 without lunch.

A 15-minute river crossing by ferry to a new road on the opposite bank gives easy access to the deserted beaches of **Santo André** and **Santo Antônio**. As yet, few tourists make it to here, but the new road is certain to change this. Hourly buses run between Santa Cruz and Porto Seguro (23 km).

South of Porto Seguro » pp396-406.

Arraial da Ajuda → *Phone code: 073. Colour map 4, B5.*

Across the Rio Buranhém, south from Porto Seguro, is the resort village of Arraial da Ajuda, the gateway to the idyllic beaches of the south coast. Set high on a cliff, there are great views of the coastline from the main square. Ajuda used to be known as a 'hippie' resort, with drugs said to be widely available, but there is nothing laid-back about the town now – it has become far larger in scale and more rave orientated. Parties are held almost every night, on the beach or in the main street, called the *Broadway*. At Brazilian holiday times (especially New Year and Carnaval) it is very crowded, almost to bursting point. There are many pousadas, from the very simple to the moderately sophisticated, as well as numerous restaurants, bars and small shops. There is also a capoeira institute; ask for directions.

Each August there is a pilgrimage to the shrine of **Nossa Senhora da Ajuda** (1549). In the church is an interesting room full of ex-voto offerings. There are good views from behind the church. Legend has it that a spring miraculously appeared during mass, aiding the construction of the Jesuit church. The spring can be seen at the foot of the steep hill leading up to the town.

The village's surrounding beaches are splending, with several protected by a coral reef. During daylight hours those closest to town are extremely busy. The nearest is 15 minutes' walk away (take Rua da Praia out of town to the south). The best are **Mucugê**, **Pitinga** (*'bronzeamento irrestrito'* or nude sunbathing) and **Taipé**. Excellent *barracas* sell good seafood, chilled drinks, and play music. It is possible to walk to Transcoso (see below) along the beach via the village of **Rio da Barra**. Allow three hours. A dirt road behind the beach follows the same route.

Ins and outs Ferries from Porto Seguro run across the Rio Buranhém to the south bank, 15 minutes, US$0.60 for foot passengers, US$3.60 for cars, every 30 minutes day and night. It is then a further 5 km to Arraial da Ajuda, US$0.50 by bus, kombis charge US$0.75 per person, taxis US$5.

Trancoso → *Phone code: 073. Colour map 4, B5.*

This once sleepy little village 15 km south of Arraial is rapidly developing as southern Bahia state's most chic resort, after Itacaré. Expensive São Paulo boutiques fill the tiny shopping centre and there are a range of smart little boutique pousadas and a handful of restaurants offering more than just fish, rice and beans. Leonardo DiCaprio is rumoured to have bought a number of properties in the exclusive condominiums to the south of town; *forró* star Elba Ramalho lives here; and Gisele Bündchen is a frequent visitor. This has inevitably pushed prices up and up.

Despite its new-found status, Trancoso remains a simple little town, with life concentrated on the long grassy main square, crowned with the little whitewashed 17th-century church of São João Batista, which looks down over the top of the cliff to the numerous beaches stretching away to the north and south. The most famous, **Praia dos Nativos**, is also the closest to town and is lined with numerous *barraca* beach bars that have begun to host rave parties during the summer months. **Coquieros** across the little river to the north is quieter. **Espelho**, a 50-minute drive along the dirt road to Caraiva, is one of the state's most beautiful, with a glassy bay fringed with white sand and rocks. Like any of the Bahian resorts, Trancoso can be packed out at this time. Be sure to book ahead. Cheap rooms tend to be in the upper city with more luxurious accommodation lining the road that runs to and along the coast.

The town divides into the upper area focused on the main square (or *quadrado*), a square kilometre of grass with a football pitch, watched over by pretty pastel-coloured colonial houses. Behind it lies the new part of town with its upmarket boutiques. The beach is about 10 minutes' walk from both across the river, along a road lined with the best of the pousadas, many of them set in their own private gardens.

Ins and outs Buses run along the newly paved road between Porto Seguro, Arraial de Ajuda and Trancoso at least once an hour in high season (US$2 from Porto Seguro, US$1.20 from Arraial). Various tour operators around the main square sell kombi, bus (and air) tickets for destinations throughout Bahia and organize day trips.

Caraíva → *Phone code: 073. Colour map 4, B5.*

This incredibly peaceful, atmospheric fishing town, 65 km south of Porto Seguro, is on the banks of the Rio Caraíva. There is no electricity or hot water and the streets are sand so there are no cars. The marvellous beaches here make a real escape from Trancoso and Porto Seguro. Despite difficulty getting there, it is increasingly popular.

There are plenty of cheap pousadas and restaurants along the rustic sandy streets. Most bars have live *forró* in the summer. There is a good walk north to **Praia do Satu** (where Señor Satu provides an endless supply of coconut milk), or 6 km south to a rather sad Pataxó indigenous village; watch the tides as you may get cut off. Horses can be hired from **Pousada Lagoa** or **Pizzeria Barra Velha**. Boats can be hired for US$40 per day from **Zé Pará** to Caruípe beach, for snorkelling at Pedra de Tatuaçu reef and Corombau (take your own mask and fins) or for diving (best December-February). **Prainha** river beach, about 30 minutes away, and mangrove swamps can also be visited by canoe or launch.

Ins and outs Caraíva is connected to Transcoso by irregular buses along a very poor dirt road. The journey involves a river crossing and can take as long as three hours in the wet season (April-June and November). The high season is December to February and July. Use flip-flops for walking along the sand streets and take a torch.

Parque Nacional de Monte Pascoal

ⓘ *Caixa Postal 076, CEP 45830-000 Itamaraju, T073-281 2419.*

The national park was set up in 1961 to preserve the flora, fauna and birdlife of the coast where Europeans first landed in Brazil. A Pataxó reservation is located at Corombau village, on the ocean shore of the park, where a small luxury resort has been built. Corombau can be reached by schooner from Porto Seguro. From Caraíva there is a river crossing by boats that are always on hand. Buses run from Itamaraju 16 km to the south, Monday to Friday at 0600.

Cumuruxatiba and Prado → *Phone code: 073. Colour map 4, B5.*

The road from Itamaraju leads to the coastal towns of **Cumuruxatiba** (www.cumuru.com.br) and **Prado** (www.acampe.com.br/prado). The latter has some 16th-century buildings and beautiful beaches both north and south.

Caravelas → *Phone code: 073. Colour map 4, B5.*

Further south still, is this charming little town in the mangroves, which was a major trading town in the 17th and 18th centuries. Caravelas is rapidly developing for tourism and the beaches are about 10 km away at the fishing village of **Barra de Caravelas** (hourly buses). There is a helpful tourist information, **Ibama Centro de Visitantes** ⓘ *Barão do Rio Branco 281.*

Parque Nacional Marinho dos Abrolhos

ⓘ *Permission from Praia do Kitombo, Caravelas, Bahia 45900, T073-297 1111, or Ibama, Av Juracy Magalhães Junior 608, CEP 40295-140, Salvador, T071-240 7322.*

The Parque Nacional Marinho dos Abrolhos is 70 km east of Caravelas. Abrolhos is an abbreviation of *Abre os olhos*, 'Open your eyes', from Amérigo Vespucci's exclamation when he first sighted the reef in 1503. Established in 1983, the park consists of five small islands (**Redonda, Siriba, Guarita, Sueste, Santa Bárbara**), which are volcanic in origin. There are also several coral reefs. Darwin visited them in 1830 and Jacques Cousteau studied the marine environment here. The islands and surrounding reefs are home to goats, birds, whales, fish, turtles and giant fire corals. The warm current and shallow waters (8-15 m in depth) form a rich undersea life, with 160 species of fish. The park is good for snorkelling and best visited October to March, when underwater visibility reaches 30 m. The waters are warmest and calmest at this time too. Humpback whales breed and give birth here from July to December. Diving is best December to February.

The archipelago is administered by **Ibama** and a navy detachment mans a lighthouse on Santa Bárbara, which is the only island that may be visited. Visitors are not allowed to spend the night on the islands, but may stay overnight on schooners.

Ins and outs Three-day, two-night packages from São Paulo cost around US$700, including return flights. The journey to the islands takes one to six hours, depending on the boat. **Mestre Onofrio Frio** in Alcobaça, T073-293 2195, is authorized by the Navy to take tourists. Tours are also available from **Abrolhos Turismo**, see page 404. One-day tours can be made in a faster boat (US$100) from Abrolhos or the Marina Porto Abrolhos. ▸▸ *See Transport, page 406.*

Sleeping

Valença *p387*

A Portal Rio Una, R Maestro Barrinha, T/F075-741 5050, www.portalhoteis.tur.br. Resort hotel by the riverside. Facilities include a pool, tennis courts and organized activities.

B Do Porto, Av Maçônica 50, T075-741 3066. Clean, helpful, safe, good breakfast and a reasonable restaurant.

B Guabim, Praça da Independência, T075-741 3408. Modest but well looked after with singles, doubles and triples.

D Valença, R Dr H Guedes Melo 15, T075-741 1807. Simple hotel with plain but well-kept rooms and a good breakfast. Recommended.

Tinharé and Morro de São Paulo *p387*

In Morro de São Paulo, there are many cheap pousadas and rooms to rent near the fountain (Fonte Grande), but this part of town is very hot at night.

There are 4 beaches next to Morro town, which are quieter the further from town you go. The 1st and 2nd beaches, Primeira and Segunda Praia are designated party areas, with throbbing bars and many beachside shacks selling food and drinks well into the night. There are only pousadas and a few restaurants on the final 2 beaches. To reach the beaches turn right at the end of the main street; there is only one trail out of town. You'll have to walk as there are no cars on the island – porters can be hired to wheel your luggage to the hotel in a barrow.

A Pousada Catavento, 4th beach, T/F075-3652 1052, www.cataventopraiahotel.com.br. One of the most luxurious and secluded of the hotels on the island, with well-appointed mock-colonial rooms arranged around a beautiful sculpted swimming pool, a decent restaurant and good service.

A Pousada Fazenda Caeira, 3rd beach, T075-3652 1042, www.fazendacaeira.com.br. Very spacious and airy chalets in a large coconut grove overlooking the sea. Good breakfasts, a well-stocked library and a games room with snooker and board games.

A Pousada Vistabella, 1st beach, T075-3652 1001, www.vistabelapousada.com. Good rooms, those to the front have good views and are cooler and all have fans and hammocks. The owner Petruska is very welcoming. Recommended.

A-C Fazenda Vila Guaiamú, 3rd beach, T075-3652 1035, www.vilaguaiamu.com.br. 7 tastefully decorated chalets of various sizes and styles set in their own tropical gardens and visited by marmosets, tanagers and rare cotingas. The hotel has a spa service with wonderful massage. The Italian photographer owner runs an ecotourism project protecting a rare species of crab, which live in the river that runs through the *fazenda*. Guided rainforest walks available. Excellent food. The best option for nature lovers. Highly recommended.

B Pousada Colibri, R do Porto de Cima s/n, Centro, near the fountain. In Morro de São Paulo, which stays cool. 6 apartments with pleasant sea views. Helmut, the owner, speaks English and German.

B Pousada Farol do Morro, 1st beach, T075-3652 1036, www.faroldomorro.com.br. Little huts running up the hill all with a sea view and served by a private funicular railway. The pool sits perched on the edge of the hill.

C Pousada Gaúcho, near the fountain. With a huge breakfast and shared bathrooms.

C Pousada Ilha da Saudade, 1st beach, T075-3652 1015, www.ilhadasaudade.com.br. Elegant hillside pousada with a beautiful pool with a view, a small gym and deluxe suites with jacuzzis. Restaurant, bar and good breakfast.

C Pousada Ilha do Sol, 1st beach. Modest but scrupulously clean little pousada with good views. Recommended.

C-D Pousada Grauça, 3rd beach, T075-3652 1099, www.pousadagrauca.com.br. Simple but well-kept a/c and fan-cooled rooms with en suites in concrete cabanas away from the beach. Formerly called the Aradhia. Recommended.

D Pousada Oxum, 2nd beach, T075-3652 1048. Newly renovated, very simple fan-cooled rooms and a campsite make this little pousada very popular with young Bahianos and Paulistanos.

Ilha de Boipeba *p388*

Accommodation is split between the little town where the riverboat ferry arrives; the adjacent beach, Boca da Barra, which is more idyllic; and the fishing village of Moreré ½-hr boat ride to the south (high tide only).

A Pousada Tassimirim, (reservations: T075-9981 2378, R Com Madureira 40, Valença), Tassimirim Beach, 30-min walk south of town. A coconut grove shading bungalows, bar, restaurant and pool. The price includes breakfast and dinner. Secluded and very tranquil.

A-B Vila Sereia, Boca da Barra beach, T075-3635 6045. Elegantly simple duplex wooden chalets overlooking the beach. Breakfast on your own private veranda. Very romantic.

A-C Santa Clara, Boca da Barra beach, T075-3653 6085, www.santaclaraboipeba.com. Californian-owned pousada with the island's best restaurant and large, tastefully decorated duplex *cabañas*. Very good value room for 4 at **D** per person. Superlative therapeutic massages available. Both are highly recommended.

B-D Horizonte Azul, Boca da Barra beach, T075-3653 6080, ww.amabo.org.br/horizonteazul.html. Pretty little pousada next door to **Santa Clara**, with a range of chalets – from very comfortable to fairly simple. The hillside garden is visited by hundreds of rare birds from the nearby Atlantic Coast rainforest. Very friendly owners who speak English and good French. Highly recommended. Lunch available.

D Cheiro do Mar, Moreré town, just north of the **Pousada Moreré**. Hillside cabins, the best of which has a breathtaking view. Ask for Fatima or João.

D Mar e Coco, Moreré, T075-3653 6013. A couple of very simple rooms with a Bahian family and a wonderful seafood restaurant. 5 mins north of town. The restaurant **Paraiso** next door is as good and also rents a room (**D**). Ask for Gentil or Angelica.

D Pousada Luar das Águas, T075-9981 1012. Simple and good value.

D Pousada Moreré, Moreré town, T075-9987 1513. Simple fan-cooled rooms, some of which are a little musty. Good restaurant which doubles up as the town's only bar. The owner is the island's *prefeito*.

Ituberá and Camamu *p389*

C Rio Acaraí, Praça Dr Francisco Xavier, T073-255 2315, www.hotelrioacarai.com.br. Ugly modern pousada with a pool and restaurant.

D Tropical, Av Hildebrando Araújo Góes 270, Ituberá, T073-256 2233. Standard, simple, small town pousada with a/c rooms, a restaurant, bar and pool.

E Green House, next to the *rodovíaria*, T073-255 2178. Very basic and friendly with breakfast and a simple restaurant.

Barra Grande and the Peninsula de Maraú *p389*

LL Kiaroa, Praia Taipus de Fora, T073-258 6215, www.kiaroa.com.br. One of the country's most luxurious resorts, set on a glorious beach, with a range of beautifully appointed rooms and excellent restaurant, pampering and various organized activities.

AL-A Lagoa do Cassange, Praia do Cassange, T073-258 2166, www.maris.com.br. Family resort with a pool, restaurant and 14 individual chalets overlooking the beach.

AL-A Taipú de Fora, Praia Taipus de Fora, T073-225 2276, www.taipudefora.com.br. Small upscale mini-resort with a good range of activities including diving and kayaking.

D Meu Sossego, R Dr Chiquinho 17, Barra town, T073-258 6012, www.meusossego.com. 19 plain a/c rooms with fridges.

Itacaré *p389*

The area is becoming very popular and prices are going up all the time. Book well ahead in high season.

LL Txai Resort, Praia de Itacarezinho, T073-634 6956, www.txai.com.br. The most exclusive and luxurious resort in Bahia. Set on a deserted beach with very spacious and tastefully appointed bungalows overlooking a long, deep-blue pool shaded by its own stand of palms. Excellent spa and a full range of activities including diving and horse riding.

AL-A Sage Point, Praia de Tiririca, T073-251 2030, www.pousadasagepoint.com.br. Oceanfront pousada with smart wooden chalets in a tropical garden overlooking the sea, each with their own hammock-strewn terraces. Some are a little small but all have wonderful views. The Cuban owner, Ana, speaks English and can organize trips to nearby beaches.

AL-A Vila de Ocaporan, T073-251 2470, www.viladeocaporan.com.br. Brightly coloured, spacious chalets gathered around a charming little pool in a hammock-filled garden. Between the town and Praia da Concha. Good Bahian restaurant.

A-B Art Jungle, T073-9996 2167, www.artjungle.org. A modern sculpture garden with 6 tree houses in the middle of the forest. All have views out to the sea and to the Rio de Contas. A favourite with celebrities – Sean Penn, Jade Jagger and Gisele Bündchen all come here.

B-C Pousada da Lua, Praia da Concha, T073-251 2209, www.itacare.com.br/pousadadalua. A handful of little chalets in a forest filled with marmosets and parakeets. Great breakfast.

C Pousada Litoral, R de Souza 81, 1 block from where buses stop. The owner João Cravo speaks English and can organize tours to remote beaches and hire fishing boats.

C-D Estrela, R Pedro Longo 34, Centro, T073-3251 2006, pousadaestrela@backpacker.com.br. A range of well-maintained, simple rooms and an excellent home-made breakfast with a huge choice. Very friendly.

Ilhéus and around *p389, map p390*

There are plenty of cheap hotels in Ilhéus near the municipal *rodoviária* in centre; not all are desirable (check for hot pillows!).

AL Hotel Jardim Atlântico, Pontal, near Ilhéus, T073-632 2222. Sports facilities, restaurant, bar.

A Hotel Barravento, on Malhado beach, R Nossa Senhora das Graças 276, Ilhéus, T/F073-634 3223. Ask for the penthouse – there is usually no extra charge, includes breakfast and a fridge.

A Ilhéus Praia, Praça Dom Eduardo (on the beach), Ilhéus, T073-634 2533. With a pool and helpful staff. Recommended.

A Pontal Praia, Av Lomanto Júnior 1358, Praia do Pontal, Ilhéus, T/F073-634 3033. A little outside city but with frequent buses passing. Unpretentious family hotel with a/c rooms and a swimming pool.

A Tarik Plaza, Av Aziz Maron, Itabuna, T073-211 8800, www.tarikplaza.com.br. The best in town; modern with a pool and fairly good restaurant.

B Pousada Sol Atlântico, Av Lomanto Júnior 1450, Pontal, T073-231 8059. Rooms with views over bay, fan, TVs and balconies.

B São Marino, 28 de Junho 29, Ilhéus, T073-231 6511 and at 28 de Junho 16.

C Britânia, Ilhéus, T073-634 1722. Cheap and fairly cheerful with breakfast.

D Hotel Atlântico Sul, R Bento Berilo 224, Ilhéus Centro, T073-231 4668. Good value with a bar/restaurant. Recommended.

D JG, Jardim Grapiúna, Itabuna, T/F073-211 2858, www.bahiaclick.com.br/jg. Basic hotel with plain a/c and fan-cooled rooms and a pool.

E Fazenda Tororomba, R Luiz Eduardo Magalhães s/n, Olivença centre, near Ilhéus, T073-269 1139. Youth hostel.

Camping

Estância das Fontes, 19 km on road south to Olivença, T073-212 2505. Cheap, shady. Recommended.

Porto Seguro *p392, map p392*

Prices rise steeply Dec-Feb and Jul. Off-season rates can drop by 50%, negotiate the rate for stays of more than 3 nights. Room capacity is greater than that of Salvador. Outside Dec-Feb, rooms with bath and hot water can be rented for about US$150 per month.

A Estalagem Porto Seguro, R Mcal Deodoro 66, T073-288 2095, F288 3692. In an old colonial house with a tranquil atmosphere, a/c, TV, pool, good breakfast.

A Pousada Alegrete, Av dos Navegantes 567, T/F073-288 1738. Simple rooms and very friendly and helpful staff. Recommended.

A Pousada Casa Azul, 15 de Novembro 11, T/F073-288 2180. TV, a/c, good pool and garden, quiet part of town.

A Pousada Gaivota, Av dos Navegantes 333, Centro, T/F073-288 2826. A/c rooms in a hotel with, pool, sauna, parking facilities.

A Pousada Imperador, Estrada do Aeroporto, T073-288 2759, F288 2900. Modest 4-star with views out over the city, especially from the pool deck.

A Toca do Marlin, Estrada BA 001, Km 40.5, Santo André, Santa Cruz Cabrália, T073-3671 5009, ww.tocadomarlin.com.br. One of the most luxurious beach resorts in South America, with spacious a/c *cabañas* next to a ranch overlooking a quiet, beautiful beach some 50km north of Porto Seguro. Excellent food and excursions.

A Vela Branca, R Dr Antonio Ricaldi , Cidade Alta, T073-288 2318, www.velabranca.com.br. Luxury resort with a wonderful view out over the water. Beautiful pool, tennis courts, sauna and spacious a/c rooms.

B Pousada Las Palmas, Praça Antônio Carlos Magalhães 102, T/F073-288 2643. A/c rooms with TVs in a little hotel with no pool, but highly recommended.

B-D Pousada dos Raizes, Praça dos Pataxós 196, T/F073-288 4717. Well-kept unpretentious city hotel with helpful staff. Cheaper without breakfast. Recommended.

C Pousada Alcantara, R das Papagaias 70, T/F073-288 1657. Centrally located with fan-cooled rooms only. Well looked after.

C Pousada Coral, R Assis Chateaubriand 74, T/F073-288 2630. A/c rooms with a TV in a dull building but in a good location.

C Pousada da Orla, Av Portugal 404, T/F073-288 1131. Fan-cooled simple rooms and a good breakfast. Great location. Highly recommended.

C Pousada dos Navegantes, Av 22 de Abril 212, T073-288 2390, www.portonet.com.br/navegantes. A/c rooms, with en suites and TVs, crowding over a little pool.

C Pousada Jandaias, R das Jandaias 112, T073-288 2611, F288 2738. Fan-cooled rooms and a great breakfast, tranquil. Recommended.

D Estalagem da Ivonne, R Mcal Deodoro 298, T073-288 1515. Basic hotel with some a/c rooms.

D Maracaia, Coroa Vermelha, on road to Santa Cruz Cabrália, T073-872 1155, F872 1156. IYHA hostel. Price per person.

D Porto Seguro, R Cova da Moça 720, T/F073-288 1742. IYHA hostel. Price per person.

D Pousada Aquarius, R Pedro Álvares Cabral 174, T/F073-288 2738. No breakfast but clean, family run, friendly and central.

E Porto Brasília, Praça Antônio Carlos Magalhães 234. Fans, mosquito nets, with breakfast.

F Pousada Casa Grande, Av dos Navegantes 107, Centro, T073-288 2003. Comfortable, very simple with helpful multilingual staff and a hearty breakfast.

Camping

Camping da Gringa, Praia do Cruzeiro, T073-288 2076. Laundry, café, pool, excellent, US$5 per night.

Camping do Sítio, R da Vala. Mosquitoes can be a problem here.

Camping dos Marajas, Av Getúlio Vargas. Central.

Camping Mundaí Praia, T073-879 2287. US$8 per night.

Tabapiri Country, BR-367, Km 61.5, next to the *rodoviária* on the road leading to the Cidade Histórica, T073-288 2269.

Santa Cruz Cabrália *p394*

A-B Baía Cabrália, R Sidrack de Carvalho 141, centro, T/F073-282 1111, www.baiacabralia.com.br. Medium-size family resort with a large pool, sauna and gym.

B-C Victor Hugo, Villa de Santo André, Km 3, Santa Cruz Cabrália, T073-671 4064, www.portonet.com.br/victorhugo. Smart, tastefully decorated little pousada right on the beach. Rooms are plain and scrupulously clean, with whitewashed walls and dark wood floors.

C Pousada do Mineiro, T073-282 1042. A/c rooms around a pool and with a sauna, friendly staff and a *churrascaria* barbecue. Recommended.

C Tribo da Praia, Av Beira de Santo André, T073-282 1620. Pousada with a helpful American owner.

Arraial da Ajuda *p394*

At busy times such as New Year's Eve and Carnaval, don't expect to find anything under US$15 per person in a shared room, with a minimum stay of 5-7 days.

Note We have received warnings about Pousada da Anginha and would advise travellers to avoid staying there. For more information contact the Porto Seguro Delegacia de Proteçao ao Turista.

A Pousada Pitinga, Praia Pitinga, T073-575 1067, www.pousadapitinga.com.br. Wooden chalets in a coconut-filled rainforest garden on a hill overlooking the sea. Tranquil atmosphere, great food and a pool A member of the **Roteiros de Charme** group, see page 50. Recommended.

A-C Pousada Canto d'Alvorada, on the road to Ajuda, T073-875 1218, www.cantodalvorada.com.br. Cheaper out of season. Pretty, Swiss-run pousada a little out of town with 7 cabins, a restaurant, pool, sauna and laundry facilities.

B Ivy Marey, near the centre on the road to the beach, T073-875 1106. Franco-Brazilian pousada, tastefuly decorated, 4 rooms and 2 bungalows.

B Pousada do Robalo, T073-875 1053/1528, F875 1078. Welcoming pousada with a nice pool set in pleasant garden surroundings.

B Sole Mio, T073-875 1115, just off the beach road leading from the ferry to Arraial. French owners, English spoken, laid-back with 4 chalets and an excellent pizzeria.

C Pousada Erva Doce, Estrada do Mucugê 200, T073-875 1113. Well-appointed chalets and a decent restaurant. Highly recommended.

C Pousada Mar Aberto, Estrada do Mucugê 554, T/F073-875 1153, Pretty little pousada set in lush gardens very near Mucugê beach, 400 m from the centre.

C Pousada Tubarão, R Bela Vista, beyond the church on the right, T073-875 1086. With sweeping views of the sea, a cool sea breeze and a reasonable restaurant.

C-E O Cantinho, Praça São Bras, T073-575 1131, www.arraialnet.com.br/pousada cantinho. Terraces of smart a/c and fan-cooled rooms around a fruit tree garden courtyard. Excellent breakfast, pleasant public areas and off-season discounts.

D Pousada Corujão, T/F073-875 1508. Basic bungalows on the way to the beach with cooking facilities, a laundry, restaurant and book exchange.

D Pousada do Mel, Praça São Bras, T073-875 1309. Simple but clean and with a good breakfast. Recommended.

D Pousada Flamboyant, Estrada Mucugê 89, T073-875 1025. Rooms arranged around a little courtyard. Good breakfast and a pool.

E-F Daunbailó, Estrada do Mucugê 125, T073-575 1194, linobeto@yahoo.com. Very simple backpacker-orientated pousada with tiny but well-kept rooms, some with a/c.

E-F Good's, Estrada do Mucugê 69, T073-575 1998, www.arraialdajudahostel.com.br. Price per person. Backpacker hostel with IYHA discount, snack bar, internet and book exchange. Very good location.

Camping

Generally, Arraial da Ajuda is better for camping than Porto Seguro.

Chão do Arraial, 5 mins from Mucugê beach. Shady, good snack bar, also rents out tents. Recommended.

Praia, on Mucugê beach. Good position and facilities.

Trancoso *p395*

As well as the pousadas, there are many houses to rent; contact Clea at **Restaurant Abacaxi** on the main square on the right.

A Caipim Santo, to the left of the main square, T073-668 1122. Pleasant pousada with one of the better restaurants in Trancoso. Recommended.

A Pousada Brasília, Estrada do Arraial, T073-668 1128. Party pousada popular with young and well-to-do Paulistanos. Not for seekers of tranquility.

A-B Mata N'ativa, Estrada Velha do Arraial (next to the river on the way to the beach), T073-668 1830, www.matanativa pousada.com.br. The best in town, with a series of elegant cabins gathered in a lovingly maintained orchid and heliconia garden by the riverside. Owners Daniel and Daniela are very hospitable. Good English, Spanish and Italian.

B Pousada Calypso, Parque Municipal, T073-668 1113, www.pousadacalypso.com.br. Comfortable, spacious rooms, a library and sitting area and helpful staff who speak German and English. Recommended.

C Gulab Mahal, on the main square. Mock-oriental and set in a little tropical garden. Vast breakfast. Highly recommended.

C Pousada do Bosque, Estrada Velha do Arraial (on the way to the beach). Simple pousada in a garden and with camping facilities. English, German and Spanish spoken. Decent breakfast.

D Luana Pousa, in the *invasão* (the newer part of Trancoso), further along on the left from **Quarto Crescente**. With well-ventilated modest rooms. Recommended.

D Pousada Quarto Crescente, About 500 m inland, away from main square, in the *invasão*, with cooking facilities, laundry and helpful owners who speak English, German, Dutch and Spanish. Highly recommended.

E Pousada Beira Mar. Very simple rooms with bath and an equally simple restaurant serving *prato feito*.

Caraiva *p395*

D Pousada da Barra, at the far end of the village. Simple rooms, breakfast included.

D Pousada da Canoa, attached to **Bar do Pará**, by the river. Simple fan cooled rooms and a restaurant serving the best fish in the village, US$7-8 (try *sashimi* or *moqueca*).

D Pousada da Terra, far end of the village near the indigenous reserve. Simple rooms with breakfast. Recommended.

D Pousada Lagoa, T/F073-9965 6662. Chalets and bungalows under cashew trees, good restaurant, own generator; the owner, Hermínia, speaks English, is very helpful and can arrange local trips and excursions.

Cumuruxatiba and Prado *p396*

C Casa de Maria, R Seis, Novo Prado, Prado, T073-298 1424, www.casademaria.com.br. Simple beachside pousada with a pool. Claims to serve the best breakfast in southern Bahia.

C-D Novo Prado, Praia Novo Prado, Prado, T073-298 1455, www.novoprado.com.br.

Pleasant beach hotel with a pool, sauna and a range of a/c and fan-cooled rooms.

D **Pousada Guainamby**, R Bela Vista, CEP 45983, Cumuruxatiba. German and Brazilian owned with small, clean, comfortable chalets and good views out over the long beach, a good breakfast and a restaurant with fish and Italian meals. Recommended.

E **Praia de Cumuruxatiba**, Av Beira Mar s/n, Cumuruxatiba, T073-873 1020, F873 1004. Basic beachside hostel.

Caravelas *p396*

A **Marina Porto Abrolhos**, R da Baleia, T073-674 1082, www.marinaporto abrolhos.com.br. Luxurious beachfront family resort with 34 apartments, a pool, sauna and a range of activities.

C **Pousada Caravelense**, 50 m from the *rodoviária*, T073-297 1182. Plain rooms with a TV, fridge, a good breakfast and an excellent restaurant. Recommended.

D **Shangri-la**, Barão do Rio Branco 216. Simple rooms with en suites and breakfast.

E **Pousada Jaquita**, Barra de Caravelas. Basic with the use of a kitchen, big breakfast, bath, airy rooms. The owner, Secka, speaks English. There are some food shops nearby as well as restaurants and bars.

Eating

Tinharé and Morro de São Paulo *p387*

There are plenty of restaurants in Morro de São Paulo town and on the 2nd and 3rd beaches. Most of them are okay though somewhat overpriced. For cheap eats stay in a pousada that includes breakfast, stock up at the supermarket and buy seafood snacks at the *barracas* on the 2nd beach.

ΨΨ **Belladonna**, Morro town. Decent Italian restaurant with live music and a good meeting point. The owner Guido speaks Italian, English and French. Evenings only.

ΨΨ **Bianco e Nero**, Morro town. Reasonably good pizza, pasta and grilled food.

ΨΨ **Chez Max**, Morro town, 3rd beach. Simple but decent seafood in a pretty restaurant overlooking the sea.

ΨΨ **Fazenda Vila Guaiamú** (see page 397), Morro town. Excellent seafood restaurant that must be booked in advance for non-guests.

ΨΨ **Piscina**, Morro town, 4th beach, T075-483 1072. One of Morro's few good, as opposed to adequate, seafood restaurants.

Ψ **Comida Natural**, Morro town, on the main street. Good breakfasts, pay-by-weight lunches and juices.

Ilha de Boipeba *p388*

Boipeba has cheap eats in the town and surpirisingly good food at the **Pousada Santa Clara** and the rustic restaurants in Moreré.

ΨΨ **Santa Clara** (see page 397), Boipeba. San Francisco panache in rustic but elegantly decorated tropical surrounds. Come for dinner. Highly recommended.

Ψ **Mar e Coco** (see page 398), Boipeba. Very fresh seafood in idyllic surroundings, shaded by coconuts and next to a gently lapping bath-warm sea.

Itacaré *p389*

There are plenty of restaurants in Itacaré, most of them on **R Lodônio Almeida**. Menus here are increasingly chic and often include a respectable wine list.

ΨΨΨ **Casa Sapucaia**, R Lodônio Almeida, T073-251 3091. Sophisticated Bahian food with an international twist from 2 ex-round-the-world sailors. Try the delicious king prawn caramelized with ginger.

ΨΨΨ **Dedo de Moça**, R Plinio Soares (next to the São Miguel church), T073-251 3391. One of Bahia's best restaurants. Chef Vagner Aguiar trained at São Paulo's award-winning **Laurent** restaurant and cooks dishes that combine Brazilian ingredients with French and Oriental techniques. Offerings include tempura with pear rice cooked in port wine, lightly caramelized with balsamic vinegar.

ΨΨΨ **O Casarão Amarelo**, Praia da Coroinha, T073-9996 0599. Swiss-owned restaurant in one of the most beautiful colonial buildings in the town. International menu which is good in parts. The fish is always a reliable choice.

ΨΨ **Boca de Forno**, R Lodônio Almeida 134, T073-251 2174. The busiest restaurant in Itacaré, serving good wood-fired pizzas in tastefully decorated surroundings to a well-dressed post-beach crowd.

Ψ **O Restaurante**, R Pedro Longo 150, T073-251 2012. One of the few restaurants with a *prato feto*, alongside a mixed seafood menu.

Ilhéus and around *p389, map p390*
Specialities include the local drink, *coquinho*, coconut filled with *cachaça*, which is only for the strongest heads. There are cheap eats from the various seafood stalls on the praça and near the cathedral.

Vesúvio, Praça Dom Eduardo, T073-634 4724. Next to the cathedral, made famous by Amado's novel (see box page 391), now Swiss- owned. Very good but pricey.

Os Velhos Marinheiros, Av 2 de Julho. Decent seafood and juices on the waterfront. Recommended.

Come Bem, near Praça Cairu. Cheap but good Bahian food.

Nogar, Av Bahia 377. Close to the sea. Decent pizzas and pasta.

Porto Seguro and around *p392, map p392*

Cruz de Malta, R Getúlio Vargas 358. Good seafood in pleasant surrounds.

Anti-Caro, R Assis Chateaubriand 26. Good food in a working antique shop, great atmosphere.

Les Agapornis, Av dos Navegantes 180. Wide selection of crêpes and pizzas.

Prima Dona, No 247. Decent pasta, pizza and other Italian dishes.

Tres Vintens, Av Portugal 246. Good imaginative seafood dishes. Recommended.

Vida Verde, R Dois de Julho 92, T073 288 2766. Reasonable vegetarian food, one of few that serve it. Mon-Sat 1100-2100.

Da Japonêsa, Praça Pataxós 38. Excellent value with a varied Brazilian and Japanese menu, open 0800-2300. Recommended.

Pau Brasil, Praça dos Pataxós. Simple café with good breakfast.

Ponto do Encontro, Praça Pataxós 106. Good simple food, the owners also rent rooms, open 0800-2400.

Preto Velho, Praça da Bandeira. Good value for à la carte or self-service.

Arraial da Ajuda *p394*
Food in Arraial is pricey and restaurants tend to look better than the dishes they serve. Recommended *barracas* are **Tem Q Dá** and **Agito** on Mucugê beach, as well as **Barraca de Pitinga** and **Barraca do Genésio** on Pitinga.

Don Fabrizio, Estrada do Mucugê 402, T073-575 1123. The best Italian in town, in an upmarket open air-restaurant with live music and reasonable wine.

Manguti, Estrada do Mucugê, T073-575 2270, www.manguti.com.br. Reputedly the best in town, though the food looks like mutton dressed as lamb. Meat, pasta, fish served as comfort food alongside other Brazilian dishes. Very popular and informal.

Nipo, Estrada do Mucugê 250, T073-575 3033. Reasonably priced but decent Japanese with hotel delivery.

Pizzaria do Arraial, Praça São Bras s/n. Basic pizzeria and pay-by-weight restaurant.

Mineirissima, Estrada do Mucugê, T073-575 3790. Good value pay-by-weight with filling Minas Gerais food and *moquecas*. Opens until late but menu service only after 1800.

Paulinho Pescador, Estrada do Mucugê. Excellent seafood, also chicken and meat, one price (US$5), English spoken, good service. *Bobó de camarão* highly recommended. Very popular, there are often queues for tables. Open 1200-2200.

Trancoso *p395*
Food in Trancoso is expensive. Those on a tight budget should shop at the supermarket between the main square and the new part of town. There are numerous fish restaurants in the *barracas* on the beach. None are cheap. Elba Ramalho, when in town, gigs at her restaurant, **Para Raio**.

Cacão, main square, T073-668 1266. One of the best in town with a varied international and Brazilian menu. Pleasant surrounds.

Laila, in the new shopping area just before the main square. Elegant little restaurant serving good Moroccan and Lebanese food.

Silvana e Cia in the historical centre. Respectable Bahian food at a fair price.

Portinha, on the main square. The only place serving food at a reasonable price. Excellent pay-by-weight options and good if over-priced juices.

Bars and clubs

Tinharé and Morro de São Paulo *p387*
There is always plenty going on in Morro. The liveliest bars are **87** and **Jamaica**; both on the 2nd beach. These tend to get going after 2300 when the restaurants in town empty.

Ilha de Boipeba *p388*

Nightlife on Boipeba is limited to watching the stars or having a beer at the reggae bar in town.

Itacaré *p389*

The liveliest bars of the moment are **Toca do Calango**, **Praça dos Cachorros** and **Mar e Mel** on the Praia das Conchas. The **Casarão Amarelo** restaurant becomes a dance club after 2300 on weekends. There is frequent extemporaneous *forró* and other live music all over the city and most restaurants and bars have some kind of music Oct-Apr.

Porto Seguro *p392, map p392*

Porto Seguro is famous for the *lambada* (see Music, page 689). A good bar for live music is **Porto Prego**, R Pedro Álvares Cabral, which has a small cover charge. **Sotton Bar**, Praça de Bandeira, is lively, as are **Pronto Socorro do Choppe**, **Doce Letal 50** and **Studio Video Bar**. There are bars and street cafés on Av Portugal.

Arraial da Ajuda *p394*

The *lambada* is danced at the **Jatobar** bar (summer only), by the church on the main square (opens 2300 – *pensão* at the back is cheap, clean and friendly). **Limelight** has raves all year round. Many top Brazilian bands play at the beach clubs at **Praia do Parracho** during the summer, entry is about US$20. Entry to other beach parties is about US$10.

❂ Festivals and events

Ilhéus and around *p389, map p390*

17-20 Jan Festa de São Sebastião.
Feb Shrove Tue, Carnaval.
23 Apr Festa de São Jorge.
28 Jun Foundation day.
Oct Festa do Cacau.

▲ Activities and tours

Itacaré *p389*

Bahia Alegria, T073-251 3461, and **Itacaré Ecoturismo**, T73-251 2224, organize abseiling trips and other activities.

Porto Seguro *p392, map p392*

Diving and snorkelling

Companhia do Mar, Praça dos Pataxós, T073-288 2981. Daily trips by schooner to coral reefs off the coast. The most popular is to Recife de Fora, with good snorkelling (it leaves daily at 1000, returns at 1630, about US$18, US$3 extra for snorkelling gear).
Portomar Ltda, R Dois de Julho 178. Equipment hire, also arranges diving and snorkelling trips to the coral reefs offshore, professional instructors.

Tour operators

Dugout canoes fish on the Rio Burnahém and trips can be taken by canoe to explore the mangroves. There are several agencies at the airport, including **Grou Turismo**, T073-288 4155, **Soletur**, T073-288 1736, and **Viagens Costa**, T073-288 5288.
BPS, at the Shopping Centre, T073-288 2373. Offers guided tours of the area.
Brazil Travel, Av 22 de Abril 200, T/F073-288 1824 and braziltravel@braziltravel.tur.br. Dutch-run travel agency, all types of trips organized. English, German, Dutch, French and Spanish spoken.

Arraial da Ajuda *p394*

Eco Calicute, T073-9979 5452, www.calicute.com.br. Not 'eco' at all; as usual in Brazil the word translates as mucking about in nature, in this case with a 4WD, glider, quad bike, horse or scuba gear. Don't expect guides to know anything about wildlife or show any interest in it.

Trancoso *p395*

Joáçio, T073-668 1270, or ask at **Bouganvillea** restaurant on the main square. Good day trips to Espelho Beach, Caraíva and other beaches and forested areas in the area. Expect to pay US$10-15 per person depending on group size and distance.

Caravelas *p396*

Teresa and **Ernesto** (from Austria) organize boat trips (US$40 per day), jeep and horse hire (turn left between the bridge and the small supermarket).
Abrolhos Turismo, Praça Dr Imbassahi 8, T073-297 1149. 'Alternative' beach holidays (organic vegetarian food, yoga, meditation, other activities) with Beky and Eno on the unspoilt island of Coçumba, recommended. Also rents diving gear and arranges boat trips.

Transport

Valença *p387*
Air Flights mainly go to **Salvador** from where there are connections with other towns.

Bus Long-distance buses run from the new *rodoviária* on Av Maçônica. Many buses a day to **Salvador**, 5 hrs, US$6, several companies, including **Aguia Branca**, T075-450 4400. **São Jorge** to **Itabuna**, 5 hrs, US$5, very slow. For the shortest route to **Salvador**, take a bus via Nazaré das Farinhas to Bom Despacho (130 km), and take a ferry from there to the São Joaquim ferry terminal (see page 372). To **Bom Despacho** on Itaparica, **Camarujipe** and **Águia Branca** companies, 16 a day, 1 hr 45 mins, US$3.60.

Ferry There are boats to **Gamboa** (1½ hrs) and **Morro de São Paulo** (1½ hrs) from the main bridge in Valença, 5 times a day (signalled by a loud whistle). The fare is US$2.50. The *lancha rápida* takes 25 mins and costs US$8. Only Salvador–Valença buses leaving 0530-1100 connect with ferries. If not stopping in Valença, get out of the bus by the main bridge in town, don't wait until you get to the *rodoviária*, which is a long way from the ferry. Private boat hire can be arranged if you miss the ferry schedule. A responsible local boatman is **Jario**, T075-741 1681; he can be contacted to meet travellers arriving at the *rodoviária* for transfer to Morro. He also offers excursions to other islands, especially Boipeba. There is a regular boat from Valença to **Boipeba** on weekdays 1000-1230 depending on tide, return 1500-1700, 3-4 hrs.

Tinharé and Morro de São Paulo *p387*
Air There are several daily direct flights from the 2rd beach at Morro de São Paulo to **Salvador**. These cost US$50 one way. Times vary seasonally and from year to year but are usually as follows: Salvador–Morro (0815, 1430, 1500), Morro–Salvador (0900, 1015, 1315, 1715). For further details ask your hotel to contact **Addey** T071-377 1993, www.addey.com.br, or drop into the airport office next to the landing strip on Morro.

Ferry Several companies run catamarans from Morro de São Paulo to the Terminal Marítimo in front of the Mercado Modelo in **Salvador** (1½ hrs). Times vary according to the season and weather but there are usually several a day 0800-1400; check with the tourist office or **Catamarã Gamboa do Morro**, T071-9975 6395. There are also water taxis.

Boats from Morro de São Paulo and **Gamboa** run to the main bridge in **Valença** (1½ hrs) 5 times a day, US$2.50 (see under Valença, above). There is also a *lancha rápida* which takes 25 mins and costs US$8. Private boat hire can also be arranged, contact **Jario**, T075-741 1681.

Ilha de Boipeba *p388*
Boat Day trips to the island run from Morro de São Paulo (see page 387). There is a regular boat from Boipeba to **Valença** on weekdays 1500-1700, 3-4 hrs. Overnight excursions to the village are possible. Contact **Zé Balacha** T075-9148 0343 or book through your pousada in Morro or Boipeba.

Itacaré *p389*
Bus Frequent buses to **Ilhéus** (the nearest town with an airport), 45 mins, US$7 along the newly paved road. To **Salvador**, change at Ubaitaba (3 hrs, US$3), Ubaitaba–Salvador, 6 hrs, US$12, several daily.

Ilhéus and around *p389, map p390*
Bus The **Itabuna–Olivença** bus goes through the centre of Ilhéus. Several buses run daily to **Salvador**, 7 hrs, US$14.40 (*leito* US$29, **Expresso São Jorge**), the 0620 bus goes via **Itaparica**, leaving passengers at Bom Despacho ferry station on the island from where it is a 50-min ferry to **Salvador**. To **Itacaré**, 4 hrs, US$5. To **Eunápolis**, 5 hrs, US$5.40, this bus also leaves from the central bus terminal. Local buses leave from Praça Cairu.

Taxi Insist that taxi drivers have meters and price charts.

Porto Seguro and around *p392, map p392*
Air Flights to **Belo Horizonte**, **Rio de Janeiro**, **Salvador** and **São Paulo**. Taxi to airport US$7.

Bus At Brazilian holiday times, all transport should be booked well in advance. **Expresso Brasileiro** buses run from Praça dos

Pataxós along the BR-367 stopping at the beaches north of town.

To **Salvador** (Águia Branca), daily, 12 hrs, US$22.25. To **Vitória**, daily, 11 hrs, US$18. **Ilhéus**, daily 0730, 5½ hrs, US$11. To **Eunápolis**, 1 hr, US$2. For **Rio** direct buses (São Geraldo), leaving at 1745, US$35 (*leito* 70), 18 hrs, from Rio direct at 1600 (very cold a/c, take warm clothes), or take 1800 for Ilhéus and change at Eunápolis. To **Belo Horizonte**, daily, direct, US$33 (São Geraldo). To **São Paulo** direct, 1045, 25 hrs, not advisable, very slow, much better to go to Rio then take Rio–São Paulo express. Other services via Eunápolis (those going north avoid Salvador) or Itabuna (5 hrs, US$9).

Car hire Several companies located at the airport, including Localiza, T073-288 1488 (and R Cova da Moça 620, T073-288 1488) and Nacional, T073-288 4291.

Cycle hire Oficina de Bicicleta, Av Getúlio Vargas e R São Pedro. US$10 for 24 hrs, also at Praça de Bandeira and at 2 de Julho 242.

Arraial da Ajuda *p394*
Ferry Take a bus or kombi to **Rio Buranhém**, from where boats cross the river to **Porto Seguro**, on the north bank, 15 mins, US$0.60 for foot passengers, US$3.60 for cars, every 30 mins day and night.

Caravelas *p396*
Air There are flights to **Belo Horizonte**, **São Paulo** and **Salvador**. Another option is to fly via **Porto Seguro**.

Bus Caravelas is well connected, with buses to **Texeira de Freitas** (4 a day), **Salvador**, **Nanuque** and **Prado**.

Train There are rail connections to **Minas Gerais**.

Parque Nacional Marinho dos Abrolhos *p396*
Boat See Ins and outs, page 396. The journey to the mainland takes 1-6 hrs. Contact Mestre Onofrio Frio in Alcobaça, Bahia, T073-293 2195 or Abrolhos Turismo, see page 404.

Directory

Valença *p387*
Banks There is a Bradesco and Banco do Brasil in town, which have ATMs and *cambios*.

Tinharé and Morro de São Paulo *p387*
Banks There are no banks on the island, but cash dollars can be exchanged in *casas de cambio* in the village. **Internet** There is access in the town in several cafés.

Ilhéus and around *p389, map p390*
Banks Empresa de Cambio e Turismo, T073-634 3900, will change money.

Porto Seguro *p392, map p392*
Banks Agência do Descobrimento, Av Getúlio Vargas, also arranges flight tickets and house rental. Banco do Brasil, Av Beira Mar, 1000-1500, changes TCs and US$ cash, also Visa ATMs. Also at airport. Bradesco, Av Getulio Vargas, Visa ATMs. Deltur, in the new shopping centre, near Banco do Brasil. **Laundry** New Porto, Shopping Av, daily 0900-2230, priced per item. **Post office** In the mini-shopping centre on the corner of R das Jandaias and Av dos Navegantes. **Telephone** Shopping Av, daily 0700-2300, corner of Av dos Navegantes and Av Beira Mar, also at Praça dos Pataxós, beside ferry terminal. Daily 0700-2200, cheap rates after 2000, receives and holds faxes, F288 3915.

Arraial da Ajuda *p394*
Banks There is a Banco do Brasil with a cambio and ATM in the small shopping centre on Estrada do Mucugê. Several bars on Broadway change US$ cash, but rates are poor. **Internet** Dotted throughout town. **Post office** Praça São Bras. **Telephone** Telemar on the main square. Daily 0800-2200, number for receiving faxes is F875 1309, US$1.

Trancoso *p395*
There are internet cafés on the main square but no bank.

Caravelas *p396*
Banks The Banco do Brasil, Praça Dr Imbassahi, does not change money but has an ATM.

Linha Verde and the northern coast

Heading north from Salvador airport, the coast road (BA-099), or Estrada de Coco (Coconut Highway), passes many coconut plantations and 50 km of beautiful beaches. From south to north the best known are Ipitanga (famous for its reefs), Buraquinho, Jauá, Arembepe, Guarajuba, Itacimirim, Castelo Garcia D'Ávila (where there is a 16th-century fort) and Forte. North of the smart mini-resort town of Praia do Forte, the road is called the Linha Verde (Green Line), which runs for 142 km to the Sergipe state border. The road is more scenic than the BR-101, especially near Conde. There are very few hotels or pousadas in the more remote villages. Among the most picturesque are Subaúma and Baixio; the latter, where the Rio Inhambupe meets the sea, is very beautiful. Buses serve most of these destinations. ▸▸ *For Sleeping, Eating and other listings, see pages 408-410.*

Linha Verde

Arembepe

➔ *Phone code: 071. Colour map 4, A6.*

Some 45 km north of Salvador, this former fishing village is now a quiet resort. There is an 'alternative' village of palm huts, 30 minutes' walk along the beach, behind the sand dunes, with a café and swimming. The best beaches are 2 km north of town. A music festival is held the weekend after Carnaval.

Praia do Forte

➔ *Phone code: 071. Colour map 4, A6.*

About 80 km north of Salvador, is this pleasant mini resort town much beloved of wealthy people from Salvador. Praia may no longer be a fishing village but it still feels low key. Aside from the town's main street, Alameda do Sol, most of the streets are sand. Much of the area around the town is protected, with turtle-nesting beaches, remnant coastal *restinga* forest, and a small area of marshland, which is home to a large number of birds, caymans and other animals. Bird-watching trips on the Pantanal are rewarding and can be organized through the town's large-scale 'eco' resort.

The **Projeto Tamar** ⓘ *Caixa Postal 2219, Rio Vermelho, Salvador, Bahia, T071-876 1045, F876 1067*, is a national project that studies and preserves the sea turtles that lay their eggs in the area. Praia do Forte is the headquarters of the **national turtle preservation programme** and is funded by the Worldwide Fund for

Nature. There is a visitor centre at the project (US$1.50 for turtle sanctuary). The coast here is ideal for windsurfing and sailing, owing to constant fresh Atlantic breezes.

Praia do Forte takes its name from the castle built by a Portuguese settler, Garcia D'Ávila, in 1556, to warn the city to the south of enemy invasion. He was given a huge area of land, from Praia do Forte to Maranhão, on which he made the first farm in Brazil. He brought the first herd of cattle to the country, cleared the virgin Atlantic forest and brought the first coconut and mango trees to Brazil.

Imbassaí → *Phone code: 071. Colour map 4, A6.*

About 14 km from Praia do Forte is the simple village of Imbassaí, which has a beach at the mouth of the Rio Barroso. Other nearby beaches are **Praia de Santo Antônio**, 4 km away, with sand dunes and a small fishing village, and **Porto Sauípe**, 22 km north, which has recently been transformed into an ugly and old-fashioned mega-resort modelled on those which infected southern Spain in the 1980s. It caters almost exclusively to the worst kind of national and international package tourism.

Sítio do Conde → *Phone code: 075. Colour map 2, C5.*

Situated on the coast, 6 km from Conde, Sítio do Conde is a site for **Projeto Tamar** (see Praia do Forte, page 407). The beaches are not very good but it's an ideal base to explore other beaches at **Barra do Itariri**, 12 km south, at the mouth of a river, and has fine sunsets. The road passes unspoilt beaches; the best are **Corre Nu** and **Jacaré**. You can also go to **Seribinha,** 13 km north of Sítio do Conde. The road goes along the beach through coconut groves and mangroves; at Seribinha are beach huts serving cool drinks or food.

Mangue Seco → *Phone code: 075. Colour map 2, C5.*

The last stop on the Linha Verde is Mangue Seco. The town was immortalized in Jorge Amado's book *Tieta*. A steep hill rises behind the village to white sand dunes that offer superb views of the coast. The encroaching dunes have caused the mangrove to dry up.

The peninsula is connected to Pontal in the state of Sergipe by boat or canoe on the Rio Real (10-minute crossing). Buses run between Pontal and Estancia twice a day. The ferry across the river usually leaves before 1000 in the morning. A private launch will cost US$10, but it is usually possible to find someone to share the ride and cost.

Sleeping

Arembepe *p407*

B-C Arembepe Refúgio Ecológico, Estrada Aldeia Hippie, T071-624 1031, www.aldeia arembepe.com.br. 11 well-appointed a/c chalets around a pool in a protected area by the Tamar turtle project. Very peaceful.

C-D Gipsy, R Eduardo Pinto, Km 3, T071-624 3266, www.gipsy.com.br. 40-room hotel with a/c rooms and a pool.

Praia do Forte *p407*

Prices rise steeply in the summer season. It can be difficult to find cheap accommodation. Bahia Forte Imoveis, main street, No 48, above AO Europeu restaurant, T071-3676 1433, www.bahiaforte.com, are property agents dealing in local rental accommodation; experienced staff speak many languages and offer an efficient service.

LL-AL Praia do Forte EcoResort, Av do Farol, T071-676 4000, reservas@pfr.com.br. Large-scale family resort set in tropical gardens on the beach and with programmes to visit the nearby protected areas. Rooms are spacious, well appointed and comfortable. There is a spa and service is excellent. Beautiful pool.

AL Pousada Solar da Lagoa, R do Forte, T071-3676 1271. Smart chalets with room enough for 4, a decent pool and excellent service. The price is for full board.

A Pousada Praia do Forte, Av do Farol, T071-3676 1116, www.pousadapraiado forte.com.br. Chalets in peaceful setting, in ideal position on beach. Recommended.

A-B **Sobrado da Vila**, Av do Sol, T/F071-3676 1152, www.sobradodavila.com.br. The best pousada in the village itself with a range of individually decorated rooms with balconies and a good-value restaurant. Very convenient for the restaurants.

B **Ogum Marinho**, Av Alameda do Sol, T071-3676 1165, www.ogummarinho.com.br. A/c or cheaper fan-cooled rooms in a mock colonial house with a nice little courtyard garden. Good restaurant and service.

B-C **Pousada dos Artistas**, Praça dos Artistas s/n, T071-3676 1147, www.pousadados artistas.tur.br. One of the best in town with a/c or fan-cooled rooms with balconies overlooking a little courtyard. Friendly staff and a stroll from the sea and the main street.

B-C **Pousada João Sol**, R da Corvina, T071-3676 1054, www.pousadajoaosol.com.br. 6 well-appointed and newly refurbished chalets. The owner speaks English, Spanish and German. Great breakfast.

C **Pousada Tatuapara**, Praça dos Artistas, T071-3676 1015. Spacious and well-maintained, fan-cooled rooms with a fridge. Good breakfast.

D **Albergue da Juventude**, Praia do Forte, R da Aurora 3, T071-3676 1094, praiadoforte@ albergue.com.br. Smart youth hostel with decent rooms with en suites, a large breakfast, Private bathroom, fan, breakfast, kitchen and shop, more expensive for non-IYHA members.

D **Tia Helena**, just east of the Praça dos Artistas. Helena, the motherly proprietor, provides an excellent meal and enormous breakfast. The rooms are simple but well kept and the price reduced for 3-day stays.

Imbassaí *p408*

B **Pousada Caminho do Mar**, T/F071-832 2499. Bungalows with a/c, restaurant, German-run.

B **Pousada Imbassaí**, T/F071-876 1313. A/c chalets and apartments.

C **Pousada Lagoa da Pedra**, T071-248 5914. Chalets set in large grounds, some English spoken, friendly.

D **Pousada Anzol de Ouro**, T071-322 4422. Modest fan-cooled chalets around a simple pool.

Sítio do Conde *p408*

A **Hotel Praia do Conde**, T075-429 1129 (in Salvador T071-321 2542). Smart a/c chalets with en suites around a pool.

C **Pousada Oasis**, T075-421 2397. Very simple, plain accommodation either fan-cooled or a/c rooms. With breakfast.

Mangue Seco *p408*

There are plenty of small cheap places in Mangue Seco along the seafront from the jetty, none with addresses or phone numbers (the village is tiny). There are simple restaurants around the main square next to the church. The beach has a handful of *barracas* serving cheap fish.

B-C **Asa Branca**, T075-445 9054, www.infonet.com.br/asabranca. The plushest in town with a range of simple a/c rooms in terraces overlooking a rectangular pool. Good restaurant.

Eating

Arembepe *p407*

TT **Mar Aberto**, Lg de São Francisco 43, T071-824 1257. Good seafood with a French twist.

Praia do Forte *p407*

TTT **Sabor da Vila**, Alameda do Sol, T071-676 1156. International menu with good Bahian cooking and seafood.

TT **Bar Da Souza**, Av do Sol (on the right as you enter the village). Excellent seafood and live music at weekends. Recommended. Reasonably priced.

TT **O Europeu**, Alameda do Sol 48, T071-3676 0232, oeuropeu@gmail.com. Stylishly decorated English-owned restaurant with the most adventurous menu in town. International cuisine is served with a Bahian touch, alongside risotto, steak, salads and desserts. The owner, William, is affable and knowledgeable about the area.

T **Cafe Tango**, Praça das Artistas. Pleasant open-air tea and coffee bar with great pastries and cakes.

T **La Crêperie**, Alameda do Sol. Excellent savoury and sweet crêpes, Tue-Sun, good music. The owner, Kleber, is very friendly.

T **Pizzeria Le Gaston**, Alameda do Sol. Good pizza, pasta and home-made ice cream, open daily.

Shopping

Praia do Forte *p407*

Afro-Bahia, Alameda do Sol. Funky T-shirts.
Boutique Ogum Marinho, Alameda do Sol. Quirky woodcarvings by local artists.
Kennedy Bahia, Alameda do Sol. Gallery run by a family of Irish-Brazilian artists. Recommended.
Vivire, Alameda do Sol. High-quality swimwear from a Bahian brand.

Activities and tours

Praia do Forte *p407, phone code 071*

Odara Turismo, in the EcoResort Hotel, T071-676 1080, F676 1018, runs imaginative tours to surrounding areas and outlying villages and beaches using 4WD vehicles. Very friendly and informative, recommended. Owners, Norbert and Papy, speak English and German.

Transport

Arembepe *p407*

Bus To the Terminal Francês in **Salvador**, every 2 hrs, 1½ hrs, US$2, last bus at 1700. Buses also run to **Itapoã**.

Praia do Forte *p407*

Bus It is easy to flag down buses from the crossroads on the main highway out of town. To get there take a kombi (every 15 mins, US$0.25) from town. Taxis are a rip-off. To **Salvador** Santa Maria/Catuense runs 5 times daily, 1½ hrs, US$2. To **Estancia** in Sergipe, 4-5 daily, US$5.

Sítio do Conde *p408*

Bus To **Salvador** with São Luís, T071-358 4582, 3 a day, 4 on Fri, US$7.25.

Chapada Diamantina and the sertão

→ *Colour map 4, A5.*

The beautiful Chapada Diamantina national park comprises a series of escarpments swathed in tropical forest, dripping with waterfalls and dotted with dramatic caverns. It is one of the highlights of inland Bahia. Although little of the forest is original, there is still much wildlife here, including jaguar and maned wolf, and the area is good for birdwatching. Various trails cut through the park offering walks from a few hours to a few days. The road from Salvador to the Chapada passes through Feira de Santana, famous for its Micareta, *an extremely popular out-of-season carnival, before arriving at Lençóis. This small colonial town, once a main centre for diamond prospectors, is the most convenient base for exploring the national park.*

The harsh beauty of the sertão *and its hospitable people are the reward for those wanting to get off the beaten track. The region has been scarred by droughts and a violent history of bandits, rebellions and religious leaders. Euclides da Cunha and Canudos are good places to start exploring this history. The Raso da Catarina, once a hiding place for Lampião, and the impressive Paulo Afonso waterfalls, can both be visited from the town of Paulo Afonso located on the Rio São Francisco. This important river continues through the* sertão, *linking agricultural settlements such as Juazeiro, Ibotirama and Bom Jesus de Lapa before entering northern Minas Gerais.* » *For Sleeping, Eating and other listings, see pages 414-416.*

Parque Nacional da Chapada Diamantina

The park was founded in 1985 and comprises 1500 sq km of mountainous country. It forms part of the Brazilian shield, like the Guayana Highlands – a geological remnant of when the world was only one land mass. There is an abundance of endemic plants, waterfalls, rivers with natural swimming pools and good walking tours. There are also a number of large caves, which can be explored but are hard to find without a guide as there are no signs. Take a strong torch and be careful.

The trails in the park are not always well marked, and can involve a lot of clambering over rocks and stepping stones. A reasonable level of physical fitness is advisable. Walking boots are preferable but good training shoes are adequate. Avoid using new shoes, which give less grip on rocks. The most essential item for any trek is a flashlight with strong beam. Some of the walking may be after nightfall, but guides take trouble to avoid this. There are a lot of mosquitos in the encampment areas, so carry repellent. For guides and tours, see Lençois tour operators, page 416.

For overnight trips it is highly advisable to bring a sleeping bag and/or a blanket and roll-up mattress as nights in the 'winter' months can be cold. Sometimes, guides can arrange these. A tent is useful but optional; many camps are beside reasonably hospitable caves. Matches and paper for kindling camp fires, as well as a first aid kit, are necessary.

Ins and outs

Getting there There is a small **airport** ⓘ *Km 209, BR-242, 20 km from Lençois, T075-625 6497*, however most people choose to visit on an organized tour.

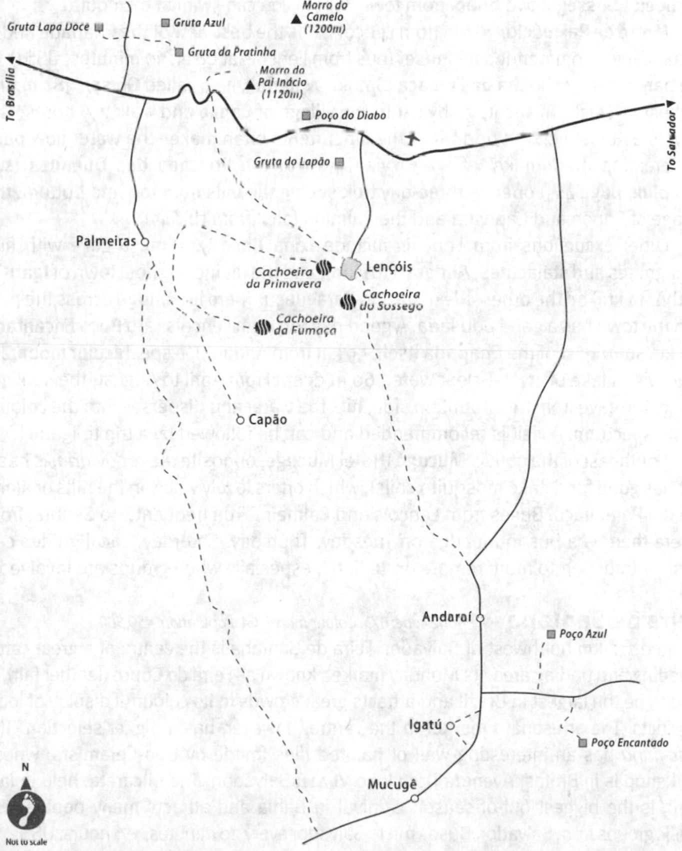

Tourist information The park headquarters is at Palmeiras, 50 km from Lençois. For Information call T075-332 2175, or contact **Ibama** in Salvador. There is a tourist office, **Sectur** ⓘ *Praça Oscar Maciel, Lençois, T075-334 1327*, next to the church across the river from town.

Lençóis → *Phone code: 075. Colour map 4, A5. Population: 9000.*

Set right in the middle of the park, this pretty colonial mining town is the area's main tourist centre. It was founded in 1844 to exploit the diamonds in the region; the tents assembled by the prospectors who first arrived there looked like sheets, *lençóis* in Portuguese, when seen from the hills. While there are still some *garimpeiros* (gold prospectors) left, it is not precious metals that attracts most visitors, but the cool climate, the relaxed atmosphere and the wonderful trekking in the hills of the Chapada Diamantina. This is also a good place for buying handicrafts.

Around Lençóis

Near Lençóis, the **Serrano** has wonderful natural pools in the riverbed, which give a great hydromassage. A little further away is the **Salão de Areia**, where the coloured sands for the bottle paintings come from. **Ribeirão do Meio** is a 45-minute walk from town; here locals bathe in the river and slide down a long natural water-chute into a big pool. The **Gruta do Lapão**, three hours from Lençóis, is a cave formed in quartz rock and therefore has no stalagmites (guide essential, some light rock climbing required). Also recommended are the pretty waterfalls of **Cachoeira da Primavera**, close to town; and **Cachoeira Sossego**, two hours from town, where you can swim in the pool.

Morro de Pai Inácio, 30 km from Lençóis, has the best view of the Chapada and is particularly recommended at sunset (bus from Lençois at 0815, 30 minutes, US$1). In the park is the **Cachoeira da Fumaça** (Smoke Waterfall, also called **Glass**), 384 m, the highest in Brazil. To see it, go by car to the village of **Capão** and walk 2½ hours. The view is astonishing; the updraft of the air currents often makes the water flow back up, creating the 'smoke' effect. Olivia Taylor at the **Pousada dos Duendes** (see Sleeping, page 415) offers a three-day trek seeing the falls from top and bottom, the village of Capão and Capivara and the Palmital falls (from US$45).

Other excursions from Lençois include **Lapa Doce** (70 km), a cave with fine stalagmites and stalactites, **Andaraí** (101 km), and the diamond ghost town of **Igatu** (a further 14 km) on the other side of the Rio Paraguaçu. There is a bridge across the river and the town has a good pousada. A good day trip from Lençóis is to **Poço Encantado** (23 km southeast of the Chapada itself, 55 km from Andaraî), a spectacular mountain cave with a lake of crystal-clear water, 60 m deep. From April to August, the sunlight enters the cave from the mountain side, hits the water and disperses into the colours of the spectrum. A visit is recommended and can be followed by a trip to Igatu.

Southeast of the park is **Mucugé** (**Hotel Mucugé**, opposite the *rodoviária*, is basic but has good food, take mosquito coils), which offers lovely walks in the hills or along the Rio Paraguaçu. Buses from Lençois and Palmeiras run frequently to Seabra, from where there is a bus to Mucugé on Tuesday, Thursday, Saturday. Local guides can arrange transport to more remote excursions, especially when groups are involved.

Feira de Santana → *Phone code: 075. Colour map 2, C4. Population: 450,500.*

Located 112 km northwest of Salvador, Feira de Santana is the centre of a great cattle breeding and trading area. Its Monday market, known as **Feira do Couro** (leather fair), is said to be the largest in Brazil and attracts great crowds to its colourful display of local products. The **artesanato market** in the centre, however, has a bigger selection. The *rodoviária* has an interesting wall of painted tiles (made by **Udo-Ceramista**, whose workshop is in Brotas, Avenida Dom João VI 411, Salvador). The **Micareta**, held in late April, is the biggest out-of-season carnival in Bahia and attracts many popular *axé* music groups from Salvador. Buses run to Salvador every 20 minutes, 1½ hours, US$3.

The sertão → *Colour map 2, C4.*

Situated 250 km from Salvador, and surrounded by the dry Bahian *sertão*, are the spa towns of **Cipó**, on the banks of the Rio Itapicuru, and nearby **Caldas do Jorro**. Both are popular for their thermal springs and have hotels (see www.thermaspousadahpg.com.br and www.pousadadojorro.com.br).

Euclides da Cunha and Monte Santo → *Phone code: 075.*

North of Feira da Santana, at Km 225 on the BR-116 road to Fortaleza, **Euclides da Cunha**, is a good base for exploring the Canudos area with a couple of standard hotels. The bus station is on the BR-116, T075-271 1365.

About 38 km west is the famous hill shrine of **Monte Santo** in the sertão, reached by 3½ km of steps cut into the rocks of the **Serra do Picaraça**. It takes about 45 minutes' walk each way, so set out early. This is the scene of pilgrimages and great religious devotion during Holy Week. The shrine was built by an Italian who had a vision of the cross on the mountain in 1765. One block north of the bottom of the stairs is the **Museu do Sertão**, with pictures from the 1897 Canudos rebellion.

Canudos → *Phone code: 075.*

Canudos itself is 100 km away. Religious rebels, led by Antônio Conselheiro, defeated three expeditions sent against them in 1897 before being overwhelmed. The Rio Vaza Barris, which runs through Canudos, has been dammed, and the town has been moved to **Nova Canudos** by the dam. Part of the old town is still located 10 km west in the **Parque Estadual de Canudos**, created in 1997. For tourist information, contact the **Prefeitura** ⓘ *T075-894 2165*. There are direct buses to Canudos from Salvador.

Paulo Afonso and Parque Nacional de Paulo Afonso

→ *Phone code: 075. Colour map 2, C5. Population: 94,000.*

Part of the northern border of Bahia is formed by the Rio São Francisco. From Salvador, the paved BR-110 runs 471 km north to the river at **Paulo Afonso**. The town was founded in 1913 when a large dam was constructed. Handicrafts (embroidery, fabrics) are available from **Núcleo de Produção Artesanal** ⓘ *Av Apolônio Sales 1059*. Nearby is the **Raso da Catarina** ⓘ *T075-281 3347*, a series of trails in the *caatinga* that was used as a hideout by the bandit Lampião. A guide and a 4WD vehicle are recommended for exploring the trails, due to the heat and lack of shade.

About 25 km northwest of the town is the Parque Nacional de Paulo Afonso, an oasis of trees amid a desert of brown scrub and cactus. The **Cachoeira de Paulo Afonso** ⓘ *in a security area, admission 0800-1100 only, by car or taxi, accompanied by a guide from the tourist information office, T075-282 1717, 2 hrs, US$6 per car*, was once one of the great waterfalls of the world but is now exploited for hydroelectric power. The falls are 270 km from the mouth of the São Francisco river, which drains a valley three times the size of Great Britain. The source of the river is 2575 km upstream in Minas Gerais. The 19th-century British linguist and explorer, Sir Richard Burton, took an expedition down the river and negotiated some of its treacherous rapids. Below the falls is a deep, rock gorge through which the water rushes. The best time to visit the falls is in the rainy season (January-February); only then does much water pass over them, as almost all the flow now goes through the power plant. The best view is from the northern (Alagoas) bank.

The Rio São Francisco is navigable above the falls from above the thriving twin towns (linked by a bridge) of Juazeiro, in Bahia, and Petrolina, in Pernambuco. Navigation is possible as far as **Pirapora** in Minas Gerais, linked by road to the Belo Horizonte-Brasília highway (see page 270).

Ins and outs The **airport** ⓘ *4 km from town*, receives flights from Recife and Salvador. The **rodoviária** ⓘ *Av Apolônio Sales*, has connections to Maceió, Recife and Salvador. For information and tours, contact **InfoTur** ⓘ *Av Apolonio Sales s/n, T075-2812 7757*.

Juazeiro → *Phone code: 074. Colour map 2, C4. Population: 172,500.*

Juazeiro is located at an important crossroads where the BR-407 meets the Rio São Francisco. For information on river transport, T075-811 2465. On the opposite bank in Pernambuco is Petrolina (see page 442). The local economy revolves around agriculture and its exportation. There is a market on Friday and Saturday and simple hotels in town, see www.juazeiro.ba.gov.br. The bus from Canudos (five hours) gets crowded; buy tickets early to ensure a seat. The second half of the route is unpaved.

Xique-Xique and Ibotirama → *Phone code: 074. Colour map 2, C2.*

The next major town upriver is Xique-Xique, an agricultural town 587 km from Salvador. The remains of what may be a pre-Neanderthal man have been found in the nearby **Grotto of the Cosmos**, whose cave paintings suggest that it could well have been used as an observatory.

The next town upriver, **Ibotirama**, 650 km from Salvador on the BR-242, is famous for its fishing, especially for *surubim* and *pocomã*. There are a few moderately priced hotels with restaurants.

Bom Jesus de Lapa → *Phone code: 077. Colour map 4, A4.*

An important stop on the Rio São Francisco and 148 km from Ibotirama on the BR-242 is **Bom Jesus de Lapa**. The **Igreja Nossa Senhora da Soledad** is situated within a grotto near to Praça da Bandeira. This sanctuary, discovered by a monk in the 17th century, is the centre of a *romaria* between July and September, which attracts thousands of visitors to the town. There are a few places to stay and a bank in town. The **airport** is at Avenida Manuel Novais, T077-481 4519.

Sleeping

Lençois *p412*

A Portal de Lençóis, R Chacara Grota, at the top of the town, T075-334 1233, www.portalhoteis.tur.br. 15 smart chalets in a mini-resort on the edge of the park, with a pool, sauna, restaurant, bar and play area for kids. Activities and walks organized.

A-B Pousada de Lençóis, R Altinha Alves 747, T/F075-334 1102, www.hoteldelencois.com.br. Plain, dark wood and white-tiled rooms with terracota roofs set in a grassy garden on the edge of the park. Good breakfast, pool and a restaurant.

B Canto das Águas, Av Senhor dos Passos, T/F075-334 1154, www.lencois.com.br. Medium-size riverside hotel with modest a/c or fan-cooled rooms, a pool and efficient service. The best rooms are in the new wing. Others can be musty.

C Aguas Claras, R P Benjamin, T075-334 1471 (100 m from the *rodoviária*). Simple pousada with plain but well-looked-after rooms; some with a fridge.

C Fazenda Guaxo, Rodoviária Ba 850, s/n, T075-334 1356. Simple and tranquil mock-ranch house hotel a little outside the town.

C O Casarão, Av 7 de Setembro 83, T075-334 1198. Modest pousada with a/c or fan-cooled rooms with a fridge. Recommended.

C-D Estalagem de Alcino, R Gen Vieira de Morais 139, T075-334 1171. An enchanting and beautifully restored period house with a range of rooms furnished with 19th-century antiques. Most have shared bathrooms. The superb breakfast is served in the little hummingbird-filled garden. Highly recommended.

C-D Pousalegre, R Boa Vista 95, T075-334 1124. Dormitories only with hot shared showers, a tasty breakfast and a good vegetarian restaurant.

D Casa da Geleia, R Gen Viveiros 187, T075-334 1151. A handful of smart chalets set in a huge garden at the entrance to the town. English spoken, good breakfast. Ze Carlos is a keen birdwatcher and an authority on the region, Lia makes excellent jams.

D Casa de Hélia, R da Muritiba, T075-334 1143. Attractive and welcoming little guesthouse. English spoken. Good facilities, legendary breakfast. Recommended.

D Tradição, R José Florêncio, T075-334 1137. Plain rooms with TV, breakfast, fridge and mosquito nets. Friendly service.

E Pousada dos Duendes, R do Pires, T/F075-334 1229. English-run pousada with rooms with shared showers and breakfast. Their tour agency (**Saturno** on R Miguel Calmon) arranges tours and treks from 1-11 days.

House rental

There are mostly very simple houses to rent throughout Lençóis. **Juanita** on R do Rosário rents rooms with access to washing and cooking facilities, US$3.50 per person. **Claudia and Isabel**, R da Baderna 95, T075-334 1229, rent houses all over the town; both for around US$4 per person without breakfast.

Camping

Alquimia, at the entrance to Lençóis, T075- 334 1213.

Camping Lumiar, near the Rosário church in the town centre, T075-334 1241, and with a popular restaurant. Friendly, recommended.

Around Lençóis *p412*

C Candombá, Capão, F332 2176 or contact through **Tatur Turismo** in Salvador, T075 450 7216, www.tatur.com.br. Good breakfast, excellent food, home-grown vegetables, run by Claude and Suzana. Claude speaks French and English and guides in the region.

D Pousada Verde, at entrance to Capão. Very good breakfast. Recommended.

E Pouso Riacho do Ou, Capão. Simple and friendly. Recommended.

E Tatu Feliz, Capão. Very basic with no breakfast, but adequate.

Feira de Santana *p412*

There are several cheap hotels in Praça da Matriz and near the *rodoviária* (quite near the centre).

A Feira Palace, Av Maria Quitéria 1572, T075 221 5011, www.feirapalacehotel.com.br. Blocky 1970s hotel in need of renovation, but the best in town; with a restaurant and pool.

B-C Acalanto, R Torres 77, T075-625 3612, www.hotelalacanto.com.br. Modern, standard, small-town hotel with around 50 modest rooms with en suites.

D Paládio, Av Getúlio Vargas 294, T075-623 8899. Far less grand than its name but well kept and less than 10 years old.

Euclides da Cunha and Monte Santo *p413*

B Do Conselheiro, Av Mcal Juarez Tavora 187, Euclides, T075-275 1814. Standard town hotel with breakfast in the price.

C Grapiuna, Praça Monsenhor Berenguer 401, Euclides, T075-275 1157. Basic rooms with a/c and cheaper options without bath. Recommended.

Canudos *p413*

E Brasil, Nova Canudos. Very simple rooms with en suites and fans. Cheaper without breakfast.

Paulo Afonso and Parque Nacional de Paulo Afonso *p413*

B Belvedere, Av Apolônio Sales 457, Paulo Afonso, T075-281 3314. Plain rooms with a/c and pool.

B Grande Hotel de Paulo Afonso, Parque Nacional Paulo Afonso, at the falls. T075-281 1914, F281 1915. A/c rooms and a pool. There are simple rooms in the adjacent guesthouse (reservations recommended).

B Palace, Av Apolônio Sales (next door to Belvedere), Paulo Afonso, T075-281 4521. The best in town with a/c rooms and a pool.

Xique-Xique and Ibotirama *p414*

B Carranca Grande, Xique-Xique, Km 1, T/F074-661 1671. Standard blocky hotel with a pool and restaurant.

Eating

Lençóis *p412*

₸₸ A Picanha da Praça, on the main praça. The best steaks in town.

₸₸ Artistas da Massa, R Miguel Calmon. Reasonable pasta and pizza, with a sprinkling of other Italian dishes.

₸₸ Raizes Arte Culinaria, R das Pedras 79. Tasty regional dishes and good service.

₸ Goody, R da Rodoviária. Very simple dishes in generous portions.

Lanchonette Zacão, Main *praça*. Natural yoghurts, juices and *bolinhos de queijo*, fried balls of dough filled with melted cheese. Recommended.

Feira de Santana *p412*

Panela de Barro, R Sen Quintino 259. Good Bahian food.

Bars and clubs

Lençóis *p412*

Bar Lençóis on the main praça. Good *cachaça* and *caipirinhas*. Recommended.

Clube Sete, R das Pedras. Little dance club open Fri and Sat nights.

Doce Barbaros, R das Pedras, 21. Lively little bar almost any night of the week.

Shopping

Lençóis *p412*

Artesanato Areias Coloridas, R das Pedras, owned by Taurino, is the best place for local sand paintings made in bottles. These are inexpensive and fascinating to see being made. For ceramic work, the most original is **Jota**, who has a workshop which can be visited. Take the steps to the left of the school near the **Pousada Lençóis**. The market on Mon and Fri mornings is recommended. There are *artesanato* stalls in the main square.

Activities and tours

Lençóis *p412*

Guides

There are guides offering their services at most pousadas (about US$20-30 per trip); most of them are very young. The following are recommended:

Edmilson (known locally as Mil), R Domingos B Souza 70, T075-334 1319. Knows the region extremely well and is very knowledgeable and reliable.

Ereas, R Jose Florencio 60, T075-334 1155. The only specialist birding guide in the town.

Índio, contact at **Pousada Diangela**, R dos Minheiros 60, Centro Histórico. Reliable, will take you off the beaten track.

Luiz Krug, contact via **Pousada de Lençois**, T075-334 1102. An independent guide specializing in geology and speleology (caving). He speaks English.

Roy Funch, T/F075-334 1305, royfunch@ ligbr.com.br. The ex-director of the Chapada Diamantina national park is an excellent guide and has written a visitor's guide. It is the best for information on the geography and trails of the Chapada. Highly recommended. He can be booked through www.ela brasil.com from the USA or UK.

Trajano, contact via **Casa da Helia**, T075-334 1143. Speaks English and is a good-humoured guide for treks to the bottom of the Cachoeira da Fumaça.

Tour operators

Cirtur, R da Baderna 41, T075-334 1133, cirtur@neth.com.br. Speak to Paulo who organizes day trips to nearby caves and to see the sunset at Morro do Pai Inácio.

Pé de Trilha Turismo Aventura, Praça 7 de Setembro, T075-334 1124. Guiding, trekking and camping equipment. Can make reservations for most of the pousadas in the Chapada Diamantina, represented in Salvador by **Tatur Turismo** (see page 383).

Transport

Lençóis *p412*

Bus Real Expresso runs to **Salvador** 3 times daily, US$17, *comercial*. Book in advance, especially at weekends and holidays. To **Feira de Santana**, returns at 0900, 2100. Buses also to **Recife**, **Ibotirama**, **Barreiras** or **Brasília**, 16 hrs, US$33 (take irregular bus to Seabra, then 2 a day to Brasília).

Paulo Afonso and Parque Nacional de Paulo Afonso *p413*

Air Flights to **Recife** and **Salvador** with **Varig**, see www.varig.com.br.

Bus Connections with **Maceió**, **Recife** and **Salvador**.

Directory

Lençóis *p412*

Banks Several banks with ATMs and *cambios*, including **Banco do Brasil** and **Bradesco**.

Feira de Santana *p412*

Banks **Banco 24 Horas**, Av Senhor dos Passos 1332. **Banco do Brasil**, Av Getúlio Vargas 897.

Recife and the northeast coast

Footprint features

Introduction

The four states that comprise this region – Sergipe, Alagoas, Pernambuco and Paraíba – are often overlooked by visitors. Most travellers whizz through, perhaps stopping for a beach break at Porto de Galinhas or Fernando de Noronha, and a few days in colourful, colonial Olinda. But those who spend time in the region, exploring its buildings, sampling the music and arts scene in Recife or getting lost in the crowds at the great festivals in the *sertão* find it one of the most interesting, diverse and least spoilt parts of Brazil.

In the first centuries of its colonial history, the region grew rich through sugar and became the commercial and intellectual centre of Brazil. Pernambuco, in particular, retains many magnificent buildings from that period, while the convents in Olinda and Igarassu are fine examples of Iberian baroque. In the late 19th century, the sugar boom subsided and poverty began to spread across the state. Yet the proud intellectual tradition continued, with notables such as Marechal Deodoro, the founder of the Brazilian republic, Gilberto Freyre, who helped forge Brazil's identity and Francisco Brennand, the surreal artist, all from the area.

The region has never been more culturally exciting than today. In the 1980s Recife saw the explosion of an artistic movement called *mangue beat* which sought to fuse the rich heritage of Pernambuco folk art and music with social activism and post-modernism. The resulting cultural fluorescence has helped to make Pernambuco Brazil's most vibrant cultural state. Artists have ateliers on every other corner in Olinda, while numerous festivals showcase the country's most innovative film making and resurrect popular culture. Carnival in Recife or Olinda is considered by many to be the best and most traditional in the country.

★ Don't miss...

1. **Olinda** Wander the streets of this World Heritage site, with its fine colonial buildings, page 436.
2. **Carnaval** Revel at the best traditional street carnival north of Salvador, page 448.
3. **Fernando de Noronha** Explore the archipelago of rugged islands set in crystal-clear waters and said by Brazilians to have the most beautiful beaches in the country, page 452.
4. **Cariri** Wonder at the haunting, mystical landscape of hollowed-out boulders strewn across a giant rocky plain in the middle of the *sertão*, page 462.
5. **Souza** Follow in the footsteps of dinosaurs at one of a handful of places in the world where their imprints have been preserved in fossilized mud, page 463.
6. **São João celebrations in Campina Grande** Let your hair down at the biggest *forró* party in Brazil, page 466.

Sergipe and Alagoas

The state of Sergipe has beautiful beaches around its capital Aracaju, as well as some interesting towns such as colonial São Cristóvão and imperial Laranjeiras, making it worth a short stop en route along the coastal highway between Salvador and Recife. Most of the population lives near the coast. The Rio São Francisco forms the border with Alagoas to the north, while the Rio Real defines the southern border with Bahia. The area of sertão *is quite small in this state compared with other parts of the northeast.*

The state of Alagoas has a pleasant capital, Maceió, with many beaches. There is also the interesting river culture of Penedo at the mouth of the important Rio São Francisco, which flows from Minas Gerais through the arid interior to meet the Atlantic Ocean. It is one of the poorest and least-developed states; most people live near the coastal strip and in the capital. » For Sleeping, Eating and other listings, see pages 426-430.

Aracaju » pp426-430.

➔ Phone code: 079. Colour map 2, C5. Population: 462,600.

Founded in 1855, the state capital stands on the south bank of the Rio Sergipe, about 10 km from its mouth and 327 km north of Salvador. In the centre is a group of linked, beautiful parks: **Praça Olímpio Campos**, in which stands the cathedral, **Praça Almirante Barroso**, with the Palácio do Governo, and praças **Fausto Cardoso** and **Camerino**. Across Avenida Rio Branco is the river. The streets are clean and parts of Laranjeiras and João Pessoa, in the centre, are reserved for pedestrians. There is a handicraft centre, the **Centro do Turismo** ⓘ *Praça Olímpio Campos, R 24 Horas, 0900- 1300, 1400-1900*, in the restored Escola Normal; the stalls are arranged by type (wood, leather etc). The commercial area is on Rua Itabaianinha and Rua João Pessoa, leading up to Rua Divina Pastora and Praça General Valadão. At Rua Itabaianinha 41 is the **Instituto Geográfico e Histórico de Sergipe** ⓘ *Mon-Fri 0800-1200, 1400-1700.*

Ins and outs

Getting there **Santa Maria airport** ⓘ *11 km from the centre, Av Sen Júlio César Leite, Atalaia, T079-243 1388*, receives flights from Maceió, Rio de Janeiro and Salvador. Interstate buses arrive at the *rodoviária*, 4 km west of the centre, linked by local buses from the adjacent terminal (buy a ticket before going on to the platform). Bus 004 'T Rod/L Batista' goes to the centre, US$0.50. Buses from Laranjeiras and São Cristóvão (45 minutes) arrive at the old bus terminal at Praça João XXIII. Look for route plates on the side of buses and at bus stations in town. » *See Transport, page 429.*

Tourist information The **Bureau de Informações Turísticas de Sergipe** ⓘ *R 24 Horas, T079-224 5168*, is very friendly, helpful, and has abundant leaflets. **Emsetur** ⓘ *Trav Baltazar Gois 86, Edif Estado de Sergipe, 11th-13th floors, T079-317 1950, www.prodase.com.br/emsetur, Mon-Fri 0700-1300*, also has information. In the centre, go to **Aracatur** ⓘ *R Maruim 100, Sala 10, T079-224 1226*, which has leaflets and maps such as *Aracaju no bolso* and *Onde?*. Helpful, English spoken.

Beaches

A 16-km road leads to the fine **Atalaia** beach (although there are oil-drilling rigs offshore). Beaches continue south down the coast along the Rodovia Presidente José Sarney. This long stretch of sand is between the mouths of the Rio Sergipe and Rio Vaza Barris; the further you go from the Sergipe, the cleaner the water. There is an even better beach, **Nova Atalaia**, on Ilha de Santa Luzia across the river. It is 30 km long and is easily reached by boat from the Hidroviária (ferry station), which is across Avenida Rio Branco from Praça General Valadão. Boats cross the river to **Barra dos Coqueiros** every 15 minutes. Services are more frequent at weekends, when it is very lively. The river at Barra dos Coqueiros is busy with fishing and pleasure craft.

Excursions from Aracaju

About 23 km northwest from Aracaju is **Laranjeiras**, a small pleasant town with a ruined church on a hill. It is reached by the São Pedro bus, from the old *rodoviária* in the centre of Aracaju, 45 minutes. It has several churches from the imperial period, when it was an important sugar producer, although the town was originally founded in 1605. The 19th-century **Capela de Sant'Aninha** has a wooden altar inlaid with gold. There are three museums: **Museu Afro-Brasileiro** ⓘ *R José do Prado Franco 70, Tue-Fri 1000-1700, Sat and Sun 1300-1700*; **Museu Sacro** ⓘ *Praça Dr H Diniz Gonçalves, Tue-Sun 1000-1700*; and the **Centro de Cultura** ⓘ *João Ribeiro*.

Some 70 km west of Aracaju is **Itabaiana**, which has a famous gold market on Saturday. There are a few hotels (D) in the centre.

São Cristóvão » *pp426-430.*

→ *Phone code: 079. Colour map 2, C5. Population: 65,000.*

This is the old state capital of Sergipe, situated 17 km southwest of Aracaju on the road to Salvador. It was founded in 1590 by Cristóvão de Barros and is the fourth oldest town in Brazil. Built on top of a hill, its colonial centre is unspoiled, with the majority of buildings painted white with green shutters and woodwork.

The **Museu de Arte Sacra e Histórico de Sergipe** ⓘ *Tue-Fri 1000-1700, Sat and Sun 1300-1700*, in the **Convento de São Francisco** contains religious and other objects from the 17th to 19th centuries. Also worth visiting is the **Museu de Sergipe** (same opening hours) in the former **Palácio do Governo**; both are on Praça de São Francisco. On the same square are the churches of **Misericórdia** (1627) and the **Orfanato Imaculada Conceição** (1646, permission to visit required from the sisters), and the **Convento de São Francisco**.

On Praça Senhor dos Passos are the churches of **Senhor dos Passos** and **Terceira Ordem do Carmo** (both built 1739), while on the Praça Getúlio Vargas (formerly Praça Matriz) is the 17th-century **Igreja Matriz Nossa Senhora da Vitória** ⓘ *all are open Tue-Fri 1000-1700, Sat-Sun 1500-1700*. Also worth seeing is the old **Assembléia Legislativa** ⓘ *R Coronel Erundino Prado*.

Estância

➔ *Phone code: 079. Population: 57,000.*

Estância is 247 km north of Salvador, on the BR-101, almost midway between the Sergipe-Bahia border and Aracaju. It is one of the oldest towns in Brazil. Its colonial buildings are decorated with Portuguese tiles (none are open to the public). Its heyday was at the turn of the 20th century and it was one of the earliest places to get electricity and telephones. Estância is also called 'Cidade Jardim' because of its parks. The month-long festival of **São João** in June is a major event.

Maceió

» *pp426-430.*

➔ *Phone code: 082. Colour map 2, C6. Population: 780,000.*

The capital of the state of Alagoas is a friendly city with a low crime rate. It is mainly a sugar port, although there are also tobacco exports and a major petrochemical plant. A lighthouse (*farol*) stands in a residential area of town, 1 km from the sea. The commercial centre stretches along the seafront to the main dock and into the hills behind.

Ins and outs

Getting there Flights arrive at **Campos dos Palmares Airport** ⓘ *20 km north of the centre, To82-322 1300*, from Aracaju, Recife, Rio de Janeiro, Salvador and São Paulo.

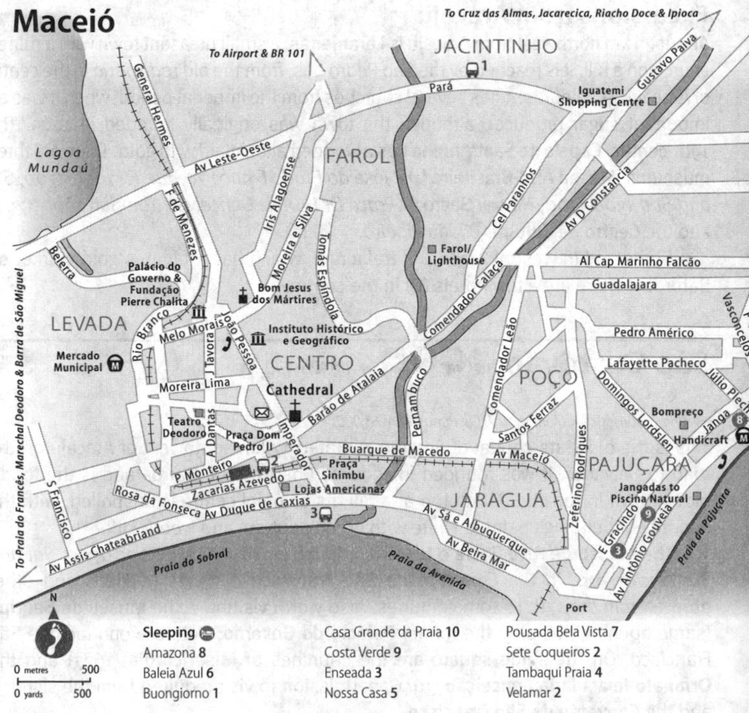

Taxis to the centre charge about US$25. Buses to the centre run from Tabuleiro dos Martins, an eight-minute walk from the airport, US$0.75. Interstate buses arrive at the *rodoviária*, which is 5 km from the centre on a hill, with good views. Luggage store is available. Take bus marked 'Ouro Preto p/centro' (taxi quicker, US$7) to Pajuçara. » *See also Transport, page 429.*

Getting around The commercial centre is easy to walk around but you need to take a bus to the main hotel and beach area of the city at Pajuçara. Frequent buses, confusingly marked, serve all parts of the city (see Transport, page 429 for details). Bus stops are not marked; it is best to ask people who look as though they are waiting. The *ferroviária* is in the centre, Rua Barão de Anádia 121. Train services are suburban.

Tourist information Ematur ⓘ *Av da Paz 2014, Centro, T082-221 9465, F221 8987*, also at the airport and *rodoviária* is helpful, has good maps and leaflets. The municipal tourist authority is **Emturma** ⓘ *R Saldanha da Gama 71, Farol, T082-223 4016*. There is an information post on Pajuçara beach, opposite **Hotel Solara**.

Sights

Two of the city's old buildings, the **Palácio do Governo**, which also houses **Fundação Pierre Chalita** (Alagoan painting and religious art) and the church of **Bom Jesus dos Mártires** (built 1870, covered in tiles) are particularly interesting. Both are on Praça dos Martírios (or Floriano Peixoto). The **cathedral**, Nossa Senhora dos Prazeres (1840) is on Praça Dom Pedro II.

The **Instituto Histórico e Geográfico** ⓘ *R João Pessoa 382, T082-223 7797*, has a good small collection of indigenous and Afro-Brazilian artefacts. **Lagoa do Mundaú**, a lagoon, whose entrance is 2 km south at **Pontal da Barra**, limits the city to the south and west. Excellent shrimp and fish are sold at its small restaurants and handicraft stalls and it's a pleasant place for a drink at sundown. Boats make excursions in the lagoon's channels (T082-231 7334).

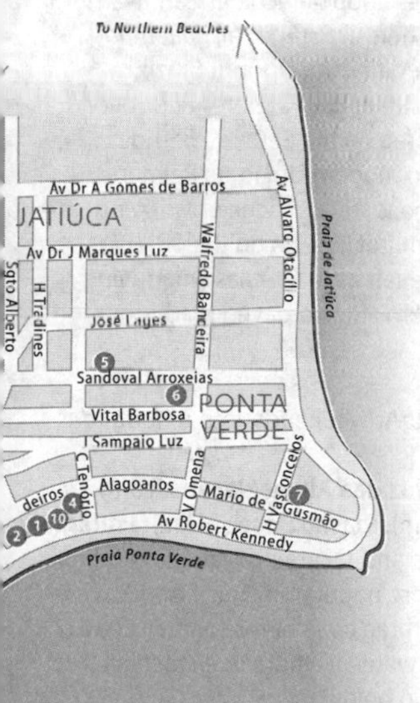

Buses
Rodoviária 1
To Marechal Deodoro & Praia do Francês 2
To Riacho Doce 3

Beaches

Beaches fronting the old city, between the Salgema terminal and the modern port area (Trapiche, Sobral), are too polluted for swimming. Beyond the city's main dock, the beachfront districts begin; within the city, the beaches are more exclusive the further from the centre you go. The first, going north, is **Pajuçara** where there is a nightly craft market. At weekends there are wandering musicians and entertainers and patrols by the cavalry on magnificent Manga Larga Marchador horses. There are periodic *candomblé* and *axé* nights and rituals to the goddess *Lemanjá*. There is a natural swimming pool 2 km off Pajuçara beach (**Piscina Natural de Pajuçara**), at low tide you can stand on the sand and rock reef (beware of sunburn). You must check the tides, there is no point going at high tide. *Jangadas* cost US$5 per person per day (or about US$20 to have a *jangada* to yourself). On Sunday or

Zumbi and Palmares

From the first days of slavery in Brazil, *fujões* (runaways) would disappear into the interior and set up villages or *mocambos*. Between the 1630s and the end of 17th century these *mocambos* prospered (especially during times of crisis such as the Dutch invasion in 1630) and together formed *quilombos*, free territories which accepted not only runaway slaves but freed ones and whites who had fallen out with the re-established Portuguese colony. The most famous of these *quilombos*, established in what is now the state of Alagoas, was called Palmares after the large number of palm trees in the area. It consisted of 30,000 people living in several *mocambos* in an area of 17,000 square miles (44,000 sq km). According to reports from Bartholomeus Lintz, the leader of a Dutch expedition in 1640, the largest settlement in Palmares had 220 buildings, a church, four smithies and a meeting house.

The political and social structures were very similar to those found in West Africa, and although Catholicism was practised, so was polyandry, mainly due to the lack of women in the republic. The leader of Palmares was Ganga-Zumba who was revered like a king, but it appears he was killed by his followers in 1680 after making some concessions to the Portuguese two years earlier. He was succeeded by the republic's brave military commander, Zumbi, who is said to have been an African king.

The existence of Palmares was a constant thorn in the side of Portuguese domination of Brazil and dozens of attempts were made to destroy it. However, Zumbi managed to defend the republic until it was finally smashed in 1695 by the Portuguese with *bandeirante* help. Zumbi was killed and his decapitated head was put on display in Recife to discourage other potential runaways and prove that he was not immortal as his followers believed. He is still remembered every year on 20 November, Brazil's Black Consciousness Day. He has also become a popular icon at Carnaval time. There are still small *quilombo* communities throughout Brazil.

The site of the Palmares Republic is situated on the Serra da Barriga, close to modern União do Palmares in Alagoas state, reached by driving north out of Maceió on the BR-101, turning left after Messias and driving for 40 km along a paved road.

local holidays in the high season it is overcrowded. At weekends lots of *jangadas* anchor at the reef, selling food and drink.

The next beach is **Ponta Verde**, then **Jatiúca**, **Cruz das Almas**, **Jacarecica** (9 km from the centre), **Guaxuma** (12 km), **Garça Torta** (14 km), **Riacho Doce** (16 km), **Pratagi** (17 km) and **Ipioca** (23 km). Jatiúca, Cruz das Almas and Jacarecica are all good for surfing. The beaches are some of the finest and most popular in Brazil and have a protecting coral reef about 1 km out. Bathing is best three days before and after a full or new moon, because tides are higher and the water is more spectacular. For beaches beyond the city, see Excursions from Maceió below.

Excursions from Maceió » *pp426-430.*

Marechal Deodoro

About 22 km south, by bus past Praia do Francês, is the attractive colonial town and former capital of Alagoas, Marechal Deodoro, which overlooks the Lagoa Manguaba.

The 17th-century **Convento de São Francisco**, Praça João XXIII, has a fine church (Santa Maria Magdalena) with a superb baroque wooden altarpiece, which has been badly damaged by termites. You can climb the church's tower for views. Adjoining it is the **Museu de Arte Sacra** ⓘ *Mon-Fri, 0900-1300, US$0.30, guided tours available, payment at your discretion*. Also open to visitors is the **Igreja Matriz de Nossa Senhora da Conceição** (1783).

The town is the birthplace of Marechal Deodoro da Fonseca, founder of the Republic. The modest **house** ⓘ *R Marechal Deodoro, Mon-Sat 0800- 1700, Sun 0800-1200, free*, where he was born is close to the waterfront. The **Restaurant São Roque** is simple but good and local lacework can be bought.

On a day's excursion, it is easy to visit the town, then spend some time at beautiful **Praia do Francês**. The northern half of the beach is protected by a reef, the southern half is open to the surf. Along the beach there are many *barracas* and bars selling drinks and seafood; try *agulhas fritas*.

Further out from Maceió is the beach of **Barra de São Miguel**, entirely protected by the reef. It gets crowded at weekends. You can make excursions to other beaches. Several good, cheap *barracas* serve food and drink (**da Amizade** is recommended) and there are some decent places to stay. Carnival here has a good reputation.

Penedo » pp426-430.

→ *Phone code: 082. Colour map 2, C5. Population: 57,000.*

A more interesting crossing into Alagoas can be made by frequent ferry crossings from **Neópolis** in Sergipe, to Penedo some 35 km from the mouth of the Rio São Francisco.

Penedo is a charming town, with a pleasant waterfront park, **Praça 12 de Abril**, with stone walkways and walls. Originally the site of the Dutch Fort Maurits (built 1637, razed to the ground by the Portuguese), the colonial town stands on a promontory above the river. Among the colonial buildings, modern structures such as the **Associação Comercial** and **Hotel São Francisco**, both on Avenida Floriano Peixoto, **do not sit easily**.

Ins and outs

The *rodoviária* is on Avenida Duque de Caxias, behind Bompreço and has connections with Salvador, Aracaju and Mació. There's a **tourist office** ⓘ *Casa da Aposentadoria, Praça Barão de Penedo, T082-551 2827, ext 23*. » *See Transport, page 430.*

Sights

On Praça Barão de Penedo is the neoclassical Igreja Matriz (closed to visitors) and the 18th-century Casa da Aposentadoria (1782). East and a little below this square is the Praça Rui Barbosa, on which are situated the **Convento de São Francisco** (1783 and later) and the church of **Santa Maria dos Anjos** ⓘ *free guided tours at 1660*. As you enter, the altar on the right depicts God's eyes on the world, surrounded by the three races (indigenous, black and white). The church has fine trompe l'oeil ceilings (1784). The convent is still in use. The church of **Rosário dos Pretos** ⓘ *Praça Marechal Deodoro* (1775-1816), is open to visitors as are **Nossa Senhora da Corrente** ⓘ *Praça 12 de Abril* (1764), and **São Gonçalo Garcia** ⓘ *Av Floriano Peixoto, Mon Fri 0800-1200, 1400- 1700* (1758-70). On the same street is the pink **Teatro 7 de Setembro** ⓘ *Av Floriano Peixoto 81, Mon-Fri 0800-1200, 1400-1730, Sat morning only*, dating from 1884. Between it and the old covered market are fruit and vegetable stalls.

The **Casa de Penedo** ⓘ *R João Pessoa 126, signs point the way up the hill from Floriano Peixoto, T082-551 2516, Tue-Sun 0800-1800*, displays photographs and books on, or by, local figures.

Very few of the long two-masted sailing vessels that used to cruise on the river can be seen now, although there are plenty of smaller craft. **Beaches** in Sergipe (for example, Arambipe) or Alagoas (for example, Peba) can be reached by boat; the latter also by road. Either side of the river mouth are turtle nesting grounds which are protected. For information contact the **Fundação Pró-Tamar** ⓘ *Reserva Biológica de Santa Isabel, CEP 49190-000, Pirambu, SE, T079-276 1201, F276 1217.*

North of Maceió » pp426-430.

There are many interesting stopping points along the coast between Maceió and Recife. At **Paripueira,** a 40-minute bus ride from the *rodoviária* in Maceió, the beach is busy only during high season. As at Pajuçara (see page 423), low tide leaves lots of natural swimming pools.

Barra de Santo Antônio

Some 45 km north is this busy fishing village, with a palm-fringed beach on a narrow peninsula, a canoe ride away. The beaches nearby are beautiful: to the south, near the village of Santa Luzia, are **Tabuba** and **Sonho Verde**. To the north is Carro Quebrado, from which you can take a buggy to **Pedra do Cebola**, or further to **Praia do Morro**, just before the mouth of the Rio Camaragibe.

Beyond Barra do Camaragibe, a coastal road, unpaved in parts, runs to the Pernambuco border and **São José da Coroa Grande**. The main highway, BR-101, heads inland from Maceió before crossing the state border to Palmares.

Sleeping

Aracaju *p420, map p420*
A Apreipê, R São Cristóvão 418, T079-211 1880. Centrally located with restaurant. Rooms include a/c, phone and fridge.
A Grande, R Itabaianinha 371, T/F079-211 1383. Centrally located with restaurant. A/c, TV and fridge in the rooms.
A Palace de Aracaju, Praça Gen Valadão, T079-224 5000. Centrally located 3-star hotel with a/c, TV and fridge in the rooms. There's a pool, restaurant and parking facilities.
A Serigy, R Santo Amaro 269, T079-211 1088. A comfortable hotel with the same management and facilities as the Aperipê.
B Brasília, R Laranjeiras 580, T079-224 8022. Modest hotel but good value and with a good breakfast. Recommended.
B Oásis, R São Cristóvão 466, T079-224 2125. Good breakfast, hot water, fair, a bit tatty.
C Amado, R Laranjeiras 532. A/c rooms, cheaper with a fan and laundry facilities.
D Turista, R Divina Pastora 411. Noisy, mosquitoes, no hot water or breakfast but at least it's friendly.

Laranjeiras *p421*
B Pousada Vale dos Outeiros, Av José do Prado Franco 124, Laranjeiras, T079-281 1027. One of several hotels, this one with 10 a/c rooms and a restaurant is recommended.

São Cristóvão *p421*
There are no hotels, but families rent rooms near the *rodoviária* at the bottom of the hill.

Estância *p422*
There are a number of cheap, very simple hotels around the Praça Barão do Rio Branco.
C Jardim, Praça Joaquim Galazans 202, T079-522 1638. A modern hotel with a/c. They serve a huge buffet breakfast. Recommended.
C Turismo Estanciano, Praça Barão do Rio Branco 176, T079-522 1404. A modest and very standard town hotel with fan and a/c rooms, some with en suites.
D Magnus, T079-522 2453. Breakfast. Rooms include TV and fridge.
D Praia Abais, T079-751 0020. Breakfast, TV, pool.
D Sawana, T079-985 1570. Has a restaurant.

Maceió *p422, map p422*
There are many hotels on Praia Pajuçara, mostly along Av Dr Antônio Gouveia and R Jangadeiros Alagoanos. It can be hard to find a room during the Dec-Mar holiday season, when prices go up.

L Matsubara, on Cruz das Almas beach, Av Brig Eduardo Gomes 1551, T082-235 3000, www.matsubarahotel.com. Resort hotel with a large pool, tennis courts and organized games. Recommended.
L Tambaqui Praia, R Eng Mário de Gusmão 176, Ponta Verde beach, T082-231 0202. Rooms with a/c, TV, phone and restaurant.
AL Enseada, Av A Gouveia 171, T082-231 4726, www.enseada.com.br. 1980s business hotel on the waterfront with a pool and restaurant. Recommended.
AL Sete Coqueiros, Av A Gouveia 1335, T082-231 8583, www.setecoqueiros.com.br. 3-star hotel with a/c, rooms with TVs and a phone. There is a pool and a popular restaurant.
A Velamar, Av A Gouveia 1359 (next door to the Coqueiros), T082-327 5488, www.hotelvelamar.com.br. A/c rooms with a TV, fridge and safe in rooms.
B Buongiorno, Av A Gouveia 1437, T082-231 7577, F231 2168. Rooms have a/c and fridge. The English-speaking owner is very helpful.
C Amazona, Av A Gouveia 1095. Modest and ordinary town hotel with a great breakfast.
C Baleia Azul, Av Sandoval Arroxeias 822, Ponta Verde beach, T082-327 4040, www.hotelbaleiaazul.com.br. Plain rooms with a/c, fridge and TV.
C Casa Grande da Praia, Av A Gouveia 1528, T082-231 3332. A/c and TV available but cheaper without. Recommended.
C Costa Verde, Av A Gouveia 429, T082-231 4745. A good family atmosphere here. Rooms have bath and fan. English, German spoken. The rooms on 1st floor are the best.
C Hospedaria de Turismo Costa Azul, Av João Davino and Manoel Gonçalves Filho 280 (not close to town centre), T082-231 6281. Rooms with a shower and fan and discounts for stays over a week. English spoken.
C Pousada Bela Vista, Av Eng Mário de Gusmão 1260, Ponta Verde beach, T082-231 8337. Well situated, excellent breakfast, a/c, TV. Recommended.
C Pousada Cavalo Marinho, R da Praia 55, Riacho Doce (15 km from town centre), facing the sea, T/F082-235 1247. Friendly pousada popular with 20-something surfers with bike canoes and body-board rental. Rooms have hot showers. German and English spoken, tropical breakfasts, Swiss owner. Very highly recommended. There are some bars and restaurants nearby.
C Pousada Shangri-La, Antônio de Mendonça 1089, T082-231 3773. Simple hotel with friendly staff, a/c rooms with optional safes.
D Mandacaru, Almte Maranenhas 85, 2 corners from the beach. Safe with simple rooms with fans, but good value.
D Pousada Saveiro, No 805. Clean, simple, good value. Rooms available with a/c, bath and TV, but it's cheaper without a/c.
D Sol de Verão, R Eng Mário do Gusmão 153, Ponta Verde beach. Small rooms without baths and some larger and more expensive a/c options with en suites.
E Nossa Casa, R Pref Abdon Arroxelas 327, Ponta Verde, T082-231 2246. IYHA hostel. Reservations required Dec-Feb, Jul and Aug.
E Pajuçara, R Quintino Bocaiúva 63, Pajuçara, T082-2310631. Youth hostel. Reservations required Dec-Feb, Jul and Aug
E Stella Maris, Av Des Valente de Lima 209, Mangabeiras, T082-325 2217. Reservations required Dec-Feb, Jul and Aug.

Camping

Camping Clube do Brasil site on Jacarecica beach, T082-235 3600. A 15-min taxi ride from the town centre.
Camping Pajuçara, Largo da Vitória 211, T082-231 7561. Clean, safe, food for sale. Recommended.

Marechal Deodoro *p424*

B Pousada Bougainville e Restaurant Chez Patrick, R Sargaço 3 T082-260 1251. A very nice pousada with a/c, rooms with TVs, a pool, seafood and international cooking.
C O Pescador, 40 m from Praia do Francês, T082-231 6959. Restaurant, beach huts, chalets with fridge, TV.

Barra de São Miguel

A Village Barra Hotel, R Sen Arnon de Mello, T082-3272 1000, www.villagebarrahotel.com.br. Pool, restaurant and runs excursions.
C Pousada da Barra, Av Oceanica 249, Praia Sta Irene, T022-2771 3109, www.pousadadabarra-rj.com.br, is also good.

Penedo *p425*

A São Francisco, Av Floriano Peixoto, T082-551 2273. A/c provided except in standard

rooms. TV and fridge also available. Recommended except for poor restaurant.
B **Pousada Colonial**, Praça 12 de Abril 21, T082-551 2355, F5513099. A spacious pousada with a good cheap restaurant. The front rooms have a view of Rio São Francisco, the *luxo* rooms and suites have phone, TV and fridge. The suites have a/c.
D **Turista**, R Siqueira Campos 143, T082-551 2237. Simple rooms with a bath, fan and hot water. Recommended.

Barra de Santo Antônio *p426*
This is a tiny place with no visible addresses. Locals will point you to pousadas but it is a struggle to get lost.
D **São Geraldo**. Very simple but very clean, and with a restaurant.
D-E **Pousada Buongiorno**, T082-231 7577 (in Maceió). 6 modest rooms to rent in a farmhouse, bathrooms but no electricity, many fruit trees.

Eating

Aracaju *p420, map p420*
¥¥¥ **O Miguel**, Av António Alves 340, Atalaia Velha, T079-2431444. Much the best restaurant in the city, serving regional food, which is heavy on meat and includes *carne de sol* – a type of jerky cooked into a stew.
¥¥ **Cacique Chá**, in the cathedral square. Good bar and restaurant. Lively at weekends.
¥¥ **Rancho Gaúcho**, Praça Olímpio Campos 692. Reasonable, very friendly *churrascaria*.
¥¥-¥ **Cantinha da Bahia**, Av Oceânica 180. Recommended for fresh crab and seafood.
¥ **Bar e Lanchonete Dom Qui Chopp**, opposite Telemar on R Laranjeiras. Very popular snack bar serving beer and drinks.
¥ **Gonzaga**, R Santo Amaro 181. Lunch only, good value, very popular, excellent traditional dishes.

São Cristóvão *p421*
¥ **Senzala do Preto Velho**, R Messias Prado 84. Recommended northeastern specialities.

Maceió *p422, map p422*
There are many good bars and restaurants in Pajuçara and Av Antônio Gouveia. For 5 km from the beginning of Pajuçara to Cruz das Almas in the north, the beaches are lined with *barracas* (thatched bars) providing music, snacks and meals until 2400 (later at weekends). Vendors on the beach sell beer and food during the day; clean and safe. There are many other bars and *barracas* at Ponto da Barra, on the lagoon side of the city. Local specialities include oysters, *pitu*, a crayfish (now scarce), and *sururu*, a type of cockle. The local ice cream, **Shups**, is recommended.
¥¥¥ **Ao Lagostão**, Av Duque de Caxias 1348. Seafood and a fixed-price menu.
¥ **Nativa**, Osvaldo Sarmento 56. Similar to O Natural but with good views.
¥ **O Natural**, R Libertadora Alagoana and R da Praia) 112. Reasonable vegetarian restaurant with a choice of hot and cold dishes.
¥ **Pizzeria Sorrisa**, Av Alagoana and J Pessoa Imperador. Very cheap and popular with good pizzas and Italian food.

Barra de Santo Antônio *p426*
¥¥ **Estrela Azul**. Good, popular with tourists.
¥ **Peixada da Rita**, try prawns with coconut sauce. Recommended for local seafood.

Bars and clubs

Aracaju *p420, map p420*
Augustu's, T079-243 2274. Nightclub, Tue-Sun.
Espaço Ernes, Av Tancredo Neves 225, T079-231 9138. Venue for live shows.
Gonzagao, Av Heraclito Rollemberg. Live shows.

Maceió *p422, map p422*
The bars here are relaxed and varied and there are nightclubs to suit most tastes.
Bar Chapéu de Couro, José Carneiro 338, Ponto da Barra. A popular music bar for young people
Calabar, Pajuçara. For *forró* and *lambada*.
Fellini, Ponta Verde. Good blues and jazz.
Ipaneminha, Pajuçara. Another popular *barraca* playing Brazilian pop.

Entertainment

Aracaju *p420, map p420*
Cinema 10-screen **Cinemark**, in Shopping Jardins.

Maceió *p422, map p 422*
Cinema Arte 1 and 2, Pajuçara and Iguatemi shopping centres. **Cinema São Luiz**, R do Comércio, in the centre.

Theatre Teatro Deodoro, Praça Mcal Deodoro, in the centre.

Festivals and events

Aracaju *p420, map p420*
1 Jan Bom de Jesus dos Navegantes, procession on the river.
1st weekend in Jan Santos Reis (Three Kings).
Jun Festas Juninas.
8 Dec Both Catholic (Nossa Senhora da Conceição) and Umbanda (*Iemenjá*) religious festivals.

Excursions from Aracaju *p421*
Jan The main festival in Laranjeiras is São Benedito in the first week of the month.

São Cristóvão *p421*
Mar Senhor dos Passos, held 15 days after Carnaval.
8 Sep Nossa Senhora de Vitória, the patron saint's day.
Oct/Nov Festival de Arte (dates varies).

Estância *p422*
Jun The month-long festival of São Joao is a major event.

Maceió *p422, map p422*
27 Aug Nossa Senhora dos Prazeres.
16 Sep Freedom of Alagoas.
8 Dec Nossa Senhora da Conceição.
15 Dec Maceiofest, a great street party with *trios elêctricos*.
24 Dec Christmas Eve.
31 Dec New Year's Eve, half-day.

Shopping

Aracaju *p420, map p420*
The *artesanato* is interesting: pottery figures and lace particularly. A fair is held in Praça Tobias Barreto every Sun afternoon. The municipal market is a block north of the *hidroviária*.

Penedo *p425*
Daily market on streets off **Av Floriano Peixoto**, good hammocks. Ceramics for sale outside **Bompreço** supermarket, on Av Duque de Caxias.

Activities and tours

Maceió *p422, map p422*
Aeroturismo, R Barão de Penedo 61, T082-326 2020, American Express representative.

Transport

Aracaju *p420, map p420*
Air There are regular flights to **Maceió**, **Rio de Janeiro** and **Salvador**.

Bus Buses run from the old bus station at Praça João XXIII to **Laranjeiras** and **São Cristóvão** (45 mins, US$1.25). Long-distance buses run from the *rodoviária*, 4 km from the centre. Buses to the *rodoviária* run from Praça João XXIII, the terminal near the Hidroviária and from Capela at the top of Praça Olímpio Campos. To **Salvador**, 6-7 hrs, 11 a day with **Bonfim**, US$11, executive service at 1215, US$14, saves 1 hr. To **Maceió**, US$9 with Bonfim. Many coastal destinations served; also **Vitória** (US$26.50), **Rio** (US$51), **São Paulo**, **Belo Horizonte** (US$35). To **Estância**, US$2, 1½ hrs. To **Recife**, 7 hrs, US$12-14, 1200 and 2400.

São Cristóvão *p421*
Bus São Pedro buses run to the old *rodoviária* in the centre of **Aracaju** (45 mins, US$1.25).

Train A tourist train runs between **Aracaju** and São Cristóvão each Sat and Sun, 0900, 3½ hrs, T079-211 3003 to check it is running – a minimum of 15 passengers is needed.

Estância *p422*
Bus Many buses stop at the *rodoviária*, on the main road. To **Salvador** 4 hrs, US$12-14.

Maceió *p422, map p422*
See also Ins and outs, page 422.
Air Flights to **Aracaju**, **Recife**, **Rio de Janeiro**, **Salvador** and **São Paulo**. Buses to the airport from near **Hotel Beiriz**, R João Pessoa 290 or in front of the *ferroviária*, signed 'Rio Largo'; alight at Tabuleiro dos Martins, then 7-8 mins' walk to the airport, bus fare US$0.75. Taxi about US$25.

Bus Local: the 'Ponte Verde/Jacintinho' bus runs via Pajuçara from the centre to the *rodoviária*, also take 'Circular' bus (25 mins Pajuçara to *rodoviária*). Taxis from town go to all the northern beaches (for example 30 mins to Riacho Doce), but buses run as far as Ipioca. The Jangadeiras bus marked 'Jacarecica-Center, via Praias' runs past all the beaches as far as **Jacarecica**. From there you can change to 'Riacho Doce-Trapiche', 'Ipioca' or 'Mirante' buses for Riacho Doce and Ipioca. These last 3 can also be caught in the centre on the seafront avenue below the Praça Sinimbu (US$0.50 to Riacho Doce). To return take any of these options, or take a bus marked 'Shopping Center' and change there for 'Jardim Vaticana' bus, which goes through Pajuçara.

Bus and kombi: to **Marechal Deodoro, Praia do Francês** and **Barra de São Miguel** leave from R Barão de Anádia, outside the *ferroviária*, opposite **Lojas Americanas**: bus US$0.75, kombi US$1 to Marechal Deodoro, 30 mins, calling at Praia do Francês in each direction. Last bus back from Praia do Francês to Maceió at 1800.

Long distance Bus to **Recife**, 10 a day, 3½ hrs express (more scenic coastal route, 5), US$9. To **Aracaju**, US$9, 5 hrs (potholed road). To **Salvador**, 10 hrs, 4 a day, US$20 (*rápido* costs more).

Car hire Localiza, Av Alvaro Otacilio 6445, Jatiuca, T082-325 6565/6553. **Rotacar**, R Quintino Bocauiva 123, Pajucara, T082-327 3388.

Penedo *p425*

Bus Daily bus to **Salvador**, 451 km (US$12-14, 6 hrs, at 0600, book in advance), at same time for **Aracaju** (US$6); buses south are more frequent from **Neópolis**, 6 a day (0630-1800) to **Aracaju**, 2 hrs, US$3.60. **Maceió**, 115 km, 5 buses a day in either direction, US$5.40-6.60, 3-4 hrs.

Ferry Frequent launches for foot passengers and bicycles across the river to **Neópolis**, 25 mins, US$0.50. The dock in Penedo is on Av Duque de Caxias, below Bompreço. The ferry makes 3 stops in Neópolis, the 2nd is closest to the *rodoviária* (which is near the **Clube Vila Nova**, opposite the Texaco station). There is also a half-hourly car ferry (US$3, take care when driving on and off).

Directory

Aracaju *p420, map p420*

Banks Visa ATMs at Shopping centres, **Banco do Brasil**, Praça Gen Valadão and **Bradesco** in the city centre. MasterCard ATMs at Banco 24 hrs, Av Francisco Porto and Av Geraldo Sobral, in the city centre close to the Shell gas station. **Embassies and consulates** France, T079-224 8610. **Italy**, T079-243 3814. **Portugal**, T079-222 6662. **Medical services** Clinica São Domingos Savio, T079-211 1344, casualty department. **São Lucas**, R Col Stanley Silveira 33, São José, T079-211 1738. **Dental emergencies**: Pronto Odonto, Av Barão de Maruim, T079-222 2927. **Post office** Laranjeiras and Itabaianinha. **Telephone** Laranjeiras 296, national and international calls until 2200, also at *rodoviária*.

Maceió *p422, map p422*

Banks Open 1000-1500. Good rates at Banespa. Cash against MasterCard at Banorte, R de Comércio, 306, Centro. **Embassies and consulates** France, T082-235 2830. **Portugal**, T082-336 4564. **Spain**, T082-241 2516. **Laundry** Lave-Sim, R Jangadas Alagoanas 962, Pajuçara. **Washouse**, R Jangadas Alagoanas 698, Pajuçara. **Medical services** Unimed, Av Antonio Brandao 395, Farol, T082-221 1177, used to be São Sebastião hospital. **Pediatria 24 horas**, R Durval Guimaraes 519, Ponta Verde, T082-231 7742/7702. **Dentist**: Pronto Socorro Odontologico de Maceio, Av Pio XV11, Jatiuca, T082-325 7534. **Post office** R João Pessoa 57, Centro, 0700-2200. **Telephones** R do Comércio 508, almost opposite **Bandepe**. There is a small post office on Pajuçara beach, opposite the **Othon** hotel. Also at the *rodoviária*.

Penedo *p425*

Banks Open 0830-1300. **Banco do Nordeste do Brasil**, on Av Floriano Peixoto. **Banco do Brasil** and **Bradesco** on Av Duque de Caxias, opposite Bompreço supermarket. **Restaurant e Bar Lulu**, Praça 12 de Abril, will change cash if conditions suit the owner, fair rates. **Post office** Av Floriano Peixoto, opposite **Hotel Imperial**. **Telephone** On Barão de Penedo.

Pernambuco

Once the main producer of the world's sugar, today the state of Pernambuco offers a variety of attractions from beaches, traditional culture, colonial cities and museums. Recife, the state capital, is the main industrial and commercial centre with a very lively cultural scene and extensive urban beaches, while Olinda offers colonial elegance and a number of magnificent churches. Towns such as Caruarú and Nova Jerusalem, in the sertão, *host very lively festivals and have some of the country's strongest artisan traditions working with clay, straw and leather handicrafts.*

Pernambuco is saturated with music. In the 1970s, musician Nana Vasconcelos took the traditional beats of forró, ciranda *and* maracatú *to New York, Miles Davis and beyond. In the 1980s and 1990s the mangue beat movement fused them with rock, electronica and trance. Many of Brazil's most famous contemporary avant-garde musicians are from Pernambuco, and Recife is considered Brazil's musical capital. Carnaval in the city of Recife and nearby Olinda is among the best in the country. Nana Vasconcelos opens the festival leading a drum orchestra that dwarfs those in Bahia, and the* maracatú *prepares the way for three days of African-Brazilian cultural processions and relentless partying.* » *For Sleeping, Eating and other listings, see pages 443-452*

Recife and around » *pp443-452.*

→ *Phone code: 081. Colour map 2, B6. Population: 1.2 million.*

Recife is one of the most attractive of Brazil's larger cities. Although from afar it looks as blighted by skyscrapers as Rio or Belo Horizonte, many fine colonial buildings from the sugar boom huddle in the shadows, watching over little shady squares or sitting on the edge of the filigree of canals and waterways, which divide up the city. The colonial heart is Recife Antigo; a no-go area like Rio's Lapa until a decade ago, but now the centre of the city's booming music and alternative culture scene. To the south of the centre are a string of urban beach suburbs – Pina, Boa Viagem and Piedade – which although swum by bull sharks are among the cleanest urban beaches in the country. The city prides itself on good food and unique fashion and has many fine restaurants and boutiques. The latter are concentrated in the shopping malls. Although they retain separate names, Recife and Olinda have long ceased to be two cities. Olinda is now Recife's colonial suburb.

Ins and outs

Getting there International and domestic flights arrive at **Gilberto Freyre Airport**, Guararapes, 12 km from the city centre, near the hotel district of Boa Viagem (airport taxis US$5 to the seafront) and 12 km from the city. Bus No 52 runs to the centre, US$0.40. The airport is modern and spacious, with a tourist office, banks, shops, post office and car rental and tour agencies. Long-distance buses arrive at the **Terminal Integrado dos Passageiros**, or TIP (pronounced 'chippy'), 12 km outside the city near the Oficina Brennand cultural museum at São Lourenço da Mata, T081-3452 1999. To get to the centre from the *rodoviária*, take the Metrô to the Central station, 30 minutes. If going to Boa Viagem, get off the Metrô at Central station (Joanna Bezerra station is unsafe) and take a bus or taxi (US$8) from there. » *See Transport, page 450.*

Getting around City **buses** cost US$0.30-0.60; they are clearly marked and run frequently until about 2230. Many central bus stops have boards showing routes. On buses, especially at night, look out for landmarks as street names are hard to see. Commuter services, known as the **Metrô** but not underground, leave from the central station; they have been extended to serve the *rodoviária* (frequent trains, 0500-2300, US$0.40 single). Integrated bus-metro routes and tickets (US$1) are explained in a leaflet issued by **CBTU Metrorec**, T081-3251 5256. Trolleybuses run in the city centre. Taxis are plentiful; fares double on Sunday, after 2100 and during holidays.

Recife orientation

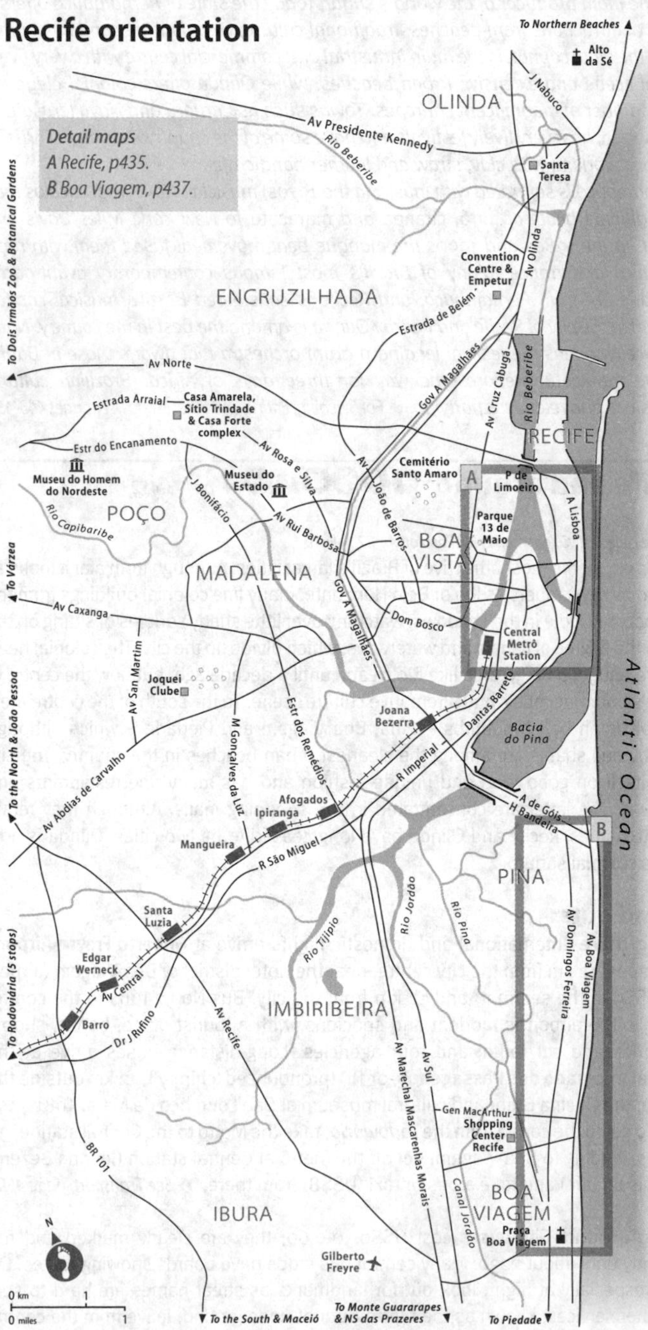

Rock in Recife

Forget Rio. Ignore São Paulo. Recife is the capital of modern Brazilian music. You'll find no re-sampled old-hat bossa nova or cheesy funk here, and no identikit Salvador carnival bands fronted by a woman in a tiny skirt. Instead, bursting from the city's various grungy streetside bars and pouring in from the rocky desert of the state's interior, is a seemingly endless diversity of bands and artists fusing the old with the new: octogenarian mouth organists playing psychedelic forró, agonized students thrashing out *maracatú* fired-glum rock, hip hopsters fusing dub with *embolada* desert poetry…

Every day there is a new name on everyone's lips and a new band tipped for stardom on the Brazilian or international stage. Some have already made it there, including Naná Vasconcelos (see page 434), Otto and DJ Dolores. But it wasn't always this way. Recife's musical revolution began in the 1980s with Chico Science and his band Nação Zumbi who invented a movement called mangue beat – a kind of Bauhaus of rock that embraced all styles in an angry shout against the conservatism and conformity that had dominated music here until then. Nação Zumbi still play regularly in Recife, sadly without Chico who died in a car accident in the 1990s.

Be sure to catch some live music while you're in Recife and check out www.manguebeat.com.br for a podcast of the latest offerings, or www.reciferock.com.br for the latest gigs. For venues see page 447.

Orientation The city centre consists of three sections: Recife proper, Santo Antônio and São José, and Boa Vista and Santo Amaro. The first two are on islands formed by the rivers Capibaribe, Beberibe and Pina, while the third is made into an island by the Canal Tacaruna, which separates it from the mainland. The centre is always very busy by day; the crowds and the narrow streets, especially in the Santo Antônio district, can make it a confusing city to walk around. But this adds to its charm. This is one of the few cities in Brazil where it is possible to get lost and chance upon a shady little square or imposing colonial church or mansion. Recife has the main dock area, with commercial buildings associated with it. South of the centre is the residential and beach district of Boa Viagem, reached by bridge across the Bacia do Pina. Olinda, the old capital, is only 7 km to the north (see page 436). Although the streets are generally too full to present danger it is wise to be vigilant where the streets are quiet. Always take a cab after dark if you are walking alone or in a pair.

Tourist information The main office for **Empetur** ⓘ *Centro de Convenções, Complexo Rodoviário de Salgadinho, T081-3427 8000, www.empetur.com.br* is between Recife and Olinda. There are other branches at the airport (T081-3224 2361, open 24 hours), they cannot book hotels, but are very helpful and offer leaflets and decent maps, English spoken, and in Boa Viagem (T081-3463 3621). Also try the **Secretaria de Turismo do Recife** ⓘ *T081-3224 7198*.

Safety Opportunistic theft is unfortunately common in the streets of Recife and Olinda (especially on the streets up to Alto da Sé). Keep hold of bags and cameras, and do not wear a watch. Prostitution is reportedly common in Boa Viagem, so choose nightclubs with care. Tourist Police, T081-3326 9603/T081-3464 4088.

Naná Vasconcelos

Brazilian music without Recife's master percussionist Naná Vasconcelos would be like jazz without Charles Mingus. Bossa Nova had been introduced into the USA by Stan Getz. But it was Naná and Paranense Airto Moreira who placed Brazilian percussion in the upper echelons of the serious jazz world. Naná was introduced to the US jazz scene by Miles Davis who went to one of the percussionist's concerts in the 1970s. And during a 25 year sojourn in New York he added his trademark berimbau and percussion to scores of records by artists like the CODONA trio (which he led with Don Cherry and Colin Walcott), Jan Garbarek, Pat Metheny, Gato Barbieri and numerous others. His most remarkable work though is purely Brazilian. Together with Egberto Gismonti and on albums like *Danca das Cabecas* (ECM), he created a new musical genre which fused jazz, classical and Brazilian styles. And his *Fragmentos* (Nucleo Contemporaneo/ Tzadik) and *Storytelling* (EMI) albums are complex, mesmerising tapestries of percussion and vocals that beautifully evoke Brazilian landscapes and local peoples.

Sights

Recife's architecture is far less celebrated than its pretty neighbour, Olinda, but it retains some very attractive buildings. Rua da Aurora, which watches over the Capibaribe river, is lined with stately palladian and neoclassical buildings. The islands that lie to the south over the filigree of bridges are dotted with imposing churches and surprisingly lavish civic structures, especially around the Praça da República. The city began with the Dutch and the twin forts on the island of Recife Antigo; or Ancient Recife. The **Forte do Brum** ⓘ *Tue-Fri 0900-1600, Sat and Sun 1400-1600, donation optional*, is now an army museum. The **Forte das Cinco Pontas**, was built by the Dutch in 1630, seven years before Maurice of Nassau sacked and burnt Olinda. The two forts controlled access to the port at the northern and southern entrances respectively. Within Forte das Cinco Pontas is the **Museu da Cidade do Recife** ⓘ *Mon-Fri 0900- 1800, Sat and Sun 1300-1700, US$0.50 donation*, which houses a cartographic history of the settlement of Recife. This part of the city is known today as **Recife Antigo** (Old Recife).

Recife is replete with churches. The most famous is the **Concatedral de São Pedro dos Clérigos** ⓘ *Pátio de São Pedro, R Barão da Vitória at Av Dantas Barreto, Mon-Fri 0800-1200 and 1400-1600, T081-3224 2954*, a towering baroque building with a beautiful painted interior, overlooking one of the city's best-preserved colonial squares. The area has recently been nominated a national historical monument, has been renovated and is filled with little shops, restaurants and bars. There are sporadic roots music and poetry shows evenings from Wednesday to Sunday. Also worth visiting is the 18th-century **Basílica e Convento de Nossa Senhora do Carmo** ⓘ *Av Dantas Barreto, Santo Antônio, T081-3224 3341, Mon-Fri 0800-1200 and 1400-1900, Sat 0700-1200, Sun 0700-1000*, named after the city's patron saint and which has a magnificent painted ceiling and high altar. The **Capela da Ordem Terceira do São Francisco** ⓘ *R do Imperador, Santo Antônio, T081-3224 0994, Mon-Fri 0800-1130 and 1400-1700, Sat 0800-1130*, (1695-1710 and 19th century), is one of the finest baroque buildings in northeast Brazil and is another national monument. The lavish façade conceals a gorgeous gilt painted interior with ceiling panels by Manuel de Jesus Pinto. The **Basílica de Nossa Senhora de Penha** ⓘ *Praça Dom Vital, São José, T081-3424 8500, Tue-Thu 0800-1200 and 1500-1700, Fri 0600-1800, Sat 1500-1700, Sun 0700-0900*, is an Italianate church that holds a traditional 'blessing of São Felix' on Fridays – attended by hundreds of sick Pernambucans in search of miracles.

West of the centre

About a kilometre to the west of the fort around the Praça 3 de Maio is a lively bar area with many live music venues thronging with a Bohemian crowd. It is to Recife what Lapa is to Rio and remains the centre of Recife's musical boom, which begun with mangue beat (see box page 433). This was named in homage to the Mangroves that fill Recife's

Recife

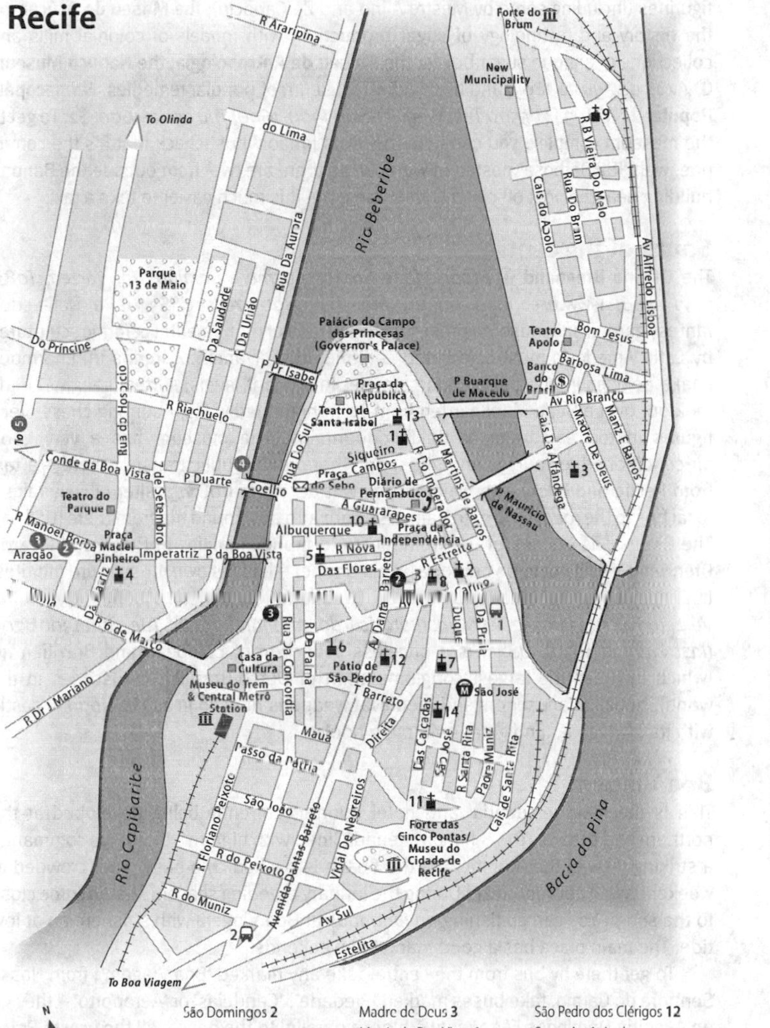

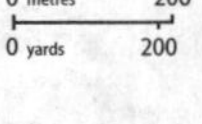

Sleeping
América 2
Central 3
Pousada Villa Boa Vista 5
Recife Plaza 4
São Domingos 2

Eating
Gelattos 2
Leite 3

Churches
Basílica de Nossa Senhora de Penha 14
Capela Dourada 1
Espírito Santo 2
Madre de Deus 3
Matriz de Boa Vista 4
Nossa Senhora da Conceição dos Militares 5
Nossa Senhora do Carmo 6
Nossa Senhora do Livramento 7
Nossa Senhora do Rosário dos Pretos 8
Pilar 9
Santo Antônio 10
São José do Ribamar 11
São Pedro dos Clérigos 12
Santo Antônio do Convento de São Francisco 13

Buses
To Itamaracá & Igarassu 1
To Porto da Galinhas 2
To Boa Viagem 3

 rivers and canals, and has spawned artists like Otto, Siba and DJ Dolores. Be sure to take a taxi there and back for safety.

Following Avenida Rui Barbosa west of the centre, the **Museu do Estado** ⓘ *Av Rui Barbosa 960, Graças, Tue-Fri 0900-1700, Sat and Sun 1400-1700,* has excellent paintings by the 19th-century landscape painter, Teles Júnior.

About 7 km west of the centre, the **Museu do Homem do Nordeste** ⓘ *Av 17 de Agosto 2223, Casa Forte,* comprises the **Museu de Arte Popular**, containing ceramic figurines (including some by Mestre Alino and Zé Caboclo); the **Museu do Açúcar**, on the history and technology of sugar production, with models of colonial mills and collections of antique sugar bowls; the **Museu de Antropologia**, the **Nabuco Museum** ⓘ *Av 17 de Agosto 1865,* and the modern museum of popular remedies, **Farmacopéia Popular** ⓘ *T081-3441 5500 Tue, Wed, Fri-Sun 1300-1600, Thu 0900-1600, $2.* To get to the museum complex, you can take the 'Dois Irmãos' bus (check that it's the correct one, with 'Rui Barbosa' posted in window, as there are two) from outside the Banorte building near the post office on Guararapes, but it is much easier to take a taxi.

South of the centre

The **Oficina Brennand** ⓘ *Propriedade Santos Cosme e Damião s/n, Várzea, T081-3271 2466, www.brennand.com.br, Mon-Fri 0800-1700, US$3,* is a Dali-esque fantasy garden and museum preserving hundreds of monumental ceramic sculptures by Latin America's most celebrated ceramic artist, Francisco Brennand. Enormous snake penises in hob-nailed boots are set in verdant lawns; surrealist egret heads look out over a Burle Marx garden from 10-m-high tiled walls; haunting chess-piece figures in top hats gaze at tinkling fountains. The museum has a very good air-conditioned restaurant and gift shop. There is no public transport here – a taxi from Recife and back, with waiting time will be around US$15; alternatively take a local bus to the *rodoviária* or to Varzea suburb and do a round trip from there (US$10). The Brennands are one of the wealthiest old money families in Brazil and Ricardo Brennand – as if not to be outdone by his brother – has his own museum 10 minutes' taxi ride away. The **Instituto Ricardo Brennand** ⓘ *Alameda Antônio Brennand, Várzea, T081-2121 0352, www.institutoricardo brennand.org.br, Tue- Sun 1300-1700 (last entry at 1630), US$3,* is a priceless collection of European and Brazilian art (which includes the largest conglomeration of Dutch-Brazilian landscapes in the world), books, manuscripts and medieval weapons housed in a fake Norman castle with its own moat...and giant swimming pool.

Boa Viagem

This is the main residential and hotel quarter, currently being developed at the northern end of town. The 8-km promenade lined with high-rise buildings commands a striking view of the Atlantic, but the beach is backed by a busy road, crowded at weekends and not very clean. During the January breeding season, sharks come close to the shore. You can go fishing on *jangadas* at Boa Viagem with a fisherman at low tide. The main praça has a good market at weekends.

To get there by bus from the centre, take any marked 'Boa Viagem'; from Nossa Senhora do Carmo, take buses marked 'Piedade', 'Candeias' or 'Aeroporto' – they go on Avenida Domingos Ferreira, two blocks parallel to the beach, all the way to Praça Boa Viagem (at Avenida Boa Viagem 500). Back to the centre take buses marked 'CDU' or 'Setubal' from Avenida Domingos Ferreira.

Olinda → *Phone code: 081. Colour map 2, B6. Population: 350,000.*

Ins and outs From Recife take any bus marked 'Rio Doce', No 981, which has a circular route around the city and beaches, or No 33 from Avenida Nossa Senhora do Carmo, US$0.60, or 'Jardim Atlântico' from the central post office at Siqueira Campos. From Boa Viagem, take bus marked 'Piedade/Rio Doce' or 'Barra de Jangada/Casa

Boa Viagem

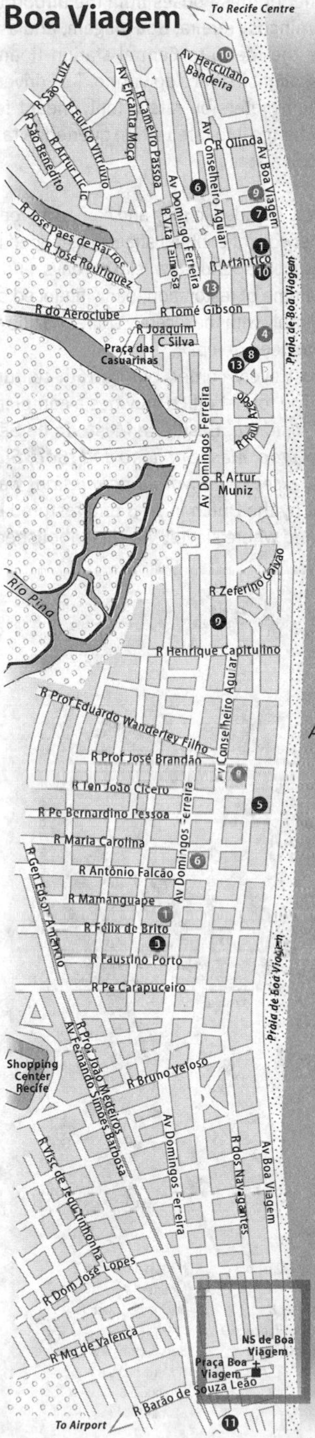

To Recife Centre
Av Herculano Bandeira
R São Luiz
R Eurico Vitrúvio
Av Encanta Moça
R Carneiro Passoa
R São Benedito
R Artur Lício
R Olinda
Av Conselheiro Aguiar
Av Boa Viagem
Av Domingo Ferreira
R Vita Tamosa
R José Paes de Barros
R José Rodriguez
R Atlântico
Praia de Boa Viagem
R do Aeroclube
R Tomé Gibson
R Joaquim C Silva
Praça das Casuarinas
R Raul Azedo
Av Domingos Ferreira
R Artur Muniz
Rio Pina
R Zeferino Galvão
R Henrique Capitulino
R Prof Eduardo Wanderley Filho
Av Conselheiro Aguiar
R Prof José Brandão
R Ten João Cícero
R Pe Bernardino Pessoa
R Maria Carolina
R Gen Edson Amaral
R Antônio Falcão
R Mamanguape
R Félix de Brito
R Faustino Porto
R Pe Carapuceiro
Praia de Boa Viagem
Shopping Center Recife
R Prof João Medeiros
Av Fernando Simões Barbosa
R Bruno Veloso
Av Domingos Ferreira
R dos Navegantes
Av Boa Viagem
R Visc de Jequitinhonha
R Dom José Lopes
R Mq de Valença
NS de Boa Viagem
Praça Boa Viagem
R Barão de Souza Leão
To Airport

Atlantic Ocean

Boa Viagem detail

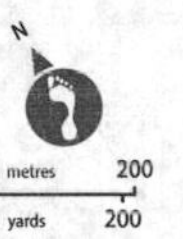

Sleeping

Aconchego **1**
Albergue do Mar **2**
Coqueiral **3**
Do Sol **4**
Maracatú do Recife **6**
Pousada da Julieta **8**
Pousada da Praia **9**
Praia **10**
Recife Monte **11**
Uzi Praia **13**

Eating

Bargaço **1**
Chica Pitanga **2**
Churrascaria Porcão **3**
Ilha da Kosta **5**
La Capannina **6**
La Maison **7**
Parraxaxa **8**
Peng **9**
Real Eza **10**
Romana **11**
Tempero Verde **12**
Tio Dadá **13**

Caiada' (US$0.60, 30 minutes). Change to either of these buses from the airport to Olinda: take the 'Aeroporto' bus to Avenida Domingos Ferreira, Boa Viagem, and ask to be let off. From the Recife *rodoviária*, take the Metrô to Central station (Joana Bezerra is unsafe) and then change. In all cases, alight in Praça do Carmo. Taxi drivers between Olinda and Recife often try to put their meters on rate 2 (only meant for Sundays, holidays and after 2100), but should change it to rate 1 when queried. A taxi from Boa Viagem should cost around US$8, US$12 at night.

Sights About 7 km north of Recife is the old capital, founded in 1537 and named a World Heritage site by UNESCO in 1982. The compact network of cobbled streets is steeped in history and invites wandering. This is a charming spot to spend a few relaxing days, and a much more appealing base than Recife. A programme of restoration, partly financed by the Dutch government, was initiated in order to comply with the recently conferred title of National Monument, but much is still in desperate need of repair.

The city boasts an ornate church on almost every corner, but its 16th-century monastery and convent are worth seeking out. The tourist office provides a complete list of all historic sites with a useful map, *Sítio Histórico*. **Basilica e Mosterio de São Bento** ⓘ *R São Bento, Mon-Fri 0830-1130, 1430-1700, Mass Sat 0630 and 1800; Sun 1000, with Gregorian chant; monastery closed except with written permission*, was founded 1582 by the Benedictine monks, burnt by the Dutch in 1631 and restored in 1761. This is the site of Brazil's first law school and where slavery was first abolished.

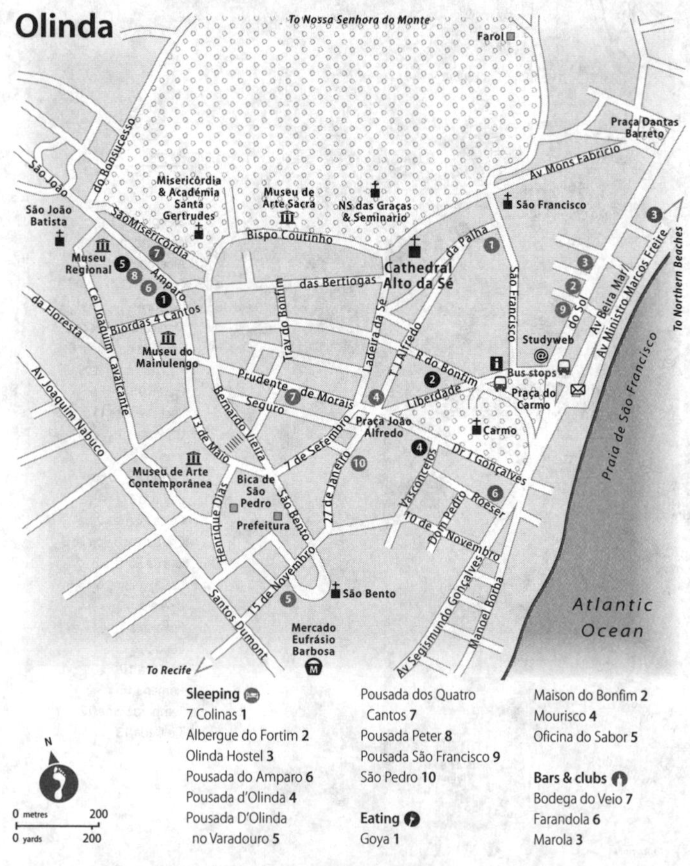

Brazilian dance

Dance is one of the world's great expanding art forms and pastimes, with salsa (which originated in Hispanic America and is little known in Brazil), probably being the most popular Latin dance worldwide. Brazil has numerous dance styles which are perhaps even more beautiful and infectious than salsa and involve similar steps over music, also in 2/4 time. The most famous and probably the most difficult is samba, which comes in varying forms and can be danced either individually or as a couple. As a rhythm, samba finds its origins in a Bahian two-time drum beat called *batucada*. In its current form it was born in the slums of Rio, where hand claps, whistles, tambourines, guitars, *cavaquinhos* and the squeaky *cuíca* drum were added to produce a fevered syncopated soup. The basic steps, particularly of the solo samba danced at Carnaval are notoriously difficult to master and tiring to dance. But they are an astoundingly beautiful combination of grace and energy, unrivalled by any other Latin American dance: head and body perfectly poised and floating over the perpetual, sensual motion of the hips.

Forró, which is the most popular beach dance for young Brazilians, especially in the northeast, is a good deal easier than samba and was especially invented for Anglo Saxons who dance like they have two left feet. The name is thought to be a corruption of 'for all', after 'For alls', which were end-of-the-week parties held by British railway workers in Pernambuco during their construction of the Brazilian Great Western Railway at the turn of the 19th century. The rhythm was brought to national popularity by Luiz Gonzaga in the 1950s and 1960s and has now become the party and carnival music of choice north of Bahia. *Forró* is also in 2/4 time but is far choppier than samba, with the driving rhythm coming from the accordion rather than from drums. It is danced in pairs.

Pernambuco has produced numerous others dances, including *frevo*, which is danced at Carnaval, *coco* and *ciranda*, all of whose rhythms can be heard underneath many *mangue beat* songs.

Most other Brazilian styles are variations of samba or *forro*; such as *pagode* which comes from the former, and lambada, from the latter. Tango is also popular, mainly in Rio where it is danced every Saturday at the antiques market on Rua do Lavradio in Lapa.

The magnificent gold altar was on loan to New York's Guggenheim Museum at the time of writing. Despite its weathered exterior, the **Convento de São Francisco** (1585), Ladeira de São Francisco, has splendid woodcarving and paintings, superb gilded stucco, and *azulejos* in the Capela de São Roque within the church of **Nossa Senhora das Neves** ⓘ *Tue-Fri 0700-1130, 1400-1700, Sat 0700-1200, US$0.40. Mass 1900 Tue, 1700 Sat and 0800 Sun*, in the same building.

Make the short, but very steep, climb up to the **Alto da Sé** for memorable views of the city and the coastline stretching all the way to Recife. Here, the simple **Igreja da Sé** ⓘ *Mon-Fri 0800-1200, 1400-1700*, (1537), a cathedral since 1677, was the first church to be built in the city. Nearby, the **Igreja da Misericórdia** ⓘ *R Bispo Coutinho, daily 1145-1230, 1800-1830*, (1540), has fine tiling and gold work but limited opening hours. On a small hill overlooking Praça do Carmo, the **Igreja do Carmo** (1581) has been closed for several years due to planned restoration.

There are some 17th-century houses with latticed balconies, heavy doors and brightly painted stucco walls, including a house in Moorish style at Praça João Alfredo 7, housing the **Mourisco** restaurant and a handicrafts shop, **Sobrado 7**. The local colony of artists means excellent examples of regional art (mainly woodcarving and terracotta figurines) may be bought in the Alto da Sé, the square on top of the hill by the cathedral, or in the handicraft shops at the **Mercado da Ribeira** ⓘ *R Bernardo Vieira de Melo*, (Vieira de Melo gave the first recorded call for independence from Portugal, in Olinda in 1710). Handicrafts are also sold at good prices at the Mercado Eufrásio Barbosa, by the junction of Avenida Segismundo Gonçalves and Santos Dumont, Varadouro. There is a **Museu de Arte Sacra** ⓘ *Alto da Sé 7, Tue-Fri 0900-1300*, in the former Palácio Episcopal (1696). The **Museu do Mamulengo** ⓘ *Amparo 59, Mon-Fri 0900-1800, Sat and Sun 1100-1800*, houses Pernambucan folk puppetry. **Corredor Artístico do Amparo**, formally identified as the cultural and artistic zone, has artists workshops, while the **Casa dos Bonecos** houses papier mâché giants.

For **tourist information** go to the **Secretaria de Turismo** ⓘ *Praça do Carmo, T081-3429 9279, daily 0900-2100*. Guides with identification cards wait in Praça do Carmo. They are former street children and half the fee for a full tour of the city (about US$12) goes to a home for street children. If you take a guide you will be safe from mugging, which does unfortunately occur.

The beaches close to Olinda are polluted, but those further north, beyond Casa Caiada – at **Janga**, and **Pau Amarelo** – are beautiful, palm-fringed and usually deserted (although the latter can be dirty at low tide). Take either a 'Janga' or 'Pau Amarela' bus, Varodouro bus to return. At many simple cafés you can eat *sururu* (clam stew in coconut sauce), *agulha frita* (fried needle-fish), *miúdo de galinha* (chicken giblets in gravy), *casquinha de carangueijo* (seasoned crabmeat) and *farinha de dendê* (served in crab shells). Visit the Dutch fort on Pau Amarelo beach where there is a small craft fair on Saturday nights.

Biological reserves

Pernambuco's two reserves are **Saltinho**, in the south of the state, which preserves some of the last vestiges of Atlantic forest in the northeast, and **Serra Negra**, in the centre of the state, which has some of the last remaining forest at higher altitude in the interior. For information contact **Ibama** ⓘ *Av 17 de Agosto 1057, Casa Forte, CEP 52060-590, T081-441 5033, F441 1380, Recife.*

Southern coast » pp443-452.

Gaibú and around

Heading south from Recife are some of the best beaches in the state. The first stop is the beautiful and quiet beach at **Gaibú**, 30 km south, where there are pousadas and cheap restaurants. The scenic **Cabo de Santo Agostinho**, with a ruined fort, is 5 km to the east. About 1 km on foot from Gaibú is the beautiful **Praia Calhetas**. The nearby beach at **Itapuama** is even emptier.

Buses to Gaibú and the beaches run frequently from **Cabo**, Pernambuco's main industrial city, which has a few interesting churches and forts and a **Museu da Abolição**. To get to Cabo take a bus signed 'Centro do Cabo' from the airport in Recife. Nearby **Suape** has many 17th-century buildings and a biological reserve.

Porto de Galinhas → *Phone code: 081.*

Sixty kilometres south of Recife, Porto de Galinhas – whose name means 'port of chickens' because slaves were smuggled here in chicken crates – was one of the first of a string of low-key beach resorts discovered in the 1990s. Back then it was little more than a beach and two sandy streets and the myth of its tranquil charm endures. But it is only a myth. Today Porto de Galinhas is as well on its way to becoming a full scale resort as its counterparts near Porto Seguro in Bahia. The sandy streets are asphalted and lined with shops and restaurants, while the beaches are backed with pousadas and resort hotels for kilometres north and south. Because of a reef close to the shore, swimming is only possible at high tide.

The **Centro de Informacões Turisticas** ⓘ *R da Esperança s/n, T081-3552 1728, www.bureaudeinformacoes.tur.br*, has maps, information on transport, hotels and tour operators and a few English-speaking staff. Buses and minivans run from Avenida Dantas Barreto and Rua do Peixoto in Recife, at least hourly. Taxis cost around US$50.

South of Porto de Galinhas

Eighty kilometres south of Recife are the beaches of **Barra do Sirinhaém**, with some tourist development and three hotels, including **Dos Cataventos** (D). Fishermen make trips to offshore islands (good views). Beyond these are the little towns of **Tamandare** and **São José da Coroa Grande** which are quieter than Porto de Galinhas and have a few simple places to stay.

Northern coast

» *pp443-452.*

Igarassu

→ *Phone code: 081. Colour map 2, B6. Population: 77,500.*

Some 39 km north of Recife on the road to João Pessoa, Igarassu has the first church built in Brazil, **SS Cosme e Damião** (1535) and the convent of **Santo Antônio**, a beautiful baroque building with some very fine gilt work and *azulejos*.

Itamaracá

→ *Phone code: 081. Population: 14,000.*

North of Igarassu the road passes through coconut plantations to Itapissuma, where there is a bridge to **Itamaracá** island. According to the locals, this is where Adam and Eve spent their holidays (so does everyone else on Sunday now). It has the old Dutch **Forte Orange**, built in 1631; an interesting penal settlement with gift shops, built round the 1747 sugar estate buildings of Engenho São João, which still have much of the old machinery, charming villages and colonial churches, as well as some fine, wide beaches. At one of them, **Praia do Forte Orange**, Ibama has a centre for the study and preservation of manatees, **Centro Nacional de Conservação e Manejo de Sirênios or Peixe-boi** ⓘ *Tue-Sun 1000-1600.*

There are pleasant trips by *jangada* from Praia do Forte Orange to **Ilha Coroa do Avião**, a recently formed sandy island (developing wildlife and migratory birds – for which there is a research station) with rustic beach bars. **Praias do Sossego** and **da Enseada** have some bars but are quiet and relatively undiscovered. The crossing is 3 km north of Itamaracá town, recommended for sun worshippers.

Further north again, two hours from Recife by bus, is **Pontas de Pedra**, an old fishing village, nice beach, fishing and diving expeditions, lots of bars.

At the Pernambuco-Paraíba border, a 27-km dirt road goes to the fishing village of **Pitimbu**, with *jangadas*, surf fishing, lobster fishing and lobster-pot making. There are no tourist facilities but camping is possible and food is available from **Bar do Jangadeiro**. To get here, take a bus from Goiana, US$1.

West of Recife

» *pp443-452.*

Bezerros

→ *Phone code: 081. Colour map 2, B6. Population: 52,000*

About 15 km further west, on the BR-232 is Bezerros, on the Rio Ipojuca. It has some old houses, fine praças and churches. Some, like the **Igreja de Nossa Senhora dos Homens Pretos, São José** and the **Capela de Nossa Senhora**, date from the 19th century. The former railway station has been converted into the **Estação da Cultura**, with shows and other cultural performances. The best known artist and poet is J Borges (born 1935), whose work has been exhibited internationally. The city's main attraction is handicrafts, which are found in the district of **Encruzilhada de São João**; items in leather, clay, wood, papier mâché and much more. Most typical are the Papangu masks, made of painted papier mâché. The masks are used at Carnaval, as interior decoration, even as key-holders. Wooden toys are also popular. About 10 km from the centre of Bezerros, near the village of Serra Negra, a small ecotourism park, **Serra Negra ecological tourism trail**, has been set up. Trails lead to caves and springs; the flora is typical of the *agreste*.

Carnaval here is famed throughout Brazil and is known as **Folia do Papangu**, see Festivals, page 449. For tourist information contact the **Departamento de Turismo** ⓘ *Praça Duque de Caxias 88, Centro, T081-328 1286, F3728 1316*. The artisans association, **Associação dos Artesãos de Bezerros**, is at the same address.

Caruaru → *Phone code: 081. Altitude: 554 m. Colour map 2, B6. Population: 254,000.*

Situated 134 km west of Recife, this small *sertão* town is famous for its huge **Festas Juninhas**, held throughout June (see Festivals, page 449), and its little clay figures (*figurinhas* or *bonecas de barro*) originated by Mestre Vitalino (1909-1963), and very typical of northeast Brazil. Most of the potters live at **Alto da Moura**, 6 km away, and you can visit a house – **Casa Museu Mestre Vitalino** – once owned by Vitalino, containing personal objects and photographs, but no examples of his work. Unesco has recognized the area as the largest centre of figurative art in the Americas. Buses run from Caruaru, a bumpy 30-minute ride, US$0.50.

Ins and outs The *rodoviária* is 4 km west of town; buses from Recife stop in the town centre. Alight here and look for the **Livraria Estudantil** on the corner of Vigário Freire and Rua Anna de Albuquerque Galvão. Go down Galvão, turn right on Rua 15 de Novembro to the first junction, 13 de Maio; turn left, cross the river to the Feira do Artesanato (the arts and crafts market).

During the Festas Juninhas, there is a tourist train, *Train do Forró*, from Recife, which is a very spirited affair with bars, and bands playing in the carriages. See www.tremdoforro.com.br for information.

Fazenda Nova and Nova Jerusalém

During Easter Week each year, various agencies run package tours to the little country town of **Fazenda Nova**, 23 km from Caruaru. Just outside the town is **Nova Jerusalém**. Every day from the day before Palm Sunday up to Easter Saturday, an annual Passion play is enacted here, on an open-air site about one third the size of the historic quarter of Jerusalem. Nine stages are used to depict scenes from the Passion of Christ, which is presented using 50 actors and 500 extras to re-enact the story with the audience following in their footsteps. *TV Globo* stars often play the starring roles and the sound and lighting effects are state of the art. Performances begin at 1800 and last for about three hours.

There is little accommodation in Nova Jerusalém/Fazenda Nova and it is usually full during the Passion. **Empetur** in Recife/Olinda have details of agencies who offer trips. During the Easter period there are direct bus services from Recife (and from Caruaru at other times).

Petrolina and the sertão

Beyond Serra Talhada the BR-232 continues to Salgueiro, where it meets the BR-116 heading north to Fortaleza. The BR-232 becomes the BR-316 and heads northwest to Araripina before entering Piauí. This part of Pernambuco was the haunt of the bandit Lampião until his death in 1938. Even today the area is still quite lawless and buses are often escorted by armed police. Cultivation of marijuana in the area between Salgueiro and Floresta means that visitors are not generally welcome.

Petrolina, on the banks of the Rio São Francisco, is best visited from Juazeiro in Bahia (see page 414). The city is famous for the production of *carrancas* (boat figureheads, mostly grotesque) of wood or ceramic, and for having the closest vineyards to the equator in the world. The city has its own airport. Near the runway is the small **Museu do Sertão,** with relics of rural life in the Northeast and the age of the *coronéis* and the bandit Lampião.

Sleeping

Recife *p431, map p435*

Boa Viagem is the main tourist district and although it has plenty of hotels it is a long way from the centre of Recife. The beach is notorious for shark attacks. For the city centre, the best pace to stay is Boa Vista. Be careful walking back to hotels in central Recife after dark.

During Carnaval and for longer stays at other times, private individuals rent rooms and houses in Recife and Olinda; listings can be found in the classified ads of *Diário de Pernambuco*. This accommodation is generally cheaper, safer and quieter than hotels.

Centro

A Pousada Villa Boa Vista, R Miguel Couto 81, Boa Vista, T081-3223 0666, www.pousadavillaboavista.com.br. The only modern hotel in town, with plain, comfortable a/c rooms (all en suites with modern bathrooms and powerful showers), around a courtyard. Quiet, safe and a 5-min taxi ride from the centre.

A Recife Plaza, R da Aurora 225, T081-3231 1200, www.recifeplazahotel.com.br, Boa Vista, overlooking the Rio Capibaribe. Comfortable old-fashioned business hotel with a reasonable restaurant, which is very popular at lunchtime.

D América, Praça Maciel Pinheiro 48, Boa Vista, T081-3221 1300. Frayed, very simple rooms with low, foamy beds, lino floors and tiny en suites. The best rooms are on the upper floors with views out over the city.

D Central, Av Manoel Borba 209, Boa Vista, T081-3222 4001. A splendid 1920s building with its original French open lifts and plain, but freshly painted rooms with parquet flooring and flat-pack furniture. The bathrooms have enormous iron tubs (without plugs). The upper floors have wonderful views of the city.

D São Domingos, Praça Maciel Pinheiro 66, Boa Vista, T081-3223 0060. An old grand dame from the 1960s now fallen on hard times. The parquet-floored rooms are scuffed and come with huge 1960s commodes. The upper rooms have good views.

Boa Viagem *p436, map p437*

The main beachfront road is Av Boa Viagem; hotels here are mostly tower blocks and tend to be more expensive.

A Recife Monte, on the corner of R Petrolina and R dos Navegantes 363, T081-3465 7422, F3465 8406. Very smart and good value for the category, caters to business travellers.

B Aconchego, Félix de Brito 382, T081-3326 2989, aconchego@novaera.com.br. Motel-style rooms around a pleasant pool area, a/c, sitting room. English-speaking owner, will collect you from the airport.

B Do Sol, Av Boa Viagem 978, T081-3465 6722, reservas@hsol.com.br. Decent, if rather bland with business facilities.

B Praia, Av Boa Viagem 9, T/F081-465 3722. Large modern block with bar, restaurant and decent sized pool.

B Setúbal, R Setúbal 932, T081-3341 4116. Helpful standard town hotel with good breakfast and fairly comfortable rooms.

C Casa da Praia, Av Beira Mar 1168, Praia de Piedade, T081-3461 1414. On a quiet street, with garden, good breakfast, owner speaks French. Recommended.

C Coquelral, R Petrolina, 43, T081-3326 5881. Dutch-owned (English and French spoken). Small, homely rooms with a/c and a pretty breakfast room. Recommended.

C Praia Mar, Av Boa Viagem 1660, T081-3465 3759. Intimate and safe. Recommended.

C Uzi Praia, Av Conselheiro Aguiar 942, T/F081-3466 9662. Plain rooms with a/c and a cosy, sister hotel across the road.

D Albergue Mandacaru, R Maria Carolina 75, T081-326 1964. Youth hostel. Stores luggage, English and German spoken, good breakfast. Recommended.

D Pousada da Julieta, R Prof José Brandao 135, T081-3326 7860, hjulieta@elogica.

com.br. Friendly and clean. One block from beach, very good value. Recommended.

D Pousada da Praia, Alcides Carneiro Leal 66, T081-3326 7085. TV, safe, a/c, rooms vary (some tiny), very helpful. Roof-top breakfast room.

E Albergue do Mar, R dos Navegantes 81, T081-3326 2196. Youth hostel with good breakfast and atmosphere.

E Maracatú do Recife, R Maria Carolina 185, T081-3326 1221, www.geocities.com/albergue maracatu. IYHA hostel. Large, well-kept dorms, simple, safe, cooking facilities and a decent breakfast.

Camping

Paraíso Camping Clube, Av Dantas Barreto 512, loja 503, T081-3224 3094. Can provide information on camping throughout the state. There is no camping within the city.

Olinda *p436, map p438*

Prices at least triple during Carnaval when 5-night packages are sold. Rooms at regular prices can often be found in Boa Viagem during this time. In the historic centre, accommodation is mostly in converted mansions, which are full of character. If you can afford it, staying in one of these pousadas is the ideal way to absorb Olinda's colonial charm. All pousadas, and most of the cheaper hotels outside the old city, have a pool.

AL 7 Colinas, Ladeira de Sao Francisco 307, T/F081-3439 6055, www.hotel7colinas.com.br. Spacious, new hotel with all mod cons, set in private, gated gardens and with a large swimming pool.

AL Pousada do Amparo, R do Amparo 199, T081-3439 1749, www.pousadoamparo.com.br. Olinda's best hotel is a gorgeous, 18th-century house, full of antiques and atmosphere in the **Roteiros do Charme** group (see page 50). Rooms have 4-poster beds and each is decorated differently. The public areas include a spacious foyer with a high ceiling decorated with art, a pool and sauna area surrounded by a little flower-filled garden and an excellent, delightfully romantic restaurant.

B-C Pousada dos Quatro Cantos, R Prudente de Morais 441, T081-3429 0220, www.pousada4cantos.com.br. A large converted townhouse with a little walled garden and terraces. The maze of bright rooms and suites are decorated with Pernambuco arts and crafts and furnished mostly with antiques. Warm, welcoming and full of character.

C Pousada São Francisco, R do Sol 127, T081-3429 2109, www.pousadasao francisco.com.br. Well-kept and airy a/c rooms with little terraces, slate floors and pokey bathrooms. The pool and bar area are set in pleasant gardens visited by humming birds in the early morning and there is a small restaurant and parking. Outside the historic centre but within walking distance.

C-D Pousada Peter, R do Amparo 215, T/F081-3439 2171, www.pousada peter.com.br. The rather pokey white-tiled a/c rooms in this converted town house contrast with the spacious lobby lounge decorated with Pernambuco crafts and colourful artwork. Breakfast is served on the terrace overlooking distant Recife and the modest pool.

C-E Olinda Hostel, R do Sol 233, T081-3429 1592, www.alberguedeolinda.com.br. IYHA youth hostel with fan-cooled 8-bed dorms with shared en suites, and doubles. The hostel has a tropical garden, TV room, and a shady area with hammocks next to a pool.

C-E Pousada d'Olinda, P João Alfredo 178, T/F081-3494 2559, www.pousadado linda.com.br. Basic but well-kept dorms and doubles around a pool, garden and communal breakfast area and lunchtime restaurant. Discount of 10% for owners of *Footprint* guides. English, French, German Arabic and Spanish spoken.

C-E Pousada d'Olinda no Varadouro, R 15 de Novembro 98, T081-3439 1163, www.pousadadolindavaradouro.com.br. Little suites in a converted townhouse and cheaper communal rooms. The best are on the upper floors. Spacious open-air dining area/restaurant and a small pool.

D São Pedro, R 27 Janeiro 95, T081-3439 9546, www.pousadapedro.com. Quiet little pousada with a walled garden, a small pool shaded by frangipani and bamboo. Has a delightful breakfast area and lobby decorated with art and antiques. The rustic rooms are tiny but tastefully decorated and all a/c. The best are on the upper floor.

D-E Albergue do Fortim, R do Sol 151, T081-3429 1939, www.pousadadofortim.com.br. Very simple but clean boxy rooms with a/c at the cheapest rates in Olinda. Some are big enough for 4. Breakfast is US$2 extra.

Camping

Olinda Camping, R Bom Sucesso 262, Amparo, T081-3429 1365. US$5 per person, space for 30 tents, 5 trailers, small huts for rent, quiet, well-shaded, town buses pass outside. Recommended.

Porto de Galinhas *p440*

There are plenty of cheap pousadas and hotels in town along R da Esperança and its continuation R Manoel Uchôa. Also along R Beijapurá which runs off R da Esperança.

L **Village Porto de Galinhas**, T081-3552 2945, www.villageportodegalinhas.com.br. All-inclusive family beach resort right on the ocean and with a large pool, restaurant, a/c rooms. Some 7km from town.

C-E **IYHA Pousada A Casa Branca**, Praça 18, T081-3552 1808, www.pousadaacasabranca.com.br. Very clean, well-kept, newly opened hostel with some a/c rooms and several dorms. To get there take the right turn (away from the sea) off R Beijupira opposite R Carauna and walk inland for 400 m. The pousada is in a little square 150 m before the Estrada Maracaipe.

C-E **La Vila delle Rose**, R Manoel Uchôa 11, T081-3552 1489, www.laviladellerose.com.br. Simple, bright and well-kept doubles and shared rooms in a large house very close to the beach. Good breakfast and friendly service. All en suites.

Igarassu *p441*

Camping

Engenho Monjope, 5 km before Igarassu coming from Recife, T081-3543 0528, US$5. A **Camping Clube do Brasil** site on an old sugar estate, now a historical monument (bus US$1, alight at the 'Camping' sign and walk 5-10 mins).

Itamaracá *p441*

B **Casa da Praia**, Av da Forte Orange, T081-3544 1255. With pool, minibar, breakfast and optional dinner.

C **Pousada Itamaracá**, R Fernando Lopes 205/210, T081-3544 1152. Away from the beach, but has a pool.

C **Pousada Jaguaribe**, R Rios 355 (close to bus terminal) near the beach. Fans and mosquito nets in all rooms, kitchen, laundry facilities, swimming pool.

Caruaru *p442, map p420*

A large number of cheap *hospedarias* can be found around the central square, Praça Getúlio Vargas.

A **Grande Hotel São Vicente de Paulo**, Av Rio Branco 365, T081-3721 5011, F3721 5290. A good, centrally located hotel with a/c, laundry, garage, bar, restaurant, pool, TV. It also houses the local cinema.

C **Centenário**, 7 de Setembro 84, T081-3722 4011, F3721 1033. Also has more expensive suites and a pool. The breakfast is good. As the hotel is in the town centre it can be noisy, but otherwise recommended.

C **Central**, R Vigario Freire 71, T081-3721 5880. Suites or rooms, all with a/c, TV, good breakfast, in the centre. Recommended.

Fazenda Nova and Nova Jerusalém *p442*

E **Grande**, Av Poeta Carlos Penha Filho, T081-732 1137. Very basic but the best in town nonetheless.

Petrolina *p442*

Choices here are poor; avoid the Central Hotel at all costs.

C **Hotel Neuman**, Av Souza Filho 444, T081-961 0595. Overpriced with pokey little a/c rooms all with en suites.

D **Pousada da Carranca**, BR-122, Km 4, T081-961 3421. Pleasant and fairly well looked after but a little inconvenient for the town.

Eating

Recife *p431, map p435*

There is a good variety of restaurants in the city and along the beach at Boa Viagem. Be careful of eating the local small crabs, known as *guaiamum*; they live in the mangrove swamps which take the drainage from Recife's *mocambos* (shanty towns).

Centro

There are many cheap *lanchonetes* catering to office workers, they tend to close in evening.

TTT **Leite** Praça Joaquim Nabuco 147/53 near the Casa de Cultura, Santo Antônio. Frequently voted the best in the city, and an institution for 130 years, with a live pianist and a varied menu of around 100 dishes.

Gelattos, Av Dantas Barreto, 230. Great *sucos* (try the delicious *guarana do amazonas* with nuts), hamburgers and sandwiches. Recommended.

Boa Viagem *p436, map p437*

Restaurants on the main beach road of Av Boa Viagem are pricier than in the centre. Venture a block or 2 inland for cheaper deals.

Bargaço, Av Boa Viagem 670. Typical northeastern menu specializing in seafood dishes. Sophisticated with small bar.

La Maison, Av Boa Viagem, 618, T081-3325 1158. Fondue restaurant in low-lit basement with an illicit feel. Appropriately cheesy and good fun, with rosé wine and peach melba on menu.

Chica Pitanga, R Petrolina, 19, T081-3465 2224. Upmarket, excellent food by weight. Be prepared to queue. Recommended.

Churrascaria Porcão, Av Eng Domingos Ferreira 4215. Good for meat- and salad-eaters alike, very popular.

Ilha da Kosta, R Pe Bernardino Pessoa, 50, T081-3466 2222. Self-service seafood, sushi, pizza and Brazilian cuisine. Nothing special, but open from 1100 until the last client leaves.

La Capannina, Av Cons Aguiar 538, T081-3465 9420. Italian pizzas, salad, pasta and sweet and savoury crêpes. Recommended.

Parraxaxa, R Baltazar Pereira, 32, T081-9108 0242. Rustic-style, award-winning buffet of northeastern cuisine, including breakfast. Recommended.

Gibi, Av Cons Aguiar, 542. Basic but popular hamburger joint.

Peng, Av Domingos Ferreira, 1957. Self-service, some Chinese dishes. Bargain, rather than gourmet food, in an area with few other restaurants.

Real Eza, Av Boa Viagem, on corner with Av Atlântico. Beachfront location, hamburgers, snacks and pizza.

Romana, R Setubal, 225. Deli/bakery with a few tables and chairs. Pastries, coffee, yoghurt for breakfast and snacks.

Tempero Verde, R SH, Cardim, opposite **Chica Pitanga**. Where the locals go for a bargain meal of beans, meat and salad, US1.50. Simple, self-service, street tables.

TioDadá, R Baltazar Pereira, 100. Loud, TV screens, good-value portions of beef.

There are many a/c cheapies in the **Shopping Center Recife**, 1000-2200, T081-3464 6000.

Cafés

Café Cordel, R Domingos José Martins. Northeastern dishes, Cordel literature, regional books (some in English), good CD collection with requests accepted.

Savoy, Av Guararapes, open since 1944 and a haunt of Pernambucan intellectuals. Simone de Beauvoir and Jean Paul Sartre once ate here according to a book written about the bar. Poetry all over the walls.

Olinda *p436, map p438*

Try *tapioca*, a local dish made of manioc with coconut or cheese. The traditional Olinda drinks, *pau do índio* (with 32 herbs) and *retetel* are manufactured on R do Amparo.

Goya, R do Amparo 157, T081-3439 4875. Regional food, particularly seafood, beautifully presented.

Oficina do Sabor, R do Amparo 355, T081-3429 3331. Probably the city's best restaurant, consistently wins awards. Pleasant terrace overlooking city, food served in hollowed-out pumpkins and lots of vegetarian options.

Maison do Bonfim, R do Bonfim 115, T081-3429 1674. Serene, fan-cooled, rustic-style restaurant. French cuisine, such as chicken chasseur and escargots, as well as Brazilian and Italian food.

Samburá, Av Min Marcos Freire 1551. With terrace, try *caldeirada* and *pitu* (crayfish), also lobster in coconut sauce or daily fish dishes, very good.

Grande Pequim, Av Min Marcos Freire 1463, Bairro Novo. Good Chinese food.

Mourisco, Praça João Alfredo. Excellent, good-value food by weight in lovely, part-covered garden. Delicious deserts. A real find. Warmly recommended.

There are a number of *lanchonetes* and fast-food options along the seafront, including **Mama Luise** and **Gibi**, Av Min Marcos Freire, and **Leque Moleque**, Av Sigismundo Gonçalves 537.

Itamaracá *p441*

Vila Velha, T081-971 2962, ask for Newton Bezerra, dealer for artist Luis Jasmim.

Those with a car and cash to spare should have lunch and a swim at this charming villa. Any art purchase comes with a free lunch, allow all afternoon for a visit.

Caruaru *p442, map p420*
Alto da Moura is a real tourist spot and gets very busy.
¥¥-¥ Catracho's, close to the São Sebastião hospital. Has a Caribbean feel and the Honduran owner mixes great cocktails.
¥¥-¥ Costela do Baiano, close to Igreja do Rosário. Very good value northeastern cooking with good seafood.
¥ A Massa, R Vidal de Negreiros. The best of a number of cheap lunch restaurants in the centre near Banco do Brasil. With respectable pizzas and pasta.

Bars and clubs

Recife *p431, map p435*
Recife Antigo is the best place in the city for weekend nightlife. Many exciting bands post Mangue Beat fusion bands and DJs play in the bars and clubs around R Tomazino (R do Burburinho); and there is always a lively crowd. The area is not safe to walk to so take a taxi. The best listings site is www.reciferock.com.br and has information on live post-Mangue beat music.
Armazém 14, Av Alfredo Lisboa, s/n, Cais do Porto, Recife Antigo. One of the top live music venues for the alternative scene. Big names like Mundo Livre and Mombojo play here.
Boratcho, Galeria Joana Darc, Pina, Recife, T081-3327 1168. Tex Mex restaurant and live music venue for alternative Mangue Beat bands. Alternative and gay crowd.
Burburinho R Tomazino s/n, T081-3224 5854. The best of the live music spots in Recife Antigo. Grungey, arty crowd and a range of sounds from psychedelic *forró* funk to *frevo* rock and all things mixed. Other bars lie near by – start here and wander.
Central, R Mamede Simões 144, Boa Vista, T081-3222 7622, www.centralrecife.com.br. The drinking hole of choice for the city's musical and artistic middle-class community. Decent bar food, lunches and breakfast.
Depois Dancing Bar, Av Rio Branco 66, T081-3424 7451. Well-established alternative dance club with live bands.
Estação Pirata, R do Apolo, Recife Antigo. Good live bands – look out for Eddie and Tine who play here.
Garagem, R Amélia at Av Ruy Barbosa, no lado da Torre. A tyre shop by day and grungy bar packed with Recife underground figures by night. Live music and electronica.

Olinda *p436, map p438*
Beginning at dusk, but best after 2100, the Alto da Sé becomes the scene of a small street fair, with arts, crafts, makeshift bars, barbecue stands, and impromptu traditional music. Every Fri night band musicians walk the streets serenading passers-by. Each Sun from 1 Jan to Carnaval there is a mini carnival in the streets of the city, with music and dancing.
Bodega do Veio, R do Amparo, T081-3429 0185. An Olinda institution with live music Thu-Sun. Sat nights are hosted by a famous local fiddle player, Mestre Saluciano, and his band, who play traditional *pe na serra forró*. Great *petiscos* (especially the *prato frio*) and *caipirinhas*.
Cantinho da Sé, Ladeira da Sé 305, T081-3439 8815. Lively, good view of Recife, food served.
Farandola, R Dom Pedro Roeser, 190, tucked away behind Igreja do Carmo church. Mellow bar with festival theme and big top-style roof. Live music nightly, plans for a circus next door. Drinks are cheap; try *bate bate de maracuja* (smooth blend of *cachaça*, passionfruit juice and honey) or *raspa raspa* fruit syrup. Warmly recommended.
Marola, Tr Av Dantas Barreto 66, T081-3429 2499. Funky wooden *barraca* on rocky shore-line specializing in seafood. Great *caiprifrutas* (frozen fruit drink with vodka – try the cashew). Can get crowded. Recommended.
Pernambucanamente, Av Min Marcos Freire 734, Bairro Novo, T081-3429 1977. Live, local music every night.

Itamaracá *p441*
Bar da Lia, R do Jaguaribe, close to the Forte Orange, weekends feature *cirandus* danced at the bar, led by the well-known singer, Dona Lia, and her band. Also serves food.

Festivals and events

Recife *p431, map p435*
For Carnival, see box on page 448.
1 Jan Universal Brotherhood.

Carnaval in Olinda and Recife

Carnaval in Olinda and Recife vies with Rio and Salvador as the best in Brazil. While Rio Carnaval moves along the dedicated arena of the Sambódromo to the sound of samba, and Salvador is a riotous two million strong street party energized by pounding *axé* music, Recife and Olinda are more traditional street celebrations powered by Pernambuco's myriad rhythms such as *frevo*, *coco* and *maracatu*. *Maracatu* is also the name given to the schools and *blocos* in Pernambuco, each of whom were originally enslaved denizens of particular African nations who used proto-Carnaval celebrations to articulate their individual identities in a foreign land – leading to intense rivalries that persist to this day. Here are the essential facts for planning your Recife Carnaval:

➔ Times and *blocos* are announced in the local press and in tourist offices (who are very helpful with all Carnaval related information; such as details of the Carnaval press offices and of where tourists can learn Carnaval dance steps).

➔ Avenida Guararapes in Recife, Pina near Boa Viagem, Largo do Amparão and Mercado Eufrásio Barbosa (Varadouro) in Olinda are the main centres for the festivities. The best place to see the groups is from the balconies of **Hotel do Parque** or **Recife Palace Hotel** in Recife and the various hotels that line the streets of Olinda. Seats in the stands and boxes can be booked up to a fortnight in advance at the central post office in Avenida Guararapes, Recife.

➔ There is a *pre-carnavalesca* week which starts with the *Bloco da Parceria* in Boa Viagem (with many top Recife acts) and the *Virgens de Bairro Novo* in Olinda led by drag queens. These are followed by carnival balls such as *Baile dos Artistas* (popular with the gay community) and the *Baile Masque* held at the Portuguese club, Rua Governador Agamemnon Magalhães.

➔ Carnaval is officially opened on the first Saturday by the *bloco* Galo da Madrugada – a giant cockerel float – and the great Recife percussionist Naná Vasconcelos usually leads the drum troupes. Crowds reach over one million. This is followed by other events between Sunday and Tuesday.

➔ The *maracatu blocos* dance at the doors of all the churches they pass; they usually go to the church of Nossa Senhora do Rosário dos Pretos, patron saint of the slaves (Rua Estreita do Rosário, Santo Antônio), before proceeding into the downtown areas. A small car at the head bears the figure of an animal and is followed by the king and queen under a large, showy umbrella. Next comes the *dama do passo* carrying a small doll, or *calunga*. After the *dama* comes the *tirador de loas* who chants to the group which replies in chorus, and last comes a band of local percussion instruments.

➔ Look out for the *caboclinhos* in indigenous costume with bright feathers round their waists and ankles, colourful cockades, bead and animal teeth necklaces and a dazzle of medals on their red tunics. The dancers beat out the rhythm with bows and arrows; others of the group play African and indigenous musical instruments. The dance is spectacular: spinning, leaping, and stooping with almost mathematical precision.

12-15 Mar Parades to mark the city's foundation.
Mid-Apr Pro-Rock Festival, a week-long celebration of rock, hip-hop and *manguebeat SP at Centro de Convenções, Complexo de Salgadinho and other venues. Check Diário de Pernambuco* or *Jornal de Comércio* for details.
Jun Festas Juninhas, see box, page 462.

11-16 Jul Nossa Senhora do Carmo, patron saint of the city.
Aug Mes do Folclore.
Oct **Recifolia**, a repetition of the Carnaval over a whole weekend; dates vary.
1-8 Dec **Festival of Lemanjá**, with typical foods and drinks, celebrations and offerings to the goddess.
8 Dec **Nossa Senhora da Conceição.**

Olinda *p436, map p438*
Feb **Carnaval**. Thousands of people dance through the narrow streets of the old city to the sound of the *frevo*, the brash energetic music that normally accompanies a lively dance performed with umbrellas. The local people decorate them with streamers and straw dolls, and form themselves into costumed groups (*blocos*), which you can join as they pass (take only essentials). Among the best-known *blocos*, which carry life-size dolls, are **O homem da meianoite** (Midnight Man), **A Corda** (a pun on 'the rope' and 'acorda' – wake up!), which parades in the early hours, **Pitombeira and Elefantes.** Olinda's carnival continues on Ash Wed, but is much more low-key, *a quarta-feira do batata* (Potato Wednesday, named after a waiter who claimed his right to celebrate Carnaval after being on duty during the official celebrations). The streets are very crowded with people dancing and drinking non-stop. The local cocktail, *capeta* (guaraná powder, sweet skimmed milk and vodka) is designed to keep you going.
12-15 Mar **Foundation Day**, 3 days of music and dancing, night-time only.

Bezerros *p441*
Feb Carnaval celebrations are famous throughout Brazil and known as **Folia do Papangu**. Papangu characters wear masks that resemble a cross between a bear and a devil and are covered from head to foot in a costume like a bear skin (a variant is an all-covering white tunic).
Jun São João.

Caruaru *p442, map p420*
Mar/Apr **Semana Santa**, Holy Week, with lots of folklore and handicraft events.
18-22 May **The city anniversary.**
13 Jun **Santo Antônio.**
24 Jun **São João**, a particularly huge *forró* festival, part of Caruaru's **Festas Juninhas**. The whole town lights up with dancing, traditional foods, parties like the **Sapadrilha**, when the women dress as men, and the **Gaydrilha**, where the men dress as women, and there is even a *Trem do Forró*, which runs from Recife to Caruaru, rocking the whole way to the rhythms.
Sep **Micaru**, a street carnival. Also in Sep is **Vaquejada**, a Brazilian cross between rodeo and bull fighting; biggest in the northeast.

Shopping

Recife *p431, map p435*
Markets
The permanent craft market is in the **Casa da Cultura**; prices for ceramic figurines are lower than Caruaru.
Cais de Alfândega, Recife Barrio. With local artisans work, first weekend of the month.
Domingo na Rua, Sun market in Recife Barrio, stalls of local *artesanato* and performances.
Hippy fair, Praça Boa Viagem, seafront. Life-sized wooden statues of saints, Sat-Sun only.
Mercado São José (1875), for local products and handicrafts.
Sítio Trindade, Casa Amarela. Sat craft fair during the feast days of 12-29 Jun, fireworks, music, dancing, local food. On 23 Apr, here and in the Pátio de São Pedro, one can see the *xangô* dance. Herbal remedies, barks and spices at Afogados market.

Shopping malls
Shopping Center Recife, between Boa Viagem and the airport, www.shopping-recife.com.br. One of the largest in the country, with clothes, CDs, bookshops and lots more.
Shopping Tacaruna, Santo Amaro. Buses to/from Olinda pass.

Bezerros *p441*
The city's main attraction is handicrafts, which are found in the district of Encruzilhada de São João; items in leather, clay, wood, papier mâché and much more.

Caruaru *p442, map p420*
Caruaru is most famous for its markets which, combined, are responsible for about 70% of the city's income. The **Feira da**

Sulanca is basically a clothes market supplied mostly by local manufacture, but also on sale are jewellery, souvenirs, food, flowers and anything else that can go for a good price. The most important day is Mon. There is also the **Feira Livre** or **do Troca-Troca** (free, or barter market). On the same site, Parque 18 de Maio, is the **Feira do Artesanato**, leather goods, ceramics, hammocks and basketware, all the popular crafts of the region; it is tourist orientated but it is on a grand scale and is open daily 0800-1800.

Activities and tours

Recife *p431, map p435*

Diving

Offshore are some 20 wrecks, including the remains of Portuguese galleons; the fauna is very rich.

Mergulhe Coma, T081-3552 2355, T081-9102 6809 (mob), atlanticdivingasr@hotmail.com. English-speaking instructors for PADI courses.

Seagate, T081-3426 1657, www.seagaterecife.com.br. Daily departures and night dives.

Football

Recife's 3 clubs are Sport, Santa Cruz and Nautico. **Sport** play at Ilha do Retiro, T081-3227 1213, take Torrões bus from the central post office on Av Guararapes. **Santa Cruz** play at Arruda, T081-3441 6811, take Casa Amarela bus from the central post office. **Nautico** play at Aflitos, T081-3423 8900, take Água Fria or Aflitos bus. Local derbies are sometimes full beyond safe capacities. Avoid *arquibancada* tickets for Santa Cruz-Sport games. For games at Arruda, dress down.

Tour operators

Jacaré e Cobra de Água Eco-Group, T081-3447 3452, 9687360 (mob), www.truenet.com.br. Regular excursions in Pernambuco.

Souto Costa Viagens e Turismo Ltda, R Felix de Brito Melo 666, T081-3465 5000, and Aeroporto de Guararapes (American Express representative).

Student Travel Bureau (STB), R Padre Bernardino Pessoa 266, T081-3465 4522, F3465 2636, stbmaster@stb.com.br. ISIC accepted, discounts on international flights but not domestic Brazilian flights.

Trilhas, T081-3222 6864, recommended for ecologically oriented excursions.

Olinda *p436, map p438*

Tour operators

Viagens Sob O Sol, Prudente de Moraes 424, T/F081-429 3303, T081-971 8102 (mob), English spoken, transport, car hire.

Victor Turismo, Av Santos Domont, 20, loja 06, T081-3494 1467. Day and night trips to Recife.

Victor Turismo, **Felitur**, R Getulio Vargas 1411, Bairro Novo, T/F081-439 1477.

Porto de Galinhas *p440*

Diving

AICA Diving, Nossa Senhora do Ó, T/F081-552 1290 or T081-968 4876 (mob), run by Mida and Miguel. For diving and canoeing trips, as well as excursions to Santo Aleixo island.

Porto Point Diving, Praça Principal de Porto de Galinhas, T081-552 1111. Diving and canoeing trips, as well as excursions to Santo Aleixo island.

Transport

Recife *p431, map p435*

Air

Bus No 52 runs to the airport, US$0.40. International flights to Lisbon and Milan. Domestic flights to **Brasília**, **Campina Grande**, **Fernando de Noronha**, **Fortaleza**, **João Pessoa**, **Juazeiro do Norte**, **Maceió**, **Natal**, **Paulo Afonso**, **Petrolina**, **Rio de Janeiro**, **Salvador** and **São Paulo**.

Airline offices BRA, T081-3421 7060, www.voebra.com.br and the airport. **Gol**, T081-3464 4793, www.voegol.com.br and the airport. **Nordeste/RioSul**, Av Domingos Ferreira 801, loja 103-5, T081-465 6799 (**RioSul**, T081-3465 6799), at airport, T081-341 3187. **Ocean Air**, www.oceanair.com.br. **TAM**, reservations T081-342 5011, at airport, T081-3462 4466. **TAP Air Portugal**, Av Conselheiro de Aguiar 1472, Boa Viagem T081-3465 8800, at airport T081-3341 0654. **Trip**, T081-3464 4610 (for flights to Noronha) www.voetrip.com.br and the airport. **United**, R Progreso 465/802, T081-3423 2444. **Varig**, R Conselheiro de Aguiar 456, Boa Viagem,

T081-3464 4440, R J E Favre 719, T081-3339 2998, at airport T081-3341 4411, cargo T081-3465 8989.

Bus

To get to the *rodoviária*, take the Metrô from the central railway station, entrance through Museu do Trem, opposite the Casa da Cultura, 2 lines leave the city, take train marked 'Rodoviária', 30 mins. From Boa Viagem a taxi all the way costs US$20, or go to central Metrô station and change there. Bus from the centre (1 hr) or from Boa Viagem. Bus tickets are sold at Cais de Santa Rita (opposite EMTU).

Buses to the nearby destinations of **Igarassu** (every 15 mins) and **Itamaracá** (every 30 mins) leave from Av Martins de Barros, in front of Grande Hotel. To **Olinda** take any bus marked 'Rio Doce', No 981, which has a circular route around the city and beaches, or No 33 from Av Nossa Senhora do Carmo, US$0.60, or 'Jardim Atlântico' from the central post office at Siqueira Campos.

To **Cabo** (every 20 mins) and beaches south of Recife from Cais de Santa Rita.

To **Salvador**, daily 1930, 12 hrs, US$18-25, 4 a day (all at night) (1 *leito*, 70). To **Fortaleza**, 12 hrs, US$20 *convencional*, US$30 *executivo*. To **Natal**, 4 hrs, US$9. To **Rio**, daily 2100, 44 hrs, US$58-65. To **São Paulo**, daily 1630, 50 hrs, US$60-70. To **Santos**, daily 1430, 52 hrs, US$60. To **Foz do Iguaçu**, Fri and Sun 1030, 55 hrs, US$90. To **Curitiba**, Fri and Sun, 52 hrs, US$76. To **Brasília**, daily 2130, 39 hrs, US$49-60. To **Belo Horizonte**, daily 2115, 34 hrs, US$41. To **São Luís**, 28 hrs, Progresso at 1430 and 1945, US$75. To **Belém**, 34 hrs (Boa Esperança bus recommended). To **João Pessoa**, every 30 mins, US$2.50. To **Caruaru**, every hour, 3 hrs, US$3. To **Maceió**, US$9, 3½ hrs (express), 6 hrs (slow), either by the main road or by the coast road daily via 'Litoral'.

Car hire

Budget, T081-3341 2505. 24 hrs, just outside Guararapes airport. **Hertz**, T081-462 3552. **Localiza**, Av Visconde de Jequitinhonha 1145, T081-3341 0287, and at Guararapes airport, T081-3341 2082, freephone, T0800-992000.

Olinda *p436, map p438*

See also Ins and outs, page 436.

To **Recife**, the No 981 bus has a circular route around the city and beaches. The No 33 runs to Av Nossa Senhora do Carmo, US$0.60. Or take the Metrô from Praça do Carmo to Central station.

Taxi to **Boa Viagem** US$8, US$12 at night. Make sure the meter is set to rate 1, except on Sun, holidays or after 2100, when rate 2 applies.

Igarassu *p441*

Bus Buses run to Cais de Santa Rita, **Recife**, 45 mins, US$1.

Itamaracá *p441*

Bus Buses run to **Recife** (Av Martins de Barros opposite the Grande Hotel), US$1.10, very crowded) and **Igarassu**.

Caruaru *p442, map p420*

Bus See also Ins and outs, page 442. Buses from the centre, at the same place as Recife bus stop, to *rodoviária*, US$0.40. Many buses run to TIP in **Recife**, 2 hrs express, US$3. Bus to **Maceió**, 0700, 5 hrs, US$9. Bus to **Fazenda Nova** 1030, 1 hr, US$2, returns to Caruaru 1330.

Directory

Recife *p431, map p435*

Banks Open 1000-1600, hours for exchange vary between 1000 and 1400, sometimes later. **Banco do Brasil**, R Barão da Souza Leão 440, Boa Viagem; Av Dantas Barreto, 541, Santo Antonio, exchange and credit/debit cards, TCs. **Bradesco**, Av Cons Aguiar 3236, Boa Viagem, T081-3465 3033; Av Conde de Boa Vista, Boa Vista; R da Concordia 148, Santo Antônio, 24-hr VISA ATMs, but no exchange. **Citibank**, Av Marquês de Olinda 126, T081-3216 1144, takes MasterCard. Av Cons Aguiar, 2024, ATM. **Lloyds Bank**, R AL Monte 96/1002. MasterCard, Av Conselheiro Aguiar 3924, Boa Viagem, cash against card. **Money changers** at **Anacor**, Shopping Center Recife, loja 52, also at Shopping Tacaruna, loja 173. **Monaco**, Praça Joaquim Nabuco, cambio, TCs and cash, all major currencies, no commission but poor rates. **Norte Cambio Turismo**, Av Boa Viagem 5000, also at Shopping Guararapes, Av Barreto de

Menezes. **Cultural centres** British Council, Av Domingos Ferreira 4150, Boa Viagem, T081-3465 7744, www.britcoun.org/br. 0800-1500, reading room with current British newspapers, very helpful. **Alliance Française**, R Amaro Bezerra 466, Derby, T081-3222 0918. **Embassies and consulates** **Denmark**, Av Marques de Olinda 85, Edif Alberto Fonseca 2nd floor, T081-3224 0311, F3224 0997 (0800- 1200, 1400-1800). **France**, Av Conselheiro Aguiar 2333, 6th floor, T081-3465 3290. **Germany**, Av Dantas Barreto 191, Edif Santo Antônio, 4th floor, T081-3425 3288. **Japan**, R Pe Carapuceiro, 733, 14th floor, T081-3327 7264. **Netherlands**, Av Conselheiro Aguiar 1313/3, Boa Viagem, T081-3326 8096. **Spain**, R Sirinhaem, 105, 2nd floor, T081-3465 0607. **Sweden**, Av Conde de Boa Vista 1450, T081-3231 2581. **Switzerland**, Av Conselheiro Aguiar 4880, loja 32, Boa Viagem, T081-3326 3144. **UK**, Av Eng Domingos Ferreira 4150, Boa Viagem, T081-3465 7744 (0800-1130). **USA**, R Gonçalves Maia 163, Boa Vista, T081-3421 2441, F3231 1906. **Internet** **Shopping Centre Recife**, Boa Viagem. Also, **Lidernet**, Shopping Boa Vista, city centre. **popul@r.net**, R Barao de Souza Leao, near junction with Av Boa Viagem, daily 0900-2100. **Laundry** **AcquaClean**, Domingos Ferreira, 4023, Boa Viagem, T081-3466 0858, Mon-Fri 0630-1900, Sat 0800-1600. **Medical services** Dengue has been resurgent in Recife. Previous sufferers should have good insurance as a 2nd infection can lead to the haemorrhagic form, requiring hospitalization. **Hospital Santa Joana**, R Joaquim Nabuco 200, Graças, T081-3421 3666. **Unicordis**, Av Conselheiro Aguiar 1980, Boa Viagem, T081-3326 5237 and Av Conselheiro Rosa de Silva 258, Aflitos, T081-3421 1000, equipped for cardiac emergencies. **Post office** Poste Restante at Central Correios, Av Guararapes 250, next to Rio Capibaribe. 0900-1700, outgoing mail leaves at 1500 each day. Also has a philately centre. Another on R 24 de Maio 59. Poste Restante also with American Express representative Souto Costa, R Félix Brito de Melo 666, T081-465 5000, and at Av Conselheiro Aguiar, Boa Viagem.

Olinda *p436, map p438*

Banks There are no facilities to change TCs, or ATMs, is the old city. **Banco do Brasil**, R Getulio Vargas 1470. Bandepe, Av Getulio Vargas, MasterCard ATMs. **Bradesco**, R Getulio Vargas 729, Visa ATMs. **Internet** **Studyo Web**, Praça do Carmo, US$1.20, 30 mins, a/c. **Olind@.com**, 15, Av Beira Mar, US$1.50, 30 mins. **Laundry** **Cooplav**, Estr dos Bultrins, cost per weight of laundry, easily visible from main road, take Bultrins bus from Olinda. **Medical services** **Prontolinda**, R José Augusto Moreira 1191, T081-432 1700, general, but also equipped for cardiac emergencies. **Post office** Praça do Carmo, open 0900-1700.

Fernando de Noronha

→ *Phone code: 081.*

This small volcanic island rising from the deep, on the eastern edge of the mid-Atlantic ridge 350 km off the coast, is the St Barts of Brazil and one of the world's great romantic destinations. It is blessed with exceptional natural beauty; rugged like the west of Ireland, covered in maquis like Corsica and fringed by some of the cleanest and most beautiful beaches in the Atlantic. Many of the beaches are exposed to the full force of the ocean and pummelled by a powerful bottle-green surf that has earned the island the nickname 'the Hawaii of the Atlantic'. Surf championships are held on Cacimba do Padre beach. However, there are numerous coves where the sea is kinder and the broad beaches are dotted with deep clear-water rock pools busy with juvenile reef fish. The water changes through shades of aquamarine to deep indigo and is as limpid as any on Earth. Diving here rivals Mexico's Cozumel and the Turks and Caicos.

Despite the fact that two thirds of the island is settled, it is an important nesting ground for turtles and marine birds, both the island itself and the seas around it are a marine park, protected by Ibama. All that is needed to make it a sanctuary of international standing is to remove the non-native feral monitor lizards (brought here in the 20th century to kill rats), goats and the island's abundant cats and dogs. Tourism, however, is controlled and only limited numbers can visit the island at any time. Book well in advance. ▸▸ *For Sleeping, Eating and other listings, see pages 454-455.*

Ins and outs

Getting there and around Flights to the island from Recife and Natal are run by **TRIP** and **Varig**. **CVC**, www.cruisevacationcenter.com, operates a small cruise liner, which sails from Recife to Noronha and then back to Recife via Fortaleza and Natal. Buggy hire, motorbike hire and jeep tours are available in town, from your pousada or the numerous pamphleteers who greet each flight. **Pousada Maravilha**, www.pousada maravilha.com.br, has free mountain bikes for guests. Hitching is easy as everyone stops. Buses run every half hour along the island's only main road.

Activities and tours There are good possibilities for hiking, horse riding and mountain biking. A guide or a ranger will take you to the marine park and to beaches like **Atalaia**, which has the best snorkelling. Trips should be booked in advance through an operator. **Locadora Ilha do Sol**, T081-3619 1132, T081-998 54051 (mob), www.pousadadovale.com, offers buggy rental and guided tours of the island.

Best time to visit The rains are from April to July. The vegetation turns brown in the dry season is August to March, but the sun shines all year round. Noronha time is one hour later than Brazilian Standard Time. There are far fewer mosquitoes here than on the coast but be sure to bring repellent (and sun cream).

Tourist information **Ibama** has imposed rigorous rules to prevent damage to the nature reserve and everything, from development to cultivation of food crops to fishing, is strictly administered, if not forbidden. Many locals are now dependent on tourism and most food is brought from the mainland; prices are about double. Entry to the island is limited and there is a tax of US$30, payable per day for the first week of your stay. In the second week the tax increases each day. Take sufficient *reais* as it's difficult to change money. For information see www.fernandonoronha.com.br.

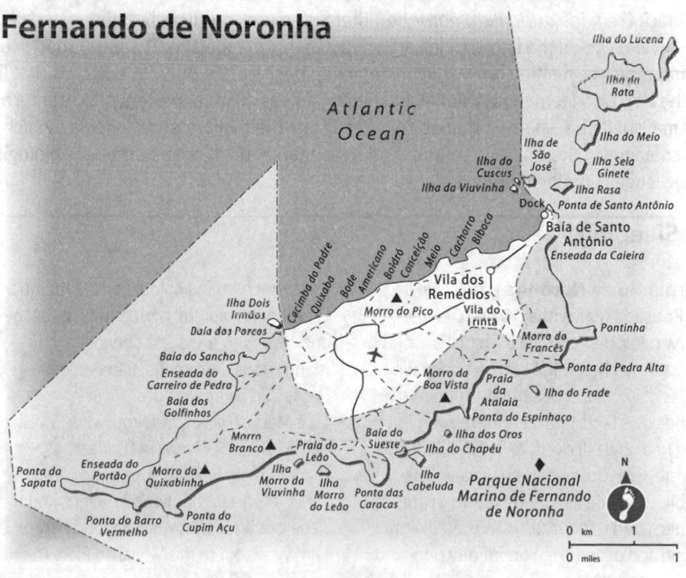

Sights

The island was discovered in 1503 by Amerigo Vespucci and was for a time a pirate lair. In 1738 the Portuguese built a charming little baroque church, **Nossa Senhora dos Remedios**, some attractive administrative buildings and a fort, **O Forte dos Remédios**, which was used as a prison for political dissidents by the military dictatorship in the late 20th century. The most famous was the communist leader Luis Carlos Prestes, who led the famous long march, the Prestes Column, in 1925-1927. Many people were tortured and murdered here. The islands were occupied by the United States during the Second World War and used as a naval base. US guns sit outside the Prefeitura in the centre of the main town, **Vila dos Remédios**, which overlooks the coast on the eastern shore.

Some of the best beaches lie immediately south of the town, clustered around an imposing granite pinnacle, the **Morro do Pico**. The most beautiful are **Conceição, Boldró, Americano, Baía do Sancho, Cacimba do Padre** and the turquoise cove at **Baía dos Porcos**, which sits on the edge of the beginning of the marine park. Beyond is the **Baía dos Golfinhos**, with a lookout point for watching the spinner dolphins in the bay. On the south, or windward side, there are fewer beaches, higher cliffs and the whole coastline and offshore islands are part of the marine park. As with dive sites, **Ibama** restricts bathing in low-tide pools and other sensitive areas to protect the environment.

Wildlife and conservation

The island is designated as a UNESCO World Heritage site, along with Atol das Rocas. It may look like an ecological paradise but it has been the victim of much degradation. Almost all of the native vegetation was chopped down in the 19th century, when the island was used as a prison, to prevent prisoners from hiding or making rafts. A giant native rodent, recorded by Amerigo Vespucci was wiped out and linseed, feral cats, dogs, goats, rats, mice, tegu lizards and cavies were introduced in the 16th century. These continue to damage bird and turtle nesting sites and native vegetation to this day. Nonetheless, the island remains an important sanctuary for sea bird species. Ruddy turnstone, black and brown noddy, sooty tern, fairy tern, masked booby, brown booby and white-tailed tropicbird all nest here. Some endemic bird species survive to this day: the Noronha vireo (*Vireo gracilirostris*); a tyrant flycatcher, the Noronha elaenia or cucuruta (*Elaenia spectabilis reidleyana*); and the Noronha eared dove or arribaçã (*Zenaida auriculata noronha*). There is an endemic lizard (*Mabuya maculate*) and at least 5% of the fish species are unique to the archipelago. The most spectacular animals are the nesting hawksbill and green turtles, and the spinner dolphins that live in the bay. Good terrestrial wildlife and birding guides are non-existent on Noronha and **Ibama** spell the species names incorrectly on their information sheets, which is discouraging. There are a number of reasonable dive shops; though biological knowledge is pretty minimal.

Sleeping

Fernando de Noronha *p452, map p453*

LL Pousada Maravilha, T081-3619 1290, www.pousadamaravilha.com.br. One of the finest beach hotels in South America with a series of luxurious, beautifully appointed bungalows (and smaller annexe rooms) perched on a hill overlooking the Bahia do Sueste. Every room has a bay view. The public areas are its tour de force in carefully understated good taste; furnished in light wood and overlooking an infinity pool and the ever-changing colours of the Atlantic. Excellent restaurant, gym, sauna, massage and help with tours and services on the island. Transfer from Rio, São Paulo or Recife can be arranged.

L Zé Maria, R Nice Cordeirol, Floresta Velha, T081-3619 1258, www.pousadaze maria.com.br. Spacious bungalows with cream tile floors, hardwood ceilings and generous beds with verandas and hammocks, with views out to the Morro do Pico. The highlight of the public areas is the delicious, but small deep-blue half-moon pool.

L-AL Solar dos Ventos, T081-3619 1347, www.pousadasolardosventos.com.br. Next door to the **Maravilha** and sharing the same spectacular view; although not in the same league. The wood, brick and tile bungalows are well-appointed, though a little small. The pousada has no pool.

AL Pousada do Vale, T081-3619 1293, www.pousadadovale.com. Friendly, well-run pousada with a range of comfortable, well-appointed rooms with bathrooms decorated with mosaics showing Noronha sea life. The best rooms are the duplex wooden bungalows. A few hundred metres from Vila dos Remedios town centre.

A-B Pousada dos Corais, Conj. Residencial Floresta Nova, Quadra 'D' Casa 07, T081-3619 1147, www.pousadacorais.com.br. 8 simple a/c rooms overlooking a small pool. One of the few 'cheaper' options.

Eating

Fernando de Noronha *p452, map p453*

TTT Ecologiku's, Estr Velha do Sueste, T081-3619 1807. Great Bahian cooking, with particularly delicious *moqueca*, served in an open-sided, mood-lit restaurant with a little garden. Good *caipirinhas*.

TTT Porto Marlin, Porto de Santo Antônio, T081-3619 1452. Good Japanese food à la carte with an all-you-can-eat buffet on Thu and Sat evenings from 1800.

T Açai e Raizes, BR363, Floresta Velha, T081-3619 0058. Roadside sandwich bar with good snacks, puddings and delicious cream of Cupuaçu and Açai.

T Cia da Lua, Bosque dos Flamboyantes, T081-3619 1631. Decent coffee, snacks, sandwiches, internet access and car and buggy rental.

T Jacaré, Praça Presidente Eurico Dutra (next to the Banco Real), T081-3619 1947. The best-value restaurant on the island with lunchtime seafood and general Brazilian buffet.

Bars and clubs

Vila dos Remédios town, which is the size of a postage stamp, has several bars including a pizzeria with lively weekend *forró* from 2200 on weekends, and a bar with live reggae nightly in high season.

Activities and tours

Fernando de Noronha *p452, map p453*

Tour and dive operators

It is possible to see hatching turtles in season. TAMAR, together with **Ibama** open nests to free turtles and invite the public to see them head for the sea. Several species nest here including hawksbill, leatherback and green turtles. For details, contact **Fundação Pró-Tamar**, Caixa Postal 50, CEP 53990-000, Fernando de Noronha, T081-3619 1269, F619 1386.

Atlantis Divers, T081-3619 1371, www.atlantisdivers.com.br. Águas Claras and Noronha Divers all offer the same dive locations around Noronha and the offshore islands, as well as dive 'baptism' for complete beginners. Diving costs US$50-75 for 2 tanks and is by far the best in Brazil aside from Atol das Rocas, 2 days off Bahia.

Barco Naonda, Vila do Porto, T081-3619 1307, www.barconaonda.com.br. One of many companies offering boat trips around the island. The best leave at lunchtime, catching the late afternoon light on their return.

Transport

Fernando de Noronha *p452, map p453*

Air Daily flights to **Recife** with **Varig** and TRIP (1 hr 20 mins, US$400 return). To **Natal** with TRIP (1 hr, US$300 return).

Paraíba

Travellers used to bypass Paraíba, but they are now beginning to discover that there are many reasons to stop. The beaches are some of Brazil's best and least spoilt. Some of the most important archaeological sites in the Americas sit in the haunting, rugged landscapes of its interior and the state capital, João Pessoa, is an attractive colonial city with a lively nightlife. Every June Campina Grande, an attractive and prosperous city on the edge of the sertão, *hosts one of the countries biggest festivals, the Festa do São João, with live music and up to a million people dancing* forró *into the small hours.*

The dense tropical forest that once covered the entire coastal strip now only survives in patches, one of which is within the city of João Pessoa; forming one of the largest areas of wilderness within any city in the world. The seaboard is marked for much of its length by offshore reefs. Inland from the coastal plain the Zona da Mata is an abrupt line of hills and plateaus, a transitional region between the moist coast and the much drier interior. Most people live in this zone, especially in and around the state capital and a couple of other industrial centres. » For Sleeping, Eating and other listings, see pages 463-468.

João Pessoa and around » pp463-468.

→ *Phone code: 083. Colour map 2, B6. Population: 598,000.*

João Pessoa is the capital of the state yet retains a small town atmosphere. It has some attractive colonial architecture and is set on the Rio Paraíba amid tropical forest. The atmosphere is restful and laid-back, yet there are plenty of bars and restaurants along the beachfront, particularly popular at weekends.

Ins and outs

Getting there and around It is a two-hour bus ride through sugar plantations on a good road from Recife (126 km) to João Pessoa. The **Presidente Castro Pinto Airport** ⓘ *11 km south of the centre, T083-232 1200*, receives flights from São Paulo, Brasília, Recife and Rio de Janeiro. A taxi from the airport to centre costs US$8, to Tambaú US$12. **Gol** will fly from São Paulo or Rio to Recife, then provide free bus transport to João Pessoa. The **rodoviária** ⓘ *R Francisco Londres, Varadouro, 10 mins west of the centre, T083-221 9611*, has a luggage store and helpful **PBTUR** information booth. A taxi to the centre costs US$1.50, to Tambaú US$5. All city buses stop at the *rodoviária* and most go by the Lagoa (Parque Solon de Lucena). From the centre, take No 510 for Tambaú, No 507 for Cabo Branco. The **ferroviária** ⓘ Av Sanhauá, Varadouro, T083-221 4257, has train connections to Bayeux and Santa Rita in the west, and Cabedelo to the north.

Tourist information There's a tourist office **PBTUR** ⓘ *Centro Turístico Almte Tamandaré 100, Tambaú, T083-214 8279 or T0800-281 9229, 0800-1900*, and others at the *rodoviária*, T083-218 6655, and airport T083-253 4010. They provide useful information, pamphlets and maps. At least one member of staff in the Tambaú centre speaks good English and some French.

Background

The Portuguese did not gain a foothold on this part of the northeast coast until the end of the 16th century. Their fort became the city of Filipéia, which grew to become the third largest in Brazil. This was later re-named Parahyba and then João Pessoa, in honour of the once state governor who refused to form alliances with other powerful politicians during the 1930s run for the vice-presidency. This led to his assassination, an event which swept his running mate, the fascist, Getúlio Vargas to power. Pessoa's '*nego*' ('I refuse') is written on the state's flag.

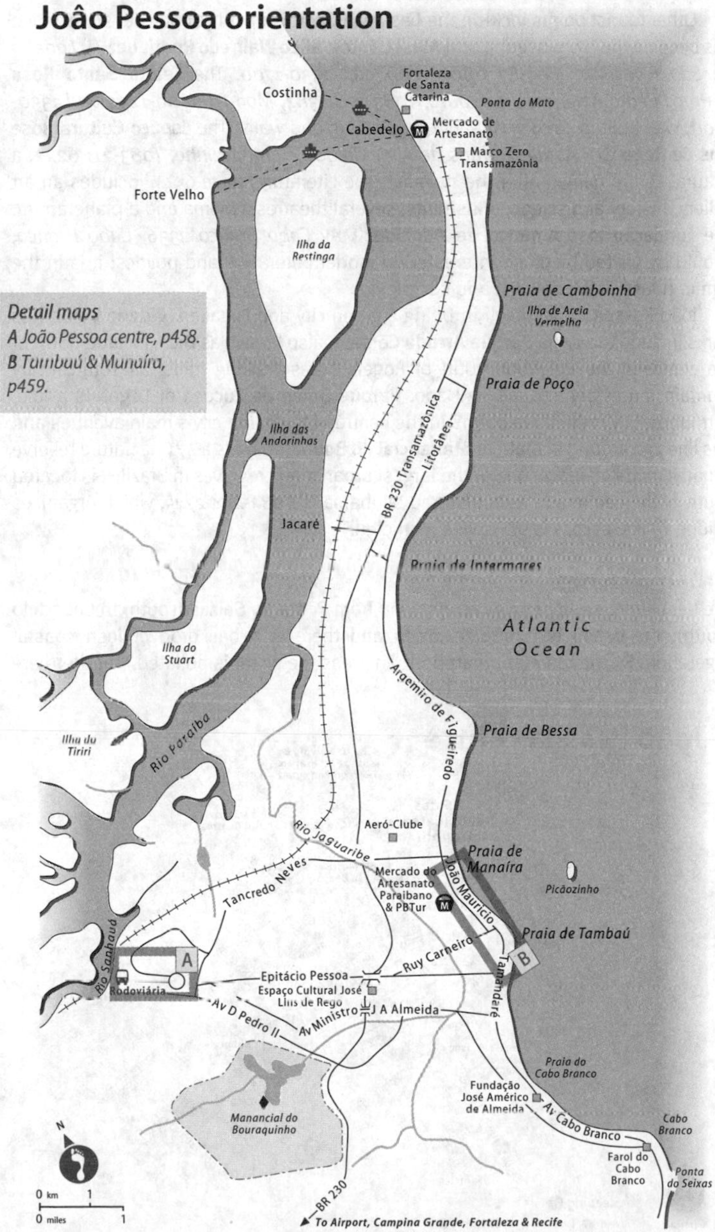

Sights

The well-preserved Centro Histórico has several churches and monasteries that are worth seeing. The **São Francisco Cultural Centre** ⓘ *Praça São Francisco 221*, one of the most important baroque structures in Brazil, includes the beautiful 16th-century church of São Francisco and the Convento de Santo Antônio, which houses the **Museu Sacro e de Arte Popular** ⓘ *Tue-Sat 0800-1100, Tue-Sun 1400-1700, T083-221 2840*, with a magnificent collection of colonial and popular artefacts. This is also the best point to see the sun set over the forest.

Other tourist points include the **Casa da Pólvora**, an old gunpowder store which has become the city museum, and **Museu Fotográfico Walfredo Rodríguez** ⓘ *Ladeira de São Francisco, Mon-Fri 0800-1200 and 1330-1700*. The **Teatro Santa Rosa** ⓘ *Praça Pedro Américo, Varadouro, T083-218 4382, Mon-Fri 0800-1200 and 1330-1800*, was built in 1886 with a wooden ceiling and walls. The **Espaço Cultural José Lins de Rego** ⓘ *R Abdias Gomes de Almeida 800, Tambauzinho, T083-211 6222*, a cultural centre named after the novelist (see Literature, page 694), includes an art gallery, history and science museums, several theatres, cinema and a planetarium. The **Fundação José Américo de Almeida** ⓘ *Av Cabo Branco 3336, Cabo Branco*, should be visited by those interested in modern literature and politics; it is in the former house of the novelist and sociologist.

João Pessoa prides itself in being a green city and is called 'Cidade Verde'. Its parks include the 17-ha **Parque Arruda Câmara**, also known as Bica, located north of the centre in the neighbourhood of Roger; it has walking trails, an 18th-century fountain, an aviary and a small zoo. **Parque Solon de Lucena** or **Lagoa** is a lake surrounded by impressive palms in the centre of town, the city's main avenues and bus lines go around it. **Mata** or **Manancial do Bouraquinho** is a 471-ha nature reserve of native *mata atlântica*, one of the largest urban forest reserves in Brazil. It is located south of the centre and administered by **Ibama** ⓘ *T083-244 2725*, which organizes guided walks; access is otherwise restricted.

Urban beaches

The beachfront stretches for some 30 km from Ponta do Seixas (south) to Cabedelo (north); the ocean is turquoise green and there is a backdrop of lush coastal vegetation. By the more populated urban areas the water is polluted, but there are

Tambaú & Manaíra

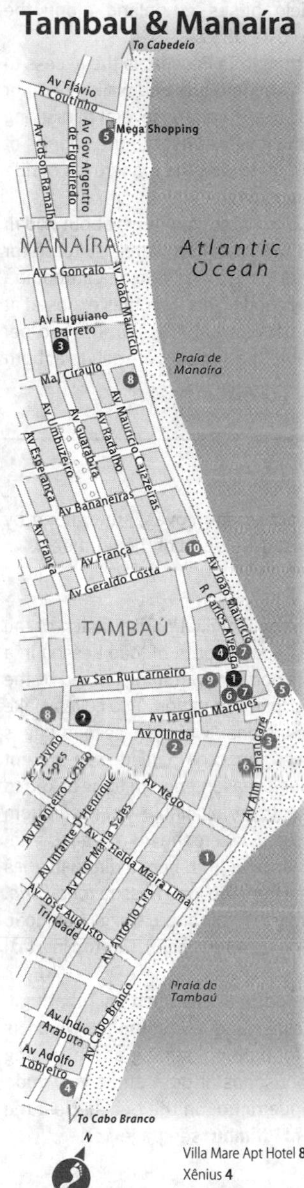

Sleeping
Caiçara 2
Littoral 1
Pousada Mar Azul 10
Royal Praia 5
Solar Filipéia 9
Tambía Praia 7
Tropical Tambaú 3
Victory Business Flat 6
Villa Mare Apt Hotel 8
Xênius 4

Eating
Adega do Alfredo 1
Cheiro Verde 4
Gulliver 2
Mangaí 3

Bars & clubs
Fashion Club 5
Incognito 6
Mr Caipira 8
Zodiaco 7

also parts away from town which are reasonably clean, some spots are calm and suitable for swimming while others are best for surfing. About 7 km from the city centre, following Avenida Presidente Epitáceo Pessoa, is the beach of **Tambaú**, which has many hotels, restaurants and the state tourism centre and is, for all intents and purposes, the centre of the city. The pier by **Hotel Tambaú** affords nice views (bus No 510 'Tambaú' from outside the rodoviária or the city centre, alight at **Hotel Tropical Tambaú**). South of Tambaú are **Praia de Cabo Branco** and **Praia do Seixas** and to the north are the beaches of **Manaíra**, **Bessa**, **Intermares**, **Poço** and **Camboinha**, before reaching the port of **Cabedelo**.

Excursions from João Pessoa

About 14 km south of the centre, down the coast, is the **Cabo Branco** lighthouse at Ponta do Seixas, the most easterly point of continental Brazil and South America (34° 46' 36" W) and thus the first place in the Americas where the sun rises; there is a panoramic view from the clifftop. **Cabo Branco** is much better for swimming than Tambaú. Take bus No 507 'Cabo Branco' from outside the *rodoviária* to the end of the line and hike up to the lighthouse from there. At low tide you can walk from Tambaú to Ponta do Seixas in about two hours.

The port of **Cabedelo**, on a peninsula between the Rio Paraíba and the Atlantic Ocean, is 18 km north by road or rail. Here, Km 0 marks the beginning of the **Transamazônica highway**. At the tip of the peninsula are the impressive, but somewhat run- down walls of the 17th-century fortress of **Santa Catarina,** amid oil storage tanks and the commercial port. The **Mercado de Artesanato** is at Praça Getúlio Vergas in the centre.

The estuary of the Rio Paraíba has several islands; there is a regular boat service between Cabedelo and the fishing villages of **Costinha** and **Forte Velho** on the north bank; Costinha had a whaling station until the early 1980s.

The beaches between João Pessoa and Cabedelo have many bars and restaurants and are very popular with the locals on summer weekends (**Bar do Sumé**, Rua Beira Mar 171, Praia Ponta do Mato, Cabedelo, has good fish and seafood). Take a bus marked

 Cabedelo-Poço for the beach as most Cabedelo buses go inland along the Transamazônica. A taxi from Tambaú to Cabedelo costs US$24.

At Km 3 of the Transamazônica, about 12 km from João Pessoa, is the access to **Jacaré**, a pleasant beach on the Rio Paraíba (take Cabedelo bus and walk 1½ km or take the train and walk 1 km, taxi from Tambaú US$10). There are several bars along the riverfront where people congregate to watch the lovely sunset to the sounds of Ravel's *Bolero*. Here you can hire a boat along the river to visit the mangroves or ride in an ultralight aircraft (see Activities and tours, page 467).

From Tambaú tour boats leave for **Picãozinho**, a group of coral reefs about 700 m from the coast which at low tide turn into pools of crystalline water, suitable for snorkelling (US$20 per person). Further north, boats leave from Praia de Camboinha to **Areia Vermelha**, a large sandbank surrounded by corals. This becomes exposed at low tide, around the full and new moon, and is a popular bathing spot (US$20 per person tour, US$5 per person transport in a *jangada*). Floating bars are set up at both locations, travel agencies arrange trips.

Paraíba coast

» *pp463-468.*

The Paraíba coastline has 117 km of beautiful beaches and coves, surrounded by cliffs and coconut groves. These are among the least developed of the northeast.

Tambaba

→ *Colour map 2, B6.*

The best-known beach of the state is Tambaba, the only official nudist beach of the northeast and one of only two in Brazil. It is located 49 km south of João Pessoa in a lovely setting: the green ocean, warm water, natural pools for swimming formed by the rocks, cliffs up to 20 m high full of caves, palms and lush vegetation. Two coves make up this famous beach: in the first bathing-suits are optional, while the second one is only for nudists. Strict rules of conduct are enforced, unaccompanied men are not allowed in this area and any inappropriate behaviour is reason enough to be asked to leave. The only infrastructure is one bar, where meals are available. Access is from **Jacumã**, via the BR-101, 20 km south from João Pessoa to where the PB-018 goes 3 km east to Conde and continues 11 km to the beach of Jacumã; from here a dirt road goes 12 km south to Tambaba. Buses run hourly to Jacumã from the João Pessoa *rodoviária*. In summer, dune buggies can be hired at Jacumã to go to Tambaba. Buggy from João Pessoa to Tambaba US$25 per person return (leave 0930, return 1730). Day trip in a taxi US$95.

Between Jacumã and Tambaba are several good beaches such as **Tabatinga**, which has many summer homes built on the cliffs, and **Coqueirinho**, which is surrounded by pleasant vegetation, and is good for bathing, surfing and exploring caves. There are plenty of cheap and mid-range pousadas at both and a very good seafood restaurant at Coqueirinho, **Canyon de Coqueirinho**, on the beach. Near the border with Pernambuco is the 10-km long beach of **Pitimbu**, see page 441.

Campina and around

The best beaches of northern Paraíba are in the vicinity of the fishing village of **Campina**; although there is little infrastructure in this area, the shore is worth a visit. Access is via a turnoff to the east at Km 73.5 of the BR-101, 42 km north of João Pessoa. It is 28 km along a dirt road (PB-025) to Praia Campina, with a wide beach of fine sand, palms and hills in the background. Nearly 3 km south is **Praia do Oiteiro**, in which the white sand stands out in contrast with the multicoloured cliffs and calm blue ocean. About 2 km north of Campina is **Barra do Mamanguape**, where **Ibama** runs a preservation centre for marine manatee.

Some 85 km from João Pessoa is **Baia da Traição**, a fishing village and access point for a number of beaches. Its name means 'Bay of Betrayal' and refers to the massacre of 500 residents of a sugar plantation in the 16th century. There is a reserve near town where wood and string crafts are made by the local indigenous people. An annual festival, **Festa do Toré** (an Indian dance), takes place on 19 April. Inho, a fisherman, offers tours by sea to the less accessible beaches in the area (US$15 per person). **Barra de Camaratuba**, about 17 km north of Baia da Traição, is a popular surfing beach.

The sertão

» pp463 468.

The semi-arid region of thorn and bush that makes up the hinterland of the northeast is known as the *sertão*. The Transamazônica runs right through the heart of the region, due west of João Pessoa as the BR-230, and along the axis of the state of Paraíba.

Campina Grande

Phone code: 083. Colour map 2, B6. Population: 340,500.

Set in the Serra da Borborema, 551 m above sea level and 130 km west of João Pessoa, the second city in Paraíba has a very pleasant climate. Known as the '*porta do sertão*' (door of the sertão), it is an important centre for light industry and an outlet for goods from most of northeast Brazil. In the 1920s it was one of the most important cotton producing areas in the world; a decline in this industry brought a decrease in prosperity in the 1940s and 1950s and the diversification of industry to areas such as sisal and leather. The city's two universities have been instrumental in technological development and reactivation of the local economy.

Ins and outs The **João Suassuna airport** ⓘ *7 km south of centre on the road to Caruaru, T083-331 1149*, receives daily flights from Recife. A taxi from the airport to the centre US$7. A city bus runs to Praça Clementino Procópio, behind Cine Capitólio. The *rodoviária* is at Avenida Argemiro de Figuereido, a 20-minute ride from the centre, T083-321 5780. Tourist information is available from **PBTUR** ⓘ *T156 for information*, and **DEMTUR** ⓘ *T083-341 3993, Municipal*.

Sights Avenida Floriano Peixoto is the main street running east-west through the entire city, with Praça da Bandeira at its centre. The **Museu de Arte Assis Chateaubriand** ⓘ *Parque do Açude Novo, T083-341 3300, Mon-Fri 0900-1200, daily 1400-2200*, has a collection of paintings and etchings by Brazilian artists and temporary exhibits. **Museu Histórico de Campina Grande** ⓘ *Av Floriano Peixoto 825, Centro, daily 0800-1130, 1300-1645*, is the city museum housed in a 19th-century building, with a photo and artefact collection reflecting the cycles of prosperity and poverty in the region. **Museu da História e Tecnologia do Algodão** ⓘ *Centro Nacional de Produção do Algodão, Oswaldo Cruz 1143, Centenário, T083-341 3608, Mon-Fri 0730- 1130, 1330-1730, Sat and Sun 0800-1200*, has machines and related equipment used in the cotton industry in the 16th and 17th centuries. **Museu Regional de São João** ⓘ *Largo da Estação Velha, Centro, T083-341 2000, daily 0800-1300*, houses an interesting collection of objects and photographs pertaining to the June celebrations.

The **Teatro Municipal Severino Cabral** ⓘ *Av Floreano Peixoto*, is a modern theatre where there are regular performances. The main parks in town are: the **Parque do Açude Novo** (Evaldo Cruz), a green area with playgrounds, fountains and restaurants; the nearby **Parque do Povo** with its *forródromo* where the main festivities of the city take place; and the **Açude Velho**, a park around a dam south of the centre. The **Mercado Central**, where a large roof has been built over several blocks of old buildings, has regional crafts and produce, is worth a visit.

The world's greatest barn dance – the Festas Juninhas

Carnaval is essentially an urban, black Brazilian celebration. The Festas Juninhas, which take place throughout Brazil during June, are a rural celebration. While carnival pounds to samba, the Juninhas pulsate to the triangle and accordion of *forró*. Rather than wearing feathers and sequins, Juninhas revellers dress up as *caipiras* (yokels) in tartan shirts and reed hats; and they eat *canjica* (maize porridge) and drink *quentão* (a Brazilian version of mulled wine). And they do it in enormous numbers. During the most important weekend of the festivals – the eve of St John's Day on the 23rd of June – over one million mock-*caipiras* descend on the little backland towns of Campina Grande in Paraíba and Caruaru in Pernambuco. Both towns are entirely taken over by *forró* bands, cowboys, stalls selling *doce de leite* and other country produce, and the percussion of fireworks and bangers. Foreign visitors are still a rare curiosity.

Excursions from Campina Grande

About 10 km north from Campina Grande is **Lagoa Seca**, where figures in wood and sacking are made, and there is a **Museu do Índio**.

Some 35 km east of Campina Grande, off the road to João Pessoa, is **Ingá**, site of the **Pedra de Itacoatiara** archaeological centre, where inscriptions dated as 10,000 years old were found on a boulder 25 m long and 3 m high. A small museum at the site contains fossils of a giant sloth and a Tyrannosaurus rex. During the June festivities there is a train service to Itacoatiara.

The **Boqueirão** dam on the Rio Paraíba, 70 km southeast of town, is where locals flock on holidays for watersports; there is a hotel-*fazenda* (T081-391 1233).

Cariri

The *sertão* proper begins near São João do Cariri an hour or so from Campina Grande. This is an area of fascinating rock formations, with giant weather-worn boulders sitting on top of gently curved expanses of rock that look out over a plain of low bushes and stunted trees. Although the vegetation is quite different to the landscape itself; the arid conditions and the size of the trees recalls the Australian outback (the rocks themselves have been compared to the Devil's Marbles). The most spectacular of all the formations sit in the private grounds of *fazenda* **Pai Mateus** (see Sleeping, page 465). Like various other sites in Paraíba and Rio Grande do Norte, boulders here are covered in important pre-Colombian rock art, some of which has been controversially dated as pre-Clovis (making it older than recent datings for the first waves of American population coming from over the Bering Strait). A famous local holy man lived inside one of the giant hollowed-out stones and the views from his former home at sunset are particularly spellbinding. The *fazenda* itself is a very pleasant place to stay and there is rich, though depleted wildlife in the area and good birdwatching. Tours can be organized with **Manary Ecotours** in Natal (see Activities and tours, page 484), who provide fascinating information about the archaeological sites but have little knowledge of the fauna in the region. The *fazenda*'s guides are informative about life in the Sertão and the use of medicinal plants, but again as ever in Brazil, knowledge of birds and animals is poor.

North of Cariri, 46 km from Campina Grande, is **Areial**, the main town of the Brejo Paraibano, a scenic region of green hills and valleys, with a pleasant climate, where colonial sugar *fazendas* have been transformed into hotels.

Patos → *Colour map2, B5. Population: 84,500.*

West of Campina Grande the landscape turns to vast, flat expanses, flanked by rolling hills and interesting rock formations; very scenic when green, but a sad sight during the prolonged *sertão* droughts. Situated 174 km from Campina Grande is Patos, the centre of a cattle-ranching and cotton-growing area. It's also an access point for the **Serra do Teixeira**, 28 km away, which includes **Pico do Jabre**, the highest point in the state, at 1130 m above sea level. There are various hotels and restaurants in Patos.

Souza → *Phone code: 081. Colour map 2, B5. Population: 59,000.*

About 130 km northwest of Patos, the pleasant *sertão* town of Souza, has high temperatures year-round and is gaining fame for the nearby dinosaur tracks and prehistoric rock carvings. The *rodoviária* is 1 km from the centre, there are no city buses, walk (hot), take a moto-taxi (US$1) or a taxi (US$5). The **Igreja do Rosário** at the Praça Matriz has paintings dating to the Dutch occupation of the area. It currently functions as a school. About 3 km from the centre, atop a hill, is a **statue of Frei Damião**, an important religious leader of the northeast who died in 1997. Frei Damião was an Italian friar who came to Brazil in the 1930s and stayed to become an inspiration for the faith of its most recent generation of dispossessed. He is seen as belonging to the same tradition as O Conselheiro and Padre Cícero.

Fossilized dinosaur prints of up to 90 different species, which inhabited the area between 110 and 80 million years ago, are found in a number of sites in the Souza region. These were extensively studied by the Italian palaeontologist Giussepe Leonardi in the 1970s and 1980s. The **Vale dos Dinossauros**, on the sedimentary river bed of the Rio do Peixe, is one of the closest sites to Souza; it has some impressive Iguanodontus prints. Access is 4 km from town along the road north to Uiraúna; the best time to visit is the dry season, July to October. The area has no infrastructure and is best visited with a guide. Try to contact Robson Marques of the **Movisaurio Association** ① *R João Rocha 7, Souza, PB 58800-610, T083-522 1065*, who is very knowledgeable; otherwise contact the Prefeitura Municipal. Tours can be organized through **Manary Ecotours** in Natal (see page 484), these can be combined with visits to Cariri.

Cajazeiras → *Colour map 2, B5. Population: 51,000.*

Some 37 km west of Souza, the Transamazônica (BR-230) reaches Cajazeiras, the centre of a cotton-growing area, with an impressive tower on the main church and various hotels. This is an access point for the **Brejo das Freiras** thermal mineral baths 32 km to the north, an oasis with natural springs in the middle of the *sertão*.

From Cajazeiras it is 17 km to the Ceará border; the Transamazônica continues west across the *sertãos* of Ceará and Piauí and on to Maranhão, Tocantins and Pará. Southwest of Cajazeiras it is 118 km to Juazeiro do Norte, an important pilgrimage centre, see page 498.

Sleeping

João Pessoa centre *p456, map p458*

The town's main attractions are its beaches, where most tourists stay. Hotels in the centre are poorer and tend to cater for business clients. The centre is very quiet after dark and it is difficult to find a restaurant. Cheaper hotels can be found near the *rodoviária*; look carefully as some are quite sleazy. The most convenient beach and the focus of nightlife and restaurants is **Tambaú**. There are good restaurants and a few hotels in **Manaíra**, to the north of Tambaú. There are also a few in the southern beach suburb of **Cabo Branco**. But this is quieter and has fewer eating and nightlife options.

C-B Hotel JR, R João Ramalho de Andrade, T083-241 6262, www.bomguia.com.br/jr. 1990s business hotel with basic facilities and a restaurant. The largest and most comfortable in the centre.

C-D Guarany, R Almeida Barreto 181 and 13 de Maio, T/F083-241 5005, guarany@

bomguia.com.br/guarany. Cheaper in low season, or without a/c and TV. A pleasant, safe, extremely good-value establishment with a self-service restaurant. Recommended.

D Aurora, Praça João Pessoa 51, T083-241 3238. A/c or cheaper fan-cooled rooms, on an attractive square.

D Ouro Preto, Idaleto 162, T083-221 5882, Varadouro near *rodoviária*. Very simple rooms with baths and a fan.

Urban beaches *p458, map p459*

Accommodation can also be found in the outer beaches such as Camboinha and Seixas, and in Cabedelo.

L Littoral, Av Cabo Branco 2172, T083-247 1100, F247 1166. A full luxury service. Low-season discounts available.

AL Caiçara, Av Olinda 235, T/F083-247 2040, www.hotcaicarara.com.br. A slick, business-orientated place with a pleasant restaurant.

AL Tropical Tambaú, Av Alm Tamandaré 229, T083-247 3660, www.tropicalhotel.com.br. An enormous round building on the seafront which looks like a rocket-launching station and has comfortable motel-style rooms around its perimeter. Good service. Recommended.

AL Xênius, Av Cabo Branco 1262, T083-226 3535, www.xeniushotel.com.br. Popular standard 4-star hotel with a pool, good restaurant. Well-kept but standard a/c rooms, low-season reductions.

A-B Royal Praia, Coração de Jesus, T083-2106 3000, www.royalhotel.com.br. Comfortable a/c rooms with fridges, pool.

A-B Victory Business Flat, Av Tamandaré 310, T083-247 3011, www.victoryflat.com.br. Furnished apartments with a pool and sauna. Cheaper in low season.

B Pouso das Águas, Av Cabo Branco 2348, Cabo Branco. A homely atmosphere with landscaped areas and a pool.

B Tambía Praia , R Carlos Alverga 36, T083-247 4101, www.tambiahotel.hpg.com.br. Centrally located and 1 block from the beach. Intimate, with balconies and sea view. Recommended.

B Villa Mare Apartment Hotel, Av Négo 707, T083-226 2142, www.pbnet.com.br/openline/george. Comfortable apartments for 2 or 3 people with full amenities per night or from US$400-500 per month. Helpful staff. Recommended.

B-C Pousada Casa Rosada, Av Cabo Branco 1710, Cabo Branco. T083-247 2470. Well-kept rooms with bath and fans run by a friendly family. Cheaper with shared bath.

C Pousada Casa Grande, R Infante Dom Henrique 750, Manaíra, T083-226 2071, www.holandahhoteisezdir.net. Well-kept, simple rooms with en suites and friendly staff in a discreet small family hotel, 2 blocks from the beach.

C-D Solar Filipéia, Av Incognito Coracão de Jesus 153, www.solarfilipeia.com.br. Brand-new, very smart hotel with large, bright rooms with bathrooms in tile and black marble and excellent service. Good value.

E Pousada Mar Azul, Av João Maurício 315, T083-226 2660. Very clean large rooms, the best are on the upper level, right on the oceanfront road. Some have a/c and private bathrooms, others have fans. Well kept, safe and a real bargain.

Youth hostels

Hostel Manaíra, R Major Ciraulo 380, Manaíra, T083-247 1962, www.manairahostel.br2.net. Friendly new hostel close to the beach, with a pool, internet, barbecue, cable TV and breakfast. A real bargain.

Camping

Camping Clube do Brasil, Praia de Seixas, 13 km from the centre, T083-247 2181.

Tambaba *p460*

B Chalé Suiço, R Chalé Suiço 120, Tabatinga, T083-981 2046. Small, shared bath, restaurant, upstairs rooms have ocean-view balconies.

B Pousada Corais de Carapebus, Av Beira Mar, Carapebus, T083-290 1179, a few kilometres south of Jacumã. With bath, pool, restaurant and a nice breeze since it is located on a cliff across from the ocean.

B Vivenda Ocean, R Sidine C Dore 254, Carapebus, T083-226 6017. Chalets for 5, with restaurant.

C Vallhalla, R Niterói, Jacumã, T083-290 1015. Away from the beach with good views. Rooms are simple with a fan as the only extra. It's Swedish run and the restaurant has a varied menu.

Camping

Camping is possible in Tambaba with permission from the guards, also in Coqueirinho; no infrastructure in either.

Campina *p460*

C **Pousada Ponto do Sol**, Dom Pedro II 537, Baia da Traição, T083-296 1050. Rooms with baths and fridges, restaurant. On the same street are the simpler pousadas **Alvorada** and 2001, T083-296 1043. Several others in town.
C **Pousada Porto das Ondas**, Barra de Camaratuba, T083-247 2054. Bath, fan, restaurant.

Campina Grande *p461*

Many hotels around Praça da Bandeira.
A **Ouro Branco**, João Lourenço Porto 20, T083-341 2929, F322 5788. Cheaper rooms are available with discounts for cash.
A **Serrano**, Tavares Cavalcante 27, T083-341 3131, F321 0635. Luxury standard with pool and restaurant. You can get discounts for cash.
B **Mahatma Gandhi**, Floriano Peixoto 338, T/F083-321 5275. With bath, a/c (cheaper with fan), fridge.
B **Souto Maior**, Floriano Peixoto 289, T083-321 8043, F321 2154. Rooms include bath a/c and fridge.
C **Regente**, Barão do Abiaí 80, T083-321 3843, F321 3843. With bath, a/c or fan, fridge.
C-D **Pérola**, Floriano Peixoto 258, T083-341 5319. With bath and a/c, cheaper with fan, parking and a very good breakfast.
D **Avenida**, Floriano Peixoto 378, T083-341 1249. With fan, good value, cheaper with shared bath.
D-E **Eliu's**, Maciel Pinheiro 31B, 1st floor, T083-321 4115. Clean, friendly, a/c and bath (cheaper with fan; cheaper still without bath), good value. Breakfast not provided.
D **Verona**, 13 de Maio 232, T083-341 1926. With bath, fan, good value, friendly service.
E **Aurora**, 7 de Setembro 120, T083-321 4874. Shared bath, very basic and run down.

Cariri *p462*

Fazenda Pai Mateus, www.paimateus.com.br, can be organized through **Manary Ecotours**, see Activities and tours, page 484.
B **Gadelha Palace**, Trav Luciana Rocha 2, Cariri, T081-521 1416. With bath, a/c, fridge, pool and restaurant.
C **Dormitório Sertanejo I**, R Col Zé Vicente, Cariri. Rooms nice and clean with bath and fan. No breakfast, but good value. Recommended.
E **Dormitório Aguiar**, R João Gualberto, Cariri. Very basic.

Cajazeiras *p463*

A **Estância Termal Brejo das Freiras**, São João do Rio do Peixe, T081-522 1515. Rooms or chalets with bath, a/c, fridge. There is a pool and restaurant.
C **Regente**, in centre, 15 mins' walk from *rodoviária*, a/c available but cheaper without. TV, bath.
E **Cacique**, near *rodoviária*, cheaper with fan.

Eating

João Pessoa *p456, map p458*

There are few eating options in the city centre. Locals eat at the stalls in Parque Solon de Lucena next to the lake, where there are a couple of simple restaurants.

Urban beaches *p458, map p459*

Every evening on the beachfront, stalls sell all kinds of snacks and barbecued meats. At Cabo Branco there are many straw huts on the beach serving cheap eats and seafood.
TTT **Adega do Alfredo**, Coração de Jesus. Very popular traditional Portuguese restaurant in the heart of the club and bar area.
TTT **Gulliver**, Av Olinda 590, Tambaú. Trendy French/Brazilian restaurant frequented by João Pessoa's upper middle classes.
TT **Cheiro Verde**, R Carlos Alverga 43. Self-service, well established, regional food.
TT **Mangaí**, Av General Édson Ramalho 696, Manaíra, T083-226 1615. This is one of the best restaurants in the northeast to sample the region's cooking. There are almost 100 different hot dishes to chose from, sitting in copper tureens over a traditional wood-fired stove some 20 m long. The open-sided dining area is very welcoming and spacious. Very good Italian too with a charming atmosphere.
TT **Sapore d'Italia**, Av Cabo Branco 1584, Standard Italian fare including pizza.

Campina Grande *p461*

R 13 de Maio by Rui Barbosa in the centre has several good restaurants. There are many bars near Parque do Povo, busy at weekends.

ΨΨ **A Cabana do Possidônio**, 13 de Maio 207 T083-341 3384. A varied menu of regional and international dishes.

ΨΨ **La Nostra Casa**, R 13 de Maio 175, T083-322 5196. Modest but friendly pasta and pizza restaurant.

Ψ **Carne & Massa**, R 13 de Maio 214, T083-322 8677. Regional cooking including *carne de sol*, pasta and a range of desserts.

Ψ **La Suissa**, Dep João Tavares 663. Good savoury and sweet snacks.

Ψ **Lanchonette Casa das Frutas**, Marquês de Herval 54. Good-value meals, fruit juices and snacks.

Ψ **Manoel da Carne de Sol**, Félix de Araújo 263. T083-321 2877. One of the city's best-value regional restaurants including an excellent *carne de sol* lunch with runner beans, *farofa* manioc flour and vegetables.

Ψ **Vila Antiga**, R 13 de Maio 164, T083-341 4718. A popular pay by weight restaurant with a broad range of regional dishes, pastas, salads and desserts.

Souza *p463*

Several restaurants are on R Col Zé Vicente.

Ψ **Diagonal**, Getúlio Vargas 2. Ordinary but reasonable pizzeria.

Bars and clubs

João Pessoa *p456, map p458*

There are many open bars on and across from the beach in Tambaú and Cabo Branco; the area known as Feirinha de Tambaú, on Av Tamandaré by the Tambaú Hotel and nearby streets, sees much movement even on weekend nights, with R Coração do Jesus being the epicentre. There are numerous little bars and *forró* places here and this is the place for a night-time browse. Other beachfront neighbourhoods also have popular bars.

Fashion Club, Mega Shopping, Manaíra. Still the most popular nightclub in the city – with a 20-something crowd and mostly techno and MPB. Large beachfront *baracca* restaurant with live music at weekends. Not as popular as it once was.

Incognito, R Coração do Jesus. A very popular and lively bar and dance club. There are many others here including KS.

Mr Caipira, Av João Maurício 1533, Manaíra, T083-246 7597. Live acoustic music, Brazilian barbecued food, *feijoada* and a smart 30-something crowd. On the seafront road.

Zodiaco, Incognito Coração do Jesus 144. One of several nightclubs in the area attracting a lively young crowd especially at the weekends.

Festivals and events

João Pessoa *p456, map p458*

Feb Pre-carnival celebrations in João Pessoa are renowned: the *bloco* Acorde Miramar opens the celebrations the Tue before Carnaval. On Wed, known as Quarta Feira de Fogo, thousands join the Muriçocas de Miramar, forming a *bloco* second only to Recife's Galo da Madrugada with as many as 300,000 people taking part.

5 Aug The street celebrations for the patroness of the city, Nossa Senhora das Neves, last for 10 days to the rhythm of *frevo*.

Campina Grande *p461*

Apr Micarande, the out-of-season Salvador-style carnival.

Jun-Jul Campina Grande boasts the largest São João celebrations in Brazil; from the beginning of Jun into the 1st week of Jul the city attracts many visitors; there are bonfires and *quadrilhas* (square dance groups) in every neighbourhood; *forró* and invited artists at the Parque do Povo; *quentão*, *pomonha* and *canjica* are consumed everywhere.

Aug The annual Congresso de Violeiros, which gathers singers and guitarists from all of the Nordeste.

Shopping

João Pessoa *p456, map p458*

Terra do Sol, R Coração do Jesus 145, T083-226 1940, www.terradosol.art.br. The best place to buy regional crafts, including lace-work, embroidery and ceramics. Very elegant, high-quality bedspreads, bath robes, hammocks and tablecloths made from natural beige cotton. The shop also sells a range of work by Paraíba artists and artisans.

Cheaper arts and crafts can be bought at **Mercado de Artesanato**, Centro de Turismo, Almte Tamandaré 100, Tambaú, daily 0800-1800; **Mercados de Artesanato Paraibano**, Av Rui Carneiro, Tambaú, daily 0900-1700; **Bosque dos Sonhos**, by the Cabo Branco lighthouse. Weekends only.

Activities and tours

João Pessoa *p456, map p458*
Cliotur, Av Alm Tamandaré 310, Sala 2, T083-247 4460. Trips to the *sertão*. Also offers light adventure activities.
Roger Turismo, Av Tamandaré 229, T083-247 1856. Half-day city tours (US$6), day trips to Tambaba (US$8) and Recife/Oldina (US$12). A large agency with some English-speaking guides and a range of other tours.

Excursions from João Pessoa *p459*
Flaviano Gouveia, Jacaré, T083-982 1604. Ultralight aircraft rides, US$19 for 8-min ride or US$115 for 1 hr.
Sea Tech, PO Box 42, João Pessoa, 56001-970, T083-245 1476, F245 2302. Run by Brian Ingram, originally from England. Boatyard and frequent port of call for international yachtspeople plying the Brazilian coast.

Transport

João Pessoa *p456, map p458*
Air A taxi to the airport costs US$8 from the centre or US$12 from Tambaú. Flights to **São Paulo, Brasília, Recife** and **Rio de Janeiro**. Gol will fly to **São Paulo** or **Rio** from Recife, and provide free bus transport from João Pessoa.

Airline offices BRA, Av Almirante Barroso 651, T083-222 6222, www.voebra.com.br and the airport. **Gol**, www.voo egol.com.br, and at the airport. **Ocean Air**, www.oceanair.com.br, **TAM**, at airport, T083-247 2400, Av Senador Rui Carneiro 512, T083-247 2400. **Varig**, Av Getúlio Vargas 183, Centro, T083-247 8383, freephone T0800-997000.
Bus From the *rodoviária* or Lagoa (Parque Solon de Lucena), take bus No 510 for **Tambaú**, No 507 for **Cabo Branco**.

Buses to **Recife** with Boa Vista or Bonfim, every 30 mins, US$2.50, 2 hrs. To **Natal** with Nordeste, every 2 hrs, US$8 *convencional*, US$7.50 *executivo*, 3 hrs. To **Fortaleza** with Nordeste, 2 daily, 10 hrs, US$18. To **Campina Grande** with Real, every 30 mins, US$4, 2 hrs. To **Juazeiro do Norte** with Transparaíba, 2 daily, US$14, 10 hrs. To **Salvador** with Progresso, 4 weekly, US$30, 14 hrs. To **Brasília** via Campina Grande, with Planalto, 2 weekly, US$57, 48 hrs. To **Rio de Janeiro with** São Geraldo, daily, US$67 *convencional*, US$80 *executivo*, 42 hrs. To **São Paulo** with **Itapemirim**, daily, US$73 *convencional*, US$76 *executivo*, 47 hrs. To **Belém** with **Guanabara**, daily, US$46, 36 hrs.

Car hire Avis, Av Nossa Senhora dos Navegantes, 402, T083-247 3050. **Localiza**, Av Epitácio Pessoa 4910, T083-247 4030, and at the airport, T0800-992000. **Tempo**, Almte Tamandaré 100, at the Centro de Turismo, T083-247 0002.

Train Regional services west to **Bayeux** and **Santa Rita**, and **Cabedelo** in the north.

Tambaba *p460*
From Tambaba a dirt road leads 12 km north to the beach of **Jacumã**, from where the PB-018 goes 11 km west to **Conde** and continues 3 km to the BR-101, which runs 20 km north to **João Pessoa**. There are hourly buses from Jacumã to **João Pessoa** *rodoviária* (0530-1900).

Campina Grande *p461*
Air Daily flights to **Recife** with **Nordeste**. Taxi to airport US$7. City bus Distrito Industrial from Praça Clementino Procópio, behind Cine Capitólio.

Bus To **João Pessoa**, with **Real**, every 30 mins, US$3, 2 hrs. To **Souza** with **Transparaíba**, 6 daily, US$7, 6 hrs. To **Juazeiro do Norte** with **Transparaíba**, 2 daily, US$10, 9 hrs. To **Natal** with **Nordeste**, 0800 daily, US$6, 18 hrs. To **Rio** with **Itapemirim**, 1600 daily, US$65, 42 hrs. To **Brasília** with **Planalto**, 2 weekly, US$55, 46 hrs.
Car hire On R Tavares Cavalcante are **Intermezzo**, No 27, T083-321 4790, F321 0835; **Kelly's**, No 301, T/F083-322 4539. Also **Localiza**, R Dr Severino Cruz 625, T083-341 4034, and at the airport, T083-331 4594.

Souza *p463*
Bus To **Campina Grande** with **Transparaíba**, 6 daily, US$7, 6 hrs. To **João Pessoa** with Transparaíba, 6 daily, US$10, 8 hrs. To **Juazeiro do Norte** with **Transparaíba** or Boa Esperança, 4 daily, US$4, 3½ hrs. To **Mossoró**, RN, with **Jardinense**, 4 daily, US$6, 4½ hrs.

Directory

João Pessoa *p456, map p458*
Banks Banco 24 horas , Av Almirante Tamandaré, 100, in front of Centro de Turismo, Tambaú, ATM for Cirrus, Visa and MasterCard. Banco do Brasil, Praça 1817, 3rd floor, Centro, Isidro Gomes 14, Tambaú, behind Centro de Turismo, helpful but poor rates. HSBC, R Peregrino de Carvalho, 162, Centre, ATM for cirrus and visa. Mondeo Tour, Av Négo 46, Tambaú, T083-226 3100. 0900-1730, cash and TCs. PB Câmbio Turismo, Visconde de Pelotas 54C, Centro, T083-221 4676, Mon-Fri 1030-1630, cash and TCs. **Internet** Cyberpointy Cafe, Av Almirante Tamandaré, 100, in Centro Turístico Tambaú, daily 0800-2100, US1.60 per hr. **Post office** Main office is at Praça Pedro Américo, Varadouro; central office is at Parque Solon de Lucena 375; also by the beach at Av Rui Carneiro, behind the Centro de Turismo. **Telephones** Calling stations at: Visconde de Pelotas and Miguel Couto, Centro; Centro de Turismo, Tambaú; Av Epitácio Pessoa 1487, Bairro dos Estados; *rodoviária* and airport.

Campina Grande *p461*
Banks Banco do Brasil, 7 de Setembro 52, cash and TCs at poor rates. Mondeo Tour, R Índios Cariris 308, T/F083-321 6965, cash at good rates and TCs, Mon-Fri 1000-1600. **Post office** R Marquês do Herval, Praça da Bandeira. **Telephone** Floriano Peixoto 410 by Praça da Bandeira in the industrial district and at the *rodoviária*.

Fortaleza

Footprint features

Introduction

Bahia may have the prettiest stretches of coastline in Brazil but the northeast has some of the most dramatic. Broken, striated cliffs and imposing dunes tower above the beaches of Natal, Genipabu, Pipa, Areia Brana and Jericoacoara, plunging into the sea and glowing deep yellow or fiery red in the setting sun.

As the coast stretches north, cliffs and dunes give way to the wetland wilderness of the Delta do Parnaíba, the largest delta in the western hemisphere, exceeded in size only by the deltas of the Ganges, Mekong and Nile. The Rio Parnaíba spreads like an outstretched palm to divide the land into myriad islands, a maze of narrow channels and an infinity of lakes. All these are ecological sanctuaries. Beyond lies the coastal desert of the Lençóis Maranhenses – a grand erg of dunes pocked with freshwater lakes. There are three wetland sites recognized by the Ramsar Convention along the Maranhão coast and, offshore, is the largest bank of coral in Atlantic South America, the Parque Estadual Marinho do Parcel Manoel Luís, which is only now beginning to open up to diving.

The state capital, São Luís, is covered in blue and white Portuguese *azulejos* and filled with decaying baroque churches. Together with neighbouring Alcântara, it is the only town of interest on this stretch of coast. São Luís is one of two World Heritage sites in the region, the other being the Parque Nacional da Serra da Capivara in Piauí, whose bizarre honeycomb domes tower over canyons covered in what may be the oldest rock painting ever to be found in the Americas.

★ Don't miss...

1 **Pipa** Sit back and relax in this laid-back little resort town which attracts an interesting arty crowd and has some great hotels and restaurants, page 475.

2 **Areia Branca** Explore this bleak, biblical landscape of plunging cliffs, shifting seas of pink and lemon-yellow dunes and seemingly endless beaches, page 477.

3 **Parque Nacional de Sete Cidades and Parque Nacional da Capivara** Seek out the 50,000 BC rock art at two of the most important archaeological sites in the Americas, perhaps the cradle of its civilization, pages 514 and 515.

4 **São Luís** Vies with Salvador and Olinda for the title of the most beautiful coastal city in the northeast, page 517.

5 **Alcântara** An unlikely fusion of pretty colonial town, coastal wilderness and rocket station, page 519.

6 **Lençóis Maranhenses** A disorientating sea of shifting dunes dotted with lakes, page 519.

7 **Delta do Parnaíba** One of the world's great wildlife locations overflowing with birds, mammals and reptiles and with miles of unspoilt coast washed by a warm tropical sea, page 520.

Rio Grande do Norte

This state is famous for its beaches and their dunes, especially around Natal. The coastline begins to change here, becoming gradually drier and less green, as it shifts from running north-south to east-west. The vast sugar cane plantations and few remaining stands of mata atlântica *(coastal forest) are replaced by the dry* caatinga *vegetation and* caju *orchards. The people are called 'Potiguares', after an indigenous tribe that once resided in the state.* »» *For Sleeping, Eating and other listings, see pages 478-485.*

Natal

»» *pp478-485.*

→ *Phone code: 084. Colour map 2, B6. Population: 713,000.*

The state capital, located on a peninsula between the Rio Potengi and the Atlantic Ocean, is pleasant enough but has few sights of interest. Most visitors head for the beaches to the north and south. During the Second World War, the city was, somewhat bizarrely, the second largest US base outside the United States and housed 8000 American pilots.

Ins and outs

Getting there Flights arrive at **Augusto Severo airport** ⓘ *Parnamirim, 15 km south of centre, T084-644 1000*. A taxi to the centre costs US$25; US$20 to Ponta Negra. Buses run every 30 minutes to the old *rodoviária* near the centre, US$0.65. Interstate buses arrive at the **rodoviária** ⓘ *Av Capitão Mor Gouveia 1237, Cidade da Esperança, 6 km southwest of the centre, T084-205 4377*. Buses from the south pass Ponta Negra first, where you can ask to alight. The city buses 'Cidade de Esperança Avenida 9', 'Areia Preta via Petrópolis' or 'Via Tirol' run from the *rodoviária* to the centre; a taxi costs US$8; US$12 to Ponta Negra. »» *See also Transport, page 484.*

Getting around Unlike most Brazilian buses, in Natal you get on the bus at the front and get off at the back. The old *rodoviária* on Avenida Junqueira Aires, by Praça Augusto Severo, Ribeira, is a central point where many bus lines converge. Buses to some of the beaches near Natal also leave from here. Taxis are expensive compared to other cities (eg four times the price of Recife); US$8 for a 10-min journey.

Tourist information The state tourist office, **SETUR** ⓘ *R Mossoró 359, Petrópolis, T084-232 2500, www.setur.rn.gov.br*, covers the whole of Rio Grande do Norte state, although their information and English is very limited, and their office is not conveniently located. However, there are tourist information booths at the airport, the bus station, on Avenida Presidente Café Filho and at Praia das Artistas beach, all open daily 0800-2100. A useful website is www.natal.com.br.

Sights

No one comes to Natal for sightseeing, but the city is not without culture. The oldest part is the **Ribeira** along the riverfront, where a programme of renovation has been started. This can be seen on Rua Chile and in public buildings restored in vivid art deco fashion, such as the **Teatro Alberto Maranhão** ⓘ *Praça Agusto Severo, T/F084-222 9935*, built 1898-1904, and the **Prefeitura** ⓘ *R Quintino Bocaiuva, Cidade Alta*. The **Cidade Alta**, or Centro, is the main commercial centre and Avenida Rio

Natal was used for African airborne operations during the Second World War.

Branco its principal artery. The main square is made up by the adjoining praças, **João Maria**, **André de Albuquerque**, **João Tibúrcio** and **7 de Setembro**. At Praça André de Albuquerque is the old **cathedral** (inaugurated 1599, restored 1996). The modern cathedral is on Avenida Deodoro, Cidade Alta. The church of **Santo Antônio** ⓘ *R Santo Antônio 683, Cidade Alta, Tue-Fri 0800-1700, Sat 0800-1400*, dates from 1766, and has a fine, carved wooden altar and a sacred art museum.

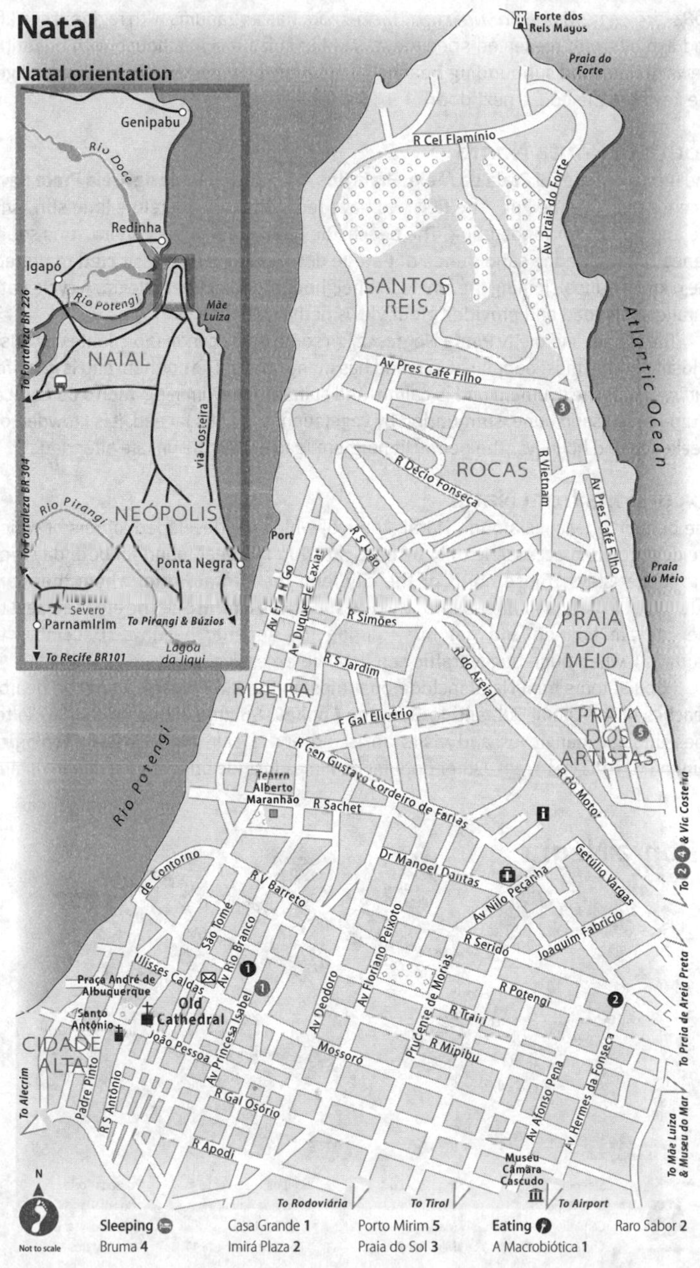

The **Museu Câmara Cascudo** ⓘ *Av Hermes de Fonseca 1440, Tirol, T084-212 2795, Tue-Fri 0800-1100, 1400-1600, Sat 1000-1600, US$1.50*, has exhibits on Umbanda rituals, archaeological digs, and the sugar, leather and petroleum industries.

The 16th-century **Forte dos Reis Magos** ⓘ *daily 0800-1645, US$1.50*, is at Praia do Forte, the tip of Natal's peninsula; between it and the city is a military installation. Walk along the beach to the fort for good views (or go on a tour, or by taxi).

Museu do Mar ⓘ *Av Dinarte Mariz (Via Costeira), Praia de Mãe Luiza, T084-215 4433, Mon-Fri 0800-1100, 1400-1700*, has aquariums with regional sea life and exhibits with preserved specimens. At Mãe Luiza is a lighthouse with beautiful views of Natal and surrounding beaches (take a city bus marked 'Mãe Luiza' and get the key from the house next door).

South to Ponta Negra

The urban beaches of **Praia do Meio, Praia dos Artistas** and **Praia de Areia Preta** have recently been cleaned up. The first two have reefs offshore, therefore little surf, and are appropriate for windsurfing. The beachside promenade, **Via Costeira**, runs south beneath the towering sand dunes of **Parque das Dunas** (access restricted to protect the 9 km of dunes), joining the city to the neighbourhood of Ponta Negra. A cycle path parallels this road and provides great views of the coastline.

The vibrant and pretty **Ponta Negra**, 12 km south of the centre (20 minutes by bus), is justifiably the most popular beach and has many hotels. The northern end is good for surfing, while the southern end is calmer and suitable for swimming. **Morro do Careca**, a 120-m-high sand dune, surrounded by vegetation, sits at its far end. It is crowded on weekends and holidays. The poorly lit northern reaches can be unsafe after dark.

Excursions from Natal

The beautiful beaches around Natal, some of which are developed, others of which are deserted and accessible only by trails, are good all year round for both day trips and longer stays. Those north of the city form the **Litoral Norte**, where there are extensive cashew plantations; those to the south, the **Litoral Sul**. The areas closest to the city are built-up and get busy during the summer holidays (December to Carnaval), when dune-buggy traffic can become excessive.

Popular tours from Natal include boat trips on the **Rio Potengi**, along the nearby beaches of the Litoral Sul, and to **Barra do Cunhaú**, 86 km south of Natal. The latter goes through mangroves and visits an island and a salt mine (**Passeio Ecológico Cunhaú** ⓘ *T084-211 1123*). Other popular pastimes include buggy tours, marlin fishing

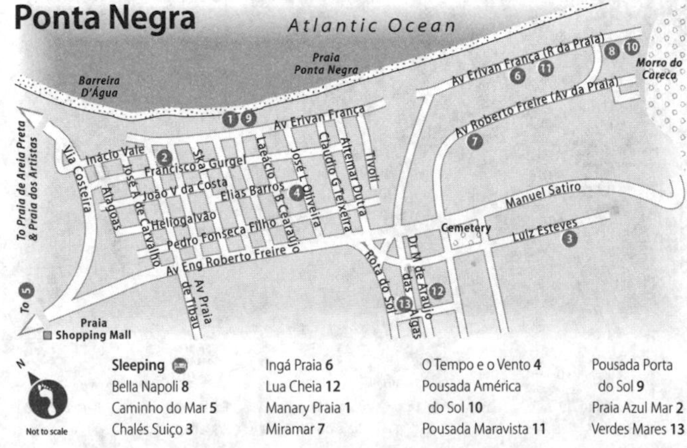

(11 km from shore, said by some to be the best in Brazil) and microlight flights over the Rio Potengi and sand dunes north of Natal. » See Activities and tours, page 484.

The **Centro de Lançamento da Barreira do Inferno** ⓘ *T084-211 4799, visits by appointment on Wed from 1400*, the launching centre for Brazil's space programme, is located 11 km south of Natal on the road to Pirangi.

Southern coast » pp478-485.

South of Natal, the Rota do Sol/Litoral Sul (RN-063) follows the coastline for some 55 km and provides access to beaches south of Ponta Negra. From here the coast becomes more remote and long curves of white sand backed by multicoloured sandstone cliffs and sweeping dunes, fragments of Atlantic forest alive with rare birds, black tea lagoons and bays filled with dolphins, make this one of the most popular stretches in the northeast. Thankfully development is small scale and it still feels relaxed (outside high season). Several species of turtles, including giant leatherbacks, still nest here, although numbers are declining as the popularity of beach buggy tourism grows. The best place to stay along this stretch of coast is Pipa, a lively little town with good pousadas and restaurants.

Rota do Sol

ⓘ *Buses run from both Natal's rodoviárias, every 30 mins in summer, along the Literal Sul, stopping at Pirangi, US$1, 1 hr, and Tabatinga US$1.50, 1¼ hrs.*

Praia do Cotovelo, 21 km from Natal, offers a view of the Barreira do Inferno rocket-launching centre to the north. At its southern end it has some cliffs and coconut palms where camping is possible.

Pirangi do Norte, 25 km from Natal (30 minutes by bus from the new *rodoviária*) has calm waters and is popular for watersports and offshore bathing (500 m out) when natural pools form between the reefs. Nearby is the world's largest cashew-nut tree (*cajueiro*); branches springing from a single trunk cover an area of some 7300 sq m. The snack bar by the tree has schedules of buses back to Natal. Pirangi has a lively Carnaval. Lacemakers here offer good bargains for clothing and tableware.

Búzios, 35 km from Natal, has a pleasant setting with vegetation-covered dunes and coconut palms. The water is mostly calm and clear, making it good for bathing.

Barra de Tabatinga, 45 km from Natal, is surrounded by cliffs used for parasailing. Waves are strong here, making it a popular surfing beach. A new 'shark park' complete with resident biologist is its latest attraction.

Camurupim and **Barreta**, 46 and 55 km from Natal respectively, have reefs near the shore, where bathing pools form at low tide; this area has many restaurants specializing in shrimp dishes. Beyond Barreta is the long, pristine beach of **Malenbar** or **Guaraíra**, accessible by walking or on a 10-minute boat ride across the Rio Tibau to the south end. A buggy tour from Natal costs US$100.

Tibau do Sul and Pipa → *Colour map 2, B6. Population 6124.*

ⓘ *From Natal there are 6 daily buses to Tibau and Pipa (2-3 hrs). From João Pessoa in Paraíba you will have to change at Goaianinha on the main road to Natal. This route is also run by combis which leave when full up and cost about 20% more than the buses. Combis connect Pipa and Tibau until around 2300.*

The little fishing town of **Tibau do Sul** has cobbled streets and sits high on a cliff between surf beaches and the manatee-filled Lago de Guaraíra. Boat trips can be arranged from here to the *lago* or to see dolphins in the calm waters offshore. Although most tourists head straight for Pipa, which is more developed, the beach *barracas* in Tibau are lively at night with *forró* and MPB. Natal's finest restaurant is also here (see page 481) and there are a handful of decent pousadas in town.

Lampião – Brazil's bloodthirsty Robin Hood

Were they subversives, common criminals or heroes? The debate rages on about the armed band led by Virgulino Ferreira da Silva, better known as Lampião. He is regarded by some as a Robin Hood of the northeast, stealing from the *coroneis* (wealthy landowners with almost feudal powers) and urban gentry, to give to the ubiquitous poor of the *sertão*. Others look on Lampião and his followers as nothing more than common criminals; looting, raping and killing as they terrorized towns in the northeast during the 1920s and 1930s. This was the *Cangaço*, the reign of banditry, which inspired so much fear and fascination throughout Brazil and attracted worldwide attention.

The controversial religious leaders of the *sertão* were also involved. Lampião claimed the spiritual protection of Padre Cícero, and the legacy of the *Cangaço* retains an unusual religious dimension. The tomb of Jararaca, for example, one of Lampião's lieutenants who was captured during the band's unsuccessful 1927 siege of Mossoró and supposedly buried alive, is attributed miraculous powers and has become a site of pilgrimage. Yet Jararaca is reputed to have been a ruthless killer.

There was even a Middle Eastern connection. Several early cinematographers from the US, Germany and France tried to film Lampião and his band, but only Lebanese-born Benjamin Abrahão was sufficiently taken into his confidence to do so. Abrahão spent almost seven months recording the day-to-day life of the *cangaceiros*. His footage was considered so subversive that he was subsequently murdered under mysterious circumstances and his film confiscated by the government of Getúlio Vargas. It languished in an official vault for 20 years, much of it destroyed by time and the elements.

Today the Sociedade Brasileira de Estudos do Cangaço is one of the organizations which collects data, anecdotes and artefacts from this important episode in the region's and the nation's history. It also carries on the unresolved debate as to whether the *cangaceiros* were really heroes or villains.

From Tibau, a series of wide crescents of white sand, separated by rocky headlands and backed by high cliffs crowned with coconut groves and remnant coastal forest, stretches south to **Pipa**. This is one of Natal's most enchanting little tourist towns, whose mix of local fishermen and settlers from all over Brazil has formed an eclectic alternative community. There are excellent pousadas and restaurants in all price ranges and the nightlife is animated. The town is becoming increasingly popular and the number of people can feel overwhelming during Carnaval and New Year.

The town beach is somewhat developed, but there are plenty of others nearby. **Praia dos Golfinhos** to the south and **Madeiro** beyond it have only a few hotels and **Praia do Amor** to the north is surrounded by cliffs and has reasonable surf. Access to the shore is down the steps built by the few clifftop hotels or by walking along the beach from Pipa at low tide. There are tours to see dolphins from US$5 per person and also around the mangrove-lined **Lagoa Guaraíra** at Tibau, particularly beautiful at sunset.

Just north of town, on a 70-m-high dune, is the **Santuário Ecológico de Pipa** ⓘ *0800-1600, US$3*, a 60-ha park created in 1986 to conserve the *mata atlântica* forest. There are several trails and lookouts over the cliffs, which afford an excellent view of the ocean and dolphins. Although larger animals like cats and howler monkeys are long gone, this is one of the few areas in the state where important indicator bird species, such as guans, can be found.

Genipabu and the northern coast » pp478-485.

The coast north of Natal is known for its many impressive, light-coloured sand dunes, some reaching a staggering 50 m in height. Genipabu, a weekend resort for the Natal middle classes, is the most famous of these and is only a very short bus ride from the city. The country beyond is well off the tourist trail, with vast long beaches backed by multicoloured sand dunes and salt lakes. It is dramatic terrain, so much so that it has been used as the backdrop to numerous biblical films. Three crosses stand over the cliffs at **Areia Branca**, left there by one of the most recent productions, *Maria, A Mãe do Filho de Deus*. Fixed dunes are protected and should not be disturbed, but shifting dunes can be visited by buggy, camel or horse. Ask locally for advice.

Ins and outs

Areia Branca and the other small towns along the northern coast are reachable from Mossoró, the second largest town in the state with little worth seeing in its own right. Galinhos, in the far north, sits on a long broad sandspit and is connected to the mainland by ferry from the little village of Guamaré. From here, there are buses to both Mossoró and Natal via the small town of Jandaíra.

Redinha → *Colour map 2, B6.*

A 25-minute ferry crossing on the Rio Potengi, or a 16-km drive from Natal up the Rota do Sol/Litoral Norte, takes you to Redinha, an urban beach with ocean and river bathing and buggies for hire. The local delicacy is fried fish with tapioca, served at the market. About 5 km north of Redinha, on a point, is **Santa Rita**. From its high dunes there is a great view of the surrounding coastline.

Genipabu and around

The best-known beach in the state, Genipabu, is 30 km north of Natal. Its major attractions are some very scenic dunes and the **Lagoa de Genipabu**, a lake surrounded by cashew trees where tables are set up on a shoal in the water and drinks are served. There are also many bars and restaurants on the seashore. Buggy rental and microlight flights can be arranged. » *See Activities and tours, page 484.*

North of Genipabu, across the Rio Ceará Mirim, are several beaches with coconut groves and dunes, lined with fishing villages and summer homes of people from Natal; access is via the town of Extremoz. One of these beaches, **Pitangui**, 35 km from Natal, is 6 km long and has a crystalline lake where colourful schools of fish can be seen. **Jacumã**, 49 km from Natal, has a small waterfall and the inland Lagoa de Jacumã, a lake surrounded by dunes where sand-skiing is popular.

Muriú, 44 km from Natal, is known for its lovely green ocean where numerous small boats and *jangadas* anchor; the beach has attractive palms (buggy tour from Natal, including shifting dunes US$100). About 5 km to the north is **Prainha** or **Coqueiro**, a beautiful cove with many coconut palms and strong waves.

Lovely beaches continue along the state's coastline; as you get further away from Natal the beaches are more distant from the main highways and access is more difficult. Around 83 km north of Natal, in the centre of a coconut and lobster producing region, is the ugly resort town of **Touros**. From here the coastline veers east-west.

Far north → *Phone code: 084.*

As the coast turns to the west, the terrain becomes more dramatic and bleak. Sheltered coves are replaced by vast beaches stretching in seemingly interminable broad curves. Behind them are pink, brown and red cliffs, or large expanses of dunes. Highlights are the sleepy little village of **Galinhos**, with its sand streets and beautiful, gentle beach washed by a calm sea, and the **Costa Branca** near the little fishing towns of **Areia Branca**, **Ponta do Mel** and **Rosadao**, where huge pink and white dunes converge behind magnificent long beaches.

The sertão → *Population: 11,000.*

The interior of Rio Grande do Norte, like that of its neighbours, is a combination of semi-desert *sertão*, with hilly areas covered in green vegetation, and pleasant temperatures of between 16°C and 25°C. The state is rich in archaeological sites, and numerous caves with primitive paintings have been found.

In the mountainous south-central region of the state is **Acari**, with the 18th-century church of Nossa Senhora da Guia. Acari is the access point for the Serra do Bico de Arara and is 221 km from Natal. South of town, in the **Seridó** area, are multicoloured cave paintings where human remains dating back 11,000 years have been discovered.

In the centre of the state, on the east shore of the Armando Rua Gonçalves dam, is **São Rafael**. The town is surrounded by granite mountains on top of which are natural waterholes of up to 3 m deep that contain many fossils of giant fauna of the Pleistocene period. There are also rock paintings and engravings on boulders in this area.

Some 76 km southwest of Mossoró is **Apodi**, a town with colonial mansions, where people make their living from agriculture, ceramics and lime extraction. About 10 km from town is **Lajedo de Soledade**, a limestone shelf, 1 km wide and 2 km long, which has been weathered into canyons, grottoes and interesting formations. Paintings of animals and geometric figures, dating from 3000 to 5000 years ago, have been found in the caves.

Sleeping

Natal *p472, map p473*
Economical hotels are easier to find in Natal than at the outlying beaches or Ponta Negra, but very few people stay here and what they save by doing so is often spent on public transport to and from the beaches.

The distinction between Praia do Meio and Praia dos Artistas is often blurred. Most hotels are on the beachfront Av Pres Café Filho, the numbering of which is illogical.

The Via Costeira is a strip of enormous, upmarket beachfront hotels, which are very isolated, with no restaurants or shops within easy walking distance.

L Maine, Av Salgado Filho 1741, Lagoa Nova, T084-206 5774, F206 5707. A business-orientated 4-star with reasonable service and a restaurant.

AL-A Imirá Plaza, Via Costeira 4077, T084-211 4104, F211 5722, cheaper in low season. On the beach and with a pool and tennis court. Recommended.

AL-C Porto Mirim, Av Pres Café Filho 68, Praia do Meio, T084-202 4200. Big luxury hotel with a rooftop pool and deck. Cheaper off season.

A Praia do Sol, Av Pres Café Filho 750, Praia do Meio, T084-211 4562, F222 6571. Quiet a/c rooms opposite beach. Recommended.

B Bruma, Av Pres Café Filho 1176, T/F084-211 4308, www.hotelbruma@zaz.com.br. Slick and intimate with beachfront balconies, pool and terrace. Recommended.

B Casa Grande, R Princesa Isabel 529, Centro, T084-211 0555. Built around a family home, popular with business visitors. A/c, cheaper without bathroom. Pleasant, good breakfast, excellent value with off-season discounts. Recommended.

B Oassis Swiss, R Joaquim Fabrício 291, Casa 08, Petrópolis, T/F084-202 2455. Swiss-owned hotel with a/c and fan-cooled rooms, cheaper with fan. Pool, massive breakfasts, off-season discounts. Exceptional value.

B Pousada Esperança, Av Capt Mor Gouveia 418, near the *rodoviária*, T084-205 1955. Rooms with or without a/c and bathrooms. Basic but respectable.

D Beira Mar, Av Pres Café Filho, Praia do Meio, T084-202 1470. Motel-style, beachfront a/c rooms, with breakfast, small pool. Good value, popular. Recommended.

D Bom Jesús, Av Rio Branco 384, Centro. Simple, popular cheapie, reasonable breakfast.

D Cidade do Sol, Piancó 31, near the *rodoviária*, T084-205 1893. Very basic rooms with or without baths and a/c.
D Fenícia, Av Rio Branco 586, Centro, T084-211 4378. Fan-cooled and more expensive a/c rooms with breakfast. English spoken, low-season discount.
D Le Bateau, Praia de Areia Preta, on the beachfront. Simple but helpful and with a good breakfast, English and French spoken.
E Meu Canto, R Manoel Dantas 424, Petrópolis, T084-211 3954. Youth hostel with private rooms and dorms. Friendly staff, highly recommended.
E Pousada Beth Shalom, R Patos 45, near the *rodoviária*, T084-205 1141. Small fan-cooled rooms and friendly service.
E Pousada Marina, Av Pte Café Filho 860, Praia do Meio, T084-202 1677, www.hotelpousadamarina.com.br. Plain and simple, with a/c, TV and fridge.
E Pousada Ponta do Morcego, R Valentin de Almeida 10, Praia dos Artistas, T084-202 2367. Basic dorm-style rooms and a handful of others. Price per person.

Camping

Camping Clube do Brasil, Sítio do Jiqui, Pirangi, T084-217 2603. Expensive.

Ponta Negra *p474, map p474*

Ponta Negra is the ideal place to stay, with its attractive beach and concentration of restaurants. The most popular hotels are those right on the beach, on Av Erivan França facing the sea, and on R Francisco Gurgel behind that street. The latter is quieter.
LL Manary Praia, R Francisco Gurgel 9067, T/F084-219 2900, www.manary.com.br. The best and most tranquil hotel facing the beach and the only one with a trace of style. The rooms, which are decorated in hardwood and pastel colours, have ample bathrooms and secluded private terraces. Good food. A member of the **Roteiros de Charme** group, see page 50.
L Ocean Paláce, Km 11, near Ponta Negra, T084-219 4144, F219 3081. Luxury hotel, rooms and facilities of suitable standard, generally well designed with lovely ocean-front pool and terrace; relaxed and friendly.
AL Praia Azul Mar, R Franscisco Gurgel 92, T084-219 3555, www.praiaazulmarhotel.com.br. Pleasant package holiday hotel, with a/c rooms and a pool.
A-B Hotel e Pousada O Tempo e o Vento, R Elias Barros 66, T/F084-219 2526, www.digicom.br/otempoeovento. A/c rooms with fridge around a pool. The *luxo* rooms are very comfortable. Cheaper with fan and in low season. Recommended.
A-C Chalés Suíço, R Luiz Esteves 2272, T084-236 3090. Simple a/c furnished cabins for up to 5 people, cheaper in low season.
B Caminho do Mar, R Des HH Gomes 365, T084-219 3363. Simple plain rooms and breakfast, a short walk from the beach.
B Ingá Praia, Av Erivan França 17, T084-219 3436, www.ingapraiahotel.com.br. A pink cube on the beach with comfortable well-kept rooms and a rooftop terrace. Recommended.
B Miramar, Av da Praia 3398, T084-236 2079. Well-maintained, family-run pousada. English spoken.
C Pousada América do Sol, R Erivan França 35, T084-219 2245, www.pousadaamericadosol.com.br. Very simple a/c rooms with pokey bathrooms and TVs. Good breakfast in a terrace overlooking the beach and substantial off-season reductions.
C Pousada Porta do Sol, R Erivan França 9057, T084-236 2555, F205 2208. Basic rooms with TV, fridge, fan and an excellent breakfast, pool, beachfront, good value. Recommended.
C-D Bella Napoli, Av Erivan França 3188, T084-219 2666, www.pousadabellanapoli.com.br. Pokey little a/c rooms with fridge, in a hotel above the restaurant of the same name. In need of renovation but it's right on the beach. Cheaper in low season.
D Lua Cheia, R Dr Manoel Augusto Bezerra de Araújo 500, T084-236 3696, www.luachela.com.br. One of the best youth hostels in Brazil; in a 'castle' with a 'medieval' **Taverna Pub** in the basement (see Bars and clubs below). IYHA, price per person, includes breakfast. Highly recommended.

For Sleeping and Eating price codes, see pages 49 and 52 or the inside front cover. For an explanation of phone codes, see page 66.

D **Pousada Maravista**, R da Praia 223, T084-236 4677, marilymar@hotmail.com. Plain and simple but with a good breakfast, English spoken, TV, fridge.

D **Verdes Mares**, R das Algas 2166, Conj Algamar, T084-236 2872, F236 2872. IYHA youth hostel, price per person, includes breakfast, discount in low season.

E **Pousada Porto Seguro**, Av Pres Café Filho 1174, T084-9412 1039. Very lively, with a beachfront terrace and small but decent rooms. Good value. Recommended.

Camping

Vale das Cascatas, Via Costeira Km 8.5, Ponta Negra beach. Little shade, swimming pool, leisure facilities.

Rota do Sol *p475*

A **Cotovelo Apart-hotel**, R Estrela D'Alva 34, Praia do Cotovelo, T084-237 2051. Rooms with kitchenettes set around a pool.

A **Colinas Chalés**, Estr de Pirangi, Praia do Cotovelo, T084-237 2168. Cabins with a fridge. Restaurant and a pool.

A-B **Chalés de Pirangi**, R Sebastião 56, Pirangi do Norte, T084-238 2241. Standard apartment hotel with a/c rooms and en suites.

B **Barreira do Sol**, Estr para Búzios, Pirangi do Sul (across the river), T084-238 2230. Modest rooms with en suites, most with a/c.

B **Portal do Kutuvelo**, Estr para Búzios, Praia do Cotovelo, T084-237 2121. Reasonable plain rooms with attached kitchen, pool.

B **Pousada Esquina do Sol**, R Dom Bosco and Av Dep Márcio Marinho, Pirangi do Norte, T084-238 2078, F211 5637. Rooms and cabins for 4. Breakfast not included.

B **Pousada Vista do Atlântico**, R do Cajueiro 141, Pirangi do Norte, T084-2382 0778. In the town itself but within walking distance of the beach. The upstairs rooms are better ventilated and have good views.

B **Varandas de Búzios**, Estr Principal, Búzios, T084-239 2121. Cabins with a fridge around pool. Reasonable restaurant.

Tibau do Sul and Pipa *p475*

In Pipa more than 30 pousadas and many private homes offer accommodation.

LL-A **Sombra e Água Fresca**, Praia do Amor, T084-246 2144, www.sombraeagua fresca.com.br. Cheaper in low season. Tastefully decorated but small chalet rooms and vast luxury suites with separate sitting and dining areas. All with magnificent views.

LL-A **Toca da Coruja**, Praia da Pipa, T084-246 2225, www.tocadacoruja.com.br. One of the best small luxury hotels in Brazil with a range of chalets set in forested gardens and decorated with northeast Brazilian antiques and art. Beautiful pool and an excellent restaurant. A member of the **Roteiros de Charme** group, see page 50.

AL **Ponta do Madeiro**, R da Praia, Estr para Pipa Km 3, T/F084-246 4220, www.pontado madeiro.com.br. Very comfortable spacious a/c chalets, beautiful pool with bar and spectacular views over the Praia do Madeiro. Excellent service and a good restaurant. Highly recommended.

AL **Village Natureza**, Estr para Pipa Km 5, T/F084-502 2325. A/c chalets overlooking the sea and Madeiro beach, a pool, pleasant grounds, lovely views.

A **Marinas Tibau Sul**, Tibau do Sul, T/F084-502 2323. Cabins for 4, pool, restaurant, watersports, horse riding and a boat dock.

A-B **Mirante de Pipa**, Rua do Mirante 1, Praia da Pipa, T084-246 2251, www.mirante depipa.com.br. Fan-cooled chalets with a veranda set in a forested garden. Wonderful views.

C **A Conchego**, R do Ceu s/n, Praia da Pipa, T084-9419 7181, www.pipa.com/aconchego. Family-run pousada with simple chalets with red-tiled roofs and terraces, in a garden filled with cashew and palm trees. Tranquil and central. Good breakfast.

D **Pousada da Pipa**, Praia da Pipa, T084-246 2217. Small rooms decorated with a personal touch. The best are upstairs and have a large shared terrace with glazed terracotta tiles, sitting areas and hammocks. Large breakfast.

D **Vera-My house**, Praia da Pipa, T084-246 2295. Good value, friendly and well maintained though simple. Rooms with bath, US$5 per person in dormitory, use of kitchen, no breakfast. Recommended.

Camping

Espaço Verde, behind restaurant, T084-988 5145, US$3 per person. Sandy, some shade.

Genipabu and around *p477*

A Genipabu, Estr de Genipabu, s/n, 2 km from beach, T084-225 2063, www.genipabu.com.br. A very relaxing spa hotel on a hillside outside of town with wonderful views out over the beaches and sea. Smart and very well-kept a/c rooms with en suites. Treatments include Ayurvedic massage, reiki, yoga, body wraps and facials. Attractive pool and a sauna.

A Pousada Sinos do Vento, Praia das Garças, Touros, 6 km from town, T084-263 2453, www.sinosdovento.com.br. Attractive seaside pousada with accommodation in 14 spacious chalets on a deserted stretch of beach and surrounded by forested gardens. Offers a range of activities including horse riding, bike rental and buggy tours.

B do Gostoso, Praia Ponta de Santo Cristo, 27 km west of town, T084-221 4399. Pleasant modern chalets and a simple restaurant.

B Mar-Azul, on the beach, Genipabu, T084-225 2065. One of many modest beachside hotels. Pleasant rooms with bath and fridge.

B Pousada Villa do Sol, Enseada do Genipabu, Km 4, T084-225 2132, www.villadosol.com.br. 20 attractive a/c chalets, the best of which are the 5 newest, with views over the river. Decent pool and restaurant with good service.

C Bangalôs Muriú, Muriú, T/F084-219 3731. Modest furnished chalets and breakfast.

C Pousada do Coruja, R Principal 100, Genipabu, T084-225 2592. In the town. Simple but adequate rooms with fan.

C Pousada Marruá, Av Beira Mar 438, Pitangui, T084-202 2404. Simple but reasonably well maintained and friendly.

C Tabuão, R Principal, Genipabu, T084-225 2134. Modest furnished bungalows in the main town. No breakfast.

D Aldeia, R Principal, Estr de Genipabu, T/F084-225 2011, www.hotelaldeia.hpg.com.br. Five comfortable and nicely decorated bungalows for up to 4 people, a pool and a decent restaurant.

E Pousada Porta Alberta, on beach, Genipabu. Basic but with a good breakfast and friendly service.

Far north *p477*

There are plenty of pousadas in **Tibau** and many restaurants and bars along the beach. Although there are some pousadas in Areia Branca, it isn't a good base for the beaches. **Ponta do Mel**, which is flanked by 2 magnificent beaches, is better and has a couple of very basic pousadas in the town.

Galinhos town is very sleepy and pousadas often close up for a few days whilst their owners go away. There are at least 7 in town so it is always possible to find a room, either on the ocean or the coastal side.

A Pousada Costa Branca, Ponta do Mel, Costa Branca, T084-332 7062, www.costabranca.com.br. The best hotel between Genipabu and Ceará with a range of cabins on a bluff with magnificent views over an endless stretch of beach. Organized tours to the dunes to the south, which are among the most spectacular in the state. Good restaurant, service and pool, and Lord Byron tribute bar with live music.

B Dunas Praia, Praia das Manoelas, Tibau, T084-326 2304. Friendly staff, a restaurant and a series of chalets, all with fridge.

B Leiria Mar, Tibau, T084-326 2541. Plain a/c rooms with fridge, around a pool. Reasonable restaurant.

D Panorama, Tibau. Very basic rooms with a bath and more expensive options with fans.

D Pousada e Restaurante Brasil Aventura, Galinhos, T084-552 0085. One of several very simple beachfront pousadas with a fish restaurant. Plain but well kept and popular with backpackers.

The sertão *p478*

C Pousada do Gargalheiras, Açude Marechal Dutra, about 5 km from Acari. With a restaurant.

D Conceição Palace Hotel, R Otávio Lamartine 432, Jardim do Seridó, some 27 km south of Acari, T084-472 2249. A simple option.

D Passeio Hotel, on the BR-405, Km 76, T084-333 2031. One-star hotel.

D Pousada Chapado, R Dep Dauto Cunha 30, Apodi, T084-333 2049. A/c, fridge and a restaurant serving regional food.

Eating

Natal *p472, map p473*

Prawns feature heavily on menus as Natal is the largest exporter of prawns in Brazil. Check out the beach *barracas* for snacks and fast food.

TTT Chaplin, Av Pres Café Filho 27, Praia dos Artistas. Traditional seafood restaurant with sea views. Part of a leisure complex with a bar, English pub and a nightclub.

TTT Doux France, R Otâvio Lamartine, Petrópolis. Authentic French cuisine, outdoor seating.

TTT Estação Trem de Minas, Av Pres Café Filho 197, Praia dos Artistas, T084-202 2099. Charming rustic style, distinctly upmarket. 40 brands of *cachaça*, live music nightly, terrace and cocktails. Self-service lunch and dinner.

TTT Raro Sabor, R Seridó 722, Petrópolis, T084-202 1857. Exclusive bistro with Russian caviar on the menu.

TT A Macrobiótica, Princesa Isabel 524, Centro. Vegetarian restaurant and shop. Lunch only.

TT Bob's, Av Sen Salgado Filho, Hamburger chain, daily 1000-2200.

TT Camarões Express, Av Sen Salgado Filho, Centro. Express prawns in 15 styles. Open for lunch only at weekends.

TT Carne de Sol Benigna Lira, R Dr José Augusto Bezerra de Medeiros 09, Praia do Meio. Traditional setting, regional cuisine.

TT Fiorentina, Augusto Bezerra de Medeiros 529, delivery T084-202 0020. An Italian pizzeria with a huge range of seafood, try the lobster with spaghetti. Friendly service, 10% tax. Warmly recommended.

TT Peixada da Comadre, R Dr José Augusto Bezerra de Medeiros 4, Praia dos Artistas. Lively seafood restaurant with popular prawn dishes.

TT Saint Antoine, R Santo Antônio 651, Cidade Alta, Centro. Mediocre self-service pay by weight establishment.

TT-T Farol Bar, Av Sílvio Pedrosa 105 (at the end of Via Costeira on Praia Areia Preta). Famous dried meat dishes – a local speciality.

Ponta Negra *p474, map p474*

TTT Manary, **Manary Praia Hotel**, R Francisco Gurgel (see page 479). The best seafood in the city in a poolside restaurant overlooking Ponta Negra beach.

TTT Roschti, Av Erivan França, T084-219 4406. International cuisine in a relaxed beachfront bistro and more formal upstairs dining room.

TTT Sobre Ondas, Av Erivan França 14, T084-219 4222. Average seafood and international dishes in an intimate beachfront setting with an underwater theme.

TT Atlântico, Av Erivan França 27, T084-219 2762. Relaxed, warm service, semi open air, beachfront. Portuguese-owned, Italian and Portugese dishes, fish and *carne do sol*. Recommended.

TT Barraca do Caranguejo, Av Erivan França 1180, T084-219 5069. Eight prawn dishes for US$8 and live music nightly from 2100.

TT Camarões, Av Eng Roberto Freire 2610. Also at Natal shopping centre. Touristy, but very good seafood.

TT Cipó Brasil, Av Erivan 3, T0800-284051. Funky little Playa del Carmen-style bar with a jungle theme, 4 levels, sand floors, lantern-lit, very atmospheric. Average food (pizzas, crêpes), good cocktails, live music from 2100.

TT Ponta Negra Grill, Av Erivan 20, T084-219 3714. A large, popular restaurant with live music and several terraces overlooking the beach. Steaks, seafood and cocktails.

T Ponta Negra Mall. Stalls sell sandwiches and snacks.

Tibau do Sul and Pipa *p475*

There are many restaurants and bars along Pipa's main street, Av Baía dos Golfinhos.

TTT Al Buchetto, Av Baía dos Golfinhos 837, Pipa, T084-246 2318. Decent, Italian-made pasta and a lively atmosphere.

TTT Camamo Beijupirá, Tibau do Sul, T084-246 4195. One of the best restaurants in Brazil with a eclectic mix of fusion dishes like prawns and slices of leek in a spicy cashew sauce with raisins and ginger, served with fervent enthusiasm by owner Tadeu Lubambo. Excellent wine list.

TTT Toca da Coruja, Praia da Pipa (see page 480). Superlative and beautifully presented regional food in a tropical garden setting. Intimate and romantic. Highly recommended.

TTT Vivendo, Av Baía dos Golfinhos, Pipa. One of the town's best seafood restaurants and a good place to watch the passers-by.

T Casa de Taipe and Shirley My House, Av Baía dos Golfinhos 1126 and 1213, Praia da Pipa. Very cheap but decent self-service restaurants, the latter owned by the sister of Vera of **Vera-My House** (see page 480).

T São Sebastião, R do Ceu, Pipa. Vegetarian and wholefood. Good value. Good juices.

T Sopa de Patrick/Chez Lisa, Av Baía dos Golfinhos s/n, Praia da Pipa. Generous portions of various delicious soups, in a little shack beyond the main square.

Tatoo Batata, R do Ceu, Pipa, T084-9419 7181. Enormous baked potatoes with fillings like cheese and sweet corn. Salads and juices too. Friendly owner. Next to **A Conchego** pousada (see Sleeping).

Bars and clubs

Natal *p472, map p473*

Dance is an important pastime in Natal. In an area in the centre known as **Ribeira**, there are a few popular bars/nightclubs in restored historic buildings in R Chile.

Amiça, Av Engenheiro Roberto Freire s/n. New club with techno and house, popular with locals and tourists.

Blackout B52, R Chile 25, T084-221 1282. Lively venue with a 1940s theme. The best night is 'Black Monday'. There is live rock, blues and MPB on other nights. The crowd is 20s and early 30s.

Budda Pub, Av Engenheiro Roberto Freire (an annexe of the Tiberius). A little bar with good bar food and a laid-back atmosphere.

Centro de Turismo (see Shopping below) has *Forró com Turista*, a chance for visitors to learn this fun dance, Thu at 2200. There are many other enjoyable venues where visitors are encouraged to join in.

Chaplin, Av Presidente Café Filho 27, Praia dos Artistas, T084-202 1188. Different zones with everything from MPB and *forró* to techno and progressive house.

Novakapital, Av Presidente Café Filho 872, Praia dos Artistas, T084-202 7111. With *forró*, live music, especially rock and foam parties, US$4, from 2400.

Ponta Negra *p474, map p474*

Although there is a handful of respectable clubs, Ponta Negra beach is now somewhat seedy. The municipal authorities are coming down very hard on the sex industry and its clients, and are installing video cameras all along the beach. Alto Punta Negra is very lively and has live music and a range of bars and clubs open until dawn.

Baraonda, Av Erivan França 44, T084-9481 3748. Live music nightly except Tue, including *forró* and MPB from 2300 until late.

Taverna Pub, R Dr Manoel, Araújo 500, Alta Ponta Negra, T084-236 3696. Medieval-style pub in youth hostel basement. Eclectic (rock, Brazilian pop, jazz, etc) live music Tue-Sun from 2200, best night Wed. Recommended.

In front of the Taverna is a cluster of small venues including **Tapiocaria Salsa Bar** and the **Calderão da Bruxa**.

Tibau do Sul and around *p475*

Tibau do Sul has various beach *barracas*. There is always something going on in Pipa, whatever the night and whatever the month.

Aruman, Av Baía dos Golfinhos s/n, Pipa. Good cocktails and a trendy crowd.

Blue Bar, Av Baía dos Golfinhos, Pipa. Live *pagodé* and samba on Wed.

Calangos, Baía dos Golfinhos s/n (at the southern end of Pipa). A club with famous DJs like Patife. Techno and MPB Thu-Sun.

Carvalho do Fogo, Tibau do Sul. *Forró* until dawn every Wed.

Reggae Bar, just off Av Baía dos Golfinhos, Pipa centre. Live reggae bands, usually on Tue.

Festivals and events

Natal *p472, map p473*

Jan **Festa de Nossa Senhora dos Navegantes**, when numerous vessels go to sea from Praia da Redinha, north of town.

Mid-Oct Country show, **Festa do Boi** (bus marked Parnamirim to the exhibition centre), gives a good insight into rural life.

Mid-Dec **Carnaval**, the Salvador-style out-of-season carnival, a lively 4-day music festival with dancing in the streets.

Shopping

Natal *p472, map p473*

Centro de Turismo, R Aderbal de Figueiredo, 980, off R Gen Cordeiro, Petrópolis, T084-212 2267. A converted prison with a wide variety of handicraft and antiques shops, art gallery and tourist information booth. Good view of the Rio Potengi and the sea, Sun-Wed 0900-1900, Thu 2200.

Centro Municipal de Artesanato, Av Pres Café Filho, Praia dos Artistas. Daily 1000-2200. Sand-in-bottle pictures are very common in Natal and there are plenty here alongside other touristy items.

Natal Shopping, Av Senador Salgado Filho, 2234, between Via Costeira and Ponta Negra. Large mall with restaurants, cinemas and 140 shops. Free shuttle service to major hotels.

Tibau do Sul and around *p475*

Pipa is a good place for raw cotton and costume jewellery made from tropical seeds.
The Bookshop (next to the Reggae Bar, see Bars and clubs). Run by the wonderfully knowledgeable and eccentric Cyntia, who rents out books from Oscar Wilde to Dostoevsky.

Activities and tours

Natal *p472, map p473*

Boat trips

Boat trips on the Rio Potengi and along the nearby beaches of the Litoral Sul. A 2-hr tour includes hotel pickup, a snack, and allows time for a swim, US$15 per person. Boat trips to Barra do Cunhaú, 86 km south of Natal, go through mangroves, visit an island and a salt mine (Passeio Ecológico Cunhaú).
Albacora Azul, T084-239 2160, F238 2204.
Marina Badauê, T084-238 2066, F238 2166.

Buggy tours

Buggy tours are by far the most popular, US$35-90, depending on the destination.
China's Turismo, R Mossoró 574, T084-222 1564, American Express representative.
Marsol Turismo, Av Senador Salgado Filho, 141, T084-206 3308.
Nataltur, Av Deodoro 424, Centro, T084-211 0117, F211 6325.

City tours

A city tour costs US$15; if it includes the northern beaches US$20-25; including southern beaches US$30-35.

Microlight flights

Ultraleve, T084-982 7348. Microlight flights over the Rio Potengi and sand dunes and beaches north of Natal are available for US$29 per person including hotel pickup.

Ponta Negra *p474, map p474*

Manary Ecotours, R Francisco Gurgel 9067, T/F084-219 2900, www.manary.com.br. Excellent tours to some of the most interesting sights in the northeastern interior, such as Souza, Cariri and the Serra da Capivara. Short on information about local fauna.

Tibau do Sul and Pipa *p475*

Buggy tours to Barra de Cunhaú US$50, from Pipa to Natal US$115.

Genipabu *p477*

Associação dos Bugueiros, T084-225 2077. US$25 for dune buggy tour. Microlight flights are also available.

Transport

Natal *p472, map p473*

See also Ins and outs, page 472.

Air Flights to **Belém**, **Brasília**, **Fernando de Noronha**, **Fortaleza**, **Recife**, **Rio de Janeiro**, **Salvador** and **São Paulo**.

Airline offices BRA, Av Prudente de Morais 507, Centro, T084-221 1155, at airport, T084-643 2068, www.voebra.com.br. **FLY**, Av Prudente de Morais 3857, T084-206 9070, at airport, T084-643 2124. **Gol**, www.voegol.com.br, at airport. **Nordeste**, at airport, T084-272 6814. **Ocean Air**, www.oceanair.com.br. **TAM**, Av Campos Sales 500, Tirol, T084-201 2020, at airport, T084-643 1624, F272 2624, freephone T0800-123100. **Trip**, T084-234 1717, freephone T0800-2747. **Varig**, R Mossoro 598, Centro, T084-201 9339, F221 1531, at airport, T084-743 1100, freephone T0800-997000.

Bus Regional tickets are sold on street level of the *rodoviária* in Cidade da Esperança, interstate tickets from the 2nd floor.

Viação Campos runs to **Pirangi**, US$0.60, 5 times a day 0630-1815, 3 on Sun 0730, 0930, 1645. In summer, buses run from both *rodoviárias*, every 30 mins to **Pirangi**, US$1, 1 hr; to **Tabatinga** US$1.50, 1¼ hrs.

From the new *rodoviária*, there are 6 buses a day to **Tibau do Sul**, US$3, 2 hrs, starting at 0600, and going on from Tibau to **Pipa**, US$4, 15 mins more.

To **Recife** with **Napoles**, 5 daily, US$6.60 *convencional*, US$9 *executivo*, 4 hrs. With **Nordeste** to **Mossoró**, US$6 *convencional*, US$10 *executivo*, 4 hrs. To **Aracati**, US$7.50, 5½ hrs. To **Fortaleza**, US$11 *convencional*, US$15.50 *executivo*, US$25 *leito*, 8 hrs. To **João Pessoa**, every 2 hrs, US$4 *convencional*, US$5 *executivo*, 3 hrs. With **São Geraldo** to **Maceió**, buses both direct and via Recife, US$14 *convencional*, US$20 *executivo*, 10 hrs. To **Salvador**, US$32.50 *executivo*, 20 hrs. To **Rio de Janeiro**, US$69.65. To **São Paulo**, US$66 *convencional*, US$84 *executivo*, 46-49 hrs. With Boa Esperança to **Teresina**, US$26 *convencional*, US$31.25 *executivo*, 17-20 hrs. To **Belém**, US$45, 32 hrs.

Car hire Avis, at airport, T084-644 2500. Buggy Mille, Av Praia de Ponta Negra 8848, T084-236 3373, F236 2382. **Dudu Locadora**, Av Rio Branco 420, Centro, T084-211 7000, F221 4694. **Hertz**, airport, T084-643 1660. Localiza, Av Nascimento de Castro 1792, T084-206 5296, or at airport, T0800-992000.

Tibau do Sul and Pipa *p475*

Bicycle hire From Blue Planet, Pipa. US$5 ½ day, US$10 full day.

Buggy It is possible to travel all the way to **Fortaleza** in Ceará by buggy with Top Buggy , T084-321 9820, www.top buggy.com.br, via the stunning Rio Grande do Norte dunes and beaches.

Bus Combis connect Pipa and Tibau until around 2300. 6 buses a day to **Natal**'s new *rodoviária*, US$3, 2 hrs, from Pipa via Tibau do Sul, leaving Pipa 0500-1600. Minivans also do this run and are easiest to catch from the beach.

Buses to **Paraíba** pass through Goianinha on the interstate road. Frequent combis connect **Goianinha** with Pipa (30 mins, US$1.50).

Taxi Carlos, T084-9977 0006, after-hours taxi, speaks basic English.

Redinha *p477*

Bus Regular bus service from the old *rodoviária* to **Genipabu**.

Ferry There is a frequent ferry service to Cais Tavares de Lira, **Ribeira**, weekdays 0530-1900, weekend and holidays 0800-1830, US$0.50 per person, US$3 for car.

Directory

Natal and Ponta Negra *p472, map p473*

Banks Banco 24 horas, Natal Shopping, Cirrus, Visa, MasterCard and Plus. Also, Av Rio Branco 510, Cidade Alta, US$ cash and TCs at poor rates, cash advances against Visa, Mon-Fri 1000-1600. **Banespa**, Av Rio Branco 704, Cidade Alta, US$ cash and TCs at **dolar turismo** rate, Mon-Fri 1000-1430. **Sunset Câmbio**, Av Hermes da Fonseca 628, Tirol, T084-212 2552, cash and TCs, 0900-1700. Dunas Câmbio, Av Roberto Freire 1776, Loja B-11, Capim Macio (east of Parque das Dunas), T084-219 3840, cash and TCs, 0900-1700. **Embassies and consulates** Germany, R Gov Sílvio Pedrosa 308, Areia Preta, T084-222 3596. **Italy**, R Auta de Souza 275, Centro, T084-222 6674. **Spain**, R Amintas Barros 4200, Lagoa Nova, T084-206 5610. **Post office** R Princesa Isabel 711, Centro; Av Rio Branco 538, Centro; Av Engenheiro Hildegrando de Góis 22, Ribeira. **Poste restante** is in Ribeira, near the old *rodoviária*, at Av Rio Branco and Av General Gustavo Cordeiro de Farias, hard to find. **Security** Tourist police (Delegacia do Turista): T084-236 3288, 24 hrs. **Telephone** R Princesa Isabel 687 and R João Pessoa, Centro, also *rodoviária*.

Ponta Negra *p474, map p474*

Banks Banco do Brasil, Seafront ATM for Cirrus, Visa, MasterCard and Plus. **Embassies and consulates** Canada, Av Roberto Freire 2951, bloco 01, loja 09-CCAB Sul, T084 219 2197. **Internet** Sobre Ondas, (also bar and restaurant, see Eating), 0900-2400, 10 centavos 1 min. **Post office** Av Praia de Ponta Negra 8920. **Telephone** Av Roberto Freire 3100, Shopping Cidade Jardim, Av Roberto Freire.

Ceará

The state which has been dubbed 'terra da luz' (land of light) is known for its 573 km of glorious coastline, beaches, dunes and almost constant sunshine. The sophisticated city of Fortaleza is still home to traditional jangadas *(rafts), while inland is the harsh* sertão *and several sites of natural and cultural interest such as Juazeiro de Norte.*

It was only during the period of Dutch rule that efforts were made to populate the interior of Ceará. Many Portuguese, fleeing the Dutch, moved into the sertão *to raise cattle. Beef and leather came to typify the region. The Cearenses participated in the republican movements that flared up in the northeast in the 1800s, but real development did not begin until the second half of the 19th century. Ceará was one of the foremost provinces in the drive to abolish slavery. It remains largely underdeveloped although tourism is increasing.*

The ocean is warm with average temperatures of 29°C and a constant breeze makes the climate pleasant. Most rain falls between March and July and, although locals refer to this period as winter, Europeans will find it warm and sunny with sporadic rainy days. One third of the coast is east of Fortaleza in the Litoral Leste or Costa Sol Nascente (Sunrise Coast), which has a fair concentration of towns and fishing villages. Two thirds of the coastline is west of Fortaleza in the Litoral Oeste or Costa Sol Poente (Sunset Coast), which has some beautiful undeveloped stretches. » *For Sleeping, Eating and other listings, see pages 499-512.*

Fortaleza » *pp499-512.*

→ *Phone code: 085. Colour map 2, A5. Population: 2.1 million.*

The fifth largest city in Brazil and capital of the state of Ceará is a busy metropolis with many high-rise buildings, an important clothes manufacturing industry, lots of hotels and restaurants and a lively nightlife. Fishermen's *jangadas* still dot the turquoise ocean across from the beach and transatlantic cruise ships call in for refuelling. The midday sun is oppressive, tempered somewhat by a constant breeze; evening temperatures are more pleasant, especially by the sea.

Ins and outs

Getting there International and domestic flights arrive at **Aeroporto Pinto Martins** ⓘ *Praça Eduardo Gomes, 6 km south of the centre*. The airport has a 24-hour tourist office, T085-477 1667, car hire, a food hall, internet facilities, **Laselva** bookstore and **Banco do Brasil**, open 1100-1500. Bus No 404 runs from the airport to Praça José de Alencar in the centre, US$0.70. **Expresso Guanabara** minibus runs to the *rodoviária* and Beira Mar (US$1), also No 066 Papicu to Parangaba and No 027 Papicu to Siqueira. Taxis charge US$6 minimum to the centre, Avenida Beira Mar or Praia do Futuro, US$7-10 at night. Use **Cooperativa Taxi Comum** or **Taxi Especial Credenciado**.

Most phone numbers outside metropolitan Fortaleza have the area code 088, but all numbers beginning with 3 must be prefixed with 085.

Interstate buses arrive at the **rodoviária** ⓘ *Av Borges de Melo 1630, Fátima, 6 km south of the centre, T085-256 2100, information from T085-256 4080 or 24-hr Disque Turismo*, which has a tourist information booth open 0600-1800, but no luggage store (only lockers). Opposite the *rodoviária* is **Hotel Amuarama**, which has a bar and restaurant; there's also a *lanchonete*. Many city buses run to the centre, US$0.65. A taxi to Praia de Iracema, or Avenida Abolição costs US$5. » *See also Transport, page 509.*

Getting around The city is spread out, with its main attractions in the centre and along the seashore; transport from one to the other can take a long time. The city bus system is efficient if a little rough. Fare US$0.70; vans also charge US$0.70. The cheapest way to get to know the city is to take the 'Circular 1' (anti-clockwise) or 'Circular 2' (clockwise) buses which pass Avenida Beira Mar, the Aldeota district, the university (UFC) and the city centre and cathedral, US$0.90. Alternatively, take the new *Top Bus* run by **Expresso Guanabara** ⓘ *T0800-991992, US$1.50*, an air-conditioned minibus starting at Avenida Abolição.

When driving outside the city, have a good map and be prepared to ask directions frequently as road signs are non-existent or are placed after junctions.

Tourist information **Secretaria do Turismo (Setur)** ⓘ *Centro Administrativo Virgílio Távora, Cambeba, T085-3101 4639, www.setur.ce.gov.br*, the main office of the state tourism agency, has map and brochures and can help with hotels and tours. There are information booths at the airport and *rodoviária* (see above), and the Farol de Mucuripe (old lighthouse), 0700-1730. The **Posta Telefônica Beira Mar** ⓘ *Av Beira Mar almost opposite Praiano Palace Hotel*, provides information, sells kombi tickets to Jericoacoara, and has a good range of postcards, as well as clothes, newspapers and magazines. **Tourist police** ⓘ *R Silva Paulet 505, Aldeota, T085-433 8171*.

Security Generally the city is safe for visitors. However, tourists should avoid the following areas: Serviluz favela between the old lighthouse (Avenida Vicente de Castro), Mucuripe and Praia do Futuro; the favela behind the railway station; the Passeio Público at night; and Avenida Abolição at its eastern (Nossa Senhora da Saúde church) and western ends.

Sights

Walking through the centre of Fortaleza, it is hard to ignore the city's history, which dates back to the 17th century. Pedestrian walkways radiate from the **Praça do Ferreira**, the heart of the commercial centre, and the whole area is dotted with shady green squares. The **Fortaleza Nossa Senhora da Assumpção** ⓘ *Av Alberto Nepomuceno, T085-255 1600 in advance for permission to visit, daily 0800-1100, 1400-1700*, originally built in 1649 by the Dutch, gave the city its name. Near the fort, on Rua Dr João Moreira, is the 19th-century **Praça Passeio Público** or Praça dos Mártires, a park with old trees and statues of Greek deities. West of here a neoclassical former prison (1866) houses a fine tourist centre, the **Centro de Turismo do Estado (Emcetur)** ⓘ *Av Senador Pompeu 350, near the waterfront, T0800-991516, closed Sun*, with museums, theatre and craft shops. It houses the renovated **Museu de Arte e Cultura Populares** and the **Museu de Minerais** ⓘ *T085-212 3566*. Further west along Rua Dr João Moreira, at **Praça Castro Carreira**, (commonly known as Praça da Estação), is the nicely refurbished train station, **Estação João Felipe** (1880), which runs commuter services.

The **Teatro José de Alencar** ⓘ *Praça José de Alencar, T085-229 1989, Mon-Fri 0800-1700, hourly tours, some English-speaking guides, US$1, Wed free*, was inaugurated in 1910 and is worth a visit. It is a magnificent iron structure imported from Scotland and decorated in neoclassical and art nouveau styles. It also houses a library and art gallery. The **Praça dos Leões** or Praça General Tibúrcio on Rua Conde D'Eu has bronze lions imported from France. Around it stand the 18th-century **Palácio da Luz** ⓘ *T085-231 5699*, former seat of the state government, and the **Igreja Nossa Senhora do Rosário**, built by slaves in the 18th century. Also here is the former provincial legislature, dating from 1871, which houses the **Museu do Ceará** ⓘ *R São Paulo, next to Praça dos Leões, T085-251 1502, Tue-Fri 0830-1730, Sat 0830-1400, US$0.80*. The museum has displays on history and anthropology. To get there, take bus marked 'Dom Luís'.

The new **cathedral** ⓘ *Praça da Sé*, completed in 1978, in Gothic style but built in concrete, with beautiful stained-glass windows, stands beside the new semi-circular **Mercado Central**.

There are several worthwhile museums to visit in and around Fortaleza. The **Museu do Maracatu** ⓘ *Rufino de Alencar 231*, at Teatro São José, has costumes of this ritual dance of African origin.

The new and exciting **Centro Dragão do Mar de Arte e Cultura** ⓘ *R Dragão do Mar 81, Praia de Iracema, T085-488 8600, www.dragaodomar.org.br, Tue-Thu 1000-1730, Fri-Sun 1400-2130, US$0.75 for entry to each museum/gallery, free on Sun*, hosts concerts, dance performances and exhibitions of art and photography. It has various entrances, from Rua Almirante Barroso, Rua Boris, and from the junction of Monsenhor Tabosa, Dom Manuel and Castelo Branco. This last one leads directly to three museums: on street level, the **Memorial da Cultura Cearense**, with changing exhibitions; on the next floor down is an art and cultural exhibition; in the basement is an excellent audio-visual **museum of El Vaqueiro**. Also at street level is the **Livraria Livro Técnico**. There is a **planetarium** with a whispering gallery underneath. The centre also houses the **Museu de Arte Contemporânea do Ceará**. This area is very lively at night.

South of the centre

The **Museu Artur Ramos** ⓘ *Av Perimetral, Messejana, 15 km from the centre, T085-229 1898, Tue-Sun 0800-1200, 1400-1700, Mon 1400-1730*, in the Casa de José de Alencar, displays artefacts of African and indigenous origin collected by the anthropologist Artur Ramos, as well as documents from the writer José de Alencar.

Beaches

The urban beaches between Barra do Ceará (west) and Ponta do Mucuripe (east) are considered polluted and not suitable for swimming. There are a number of minibus day tours to other beaches, US$4 and Jericoacoara, US$15; minibuses gather along the seafront. The agency **CPVTUR** ⓘ *Av Monsenhor Tabosa 1001*, also runs trips.

Eastern beaches Just east of the centre is **Praia de Iracema,** one of the older beach suburbs, with some original turn-of-the-century houses. It is not much of a sunbathing beach as it has little shade or facilities and swimming is unsafe, but don't miss it at night. Of its many bars and restaurants, the **Estoril,** housed in one of the earliest buildings, has become a landmark. At the shore, Ponte Metálica or Ponte dos Ingleses are good places to see the sunset and view dolphins.

East of Iracema, the **Avenida Beira Mar** (Avenida Presidente Kennedy) connects Praia do Meireles (divided into **Praia do Ideal, Praia dos Diários** and **Praia do Meireles)** with Volta da Jurema and Praia do Mucuripe; it is lined with high-rise buildings and most luxury hotels are located here. A *calçado*, or walkway, following the palm-lined shore, becomes a night-time playground as locals promenade on foot, roller skates, skate boards and bicycles. Children ride mini-motorbikes, scooters or the 'happiness' train with its real life Disney characters. Take in the spectacle while sipping an *agua de coco* or *caiprinha* on the beachfront, where there are volleyball courts, bars, open-air shows and a crafts fair in front of the **Imperial Othon Palace Hotel.**

Praia do Mucuripe, 5 km from the centre, is Fortaleza's main fishing centre, where *jangadas* (traditional rafts with triangular sails) bring in the catch; there are many

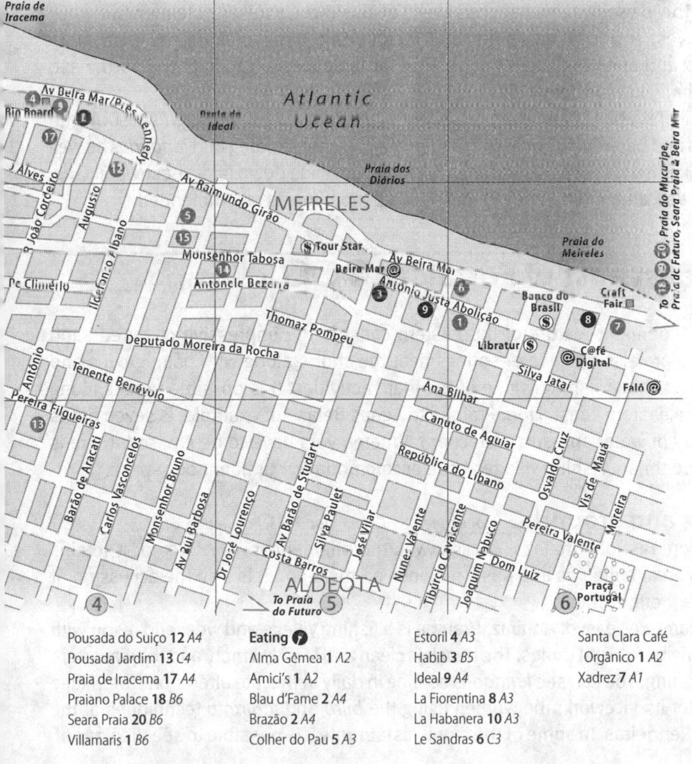

restaurants serving *peixada* and other fish specialities. The symbol of this beach is the statue of Iracema, the main character of the romance by José de Alencar (see Background, page 694). From the monument there is a good view of Mucuripe's port and bay. At Mucuripe Point is a lighthouse built by slaves in 1846, which houses the **Museu de Fortaleza** (now sadly run down and not a safe area, according to the tourist office). There is a lookout at the new lighthouse, good for viewing the *jangadas*, which return in the late afternoon, and the sunset.

Praia do Futuro, 8 km southeast of the centre, is the most popular bathing beach. It is 8 km long, with strong waves, sand dunes and freshwater showers, but no natural shade. Vendors in straw shacks serve local dishes such as crab. On Thursday nights it becomes the centre for the city's nightlife, with people enjoying live music and *forró*. The south end of the beach is known as Caça e Pesca; water here is polluted because of the outflow of the Rio Cocó. Praia do Futuro has few hotels or buildings because the salt-spray corrosion is among the strongest in the world.

At **Praia de Sabiaguaba**, 20 km southeast of the centre, is a small fishing village known for its seafood; the area has mangroves and is good for fishing.

Some 29 km southeast of the centre is **Praia Porto das Dunas**, a pleasant beach popular for watersports including surfing. Buggies and microlight tours can be arranged. The main attraction is **Beach Park** ⓘ *US$20*, the largest water park in South America, with pools, water toboggans, sports fields and restaurants.

Western beaches Northwest of the centre is **Praia Barra do Ceará**, 8 km, where the Rio Ceará flows into the sea (take a Grande Circular 1 bus). Here are the ruins of the 1603 Forte de Nossa Senhora dos Prazeres, the first Portuguese settlement in the area, partially covered by dunes, from which you can watch the beautiful sunsets. The palm-fringed beaches west of the Rio Ceará are cleaner but have strong waves. A bridge has been built across this river, making the area more accessible and open to development, as at **Praia de Icaraí**, 22 km to the northwest, and **Tabuba**, 5 km further north.

Beyond Tabuba, **Cumbuco** is a lively beach (it can be dirty in high season) with palm trees and bars. For the active, there are buggies, horse riding and *jangadas* as well as dunes (known locally as *skibunda*), which you can slide down into a freshwater lake, the **Lagoa de Parnamirim**. A buggy tour, US$7 per person, is recommended.

The coast east of Fortaleza » pp499-512.

The most prominent feature of the eastern coast is the impressive coloured sand cliffs. There are also freshwater springs near the shore, along with palm groves and mangroves. Lobster fishing is one of the main activities. It is possible to hike along much of the eastern coast. From Prainha to Águas Belas, for example, is seven hours (take plenty of water and sun protection). Where rivers have to be crossed, there is usually a boatman. Fishing villages have accommodation or hammock space.

Aquiraz and around → *Phone code: 085. Colour map 2, A5. Population: 61,000.*

Some 31 km east of Fortaleza, Aquiraz was the original capital of Ceará. It retains several colonial buildings and has a religious art museum. It is also the access point for a number of beaches.

Six kilometres east of Aquiraz, **Prainha** is a fishing village and weekend resort with a 10-km long beach and dunes. The beach is clean and largely empty and the waves are good for surfing. You can see *jangadas* coming in daily in the late afternoon. The village is known for its lacework; the women using the *bilro* and *labirinto* techniques at the **Centro** de Rendeiras. In some of the small restaurants it is possible to see displays of the *carimbó*, one of the north Brazilian dances. Just south of Prainha is **Praia do Presídio** with gentle surf, dunes, palms and *cajueiros* (cashew trees).

About 18 km southeast of Aquiraz is **Praia Iguape**, another fishing and lacework village. The beach is a large, elbow-shaped sandbank, very scenic especially at Ponta do Iguape. Nearby are high sand dunes where skiing is popular. There is a lookout at Morro do Enxerga Tudo; one hour *jangada* trips cost US$8.50. Lacework is sold at the **Centro de Rendeiras.** Locals are descendants of Dutch, Portuguese and indigenous peoples; some traditions such as the *coco-de-praia* folk dance are still practised. Some 3 km south of Iguape is **Praia Barro Preto,** a wide tranquil beach, with dunes, palms and lagoons.

Cascavel → *Phone code: 085.*

Cascavel, 62 km southeast of Fortaleza, has a Saturday crafts fair by the market. It is the access point for the beaches of Caponga and Águas Belas, where traditional fishing villages coexist with fancy weekend homes and hotels. **Caponga,** 15 km northeast of Cascavel, has a wide, 2-km-long beach lined with palms. *Jangadas* set sail in the early morning; arrangements can be made to accompany fishermen on overnight trips, a 90-minute ride costs US$14 for up to five people. There is a fish market and crafts sales (ceramics, embroidery and lacework) on the beach. A 30-minute walk south along the white-sand beach leads to **Águas Belas,** at the mouth of the Rio Mal Cozinhado, offering a combination of fresh and saltwater bathing (access also by road, 15 km from Cascavel, 4 km from Caponga). The scenery here, and 5 km further east at Barra Nova, changes with the tide. A walk north along the beach for 6 km takes you to the undeveloped **Praia do Batoque,** which is surrounded by cliffs and dunes.

Morro Branco and Praia das Fontes → *Phone code: 085.*

Beberibe, 78 km from Fortaleza, is the access point for Morro Branco and Praia das Fontes, some of the better-known beaches of the east coast.

About 4 km from Beberibe, **Morro Branco** has a spectacular beach, coloured craggy cliffs and beautiful views. *Jangadas* leave the beach at 0500, returning at 1400- 1500; lobster is the main catch in this area. The coloured sands of the dunes are bottled into beautiful designs and sold along with other crafts such as lacework, embroidery and straw goods. *Jangadas* may be hired for sailing (one hour for up to six people US$30). Beach buggies cost US$100 for a full day; taxis are also available for hire. The beach is lined with summer homes and can get very crowded during peak season.

South of Morro Branco and 6 km from Beberibe is **Praia das Fontes,** which also has coloured cliffs with freshwater springs. There is a fishing village and, at the south end, a lagoon. Near the shore is a cave, known as **Mãe de Água,** visible at low tide. Buggies and microlights can be hired on the beach. A luxury resort complex has been built here, making the area expensive.

South of Praia das Fontes are several less developed beaches including **Praia Uruaú** or **Marambaia,** about 6 km from Praia das Fontes along the beach or 21 km by road from Beberibe, via Sucatinga on a loose sand road. The beach is at the base of coloured dunes; there is a fishing village with some accommodation. Just inland is **Lagoa do Uruaú,** the largest in the state and a popular place for watersports. A buggy from Morro Branco costs US$45 for four.

About 50 km southeast of Beberibe is **Fortim,** access point to **Pontal de Maceió,** a reddish sand point at the mouth of the Rio Jaguaribe, from where there is a good view of a large section of the eastern coast. In the winter the river is high and there is fishing for shrimp, while in the summer it dries up, forming islands and freshwater beaches; boats go to the islands from Fortim. There's a fishing village about 1 km from the ocean with bars, restaurants and small pousadas.

Prainha do Canto Verde → *Phone code: 085.*

Some 120 km east of Fortaleza, in the district of Beberibe, is Prainha do Canto Verde, a small fishing village on a vast beach, which has an award-winning community tourism project. There are guesthouses or houses for rent (see Sleeping, page 502), restaurants (good food at **Sol e Mar**) and a handicraft cooperative. Each November there is a **Regata Ecológica**, with *jangadas* from up and down the coast competing. *Jangada* and catamaran cruises are offered, as well as fishing and a number of walking trails. This a simple place, where people make their living through artesanal fishing, without the use of big boats or industrial techniques. The village has built up its tourism infrastructure without any help from outside investors, and has been fighting the speculators since 1979. The people are friendly and visitors are welcome to learn about the traditional way of life, although knowledge of Portuguese is essential.

Ins and outs To get to Prainha do Canto Verde, take a São Benedito bus to Aracati or Canoa Quebrada, buy a ticket to Quatro Bocas and ask to be let off at Lagoa da Poeira, two hours from Fortaleza. If you haven't booked a transfer in advance, Márcio at the **Pantanal** restaurant at the bus stop may be able to take you, US$2.75. The website www.fortalnet.com.br/~fishnet is a good source of information. Alternatively contact René Schärer, T088-413 1426, fishnet@uol.com.br, who speaks English, or the tourism coordinator of **Lagomar**, Antônio Aires, T085-9608 8222.

Aracati → *Phone code: 088. Population: 62,000.*

Situated on the shores of the Rio Jaguaribe, Aracati is the access point to the southeasternmost beaches of Ceará. The city is best known for its Carnaval (the liveliest in the state) and for its colonial architecture, including several 18th-century churches and mansions with Portuguese tile façades. There is a religious art museum (closed lunchtime and Sunday afternoon), a Saturday morning crafts fair on Avenida Coronel Alexandrino, and a number of simple pousadas on the same street (B-E).

Canoa Quebrada → *Phone code: 088. Colour map 2, A5.*

Canoa Quebrada stands on a sand dune 10 km from Aracati. It remained an isolated fishing village until 1982, when a road was built. It is now a very popular resort, with many bars, restaurants and *forró* establishments, known for its easygoing party atmosphere (there have been reports of drug problems here). The village is also famous for its *labirinto* lacework, coloured sand sculpture and beaches. Sand skiing is popular on the dunes. Local fishermen have their homes in **Esteves**, a separate village also on top of the cliff; they still live off the sea and rides on *jangadas* can be arranged at the beach. To avoid biting insects (*bicho do pé*) it is best to wear shoes or sandals. The nearest place to change money is the **Banco do Brasil** in Aracati.

South of Canoa Quebrada

Heading south from Canoa Quebrada, **Porto Canoa** is a resort town that opened in 1996, fashioned after the Greek islands. It includes beach homes and apartments, shopping areas, restaurants and hotels, and there are facilities for watersports, horse riding, microlight flights, buggy and *jangada* outings.

South of here, **Majorlândia** is a very pleasant village with multi-coloured sand dunes, used in bottle pictures and cord crafts, and a wide beach with strong waves, good for surfing. The arrival of the fishing fleet in the evening is an important daily event; lobster is the main catch. It is a popular weekend destination with beach homes for rent and plenty of pousadas. Carnaval here is quite lively, but you will have no trouble finding a room outside the peak season. The town is easy to find your way around.

About 5 km south along the beach from Majorlândia is the village of **Quixaba**, on a beach surrounded by coloured cliffs, with reefs offshore and good fishing. At low tide you can reach the popular destination of **Lagoa do Mato**, some 4 km south. The *lagoa* can also be reached by buggy from Canoa Quebrada beach (US$30 for four). There's a hotel, restaurant and pristine beach surrounded by dunes, cliffs and palms.

Ponta Grossa → *Phone code: 088.*

Ponta Grossa, 30 km southeast of Aracati, near Icapuí, is the last municipality before Rio Grande do Norte (access from Mossoró) and is reached via a sand road just before Redonda. It's a very pretty place, nestled at the foot of the cliffs, with a beautiful beach.

Ponta Grossa has its own community tourism development. The fishing community here has many inhabitants of Dutch origin, following a shipwreck in the 19th century, and many people have fair hair. It is also one of the few places where *peixe boi marinho* (manatees) can be spotted. There's a natural lookout from the cliffs (buggy US$75 for four, four hours).

Beach trips go from Canoa Quebrada (see above) to Ponta Grossa for lunch, but if you want to stay here, it helps if you can speak Portuguese. Cabins for rent are under construction and there are restaurants/bars. For information contact the tourism coordinator, Eliabe, T088-432 5001/9964 5846. For further information on community tourism and the preservation of traditional ways of life in Ceará, contact **Instituto Terramar** ⓘ *R Pinho Pessoa 86, Joaquim Távora, Fortaleza, T085-226 4154/8804 0999, ask for Esther Neuhaus, www.terramar.org.br.*

To the south are the beaches of **Redonda**, another very pretty place, and **Barreiras**, which is good for surfing and has a handful of hotels.

The coast west of Fortaleza  » *pp499-512.*

The coast northwest of Fortaleza has many wide beaches below fixed or shifting dunes, surrounded by swathes of coconut groves. The main roads are some distance from the shore, making access to the beaches more difficult than on the eastern coast. This means the fishing villages have retained a traditional lifestyle and responsible travel is especially important.

Pecém and Taíba → *Phone code: 085. Population: 5500 (Pecém).*

Some 58 km northwest of Fortaleza, **Pecém** is a village set in a cove with a wide beach, dunes and inland lagoons. There is strong surf and surfing and fishing championships are held. From Pecém it is 19 km by road to **Taíba**, a 14-km-long beach with a long palm-covered point extending into the sea. Nearby is **Siupé**, a village that maintains colonial characteristics, where embroidered hammocks, a trademark of Ceará, are made.

Pecém and Taíba are serviced by regular buses from Fortaleza; both have a few simple pousadas. (The town's central telephone exchange can be reached on T085-344 1064 and T085-340 1328; any three-digit numbers listed are extensions on these central lines.)

Paracuru and Lagoinha → *Phone code: 085. Population: 28,000 (Paracuru).*

Some 106 km northwest of Fortaleza, **Paracuru** is a fishing port which hosts the most important Carnaval on the northwest coast, including street dancing and parades, decorated boat s, sports championships and a beauty contest. It has some lovely deserted white-sand beaches with good bathing and surfing, and the people are very friendly. There are several pousadas in the centre. Restaurant **Ronco do Mar** has good fish dishes. **Boca do Poço** bar has *forró* at weekends. There are eight daily buses from Fortaleza *rodoviária*, US$3; for information contact T085-272 4483 (in Fortaleza).

West of Paracuru and 12 km from the town of Paraipaba is **Lagoinha**, a very scenic beach with hills, dunes and palms by the shore. There's a fishing village on one of the hills and nearby are some small but pleasant waterfalls. About 3 km west of town is **Lagoa da Barra**, a lake surrounded by dunes. Local legend says that one of the hills, Morro do Cascudo, has hidden treasure left by French pirates. There are six daily buses from Fortaleza with **Brasileiro**, three hours, US$2.60 and plenty of cheap seafood restaurants.

Fleixeiras and around → *Phone code: 085. Colour map 2, A4.*

Further northwest, some 135 km from Fortaleza, is **Trairi**, access point to a series of beaches that have kept their natural beauty and, until the mid-1990s, were untouched by tourism. North of Trairi, 15 km by road, is **Fleixeiras**, where pools that are good for snorkelling form near the beach at low tide. There are three daily buses from Fortaleza to Fleixeiras (US$3.85, information T085-272 4128).

About 5 km west is **Imboaca**, a scenic beach with interesting rock formations and shifting dunes. Further west, at the mouth of the Rio Mundaú, is **Mundaú**, another beautiful area, with a beach, palms, dunes and an old working lighthouse. Take a raft across to the spit and walk for hours on deserted sands, see wind-eroded dunes or take a boat from the quay up the river to see the mangroves. Access roads from Imboaca and Cana to the south are often impassable because of shifting dunes; at low tide it is possible to reach it along the beach from Fleixeiras. There is a fishing village near the beach with some pousadas and restaurants.

Jericoacoara » pp499-512.

→ *Phone code: 088. Colour map 2, A4.*

Nestled in the dunes, the fishing community of Jericoacoara (or Jerí as the locals call it) is popular with both Brazilian and international travellers. Despite the large influx of visitors, it remains a tranquil and safe town. Visitors are rewarded with towering sand dunes, deserted beaches with little shade, cactus-covered cliffs rising from the sea, interesting rock formations and a pleasant atmosphere. Watching the sunset from the top of the large dune just west of town, followed by a display of *capoeira* on the beach, is a tradition among visitors. There is nightly *forró* in high season; Wednesday and Saturday at other times.

Jericoacoara is ostensibly part of an environmental protection area that includes a large coconut grove, lakes, dunes and hills covered in *caatinga* vegetation. However, in recent years, the relentless buggy-based tourism and proliferation of pousadas, together with local authorities who are very amenable to persuasion from business has seen this beautiful area become a little spoilt. Over-development has led to pollution and buggy tourism has disturbed the dunes and their flora and fauna. A youth group publishes *Força Jovem Jericoacoara*, a monthly newspaper providing information for visitors and covering general issues of environmental protection in the area. There are several possibilities for walking and horse riding (US$2-3 per hour). Buggy trips on the dunes are available but you can see them equally well on foot with less environmental impact. Take water and sun protection as it gets very hot and there is no shade; several hotels offer tours.

Ins and outs

There are three buses a day from Fortaleza to Jericoacoara. The journey is a fairly gruelling six hours. Be sure to take a *leito* or *executivo* bus as the last leg of the journey involves a change at either Prea or Jijoca for a 45-minute rough stretch in either the back of a truck or a ramshackle off-road bus. There are also connections with the rest of the state through Sobral.

Around Jericoacoara

Going west along the beach takes you through a succession of sand dunes and coconut groves; the views are beautiful. After 2 km is the beach of **Mangue Seco**, and 2 km beyond this is an arm of the ocean that separates it from **Guriú** (across the bridge), where there is a village on top of a fixed dune. Some of the best scenery in the area is around **Nova Tatajuba**, about 35 km west of Jerí. It is reached by land from Camocim, or along the beach by dune-buggy including a river crossing on a barge (US$20 per person, minimum four) or by sea, three hours (US$100); there are basic pousadas, see Sleeping, page 503.

A 45-minute walk to the east takes you to the **Pedra Furada**, a stone arch sculpted by the sea, one of the symbols of Jerí, accessible only at low tide (check the tide tables at the **Casa do Turismo**). In the same direction but just inland is **Serrote**, a large hill with a lighthouse on top; it is well worth walking up for the magnificent views.

About 15 km east along the shore (43 km by road via Jijoca and Caiçara) is **Praia do Preá**, with light sand and blue ocean. At low tide you can visit the **Pedra da Seréia**, a rock with natural swimming pools on top.

Some 10 km beyond Praia do Preá (62 km by road) is the beach of **Barrinha**, with access to the picturesque **Lagoa Azul**. From here it's 10 km inland through the dunes (20 km along the road) to **Lagoa Paraíso** or **Jijoca**, a turquoise, freshwater lake, great for bathing (buggy US$10 per person).

Cruz

Some 40 km east of Jijoca is Cruz, an obligatory stop if travelling by bus from Sobral to Jericoacoara. It is a small pleasant town, surrounded by a *carnauba* palm forest (used in making brooms). At the south end is a large wooden cross dating from 1825, nearby is a statue to São Francisco. There is a lively market on Sunday when, at dawn, *pau d'arara* trucks, mule carts and bicycles converge on the town. There are two very basic hotels.

Western Ceará

» pp499-512.

Sobral → *Phone code: 088. Colour map 2, A4. Population: 145,000.*

Sobral, 238 km west of Fortaleza (four hours by bus, US$5), is the principal town in western Ceará and the access point to beaches in the west of the state. The city has a handful of well-preserved colonial buildings including the **Catedral da Sé, Teatro São João** and a mansion on the Praça da Sé. There is a **Museu Diocesano** ⓘ *Praça São João*, a Cristo Redentor statue and a monument to the 1919 solar eclipse. Near town is the **Parque Ecológico Lagoa da Fazenda.**

Chapada de Ibiapaba

In the Chapada de Ibiapaba, an area of tablelands, caves, rock formations, rivers and waterfalls, is **Tianguá.** The town is surrounded by waterfalls; 3 km to the north is Cachoeira de São Gonçalo, a good place for bathing; 5 km from town are natural pools at the meeting place of seven waterfalls. About 16 km from town on the edge of the BR-222 is Cana Verde, a 30-m-high waterfall surrounded by monoliths and thick vegetation.

Some 30 km north of Tianguá is **Viçosa do Ceará**, a colonial town also within the Chapada, known for its ceramics, hang-gliding, food and drink. The Igreja de Nossa Senhora das Vitórias, a stone church on top of the 820-m-high **Morro do Céu**, is reached walking up 360 steps. There is an excellent view of the town, the surrounding highlands and the *sertão* beyond. Near the town are interesting rock formations such as the 100-m-wide **Pedra de Itagurussu** with a natural spring. There is good walking in the area. Basic walking maps are available at the **Secretaria de Turismo**, near the old theatre to the right of the *praça* on which the church stands. Ask about visiting the community that makes sun-baked earthenware pots. To get there take an **Expresso Serrana** bus from Fortaleza, six hours, US$8.40, five a day via Sobral.

Parque Nacional Ubajara → *Colour map 2, A4.*

Eighteen kilometres south of Tianguá, at an altitude of 840 m, is the town of **Ubajara** (tourist information, T085-634 1300 ext 231, www.ubajara.ce.gov.br), with an interesting Sunday morning market selling produce of the *sertão*. Some 3 km from the town is the **Parque Nacional Ubajara**, with 563 ha of native highland and *caatinga* brush. It is the smallest of Brazil's national parks and its main attraction is the **Ubajara cave** on the side of an escarpment. Fifteen chambers extending for a total of 1120 m have been mapped, of which 360 m are open to visitors. Access is along a 6-km footpath and steps (two to three hours, take water) or by a **cable car** ⓘ *T088-634 1219, 0900-1430, last up at 1500, US$1.50, locals US$0.15*, which descends the cliff to the cave entrance. Lighting has been installed in nine caverns of the complex. An **Ibama** guide leads visitors through the cave, which is completely dry and home to 14 types of bat. At one point the lights are turned out to appreciate total blackness. Several rock formations look like animals: horse's head, jacaré, snake. At the park entrance is an **Ibama office** ⓘ *5 km from the caves, T085-634 1388, www.ibama.gov.br*, and a bar by the entrance serving juices, snacks and *refrigerantes*. In the park there is a new easy walkway through the woods with stunning views at the end. Start either to the left of the park entrance or opposite the snack bar near the cable car platform. There is a good 8-km trail to the park from Araticum (7 km by bus from Ubajara). This route is used by locals and passes through *caatinga* forest.

South from Ubajara

The Chapada de Ibiapaba continues south from Ubajara for some 70 km. Other towns in the highlands are: **Ibiapina**, with the nearby Cachoeira da Ladeira, reached by a steep trail, a good place for bathing; **São Benedito**, known for its straw and ceramic crafts and a working *engenho* sugar mill; and **Carnaubal**, with waterfalls and a bathing resort.

Ipu, 80 km south of Ubajara, is a town at the foot of the Serra de Ibiapaba, on the edge of the *sertão*. It's an interesting transition as you descend from the green serra, with its sugar cane, tall *babaçu* palms and cattle, down the escarpment to the *sertão*. Ipu's main claim to fame is the **Bica do Ipu**, a 180-m waterfall plunging off the sheer edge of the serra into a pool, said to be the site of the legendary love affair between Iracema, a local *indígena*, and the founder of Fortaleza. You can cool off under the fall and there are basic facilities and a few places to stay around town

If driving, you can cross the *sertão* on good roads via **Varjota** on the large lake of the **Açude de Araras** (33 km), **Santa Quitéria** (a further 41 km) to **Canindé** (111 km on CE-257).

Monsenhor Tabosa, in the centre of the state, has the highest peak in Ceará. The area around the mountain, called **Cabeço Branco**, has been made into an environmental protection area, with *caatinga* and patches of *mata atlântica*. This remote town is very friendly, with three hotels (see Sleeping, page 504). It can get very wet in the rainy season (around March). The easiest way to get there is by car or **Horizonte** bus on the CE032 from Canindé, but there are roads from Nova Russas, south of Ipu, and the BR-020 from Boa Viagem (which is very rough).

Continuing south, the greenery of the Chapada de Ibiapaba eventually gives way to the dry **Sertão dos Inhamuns**. One of the main towns in this area is **Crateús**, about 210 km south of Sobral, a remote settlement with rich folkloric traditions seen during festivals in August (**Mergulho Folclórico**) and September (**Festival de Repentistas**); nearby are archaeological sites with rock inscriptions. There is a regular bus service on the paved road to Fortaleza (347 km). The bus service from Crateús runs along the very bad road to Teresina, every other day.

South of Fortaleza » pp499-512.

Serra de Baturité → *Phone code: 085. Colour map 2, A5. Population: 32,000. Altitude: 171 m.*

The town of **Baturité**, the largest in the area, is surrounded by the hills and waterfalls of the **Maciço de Baturité**, an irregular massif with beautiful scenery. Baturité is more in the foothills than in the serra proper. It has some colonial buildings and a historical museum. It is home to the **Pingo de Ouro** distillery, which can be visited, and there are hotels and restaurants. You can also stay in the **Jesuit Seminary** ⓘ *T085-347 0362 in advance*, where a few monks still work in the local community and tend the cloister garden (E per person, full board US$11.10 per day including morning and afternoon coffee with local fruits, ask for 'Jesuitas' if taking a taxi, or walk up). The *rodoviária* is beyond town on the way out to Guaramiranga.

Another historic town is **Redenção**. Northwest of Baturité, at 365 m above sea level, is **Guaramiranga** (16 km on a very twisty road through lush vegetation and fruit trees; lots of birdsong). There are several pousadas along the road on the way up. Guaramiranga is the centre of a fruit and flower growing area and it is packed with visitors at weekends; if you want to stay overnight you must book in advance. During Carnaval (February) it holds a **Festival de Jazz & Blues** and carnival music is forbidden! To ensure a bed in town during this time you must book in November. It also holds a **Festival Nordestino de Teatro** in September in the **Teatro Municipal Rachel de Queiroz**. This is in the centre of town and around it are a number of eating places: **Café com Flores, Taberna Portuguesa, O Alemão, Confrari** (pastas and fondues). For information contact secullguaramiranga@hotmail.com.

About 7 km further north is **Pacoti**, with large botanical gardens (*horto forestal*), trails and several waterfalls; good for a dip and for viewing the highland flora. On the main road to Pacoti, turn left at Forquilha to climb **Pico Alto** (1115 m above sea level, previously thought to be the highest peak in Ceará), which offers special views and sunsets. You can go up by car, or if you leave early in the morning you may be able to catch a lift with the school bus. Between Baturité and Guaramiranga is a turning west to Mulungu and Aratuba, a town in the south of the serra.

Canindé → *Colour map 2, A4.*

The pilgrimage centre of Canindé, 108 km southwest of Fortaleza, is located in the Sertão Central of Ceará. A large modern church stands on a hill and has carved baptistry doors and many ex-votos. It receives hundreds of thousands of pilgrims from all over the northeast between 26 September and 4 October, devotees of São Francisco das Chagas, '*O pobrezinho de Asis*', many of them dressed like Franciscan priests. The pilgrims flock to town on foot, by bus and mostly on *pau de arara* trucks. It is reputed to be second in the world, after Assisi, as a pilgrimage centre for Saint Francis. There is a regional museum with artefacts representative of northeast culture and several restaurants. There is a daily bus service from Fortaleza *rodoviária* with **Viação Nova Esperança,** three hours, and interesting dry-land vegetation along the route. From Canindé south to the Sertão Central (Quixadá), CE-456 is under repair. The majority of the road is not too bad, but there are some rough bits (95 km).

Quixadá → *Phone code: 088. Population: 64,500.*

Quixadá is on the **Serra do Estevão**, with its rocky outcrops and dry hills representative of the central *sertão*. It is one of the top hang-gliding sites in the world and is also good for climbing and trekking. The town has a dam, **Açude de Cedro,** built by ex-slaves during the empire by order of Dom Pedro II, following the terrible drought of 1877-1879. You can walk across the dam to view the surrounding scenery, including interesting rock formations such as the **Galhina Choca** (broody hen). There are restaurants and bars at the start of the dam, which you can walk across. Activities include a two-hour trail to the **Galhina Choca** (take an **ATEC** guide), and climbing and abseiling on the rocks by the dam. There is a historical museum in the town.

Nossa Senhora Inmaculada Rainha do Sertão is a pilgrimage centre 10 km from town, halfway up the highest peak in the region, **Pico do Urucum**, or Serra Preta, at 600 m. The views are tremendous. It's a modern sanctuary (inaugurated 1995) accommodating over 800 worshippers, and is decorated with the flags and images of the patron saints of every Latin American country and Italy. The main festival is 11 February, so the whole month is *super lotado*. The main launch ramp for hang-gliding ramp is just below the church.

About 21 km from Quixadá is **Gruta do Pajé**, a complex of religious buildings dating from the early 1900s (see Sleeping, page 499).

Quixeramobim is an important regional hub and the geographical centre of Ceará, 20 minutes from Quixadá. The town centre is pleasant and is being completely refurbished. It has a lovely old market building. There is a **Memorial de Antônio Conselheiro** (of Canudos), who was born here in 1830 and lived in the town until, shamed by his first wife's adultery, he left for a wandering life before becoming the religious figure famous in history and novels. The memorial has some sculptures, high-relief pictures and a tiny remnant of railway. Nearby is an old iron railway bridge, another 'postcard' view of the town and **archaeological sites** ⓘ *contact Sr Simão, R Mons Salviano Pinio 233, T088-638 0000*, with ancient inscriptions on boulders. The regional dam has been used for irrigation with good results. In August, an important musical event, the **Festival de Violas e Violeiros**, is held (see page 508).

Juazeiro do Norte

» *pp499-512.*

→ *Phone code: 088. Colour map 2, B4. Population: 200,000.*

The south of the state is known as the **Cariri region**, the name of an indigenous group which lived in the interior and resisted Portuguese colonization for a long time. The main centre in this area is Juazeiro do Norte, the second city in Ceará. Along with its two satellites, Crato and Barbalha, 10 km to the west and south respectively, they form an oasis of green in the dry *sertão*.

Juazeiro do Norte was the home of Padre Cícero Romão Batista, a controversial and very popular priest who advocated the interests of the city and its most deprived inhabitants from the 1870s to the 1930s. Even before his death, Padre Cícero had become a legend and Juazeiro do Norte an important pilgrimage site, drawing the faithful from throughout the northeast and, increasingly, from the whole nation. Today it is the most important pilgrimage centre of the region; there are six main annual pilgrimages but visitors arrive all year round. Religious tourism is the principal source of income in this otherwise poor area; prices rise during pilgrimages and there are many beggars at all times. Another cultural manifestation seen throughout the Cariri region is the *bandas cabaçais ou de pífaros*, musical groups that participate in all celebrations. As well as playing instruments, they dance, imitating animals, and perform games or fights.

On Praça do Cinquentenário the **Memorial Padre Cícero** ⓘ *Mon-Fri 0730-1130, 1330-1730, Sat and Sun 0800-1200, free*, is a museum featuring photographs and religious artefacts; a good selection of books is on sale. Nearby is the **chapel of Nossa Senhora do Perpétuo Socorro**, which houses Padre Cícero's tomb. A 27-m-high statue of him stands in the Logradouro do Horto, a park overlooking the town; either take the pilgrim trail up the hill (one hour, start early because of the heat) or take the Horto city bus. Also worth seeing is the **church of Nossa Senhora das Dores** with the adjacent pilgrimage grounds, roughly fashioned after St Peter's Square in Rome.

Ins and outs

The airport is 7 km from the centre along Avenida Virgílio Távora, T088 511 2118. A taxi to the centre costs US$5.75, motorcycle taxi US$3; taxi to the *rodoviária* US$8.40. The *rodoviária* is at Avenida Dalmiro Gouveia, on the road to Crato, T088-511 2868. A taxi to the centre costs US$3, motorcycle taxi US$0.60.

Excursions from Juazeiro do Norte

The **Chapada do Araripe**, a tableland about 850 m high, is south of Juazeiro do Norte and extends from east to west for 220 km. The area is believed to have been uplifted and numerous fossilized plants and animals including giant sloths have been found. It has one of the most important native forest reserves in the state, the **Floresta Nacional do Araripe**, 20 km from Crato, with grottoes, palaeontological sites, springs and cloudforest with ferns and orchids. Some 22 km south of Juazeiro do Norte, within the Chapada, is the **Balneário do Caldas**, a pool fed with natural spring water (0700-1700), access through Barbalha.

In the area of **Jardim**, 34 km south of Barbalha, there are several natural springs, while by **Missão Velha**, 22 km east of Barbalha, there are rapids on the Rio Salgado and an attractive waterfall. Another point pf access to the Chapada is through **Santana do Cariri**, 60 km west of Juazeiro do Norte. The main attraction here is the **Nascente dos Azedos**, a natural spring good for bathing. There is also a palaeontology museum and one basic hotel. Transport is with **Pernambucana**, daily at 1430, returning 0600, US$2.50, two hours.

Crato is an older city which lost its significance in the region, owing to the increased importance of Juazeiro do Norte. It has several pleasing praças and a small **Museu de Fósseis** ⓘ *Praça da Sé 105, Mon-Fri 0800-1200, 1400-1800, free*, housing an impressive collection of fossils from the Cretaceous period gathered in the Chapada do Araripe.

Sleeping

Fortaleza *p486, map p488*

Almost all hotels offer reduced prices in the low season. There are many pousadas in the Iracema/Meireles area, but they change frequently.

Centre

C **Caxambu**, Gen Bezerril 22, T085-226 6656. Reduction in low season. a/c, TV, fridge, room service, with breakfast, probably best bet in centre (opposite cathedral), good value.

D Passeio, Dr João Moreira 221, Centro, T085-226 9640, F253 6165. Opposite Passeio Público (which is not so enticing when the prostitutes are about) and near Centro de Turismo, homely, rooms with high ceilings, a/c or fan, gloomy passages, good value.
E Backpackers, R Dom Manuel 89, T085-3091 8997. Central, basic, shared bathrooms, no breakfast, helpful owner. Price per person.
E Big, Gen Sampaio 485, on Praça da Estação in centre, T085-212 2066. All rooms with fan, cheaper without TV, even cheaper without bath, simple breakfast, OK, but caution needed at night, right in thick of the central scrum.

Beach

LL-L Imperial Othon Palace, Av Beira Mar 2500, Meireles, T085-3466 5500, www.othon.com.br. Beachfront location, large hotel with all facilities common to this group, business and tourists catered for, pool, sauna, massage (recommended *feijoada* on Sat).
LL-L Seara Praia, Av Beira Mar 3080, Meireles, T085-4011 2200, www.hotelseara.com.br. 30% cheaper in low season, smart, comfortable luxury hotel with pool, gym, cyber café, French cuisine.
L Beira Mar, Av Beira Mar 3130, T085-3242 5000, Meireles, www.hotelbeiramar.com.br. Some seafront rooms, others side view, comfortable, safe, pool, 24-hr business centre (internet), parking, good value, especially in low season.
L Praiano Palace, Av Beira Mar 2800, Meireles, T085-4008 2200, www.praiano.com.br. Much the same services and standards, but not quite as luxurious, opposite the craft fair.
L Ponta Mar, Av Beira Mar 2200, Meireles, T085-4006 2200, www.ponta mar.com.br. Aimed more at the business market, but still a good location and similar facilities.
AL Best Western Colonial Praia, R Barão de Aracati 145, Iracema, T085-4005 4644, www.colonialpraiahotel.com.br. 4 stars, **B** in low season, pleasant grounds and big pool, low-rise, which is unusual, popular with families, laundry service.
AL-A Agua Marinha, Av Almte Barroso 701, Iracema, T085-219 0303, www.aguamarinha hotel.com.br. Less 10% in low season, a/c, TV, room safe, fridge, generally comfortable, pool, internet.
A Ibis, Atualpa Barbosa de Lima 660, Iracema, T085-3219 2121, www.accorhotels.com.br. Breakfast extra, in **Accor** style, with usual facilities, pool.
A-C Alfa Residence, Av Mons Tabosa 1320, Meireles, T085-248 2020. Associated with Coimbra Residence Flat, Prime Plus car hire, all in same block. Apartments with a/c, TV, fridge, unfussy but welcoming, can use pool and sauna at Coimbra.
B Abrolhos Praia, Av Abolição 2030, Meireles, T/F085-248 1217. Pleasant, TV, fridge, hot shower, a/c, rooms look a bit sparse but no different from others in this category, soft beds, discount in low season, 1 block from beach, internet.
B Pousada Icaraí, Praia Icaraí, just before town on curve in road, T085-318 2000. English/Brazilian owners, ask for Fiona. A good out-of-town base with beautiful gardens, lots of budgerigars flying free, pools, restaurant, near beach and bus to Fortaleza.
B Pousada Jardim, Idelfonso Albano 950, Aldeota, T085-226 9711, www.hotel jardim.com.br. No sign outside, nice garden, excursions arranged, many languages spoken. Recommended, 20% discount for *Footprint Brazil* users.
B Praia de Iracema, Raimundo Girão 430, Iracema, T085-219 2299. 20% discount in low season, a/c, TV, fridge, safe in room, coffee shop, pool, brightly coloured bedcovers, on corner so traffic outside, but OK for value and comfort.
B Villamaris, Av Abolição 2026, Meireles, T085-248 0112, www.hotelvillamaris.com.br. **C** in low season, cosy, security guard, TV, fridge, small rooftop pool, 1 block from beach.
B-C Pousada do Suiço, R Antônia Augusto 141, Iracema, T085-9992 9481 (mob), www.pension-vom-schweizer.com.br/. Must reserve mid-Oct-Feb. Very private, no sign, quiet street, variety of rooms, some with kitchens, small pool, a/c, TV, fridge, Swiss run, changes cash and TCs. Recommended.
C Pousada Atalaia, Av Beira Mar 814, Iracema, T/F085-3219 0755, www.atalaiahostel.com.br. Hostel, **E** in dormitory, a/c, fan, TV, good breakfast, prices fall in low season.

C Pousada Salinas, Av Zezé Diogo 3300, Praia do Futuro, T085-3234 3626, www.pousadasalinas.com.br. **D** in low season, popular, a/c, TV, fridge, parking, just across from sea, some English spoken.
C-D Ondas Verdes, Av Beira Mar 934, Iracema, T085-219 0871, www.centernet.psi.br/hotelondasverdes. Being refurbished, fan, TV, very good value for location, convenient for just about everything, French owner. Recommended.
C-D Pousada Beleza Tropical, R Dom Joaquim 132, Iracema, T085-219 0515. A/c, hot water, TV, fridge, breakfast by the pool, good.
D Albergue Praia de Iracema, Av Almte Barroso 998, T085-3219 3267, www.aldeota.com/albergue. Basic hostel, busy, helpful staff.

Camping

Fortaleza Camping Club, R Pedro Paulo Moreira 505, Parque Manibura, Água Fria, 12 km, T085-273 2544, many trees for shade, US$7 per person.

Aquiraz and around *p490*

In Águas Belas, there are simpler rooms available in private houses.
L New Life, Alto da Prainha, Prainha, T085-362 1314. Weight reduction centre, with fridge, pool, restaurant.
A Aquiraz Praia e Escola de Hotelaria, Estr da Prainha, Km 5, T085 362 1006. Pleasant and comfortable rooms with baths, fridges and a/c, arranged around a pool. The hotel has a reasonable restaurant.
A Marina Barro Preto, R Francisco das Chagas 10, Barro Preto, T085-370 1166. With bath, fridge, pool, restaurant.
A Village Barra Mar, Caponga, T085-334 8088, www.barramar.com. A pleasant beach hotel set in a tropical garden with a range of a/c chalets all with a fridge, restaurant, pool.
B Chalés Barra Encantada, R Francisco das Chagas 13, Barro Preto, T085-370 1466. Cabins for up to 6, fridge, pool, restaurant, large camping area with palms, US$9 per person, **Camping Club** members US$4 per person.
B Da Prainha, R Berlim, Alto da Prainha, T085-362 1122. Standard a/c rooms with a bath. The rooms on the top floor have more air, nice views.
B Do Sol, Praia do Presídio, T085-370 1222. Large rooms with bath, a/c, a couple of chalets, pool, restaurant.
B Iguape Hotel de Turismo, R 8, Praia do Presídio, T085-370 1444. Cabins, pool with spring water, restaurant.
B Jangadeiro Praia, Praia do Presídio, T085-254 6466/361 6039, www.hoteljangadeiro.com.br. With bath, fridge, restaurant, pool, nice lawns down to the beach.
B Prainha Solar, R Principal, Prainha, T085-362 1355, F362 1366. Plain rooms with fridge, restaurant, pool. Comfortable.
B Recanto da Fantasia, R Francisco das Chagas, Barro Preto, T085-239 4943. Well-equipped cabins for up to 4, no breakfast.
B Sol Leste, R São Pedro, Iguape, T/F085-370 1233. With bath, fridge, pool, restaurant, sports fields. Other hotels and pousadas also available.
C Coqueiral, R Laureano de Paula Santana 537, Caponga, T085-335 1073. Chalets with a bath and small terraces strewn with hammocks.
C Fateixa, R Laureano de Paula Santana 555, Caponga, T085-335 1122. One of several similar pousadas on this street, with a selection of chalets in a bougainvillea garden with en suites and a pool.
C Le Paradis, Águas Belas, T085-335 1050, F335 1289. Simple rooms with attached bathrooms in a hotel with a pool and restaurant.
C Mon Kapitan, R Pedro Moita on the square, Caponga, T085-335 1031. Large rooms with attached bathrooms, very helpful staff and a good restaurant.
C Praia Águas Belas, Águas Belas, T085-335 1060. A range of rooms, some in individual cabins, all with baths and a/c. The hotel has a reasonable restaurant and a pool.
D Versailles, R J Irineu Araujo, Caponga, 1.5 km from the beach, T085-335 1071. Rooms with tiny en suites. Breakfast is extra.

Camping

Barra Encantada, Praia do Barro Preto, Iguape, 42 km southeast (reservations in Fortaleza, T085-370 1173), US$9 per person, **Camping Club** members US$4 per person.

Morro Branco and Praia das Fontes *p491*

L Praia das Fontes, Av A Teixeira 1, Praia das Fontes, T085-338 1179, www.oasispraiadasfontes.com.br. Luxurious resort, watersports, horse hire, tennis courts and a simple spa. Recommended.

B Das Falésias, Av Assis Moreira 314, Praia das Fontes, T085-338 1018, www.hotelfalesias.com.br. Pleasant German-owned cliff-side pousada with a pool and well-kept rooms.

B Recanto Praiano, Morro Branco, T085-224 7118. Peaceful little pousada with a good breakfast. Recommended.

C Pousada Sereia, on the beach, Morro Branco, T085-330 1144. Lovely simple pousada with an excellent breakfast and friendly staff. Highly recommended.

D Rosalias, Morro Branco, T085-330 1131. Very simple and somewhat run down but only 50 m from bus stop, and with a shared kitchen.

Camping

Lagoa das Dunas, Uruaú (115 km southeast of Fortaleza), T085-244 2929. Access 9 km south of Beberibe on CE-004, then east from Sucatinga 5 km on a poor dirt road. Large area with grass and palms for shade, pool, restaurant, sports fields. 1 km through dunes to Praia Marambaia or Uruaú. US$4 per person for **Camping Club** members, US$9 per person for non-members; also rents rooms with shared bath (US$45 room for 4, US$55 room for 6).

Prainha do Canto Verde *p492*

E Dona Mirtes. Price includes breakfast, will negotiate other meals.

There are also houses for rent (eg **Casa Cangulo** or **Vila Marésia**). Note that prices rise by 30% for the regatta and over Christmas and Semana Santa.

Canoa Quebrada *p492*

Villagers will let you sling your hammock or will put you up cheaply. **Verónica** is recommended, European books exchanged. **Sr Miguel** rents good clean houses for US$10 a day.

A Tranqüilândia, T088-421 7012, www.tranquilandia.it. 9 a/c chalets around a pool in a tropical garden. Decent restaurant.

B Pousada Latitude, R Dragão do Mar, T323. A/c, cheaper with fan, fridge, restaurant.

B Pousada Lua Estrela, R Nascer do Sol 106, T088-421 7040, www.pousadaluaestrela.com.br. IYHA-affiliated smart hostel with fan-cooled rooms with fridges and hot showers. Great sea views.

C Pousada Alternativa, R Francisco Caraço. Rooms with or without bath. Centrally located and recommended.

C Pousada Oásis do Rei, R Nascer do Sol 112, T088-421 7081 www.oasisdorei.com. Simple rooms in a pousada with a pool. All have a fan and fridge and are set in a little tropical garden. Recommended.

C Pousada Via Láctea, off the main street (so quieter). Beautiful view of beach some 50 m away. Some rooms with hot shower, fridge, fan, good breakfast, safe parking, horse and buggy tours, English spoken. Highly recommended.

C Tenda do Cumbe, at end of the road on cliff, T088-421 1761. Thatched huts in a hotel with a restaurant. Warmly recommended.

D Beco's, R José Melancia 2300. Simple rooms with a bath all with little terraces slung with hammocks and organized around a pleasant inner courtyard.

Paracuru and Lagoinha *p493*

To call Fleixeras, dial T088-511 184, followed by the 3-digit extensions indicated below; to call Mundaú, dial T088-351 1210, followed by the 3-digit extensions indicated below.

C Monalisa, T126. Large, plain, fan-cooled rooms with attached bathrooms.

C O Milton, T102. Plain cabins on the beach with an outdoor restaurant.

D Ondas do Mar, T146. Pleasant cabins with a bath and with porches hung with hammocks. Reasonable restaurant.

Fleixeras *p494*

To call Fleixeras, dial T088-511 184, followed by the 3-digit extensions indicated below; to call Mundaú, dial T088-351 1210, followed by the 3-digit extensions indicated below.

A Solar das Fleixeras, Fleixeras, T136. Beach hotel with standard rooms with en suites, a pool and restaurant.

A-C Mundaú Dunas, Mundaú. Exceptional value, well-kept rooms with fridges, around a pool. Reasonable restaurant. Cheaper in the low season.

B Sombra dos Coqueiros, Mundaú, T200. Rooms with a bath, modest restaurant.
C Da Célia, R São Pedro, Fleixeras, T105. Plain a/c rooms with en suites and no breakfast.
D Brisa do Mar, Mundaú. Small rooms with en suite bathrooms. Breakfast is extra.
E Casa de Retiro Estrela do Mar, Mundaú, T085-351 1220, ext 154. A priest's retreat home, must reserve ahead, rooms with hammocks, some with bath, use of kitchen.

Jericoacoara *p494*
There are crowds at weekends mid-Dec to mid-Feb, in Jul and during Brazilian holidays. Many places full in low season too. For Reveillon, 4- to 5-day packages are available, but prices rise steeply.
LL-L Recanto do Barão, R do Forró 433, T088-669 2149, www.recantodobarao.com. 21 rooms mostly for 3 to 5 (ie families, groups), nicely decorated with hibiscus theme, lots of hammocks, a/c, TV, fridge, hot shower, big rooms, upper balcony for sunset, pool, 4WD tours. Good reputation.
A Avalon, R Principal, T088-669 2066, www.jericoacoara.tur.br/avalon/ index.html. Nice rooms with a fan and a pleasant restaurant.
A Casa do Turismo, R das Dunas, T088-669 2000, www.jericoacoara.com, or www.casadoturismo.com. Comfortable, well-maintained rooms, all a/c, hot shower and TV. Information, tours, horse hire, **Redenção** bus tickets (only place selling them, 1030-1400 and 1730-2200), windsurf school, kite surf, sand-board rental, telephone calls, post office, exchange.
A Hippopotamus, R do Forró, T088-268 2722. Hotel with a decent pool, with a r ange of a/c rooms all with hot water and a restaurant.
B Matusa, T085-246 7354, www.matusa.com.br. Standard package hotel: a/c rooms with a TV, fridge and hot shower, pool.
C Casa Nostra, R das Dunas, T088-669 2035, www.jericoacoara.tur.br/casanostra/ index.html. Decent rooms, good breakfast and the option to pay with US$ or German marks. Money change, Italian spoken. Recommended.
C Isalana Praia, R Principal, T088-660 1334, www.jericoacoara.tur.br/isalanapraiahotel /index.html. A/c rooms with minibars, TVs, and very helpful staff: ask for Will Louzada.
C Pousada Papagaio, Beco do Forró, T088-669 2142, www.jericoacoara.tur.br/ pousadapapagaio/index.html. Plain rooms with en suites and organized tours. Recommended.
C Pousada da Renata, T088-669 2061, www.jericoacoara.tur.br/pousadadarenata. Owned by the sister of Fernanda at **Pousada do Paulo** at Jijoca. Pleasant, simple rooms with patios strung with hammocks, breakfast, English, Italian and German spoken. They also own the **Pousada do Serrote**, 100 m from Praia da Malhada, same phone, and T088-9961 5522 (mob), www.jericoacoara.tur.br/pousadadoserrote.
D Calanda, R das Dunas, T088-669 2285, www.jericoacoara.tur.br/calanda. Plain rooms with en suite bathrooms, solar-heated water and good service from the Swiss owners and their staff. Good views, good breakfast, a full-moon party each month and German, English and Spanish spoken. Warmly recommended.
D Pousada do Véio, R Principal. T088 669 2015, www.jericoacoara.tur.br/pousada doveio. Popular pousada with a/c or fan-cooled rooms, all with baths and hot water.
E Pousada Tirol, R São Francisco 202, T088-669 2000, www.jericoacoara-tirol.com. IYHA-affiliated hostel with dorms with hot water showers and doubles (**C-D** in low season). Very friendly and popular with party loving travellers. Very busy cyber café, US$3 per hr; 10 mins free use for all guests.

Around Jericoacoara *p495*
D Pousada Azul do Mar, Praia do Preá, T088-660 3062, with bath, electricity, good food and, if you are lucky, kite surfing.

Cruz *p495*
F Hospedaria, R 6 de Abril 314. Very basic, simple little pousada with tiny rooms.
F Hotel Magalhães, R Teixeira Pinto 390. Very basic, shared bath, friendly, meals available.

Western Ceará *p495*
D Pousada Doce Lar, R Felipe Sampaio 181, Centro, Itapajé, T085-346 1432. Ask for a room with a mountain view, clean, comfortable, no restaurant. Eat in restaurants close by.

Sobral *p495*

A Beira Rio, R Conselheiro Rodrigues 400 across from the *rodoviária*, T088-613 1040. A/c (cheaper with fan), fridge.
A Visconde, Av Lúcia Saboia 473, 10 mins from the *rodoviária*, T088-611 4222, F611 4197. Friendly, a/c, cheaper with fan, good breakfast.
B Cisne, Trav do Xerez 215, T/F088-611 0171. A/c, cheaper with fan, friendly.
B Vitória, Praça Gen Tibúrcio 120, T088-613 1566. Bath, a/c, cheaper with fan, some rooms without bath (**C**), restaurant.
D Francinet's, R Col Joaquim Ribeiro 294. With fan, bath, cheaper with shared bath.

Chapada de Ibiapaba *p495*

A Serra Grande, about 2 km from town, BR-222 Km 311, T088-671 1818, F671 1477. All amenities, good.
C Complexo de Lazer Rio's, Viçosa do Ceará, Km 4.5 on the road from Tianguá, T088-632 1510/1099. Swiss-style chalets, water park, good local food in the restaurant.

Parque Nacional Ubajara *p496*

B-C Pousada da Neblina, Estrada do Teleférico, near the park, 2 km from town, T/F085-634 1270. In beautiful cloudforest, swimming pool, with breakfast (cheaper without) and private shower, restaurant open 1100-2000. Meals recommended. Campsite (US$15 per tent).
C Le Village, on Ibiapina road 4 km south from Ubajara town, T085-634 1364. Restaurant, pool, sauna, good value.
C Pousada Gruta da Ubajara, almost opposite, close to park entrance, rustic, restaurant. Recommended.
D Paraíso, in the centre, Ubajara, T085-634 1728. Reckoned to be the best in town.
D Pousada da Neuza, R Juvêncio Luís Pereira 370, Ubajara, T085-634 1261. Small restaurant.
D Sítio do Alemão, take Estrada do Teleférico 2 km from town, after the **Pousada da Neblina** turn right, signposted, 1 km to Sítio Santana, in the coffee plantation of **Herbert Klein** (Caixa Postal 33, Ubajara, CE, CEP 62350-000, T088-9961 4645). Down a path are 3 small chalets with full facilities, and 2 older ones with shared bath (**E**) , view from breakfast/hammock area to *sertão*, excursions, bicycle hire, if chalets are full Klein may accommodate visitors at the house. No meals other than breakfast but **Casa das Delícias** in Ubajara will send lasagne if necessary – it's owned by Klein's partner. Warmly recommended.

South from Ubajara *p496*

B Pousada de Inhuçu, R Gonçalo de Freitas 454, São Benedito, T088-626 1173, pool, restaurant.
D Crateús Palace Hotel, Crateús. Very reasonable and clean, with breakfast, good restaurant. **Churrascaria Pequena Cabana** is at the back of the hotel.
E Bar e Churrascaria Pousada da Bica, Ipu, T088-683 2236, serves very good, cheap *comida caseira* lunch and has rooms, with breakfast included.
E Hotel Ipu, upper town, Ipu. Basic, friendly.

A pousada is being built at the *SAT posta* on the exit to Varjota and Sobral; it also has a *churrascaria*.

There are 3 basic pousadas in **Cabeço Branco**: **dos Viajantes** and **São Sebastião**, both contactable through the phone exchange (T088-826 1150), and **Pousada Gaia**, just behind the cemetery on the road out to Santa Quitéria (T088-696 1904), ask for Márcia or Honório Júnior. Honório will draw rough walking maps and, if asked, can arrange for the *forró* band to play.

Serra de Baturité *p497*

A Estância Vale das Flores, Sítio São Francisco, Pacoti, T085-325 1233. Chalets and rooms, price includes lunch, fridge, restaurant, pool, sauna, lake, horses.
B Remanso Hotel da Serra, 5 km north of Guaramiranga, T088-325 1222. Bath, restaurant, pool, lake, sports fields.
B Senac Hotel Escola de Guaramiranga, in Guaramiranga, T/F088-321 1106, escola_hotelaria@ce.senac.br. Bath, fridge, hot water, restaurant, pool, on top of a hill in an 8-hut estate which includes forest, orchards and an old convent, it doubles as a tourism school. Lots of events held here, so it is often full. It's 500 m outside town up a road from the main street, past Parque das Trilhas.
B-C Hofbräuhaus, Estrada de Aratuba, Chapada de Lameirão, Mulungu, CEP 62754-000, T085-221 6170, www.hofbrauhaus-brasil.com. Run by

Wolfgang Helmut Rühle, who has restaurants in Guaramiranga (O Alemão), Pacoti and 2 in Fortaleza, speaks German, English, Portuguese (and maybe more). This is an exceptional place in that every room is designed in a different style (Spanish, Arabic, Japanese, etc) with all comforts, homely, very clean and smart, rooms with veranda cost a little more and prices are cheaper Mon-Thu (a bargain). The restaurant is German and Cearense. All vegetables and herbs (for all the restaurants) are grown on the property, also has a snail farm for the house speciality. Lots of flowers and grapes, far-reaching views over the *sertão*, mini-disco, small business centre, completely safe. A real surprise!

Quixadá *p497*

C **Casa de Reposo São José**, Gruta do Pajé, 21 km from Quixadá, today a popular hotel run by nuns (T088 412 0927, with bath).

C **Hotel Fazenda Parelhas**, Km 133 Rodovia do Algodão, a short distance out of Quixeramobim, just off the Quixadá road, T088-402 2847/9946 7640, aceterbr@yahoo.com.br. Ricardo Porto is the owner and set this up in 1998 as the first *turismo rural* place in Ceará. Price includes breakfast, full board is US$7.50 extra. Chalets with a/c, TV, fridge and cold water. It's a working sheep and goat farm in the *caatinga*, offering horse rides of 1½ and 3 hrs, or 30 km to Serra do Caboclo, also pony and trap rides and river bathing.

C **Pedra dos Ventos**, Near Juatama between Quixadá and Quixeramobim, T085-257 4464 /9988 4684, www.pedradosventos.com.br. Cheaper with fan, all rooms with TV, hot water, fridge. Great views (even at night) as it is built high up a rock. Good breakfast, pool, 3 trails of 30 mins each, can help with adventure sports. You need a car to get there although the **Redenção** bus passes the turn-off.

D **Hotel Fazenda Magé**, Km 3 Antiga Estrada de Baturité, T088-412 0467, nemesio@quixadanet.com.br. With breakfast in the *fazenda*, all facilities, cold water, cheaper singles with fan. Down a track is the restaurant which has tables under an overhanging rock, open Sat, Sun and once a month at full moon, has hammocks. The rock has a viewpoint, climbing and abseiling routes, equipment hire US$5.55, plus US$7.40 for instructor.

Juazeiro do Norte *p498, map p498*

You can expect prices to be higher during pilgrimages. There are many basic hotels and *hospedarias* for pilgrims on R São José and around Nossa Senhora das Dores basilica.

A Verde Vales Lazer, Av P A Castelo, 3 km from town on the road to Barbalha, T/F088-571 2544. Pool, restaurant.

B **Panorama**, Santo Agostinho 58, T088-521 3100, F512 3110. Pool, restaurant, good value.

C **Municipal**, São Francisco 220, Praça Padre Cícero, T088-512 2899. Comfortable large rooms, good value, cheaper with fan. Recommended.

C-D **Plaza**, Padre Cícero 148, T088-511 0493. With bath, a/c, cheaper with fan and cheaper still with shared bath.

C-D **Viana Palace**, São Pedro 746, T088-511 2585, F511 2476. With bath, a/c, cheaper with fan, fridge.

D **Aristocrata**, São Francisco 402, T088-511 1889. With bath, fridge, cheaper without, fridge, basic, family run, restaurant.

D **Maceló**, São José 208, T088-511 2930. With bath, cheaper with shared bath, fan, restaurant.

D-E **Pousada Cariri**, São José 218, T088-512 2079. With bath, cheaper without breakfast, basic, friendly, family run, good restaurant.

Excursions from Juazeiro do Norte *p499*

A **Hotel das Fontes**, Balneário do Caldas, T088-532 1060, with bath, fridge, restaurant.

B-D **Crato**, R Bárbara de Alencar 668, near Praça Cristo Rei, Crato, T088-521 2824. A friendly hotel with bath, a/c, cheaper with fan, restaurant.

Eating

Fortaleza *p486, map p488*

Centre

There are several options around the station.

TTT **Xadrez**, Emcetur restaurant, in the old prison. Good atmosphere, overpriced, open to 2400, reported safe to 2100.

T **Alivita**, Barão do Rio Branco 1486. Good for fish and vegetarian, lunch only, Mon-Fri.

¶ **Fonte de Saúde**, R Pedro 339. Excellent vegetarian food, sold by weight, and a wide range of fruit juices.

Iracema and Dragão do Mar

Two good areas for restaurants, with plenty of variety. There are many eateries of various styles at the junction of Tabajaras and Tremembés, mostly smart.

¶¶ **Alma Gêmea**, R Dragão do Mar 30. Bar and restaurant with good atmosphere by the cultural centre.

¶¶ **Amici's**, R Dragão do Mar 80. Pasta, pizza and lively atmosphere in music-filled street, evenings only. Some say it's the best at the cultural centre.

¶¶ **Colher do Pau**, R Tabajaras 412, Iracema. Opens daily at 1830, *sertaneja* food, seafood, indoor and outdoor seating, live music. Recommended.

¶¶ **Estoril**, R dos Tabajaras 397, Iracema. Varied food in this landmark restaurant, which is also a catering school.

¶ **Blau d'Fame**, R João Cordeiro 41, Iracema. Good self-service, serving lunch much later than others, especially on Sat.

¶ **Brazão**, R João Cordeiro corner of Av R Girão, Iracema, next to Blau d'Fame. The only place open 24 hrs, but the food is not that special.

¶ **Santa Clara Café Orgânico**, R Dragão do Mar 81, at end of red girder walkway (or upstairs depending which way you go), www.santa clara.com.br. Café, delicious organic coffees, juices, cold drinks, plus sandwiches and desserts.

Beaches

Several good fish restaurants at Praia de Mucuripe, where the boats come ashore between 1300 and 1500. Rua J Ibiapina, at the Mucuripe end of Meireles, 1 block behind beach, has pizzerias, fast food restaurants and sushi bars.

¶¶¶-¶¶ **La Fiorentina**, Osvaldo Cruz 8, corner of Av Beira Mar, Meireles. Some seafood expensive, but there's also fish, meats and pasta. Unpretentious, attentive waiters, good food, frequented by tourists and locals alike.

¶¶¶-¶¶ **Le Sandras**, Av Santos Dumont 938, Aldeota. Successor to Sandras of Praia do Futuro. Brightly painted old building, cool yellow inside, tasteful, elegant. Outdoor, indoor and a/c seating, garden, French-trained owner, *novo cearanse* and Mediterranean cooking, lobster still a speciality, good food.

¶ **Churrascaria Picanha de Veras**, R Carlos Vasconcelos 660, Aldeota. Good for chicken.

¶ **Dom Pastel**, R Carlos Vasconcelos 996, Aldeota. Pay by weight.

¶ **Habib**, Av Abolição, corner with Av Barão de Studart, Meireles (and other branches). Modern Middle Eastern fast-food restaurant, excellent service, set menus are a bargain, good desserts. Recommended.

¶ **Ideal**, Av Abolição e José Vilar, Meireles. Open 0530-2030, bakery serving lunches, small supermarket and deli, good, handy.

¶ **La Habanera**, Praça da Igreja in Iracema, Av Beira Mar e Ararius. Café, wicker chairs, marble tables, old photos of Fidel, Che, et al, coffee and cigars.

Out of town

¶¶ **Carneiro de Ordones**, R Azevedo Bolão 571, Parquelândia, near North Shopping. Crowded with locals at weekends for every kind of lamb dish.

¶¶ **Fazenda do Joe**, T085-260 1610. One of several country restaurants. German, open for lunch weekends and holidays only, also sells German breads and sausages. Has a pousada too.

¶¶ **Lá na Roça**, opposite the church, in the district of Eusêbio. Excellent *sertaneja* restaurant, very popular on Sun, pay by weight, go early to be sure of a table – all local dishes and sweets.

Eusêbio is reached from the CE 040, the road to Iguape and Aquiraz. This road out of the city is the best place for tapioca shacks. As well as the rough traditional shacks, there is a whole complex for tapioca sellers at the Estrada do Fio.

¶ **Casa de Farinha**, CE 040 Km 13. Mon-Fri 1100-1500 à la carte only, Sat, Sun and holidays 1100-1800 self-service *sertaneja* food, very good. It is also a working cassava/manioc mill and museum so you can see the whole process of making tapioca. A good place to take kids, plenty of games for them.

¶ **Delicias de Cana**, Km 18. A working sugar mill, selling *rapa dura* flavoured with fruits and nuts (cashew – of course, sesame).

Jericoacoara *p494*
There are several restaurants serving vegetarian and fish dishes.
ΨΨ **Carcará**, R do Forró, T088-669 2013. Restaurant and bar, northeastern specialities, seafood and pastas, said to be the best in town.
ΨΨ **Espaço Aberto**, R Principal, T088-669 2063. Meat dishes, delicious seafood, salads, pleasant atmosphere. Recommended.
ΨΨ **Naturalmente**. On the beach. Pleasant atmosphere, wonderful crêpes. Recommended.
ΨΨ **Pizzeria Banana**, R Principal 26, T088-669 2282. The best of many pizzerias on this street with plenty of choice of other dishes, from pasta to salads and snacks.
ΨΨ **Taverna**, R Principal. Cantina and restaurant with lovely pasta and pizza, crêpes, espresso and other drinks.
ΨΨ **Tudo na Brasa**, R Principal. Recommended *churrascaria.*
Ψ **Tempero da Terra**, R São Francisco.

Sobral *p495*
ΨΨ **Casa Grande o Louro**, R Tabelo Idelfonso Cavalcante 611. Good meat.
ΨΨ **Hotel Vitória**, good lunch buffet. Recommended.
Ψ **Chico 1000** and **2000**. Varied menu.
Ψ **Churrascaria Gaúcho**, Av Dom José. Meat.
Ψ **Lataro**. Self-service.

Quixadá *p497*
ΨΨ-Ψ **Churrascaria Drinks**, Quixeramobim, by the BR *posta* on the Quixadá road. One of the best in the city.

Juazeiro do Norte *p498, map p498*
Several restaurants around Praça Padre Cícero, more economical ones on R São José.
ΨΨ **Cheiro Verde**, S Cândido 72, varied menu.
ΨΨ **Pousada**, R São José, good food.

Bars and clubs

Fortaleza *p486, map p488*
Fortaleza is renowned for its nightlife and prides itself on having the liveliest Mon night in the country. Some of the best areas for entertainment, with many bars and restaurants, are: the Av Beira Mar, Praia de Iracema, the hill above Praia de Mucuripe and Av Dom Luís. *Forró* is the most popular dance and there is a tradition to visit certain establishments on specific nights.
Mon *Forró* is danced at the **Pirata Bar**, Iracema, US$5, open-air theme bar, from 2300, and other establishments along R dos Tabajaras and its surroundings.
Tue Live golden oldies at **Boate Oásis**, Av Santos Dumont 6061, Aldeota.
Wed Regional music and samba-reggae at **Clube do Vaqueiro**, city bypass, Km 14, by BR-116 south and E-020, at 2230.
Thu Live music, shows and crab specialities at the beach shacks in Praia do Futuro; **Chico do Caranguejo**, lively bar with some sex tourism. Recommended for crab is **Atlântico**. For music, try **Rebu** (traditional) and **Vila Galé** (for tourists).
Fri Singers and bands play regional music at **Parque do Vaqueiro**, BR-020, Km 10, past city bypass.
Sat *Forró* at **Parque Valeu Boi**, R Trezópolis, Cajueiro Torto, **Forró Três Amores**, Estrado Tapuio, Eusêbio and **Cantinho do Céu**, CE-04, Km 8.
Sun *Forró* and *música sertaneja* at **Cajueiro Drinks**, BR-116, Km 20, Eusêbio.

The streets around Centro Cultural Dragão do Mar on R Dragao do Mar are lively every night of the week. Brightly painted, historic buildings house restaurants, where musicians play to customers and the pavements are dotted with cocktail carts.
Caros Amigos, R Dragão do Mar, 22. Live music at 2030: Tue, Brazilian instrumental; Wed, jazz; Thu, samba; Sun, Beatles covers, US$1 (also shows music on the big screen).
Restaurant e Crêperie Café Crème, R Dragão do Mar 92, live music on Tue.

Jericoacoara *p494*
There are frequent parties to which visitors are welcome. About once a week in high season there is a folk dance show which includes *capoeira*. There is *forró* nightly in high season at R do Forró, Wed and Sat in low season, starts about 2200. Action moves to bars, such as **Bar Barriga da Lua** and **Pizza Reggae**, when the *forró* has stopped about 0200. After *forró*, **Padaria Santo Antônio** opens, selling special breads, coconut, banana, cheese, 0230-0700.

Entertainment

Fortaleza *p486, map p488*

Cinema For information about cinema programming, T139.

Theatre In the centre are **Teatro José de Alencar**, Praça José de Alencar (see Sights page 487), and **Teatro São José**, R Rufino de Alencar 363, T085-231 5447, both with shows all year.

Festivals and events

Fortaleza *p486, map p488*

6 Jan Epiphany.

Feb Ash Wed.

19 Mar São José.

Jul Last Sun in Jul is the **Regata Dragão do Mar**, Praia de Mucuripe, with traditional *jangada* (raft) races.

Jul During the last week of Jul, the out-of-season Salvador-style carnival, **Fortal**, takes place along Av Almte Barroso, Av Raimundo Giro and Av Beira Mar. In Caucaia, 12 km to the southeast, a **vaquejada**, traditional rodeo and country fair, takes place during the last weekend of Jul.

15 Aug, the local Umbanda *terreiros* (churches) celebrate the **Festival of Iemanjá** on Praia do Futuro, taking over the entire beach from noon till dusk, when offerings are cast into the surf. Well worth attending (members of the public may '*pegar um passo*' – enter into an inspired religious trance – at the hands of a *pai-de-santo*). Beware of pickpockets and purse-snatchers.

Mid-Oct **Ceará Music**, a 4-day festival of Brazilian music, rock and pop, is held in Marina Park.

Canoa Quebrada *p492*

Jul In the second half of the month is the **Canoarte** festival, which includes a *jangada* regatta and music festival.

Quixada *p497*

12-15 Jun Festa de Santo Antônio.

Aug **Festival de Violas e Violeiros** is an important music festival drawing participants from near and far.

Sep **Grande Vaquejada de Quixeramobim**, a typical *sertão* rodeo.

Juazeiro do Norte *p498, map p498*

6 Jan Reis Magos (Epiphany).

2 Feb Candeias (Candelmas), Nossa Senhora da Luz.

24 Mar Padre Cícero's birth.

20 Jul Padre Cícero's death.

10-15 Sep Nossa Senhora das Dores, the city's patron saint.

1-2 Nov Finados, the city receives some 600,000 visitors for the All Saints' Day pilgrimages.

Shopping

Fortaleza *p486, map p488*

Bookshops

Livraria Livro Técnico, see Dragão do Mar,, has several branches, on Dom Luís, Praça Ferreira, Shopping Norte and at UFC university.

Livraria Nobel bookstore and coffee shop in Del Paseo shopping centre in Aldeota.

Siciliano, bookstore and coffee shop in new part of Iguatemi shopping mall, with just a bookstore in the old part.

Handicrafts

Fortaleza has an excellent selection of locally manufactured textiles, which are among the cheapest in Brazil, and a wide selection of regional handicrafts. The local craft specialities are lace and embroidered textile goods; also hammocks (US$15 to over US$100), fine alto-relievo woodcarvings of northeast scenes, basket ware, leatherwork and clay figures (*bonecas de barro*). Bargaining is OK at the **Mercado Central**, Av Alberto Nepomuceno (closed Sun), and the **Emcetur Centro de Turismo** in the old prison. Crafts also available in shops near the market, while shops on R Dr João Moreira 400 block sell clothes. Every night (1800-2300) there are stalls along the beach at Praia Meireiles. Crafts also available in the commercial area along Av Monsenhor Tabosa.

Shopping centres

The biggest is **Iguatemi**, south of Meireles on way to Centro de Convenções; it also has modern cinemas. Others are **Aldeota** and **Del Paseo** in Aldeota, near Praça Portugal.

Activities and tours

Fortaleza *p486, map p488*

Diving

Projeto Netuno/Manta Diving Center, R Oswaldo Cruz 2453, Dionísio Torres, T085-3264 4114, www.pnetuno.com.br.

Surfing

Surfing is popular on a number of Ceará beaches. Kitesurfing also catching on.

Trekking

The Fortaleza chapter of the **Trekking Club do Brasil** has walks once a month to different natural areas; visitors welcome, US$20 for transport and T-shirt, T085-212 2456.

Tour operators

Many operators offer city and beach tours. Others offer adventure trips further afield, most common being off-road trips along the beaches from Natal in the east to the Lençois Maranhenses in the west.

Ceará Saveiro, Av Beira Mar 4293, T085-263 1085. *Saveiro* and yacht trips, daily 1000-1200 and 1600-1800 from Praia de Mucuripe.

Dunnas Expedições, R Silva Paulet 1100, Aldeota, T085-3264 2514, www.dunnas.com.br. Off-road tours with a fleet of white Land Rover Defenders, experienced, environmentally and culturally aware, very helpful and professional staff. Recommended.

Martur, Av Beira Mar 4260, T085 263 1203. Sailing trips, from Mucuripe, same schedule as Ceará Saveiro.

Sunny Tour, Av Prof A Nunes Freire 4097, Dionísio Torres, T085 9986 5689, also has a bus-cum-stand on Av Beira Mar near the craft fair. Offers beach tours (eg 3 in 1 day, 6 in 4 days, trips to Jericoacoara).

Windsurfing

A number of Ceará beaches are excellent for windsurfing. Equipment can be rented at some of the popular beaches such as Porto das Dunas and in the city.

Bio Board, Av Beira Mar 914, T085-3242 1642, www.bio board.com.br. Looks after equipment for you, windsurf school, Açaizeiro Café with *açai*, juices, sandwiches upstairs (opens 1000 till 2000, 1900 Sat, 1800 Sun), also travel agency.

Windclub, Av Beira Mar 2120, Praia dos Diários, T085-9982 5449. Equipment rental, lessons also available.

Jericoacoara *p494*

Buggy tours cost US$44.45 for a buggy to all the sites; contact the **Associação de Bugueiros** (ABJ), R Principal, *barraca* near Ibama. If seeking a *bugueiro* who speaks English, Spanish, Italian and French, ask for Alvaro, the school teacher, who is Uruguayan.

Clube dos Ventos, R das Dunas, T088-621 0211, www.clubedosventos.com. Windsurfing and kitesurfing at Preá and Lagoa Jijoca. Equipment hire US$18 per hr, US$44 per day for experienced, US$13 and US$31 for beginners, US$270 deposit (R$700). Basic course US$55.55, 3 hrs and up.

Jeri Off Road, T088-669 2022, T088-9961 4167 (mob), www.jeri.tur.br. João Gaúcho runs adventure trips in the area. Recommended, popular. Also has a travel agency run by Paula Salles.

Quixadá *p497*

Assossiação de Montanhismo e Escalada de Quixadá, Secretário, Henrique Cavalcante, T088-9956 4722. Climbing, up to grade 7. Henrique can help with every type of adventure sport, trekking, orienteering and historical information.

Assossiação de Turismo Ecológico (ATEC), guides for US$11.10 for a day, city tour prices depend on group size.

Sertão & Pedras, T088-412 5995, www.quixadanet.com.br/sertaopedras. For hang-gliding contact Paulo Rocha (delta wing), T088-9251 1955. For paragliding contact Sívio, T085-9979 6027. For climbing contact Kido, T088-9956 7127.

Transport

Fortaleza *p486, map p488*

See also Ins and outs, page 486.

Air

Regular international flights to **Lisbon** and **Milan**. Domestic flights to most major cities, as well as **Juazeiro do Norte**.

Airline offices BRA, T085-477 1470. Fly, Av Mons Taboso 1069, T085-219 7171. TAF (Transportes Aéreos Fortaleza), T085-272 7474, flights to Juazeiro do Norte and other places in the interior, 0900-1630. TAM, Av Santos Dumont 2849, Aldeota, T085-261 0916. **Varig**, Av Santos Dumont 2727, Aldeota, T085-266 8000, F244 0500, freephone T0800-997000.

Bus

Local Many city buses run to the *rodoviária* (US$0.65), including 'Aguanambi' 1 or 2 which go from Av Gen Sampaio, 'Barra de Fátima-Rodoviária' from Praça Coração de Jesus, 'Circular' for Av Beira Mar and the beaches, and 'Siqueira Mucuripe' from Av Abolição. A taxi from Praia de Iracema or Av Abolição costs about US$5. For the **eastern beaches** near Fortaleza (Prainha, Iguape, Barro Preto, Batoque) and towns such as **Aquiraz**, **Eusêbio** or **Pacajus**, you must take São Benedito buses, T085-272 2544, from the *rodoviária*: to **Beberibe** 10 a day US$2, **Cascavel** US$1.10, **Morro Branco** 0745, 1000, 1515, 1750, US$2.25, **Canoa Quebrada** 0830, 1100, 1340, 1540 (plus 1730 on Sun) US$4.25, **Aracati** 0630, 0830, 1100, 1340, 1540, 1900 last back at 1800, US$3.90.

Long-distance Nordeste to **Mossoró**, 10 a day, US$8.75; **Natal**, 8 daily, US$17.75 *semi-leito*, US$25.15 *executivo*, US$40 *leito*, 7½ hrs; **João Pessoa**, 2 daily, US$26.35 *semi-leito*, US$36 *leito*, 10 hrs. Boa Esperança stops at Fortaleza on its **Belém–Natal** route only. Itapemirim to **Salvador**, US$57.40, 1900, 23 hrs. Guanabara to **Recife**, 5 daily, US$29 *executivo*, US$41.50 *leito*, 12 hrs, book early for weekend travel; to **Teresina**, several daily, US$20.35, *leito* US$35.55, 10 hrs; to **Parnaíba** US$18.15; to **Belém**, 2 daily, US$49 *executivo*, 23 hrs; to **São Luís**, 3 daily, US$33.35, 18 hrs; **Sobral** US$5.55; **Ubajara** 0800, 1800, return 0800, 1600, 6 hrs, US$8.15; to Piripiri for **Parque Nacional de Sete Cidades,** US$15.20, 9 hrs, a good stop en route to **Belém.**

Ipu Brasília to **Sobral**, US$9.25, and to **Camocim**, 1120, 1530. To **Majorlândia**, US$4, **Campina Grande**, US$22.20, 13 hrs.

To **Juazeiro do Norte**, Rio Grande/Rápido **Juazeiro**, 5 a day from 1230-2145, 8-9 hrs, US$36.55, *leito* US$73. **Redenção** to **Quixadá**, many daily, US$4, also **Redentora**, 0600,1200 via Baturité. **Redenção** to **Almofala** 0700, 1730, US$6.65, **Cruz** 0900, 1030, 1630, 1830, US$6.40. **Redenção** from *rodoviária* to **Gijoca**, US$7.60, 1030, 1830 and **Jeri**, 0900, 1830, US$10. Tickets are also sold at the **Posta Telefônica** Beira Mar, on Beira Mar almost opposite **Praiano Palace**.

Long-distance bus companies Açailândia, T085-256 8525; **Boa Esperança**, T085-256 5006; **Eucatur/União Cascavel**, T085-256 4889, run Pantanal–Palmas, Gontijo–São Paulo, São Gonçalo–Belo Horizonte; **Guanabara**, T085-256 0214; **Nordeste**, T085-256 2342; **Rio Grande/Rápido Juazeiro**, T085-254 3600; **Transbrasiliana**, T085-256 1306.

Car hire

Many car hire places on Av Monsenhor Tabosa: **Amazônia**, No 1055, T085-219 0800; **Reta**, No 1171, T085-219 5555; **Shop**, No 1181, T085-219 7788, and many more at the junction with Ildefonso Albano. **Brasil Rent a Car**, Av Abolição 2300, T085-242 0868, www.brasillocadora.com.br. **Localiza**, Av Abolição 2236, T0800-992020. There are also many buggy rental shops.

The coast east of Fortaleza *p490*

Bus

Daily bus service from Fortaleza *rodoviária* to **Prainha**, 11 daily, US$1; **Iguape**, hourly 0600-1900, US$1.10. To **Caponga**: direct bus from Fortaleza *rodoviária* (4 a day, US$1.30) or take a bus from Fortaleza to Cascavel (80 mins) then a bus from Cascavel (20 mins); bus information in Caponga T088-334 1485. For bus information in Fortaleza, **São Benedito**, T088-272 2544, at *rodoviária*: to **Beberibe**, 10 a day, US$2; **Cascavel**, US$1.10; **Morro Branco**, 0745, 1000, 1515, 1750, US$2.25; **Canoa Quebrada**, 0830, 1100, 1340, 1540 (plus 1730 Sun), US$4.25; **Aracati**, 0630, 0830, 1100, 1340, 1540, 1900, last back at 1800, US$3.90. Natal–Aracati bus via Mossoró, 6 hrs, US$7.50; from Mossoró (90 km) US$2.50, 2 hrs; Fortaleza–Aracati (142 km), besides **São Benedito**, **Guanabara** or **Nordeste** many daily, US$4, 2 hrs; Aracati–**Canoa Quebrada** from Gen Pompeu e João Paulo, US$0.60; taxi US$3.60.

Pecém and Taíba *p493*
There are 11 daily buses to **Fortaleza** and 4 daily buses to **Siupé**.

Paracuru and Lagoinha *p493*
There are 8 daily buses to **Fortaleza** *rodoviária*, US$3 to **Paracuru**. For information contact T085-272 4483 (in Fortaleza).

Jericoacoara *p494*
Bus Redenção buses from Fortaleza to **Jijoca** and **Jericoacoara** from the *rodoviária* 0900, 1700 and the Av Beira Mar at the Posta Telefônica opposite **Praiano Palace Hotel** 30 mins later. The day bus goes via Jijoca and the night bus via Preá. The journey takes 6 hrs and costs US$10 one way. Always check times of the **Redençao** buses from Fortaleza as they change with the season. The night bus requires an overnight stop in Preá; make your own way to Jeri next day. A *jardineira* (open-sided 4WD truck) meets the **Redenção** bus from Fortaleza, at Jijoca (included in the **Redenção** price). Buses return from Jeri at 1400 (via Preá) and 2230 (via Jijoca); the *jardineira* leaves from **Casa do Turismo** (see page 503 for ticket sale times). Hotels and tour operators run 2- or 3-day tours to Jeri from Fortaleza. If not on Redençao or a tour, 'guides' will besiege new arrivals in Jijoca with offers of buggies, or guiding cars through the tracks and dunes to Jeri for US$5.55. If you don't want to do this, ask if a pickup is going: try Francisco Nascimento, O Chicão, at **Posta do Dê**, or T088-669 1356, US$3.70 per person up front, 22 km, 30 mins (but some only charge US$1.50 per person). A buggy is US$16.65.

If coming from **Belém** or other points north and west, go via Sobral (from Belém US$28.25, 20 hrs), where you change for Cruz, 40 km east of Jijoca, a small pleasant town with basic hotels (there is only one bus a day Sobral–Cruz, US$7.25, 3-4 hrs, but Redenção runs to **Cruz** from Fortaleza 0900, 1030, 1630, 1830, US$6.40. Either continue to **Jijoca** the next day (Cruz–Jijoca, daily about 1400, US$1.25, meets *jardineira* for Jeri, Cruz-Jericoacoara, US$2.20) or take an *horário* pick-up Cruz–Jijoca.

An alternative from the west, especially if going through **Parnaíba**, is by buggy or *jardineira* from **Camocim**, which is 1½ hrs by road from Parnaíba. They leave 0900-1030. You can break the journey from Camocim to Jericoacoara at villages such as Nova Tatajuba (see below), or **Guriú**, where hammock space can be found. There is good birdwatching here. The village musician sings his own songs in the bar. Walk 4 hrs, or take a boat across the bay to Jericoacoara. The journey along the beach has beautiful scenery. In Jericoacoara ask around for buggy or *jardineira* rides to **Camocim**, about US$11-15 per person. Inland, there is an unmade road from Jijoca through cashew plantations to **Granja** (61 km), on the CE-364, which heads north 21 km to Camocim. If driving, ask the way frequently.

Motorcycle If on a motorcycle, it is not possible to ride from Jijoca to Jericoacoara (unless you are an expert in desert conditions). Safe parking for bikes in Jijoca is not a problem.

Cruz *p495*
Bus The bus to **Jijoca** goes through town at about 1400, US$2 or US$3.50 to **Jericoacoara**, wait for the bus by 1330.

Chapada de Ibiapaba *p495*
Bus To **Fortaleza** US$8; to **Belém** US$30.

Serra de Baturité *p497*
Bus Redentora bus from **Fortaleza** *rodoviária*, T085-256 2729, to **Baturité**, 4 a day (plus 1300 on Sat), 3 hrs. To **Guaramiranga** Mon-Fri 0830, daily 1030, 1700, also to **Aratuba**. Pinheiro, T085-256 3729, also runs to **Guaramiranga** and **Aratuba**.

Quixadá *p497*
Bus Redenção bus to **Fortaleza** *rodoviária*, many daily, 3 hrs, US$4. Redentora, to **Fortaleza** 0600, 1200 via **Baturité**. Redenção to **Quixeramobim**, 4 hrs, US$7.

Juazeiro do Norte *p498, map p498*
Air There are connections with **Fortaleza**, **Petrolina** and **Recife** with TAF (Táxi Aéreo Fortaleza), T088-511 0699.
Bus To **Fortaleza** with Rio Negro, 2 daily, US$13.50 *convencional*, US$17.50 *executivo*, 8 hrs. To **Picos** with Boa Esperança, 2 daily, US$5.75, 5 hrs. To **Teresina** with Boa Esperança, Progresso or Aparecida, 3 daily, US$11-12, 11 hrs. To **São Luís** with **Progresso**,

US$20, 16 hrs. To **Belém** with Boa Esperança, 1 daily (often full), US$30, 25 hrs. To **Campina Grande** with Transparaiba, 2 daily, US$9, 9 hrs. To **João Pessoa** with Braga, 1 daily, US$12, 10 hrs. To **Recife** with Braga, 1 daily, US$14, 11 hrs. To **Salvador** with Itapermirim, 2 weekly, US$17.50, 14 hrs. To **São Paulo** with Itapemirim, 1 daily, US$63, 40 hrs.

Car hire IBM, Santo Agostinho 58, T088-511 0542. Localiza, at the airport and at Av Padre Cícero Km 3, No 3375, T088-571 2668. Unidas, Av Padre Cícero, Km 2 on road to Crato, T088-571 1226, F571 1855.

Directory

Fortaleza *p486, map p488*

Banks Banco do Nordeste, R Major Facundo 372, a/c, helpful, recommended. TCs exchanged and cash with Visa at Banco do Brasil, R Barão do Rio Branco 1500, also on Av Abolição (high commission on TCs). ATM for Cirrus, Visa and MasterCard outside cinema at Centro Cultural Dragão do Mar. Also at Av Antonio Sales and Iguatemi Shopping. Banco Mercantil do Brasil, R Mayor Facundo 484, Centro, Praça do Ferreira, cash against MasterCard. Exchange at Tropical Viagens, R Barão do Rio Branco 1233, T085-221 3344, English spoken. Libratur, Av Abolição 2194, T085-248 3355, Mon-Fri 0900-1800, Sat 0800-1200; also has kiosk outside Othon hotel on Av Beira Mar which is open every day till 2300. Recommended. More *câmbios* on Av Mons Tabosa: eg TourStar, No 1587, Sdoc, No 1073, T085-219 7993. **Embassies and consulates** Belgium, R Eduardo Garcia 909, Aldeota, T085-261 2451, nattur@secrel.com.br. France, R Bóris 90, Centro, T085-254 2822. Germany, R Dr Lourenço 2244, Meireles, T085-246 2833, gja435@sec.secrel.com.br. Italy, Rua E 80, Parque Wáshington Soares, T085-273 2606. Netherlands, Av Pe Antônio Tomás 386, T085-461 2331. Sweden and Norway, R Leonardo Mota 501, Aldeota, T085-242 0888, marcos@emitrade.com.br. Switzerland, R Dona Leopoldina 697, Centro, T085-226 9444. UK, c/o Grupo Edson Queiroz, Praça da Imprensa s/n, Aldeota, T085-466 8888, annette@edsonqueiroz.com.br. US, Nogueira Acioli 891, Centro, T085-252 1539. **Internet** Many internet cafés around the city. Beira Mar Internet Café, Av Beira Mar 2120A, Meireles, 0800-0200, US$2.60 per hr (discounts with receipt from Habib's), also international phones, coffee. Outside Av Shopping, Av Dom Luís 300, US$2.50 per hr. Abrolhos Praia, Av Abolição 2030, Meireles, part of hotel of same name, US$1.25 per hr, Mon-Fri 0800-2000, Sat 0800-1400. Cearápontocom, Av Beira Mar e R dos Ararius, across from La Habanera. US$3 per hr, popular, cafés around it. Cyber Net, Av Beira Mar 3120 in small mall, smart, US$2.20 per hr. Ligue.com, Osvaldo Cruz in Beira Mar Trade Center. Internet Express, R Barão de Aracati opposite Colonial Praia, opens 0800. Via Veneto Flat, Av Abolição 2324, has C@fé Digital, US$2.25 per hr, open Sun evening. 2 doors from Pousada Casa Nossa is Falô, Av Abolição 2600 block, daily 0800-2000, US$1.50 per hr, also phones. Others in Pôlo Comercial at Av Mons Tabosa e Ildefonso Albano. **Laundry** Laundromat, Av Abolição 3038, Meireles. **Medical services** Instituto Dr José Frota (IJF), R Barão do Rio Branco 1866, T085-255 5000, recommended public hospital. **Post office** Main branch at R Senador Alencar 38, Centro; Av Monsenhor Tabosa 1109 and 1581, Iracema; at train station; opposite the *rodoviária*. Parcels must be taken to Receita Federal office at Barão de Aracati 909, Aldeota (take 'Dom Luís' bus). **Telephone** International calls from Emcetur hut on Iracema beach and from Telemar offices: R Floriano Peixoto 99, corner of R João Moreira, Centro; R José Vilar 375, Aldeota; Av Beira Mar 736, Iracema; Av Beira Mar 3821, Meireles; Av César Cals 1297, Praia do Futuro; at *rodoviária* and airport.

Juazeiro do Norte *p498, map p498*

Banks Banco do Brasil, R São Francisco, near Praça Pradre Cícero, poor rates, Mon-Fri 1100-1600. No *câmbios* in town. **Post office** R Conceição 354 and at *rodoviária*. **Telephone** R São Pedro 204, half a block from Praça Padre Cícero and at *rodoviária*.

Piauí and Maranhão

Piauí is possibly the poorest state in Brazil. Its population is about 2.7 million, but many leave to seek work elsewhere. The economy is almost completely dependent upon agriculture and livestock, both of which in turn depend on how much rain, if any, falls.

Maranhão state is about the size of Italy, with flat and low-lying land and highlands to the south. The Atlantic coastline – a mass of sandbanks and creeks and sandy islands – is 480 km long. On one of the islands stands São Luís, the state capital, whose colonial centre, decorated with ceramic tiles, has been restored. It is now part of UNESCO's list of sites of worldwide cultural importance. The Bumba-Meu-Boi is typical of the region and the African influence harks back to the days when slaves were imported into the city, which is also considered Brazil's reggae capital.

The coast to the east, stretching to the Parnaíba delta, contains an area of sand dunes and freshwater lakes, the Lençóis Maranhenses, which deserves a visit for its beauty and remoteness. The area around Carolina, south of Imperatriz, is renowned for its mountain scenery and spectacular waterfalls. » *For Sleeping, Eating and other listings, see pages 522-526.*

Background

Much of Piauí's history springs from cattle farmers who moved into the interior from Bahia at the beginning in the 17th century. Until the early 19th century though, the state was under the control of neighbouring Maranhão. At Independence, there was bitter fighting between the Portuguese supporters of the colony and the Brazilians who sought their freedom.

Initially, the Portuguese did not show much interest in this part of the northeast, and the French were the first to set up colonies. By the end of the 16th century, the Portuguese had taken over, although their rule was interrupted by a brief period of Dutch dominance in the early 1640s. The Companhia Geral do Comércio do Maranhão e Grão-Pará, 1685-1777, was the major influence in the area, but after its demise, there was unrest until Maranhão finally bowed to the Independence movement.

Teresina » *pp522-526.*

→ *Phone code: 086. Colour map 2, A3. Population: 716,000.*

The capital of Piauí state is about 435 km from the coast, on the Rio Parnaíba. The city itself is reputed to be the hottest after Manaus, with temperatures up to 42°C. There are a few sights of interest.

The **Palácio de Karnak** ⓘ *just west of Praça Frei Serafim, Mon-Fri 1530-1730*, the old governor's palace, contains lithographs of the Middle East in 1839 by David Roberts RA. Also see the **Museu do Piauí** ⓘ *Praça Marechal Deodoro, Tue-Fri 0800-1730, Sat and Sun 0800-1200, US$0.60*, which has displays on the history of the state (in Portuguese) and an impressive and extensive collection of fossils.

There is an interesting open market by the Praça Marechal Deodoro; it's a good place to buy hammocks, but bargain hard. Every morning along the picturesque river, with washing laid out to dry on its banks, there is the *troca-troca*, where people buy, sell and swap. An undercover complex, **Mercado Central do Artesanato** ⓘ *R Paissandu 1276, Praça Dom Pedro II, Mon-Fri 0800-2200*, has also been built. Most of the year the river is low, leaving sandbanks known as *coroas* (crowns).

Ins and outs

There are paved road and rail connections (freight only) with the neighbouring state capitals. Outside the airport, buses run straight into town and to the *rodoviária*.

For tourist information there are several options: **Piemtur** ⓘ *R Álvaro Mendes 2003, Caixa Postal 36*; *R Magalhães Filho, next to 55 N, English spoken, and R Acre, Convention Centre, T086-221 7100*. There are also kiosks at the rodoviária and the airport. The Sindicato dos Guiás de Turismo de Piauí, **Singtur** ⓘ *R Paissandu 1276, T086-221 2175*, has information booths at the Centro de Artesanato, Praça Dom Pedro II (helpful, friendly), the Encontro das Águas, Poty Velho and on the shores of the Rio Poty. Another office is **Ana Turismo** ⓘ *R Álvaro Mendes 1961, Centro, T/F086- 223 3970*.

Parque Nacional de Sete Cidades → *Colour map 2, A3.*

Some 190 km northeast of Teresina, this interesting park has strange eroded rock formations which, from the ground, look like a medley of weird monuments. The inscriptions on some of the rocks have never been deciphered. One theory suggests links with the Phoenicians, and the Argentine Professor Jacques de Mahieu considers them to be Nordic runes left by the Vikings. Within the 20 sq km of the park, there is plenty of birdlife and iguanas, which descend from their trees in the afternoon. If hiking in the park, beware of rattlesnakes. A small booklet with a sketch map is available from Ibama, but is not really good enough for walking. Local food is limited and monotonous, so bring a few treats, especially fruit. Some 50 km away, **Pedro Segundo** is a good place to buy opals.

Ins and outs Information is available from **Ibama** ⓘ *Av Homero Castelo Branco 2240, Teresina, 64048-400, T086-232 1142, US$30*. A free bus service leaves the Praça da Bandeira in Piripiri (by the **Telemar** office) at 0700, passing **Hotel Fazenda Sete Cidades** at 0800, reaching the park 10 minutes later; return at 1630, or hitchhike. A taxi from Piripiri costs US$15; from Piracuruca, US$20. To get to Piripiri, take a bus from Teresina, São Luís, Fortaleza or Ubajara (marked 'São Benedito', or 'Crateús'), a beautiful trip.

Parnaíba and around → *Phone code: 086. Colour map 2, A3. Population: 133,000.*

Between the states of Maranhão and Piauí runs the Rio Parnaíba. Near the river mouth is the anchorage of Luís Correia, where large ships are unloaded for final delivery by tugs and lighters at Parnaíba, 15 km upriver. This is the collection and distribution centre for the trade of Piauí (tropical products and cattle). Parnaíba is partly encircled by shifting white sand dunes up to 30 m high. The town is a relaxed,

Cabeça-de-Cuia

Crispim was a fisherman who lived in Teresina, at the confluence of the rivers Poti and Parnaíba. One day, returning home after a hard day's fishing with no catch whatsoever, he discovered that there was no food in the house. Infuriated, he grabbed a large bone which was lying nearby and beat his mother to death. Her dying curse was that Crispim should live out his days as a hideous monster with an enormous head.

A young and single man, Crispim was driven to despair by his now terrifying appearance. He drowned himself in the Parnaíba. Legend has it that Crispim's life and good looks will be restored, when he has managed to eat seven virgins named Maria. Young laundresses, when they go to the river, are still afraid of him.

Cabeça-de-Cuia means 'head of a gourd'. Carvings of this strange figure are a common sight in Teresina.

friendly place. If crossing the delta, buy all provisions here. There are beaches at **Luís Correia**, 14 km from Parnaíba, with radioactive sands. About 18 km from Parnaíba is **Pedra do Sal**, with dark blue lagoons and palm trees. At **Lagoa de Portinho**, 12 km from Parnaíba, there are bungalows, a bar, restaurant and canoes for hire; it is possible to camp. **Praia do Coqueiro** is a small fishing village with natural pools formed at low tide. Seafood is good at **Alô Brasil** and **Bar da Cota.**

Ins and outs There is a regular connection from here with Tutóia, for boats across the Parnaíba delta; a tour in the delta costs US$20 per person. For tourist information, there's **Piemtur** ⓘ *To86-321 1532*, and the **Secretaria de Turismo e Meio Ambiente** ⓘ *To86-323 1715*, both at Porto das Barcas.

Southern Piauí » *pp522-526.*

In **Oeiras**, the old capital of Piauí, the state government is restoring some of the old buildings, such as the bishop's palace and the church of Nossa Senhora da Vitória.

Parque Nacional Serra da Capivara → *Colour map 2, B3.*

About 500 km south of Teresina is this 130,000-ha park, on the UNESCO World Heritage list. Some 30,000 prehistoric rock paintings on limestone have been found, dating from between 6000 and 12,000 years ago. The paintings are of daily life, festivities and celebrations, as well as hunting and sex scenes. Excavations by Brazilian and French archaeologists have uncovered fossilized remains of extinct animals such as the sabre-toothed tiger, giant sloths larger than elephants and armadillos the size of a car.

Nearly 400 archaeological sites have been identified in the park since research began in 1970. About 22 of them have been set up to receive tourists. Roads and all-weather paths allow visitors to view the sites with ease. Specially trained guides are available. The area is good for hiking in the *caatinga*, with its canyons and mesas. It is also possible to see much of the *caatinga* wildlife, in particular the birds.

Much investment has gone into the park, not just for visitors' facilities, but also to educate the local population about protecting the paintings and to establish a beekeeping project to provide income in times of drought. The **Museu do Homen Americano** ⓘ *Centro Cultural Sérgio Motta, Bairro Campestre, To89-582 1612, www.fumdham.org.br*, has a fascinating collection of artefacts found in the serra. These are well displayed, though the information in English is poor. The museum is in the town of São Raimundo Nonato, 35 km from the park.

Bumba-meu-boi

Throughout the month of June the streets of São Luís are alive to the sound of *tambores* and dancers recreating the legend of Catirina, Pai Francisco and his master's bull. Although this mixture of African, indigenous and Portuguese traditions exists throughout the north, it is in Maranhão that it is most developed, with around 100 groups in São Luís alone. Here there are various styles called *sotaques*, which have different costumes, dances, instruments and *toadas*. These are Boi de Matraca da Ilha and Boi de Pindaré, both accompanied by small percussion instruments called *matracas*, Boi de Zabumba marked by the use of a type of drum, and Boi de Orquestra accompanied by string and wind instruments. Although there are presentations throughout June the highlights are the 24th (São João) and the 29th (São Pedro) with the closing ceremony lasting throughout the 30th (São Marçal), particularly in the *bairro* João Paulo. The shows take place in an *arraial*, which are found all over the city, with the ones at Projeto Reviver and Ceprama being more geared towards tourists (however be aware that a livelier more authentic atmosphere is to be found elsewhere in other *bairros*, such as Madre Deus). The Centro de Cultura Popular Domingos Vieira Filho at Rua do Giz 221, Praia Grande is the place to learn more about these variations as well as many other local festivals and traditions such as Tambor de Crioula or Cacuriá, both sensual dances derived from Africa. A good location to see these dances and *capoeira* practised is *Labouarte*, Rua Jansen Muller, Centro (Cacuriá de Dona Tetê is particularly recommended, with participation encouraged).

Ins and outs Access is from São Raimundo Nonato on the BR-324, or from Petrolina in Pernambuco. A taxi from Petrolina airport (290 km) will cost about US$200 one way, or there are buses. For information, the main organization is the **Fundação do Homem Americano (Fumdham)** ⓘ *R Abdias Neves 551, CEP 64770-000, São Raimundo Nonato, Piauí, T086-582 1612/1389, F582 1656*, which has a museum for scientists. For further information on the park and reservations in local hotels, contact Dr Niéde Guidon, Fumdham Parque Nacional, at the same address.

Hyacinth Site

In the far southwest of the state, 20 km from **São Gonçalo do Piauí**, is one of the best places for seeing hyacinth macaws. The Hyacinth Site is on private land in a region of *cerrado* with red sandstone cliffs where the macaws nest. This used to be an area in which an illegal bird trade flourished, but the local people now guard the site, which is supported by the **Kaytee Avian Foundation** (USA) and others. Many other *cerrado* birds may be seen, together with black-and-gold howlers and, less commonly, maned wolves and giant anteaters. Accommodation is in very simple huts with mosquito nets, sand floors and shared bathrooms. Meals are served at the site. Access is via the airport at Barreiras in Western Bahia, 340 km south, five or six hours' drive away. Tours are only possible through **Focus Tours**, see Essentials page 24.

São Luís » pp522-526.

→ *Colour map 2, A2. Phone code: 098. Population: 870,000.*

The capital and port of Maranhão state, founded in 1612 by the French and named after St Louis of France, stands upon São Luís island between the bays of São Marcos and São José. The urban area extends to São Francisco island, connected with São Luís by three bridges. The historic centre is being restored with UNESCO support and the splendid results rival the Pelourinho in Salvador. An old slaving port, the city has retained much African culture. The area is subject to heavy tropical rains, but a large proportion of the surrounding deep forest has been cut down to be replaced by *babaçu* palms, the nuts and oils of which are the state's most important products.

Ins and outs

Getting there **Marechal Cunha Machado airport** ⓘ *15 km from centre, Av Santos Dumont, T098-245 1688*, receives flights from Belém, Fortaleza, Imperatriz, Parnaíba and Teresina. **São Cristovão** buses run to the city until midnight, US$0.75; a taxi costs US$12.50. The *rodoviária* is 12 km from the centre on the airport road. Take the 'Rodoviária via Alemanha' bus to the centre (Praça João Lisboa), US$0.50. There are three trains a week from Parauapebas. Ferries cross the bay daily from Porto do Itaqui to Porto do Cujupe. T098-222 8431 for times. US$3 foot passenger, US$15 car.

Tourist information **Fumtur** ⓘ *Praça Benedito Leite, T098-222 5281*, and **Maratur** ⓘ *Praça João Lisboa 66, T098-231 2000, maratur@geplan.ma.gov.br.*

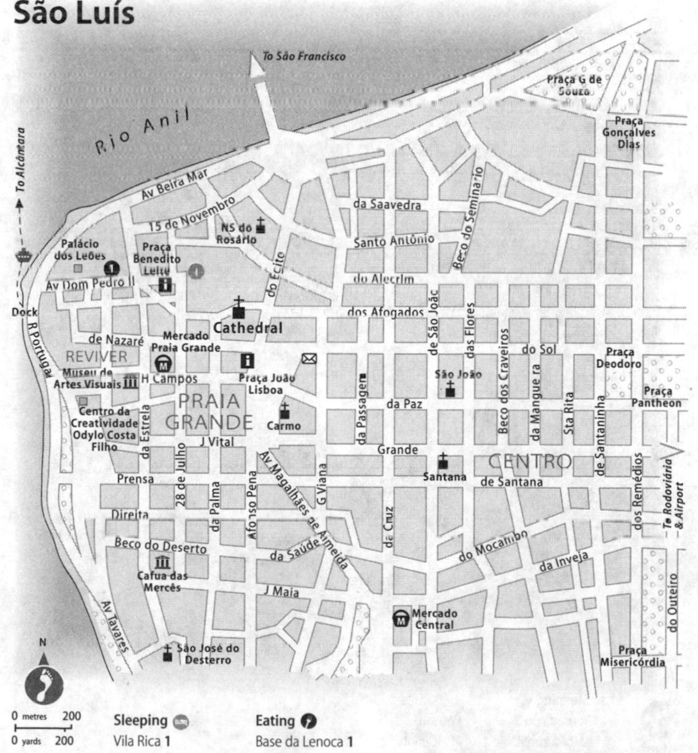

Sights

The old part of the city, on very hilly ground with many steep streets, is wonderfully preserved and full of colonial buildings. The damp climate encouraged the use of ceramic tiles for exterior walls and São Luís displays a greater variety of such tiles than anywhere else in Brazil, with Portuguese, French and Dutch styles. The commercial quarter (Rua Portugal, also called Rua Trapiche) is still much as it was in the 17th century. The best shopping area is Rua de Santana near Praça João Lisboa.

The **Palácio dos Leões** ⓘ *Av Dom Pedro II, Mon, Wed and Fri 1500-1800*, the governor's palace, has beautiful floors of dark wood (*jacarandá*) and light (*cerejeira*). There are marvellous views from the terrace. The restored **Fortaleza de Santo Antônio**, built originally by the French in 1614, is on the bank of the Rio Anil at Ponta d'Areia.

The **Fábrica Canhamo** ⓘ *R São Pantaleão 1232, Madre de Deus, near Praia Grande, T098-232 2187, Mon-Fri 0900-1900*, is a restored factory and houses an arts and crafts centre. The **Centro da Creatividade Odylo Costa Filho** ⓘ *R da Alfândego 200, Praia Grande, T098-231 4058, Mon-Fri 0800-2200*, is an arts centre with theatre, cinema and music, a bar and café – a good meeting place.

The best colonial churches in town are the **cathedral** on Praça Dom Pedro II (1629), and the churches of **Carmo** on Praça João Lisboa (1627), **São João Batista** on Largo São João (1665), **Nossa Senhora do Rosário** on R do Egito (1717), and the 18th-century **Santana** on R de Santana. On Largo do Desterro is the **church of São José do Desterro**, which was finished in 1863, but has much older parts.

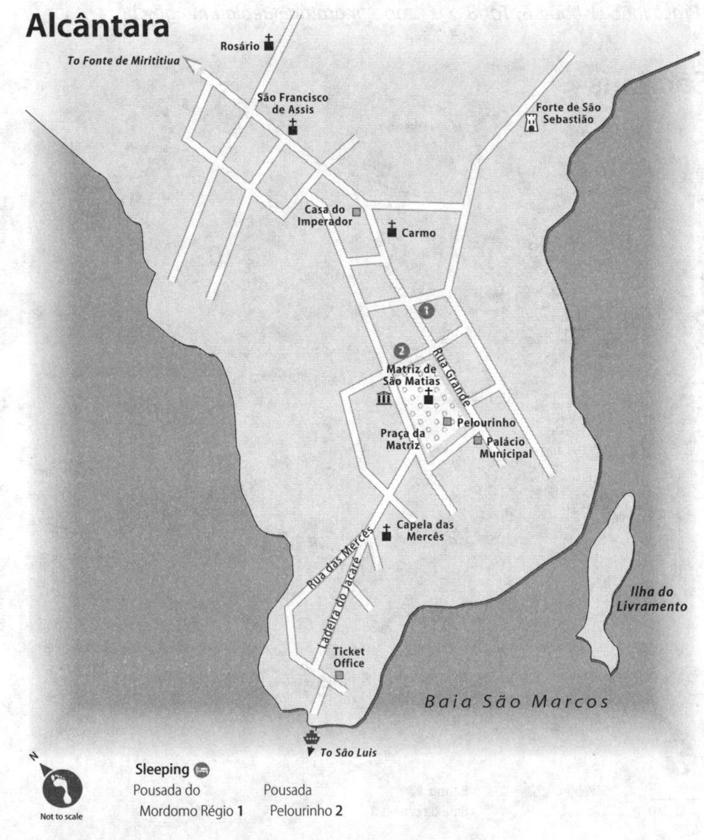

As for museums, the **Cafua das Mercês** ⓘ *R Jacinto Maia 43, Mon-Fri 1330-1700*, is housed in the old slave market, in a small building opposite the *quartel militar*. It is a space devoted to the history of African culture in Maranhao. The various exhibits include pieces of African art, musical instruments and ritual objects, alongside displays about Afro-Brazilian history and life. Information is in Portuguese. It is well worth the effort to find it. Also worth a visit is the **Casa dos Negros** next door. The **Museu Histórico e Artístico do Estado** ⓘ *R do Sol 302*, is housed in a fine early 19th-century mansion, complete with slave quarters. Also on the Rua do Sol is the **Teatro Artur Azevedo** (1816).

The **Museu de Artes Visuais** ⓘ *Av Portugal 289, Mon-Fri 0800-1300, 1600-1800*, shows ceramics and post-war art.

Excursions from São Luís

Calhau is a huge beach, 10 km away. **Ponta D'Areia** is nearer to São Luís but more crowded. **Raposa**, a fishing village built on stilts, is a good place to buy handicrafts; there are a few places to stay on Avenida Principal. To get there, take a bus from the Mercado Central in São Luís (one hour with **Viação Santa Maria**, every 30 minutes).

Another fishing village is **São José de Ribamar**, whose church dedicated to the patron saint is a centre for *romeiros* in September. Many bars on the seafront serve local specialities such as fried stonefish. It is a 30-minute bus ride with **Maranhense** from the market in São Luís.

Alcântara → *Phone code: 098. Colour map 2, A2. Population: 22,000.*

The former state capital, Alcântara, is on the mainland bay of São Marcos, 22 km by boat from São Luís. Construction of the city started at the beginning of the 17th century and it is now a historical monument. There are many old churches, such as the ruined **Matriz de São Matias** (1648), and colonial mansions, including the **Casa** and **Segunda Casa do Imperador**, and the old cotton barons' mansions with their blue, Portuguese- tiled façades. In the Praça da Matriz is the **Pelourinho** ⓘ *0900-1330, US$0.75*, (1648), the traditional pillory, and a small museum. You can also see the **Forte de São Sebastião** (1663), now in ruins, and the **Fonte de Mirititiua** (1747).

Canoe trips go to **Ilha do Livramento**, where there are good beaches and walks around the coast. It can be muddy after rain, and watch out for mosquitoes after dark. A rocket-launching site has been built nearby!

Ins and outs Launches leave São Luís dock at about 0700 and 0930, returning from Alcântara about 0815 and 1615; check time and buy the ticket the day before at the *hidroviária*, west end of Rua Portugal, T098-232 0692, as departure depends on the tides. The journey takes 1½ hours, a return ticket costs US$15. The sea can be very rough between September and December. Old wooden boats, the *Newton Bello* and *Mensageiro da Fé*, leave São Luís at 0630 and 1600, returning at 0730 and 1700 (1½ hrs, US$5 return). There are sometimes catamaran tours bookable through tour operators in São Luís (see page 525).

Parque Nacional Lençóis Maranhenses

» *pp522-526.*

→ *Phone code: 098 Colour map 2, A3.*

To the east of São Luís, on the Atlantic Coast, is the beautiful Parque Nacional Lençóis Maranhenses, whose 155,000 ha of beaches and dunes are sprinkled with freshwater lagoons. There is very little vegetation and the wildlife remains largely unstudied. Despite its remoteness, Lençóis Maranhenses (which means 'sheets of Maranhão') is not difficult to visit. Travellers with a few days to spare are rewarded by an amazing panorama of dunes reaching from horizon to horizon, deserted beaches, boat rides on the aptly named **Rio Preguiça** (Lazy River), and tiny, quiet hamlets where strangers are still a novelty. However, the region is starting to become popular with Brazilian holidaymakers (and developers).

A strange landscape of shifting white dunes, stretching for about 140 km along the coast between **Tutóia** and Primeira Cruz, west of **Barreirinhas**, has created a unique and delicate ecosystem that has been protected since 1981. The sand, which extends up to 50 km inland from the coast, is advancing by as much as 200 m a year in some places. Dumped by the sea and blown by the wind, it forms ridges 50 m high in long flowing patterns which change constantly. The best time to visit is during the rainy season (June to September), when the dune valleys fill with water. Reflections of the sky make the water appear vivid blue, providing a spectacular contrast with the brilliant white sand.

Barely visited until recently, Lençóis Maranhenses provides a refuge for severely endangered species. Giant turtles come here to lay their eggs and among the resident mammals are paca, deer and sea cow. There are almost-extinct varieties of fish such as the camurupim, which likes both salt and fresh water. The dunes are a breeding ground for migratory birds and recent studies have shown the sparse vegetation to include grasses unknown elsewhere. Excavations were begun in 1995 on the supposed site of a Jesuit settlement which, according to local rumour, was buried intact by a sandstorm.

Ins and outs

To get to the park, take a bus from São Jose to Barreirinhas (eight hours, US$5), where there are some pousadas and restaurants. From Barreirinhas it is a four-hour boat ride along the Rio Preguiça and then a one-hour walk; allow at least two hours in the dunes, US$12. It is also possible to hire a speedboat, or get a lift from a fisherman. Tours can be organized from São Jose (see page 525) or at Barreirinhas with **Pousada Lins** (see page 523), **Parna Lençóis Maranhenses** and **Pocof Barreirinhas**, both at Rua Cazuza Ramos 3, T098-349 1155.

The only forms of transport that can get across the dunes right into the park are a jeep or a horse. Allow two days by jeep, staying overnight at Paulino Neves (US$20). From Tutóia, José Neves Rodrigues, known as 'O Anjo' (the Angel), does the trip for around US$40 per passenger. A very bad road passing inland links Tutóia and Barreirinhas: hardy drivers could stop at Rio Novo and explore the dunes from there.

» *See also Activities and tours, page 525, and Transport, page 525.*

Traversing Lençóis Maranhenses

The area to the west of Rio Preguiça is the park proper. The dunes east of the river form a protected area, which is easier to travel through, and has several small, friendly settlements. It is possible to walk along the coast between Barreirinhas and Tutóia in either direction; allow about three days. Camping is permitted, but you must take all supplies with you including water, since some dune lakes are salty. Because of the hot and sandy conditions, this is a punitive trek, only for the very hardy. Do not try the treacherous hike inland across the dunes.

Delta do Parnaíba » *pp522-526.*

The extensive Parnaíba delta contains 70 islets covered in forest, palms or dunes. River and salt water flow side by side through its channels. Catch a boat in Parnaíba, hook up your hammock, and pass a few desultory hours watching herons nesting in the trees and fishermen asleep in their rowing boats or admiring the daily crab harvest.

When you arrive at the delta mouth you can either stop at Ilha do Caju, which gets its name from the hundreds of cashew trees that grow there, or continue to **Tutóia**, where millions of birds populate freshwater lakes, formed by rain collecting between massive white dunes. Both are protected areas of outstanding natural beauty. Good food and accommodation are available on the island and in Tutóia, but many people in this region live as they have done for generations, in adobe houses, on a diet of fish cooked in baked-earth ovens. Illiteracy is the norm. Travel is by jeep or, more commonly, by horse. There is no mains electricity and the nearest shopping is at Parnaíba.

Crossing the Parnaíba delta, which separates Piauí from Maranhão, is possible by boat, arriving in Tutóia; an interesting trip through swamps sheltering many birds. Trucks from Tutóia go to Barreirinhas, gateway to the **Parque Nacional dos Lençóis Maranhenses**, a vast area of sand dunes with rare birds and other wildlife, see above.

Ilha do Caju → *Population: 70, www.ilhadocaju.com.br.*

Virtually unchanged for four centuries, Ilha do Caju has an astonishing variety of terrain, with lakes, forest, marshes and an expanse of white dunes to the northwest. Much of the water, including the sea, is *salobre* – a mixture of fresh and salt. Swimming is possible from the vast, shimmering beach, through currents of alternating sea and river water, a heartily recommended experience. There are lakes on the island, caused by flooding, in which trees (killed by the brine content) stand bleached and knotted, an unnerving image of lifelessness surrounded by vigorous vegetation. Nesting herons and peregrines take off in clouds of flashing green feathers as you pass; tiny, long-legged cafézinho birds hop from leaf to leaf on the water lilies; and myriad butterflies hover around your head as you walk through the forest surrounding the lake. The whole island is environmentally protected and no chemical pesticides are used.

Caxias → *Population: 149,500.*

The main road from Teresina passes through the Maranhense town of Caxias, a battle site during the Balaiada rebellion in 1838. It has a good *churrascaria*, **Selva do Braz**, Avenida Central 601, with live music in the evening. About 3 km from the town on the Buriti Bravo road is a spring for medicinal bathing, with a restaurant serving regional food.

Southern Maranhão » *pp522-526.*

Imperatriz → *Phone code: 098. Colour map 2, A1. Population: 295,000.*

On the eastern bank of the Rio Tocantins, at Maranhão's western border with Tocantins, is Imperatriz, a city serving a large cattle region. Founded in 1851, the **Igreja de Santa Tereza D'Ávila** ⓘ *R 15 de Novembro*, is dedicated to the city's patron saint. River beaches appear between July and October when the river is low. The town can be quite a rough place and it is wise to exercise caution, especially at night.

Ins and outs The **airport**, T098-722 4666, receives flights from Altamira, Araguaína, Belém, Brasília and São Luís. Lying on the BR-010 Belém–Brasília highway, Imperatriz has bus connections with both cities, as well as Teresina; the *rodoviária* is at R Lias Barros, Nova Carolina, T098-731 1195. There is a **ferroviária**, T098-723 2260, with trains from Pará and other towns in Maranhão.

Carolina → *Phone code: 098. Population: 26,000.*

South of Imperatriz, also on the Rio Tocantins, Carolina is set in an area of spectacular waterfalls and mountain scenery. Near to the **Cachoeira da Prata**, on the Rio Farinha, is **Morro das Figuras**, which has rock inscriptions. Access is by unsealed road from the BR-230, requiring a 4WD. Some 35 km south of Carolina, on the road to Estreito, is **Cachoeria de Pedra Caída**. For information contact **Secretaria de Turismo** ⓘ *R Duque de Caxias 522, T098-731 1613, Mon-Fri 0800-1300.*

Sleeping

Teresina *p513, map p514*

L **Rio Poty**, Av Mcal Castelo Branco 555, Ilhota, T086-223 1500, F222 6671. 5 stars. Recommended.

A **Real Pálace**, R Lizandro Nogueira 1208, T086-221 2768, F221 7740. A/c, pool, restaurant.

A **São José**, João Cabral 340, T086-223 2176, F223 2223. Reasonable restaurant.

B **Royal Pálace**, R 13 de Maio 233N, T/F086-221 7707. A/c, restaurant.

B **Sambaíba**, R Gabriel Ferreira 230-N, T086-222 6711. 2 stars, central, good.

D **Fortaleza**, Felix Pacheco 1101, Praça Saraiva, T086-222 2984. Fan, basic. Recommended.

D **Grande**, Firmino Pires 73. Very friendly staff, clean.

D **Santa Terezinha**, Av Getúlio Vargas 2885, opposite *rodoviária*, T086-219 5918. With a/c or fan, clean, friendly.

Many cheap places in R São Pedro and R Alvaro Mendes, such as **Glória**, 823 (clean, best), blocks 800 and 900 on each street. Other cheap hotels and *dormitórios* around Praça Saraiva.

Parque Nacional de Sete Cidades *p514*

Piripiri, 26 km from the park, is a cheap place to break the Belém-Fortaleza journey. As well as those listed, there are other options near bus offices and behind the church.

B **Hotel Sete Cidades**, Km 63 on BR-222, 6 km from the park entrance, T086-276 2222. Chalets with private bath, swimming pool, good restaurant and bicycle or horse transport; also has a free pickup to the park (and a most unpleasant zoo).

E **Ibama hostel**, in the park, T086-343 1342. Price per person. Rooms with bath, pleasant, good restaurant, natural pool nearby, camping. Recommended.

E **Novo Hotel Central**, town centre, Piripiri. With fan, bath, breakfast and safe parking, friendly. Recommended.

Parnaíba and around *p514*

L **Cívico**, Av Gov Chagas Rodrigues 474, Parnaíba, T086-322 2470. Restaurant, pool, good breakfast. Recommended.

A **Pousada dos Ventos**, Av São Sebastião 2586, Universidade, Parnaíba, T086-322 2177, F322 4880. Pool. Recommended.

A **Rio Poty Praia**, Av dos Magistrados 2350, Luís Correia, T/F086-367 1277. Bar, restaurant, pool.

D **Rodoviária**, and other basic hotels in the centre of Parnaíba.

São Luís *p517, map p517*

Many cheap hotels can be found in R das Palmas, very central, and R Formosa.

AL **La Ravadière**, Av Mcal Castelo Branco 375, São Francisco, T098-235 2255, F235 2217. Pool, restaurant, sauna.

AL-A **Praia Mar**, Av São Marcos, Ponta d'Areia, T098-235 2328. On the beach.

B **Deodoro**, R de Santaninha 535, T098-231 5811. A/c, parking, good.

B **Ponta D'Areia**, Av dos Holandeses, Ponta D'Areia, T098-235 3232, F227 2892. Pool.

B **Pousada Colonial**, R Afonso Pena 112, T098-232 2834. In a beautiful restored, tiled house. Recommended.

B **São Marcos**, R da Saúde 178, T098-232 3768, F231 7777. Restored colonial house, a/c, family run. Recommended.

B **Vila Rica**, Praça Dom Pedro II 299, T098-232 3535, www.hotelvilarica.com.br Central, pool, business centre with internet connection. Recommended.

C **Lord**, R de Nazaré 258, facing Praça Benedito Leite, T/F098-221 4655. A/c, comfortable, good value, good breakfast. Recommended.

D **Hotel Casa Grande**, R Isaac Martins 94, Centro, T098-232 2432. Clean and basic single, double or triple rooms. Recommended.

D **Pousada Solar dos Nobres**, R 13 de Maio 82, Centro, T098-232 5705. Bright, welcoming, superb breakfast, very good.

D **Pousada Turismo Jansen Müller**, R Jansen Müller 270, T098-231 0997. With breakfast and bath.

E-F **Dois Continentes**, R 28 de Julho 129, Praia Grande, T/F098-222 6286. Family-run youth hostel.

E-F **Solar das Pedras**, R da Palma 127, T/F098-232 6694. Youth hostel.

G **Pousada Ilha Bela**, R Formosa. Safe.

Excursions from São Luís *p519*

In Raposa there are some places to stay on Av Principal.

C Hotel Sol e Mar, Av Gonçalves Dias 320, São José de Ribamar, with a restaurant.

Alcântara *p519, map p518*

B Pousada dos Guarás, Praia da Baronesa, T098-337 1339. Bungalows with bath, good restaurant, canoe hire.

C Pousada do Mordomo Régio, R Grande 134, T098-337 1197. TV, fridge, good restaurant.

D Pousada Pelourinho, Praça da Matriz 55, T098-337 1257. Breakfast, good restaurant, shared bathroom. Recommended.

E Pousada da Josefa, R Direita, T098-337 1109. Restaurant. Ask for hammock space or rooms in private houses, friendly but no great comfort, provide your own mineral water.

Parque Nacional Lençóis Maranhenses *p519*

There are pousadas and restaurants at Rio Novo and Paulino Neves, in Tutóia.

C Tutóia Palace Hotel, Av Paulino Neves 1100, Tutóia, T098-479 1247. Crumbling mock colonial hotel in garish pink with 12 fading rooms, 5 of which have a/c.

D Pousada do Balaho, R Col Godinho, Barreirinhas, T098-349 1110. Many others.

D Pousada Em-Bar-Cação, R Magalhães de Almeida 1064, T098-479 1219, on the beach. Breakfast US$3, friendly, good food and *tiquira*, a drink made from manioc.

D Pousada Lins, Av Joaquim Soeiro de Carvalho, Barreirinhas, T098-349 1203. Good, but shop around before taking their tours. Restaurant.

Delta do Parnaíba *p520*

AL Pousada Ecológica Ilha do Caju, contact address: Av Presidente Vargas 235, Centro, Parnaíba, Piauí, T086-322 2380, F321 1308. The pousada is an attractive converted farmhouse with thatched guesthouses in the grounds; each has its own hammock outside, but inside there is a huge bed, handmade by the same craftsmen who made much of the pousada's highly individual furniture. The owner, Ingrid, and senior staff speak English and are helpful and welcoming. Children must be aged 12 or over.

Imperatriz *p521*

Many cheap hotels near the *rodoviária*.

A Imperatriz Park, BR-010, Km 1347, opposite *rodoviária*, T086-723 2950. Pool.

A Posseidon, R Paraíba 740, T086-723 2323. Central, the best, pool. Recommended.

Carolina *p521*

B Pousada Pedra Caída, BR-010, Km 30, T098-731 1318. Chalets with fan, restaurant, natural pool and 3 waterfalls.

B Pousada do Rio Lages, BR-230, Km 2, T098-731 1499. Chalets with a/c.

B-C Cafuné, BR-230 Km 2. Local food.

Eating

Teresina *p513, map p514*

There are many places for all budgets in Praça Dom Pedro II.

TTT Camarão do Elias, Av Pedro Almeida 457, T086-232 5025. Best restaurant in the city, with fish and prawn dishes. Try the fish of the day in caper and lemon sauce.

TT Pesqueirinho, R Domingos Jorge Velho 6889, in Poty Velho district, T086-225 2268. Excellent fish restaurant on the riverbank.

T Sabores Rotisserie, R Simplício Mendes 78, Centro. By the kg, good quality and variety.

Parnaíba and around *p514*

T Recanto Gaúcho, Trav Costa Fernandes, next to the university. *Churrasco*.

T Renatinho, Av das Nações Unidas, Beira Rio. Crab and seafood.

T Sorveteria Araújo, R Pires Ferreira 615. Good ice cream made from local fruits.

São Luís *p517, map p517*

Bases provide home cooking in simple surroundings, although most are found away from the centre and beaches. Typical dishes are *arroz de cuxá* and *torta de camarão* and desserts or liquors made from local fruits. Try the local soft drink called *Jesús* or *Jenève*.

TT Base do Edilson, R João Damasceno 21, Ponta do Farol. Excellent for prawns.

TT Base do Germano, Av Venceslau Brás, Camboa. Excellent shrimp stew.

T Base da Lenoca, Av Dom Pedro II 181. Good view, big portions.

T Beiruth 2, Av Mcal Castelo Branco 751B. Recommended.

Ỷ **Naturalista Alimentos**, R do Sol 517. Very good, natural food shops and restaurants.

Ỷ **Senac**, R Nazaré 242, next to hotel **Lord**. Tourism school restaurant, good food in a beautifully restored mansion.

Ỷ **Tia Maria**, Av Nina Rodrigues 1, Ponta d'Areia. Recommended for fried fish with *castanha* and *caju*.

Alcântara *p519, map p518*

Ỷ **Bar do Lobato**, Praça da Matriz. Pleasant with good simple food, fried shrimps highly recommended.

Imperatriz *p521*

ỶỶ **Rafaello Grill**, in Imperatriz Shopping, Av Dorgival Pinheiro Sousa 1400. Self-service. Modest *churrascaria* with a reasonable choice of side dishes.

Ỷ **Fogão Mineiro**, Av Getúlio Vargas 2234. Minas Gerais wood-oven cooking with a range of heavy, meaty dishes and side vegetables like squash.

Bars and clubs

Teresina *p513, map p514*

Centro Cultural Porto das Barcas, a pleasant shopping and entertainment complex with several good restaurants and a large open-air bar on the riverside.

São Luís *p517, map p517*

Antigamente, Praia Grande. Live music Thu-Sat.

Coqueiro Bar, Av dos Holandeses, Praia da Ponta D'Areia. Reggae on Thu.

Extravagance, Av Conselheiro Hilton Rodrigues, Calhau. A good nightclub.

Poeme-Sei, R João Gualberto 52, Praia Grande, is a bar/gallery open in the evening, good atmosphere, no food.

Senac (see Eating, above). Piano bar Thu-Sat.

Tombo da Ladeira, Praia Grande. Good for reggae on Wed.

Imperatriz *p521*

Fly Back Disco Club, Beira Rio, north of the ferry crossing. 2 dance floors, 1 fast, 1 slow (for couples only), good.

Entertainment

São Luís *p517, map p517*

Cinema Colossal, Av Mcal Castelo Branco 92, São Francisco. **Passeio**, R Oswaldo Cruz 806.

Theatre **Teatro Artur Azevedo**, see page 519. **Teatro Viriato Correa**, Av Getúlio Vargas, Monte Castelo, T098-218 9019.

Festivals and events

Teresina *p513, map p514*

Feb/Mar Teresina is proud of its **Carnaval**, which is then followed by **Micarina**, a local carnival in Mar.

Jul/Aug Much music and dancing at the Bumba-Meu-Boi, a Teresina dance festival, **Festidanças**, and a convention of itinerant guitarists.

São Luís *p517, map p517*

24 Jun (São João) is the **Bumba-Meu-Boi**, see box, page 516. For several days before the festival, street bands parade, particularly in front of São João and São Benedito churches. There are dances somewhere in the city almost every night in Jun.

Aug **São Benedito**, at the Rosário church.

Oct Festival with dancing, at **Vila Palmeira** suburb (take bus of same name).

Alcântara *p519, map p518*

Jun **Festa do Divino**, at Pentecost (Whitsun). On 29 Jun is **São Pedro** saint day.

Aug São Benedito.

Shopping

Teresina *p513, map p514*

Crafts Teresina is an excellent and cheap source of northeastern *artesanato*, for which Piauí is renowned throughout Brazil. Panels of carved and painted hardwood, either representing stylized country scenes or images of religious significance, are a good buy, as are clay or wooden models of traditional rural characters. Many of these eccentric figures come from the region's rich fund of myths and legends. Hammocks, straw and basket ware are also made here, as well as leather and clothes.

Parnaíba and around *p514*

Crafts Artesanato de Parnaíba, R Dom Pedro II 1140 and Cooperativa Artesanal Mista de Parnaíba, R Alcenor Candeira, for local handicrafts.

São Luís *p517, map p517*

Crafts Ceprama, R de São Pantaleão 1232, Madre Deus, handicraft shops in an old colonial house.

Activities and tours

São Luís *p517, map p517*

Tour operators

Babaçu Viagens, Av Dom Pedro II 258, lojas A/B/C, T/F098-231 4747. Good.
Taguatur, R do Sol 141, loja 15, T098-232 0906, F232 1814.

Tours to Parque Nacional Lençois Marahenses

See also Ins and outs, page 520.
Ribamar at Ibama, Av Jaime Tavares 25, São Luís, T098-222 3066/3006 (also at Av Alexandre Mowa 25, Centro, T098-231 3010, F231 4332), is helpful for walks and horse rides along lesser routes.

Agencies running tours to the dunes include: **Baluz Turismo**, T098-222 6658; **Jaguarema**, T098-222 4764; **Maratur**, T098-221 1231. **Nasaturismo**, T098-235 4429; **Sunset Turismo** at the airport.

Tours often stop at the Mandacuru lighthouse for impressive views of the park. Organized bus tours cost US$22.50. To see the dunes by plane (single propeller), contact pilot Amirton, T098-225 2882, 1 hr, US$75. Tours with a flight cost US$200. This is a fabulous experience, with panoramic views of the dunes, recommended.

Transport

Teresina *p513, map p514*

Air Flights to **Fortaleza**, **Brasília**, **Rio de Janeiro**, **São Paulo**, **Goiânia** and **São Luís**.

Bus The bus trip to **Fortaleza** is scenic and takes 9 hrs (US$13.50). There are direct buses to **Belém** (13 hrs, US$23.40), **Recife** (16 hrs, US$27) and **São Luís** (7 hrs, US$12).

São Luís *p517, map p517*

Air Flights to **Belém**, **Fortaleza**, **Imperatriz**, **Parnaíba** and **Teresina**.

Airline offices TAM, T098-244 0461. Transbrasil, Praça João Lisboa 432, T098-232 1414. **Varig/Nordeste**, Av Dom Pedro II 267, T098-231 5066.

Bus To **Fortaleza**, US$270, 4 a day, 18 hrs. To **Belém**, 13 hrs, US$20, **Transbrasiliana** at 1900 and 2000 (no *leito*). Also to **Recife**, US$45, 25 hrs, all other major cities and local towns. To **Barreirinhas**, 8 hrs on an awful road US$12. Slightly more comfortable on a private bus, US$24.

Ferry These cross the bay daily between **Porto do Itaqui** and **Porto do Cujupe**. T098-222 8431 for times. US$3 foot passenger, US$15 car. Also launches to **Alcântara**, see page 519.

Trains 3 trains a week on the Carajás railway to **Parauapebas**, 13½ hrs, 890 km, leave São Luís 0800, Mon, Wed, Fri, return 0800, Tue, Thu, Sat (crowded, take your own food). For the station take 'Vila Nova' or 'Anjo da Guarda' bus.

Parque Nacional Lençóis Maranhenses *p519*

See also Ins and outs page 520.
Boat River boat up the Parnaíba delta, 8 hrs, US$6. Recommended. Private boat hire is also possible. A regular boat service plies the river between Tutóia and Paulino Neves/Rio Novo, and between there and Barreirinhas (both 4 hrs, US$10). Speedboats can be organized at Barreirinhas through Claúdio, T098-549 1183, or Sr Carlos, T098-349 1203, who also have a combi, US$150 for up to 15 people.

Bus **Parnaíba–Tutóia**, 4 hrs, US$6. **São Luís–Barreirinhas**: bus, 8 hrs on an awful road, US$12. Slightly more comfortable on a private bus, US$24 or on a tour.

Imperatriz *p521*

Air Flights to **Altamira**, **Araguaína**, **Belém**, **Brasília** and **São Luís**. Air taxi: Heringer, at airport, T098-722 3009.

Airline offices Penta, R Luís Domingues 1420, T098-723 1073. TAM, R Ceará 678, T098-722 3148. Varig/RioSul, R Luís Domingues 1471, T098-723 2155.

Bus Regular bus connections to **Belém** and **Brasília** along the BR-010, There is a slow, crowded bus service to **Teresina**. To get to **Marabá** on the Transamazônica, you can either take a **Transbrasiliana** bus direct, 7-10 hrs (starting on the Belém highway, the bus then turns west along a poorer road, passing finally through destroyed forest, new *fazendas* and unplanned cities), or a faster route, involving taking a ferry across the river in the early morning (0600-0700) to catch a pickup on the other side, takes about 5 hrs, but is more expensive. To get to the ferry across the river, go along R Luís Domingues, which runs parallel to Av Getúlio Vargas.

Car hire Interlocadora, Av Dorgival Pinheiro de Souza 990, T098-722 3050. Localiza, BR-010, Setor *rodoviária*, T098-721 4507, and at airport, T098-721 8611.

Train Trains to **Pará** and **Maranhão**.

Directory

Teresina *p513, map p514*
Banks Banks with ATMs: Banco do Brasil and Unibanco, Av Nossa Senhora de Fátima, in front of Caixa Econômica Federal. Itaú, in same avenue at P Center Shopping. Bradesco, Av Frei Serafim, at corner of 1 de Maio. Mirante Câmbio, Av Frei Serafim 2150, T086-223 3633. Alda Tur, R A de Abreu 1226.

Parnaíba and around *p514*
Banks Banco do Brasil, Praça da Graça 340. Bradesco, Av Pres Getúlio Vargas 403. **Medical services** Pró-Médica, Av Pres Vargas 799, T086-322 3645, 24-hr emergency ward. **Post office** Praça da Graça. **Telephone** Av Pres Getúlio Vargas 390.

São Luís *p517, map p517*
Banks Banco do Brasil, Praça Deodoro, for TCs and Visa ATMs. HSBC, off Praça João Lisboa, accepts MasterCard/Cirrus/Maestro. Agetur, R do Sol 33A. **Embassies and consulates** Denmark, Av Colares Moreira 444, Monumental Shopping, Sala 220, T098-235 7033. France, R Santo Antônio 259, T098-231 4459. Germany, Praça Gonçalves Dias 301, T098-232 7766. Italy, R do Genipapeiro, Jardim São Francisco, T098-227 0270. Spain, Praça Duque de Caxias 3, João Paulo, T098-223 2846. USA, Av Daniel de La Touche, Jardim Buriti, T098-248 1769. **Internet** HCG, R Paparaúbas 11, São Francisco. **Language courses** Senhora Amin Castro, T098-227 1527, for Portuguese lessons. Recommended. **Laundry** Nova China, R da Paz 518. **Libraries** Arquivo Público, R de Nazaré 218, rare documents on local history. **Medical services** Clínica São Marcelo, R do Passeio 546, English-speaking doctor. Hospital Monte Sinai, R Rio Branco 156, T098-232 3260, 24 hrs. **Post office** Praça João Lisboa 292. **Telephone** Embratel, Av Dom Pedro II 190.

Alcântara *p519, map p518*
Banks Banco do Estado do Maranhão, R Grande 76, changes US$ and TCs. **Post office** R Direita off Praça da Matriz. **Telephone** Telemar, R Grande, 0700-2200.

Imperatriz *p521*
Banks Banco do Brasil, Av Getúlio Vargas 1935. **Medical services** Santa Mônica, R Piauí, T098-722 3415, 24-hr emergency ward. **Telephone** R Rio Grande do Norte 740, a side street off Av Getúlio Vargas, near Hotel Posseidon, 0630-2400.

Carolina *p521*
Banks Banco do Brasil, A Mascarenhas 159. **Medical services** FNS, R Benedito Leite 57, T098-731 1271. **Telephone** Av E Barros, 0730-2230.

The Amazon

Footprint features

Introduction

The Amazon is a region of great geographical diversity. In the north, along the border with Venezuela, are the forests and savannahs of the Guiana Shield – the ancient heart of the South American continent, covered in a forest that grows like a giant filigree over white sand and recycles 99.9% of all its water and nutrients. Giant boulders the size of mountains break intermittently through the canopy.

In the east lie the expansive Amazon savannahs, which stretch across Roraima and southern Venezuela into the Rupununi of Guyana. The world's largest table-top mountains tower over them, their brows heavy with perpetual thunder cloud. South of here, the Amazon pours out into the ocean leaving an island of silt the size of Denmark in its wake and turning the Atlantic fresh for 100 miles offshore. The forest gets thicker and more vibrant and the mud on which it grows is as red and sticky as blood.

In the far west, the forest it is gentler and more fertile; filled with life around the magical Rio Javarí, where the trees seem permanently full of parrots, macaws and monkeys and where grey and pink dolphins surface from the deep, languid brown. To the south, the trees are broken by the squares of giant fields which cut into the green with greedy geometric order, and the Amazon exists as mere segments.

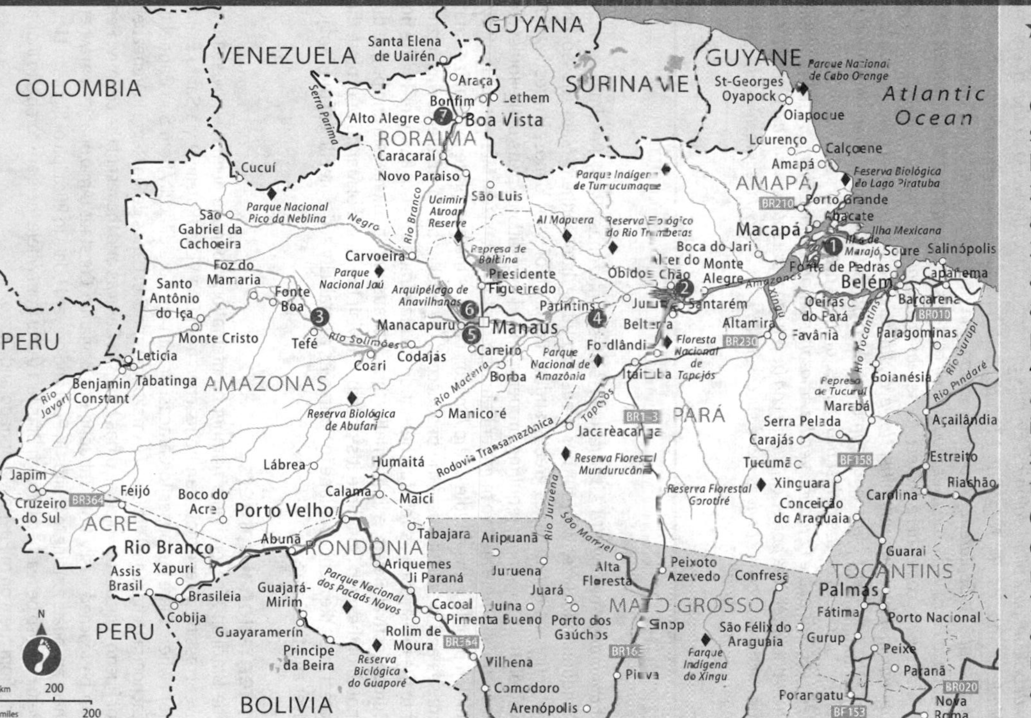

★ Don't miss...

1 Islands of Pará From Marajó, the size of Denmark and covered in forest and swamp, to Algodoal, a laid-back little beach getaway, pages 541 and 542.

2 Alter do Chão Blue rivers, pink dolphins and 10-km-long beaches, page 547.

3 Amazon Clipper Cruise the Rio Negro and see wildlife and river communities and visit the Analvilahans archipelago, pages 567 and 578.

4 Boi Bumba festival As colourful, frenetic and exciting as the Rio Carnaval, but on an island in the middle of the river, page 568.

5 Mamirauá Ecological Reserve One of the best wildlife spots, page 569.

6 Amazon Ecopark Lodge The most ecologically aware and most comfortable rainforest lodge close to Manaus, page 574.

7 Boa Vista A wild off-season carnival and a city surrounded by even wilder rainforests, waterfalls, table-top mountains and savannah, page 584.

The Amazon

Many people imagine the Amazon as a single river but, in reality, it is a huge network of rivers extending into nine countries. Before the Andes were formed, some 15 million years ago, the Amazon flowed west into the Pacific. But as the crash of continental plates pushed up the mountains, the river was cut off from its ocean and became a vast inland sea, hemmed in by the Guiana Shield to the east. Over millions of years this sea eroded the ancient sandstone shield, until it eventually burst through into the Atlantic. It left behind a vast filigree of veins which today make up the Amazon river system, populated by prehistoric air-breathing fish and unique freshwater species such as the Amazon stingray, whose closest relatives still live in the Pacific.

The Amazon contains a third of the world's fresh running water, whose colours range from vodka clear and tea black to coffee with milk and opaque aquamarines sprinkled with brilliant pink blind dolphins. Even its tributaries dwarf the world's other rivers: the Madeira, Tapajos, Rio Negro and Tocantins all have flows far greater than that of the Mississippi. At Santarem, 800 miles inland, the river spans a distance greater than London to Paris, while the river mouth itself contains an island the size of Denmark.

Many who come here expect to see animals, and common sightings include caiman, monkeys and dolphins. However, the forest offers plenty of cover for lowland animals, and most birds and primates live high in the canopy. Even in the small rainforest lodges on the tiniest tributaries, animals are hard to spot. Far more can be seen in Goiás or the Pantanal, yet the Amazon is unforgettable. There are few places in the world where the power of Nature can be felt more potently or where a way of life in tune with that power survives more successfully. ▸▸ *For history and environmental issues see Background page 717.*

Ins and outs

The Amazon belongs to six Brazilian states: Amazonas, Pará, Roraima, Amapá, Rondônia and Acre, with further areas extending into northern Mato Grosso and Tocantins. Its terrain varies greatly and, while much of what is most interesting lies well off the tourist trail, requiring properly funded expeditions, parts of the forest are easy to visit. There are two major entrance points to the Amazon: **Manaus**, a city of 1½ million people in the middle of the Amazon basin, is the best place to organize safari cruises and lodges. It offers the best access (by boat or air) to smaller towns further into the forest, such as Tefé for the wonderful **Mamirauá** lodge or Parintins for the **Boi Bumba** festival. **Belém**, a little smaller than Manaus, was a colonial slaving port at the mouth of the river. From here it's possible to visit the island of Marajó or explore the forest and take a boat or plane to Santarém, a small city at the meeting of the Tapajós river and the Amazon.

International borders

The Brazilian Amazon has a number of international borders permitting overland or river crossings. **Venezuela** can be reached from Boa Vista (Roraima) via Santa Elena, from where there are buses to Caracas; or with far more difficulty from São Gabriel da Cachoeira (Amazonas) via Cucuí (Amazonas) and San Carlos de Río Negro in Venezuela for Puerto Ayacucho, which also has buses to Caracas and the rest of the country. **Peru** can be reached easily from Tabatinga or Benjamin Constant (Amazonas), from where there are boats running to Iquitos in Peru and onward boats to Pucallpa or flights to Lima. Peru can also be reached through Brasiléia (Acre) from where there are combis to Iñapari and from there on to Puerto Maldonado and Cuzco.

“”...colours range from vodka clear and tea black to coffee with milk and opaque aquamarine sprinkled with brilliant pink blind dolphins.

Bolivia is easily reached from Guajará-Mirim (Rondônia); from where launches cross the river to Guayará Merin in Bolivia for buses to Rurrenabaque and La Paz.

Colombia is easily reached from Tabatinga (Amazonas) which is twinned and contiguous with the Colombian city of Leticia, from where there are flights to Bogotá.

French Guiana (Guyane) can be reached from Macapá (Amapá) by bus to Oiapoque, from where there are onward combis to St-Georges Oyapock (French Guiana), onward to Cayenne and all the way through Suriname to Guyana.

Guyana is easily reached by bus from Boa Vista via Bonfim (Roraima) to Lethem (Guyana), from where there are buses to Georgetown.

Getting around the Amazon

By road Aside from routes to Belém from the Atlantic Coast and from Tocantins, bus routes are limited to the following. **Amazonas/Roraima**: Manaus–Boa Vista (via Presidente Figuieredo), paved. **Roraima:** Boa Vista–Venezuela, paved. Boa Vista–Guyana, paved. **Amazonas**: São Gabriel da Cachoeira–Cucuí, paved and dirt. **Amapá**: Macapá–Oiapoque (from where there is boat and road access to French Guiana), dirt. **Pará**: Santarém–Cuiabá (in the Pantanal) is being improved and buses will be running along it by 2007. It will run through Pará into Mato Grosso and there are changes at Itauba for Alta Floresta and the Rio Cristalino (see page), paved and dirt. **Amazonas/ Rondônia**: Humaitá–Porto Velho. **Rondônia/Acre**: Porto Velho–Rio Branco with onward buses to Cruzeiro do Sul and Peru, weather permitting. There are services to Guajará Mirim along a small branch road, paved and dirt. **Rodônia/Mato Grosso**: Porto Velho– Cuiabá and onwards to the rest of Brazil, paved. There are dirt roads Manaus–Porto Velho, and Santarém–Porto Velho, but these are currently overgrown and impassable.

By plane There are reasonable flight networks within the Amazon. **Rico** www.voerico.com.br, fly between all the Amazon state capitals (often via Manaus) except Boa Vista and Macapá. They also fly Manaus–Tabatinga via Tefé (for Mamirauá), Manaus–Parintins (for the Boi Bumba) and Manaus–Santarém. **Trip**, www.airtrip.com.br, fly Manaus–São Gabriel da Cachoeira via Barcelos, and Manaus–Tabatinga via Tefé. They also link Manaus with Brasílla, Cuiabá and Campo Grande. **Meta,** www.voemeta.com, fly Belém–Boa Vista, Belém–Georgetown (Guyana) via Paramaribo (Suriname), Belém–Santarém, Boa Vista–Georgetown and Boa Vista–Paramaribo. **TAM,** www.tam.com.br, fly Manaus–Boa Vista and Belém–Macapá and to Porto Velho and Rio Branco. **GOL,** www.voegol.com.br, fly Belém–Santarém and Manaus–Boa Vista.

Flight schedules are constantly changing and routes frequently close and re-open. Check websites for the latest details and for prices.

By boat River boats are the buses of the Amazon and serve an extensive network, connecting both major and minor settlements. You won't see a great deal from the deck, especially if travelling downstream, as the boats stay in the middle of the river to catch the current. Going upstream, you will see little but an endless line of trees broken by the occasional village. However, the atmosphere on board is lively. Food is served, usually consisting of meat, beans and rice (which is brown as it is cooked in river water) and there is often a bar serving drinks and snacks. The size and quality of the boats varies greatly. The best boats ply the busiest routes: Manaus–Santarém–Belém and Manaus–Tabatinga. Overcrowding can be a problem.

The cheapest way to travel is **hammock class**, out in the open on the deck. Be sure to take water, a cable and padlock for your bags, a jumper (nights on the water can be cool) a fat novel and, most importantly, a hammock with two pieces of rope (each about 1 m long) to string it up across the beams. You may also want to buy a mosquito net for your hammock (*mosquiteiro para rede*). Arrive early to get a good spot. Some boats also have air-conditioned berths and **cabins** and, for a higher price, **suites** with attached bathroom.

Many boats ply the following routes: Manaus–Belém via Parintins, Óbidos and Santarém (four days); Manaus–São Gabriel da Cachoeira via Barcelos and Santa Isabel (six days); Manaus–Porto Velho via Manicoré and Humaitá (four days); Manaus–Tefé (36 hours); Manaus–Parintins (20 hours); Manaus–Tabatinga (six days); Belém–Santarém (two to three days); Belém–Macapá (36 hours); Macapá–Manaus (seven to 10 days). For more details see page 579.

Health

There is a danger of **malaria** in Amazônia, especially on the brown-water rivers. Mosquito larvae do not breed well in the black-water rivers as they are too acidic. Mosquito nets are not required when in motion as boats travel away from the banks and are too fast for mosquitoes to settle. However, nets and repellent can be useful for night stops. Wear long, loose trousers (tight ones are easy to bite through) and a baggy shirt at night and put repellent around shirt collars, cuffs and the tops of socks. **Johnsons Off** is an effective brand and is available in pharmacies throughout Brazil. Deet is not recommended as it melts plastic and is no more effective.

A **yellow fever** inoculation is strongly advised. It is compulsory to have a certificate when crossing borders and those without one will have to get inoculated and wait 10 days before travelling. Other common infections in the Amazon are **cutaneous larva migrans** (a spot that appears to move), which is easily treated with **Thiabendazole**, and **tropical ulcers**, caught by scratching mosquito bites, which then get dirty and become infected. ⏩ *See also Essentials, page 61.*

Amazon food

The Amazon has a distinctive range of dishes that make use of the thousands of fruits and vegetables and the abundant unique fish. Must-tries include *tacacá*, a soup made with jambo leaves, which numbs the tongue as and stimulates energy. The best fish are pacu and tambaqui, both types of vegetarian piranha; the carnivorous ones can be eaten too. Pirarucu, one of the world's largest freshwater fish, is delicious; however, due to overfishing it is in danger of becoming extinct. Specialities of Pará state include duck, often served as *pato no tucupi*, in a yellow soup made from the juice of the root of the manioc (*tucupí*) and served with jambo. *Maniçoba* is made with the poisonous leaves of the bitter manioc (*cassava*), simmered for eight days to get rid of the cyanide. *Caldeirada* is a fish and vegetable soup, served with *pirão* (manioc puree), and is a speciality of Amazonas. There is also an enormous variety of tropical and jungle fruits, many unique to the region. Try them fresh, or in ice creams or juices. The best include tapereba, cupuaçu, cajú (the fruit of the cashew nut), cacão (the fruit of the cocoa bean) and camu camu, which has the highest vitamin C content of any fruit in the world. Avoid food from street vendors, except those selling *tacacá* at the Boi Bumba.

Banks

There are plenty of ATM facilities in all the Amazon's main towns and whenever there is a **Bradesco** or **Banco 24 horas**. Small amounts of US dollars cash can usually be exchanged away from banks at a poor rate, but are not accepted as local currency. The rate of exchange for exchange traveller's cheques is appalling.

The Amazon and the theory of evolution

While the Spanish and Portuguese came to the Amazon to plunder, pillage and enslave, the Europeans who followed them in the 18th and 19th centuries were more interested in beetles and botany than gold. Among the first was the Frenchman Charles Marie de la Condamine, who came to the Andes in the mid-1700s to ascertain whether the Earth was orange shaped or a perfect sphere. He narrowly escaped being stoned by a superstitious mob in Cuenca, Ecuador, and fled to Cayenne. In doing so he was obliged to cross the Amazon, producing the first accurate map of the basin along the way and bringing rubber back to Europe. La Condamine inspired other Enlightenment scientists to follow him. The greatest was Alexander von Humboldt, today known for the Humboldt Current (which he did not discover) and the Humboldt River (which he never saw), but who, in his time, was considered the pre-eminent scientist in Europe. During his stay on the upper Rio Negro, this great German collected some 12,000 specimens and survived shocks by electric eels, *curaré* poison and bathing with piranhas. He captured and dissected a 7-m caiman and established the region as the best in the world for the study of natural sciences. The English followed him: Henry Bates, Richard Spruce and, in 1848, Alfred Russel Wallace, who wrote: "I'd be an Indian here, and live content, to fish and hunt, and paddle my canoe, and see my children grow, like wild young fawns, In health of body and peace of mind, rich without wealth, and happy without gold! "

The seemingly infinite variety of plants and animals in the Amazon caused Wallace to reflect on how all this variety had come about: so alike in design yet so changeable in detail? "Places not more than fifty or a hundred miles apart have species of insects and birds at the one which are not found at the other. There must be some boundary which determines the range of each species, some external peculiarity to mark the line which each one does not pass."

Charles Darwin had the same thought two years earlier after his return from Brazil and while reading an essay by Thomas Malthus on population. In his essay the economist argued that the realization of a happy society will always be hindered by its tendencies to expand more quickly than its means of subsistence. If this is true of animals, thought Darwin, then they must compete to survive and Nature must act as a selective force, killing off the weak, and species must evolve each from another through this process. Darwin was terrified by the implications of his thought and did not commit it to paper for six years, then sealing it and handing it to his wife with instructions to publish it after his death.

Alfred Russel Wallace was younger and less timid. While in a high fever on a field trip in Indonesia he was pondering over the thoughts that had haunted him since his days on the Amazon, and he too recalled the same essays by Malthus. The same thought which had struck Darwin, flashed into his own mind: "I saw at once that the ever- present variability of all living things would furnish the material from which, by the mere weeding out of those less adapted to the actual conditions, the fittest alone would survive the race." Wallace wrote to Darwin who was, at that time, the most famous natural scientist in Britain, explaining his theory and asking for his advice. Darwin's hand was forced and, after papers written by both scientists were presented at the Linnean Society on the same day, the theory of evolution was born.

Amapá and Pará

Sometimes called Brazilian Guyana, the isolated border state of Amapá was once exploited for its natural resources and suffered from heavy deforestation. However, efforts are now being made towards sustainable development. Located near the French territory of Guyane, with its cheap air links to Paris, it is another good port of entry into northern Brazil. Tourist infrastructure outside the provincial riverside capital of Macapá is negligible. The state is a quarter the size of France, but has a population of just under half a million.

Pará is just across the river from Amapá – a distance that would span Switzerland. The state capital, Belém, has gone from dangerous and down at heel in the 1990s to a refurbished, attractive colonial city in the new millennium. The state itself is barely aware of the existence of tourists. Although there are many beautiful natural sights – such as the vast river island of Marajó in the Amazon delta and the Amazônia National Park on the River Tapajós – infrastructure is poor, with no jungle lodges at all in the extensive rainforests. And while areas north of the Amazon have been afforded at least nominal protection since 2006, in the south of the state rapid deforestation is making space for vast soya plantations. Santarém, a quiet little town at the junction of the Tapajós and Amazon rivers, is the world's largest soya-export port. Thankfully ecotourism is gradually catching on here: a few tour companies offer trips to the river beaches at Alter do Chao and the failed rubber plantation towns of Belterra and Fordlândia – set up by Henry Ford in the early 20th century. Monte Alegre, whose caves have revealed evidence of a significant pre- Colombian Amazon culture, are a day's boat ride away upstream. Travel in Para takes time (as it does anywhere in the Amazon) and the more isolated parts of the state are often linked only by boat and air. Even when there are roads, rain and forest encroachment makes even asphalted areas impassable. ›› *For Sleeping, Eating and other listings, see pages 549-558.*

Macapá ›› *pp549-558.*

→ *Phone code: 096. Colour map 1, A5. Population: 284,000.*

The capital of Amapá is a pleasant city on the banks of the northern channel of the Amazon delta. It has an impressive fortress as well as a monument to the equator, which divides the city. There is a museum detailing the research being carried out in the rainforest and at nearby Curiaú, a village originally formed by escaped slaves.

The town was founded around the first Forte de São José do Macapá, built in 1688. In 1751 more settlers from the Azores arrived to defend the region from Dutch, English and French invasions and the *aldea* became a *vila* in 1758. Many slaves were later brought from Africa for the construction of the fort.

Ins and outs

Getting there The **airport** ⓘ *R Hildemar Maia, 4 km from centre, T096-223 2323*, receives flights from Brazil's main cities, and has international connections with Cayenne (Guyane) and Paramaribo (Suriname). The centre is a short taxi ride.

Buses arrive at the new **rodoviária** ⓘ *on the BR-156, 3 km north of Macapá*. Buses from Oiapoque pass through the city centre after a long and uncomfortable journey over mainly unsurfaced roads. This journey can take even longer during the rainy season (January to May). Boats from Belém and Santarém arrive at nearby Porto Santana, which is linked to Macapá by bus or taxi. ›› *See also Transport, page 555.*

Getting around There is an air-taxi service to some towns, however, most are linked by the trucks, buses and community minibuses, which leave from the new *rodoviária*. Buses to other parts of the city leave from a bus station near the fort. The centre and the waterfront are easily explored on foot.

Tourist information Detur ⓘ *Av Raimundo Álvares da Costa 18, Centro, CEP 68906-020, T096-223 0627, www.detur.ap.gov.br*, also has a branch at the airport. **Ibama** ⓘ *R Hamilton Silva 1570, Santa Rita, CEP 68906-440, Macapá, T/F096-214 1100.*

Sights

Each brick of the **Fortaleza de São José do Macapá**, built between 1764 and 1782, was brought from Portugal as ballast. Fifty iron cannon still remain and there is a museum. The *fortaleza* is used for concerts, exhibitions and colourful festivities on the anniversary of the city's founding on 4 February. **São José cathedral**, inaugurated by the Jesuits in 1761, is the city's oldest landmark. The **Centro de Cultura Negra** ⓘ *R General Rondon*, has a museum and holds frequent events. The **Museu do Desenvolvimento Sustentável** ⓘ *Av Feliciano Coelho 1509, Tue-Fri 0830-1200, 1500-1800, Mon and Sat 1500-1800*, exhibits research on sustainable development and traditional community life in Amazônia. The museum shop sells arts and crafts.

The riverfront has been landscaped with trees, lawns and paths and is a very pleasant place for an evening stroll. The **Complexo Beira Rio** has food and drink kiosks and a nice lively atmosphere. The recently rebuilt pier (*trapiche*) is a lovely spot for savouring the cool of the evening breeze, or watching the sun rise over the Amazon.

There is a monument to the equator, **Marco Zero** (take Fazendinha bus from Avenida Mendonça Furtado). The equator also divides the enormous football stadium nearby, aptly named O Zerão. The Sambódromo stadium is located nearby. South of here are the **botanical gardens** ⓘ *Rodovia Juscelino Kubitschek, Km 12, Tue-Sun 0900-1700.*

Excursions from Macapá

Some 16 km from the centre, **Fazendinha** is a popular local beach, which is very busy on Sunday and has many seafood restaurants. **Curiaú**, 8 km from Macapá, is inhabited by the descendants of African slaves, who have maintained many of the customs of their ancestors. They are analogous to the Bush Negroes of Suriname, making the village the only one of its kind in Brazil. It is popular at weekends for dancing and swimming. The surrounding area is an environmental reserve with many water buffalo.

North of Macapá » pp549-558.

Only the first section of the road north to the Guyane border (BR-156) is paved. Although precarious in places, it is open throughout the year with buses and pickups operating even in the wet season. At all times, however, take food and water for the journey as services are scarce. Petrol and diesel are available along the road, but drivers should take extra fuel from Macapá.

North of Macapá the road divides at **Porto Grande**, and a branch heads northwest to Serra do Navio where manganese extraction has now ended (**Hotel Serra do Navio** and several bars and restaurants). The BR-156 continues north, passing the turnings for two jungle hotels. The paved road goes as far as **Ferreira Gomes** on the shores of the Rio Araguari. Further on is **Amapá**, formerly the territorial capital and location of a Second World War American airbase. There are a few hotels. Beyond Amapá is **Calçoene**, with a government-owned hotel that serves expensive food in an adjoining canteen; very cheap sleeping space is also advertised in a café on the Oiapoque road. North of Calçoene a road branches west to **Lourenço**, whose goldfields still produce even after decades of prospecting. The main road continues north across the Rio Caciporé and on to the border with French Guyane at **Oiapoque**, on the river of the same name. About 7 km west is Clevelândia do Norte, a military outpost and the end of the road in Brazil.

Oiapoque → *Colour map 1, A5. Population: 13,000.*

This is a ramshackle little gold-mining town with dirt streets lined with little guest-houses, spit-and-sawdust bars and shops buying the precious metal by the gram. It lies 90 km inland from **Cabo Orange**, Brazil's northernmost point on the Atlantic Coast and the site of one of its wildest and remotest national parks. Access to the park is very difficult although guides can sometimes be arranged through the baotmen on the river docks in Oiapoque.

Oiapoque town has its share of contraband, illegal migration and drug trafficking and can be a little rough; visitors should be cautious, especially late at night. With the building of the road between St-Georges Oyapock and Cayenne, the town has become a popular spot for French Guianan weekenders, most of them single men and in search of more than a drink. The **Cachoeira Grande Roche** rapids can be visited, upstream along the Oiapoque river, where it is possible to swim, US$30 by motor boat. The **Associação dos Povos Indígenas de Oiapoque**, in front of the Banco do Brasil, gives information about the indigenous peoples that live in the area, and the Uaçá Indian Reserve.

Ins and outs There are plenty of cheap hotels, but none of them are well maintained. There are frequent launches from Guyane across the river (US$5, 10 minutes) and at least two buses a day from Macapá. A bridge is being built and should be complete in 2007, and there are plans to asphalt the road all the way to Amapá. (It is currently asphalted as far as Cayenne.) The road construction has led to significant environmental damage with much deforestation along the Brazilian side of the road in Amapá, and Brazilian *garimpeiros* and hunters illegally flooding into Guyane have been causing havoc in pristine forests. Combis to Cayenne leave from St-Georges Oyapock before lunch so be ready by 1000. For further details, see the *South American Handbook*.

Belém

» pp549-558.

→ *Phone code: 091. Colour map 1, A6. Population: 1.3 million.*

Belém do Pará is the great port of the Amazon. The city has much of cultural interest, a fascinating market, and is the starting point for trips along the river. With mean temperatures of 26°C, it is hot, but frequent showers freshen the streets. The city has its share of crime and is prone to gang violence. Take sensible precautions, especially at night.

Ins and outs

Getting there The **Val-de-Cans airport** ⓘ *12 km from the city, T091-210 6272*, receives international flights from Cayenne, Miama and Paramaribo, as well as domestic flights from all major cities in Brazil. Buses take 40 minutes to the centre and charge US$0.50. Taxis cost US$10-15 (ordinary taxis are cheaper than co-operatives, buy ticket in advance in Departures side of airport). There are ATMs in the terminal.

There are road connections from São Luís and the northeastern coast as well as a three-day bus link from São Paulo via Brasília. Interstate buses arrive at the **rodoviária** ⓘ *end of Av Gov José Malcher, 3 km from the centre*. There are showers (US$0.10), a good snack bar, and agencies with information and tickets for riverboats. Buses to the centre cost US$0.50; taxis charge US$5-7. At the *rodoviária* you are given a ticket with the taxi's number on it; threaten to go to the authorities if the driver tries to overcharge.

Boats arrive at the port from Macapá, Manaus and Santarém as well as other parts of the Amazon region and delta. » *See also Transport, page 556.*

Getting around The city centre is easily explored on foot. City buses and taxis run to all the sites of interest and to transport hubs away from the centre.

Belém orientation

 Tourist information Belemtur ⓘ *Av Gov José Malcher 592, T091-3242 0900, belemtur@cinbesa.com.br*, also at the airport. **Paratur** ⓘ *Praça Waldemar Henrique on the waterfront, T091-3223 2130, F3223 6198*, by the handicraft shop. Helpful, many languages spoken, can provide a good map of Belém in many languages (some references are incorrect). A town guidebook costs US$2.75. **Ibama** ⓘ *Av Conselheiro Furtado 1303, Batista Campos, CEP 66035-350, T091-3241 2621, F3223 1299.*

Background

Established in 1616 because of its strategic position, Belém soon became the centre for slaving expeditions into the Amazon basin. The Portuguese of Pará, together with those of Maranhão, treated the *indígena* abominably. Their isolation from the longer-established colonies allowed both places to become relatively lawless. In 1655, the Jesuits, under Antônio Vieira, attempted to lessen the abuses, while enticing the *indígena* to descend to the *aldeias* around Belém. This unfortunately led to further misery when smallpox spread from the south, striking the Pará *aldeias* in the 1660s.

Soon after Brazil's Independence, the Revolta da Cabanagem, a rebellion by the poor blacks, *indígena* and mixed-race *cabanos*, was led against the Portuguese-born class that dominated the economy. The movement came to an end in 1840 when the *cabanos* finally surrendered, but the worst years of violence were 1835-1836. Some estimates say 30,000 were killed. The state's strategic location once again became important during the Second World War, when Belém was used as an airbase by the Americans to hunt German submarines in the Atlantic.

Sights

Belém used to be called the 'city of mango trees' and there are still many such trees remaining. There are some fine squares and restored historic buildings set along broad avenues. The largest square is the **Praça da República**, where there are free afternoon concerts; the main business and shopping area is along the wide Avenida Presidente Vargas, leading to the river, and the narrow streets which parallel it.

The recently restored neoclassical **Teatro da Paz** ⓘ *Tue-Fri 0900-1800, tours US$1.50*, (1874), is one of the largest theatres in the country and worth a visit. It stages performances by national and international stars, and offers free concerts and shows.

West of here, at the **Estação das Docas**, the abandoned warehouses of the port have been restored into a complex with an air-conditioned interior and restaurants outside. The Terminal Marítimo has an office of **Valverde Tours**, which offers sunset and night cruises. The Boulevard das Artes contains the **Cervejaria Amazon** (brewery), with good beer and simple meals, an archaeological museum and arts and crafts shops. The Boulevard de Gastronomia has smart restaurants and the five-star **Cairu** ice cream parlour (try *açaí* or the *pavê de capuaçu*). In the Boulevard das Feiras there are trade fairs. Live music is transported between the pavilions on a moving stage. Also in the complex are ATMs, internet café, phones and good toilets.

Heading south, the 17th-century **Mercês church** (1640) is the oldest in Belém. It forms part of an architectural group known as the Mercedário, the rest of which was heavily damaged by fire in 1978 and has now been restored.

Near the church, the Belém market, known as **Ver-o-Peso**, was the Portuguese Posto Fiscal, where goods were weighed to gauge taxes due, hence the name: 'see the weight'. It now has lots of gift shops selling charms for the local African-derived religion, *umbanda*, and interesting medicinal herb and natural perfume stalls. You can see giant river fish being unloaded around 0530, with frenzied wholesale buying for the next hour. A new dock for the fishing boats has been built just upriver from the market. The whole area swarms with people, including many armed thieves and pickpockets.

Around Praça Dom Pedro II is a cluster of interesting buildings. The **Palácio Lauro Sodré** and **Museu do Estado do Pará** ⓘ *Praça Dom Pedro II, T091-3225 3853, Mon-Fri 0900-1800, Sat 1000-1800*, is a gracious 18th-century Italianate building. It contains

Brazil's largest framed painting, *The Conquest of Amazônia*, by Domenico de Angelis. The building was the work of the Italian architect Antônio Landi, who also designed the cathedral, and was the administrative seat of the colonial government. During the rubber boom many new decorative features were added. Also on Praça Dom Pedro II is the **Palácio Antônio Lemos**, which houses the **Museu de Arte de Belém** as well as the **Prefeitura** ⓘ *Tue-Fri 0900-1200, 1400-1800, Sat and Sun 0900-1300*. It was originally built as the Palácio Municipal between 1868 and 1883, and is a fine example of the Imperial neoclassical style. In the downstairs rooms there are old views of Belém; upstairs, the historic rooms, beautifully renovated, contain furniture and paintings, which are all well explained.

The **cathedral** ⓘ *Praça Frei Caetano Brandão, Mon 1500-1800, Tue-Fri 0800-1100, 1530-1800*, (1748), is also neoclassical, and contains several remarkable paintings. Directly opposite is the restored 18th-century **Santo Aleixandre church**, which is noted for its woodcarving.

Also in the old town is the **Forte do Castelo** ⓘ *Praça Frei Caetano Brandão 117, T091-223 0041, daily 0800-2300*, which was rebuilt in 1878. The fort overlooks the confluence of the Rio Guamá and the Baía do Guajará and was where the Portuguese first set up their defences. There is a good restaurant, the **Boteco Onze**, where you can watch the sunset (entry US$1, drinks and *salgadinhos* served on the ramparts from 1800). At the square on the waterfront below the fort, the açaí berries are landed

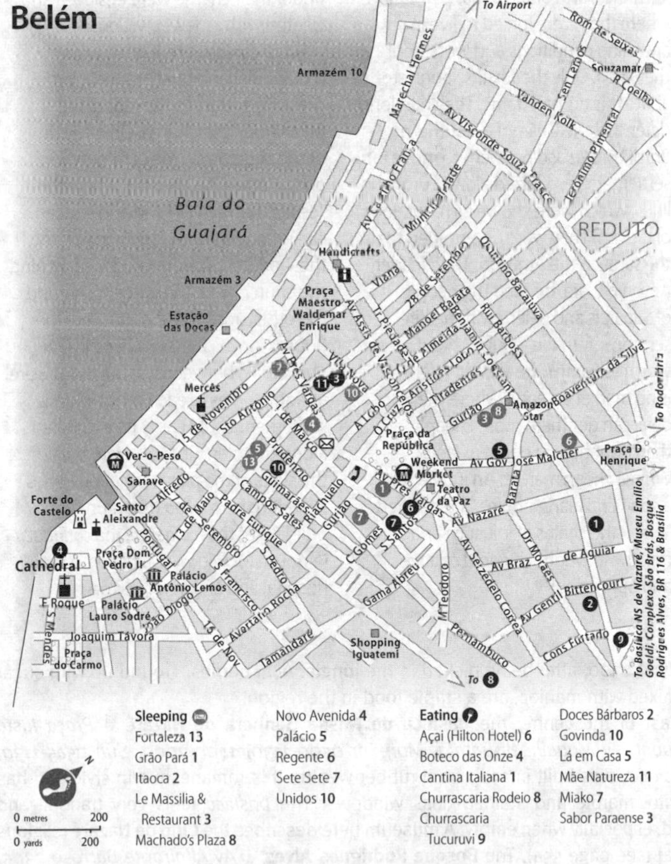

The Jesuits and the slave trade

Cristobal de Acuna, a Jesuit who visited the Amazon in the 1620s, describes an incredible density of villages along the lower Amazon. He writes of the happy and abundant life of the Omagua people, the largest of the tribal nations, who lived in large towns with handsome houses, fired pottery as fine as any in Europe, baked bread, wove cotton and farmed turtles. Within 100 years of his visit they and all the *indígena* of the lower Amazon nations were killed and their cultures and achievements lost for ever.

The were lost to 'Red Gold', the little-known Amazon slave trade. The *indígena* were rounded up in droves and brought to São Luís and Belém to farm the burgeoning sugar plantations where they were forced to live in appalling conditions and work until they died. Only the Jesuits sought to abate this human traffic. They had long defended the Guaraní in southern Brazil by persuading them to move into settlements organized along European lines, which were known as reductions or *aldeias*. They were determined to do the same in the Amazon. Their leader, Antônio Viera, berated the people of São Luís and Belém with hellfire sermons: "What is a human soul worth to Satan?" he asked; "There is no market on earth where the devil can get them more cheaply than right here in our own land… What a cheap market! An Indian for a soul! Christians, nobles," he begged "break the chains of injustice and free those whom you hold captive and oppressed!"

Viera was successful... for a while. The captive *indígena* would be sent to Jesuit reductions from where they would be on loan to plantation owners for six months of the year. The *indígena* were certainly treated with less cruelty by the Jesuits. However, the Order were, in effect, equally responsible for the loss of indigenous life and culture. The reductions were breeding grounds for European disease and the *indígena* were forced to abandon completely their religious and social practices. And when the Order was forced to leave Iberian America after a campaign against them by Portugal's Marquis de Pombal, the *indígena* who had been under their charge were enslaved and treated with renewed viciousness.

A typical Jesuit reduction was rectangular and built around a large praça de armas. To the rear of the plaza stood the church. On one side of the church was the cemetery and on the other the claustro, where the Jesuits themselves lived and studied. Near this were the workshops in which the works of art were produced. Behind the church were the gardens. Around the other sides of the plaza were the houses in which the *indígena* lived. The streets between the buildings were at right angles to each other and the settlement could easily be expanded along this plan. Chapels were built on the sides of the plaza. Other buildings included the *cabildo* (the municipal building of the *indígena*), the *cotiguazu* (a house for widows), a prison, a hospital and an inn for visitors.

nightly at 2300, after being picked in the jungle. Açaí berries, ground up with sugar and mixed with manioc, are a staple food in the region.

East of the centre, the **Basílica de Nossa Senhora de Nazaré** ⓘ *Praça Justo Chermont, Av Magalhães Barata, Mon-Sat 0500-1130, 1400-2000, Sun 0545-1130, 1430-2000,* was built in 1909 from rubber wealth. It is romanesque in style and has beautiful marble and stained-glass windows. The *basílica* feels very tranquil and sacred, especially when empty. A museum here describes the **Círio de Nazaré** religious festival (see page 554). The **Bosque Rodrigues Alves** ⓘ *Av Almirante Barroso 2305,*

T091-226 2308, Tue-Sun 0800-1700, is a 16-ha public garden (really a preserved area of original flora), with a small animal collection. To get there, take the yellow bus marked 'Souza' or 'Cidade Nova' (any number), 30 minutes from Ver-o- Peso market, or from the cathedral. The **Museu Emílio Goeldi** ⓘ *Av Magalhães Barata 376, Tue-Thu 0900- 1200, 1400-1700, Fri 0900-1200, Sat and Sun 0900-1700, US$1*, takes up an entire city block and consists of the museum proper (with a fine collection of indigenous Marajó pottery and an excellent exhibition of Mebengokre tribal lifestyle), a zoological garden (including manatees) and botanical exhibits including Victoria Régia lilies. Buses run from the cathedral.

The **Murucutu** ruins, an old Jesuit foundation, are reached by the Ceará bus from Praça da República; entry is via an unmarked door on the right of the Ceará bus station.

Around Belém » pp549-558.

A passenger ferry (*foca*) to the small town of **Barcarena** ⓘ *daily departures from Ver-o-Peso, but best Tue-Fri, US$1*, makes an interesting half-day trip. A return trip on the ferry from Ver-o-Peso to Icaoraci provides a good view of the river. Several restaurants here serve excellent seafood; you can eat shrimp and drink coconut water and appreciate the breeze coming off the river. **Icaoraci** is 20 km east of the city and is well known as a centre of ceramic production. The pottery is in Marajóara and Tapajonica style. Artisans are friendly and helpful, will accept commissions and send purchases overseas. A bus from Avenida Presidente Vargas in Belém runs to Icoaraci.

The nearest beach to Belém is at **Outeiro** (35 km), on an island near Icoaraci. It takes about an hour by bus and ferry (the bus may be caught near the **Maloca**, an indigenous-style hut near the docks that serves as a nightclub). A bus from Icoaraci to Outeiro takes 30 minutes.

Further north is the island of **Mosqueiro** (86 km), accessible by bridge and an excellent highway, with many beautiful sandy beaches and jungle inland. It is popular in July and at weekends, when traffic can be heavy and the beaches get crowded and polluted. Buses from Belém to Mosqueiro run every hour from the *rodoviária* (US$1.50, 80 minutes). There is also a ferry from Porto do Sal, on the street between Forte do Castelo and the cathedral. It takes about two hours. There are many hotels and weekend villas in the villages of Mosqueiro and Vila, which are recommended, but these may be full during peak times.

Ilha de Marajó → Colour map 1, A5.

This is the world's largest river island (although some claim the Bananal is larger), which is partly flooded in the rainy season from January to June. It provides a suitable habitat for large numbers of water buffalo, which are said to have swum ashore after a shipwreck. Many are now farmed; try the cheese and milk. Marajó is also home to numerous bird species, including thousands of roseate spoonbills, and black caiman, river turtles and other wildlife. The island was the site of the pre-Columbian Marajóaras culture, celebrated for its ceramics. It gets very busy in the July holiday season.

The capital of the island is **Soure**. There are fine beaches: **Araruna**, 2 km away; take supplies and supplement with coconuts and crabs, beautiful walks along the shore; **do Pesqueiro**, 13 km away (bus from Praça da Matriz at 1030, returns 1600, food available at Maloca, a deserted beach); and **Caju-Una** (15 km).

At the entrance to the Marajó archipelago is the little town of **Ponta de Pedras**, which has a few colonial buildings and a fine beach. There are boats every Tuesday, Thursday and Saturday at 0800 from Arapari island port, 9 km from Belém. In Ponta de Pedras is **Hotel Ponta de Pedras** (D) which serves good meals. Bicycles can be hired at US$1 per hour to explore beaches and the interior of the island. Fishing boats make the eight-hour trip to **Cachoeira do Arari** (one hotel, D), where there is a

The legend of the rubber tree

Once upon a time, an Amazonian *indígena* called Maitá was unfairly accused of theft. As a punishment, the chief of his tribe curelly condemned him to a very peculiar task: to empty a small lake by using a wicker basket. The work was of course extremely unproductive, as the water always flowed through the holes of the basket. Maitá soon realized that he would have to work for the rest of his life and still never empty the lake.

Knowing that Maitá was innocent, a forest fairy approached the poor *indígena* and asked him to follow her. They walked in the jungle until they reached a very large tree. There, she showed Maitá how to make some cuts in the tree and, as he did, he noticed that a milk-like liquid started to flow. The tree was a rubber tree and the liquid was natural latex. Then the fairy told him to spread the sticky liquid over the basket and wait for a while. As the liquid started to dry, he realized that a thin layer of a water resistant material (rubber) was covering all the holes. On returning to the lake, he was very pleased to see that he had no problem in scooping out large amounts of the lake's water. He gratefully thanked the fairy and finished his task in a few days.

As in all good fairy tales, there was a happy ending. The chief discovered he had made a mistake and apologized to Maitá on his return to the tribe. A big party was held to celebrate Maitá's return and, most of all, an important secret had been revealed: the secret of the rubber tree.

fascinating **Marajó museum**. A 10-hour boat trip from Ponta de Pedras goes to the **Arari lake** where there are two villages: **Jenipapo** and **Santa Cruz**, which is less primitive, but less interesting; a hammock and a mosquito net are essential.

Ins and outs A ferry from Belém sails at weekends (four hours, US$5). Small craft await passengers from the **Enasa** boats, for **Salvaterra** village (good beaches, bars and seafood), US$12, 10 minutes. There is a ferry to Porto do Cámara (three hours). Then take a bus to Salvaterra and a ferry to Soure. There is a taxi-plane service to Soure. The **Banco do Brasil** has an ATM. Changing money is only possible at very poor rates. Take plenty of insect repellent.

Other islands around Belém

The **Ilha do Mosqueiro**, close to Belém, is the city's weekend escape and is particularly crowded at Christmas and during Carnaval. The beaches are nothing special and there is a handful of hotels in the port town. More remote are the **Ilha da Mexiana** in the Marajó archipelago, and the broad beaches of the **Ilha de Maiandeua**, a three-hour bus and boat journey on the Atlantic Coast. The island is a semi-protected area at the junction of the sea, the Amazon and the Rio Maracanã. It's very quiet and has sand dunes, small lakes and a number of isolated beaches lapped by an Atlantic heavy with the silt of the Amazon. The main town is called **Vila do Algodoal** and this name is often used for the island as a whole. Most of the accommodation is concentrated here, although there are pousadas on the other beaches. Hotels are low-key and simple and the island, which is popular with French visitors from Guyane, has a hippy feel.

Ins and outs Algodoal is reached by taking a bus from Belém to Marudá from where you catch a ferry. It is easy to find a room on arrival, except for weekends and holidays.

Salinópolis ➔ *Colour map 1, A6. Population: 33,500.*

Some 223 km from Belém, at the extreme eastern end of the Amazon delta, this seaside resort has many small places where you can eat and drink at night by the waterfront. There is a fine sandy beach nearby (buses and cars drive onto the beach) but the water is murky. It is a peaceful place mid-week but very busy at weekends and in high season and is at its peak during the holiday month of July. **Atalaia**, an island opposite Salinópolis, is pleasant and can be reached by taxi (US$6) or by boat. Salinópolis is four hours from Belém by bus on a good road, US$6.

The little riverside village of **Tomé-Açu**, south of Belém on the Rio Acará-Mirim, affords a view of life on a smaller river than the Amazon. Three buses a day run from Belém, US$8. The **Hotel Las Vegas** has a friendly owner, Fernando. The boat back to Belém on Sunday leaves at 1100, arriving 1800, US$5.

South of Belém

» *pp549-558.*

Marabá and around ➔ *Phone code: 094. Colour map 1, B5. Population: 170,000. Altitude: 84 m.*

Near Marabá are beaches on the Tocantins and Itacaiúnas rivers, which are best visited from June to October. There is a bridge across the Tocantins at Marabá. The town was moved as a result of the Tucuruí dam, but it still suffers from flooding. There are essentially three parts of the town: **Marabá Velha** (also called Marabá Pioneira), **Marabá Nova** and **Cidade Nova**. The distance between Marabá Nova and Velha is about 2½ km. A good travel agent is **IBR Travel** on the main street of Marabá Velha. **Banco do Brasil** will not cash traveller's cheques; the parallel market operates in larger stores, such as **Supermercado Bato Logo.**

The **Serra Pelada** gold mines, made famous by Sebastião Salgado, whose images made them look like the circles of Hell, are now worked by heavy machinery. This massive excavation was the scene of much human misery and also some fabulous fortunes. To get there, take a bus to Km 6 and change for the Serra Pelada bus, US$6, three hours, last bus back 1400. About 11 km before the town is a police post where searches are carried out for weapons and alcohol (forbidden). There is a second search point at the airport, 2 km from the mine.

Ins and outs The nearest airport is in the Cidade Nova, 3 km from the centre, and receives direct flights from Belém, São Luís and Imperatriz. The **rodoviária** ⓘ *Nova Marabá, 4 km on PA-150, T094-321 1892*, has bus connections with the main regional cities as well as Rio de Janeiro and São Paulo.

Carajás

The main attraction here is an impressive iron ore mine, operated by the **Companhia Vale Rio Doce (CVRD)** ⓘ *T091-327 5300, or enquire in Marabá, São Luís, São Paulo or Rio: Av Graça Aranha 26, 16th floor, Centro, Rio de Janeiro, attention of Dr Hugo Mourão*. The mine is a giant red hole in a green jungle and the ore is almost pure iron oxide and therefore extremely profitable. It is ground, washed and shipped to São Luís by trains up to 2 km long, without further treatment or chemical processing. Apart from iron ore, other metals such as manganese are also mined by the CVRD in the area. As a result of the mining, a city has built up around Carajás, but most of it is within CVRD bounds. To get into Carajás (the Núcleo and to visit the mine) and to pass the checkpoint 35 km from the project, you must have a permit, available from CVRD. You need to apply in advance and have a good reason for visiting. There is accommodation in **Parauapebas**, built as a temporary settlement for the Carajás construction workers, and now a town in its own right.

Roads to nowhere

In the early 1970s, Brazil's military rulers became increasingly unnerved by what they saw as foreign designs upon the resources of the Amazon basin. This real or imaginary fear of invasion was directed against not only the rich, developed countries, but also Brazil's neighbours, who the Brazilians felt were slowly encroaching upon the country's borders. In the early 1960s, Peru's president, Fernando Belaunde Terry, had proposed the construction of the Carretera Marginal in order to link Peru's jungle with the rest of the country. Under the slogan '*Integrar para não entregar*' (takeover not handover), the Brazilian military announced the construction of the **Transamazônica Highway**. The road was originally designed to link João Pessoa, Paraíba, with Acre, thence to link up with the Peruvian road system to complete a road route across South America to the Pacific and open up Brazilian products to Asian markets. The Transamazônica itself would be 5400 km and would unify Amazônia from east to west and integrate it with the rest of the nation. In addition, it would give opportunities for people from the northeast to resettle in areas not affected by drought and to become economically active in small agricultural schemes. In the often-quoted words of President Emílio Garrastazu Médici, it would move "*Homens sem terra para terras sem homens*"' (men without land to land without men). All along the highway, purpose-built *agrovilas* would offer Brazil's poor a new life. The project was proposed in 1970; huge financial investment failed to make the it work. Not only did fewer than anticipated northeasterners take up the offer, but those that did found that the Amazonian soils did not permit the type of rewards that they had been led to expect. The colonizers also found that the social infrastructure did not meet their needs and both the road and the

West of Belém

Along the Transamazônica

The Transamazônica – an almost impassable dirt road riddled with potholes and infringing forest throughout its 5000 km – connects Brazil's eastern and western extremities. And for no good reason. Millions of dollars were spent on constructing this road, while others of real economic importance in the east of the country were left to crumble. Together with grandiose and unnecessary schemes such as the Amazon dams, the Transamazônica was a major contributor to the country's national debt and to deforestation (see box, above).

The Transamazônica crosses the Rio Xingu at **Favânia,** 41 km east of Altamira, a busy, booming Amazonian town with many gold dealers. A road is being paved 46 km north to the fishing village of Vitória on the lower Xingu, from which boats go to Belém. The dock is a good place to watch *garimpeiros*, who have been responsible for destroying huge areas of the forest, working below the last rapids. There are no organized trips but a boat can be hired, US$25 per day, for a trip up the Xingu, which is highly recommended. Many animals can be seen. The area is an indigenous Assurine reservation and it is forbidden to enter villages without permission; buy food in Altamira.

project began to deteriorate. By the late 1980s, a 'Movement for Survival' along the Transamazônica had been set up by the farmers.

Another road which was intended to promote development in the Amazon region was the **BR-364**, from Cuiabá to Acre state . In the mid-1970s, the government hoped that the road would reinvigorate settlement in the Amazon, in a way that the Transamazônica had failed to do. Like the latter, the BR-364 was supposed to encourage small landholders to follow the building of the main highway and its feeder roads, but in Rondônia the main colonizers were cattle ranchers and land speculators who speeded up the process of deforestation and caused land conflicts with the traditional cultivators, forest farmers and indigenous people.

A third road in the Amazon which has come to grief, even more so than the other two, is the **BR-319** from Manaus to Humaitá on the Transamazônica. Planned in 1960 and opened to traffic in 1975, the road has become a route from nothing to nowhere. The people living along it have been deserted, the only maintenance being the occasional team from Embratel who come to look at the telephone lines which follow the road. Initially there were farms, hotels, petrol stations and restaurants along the BR-319. Most have now gone. Access to health clinics and schools is all but impossible and the only public transport on the southern part of the road is a once-weekly truck. The only people to benefit are the shipping owners who take the traffic, which would have used the road, on barges along the Rio Madeira. The journalist Giuliano Cedroni tried to drive the BR-319 in the late 1990s. He and his companions made it through, but not without a tow from the weekly truck after their jeep broke down. One inhabitant of the region pleaded with him: "Tell the people down there [in the south] what is happening in the north. This here is not a life."

Ins and outs It is possible to make your way along sections of the road using public transport, but there is no predicting whether the route will be open. Some sections are totally impassable throughout the rainy season. Others have sporadic scheduled bus services. Conditions change constantly so detailed local enquiry is essential before heading out. Driving the road is sometimes possible in a 4WD, but it is challenging and can be dangerous. Do not leave without spare tyres, 20 litres of water, food for a day and plenty of reais. It is essential to speak some Portuguese as you will need to enquire about road conditions along the way.

There are flights to Carajás from Belém, Marabá and Tucuruí and trains to **Marabá**, (leave at 1930; two hrs, US$4) and to **São Luís**, see page 525. Buses run to cities as far away as Rio and São Paulo.

Itaituba → *Colour map 1, B4.*

This *garimpeiro* town is the jumping-off place for the **Amazônia National Park**. Father Paul Zoderer, who can be found at the church on the waterfront, may help to arrange a visit. Information is available from **Ibama** ⓘ *Av Marechal Rondon, CEP 681811-970, Itaituba, T093-518 1530.*

There is accommodation in a number of hotels (B-D) on and around the main praça. **Varig** fly here and there are buses to Marabá, (about 34 hours, US$45), Santarém via Rurópolis (11 hours, US$20) and Jacarèacanga and Humaitá.

Towards Amazonas state » pp549-558.

Santarém → *Phone code: 093. Colour map 1, B4. Population: 262,500.*

The third largest city on the Brazilian Amazon is nonetheless small enough to walk around in a morning. It was founded in 1661 as the Jesuit mission of Tapajós; the name was changed to Santarém in 1758. There was once a fort here, and attractive colonial squares overlooking the waterfront still remain. Standing at the confluence of the Rio Tapajós with the Amazon, on the southern bank, Santarém is halfway (three days by boat) between Belém and Manaus. Most visitors breeze in and out on a stopover.

In front of the market square, the yellow Amazon water swirls alongside the green-blue Tapajós river at the **meeting of the waters**, which is nearly as impressive as that of the Negro and Solimões near Manaus. A small **Museu dos Tapajós** in the old city hall (now the **Centro Cultural João Fora**) on the waterfront, downriver from where the boats dock, has a collection of ancient Tapajós ceramics, as well as various 19th-century artefacts. The unloading of the fish catch between 0500 and 0700 on the waterfront is interesting. There are good beaches nearby on the Rio Tapajós. **Prainha**, a small beach, is between town and the port, by a park with many mango trees (Floresta-Prainha bus from centre). On the outskirts of town is **Maracanã**, with sandy bays (when the Tapajós is low) and some trees for shade (Maracanã bus from centre, 20 minutes).

Ins and outs The port is in right in the centre of town; a taxi to any of the hotels in this area is around $US2. The **airport** ⓘ *15 km from town, T093-523 1021*, receives internal flights only. The **rodoviária** ⓘ *outskirts of town, T093-522 3392*, buses run to the waterfront near the market, US$0.35. The tourist office, **Comtur** ⓘ *R Floriano Peixoto 434, T/F093-523 2434*, has good information available in English.

Alter do Chão → *Colour map1, B4.*

Alter do Chão is a friendly village on the Rio Tapajós, at the outlet of Lago Verde, 34 km west. Of particular interest is the **Centro do Preservação da Arte Indígena** ⓘ *R Dom Macedo Costa, T093-527 1110*, which has a substantial collection of artefacts from tribes of Amazônia and Mato Grosso. There is good swimming in the Tapajós from the beautiful clean beach. Close to Alter do Chão (30 minutes by boat), the joining of the Rio Tapajós with the Aruã and the Arapiuns creates an island surrounded by clean rivers of differing colours, each teeming with life. The forested island is being developed as an ecopark, **Parque Ecoturístico Arapiuns**, with accommodation for visitors; it is already becoming popular. Monkeys and birds inhabit the woodlands, protected more for commercial reasons than any other. For information, contact **Paratur** ⓘ *T091-223 2130, in Belém.*

Floresta Nacional do Tapajós → *Colour map1, B4.*

ⓘ *Ibama, T091-224 5899, or Av Tapajos 2267, Aldeia, Santarém, T093-523 2964.*
At Km 123, south of Santarém on BR-163, there is a section of the Floresta Nacional do Tapajós which has a vehicle track running due west through it. It is beautiful rainforest which can be entered with permission from **Ibama** if accompanied by one of their guides. It is well worth a visit if only to see the butterflies.

Belterra and Fordlândia → *Phone code 093. Colour map1, B4.*

Fordlândia, 300 km south of Santarém, was Henry Ford's first rubber plantation. He founded it in 1926 in an attempt to provide a cheaper source of rubber for his Ford Motor Company than the British and Dutch controlled plantations in Malaya. There is **Hotel Zebu**, in old Vila Americana (turn right from the dock, then left up the hill), one restaurant, two bars and three shops on the town square. A little pebble beach is north of the town.

Closer to Santarém, 37 km south on a dirt road, is **Belterra**, where Henry Ford established his second rubber plantation. In the highlands overlooking the Rio Tapajós. It is nearer to the town than his first project, which was turned into a research

Around Santarém

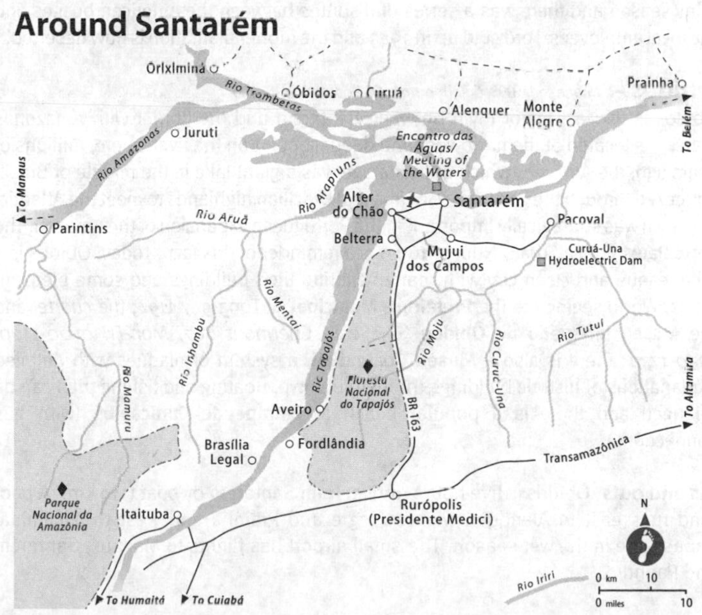

Monte Alegre

Monte Alegre is the site of archaeological discoveries that have threatened to radically alter current views of the spread of civilization in South America. In the 1990s, Dr Anna C Roosevelt, of the Field Museum of Natural History, Chicago, found pottery fragments in a cave which, according to radiocarbon dating, appear to be from 7000-8000 BC. This predates by some 3000 years what was thought to be the earliest ceramic ware in South America (from Colombia and Ecuador). Subsequent artefacts discovered here, however, have radiocarbon dates of 15,000 BC, which calls for a significant rethink of the original idea that people moved from the Andes into the Amazon basin. If nothing else, these finds suggest that the story of the people of the Americas is more diverse than hitherto understood. The cave that Dr Roosevelt excavated is called Caverna da Pedra Pintada. Also in the area are pictographs, with large designs of human and animal figures and geometric shapes. Trips can be arranged.

Many thanks to to Philip W Hummer, who sent us a description of a tour to the region, led by Dr Anna Roosevelt.

station. At Belterra, Ford built a well laid-out new town, where the houses resemble the cottages of Michigan summer resorts, many with white paint and green trim. The town centre has a large central plaza that includes a bandstand, the church of Santo Antônio (circa 1951), a Baptist church and a large educational and sports complex. A major hospital, which at one time was staffed by physicians from North America, is now closed.

Ford's project, the first modern attempt to invest in the Amazon, was unsuccessful. It was difficult to grow the rubber tree in plantation conditions, where it was unprotected from the heavy rains and harsh sun, and indigenous parasites were attracted by the concentratiosn of trees. Boats could only come this far upriver in the rainy season and there was a series of disputes between the American bosses and the local employees. Ford sold up in 1945 and the rubber plantation is now deserted.

Óbidos → *Phone code: 093. Colour map1, A4. Population: 46,500.*

Óbidos is the last major town between Santarém and the border with Amazonas state. It is located at the narrowest and deepest point on the river where, millions of years ago, the Amazon (which at that stage was a giant lake in the middle of Brazil) squeezed through the gap in the Guyana and Brazilian highlands to meet the Atlantic. The town was strategically important in the Portuguese expansion of the Amazon. The **Forte Pauxi** (Praça Coracy Nunes, 1697) is a reminder of this fact . Today, Óbidos is a picturesque and clean city with many beautiful tiled buildings and some pleasant parks. Worth seeing are the **Prefeitura Municipal** ⓘ *T093-547 1194*, the *cuartel* and the **Museu Integrado de Ôbidus** ⓘ *R Justo Chermont 607, Mon-Fri 0700-1100, 1330-1730*. There is also a **Museu Contextual**, a system of plaques with detailed explanations of historic buildings throughout town. Boating and fishing trips can be arranged and there is a popular beach at **Igarapé de Curuçambá** (with bus connections).

Ins and outs Óbidos is five hours upriver from Santarém by boat (110 km). A poor road runs east to Alenquer, Monte Alegre and Prainha and west to Oriximiná, impassable in the wet season. The small airport has flights to Manaus, Santarém and Parintins.

Sleeping

Macapá *p534, map p535*

AL Ceta Ecotel, R do Matodouro 640, Fazendinha, T096-3277 3396, www.ecotel.com.br. A rainforest-themed hotel with sloths and monkeys in the trees and a series of trails. All the furniture is made on site. 20 mins from the town by taxi.

AL-A Atalanta, Av. Coracy Nunes 1148, T096-3223 1612, www.atalanta.com.br. By far the best hotel in town with a rooftop pool and comfortable modern a/c rooms with bathrooms. Includes a generous breakfast. 10 mins' walk from the river.

A Macapá, Av Francisco Azarias Neto 17, on the waterfront, T096-3217 1350. The city's grandest hotel, overlooking the river, with a pool, tennis courts and a children's play area. Rooms are past their best and showers have electric heads. Popular with families from Guyane.

A-B Pousada Ekinox, R Jovino Dinoá 1693, T096-3223 0086, www.ekinox.com.br. One of the best in town, with chalets set in a little tropical garden and with a library. Helpful, French-speaking staff and a good restaurant.

B Frota Palace, R Tiradentes 1104, T096-3223 3999, frotapalacehotel@bol.com.br. Plain, faded rooms with en suites. Airport pickup service for US$2.50.

C Gloria, Leopoldo Machado 2085, T096-3222 0984. A clean, well-kept, simple hotel with a/c rooms all with en suite, TV and hot water. Breakfast included in the price.

D Mercúrio, R Cândido Mendes 1300, 2nd floor, T096-3224 2766. Very basic, but close to Praça São José (where the bus from Porto Santana stops).

D-E Holliday, Av Henrique Gallúcio 1623, T096-3223 3122. Very simple, though recently repainted, little boxy a/c rooms 20 mins' walk from the river. Breakfast included.

D-E Vista Amazônica, Av Beira Rio 1298 (about 1½ km beyond the Cantino Baiano restaurant away from town), T096-3222 6851. A simple pousada and restaurant sitting right opposite the Amazon, with simple but well-maintained tiled rooms with en suites.

E-F Santo Antônio, Av Coriolano Jucá 485, T096-3222 0226. Very simple and slightly musty downstairs rooms and brighter a/c rooms upstairs.

Oiapoque *p536*

There are plenty of cheap hotels in Oiapoque, all in the same league. The noisiest and least reputable are closest to the river; the best a few blocks behind.

Belém *p537, map p539*

A series of new openings and renovations has seen Belém's hotels improve greatly, although they are still not up to much. All are fully booked during **Círio** (see Festivals, page 554). There are many cheap hotels close to the waterfront (none too safe) and several others near the *rodoviária* (generally okay).

A Itaoca, Av Pres Vargas 132, T091-4009 2400, www.pousadadosguaras.com. Well-kept, bright, no-nonsense a/c rooms with writing desks and en suites. The best are on the upper floors away from the street noise, and with river views. Decent breakfast.

A Machado's Plaza, R Henrique Gurjão 200, T091-4008 9800. Bright, brand-new boutique hotel with smart and tastefully decorated a/c rooms, a small business centre, plunge pool and a pleasant a/c breakfast area. Good value.

A Regente, Av Gov José Malcher 485, T091-3181 5000, www.hotelregente.com.br. Small, newly refurbished a/c rooms decorated in cream and white tile and with standard 3-star fittings, above a noisy street. Popular with US tour groups.

B Le Massilia, R Henrique Gurjão 236, T091-3224 2834, www.massilia.com.br. An intimate, French-owned boutique hotel with chic little duplexes and more ordinary doubles. Excellent French restaurant and a tasty French breakfast.

C-D Grão Pará, Av Pres Vargas 718, T091-3224 9600. Well-kept, new a/c rooms with contemporary fittings and smart en suites in black marble, and a boiler for hot water. The best have superb river views. Excellent breakfast. Great value.

D Novo Avenida, Av Pres Vargas 404, T091-3223 8893, www.hotelnovoavenida.com.br. Slightly frayed but spruce en suite rooms. Decent breakfast. Groups can sleep in large rooms for **E-F** per person. Good value.

D Sete Sete, Trav 1 de Março 673, T091-3222 7730. Newly refurbished, clean but still

gloomy little rooms. Decent breakfast and convenient location. Be careful after dark.
D Unidos, Ó de Almeida 545, T091-3229 0600. Simple but spruce, spacious a/c rooms with cable TV and clean en suites.
E-F Fortaleza, Trav Frutuoso Guimarães 276, T091-3212 1055. Unkempt hotel with a range of very simple wood-floor rooms and dorms around a communal sitting area. Popular with backpackers. Be careful in this area after dark.
E-F Palácio, Trav Frutuoso Guimarães, T091-3212 8422. Opposite and almost identical to the Fortaleza, though with scruffier communal areas and slightly cleaner rooms, and a restaurant/snack bar. Be careful in this area after dark.

Ilha de Marajó *p541*

A Pousada dos Guarãs, Av Beira Mar, Salvaterra, T/F091-3765 1133, www.pousadadosguaras.com.br. Well-equipped little resort hotel on the beach with an extensive tour programme.
B Hotel Ilha do Marajó, 2a Travessa 10, T091-741 1315 (Belém T091-241 3218), himarajó@interconect.com.br. Simple hotel popular with weekenders from Belém. Friendly staff.
C Soure, R 3 Centro. Basic, with a/c rooms.
C Waldeck, Trav 12, T091-741 1414. Basic but friendly, with only 4 rooms.
E Pensão, at 2a R 575, (**Bar Guarani**). Simple but well-run and recommended.

Other islands around Belém *p541*

Mosqueiro

There are plenty of opportunities for camping on Mosqueiro.
B Farol, Praia Farol, Olha do Mosqueiro, T091-771 1219. 1920s architecture in good repair, small restaurant, rooms face beach, good views.

Vila do Algodoal

B-C Jardim do Éden, http://onlinehotel.com.br/para/ilha-do-algodoal/jardim-do-eden-pousada/index.htm. A series of bizarre neo-Gothic brick cabanas with kitchenettes overlooking the beach on Praia do Farol. Well kept and well run and with more personality than most on the island. Tours available and camping in the grounds (on the beach). Discounts available online.
B-C Pousada Bela-Mar, Av Beira Mar, Vila do Algodoal beach, T091-3854 1128, www.belamar.hpgvip.com.br. A very simple beachside hotel with tiny rooms, set in a garden. Close to the boat jetty.
B-C Pousada Chalés do Atlântico, Vila do Algodoal, T091-3854 1114. Recently renovated. 11 simple little cabanas with mosquito screening, en suites and cold showers.

Salinópolis *p543*

A Atalaia, Ilha Atalaia, 15 km from Salinópolis, T/F091-464 1122. A simple pousada in a pleasant setting. Reserve in advance for the weekend, take a taxi.
A Joana d'Arc, Av João Pessoa 555, T/F091-823 1422. Modest but well looked after and with a generous breakfast.
A Solar, Av Beira Mar, T091-823 1823. The best in town with smart en suite rooms and a good restaurant.
B Diolindina, Av Pres Médici 424, Capanema, T091-821 1667. Small clean a/c rooms with fridge and bath. The price includes breakfast and safe parking. Recommended. There are good restaurants and a supermarket opposite.

Marabá and around *p543*

There are various slightly seedy cheap hotels near the *rodoviária*.
A Del Príncipe, Av Marechal Rondon 95, Cidade Nova, T094-324 1175. A/c rooms with TV and fridge in modest hotel with a restaurant and games room.
A Vale do Tocantins, Folha 29, Cidade Nova, 7 km, T094-322 2321, F322 1841. Modern and characterless, with a restaurant and travel agency.
B Dallas, Nova Marabá. Well run and convenient for the *rodoviária* (immediately next door). Recommended.
B Plaza, Folha 32, quadra 10, lote 06, T094-322 3543, F322 1610. Fan-cooled rooms in a quiet and friendly hostel serving a very good breakfast. Some English spoken. Recommended.

Santarém *p546, map p546*

All hotels, except **Amazon Park**, are in the compact grid of streets in the heart of the city near the waterfront.
A Amazon Park, Av Mendonça Furtado 4120, T091-523 2800, amazon@stm.interconect.com.br. Large 1970s hotel, 4 km from

Natural energy drinks

There is nowhere better for fruit juices than Brazil: the choice is staggering. Some juice bars in the Amazon and in Rio's beach suburbs have over 30 different flavours to choose from – many from fruits that are unknown and unavailable outside of South America. Must-tries include *cupuaçu*, a fragrant, pungent juice extracted from a relative of the *cacão* bean; *cajú* made from the fruit of the cashew nut tree; and *tapereba* – tangy, deliciously refreshing and made from an Amazon fruit related to the Brazil nut. If you are looking to top up your energy levels opt for an *açai an acerola* or a *camu camu*. *Açai* is a meal in itself, served thick, sweet, icy cold and dark maroon, and packed with electrolytes and vitamins. *Acerola*, which comes originally from the Yucatán, is a tropical cherry with a sharp, refreshing flavour and what was thought until recently to be the highest of all naturally occurring levels of vitamin C. This accolade is now accorded to *camu camu*, a light-orange fruit from the Amazon which on average contains about 2g of vitamin C per 100g – 30 times as much as an average orange. *Camu camu* is also a significant source of vitamin B, phosphorus, potassium and iron, together with the full complement of other minerals and amino acids which aid the absorption of vitamin C.

Many of these juices are available as constituents of various non-alcoholic cocktails or *vitaminas*; made up with either water or milk, sugar and often *guaraná* powder - a naturally occurring stimulant made from a pounded Amazon nut. Some are used in *batidas* – vodka and fruit juice infusions. More standard fruits such as limes (*limao*), passion fruit (*maracuja*) and strawberries (*morango*) are used to flavour *caipirinhas* and their vodka and sake counterparts, the *caipiroska* and *caipisake/sakirinha*.

the centre, with a swimming pool and friendly, competent staff.

C **Brasil Grande Hotel**, Trav 15 de Agosto 213, T091-522 5660. Family-run. Restaurant.

C **New City**, Trav Francisco Corrêa 200, T091-523 3149. Standard town hotel with plain a/c rooms and an airport pickup service. River trips can be organized from here.

C-D **Santarém Palace**, Rui Barbosa 726, T091-523 2820, F522 1779. A 1980s hotel with 44 comfortable but simple a/c rooms with TV and fridge.

D **Brasil**, Trav dos Mártires 30, T091-523 5177. Pleasant, family-run, with fan cooled rooms with shared bathrooms, breakfast and a small restaurant.

D **Mirante**, Trav Francisco Correa 115, T091-523 3054, freephone T0800-707 3054, www.mirantehotel.com. One of the new and cleaner cheapies. A/c rooms with fridges, TVs, and some with a balcony and individual safes. Internet facilities available. Recommended.

D-F **Horizonte**, Trav Senador Lemos, 737, T091-522 5437, horizontehotel@bol.com.br. Plain, simple, well-kept rooms with a/c or fan.

E **Grão Rios**, in a little alley off Av Tapajós between Trav dos Mártires and 15 de Agosto. Well-kept a/c rooms, some with a river view.

Alter do Chão *p547*

B **Pousada Tupaiulândia**, R Pedro Teixera 300, next to telephone office opposite bus stop, T091-527 1157. Unprepossessing but adequate, with plain and boxy a/c rooms and very helpful, friendly staff. Good breakfast.

D **Alter do Chão**, R Lauro Sodré 74, T091-527 1215. Simple with a reasonable restaurant and a little orchid garden.

D **Tia Marilda**, Trav Agostinho Lobato, T091-527 1144. A/c and cheaper fan-cooled rooms.

Belterra and Fordlândia *p547*

E **Hotel Seringueira**, Belterra. 8 simple fan-cooled rooms and a pleasant restaurant.

Óbidos *p548*
C Braz Bello, R Corrêia Pinto, on top of the hill. Clean rooms with shared bathrooms. Optional full board.
C-D Pousada Brasil, R Corrêia Pinto. Basic with fan-cooled rooms with en suites or shared bathrooms.

Eating

Macapá *p534, map p535*
The waterfront praça has many open-air restaurants and bars, concentrated at the Trapiche (pier). These are lively after 1800, especially at weekends.
TTT **Chalé**, Av Pres Vargas 499, T096-3222 1970. The best restaurant in the city with good fish, Brazilian dishes and a pleasant atmosphere.
TT **Cantinho Baiano**, Av Beira-Rio 1, T096-3223 4153. Overlooking the river 10 mins' walk south of the fort and with some of the best river fish in town. There are many other restaurants along this stretch about 1½ km beyond the Cantinho Baiano.
TT **Flora**, Rodovia Salvador de Diniz 1370-A, Km 15, T096-3283 2858. A lively little restaurant on the riverside next to a little marina 15 km from the fort (travelling away from town). Good fish and local dishes; try the fish infused with energetic Amazon fruits.
T **Bom Paladar Kilo's**, Av Pres Vargas 456, T096-223 0555. Pay-by-weight buffet with excellent ice cream made from local fruits; make sure you try the *cupuaçu*.
T **Divina Arte**, Av Pres Vargas 969, T096- 3222 1877. A decent lunchtime menu restaurant and per kilo buffet. Plenty of choice.
T **Divina Gula**, Av Pres Vargas 993, T096-3083 2091. Pleasant little café serving coffee, cakes and snacks.
T **Sarney**, R Gal Rondon 1501. Simple but very cheap and filling per kilo restaurant. Good value. Lunchtime only.

Oiapoque *p536*
Gourmets will find themselves in a desert but there are many cheap places serving fish, beans and rice, and several spit-and-sawdust bars in the blocks around the river.

Belém *p537, map p539*
All the major hotels have upmarket restaurants. There are numerous outdoor snack bars serving far cheaper meals. Good snack bars serving *vatapá* (Bahian dish) and *tapioca* rolls are concentrated on Assis de Vasconcelos on the eastern side of the Praça da República. There are many decent a/c restaurant, bar and café options in the smart and newly renovated Estação das Docas on the riverfront where the boats dock.
TTT **Açaí, Hilton Hotel**, Av Pres Vargas 882, T091-242 6500. Regional dishes such as roasted duck with tucupi sauce and jambo leaves. Come for lunch or dinner daily, or Sun brunch.
TTT **Boteco das Onze**, Praça FC Brandão s/n, T091-3224 8599. Just about the best regional cooking in Belém with live music every night and a view out over the river. Try the *filetena brasa* or the excellent *tambaqui*.
TTT **Churrascaria Rodeio**, Rodovia Augusto Montenegro, Km 4, T091-3248 2004. A choice of 20 cuts of meat and 30 buffet dishes for a set price. Well worth the short taxi ride to eat all you can.
TTT **Churrascaria Tucuruvi**, Trav Benjamin Constant 1843, Nazaré, T091-3235 0341. Enormous slabs of pork, beef, lamb and a range of sausages; all in vast portions and served with salads and accompaniments.
TTT **Lá em Casa**, Av Gov José Malcher 247, T091-223 1212. Respectable local cooking, especially the *menu paraense*. Fashionable.
TTT **Miako**, Trav 1 de Março 766, behind Praça da República, T091-3242 2355. Japanese, oriental and international food in a vast dining room tucked away behind the **Hilton**.
TTT-TT **Le Massilia**, see Sleeping. French-owned and run with dishes including frogs' legs, *sole meunière* and *magret de canard*. Excellent cocktails.
TT **Cantina Italiana** Trav Benjamin Constant 1401, T091-225 2033. Excellent Italian, with hotel delivery.
TT **Sabor Paraense,** , R Sen Manoel Barata 897, T091-3241 4391. A variety of fish and meat dishes such as crab in coconut milk served in a bright, light dining room.
TT-T **Mãe Natureza**, R Manoel Barata 889, T091-3212 8032. Vegetarian and wholefood dishes in a bright clean dining room. Lunch only.
T **Doces Bárbaros**, R Benjamin Constant 1658, T091-3224 0576. Cakes, snacks, sandwiches and decent coffee in a/c surrounds. Lunch only.

Ⲯ **Govinda**, R Ó de Almeida 198. Basic but tasty vegetarian food. Lunch only.

Ilha de Marajó *p541*
There are a number of cheap places to eat in Soure but few restaurants of any distinction.
Ⲯ **Canecão**, Praça da Matriz, Soure. Sandwiches and standard beans, rice and cheap meals. Recommended.

Other islands around Belém *p541*
ⲮⲮ **Hotel Ilha Bela**, Av 16 de Novembro 409, Mosqueiro. Recommended for fish, no evening meals.
ⲮⲮ **Marésia**, Praia Chapeu Virado, Mosqueiro. Highly recommended.
Ⲯ **Sorveteria Delícia**, Av 16 de Novembro, Mosqueiro. Serves good local fruit ice creams and the owner buys dollars.

Salinópolis *p543*
Ⲯ **Bife de Ouro**, Av Dr Miguel Santa Brigida, opposite petrol station. Simple, but excellent for fish and shrimp. Always busy at lunchtime.
Ⲯ **Gringo Louco**, 15 km (take taxi or hitch), at Cuiarana beach (follow signs). The US owner serves good, unusual dishes, and some 'wild' drinks known as 'bombs'. Popular.

Marabá and around *p543*
There are a few good *churrascarias* around the central praça.
ⲮⲮ **Bambu**, Pedro Carneiro 111, Cidade Nova, 3 km. Mainly fish, clean, good value, 1100-1500, 1800-2300.
ⲮⲮ **Lanchonete Domino**, opposite the *rodoviária*. Recommended.

Santarém *p546, map p546*
As with other small towns in the interior of Brazil, most restaurants in Santarém serve basic café-style food, lunch (consisting of rice, beans, chips and a choice of beef, chicken or fish) and juices. The best choice is to be found along the waterfront in the centre.
ⲮⲮ **Mascote**, Praça do Pescador 10, T091-523 2844. Open 1000-2330. Fish-orientated restaurant with a bar and ice cream parlour. Avoid *piraracu*.
ⲮⲮ **Mascotinho**, Praça Manoel de Jesus Moraes, on riverfront. Bar and pizzeria attracting a lively crowd at sunset. Great river view.
ⲮⲮ **Santo Antônio**, Av Tapajós 2061, T091-523 2356. Barbecued meat and fish.
Ⲯ **Lucy**, Praça do Pescador. Good juices and pastries. Recommended.

Alter do Chão *p547*
Ⲯ **Lago Verde**, Praça 7 de Setembro. Good fresh fish, try *calderada de tucunaré*.

Óbidos *p548*
There are plenty of cheap fish restaurants near the waterfront and in the upper town.

Bars and clubs

Macapá *p534, map p535*
The food and drink kiosks in **Complexo Beira Rio** have live music most evenings. **ETNA** is the current dance club of choice, vibrating to the frenetic local rhythm *brega*, which sounds like *forró* on speed.

Belém *p537, map p539*
There are many dance venues around **Av Doca de Souza Franco**, (often just called 'Doca'); Thu is the best night. The **Reduto** district is becoming the most fashionable nightlife area in the city.
African Bar, Praça Waldemar Henrique 2. Rock or samba at weekends only.
Baixo Reduto, R Quintino Bocaiúva, Reduto, T091-242 6282. Live blues on Wed, MPB on Thu, rock on Fri and jazz on Sat.
Bar Teatro Bora Bora, R Bernal do Couto 38, T091-241 5848. Restaurant, bar and nightclub with MPB and pagode. Open from 2100 until late Thu-Sun.
Colarinho Branco Chopperia, Av Visconde de Souza Franco 80, near the river. Tue-Sun, 1800 to last customer. Excellent draught beer and live MPB. Very popular.
Escapóle, Rodovia Augusto Montenegro 400. Huge dance hall with various styles of music from live bands and DJs. Open Wed-Sat from 2200 (take a radio taxi for safety), no a/c, dress informally.
Olê Olá, Av Tavares Bastos, 1234, T091-243 2340. Live music and a DJ driven dance floor. Thu-Sun only, 2230 to last customer.

Entertainment

Macapá *p534, map p535*
Art galleries **Cândido Portinari**, corner of R Cândido Mendes and Av Raimundo Álvares da Costa. Exhibitions of local art.

Cinemas In Macapá Shopping, R Leopoldo Machado 2334.

Theatre **Teatro das Bacabeiras**, R Cândido Mendes. Concerts, poetry and plays.

Belém *p537, map p539*
Art galleries **Debret**, R Arcipreste Manoel Theodoro 630, Batista Campos, T091-222 4046. Contemporary painting and sculpture, also has library specializing in art and philosophy.
Casa das 11 Janelas (1768), Praça Frei Caetano Brandão, T091-219 1105. Cultural performances and art exhibitions, panoramic view.

Cinema **Olímpia**, Av Pres Vargas 918, T091-223 1882. The first cinema in Belém, opened over 80 years ago. It now shows films for lonely men. But **Nazaré** a few doors down is respectable and there are plenty of multiplexes in the city's shopping malls.

Theatre **Margarida Schiwwazappa**, Av Gentil Bittencourt 650, T091-222 2923.

Santarém *p546, map p546*
Cinema Av Rui Barbosa 183.

Festivals and events

Macapá *p534, map p535*
Apr/May **Marabaixo** is the traditional music and dance festival held for 40 days after Easter.
Jun The Sambódromo has parades of Escolas de Samba at **Carnaval** and **Quadrilhas** during **São João**.
14 Aug **Festa de São Joaquim** held in Curiaú.

Belém *p537, map p539*
Apr Maundy Thu, half-day; **Good Fri**, all shops closed, all churches open and there are processions.
9 Jun Corpus Christi.
15 Aug Accession of Pará to Independent Brazil.
7 Sep **Independence Day**, commemorated on the day with a military parade, and with a students' parade on the preceding Sun.
30 Oct **Círio**. The festival of candles, based on the legend of Nossa Senhora de Nazaré whose image was found on the site of her Basílica around 1700. On the 2nd Sun in Oct a procession carries the Virgin's image from the Basílica to the cathedral; it is returned 2 weeks later. The festival attracts many artists and musicians and has become a massive national celebration with carnival performers and rock groups. Highly recommended.
2 Nov All Souls' Day.
8 Dec Immaculate Conception.
24 Dec Christmas Eve, half-day.

Santarém *p546, map p546*
22 Jun Foundation of the city.
29 Jun São Pedro, with processions of boats on the river and Boi-Bumba dance dramas.
8 Dec **Nossa Senhora da Conceição**, tthe city's patron saint.

Alter do Chão *p547*
2nd week in Sep Festa do Çairé, religious processions and folkloric events. Recommended.

Shopping

Macapá *p534, map p535*
Macapá and Porto Santana were declared a customs-free zone in 1992. There are now many cheap imported goods available from shops in the centre. In the handicraft complex **Casa do Artesão**, Av Azárias Neto, Mon-Sat 0800-1900, craftsmen produce their wares on site. A feature is pottery decorated with local manganese ore, also woodcarvings and leatherwork.

Belém *p537, map p539*
There is an arts and crafts market in the Praça da República every weekend selling attractive seed and bead jewellery, wicker, hammocks and raw cotton weave work, toys and other knick-knacks. Belém is a good place to buy hammocks: look in the street parallel to the river, 1 block inland from **Ver-o-Peso**. Bookshop with English titles in the arcade on Av Pres Vargas.
Complexo São Brás, Praça Lauro Sodré. Has a handicraft market and folkloric shows in a building dating from 1911.
Parfumaria Orion, Trav Frutuoso Guimarães 268. Has a wide variety of perfumes and essences from Amazonian plants, much cheaper than tourist shops.
Shopping Iguatemi, Trav Padre Eutique 1078.

Santarém *p546, map p546*
Muiraquitã, R Lameira Bittencourt 131. Good for ceramics, woodcarvings and baskets.

Activities and tours

Macapá *p534, map p535*
Tour operators
Amapá Turismo, Hotel Macapá, T096-223 2667.
Fénix, R Cãndido Mendes 374, T/F096-223 8200, and R Jovino Dinoá 1489, T096-223 5353.

Belém *p537, map p539*
Tour operators
Amazon Star, R Henrique Gurjão 236, T091-3241 8624, T091-982 7911 (mob), amazstar@interconect.com.br. Offers 3-hr city tours and river tours. The company also books airline tickets and hotel on Marajó.
Amazônia Sport and Ação, Av 25 de Setembro 2345, T091-226 8442. Extreme sports, diving, rock climbing.
Iate Clube do Pará, Av Bernardo Sayão 3324, T091-229 7599. Swimming pools, gym and sports courts.

Santarém *p546, map p546*
Tour operators
Amazon Tours, Trav Turiano Meira 1084, T091-522 1928, T091-975 1981 (mob), www.amazonriver.com. Owner Steve Alexander is very friendly and helpful and has lots of tips on what to do, he also organizes excursions for groups to Bosque Santa Lúcia with ecological trails. Recommended.
Coruá-Una Turismo, R Dr Hugo Mendonça 600, T091-518 1014, F523 2670. Various tours, Pierre d'Arcy speaks French. Recommended.
Gil Serique, Praça do Pescador 131, T091-522 5174, English-speaking guide, recommended.
Santarém Tur, R Adriano Pimental 44, T091-522 4847, www.santaremtur.com.br. Branch in **Amazon Park Hotel** (see Sleeping, page 550). Friendly, helpful foreign-owned company offering individual and group tours (US$50 per person per day for a group of 5), to Tapajós National Forest, Maiça Lake and Fordlândia. Recommended.

Transport

Macapá *p534, map p535*
See also Ins and outs, page 534.

Air Flights to **Belém, Belo Horizonte, Boa Vista, Brasília, Breves, Manaus, Oiapoque, Rio de Janeiro**, **Santarém** and **São Paulo**.

Airline offices Gol, www.voegol.com.br. META, airport, T0300-789 5503 www.voemeta.com. **Puma Air**, T096-3039 3939, www.pumaair.com.br. **TAM**, airport, T096-4002 5700, www.tam.com.br. **Varig**, R Cândido Mendes 1039, T096-3223 4612, www.varig.com.br.

Boat To **Belém**, *Atlântica*, fast catamaran 8 hrs, 3 times a week, US$30, reservations at **Martinica**, Jovino Dinoá 2010, T096-2235 777, F222 3569. Slower but slightly cheaper boats are *Bom Jesus*, *Comandante Solon*, *São Francisco de Paulo*, *Silja e Souza* of **Souzamar**, Cláudio Lúcio Monteiro 1375, Porto Santana, T096-281 1946, car ferry with **Silnave**, T096-223 4011. Purchase tickets from offices 2 days in advance (**Agencia Sonave**, R São José 2145, T096-223 9090, sells tickets for all boats). Also smaller boats to **Breves** as well as a regular direct service to **Santarém**).

Bus Estrela de Ouro, office on the main square in front of the cathedral, leaves daily at 2000; and **Cattani**, office on Nunes between São José and Cândido Mendes, leaves daily at 0630 to **Amapá** (US$20), **Calçoene** (US$25, 7 hrs) and **Oiapoque** (12 hrs in the dry season with several rest stops, 14-24 hrs in rainy season, US$35). The Oiapoque bus does not go into Amapá or Calçoene and it is therefore inconvenient to break the trip at these places.

Pickup trucks run daily to various locations throughout Amapá: crowded on narrow benches in the back, or pay more to ride in the cab. Despite posted schedules, they leave when full. To **Oiapoque** at 0800, 10-12 hrs, US$35 cab, US$15 in back, to **Lourenço** at 0900.

Car hire Localiza, R Independência 30, T096-223 2799, and airport T096-224 2336. **Sila Rent a Car**, Av Procópio Rola 1346, T096-224 1443.

Train Limited services between **Porto Santana** and **Serra do Navio**.

Oiapoque *p536*
Air Flights to **Macapá** 3 times a week.
Boat Occasional cargo vessels to **Belém** or **Macapá** (Porto Santana).

Bus Estrela de Ouro leaves for **Macapá** from the waterfront, twice daily at 1000 and after lunch, 10-12 hrs (dry season), 14-24 hrs (wet season), US$35, also **Cattani**. Pickup trucks depart from the same area when full, US$35 in cab, US$15 in the back.

Belém *p537, map p539*
See also Ins and outs, page 537

Air To get to the airport take bus 'Perpétuo Socorro-Telégrafo' or 'Icoaraci', every 15 mins from the Prefeitura, Praça Felipe Patroni, 40 mins, US$1. A taxi to the airport costs US$15.

Airline offices BRA, www.voebra.com.br. **Gol**, www.voegol.com.br. META, airport, T0300-789 5503 www.voemeta.com. **Puma Air**, T091-3039 3939, www.pumaair.com.br. **TAM**, at airport, T091-4002 5700, www.tam.com.br. **Varig**, R Cândido Mendes 1039, T091-3223 4612, www.varig.com.br.

Boat River services to **Santarém, Manaus**, and intermediate ports (see Routes in Amazônia, page 579). The larger ships berth at **Portobrás/Docas do Pará** (the main commercial port), either at Armazém (warehouse) No 3 at the foot of Av Pres Vargas, or at Armazém No 10, a few blocks further north (entrance on Av Marechal Hermes, corner of Av Visconde de Souza Franco). The guards will sometimes ask to see your ticket before letting you into the port area, but tell them you are going to speak with a ship's captain. Ignore the touts who approach you. Smaller vessels (sometimes cheaper, usually not as clean, comfortable or safe) sail from small docks along the **Estrada Nova** (not a safe part of town). Take a **Cremação** bus from Ver-o-Peso.

To **Macapá** (Porto Santana) daily service: Silja e Souza of **Souzamar**, Trav Dom Romualdo Seixas, corner of R Jerônimo Pimentel, T091-222 0719, and Comandante Solon of **Sanave (Serviço Amapaense de** Navegação, Av Castilho Franca 234, opposite Ver-o-Peso, T091-222 7810). Via **Breves**, ENAL, T091-224 5210. There are 2 desks selling tickets for private boats in the *rodoviária*; some hotels (eg **Fortaleza**) recommend agents for tickets. Purchase tickets from offices 2 days in advance. Smaller boats to Macapá also sail from Estrada Nova.

Bus To get to the *rodoviária* take **Aeroclube**, Cidade Novo, No 20 bus, or **Arsenal** or **Canudos** buses, US$0.50, or taxi, US$5 (day), US$7 (night).

Regular bus services to all major cities: **Transbrasiliana** go direct to **Marabá**, US$20 (16 hrs). To **Santarém**, via Marabá once a week (US$45, more expensive than by boat and can take longer, goes only in dry season). To **São Luís**, 2 a day, US$20, 13 hrs, interesting journey through marshlands. To **Fortaleza**, US$35-40 (24 hrs), several companies. To **Salvador**, US$50.

Car hire Avis, R Antônio Barreto 1653, T091-230 2000, also at airport, freephone T0800-558 066. **Localiza**, Av Pedro Álvares Cabral 200, T091-212 2700, and at airport, T091-257 1541.

Marabá and around *p543*
Air There are no direct flights to Altamira or Santarém, only via **Belém** with **Brasil Central** or **Varig**. **Brasil Central** flies to several local destinations, eg **São Luís**, **Imperatriz**.

Airline offices TAM, T091-324 3644. **Varig**, T091-322 1965.

Boat River services to **Belém** (24 hrs) and **Santarém** (18 hrs).

Bus Buses leave daily for **Belém** (654 km, paved, US$20), for **Santarém** (34 hrs) and many daily for **Imperatriz** (7-10 hrs, US$10. There is also a pickup to the bank of the Tocantins river opposite Imperatriz, 5 hrs, but more expensive). Buses can be caught going south at Tocantinópolis, opposite Porto Franco on the Belém–Brasília road. Also a bus can be taken to **Araguaína**, 12½ hrs, US$20; to **Goiânia** (change at Araguaína); to **Santa Inês** (Maranhão, on the Belém- Teresina road), 19 hrs, US$55. **Transbrasiliana** bus to **Altamira** daily, 1300 (if road is passable), 15 hrs, US$30. There are direct buses to **Rio** and **São Paulo**. On these bus trips take plenty of food and drink as local supplies are expensive. From the *rodoviária* to the railway station for trains on the São Luís-Parauapebas line, take a *colectivo* bus US$0.75 from opposite the *rodoviária* to Km 6 (a kind of suburb of Marabá), then another *colectivo* bus, US$0.75, to the Estação Ferrovia. The *colectivos* are infrequent and crowded. Alternatively, taxis, which can be shared, cost US$15 from the railway station to town.

Santarém *p546, map p546*

Air

The bus to the airport from the centre leaves in front of the cinema in Rui Barbosa every 80 mins, 0550-1910, or taxis (US$8). The hotels **Amazon Park, New City and Rio Dourado** have free buses for guests; you may be able to take these.

Internal flights to **Belém** and **Manaus**.

Airline offices META, R Siqueira Campos 162, T091-522 6222. Penta, Trav 15 de Novembro 183, T091-523 2532.

Bus

To get to the *rodoviária* take the 'Rodagem' bus from the waterfront near the market, US$0.35. To **Itaituba**, US$11, 11 hrs, 2 a day. To **Marabá** on the Rio Tocantins (via **Rurópolis** US$7.50, 6 hrs, and **Altamira** US$23, 28 hrs), 36 hrs (can be up to 6 days), US$41, with **Transbrasiliana**. Also to **Imperatriz**, via Marabá; office on Av Getúlio Vargas and at the *rodoviária*. Enquire at the *rodoviária* for other destinations. Beware of vehicles that offer a lift, which frequently turn out to be taxis. Road travel during the rainy season is always difficult, often impossible.

Boats

Shipping services to **Manaus, Belém, Macapá, Itaituba** and intermediate ports (Routes in Amazônia, page 579). Boats to Belém and Manaus dock at the Cais do Porto, 1 km west, take 'Floresta-Prainha', 'Circular' or 'Circular Externo' bus; taxi US$4. Boats to other destinations, including Macapá, dock by the waterfront near the centre of town. Local service to **Óbidos**, US$10, 4 hrs, **Oriximiná** (US$12.50), **Alenquer**, and **Monte Alegre** (US$10, 5-8 hrs).

Alter do Chão *p547*

Bus Tickets and information from the bus company kiosk opposite **Pousada Tupaiulândia**. From **Santarém**: bus stop on Av São Sebastião, in front of Colégio Santa Clara, US$1, about 1 hr.

Belterra and Fordlândia *p547*

Bus Bus from **Santarém** to Belterra (from Trav Silvino Pinto between Rui Barbosa and São Sebastião), 1000 and 1230, Mon-Sat, return 1300 and 1530, US$4, about 2 hrs. There is a 1-hr time difference between Santarém and Belterra, so if you take the 1230 bus you'll miss the 1530 return.

Boat Boats from **Santarém** to **Itaituba** stop at Fordlândia if you ask (leave Santarém 1800, arrive 0500-0600, US$12 for 1st-class hammock space); ask the captain to stop for you on return journey, about 2300. The alternative is to take a tour with a Santarém travel agent.

Directory

Macapá *p534, map p535*

Banks Banco do Brasil, R Independência 250, and Bradesco, R Cândido Mendes 1316, have Plus ATMs for VISA withdrawals. For *câmbios* (cash only), Casa Francesa, R Independência 232. **Monopólio**, Av Isaac Alcoubre 80. Both US$ and euros can be exchanged here. Best to buy euros in Belém if heading for Guyane as *câmbios* in Macapá are reluctant to sell them and they are more expensive and hard to obtain at the border. **Embassies and consulates** France, at Pousada Ekinox (see Sleeping, page 549). Visas are not issued for non-Brazilians. **Internet** @llnet in Macapá Shopping. **Medical services** Hospital Geral, Av FAB, T096-212 6127. Hospital São Camila & São Luiz, R Marcelo Candia 742, T096-223 1514. **Post office** Av Corialano Jucá. **Telephone** R São José 2050, open 0730-2200.

Oiapoque *p536*

Banks It is possible to exchange US dollars and reais to euros, but dollar rates are low and TCs are not accepted anywhere. **Banco do Brasil**, Av Barão do Rio Branco, 1000-1500, reais to euros and Visa facilities. Visa users can

also withdraw reais at Bradesco, exchanging these to euros. Gold merchants, such as Casa Francesa on the riverfront and a *câmbio* in the market, will sell reais for US$ or euros. Rates are even worse in St-Georges. Best to buy euros in Belém, or abroad.
Immigration Polícia Federal for Brazilian exit stamp is on the road to Calçoene, about 500 m from the river. **Post office** Av Barão do Rio Branco, open 0900-1200, 1400-1700.

Belém *p537, map p539*
Banks Banks open 0900-1630, but foreign exchange only until 1300. Banco do Brasil, Av Pres Vargas, near Hotel Itaoca, good rates, ATMs; other Brazilian banks (0900-1630, but foreign exchange only until 1300). HSBC, Av Pres Vargas near Praça da República has MasterCard Cirrus and Amex ATMs. Banco de Amazônia (Basa), on Pres Vargas, gives good rates for TCs (Amex or Citicorp only), but does not change cash. Itaú, R Boaventura 580, good TCs and cash rates. Officially, money can only be changed at banks during the week. At weekends hotels will only exchange for their guests, while restaurants may change money, but at poor rates. **Embassies and consulates** Denmark (Consul Arne Hvidbo), R Senador Barata 704, sala 1503, T091-2411 588 (PO box 826). Finland and Sweden, Av Senador Lemos 529, Umarizal, T091-222 0148. France, www.ambafrance.org.br. Germany, www.alemanha.org.br. Italy, www.emb italia.org.br. UK, Edif Palladium Centre, room 410, Av Gov José Malcher 815, T091-220 0274. USA, www.embaixada.americana.org.br. Venezuela, opposite French Consulate, R Pres Pernambuco 270, T091-222 6396 (Venezuelan visa takes 3 hrs, costs US$30 for most nationalities, but we are told that it is better to get a visa at Manaus; latest reports indicate that a yellow fever vaccination certificate is not required but it is best to check in advance – see also medical services, below).
Internet Amazon, 2nd floor of Estação das Docas. InterBelém, Av Jose Malcher 189, US$1 per hr, helpful South African owner, English spoken. Convert, Shopping Iguatemi, 3rd floor, US$1.40 per hr. **Language schools** Unipop, Av Sen Lemos 557, T091-224 9074, Portuguese course for foreigners. **Laundry** Lav e Lev, R Dr Moraes 576. Lavanderia Paraense, Trav Dom Pedro 1104, T091-222 0057, dry and steam cleaning. **Libraries** UFPA, Av Augusto Correa 1, T091-211 1140, university library with many titles on Amazônia. **Medical services** A yellow fever certificate of inoculation is mandatory. It is best to get one at home (always have your certificate handy) and avoid the risk of recycled needles. Medications for malaria prophylaxis are not sold in Belém pharmacies. You can theoretically get them through the public health service, but this is hopelessly complicated. Such drugs are sometimes available at pharmacies in smaller centres, eg Santarém and Macapá. Bring an adequate supply from home. Clínica de Medicina Preventativa, Av Bras de Aguiar 410 (T091-222 1434), will give injections, English spoken, open 0730-1200, 1430-1900 (Sat 0800-1100). Hospital da Ordem Terceira, Trav Frei Gil de Vila Nova 59, T091-212 2777, doctors speak some English, free consultation. Surgery Mon 1300-1900, Tue-Thu 0700-1100, 24 hrs for emergencies. The British consul has a list of English-speaking doctors. **Police** for reporting crimes, R Santo Antônio and Trav Frei Gil de Vila Nova. **Post office** Av Pres Vargas 498. Also handles telegrams and fax. **Telephone** Telemar, Av Pres Vargas.

Marabá and around *p543*
Banks Banco do Brasil, Praça Duque de Caxias 966. **Hospitals** Celina Gonçalves, T091-322 1031.

Santarém *p546, map p546*
Banks Banco do Brasil, Av Rui Barbosa 794, exchanges TCs and cash, also withdrawals on Visa. **Internet** Tapajos On Line, Mendonça Furtado 2454, US$3.50 per hr.
Laundry Storil, Trav Turiano Meira 167, 1st floor. **Post office** Praça da Bandeira 81.
Medical services Hospital São Raimundo Nonato, Av Mendonça Furtado 1993, T091-523 1176. **Telephone** Posto Trin, R Siqueira Campos 511. Mon-Sat 0700-1900, Sun 0700-2100.

Amazonas and the Amazon River

Amazonas is the largest state in Brazil (1.6 million sq km), bigger than any country in South America except Argentina, but with a population of just 2.8 million. Half of the inhabitants live in the capital, Manaus, with the rest spread out in remote communities often linked only by air and river.

The scenery in Amazonas is magnificent. Nothing can prepare you for the vast skies, the pure air, the endless shades of green, and rivers that stretch to the horizon. Nowhere does the Amazon feel more like the inland sea it once was than here. Rivers merge in vast swirls of myriad shades – from the translucent black of strong iced tea to café-au-lait brown – through vast forest-fringed lakes covered with giant water lilies or through eerie strands of flooded igapó *or* varzea *forest. And in the rivers' depths swim 4-m-long horny-tongued fish, bull sharks, dolphins, stingrays and catfish big enough to swallow a man whole.*

Amazonas state preserves Brazil's most extensive and unspoilt areas of lowland tropical forest, and the tourist industry here is developing fast. Most tours and trips to jungle lodges begin in Manaus, a sprawling rubber-boom town with good national and international connections. Beyond Manaus are the giant boulder mountains of the upper Rio Negro, which rise to Brazil's highest peak, the flooded wilds of Mamirauá near Tefé, and the Javari near Tabatinga, which are among the best places in the Amazon for spotting wildlife.

But the vast forests of Amazonas are not uninhabited. Civilizations have been living here from anywhere between 11,000 and 5000 BC and these people and their caboclo *descendants maintain a rich cultural life. Although indigenous villages are very difficult to visit, their heritage can be experienced at the festivals in São Gabriel and the Boi Bumba in Parintins. The latter is the largest and most spectacular in the country after Carnaval and takes place on an island in the middle of the Amazon river at the end of June.* ▸▸ *For Sleeping, Eating and other listings, see pages 573-583.*

Visiting the forest

What to visit

A visit to the Amazon is about experiencing the spectacular scenery and vastness of the landscapes. Animals are very difficult to see in the rainforest, far more so than on the African savannah or in the Pantanal. The scenery is at its best on the **Rio Negro**, especially around the Anavilhanas, and further upstream where the mountains of the Guiana Shield punctuate the forest like giant worn crocodile teeth. However, the Rio Negro is an acidic, black-water river and consequently has a lower level of biodiversity than the more ph-neutral brown-water rivers like the Solimões (Amazon). So if you are intent above all on seeing wildlife, you will see far more in the regions **south of Manaus**, on the smaller river tributaries, creeks (*igarapés*) and flooded forest areas (*varzea* and *igapós*). The best places of all are those farthest from people, and certainly far from Manaus. Of all the readily accessible locations, the best is **Mamirauá** near Tefé, a flight away from Manaus. Some of the lodges around Manaus have their own reserves, which have been populated with rescued primates and birds. The best of these is the **Amazon Ecopark** (see page 574). Others, such as those around Lago Piranha or Lago Mamori, are in semi-protected areas where species levels are recovering.

When to visit

There is no best time to visit the forest; it depends what you want to see. The Amazon around Manaus is far more than a big river; think of it rather as an inland sea. Water is everywhere, especially during the **wet season**, which lasts from November to May. During the floods, the water rises by 5-10 m and the forests around the main rivers form areas known as *varzea* (on brown-water rivers) and *igapó* (on black-water rivers). Trees are submerged almost to their canopies and it is possible to canoe between their trunks in search of wildlife. In the morning you can often hear the booming call of huge black caiman and the snort of dolphins. And as the boats pass through the trees, startled hatchet fish jump into the bows. It is possible to canoe for tens of kilometres away from the main river flow, as *varzea* and *igapós* often connect one river to another, often via oxbow lakes covered in giant lilies. The lakes are formed when a meandering river changes course and leaves part of its previous flow cut off from the stream. In the **dry season** the rivers retreat into their main flow, exposing broad mudflats (on the brown-water rivers) or long beaches of fine white sand. Caiman and giant river turtles can often be seen basking on these in the evening sun, and wildlife spotting is generally a little easier at this time of year. Trees in the Amazon bear fruit at different times throughout the year; whenever a particular tree is in fruit it attracts large parrots, macaws and primates.

Choosing a tour or lodge

Once you have decided on when and where to go, the next decision is to choose a lodge or an operator. Those used to the quality of wildlife information supplied by rainforest tour operators in Costa Rica, Peru, Ecuador or Bolivia will be disappointed by the lack of professional wildlife knowledge and ecotourism services offered by many of the operators in Manaus. If you are interested first and foremost in wildlife and want accurate information, be sure to request a specialist wildlife guide (see page 579) and question your tour company carefully to test their knowledge. A good way of doing this is to ask whether they can supply a species list for the area around their lodge or for the forests they visit during their tours. Few can. Serious wildlife enthusiasts and birders looking to visit the Brazilian Amazon should think about heading for Mamirauá near Tefé or **Cristalino Jungle Lodge** (see page 666) in Mato Grosso.

Standard tours from Manaus or the rainforest lodges involve a walk through the forest looking at plants and their usage, caiman spotting at night (many guides drag caiman out of the water, which has negative long-term effects and should be discouraged), piranha fishing and boat trips through the *igapós* or the creeks (*igarapés*). They may also visit a *caboclo* (river village) or one of the newly established indigenous villages around the city. Other trips involve light adventure such as rainforest survival, which involves learning how to find water and food in the forest, and how to make a shelter and string up a hammock for a secure night's sleep.

Trips vary in length. A half-day or a day trip will usually involve a trip to the 'meeting of the waters' and the Lago de Janauri nature reserve, where you are likely to see plenty of birds, some primates and river dolphins. The reserve was set up to receive large numbers of tourists so there are captive parrots on display and numerous tourist shops. Yet ecologists agree that the reserve helps relieve pressure on other parts of the river. Boats for day trippers leave the harbour in Manaus constantly throughout the day, but are best booked at one of the larger operators. Those with more time can take the longer cruises with a company like **Amazon Clipper** (see page 578) or stay in one of the rainforest lodges. To see virgin rainforest, a five-day trip by boat is needed.

Prices vary but usually include lodging, guide, transport, meals (but not drinks) and activities. The recommended companies charge US$60-95 per person for a day trip, or US$195-285 for three days.

Beware of the touts

There are many hustlers at the airport in Manaus and on the street (particularly around the hotels and bars on Joaquim Nabuco and Miranda Leão), and even at hotel receptions. It is not wise to go on a tour with the first friendly face you meet; all go-betweens earn a commission so recommendations cannot be taken at face value and employing a freelance guide not attached to a company is potentially dangerous as they may not be qualified; check out their credentials. Tourist offices are not allowed by law to recommend guides, but can provide you with a list of legally registered companies. Unfortunately, disreputable companies are rarely dealt with in any satisfactory manner, and most continue to operate. Book direct with the company itself and ask for a detailed, written contract if you have any doubts.

What to take

Leave luggage with your tour operator or hotel in Manaus and only take what is necessary for your trip. Long-sleeved shirts, long trousers, walking boots and insect repellent are advisable for treks in the jungle, where insects can be voracious. A hat offers protection from the sun on boat trips. Powerful binoculars are essential for spotting wildlife (at least 7x magnification is recommended, with the ability to focus at between 2.5m and infinity). Buying bottled water at the local villages is a sure way to help the local economy, but it can be expensive in the lodges. A hammock mosquito net is useful for treks, and a bed mosquito net is a good idea for the cheaper lodges where the provided net may have holes.

Lodges → *See page 574 for a list of recommended lodges.*

Most of the lodges around Manaus do not adhere to proper ecotouristic practice; this guide lists the exceptions. Good practice includes integration and employment for the local community, education support, recycling and proper rubbish disposal, and trained guides with good wildlife lodges. Ecotourism in Brazil is often a badge for adventure tourism in a natural setting and few operators conform to the best practices of the **International Ecotourism Society,** www.ecotourism.org. Neither the environment nor the local communities receive much from Brazilian 'ecotourism'. In Manaus, a relatively small number of communities have benefited from a boom which has seen the total number of beds rise from just six in 1979 to over 1000 today. Only 27% of labour derives from local communities and very few of the lodges are locally owned.

Manaus » *pp573-583.*

→ *Phone code: 092. Colour map 1, B3. Population: 1.4 million.*

Manaus, the state capital, sits at 32 m above sea level some 1600 km from the Atlantic. The city sprawls over a series of eroded and gently sloping hills divided by numerous creeks, and stands at the junction of the liquorice-black Rio Negro and the toffee-coloured Solimões, whose waters flow side by side in two distinct streams within the same river. The city is the commercial hub for a vast area including parts of Peru, Bolivia and Colombia, and ocean-going container vessels often dock here.

New-found wealth has turned Manaus from tawdry to tourist-friendly in the last five years. The historic centre, which huddles around the green and gold mock-Byzantine dome of the opera house, has been tastefully refurbished and now verges on elegant. The area is a pleasant place to stroll around and sip a cool juice or a strong coffee, and many of the best hotels and guesthouses are found here. There are plenty of restaurants, bars and clubs, which support a lively, colourful nightlife.

Despite the city's size, the forest is ever present on the horizon and always feels just a short boat trip away. Beaches fringe its western extremities at Ponta Negra, whose sands are increasingly backed by towering blocks of flats, making it feel like a kind of Amazonian Ipanema.

There are plenty of sights near Manaus. The most vaunted are generally the least interesting. However, the Anavilhanas – the largest river archipelago in the world, comprising a beautiful labyrinth of forested islands fringed with white-sand beaches lapped by the jet-black waters of the Rio Negro – should not be missed. Try to be there for sunset when thousands of swifts descend to roost and the light is a deep, rich gold.

Manaus is also the main departure point for rainforest tours. There are many lodges around the city, from 20 minutes to four hours away. And although animals here are not as easy to see as in Tefé or on the Rio Javari, the scenery is breathtaking.

Ins and outs

Getting there The only usable road runs north to Boa Vista, Guyana and Venezuela. Visitors almost invariably arrive by plane or boat. The modern **Eduardo Gomes airport** ⓘ *10 km north of the city centre, T092-652 1120*, receives flights from all of Brazil's principal cities and there are international connections with Germany and Miami. The restaurant serves good à la carte and buffet food throughout the day. A taxi to the

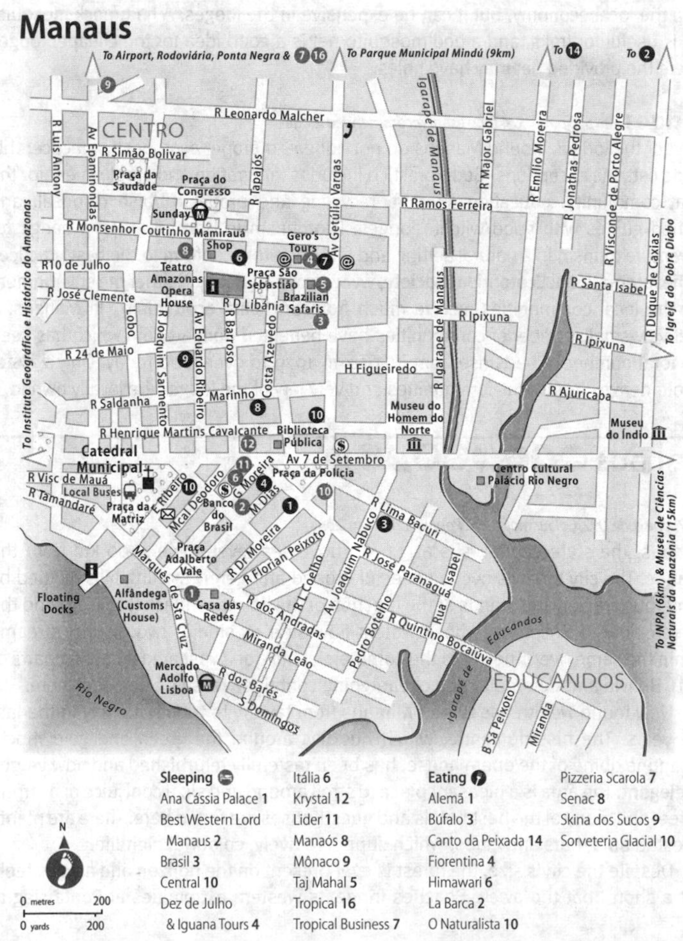

centre costs around US$17.50 on the meter. Taxi drivers often tell arrivals that no bus to town is available, be warned.

The only long-distance buses arriving in Manaus **rodoviária** ⓘ *5 km out of town at the intersection of Av Constantino Nery and R Recife*, are from Boa Vista, Presidente Figueiredo and Itacoatiara. Local buses from the airport to the city cost US$1, but there are none between 2330 and 0500.

Boat passengers arrive at the newly renovated **floating docks** ⓘ *in the centre, a couple of blocks south of Praça da Matriz*, with direct access to the main artery of Avenida Eduardo Ribeiro, and 10 minutes' walk from the opera house and main hotel area. Other towns in the state are best visited by air or boat, especially during the November to May wet season when road travel is next to impossible. Those arriving by boat (eg from Leticia) who have not already had their passports stamped, must go to the immigration office on the first of the floating docks next to the tourist office. To get there, take the dock entrance opposite the cathedral, bear right, after 50 m left, pass through a warehouse to a group of buildings on a T-section. ▸▸ *See also Transport, page 580.*

Getting around The city centre is easily explored on foot. All city bus routes start on Marques da Santa Cruz next to the Praça da Matriz. Information on local buses can be found on www.embarque.com.br. Taxis can be found near the opera house, at the *rodoviária*, airport and in Ponta Negra. Many of the upmarket hotels are in Ponta Negra, which is 13 km from the city centre and can feel somewhat isolated.

Tourist information There are several **Centros de Atendimento ao Turista** (**CAT**) throughout the city. The main office is 50 m south of the opera house ⓘ *Av Eduardo Ribeiro 666, T092-622 0767, Mon-Fri 0800-1700, Sat 0800-1200*. There are also offices in **Amazonas Shopping** ⓘ *Av Djalma Batist 482, Chapada, T096-236 5154, Mon-Sat 0900-2200, Sun 1500-2100*; at the **airport** ⓘ *T096-652 1120 or T0800-280 0820, daily 0700-2300*, at the **port** ⓘ *regional terminal, R Marquês de Santa Cruz, armazém 07, Mon-Fri 0800-1700*, and ⓘ *international terminal, R Marquês de Santa Cruz, armazém 10*, which opens only when cruise liners dock. There is a **CAT** trailer in the **rodoviária** ⓘ *R Recife s/n, Flores, Mon-Sat 0800-1200*. The website for Amazonas tourism is www.amazonastur.am.gov.br. It has extensive information on accommodation throughout the state in Portuguese and English. *A Crítica* newspaper lists local entertainment and events.

Centro histórico

The colonial streets that spread out from Praça São Sebastião are a reminder of Manaus's brief dalliance with wealth and luxury. Eduardo Ribeiro, the state governor who presided over these golden years, was determined to make 19th-century Manaus the envy of the world: a fine European city in which the nouveau riche could parade their linen and lace. He spared no expense. Trams were running in Manaus before they were in Manchester or Boston and its roads were lit by the first electric street lights in the world. The city's confidence grew with its majesty. Champagne flowed under the crystal chandeliers and prices rose to four times those of contemporaneous New York. Extravagance begot extravagance and rubber barons eager to compete in statements of affluent vulgarity fed their horses vintage wine or bought lions as guard cats.

In the 1890s, Ribeiro decided to put the icing on his cake, commissioning Portuguese architect Domenico de Angelis to build an Italianate opera house, the **Teatro Amazonas** ⓘ *Praça São Sebastião, T096-622 1880, Mon-Sat 0900-1600, 20-min tour US$7, students US$2.50*, and to surround it with stone-cobbled streets lined with elegant houses, plazas, and gardens replete with ornate fountains and gilded cherubs. Masks adorning the theatre walls were made in homage to four great European artists: Shakespeare, Mozart, Verdi and Molière. The stage curtain depicted the meeting of the waters and *Iara*, the spirit of the river Amazon, and the driveway was paved in rubber to prevent the sound of carriage wheels spoiling performances. After the theatre doors were opened in 1896, Caruso sang here and Pavlova danced. But for all its beauty and expense the theatre was used for little more than a decade. In the early 20th century the rubber economy collapsed. Seeds smuggled by Englishman Henry Wickham, to the Imperial Gardens at Kew and thence to Malaysia, were producing a higher yield. The wild-rubber economy dwindled and the doors to the opera house closed. Over the decades, the French tiles on the dome began to crack, the Italian marble darkened and the fine French furniture and English china slowly began to decay. What you see today is the product of careful restoration, which has returned the *teatro* to its original glory. There are regular performances, which sell out very quickly, and an arts festival every April. Until less than 10 years ago the streets around the opera house were down at heel and seedy, but they have now been refurbished. The colonial houses have all been freshly painted; several are now little cafés and souvenir shops and the area is a safe and pleasant place to while away an hour or two.

The city's other sights are huddled around the waterfront. The **Mercado Adolfo Lisboa** ⓘ *R dos Barés 46*, was built in 1882 as a miniature copy of the now-demolished Parisian Les Halles. The wrought ironwork, which forms much of the structure, was imported from Europe and is said to have been designed by Eiffel. It's worth coming here if only to see the astonishing array of bizarre fish from tiger-striped catfish to enormous *piraíba* (said to be able to eat a man) and *pacu*, a large vegetarian piranha with molars powerful enough to crack a Brazil nut.

The remarkable **harbour installations**, completed in 1902, were designed and built by a Scottish engineer to cope with the Rio Negro's annual rise and fall of up to 14 m. The large **floating dock** is connected to street level by a 150-m-long floating ramp, at the end of which, on the harbour wall, can be seen the high-water mark for each year since it was built. When the river is high, the roadway floats on a series of large iron tanks measuring 2½ m in diameter. The large beige **Alfândega** (Customs House) ⓘ *R Marquês de Santa Cruz, Mon-Fri 0800-1300*, stands at the entrance to the city when arriving by boat. Said to be have been modelled on the one in Delhi, it was entirely prefabricated in England, and the tower once acted as a lighthouse.

Dominating the streets between the opera house and the waterfront; and right next to the local bus station, is the **Catedral Municipal**, on Praça Osvaldo Cruz, built in simple Jesuit style and very plain inside and out. Originally constructed in 1695 in wood and straw, it was burnt down in 1850 and rebuilt in neoclassical style. Nearby is the main shopping and business area, the tree-lined **Avenida Eduardo Ribeiro**, crossed by Avenida 7 de Setembro and bordered by ficus trees. There are a few other interesting buildings worth visiting if you have time to spare.

The **Biblioteca Pública** (Public Library) ⓘ *R Barroso 57, Mon-Fri 0730-1730, T096-234 0588*, inaugurated in 1871, is part of the city's architectural heritage. Featuring an ornate European cast-iron staircase, it is well stocked with 19th-century newspapers, rare books and old photographs, and is worth a visit.

The **Museu do Homem do Norte** ⓘ *Av 7 de Setembro 1385, near Av Joaquim Nabuco, T096-232 5373, Mon-Thu 0900-1200, 1300-1700, Fri 1300-1700, US$1*, is an interesting review of the way of life of the Amazonian population, or 'men of the north', although it has deteriorated in recent years. Social, cultural and economic aspects are displayed with photographs, models and other exhibits.

The **Centro Cultural Palácio Rio Negro (Museu de Imagem e Son)** ⓘ *Av 7 de Setembro 1546, T096-233 2850, Tue-Fri 1000-1700, Sat and Sun 1600-2100*, was the residence of a German rubber merchant until 1917 and later because the state government palace. It now holds various cultural events, including exhibitions, shows and films. There is also a café.

The **Museu do Índio** ⓘ *R Duque de Caxias 296, near Av 7 Setembro, T096-234 1422, Mon-Fri 0830-1200 and 1400-1700, Sat 0800-1130, US$3*, is managed by the

Salesian missionaries who have been responsible for the ravaging of much of the indigenous culture of the upper Rio Negro. It is rather run down and betrays a Victorian view of indigenous culture. The displays are dusty but there are plenty of artefacts, including handicrafts, ceramics, clothing, utensils and ritual objects from the various indigenous tribes of the upper Rio Negro. There is also a small craft shop.

North of the centre

The **Parque Municipal do Mindú** ⓘ *R Perimetral s/n, Parque Dez suburb, T096-236 7702, Tue-Sun 0900-1700; take bus No 423 or 433 from Praça da Matriz*, is a 33-ha ecological reserve and education centre with a system of trails, elevated walkways, a little amphitheatre and orchid gardens. If you are very lucky you may catch a glimpse of one of the world's rarest monkeys, the pied bare-face tamarin (*Saguinus bicolor bicolor*), a subspecies of bare-faced tamarin thought to live only near Manaus and threatened with extinction.

The **Jardim Botânico Chico Mendes** (Horto Municipal) ⓘ *Av André Araujo s/n, daily 0800-1200 and 1400-1700; take bus for 'Aleixo' or 'Coroado'*, contains a collection of plants from the Amazon region.

West of the centre

The **Instituto Geográfico e Histórico do Amazonas** ⓘ *R Bernardo Ramos 117, near the Prefeitura, T096-232 7077, Mon-Fri 0900-1200 and 1300-1600, US$0.20*, is located in a fascinating older district of central Manaus. It houses a museum and library of over 10,000 books, which thoroughly document Amazonian life through the ages.

The **zoo** ⓘ *Estrada Ponta Negra 750, T096-625 2044, Tue-Sun 0900-1630, US$3, free on Sun, take bus No 120 from R Tamandaré by the cathedral, US$0.70, every 30 mins, get off 400 m past the first infantry barracks, a big white building*, is run by **CIGS**, the Brazilian Army Unit specializing in jungle survival. It has recently been expanded and improved. About 300 Amazonian animals are kept in the gardens, including anacondas in a huge pit.

Just north of the centre, the **Hotel Tropical** has a small zoo and many kinds of birds can be seen in and around the grounds, including flycatchers (kingbirds and kiskadees), swallows, yellow-browed sparrows, aracaris (a member of the toucan family), woodpeckers, woodcreepers, thrushes, anis, three species of tanager and two types of parrot (dusky and blue-headed). Sloths and monkeys may also be seen. For further information, contact Moacir Fortes or Andrew Whittaker, birding@internext.com.br.

East of the centre

There is a curious little church, **Igreja do Pobre Diabo**, at the corner of Avenida Borba and Avenida Ipixuna, in the suburb of Cachoeirinha. It is only 4 m wide by 5 m long, and was built by a local trader, the 'poor devil' of the name. To get there, take the 'Circular 7 de Setembro Cachoeirinha' bus from the cathedral to Hospital Militar.

The **botanic gardens** are maintained by the **Instituto Nacional de Pesquisas da Amazônia (INPA)** ⓘ *Estrada do Aleixo, Km 3, near the natural science museum, see below, T096-643 3377, Mon-Fri 0900-1100, 1400-1630, Sat and Sun 0900-1600, US$2; take bus No 519 from the local bus depot by the cathedral*, which conducts research into all aspects of the Amazon. There is a small park that is good for a taste of rainforest flora and fauna before you head out to the forest. The animals here are kept in less distressing conditions than in the city zoo. Paca (*Agouti paca*), agouti (*Myoprocta exilis*), squirrel monkeys (*Saimiri scicureus*) and tamarins (*Saguinus sp*) roam free, and among the other animals on display are Amazonian manatee (*Trichechus inunguis*) and giant otter (*Pternura brasiliensis*).

The **Museu de Ciências Naturais da Amazônia** (natural science museum) ⓘ *Al Cosme Ferreira, Cachoeira Grande suburb, 15 km from centre, T096-644 2799, Mon-*

 Sat 0900-1700, US$4, best to combine with a visit to INPA, and take a taxi from there (see above), is one of the city's little-known treasures. The remote museum is run by Japanese, with characteristic efficiency, and the exhibits are beautifully displayed and clearly labelled in Japanese, Portuguese and English. The main building houses hundreds of preserved Amazon insects and butterflies, together with stuffed specimens of a selection of the river's bizarre fish. You can also see live versions, including the endangered pirarucu (*Arapaima gigas*), which can grow up to 3½ m, and a primitive osteoglottid fish that breathes air.

Beaches

Manaus has two sandy beaches on the outskirts of the city. The **Praia da Ponta Negra**, which lies upstream of the city's pollution, is the most popular and the most heavily developed. It is backed by high-rise flats and lined with open-air restaurants, bars and areas for beach volleyball and football. Nightlife here is lively, especially at weekends. However, on most nights at least one of the bars (such as **O Laranjinha**, see page 576) will have Boi Bumba dance shows. Many of the better hotels, including the **Tropical**, are situated here. To get here take any bus marked 'Ponta Negra' (eg No 120) from the local bus station next to the cathedral. The beach can also be reached on the Tropical's shuttle bus (see Sleeping, page 573).

The city's other beach, **Praia Amarelinho**, in the Educandos neighbourhood, is a little too close to the centre to avoid pollution and is not recommended.

The meeting of the waters

About 15 km from Manaus is the confluence of the coffee-coloured **Rio Solimões** (Amazon) and the black-tea coloured **Rio Negro**, which is itself some 8 km wide. The

Around Manaus

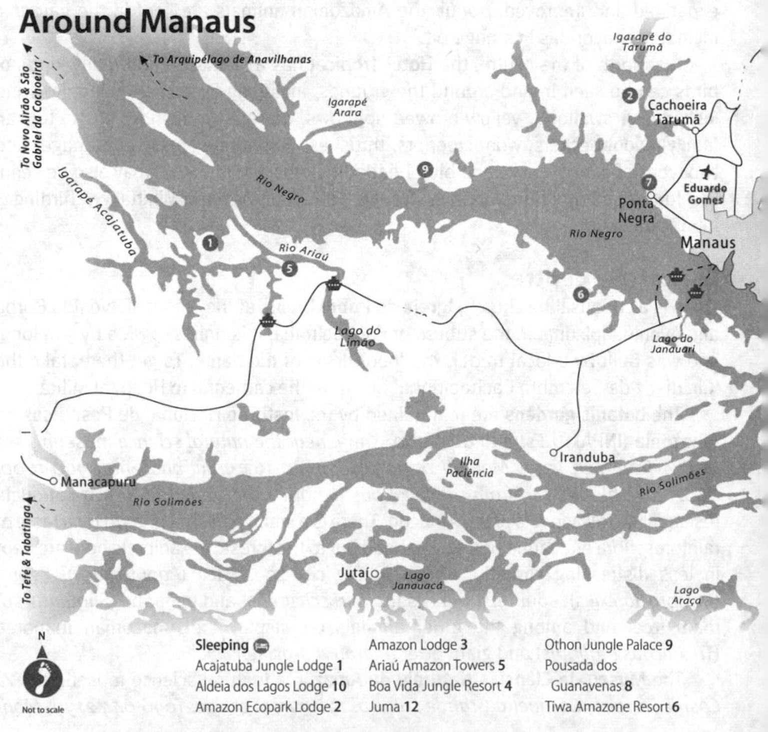

two rivers run side by side for about 6 km without their waters mingling. This phenomenon is caused by differences in the temperature, density and velocity of the two rivers. Tourist agencies run boat trips to this spot (US$60-160). The simplest route is to take a taxi or bus No 713 'Vila Buriti' to the Careiro dock, and take the car ferry across. The boat is very basic with no shelter on deck and departs at 0700 returning 1000, and 1500 returning 1800. There are also small private launches, which take 40 minutes and cost about US$10-15 per seat; ask for the engine to be shut off at the confluence. You should see dolphins, especially in the early morning. Alternatively, hire a motorized canoe from near the market (about US$15; allow three to four hours to experience the meeting properly). A 2-km walk along the Porto Velho road from the Careiro ferry terminal leads to some ponds, some way from the road, in which huge Victoria Regia water lilies can be seen from April to September.

Excursions from Manaus

Manacapuru → *Colour map 1, B3.*

This typical Amazon market town is situated on the Solimões 110 km west of Manaus. It has three basic hotels and **Il Maccarone** pizzeria (Avenida Eduardo Ribeiro 1000). It is 84 km by road (four buses daily, US$5, two hours including ferry crossing) on the AM-070. Around 25 km from Manaus is the **Piranha Lake Sustainable Development Reserve**, comprising a series of lakes and protecting large areas of *varzea* forest, dotted with gigantic trees such as sumaumeira. The area is a refuge for migratory birds and a breeding ground for many endemic herons, storks, egrets and ducks. There is excellent sport fishing.

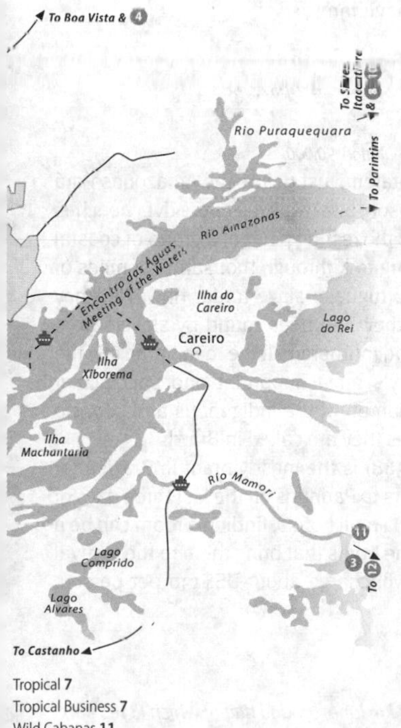

Araça

This village on the Rio Mamori has plenty of wildlife close at hand, and canoes can be hired to spot animals from the river. Many of the jungle lodges lie a little upstream on the Rio Mamori, around lake Mamori. There is malaria in this area. To get here, take bus No 11 from the Manaus *rodoviária* in the direction of Castanho. The journey takes three hours, including the ferry at the confluence of the Negro and Solimões, and costs US$1.50. Buses leave Manaus at 0600 and 1100.

Arquipélago de Anavilhanas

This filigree of more than 350 brilliant-green islands in the jet-black Rio Negro – some fringed with white-sand beaches, others anchored only by their roots – is one of the areas's must-see sights. The scene is particularly beautiful at the end of the day when the sky looks vast and warm and the light on the trunks of the partially submerged trees is a thick orange-yellow. Birds fly into the Anavilhanas to roost and millions of bats leave for their night hunt. The air is silent

Festa do Boi Bumba

The Boi Bumba festival in Parintins is a competition between two rival groups, similar to the samba schools in Rio, called Caprichoso (whose colour is blue) and Garantido (red). The two teams present a pageant, which originates from Braga in Portugal, but has been heavily syncretized with indigenous and Afro-Brazilian themes. It was brought to Parintins in the early 20th century by settlers from São Luís in Maranhão. The pageant tells the story of Pai Francisco and his wife Mãe Catirina who steal the prize bull from the landowner that they work for, and kill it. The landowner discovers this and threatens to kill them if they fail to resurrect his bull by midnight. The couple employ the talents of a shaman, a priest and an African *pai santo*, and these characters invoke the female spirit of rainforest fertility, the Cunhã-poranga, played by a beautiful young dancer. The story is told to the backdrop of vast four-storey floats with moving parts and troupes of hundreds of dancers. It is performed in the purpose-built *bumbódromo* stadium which holds almost 40,000 spectators. Previews of the festival in miniature are held in the **Hotel Tropical** in Manaus throughout the year and there are always Boi Bumba dancers on weekend evenings in the Ponta Negra bars in Manaus.

but for bird calls, the lapping of the river and the bluster of river dolphins surfacing for air. The islands are 80 km upstream of Manaus. Several companies arrange visits to the archipelago (US$195-285, one day) as can most of the Rio Negro lodges. Rio Negro safari cruises almost all visit the Anavilhanas.

Downstream from Manaus » pp573-583.

Parintins → *Phone code: 092. Colour map 1, B4. Population: 90,000.*

Parintins is situated between Manaus and Santarém, just before the Amazonas-Pará border, on the Ilha Tupinambana. In the dry season, boat trips run to the river beaches and to nearby lakes. In colonial times, this was the resting point of a group of coastal indigenous Brazilians who made an astonishing trek through thousands of miles of dense forest to escape the ravages of the Portuguese slave trade. However, they didn't evade it for long. Within a generation they had been found by slavers from Belém who took all the women and children and murdered all the men. Ironically the island is now the site of one of the country's most important and spectacular festivals, Boi Bumba, which celebrates the triumph of the indigenous and *caboclo* poor over a tyrannical landowner, or *coronel*, as they are called in Brazil.

The **Festa do Boi Bumba** (see box, page 568) is the most vibrant in Brazil after Carnaval and draws tens of thousands of visitors to Parintins on the last three days of June each year. But since the town has only two small hotels, finding a room can be a challenge. Everyone sleeps in hammocks on the boats that bring them to the festival from Manaus and Santarém (a large vessel will charge about US$130 per person, including breakfast, for the duration).

The mighty Amazon system is a staggering 6577 km long, around half of which (3165 km) is in Brazilian territory. Ships of up to 5000 tons regularly negotiate the waterway as far as Iquitos in Peru, 3646 km from Manaus.

Upstream from Manaus » pp573-583.

Tefé → *Phone code: 097. Colour map 1, B2. Population: 65,000.*

Tefé is a scruffy town roughly halfway between Manaus and the Colombian border. The local airport authorities confiscated all of the city's rubbish lorries in a dispute over the municipal dump, and now it is piled up willy-nilly. But few come here for the town itself, for this is the access point to one of the world's most important primate and waterfowl reserves, the **Mamirauá Ecological Reserve** ⓘ *T097-3343 4160, www.mamiraua.org.br*. This is a **Ramsar** (Convention on wetlands, www.ramsar.org) site set up with British support to protect huge areas of terra firme, gallery, *varzea* and *igapó* forest at the confluence of the Solimões and Japurá rivers, and to manage them sustainably with the local riverine people. There are abundant birds including numerous rare trogons, cotingas, currasows, five species of macaw, hoatzin and harpy eagle. There are black caiman (one of which lives under the floating lodge), both species of Amazon dolphin, and numerous rare primates – the most spectacular of which are the endemic black-headed squirrel monkey and the endangered white uakari, known locally as the 'macaco Ingles' because of its red complexion. A visit is unforgettable.

The reserve has a small floating lodge, the **Pousada Uacari** on the Mamirauá river and visitors stay here in simple but elegant wooden rooms. Trips include walks in terra firme forest, boat and canoe trips to *igarpe* creeks, *varzea* and *igapó* forest and the vast Mamirauá lake. Visits must be booked in advance.

Ins and outs Tefé is connected to Manaus by air three times a week on Rico, with onward flights to Tabatinga. There are regular boats (at least one a day) from Manaus or from Tabatinga. The town is small enough to negotiate on foot.

Benjamin Constant → *Phone code: 097. Colour map 1, B1. Population: 23,000.*

This tiny town, with a big sawmill and a series of little tiled houses set in bougainvillea gardens, sits on the frontier with Peru, just opposite Leticia in Colombia. There is an interesting **Ticuna indigenous cultural centre and museum** ⓘ *Av Castelo Branco 396, T096-415 5624*, with artefacts, information panels and a gift shop. The music is haunting but sadly not for sale. Ticuna people run the museum. There are boat services from Manaus (seven days or more), to Manaus (four days or more) and to Iquitos.

Tabatinga → *Phone code: 097. Colour map 1, B1. Population: 38,000.*

Tabatinga is theoretically 4 km from Leticia (in Colombia) but, in reality, it is the scruffy half of the same town – a long street buzzing with mopeds, a port and some untidy houses in between. There is an important Ticuna centre here, and the town is the headquarters of one of the country's most important indigenous NGOs, **FIUPAM** (fiupam@yahoo.com.br.). However, there is little of interest for tourists, who are better off staying in Leticia. Flights arrive in Leticia (see below) from where a minibus to Tabatinga costs US$1.

Border crossing No visas or entry stamps are required to pass between Tabatinga and Leticia, but immigration and customs in and out of Tabatinga by air can be very rigorous. The port area is called Marco and the port captain is very helpful and speaks good English. A good hammock will cost US$15 in Tabatinga (try Esplanada Teocides) or Benjamin Constant. A mosquito net for a hammock is essential if sailing upstream from Tabatinga, much less so downstream. There are regular boats to Manaus and to Benjamin Constant, across the water, and onwards to Iquitos in Peru. The best way to get to Leticia is to walk or take a cab or minibus (US$0.60).

Leticia (Colombia) → *Phone code: 9859. Colour map 1, B1. Population: 27,000.*

This riverside city is clean and modern, though run down, and is rapidly merging into one town with neighbouring Marco in Brazil. Leticia is a good place to buy indigenous products typical of the Amazon, and tourist services are better than in Tabatinga or Benjamin Constant. The best time to visit the area is in July or August, the early months of the dry season. At weekends, accommodation may be difficult to find.

The **museum** ⓘ *Cra 11 y Calle 9*, set up by **Banco de la República**, covers local ethnography and archaeology and is set in a beautiful building with a library and a terrace overlooking the Amazon. There is a small **Amazonian zoo** ⓘ *US$1*, and botanical garden on the road to the airport, within walking distance of town (20 minutes).

Ins and outs The **airport** ⓘ *1½ km from town*, receives flights from Manaus (three times a week with **Rico**) via Tefé. It is a small terminal with few facilities. A taxi to the centre costs US$1.60. There is a **tourist office** ⓘ *C 10, No 9-86, Ministerio del Medio Ambiente, Cra 11, No 12-05*, for general information on national parks.

Border with Colombia and Peru

It is advisable to check requirements and procedures before arriving at this multiple border. No foreign boats are allowed to dock at the Brazilian, Colombian and Peruvian ports, so travellers should enquire carefully about embarkation/disembarkation points and where to go through immigration formalities. If waiting for transport, the best place for accommodation, exchange and other facilities is Leticia in Colombia. Details of travel between Colombia, Brazil and Peru are given below. Travel to/from Colombia is detailed under Leticia (see above and Transport, page 582).

Brazil

Brazilian immigration Entry and exit stamps are given at the Polícia Federal, 10 minutes' walk from the Tabatinga docks (Monday to Friday 0800-1200, 1400-1800), through the docks to the end of the road, turn right at this T-junction for one block to a white building opposite **Café dos Navegantes**; also at the airport, Wednesday and Saturday only. Proof of sufficient funds (US$500) or an onward ticket may be asked for. There are no facilities in Benjamin Constant, but it is possible to buy supplies for boat journeys. One week's transit in Tabatinga is permitted. In this area, carry your passport at all times. If coming from Peru, you must have a Peruvian exit stamp and a yellow fever certificate.

The **Colombian consulate** (0800-1400) is near the border on the road from Tabatinga to Leticia, opposite **Restaurant El Canto de las Peixadas**. Tourist cards are issued on presentation of two passport photos.

Transport Travel between Tabatinga and Leticia is very informal. Taxis between the towns charge US$5 (more if you want to stop at immigration offices or change money), or US$0.80 in a *colectivo* (more after 1800). Beware of taxi drivers who want to rush you expensively over the border before it 'closes'). It is not advisable to walk the muddy path between Tabatinga and Leticia as robberies occur here.

Boats from Manaus to Benjamin Constant normally go on to Tabatinga and start from there when going to Manaus. They usually wait one or two days in both Tabatinga and Benjamin Constant before returning to Manaus; you can stay on board. Tabatinga and Leticia are 1½ to two hours from Benjamin Constant (ferry/*recreio* US$2; 25 minutes by speedboat, US$4 per person, cheaper if more passengers). ➤ *For boats to/from Manaus, see Routes in Amazônia, page 579.*

Colombia → *International phone code +57.*

Colombian immigration DAS ① *C 9, No 8-32, Leticia*, and at the airport. Exit stamps to leave Colombia by air or overland are given only at the airport. If flying into Leticia prior to leaving for Brazil or Peru, get an exit stamp while at the airport. Check both offices for entry stamps before flying into Colombia.

Entering Colombia To enter Colombia you must have a tourist card to obtain an entry stamp, even if you are passing through Leticia en route between Brazil and Peru (the Colombian consul in Manaus may tell you otherwise; try to get a tourist card elsewhere). The Colombian consular office in Tabatinga issues tourist cards; 24 hour transit stamps can be obtained at the **DAS** office. If visiting Leticia without intending to go anywhere else in Colombia, you may be allowed to enter without immigration or customs formalities (but traveller's cheques cannot be changed without an entry stamp).

Consulates Brazilian ① *C 11, No 10-70, Mon-Fri 1000-1600*, efficient, helpful; onward ticket and two black- and-white photos needed for visa (photographer nearby); allow 36 hours. **Peruvian** ① *Cra 11, No 6-80, 0830-1430*; no entry or exit permits are given here.

Peru → *International phone code +51.*

Peruvian immigration Entry/exit formalities take place at Santa Rosa. Every boat leaving Peru stops here. There an **immigration office** ① *Malecón Tarapacá 382*, in Iquitos, where procedures for leaving can be checked. Exchange is available at Islandia.

Consulates In Iquitos there are consulates for **Brazil** ① *C Sargento Lores 363, T005194-232081*, and **Colombia** ① *C Putumayo 247*.

Transport Boats sail from Iquitos to a mudbank called **Islandia**, on the Peruvian side of a narrow creek, a few metres from the Brazilian port of Benjamin Constant. The journey takes a minimum of two days upstream, eight to 36 hours downstream, depending on the speed of the boat. On ordinary boats, fares range from US$30-40 per person, depending on standard of accommodation, food extra. Speedboats charge US$75 per person, three a week are run by **Amazon Tours and Cruises.** Passengers leaving Peru must visit immigration at Santa Rosa when the boat stops there. For entry into Brazil, formalities are carried out in Tabatinga; for Colombia, in Leticia. Boats to Peru leave from Islandia, calling at Santa Rosa (two to three days upstream to Iquitos). **Amazon Tours and Cruises** also operate a luxury service between Iquitos and Tabatinga leaving Sunday, returning from Tabatinga on Wednesday, US$695 per person in the Río Amazonas. Also *Arca* US$495 per person, return journey Wednesday to Saturday.

Up the Rio Negro

It is possible to get a public passenger boat (from Sao Raimundo port on the outskirts of Manaus) up the Rio Negro; see Routes in Amazônia, page 579 . There are hardly any villages of more than a few houses, but these places are important in terms of communications and food resources. It is vital to be self-sufficient in terms of food and cash and to be able to speak Portuguese or have a Brazilian guide. **Nova Airão,** on the west bank of the Negro, is an overnight, eight-hour boat trip upstream. It has a large boat-building centre at the south end, and a fish and vegetable market at the north end. Ice and bread can also be purchased here. It has a telephone, from which international calls can usually be made. There is road access and a bus service from Manaus.

It's two days from Nova Airão to the **Parque Nacional Jaú**. The only way to get here is with a tour; there is no transport or facilities. Permits are necessary; contact **Ibama** ⓘ *R Ministro João Gonçalves de Souza, BR-319, Km 1, Distrito Industrial, Caixa Postal 185, Manaus, CEP 69900, T096-237 3718/3710, F237 5177.*

Moura is about five days upstream from Manaus. It has basic medical facilities and the military base has an airstrip (only usable September to December) and telecommunications. About a day further upstream is **Carvoeira**, almost opposite the mouth of the Rio Branco. There is a vibrant festival in the first week of August. More than a day beyond is **Barcelos**, with a daily air service, except Sundays, the centre for bass fishing on the Amazon. There are a couple of places to stay here.

São Gabriel da Cachoeira → *Colour map 1, A2.*

A great distance further upstream is São Gabriel da Cachoeira – some 900 km and 10 days from Manaus by boat. The city is tiny and sits under a hulking boulder mountain in front of a series of dramatic rapids. There are fine white-sand beaches on the Negro during the dry season. São Gabriel is near the **Pico da Neblina National Park**, named after the highest mountain in Brazil (3014 m). Contact the **Ibama** office in Manaus for more information and details of guides and trips to indigenous villages (not very traditional any more).

Ins and outs There are flights four times a week with **Trip**, www.airtrip.com.br. You can continue from São Gabriel to Venezuela or to Colombia; be sure to get an exit stamp for Brazil here and an entry stamp for Colombia. Visas for Venezuela must be obtained in Manaus. There is a Colombian consulate in São Gabriel near the **FOIRN** indigenous headquarters. In São Gabriel there are two banks but no exchange facilities and the **Vaupes** hotel (E). Cargo boats go to **Cucuí** at the border between Brazil, Colombia and Venezuela. There is also a twice-weekly bus, US$5 (one hotel, ask for Elias, no restaurants). From Cucuí there are daily boats to Guadalupe (Colombia) and infrequent boats to Santa Lucía (Venezuela).

South on the Rio Madeira

Humaitá → *Phone code: 097. Colour map 1, B3. Population: 33,000.*

Humaitá is situated at the crossroads of the Rio Madeira with the Transamazônica highway and the BR-319 north to Manaus. Cattle ranching has begun in the area around the town. There are several basic hotels on the eastern edge of town and the Soltur *rodoviária* in the centre.

Ins and outs There is very little traffic on the Transamazônica from Humaitá east to Itaituba (1025 km); local drivers may give lifts. A ferry crosses the Rio Aripuanã at Vila do Carmo. The road is good for about 350 km from Humaitá, then it deteriorates badly. It is hilly, narrow, and the jungle usually grows over the side of the road. Buses run to **Apuí** (**Hotel Goaino**, basic), 458 km, about 12 hours, US$36; and to **Jacarèacanga**, erratic service, another 222 km (the town is 8 km off the highway). You need to stay overnight and catch the Transbrasiliana bus to Itaituba (24 hours, schedule erratic, the bus is replaced occasionally by a truck). **Hotel São Cristóvão** (D) has a good restaurant, or try the filling station, on the Transamazônica near the Jacarèacanga turning, for hammock space. Travel times depend on the weather conditions, the condition of the bus, and whether the driver decides to stop somewhere for the night. There are flights from Jacarèacanga to Itaituba.

It is also possible to travel to Itaituba by boat; not daily, ticket from fuel station, US$25, 1½ days, very basic, hammock space only. About 70 km before Itaituba there are rapids; the rest of the journey is done by pickup, US$10.

Sleeping

Manaus *p561, map p562*
Although the area around **Av Joaquim Nabuco** and **R dos Andradas** has lots of cheap hotels, this is a low-key red-light district and not particularly safe at night. A better alternative is the nearby **Zona Franca**, which is convenient for shops, banks, restaurants and the port area. However, Zona Franca is very quiet at night and not too safe. The best area to stay now is around the **Teatro Amazonas**, where the Italianate colonial houses and cobbled squares have been newly refurbished.

L Tropical, Av Coronel Teixeira 1320, Ponta Negra, T092-3659 5000, www.tropicalhotel.com.br. A lavish 5-star hotel 20 km outside the city in a semi-forested parkland setting next to the river. The hotel has a private beach, tennis court and a large pool with wave machine. There are several restaurants including a decent *churrascaria*. The river dock is a departure point for many river cruises. To get here take a minibus from R José Paranaguá in front of the Petrobras building at the corner of Dr Moreira, US$5 return, 0830, 0930, 1130 to hotel, 1200, 1400, 1500, 1800 to town, or take a Ponta Negra bus, US$0.70, then walk. A taxi to the centre costs around US$20. The hotel charges a 12% service tax and offers substantial discounts for those arriving on **Varig** flights. Service can be slow. The hotel tour agency organizes excursions.

L Tropical Business, Av Coronel Teixeira 1320, Ponta Negra, T092-2123 3000, www.tropicalhotel.com.br. The business companion to the **Tropical** and just a few doors away. Rooms and suites are modern and well appointed, housed in a large tower block with great views out over the river from the upper floors. The hotel has the best business facilities in the city.

AL Taj Mahal Hotel, Av Getúlio Vargas 741, Centre, T092-3627 3737. A large, well-run business hotel near the opera house in the centre. Facilities include a tour agency, revolving restaurant and a spa.

A Ana Cássia Palace, R dos Andradas 14, Centre, T092-3622 3637, hacassia@internext.com.br. Gloriously faded large rooms, some with great views of the port. The hotel has a decent restaurant and pool.

A Best Western Lord Manaus, R Marcílio Dias 217, T092-3622 2844, http://book.bestwestern.com/bestwestern. Pleasant, spacious lobby and standard well-kept a/c rooms. Conveniently located for boats and shops, in the heart of the Zona Franca.

A Manaós, Av Eduardo Ribeiro 881, T092-3633 5744, www.hotelmanaos.com.br. Recently renovated and right next to the Teatro Amazonas. Spruce a/c rooms with marble floors and smart bathrooms. Decent breakfast.

A-B Mônaco, R Silva Ramos 20, T092-2121 0004, www.hotelmonaco.tur.br. Clunky 1970s mock art deco old hotel decked out with ugly furniture and plastic pot plants but with wonderful views from the top-floor rooms, restaurant and little rooftop pool.

B-C Lider, Av 7 de Setembro 827, T092-3621 9700, www.liderhotelmanaus.com.br. Small modern a/c rooms with marble floors, little breakfast tables and en suite bathrooms. The best are at the front of the hotel on the upper floors. Very well kept.

B-C Krystal, R Barroso 54, T092-3233 7535, www.krystalhotel.com.br. A range of small though business-like, well-maintained modern a/c rooms.

B-C Central, R Dr Moreira 202, T092-3622 2600, www.hotelcentralmanaus.com.br. A business hotel in the heart of the Zona Franca with a range of rooms, many very scruffy although some well kept; look at a few. Excellent large breakfast.

C-D Brasil, Av Getúlio Vargas 657, T092-2123 6575, hotel-brasil@internext.com.br. Faded cavernous a/c rooms decorated with tacky art and with tiny en suite bathrooms and even tinier balconies. Small pool.

D Dez de Julho, R 10 de Julho 679, T092-3232 6280, www.hoteldezdejulho.com. Much the best cheap option, very clean though simple rooms (some with a/c and hot water), with laundry, tour operator and efficient, English-speaking staff. There have been complaints about security recently.

D Itália, R Guilherme Moreira 325, T092-3234 7934. Very simple but well-kept rooms in the heart of the Zona Franca. The best are on the upper floors. Generous breakfast.

Lodges accessible from Manaus

LL-L Othon Jungle Palace, office at R Saldanha Marinho 700, Manaus, T092-3633 6051, www.junglepalace.com.br or book through **Iguana Tours** or **Gero's Tours** in Manaus. A floating lodge with very comfortable a/c 4-star rooms and a pool, on a black-water tributary of the Rio Negro some 5 km from the Anavilhanas. Excellent guides and service but, as ever with lodges close to Manaus, somewhat depleted forest.

L Acajatuba Jungle Lodge, Lago Acajatuba, 4 hrs up the Rio Negro from Manaus. Office at Conjunto Vila Municipal, R 07 No 87, Adrianópolis, Manaus, T092-3642 0358, www.acajatuba.com.br. 40 apartments with showers, a bar and a restaurant. About as comfortable as a damp forest can get but with pet wild animals, so hardly best practice ecologically.

L Ariaú Amazon Towers, 60 km and 2 hrs by boat from Manaus, on the Rio Ariaú, 2 km from Archipélago de Anavilhanas. Office at R Leonardo Malcher 699, Manaus, T092-2121 5000, www.ariautowers.com.br. With 271 rooms in complex of towers connected by walkways, a pool, meditation centre, large restaurant and gift shop, this is a jungle hotel more than a jungle lodge. If you are after intimacy with the forest you won't find it here. But the hotel is a good option for older people or those with small children. The guided tours are generally well run, although specialist wildlife guides are not available and tame wildlife hangs around the lodge.

L Pousada dos Guanavenas, Ilha de Silves, 300 km from Manaus on the road to Itacoatiara, then by boat along the Rio Urubu. T092-3656 1500, www.guana venas.com.br, book through **Iguana Tours** or **Gero's Tours**. A large lodge in cleared grounds overlooking the black-water Lago Canacari, some 4-5 hrs from Manaus. The hotel has a pool, excellent restaurant and very comfortable a/c rooms with hot water. The hotel's tours run like clockwork – sometimes too much so.

L-AL Amazon Ecopark Lodge, Igarapé do Tarumã, 20 km from Manaus, 15 mins by boat, T092-2547 7742 or T092-9146 0594 www.amazonecopark.com.br. Book through **Gero's Tours** in Manaus. The best lodge close to Manaus, in a private reserve that would otherwise have been destroyed. The lodge makes a real effort at conservation and good practice. The apartment cabins are very comfortable (with hot showers) and are set in the forest. The lodge has a lovely white-sand beach and is close to the **Amazon Monkey Jungle**, an ecological park where many primate species (including white uakari) are treated and rehabilitated in natural surroundings. The **Living Rainforest Foundation**, which administers the ecopark, also offers educational jungle trips and overnight camps (bring your own food), entrance US$15.

A Amazon Lodge, T092-656 3878, F656 6101, Lago do Juma, 80 km from Manaus, 30 mins by Careiro ferry, then 1½ hrs by bus, then 2 hrs by boat. A floating lodge with 12 basic apartments (cold showers), restaurant, good excursions. Highly recommended.

A Boa Vida Jungle Resort, Rodovia AM-010, KM 53; 53 km from Manaus on the AM-010 highway towards Itacoatiara,T092-3231 1661, www.boavidahotel.com.br or through **Iguana Tours** or **Gero's Tours** in Manaus. A very small, intimate lodge with just 7 apartments and 6 chalets all with showers and fridges and a communal bar and restaurant. In an area with good wildlife and few tourists.

A Juma, Lago da Juma, T092-3232 2707, www.jumalodge.com or through **Gero's Tours** in Manaus. Newly refurbished lodge in a beautiful location, with a burgeoning interest in birdwatching and proper wildlife tours.

A Tiwa Amazone Resort, Lago Salvador, 10 minutes immediately across the Solimões from Ponta Negra, T092-3088 4676, T092-9995 7892, www.tiwaamazone.com or through **Iguana Tours** or **Gero's Tours** in Manaus. A medium-sized resort lodge with very comfortable spacious cabanas, all with en suites and a/c, built out over a small caiman-filled lake. The resort itself has a large pool and bar. Too close to Manaus for much wildlife, but an option as an alternative city hotel, especially for a business trip. Good tours.

A Wild Cabanas, 80 km from Manaus, book through **Brazilian Safaris**. Comfortable rooms and hammock space in a large *maloca*-style building on a caiman- filled lake close to the Rio Mamori. Popular with backpackers.

A-B Aldeia dos Lagos Lodge, near Silves, run by the **Silves Project**, T092-3248 9988, www.viverde.com.br/aldeia. A community-based eco-project with WWF support. Set in a system of lakes with high environmental diversity. Good for birds and caiman.

Tefé *p569*

L Uacari Lodge, T097-3343 4672 or T097-3343 4160, www.mamiraua.org. Together with **Cristalino Jungle Lodge** (see page 666), this is the best lodge for wildlife, guiding and ecotouristic practice in the Brazilian Amazon. The lodge is in a magical location in the Mamirauá reserve, floating on a river, with 10 suites of 25 sq m each linked by floating bridges. Tours are excellent. Look out for the friendly black caiman which lives in the water under the restaurant. The lodge and the trips in the reserve can be booked in Manaus through **Iguana Tours**, at either their shop or their office in Manaus airport. Book well in advance.

D Anilce, Praça Santa Teresa 294. Clean, a/c rooms, very helpful. Don't leave valuables in your room.

E Hotel Panorama, R Floriano Peixoto 90. Recommended, with a good restaurant.

Benjamin Constant *p569*

There are a number of very cheap and very simple pousadas in town.

B Benjamin Constant, R Getúlio Vargas 36, beside the ferry, T092-415 5638; postal address Apdo Aéreo 219, Leticia, Colombia. All rooms have a/c, some with hot water and TV. Good restaurant, arranges tours.

Tabatinga *p569*

C Pousada do Sol, General Sampaio, T092-412 3355. Simple rooms but in a hotel with a sauna and a pool. Friendly owners.

D-E Travellers Jungle Home, R Marechal Rondon 86. A little hostel and tour operator with Brazilian/French owners and a pet snake.

Leticia (Colombia) *p570*

The international phone code for Colombia is +57. The code for Leticia is 9819.

AL Anaconda, Cra 11 No 7-34, T9819-27119. The plushest in town with large a/c rooms, hot water, a restaurant, good terrace and swimming pool.

B Colonial, Cra 10 No 7-08, T9819-27164. A/c or fans, swimming pool, cafeteria, noisy.

C-D Residencias Fernando, Cra 9, No 8-80, T9819-27362. Simple but well appointed and clean. Recommended.

D Residencias La Manigua, C 8 No 9-22, T27121. Friendly staff and modest but well-maintained rooms.

D Residencias Marina, Cra 9 No 9-29, T9819-26014. Standard cheap hotel rooms, TV, some with a/c, cold water, good breakfast and meals at attached restaurant.

E Residencia Internacional, Av Internacional, between the centre and the Brazilian border. Basic rooms with attached bathrooms and fans. Hard beds.

F Residencias Colombia, C 10 at C 8. Very basic rooms with a shared bathroom. Good value.

Eating

Manaus *p561, map p562*

Many restaurants close Sun night and Mon.

TTT Himawari, R 10 de Julho 618, opposite **Teatro Amazonas**, T092-3233 2208. Swish restaurant serving sushi and Japanese food. Attentive service, open Sun night when many restaurants close. Recommended.

TTT La Barca, R Recife 684, T092-3642 3040. Very swanky and popular, with a wide variety of fish dishes. Often has live music.

TTT Restaurant Tarumã in Hotel Tropical (see page 573). The best restaurant in town, formal and open for dinner only.

TT Búfalo, Av Joaquim Nabuco 628, T092- 3633 3733, www.churrascariabufalo.com.br. The best *churrascaria* in Manaus, with a US$8 all you-can-eat Brazilian barbecue and a vast choice of meat. Come with an empty stomach.

TT Canto da Peixada, R Emílio Moreira 1677 (Praça 14 de Janeiro), T092-3234 3021. Superb fish dishes, lively atmosphere, unpretentious, a short taxi ride from the centre.

TT Fiorentina, R José Paranaguá 44, Praça da Polícia, T092-3232 1295. Fan-cooled traditional Italian with cheesy vegetarian dishes and even cheesier piped music. Great *feijoada* on Sat, half-price on Sun. Dishes are served with mugs of wine.

TT Pizzeria Scarola, R 10 de Julho 739, corner with Av Getúlio Vargas, T092-3232 6503. Standard Brazilian menu and pizza delivery, popular.

ꝩ **Alemã**, R José Paranaguá, Praça da Polícia. Food by weight with great pastries, hamburgers, juices, sandwiches.

ꝩ **O Naturalista**, R 7 de Setembro 752, 2nd floor. The best pay-by-weight vegetarian in the city, open for lunch only.

ꝩ **Senac**, R Saldanha Marinho 644, T092-633 2277. Cookery school with a self-service restaurant. Open daily, lunch only. Highly recommended.

ꝩ **Skina dos Sucos**, Eduardo Ribeiro and 24 de Maio. A large choice of Amazonian fruit juices and bar snacks.

ꝩ **Sorveteria Glacial**, Av Getúlio Vargas 161, and other locations. Recommended for unusual ice creams such as *açai* and *cupuaçu*.

Tefé *p569*

ꝩꝩ-ꝩ **Au Bec d'Or** by the port. With simple but very tasty French cuisine using Amazon ingredients.

Leticia (Colombia) *p570*

There are plenty of lunchtime *almuerzo* restaurants serving cheap dishes of the day in the centre of town. Fried banana and meat, fish and fruit is sold at the market near the harbour and there are many cheap café/bars overlooking the market on the river bank. Take your own drinking water or beer.

ꝩ **Sancho Panza**, Cra 10 No 8-72. Good-value meat dishes, big portions, Brazilian beer.

Bars and clubs

Manaus *p561, map p562*

Manaus has lively nightlife with something going on every night. **O Laranjinha** in Ponta Negra is popular any week night and has a live *Boi Bumba* dance show on Wed. Be wary of piranhas of the female, human kind after 2400.

DJ (Djalma) Oliveira, T092-9112 3942 (or book through **Gero's Tours**), will take visitors out to sample Manaus club life. He is cheaper than a taxi and speaks a little English.

Mon **Coração Blue**, Estrada Ponta Negra. Live *forró* and general dance in a large club. US$2 entrance.

Tue **Hollywood Rock**, Estrada Ponta Negra. Live *pagodé*. US$2 entrance.

Wed **Antares**, Estrada Dom Pedro, Kisia. Live *brega* (a frenetic northern Brazilian form of *forró*), US$2.

Thu **Clube do Forró**, Estrada do Aleixo. Live *forró*, US$2.

Fri **Simbola**, Estrada Ponta Negra, Big club with 3 floors playing a mix of club music, *forró* and *pagodé*, US$3.50.

Sat Numerous clubs especially **Simbola** and **Talismã Forró Club** in Cachoeirinha. There are a number of other bars in Cachoeirinha offering music and dancing.

Sun **Hollywood Rock** and **Simbola**.

Entertainment

Manaus *p561, map p562*

Cinema

In R 10 de Julho and 8 screens at the **Amazonas Shopping Centre**, bus 'Cidade Nova 5', or Nos 204, 207, 208, 307. Most foreign films are shown with original soundtrack and Portuguese subtitles. Afternoon performances are recommended as long queues often form in the evenings.

Performing Arts

For **Teatro Amazonas** and **Centro Cultural Pálacio Rio Negro**, see pages 563 and 564. In Praça da Saudade, R Ramos Ferreira, there is a Sun **funfair** from 1700; try prawns and *calaloo* dipped in *tacaca* sauce. A 'train' circling the old town with loud music and cartoon characters is good fun for children.

Teatro da Instalação, R Frei José dos Inocentes, T/F092-234 4096. Performance space in recently restored historic buildings with free music and dance (everything from ballet to jazz), May-Dec Mon-Fri at 1800. Charge for performances at weekends. Recommended.

Festivals

Manaus *p561, map p562*

6 Jan Epiphany.

Feb **Carnaval** in Manaus has spectacular parades in a sambódromo modelled on Rio's, but with 3 times the capacity. Tourists may purchase grandstand seats, but admission at ground level is free (don't take valuables). Carnaval lasts for 5 days, culminating in the parade of the samba schools.

3rd week in Apr **Week of the Indígena**, indigenous handicrafts.

Jun **Festival do Amazonas**, a celebration of all the cultural aspects of Amazonas life, indigenous, Portuguese and from the northeast, especially dancing. Also in Jun is the **Festival Marquesiano**, with typical dances from those regions of the world which have sent immigrants to Amazonas, performed by the students of the Colégio Marquês de Santa Cruz.

29 Jun São Pedro, boat processions on the Rio Negro.

Sep **Festival de Verão do Parque Dez**, 2nd fortnight, festival with music, fashion shows, beauty contests and local foods at the Centro Social Urbano do Parque Dez. In the last week of Sep is the **Festival da Bondade**, with stalls from neighbouring states and countries offering food, handicrafts, music and dancing at SESI, Estr do Aleixo, Km 5.

Oct **Festival Universitário de Música (FUM)**, the most traditional festival of music in Amazonas, organized by the university students, on the university campus.

8 Dec **Procissão de Nossa Senhora da** Conceicão, from the Igreja Matriz through the city centre and returning to Igreja Matriz for a solemn mass.

Parintins *p568*

Jun Festa do Boi Bumba. Huge 3-day festival attracting 40,000 people (see box, page 568).

24 Dec-6 Jan Parintins' other main festival is the **Pastorinhas**.

São Gabriel de Cachoeira *p572*

Oct Festribal is a very lively indigenous festival in the city.

Shopping

Manaus *p561, map p562*

All shops close at 1400 on Sat and all day Sun. Since Manaus is a free port, the whole area a few blocks off the riverfront is full of electronics shops. This area, known as the **Zona Franca**, is the commercial centre, where the shops, banks and hotels are concentrated.

Bookshops

Livraria Nacional, R 24 de Maio 415. Stocks some French books.

Usados CDs e Livros, Av Getúlio Vargas 766. Selection of used books, English, German, French and Spanish.

Valer, R Ramos Ferreira 1195. A few English classics stocked. The best in the city.

Markets and souvenirs

To buy a hammock head to the **Casa das Redes** and other shops on R dos Andradas. There are now many handicrafts shops in the area around the theatre. The souvenir shop at the **INPA** (see page 565) has some interesting Amazonian products on sale. The markets near the docks are best in the early morning. There is a very good Sun market in the **Praça do Congresso**, Av E Ribeiro. **Ponta Negra** beach boasts a small 'hippy' market, very lively at weekends. There is a good supermarket at the corner of Av Joaquim Nabuco and R Sete de Setembro.

Artesanato da Amazônia, R José Clemente, 500, loja A, opposite Teatro Amazonas, has a good, reasonably priced selection of regional products.

Central Artesanato, R Recife, near Detran. Local craftwork.

Ecoshop, 10 de Julho 509a, near the theatre, www.ecoshop.com.br. Good little a/c café.

Mamirauá Shop, R 10 de Julho 495, near the theatre. Range of indigenous crafts and books and information on the Mamirauá Reserve.

Mercado Adolfo Lisboa (see page 564), Mon-Sat 0500-1800, Sun and holidays 0500-1200. Go early in the morning when it is full of good-quality regional produce, food and handicrafts. Look out for *guaraná* powder or sticks, scales of *pirarucu* fish (used for manicure), and its tongue (used for rasping *guaraná*).

Selva Amazônica, Mercado Municipal. For woodcarvings and bark fabric.

Activities and tours

Manaus *p561, map p562*

Swimming

Swimming is possible at **Ponta Negra** beach, 13 km from the centre (Soltur bus, US$0.70), although the beach virtually disappears beneath the water Apr-Aug.

There is good swimming at waterfalls on the **Rio Tarumã**, where lunch is available, shade, crowded at weekends. Take the Tarumã bus from R Tamandaré or R Frei J dos Inocentes, 30 mins, US$0.70 (very few on weekdays), getting off at the police checkpoint on the road to Itacoatiara. There is also superb swimming in the natural pools and under falls of clear water in the little streams which rush through the woods, but take locals' advice on swimming in the river; electric eels and various other kinds of unpleasant fish, apart from the notorious piranhas, abound, and industrial pollution of the river is growing.

Every Sun, boats depart from the port in front of the market for beaches along Rio Negro, US$2, leaving when full and returning at the end of the day. This is a real locals' day out, with loud music and foodstalls on the sand.

Amazon tours

Amazon Clipper, T092-3656 1246, www.amazonclipper.com.br. The leading small boat cruise operator. Excellent trips along the Rio Negro with knowledgeable widlife guides.

Amazon Explorers, R Nhamundá 21, Praça NS Auxiliadora, T092-633 3319, www.amazonexplorers.com.br. Day tours including the 'meeting of the waters', Lago do Janauari, rubber collecting and lunch, (US$60). Highly recommended. The *Amazon Explorer* boat is available for hire at about US$230 per day.

Amazonas Indian Turismo, R dos Andradas 311, T/F092-633 5578. Offers a different, authentic experience, staying with local river people, for around US$60 per day.

Amazonatours, T092-323 28271 or in Spain T+34-61-521 9070, www.amazonatours.com. Spanish/Brazilian-run agency offering trips further afield and to their small lodge in the Tupana Natural Reserve.

Brazilian Safaris, R 10 de Julho 632, T092-3232 6830, braziliansafaris@hotmail.com. Ground operator for many of the smaller agencies and with their own lodge off the Rio Mamori and a range of good budget trips.

Gero's Tours, R10 de Julho 679, T092-3232 4755 or T092-9983 6273, www.amazon gerotours.com. Backpacker-orientated tours south of the Solimões and bookings made for lodges everywhere. Gero, the owner is very friendly and dedicated.

Heliconia, R Col Salgado 63, Aparecida, T092-3234 5915, www.heliconia-amazon.com. Run by French researcher Thérèse Aubreton.

Iguana Tour, R 10 de Julho 679, T092-3663 6507, www.amazonbrasil.com.br. Offers an extensive range of trips of various lengths. Good facilities including riverboat and campsite in the forest. Also has an office at the airport in Manaus.

Swallows and Amazons Tours, R Quintino Bocaiuva 189, Suite 13, T092-622 1246, www.swallowsandamazonstours.com.

Guides

Guides sometimes work individually as well as for tour agencies, and the best ones will normally be booked up in advance. Some will only accompany longer expeditions and often subcontract shorter trips. The easiest way to find a guide, however, is through an agency. Advance notice and a minimum of 3 people for all trips is required by the following guides, who are among the best in the city.

Matthias Raymond, T092-8115 5716, raymathias@hotmail.com. A Waipixana indigenous guide offering trips to further reaches of the forest including the Pico da Neblina (book in advance). Many languages.

Moreno Ortelli, T092-9605 0519, morenojivaro@hotmail.com. One of the few guides in Manaus who knows his birds. Excellent knowledge of indigenous culture and fascinating trips. Many languages.

Samuel Basilio, T092-3635 7740 or T092-9616 3124 (mob), samuelbasilio@hotmail.com. A guide from the upper Rio Negro specializing in long expeditions; has worked on many BBC documentaries as a location finder.

Leticia (Colombia) *p570*

Amazon Jungle trips, Av Internacional, 6-25, T9819-27377. Lodge-based tours offering a variety of adventure options.

Anaconda Tours, Hotel Anaconda, T9819-27119. Tours to Amacayacu, Isla de los Micos and **Sacambu Lodge**.

Elvis Cuevas, Av Internacional, 6-06, T0819-27780. An independent guide offering trips to Amacayacu and indigenous communities nearby.

Transport

Routes in Amazônia

Belém–Manaus Via **Breves, Almeirim, Prainha, Monte Alegre, Curua-Uná, Santarém, Alenquer, Óbidos, Juruti** and **Parintins** on the lower Amazon. 5 days upriver, 4 days downriver, including an 18-hr stop in Santarém, suite US$350 upriver, US$250 down, double berth US$180 upriver, US$150 down, hammock space US$75 upriver, US$65 down. Vehicles: small car US$250, kombi US$320 usually including driver, other passengers extra, 4WD US$450 with 2 passengers, motorcycle US$80. *Nélio Correa* is best on this route. *Defard Vieira*, very good and clean, US$75. *São Francisco* is largest, new and modern, but toilets smelly. *Cisne Branco* of similar quality. *Cidade de Bairreirinha* is the newest on the route, a/c berths. *Lider II* has good food and pleasant atmosphere. *Santarém* is clean, well organized and recommended. *João Pessoa Lopes* is also recommended. The Belém–Manaus route is very busy. Try to get a cabin if you can.

Belém–Santarém Same intermediate stops as above. 2½ days upriver, 1½ days downriver, suite US$130, berth US$135, hammock US$45 upriver, US$38 down. All vessels sailing Belém–Manaus will call at Santarém.

Santarém–Manaus Same intermediate stops as above. 2 days upriver, 1½ days downriver, fares berth US$85, hammock US$30. All vessels sailing Belém–Manaus will call in Santarém and there are others operating only the Santarém–Manaus route, including: *Cidade de Terezinha III* and *IV*, good. *Miranda Dias*, family-run and friendly. Speedboats (*lanchas*) are sometimes available on this route, 16 hrs sitting, no hammock space, US$35.

Belém–Macapá (Porto Santana) Non-stop, 8 hrs on fast catamaran, **Atlântica**, US$30, 3 days a week, or 24 hrs on large ships, double berth US$110, hammock space US$30 per person, meals not included but can be purchased onboard (expensive), vehicle US$90, driver not included. *Silja e Souza* (Wed) is best. *Comandante Solon* (Sat) is state run, slightly cheaper, crowded and not as nice. Same voyage via Breves, 36-48 hrs on smaller riverboats, hammock space US$25 per person including meals. *ENAL* (Sat); *Macamazônia* (every day except Thu), slower and more basic; *Bartolomeu I* of Enavi, food and sanitary conditions OK, 30 hrs; *Rodrigues Alves* has been recommended. *Golfinho do Mar* is said to be the fastest.

Macapá (Porto Santana)–Santarém
Via **Vida Nova**, **Boca do Jari**, **Almeirim**, **Prainha**, and **Monte Alegre** on the lower Amazon (does not call at Belém). 2 days upriver, 1½ days downriver, berth US$130, hammock US$40. Boats include *Viageiro V* (nice) and *São Francisco de Paula*.

Santarém–Itaituba Along the Rio Tapajós, 24 hrs (bus service on this route is making the river trip less common).

Manaus–Porto Velho Via **Borba**, **Manicoré** and **Humaitá** on the Rio Madeira. 4 days upriver, 3½ days downriver (up to 7 days when the river is low), double berth US$180, hammock space US$65 per person. Recommended boats are *Almirante Moreira II*, friendly owner, clean; *Lord Scania*, friendly; *Ana Maria VIII*, modern. The *Eclipse II* is a very nice boat which sails Manaus– Manicoré (2 days, US$80 double berth, US$20 hammock). Many passengers go only as far as Humaitá and take a bus from there to Porto Velho, much faster.

Manaus–Tefé Via **Codajás** and **Coari**, 24-36 hrs, double berth US$70, 1st-class hammock space US$20 per person. *Capitão Nunes* is good. *Jean Filho* also okay. Note that it is difficult to continue west from Tefé to Tabatinga without first returning to Manaus.

Manaus–Tabatinga Via **Fonte Boa**, **Foz do Mamaria**, **Tonantins**, **Santo Antônio do Içá**, **Amataura**, **Monte Cristo**, **São Paulo de Olivença** and **Benjamin Constant** along the Rio Solimões. Up to 8 days upriver (depending on cargo), 3 days downriver, double berth US$220, hammock space US$65 per person (can be cheaper downriver). When going from Peru into Brazil, there is a thorough police check some 5 hrs into Brazil. *Voyagers*, *Voyagers II* and *III* recommended; *Almirante Monteiro*, *Avelino Leal* and *Capitão Nunes VIII* all acceptable; *Dom Manoel*, cheaper, acceptable but overcrowded.

Manaus–Caracaraí (for Boa Vista)
Along the Rio Branco, 4 days upriver, 2 days downriver, many sandbars, impassable during the dry season. Now that the BR-174 (Manaus-Boa Vista) has been paved, it is almost impossible to get a passage on a boat. The only tourist boat is erratic.

Manaus–São Gabriel da Cachoeira
Via **Novo Airão**, **Moura**, **Carvoeiro**, **Barcelos** and **Santa Isabel do Rio Negro** along the Rio Negro. Berth US$180, hammock US$60, most locals prefer to travel by road. Boats on this route: *Almirante Martins I* and *II*, *Capricho de Deus*, *Manoel Rodrigues*, *Tanaka Netto* departing from São Raimundo dock, north of main port.

Manaus *p561, map p562*
See also Ins and outs, page 562.

Air
Taxi fare to airport US$7.25, fixed rate, or take bus marked 'Aeroporto Internacional' from Marquês de Santa Cruz at Praça Adalberto Vale, near the cathedral, US$0.70, or from Ed Garagem on Av Getúlio Vargas every 30 mins. No buses 2200-0700. It is sometimes possible to use the more regular, faster service run by the **Hotel Tropical**; many tour agencies offer free transfers without obligation. Check all connections on arrival. Allow plenty of time at Manaus airport, formalities are very slow especially if you have purchased duty-free goods.

Many flights depart in the middle of the night and while there are many snack bars there is nowhere to rest. Local flights leave from Terminal 2. Check in advance which terminal you leave from.

There are international flights to **Guayaquil** and **Quito** (Ecuador), **La Paz** (Bolivia), **Mexico City**, **Miami**, **Orlando** and **Santa Cruz**. For the **Guianas**, a connection must be made in Boa Vista. Domestic flights to **Belém**, **Boa Vista**, **Brasília**, **Cruzeiro do Sul**, **Macapá**, **Parantins**, **Porto Velho**, **Rio Branco**, **Rio de Janeiro**, **Santarém**, **São Paulo**, **Tabatinga**, **Tefé** and **Trombetas**.

Make reservations as early as possible; flights get booked up quickly. Do not rely on travel agency waiting lists; go to the airport 15 hrs early and get on the airport waiting list. Domestic airport tax US$7.

Airline offices BRA , T011-6445 4607, www.voebra.com.br. **GOL**, T0800-701 2131, www.voegol.com.br. **TAM** T0800-123100, www.tam.com.br. **Varig**, T0800-997000, www.varig.com.br.

Regional airlines include: **Meta**, T0300-789 5503, www.voemeta.com; **RICO**, T092-3633 5155, www.voerico.com.br; **Trip**, T0300-789 8747, www.airtrip.com.br; **Total**, T092-4004 1464, www.total.com.br.

Boat

See also Routes in Amazônia, page 579. Boats run to **Santarém**, **Belém**, **Porto Velho**, **Tefé**, **Tabatinga** (for Colombia and Peru), **São Gabriel da Cachoeira**, and intermediate ports. Almost all vessels now berth at the first (downstream) of the floating docks, which is open to the public 24 hrs a day. Bookings can be made up to 2 weeks in advance at the ticket sales area by the port's pedestrian entrance (bear left on entry). The names and itineraries of departing vessels are displayed here as well as on the docked boats themselves. Touts will engulf you when you arrive at the pedestrian entry; be calm, patient and friendly. Travellers still recommend buying tickets from the captain on the boat itself. The port is relatively clean, well organized, and has a pleasant atmosphere.

ENASA (the state shipping company) sells tickets for private boats at its office in town (prices tend to be high here), T092-633 3280. Local boats and some cargo barges still berth by the concrete retaining wall between the market and Montecristi. Boats for São Gabriel da Cachoeira, Novo Airão, and Caracaraí go from São Raimundo, upriver from the main port. Take bus No 101 'São Raimundo', No 112 'Santo Antônio' or No 110, 40 mins; there are 2 docking areas separated by a hill, the São Raimundo *balsa*, where the ferry to Novo Airão, on the Rio Negro, leaves every afternoon (US$10); and the Porto Beira Mar de São Raimundo, where the São Gabriel da Cachoeira boats dock (most departures Fri).

Manaus–São Paulo it is cheaper to go by boat from Manaus to Porto Velho, then bus to São Paulo, than to fly direct or go by boat to Belém then bus. Departures to the less important destinations are not always known at the **Capitânia do Porto**, Av Santa Cruz 265, Manaus. Be careful of people who wander around boats after they've arrived at a port; they are almost certainly looking for something to steal.

Bus

To get to the *rodoviária* take a local bus from the centre, US$0.70, marked 'Aeroporto Internacional' or 'Cidade Nova' (or taxi, US$5). There are many daily services to **Boa Vista** on Eucatur; the best are at night leaving at 2030 and 2100 (10 hrs, $28). Most go via **Presidente Figueiredo** (3 hrs, $10). There are also 8 daily buses to **Itacoatiara** (4 hrs, $15).

Car

The road north from Manaus to **Boa Vista** (770 km) is described on page 583.

The Catire Highway (BR-319), from Manaus to **Porto Velho** (868 km), has been officially closed since 1990. Several bridges are out and there is no repair in sight. The alternative for drivers is to ship a car down river on a barge, others have to travel by boat (see below).

To **Itacoatiara**, 285 km east on the Amazon; now paved route AM-010, 266 km, through Rio Preto da Eva.

Car hire Localiza, R Major Gabriel 1558, T092-233 4141, and airport, T092-652 1176.

Hitchhiking

Common, but not recommended for women travelling alone. To hitch, take a Tarumã bus to the customs building and hitch from there, or try at 'posta 5', 2 km beyond the *rodoviária*.

Parintins *p568*

Air Flights to **Manaus** (1¼ hrs), **Óbidos** and **Santarém** (1 hr 20 mins).

Boat Boats call on the Belém-Manaus route: 60 hrs to **Belém** (depending on boat and if going up or down river), 10-26 passengers. There are irregular sailings to **Óbidos** (ask at the port), 12-15 hrs. A boat to **Santarém** takes 20 hrs.

Tefé *p569*
Air The airport has a connection to **Manaus** with **Varig**. If travelling on to **Tabatinga**, note that Manaus–Tabatinga boats do not usually stop at Tefé. You must hire a canoe to take you out to the main channel and try to flag down the approaching ship.

Leticia (Colombia) *p570*
Air Expect to be searched before leaving Leticia airport, and on arrival in Bogotá from Leticia. To Bogotá, Mon and Fri, SAM. Also flights to **Tefé**.

Directory

Manaus *p561, map p562*
Banks **Banco do Brasil**, Guia Moreira, and airport changes US$ cash, 8% commission, both with ATMs for Visa, Cirrus, MasterCard and Plus. Most offices shut at 1500; foreign exchange operations 0900-1200 only, or even as early as 1100. **Bradesco**, Av 7 de Setembro 895/293, for Visa ATM. **Credicard**, Av Getúlio Vargas 222 for **Diner**'s cash advances. Cash at main hotels; **Câmbio Cortez**, 7 de Setembro 1199, converts TCs into US$ cash, good rates, no commission. **HSBC**, R Dr Moreira 226, ATM for Visa, Cirrus, MasterCard and Plus. Do not change money on the streets. **Embassies and consulates** Most open in the morning only. **Austria**, R 5, Qd E No 4, Jardim Primeravera II, T092-642 1939, F642 1582. **Belgium**, Conj Murici, Qd D No 13, Parque 10, T092-236 1452. **Bolivia**, Av Efigênio Sales 2226, Qd B No 20, T092-236 9988. **Colombia**, R 24 de Maio 220, Rio Negro Centre, T092-234 6777, check whether a Colombian tourist card can be obtained at the border. **Denmark**, Estr da Refinaria, T092-615 1555, also handles Norway. **France**, Av Joaquim Nabuco 1846, T092-234 2947. **Finland**, R Marcílio Dias 131, T092-622 6686. **Germany**, R 24 Maio 220, Rio Negro Centre, sala 812, T092-234 9045, 1000-1200. **Italy**, R Belo Horizonte 240, Adrianópolis, T092-611 4877. **Japan**, R Fortaleza 460, T092-232 2000. **Netherlands**, R Miranda Leão 41, T092-622 1366. **Peru**, R A, casa 1, Conj Aristocrático, Chapada, T092-236 3012. **Portugal**, R Terezina 193, T092-234 5777. **Spain**, Al Cosme Ferreira 1225, Aleixo, T092-644 3800. **UK**, R Paraquê 240, T092-237 7869. **USA**, R Recife 1010, Adrianópolis, T092-633 4907, will supply letters of introduction for US citizens. **Venezuela**, R Ferreira Pena 179, T092-233 6004, F233 0481, (0800-1200), everyone entering Venezuela overland needs a visa. The requirements are 1 passport photo, an onward ticket and the fee, usually US$30 (check in advance for changes to these regulations – it is reported that a yellow fever certificate is not needed). Takes 24 hrs. **Immigration** To extend or replace a Brazilian visa, take bus from Praça Adalberto Vale to Kissia Dom Pedro for Polícia Federal post; people in shorts not admitted.
Internet Many around the Teatro, including **Loginet**, R 10 de Julho 625. **Amazon Cyber Cafe**, Av Getúlio Vargas, 626, corner with R 10 de Julho, US$1.50 per hr. **Discover Internet**, R Marcílio Dias 304, next to Praça da Polícia, cabins in back of shop with internet phones and scanners, US$1.50 per hr. Free internet access is available from all public libraries in city, eg **Biblioteca Arthur Reis**, Av 7 de Setembro 444, open 0800-1200 and 1400-1700, with virtual Amazon library and English books. **Laundry** **Lavanderia Amazonas**, Costa Azevedo 63, near Teatro Amazonas, US$0.40 per item, closed Sat afternoon and Sun. **Lavanderia Central**, R Quintino Bocaiúva 602. **Lavalux**, R Mundurucus 77, fast service washes. **Lavlev**, Av Sen A Maia 1108. One of few self-service laundries is opposite the cemetery, open Sun, a taxi ride away. **Medical services** **Clinica Sao Lucas**, R Alexandre Amorin 470, T092-622 3678, reasonably priced, some English spoken, good service, take a taxi. **Hospital Tropical**, Av Pedro Teixeira (D Pedro I) 25, T092-656 1441. Centre for tropical medicine, not for general complaints, treatment free, some doctors speak a little English. Take bus Nos 201 or 214 from Av 7 de Setembro in the city centre. **Pronto Soccoro 28 de Agosto**, R Recife, free for emergencies. **Post office** Main office including poste restante on Mcal Deodoro. On the 1st floor is the philatelic counter where stamps are sold, avoiding the long queues downstairs. Staff don't speak English but are used to dealing with tourists. For airfreight and shipping, **Alfândega**, Av Marquês Santa Cruz (corner of Marechal Deodoro), sala 106. For airfreight and sea mail, **Correio Internacional**, R Monsenhor Coutinho and Av Eduardo Ribeiro (bring your own packaging). **UPS**, T092-232 9849 (Custódio). **Telephone** International calls can be made from local call

boxes with an international card. Also at Telemar, Av Getúlio Vargas 950.

Tabatinga *p569*
Banks There is a Banco do Brasil, Av da Amizade, which changes TCs at a poor rate and has a Visa ATM. It is easier to get Peruvian money for reais in Leticia.
Internet Infocenter, Av Amizade 1581.

Leticia (Colombia) *p570*
Banks Banco de Bogotá, will cash TCs, has ATM on Cirrus network, good rates for Brazilian reais. Banco Ganadero, Cra 11, has a Visa ATM. There are street money changers, plenty of *câmbios*, and banks for exchange. Shop around. **Post office** Avianca office, Cra 11 No 7-58. **Telephone** Cra 11/C 9, near Parque Santander.

Roraima

This extreme northern state is one of the country's newest and is only just beginning to exploit its strategic position on the border with Gran Sabana in Venezuela and the stunning Parakaima mountains in Guyana. The state capital is Boa Vista, a safe, tidy modern city with a very lively out-of-season carnival.

Beyond the city, the rainforest gives way to extensive grasslands overlooked by precipitous table-top mountains. The most famous of these is Conan Doyle's lost world – Roraima – which can be visited from Boa Vista. Others, such as Tepequen and those on the upper Rio Branco, are more remote and less visited, their wildernesses replete with wildlife.

Guyana and Venezuela are a couple of hours from Boa Vista and all visa formalities can be sorted out in that city. Contrary to popular belief, crossing into both countries is easy and painless and there are excellent onward transport services to Caracas or Georgetown. ▸▸ *For Sleeping, Eating and other listings, see pages 586-588.*

Background

Roraima covers an area nearly twice the size of England but supports a population of just 325,000. Land grants in the 1970s to encourage agricultural development caused the population to grow quickly from only 25,000 in 1960. Then, in the late 1980s a gold rush in the northwest of Roraima drew prospectors from all over the country. The mining took place on the Yanomami Indian Reserve, devastating their traditional way of life. Further tragedy came in January 1998 when forest fires spread across the state, causing massive destruction until extinguished by rains in March.

The forest cover gives way to grasslands in the northeast and there is a pronounced dry season. The *várzea* (flood plain) along the main rivers irrigates the southeast of the state. Cattle ranching is important as is rice cultivation on the flood plain of the Rio Branco. Other crops are maize, beans, manioc and banana. Some gold mining still continues but at a reduced level.

Towards Boa Vista

The road that connects Manaus and Boa Vista (a ferry crosses the Rio Branco at Caracaraí) is fully paved and regularly maintained. There are service stations with toilets and camping sites every 150-180 km; all petrol is low octane. At Km 100 is **Presidente Figueiredo,** with many waterfalls and a famous cave with bats. There are also shops and a restaurant. About 100 km further on is a service station at the entrance to the **Uaimiri Atroari Indian Reserve,** which straddles the road for about 120 km. Private cars and trucks are not allowed to enter the reserve between sunset and sunrise, but buses are exempt from this regulation. Nobody is allowed to stop within the reserve at any time. At the northern entrance to the reserve there are toilets and a place to hang your hammock (usually crowded with truckers overnight). At Km 327 is the village of **Vila Colina** where **Restaurante Paulista** is clean with good food, and you can use the shower and hang your hammock. At Km 359 there is a monument to mark the **equator**. At Km 434 is the clean and pleasant **Restaurant Goaio**. Just south of Km 500 is **Bar Restaurante D'Jonas**, a good place to eat; you can also camp or sling a hammock. Beyond here, large tracts of forest have been destroyed for settlement, but already many homes have been abandoned.

Boa Vista

» *pp586-588.*

→ *Colour map 1, A3. Phone code: 095. Population: 200,000.*

The capital of the extreme northern state of Roraima, 759 km north of Manaus, is a very pleasant, clean, laid-back little town on the Rio Branco. Tourism is beginning here and there are a number of interesting new destinations opening up, many offering a chance to explore far wilder country than that around Manaus, with correspondingly richer wildlife. The landscape is more diverse, too, with a mix of tropical forest, savannah and highlands dotted with waterfalls. However, the area immediately around the city has been heavily deforested.

Boa Vista lies within easy access of both Venezuela and Guyana and crossing the border to either is straightforward. When the river is low, it is possible to swim in the Rio Branco, 15 minutes by bus from the town centre (too polluted in Boa Vista). As a result of heavy international pressure, the Brazilian government expelled some 40,000 gold prospectors from the Yanomami Reserve in the west of the state in the early 1990s. The economic consequences were very severe for Boa Vista, which went from boom to bust. An increase in cattle ranching in the area has not taken up the slack.

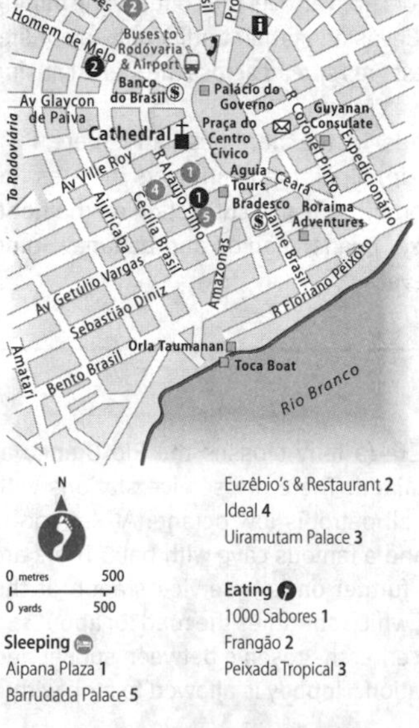

Boa Vista

Sleeping
Aipana Plaza **1**
Barrudada Palace **5**
Euzêbio's & Restaurant **2**
Ideal **4**
Uiramutam Palace **3**

Eating
1000 Sabores **1**
Frangão **2**
Peixada Tropical **3**

Ins and outs

The **airport** ⓘ *4 km from the centre*, receives national and international flights. There are no exchange or left luggage facilities. A taxi to the centre costs US$12; to the *rodoviária*, US$10. There is a bus to the centre, US$0.40, or a 45-minute walk.

The **rodoviária** ⓘ *Av das Guianas, 3 km out of town at the end of Av Ville Roy, T095-3224 0606*, receives several daily buses from Manaus, Bonfim (from the Guyanese border) and Santa Elena in Venezuela. A taxi to the centre costs US$5, or the 10-minute bus ride costs US$0.45. The local bus terminal is on Avenida Amazonas, by Rua Cecília Brasil, near the central praça.

The city has a modern functional plan, which often means long hot treks from one place to another. There's a very ineffectual **tourist office** ⓘ *R Brigadeiro Eduardo Gomes, Centro, T095-3623 1230*, with booths at the *rodoviária*, T095-623 1238 and the airport.

To Venezuela and Guyana » pp586-588.

Boa Vista has road connections with the Venezuelan frontier at **Santa Elena de Uairén**, 237 km away. The road is paved, but the only petrol available is 110 km south of Santa Elena. Boa Vista is also linked to Bonfim for the Guyanese border at **Lethem**. Both roads are open all year.

Border with Venezuela

Immigration and customs Searches are thorough and frequent at this border crossing. It is essential to have a yellow fever vaccination to leave Brazil and to enter Venezuela and vice versa. Officials may give only two months' stay and car drivers may be asked to purchase an unnecessary permit; ask to see the legal documentation. Everyone who crosses the border must have a visa for Venezuela. The current procedure is to take a filled-out visa form, onward ticket, passport photo and deposit slip from the **Banco do Brasil** (US$30) to the Venezuelan consulate in Boa Vista; be prepared to wait an hour. It may be possible to get a visa at the border; check requirements in advance. There is also a Venezuelan consulate in Manaus which issues one-year, multiple entry visas (see page 582).

Buses leave Boa Vista *rodoviária* at 0730, 1000 and 1400 for Santa Elena de Uairén, stopping at all checkpoints, US$7.50, 3½ to six hours, take water.

Santa Elena de Uairén (Venezuela) → *International phone code +58.*

Santa Elena de Uairén is the gateway to the Venezuelan Highlands for those entering the country from Brazil. It is a pleasant frontier town, 10-12 hours by bus from Ciudad Bolívar, which is nine hours from Caracas. The road is paved all the way and there are also flights. The landscape is beautiful, an ancient land of flat- topped mountains and waterfalls. The road skirts the **Parque Nacional Canaima,** in which is the highest waterfall in the world, the **Angel Falls** (Salto Angel). Not far north of Santa Elena is the route to Mount Roraima.

Around Boa Vista

The river of doubt

In 1913, Colonel Rondon invited the former US president Theodore Roosevelt to accompany him on one of his surveys. Together they explored the Rio da Dúvida – the River of Doubt – in 1914, following it to the Rio Aripuanã, thence to the Madeira. On the expedition they suffered great difficulties on the river itself, and Roosevelt contracted a fever which incapacitated him on the voyage and from which he never fully recovered. Rondon rechristened the Rio da Dúvida the Rio Roosevelt. The former president's account is told in *Through the Brazilian Wilderness* (London: John Murray, 1914), which contains photographs of the expedition. Further insights into the project are found in the *Mato Grosso ao Amazonas* telegraph by Coronel Cãndido Mariano da Silva Rondon, 1907-1915, which has photos and includes details of the Roosevelt-Rondon expedition.

Written in 1993, Sam Moses' *Down the River of Doubt* (*Travelers' Tales Brazil*) gives an account of an expedition following in Roosevelt's footsteps, which highlighted the effects of the late 20th-century mahogany trade on the Cinta Larga tribe who live on the Rio Roosevelt.

Santa Elena has plenty of hotels and places to eat, as well as money-changing facilities, a phone office with international connections, and tour companies for trips into the Gran Sabana – as the region is known.

Ins and outs The **rodoviária** ⓘ *C Mcal Sucre*, receives arrivals from Ciudad Bolívar (Venezuela) several times daily; the journey takes 10-12 hours and buses are run by a number of companies. The **Brazilian consulate** is near the bus terminal opposite the Corpoven petrol station (open 0800-1200, 1400-1800). Full details on this region, and the rest of the country, can be found in the *South American Handbook*.

Border with Guyana

The main border crossing between Brazil and Guyana is from **Bonfim**, 125 km (all paved) northeast of Boa Vista, to Lethem. The towns are separated by the Rio Tacutu, which is crossed by small boats for foot passengers (five minutes, US$2). Vehicles cross by ferry on demand, US$4, or drive across in the dry season. The river crossing is 2½ km from Bonfim, about 1½ km north of Lethem. A bridge is under construction. It is essential to have a yellow fever vaccination both to leave Brazil and to enter Guyana. The bus passes through **Brazilian immigration** where you receive your exit stamp before crossing the river. On the other side, there are taxis to take you to **Guayanese immigration** office (US$3). You are given a visa for the exact amount of time you stipulate. The border is open 24 hours but officials tend to leave immigration after 1800. There is another border crossing at **Laramonta** from where it is a hard but rewarding walk to the Guyanese town of Orinduik.

Sleeping

Boa Vista *p584, map p584*

B **Aipana Plaza**, Joaquim Nabuco 53, Praça do Centro Cívico, T095-3224 4116. The best in town with plain rooms decorated in cream and dark tiles, and photos of Roraima. Hot water, a/c, marble bathrooms and cable TV. Attractive pool area with a shady little bar.

B **Uiramutam Palace**, Av Capt Ene Garcez 427, T095-3624 4700, uiramutam@technet.com.br. A business hotel with modest

a/c rooms with writing desk and armchair, cable TV and large bathrooms. Decent pool.
C Barrudada Palace Hotel, R Araújo Filho 228, T095-3623 9335. Simple a/c rooms in a modern tower block very close to the centre. Rooms on the upper floors have views of the river. Breakfast and lunch included.
D Euzébio's, R Cecília Brasil 1107, T095-3623 0300, F623 9131. Spruce, modest rooms with a/c and en suites with cold showers. The best are airy and on the upper floors. Pleasant pool and a laundry service.
F Hotel Ideal, R Araújo Filho 481, T095-3224 6342. Very simple but well-kept rooms with en suites. Some have a/c. Friendly staff and generous breakfast. Convenient for the centre.

Camping

Rio Caaumé, 3 km north of town. Pleasant unofficial site with small bar and clean river.

Border with Venezuela *p585*

On the Brazilian side there is one basic hotel; across the border there are many far better options in Santa Elena de Uairén (see the *South American Handbook*).

Border with Guyana *p586*

Electricity in Lethem is officially turned off 2200-0700; take a torch or candles. There are plenty of cheap places to stay; see the *South American Handbook* for details. There is a café at the *rodoviária*, opposite the church, whose owner speaks English and can provide information.

Mr Myers, who speaks English and is very helpful, offers rooms (**D**) with fan and shower.

Eating

Boa Vista *p584, map p584*

Most restaurants close at night, except for pizzerias. There are a number of restaurants serving snacks and juices on the riverside along R Floriano Peixoto and several open-air restaurants and cafés on the Orla Taumanan, a complex of little bars and eating places overlooking the river. Nightlife and bars are concentrated here; it is quiet during the week but livelier at weekends. There are many little juice stands around Praça do Centro Cívico.

TT Churrascaria La Carreta, R Pedro Rodrigues 185, 500 m from **Euzébio's**. Good. US$3 buffet, nice atmosphere. Recommended.
TT Euzébio's (see Sleeping, above). A/c restaurant with decent fish, *feijoada* and meat dishes. Breakfasts are generous.
TT Peixada Tropical, R Pedro Rodrigues at Ajuricaba, T095-224 6040. A range of river fish dishes in a variety of styles from Bahian sauces to *milanesa* accompanied by beans, rice and salads.
T 1000 Sabores, R Araújo Filho at Benjamin Constant. Pizzas, snacks and juices. Opens early and closes late.
T Frangão, R Homem de Melo at Cecília Brasil. Barbecued chicken and river fish with salads, rice, beans. Canned drinks only.

Border with Guyana *p586*

T Restaurante Internacional, opposite the *rodoviária* in Lethem, on the other side from the church. Another restaurant, further down from the *rodoviária*, serves good food.

Bars and clubs

Boa Vista *p584, map p584*

R Floriano Peixoto is lively after dark at weekends when there is live music in and around the Orla Taumanan.
Toca Boat, Orla Taumanan, T095-9971 5454. River cruises and parties with live music and dancing

Activities and tours

Boa Vista *p584, map p584*

Aguia Tours, R Benjamin Constant 1683, T095-3624 1516. Can book buses and flights and the owner speaks some English.
Roraima Adventures, R Sebastião Diniz 787, T095-3624 9611, T095-9115 4171 (mob), www.roraima-brasil.com.br. A range of interesting trips to little-known and little-visited parts of Roraima state including the spectacular Tepequem and Serra Grande mountains and the Rio Uraricoera, which is replete with wildlife. Groups get the best prices, which are competitive with those in Manaus. Helpful with visas for Venezuela.

For Sleeping and Eating price codes, see pages 49 and 52 or the inside front cover. For an explanation of phone codes, see page 66.

Transport

Boa Vista *p584, map p584*

Air

Flights and buses can be booked through Aguia Tours (see above).

Flights to the **Guianas**, **Belém**, **Brasília**, **Macapá**, **Manaus**, **Santarém** and **São Paulo.** Confirm flights before reaching Boa Vista as they are often fully booked. Air taxis with Rondônia, Praça Santos Dumond, T095-224 5068.

Airline offices GOL, www.voegol.com.br. META, Praça Santos Dumond 100, T095-224 7677, www.voemeta.com.br. TAM, www.tam.com.br.

Bus

Note that it is difficult to get a taxi or bus to the *rodoviária* in time for early morning departures; as it's a 25-min walk, book a taxi the previous evening. To **Manaus**, with **Eucatur**, US$28, 10-12 hrs, 4 daily each way, can be crowded, advisable to book at least a few hours in advance. To **Caracaraí** US$9, 3 hrs. **Amatur** to **Bonfim**, daily 0730, 1430, 1700, 2 hrs, US$3.70.

Car hire

Localiza, Av Benjamin Constant 291E, T/F095-224 5222. **Yes**, Av Maj Williams 538, T/F095-224 3723.

Hitchhiking

Hitching to **Santa Elena** (Venezuela) can be difficult; either wait at the bridge and police checkpoint on the road to the border, or try to find a Venezuelan driver on the square. Hitching from Boa Vista to **Manaus** is fairly easy on the many trucks travelling south; try from the service station near the *rodoviária*. You may have to change trucks at Caracaraí. At the ferry crossing over the Rio Branco there is usually a long queue of waiting hikers; try to arrange a lift on the ferry. Truck drivers ask for approximately half the bus fare to take passengers in the cab, which is a bargain; it's even cheaper or free in the back. The view from the truck is usually better than from the bus and you can see the virgin forest of the indigenous reserve in daylight. Take some food and water.

Taxis

For radio taxis contact **Tupã**, R Monte Castelo 318, T095-224 9150.

Border with Venezuela *p585*

Bus Buses from Santa Elena to **Boa Vista** leave at 0830, 1200, 1500 and 1600, stopping at all checkpoints, US$7.50, 3½-6 hrs, take water. It is possible to share a taxi.

Border with Guyana

Bus **Bonfim–Boa Vista** at least 3 a day, US$3.70. Weekly jeep **Laramonta–Boa Vista** US$30.

Boat To cross the river, take a canoe, US$0.25. No boats at night.

Directory

Boa Vista *p584, map p584*

Banks US dollars and Guyanese notes can be changed in Boa Vista. TCs and cash in **Banco do Brasil**, Av Galycon de Paiva 56, 1000-1300 (minimum US$200),will not change bolívares. There is no official exchange agency and the local rates for bolivares are low. **Bradesco**, Jaime Brasil e Getúlio Vargas, Visa ATM. Best rate for dollars, **Casa Pedro José**, R Araújo Filho 287, T095-224 4277, also changes TCs and bolivares. **Timbo's** (gold and jewellery shop), on the corner of R Cecília Brasil e Av Getúlio Vargas, will change money. **Embassies and consulates** Venezuela, Av Benjamin Constant 1675, open mornings only. Visas available. Laid-back service. Allow 24-48 hrs. **Guyana**, R Benjamin Constant 1171, T095-9112 7017, open mornings only. **Medical services** Geral, Av Brig Eduardo Gomes, T095-623 2068. Yellow fever inoculations are free at a clinic near the hospital.

Border with Guyana *p586*

Banks Reais can be changed into Guyanese dollars in Boa Vista. There are no exchange facilities in Lethem, but reais are accepted in town. **Embassies and consulates** Guyana, there is no consul in Boa Vista, so if you need a visa for Guyana, you must get it in São Paulo or Brasília.

Rondônia and Acre

The state of Rondônia is largely populated by migrants from other parts of Brazil. Foreigners are welcomed without question or curiosity and there is no regional accent. A local academic described the state as 'a land where nobody has a name and everyone can have a dream'. Most visitors tend to arrive via the BR-364 from Cuiabá or the Rio Madeira from Manaus.

The intriguing state of Acre, rich in natural beauty, history and the seringueiro *culture, is still very much off the beaten track. The area is beginning to develop its considerable potential for adventure, as links are opening up with neighbouring Peru and Bolivia.* ▸▸ *For Sleeping, Eating and other listings, see pages 596-600.*

Background

Rondônia

When the Portuguese first arrived in Rondônia, they thought the land they had found was an enormous island. The Madeira, Guaporé and Amazon rivers do almost form a circle, but the Guaporé was thought, erroneously, to link with the Rio Paraguai on the southwestern side. A group of indigenous Tupinambá, who fled from the Portuguese colonists on the Atlantic Coast, migrated up the Rio São Francisco to the Madeira, settling eventually on the Ilha de Tupinambaranas near the river's mouth. It was probably their accounts of the rivers in this region which encouraged the idea that the Amazon and Río de la Plata systems were linked, making Brazil an island.

Slave and gold hunters in the 18th century used the Guaporé and Madeira rivers for their expeditions. As a frontier area between Portuguese and Spanish colonization, the rivers were scenes of tension between the opposing powers, as well as of conflicts between indigenous tribes and slave-traders, and *bandeirantes* and Jesuits.

Rondônia became a state in 1981 after the central government's push to open up the unpopulated, undeveloped far west brought roads and settlers to the region. The destructive effects of this are well documented (see box, page 544). One of those roads, the BR-364 highway, which was prompted by plans for exaggerated growth, led to widespread deforestation and the erosion of the way of life of many indigenous groups.

The state was named after Colonel Cândido Mariano da Silva Rondon, who founded the **Indian Protection Service (SPI)** in 1910. Rondon was of partly indigenous origin and the policies that he incorporated into the SPI included respect for native institutions, guarantee of permanent ownership by the *indígena* of their land, the right to exclusive use of natural resources on their land, and protection against rapid change once contact between indigenous and 'civilized' worlds had been made. The pressures of contact between the *indígena* and the people who subsequently encroached on their world (ranchers, gold prospectors, rubber tappers, Brazil nut gatherers and so on) made the SPI's task very difficult.

Rondônia falls within the same climatic zone as the rest of western Amazônia, with average temperatures of 24-26°C and 2000-3000 mm of rain a year. The wettest months are November to April, the driest June and August. Rondônia can be subject to the phenomenon known as the *friagem*, a sudden drop in temperature to about 6°C, as a result of low pressure over the Amazon basin attracting polar air from the South Atlantic. The cold weather can last for a week or more and occurs in the winter months. It is said to be an effect of El Niño, the changing patterns in ocean currents in the Pacific at Christmas time.

A voice from the Amazon

Humanity finds itself at a critical point. Can science solve the mounting problems which confront us in every corner of the globe? Soon after human beings lost themselves to the blind, unconscious forces of systematic self-interest and greed, we, the Indians, found ourselves robbed both of what lay buried beneath our lands and of our lands themselves.

Thankfully, through the power of memory our history has been preserved, continues, and is passed on from generation to generation. Thankfully, the memory of Indians cannot be blotted out so easily.

We Indians have the power to see the truth behind history. Just as we have cures for those abounding problems which then, as now, are the consequence of systematic self-interest and greed.

The United Nations have not succeeded in bringing peace to our world. This is because wars do not begin with nations. They begin inside each and every one of us. What we must do, and with urgency, is to reintegrate humankind with its spiritual leaders and with them bring about a cure in the interior life and the repayment of our interior debts.

In much of the world tourism continues a destructive path without thinking of the consequences of its actions for future generations. But whilst this is happening there are many individual tourists who after speaking with true spiritual masters and shamans find truth and a solution to eternal problems.

Manoel Fernandes Moura, head of FIUPAM, an organization seeking to unite indigenous spiritual leaders from around the world and based in Tabatinga in the Amazon, is one of the leading indigenous rights campaigners of his generation. He was instrumental in helping to halt the Calha Norte northern perimeter road project in Roraima and Amazonas states. Moura is the seventh son of seven generations of shamans. FIUPAM, fiupam@yahoo.com.br.

Acre

In the mid-19th century, what is now Acre was disputed land between Brazil and Bolivia. The Treaty of Ayacucho, 1866, gave the territory to Bolivia. However, the onset of the rubber boom in the 1880s upset this arrangement because many of the landowners who were exporting rubber from Acre and down the Rio Madeira were Brazilian. They resented the fact that the Bolivian government had nominal control, exacting duties, but had signed economic rights over to North American interests. Many *Nordestinos* also migrated to this western frontier at the time in search of fortune. In 1899 the Brazilians rebelled. Four years later the Bolivian government yielded the territory to Brazil under the Treaty of Petrópolis and the American company received US$2 million compensation. In 1913, Rio Branco became capital of the new Território Federal do Acre, which attained statehood in 1962.

Acre has a population of only 500,000 but, as its land is much more productive than that of Rondônia. In the 1990s there was a flood of migration from Acre's landless south into the its neighbouring state, and conditions have yet to be improved. Acre is slightly drier than Rondônia, with 1500-2000 mm of rain a year.

Porto Velho » pp596-600.

→ *Phone code: 069. Colour map 1, B2. Population: 330,000.*

Porto Velho stands on a high bluff overlooking a curve of the Rio Madeira, one of the Amazon's main tributaries. The city has seen the rubber, gold and timber booms come and go. Service and IT industries are now the major employers. Today the city is a large sprawl of streets, laid out in blocks stretching 8 km into the interior. The lack of town planning means that many of the best shops, hotels and banks are now a fair distance from the old centre near the river.

Ins and outs

Getting there Domestic flights arrive at the **airport** ⓘ *8 km west of town, T069-225 1755*. A taxi to downtown costs US$15. Interstate buses from Rio Branco and Cuiabá arrive at the **rodoviária** ⓘ *east of the centre, Jorge Teixeira, between Carlos Gomes and Dom Pedro II*. There are buses to downtown. » *See also Transport, page 598.*

Getting around Urban bus services are good. Consider hiring a car if you're going to stay for some time. Be patient as even local residents get confused with directions. Taxis in town are cheap and plentiful. Find your favourite driver and stick with him; all have mobile phones and work with partners to give prompt 24-hour service.

Tourist offices **Funcetur** ⓘ *Av 7 de Setembro, above Museu Estadual, T069-221 1881, seplan@ronet.com.br*, is very helpful and publishes a free annual events list, *Calendario do Porto Velho*. Also useful is the **Departamento de Turismo** ⓘ *R Padre Chiquinho 670, Esplanada das Secretarias, CEP 78904-060, T069-221 1499, F225 2827*. The **Fundação Cultural do Estado de Rondônia (Funcer)** is at the same address. Street maps are hard to find. For a free map go to the **Teleron office** ⓘ *Av Pres Dutra 3023, 0600-2300*, and ask for the *Guia de Porto Velho*, which includes a map and city services listings.

Security The city is relatively safe for tourists despite rising crime and unemployment. Caution is advised in the evenings and at all times near the railway station and port.

Sights → *See map page 596.*

At the top of the hill on Praça João Nicoletti is the **cathedral**, built in 1930, with beautiful stained-glass windows. The **Prefeitura** (town hall) is across the street. The principal commercial street is Avenida 7 de Setembro, which runs from the railway station to the upper level of the city, near the *rodoviária*. The centre is hot and noisy, but not without its charm, and the port and old railway installations are interesting. As well as the **Museu Ferroviário**, there is a **Museu Geológico** ⓘ *both open 0800-1800*, at the old railway yards, known as Praça Madeira-Mamoré. Also here is the **Casa do Artesão** (see Shopping, page 598) and a promenade with riverside bars; a good place to watch the sunset.

The neoclassical **Palácio do Governo** faces Praça Getúlio Vargas, while Praça Marechal Rondon is spacious and modern. There are several popular viewpoints overlooking the river and railway yards. **Mirante I** (with restaurant) is at the end of Rua Carlos Gomes; **Mirante II** (with a bar and ice cream parlour) is at the end of Rua Dom Pedro II and **Mirante III** (with restaurant) is at the end of Benjamin Constant.

It is possible to visit the **cemetery**, where many of the people who died during the construction of the railway are buried. It's about 3 km from the railway station and best to go with a local guide, as it is located in a poorer part of town and difficult to find. It is an eerie place, with many of the tombstones overgrown, some of which have been tampered with by practitioners of *macumba*, and there are rumoured to be ghosts.

Parque Nacional Municipal de Porto Velho ⓘ *Av Rio Madeira s/n, 10 km, T069-221 2769, Thu-Sun, volunteer guides*, is a small zoo with 12 km of marked trails.

Excursions from Porto Velho

The **Cachoeira de Santo Antônio**, a series of rapids on the Rio Madeira, 7 km upriver from Porto Velho, is a popular destination for a swim during the dry season. In the rainy season the rapids may be underwater and swimming is dangerous. Access is by boat from Porto Cai N'Água (one hour); or by city bus No 102, 'Triângulo' (every 50 minutes from the city bus terminus or from the bus stop on Rua Rogério Weber, across from Praça Marechal Rondon). Gold dredges may be seen working near Porto Velho.

The **Banho do Souza** is a bar, restaurant and swimming area, 36 km out of town on the BR-364. A coolbox of beers and soft drinks is left by your table and you pay for what you've drunk at the end of the afternoon, swimming is free.

Along the BR-364 » *pp596-600.*

The **Marechal Rondon Highway**, BR-364, runs 1550 km from Porto Velho to Cuiabá in Mato Grosso. The paving of this road has led to the development of farms and towns. Cattle ranches can be seen all along the road, with the lowest population density in the south between Pimenta Bueno and Vilhena.

Pousada Ecológica Rancho Grande ⓘ *contact Caixa Postal 361, Ariquemes, Rondônia 78914, T/F069-535 4301, pousada@ ariquemes.com.br*, is a working *fazenda* about 250 km south of Porto Velho. It contains millions of rare butterflies, about 450 bird species and numerous mammals, all of which can be seen on the 20 km of trails. Owner, Harald Schmitz, speaks English, German and Spanish. Highly recommended, especially for butterfly lovers. Reservations and tours can be arranged through **Focus Tours**, see Tours operators, page 24. The **Bradesco** changes money and has an ATM.

Ji Paraná → *Phone code: 069. Colour map 1, B3. Population: 95,500.*

On the shores of the Rio Machado, 376 km from Porto Velho and halfway to Cuiabá is this pleasant town with a small riverside promenade and several bars, which are lively at night. There is swimming in the river, beware of the current, and a **telegraph museum** on Avenida Marechal Rondon.

Parque Nacional dos Pacaás Novos → *Colour map 1, B2.*

Pacaás Novos protects some 765,800 ha of *cerrado*, rainforest and tropical savannah and lies west of the BR-364. The fauna includes all the spectacular mammals such as jaguar, brocket deer, puma, tapir, peccary and maned wolf. The average annual temperature is 23°C, but this can fall as low as 5°C when the cold front known as the *friagem* blows up from the south pole. Information is available from **Ibama** ⓘ *Av Jorge Teixeira 3477, CEP 78904-320, T069-223 2599/3597, Porto Velho, or R João Batista Rios, CEP 78958-000 Pacaás Novas-RO*. Also enquire here about the **Jaru Biological Reserve** in the east of the state.

Reserva Biológica do Guaporé → *Colour map 1, C3.*

On the Rio Guaporé is the **Guaporé Biological Reserve** ⓘ *Av Limoeira, CEP 78971, Guaporé, T069-651 2239*, which contains the Forte Príncipe da Beira. The fort was constructed in 1777 to defend the border with Bolivia and is currently being restored. It can be reached from Costa Marques (20 km by road), which is some 345 km by unpaved road west of **Rolim de Moura**. This unplanned town, 40 km west of Pimenta Bueno, relies on agriculture, livestock and a small furniture industry. There are a few basic hotels and guesthouses, which are easy to find and do not require reservations.

Guajará-Mirim » pp596-600.

→ *Phone code: 069. Colour map 1, C2. Population: 39,000.*

From Porto Velho, the paved BR-364 continues 220 km southwest to **Abunã** (with a few cheap hotels), where the BR-425 branches south to Guajará-Mirim. About 9 km east of Abunã is a ferry crossing over the Rio Madeira, where it receives the waters of the Rio Abunã. The BR-425 is a fair road, partly paved, which uses the former rail bridges. It is sometimes closed from March to May. Across the Mamoré from Guajará-Mirim is the Bolivian town of **Guayaramerín**, which is connected by road to Riberalta, from where there are air services to other Bolivian cities.

Guajará-Mirim is a charming town. The **Museu Municipal** ① *T069-541 3362, 0500-1200, 1400-1800*, at the old Guajará-Mirim railway station beside the ferry landing, is interesting, diverse, and recommended. An ancient stern wheeler plies the Guaporé. Return trips of 1250 km, taking 26 days, can be made from Guajará-Mirim to Vila Bela in Mato Grosso; the fare includes food.

Border with Bolivia

Immigration Brazilian exit/entry stamps can be obtained from the **Polícia Federal** ① *Av Pres Dutra 70, corner of Av Quintino Bocaiúva, T069-541 4021.*

Getting there Speedboats take five minutes to cross the Rio Mamoré (border), US$1.65, and run all day; tickets can be bought at the waterside. There is also a 20-minute ferry crossing for vehicles, T069-541 3811, Monday to Saturday 0800-1200, Monday to Friday 1400-1600.

Guayaramerín (Bolivia) → *International phone code +591*

The Bolivian town of Guayaramerín is a cheerful, prosperous little place, on the bank of the Río Mamoré. It has an important **Zona Libre**. There are flights to Trinidad, La Paz, Cobija, Cochabamba and Santa Cruz, as well as buses to La Paz, Santa Cruz, Trinidad, Cobija and other destinations, but the roads are in poor shape and appalling in the wet season. Boats sail to Trinidad. For details, see the *South American Handbook*.

Rio Branco » pp596-600.

→ *Phone code: 068. Colour map 1, B2. Population: 253,000.*

The Rio Acre is navigable upstream as far as the borders with Peru and Bolivia. It divides Rio Branco, the state capital, into two districts called Primeiro (west) and Segundo (east), on either side of the river, linked by two bridges. The central Primeiro district contains most of the sights including the shady main square, **Praça Plácido de Castro**. Nearby, along Avenida Brasil, is the **cathedral**, Nossa Senhora de Nazaré. On the same street, the **Casa do Seringueiro** ① *Av Brasil 216, corner of Avenida Getúlio Vargas, Mon-Fri 0700-1200, 1400-1700*, has a good exhibition on rubber tappers and on Chico Mendes in particular; the Hélio Melo room has a display of Melo's paintings, mainly on the theme of the forest. Just around the corner, the neoclassical **Palácio Rio Branco** is on Rua Benjamin Constant, across from Praça Eurico Gaspar Dutra. North of Praça Plácido de Castro, the **Museu da Borracha** (rubber museum) ① *Av Ceará 1177, Mon-Fri 0900-1700*, is housed in a lovely old building with a tiled façade. It has information about the rubber boom, archaeological artefacts, a section about indigenous Acreano, documents and memorabilia from the annexation and a display about the Santo Daime doctrine (see Excursions from Rio Branco, page 594), recommended.

In the Segundo district is the **Calçadão da Gameleira**, a pleasant promenade along the shore, with plaques and an old tree marking the location of the original settlement.

There are several large parks in the city. The **Horto Forestal**, in Vila Ivonete (Primeiro), 3 km north of the centre, is popular with joggers and has native Amazonian trees, a small lake, walking paths and picnic areas (take a city bus to 'Conjunto Procon' or 'Vila Ivonete'). The **Parque Zoo-Botânico**, on the UFAC campus is 5 km from the centre, along the BR-364.

Ins and outs

Getting there The **airport** ⓘ *on the AC-40, Km 1.2, in the Segundo distrito, T068-224 6833*, receives flights from several Brazilian cities. A taxi from the airport to the centre costs a flat rate of US$20, or take a bus marked 'Norte–Sul' or 'Vila Acre'. Buses arrive at the **rodoviária** ⓘ *Av Uirapuru, Cidade Nova, Segundo distrito, T069-224 1182*. To get to the centre, take a city bus marked 'Norte–Sul'.

Tourist information Contact the **Secretaria de Indústria e Comércio** ⓘ *Av Getúlio Vargas 659, Centro*, or the **Departamento de Turismo** ⓘ *BR-364, Km 05, Distrito Industrial, T068-224 3997*.

Security Despite improved air and road links, Rio Branco remains at the 'end of the line', a frontier outpost whose depressed economy, high unemployment and prevalent drug-running make the city unsafe at night, and some caution is advised at all hours.

Excursions from Rio Branco

About 8 km southeast of town, upriver on the Rio Acre, is **Lago do Amapá**, a U-shaped lake good for boating and water sports; access is by river or by land via route AC-40. About 2 km beyond along the AC-40 is **Praia do Amapá**, a bathing beach on the Rio Acre; an annual arts festival is held here in September. Excursions can be made to **rubber plantations** and rubber extraction areas in native forest (*seringais nativos*).

Chico Mendes – the first eco-martyr

The most famous *seringueiro* (rubber tapper) was Francisco (Chico) Alves Mendes, born in 1944. Chico's father had come to Acre from northeast Brazil as a *soldado da borracha*, engaged in providing rubber for the Allies during the Second World War. Chico learnt the trade of his father, became a leader of the Xapuri Rural Workers' Union and was a founder member of the CNS. He was instrumental in setting up a number of extractive reserves, parcels of land preserved for sustainable exploitation by those that lived there. He was shot dead on 22 December 1988 by cattle ranchers, to whose land-grabbing Mendes was in open opposition. He was by no means the only *seringueiro* who had been killed in such circumstances (he was the 90th rubber tapper to be killed in 1988 alone), but his murder was the culmination of a decade of *fazendeiro-seringueiro* confrontation. Over 4000 people attended his funeral; the world's media latched onto the story and Chico Mendes became the first globally-recognized eco-martyr. He was honoured by the United Nations for his efforts to stop the destruction of the rainforest. The universal outcry at his assassination led to the arrest, trial and imprisonment of his killers, members of the family of Darly Alves da Silva; a rare event in the history of Amazon land disputes. His death inspired changes in government policy on environmental protection, greater involvement of rubber tappers and other forest workers in local organizations, and the development of extractive reserves, first promoted in 1985 as protected areas for the *seringueiros*. Father Andre Ficarelli, assistant to the Bishop of Acre, said that Mendes' murder was like "the lancing of a tumour, exposing all the corruption and problems which the government [chose] to ignore". To others it was an opportunity to portray the whole affair in Hollywood-style melodrama; there was fierce competition for the film rights to Mendes' life story.

Some 13 km from Rio Branco is **Colônia Cinco Mill** (access along AC-10), a religious centre of the followers of the Santo Daime doctrine. Its members, many originally from outside Acre and Brazil, live a communal life, working in agriculture and producing crafts made of latex. The religion centres around the use of *ayahuasca*, a hallucinogenic potion adopted from local *indígena*. Visitors are usually welcome, but enquire beforehand.

Cruzeiro do Sul → *Colour map 1, B1. Population: 65,000.*

From Rio Branco, the BR-364 continues west (in principle) to Cruzeiro do Sul and Japim, with a view to reaching the Peruvian frontier when completed. It is very difficult to get from Rio Branco to Cruzeiro do Sul by road because there is no bus service, but the occasional truck travels through, mainly in the dry season. The road is frequently impassable and open, on average, around 20 days a year.

Cruzeiro do Sul is an isolated Amazonian town on the Rio Juruá in western Acre. Cheap excursions can be made on the river, for example to the village of **Rodrigues Alves,** two to three hours' return by boat or 15 km by road. In the jungle it's possible to see rubber tapping and the collecting of latex in *borrachas*. It's very difficult to change money in Cruzeiro do Sul.

Ins and outs Flights connect the town with Rio Branco (**Varig**) and Pucallpa in Peru. In the wet season there are sporadic boats to Manaus. There are a few basic boxy hotels in town (near the cathedral and facing the river), many offer full board.

Border with Bolivia and Peru

The BR-317 from Rio Branco heads south and later southwest, parallel to the Rio Acre; it is paved as far as **Xapuri**. Here is the **Fundação Chico Mendes**, with very basic lodging and two restaurants. The road continues to **Brasiléia**, opposite the Bolivian town of Cobija, on the Rio Acre. In Brasiléia is a handful of hotels and restaurants. The polícia federal give entry/exit stamps. There are three buses daily to and from Rio Branco, five hours in the wet season, US$10. It is possible to stay in **Epitaciolândia** (**Hotel Kanda, D**, five minutes' walk from the police post) and cross the border into Bolivia early in the morning. There are two official crossings between Cobija and Brasiléia: one is by ferry to Cobija's boat wharf, just off Calle Bolívar, at the west end of town. The other is via the international bridge, east of the ferry. The former is often quicker, and certainly cheaper (US$0.35), as taxis are expensive (US$12). All visitors must carry a yellow fever certificate.

The road ends at **Assis Brasil**, where the Peruvian, Bolivian and Brazilian frontiers meet. Across the Rio Acre are **Iñapari** (Peru), where the border crossing is difficult, even out of the wet season, and **Bolpebra** (Bolivia). A bus service operates only in the dry season beyond Brasiléia to Assis Brasil; access in the wet season is by river. In Assis Brasil there is one basic but clean hotel. It is sometimes possible to wade across the river between Iñapari and Assis Brasil. There is no *polícia federal* in the village, get entry/exit stamps in Brasiléia. Take small denomination bills or Peruvian soles as there is nowhere to change money on the Peruvian side.

Cobija is roughly 500 km northwest of La Paz and there are air and road connections. The town is popular with Brazilians and Peruvians for duty-free shopping. For more details, see the *South American Handbook*.

Sleeping

Porto Velho *p591, map p596*

AL Vila Rica, Av Carlos Gomes 1616, T/F069-224 3433, www.hotelvilarica.com.br. Tower block hotel with a restaurant, pool and sauna.

A Rondon Palace, Av Gov Jorge Teixeira, 491, corner R Jacy Paraná, away from the centre, T/F069-224 2718. Business-orientated hotel with a restaurant, pool and travel agency.

B Central, R Tenreiro Aranha 2472, T069-224 2099, www.enter-net.com.br/hcentral. Clean and friendly hotel with a/c rooms with TVs and fridges. Good breakfast. Highly recommended.

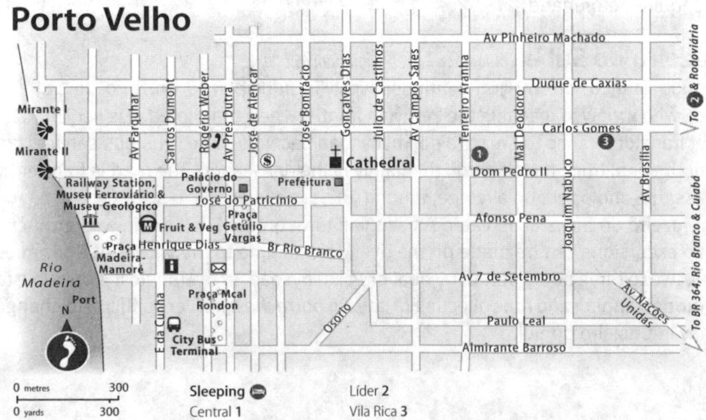

C Vitória Palace, R Duque de Caxias 745. A/c and cheaper fan-cooled rooms. Basic, clean and friendly.

D Líder, Av Carlos Gomes near the *rodoviária*. Honest and welcoming but only reasonably clean. Rooms are fan cooled.

E Tía Carmen, Av Campos Sales 2995, T069-221 7910. Very friendly and with simple well-kept rooms. The snack bar in front of the hotel serves good cakes. Highly recommended.

Ji Paraná *p592*

There are a number of hotels in the town, which is tiny and easy to negotiate. Reservations are not necessary.

Guajará-Mirim *p593*

A Pakaas Palafitas Lodge, Km 18, Estrada do Palheta, T/F069-541 3058, www.pakaas.com.br. 28 smart bungalows in a beautiful natural setting out of town.

C Jamaica, Av Leopoldo de Matos 755, T/F069- 541 3721. Simple but the best hotel in town. Rooms have a/c and fridges. Parking.

C Lima Palace, Av 15 de Novembro 1613, T069-541 3421, F541 2122. Similar to the Jamaica but with slightly scruffier rooms.

D Chile, Av Q Bocaiúva. Basic but well run. Includes breakfast, good value.

D Mamoré, R Mascarenhas de Moraes 1105, T069-541 3753. Clean, friendly and popular with backpackers.

Rio Branco *p593, map p594*

There are few economical hotels in the centre, but a reasonable selection by the *rodoviária*.

A Pinheiro Palace, R Rui Barbosa 91, 1st district (west bank), T068-224 7191, pinheiro@mdnet.com.br. Business-orientated hotel with a pool. Recommended.

B Rio Branco, R Rui Barbosa 193, by Praça Plácido de Castro, 1st district (west bank), T068-224 1785, F224 2681. Simple but well-looked-after hotel with a/c rooms all with fridges and TVs.

B-D Rodoviária, R Palmeiral 268, Cidade Nova by the *rodoviária*, T068-224 4434. Convenient and with a range of plain a/c rooms with fridge and TV, and cheaper options with shared baths and fans. Good value.

C Inácio Palace, R Rui Barbosa 72, 1st district (west bank), T068-224 6397. The budget sister hotel to the **Pinheiro Palace** (same email) with a/c rooms and a modest restaurant.

C Triângulo, R Floriano Peixoto 727, 1st district (west bank), T068-224 9265, F224 4117. Simple a/c rooms with TV and fridge.

C-D Albemar, R Franco Ribeiro 99, 1st district (west bank), T068-224 1938. Well-kept a/c rooms with a fridge and TV and a good breakfast. Recommended.

D-F Nacional, R Palmeiral 496, 2nd district, Cidade Nova, T068-224 4822. Fan-cooled rooms and options with a shared bath.

Eating

Porto Velho *p591, map p596*

Avoid eating too much fish because of mercury contamination. There are a number of good restaurants around the intersection of Dom Pedro II and Av Joaquim Nabuco, and plenty of snack bars and *padarias* throughout the city for those on a budget.

TTT Carovela do Madeira, R José Camacho 104. The city's business lunch venue, with a/c. Reasonable international menu.

TT Almanara, R José de Alencar 2624. Good authentic Lebanese food, popular but not cheap. Recommended.

TT Bella Italia, Av Joaquim Nabuco 2205. Pasta, pizza and other basic Italian fare alongside Brazilian home cooking

T Bar do Dico, Av Joaquim Nabuco 955. The best fish in town and lively in the evenings.

T Natal, Av Carlos Gomes 2783. Standard *churrascaria* with decent side dishes.

T Ponto Certo, Av Rio Madeira 45. Excellent view of river and the best *churrascaria* cuts in town, closed Mon.

Rio Branco *p593, map p594*

There are boats on the river serving cheap but good food. The local delicacy is *tacacá*: a soup served piping hot in a gourd (*cuia*), made from manioc starch (*goma*), cooked *jambu* leaves which

For Sleeping and Eating price codes, see pages 49 and 52 or the inside front cover. For an explanation of phone codes, see page 66.

numb the mouth and tongue, shrimp, spices and hot pepper sauce.

Kaxinawa, Av Brasil at the corner of Praça Plácido de Castro. The best in town for Acreano regional food.

Pizzeria Tutti Frutti, Av Ceará 1132, across from the Museu da Borracha. Expensive pizzas and exotic ice cream.

Anexos, R Franco Ribeiro 99, next door to Albemar Hotel. Popular with young people and families for meals and drinks.

Churrascaria Triângulo, R Floriano Peixoto 727. As much charcoal-grilled meat as you can eat. Recommended.

Remanso do Tucunaré, R José de Melo 481, Bairro Bosque. Excellent river fish – though avoid the *piraracu*.

Sorveteria Arte Sabor, Trav Santa Inés 28, corner Aviario, 1st district (west bank), 15 mins' walk from the centre. Excellent home-made ice cream, many jungle fruit flavours. Highly recommended.

Bars and clubs

Porto Velho *p591, map p596*

Maria Fumaça collective, T069-224 4385. Organizes regular raves, concerts and *festas* around town. Check radio and newspapers for details.

Tom Brasil, club at Peixe Noturnos, near airport (taxi US$15, essential to book return fare). Every Sun night from 2200, US$3 entry for men.

Shopping

Porto Velho *p591, map p596*

Indigenous handicrafts

Hammocks are pricier than in Manaus.

Casa do Artesão, Praça Madeira-Mamoré, behind the railway station, Thu-Sun 0800-1800.

Casa do Índio, R Rui Barbosa 1407.

Markets

There is a clean fruit and vegetable market at the corner of R Henrique Dias and Av Farquhar and a dry goods market 3 blocks to the south, near the port. On Sun there is a general market off Av Rogério Weber near port, excellent bargains but no souvenirs. Watch out for pickpockets.

Rio Branco *p593, map p594*

Arts and crafts

Fair in Praça do Seringueiro on Sun evenings. Market in 1st district (west bank), off R Epaminondas Jácome.

Activities and tours

Porto Velho *p591, map p596*

Ecoporé, R Rafael Vaz e Silva 3335, Bairro Liberdade, T069-221 5021, carol@ronet.com.br. For ecotourism projects in rubber tappers' communities on the Brazil/Bolivia border, US$50 per person per day, full details from Carol Doria, who speaks English.

Guajará-Mirim *p593*

Alfatur, Av 15 de Novembro 106, T/F069-541 2853. Tour operator.

Rio Branco *p593, map p594*

Tour operators

Inácio's Tur, R Rui Barbosa 91, at Hotel Pinheiro Palace, T068-224 9626.

Nilce's Tour, R Quintino Bocaiúva 20, T/F068-223 2611, for airline tickets, helpful, 15 mins' walk from the centre.

Serra's Tur, R Silvestre Coelho 372, T068-224 4629.

Transport

Porto Velho *p591, map p596*

See also Ins and outs, page 591.

Air

To get to the airport take bus 'Aeroporto' (last one between 2400 and 0100). Flights to **Brasília**, **Manaus** and **Rio Branco**.

Airline offices TAM, R J Castilho 530, T069-224 2180. **Varig**, Av Campos Sales 2666, T069-224 2262, F224 2278, English spoken.

Boat

See Routes in Amazônia, page 579. There is a passenger service to **Porto Cai N'Água** (which means 'fall in the water'). For the best price buy directly on the boat, avoid touts on the shore. The Rio Madeira is fairly narrow, so the banks can be seen and there are several 'meetings of waters'.

Shipping a car São Matheus Ltda, Av Terminal dos Milagros 400, Balsa, takes vehicles on pontoons, meals, showers, toilets, cooking and sleeping in your car is permitted. 6 days a week a boat leaves at 1800 for **Manaus** from Manicoré, at the confluence of the Rio Madeira and Rio Manicoré, 2 nights and 1 day's journey, food included. There are boats from Porto Velho to **Manicoré** on Mon, Wed and Sat (1800, arrives 0200, but you can sleep on board), connecting with Manicoré-Manaus boats (a recommended boat is *Orlandina*).

Bus
To get to the *rodoviária* from town take 'Presidente Roosevelt' bus No 301 (if on Av 7 de Setembro, the bus turns at Av Mcal Deodoro); 'Aeroporto' and 'Hospital Base' (No 400) also go to *rodoviária*. Health and other controls at the Rondônia-Mato Grosso border are strict. To break up a long trip is much more expensive than doing it all in one stretch.

Buses run to **Humaitá**, US$5, 3 hrs. To **São Paulo**, 60-plus hrs, US$75. To **Cuiabá**, 23 hrs, US$45, expensive food and drink is available en route. To **Guajará-Mirim**, see below. To **Rio Branco**, Viação Rondônia, 5 daily, 8 hrs, US$12.50. Daily bus with Eucatur from **Cascavel** (Paraná, connections for Foz do Iguaçu) via **Maringá**, **Presidente Prudente**, **Campo Grande** and **Cuiabá** to Porto Velho (Porto Velho-**Campo Grande** 36 hrs, US$60). To **Cáceres** for the Pantanal, 18 hrs, US$30.

Car
To **Cuiabá** is 1550 km on the BR-364 (Marechal Rondon highway), fully paved; see below and page 659. To **Rio Branco**, 554 km, BR-364, poorly paved; north to **Humaitá** (205 km) on the Madeira river or the BR-319, paved, connecting with the Transamazônica, BR-230 (frequently closed, ascertain conditions before travelling). The BR-319 north from Humaitá to **Manaus** is closed indefinitely. Road journeys are best done in the dry season, the 2nd half of the year.

Car hire LeMans, Av Nações Unidas 1200, T069-224 2012. **Silva Car**, R Almte Barroso 1528, T069-221 1423/6040. **Ximenes**, Av Carlos Gomes 1055, T069-224 5766.

Taxi
Radio Taxi: **Marmoré**, T069-224 7070.

Ji Paraná *p592*
Bus The bus station, R dos Mineiros, T069-422 2233, has services to **Porto Velho**, US$16.25, 16 hrs. To **Cuiabá**, 15 hrs.

Guajará-Mirim *p593*
Bus To **Porto Velho**, 5½ hrs or more depending on season, 8 a day with **Viação Rondônia**, US$18. A taxi to the Porto Velho *rodoviária* costs US$25 per person for 4-5 people, 3 hrs, and leaves when full.

Rio Branco *p593, map p594*
Air Taxis to the airport use the meter and usually cost around US$15. There are flights to **Porto Velho**, **Manaus**, **Brasília**, **São Paulo**, **Cuiabá** and **Campo Grande**; once a week to **Cruzeiro do Sul**.

Airline offices Varig, T068-211 1000.

Bus To **Porto Velho**, Viação Rondônia, 5 daily, 8 hrs, US$12.50. To **Guajará-Mirim**, daily with **Rondônia** at 1130 and 2200, 5-6 hrs, US$10; or take **Inácio's Tur** shopping trip, 3 per week.

Car hire Car rentals with nationwide agencies are more expensive in Acre than other states. Locabem, Rodovia AC-40, Km 0, 2nd district, T069-223 3000, F224 5222. **Localiza**, R Rio Grande do Sul 310, T069-224 7746, airport T069-224 8478. **Unidas**, T069-224 5044.

Directory

Porto Velho *p591, map p596*
Banks Open in the morning only. **Banco do Brasil**, Dom Pedro II 607 and Av José de Alencar, cash and TCs with 2% commission, minimum commission US$10, minimum amount exchanged US$200. **Marco Aurélio Câmbio**, R José de Alencar 3353, T069-223 2551, very quick, efficient, good rates for US$ cash, Mon-Fri 0900-1500. **Parmetal** (gold merchants), R Joaquim Nabuco 2265, T069-221 1566, cash only, good rates, open Mon-Fri 0730-1800, Sat 0730-1300. Local radio and newspapers publish exchange

rates. Exchange is difficult elsewhere in Rondônia. **Laundry** Lavanderia Marmoré, Pinheiro Machado 1455B. **Medical services** Hospital Central, R Júlio de Castilho 149, T/F069-224 4389, 24-hr emergencies. Dentist at Carlos Gomes 2577; 24-hr clinic opposite. **Post office** Av Pres Dutra 2701, corner of Av 7 de Setembro. **Telephones** Av Pres Dutra 3023 and Dom Pedro II, daily 0600-2300.

Guajará-Mirim *p593*

Banks Banco do Brasil, foreign exchange in the morning only. Loja Nogueira, Av Pres Dutra, corner Leopoldo de Matos, cash only. There is no market in Brazil for bolivianos. **Embassies and consulates** Bolivia, Av C Marquês 495, T069-541 2862, visas are given here. **Medical services** Regional, Av Mcal Deodoro, T069-541 2651. **Post office** Av Pres Dutra. **Telephone** Av B Ménzies 751.

Rio Branco *p593, map p594*

Banks There are no banks but the hotel owner may be persuaded to oblige. **Hospitals** Santa Casa, R Alvorada 178, T068-224 6297. **Post office** On the corner of R Epaminondas Jácome and Av Getúlio Vargas. **Telephone** Av Brasil between Mcal Deodoro and Av Getúlio Vargas, long delays for international calls.

Brasília, Goiás and Tocantins

Footprint features

Introduction

The country's capital, Brasília, is the symbol of the nation's commitment to its empty centre. Although not generally viewed as a tourist attraction, it is interesting as a city of pure invention similar to Australia's Canberra or Washington in the United States. Its central position makes it a natural crossroads for visiting the north and interior of Brazil and, when passing through, it is well worth undertaking a city tour to view its innovative modern design.

Like Brasília, Goiás is rarely on the itinerary for first-time visitors to Brazil. But those who know it well often consider it their favourite state in the country. There is so much here: colonial cities as beautiful as any in Minas and far less visited; colourful and bizarre festivals; national parks as wild as the Pantanal; and trekking, wildlife and birdwatching that is second only to the Pantanal and the Amazon. Its people are among the country's most welcoming. They are quietly spoken, poetic and obsessed with dreadful *sertanejo* music, which laments lost love through videos of girls in little shorts intercut with prize bulls. The state is easily visited from Brasília or on the way to or from the Pantanal and the coast.

Further north is the state of Tocantins, dominated by vast rivers, *cerrado* forests and, increasingly, soya plantations. The deserts of Jalapão lie here; landscapes which at first sight seem a strange fusion of north Africa and outback Australia but which, unlike both, are broken by myriad lakes and waterfalls. Further to the west on the frontier of Mato Grosso is the Bananal – one of the largest river islands in the world and home to large groups of indigenous Brazilians.

★ Don't miss...

1 **Brasília** Love or hate the country's purpose-built capital, page 604.
2 **Cidade de Goiás** Visit Brazil's best-preserved colonial town, page 617.
3 **Pirenópolis** A pretty colonial town set in *cerrado*-covered hills, with great restaurants and one of the best festivals in the country, page 618.
4 **Chapada dos Veadeiros** A breathtaking series of escarpments coarsed by rivers, with excellent hiking and adventure sports, page 619.
5 **Jalapão** Central Brazil's least spoilt wilderness, with *cerrado* forests and savannahs filled with rare birds stretching to endless horizons, page 628.
6 **Ilha do Bananal** Visit one of the world's largest river islands, home to large indigenous communities and a Ramsar-listed wetland, page 628.

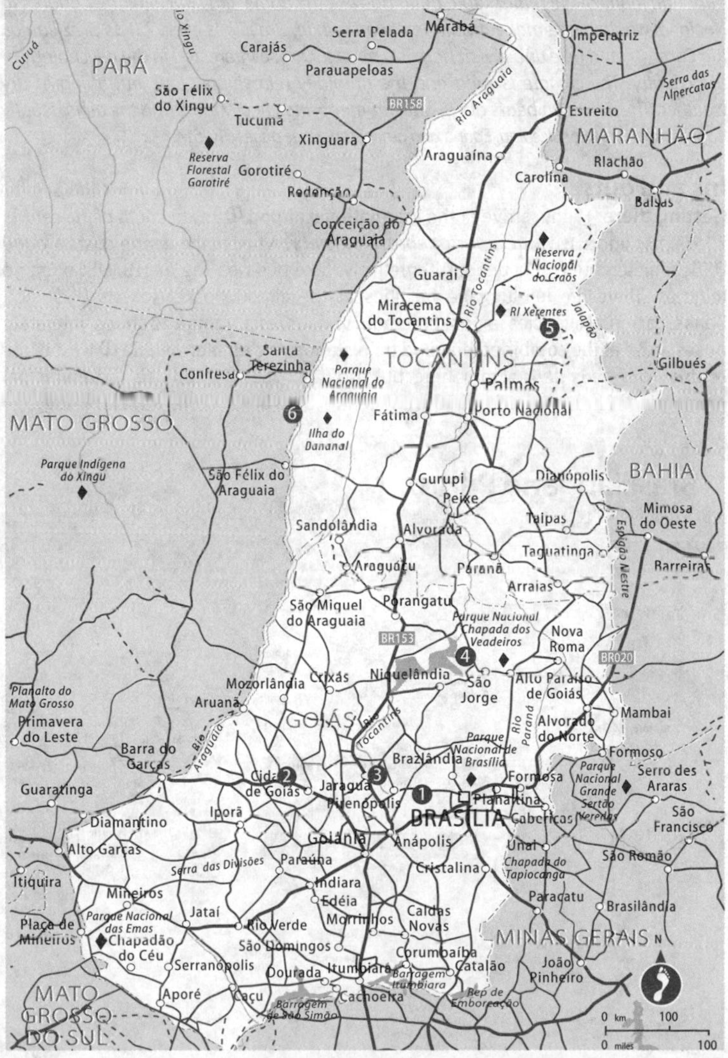

Brasília

➔ *Phone code: 061. Colour map 4, A2. Population: 2.1 million.*

This planned and impersonal capital city, sitting like a monument to the space age in a vast plain and surrounded by the ever expanding favelas and chaos of the real Brazil, may seem very un-Brazilian to those who are new to the country. This is, after all, a nation famous for its laissez-faire attitude. But it also has 'Order and Progress' written proudly on its flag, in homage to the ideas of Comte. And the grandiose schemes of many of its 20th-century leaders have long been influenced by a desire to propel the country into a Positivist vision of the future. Brazil's capital was intended by its conceivers, Lúcio Costa and Oscar Niemeyer, and their then president, Juscelino Kubitschek, as a statement of that future in concrete; an attempt perhaps to make real the cliché repeated by every other Brazilian leader that this is 'the country of the future'. Although many of the remarkable buildings like the dome and saucer of the Congresso Nacional would alone make a visit here worthwhile, Brasília is every bit as Brazilian as Rio Carnaval and Pelé and a visit here is a must for those interested in the psychology of the country. The climate is mild and the humidity refreshingly low, but trying in dry weather. The noon sun beats hard, but summer brings heavy rains and the air is usually cool by night. ▸▸ *For Sleeping, Eating and other listings, see pages 610-614.*

Ins and outs

Getting there Flights arrive at the **international airport** ⓘ *12 km south of the centre, T061-3364 9000, www.aeroportodebrasilia.gov.br*. A taxi to the centre costs around US$10, meter rate two is used. Alternatively, take bus Nos 102 or 118, US$0.65, 30 minutes. There are left-luggage facilities at the airport (locker tokens US$0.50), banks, car rental agencies, a post office and various restaurants and shops. Interstate buses arrive at the combined bus and train station, the **rodoferroviária** ⓘ *west of the centre, T061-3363 2281*. From here bus No 131, US$1.25, runs to the **municipal rodoviária** ⓘ *T061-3327 4631*, in the city centre. Both bus stations have large luggage

Brasília: Plano Piloto

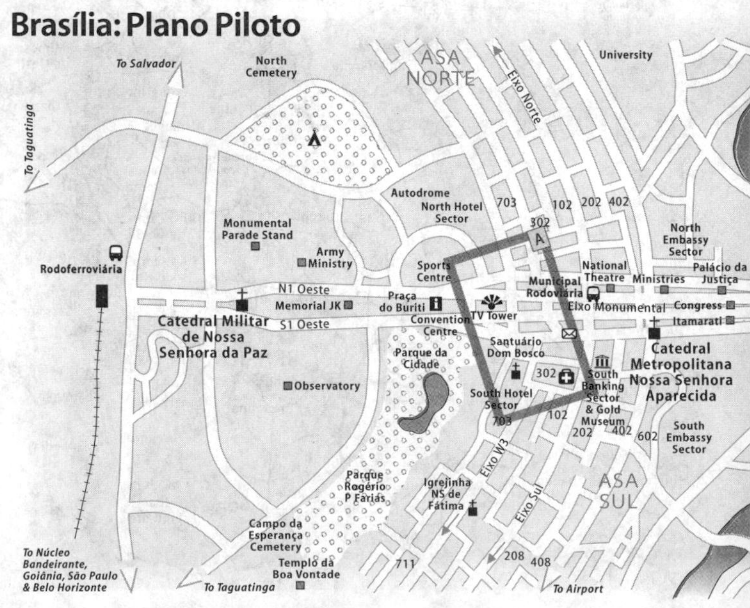

lockers. The *rodoviária* has a post office, telephone facilities and showers (US$0.50). A taxi to the northern hotel zone (Setor Hoteleiro Norte) costs US$9.

Getting around A good and cheap way of seeing Brasília is by taking bus rides from the municipal *rodoviária* at the centre: the destinations are clearly marked. The circular bus routes Nos 106, 108 and 131 go round the city's perimeter. If you go around the lake by bus, you must change at the Paranoá dam; to or from Paranoá Norte take bus No 101, 'Rodoviária', and to and from Sul, bus No 100, bypassing the airport. If staying in a hotel outside the centre, it's worth contacting them in advance to ask how to get there. A new urban railway, the Metrô, runs to the southwest suburbs but is very limited. » *See also Transport, page 613.*

Tourist information The tourist office, **Adetur** ⓘ *Centro de Convenções, 3rd floor, T061-3325 5700, 0800-1200 and 1300-1800*, is helpful, can provide a good map of Brasília and has English-speaking staff. There are other branches at the *rodoferroviária* ⓘ *daily 0800-2000*, and at the airport ⓘ *T061-3325 5730, daily 0730-2230*, which have more limited information but will book hotels and provide city maps. **Infraero** on the second floor of the airport is open 24 hours and useful for information on airport buses. **Embratur** ⓘ *Setor Comercial Norte, Quadra 02, bloco G, CEP 70710-500, T061-224 9100, www.braziltour.com*, also has a branch at the airport. The information office in the centre of Praça dos Tres Poderes has a colourful map and lots of information. The staff are friendly and have interesting information about Brasília and other places in Goiás, but only Portuguese is spoken. Other useful information is available from www.infobrasilia.com.br, www.dicasdebrasilia.com.br and www.aboutbrasilia.com

There is some gang violence in the city, so caution is advised at night.

Maps Maps of Brasília showing individual streets are almost impossible to find. But city maps with each *quadra* marked are available from larger newsagents and at the airport. Slightly less detailed maps are available from **Adetur**.

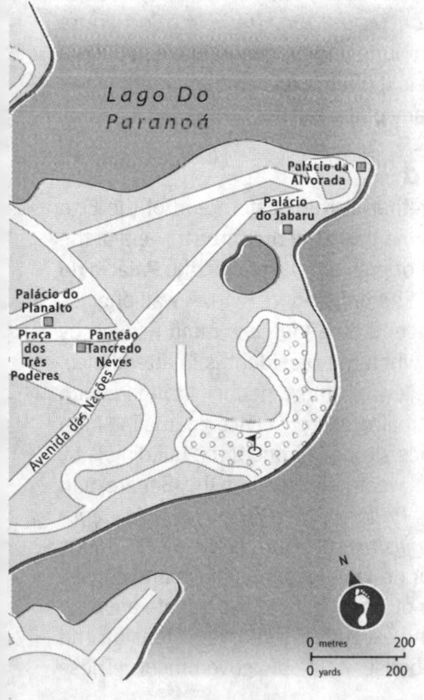

Orientation A competition for the best general plan was won by Professor Lúcio Costa, who laid out the city in the shape of a bent bow and arrow. It is also described as a bird or aeroplane in flight. The official name for central Brasília is the **Plano Piloto.**

The **Eixo Monumental** divides the city into **Asa Norte** and **Asa Sul** (north and south wings) and the **Eixo Rodoviário** divides it east and west. Buildings are numbered according to their relation to them. For example, 116 Sul and 116 Norte are at the extreme opposite ends of the city. The 100s and 300s lie west of the Eixo and the 200s and 400s to the east; *quadras* 302, 102, 202 and 402 are nearest the centre, and 316, 116, 216 and 416 mark the end of the Plano Piloto.

Residential areas are made up of large six-storey apartment blocks, called the 'Super-Quadras'. Each Super-Quadra houses 3000 people and has a primary school and playgroup. Each group of four Super-Quadras should have a library, police station, club, supermarket and secondary school. All *quadras* are separated by feeder roads, along which are the local shops. There are also a number of schools, parks and cinemas in the spaces between the *quadras* (especially in Asa Sul), though not as systematically as was originally envisaged. On the outer side of the 300s and extending the length of the city is the **Avenida W3**, and on the outer side of the 400s is the **Avenida L2**, both of these being similarly divided into north and south according to the part of the city they are in.

Asa Norte is growing very fast, with standards of architecture and urbanization that promise to make it more attractive than Asa Sul in the near future. The main shopping areas, which have more cinemas, restaurants and other facilities, are situated on either side of the old bus station (*rodoviária*). There are now several parks and green areas. The private residential areas are west of the Super-Quadras, and on the other side of the lake.

At right angles to these residential areas is the 'arrow', the 8-km long, 250-m wide **Eixo Monumental**. The main north-south road (Eixo Rodoviário), in which fast-moving traffic is segregated, follows the curve of the bow; the radial road is along the line of the arrow – intersections are avoided by means of underpasses and cloverleaves. Motor and pedestrian traffic is segregated in the residential areas.

Background

Brasília was a project powered by the indefatigable will of one man. Plans to build a new capital in the centre of the country had been drawn up as early as 1822. But it took Juscelino Kubitschek, Brazil's self-proclaimed great modernizer – whose famous election winning catchphrase was "50 years in five" – to realise the dream. His capital was rushed through from start to finish within one term of presidential office. The blueprint was cleared by Congress in 1956. Work began the following year and by the time Eisenhower laid the cornerstone of the US embassy in February 1960, accompanied by a great media fanfare, the new capital was largely complete.

Sights

Most of the interesting sights are concentrated on or around the **Eixo Monumental**, an inner-city highway forming the 'arrow' of Brasília's bow. They can be visited by car, taxi or tour in a morning. The **television tower** ⓘ *Mon 1400-2000, Tue-Sun 0800-2000, closed Mon morning,* between the Setor Hoteleiro Norte and the Setor Hoteleiro Sul is a good place to begin a tour and to orientate oneself. It offers excellent panoramic views from the observation platform 75 m up, as do many of the tall hotels nearby.

Praça dos Três Poderes and around

The most important buildings are clustered together at the western end of the Eixo Monumental around the Praça dos Três Poderes; named after the three powers of the federal state that flank it. To the north is the seat of presidential power, the **Palácio do Planalto** ⓘ *Praça dos Três Poderes, ½-hr tours, Sun only, 0930-1330*. A wall of glass between twin white concrete platforms, it is reached by a long low ramp flanked by guards in red and white uniforms. The flag flies when the president is in attendance. Opposite, the **Supremo Tribunal Federal** is smaller and more perfectly formed, with Niemeyer's trademark fluted columns hiding patrolling secret service guards in sharp suits. The famous modernist statue of blind justice sitting in front of the building is by the Mineiro sculptor Alfredo Ceschiatti. To the west, the seat of the Senate and Congress, **Congresso Nacional** ⓘ *Praça dos Três Poderes, Mon-Fri 0930-1200, 1430-1630, take your passport, free guided tour, in English 1400-1600*, is the most famous and stately group of buildings in Brasília – a tour de force of simple lines and curves. The concave and convex domes of the Chamber of Deputies and the Senate are both juxtaposed and balanced by the twin towers of the executive: a geometric tension and harmony which Niemeyer intended to symbolise that of government. These

Oscar Niemeyer and Brasília

Oscar Niemeyer Soares Filho (born 1907 in Rio de Janeiro) was educated at the Escola Nacional de Belas Artes and in 1936 joined the group of architects charged with developing Le Corbusier's project for the Ministry of Education and Health building in Rio de Janeiro. His first international project was the Brazilian pavilion at the New York International Fair in 1939 in partnership with Lúcio Costa. In the 1940s he was one of the main designers of Pampulha (see under Belo Horizonte) and in 1947 he worked on the United Nations headquarters in New York. This was the period in which he affirmed his style, integrating architecture with painting and sculpture. He transformed utilitarian constructions with the lightness of his designs, his freedom of invention and the use of complex, curved surfaces. Throughout the 1950s he was commissioned to design a wide variety of national and international projects, but it was the years 1956-1959 that stamped his signature on the architectural world. This was when he worked on Brasília, specifically the Palácio da Alvorada, the ministries, the Praça dos Três Poderes, the cathedral, university and, in 1967, the Palácio dos Arcos e da Justiça. After Brasília Niemeyer continued to work at home and abroad; among his more famous later projects were the Sambódromo in Rio (1984) and the Memorial da América Latina in São Paulo (1989). The Royal Institute of British Architects awarded him the prestigious Royal Gold Medal for Architecture in 1998.

Many of Brazil's most famous architects, sculptors and designers were involved in Brasília. The city was built during Juscelino Kubitschek's term as president (1955-1960) and was unparalleled in scale and architectural importance in Latin America at that time. A description of the city, and its effect on the economy at the time of its construction are dealt with elsewhere in the book. Niemeyer was appointed chief architecture and technical adviser to Novacap, the government authority which oversaw the new capital. But while it is common knowledge who the famous names were, it is also worth noting that 30,000 workers were involved in bringing the plan to reality. Most of them came from the Northeast. The city has been honoured not just for its architecture, but also for being the first purpose-built capital of the 20th century. In 1987 it was named a Unesco World Cultural Heritage site, the first contemporary city to gain such protection from the United Nations.

Niemeyer himself has said "The modern city lacks harmony and a sense of occasion. Brasília will never lack these". And it is true that the principal buildings, and the overall plan itself, are strikingly powerful. The whole enterprise is deeply rooted in the 20th century, not just in its design, but also in the idea that it is a city you jet into and out of. If you arrive by road (which most people do not), the experience is even more fantastic. After hours and hours in the bus, travelling across the unpopulated central plateau, you come to this collection of remarkable buildings and sculptures in the middle of nowhere. The vastness of the landscape demands a grand city and yet, for all its harmony, it is almost as if not even Brasília can compete with the sky and the horizon.

Niemeyer is still working in his late nineties. In 2002, a museum about Niemeyer, designed by the architect himself opened in Curitiba. It is spectacular, sitting like a giant black eye on a pedestal in one of the city's parks, fully living up to Niemeyer's proclamation that 'the most important element in any work of art is to surprise, to startle'. His mostly recently opened grand buildings are the Biblioteca Nacional and the dome-shaped and Oca-like Museum of Brasília, which opened in the capital in 2006.

Bingo!

Visitors to Brazil may be surprised to see bingo halls all over the major cities. But these are not mere temples to blue-rinse gambling. Brazil's bingo halls are the stuff of scandal. People have suspected for a long time that many of the bingo halls were rackets for drug and car theft money laundering. In 2004 their influence was seen to extend to the highest level, shaking the (until then) squeaky clean reputation of the country's president Luis Inácio Lula da Silva. *Epoca* magazine revealed that one of his senior aides, Waldomiro Diniz, had accepted bribes from a notorious Rio bingo moghul, known as 'Carlinhos the Waterfall' shortly after the 2002 election. 'The Waterfall' has long been regarded as a kingpin in the Rio numbers game; a Brazilian form of street bingo based on animal names which is hugely lucrative for those who run it. Within a week, Brazil's stock market crashed 10% and the *Real* fell almost 2% against the dollar, prompting Lula to fire Diniz and promise a full enquiry. There were further pledges to ban the bingo halls. But as usual in Brazil it was all sound and fury… The report was a whitewash declaring the bingo halls models of propriety. They remain open and Brazil awaits the discovery of yet further scandal.

monumental buildings are offset beautifully by the vast expanse of the square, the artificial ponds and the lawns.

There are a handful of other interesting buildings in the plaza: the **Espaço Lucio Costa** ⓘ *Tue-Sun 0900-1800, free*, with a scale model of the city; a monument to Juscelino Kubitschek; the **Panteão da Liberdade e Democracia** built in homage to Democracy and Liberty; and, most notably, Bruno Giorgio's **Candangos** – twin bronze figures sculpted in homage to the Candango workers who built the city from nothing in the middle of what was a vast plain, and who received the satellite *favelas* that ring the city as their reward.

Beyond the praça to the east and on the shores of Lago Paranoá is the **Palácio Alvorada**, residence of the president and not open to the public.

Less than a kilometre west of the praça are two further Niemeyer buildings of note. The **Palácio de Itamarati** is one the finest pieces of modernist architecture in Brazil; its elegant columns rising from a lily pond, which acts like a huge mirror for the entire building. Inside are a series of rooms decorated with fine sculpture and paintings including Pedro Américo's *O Grito de Ipiranga*, showing the moment when Dom Pedro shouted his declaration of Brazilian Independence, and Jean-Baptiste Debret's painting of the emperor's subsequent coronation. There are also works by Brazilian modernists Alfredo Volpi, Candido Portinari and Pedro Correia de Araújo. The building is named after the Conde de Itamaraty. Opposite Itamarati is the **Palácio da Justiça** ⓘ *Mon-Fri 0900-1200, 1500-1700*, its walls broken by a series of broad fountains that climb up the façade of the building and drop water into the pond that sits at the building's feet.

West along the Eixo Monumental

The Eixo stretches for some 8 km west of Praça dos Três Poderes eventually reaching the *rodoferroviária*. Almost all of the city's other important monuments lie on either side of the road. We follow them here from east to west.

The government ministry buildings line the Eixo west of the praça like dominos, or a series of commissars standing to attention. Eventually they reach Niemeyer's striking **Catedral Metropolitana Nossa Senhora Aparecida** ⓘ *Esplanada dos*

Ministérios, Eixo Monumental, T061-3224 4073, 0800-1930; a crown of thorns in concrete and glass sitting in a toroidal lake and watched over by Alfredo Ceschiatti's four evangelists, standing sentinel-like in concrete. The entrance to the cathedral is via a subterranean tunnel, emerging from relative darkness into an arena bright with stained glass and light marble.

Next to the cathedral are two of the most recently built Niemeyer buildings; yet to open to the public in early 2007: the **Museu Nacional de Brasília**, a striking dome-shaped building with an entrance halfway up its side reached by a snaking ramp; and the cuboid **Biblioteca Nacional** next door. Less than a kilometre west, a few blocks south along the Via W3 Sul, is the **Santuário Dom Bosco** ⓘ *Av W3 Sul, Quadra 702, T061 3223 6542, 0800-1800,* a modernist cube with tall Gothic arches filled with stained glass, which shades from light to dark blue and indigo as it ascends. It is particularly beautiful in the late afternoon when shafts of light penetrate the building. The church is named after the 19th-century saint and founder of the Salesian order, who proclaimed that a new civilization would arise in the third millennium between the 15th and 16th parallels and on the edge of an artificial lake. The trunk of the enormous cross hanging over the altar was carved from a single piece of tropical cedar.

Beyond the TV tower, which lies at the intersection of the Eixo and the hotel zones, are two other interesting groups of buildings. The **Memorial Juscelino Kubitschek (JK)** ⓘ *Tue-Sun 0900-1800, US$1.50, toilets and café*, stands high above a marble plinth waving towards the Praça dos Três Poderes. The former president's tomb lies beneath the marble together with a collection of memorabilia. In front of the memorial is the **Memorial dos Povos Indigenas** ⓘ *Tue-Sun 0900-1800, US$2*; a round concrete building shaped like a *Bororo* communal house or *maloca* and reached by a tongue-like ramp. Inside is a small but fascinating collection of indigenous art and cultural artefacts. On the other side of the Memorial JK, east of Praça do Cruzeiro, is the city's second Niemeyer cathedral – the **Catedral Militar de Nossa Senhora da Paz** ⓘ *Tue-Sun 0900-1800*. This is a brilliant white wedge of concrete cut with jagged windows, whose design echoes Notre Dame du Haut, designed by Niemeyer's mentor, Le Corbusier. The church marks the entrance to the **Quartel General do Exército**; an enormous and imposing complex of military buildings centred on an elliptical auditorium made of a single wave of concrete and added to Brasília during the military dictatorship, as if to compensate for the lack of army presence on the Praça dos Três Poderes. All are by Niemeyer. There is a small **military museum** ⓘ *Tue-Sun 0900-1800*, on the site.

The **Templo da Boa Vontade** ⓘ *Setor Garagem Sul 915, lotes 75/76, T061-245 1070, open 24 hrs*, is a seven-faced pyramid dedicated to all philosophies and religions topped by one of the world's largest rock crystals. To get there, take bus 151 from outside the Centro do Convenções or on Eixo Sul to Centro Médico.

The **Panteão Tancredo Neves** is a 'temple of freedom and democracy', built 1985-1986 by Niemeyer. It includes an impressive homage to Tiradentes (see box, page).

The **Monumental Parade Stand** has unique and mysterious acoustics (the complex is north of the Eixo Monumental, between the 'Memorial JK' and the *rodoferroviária*). There are remarkable stained-glass panels, each representing a state of the Federation, on the ground floor of the Caixa Econômica Federal.

Around Brasília

About 15 km along the Belo Horizonte road is the small wooden house, designed by Niemeyer, erected in only 10 days and known as **O Catetinho**. President Kubitschek stayed here in the late 1950s during his visits to the city when it was under construction; it is open to visitors and houses memorabilia and some of JK's furniture and personal items.

Some 40 km northeast of the Plano Piloto via Saída Norte is **Planaltina**, originally a settlement on the colonial pack route from the mines of Goiás and Cuiabá to the coast. The old part still contains many colonial buildings. There are two good *churrascarias* on the main street and it is a good place for a rural Sunday lunch. About 5 km outside Planaltina is the Pedra Fundamental, the foundation stone laid by President Epitácio Pessoa in 1922 to mark the site that was originally chosen for the new capital.

Also outside Planaltina, at Km 30 on the BR-020, lies **Águas Emendadas**. From the same point spring two streams that flow in opposite directions to form part of the two great river systems, the Amazon and the Plate. Permission from the biological institute in Brasília is required to visit. At Km 70 is **Formosa**. Some 20 km north of the town is the **Itiquira waterfall** (158 m high). From the top are spectacular views and the pools at the bottom offer good bathing, but it gets crowded at weekends. There are four smaller falls in the area and camping is possible. To get there from the centre of Formosa, follow the signs or ask. The only bus from Formosa to Itiquira leaves at 0730 and returns at 1700.

Parque Nacional de Brasília → *Colour map 3, A6.*

ⓘ *Contact Ibama, SAIN, Av L/4 Lote 04/08, Ed Sede do Ibama, T061-316 1080, or the park's office, Via Epia SMU, T061-233 3251, F233 5543.*

Northwest of Brasília, but only 15 minutes by car from the centre, is this park of some 28,000 ha, founded in 1961 to conserve the flora and fauna of the Federal Capital. Only a portion of the park is open to the public without a permit. There is a swimming pool fed by clear river water, a snack bar and a series of trails through gallery forest, which is popular with joggers in the early morning and at weekends. The rest of the park is rolling grassland, gallery forest and *cerrado* vegetation. Large mammals include tapir, maned wolf and pampas deer; birdwatching is good, especially for Brasília tapaculo, horned sungem, yellow-faced parrot and least nighthawk.

Sleeping

Brasília *p604, map p604*

The best area to base yourself is in the northern hotel zone, which has lots of shops and restaurants nearby. Prices usually include breakfast. Weekend discounts of 30% are often available if you ask. The best area for cheap accommodation is around W3 703 and 704 in the Asa Sul where many residential houses have been turned into hostels. The quietest areas are northwest of the main Av W3 Sul. Beware of bus station touts. The tourist office has a list of *pensões*.

Southern hotel zone

L Nacional, quadra 1, bloco A, T061-3321 7575, www.hotelnacional.com.br. This huge old-fashioned city landmark was *the* place to stay in the 1970s and 1980s. Now rooms look rather old-fashioned, but on the upper floors they offer sweeping views. Several restaurants.

A Alvorada, quadra 4, bloco A, T061-2195 1122, www.alvoradahotel.com.br. Another relic with simple, well-kept small rooms and good views from the roof terrace. Avoid the noisy streetside rooms on the lower floors.

C-E Pousada Dom Bosco, 703 Sul, bloco N, casa 34, T061-3225 5021; with another branch at W3704, M casa 9, T061-3213 1133. The best of the cheapies, with simple but neat rooms, some spacious and airy, some small and windowless. Owner Getúlio Valente will pick up from airport or bus station if you phone ahead. There are a range of other rooms around the city as well as cheap city tours (in Portuguese only).

D Pousada da Nilza, W3 Sul 703, bloco A, T061-3225 5786. Pokey and slightly musty dorms and doubles but popular with travellers. There are various similar options next door.

D-E Pousada 47, 703 Sul, bloco A, casa 97, T061-3323 5718, www.pousada47.hpg.com.br. Very simple fan-cooled dorms and doubles; the best of which are at the front. Internet.

D-E Pousada do Sol, 703 Sul, bloco K, casa 3, T061-3224 9703/9969 6636. A range of simple dorms and doubles for up to 5, some without windows.

Northern hotel zone

LL-L Kubitschek Plaza, quadra 2, bloco E, T061-3329 3333, www.kubitschek.com.br . Popular business hotel with modern rooms and excellent facilities; broadband in rooms, pool, sauna and gym. The sister hotel, **Manhattan Plaza**, www.manhattan.com.br, next door is very similar.

AL-A Aristus, quadra 2, bloco O, T061-3328 8675, www.aristushotel.com.br. Newly painted and delightfully dated 1970s block with simple a/c rooms and breakfast.

A Casablanca, quadra 3, bloco A, T061-3328 8586, www.casablancabrasilia.com.br. A mock-Niemeyer block complete with modernist Gothic arches echoing the Palácio do Itamarati. Room are newly refurbished 1970s shells with standard catalogue furniture. The best are on the upper floors.

B El Pilar, quadra 3, bloco F, T061-3328 5915, www.elpilar.com.br. Plain, well-kept fan-cooled and a/c rooms with tiled floors and en suites. Avoid those below street level as they collect car fumes.

Brasília hotel zone

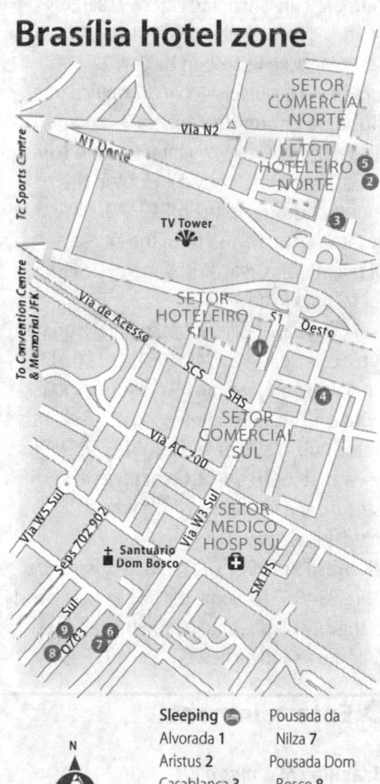

Sleeping
Alvorada **1**
Aristus **2**
Casablanca **3**
El Pilar **5**
Nacional **4**
Pousada 47 **6**
Pousada da Nilza **7**
Pousada Dom Bosco **8**
Pousada do Sol **9**

N

0 metres 100
0 yards 100

C Mirage, quadra 2, bloco N, T/F061-3328 7150. Simple rooms with a fan but good value for the area.

Other areas

LL-L Blue Tree Park, Trecho 1, lt 1-B, Bl C (Lago Norte), T062-3424 7000, www.bluetree.com.br. The city's newest, most luxurious business hotel, with rooms in a giant red horseshoe overlooking the lake, an enormous pool and excellent, good business facilities.

Eating

Brasília *p604, map p604*

The Southern Hotel Sector has more restaurants than the north. At weekends, few restaurants in central Brasília are open. There is plenty of choice in all price brackets in the **Pier 21** entertainment mall on the lakeshore. Other cheaper options are along R 405/406.

Snack bars serving *prato feito* or *comercial* (cheap set meals) can be found all over the city, especially on **Av W3** and in the **Setor Comercial Sul**. Other good bets are the **Conjunto Nacional** and the **Conjunto Venâncio**, 2 shopping/office complexes on either side of the municipal *rodoviária*. Tropical fruit flavour ice cream can be found in various parlours, eg **Av W3 Norte 302**. Freshly made fruit juices are available in all bars.

Asa Sul

There are good mid-range options on and around Av Anhaguera between Tocantins and Goiás; but by far the best choice is on and around **Praça Tamandaré** and **Av República Líbano**. For cheap bars/restaurants, try around Praça Tamandaré and on R 68 in the centre. There are many cheap places on **Av W3 Sul**, eg at **Blocos 502** and **506**.

TTT Kosui, SCES, Trecho 4, lote 1B, Academia de Tênis, T061-3316 6900. The best of the city's Japanese food, from Tokyo-born chef Ryozo Koniya. Great Japanese banquet.

TTT La Chaumière, Av W3 Sul, quadra 408, bloco A, loja 13, T061-3242 7599, lunch only on Sun. The city's favourite French cuisine in classical surroundings.

TTT Le Français, Av W3 Sul, quadra 404, bloco B, loja 27, T061-3225 4583. French food served in bistro atmosphere, classic and modern dishes, 40-bottle wine list.

¥¥¥ O Convento, SHIS, QI 9, conjunto 9, casa 4, T061-3248 1211, www.oconvento.com.br. The best for regional and Brazilian cuisine in a mock-farmhouse dining room decorated with antiques and arts and crafts.

¥¥¥ Piantella, SCLS 202, bloco A, loja 34, T061-3224 9408, www.piantella.com.br. A favourite of senior politicians for decades and is a good place to watch power lunches in action. The vast menu combines *feijoada*, Italian food, steaks and seafood. The wine list is excellent.

¥¥¥ Porcão, Sector de Clubes Sul, Trecho 2, cj 35, rest. 3, T061-3223 2002, www.porcao.com.br. Upmarket chain restaurant specializing in *churrasco*, piano bar, large veranda.

¥¥ O Espanhol, Av W3 Sul, quadra 404, bloco C, loja 07, T061-3224 2002. Open daily. Host to the city's annual Spanish festival and serving respectable seafood.

¥¥ Oca da Tribo, SCES Trecho 2, opposite Agepol, T061-3226 9880, www.ocadatribo.com.br. A wholefood restaurant in a mock-indigenous communal house decorated with artefacts from the Xingu. Plenty of vegetarian options and others by Dutch Cordon Bleu chef Gabriel Fleijsman and a good lunch buffet.

¥¥ Vercelli, SCLS 410, bloco D, loja 34, T061-3443 0100, www.vercelli.com.br. Lunch only. Pizzas, pastas and lots more on a huge menu.

¥ Naturama, SCLS 102, bloco B, loja 9, T061-3225 5125. Vegetarian and wholefood dishes. Lunchtime only.

Asa Norte

All of the large hotels in this area have upmarket restaurants.

¥¥¥ Alice, SHIN, Qi 11, conjunto 9, casa 17, Lago Norte, T061-3368 1099, www.restaurantealice.com.br. Voted the best restaurant in the by *Veja* magazine innumerable times with a menu of French and Brazilian-French fusion cooking. Excellent wine list.

¥¥¥ Trattoria da Rosario, SHIS QI 17, bloco H, Loja 215, Lago Sul, Fashion Park, T061-3248 1672, closed Mon, lunch only on Sun. Northern Italian food from chef Rosario Tessier. Excellent Uruguayan lamb.

¥¥¥ Universal Diner, SCLS 210, bloco B, loja 30, T061-3443 2089 (lunch only on Sun), www.universaldiner.com.br. One of the city's best contemporary restaurants with strong Asian influences from New York-trained chef Mara Alcamim.

¥¥ Boa Saúde, Av W3 Norte, quadra 702, edif Brasília Rádio Center. Sun-Fri 0800-2000. Respectable vegetarian with a range of salads, quiches and pies.

¥¥ Bom Demais, Av W3 Norte, quadra 706. Comfortable, serving fish, beef and rice, live music at weekends (cover charge US$0.50).

¥ Conjunto Nacional, SDN, Cj A. Enormous mall and food court with 50 restaurants.

Bars and clubs

Brasília *p604, map p604*

Arena Café, CA 7, bloco F1, loja 33, T061-3468 1141, www.cafearena.hpg.com.br. Popular gay bar with DJs from Thu to Sat.

Bar Brasília, SHC/S CR, quadra 506, bloco A, loja 15, parte A, T061-3443 4323. Little *boteco* with 1950s decor, draught beer and wooden tables. Lively after 1900, especially Fri.

Bier Fass, SHIS, quadra 5, bloco E, loja 52/53, T061-3248 1519, www.bierfass.com.br. Cavernous bar/restaurant with live music Tue-Sun and 20/30s crowd. Happy hour from 1800.

Café Cancún, Shopping Liberty Mall, SCN, Quadra 3, bloco D, loja 52, T061-3327 1566. Tacky Mexican restaurant by day, 20-something beautiful people club after dark.

Clube de Choro, SDC, quadra 3, bloco G, T061-3327 0494, www.clubedechoro.com.br. (Wed-Sat). One of the best clubs in the country devoted to the music that gave rise to samba. Top names from the city and all over Brazil. Great atmosphere. Tickets sold 9 days in advance.

Frei Caneca, Brasília Shopping, SCN, quadra 5, bloco A, lojas 82s/94s, T061-3327 0202. Similar to **Café Cancún**. Dreadful 'flashback' night on Thu. Most interesting at weekends.

Gates Pub, Av W3 Sul 403, T061-3225 4576, www.gatespub.com.br. Great for *forró* dancing and live music with a young middle-class crowd.

UK Brasil Pub, SCLS 411, bloco B, loja 28, T061-3346 5214. Some of the best live bands in the city play here to a crowd of all ages. Guinness, sandwiches.

Entertainment

Brasília *p604, map p604*

Information about entertainment is available in 2 daily papers, *Jornal de Brasília* and *Correio Brasiliense*. Any student card

(provided it has a photograph) will get you a 50% discount at the cinema/theatre/concert hall. Ask for '*uma meia*' at the box office.
Pier 21, SCSS, Trecho 2, Cj 32/33. An enormous complex with 13 cinema screens, nightclubs, restaurants, video bars and children's theme park.

Cinema There are 15 cinemas in the Plano Piloto. For programme details call T139. Entrance is half price on Wed.

Live music Concerts are given at the **Escola Parque** (Quadras 507-508 Sul), the **Ginásio Presidente Médici** (Eixo Monumental, near TV tower), the **Escola de Música** (Av L2 Sul, Quadra 602) and the outdoor **Concha Acústica** (edge of lake in the Northern hotel zone).

Theatre **Teatro Nacional**, Setor Cultural Norte, Via N 2, next to the bus station, T061-325 6109, foyer open 0900-2000, box office opens at 1400. There are 3 auditoria: the **Sala Villa- Lobos** (1300 seats), the **Sala Martins Pena** (450), and the **Sala Padre José Maurício** (120). The building is in the shape of an Aztec pyramid.

The Federal District authorities have 2 theatres, the **Galpão** and **Galpãozinho**, between Quadra 308 Sul and Av W3 Sul.

Other **Planetarium**, Setor de Divulgaoção Cultural, T061-325 6245, next to the TV tower. Being restored at time of writing.

Festivals and events

Brasília *p604, map p604*
Feb Ash Wed.
Apr Maundy Thu (half-day).
8 Dec Immaculate Conception.
24 Dec Christmas Eve.

Shopping

Brasília *p604, map p604*
Books There's a good selection of English books at **Livraria Sodiler** in Conjunto Nacional and at the airport.

Handicrafts For handicrafts from all the Brazilian states try **Galeria dos Estados** (which runs underneath the *eixo* from Setor Comercial Sul to Setor Bancário Sul, 10 mins' walk from the municipal *rodoviária*, south along Eixo Rodoviário Sul). For Amerindian handicrafts, **Artíndia** SRTVS, Quadra 702, also in the *rodoviária* and at the airport. There is a **feira hippy** at the base of the TV tower at weekends and holidays selling leather goods, woodcarvings, jewellery and bronzes.

Jewellery **H Stern**, branches in the **Nacional** and **Carlton** hotels and at the **Conjunto Nacional** and **Parkshopping**. Fine jewellery.

Shopping centres The best shopping centres are **Shopping Brasília** below the southern hotel zone and **Patio Brasília** below the northern hotel zone. Both have a wide range of boutiques and fast food restaurants. Others include the vast **Conjunto Nacional** on the north side of the rodoviária, the **Conjunto Venâncio** on the south side, the **Centro Venâncio 2000** at the beginning of Av W3 Sul, the **Centro Venâncio 3000** in the Setor Comercial Norte, **Parkshopping** and the **Carrefour** hypermarket just off the exit to Guará, 12 km from the centre.

Activities and tours

Brasília *p604, map p604*
Tour operators
Many tour operators have their offices in the shopping arcade of the **Hotel Nacional**.
Buriti Turismo, SCLS 402, bloco A, lojas 27/33, Asa Sul, T061-225 2686, American Express representative.
Presmic Turismo, SHS Q 1, bloco A, loja, 35, T061-3233 0115, www.presmic.com.br. Full, half-day and night-time city tours (0845, 1400 and 1930 respectively). 3 to 4-hr city tours with English commentary can also be booked on arrival at the airport – a convenient way of getting to your hotel if you have heavy baggage. Some tours criticized as too short, others that the guides speak poor English, and for night-time tours, the floodlighting is inadequate on many buildings.

Transport

Brasília *p604, map p604*
Air See also Ins and outs, page 604. Brasília airport has connections with most

major cities in Brazil and a number of international destinations.

Airline offices BRA, SHS quadra 1, bloco A, loja 71/72, in front of Hotel Nacional, and in Shopping Flamingo and Shopping Sia, T061-2105 0909, www.voebra.com.br. **GOL**, airport, T061-3364 9370, premium rate number, T0300-789 2121, www.voegol.com.br. **Ocean Air**, T0300-789 8160, www.oceanair.com.br. **TAM/Brasil Central**, SHN Hotel Nacional, Gallery Store, 36/37, T061-3325 1300; airport, T061-3365 1000, www.tam.com.br. **Varig**, SCN Quadra 4, bloco B, T061-3329 1240; airport, T061-3364 9219, www.varig.com.br.

Bus All major destinations served. Bus tickets for major companies are sold in a subsidiary office in Taguatinga, Centro Oeste, C8, Lotes 1 and 2, Loja 1; and at the city *rodoviária*.

To **Rio**, 17 hrs, 6 *comuns* (US$32) and 3 *leitos* (about US$64) daily. To **São Paulo**, 16 hrs, 7 *comuns* (about US$30) and 2 *leitos* (about US$60) daily (**Rápido Federal** recommended). To **Goiânia**, numerous daily. Change in Goiânia for Cidade de Goiás. To **Pirenópolis**, 2 daily. The quickest in the morning. To **Palmas**, 2 daily, best in the afternoon; via Alto Paraíso in the Chapada dos Veadeiros. To **Belo Horizonte**, 12 hrs, 9 *comuns* (US$20) and 2 *leitos* (US$40) daily. To **Belém**, 36 hrs, 4 daily (US$55, **Trans Brasília**, T061-233 7589, buses poorly maintained, but no alternative). To **Recife**, 40 hrs, US$49-60. To **Salvador**, 24 hrs, 3 daily (US$27). To **Campo Grande**, **São Luís**, 15 hrs, 1915, US$30, or **Viação Motta** via São Paulo 0930, 1930, or 1820 direct. To **Corumbá**, US$46. To **Cuiabá**, 17½ hrs (US$30) daily at 1200 with São Luís. **Mato Grosso**, generally Goiânia seems to be the better place for Mato Grosso destinations. **Barra do Garças**, 0830 and 2000, takes 9 hrs with **Araguarina**, T061-3233 7598, US$13.20 return.

Car hire All large companies are represented at the airport and the car rental sector. **Avis**, airport, T/F061-3365 2780. **Interlocadora**, airport, T061-3365 2511 and **Localiza**, Setor Locadoras, T061-3365 1616, also at airport, T0800-992000. **Unidas**, T061-365 3343, and at airport, T061-3365 1412.

Directory

Brasília *p604, map p604*

Banks Foreign currency can be exchanged at branches of **Banco Regional de Brasília** and **Banco do Brasil**, Setor Bancário Sul, latter also at airport, US$20 commission for TCs. **American Express**, Buriti Turismo, CLS 402 bloco A, lojas 27/33, T061-3225 2686. **Diners Club**, Av W3 Norte 502. **MasterCard**, for cash against a card, SCRN 502, bloco B, lojas 30 e 31, Asa Norte. Good exchange rates at **Hotel Nacional** and from hotels with 'exchange-turismo' sign. **HSBC**, SCRS 502, bloco A, lojas 7/12, ATM. **Cultural centres** **Aliança Francesa**, Sul Entrequadra 707-907, bloco A, T061-3242 7500. **American Library**, Casa Thomas Jefferson, Av W4 Sul, quadra 706, T061-3243 6588. **British Council**, Setor C Sul, quadra 01, bloco H, 8th floor, Morro Vermelho building, T061-3323 6080. **Cultura Inglesa**, SEPS 709/908 Conj B, T061-3243 3065. **Instituto Cultural Goethe**, Edif Dom Bosco, Setor Garagem Sul 902, lote 73, bloco C, T061-3224 6773. Mon-Fri, 0800-1200, also Mon, Wed, Thu 1600-2000. **Embassies and consulates** Australia, Caixa Postal 11-1256, SHIS QI-09, Conj 16, Casa 1, T061-3248 5569. **Austria**, SES, Av das Nações 40, T061-3243 3111. **Canada**, SES, Av das Nações 16, T061-321 2171. **Denmark**, Av das Nações 26, T061-34438 188 (0900-1200, 1400-1700). **Germany**, SES, Av das Nações 25, T061-443 7330. **Guyana**, SDS, Edif Venâncio III, 4th floor, sala 410/404, T061-3224 9229. **Netherlands**, SES, Av das Nações 5, T061-3321 4769. **South Africa**, SES, Av das Nações, lote 06, T061-3312 9503. **Sweden**, Av das Nações 29, Caixa Postal 07-0419, T061-3243 1444. **Switzerland**, SES, Av das Nações 41, T061-3443 5500. **UK**, SES, Quadra 801, Conjunto K, or Av das Nações, Caixa Postal 070586, T061- 3225 2710. **USA**, SES, Av das Nações 3, T061- 321 7272. **Venezuela**, SES, Av das Nações 13, T061-223 9325. **Internet** **Café.Com.Tato**, CLS 505, bloco C, loja 17, Asa Sul, open daily. **Liverpool Coffee Shop**, CLS 108, R da Igreijinha. **Laundry** **Lavanderia Laundromat**, CLN 104, bloco C, loja 106, Asa Norte. Self-service. **Post office** **Poste restante**, Central Correio, 70001; SBN-Cj 03, BL-A, Edif Sede da ECT, the central office is in the Setor Hoteleiro Sul, between hotels **Nacional** and **St Paul**. Also at Ed Brasília Rádio, Av 3 Norte.

Goiás

With an area of 364,714 sq km and some four million inhabitants, Goiás is one of Brazil's most rapidly developing frontier agricultural areas. The land is used for producing coffee, soya and rice, most of Brazil's tin and tungsten, and for raising beef on some of the country's largest cattle ranches. ▸▸ *For Sleeping, Eating and other listings, see pages 621-627.*

Goiânia ▸▸ *pp621-627.*

→ *Phone code: 062. Colour map 3, B5. Population: 1.1 million.*

Just off the BR-060, 209 km southwest of Brasília, is the second of Brazil's planned state capitals, after Belo Horizonte. Goiânia was founded in 1933 and replaced Goiás Velho as capital four years later. The city is famous for its street cafés and is a good place to stop between Brasília and the rest of the Centro-Oeste. Tourism is not as developed here as in other parts of the country, but the city is pleasant and there are some interesting sights within easy reach. Goiânia is spacious with more parks and gardens than any other of Brazil's large cities and many are filled with interesting forest and *cerrado* plants, as well as marmosets and remarkably large numbers of birds.

Ins and outs

Santa Genoveva Airport ⓘ *6 km northeast off R 57, T062-207 1288*, receives flights from Brasília, Campinas, São Paulo, Uberaba and Uberlândia. There are several car hire firms at the airport. A taxi to the centre costs US$6. Buses arrive at the **rodoviária** ⓘ *R 44, No 399 in the Norte Ferroviário sector, T062-224 8466.* Buses to the centre 'Rodoviária-Centro' (No 404) and 'Vila União Centro' (No 163) leave from the stop on the city side of the terminal, US$0.80; No 163 goes on to the Praça Tamandaré.

Tourist information is available from **Sictur** ⓘ *Centro Administrativo, Praça Cívica, 7th floor, CEP 74319-000, T062-223 0669, F223 3911*, and **Dirtur** ⓘ *R 30 corner of R 4, Centro de Convençoes, CEP 74025-020, T062-217 1121, F217 2256.* Extensive information, maps and bus routes can be found in *Novo Guia Turístico de Goiás*, readily available at news-stands, US$2.25.

Sights

The centre of the city is **Praça Cívica**, with well-lit main avenues radiating out in all directions. On the praça stand the government palace, the main post office and the **Museu Zoroastro Artiaga** ⓘ *Praça Cívica 13, T062-201 4676*. The museum has a small but interesting collection of historical objects, fossils and religious items as well as cases depicting indigenous and early settler life in Goiás. The museum was twice the size before it was cherry-picked by local politicians for their private collections.

From the praça, Avenida Araguaia runs northeast to the shady **Parque Mutirama**, with recreational facilities and a **planetarium** ⓘ *Sun 1530 and 1630*.

More tranquil is the **Bosque dos Buritis** ⓘ *1 km west of the Praça Cívica along R 10*, which has shaded walks in *buriti*-filled tropical gardens and a turtle-filled pond. In the gardens of the Bosque dos Buritis is the **Museu de Arte de Goiânia** ⓘ *R 1 605, T5241190, Mon-Fri 0800-1700, Sat 0800-1300, free*, which showcases the work of a number of local artists including Siron Franco, who is nationally renowned. The **Parque Zoólogico** ⓘ *Av Anhangüera, Tue-Sun 0700-1800*, 1 km west of the **Castro's Park** hotel is set in large gardens and is a good place to while away an afternoon.

A kilometre east of Praça Cívica, the **Museu Antropológico do UFG** ⓘ *Praça Universitária, Mon-Fri 0900-1700*, houses wide-ranging ethnographic displays on the *indígena* of the Centre West.

The **Casa do Indio** ⓘ *Av Jamel Cecílio 2000, Pedro ludovico*, is a centre for indigenous arts and craft production and an important meeting place for indigenous peoples like the Xavantes. The shop there sells a variety of handicrafts.

The **Memorial do Cerrado Museum** ⓘ *Av Bela Vista, Km 2, Jd Olímpico, T062-562 4141, Mon-Sat 0800-2200, Sun 0800-1800, US$2*, just outside the city towards Cidade de Goiás, provides an interesting introduction to *cerrado* life, with reconstructions of indigenous villages, *quilombos* and colonial streets as well as planted *cerrado* vegetation.

Excursions from Goîania

The thermal springs at **Cachoeira Dourada**, 240 km south on the Rio Paranaíba, are worth a visit, as are the fantastic rock formations of the Serra das Galés at **Paraúna,** 160 km south-southwest off BR-060. There are a host of delightful, colonial mining villages within two hours' drive on good (often paved) roads. Travel agents in town can arrange day tours, see Activities and tours, page 613.

Caldas Novas → *Phone code: 062. Colour map 3, B5. Population: 40,000.*

Goiás's most beloved resort is a hot-water theme park for families and weekenders. Hundreds of hotels line the hot river and are dotted around the various thermal springs at **Fontes de Pirapetinga** (7 km from town) and **Rio Quente** (29 km from the town, bus from Caldas Novas). There are many buses from Goiânia; best reached from Morrinhos on BR-153 (Goiânia-São Paulo). The bus from Morrinhos costs US$1, 30 minutes.

Anápolis and Cristalina → *Phone code: 062. Colour map 3, B5/6.*

Anápolis, a busy but uninteresting trading centre, is 57 km closer to Brasília than Goiânia. The **Centro de Gemologia de Goiás** ⓘ *Quadra 2, Módulo 13, Daia, Mon-Fri 0730-1630*, about 10 km out on the Brasília highway (near the Embratel tower), has a fine collection of gemstones, library, sales and lapidary courses, and will show visitors how real and synthetic gemstones are distinguished.

The scruffy, unpleasant town of **Cristalina** is also famous for its semi-precious stones, which can be bought cheaply in local shops. An interesting excursion is to the panning and mining sites amid magnificent rock formations, about 6 km away. Take the BR-040 (Brasília-Belo Horizonte road) and at Km 104 turn left along a dirt road, just after the highway police post, to the **Cristalina waterfall** (11 km along this road).

Cidade de Goiás (Goiás Velho) » pp621-627.

→ *Phone code: 062. Colour map 3, A5. Population: 30,000.*

This delightful town, nestled in the midst of *cerrado*-covered ridges, is one of central Brazil's hidden beauties. Cobbled streets lined with colourful yellow and blue Portuguese buildings gather around a little river watched over by a collection of elegantly simple baroque churches. Horses and old VWs clatter along the heavy stone flags and the local residents go about their day-to-day business as they always have done, treating visitors like guests or curiosities rather than tourists. All this may change as Cidade de Goiás was recently awarded UNESCO World Heritage status.

The town was founded in 1727 as Vila Boa and, like its Minas counterparts, became rich on gold, before becoming the capital of Goiás state, which it remained until just before the Second World War. But while towns like Ouro Preto and Tiradentes lavished their churches in gilt, Goiás chose modesty, erecting simple façades whose more classical lines stand strong against the intense blue of the sky. Interiors, too, were plain with simple panelling that beautifully offset both the richly painted wooden ceilings and the virtuoso sculpture of the *Goiás Aleijudinho* by Veiga Valle.

Ins and outs

Cidade de Goiás is well connected by bus to Goiânia, about 130 km away, but there are few services from anywhere else. The *rodoviária* is 2 km out of town at Avenida Dario da Paiva, in Bairro João Francisco. All buses also stop at the old bus station (*rodoviária velha*) next to the Mercado Municipal, 500 m west of the central Praça do Coreto. The **tourist office** ⓘ *daily 0900-1700, T062-3371 4564*, is housed in the Quartel do Vinte, (a former barracks where many of the German soldiers who fought for Brazil in the Paraguayan war were housed) on the Praça Brasil Caiado (also known as Largo do Chafariz). However, the Museu Casa de Cora Coralina is a better source of information.

Sights

The most interesting streets in the colonial part of town spread out from the two principal *praças*: **Praça Brasil Caiado** and immediately below it towards the river **Praça do Coreto**. The former is dominated by the Chafariz de Cauda, a lavish baroque fountain, which once supplied all the town's water. The best of the churches and museums are in the small cobbled town centre which radiates out from the two central plazas and spreads a little way along the riverbank. It is easily navigable on foot. The oldest church, **São Francisco de Paula** ⓘ *Praça Zacheu Alves de Castro* (1763), sits on a platform overlooking the market and the Rio Vermelho. It has a beautiful 19th-century painted ceiling by André Antônio da Conceição, depicting the life of St Francis de Paula. **Nossa Senhora da Abadia** ⓘ *R Abadia s/n*, has a similarly understated but impressive painted ceiling, while the other 18th-century churches like **Nossa Senhora do Carmo** ⓘ *R do Carmo*, on the riverside, and **Santa Bárbara** ⓘ *R Passo da Pátria*, are almost Protestant in their simplicity. The latter sits on a hill a kilometre or so east of the town from where there are wonderful sunset views.

Cidade de Goiás has a handful of interesting museums. The **Museu das Bandeiras** ⓘ *Praça Brasil Caiado/Largo do Chafariz, T062-3371 1087, Tue-Fri 0900-1700, Sat 1200-1700, Sun 0900-1300, US$1*, was once the centre of local government. The museum tells the story of the Goiás Bandeira exhibitions, which sit over a small but forbidding dungeon. The old governor's palace, the **Palácio Conde dos Arcos** ⓘ *Praça do Coreto, T062-3371 1200, Tue-Sat 0800-1700, Sun 0900-1300, US$1*, which sits in the square below Praça Brasil Caiado, was the governor's palace before the state capital moved to Goiânia. It has a display of 19th-century furniture, portraits of all the governors, and a pretty little walled garden. Across the way the **Museu de Artes Sacras** ⓘ *Praça do Coreto, T062-3371 1207, Tue-Sat 0800-1700, Sun 0900-1300, US$1*, houses some clanky 18th-century church silverware and a series of painted wooden statues by one of Brazil's most important religious sculptors, Jose Joaquim da Veiga Valle. Veiga Valle was entirely self taught with little knowledge or access to the Latin American baroque style that he was later seen to represent. Look out for the double 'V' signatures in the patterns of the fingers and the uncannily realistic stained-glass eyes.

A stroll from the Praça do Coreto, downhill and across the river, will bring you to the **Museu Casa de Cora Coralina** ⓘ *R do Candido 20, T062-3371 1990, Tue-Sun 0900-1700, US$1*, the former home of Goiás's most respected writer, with a collection of her belongings and a beautifully kept riverside garden at the back. Staff here are extremely helpful and knowledgeable about the city, though they speak no English. The 18th-century **Mercado Municipal**, next to the old *rodoviária*, is a wonderful spot for a snack and photography. All manner of interesting characters gather here and the small stall shops sell everything from shanks of beef to Catholic kitsch. **Espaço Cultural Goiandira do Couto** ⓘ *R Joaquim Bonifacio 19, T062-3371 1303, Tue-Sun 0900-1700, US$1*, has chocolate box-style paintings of the city made entirely from different coloured sands from the surrounding *serra*. The artist, now in her 80s, has exhibited all over the world.

Pirenópolis

» *pp621-627.*

➔ *Phone code: 062. Colour map 3, grid A/B5. Population: 23,000. Altitude: 770 m.*

This lovely colonial silver mining town, 165 km due west of Brasília, sits in the midst of rugged hills dripping with waterfalls and covered in rapidly disappearing but still pristine *cerrado*. Like Cidade de Goiás it was founded by *bandeirantes* in search of gold and then by small-scale cattle ranchers. Its centre remains well preserved and only a little less pretty than Cidade de Goiás, leading it to be declared a National Heritage site in 1989. Pirenópolis's proximity to Brasília has made it a favourite weekend playground for the capital's middle classes who congregate in the lively restaurants and bars, which line the northern end of Rua do Rosario. But the town's home-grown culture still thrives; one of Central Brazil's most unusual and vibrant festival takes place here every May/June (see Festivals and events, page 625) and on weekends the Praça Central fills to the brim with *peões* in stetsons and spurs blasting out *sertanejo* music from their souped-up cars. Pirenópolis is a great place to pass a few days or even weeks. The surrounding countryside offers good walking and light adventure activities and there are plenty of tour operators, though as elsewhere in Brazil, little English is spoken.

Ins and outs

Pirenópolis is served by two buses a day from Brasília. Tourist information is available at the **Centro de Atendimento ao Turista** ⓘ *R do Bonfim, Centro Historico, T062-3331 2729*, but they don't speak much English.

Sights

The **Igreja Matriz Nossa Senhora do Rosário** has undergone restoration after being gutted by a fire in 2002. It is the oldest church in the state, dating from 1728, and before the fire had one of the most magnificent painted interiors in Goiás; sadly unrestored. **Nosso Senhor do Bonfim** (1750-1754), which houses an impressive life-size crucifix from Bahia, was transported here on the backs of 260 slaves. The more subtly beautiful image of Our Lady is Portuguese. The church of **Nossa Senhora do Carmo** ⓘ *daily 1300-1700*, serves as a museum of religious art (closed in early 2007). Another, the **Museu Família Pompeu** ⓘ *R Nova 33, Tue-Fri 1300-1700, Sat 1300-1500, Sun 0900-1200*, displays regional historical items and documents. The tiny, privately owned **Museu das Cavalhadas** ⓘ *R Direita 37, Fri and Sat 0800-1700, US$1*, has a collection of masks, photographs and costumes from the Festa do Divino. **Fazenda Babilônia** ⓘ *25 km southwest, no public transport, Sat and Sun 0800-1700, US$2*, is a fine example of an 18th-century sugar *fazenda*. It's now a small museum with the original mill and a lovely little chapel.

Pirenópolis is Brazil's unofficial silver capital and is a good place to stock up on presents.

Around Pirenópolis

The *cerrado* and hills around the town have so far managed to resist the onslaught of soya and there are still opportunities to get out into the midst of some genuine wild country. There are plenty of walks and adventure activities on offer, birdwatching is good and there is a reasonably healthy population of maned wolf and various South American cats, including jaguar. The landscape is rugged, with many waterfalls and canyons. Guides are essential as many of the attractions are well off the beaten track.

Santuário de Vida Silvestre Vagafogo ⓘ *T062-3335 8490, visits through Drena, see page 626*, is the labour of love of Evandro Engel Ayer who bought an area of the *cerrado* intending to start a farm. After falling in love with the plants and animals living here he instead decided to create a wildlife reserve. There is good birdwatching, with various rare species, a species list and a library. Mammals seen here include ocelot, brown capuchin and a rare subspecies of tufted-eared marmoset. Evandro is helpful and knowledgeable, speaks good English and serves one of the best lunches in Goiás.

The **Mosteiro Buddhisto** ⓘ *information through Drena, see page 626*, is a simple Zen monastery near a series of beautiful waterfalls in the heart of pristine *cerrado* forest. Day visits can be arranged with light walks or longer term retreats. This is particularly magical at sunset.

Chapada dos Veadeiros » *pp621-627.*

→ *Colour map 3, A6.*

ⓘ *Entry only with a guide. The park is reached by paved state highway BR118. Tours can be arranged from Alto Paraíso de Goiás or São Jorge, see below.*

These table-top mountains, drained by countless fast-flowing rivers that rush through deep gorges and plummet over spectacular waterfalls, are less famous than Diamantina or Guimarães, but are less spoilt and more subtly beautiful. The national park, which protects only a fraction of their area, is almost twice the size of Diamantina and eight times the size of Guimarães. And unlike both those areas, its forests have never been felled. It was designated a World Heritage site by UNESCO in 2001. At present trips within the park itself are limited to day visits only; but there are plans to change this. Walks of up to nine days can be easily organized at a good price within the wilderness areas in the park's environs, together with a range of adventure activities from canyoning to rappelling. There is plenty of accommodation in Alto Paraíso and São Jorge and transport to and from Brasília is straightforward.

Like most of wild Goiás, the Chapada is covered in *cerrado* forest – a habitat of such floral diversity that it has recently been declared a biological hot-spot by **Conservation International.** Rare mammals including jaguar, maned wolf, puma, tapir, ocelot and giant anteater are abundant and, although no one has yet compiled a serious bird list, spectaculars and rarities include red-shouldered macaw, coal-crested finch, helmeted manakin and various key indicator species like rusty-margined guan and bare-face currasow; king vultures are abundant.

Alto Paraíso and São Jorge → *Colour map 3, A6.*

The ramshackle town of **Alto Paraíso de Goiás** is filled with crystal shops and has become famous over the years as a centre for alternative therapies. Judging only by appearance many of these seem superficial. But there are some serious practitioners here doing excellent work, and at a fraction of the price of those in other parts of the world. The town is connected to Brasília and the rest of Goiás state by the paved state highway BR118. There are bus connections to Brasília and to Palmas in Tocantins. Alto Paraíso is the best point to stock up on provisions before a trek in the Chapada dos Veadeiros (see above) and has the best of the tour operators and hotels. Access to the eastern attractions like the Vale de Lua are only really possible from Alto Paraíso. There is a small **tourist booth** on the main street (no English).

The tiny village of **São Jorge** is 40 km from Alto Paraíso on a partly paved road. With its three dirt streets, it is smaller and prettier than Alto Paraíso but has fewer restaurants and tour services. Several buses run daily between Alto Paraíso and São Jorge. The town lies only 1 km from the park entrance itself but has poorer guides.

Southwest Goiás state » pp621-627.

Serranópolis → *Colour map 3, B4.*

This little town is close to some remnant *cerrado* forest that clings to a series of small table-top mountains in the flat sea of soya, which is gradually taking over Goiás. Important cave paintings have been found here; these are now carefully protected and can be reached via a series of well-maintained trails. There are a few simple hotels in town and two excellent forest pousadas here: carefully designed, wonderfully peaceful and great for birdwatching or just relaxing.

Parque Nacional das Emas → *Colour map 3, B4.*

This 133,000-ha park, protecting low *campo sujo cerrado* forests, black water rivers and savannah is Goiás's third UNESCO World Heritage site – the others being Chapada dos Veadeiros and Cidade de Goiás. The park protects large populations of maned wolf, puma and jaguar as well as many rare *cerrado* bird species. These include red-shouldered and blue-winged macaw, greater rhea, bare-face currasow and diverse tyrant flycatchers and woodpeckers, as well as several species of macaw. It is a favourite destination for wildlife documentary film crews.

Ins and outs The most convenient base for visiting the park is **Chapadão do Céu**, www.chapadaodoceu.go.gov.br, about 30 minutes to the east. This newly created soya town has some decent hotels and tour operators to take visitors to the park. Four-day, three-night visits to the park can be arranged through agencies and tour operators such as **Drena** in Pirenópolis, www.drena.tur.br (see page 626), the **Pantanal Bird Club** in Cuiabá (see page 668), or **Focus Tours** (see page 20).

Aruanã and the Rio Araguaia » pp621-627.

➔ *Colour map 3, A5.*

Any Brazilian will tell you that the 2630-km-long Rio Araguaia is richer in fish than any other in the world, and a visit to the 220-km stretch between Aruanã and the Ilha do Bananal during the fishing season is quite an experience. As the receding waters in May reveal sparkling white beaches, thousands of Brazilian and international enthusiasts pour into the area, intent on getting the best camping spots. As many as 400 tent cities spring up, and vast quantities of fish are hauled in before the phenomenon winds down in September, when the rivers begin to rise again and flood the surrounding plains. Without Brazilian contacts, the best way of experiencing this annual event is with one of the specialist tour operators.

A yellow fever vaccination is recommended for the region; borrachudas, tiny biting insects, are an unavoidable fact of life in central Brazil in June and July; repellent helps a little.

The Araguaia is most readily accessible from Aruanã, a port 180 km northwest of Goiás Velho by paved highway, which sees little excitement outside the winter fishing season when its comfortable hotels are booked up for months. Boats can be rented to visit some of the beautiful lakes and beaches nearby. Buses from the *rodoviária* serve Araguapaz, Britânia and Goiânia. Brazilian Canoeing Championships are also held along the river.

Sleeping

Goiânia *p615, map p616*

The best hotels are 1 km from the centre in the Setor Oeste with restaurants and bars. Hotels in the centre are frayed 1970s blocks.

L Castro's Park, Av República do Líbano 1520, Setor Oeste, T062-3212 4428, www.castrospark.com.br. A 5-star hotel in a tower a few blocks from the centre with gym and swimming pool.

L-A Address Hotel, Av República do Líbano, 2526, Setor Oeste T062-3257 1000, www.addresshotel.com.br. The best hotel in the city with good promotional rates. Modern suites with comfortable beds; the best with separate living areas and good views. Excellent business facilities. Plenty of restaurants and bars nearby.

AL-A Papillon, Av República do Líbano 1824, T062-3219 1500, www.papillonhotel.com.br. A tower in the new centre with modern tiled rooms and suites, a pool, gym, sauna, business facilities and 24-hr room service. Very popular, book ahead.

B Oeste Plaza, R 2 No 389 Setor Oeste, T062-3224 5012. Well-maintained modern tower with small a/c rooms with tiled floors and en suites. Those on the higher floors have good views. Small pool and gym.

C Augustus, Praça Antônio Lisita 702, T062-3224 1022, www.augustus-hotel.com.br. Blocky B-grade 1970s business hotel with rather gloomy apartment rooms, a pool, sauna and gym. Conveniently located for the centre. Official rates higher but these are not adhered to.

D Karajás, Av Goiás and R 3 No 860, T062-3224 9666, www.hotelkarajas.com.br. Good value 1980s hotel rooms in a once-luxury hotel that has now fallen somewhat from grace. Convenient for the centre.

D Rio Vermelho, R 4 No 26, T062-3213 2555, www.hotelriovermelho.com.br. Simple hotel in a quiet street with lots of cheap restaurants. The cheapest rooms are fan cooled. With breakfast. Close to the centre.

D-F Goiânia Palace, Av Anhangüera 5195, T062-3224 4874, goiâniapalace@terra.com.br. Art-deco building with a range of rooms from simple fan-cooled doubles to suites. Good breakfast. Friendly and well located.

F Antoninho's, R 68 No 41, T062-3223 1815. Very basic but clean and well looked after. Only a few rooms have windows. Friendly, safe and with good breakfasts.

F Paissandú, Av Goiás 1290 at R 55, T062-3224 4925. Very simple fan-cooled or a/c rooms 8 blocks north of the centre. Breakfast.

Camping

Itanhangá municipal site, Av Princesa Carolina, Km 13, T062-292 1145. Attractive wooded location, reasonable facilities.

Caldas Novas *p617*

L-AL Pousada do Rio Quente, T062-3452 1122, www.caldasnovas.com.br. 4-star complex at Rio Quente. Breakfast and lunch, transport to main pools and recreation facilities included in price. Good accommodation in main buildings or chalets, the **Turismo** has a private airstrip.

Camping

At Esplanada, and **Camping Clube do Brasil** site on the Ipameri Rd, 5 km from the centre.

Anápolis and Cristalina *p617*

AL Estância Park, in a parkland setting 6 km northeast of Anápolis, T062-318 1200, F318 1300. Pool, tennis court and an unpleasant mini-zoo, but the best in town.
C Hotel Goyás, R da Saudade 41, Cristalina. With fan and fridge.
D Serra Dourada, Av Brasil 375, Anápolis, T062-324 0051. One of many cheap hotels around the *rodoviária* (Av Brasil-Norte). Restaurant, parking, fans, good value.

Cidade de Goiás *p617*

AL Fazenda Manduzanzan, on the road to Cachoeira das Andorinhas, 8 km, T062-9982 3373, www.manduzanzan.com.br. 10 apartments set in the *cerrado* near the region's prettiest waterfalls. Sauna, horse riding, spring-water swimming pools. Lunch included in the price.
AL-B Vila Boa, Av Dr Deusdete Ferreira de Moura, 1 km southeast on the Morro do Chapéu do Padre, T062-3371 1000. The best option, but out of town and inconvenient for the centre. Pool, bar, restaurant and good views. The best rooms are the 4 suites.
B Casa da Ponte, R Moretti Foggia s/n, T062-3371 4467. An art-deco building next to the bridge across the Rio Vermelho with small well-maintained a/c rooms with en suites and parquet flooring. The best overlook the river.
C-D Pousada do Ipê, R Cel Guedes de Amorim 22, T062-3371 2065. Cloisters of rooms gathered around a courtyard dominated by a huge mango tree. The annexe has a swimming pool and bar area. Breakfast is included.
C-D Pousada do Vovô Jura, R Sta Barbara 38, T062-3371 1746. A colonial house set in a little garden with views out over the river and *serra*.
D-E Pousada do Sol, R Americano do Brasil, T062-3371 1717. Well-maintained, plain, fan-cooled rooms with lino or wood floors.
E Pousada do Sonho, R 15 Novembro 22, T062-3372 1224. A simple, well-kept residential house with plain rooms with shared bathrooms. Good breakfast.
E Pousada Reis, R 15 Novembro 41, T062-371 1565. A simple cheapie next to the *Sonho* offering similar rooms to **Pousada do Sonho** but shoddier service.

Camping

Attractive, well-run **Cachoeira Grande** campground, 7 km along the BR-070 to Jussara (near the tiny airport), with bathing place and snack bar. More basic site (**Chafariz da Carioca**) in town by the river.

Pirenópolis *p618*

There are plenty of rooms in town, but they fill up during Festa do Divino so book ahead or visit from Brasília (about a 90-min drive).
A Casa Grande, R Aurora 41, T062-3331 1758, www.casagrandepousada.com.br. A big old house near the centre decorated with colonial furniture and with chalet rooms in a small garden visited by many birds.
A O Casarão, R Direita 79, T062-3331 2662, www.ocasarao.pirenopolis.tur.br. A colonial home decorated with period furniture, there's a little pool set in heliconia-filled gardens. Rooms have 4-poster beds and mosquito nets.
B-C Do Arvoredo, R Direita s/n, T062-3331 3479, www.arvoredo.tur.br. Peaceful little pousada set in a little wood. Clean, modest fan-cooled rooms are set around a small pool and there are good rates on weekdays.
C Pouso do Sô Vigario, R Nova 25, T062-3331 1206, www.pousadaspirenopolis.com.br. Small rooms but pleasant public spaces with objets d'art and posters from European painting exhibitions. Good location. Decent breakfast in a little garden next to the pool.
E Rex, Praça da Matriz 15, T062-3331 1121. 5 rooms, all with fridge and TV, around a courtyard. Good breakfast and location.

Camping

Camping Roots, R dos Pireneus 96, T062-3331 2105, camproots@yahoo.com. Sites with electricity, hot showers and English-speaking staff. 10-min walk from the centre.

Alto Paraíso and São Jorge *p620*

Prices in São Jorge often go up at weekends.

AL Casa das Flores, T061-9976 0603, São Jorge, www.pousadacasadasflores.com.br. Elegant little pousada with tasteful rooms (lit only by candlelight), sauna, pool and great breakfast in the decent attached restaurant. The best in town, but overpriced.

A-B Camelot, on the main road just north of Alto Paraíso, T061 3446 1581, www.pousada camelot.com.br. Delightfully kitsch mock-Arthurian castle with proper hot showers and comfortable a/c rooms with satellite TV.

A-B Portal da Chapada, 9 km along the road from Alto Paraíso to São Jorge, T061-3446 1820, www.portaldachapada.com.br. The best choice for birdwatchers – with comfortable with a/c wooden cabins in the midst of the *cerrado*.

B Casa Rosa, R Gumersindo 233, Alto Paraíso, T061-3446 1319, www.pousadacasarosa.com.br. The best in town with a range of well-kept a/c rooms, the best are in chalets near the pool. Also known as 'As Cerejeiras'.

B Trilha Violeta, São Jorge, T061-3455 1088, www.trilhavioleta.com.br. Fan-cooled violet rooms with private bathrooms around a bougainvillea-filled garden. Reasonable restaurant. Friendly.

B-C Aquas de Março, São Jorge, T061-3347 2082, www.chapadadosveadeiros.com.br. Simple duplex rooms decorated with paintings by local artist, Moacir. Pleasant garden, saunas, *oforo* baths and decent breakfast.

D-E Pousada do Sol, R Gumersindo 2911, Alto Paraíso, T061-446 1201. Small and simple, with a range of rooms, the best with balconies and fridges.

E Casa Grande, São Jorge, T061-9623 5515, www.pousadacasagrande.com.br. Simple but well-kept rooms and a good breakfast.

Camping

Tattoo, at the top of São Jorge, tattoo@travessia.tur.br. Powered sites from only US$3. Decent wood-fired pizzas and a small bar. English spoken. Very friendly and helpful.

Parque Nacional das Emas *p620*

A Fazenda Santa Amélia, Estrada Serranópolis, Chapadão do Céu, T064-3634 1380. A working *fazenda* with a range of wildlife tours in the property's remnant *cerrado* forest (none in Emas except with special arrangement). Comfortable chalets, a pool and full board in the price.

D Paraná, Av Indiaiá, Chapadão do Céu , T064-3634 1227. Simple, clean and well run with fan-cooled rooms.

E Rafael, Av Indiaiá, Chapadão do Céu , T064-3634 1247. Very simple and clean with fan-cooled rooms and shared bathrooms.

Serranópolis *p620*

A-B Aldeia Ecológica Guardiões do Cerrado, about 15 km south of Serranópolis at Km 70 off the BR184, take a taxi from the town (about US$20). A magical forest pousada with a ring of beautifully appointed chalets all decorated individually, many with Xavantes indigenous art and tasteful photographs. Great food and walks and much wildlife. Currasows and maned wolf visit the camp for breakfast each morning.

A-B Araras, T064-3668 1054, www.pousada dasararas.com. Tasteful little chalets in an armadillo-filled garden next to a clear-water river with a natural swimming area. Trails lead to the various archaeological sites.

Eating

Goiânia *p615, map p616*

Goiânian cooking is like that of Minas – lots of meat with huge portions of vegetable dishes and, of course, beans and rice. Local specialities include *arroz com piqui*, rice with a cruel *cerrado* fruit, a practical joke of evolution whose outer flesh is soft and sweet but if bitten leaves the mouth full of sharp spines that have to be surgically removed. Beware!

The city has a good range of restaurants and bars, especially around **Praça Tamandaré** and **Av República Líbano** in the Setor Oeste where there are options in all price brackets.

Street stands (*pamonharías*) sell *pamonha* snacks, tasty pastries made with green corn, sweet, savoury, or *picante* (spicy); all are served hot and have cheese in the middle, some include sausage.

TTT Bella Luna, R 10 704, Praça Tamandaré, T062-3214 3562. Some of the best Italian food in Goiânia, including excellent pizza, pasta and northern Italian seafood dishes.

TTT Celson & Cia, R 15 539 at C 22, T062-3215 3043, www.celsonecia.com.br. Very popular meat restaurant with a good cold buffet. Evenings only except at weekends.

ŸŸŸ Chão Nativo, Av República Líbano 1809 (opposite hotel **Papillon**), T062-3223 5396. The city's most famous Goiânian restaurant also serving local and Mineira food. Lively after 2000 and lunchtime on weekends.

ŸŸ Tribo do Açai, R 36 590, T062-3281 6971. Buzzing little fruit juice bar with excellent buffet salads and health food. Just round the corner from **Shopping Bougainville**.

ŸŸ Walmor, R 3 1062 at R 25-B, T062-3215 5555, www.churrasciariadowalmor.com.br. Large portions of excellent steaks served in an attractive open-air dining area.

ŸŸ-Ÿ Floresta, R 2 at R 9, T062-3224 9560. Lively corner bar with grilled steaks, standard rice and beans dishes, and snacks. Open until late. Good draft lager.

Ÿ Buffalo's Grill, Praça Tamandaré, T062-3215 3935. Pizzas, grilled meat and chicken, sandwiches and crêpes. Open 24 hrs.

Ÿ Giraffa, Av República Líbano 1592, T062-3225 1969. Fast food joint with some sumptuous set plates including steak/chicken with rice, beans and chips.

Ÿ Mineiro, R 4 53 (opposite **Rio Vermelho**, see Sleeping), T062-3224 9113. Cheap, good per kilo buffet with lots of choice and some veggie options. One of several on this block.

Ÿ Primo Patio, Av República Líbano (opposite Castro's Plaza), T062-3213 3366, Pizza, pasta and grilled steak and chicken (with the inevitable rice, beans and chips).

Cidade de Goiás *p617*

For the best very cheap options head for the **Mercado Municipal** between the São Francisco church and the river.

ŸŸ Dali, R 13 de Maio 26, T062-3372 1640. Riverside restaurant with a little patio offering a wide range of international and local dishes.

ŸŸ Flor do Ipê, Praça da Boa Vista 32, end of the road leading from the centre across the bridge, T062-3372 1133. The best in town for Goiânian food, with an enormous variety on offer, a lovely garden setting with views of the river and *serra*. Highly recommended.

Ÿ Degus't Fun Pizzaria, R Quinta Bocaiuva, next to Praça do Coreto, T062-3371 2800. Pizza, casseroles, soups and very friendly service from a mother-and-daughter team.

Pirenópolis *p618*

There are plenty of options along **R do Rosário**, serving a surprising range of international food including some vegetarian and Asian options. Many have live music at night (and an undisclosed cover charge – be sure to ask). There are cheaper options near the Igreja Bonfim in the upper part of town.

ŸŸ Caffe Tarsia, R do Rosário 34, T062-3331 1274, www.caffetarsia.com.br. Much the best in town with a menu of Mediterranean dishes, Goiás food and steaks. Live music and weekends. Good *caipirinhas*.

ŸŸ Chiquinha, R do Rosário 19, T062-3331 3052. Local cuisine with an emphasis on meat.

ŸŸ Emporio do Cerrado, R do Rosário 21, T062-3331 3874. Great Goiás food like Pequi risotto with chicken in orange sauce served in a dining room decorated with black and white photos. Live music at weekends.

Ÿ Alma Vegetariana, R dos Pireneus at Praça do Correto, T062-3331 2938. Vegetarian pies, pastas, sandwiches and good juices.

Ÿ O Cafeteria, R do Rosário 38, T062-9972 7953. Light food and about the cheapest option in town.

Alto Paraíso *p620*

The best of the restaurants are in Alto Paraíso. São Jorge has a few basic options.

ŸŸ-Ÿ Oca Lila, Av João Bernades Rabelo 449, T061-3446 1773. Decent pizza and sandwiches, live music at the weekend, good atmosphere and a decent veggie buffet at lunch.

Ÿ Jatô, R Coleto Paulino 522, T061-3446 1339. Open Thu-Sun. Self-service; veggie options.

Ÿ Pizza 2000, Av Ari Valadão 659, T061-3446 1814. The centre of the town's early evening social life. Respectable pizzas.

Bars and clubs

Goiânia *p615, map p616*

Goiânia is surprisingly lively, with some of the best nightlife in central Brazil. This is especially true during the various festivals and Carnaval. There is an active gay scene and plenty of choices of clubs and bars. Most locals tend to drink in the restaurants (many of which double up as bars) before heading to a club at around 2300.

Café Cancún, Shopping Flamboyant and Av Jamel Cecilio 3, T062-3546 2035, www.cafecancun.com.br. With a lively *forró* night on Wed and a mix of club music on others.

It's, Av 136, 960, Edifício Executive Tower, Térreo, Setor Marista, T062-3241 8477,

www.its.art.br. The city's current favourite with a range of different music on different nights – from techno and hip hop to MPB.
Pulse, R9 1087, T062-215 6133, www.pulse.com.br. Crowded little club with a small sound system and rather tired decoration. Sweaty and packed on Sat.

Pirenópolis *p618*
Bars along **R do Rosário** cater for those from Brasília and the children of the hippies who migrated here in the 1970s. Locals hang out near the **Igreja Bonfim** where there are 2 spit-and-sawdust bars and booming car stereos.

Festivals

Cidade de Goiás *p617*
Feb Carnaval is joyous and still little known to outsiders. There are plans to make it into a traditional 19th-century masked parade with formal balls.
Apr The streets of Cidade de Goiás blaze with torches during the solemn **Fogaréu processions of Holy Week**, when hooded figures re-enact Christ's descent from the cross and burial.
Apr-May **Festa Divino Espírito Santo** processions, serenades and the formal distribution of food to the poor.
May **Encontro Afro Brasileiro** a celebration of black Brazilian culture with live music, Afro-Brazilian food. Attended by people come from all over Brazil.
Jun **International Film Festival**, Live music by acts like Gilberto Gil and Titãs and films from almost 100 different countries and especially from Latin America.
24-26 Jul **Birthday of the City**. The city becomes once more the capital of the state and there are processions in homage to the patron saint, Santa Ana, and various shows.

Pirenópolis *p618*
May/Jun **Festa do Divino Espírito Santo**, held 45 days after Easter (Pentecost), is one of Brazil's most famous and extraordinary folkloric/religious celebrations. It lasts 3 days, with medieval costumes, tournaments, dances and mock battles between Moors and Christians, a tradition held annually since 1819. The city throbs with life over this period and there are numerous and frequent extemporaneous *forró* and *sertanejo* parties.

Shopping

Goiânia *p615, map p616*
Ceramic, sisal and wooden handicrafts from **Centro Estadual do Artesanato**, Praça do Trabalhador (0800-1800); **Sun handicrafts markets** at the Praça Cívica (morning) and Praça do Sol (afternoon). The latter starts after 1530, until 2100, known as the **Honey Fair** as all types of honey are sold; also good for a Sun snack, with many sweets and tarts sold along the street. See also **Casa do Indio**, page 616.

Cidade de Goiás *p617*
There are little artisan shops springing up all over the town.
Frutos da Terra, R Dom Cândido Penso 30, next to Cora Coralina Museum. Wide range of items from bags and belts to leather sandals and ceramics. Most is made in the town.

Pirenópolis *p618*
There are many jewellery and arts and crafts shops in the streets in the historic centre.

Activities and tours

Goiânia *p615, map p616*
There are many sporting facilities throughout Goiânia and visitors welcome. For sunbathing, swimming and waterskiing try the **Jaó Club**, T062-261 2122, on a reservoir near the city.
Turisplan Turismo, R 8 Q 7, 388 lt 50 s 1 - Setor Central, T062-3224 7076. Arranges tours to Paraúna and the mining villages. Also sells bus tickets.

Cidade de Goiás *p617*
Massage and treatments
Cleonice Albino, T062-3372 1119/062-9902 7344. Very good-value Ayurvedic massage and colour therapy. Visits to hotels or at the therapist's clinic.

Wildlife and adventure tours
Frans and Susana Leeuweenberg, contact through **Serra Dourada**, below. A husband-and-wife team of biologists who have been working hard to protect the *cerrado* for many years. English, French and Dutch spoken.
Serra Dourada Aventura, T062-3371 4277/ T062-9238 5195, www.vilaboadegoias.com.br. Hikes in the surrounding forest and within the

state park, visits to waterfalls, kayaking and canyoning and longer distance trips to the Rio Araguiaia. Very good value.

Pirenópolis *p618*

Drena, R do Carmo 11, across the bridge and up the hill, on the left, T062-3331 3336, www.drena.tur.br. Walks, adventure activities and visits to the Vagafogo private reserve and the Mosteiro Buddhisto and trips further afield to destinations like Emás and the Rio Araguiaia. Good value, well organized and excellent English spoken.

Chapada dos Veadeiros *p619*

Alternativas, T062-3446 1000, www.alternativas.tur.br. Very well-organized tours, walks and adventure trips including canyoning, rapelling and abseiling, throughout the region. Enthusiastic guides, some of whom speak English and the only tour operator in the region owned and run by locals.
Alpatour, R dos Nascentes, T062-3446 1820, www.altoparaiso.com. Van-based tours to the principal sights. Suitable for all ages.
Chapada Ecotours, T062-3446 1345, www.transchapada.com.br. Light adventure and visits to the major sights.
Travessia, T062-3446 1595, www.travessia.tur.br. Treks from a few days to over a week with rappelling and canyoning from one of the most respected instructors, Ion David.

Alto Paraíso and São Jorge *p620*

Massage and treatments

Atash, R do Segredo 37, Alto Paraíso, T061-3446 1028. Ayurvedic and classical Thai massage and breathing meditation from a long-experienced practitioner.
Sílvia Luz, R 12 Dezembro 217, Alto Paraíso, T061-3446 1585, T061-9956 9685, silviapraxis@hotmail.com. One of the best Ayurvedic and Reiki practitioners in the country. Also works with Tuiná and Shiatsu. Highly recommended

Parque Nacional das Emas *p620*

Tours are available through **Drena** (see above), www.drena.tur.br. Alternatively, contact the tourist office in the Prefeitura Municipal, Chapadão do Céu, www.chapadaodo ceu.go.gov.br, for a list of authorized tour operators. Interest is growing but visits to Emas are still in the early stages.

Aruanã and the Rio Araguaia *p621*

Boats trips

US$25 per hr. Wildlife guides can be hired in Aruanã, Britânia, Barra do Garças or Porto Luís Alves. Interesting walks in surrounding jungle with Joel, ask at the hotel.

Tour operators

KR International Travel, R Mexico 8th floor, S 801, Rio de Janeiro, T021-210 1238. Ex-Peace Corps manager, good for information on the centre-west region.
Serra Dourada Aventura, T062-3371 4277, www.vilaboadegoias.com.br. Boat and walking trips along the Rio Araguiaia. Very good value. Book at least 10 days in advance.
Transworld, R 3 No 546, Goiânia, T062-224 4340, F212 1047. One-week group trips in a 'botel' out of Aruanã to Bananal.

Transport

Goiânia *p615, map p616*

Air Flights to **Brasília**, **Campinas**, **São Paulo**, **Uberaba** and **Uberlândia**.

Airline offices Varig, Av Goiás 285, T062- 224 5059, www.varig,com.br, and at the airport. Also at the airport are **Gol**, www.voegol.com.br and **TAM**, www.tam.com.br.

Bus To **Brasília**, 207 km, at least 15 departures a day, 2½ hrs, US$5, and **São Paulo**, 900 km via Barretos, US$25, 14½ hrs, *leito* services at night. To **Goiás Velho**, 136 km, hourly from 0500, 2½ hrs, US$5. **Pirenópolis**, 0700 and 1700, 2 hrs, US$5. **Campo Grande**, 935 km, 4 services daily, 18 hrs, US$30. To **Cuiabá** (Mato Grosso), 916 km on BR-158/070 via Barra do Garças, or 928 km on BR-060/364 via Jataí (both routes paved, most buses use the latter route), 4 buses a day, US$25, 15-16 hrs, continuing to Porto Velho (**Rondônia**) and Rio Branco (Acre), a very trying journey.

Car hire Millenium, T062-9612 7842 (24 hrs); Siga, T062-207 8388.

Cidade de Goiás *p617*

Bus Hourly bus services to **Goiânia** (2½ hrs) 0530-2000, change here for other places.

Pirenópolis *p618*

Bus 2 buses a day to **Brasília** (2½-4 hrs).

Chapada dos Veadeiros *p619*
Bus **Brasília–Alto Paraíso–São Jorge** leaves at 1100 (3-4hrs), returning 0900. There is a night bus **Palmas–Brasília**, arriving from Brasília 2200.

Parque Nacional das Emas *p620*
Bus One daily bus from **Serranópolis** to Chapadão do Céu , leaving at 0800. To get to Chapadão do Céu from Campo Grande, go via Costa Rica or Chapada do Sul.

Directory

Goiânia *p615, map p616*
Banks In the centre and along Av Rep Líbano. Travel agents will exchange cash, poor rates for TCs. **Immigration** Immigration office, R 235, Setor Universitário.

Parque Nacional das Emas *p620*
Banks There is a Banco do Brasil with a Visa ATM in Chapadão do Céu .

Tocantins

Tocantins is not yet on the tourist track, yet it offers some of the most exciting opportunities for adventure tourism in Brazil's interior. Jalapão – an enormous wilderness of cerrado *forest, table-top mountains, dune deserts, waterfalls and whitewater rivers – lies on the borders of Tocantins and Piauí. It is as spectacularly beautiful as the Chapada dos Veadeiros or the Chapada Diamantina but far less visited. The world's largest river island, Ilha do Bananal, lies at the southern end of the state. Its northern extremes are almost as rich in wildlife as the Pantanal and the interior of the island is home to numerous indigenous groups (who cannot be visited without authorisation from FUNAI). The* serra *around the planned modern capital, Palmas, is covered with rainforest dotted with beautiful waterfalls. The northwestern corner of the state sees the end of the* cerrado *and the beginnings of the Amazon rainforest.* *» For Sleeping, Eating and other listings, see pages 629-630.*

Palmas *» pp629-630.*

→ Phone code: 063. Colour map 1, B5. Population: 130,000.

Palmas is Brazil's newest capital city in the country's newest state – Tocantins was carved out of Goiás in the late 1980s. It sits on the banks of the flooded Tocantins river at the feet of low forested mountains, which are bathed in a rich yellow tropical light at dusk. It is a city built for mathematicians and cars, with an arcane street numbering system and wide, long avenues broken by roundabouts. Rather fascistic monuments to the autocrat who founded the state (and whose family still largely run Tocantins like a private fiefdom) litter the capital's empty spaces, especially around Praça dos Girassóis in the city centre. Palmas is an essential jumping-off point for trips to Bananal and Jalapão and there are many waterfalls and forest trails in the surrounding hills.

Ins and outs

Palmas airport ⓘ *Av NS 5, T063-321 61237*, receives flights from Brasília, São Paulo and Belem. The airport is more than 20 km out of the town centre; taxis are around US$20 and there is an irregular shuttle bus. The **rodoviária** ⓘ *ACSUSO 40, T061-216 1603*, is 10 km from the centre; city buses are plentiful and cheap.

The city is divided into four sectors: **Noroeste** (NO), **Nordeste** (NE), **Sudoeste** (SO) and **Sudeste** (SE). Like Brasília, the different blocks are named by use and location. Some address abbreviations are **Área Central** (AC), **Área de Comércio** and **Serviço Urbano** (ACSU) and **Área Administrativa** (AA).

Tourist information is available from **ADETUR** ⓘ *Praça dos Girassóis, T061-3218 2015*, on the northeast side of the *praça*.

Sights

It is worth spending a few hours wandering across the **Praça dos Girassóis**, which lies in the city centre – an enormous grassy square dotted with monuments and imposing public buildings. The most impressive is the **Palácio Araguaia** ⓘ *Praça dos Girassóis*, a massive government palace topped with a golden globe that looks like it has been dragged here from North Korea. It is surrounded by other monuments; most whiff of totalitarianism. The state's founding *caboclo* pioneers hold their arms up in adulation as if they had discovered the promised land; Carlos Prestes – the communist leader who was, bizarrely, much admired by the fascist governor and state founder, José Wilson Siqueira Campos – stands with his troops around a tattered flag. And Siqueira Campos is everywhere, immortalized by himself out of love for the people of Tocantins, on plaques and public buildings. There's a forgotten Niemeyer building too – a long low rectangle next to the Prestes sculpture, also built in homage to the leader.

Excursions from Palmas

» 629-630.

There are numerous waterfalls in the nearby **Serra do Lajeado**, most of them reached via light trails through primary rainforest rich with birdlife. These include the **Cachoeira de Taquaruçu** near the town of the same name, **Macaco** and **Brejo do Chiqueiro**. The first trail to the falls is at Km 18 on the Estrada do Rio Negro. At Km 36 there are trails along the river to the **Brejo da Lagoa** waterfall and eventually to the 60-m-high **Cachoeira do Roncador**. Most of the falls have deep pools good for swimming. About 8 km away at Canelas is the **Praia da Graciosa**, a beach on the River Tocantins, with floating bars, sports courts, shows, and a campsite. It is particularly busy at weekends.

Jalapão

→ *Colour map 1, B5.* *Phone code 062.*

Jalapão is one of the highlights of a visit to the Brazilian interior: table-top mountains tower over seemingly endless plains covered in *caatinga* and *cerrado* forest, fast-flowing blackwater rivers lead to plunging waterfalls, sweeping sand dunes, bubbling clear-water springs and sleepy *caboclo* villages. The air so clear you can see clearly for over 100 km and, other than the Serra dos Confusões in Piauí, there is probably nowhere in Brazil where *sertão* and *cerrado* is more pristine. It is still possible to see the world's rarest large parrot, spix's macaw, in the stands of *buriti* palms and one of the world's rarest water birds, the Brazilian merganser duck, on the smaller rivers. There's plenty of other wildlife too, best seen at dawn and in silence (avoid trips with Brazilian groups if possible). Maned wolf, giant anteater and white-tailed deer are numerous and there is a healthy population of all the larger cat species.

Jalapão is a six-hour drive from Palmas on the border of Tocantins, Piauí, Maranhão and Bahia. At present only **Korubo**, www.korubo.com.br, offers trips here, staying at their very comfortable safari camp next to one of the larger rivers (see page 630 for details.). Self-drive is possible, though only with a 4WD; prepare as if for the Australian outback, with plenty of spare fuel, two ropes and at least 20 litres of water. There is simple accommodation in the scattered small towns.

Ilha do Bananal

→ *Colour map 1, B5.* *Phone code 062.*

ⓘ *Permission to visit the park should be obtained in advance from Ibama, R 219, No 95, Setor Universitário, 74605-800, Goiânia. Access is through the small but pleasant town of Santa Teresinha (see page 664). It is far easier, however to visit on an organized trip with Bananal Ecotour in Palmas, www.bananalecotour.com.br.*

Bananal is the world's largest river island and is located on the northeastern border of Mato Grosso. The island is formed by a division in the south of the Rio Araguaia and is approximately 320 km long. The entire island was originally a national park (called Parque Nacional Araguaia), which was then cut in half and later further reduced to its current size of 562,312 ha. But there are still plenty of wild areas that are rich in fauna, several permanent lakes, marshland areas and seasonally flooded habitats similar to those in the Pantanal. The vegetation is a transition zone between the *cerrado* (woody savannah), *varzea*, *igapó*, Amazon *terra firme* forest and gallery forest.

The fauna is also transitional. More than 300 bird species are found here, including the hoatzin, hyacinth macaw, harpy eagle and black-fronted piping guan. The giant anteater, maned wolf, bush dog, giant otter, jaguar, puma, marsh deer, pampas deer, Brazilian tapir, yellow anaconda and South American river turtle can also be spotted. The island is flooded most of the year, with the prime visiting time being the dry season from June to early October, when the beaches are exposed.

Sleeping

Palmas *p627, map p627*

AL Pousada das Artes, 103 Sul, Av, LO1 78, T063-3219 1500, www.arteshotel.com.br. Very comfortable, well-kept a/c rooms with marble and mosaic bathrooms, restaurant, sauna and swimming pool. Only the master suite has external windows.

A Hotel Arataú, Av JK 104 Norte 123, T063-3215 5323, hotelaratau@bol.com.br. Newly opened hotel with spacious tiled rooms; the best are on the upper floors.

A Pousada dos Girassois, Av NS 1, 103 Sul, conj 03, lote 44, T063-3219 4500, www.pousadadosgirassois.com.br. Overlooking the main grassy square. Rooms are small and modern with a/c and cable TV but tiny windows. Very good restaurant. The departure point for **Korubo**'s Jalapão tours.

B Hotel Roma, Av LO2-104 Norte, lote 23, T063-3215 3033. Pleasant, intimate little hotel with bright and airy tiled rooms in terracotta and cream. Internet access.

C Carvalho's, Av 103 Sul, SOO1, lote 11, T063-3215 5758. Modest, well-kept a/c en suites some with no external windows.

D-E Alfredo's, Av JK, 103 Sul, Qd 101, lotes 23/24, T063-3215 3036. Simple fan-cooled and a/c rooms gathered around a little garden courtyard visited by hummingbirds. Trips to the Ilha do Bananal and Jalapão. Cheapest with 4 or more people.

Ilha do Bananal *p628*

A Bananal, Praça Tarcila Braga 106, CEP 78395 (Mato Grosso), with full board. There is only room for 10 people so reserve well in advance, either by mail, allowing several months for the mail to get through.

There is some simple accommodation for scientists at the park, which can sometimes

be reserved at the address above or from the national parks department in Brasília. Bring your own food and bedding. The severely underpaid but dedicated staff appreciate any extra food or financial help, although it will not be solicited. A boat to the park can be arranged at **Hotel Bananal**, above.

Eating

Palmas *p627, map p629*

TT Cabana do Lago, Praia da Graciosa, T063-3215 6055. Local fish grills and sauce dishes like *tucunaré* (peacock bass) and Goiás meat dishes like *carne do sol* beef and guinea fowl in coconut milk. Overlooking the river.

T Dom Virgilio, Av JK 103, Norte 159, T063-3212 1400. Great buffet lunch with generous salads and pizzas in the evening.

T Paço do Pão, Av JK 154, 103 Sul, T063- 3215 5665. Very good, large wood-fired pizzas.

Shopping

Palmas *p627, map p629*

Na Natureza, Av JK 103 Sul, Conj 01, lote 150, Sala 04, T063-3215 2391. Beautiful baskets and earrings in Capim Dourado, indigenous ceramics and bead necklaces and bracelets made with Amazonian and *cerrado* seeds.

Palm Blue Shopping, ACSUSO 10, Conj 2.

Activities and tours

Palmas *p627, map p629*

Tour operators

Also see pousada **Carvalho's**, Sleeping, above.

Bananal Ecotour, quadra 103 Sul Conjunto 02, lote 02, sala 03, T063-3219 4200/ T063-3219 4201, www.bananalecotour.com.br. Expeditions to Bananal and to the waterfalls and trails around Palmas.

Korubo Expeditions, São Paulo, T011-3667 5053, www.korubo.com.br. Excellent but expensive tours into Jalapão. Guides are very good (specialist wildlife guides should be booked in advance) and accommodation is in very comfortable African-style safari tents with beds. Activities available and included in the price are whitewater rafting, treks, 4WD tours, wildlife spotting and visits to typical Jalapão villages. Avoid going with a large group of Brazilians as noise means wildlife spotting is difficult.

Ilha do Bananal *p628*

See **Bananal Ecotour** in Palmas, above. Bananal can be visited from São Félix do Araguaia (with permission from Funai in the town) by crossing the river to the Carajá village of Santa Isabela de Morra and asking to see the chief, who can tell you the history of the tribe. The island can be crossed from São Félix to São Miguel de Araguaia by taking an 8-hr trip. From São Miguel, a 5-hr bus trip brings you to Porangatu (**D Hotel Mauriti**, restaurant) on the Belém-Brasília highway.

Transport

Palmas *p627, map p629*

Air Daily flights to **Brasília**, **São Paulo** and **Belem** with Gol, www.voe gol.com.br and TAM, www.tam.com.br. Offices at the airport.

Boat The port is 9 km from the city. Ferries to **Miracema do Tocantins** and **Paraíso do Tocantins**.

Bus Buses to Brasília often run via the Chapada dos Veadeiros. To **Brasília** (12 hrs), **Belem** (10 hrs), **Goiânia** (14 hrs), **Salvador** (20 hrs), **São Luís** (14 hrs) and **Teresina** (12 hrs).

Car hire Hertz, Av Nossa Senhora, T063-3978 1900, F215 1900, and **Localiza**, ACSO 11-CL02, lote 41, Setor comercial, T063-216 1104, and airport. **Rentauto**, Av Joaquim Teotônio Segurado (ASUSE10), Conj 1, Lt 6, T/F063-215 1900.

Taxi Rádio Táxi Palmas, T063-213 2001.

Directory

Palmas *p627, map p629*

Medical services Dentist Dra Adriana Helena Toledo, ACNO 11, Conj 3, lote 38, T063-215 3201. **Hospital Regional**, Praça ARSE, Quadra 51, Setor Serrano, T063-214 1424.

Post office Av Joaquim Teotônio Segurado.

The Pantanal

Footprint features

Introduction

The Pantanal, which is an enormous seasonally-flooded wetland on the borders of Brazil, Paraguay and Bolivia, is the best place in the Americas for spotting wild animals, and one of the best places in the world to see birds. Capybara, anaconda, peccary, giant otter, metre-long macaws and ocelots are common sights and it is even possible to see that most elusive of South American mammals, the jaguar. At the end of the dry season, between June and August, the number of water birds, raptors and parrots has to be seen to be believed. Visiting the wetlands is easy with a large choice of camping tours from Campo Grande, Cuiabá, Corumbá or Miranda; or the more comfortable option of staying at one of the *fazenda* ranch houses that are increasingly opening their doors to tourists. Families with children will enjoy the little resort town of Bonito, which is famous for its clear-water rivers and caves, and makes a good base for visiting the Pantanal.

The Pantanal lies within two Brazilian states: Mato Grosso do Sul and Mato Grosso. Until the second half of the 20th century these were little-explored wildernesses of table-top mountains, *cerrado*, savannah and dense rainforest. The famous British explorer, Colonel Percy Fawcett, was lost, and perhaps murdered, in the forests of the Xingu, and Theodore Roosevelt contracted a fatal disease on an expedition here in previously uncharted territory. These days, even the Pantanal is grazed by cattle, and the great Amazonian forests of northern Mato Grosso state are steadily giving way to soya beans, planted for the vegetarians of the USA and Europe and the kitchens of China. However, substantial pockets of forest still remain for now, particularly around the Rio Cristalino near the town of Alta Floresta, where one of the best jungle lodges in the Americas can be found.

★ Don't miss...

1 **Fazendas around Miranda** Stay on a working ranch and see thousands of birds, caiman and capybara. On a night safari you might be lucky enough to spot jaguars and ocelots, page 651.

2 **Camping in Nhecolândia** Set off on a camping and trekking trip from Corumbá to see a wealth of wildlife from giant anteaters to capybara, page 655.

3 **The Transpantaneira** Drive along this dirt road through the heart of the Pantanal for great wildlife-watching and stay overnight in a *fazenda*, page 662.

4 **Alta Floresta and the Rio Cristalino** Stay in comfort in a rainforest hotel or jungle lodge on a small Amazon tributary and enjoy some of the best bird and wildlife watching in the Amazon Basin, page 663.

The Pantanal

The Pantanal UNESCO biosphere reserve is the world's largest freshwater wetland and one of the best places on Earth for seeing wildlife, particularly birds. Within Brazil it comprises a plain of around 21,000 sq km but the Pantanal extends beyond Brazil into Bolivia, Paraguay and Argentina to form an area totalling 100,000 sq km. The plain slopes 1 cm in every kilometre north to south and west to east to the basin of the Rio Paraguai and is rimmed by low mountains. From these, 175 rivers flow into the Pantanal and after the heavy summer rains they burst their banks, as does the Paraguai itself, to create vast shallow lakes broken by patches of high ground and stands of cerrado *forest. Plankton then swarm on the water to form a biological soup that contains as many as 500 million micro algae per litre. Millions of amphibians and fish spawn or migrate to consume them. And these in turn are preyed upon by waterbirds and reptiles. Herbivorous mammals graze on the stands of water hyacinth, sedge and savannah grass and at the top of the food chain lie South America's great predators – the jaguar, ocelot, maned wolf and yellow anaconda. In June, at the end of the wet season, when the sheets of water have reduced, wildlife concentrates around the small lakes or canals and then there is nowhere on Earth where you will see such vast quantities of birds or such enormous numbers of crocodilians. Only the plains of Africa can compete for mammals and your chances of seeing a jaguar or one of Brazil's seven other species of wild cat are greater here than anywhere else on the continent.*

Background

To the indigenous groups who arrived in the area tens of thousands of years before the Europeans, the Pantanal was a sea, which they called Xaraes. Myths about this sea quickly reached the ears of the Spanish and Portuguese *conquistadores*, who set out to explore it. As if to presage the future, the first to arrive, in 1543, was a Spaniard called Cabeza de Vaca (Cow Head) who complained about the swarms of mosquitoes and vampire bats and promptly turned westward into the Paraguayan *chaco*. The fate of the Pantanal and its myriad indigenous residents was left to the ruthless Portuguese and their *bandeirantes*. Apart from a few skirmishes they left the Pantanal alone for 200 years but, then, gold was discovered glittering in a stream called the 'river of stars', or Cuiabá, by the local people. A settlement was established and soon the Portuguese were scouring the area for native slave labour for their mines. The *indígena* were understandably aggrieved at this and two of the fiercest tribes, the Guaicurú and the Paiaguá, combined forces to attack the Portuguese. Their tactics were highly effective: they worked in small guerrilla bands, laying ambushes when the Europeans least expected it. The Guiacurú were horsemen, charging into battle naked but for jaguar skins, clubs, lances and machetes; crouched low on their stolen Andalusian horses, or riding on the horse's sides rather than their backs and thus invisible to the Portuguese. They used no saddles or stirrups and had just two chords for reins. The Paiaguá attacked by water and were excellent swimmers, advancing in their canoes and then leaping into the water and using the sides of the boats as shields. They would then suddenly right their boats and fire several volleys of arrows during the time the *bandeirantes* fired one. They soon defeated the Europeans, regaining control of the Pantanal for almost 100 years. The Portuguese were furious and accused the Guaicurú in particular of dishonourable tactics. "They fight only to win," the Portuguese claimed, "attacking only when the enemy seemed weaker". The Guiacurú responded by exposing the hypocrisy of the Portuguese: "Since the Portuguese and Spaniards claim to go to heaven when they die, they do well to die quickly. But, since they also claim

The plight of the Guaraní

"On my land, cattle is worth more than Indians. The cattle stomp on their gardens and tractors knock down their houses. The rivers are dirty with the waste from large farms in the region; pesticides, mercury. They finished with our forests, they are finishing with what is left of our savannahs. For this reason young Guaraní are killing themselves, they are searching for the end, hanging themselves." (Marta Silva Vito Guaraní, President of the Kaguateca Association for Displaced Indians in an address to the US House of Representatives, 10 May 1994.)

The Guaraní in Brazil, one of the country's largest indigenous groups, are suffering terribly from the theft of almost all their land. Nowhere is their plight more urgent than in the Pantanal, where thousands of Guaraní-Kaiowá live crowded onto tiny plots hemmed in by ranches and plantations. The surrounding ranch land has long been hunted and farmed by the tribe but has been forcibly taken from them by gunmen hired by ranch owners. One community, which has a federal act recognizing its right to 1240 ha of land, is crammed into an area of barely 60 ha, hemmed in by electric fences and patrolled by armed guards. They are forced by these men to work as cheap labour on the land that has been stolen from them. The situation has proved intolerable for many young Guaraní. More than 300 have committed suicide since 1986, drinking a mixture of rum and pesticide. The youngest was only nine years old.

In desperation, the tribe began to campaign internationally in the 1990s, and one group was granted land rights by the Brazilian government in 2002. But the law has not been upheld. Many Guaraní groups were forced from the little land they had, their homes were burnt and, in early 2003, Marcos Veron, a 70-year-old shaman, leader of the Guaraní-Kaiowá and land rights campaigner, was beaten to death by thugs employed by the ranchers who had taken over his homeland, Takuára.

In January 2004 a group of several thousand *indígena*, enraged by lack of activity from the government, invaded several farms close to Brazil's border with Paraguay. The ranch owners fled in fear. The invasions were widely reported in the international press, forcing the Brazilian government to promise to review the tribe's land rights in Matto Grosso do Sul. What will happen remains to be seen.

that the Guiacurú go to hell after death, in that case the Guiacurú want to die as late as possible." (John Hemming, *Red Gold*).

But through subterfuge the pact was broken and in 1734 the Portuguese regained control by means of a devastating ambush which decimated the Paiaguá. The tribes then retreated into the depths of the Pantanal where their numbers slowly diminished as a result of punitive *bandeirantes* expeditions, inter-tribal conflict and European diseases. Today Pantaneiros boast of their proud traditions, which are barely three generations old. Nearly 25 million of their cattle roam the Pantanal and the true indigenous Pantaneiros have largely disappeared. Of the 25,000 Guiacurú present in 1500, some 200 survive in their Kadiweu and Mbayá subgroups. The Paiaguá have been reduced to a sad remnant living on an island reservation near Asunción in Paraguay. Other tribes, such as the Parecis, who were enslaved in the mines, fared even worse and, of the great indigenous groups of the Pantanal, only the Bororo, who allied with the Portuguese, retain any significant numbers. Even their traditions have been greatly damaged by the aggressive missionary tactics of the Salesians in the 20th century.

Wildlife and vegetation → See also Ecology and conservation, page 638.

Wildlife

Mammals Outside Africa there is nowhere better for seeing wild mammals than the Pantanal, especially between July and late September. During this time, there are groups of capybara – the world's largest rodent – at just about every turn. Critically endangered marsh deer (who have webbed feet to help them run through the swamp), or their more timid cousins, the red brocket, and the pampas deer wander in every other stretch of savannah alongside giant anteaters. Few visitors leave without having seen both species of wild pig (the solitary collared and herd-living white-lipped peccaries), giant otters and at least one species of cat. Lucky visitors may even see a jaguar or tapir. There are at least 102 mammal species here and, although most of them are bats (including vampires), the list includes eight of South America's 10 wild cats, four dog species and numerous primates ranging from the tiny palm-sized pygmy marmoset to South America's second largest primate, the red howler monkey. For further information on the best places to watch wildlife in Brazil, see page 58.

The cats are usually top of everyone's most-wanted list. The largest is the jaguar (most easily seen here at **Fazenda San Francisco**, in the south or on the Transpantaneira), followed by the more elusive puma, which has the widest distribution of any feline in the world. Even more common is the retriever-sized ocelot and the tawny or black jaguarundi, which is about twice the size of a domestic cat, though more slender. The most elusive creature is the pampas cat, which has a fawn body and striped legs, but scientists are yet to agree on its species. The other cats are all spotted and are, in size order, the margay, geoffroy's cat (the most hunted in the America's) and, the most beautiful of all, the oncilla or tiger cat.

Other carnivores include crab-eating foxes, coatis and racoons (who often hang around the *fazendas* at night), the maned wolf, and short-eared and bush dogs (found in the drier semi-deciduous forests). Monkeys are not as varied here as they are in the Amazon, but visitors will hear or see red or black howlers, the smaller brown capuchin and possibly the pygmy or silvery marmoset. Other species present include various titi monkeys and night monkeys, which are most easily seen around **Fazenda Bela Vista** on the Estrada Parque in the south. Woolly monkeys can be found in the dry forests.

Reptiles After birds, the easiest animals to see in the Pantanal are caimans, of which the dominant species is the jacaré caiman, a smaller sub-species of the spectacled caiman found in the Amazon. Jacaré caiman reach a maximum length of about 1½ m. Yellow anaconda, the world's heaviest snake, are abundant but difficult to see; your best chance is on the Estrada Parque in the south, which they frequently cross during the day. Other snakes, the majority of which are not venomous, are also abundant but hard to spot. The venomous species, which include pit vipers, such as the fer de lance or jararaca, are nocturnal.

Birds There are over 700 resident and migratory bird species in the Pantanal. Birding on the Transpantaneira road in the north or at one of the *fazendas* in the south can yield as many as 100 species a day. From late June to early October the vast numbers of birds have to be seen to be believed. Try to visit as many habitat types as possible and, as well as trail-walking, jeep rides and horseback excursions, be sure to include river trips in your itinerary. Night safaris will maximize sightings of rarer herons, such as the boat-billed, agami and zigzag, and the numerous nightjars and potoos. Specialities in the Pantanal include the world's largest parrot – the metre-long hyacinth macaw, the golden-collared macaw, blue-fronted parrot, blue-crowned nanday, blaze-winged and green-cheeked parakeets, the giant flightless rhea, chestnut-bellied and spix's guan, crowned eagle, bare faced currasow and helmeted manakin.

Remember to bring good optical gear and a field guide. A book such as Nigel Wheatley's *Where to watch birds in South America* can give far greater detail than this book has space for. ▸▸ *For other recommended birding guides, see Books, page 714.*

Vegetation

Although the Pantanal is often described as an ecosystem in its own right, it is actually made up of many habitats, which have their own, often distinct, biological communities. The Pantanal is of recent geological origin and has very few endemic plant species. Botanically it is a mosaic: a mixture of elements from the Amazon region including *varzea* and gallery forests and tropical savannah, the *cerrado* of central Brazil and the dry *chaco* region of Paraguay.

Pantanal cerrado forest The *cerrado* is found both in the upland areas, which are not prone to flooding, and in some areas that may be inundated for a short period. It is dominated by the cerrado pequi tree (*Caryocar brasiliense*) whose fruits have a famous spiny interior, the legume *Bowdichia virgiloides* and the sandpaper tree (*Curatella americana*). But the most conspicuous trees in the *cerrado* are Tabebuia (*ipê* or trumpet trees); these are characterized by their brilliant colours (indigo in *Tabebuia impetignosa* and yellow in *Tabebuia aurea*) and no leaves in the dry season. Sometimes these trees stand as the dominant species in vast areas of semi-agrarian parkland. Within the dry *cerrado* are numerous stands of bocaiúva palm (*Acrocomia aculeate*) characterized by its very spiny trunk and leaves. Its fruit is an important food source for macaws and larger parrots. In the wetter *cerrado* are numerous islands of dense savannah forest or *cerradão*, often thick with acuri palm (*Attalea phalerata*), whose woody fruit is the principal food for the hyacinth macaw and, when fallen, for peccaries (bush pigs or, in Portuguese, *javalo*) and agouti (rabbit-sized, tailless rodents; *cutia* in Portuguese). *Cerrado* habitats are also important refuges for the larger sheltering mammals, such as jaguar and tapir, who will flee into the densest wet *cerrado* to escape predators.

Semi-deciduous tropical forest This taller, denser forest occurs on higher ground such as the Serra do Bodoquena south of Miranda, and comprises a mix of species from the Paraguayan *chaco* and the Amazon. For instance jutai (*Hymenaea courbaril*), from which the sacred copal resin is extracted, comes from the Amazon; whilst the monkey-ear plant (*Enterolobium contortisquam*), easily recognized by its curved seed pods, is a common *chaco* species. More primate species can be found here than elsewhere in the Pantanal, together with many smaller toucans, such as the chestnut eared aracari, and rare mammals, like bush dog (*Cachorro vinaigre*) and tayra (*Iara*).

Swamp and seasonally flooded land This varies greatly, from Amazonian habitats characterized by riverine forests such as *varzea* (seasonally flooded riverbank forest) to seasonally flooded grassland and palm savannah dominated by carunda palm trees. Alongside these are permanently marshy areas and open lakes and oxbows thick with floating plants. This diversity of habitatsmeans a great diversity of species and nowhere is better than these areas for seeing large concentrations of birds and mammals. *Varzea*, which is best seen by canoe or paddle boat, is good for mammals such as tapir and giant otter, and for riverine birds like the southern screamer (*tachã*), the five species of Brazilian kingfisher (*Martim pescador*), black-collared hawks (*Gaviao belo*) and the myriad species of heron and stork, including the giant 1.2-m-tall jabiru (*tuiuiu*). Apart from *varzea*, much swampland is dominated by the papyrus-like sedge *cyperus giganteus* or reed mace (*Typha dominguensis*) or by floating plants like water hyacinth (*Eichhornia crassipes*), which caiman and capybara use as cover.

For a full list of species recorded in the Pantanal, see WWF's wildfinder web page, www.worldwildlife.org/wildfinder.

 Xeric vegetation This permanently dry scrub forest found in elevated areas is dominated by *chaco* species such as various types of cacti (such as *Cereus peruvianus* and *Opuntia stenarthra*) together with the swollen-trunked, baobab-like pot-bellied chorisia (*bombacaceae*). Many distinct species occur here, including one of the world's rarest cats, the pampas cat, and rare birds, such as black-legged seriemas and *chaco* earthcreepers.

Ecology and conservation

Only one area of the Pantanal is officially a national park, the 135,000-ha **Parque Nacional do Pantanal Matogrossense** in the municipality of Poconé, only accessible by air or river. You can obtain permission to visit from **Ibama** ⓘ *R Rubens de Mendonça, Cuiabá, T065-644 1511/1581*. Hunting is strictly forbidden throughout the Pantanal and is punishable by four years' imprisonment. However, most *fazendeiros* regularly shoot and kill jaguar, many locals still offer their services as jaguar hunters and some landowners even allow illegal private hunts. Fishing is allowed with a licence, US$25, according to strict quotas. It is not permitted in the spawning season or *piracema* (1 October to 1 February in Mato Grosso do Sul; 1 November to 1 March in Mato Grosso). There are also restrictions on the size of fish that may be caught, but poaching is rife and there are plans to halt all fishing for four years due to severe stock depletion. Application forms are available from **Banco do Brasil** or **Ibama Campo** ⓘ *T067-3782 2966, www.sema.ms.gov.br*, or ask travel agents for latest details; see Fishing, page 57. Catch and release is the only kind of fishing allowed on rivers Abobral, Negro, Perdido and Vermelho. Like other wilderness areas, the Pantanal faces significant threats to its integrity. Agrochemicals and *garimpo* mercury, washed down from the neighbouring *planalto*, are a hazard to wildlife.

The **International Union for the Conservation of Nature** (**IUCN**), www.iucn.org, is concerned at the amount of poaching, particularly of *jacaré* skins, birds and capybara. The forestry police have built control points on all major access roads to the Pantanal. Biologists interested in research projects in the area should contact the **Coordenador de Estudos do Pantanal** ⓘ *Departamento de Biologia, Universidade Federal do Mato Grosso do Sul, Campo Grande, T067-3787 3311 ext 2113*, or the **IUCN** about their **Fazenda Rio Negro programme** ⓘ *T067-3326 0002, www.fazendarionegro.com.br*, or **Projeto Gadonça** ⓘ *Fazenda San Francisco, www.fazendasanfrancisco.tur.br*.

Visitors can make an important contribution to protecting the Pantanal by acting responsibly and choosing guides accordingly. Take your rubbish away with you, don't fish out of season, don't let guides kill or disturb fauna, don't buy products made from endangered species, don't buy live birds or monkeys, and report any violation to the authorities. The practice of catching caiman, even though they are then released, is traumatic for the animals and has potentially disruptive long-term effects.

Ins and outs

Getting there and around

The Pantanal can be reached from both Mato Grosso and Mato Grosso do Sul states. In Mato Grosso access is from the capital city, Cuiabá (which has an airport). In Mato Grosso do Sul it is from either the state capital, Campo Grande (where there is also an airport); from Corumbá (connected to the rest of Brazil by bus and train and on the border with Bolivia); or from the little cattle ranching town of Miranda (connected to the rest of Brazil by bus and train), which lies between them.

There are three ways to visit the Pantanal. The cheapest (and most popular with backpackers) is to take an **organized tour**. These generally involve camping, with a possible night or so in a *fazenda* (or ranch house), and a range of activities, including hiking, canoeing and wildlife and birdwatching. Guides tend to emphasise light adventure and have reasonable general knowledge of the Pantanal but poor knowledge of specific plants or animals.

Another option is to organize a tour through a **fazenda**. Although some are very modest, *fazendas* are generally comfortable with air-conditioned rooms and good home cooking. Many (if requested in advance) can organize decent wildlife guides who know English and scientific names for birds and animals. *Fazendas* can also be booked through tour operators, such as **Impactotour** in Campo Grande, **Aguas do Pantanal** in Miranda or **Natureco** in Cuiabá.

It is also possible to visit the Pantanal on a **self-drive tour**, by hiring a 4WD in Cuiabá or Campo Grande. Those considering this option should speak good Portuguese and stick to the two principal dirt roads that enter the Pantanal – the Transpantaneira in Mato Grosso and the Estrada Parque in Mato Grosso do Sul.

For further information on the Pantanal, consult www.braziltour.com, www.braziltourism.org, www.turismo.ms.gov.br, www.sedtur.mt.gov.br.

Visiting the Southern Pantanal → *For details see Mato Grosso do Sul, page 641.*

Access to the southern Pantanal is from Campo Grande (see page 629), Miranda (see page 646) and Corumbá (see page 646), all in Mato Grosso do Sul.

Campo Grande offers most of the tours, both upmarket (through agencies such as **Impacto**) and budget (**Ecological Expeditions** or **Green Track**). Touts for the budget operators are ready and waiting for buses arriving from destinations in eastern Brazil like Foz do Iguaçu.

Corumbá, near the Bolivian border, was once the capital of backpacker tourism in the Pantanal but, although many of the budget operators maintain offices here and cheap tours can be readily organized, the town is now used more as a departure point for boat trips. (For more information on this, see Choosing a budget tour, page 640.)

Miranda lies half way between Campo Grande and Corumbá at the turn off to Bonito. It is still a Pantanal ranching town free of touts, and the best of the *fazendas* (ranch house safari hotels) are situated close to here. There are two excellent operators and the town is friendly and relaxed. Although there are excellent *fazendas* off the Estrada Parque road, there are also an increasing number opening up to tourism around Miranda. These include the stylish, upmarket **Refúgio Ecológico Caiman**, the closest thing central Brazil has to a Mexican hacienda (and similarly beloved of the chic) and **Fazenda San Francisco**, which is probably the best spot in the entire Pantanal for big cats, especially ocelot, which you can almost be guaranteed to see. ⏩ *For further information, see Sleeping, page 650, and Activities and tours, page 654.*

Many of the tours and some of the *fazendas* lie off a dirt road running off the BR262 Campo Grande to Corumbá highway. This road, which is known as the **Estrada Parque**, begins halfway between Miranda and Corumbá at a turn-off called Buraco da Piranha (the Piranha hole), heads north into the Pantanal and then, after 51 km, turns west to Corumbá at a point called the Curva do Leque. This is the overland access point to **Nhecolândia** – a region particularly rich in wildlife. Four-wheel drives run by the tour operators or the *fazendeiros* wait at the Buraco da Piranha to meet tour buses arriving from Campo Grande. They then take visitors either to *fazendas* or to campsites in Nhecolândia. *Fazendas* in this area include **Fazenda Rio Negro**, a project run in conjunction with Conservation International; **Fazenda Bela Vista**, which has a wealth of primates; and **Fazenda Rio Vermelho**, which is famous for sightings of the larger carnivores.

Choosing a budget tour

Most tours include accommodation in lodges and activities such as 'safari' jeep trips, riverboat trips, piranha fishing and horse riding. A two-day trip, with a full day taken up with travel, allows you to experience most of what is on offer. Extended tours tend to have the same activities spread out over a longer period of time. The best way to enjoy a tour is not to have fixed expectations about what you will see, but to take in the whole experience that is the Pantanal.

Budget travellers are often approached in the streets or at the cheaper hotels by salesmen who speak their language and promise tours at low prices; they then hand their clients over to agencies, who often speak only Portuguese, and may deliver something quite different. Some travellers have reported unpleasant experiences, so it is important to select a guide with great care. Although we list a few of the most reputable guides, there are other good ones and most travellers enjoy a pleasant experience.

➔ Speak with other travellers who have just returned from a tour and ask for recommendations. Most guides also have a book containing comments from their former clients.
➔ Do not rush to sign up when first approached; always compare several available alternatives.
➔ Always ask who will lead the party and how big it will be. Less than four is not economical; there will be cuts in boats or guides.
➔ Do not pay everything in advance and try to deal directly with agencies or guides, not salesmen (it can be difficult to tell who is who).
➔ Discuss the planned itinerary carefully and try to get it in writing (this is seldom possible); threaten to go to someone else if necessary.
➔ Always get an itemized receipt.
➔ Act responsibly and don't expect to get something for nothing.

What to take Most tours arrange for you to leave your baggage in town, so you need only bring what is necessary for the tour. In winter (June-August), temperatures fall to 10°C; warm clothing and sleeping bag are needed at night. It's very hot and humid during summer and a hat and high-factor sun protection is vital. This is available cheaply in the larger towns. Wear long sleeves and long trousers and spray clothes as well as skin with insect repellent. Insects are less of a problem in July and August. Take insect repellent from home as mosquitoes, especially in the northern Pantanal, are becoming immune to local brands. Drinks are not included in the price of packages and tend to be overpriced, so if you are on a tight budget bring your own. Most importantly, make sure you take a pair of binoculars. See also Tour operators, pages 654 and 667.

Visiting the Northern Pantanal ➔ *For details see Mato Grosso, pages 658.*

There are two main access points to the northern Pantanal: the **Transpantaneira road** (see page 662), which cuts through the wetland and is lined with *fazendas*; and the town of **Barão de Melgaço** (see page 663), which is surrounded by large lakes and rivers and is not as good for wildlife. Both are reached from Cuiabá in Mato Grosso.

The Transpantaneira was built in 1976 and was originally planned to connect Cuiabá with Corumbá, but it currently goes only as far as the border at Porto Jofre on the Rio Cuiabá. Work was suspended indefinitely ostensibly because of the division of the two Mato Grosso states. The road is a superb spot for wildlife watching. Hundreds of thousands of birds congregate here (particularly between June and September) to wade through the shallow wetlands to either side of the road. And at any time of year there seems to be a raptor on every other fence post. Mammals and reptiles can often be spotted crossing the road or even sitting on it, particularly at dawn and dusk. Most of the northern Pantanal's tourist-orientated *fazendas* are found here. The road is unpaved, potholed and punctuated by numerous rickety wooden bridges and, although it can be driven in a standard hire car, progress is slow. It is probably better to see the Transpantaneira via a tour as most of the guides have access to the *fazendas* along the way. If you choose to go alone, be sure to book in advance; private individuals who turn up unannounced may or may not be welcome, depending on the *fazenda*.

The easiest access is in the dry season (July to September). In the wet, especially January and February, there is no guarantee that you will get all the way to Porto Jofre. Bring plenty of water and some extra fuel as petrol stations often run out. If you choose not to take a tour or hire a car you can hitch a ride along the Transpantaneira from Poconé. Do not travel alone and be prepared for a bumpy ride in the back of a truck. ▸▸ *For further information, see Sleeping, page 664, Activities and tours, page 667, and Transport, page 669.*

When to go

The Pantanal is worth visiting at any time of year. However, the dry season from June to October is the ideal time for wildlife as animals and birds congregate at the few remaining areas of water. This is also the breeding season, when birds form vast nesting areas, with thousands crowding the trees, creating an almost unbearable cacophony of sounds. The white-sand river beaches are exposed, *jacarés* bask in the sun, and capybara frolic in the grass. During these months you are most likely to see jaguars. July sees lots of Brazilian visitors and the increased activity decreases the chances of sightings. From the end of November to the end of March (wettest in February), most of the area, which is crossed by many rivers, is subject to flooding. At this time mosquitoes abound and cattle crowd onto the few islands remaining above water. In the southern part, many wild animals leave the area, but in the north, which is slightly higher, the animals remain.

Mato Grosso do Sul

Mato Grosso do Sul is dominated by the Pantanal wetlands in the north and by the low Serra da Bodoquena mountains in the south, which surround the family-orientated ecotourism town of Bonito. The mountains are honeycombed by caves and cut by numerous glassy clear streams. There are only a few towns of any size and the state is a centre of soya plantations and cattle ranching. Many of the designated backpacker tours of the Pantanal leave from the state capital, Campo Grande, which is a prosperous, modern city with lively nightlife. However, they take half a day to reach the Pantanal itself, which begins in earnest east of Campo Grande, near the cattle-ranching town of Miranda. Many of the best fazenda ranch houses in the Pantanal lie near this town and there are a handful of small, upmarket tour operators. Miranda also has one of the Pantanal's liveliest festivals, O Festa do Homen Pantaneiro, in November. The town of Corumbá, on the banks of the Rio Paraguai, is another popular departure point for the Pantanal, and lies close to the Estrada Parque dirt road (which runs through the wetlands) and to Nhecolândia, a wilderness area visited by most of the Campo Grande backpacker tours. ▸▸ *For Sleeping, Eating and other listings, see pages 648-657.*

Campo Grande

» pp648-657.

→ *Phone code: 067. Colour map 3, C3. Population: 665,000.*

A major gateway to the Pantanal, Campo Grande is a pleasant, modern city on a grid system, with wide avenues. It was founded in 1899 and became the state capital in 1979. Because of the *terra roxa* (red earth), it is called the 'Cidade Morena'.

In the centre is a shady park, the **Praça República**, commonly called the Praça do Rádio after the Rádio Clube on one of its corners. Three blocks west is **Praça Ari Coelho**. Linking the two squares, and running east–west through the city, is the broad Avenida Afonso Pena; much of its central reservation is planted with yellow *ypé* trees. In spring, their blossom covers the avenue, and much of the city besides. The Avenida's eastern reaches are the centre of a burgeoning restaurant and nightlife scene. City tours are on offer everywhere but they are generally expensive and there are few obvious sights.

Ins and outs

Getting there The **airport** ⓘ *Av Duque de Caxias, 7 km, T067-3368 6000*, receives flights from Cuiabá, Londrina, São Paulo and Santa Cruz in Bolivia. A bus leaves every 10 minutes from outside the airport terminal for the city centre and bus station. A taxi costs US$6, 10 minutes. It is safe to spend the night at the airport if you arrive late. Banco do Brasil at the airport exchanges dollars; the Bradesco just outside has a Visa ATM. The airport also has a tourist information booth (little English, many pamphlets), a post office, car rental and airline offices.

Campo Grande is well connected by bus to cities in the southern Pantanal and onwards to Bolivia and Paraguay, and to São Paulo, Cuiabá and Brasília/Goiânia. The **rodoviária** ⓘ *in the block bounded by R Barão do Rio Branco, R Vasconcelos Fernandes, R Dom Aquino and R Joaquim Nabuco, T067-3383 1678*, has shops, *lanchonetes* and a cinema, US$1.25, together with a number of budget tour operators for the Pantanal. At

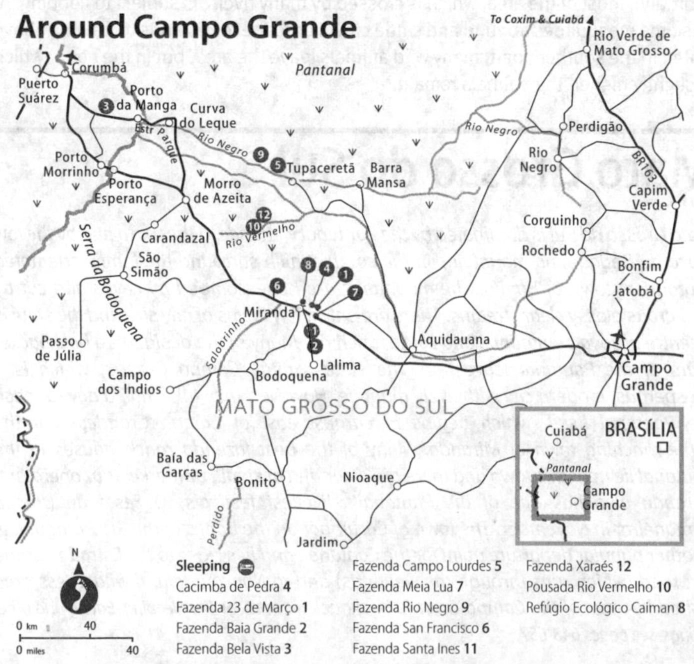

The Pantanal Mato Grosso do Sul

the Rua Vasconcelos Fernandes end are town buses, at the Rua Joaquim Nabuco end state and interstate buses. A taxi to Praça República costs US$4, or it's a 1-km walk.

The BR-262 is paved most of the way from Campo Grande to Corumbá and the Bolivian border; a rail service along this route is due to recommence in early 2007 and is likely to be expensive. It is best to make this journey during the day to take advantage of the marvellous scenery. ▸▸ *See Transport, page 656.*

Tourist information The municipal **Centro de Informação Turística e Cultural** ⓘ *Av Noroeste 5140, corner of Afonso Pena, T067-324 5830, Tue-Sat 0800-1900, Sun 0900-1200*, is housed in Pensão Pimentel, a beautiful mansion built in 1913. It sells maps and books and has a database of services in the city and cultural information.

Sights

Just north of the Praça República, is the **Museu Dom Bosco** ⓘ *Av Alfonso Pena, Parque Naçoes Indígenas, T067-3312 6491, www.museu.ucdb.br, Tue-Sat 0800-1800, Sun 0800-1200 and 1400-1700, US$1.50*, which contains relics of the tribes who suffered at the hands of aggressive Salesian missionaries in the early and mid-20th century. The largest collections are from the Tukano and Bororo people from the upper Rio Negro and Mato Grosso respectively, both of whose cultures the Salesians were responsible

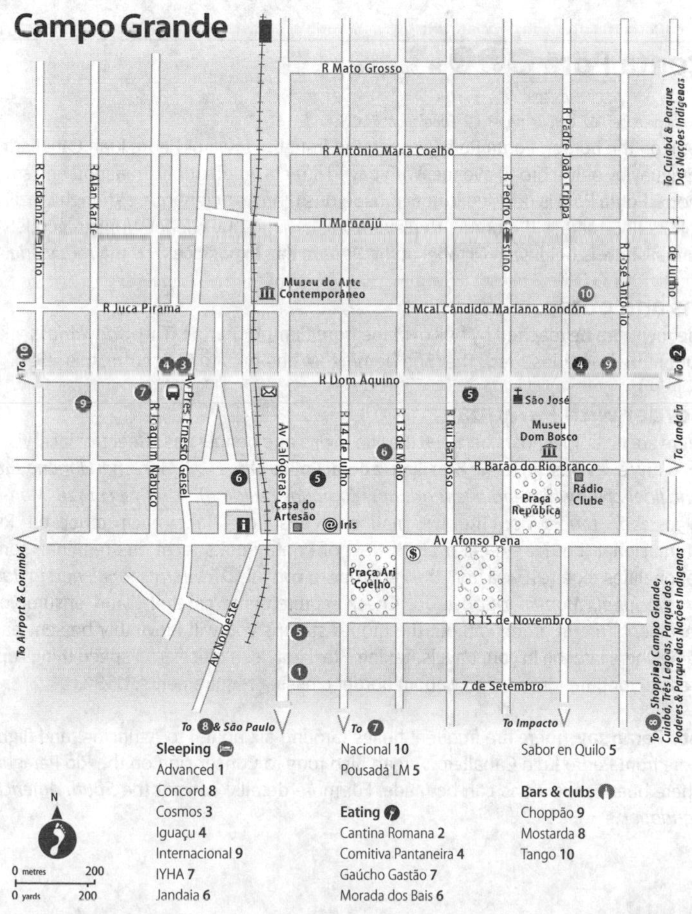

Sleeping
Advanced 1
Concord 8
Cosmos 3
Iguaçu 4
Internacional 9
IYHA 7
Jandaia 6
Nacional 10
Pousada LM 5

Eating
Cantina Romana 2
Comitiva Pantaneira 4
Gaúcho Gastão 7
Morada dos Bais 6
Sabor en Quilo 5

Bars & clubs
Choppão 9
Mostarda 8
Tango 10

for almost completely wiping out. Traditional practices such as sleeping in *malocas* or wearing indigenous clothing were banned, and the *indígena* were indoctrinated in rigorous, literalistic pre-Vatican II Catholicism. These exhibits sit alongside a rather depressing display of stuffed endangered species (mostly from the Pantanal), as well as peculiarities such as a two-headed calf, and seashells from around the world.

Next to the railway line, the **Museu do Arte Contemporâneo** ⓘ *Marechal Rondón and Av Calógeras, Mon-Fri 1300-1800, free*, displays modern art from the region.

The **Parque dos Poderes**, a long way from the centre, covers several hectares. As well as the Palácio do Governo and state secretariats, there is a small zoo for rehabilitating animals from the Pantanal. Contact the **Centro de Reabilitação Silvestres (CRAS)** ⓘ *T067-3326 1370*, to arrange a visit. There are many lovely trees in the park, along with cycling and jogging tracks. Plenty of capybara live in the lakes.

Coxim

➔*Phone code: 067. Population: 28,500.*

Coxim, 242 km north of Campo Grande on the BR-163 and halfway between Campo Grande and Rondonópolis, also provides access to the Pantanal. It sits in a green bowl, on the shores of the Rio Taquari. The area has great potential for tourism, with waterfalls nearby at Palmeiras, and the Pantanal in close proximity. But as yet there are no official tours other than a few small charter boat operators at the town port. There are a few hotels including some cheap options around the bus station.

Ponta Porã

» pp648-657.

➔*Phone code: 067. Colour map 3, C2. Population: 54,000.*

Right on the border, Ponta Porã is separated from the town of Pedro Juan Caballero in Paraguay by only a broad avenue. With paved streets, good public transport and smart shops, Ponta Porã is decidedly more prosperous than its neighbour, although Brazilian visitors flock across the border to play the casino and buy cheaper foreign goods. An animal show is held each October at the **Parque das Exposições**, by the *rodoviária*.

Ins and outs

The town can be reached by bus or plane from Campo Grande. The *rodoviária* is 3 km out on the Dourados road. The 'São Domingos' bus runs to the centre, taxi US$3.

Border with Paraguay

There are no border posts between the two towns and people pass freely for local visits. For entry/exit visas, go to the **Brazilian Federal Police office** ⓘ *R Marechal Floriano 1483 (2nd floor of the white engineering supply company building), T067-3431 1428, Mon-Fri 0730-1130, 1400-1700.* The two nations' consulates face each other on Rua Internacional (border street), a block west of Ponta Porã's local bus terminal; some nationalities require a visa from the **Paraguayan consul** ⓘ *R Internacional, next to Hotel Internacional, Mon-Fri 0800-1200*. Check requirements carefully, and ensure your documents are in order; without the proper stamps you will inevitably be sent back somewhere later on in your travels. Taking a taxi between offices can speed things up if pressed for time; drivers know about border crossing requirements, US$7.

Into Paraguay There are frequent buses (around six hours) to Asunción, and flights there from Pedro Juan Caballero. A road also runs to Concepción on the Rio Paraguai, where boat connections can be made. For more details, consult the *South American Handbook*.

Bonito and around » pp648-657.

→Phone code: 067. *See also map page 649. Colour map 3, C2. Population: 17,000.*

The designated tourist town of Bonito lies just south of the Pantanal in the **Serra da Bodoquena** hills. It is surrounded by beautiful *cerrado* forest cut by clear-water rivers rich with fish and dotted with plunging waterfalls and deep caves. The town was 'discovered' by *Globo* television in the 1980s and has since grown to become Brazil's foremost ecotourism destination. There are plenty of opportunities for gentle adventure activities such as caving, rafting and snorkelling, all with proper safety measures and great even for very small children. Those looking to see animals and contemplate nature should opt for the forest walks of the Sucuri river. Despite the heavy influx of visitors, plenty of wildlife appear on and around the trails when it is quiet. Paca and agouti (large, tailless foraging rodents), brown capuchin monkeys and toco toucans are abundant, as are endangered species like the tiny and aggressive bush dog and cats such as ocelot and jaguarundi. Bare-faced currasows (magnificent turkey-sized forest floor birds) can often be seen strutting around the pathways. Rarely seen small toucans like the chestnut-eared aracari are relatively easy to spot here, flitting in and out of the trees.

Ins and outs

Getting there and around The *rodoviária* is on the edge of town. Several buses daily run to/from Campo Grande (five hours), Miranda and Corumbá. Bonito town is a grid based around one principal street – Rua Coronel Pilad Rebuá which extends for about 2 km and is easily negotiated on foot. » *See Transport, page 656.*

Tourist information The **tourist office** ⓘ *Praça Rachid Jauli, www.bonito-ms. com.br* or www.guiabonitopantanal.com.br, has limited information and staff do not speak English. Prices in Bonito have risen sharply over the years, making the area prohibitively expensive for those on a budget. Local attractions can only be visited with prior booking through one of the town's numerous travel agents. With the exception of specialist activities like cave diving, all agents offer exactly the same products at exactly the same price, but only a few offer transport, see Activities and tours, page 655. Taxis to the sights are exorbitantly expensive; an alternative would be to hire a car (see page 656).

Best time to visit The number of visitors to Bonito is limited so pre-booking is essential during December and January, Carnaval, Easter and July; prices during these times are very high. The wet season is in January and February; December to February are the hottest months; July and August coolest.

Sights

Lagoa Azul ⓘ *26 km from Bonito, US$10 municipal tax*, is a cave with a lake 50 m long and 110 m wide, 75 m below ground level. The water's temperature is 20°C, and it is a jewel-like blue, as light from the opening is refracted through limestone and magnesium. Prehistoric animal bones have been found in the lake. The light is at its best in January and February, from 0700 to 0900, but is fine at other times. A 25-ha park surrounds the cave. **Nossa Senhora Aparecida cave** has superb stalactites and stalagmites and can be visited, although there is no tourism infrastructure.

The **Balneário Municipal** ⓘ *on the Rio Formoso, 7 km on road to Jardim, US$4*, has changing rooms, toilets, camping, swimming in clear water and plenty of colourful fish to see. Strenuous efforts are made to keep the water and shore clean. **Horminio waterfalls** ⓘ *US$1*, consist of eight falls on the Rio Formoso, suitable for swimming. There's a bar and camping is possible. **Rafting** is also a popular activity (see Activities and tours, page 655). The 2½-hour trip combines floating peacefully downriver, swimming and shooting down the four waterfalls.

The **Aquário Natural** ⓘ *US$25*, is one of the springs of the Rio Formoso. Here you can swim and snorkel with five types of fish (remove suntan oil before swimming). Birding and swimming or snorkelling in crystal-clear water from the springs of the **Rio Sucuri** to its meeting with the Formoso makes for a peaceful tour (US$10). Other tours include **Aquidaban**, a series of waterfalls in dense forest, and **Rio da Prata** ⓘ *US$24*, a beautiful spring with underground snorkelling for 2 km. Parrots and animals can be seen on the trip. There are also plenty of chances for walking along ecological trails, horse riding and fishing trips. The **fishing** season is from 1 March to 31 October. In late October and early November is the *piracema* (fish run). The fish return to the spawning grounds and hundreds can be seen jumping the falls.

Jardim

Jardim, reached by paved road (60 km from Bonito), has a wide, tree-lined main street. There is a handful of hotels and basic café-restaurants in town. The *rodoviária* operates **Cruzeiro do Sul** buses. From Bonito a road leads to **Porto Murtinho**, where a boat crosses to Isla Margarita in Paraguay (entry stamp available on the island).

Miranda » pp648-657.

→ Colour map 3, B2. See also map page 650. Population: 23,000.

This little farming town built around a now disused mill and a railway station lies some 200 km west of Campo Grande at the turn-off to Bonito. It has long been overlooked as a gateway to the Pantanal and Bonito, but is actually far closer to both than either Corumbá or Campo Grande. Many of the best of the southern Pantanal *fazendas* are found here: **San Francisco** has an impressive big cat project and almost guaranteed ocelot or jaguar sightings, while **Refúgio Ecológico Caiman** would sit comfortably within the pages of *Condé Nast Traveller*. Miranda is also a real town, preoccupied more with its own local economy and culture than it is with tourism. It lies in the heart of indigenous Terena land and the communities have a large **cultural and arts centre** ⓘ *at the entrance to town, Mon-Fri 0700-2200, Sat and Sun 0800-2200, free*, with panels on Terena history and arts and crafts for sale. Every October Miranda throws the spectacular **Festa do Homem Pantaneiro**: four days of rodeos, lassoing and general revelry that combine well with the water festival in Corumbá. For dates ask tour operators (see page 655). The crystal-clear river Salobrinho just outside town has great birdlife and a community of giant otters. There is a wonderful British girder bridge just west of town given as a gift to Brazil by King George V.

Ins and outs The Campo Grande–Corumbá road crosses the Rio Miranda bridge (two service stations before it), then continues paved all the way to cross the Rio Paraguai. Miranda is served by numerous daily buses from Corumbá, Campo Grande and Bonito. There is a tourist booth just outside the *rodoviária*, opposite the **Zero Hora** bakery and supermarket. Rail services to Corumbá, onwards to Bolivia and eventually to Campo Grande are due to recommence in 2006/2007. The town is tiny and can be walked from end to end in less than 10 minutes.

Corumbá » pp648-657.

→ Phone code: 067. Colour map 3, B1. Population: 95,000.

Situated on the south bank of the Rio Paraguai, by a broad bend, 15 minutes from the Bolivian border, Corumbá has long been considered the best starting point for visiting the southern part of the Pantanal. While many tour operators have moved to Campo Grande, Corumbá offers trips by boat or jeep and access to the major hotel and farm accommodation. Almost all of the Campo Grande agencies have offices here and there are still a number of upmarket cruise companies along the waterfront.

Corumbá was one of South America's most important river ports in the 19th century and has beautiful views along the river, especially at sunset, and some remnant colonial architecture. The compact streets include the spacious **Praça da Independência** and **Avenida General Rondon** (between Frei Mariano and 7 de Septembro), which has a palm-lined promenade that comes to life in the evenings. The **Forte Junqueira,** the city's most historic building, which may be visited only through a tour agency, was built in 1772. In the Serra do Urucum hills to the south is the world's greatest reserve of manganese, now being worked.

Ins and outs

The **airport** is 4 km west of town and receives flights from Campo Grande, Cuiabá, Londrina and São Paulo (via Campo Grande). There is no public transport from the airport to town; you have to take a taxi, US$6. The **rodoviária** is on Rua Porto Carreiro at the south end of Rua Tiradentes, next to the railway station. A city bus to Praça da República costs US$0.80. Taxis are extortionate, but moto-taxis charge only US$0.65. Corumbá is well connected by bus to Campo Grande (see page 629) and Bolivia.

The municipal tourist office, **Sematur** ⓘ*R América 969, T067-231 7336*, provides general information and city maps. The combination of economic hard times since 1994 and drug running make the city unsafe late at night.

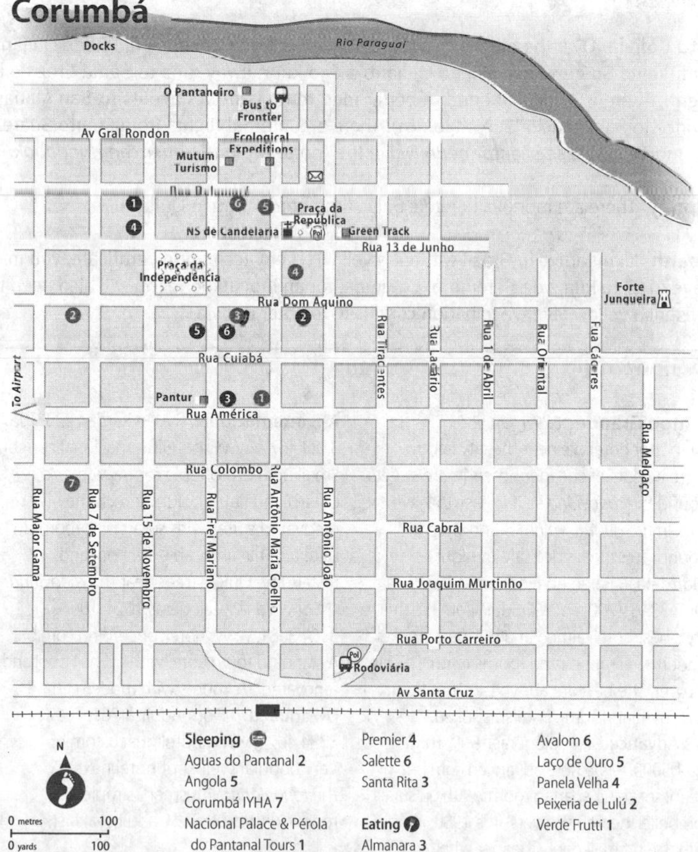

There is a lively festival every October. Corumbá is hot (particularly between September and January), with 70% humidity; June and July are cooler. Mosquitoes can be a real problem from December to February.

Border with Bolivia

Immigration Immigration formalities are constantly changing, so check procedures in advance at the tourist office or *polícia federal*. At present passports are stamped at the *rodoviária* Monday to Friday 0800-1130 and 1330-1700, and at the **Brazilian Polícia Federal** (Praça da República 37, Corumbá) at weekends 0800-1130 and 1330-1700. The visa must be obtained on the day of departure. If exiting Brazil in order to get a new visa, remember that exit and entry must not be on the same day.

Transport Leaving Brazil, take Canarinho city bus marked 'Fronteira' from the port end of Rua Antônio Maria Coelho to the Bolivian border (15 minutes, US$0.35), walk over the bridge to Bolivian immigration (blue building), then take a *colectivo* to Quijarro or Puerto Suárez. Taxis to the border cost US$6-8.

When entering Brazil from Quijarro, take a taxi or walk to the Bolivian border to go through formalities. Just past the bridge, on a small side street to the right, is the bus stop for Corumbá. Take bus marked 'Fronteira' or 'Tamengo' to Praça da República (US$0.80, every 45 minutes 0630-1915); don't believe taxi drivers who say there is no bus. Taxi to the centre US$6. Find a hotel then take care of Brazilian immigration formalities at the *polícia federal*, see above.

Into Bolivia Over the border from Corumbá are Arroyo Concepción, Puerto Quijarro and Puerto Suárez. From Puerto Quijarro a 650-km railway runs to Santa Cruz de la Sierra. There is a road of sorts. A better road route is from Cáceres to San Matías, thence to San Ignacio (see page 661). There are internal flights from Puerto Suárez. For more details, see *Footprint Bolivia* or the *Footprint South American Handbook*.

Money There are money changers only at the border and in Quijarro.

Health If you arrive in Brazil without a yellow fever vaccination certificate, you may have to go to Rua 7 de Setembro, Corumbá, for an inoculation. You will also need to present a yellow fever vaccination certificate to enter Bolivia.

Sleeping

Campo Grande *p629, map p643*
The better hotels lie near the city centre. There are lots of cheaper hotels in the streets around the *rodoviária* so it is easy to leave bags in the *guarda volumes* and shop around. This area is not safe at night.

L Jandaia, R Barão do Rio Branco 1271, T067-3316 7700, www.jandaia.com.br. The city's best hotel, aimed at a business market. Modern well-appointed rooms (with IDSL) in a tower. The best are above the 10th floor. Pool, gym and some English spoken.

A-B Advanced, Av Calógeras 1909, T067-3321 5000, www.hoteladvanced.com.br. Clean, spacious, spartan rooms with en suites and boiler-heated showers, in a 1980s block with a very small pool. Cheaper with fan.

A-B Internacional, R Alan Kardec 223, T067-3384 4677, www.hotelinternacional.com.br. Small but comfortable rooms with a/c or fans and flatpack furniture, or newly renovated suites with smart bathrooms in slate and tile and cable TV. Pool and restaurant. Quiet street near the *rodoviária*.

C Concord, Av Calógeras 1624, T067-3384 3081, www.hotelconcordinn.com.br. A standard town hotel with a small pool and renovated a/c rooms with modern fittings.

D-E Iguaçu, R Dom Aquino 761, T067-3384 4621, www.hoteliguacu.com.br. Very popular well-kept hotel next to the *rodoviária* with smart, simple a/c rooms with cable TV. Good breakfast.

D-E Nacional, R Dom Aquino 610, T067-3383 2461, hotelnacional@ig.com.br. Quiet, well-kept hotel with simple rooms with fans and proper mattresses. Some en suites. TV room and internet. Better value than the nearby IYHA.

E IYHA, R Joaquim Nabuco 185, opposite *rodoviária*, T067-3321 0505, ajcampo grande@hotmail.com. Simple, musty little rooms with saggy foam mattress beds and frayed en suites. Laundry, kitchen, internet, reception open 24 hrs. **Ecological Expeditions** (see Activities and tours) offers Pantanal trips from their office next door. The other IYHA at R Barão Rio Branco 343, T067-3325 6874, has marginally better rooms for 10% more, but the mattresses are still hot and foamy.

E-F Cosmos, R Dom Aquino 771, near the *rodoviária*, T067-3384 4270. Very simple but bright and well-kept 1980s rooms with decent mattresses and en suites.

E-F Pousada LM, R 15 de Novembro 201, by Praça Ari Coelho, T067-3321 5207, www.lmhotel.com.br. Tiny, basic en suites set around a courtyard, all with TV and fridge, some with terraces. Cheaper with fan.

Ponta Porã *p644*

Brazilian hotels include breakfast in tariff; Paraguayan ones do not.

A-B Barcelona, R Guia Lopes 45, T067-3431 3061, www.hotelbarcelonapp.com.br. Simple but well kept, with a/c or fan-cooled rooms. Bar and sauna.

C Alvorada, Av Brasil 2977, T067-3431 5866. With a good café, close to post office, good value but often full.

C-D Internacional, R Internacional 1267, T067-3431 1243. Cheaper without a/c. Hot water, good breakfast. Recommended.

E Dos Viajantes, across park opposite the railway station. Very basic and only for those on the tightest budget.

Bonito *p645, map p649*

AL Pira Miuna, R Luís da Costa Leite 1792, T067-3255 1058, www.piramiunahotel.com.br. Huge, ugly brick building with the most comfortable a/c rooms in the centre and a large pool area with jacuzzis and a bar.

AL Pousada Olho d'Água, Rod Três Morros, Km 1, T067-255 1430, olhodagua@vip2000.net. Comfortable accommodation in fan-cooled cabins set in an orchard next to a small lake. Horse riding, bike rental, solar-powered hot water and great food from the vegetable garden. Recommended.

A Tapera, Estrada Ilha do Padre, Km 10, on the hill above the Shell station on the road to Jardim, T/F067-3255 1700. Peaceful location with fine views and cool breezes. Very comfortable, but own transport an advantage.

C Canaã, R Col Pilad Rebuá 1376, T067-255 1282. A scruffy lobby leads to gloomy though reasonably well-maintained 1980s motel-style rooms with a/c and en suites.

C-E Albergue do Bonito, R Lúcio Borralho 716, Vila Donária, T/F067-255 1462, www.ajbonito.com.br. **IYHA** youth hostel. Pool, kitchen and laundry facilities. English spoken, very friendly. Price per person for dorms.

C-E São Jorge Hostel, R Col Pilad Rebuá 1605, T067-3255 1956, www.pousadasaojorge.com.br. Clean dorms with bunks and en suites (the best with 2 bathrooms) and a pleasant public dining area with snack bar. Price per person for dorms.

D Pousada Muito Bonito, R Col Pilad Rebuá 1448, T/F067-3255 1645. Price per person in en suites or dorm-style rooms with bunk beds, all with a nice shared patio. Clean, excellent and with helpful owners. The price includes breakfast. Mario Doblack at the pousada's tour office speaks English, French and Spanish. Warmly recommended.

Camping

Ilha do Padre, 12 km north of Bonito, US$10 by taxi, T/F067-255 1430. On an island with natural pools, very pleasant, no regular transport. 4 rustic cabins with either 4 bunk beds or 2 bunks and a double, US$10 per person. Youth hostel with dorms, US$6 per person, same price for camping. Toilets, showers, clothes washing, meals available, bar, electricity, lots of trees. You can swim anywhere. To enter the island for a day US$3.

Poliana, on Rio Formosa, 100 m past Ilha do Padre, T067-2551267. Very pleasant site.

Miranda *p646, map p650*

A-D Aguas do Pantanal, Av Afonso Pena 367, T067-242 1242, www.aguasdopantanal.com.br. Much the best in town with a good range of very comfortable a/c rooms and cheaper backpacker accommodation, an attractive pool surrounded by tropical flowers and a very helpful travel agency (see page 655). They usually have a rep waiting at the *rodoviária*.

C Hotel Chalé, Av Barão do Rio Branco 685, T067-242 1216, hotelchale@star5.com.br. Plain a/c motel-like rooms with tiled floors and en suites, and a pool.

C Pantanal Hotel, Av Barão do Rio Branco 609, T067-3242 1068. Standard town hotel with pool and well-maintained a/c rooms with en suite, set along a gloomy corridor.

D-E Diogo, Av Barão do Rio Branco s/n, T067-242 1468. Very simple but well-kept doubles, triples and quadruples, some with a/c.

Fazendas around Miranda

Prices below include accommodation, all food and at least 2 guided trips per day. Standard packages include jeep trips, trail walks, horse riding, boat trips (where the *fazenda* has a river) and night safaris. They do not always include transfer from Miranda or the Buraco da Onca and this should be checked when booking. Unless otherwise indicated the standard of wildlife guiding will be poor, with common familial or generic names known only for animals and little awareness of species diversity or numbers. If you are looking for a specialist guide it is best to bring your own. Keen birdwatchers should request a specialist birding guide through their tour operator or *fazenda*. Also take a good pair of binoculars and some field guides (see Books, page 722). The following *fazendas* can be booked through **Impacto** in Campo Grande, page 655, or **Aguas do Pantanal Turismo** in Miranda, page 655. Tours are the same price even if you are on your own, but there are almost always other guests.

LL Refúgio Ecológico Caiman, 36 km from Miranda, reservations: T011-3706 1800, www.caiman.com.br. The most comfortable, stylish accommodation in the Pantanal in a hotel reminiscent of a Mexican hacienda. Tours and guiding are excellent. Part of the **Roteiros de Charme** group (see page 50).

AL Cacimba de Pedra, Estr Agachi, T067-9982 4655, www.cacimbadepedra.com.br. A Jacaré caiman farm and pousada in beautiful dry deciduous forest cut by trails and dotted with lakes. A/c rooms are simple but spruce and sit in front of an inviting pool. The forest is abundant with wildlife. There is a hyacinth macaw nest on the farm and tapir sightings are common.

AL Fazenda Campo Lourdes, T067-3026 5786, www.campolourdes.com.br. One of the remotest *fazendas* in the heart of wild country. Rustic but comfortable accommodation.

AL Fazenda San Francisco, turn off BR 262 30 km west of Miranda, T067-3242 3333, www.fazendasanfrancisco.tur.br. One of the best places in the Pantanal to see wild cats, which are preserved through Roberto Coelho's imaginative **Gadonça** project, www.procarnivoros.org.br, a pioneering initiative which encourages the preservation of natural big cat prey to reduce losses from jaguar kills on cattle. The scheme has been a great success. Birding is also excellent. Accommodation is simple but very well kept in rustic a/c cabins around a pool in a garden filled with rheas. There are plans to build chic new cabins. Food and guides are excellent. Birdwatchers should request Alyson (see Activities and tours, page 655) at least a week in advance.

AL Fazenda Santa Ines, Estr La Lima, Km 19, www.fazendasantaines.com.br. A very comfortable family-orientated *fazenda* overlooking an artificial lake. Tours are aimed firmly at the Campo Grande weekend market and although there is little wildlife here, food is excellent and there is a range of light adventure activities for kids.

AL-A Fazenda Baia Grande, Estr La Lima, Km 19, T067-3382 4223, www.fazendabaiagrande.com.br. Very comfortable a/c rooms set around a pool in a bougainvillea and *ipê*-filled garden. The *fazenda* is surrounded by savannah and stands of *cerrado* broken by large lakes. The owner, Alex, is very friendly, eager to please and enthusiastic.

AL-A Fazenda Meia Lua, BR-262 Km 551, T067-9988 2284, www.fazendameialua.com.br. Charming new *fazenda* with a pool, lovely garden filled with hummingbirds and accommodation in chic a/c cabins or simple a/c rooms. The owners are very friendly and attentive. Only 10 mins from Miranda, a good option for those attending the Festa do Homem Pantaneiro.

A Fazenda 23 de Março, T067-3321 4737, www.fazenda23demarco.com.br. Simple rustic *fazenda* with only 4 rooms. There are programmes orientated to budget travellers, and **Centrapan**, a centre for the preservation of Pantanal culture, where visitors can learn to lasso, ride a bronco and turn their hand to other Pantanal cowboy activities.

Fazendas on the Estrada Parque

LL-L Fazenda Xaraés, www.xaraes.com.br. One of the most luxurious *fazendas*, with a pool, tennis court, sauna, airstrip and modest but well-appointed a/c rooms in cream and terracotta. The immediate environs have been extensively cleared, but there are some wild areas of savannah and *cerrado* nearby and there are giant otter in the neighbouring Rio Abodrai.

L-AL Fazenda Bela Vista, www.pousada belavista.com.br. 12 comfortable rooms in a *fazenda* on the banks of the Rio Papagaio in the foothills of the Serra do Urucum hills. This is a transition zone between Pantanal and higher ground and the range of habitats is one of the best in the southern Pantanal, with oxbows, savannah, *cerrado*, dry deciduous forest and xeric vegetation. Bird and primate life is very rich. Guiding is good if visitors stipulate their interest in wildlife in advance.

L-AL Fazenda Rio Negro, T067-3326 0002, www.fazendarionegro.com.br. A **Conservation International** project based at a 13,000-ha farm on the shores of the Rio Negro. This is one of the oldest *fazendas* in the Pantanal with farm buildings dating from 1920. The surrounding area has stands of *cerrado* set in seasonally flooded savannah cut by the river. Guiding is good but stipulate your interest in wildlife in advance.

AL Pousada Rio Vermelho, T067-3321 4737, www.pousadariovermelho.com.br. A rustic *fazenda* in a wild area on the banks of a river famous for its population of jaguars. Simple but well-kept a/c rooms, with fridge. Organize your trip well in advance as the *fazenda* lies a long way off the Parque Estrada road.

Corumbá *p646, map p647*

There are hostels around the bus station, however this is a 10-min walk from the centre of town where most of the hotels, restaurants and tour agencies are found.

A-B Aguas do Pantanal, R Dom Aquino Corrêa 1457, T067-3231 6582, www.aguasdo pantanalhotel.com.br. The smartest in town together with the **Nacional Palace**, with a/c rooms in a 1980s tower, a pool and sauna.

A-B Nacional Palace, R América 936, T067-3234 6000, www.hnacional.com.br. Smart, modern a/c rooms, a decent pool and parking.

C-D Angola, R Antônio Maria Coelho 124, T067-3231 7727. Huge, scruffy a/c and fan-cooled rooms with en suites. Internet access. Safe as it lies in front of the *polícia federal*.

C-E Salette, R Delamaré 893, T067-3231 6246, F231 4948. Cheap and cheerful with a range of rooms, the cheapest with fans and shared bathrooms. Recommended.

D Premier, R Antônio Maria Coelho 389, T067-3231 4937. Basic pousada with small a/c rooms without windows. Prices negotiable.

D Santa Rita, R Dom Aquino 860, T067-3231 5453. Modern, well-kept hotel with a/c rooms, all with TVs and en suites.

D-E Corumbá IYHA, R Colombo 1419, T067-3231 1005, www.corumbahostel.com.br. A newly opened, well-equipped modern hostel with helpful staff and a pool. A/c or fan-cooled rooms and dorms.

Eating

Campo Grande *p629, map p643*

Local specialities include *caldo de piranha* (soup), *chipa* (Paraguayan cheese bread, sold on the streets, delicious when hot) and the local liqueur, *pequi com caju*, which contains *cachaça* (sugar-cane rum). There are many cheap restaurants around the *rodoviária* and many others in the **Shopping Campo Grande** mall, see Shopping below.

TTT Comitiva Pantaneira, R Dom Aquino 2221, T067-3383 8799. Hearty, tasty and very meaty regional dishes served by waiters in cowboy gear or as a buffet. Lunchtime only.

TTT Gaúcho Gastão, R 14 de Julho 775, T067-3384 4326. The best *churrascaria* in town, famous for its beef. Comfortable. Lunch only.

TT Cantina Romana, R da Paz, 237, T067-3324 9777. Established for more than 20 years, Italian dishes, salads and a lunchtime buffet, good atmosphere.

TT-T Sabor en Quilo, R Barão do Rio Branco 1118 and R Dom Aquino 1786, T067-3383 3911/3325 5102. Self-service per kg restaurants with plenty of choice including sushi on Sat. Lunchtime only.

T Morada dos Bais, Av Noroeste, 5140, corner with Afonso Pena, behind tourist office. Brazilian and Italian dishes, snacks and coffee served in a pretty courtyard, Lunchtime only.

Miranda *p646, map p650*
₸₸Cantina Dell'Amore, Av Barão do Rio Branco 515, T067-3242 2826. The best in town with fish, pasta and *jacaré* steak.
₸Zero Hora, Av Barão do Rio Branco at the *rodoviária*, T067-3242 1330. 24-hr snack bar, provision shop and, at the back, there's an average but good-value per kilo restaurant, with its own private waterfall.

Bonito *p645, map p649*
₸₸₸-₸₸Santa Esmeralda, R Col Pilad Rebuá 1831. Respectable Italian food in one of the few a/c dining rooms.
₸₸Cantinho do Peixe, R 31 de Março 1918, T067-3255 3381. Á la carte Pantanal fish dishes including good *pintado na telha* (grilled surubim).
₸₸Tapera, R Col Pilad Rebuá 480, T067-3255 1110. Good, home-grown vegetables, breakfast, lunch, pizzas, meat and fish dishes, opens 1900 for evening meal.
₸Da Vovó, R Sen F Muller 570, T067-3255 2723. A great per kg restaurant serving Minas and local food all cooked in a traditional wood-burning aga. Plenty of vegetables and salads.
₸Mercado da Praça, R 15 Novembro 376, T067-3255 2317. The cheapest in town – a snack bar housed in the local supermarket, offering sandwiches and juices 0600-2400.

Corumbá *p646, map p647*
Local specialities include *peixadas corumbaenses*, a variety of fish dishes prepared with the catch of the day; as well as ice cream, liquor and sweets made of *bocaiúva*, a small yellow palm fruit, in season Sep-Feb. There is a range of decent restaurants in R Frei Mariano including a number of *churrascarias* and pasta restaurants. You'll find plenty of good simple fish restaurant bars on the waterfront.
₸₸₸-₸₸Avalom, R Frei Mariano 499, T067-3231 4430. Chic little restaurant bar with streetside tables and decent pasta, pizza and fish. Buzzing with a young middle-class crowd, especially after 2100 on Fri.
₸₸Almanara, R América 961. Arabic and Turkish food from felafel to *baba ganoush*.
₸₸Laço de Ouro, R Frei Mariano 556, T067-3231 7371. Very popular fish restaurant with a lively atmosphere and tables spilling out onto the street. Similar crowd to **Avalom**.
₸₸-₸Peixeria de Lulú, R Dom Aquino 700, T067-3232 2142. A local institution that has been selling good river fish for many years.
₸Panela Velha, R 15 de Novembro 156, T067-3232 5650. Popular lunchtime restaurant with a decent, cheap all-you-can-eat buffet.
₸Verde Frutti, R Delamaré 1164, T067-3231 3032. A snack bar with a wide variety of juices and great, ice-cold *acai na tigela*.

Bars and clubs

Campo Grande *p629, map p643*
The best of the chic bars are on R Afonso Pena, beyond the monument, and along the streets to the north of Afonso Pena.
Choppão , R Dom Aquino 2331, T067-3383 9471. Lively open-sided bar with live music from Thu to Sat.
Morada dos Bais, see Eating, above. Restaurant and *choperia*, live music in the courtyard, daily from 2030, free.
Mostarda, Av Afonso Pena 3952, T067-3026 8469. Popular 20- and 30-something bar which is always lively after 2200 and hosts live music at weekends.

Clubs
There are a number of clubs open Thu-Sat, including **Tango**, R Cândido Mariano 2181, www.tangobar.com.br, and for something a little more alternative try **Bazar** or **Garagem**, R Doutor Temístocles 94.

Bonito *p645, map p649*
Bollicho Bar, R Col Pilad Rebuá 1996, T067 3255 3299. Always thronging with young people any night of the week and serving hot chocolate, *caipirinhas*, snacks and *chopp* to the sound of live music at weekends.
O Taboa, R Col Pilad Rebuá 1837, T067-3255 1862. The liveliest in town with occasional bands and good *caipirinhas* and *chopp*.

Festivals

Miranda *p646, map p650*
Mid-Oct Festa do Homem Pantaneiro, rodeos, lasso competitions, live *sertanejo* bands, barn dances and 4 days of cowboy revelry. Can be combined with Corumbá's water festival. For dates contact **Aguas do Pantanal** in Miranda (see page 655).

Corumbá *p646, map p647*
2 Feb Festa de Nossa Senhora da Candelária, Corumbá's patron saint, all offices and shops are closed.
24 Jun Festa do Arraial do Banho de São João, fireworks, parades, traditional food, processions and the main event – the bathing of the image of the saint in the Rio Paraguai.
21 Sep Corumbá's anniversary, includes a Pantanal **fishing festival** held on the eve.
Mid-Oct Festival Pantanal das Águas, with street parades featuring giant puppets, street dancing and occasional water fights.

Shopping

Campo Grande *p629, map p643*
Local native crafts, including ceramics, tapestry and jewellery, are of good quality. A local speciality is *os bugres da conceição*, squat wooden statues covered in moulded wax. Very good selections are found at **Casa do Artesão**, Av Calógeras 2050, on corner with Av Afonso Pena. Mon-Fri 0800- 2000, Sat 0800-1200. Also try: **Barroarte**, Av Afonso Pena 4329, and **Arte do Pantanal**, Av Afonso Pena 1743. There is a market (*Feira Livre*) on Wed and Sat. **Shopping Campo Grande**, Av Afonso Pena 4909, www.shoppingcampo grande.com.br, is the largest shopping mall in town, on its eastern edge.

Corumbá *p646, map p647*
Shops tend to open early and close by 1700. **Casa do Artesão**, R Dom Aquino 405, in a converted prison. Mon-Fri 0800-1200, 1400-1800, Sat 0800-1200, good selection of handicrafts and a small bookshop.
CorumbArte, Av Gen Rondon 1011. Good silk-screen T-shirts with Pantanal motifs.
Frutal, R 13 de Junho 538. Open 0800-2000. Supermarket.
Livraria Corumbaense, R Delamaré 1080. Useful for state maps.
Ohara, Dom Aquino 621, corner Antônio João. Supermarket.

Activities and tours

See also tour operators and guides for the northern Pantanal, page 667.

Wildlife guides for the Pantanal
Alyson is a Londrina-based birding guide who works with **Neblina Forest Tours**; available through Fazenda San Francisco.
Juan Mazar Barnett, T+54 (0)11-4312 6345, www.seriematours.com. Very experienced Buenos Aires-based birding guide and editor of *Cotinga* magazine. Expert on *chaco* and Pantanal birds. Book well ahead – expensive.

Campo Grande *p629*
City Tour, T067-3321 0800, or through the Campo Grande Pantanal visitor centre and most larger hotels. Half-day tours of the city's sights including the Museu Dom Bosco and the Parque das Nações Indígenas.

Tours to the southern Pantanal
Ecological Expeditions, R Joaquim Nabuco 185, T067-321 0505, www.pantanal

trekking.com. (Also in Corumbá; see below.) Attached to the youth hostel at the bus station. Budget camping trips and lodge-based trips in Nhecolândia (sleeping bag needed) for 3, 4 or 5 days ending in Corumbá. The first day, which involves travel to the Buraco da Piranha, is free.

Impacto, R Padre João Crippa 686, T067-3325 1333, www.impactotour.com.br. Very helpful Pantanal and Bonito tour operators established over 10 years. Prices vary according to standard of accommodation; a wide range is offered. 2-day packages for 2 people US$190-600. Transfers and insurance included. English spoken.

Open Door, R Alan Kardec 87, Galeria Maria Auxiliadora, sala 4, 79008-330, T067-3321 8303, www.opendoortur.com.br. Specialists in the southern Pantanal and Amazon. Booking agents for flights and buses.

Bonito and around *p645, map p649*

There is very little to choose between agencies in Bonito, who offer the same packages for the same price. English speakers are hard to come by. We list only those who also offer transport or a specialist service such as cave diving. Rafting trips cost US$15 per person, minimum 4 people for a 2½-hr trip.

Impacto, R Col Pilad Rebuá 1515, T067-3255 1414. English-speaking staff. Can be pre-booked through their efficient head office in Campo Grande or through **Aguas do Pantanal Turismo** in Miranda (see below).

Ygarapé, R Col Pilad Rebuá 1956, T067-3255 1733, www.ygarape.com.br. English spoken. PDSE accredited cave diving.

Miranda *p646, map p650*

Tours to the southern Pantanal

Both of the operators below can organize accommodation during the Festa do Homen Pantaneiro (see Festivals and events, above).

Aguas do Pantanal Turismo, Aguas do Pantanal hotel, Av Afonso Pena 367, T067-3242 1242, www.aguasdopantanal.com.br. Very well-organized tours to the *fazendas* around Miranda, to those on the Estrada Parque, and to the sights around Bonito. They also run exclusive 1- or 2-day trips on the Rio Salobrinha to the Sanctuario Baía Negra. This is a little-visited clear water river that's great for snorkelling and teeming with life – particularly birds. Expect to see 4 species of kingfisher, screamers, bare-faced currasow and cocoi, boat-billed heron and numerous other varieties, storks and ibises. Bring insect repellent. Can also organize scenic flights.

Explore Pantanal, R General Camisão 226, T067-9638 3520, www.explorepantanal.com. Run by a Kadiweu indigenous guide and his Swiss partner, with many years experience. Very good English, French, Spanish and Italian and decent Hebrew. Great for small groups who want to get off the beaten track. Prices are competitive with budget operators in Campo Grande and Corumbá.

Corumbá *p646, map p647*

Tours to the southern Pantanal

Ecological Expeditions, R Antônio Maria Coelho 78. Main office in Campo Grande.

Green Track, R Antônio João, T067-3231 2258, http://mitglied.lycos.de, with representatives in Campo Grande at their bus station office. One of the longest-established budget operators offering camping and lodge based trips to Nhecolândia starting in Campo Grande or Corumbá, where they have a budget hostel – for details see their web site.

Mutum Turismo, R Frei Mariano 17, T067-3231 1818, www.mutumturismo.com.br. Cruises and upmarket tours (mostly aimed at the Brazilian market) and help with airline, train and bus reservations.

Pantur, R América 969, T067-3231 2000, www.pantur.com.br. Packages to Bonito and the *fazendas* on the Estrada Parque, including some of the less visited, such as **Bela Vista** (the best for primates) and the luxurious **Xaraes**. Flights and bus tickets can be booked here too. Confusing website; click on the flags for tour details.

Pantanal fishing and river cruises

Pérola do Pantanal, Nacional Palace (see Sleeping), T067-3231 1470, www.peroladopantanal.com.br. Fishing and 'eco' tours on their large river boat, *Kalypso*, with options of added jeep trips on the Estrada Parque.

O Pantaneiro, R Manoel Cavassa 225, quays, T067-3231 3372, www.opantaneiro tur.com.br. Cruises on by far the most comfortable modern boat sailing out of Corumbá, with day excursions in small launches.

Transport

Campo Grande *p629, map p643*

Air City bus No 158 stops outside the airport; taxi US$6. Flights to **Cuiabá**, **Londrina**, **São Paulo** and **Santa Cruz** in Bolivia.

Airline offices The cheapest flights can be booked on line or through agencies (many in front of the *rodoviária*). BRA, www.voebra.com.br; GOL, www.voegol.com.br; TAM, airport, T067-3363 0000, www.tam.com.br; Trip, www.voetrip.com.br, airport; Varig, airport, T067-336 3487, www.varig.com.br, and at R Barão do Rio Branco 1356, Centro, T067-3325 4070.

Bus Town buses leave from the R Vasconcelos Fernandes end of the *rodaviária*, while state and interstate buses leave from the R Joaquim Nabuco end.

To **São Paulo**, US$40, 14 hrs, 9 buses daily, first at 0800, last at 2400, 3 *leito* buses US$45. To **Cuiabá**, US$25, 10 hrs, 12 buses daily, *leito* at 2100 and 2200, US$50. To **Brasília**, US$38, 23 hrs at 1000 and 2000. To **Goiânia**, with São Luís at 1100, 2000, 15 hrs on 1900 service, US$45, others 24 hrs, US$1 cheaper. **Rio de Janeiro**, US$60, 21 hrs, 4 buses daily, *leito* at 1540, US$64. To **Belo Horizonte**, 22 hrs, US$40. To **Corumbá**, with Andorinha, 8 daily from 0600, 6 hrs, US$15. Campo Grande–Corumbá buses connect with those from Rio and São Paulo, similarly those from Corumbá through to Rio and São Paulo. To **Ponta Porã**, 5 hrs, 9 buses daily, US$12. To **Dourados**, 4 hrs, 14 daily (Queiroz), US$7. Beyond Dourados is **Mundo Novo**, from where buses go to **Ponta Porã** (0530) and to **Porto Frajelli** (very frequent). From Mundo Novo, ferries for cars and passengers go to **Guaíra** for US$1. Twice daily direct service to **Foz do Iguaçu** (17 hrs) with Integração, 1600, US$27; same company goes to **Cascavel**, US$20. To **Pedro Juan Caballero** (Paraguay), **del** Amambay company, 0600, US$8.50. Amambay goes every Sun morning to **Asunción** (Paraguay).

Car hire Hertz, Av Afonso Pena 2620, T067-3383 5331. Locagrande, Av Afonso Pena 466, T067-3721 3282, F3721 3282. Localiza, Av Afonso Pena 318, T067-3382 8786, and at the airport, along with various others T0800- 992000. Unidas, Av Afonso Pena 829, T067-3384 5626, F3384 6115, at airport, T067-3363 2145.

Ponta Porã *p644*

Air Services to **Campo Grande**, **São Paulo**, **Dourados**, **Marília** and **Presidente Prudente**. See www.voetrip.com.br.

Bus To **Campo Grande**, 9 a day 0100-2130, 4 hrs, US$5.

Bonito *p645, map p649*

Bus From **Campo Grande**, US$11, 5½-6 hrs, 1500, returns at 0530. Bus uses MS-345, with a stop at Autoposto Santa Cruz, Km 60 (all types of fuel, food and drinks available). Several each day to **Miranda**. Bus Corumbá–Miranda–Bonito–Jardim–**Ponta Porã**, Mon-Sat, leaves either end at 0600, arriving Bonito 1230 for Ponta Porã, 1300 for Miranda; can change in Jardim (1400 for 1700 bus) or Miranda (better connections) for **Campo Grande**; fare Corumbá–Bonito US$12.50. Also connections on 1230 route in Bela Vista at 2000 for **Asunción** (Paraguay) and **Col Oviedo** (Paraguay). Ticket office opens at 1200.

Car hire Unidas, R das Flores s/n, T067-255 1066. Yes Rent a Car, R Senador Filinto Muller 656, T067-255 1702.

Jardim *p646*

Bus To **Campo Grande**, 0530, 1200, 1600 and 2 at night, US$10, 5 hrs. To **Bonito** (US$3.50), **Miranda** and **Corumbá** at 1130. To **Dourados**, 0600. To **Bela Vista** (Paraguayan border) 0200, 1030, 1500, 1930. To **Porto Murtinho**, 0010 and 1530 (bus from Bonito connects). To **Ponta Porã**, 0600, 1500; Sun only at 1400 to **São Paulo**.

Miranda *p646, map p650*

Bus Miranda-**Campo Grande**, 12 a day (2-3 hrs), US$12. To **Corumbá**; 10 daily (3-4 hrs), US$12. To **Bonito**, 1 daily (2-3 hrs), US$8 at 1630.

Car hire Mavel, Av Afonso Pena 31, T067-3242 1734 or through Aguas do Pantanal hotel.

Corumbá *p646, map p647*

Air Flights to **Campo Grande**, **Cuiabá**, **Londrina** and **São Paulo** (via Campo Grande).

Check whether flights between Corumbá and **Santa Cruz** (Bolivia), are still operating. If in doubt, fly to **Puerto Suárez** in Bolivia.

Airline offices TAM, T067-231 7299. Visa, T067-231 1745.

Boat The *Acurí*, a luxury vessel, sails between Corumbá and **Cáceres** once a week, US$600 including return by air. For further details, see Cáceres, page 669.

Bus Andorinha services to all points east. To **Campo Grande**, 7 hrs, US$22, 13 buses daily 0630-2400, interesting journey ('an excursion in itself') – take an early bus to see wildlife, connections from Campo Grande to all parts of Brazil. To **São Paulo** direct, 22 hrs, US$50, 1100 and 1500, confirm bus times in advance as these change (T067-231 2033). To **Rio de Janeiro** direct, 30 hrs, US$55, daily 1100. **Cruzeiro do Sul** operates the route south to the **Paraguayan border**. To **Ponta Porã**, 12 hrs, US$20, via Bonito (6 hrs, US$12.50) and Jardim (9 hrs, US$15), Mon-Sat at 0600; ticket office open 0500-0600 only, at other times call T067-231 2383.

Car hire **Localiza**, airport and R Cabral 2064, T067-231 6000. **Unidas**, R Frei Mariano 633, T/F067-231 3124.

Directory

Campo Grande *p629, map p643*
Banks **Banco do Brasil**, 13 de Maio and Av Afonso Pena, open 1100-1600, charges commission US$10 for cash, US$20 for TCs, regardless of amount exchanged. Visa ATMs at **Bradesco**, 13 de Maio and Av Afonso Pena; at **HSBC**, R 13 de Maio 2837; and at **Banco 24 horas**, R Maracaju, on corner with 13 de Junho. Also at R Dom Aquino and Joaquim Nabuco. **Overcash Câmbio**, R Rui Barbosa 2750, Mon-Fri 1000-1600. **Embassies and consulates** **Bolivia**, R João Pedro de Souza 798, T067-382 2190. **Paraguay**, R 26 Agosto 384, T067-324 4934. **Internet** **Cyber Café Iris**, Av Afonso Pena 1975, and **Cyber Café**, R Alan Kardec 374, T067-3384 5963 near the Hotel Turis. Also in the IYHA. **Medical services** Yellow and dengue fevers are both present in Mato Grosso do Sul; the former only in very remote areas. There is a clinic at the railway station, but it's not very hygienic, best to get your immunizations at home. **Post office** On corner of R Dom Aquino and Av Calógeras 2309, and Barão do Rio Branco on corner of Ernesto Geisel, both locations offer fax service, US$2.10 per page within Brazil. **Telephone** Telems, R 13 de Maio and R 15 de Novembro, daily 0600-2200.

Ponta Porã *p644*
Banks **Banco do Brasil** changes TCs. Many in the centre of town (but on Sun change money in hotels). **Bradesco** has a Visa ATM.

Bonito *p645, map p649*
Banks **Banco do Brasil**, R Luís da Costa Leite 2279 for Visa. There are no **Banco 24 Horas**. Some hoteliers and taxi drivers may change money. **Post office** R Col Pilad Rebuá. **Telephone** Santana do Paraíso.

Jardim *p646*
Banks Elia, a taxi driver, will change money; ask around.

Miranda *p646, map p650*
Banks The town has both a **Bradesco** and a **Banco do Brasil**. **Internet** **Star Informatica**, R Francisco Rebúa 149, T067-3242 2100.

Corumbá *p646, map p647*
Banks **Banco do Brasil**, R 13 de Junho 914, ATM. **HSBC**, R Delamaré 1068, ATM. **HSBC**, R Delamaré 1068, ATM. **Câmbio Mattos**, R 15 de Novembro 140, Mon-Fri 0800-1700, good rates for US$ cash, US$5 commission on TCs. **Câmbio Rau**, R 15 de Novembro 212, Mon-Fri 0800-1700, Sat 0900-1200, cash only, good rates. **Embassies and consulates** **Bolivia**, R Antônio Maria Coelho 881, T067-231 5605, Mon-Fri 0700-1100, 1500-1730. A fee is charged to citizens of those countries that require a visa. A yellow fever vaccination certificate is also required. **Internet** **Pantanalnet**, R América 430, US$2.50 per hr. **Laundry** Apae, R 13 de Junho 1377, same day service. **Post office** Main office at R Delamaré 708, fax service. Branch at R 15 de Novembro 229. **Telephone** R Dom Aquino 951, near Praça da Independência, daily 0700-2200. To phone Quijarro/Puerto Suárez, Bolivia, costs slightly more than a local call; dial 214 + the Bolivian number.

Mato Grosso

Mato Grosso, immediately to the north of Mato Grosso do Sul, shares the Pantanal with that state and has equally well-developed tourism facilities. Although there are just as many opportunities for seeing wildlife, trips to the Pantanal near the state capital, Cuiabá, tend to be more upmarket than those leaving from Corumbá in Mato Grosso do Sul.

The state also has abundant though rapidly depleting areas of Amazon forest, and Alta Floresta, in the north, has an excellent birdwatching and wildlife lodge. The much-vaunted Chapada dos Guimarães hills near Cuiabá afford reasonable walking and birdwatching, although the natural landscape has been greatly damaged by farming and development.

The area that is now Mato Grosso and Mato Grosso do Sul was first demarcated as Spanish territory, but it was the Portuguese Aleixo Garcia who was the first to explore it in 1525. Jesuits and then bandeirantes *entered the Mato Grosso for their different ends during the 17th and early 18th centuries, and, when gold was discovered near Cuiabá, a new influx of explorers began. Mato Grosso became a captaincy in 1748 and the borders between Portuguese and Spanish territories were decided in the following years. Throughout the 19th century, after the decline in gold extraction, the province's economy stagnated and its population dwindled. This trend was reversed when the rubber boom brought immigrants in the early 20th century to the north of the region. Getúlio Vargas's 'March to the West' in the 1940s brought added development, accompanied first by the splitting off of Rondônia and by the formation of Mato Grosso do Sul in 1977.* *▸▸ For Sleeping, Eating and other listings, see pages 664-670.*

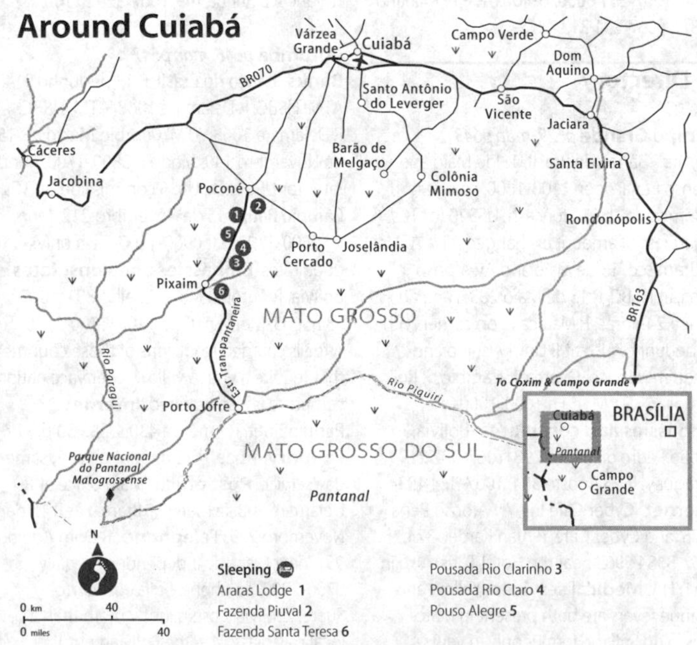

Cuiabá » pp664-670.

→ *Phone code: 065. Colour map 3, A2. Population: 470,000.*

An important starting point for trips into the Pantanal, Cuiabá is the state capital and a visibly wealthy city. It has a number of leafy praças and is known as the 'Cidade Verde' (green city). Situated on the Rio Cuiabá, an upper tributary of the Rio Paraguai, it is in fact two cities: Cuiabá on the east bank of the river, and Várzea Grande on the west. It is very hot; the coolest months for a visit are June, July and August in the dry season.

Ins and outs

Getting there Flights arrive at the **airport** in Várzea Grande, T065-682 2213. There are ATMS outside the airport, as well as a post office and **Sedtur** office. To get to the centre, take any white **Tuiuiú** bus, name written on the side, from in front of the airport to Avenida Tenente Coronel Duarte. Taxis cost US$15. Interstate buses arrive at the **rodoviária**, north of the centre at Rua Jules Rimet, Bairro Alvorada. Town buses (see below) stop at the entrance of the *rodoviária*. » *See also Transport, page 669.*

Getting around Many bus routes have stops in the vicinity of Praça Ipiranga. Bus Nos 501 or 505 ('Universidade') to the university museums and zoo (ask for 'Teatro') leave from Avenida Tenente Coronel Duarte by Praça Bispo Dom José, a triangular park just east of Praça Ipiranga.

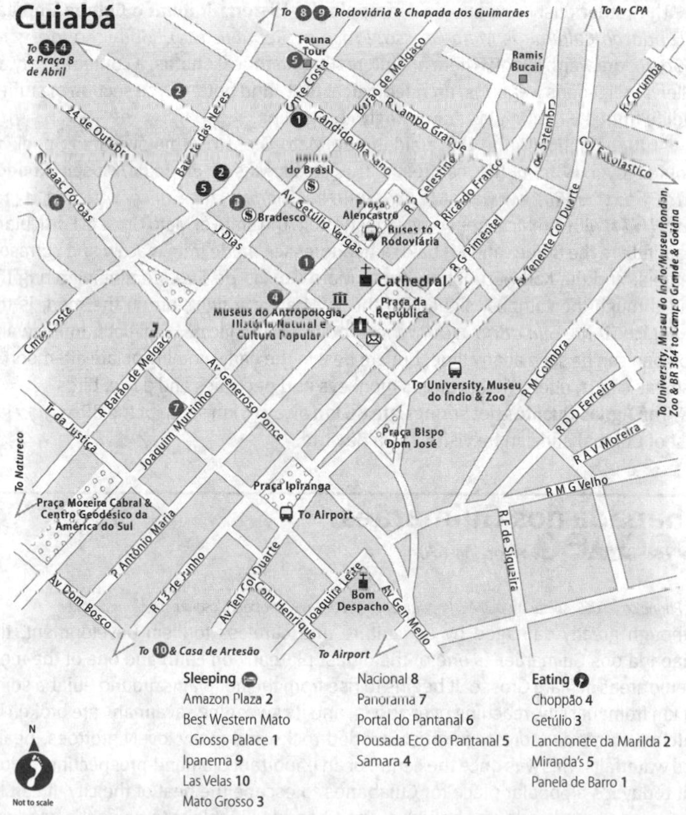

Tourist information Sedtur ⓘ *Praça da República 131, next to the post office building, T/F065-624 9060, Mon-Fri 0700-1800*, provides maps and general information on hotels and car hire. Staff are friendly and speak English and Spanish. They are very helpful in settling disputes with local tour companies. **Ramis Bucair** ⓘ *R Pedro Celestino 280*, is good for detailed maps of the region.

Sights

The most pleasant public space in Cuiabá is the lush **Praça da República** which is surrounded by a cluster of imposing buildings and dotted with sculptures and shady trees. Other pedestrian shopping streets and further squares lead off the praça. The brutalist façade of the **cathedral**, flanked by two functionalist clock towers, dominates the square. Until the late 1960s a beautiful 18th-century baroque church stood here but this was demolished to make way for the current building in a sweep of modernization that saw almost all the city's colonial charm destroyed.

On **Praça Ipiranga**, at the junction of avenidas Isaac Póvoas and Tenente Coronel Duarte, a few blocks southwest of the central squares, there are market stalls and an iron bandstand from Huddersfield in the UK, or Hamburg in Germany, depending on which story you believe.

On a hill beyond the square is the extraordinary church of **Bom Despacho**, built in the style of Notre Dame. It is best viewed from afar as it is sadly run down and not open to visitors. In front of the Assembléia Legislativa, Praça Moreira Cabral, is a point marking the **Geodesic Centre of South America** (see also under Chapada dos Guimarães, below).

The rather dusty **Museus de Antropologia, História Natural e Cultura Popular** ⓘ *Fundação Cultural de Mato Grosso, Praça da República 151, Mon-Fri 0800-1730, US$0.50*, are worth a look. There are interesting historical photos, a contemporary art gallery, indigenous weapons, archaeological finds and pottery. The section of stuffed wildlife from the Pantanal is disturbingly compelling.

At the entrance to the Universidade de Mato Grosso by the swimming pool, 10 minutes by bus from the centre, is the small **Museu do Índio/Museu Rondon** ⓘ *T065-3615 8489, www.ufmt.br/ichs/museu_rondon, Tue-Sun 0800-1100, 1330-1700, US$1*, with artefacts from tribes mostly from the state of Mato Grosso. Particularly beautiful are the Bororo and Rikbaktsa headdresses made from macaw and currasow feathers, and the Kadiwéu pottery (from Mato Grosso do Sul). Continuing along the road through the campus, signed on the left before a right turn in the road, is the **Zoológico** ⓘ *Tue-Sun 0800-1100, 1330-1700, free*. The jacaré, capybara, tortoise and tapir pen can be seen at any time, but are best in the early morning or late afternoon. It also has coatis, otters, rhea, various monkeys and peccaries and a few, birds.

The **Águas Quentes** hot springs are 86 km away (9 km south of the BR-163, 77 km east of Cuiabá) and can be visited as a day trip.

Chapada dos Guimarães

» *pp664-670.*

→ *Phone code: 065. Colour map 3, A2. Population: 13,500. www.chapadadosguimaraes.amm.org.br*

Although greatly damaged by agriculture and careless tourism development, the Chapada dos Guimarães is one of the oldest plateaux on Earth and one of the most scenic areas in Mato Grosso. It begins to rise from the hot plains around Cuiabá some 50 km from that city, reaching over 700 m, and its sweeping savannahs are broken by patches of *cerrado* forest, curiously eroded rocks and many lovely grottoes, peaks and waterfalls. This was once the centre of an important diamond-prospecting region, but today it's a popular place for Cuiabanos to escape the heat of the city. It can be very busy on weekends and holidays. The Chapada lays claim to being the geodesic heart of the South American continent and about 8 km east of Chapada dos Guimarães town, at the **Mirante do Ponto Geodésico**, there is a monument officially marking this. It overlooks a great canyon with views of the surrounding plains, the Pantanal and Cuiabá's skyline on the horizon. The region is shrouded in lore. Crystals abound, as do UFO spotters, and the rocks are said to have peculiar energizing properties. All is not as far fetched as it may at first seem: a local magnetic force that reduces the speed of cars has been documented here.

When travelling north of Cuiabá, yellow fever vaccination is obligatory; if you do not have a certificate, you may need to be (re)vaccinated.

Birdwatching here is fruitful, particularly as enthusiasts will find that the plateau, grassland and *cerrado* species complement those found in Alta Floresta and the Pantanal. Guides listed under the northern Pantanal (see page 668) can organize one- or two-day trips here and many are even based in the little town of Chapada dos Guimarães. Mammals, such as puma, jaguarundi, giant river otter and black-tailed marmoset can also be seen.

Chapada dos Guimarães town

The pleasant town of Chapada dos Guimarães, 68 km northeast of Cuiabá, is the most convenient and comfortable base for excursions. It has the oldest church in the Mato Grosso, **Nossa Senhora de Santana** (1779), a bizarre blending of Portuguese and French baroque styles, and a huge spring water public **swimming pool** ⓘ *R Dr Pem Gomes, behind the town.*

Ins and outs

Frequent, regular buses run between Cuiabá and Chapada dos Guimarães town (1-1½ hrs). The Chapada can be visited in a long day trip either by self drive (although access is via rough dirt roads that may deteriorate in the rainy season), bus or most easily through agencies such as **Fauna Tour** and **Natureco** (see page 668). The **tourist office** ⓘ *R Quinco Caldas 100, near the praça,* provides a useful map of the region and can help organize tours. The **Festival de Inverno** is held in the last week of July, and this festival and **Carnaval** are very busy with accommodation scarce and expensive.

Parque Nacional da Chapada dos Guimarães

This begins just west of Chapada dos Guimarães town, near where the Salgadeira tourist centre offers bathing, camping (and an unsightly restaurant right beneath the **Salgadeira waterfall**). The beautiful 85-m **Véu da Noiva waterfall** (Bridal Veil), 12 km from the town, near Buriti (well signposted, ask bus from Cuiabá to let you off), is less blighted and can be reached by either a short route or a longer one through forest. Other sights include: the **Mutuca** beauty spot, named after a vicious horsefly which preys on tourists there; **Rio Claro**, a viewpoint over the breathtaking 80-m-deep **Portão do Inferno gorge**; and the **Cachoeirinha falls**, where there is another small restaurant.

An excursion can be made to the **Cidade de Pedra** rock formations, 25 km from town along the road to the diamond prospecting town of Água Fria. Nearby is a 300-m wall formed by the Rio Claro. About 60 km from town are the **Pingador** and **Bom Jardim** archaeological sites – caverns with petroglyphs dating back some 4000 years.

Cáceres » pp664-670.

→ *Phone code: 065. Colour map 3, A1. Population: 86,000.*

Cáceres is a very hot but kempt and hospitable town on the banks of the Rio Paraguai, 200 km west of Cuiabá. It has a number of well-preserved 19th-century buildings painted in pastel colours and is known for its many bicycles. Until 1960, Cáceres used to have regular boat traffic; today it is limited to a few tour boats and pleasure craft. River trips from Cuiabá to Corumbá are very difficult since boats on the Cuiabá river are few and irregular, but you can sometimes get to Corumbá by river from here; be prepared to wait around for a few days and travel in a pair or group if possible.

The **Museu de Cáceres** ⓘ *R Antônio Maria by Praça Major João Carlos*, is a small local history museum. Exhibits include indigenous funerary urns. The main square, **Praça Barão de Rio Branco,** has one of the original border markers from the Treaty of Tordesillas, which divided South America between Spain and Portugal. The *praça* is pleasant and shady during the day and, in the evenings between November and March, the trees are packed with thousands of chirping swallows (*andorinhas*); beware of droppings. The square is full of bars, restaurants and ice-cream parlours and comes to life at night.

The beautiful **Serra da Mangabeira** is about 15 km east, crossed by the road from Cuiabá; the town is also at the edge of the Pantanal. Vitória Regia lilies can be seen north of town, just across the bridge over the Rio Paraguai along the BR-174. There are archaeological sites on the river's edge north of the city.

Ins and outs

Aeroporto de Cáceres ⓘ *Av Tancredo Neves, T065-223 6474*, receives flights from Cuiabá. The **rodoviária** ⓘ *Terminal da Japonesa, T065-224 1261*, has bus connections with Cuiabá and Porto Velho. It is also possible to arrive on the *Acuri*, a luxury boat that travels between Corumbá and Cuiabá. At the waterfront you can hire a boat for a day trip, US$5 per person per hour, minimum three people; on holidays and some weekends there are organized day trips on the river. » *For further details, see Transport, page 669.*

Border with Bolivia

An unpaved road runs from Cáceres to the Bolivian border at San Matías. Exit and entry formalities are carried out at **Brazilian immigration** ⓘ *R Col Farías, Cáceres, closed Sun*. When closed, go to the **Polícia Federal** ⓘ *Av Rubens de Medarca 909*.

Into Bolivia San Matías is a busy little town with hotels, restaurants and a bank. The next major town in Bolivia is San Ignacio de Velasco, which is on the road route to Santa Cruz de la Sierra. Buses run from San Matías to San Ignacio and San Ignacio to Santa Cruz; also flights. For details, see *Footprint Bolivia* or the *South American Handbook*.

Into Brazil Leaving Bolivia, get your passport stamped at **Bolivian immigration** (1000-1200, 1500-1700), then again at Cáceres. There are three luggage checks for drugs before arriving in Brazil.

Along the Transpantaneira » *pp664-670.*

Poconé to Porto Jofre

→ *Phone code: 065. Colour map 3, A2.*

A paved road turns south off the main Cuiabá to Cáceres road to **Poconé**, a scruffy town founded in 1781 and known as the 'Cidade Rosa' (pink city). Until 1995 there was much *garimpo* activity north of town and many slag heaps can be seen from the road. There are numerous cheap hotels in town but there is no real advantage in staying here and most travellers pass through after organizing their tours direct with *fazendas* or through agents in Cuiabá (see page 667).

From Poconé it is 63-km south to Pixaim, a journey of two hours in the dry season and up to five in the wet. This is the only easily accessible settlement in the northern Pantanal with any tourist infrastructure – amounting to two hotels, a fuel station and a tyre-repair shop.

Barão de Melgaço and around → *Colour map 3, A2.*

Barão de Melgaço, 130 km from Cuiabá on the banks of the Rio Cuiabá, is far less visited than the Transpantaneira. Standing on the edge of extensive areas of lakeland and seasonally flooded *cerrado*, it is reachable by two roads. The shorter, via Santo Antônio do Leverger, is unpaved from Santo Antônio to Barão (closed in the wet season). The route via São Vicente is longer but is more extensively paved.

The best way to see the Pantanal from here is by boat down the Rio Cuiabá. Near the town, the riverbanks are lined with farms and small residences but become increasingly forested with lovely combinations of flowering trees (best seen September to October). After a while, a small river to the left leads to the Chacororé and Sia Mariana lakes, which join up via an artificial canal. The canal has resulted in the larger of the two lakes draining into the smaller one, and it has begun to dry out. Boats can continue beyond the lakes to the Rio Mutum, but a guide is essential because there are many dead ends. The area is rich in birdlife and the waterscapes are beautiful.

Boat hire costs up to US$85 for a full day and is available from **Restaurant Peixe Vivo** on the waterfront, or enquire with travel agencies in Cuiabá. The best time for a boat trip is sunset, but this will involve a return trip in the dark.

North of Cuiabá » *pp664-670.*

Some 145 km north of Cuiabá is the little town of **Nobres**, which, like Bonito in Mato Grosso do Sul (see page 645), is surrounded by clear water rivers full of dourado fish, and many beautiful caves. Unlike Bonito, there are few tourists and the attractions are accordingly cheaper and less spoilt. The most spectacular cave is the **Gruta do Lagoa Azul**, which is open according to the whims of **Ibama**, Brazil's environmental protection agency; consult www.ibama.com. The town is served by regular buses from Cuiabá and Sinop/Alta Floresta, and **Natureco** (see Cuibá, page 668) offers trips here.

Alta Floresta → *Phone code: 065. Colour map 1, B4. Population: 71,500.*

The road that runs due north from Cuiabá to Santarém (1777 km) is passable in all weather conditions as far as **Sinop**, but only in the dry from here to Santarém. Plans to asphalt the rest of the road, to enable soya from Mato Grosso to be shipped via the Amazon to the Atlantic, have been announced. Cargill have already built an enormous plant in Santarém in anticipation. The areas around the road are among the principal victims of active deforestation, with land being cleared for cattle and soya farms. Soya is spreading beyond Mato Grosso into southern Pará.

There are, however, still extensive tracts of forest intact, especially near the **Rio Cristalino**, above which there is an extensive park and a vast military area. The rivers here are tributaries of the Tapajós and are mostly clear or black water, fairly mosquito free and overflowing with wildlife. Harpy eagles nest in the grounds of the **Floresta Amazônica** hotel in Alta Floresta town and can also be seen, along with other spectacular species, around the **Cristalino Jungle Lodge**, one of the best wildlife and birding lodges in the Brazilian Amazon (see Sleeping, page 666)

Ins and outs There are daily overnight buses from Cuiabá, 12 hours. On weekdays there are flights with **Trip**, www.voetrip.com.br, and **Mega**, www.voemega.com.br. **Cruiser**, www.voecruiser.com.br, flies to Guarantã do Norte which is connected to Alta Floresta by bus (two to three hours). The town was built in the late 1970s and laid out on a grid pattern. Finding your way around in straightforward. **Cristalino Jungle Lodge** representatives will meet you at the airport or bus station and transfer you to their hotels by 4WD.

East of Cuiabá

» pp664-670.

São Félix do Araguaia → *Colour map 1, C5, Population: 14,500.*

This town has a high population of indigenous Carajás, whose handicrafts can be found between the pizzeria and **Mini Hotel** on Avenida Araguaia. There is some infrastructure for fishing.

Mosquito nets are strongly recommended in São Félix, as there is a high incidence of malaria.

Indigenous *fazenda* owners may invite you as their guest. If you accept, remember to take a gift: pencils, radio batteries, a few sacks of beans or rice, or a live cockerel will be much appreciated. Many river trips are available for fishing or wildlife spotting. » *For further details, see Activities and tours, page 668.*

Ins and outs Access to São Félix and Santa Teresinha is by bus from Cuiabá. The *rodoviária* is 3 km from the centre and waterfront, taxi US$5.

Sleeping

Cuiabá *p659, map p659*

L Amazon Plaza, Av Getúlio Vargas 600, T065-2121 2000, www.hotelamazon.com.br. By far the best in the centre with very smart modern rooms in a tower with good views. The chairs and decking in the relaxing, shady pool area are painted with pictures of Amazon wildlife. Excellent service. Broadband in all rooms.

L Hotel Águas Quentes at Águas Quentes spring, 86 km from Cuiabá, see page 660, whose pools of thermal waters are 36-42°C.

AL Best Western Mato Grosso Palace, Joaquim Murtinho 170, T065-3624 7747, www.hotelmatogrosso.com.br. Conveniently located behind Praça República. Practical, clean, standard 3-star rooms with cable TVs, fridges and excellent boiler-heated showers.

A Las Velas, Av Felinto Muller 62, T065-3682 3840, resvelas@terra.com.br. Less than 100 m from the airport. Clean, spacious a/c rooms (the executive ones are best and only a little more expensive) with newly renovated bathrooms, cable TV and boiler-heated showers. Free airport transfer for luggage.

B Nacional, Av Jules Rimet 22, T065-3621 3277. Opposite the front of the bus station and convenient for those who are just passing through. Plain a/c rooms with newly renovated en suites.

B-C Mato Grosso, R Comandante Costa 643, T065-3614 7777, www.hotel matogrosso.com.br. The best-value mid-range option in the centre with newly renovated a/c or fan-cooled rooms with tiled floors and chintzy beds, the brightest of which are on the 2nd floor or above.

B-C Panorama, Praça Moreira Cabral 286, T065-3322 0072. A frayed 1980s tower with very simple, plain a/c or fan-cooled rooms with en suites; some have good views.

C Ipanema, Av Jules Rimet 12, T065-3621 3069. Opposite the front of the bus station. Very well-kept a/c or fan-cooled rooms, some with armchairs, cable TVs and smart en suites. Internet access and a huge lobby TV for films or football. Many other options between here and the **Nacional**.

C Portal do Pantanal, Av Isaac Póvoas 655, T/F065-3624 8999, www.portaldo pantanal.com.br. Youth hostel. Price per person, breakfast included, internet access (US$2.50 per hr), laundry, kitchen.

C Pousada Eco do Pantanal, R Campo Grande 487, T065-3624 1966, www.fauna tour.com.br. The best-value economy option with well-kept, clean rooms with spacious en suites in a converted town house. Facilities include excellent tour agency, laundry service, internet and free airport/bus station pickup (with 12 hrs' notice).

C Samara, R Joaquim Murtinho 270, T065-322 6001. Very simple, scruffy rooms with en suite cold showers. No breakfast. Only come here if the other options are full.

Chapada dos Guimarães *p660*

L Pousada Penhasco, 2½ km on Av Penhasco, Bom Clima, T065-3301 1555. Good views out over the plain from the *chapada*.

40 a/c rooms, tennis courts, swimming pool and a games area for children.

AL Solar do Inglês, R Cipriano Curvo 142, Centro, T065-3301 1389, www.chapadadosguimaraes.com.br. In an old converted house near town centre with 7 rooms, each with private bathroom, TV and frigobar. Garden, swimming pool and sauna. Breakfast and afternoon tea included.

A Estância San Francisco, at the entrance to town from Cuiabá (MT-251, Km 61), T065-3791 1102, F3791 1537. On a 42-ha farm with 2 lakes, said to have the best breakfast in town fresh from the farm. Good for birding.

B Turismo, R Fernando Corrêa 1065, a block from the *rodoviária*, T065-3791 1176, F3791 1383. A/c rooms with a fridge, cheaper with fan, restaurant, breakfast and lunch excellent, very popular, German run. Ralf Goebel, the owner, is very helpful in arranging excursions.

B-C Rio's Hotel, R Tiradentes 333, T065-3791 1126. A/c rooms with a fridge, cheaper with fan, cheaper with shared bath, good breakfast.

C Pousada Bom Jardim, Praça Bispo Dom Wunibaldo, T065-3791 1244. Comfortable fan-cooled rooms with parking and good breakfast.

D São José, R Vereador José de Souza 50, T065-3791 1152. Fan-cooled rooms. Cheaper with a shared bath and no fan, hot showers, basic, good, owner Mário sometimes runs excursions.

Camping

Aldeia Velha, in the Aldeia Velha neighbourhood at the entrance to town from Cuiabá, T065-322 7178 (Cuiabá). Fenced area with bath, hot shower, some shade, guard.

Salgadeira, camping is possible 16 km from town at the tourist centre, watch out for your belongings.

Cáceres *p661*

A Caiçaras, R dos Operários 745 corner R Gen Osório, T065 3223 3187, F223 2692. Modern town hotel with a/c rooms and cheaper options without a fridge.

B Ipanema, R Gen Osório 540, T065-3223 1177, www.ipanemahotelmt.com.br. Simple town hotel with a/c rooms, a pool and a restaurant.

B-D Rio, Praça Major João Carlos 61, T065-3223 3387, F3223 3084. A range of rooms – the cheapest with no a/c and shared bathrooms.

C-D Charm, Col José Dulce 405, T/F065-3223 4949. A/c and fan-cooled rooms, with or without a shared bath.

D-E União, R 7 de Setembro 340. Fan-cooled rooms, cheaper with shared bath, basic but good value.

Along the Transpantaneira *p662*

Fazendas

See also page 650. Distances are given in km from Poconé town. For tour operators, see Activities and tours, page 667.

L Fazenda Santa Teresa, Km 75. A working *fazenda* with rustic a/c or fan-cooled accommodation, a pool and hearty food. There are giant otters in the river adjacent to the farm which are fed daily for show, making sightings almost guaranteed.

L Pousada Rio Clarinho, Km 42, book through **Fauna Tour**. Charming option on the river Clarinho; what it lacks in infrastructure, it makes up for in wildlife. The river has rare waterbirds such as agami heron and nesting hyacinth macaw, as well as river and giant otters and, occasionally, tapir. The boatman, Wander, has very sharp eyes.

L Pousada Rio Claro, Km 42, book through **Natureco**. Comfortable *fazenda* with a pool and simple a/c rooms on the banks of the Rio Claro, which has a resident colony of giant otters.

L Pouso Alegre, Km 36, T065-626 1545, www.pousalegre.com.br, alegre.p@terra.com.br. Rustic pousada with simple a/c or fan-cooled accommodation on one of the Pantanal's largest *fazendas*. It's overflowing with wildlife and particularly good for birds (especially on the morning horseback trail). Many new species have been catalogued here. The remote oxbow lake is particularly good for waterbirds (including agami and zigzag herons). The lodge is used by **Ornitholidays** and **Neblina** tours. Proper birding guides can be provided with advance notice. Best at weekends when the very knowledgeable owner Luís Vicente is there.

For Sleeping and Eating price codes, see pages 49 and 52 or the inside front cover. For an explanation of phone codes, see page 66.

AAraras Lodge, Km 32, T065-682 2800, www.araraslodge.com.br. Book direct or through **Fauna Tour** or **Natureco**. One of the most comfortable places to stay with 14 a/c rooms. Excellent tours and food, home-made *cachaça*, a pool and a walkway over a private patch of wetland filled with capybara and caiman. Very popular with small tour groups from Europe. Book ahead.

AFazenda Piuval, Km 10, T065-3345 1338, www.pousadapiuval.com.br. The first *fazenda* on the Transpantaneira and one of the most touristy, with scores of day visitors at weekends. Rustic farmhouse accommodation, a pool, excellent horseback and walking trails as well as boat trips on their vast lake. Very good for spotting hyacinth macaw.

Barão de Melgaço *p663*

LPousada Passárgada, www.pousadapassargada.com, reservations through **Nature Safaris**, or through agencies in Cuiabá, São Paulo (T011- 284 5434) or Rio (T021-287 3390). Much cheaper if booked direct with the owner, Maré Sigaud, Mato Grosso, CEP 786807, Pousada Passárgada, Barão de Melgaço. Programmes are for a minimum of 3 days and include full board, boat, 4WD and trekking expeditions. Transport from Barão de Melgaço either by boat or 4WD can be arranged with the owner who speaks English, French and German. Closed Dec-Feb.

CBarão Tour Hotel, in Barão de Melgaço town. Apartments with a/c, restaurant, boat trips and excursions (contact the owner in Cuiabá T065-322 1568). There is a handful of cheaper options near the waterfront.

Alta Floresta *p663*

LCristalino Jungle Lodge, reservations Av Perimetral Oeste 2001, T065-512 7100, www.cristalinolodge.com.br. A beautifully situated and well-run lodge. Trips from the lodge include canoeing and snorkelling in clear-water rivers, as well as the usual caiman spotting and piranha fishing. Also more adventurous options such as rapelling and canyoning. Birding is superb and the lodge has a lookout with a view over the canopy.

BFloresta Amazônica, Av Perimetral Oeste 2001, T065-521 3601, F521 3801. In the park with lovely views, pool, sports, all facilities.

CItalian Palace, Av das Figueras 493, Sinop, T065-531 2109. With a restaurant, bar, sauna.

CPirâmide Palace, Av do Aeroporto 445, T065- 521 2400. A/c rooms with fridges, restaurant.

DGrande Hotel Coroados, R F1 No118, T065-521 3022. Not very well kept but has a/c, pool and bar.

São Félix do Araguaia *p664*

CXavante, Av Severiano Neves 391, T062-522 1305. A/c, frigobar, excellent breakfast, delicious *cajá* juice, the owners are very hospitable. Recommended.

EPizzeria Cantinho da Peixada, Av Araguaia, next to the Texaco station, overlooking the river, T062-522 1320. Rooms to let by the owner of the restaurant, better than hotels. He also arranges fishing trips.

Eating

Cuiabá *p659, map p659*

Many of the restaurants in the centre are only open weekdays for lunch. On Av CPA there are many good restaurants and small snack bars. There are several cheap restaurants and *lanchonetes* on R Jules Rimet across from the *rodoviária*.

TTTGetúlio, Av Getúlio Vargas 1147, at São Sebastião, T065-3264 9992. An a/c haven to escape from the heat. Black-tie waiters, excellent food with meat specialities and pizza, and a good buffet lunch on Sun. Live music upstairs on Fri and Sat from significant Brazilian acts.

TTT-TTChoppão, Praça 8 de Abril, T065-3623 9101. Established 30 years ago, this local institution is buzzing at any time of day or night. Huge portions of delicious food or *chopp*. The house speciality chicken soup promises to give diners drinking strength in the early hours and is a meal in itself. Warmly recommended.

TTPanela de Barro, R Cmte Costa 543. Self-service, a/c lunchtime restaurant with a choice of tasty regional dishes.

TT-TMiranda's, R Cmte Costa 716. Decent self-service per kg lunchtime restaurant with good value specials.

TLanchonete da Marilda, R Cmte Costa 675. Simple lunchtime snack bar with generous *prato feito*.

Chapada dos Guimarães *p660*
Pequi is a regional palm fruit with a deadly spiky interior used to season many foods; *arroz com pequi* is a popular local rice and chicken dish.
Nivios, Praça Dom Wunibaldo 631. The best place for good regional food.
O Mestrinho, R Quinco Caldas 119. Meat, regional dishes, *rodízio* at weekends.
Trapiche, R Cipriano Curvo 580. Pizza, drinks, regional dishes.
Choppada (**O Chopp da Chapada**), R Cipriano Curvo near the praça. Drinks and meals, regional dishes, live music at weekends.
Fogão da Roça, Praça Dom Wunibaldo 488. Good *comida mineira* in generous portions. Recommended.

Cáceres *p661*
Corimbá, R 15 de Novembro s/n, on the riverfront. Fish and general Brazilian food.
Gulla's, R Col José Dulce 250. Per kg buffet, good quality and variety. Recommended.
Panela de Barro, R Frei Ambrósio 34, near the *rodoviária*. Brazilian home cooking (*comida caseira*) with the usual range of meat dishes with squash, rice, black beans and salads.

São Félix do Araguaia *p664*
Pizzeria Cantinho da Peixada, Av Araguaia, next to the Texaco station, overlooking the river. As well as serving pizza, the owner, Klaus, also rents rooms (see Sleeping).

Bars and clubs

Cuiabá *p659, map p659*
Cuiabá is quite lively at night, bars with live music and dance on Av CPA.
Café Cancun, R Candido Mariano at São Sebastião. One of a chain of popular Brazilian club-bars attracting a mid-20s to 40s crowd.
Choppão, see Eating above.
Rush, Isaac Póvoas at Presidente Marquês. Teen and 20-something techno bar.
Tucano, Av CPA, bar-restaurant specializing in pizza, with beautiful view, open daily 1800-2300.

Entertainment

Cáceres *p661*
Traditional folkloric dance groups: **Chalana**, T065-223 3317, and **Tradição**, T065-223 4505, perform shows at different locations.

Festivals

Cáceres *p661*
Mid-Mar Piranha Festival.
Mid-Sep International Fishing Festival.
There's also an annual cattle fair.

Shopping

Cuiabá *p659, map p659*
Local handicrafts in wood, straw, netting, leather, skins, Pequi liquor, crystallized caju fruit, compressed guaraná fruit and indigenous crafts are on sale at the airport, *rodoviária*, craft shops in the centre and at the daily market in the Praça da República, interesting. There's a picturesque fish and vegetable market at the riverside.
Casa de Artesão, Praça do Expedicionário 315, T065-321 0603. All types of local crafts in a restored building.

Chapada dos Guimarães *p660*
Casa de Artes e Artesanato Mato Grossense, Praça Dom Wunibaldo. Crafts, indigenous artefacts, sweets and locally made honey.
Doceria Olho de Sogra, Praça Dom Wunibaldo 21. Regional sweets.
João Eloy de Souza Neves is a local artist; his paintings, music and history of Chapada (*Chapada dos Guimarães da descoberta aos dias atuais*) are on sale at Pousada Bom Jardim.

Cáceres *p661*
Náutica Turismo, R Bom Jardim 119A, by the waterfront. For fishing/camping supplies and boat repairs.

Activities and tours

Cuiabá *p659, map p659*
Travel agencies in Cuiabá also offer trips to the Chapada.

Tours to the northern Pantanal

You should expect to pay US$60-90 per person per day for tours in the Pantanal. Budget trips are marginally more expensive (around US$10 per day) than those in the southern Pantanal, but accommodation in the *fazendas* is more comfortable. For longer tours or special programmes, book in advance.

Fauna Tour, R Campo Grande 487, T065- 3624 1996, T065-9974 2622 (mob), faunatour@terra.com.br or pousada ecopantanal@gmail.com. One of several budget operators in town, but much the best option. 2- to 5-day tours to the Pantanal, Chapada and Rio Xingu with excellent wildlife guides; ask for Alex Gomes Ramos (T065-9204 5827). Camping trips available Jun-Oct with advance notice.

Natureco, R Benedito Leite 570, Cuiabá, T065-3321 1001, www.pantanaltour.net. A range of *fazenda*-based Pantanal tours, trips to the Chapada dos Guimarães and to the caves at Nobres. Specialist wildlife guides available with advance notice. Some English spoken.

Pantanal wildlife guides

All guides work freelance; companies employ extra guides for trips when busy. Most guides wait at the airport for incoming flights; compare prices and services in town if you don't want to commit yourself. The tourist office recommends guides, however, their advice is not always impartial.

Boute Expeditions, R Getúlio Vargas 64, Várzea Grande, near airport, T065-3686 2231, pauloboute@uol.com.br. Paulo Boute is one of the most experienced birding guides in the Pantanal; works from home and speaks good English and French.

Fabricio Dorileo, fabriciodorileo18@yahoo.com.br or through Eduardo Falcão – rejaguar@bol.com.br. Excellent birding guide with good equipment, good English and many years experience in the Pantanal and Chapada dos Guimarães. Trained in the USA.

Giuliano Bernardon, T065-8115 6189, giubernardon@gmail.com. Young birding guide from the Chapada dos Guimarães, with a good depth of knowledge and experience in the Chapada, Pantanal, Mato Grosso, Amazon and Atlantic coastal forest.

Pantanal Bird Club, T065-3624 1930, www.pantanalbirdclub.org. Recommended for even the most exacting clients, PBC are the most illustrious birders in Brazil with many years of experience. Braulio Carlos, the owner, has worked with Robert Ridgely and Guy Tudor and his chief guide, Juan Mazar Barnett, is one of the editors of *Cotinga* magazine. Tours throughout the area and to various parts of Brazil.

Chapada dos Guimarães *p660*

AC Tour, R Tiradentes 28, T065-3791 1122. Cássio Martins often waits at the *rodoviária*. 4-hr tours are from US$20 per person; 7-8 hrs, US$25; a horse riding day tour, costs around US$25 per person. Guided hikes, 8-10 kms, US$20 per person. Bicycle tour with guide, US$20 per person.

Ecoturismo Cultural, Praça Dom Wunibaldo 464, T/F065-3791 1393. Recommended tours with Jorge Belfort Mattos who speaks English and knows the area well; several itineraries, 4-6 hrs, US$20-50 per person.

José Paulino dos Santos is a guide working with the tourist office, Mon-Fri 0800-1100, 1300-1800, T065-3791 1245.

Cáceres *p661*

Cáceres, Av Getúlio Vargas 408, T065-223 1428, F223 2440. Fishing and photo tours to Pantanal, also boat hire. Cláudio Duarte is a helpful guide.

Pantanal Tour, R Col Fária 180, T065-223 1200. Boat hire, fishing trips, tickets.

Vereda Turismo, R Padre Cassemiro 1121, T065-223 4360. Tours, boat hire, fishing.

São Félix do Araguaia *p664*

Boat trips

Icuryala, Goiânia, T062-223 9518. Excellent food and service, US$100 per day, independent visitors welcome. Recommended.

Juracy Lopes, contact through **Hotel Xavante** (see Sleeping). A very experienced guide with many friends, including the chief and council in Santa Isabela. Trips to the village or to see wildlife cost US$15 for 2; longer trips can be made to the meeting of the waters with the Rio das Mortes, or for a night in the jungle sleeping in hammocks.

Transport

Cuiabá *p659, map p659*

See also Ins and outs, page 659.

Air A taxi to the airport costs US$15, or take the 'Aeroporto' bus from Praça Ipiranga, US$0.50. Flights can be booked in the airline offices at the airport or through **Fauna Tour** (see page 668), who also handle bus tickets.

Flights to **São Paulo**, **Brasília**, and other major cities are offered by **Gol**, www.voegol.com.br, **TAM**, www.tam.com.br, or **Varig**, T065-682 1140, www.varig.com.br. **Trip**, www.voetrip.com.br, flies to **Alta Floresta**. **Cruiser**, www.voecruiser.com.br, flies to **Santarém** and destinations in the Pantanal, as well as to **Guaranta do Norte** for connecting bus to Alta Floresta. **Mega**, www.voemega.com.br, to **Alta Floresta**, **Sinop**, **Xingu**, **Santarém**.

Airline offices All the major airlines have offices at the airport. **Varig** also has an office in town at R 15 de Novembro 230, Bairro Porto, T065-624 6498. It's easier to book through an agency like **Fauna Tour**, see page 668.

Bus Bus No 202 runs to the *rodoviária* from R Joaquim Murtinho by the cathedral, 20 mins.

Comfortable buses (toilets) to **Campo Grande**, 10 hrs, US$20, 12 buses daily, *leito* at 2000 and 2100, US$50. To **Goiânia**, 14 hrs, US$25. Direct to **Brasília**, 24 hrs, US$30, *leito* US$60. To **Porto Velho**, 6 **União Cascavel** buses a day, US$45, 21 hrs. **Andorinha** 1700 bus **São Paulo** connects with **Porto Velho** service. Several to **São Paulo**, eg **Motta**, US$42. To **Rio de Janeiro**, US$57. To **Barra do Garças**, **Xavante** 0800, 1300 and 2030, US$15, also **Barattur**. Connections to all major cities.

Car hire **Atlântida**, Av Isaac Póvoas, T065-623 0700. **Localiza**, Av Dom Bosco 965, T065-624 7979, and at airport, T065-682 7900. **Unidas**, airport, T065-682 4062. **Vitória**, R Comandante Costa 1350, T065-322 7122.

Chapada dos Guimarães *p660*

Bus 7 departures daily to **Cuiabá** (**Rubi**, 0700-1900, last return 1800), 1½ hrs, US$0.75.

Cáceres *p661*

Bus **Colibrí/União Cascavel** buses to **Cuiabá**, US$9, many daily 0630-2400 from the *rodoviária*, (book in advance, very crowded), 3½ hrs. To **Porto Velho**, US$32.

Boat The *Acurí*, a luxury tourist vessel, sails to **Corumbá**, 1-week cruise including return by air from Corumbá to Cuiabá, US$600 per person. For information on other boat sailings, ask at the Capitânia dos Portos, on the corner of the main square at the waterfront. Try to phone in advance to Cáceres, Posto Arrunda, T065-221 1707, to find out if any boats are going. Also **Portobrás** on the outskirts at the waterfront (T065-221 1728). In the dry season there are practically no boats to Corumbá.

Car hire **Localiza**, R Padre Cassimiro 630, T065-223 1330, and at airport. **Locavel**, Av São Luís 300, T065-223 1212.

Border with Bolivia *p662*

Bus From Cáceres to **San Matías**, US$9 with **Transical-Velásquez**, Mon-Sat at 0630 and 1500, Sun 1500 only (return at same times). **Trans Bolivia** to **San Matías**, Sun, Mon, Fri at 1500, Tue, Wed, Thu and Sat at 0700.

Along the Transpantaneira *p662*

Bus From Poconé to **Cuiabá**, US$7.50 with **TUT**, T065-322 4985, 6 a day 0600-1900.

Car Poconé has a 24-hr petrol station with all types of fuel, but closed on Sun.

São Félix do Araguaia *p664*

Bus To **Barra do Garças** at 0500, arrive 2300; or 1730, arrive 1100 next day. Also to **Tucumã**, 6-8 hrs, and to **São José do Xingu**, 10 hrs. No buses to Marabá.

Directory

Cuiabá *p659, map p659*

Banks **Banco do Brasil**, Av Getúlio Vargas and R Barão de Melgaço, commission US$10 for cash, US$20 per transaction for TCs (very slow for TCs, but best rates). **Incomep Câmbio**, R Gen Neves 155, good rates. The following travel agents or gold dealers change cash only at poor rates (generally Mon-Fri): Mattos-Tur, R Cândido Mariano 465. Goldmine, R Cândido Mariano 400, 0800-1600. Ourominas, R Cândido Mariano 401, 0800-1700, may change on Sat 0800-1200 if cash is available, enquire first, T065 -624 9400. Portobello, R Comandante Costa 555, 0900-1600. It is difficult to get cash advances on credit cards especially MasterCard; for Visa try Banco do Brasil or Bradesco. **Embassies and consulates** Bolivia, Av Isaac Póvoas 117, T065-623 5094, Mon-Fri. **Internet** Copy Grafic, Praça Alencastro 32, fax and email, English spoken, friendly. **Post office** Main branch at Praça da República, fax service. **Telephone** R Barão de Melgaço 3209, 0700-2200, also at *rodoviária*, 0600-2130, international service.

Chapada dos Guimarães *p660*

Post office R Fernando Corrêa 848.

Cáceres *p661*

Banks Banco do Brasil, R Col Jose Dulcé 234. HSBC, R Col Jose Dulcé 145. Casa de Câmbio Mattos, Comte Bauduino 180, next to main *praça*, changes cash and TCs at good rates. **Telephone** Praça Barão de Rio Branco.

Background

Footprint features

History

Indigenous peoples

Origins

Some 50,000 years ago the very first peoples crossed the temporary land bridge spanning Asia and America at the Bering Straits, and began a long migration southwards. They were hunters and foragers, following in the path of huge herds of now extinct animals, such as mammoth, giant ground sloth and antecedents of the camel and horse. The first signs that these people had reached South America date from around 10,000 BC, if not earlier.

Archaeological evidence

The major handicap to archaeological study of tropical cultures is that most material remains deteriorate rapidly in the warm, humid climate. Since the majority of cultural output from Brazil was in perishable materials such as feathers, wood, baskets, and woven textiles, little has survived for modern analysis. Nevertheless various artefacts have been discovered from all around the country, showing considerable artistic and technical skill. The pottery produced by the early peoples was of a high standard, admired by the European newcomers. Early ceramics have been found on Marajó island at the mouth of the Amazon. The Annatuba culture lived here in small villages by the river. Most of their ceramics found are round bowls and jars, including huge funeral urns, which have been dated with increasing antiquity; the earliest from around 980 BC. Textile production was done mainly with hand-twisted fibres, using both cotton and bast. Objects found in Rio Grande do Sul, dating from AD 550 or earlier, included twined bags, nets and ropes. Most of the textiles found throughout Brazil were simple everyday items, such as hammocks and straps, with little decoration.

It was assumed that the first humans in Brazil came down to the lowlands from the Andean chain, following the east-facing river valleys. Some very early human remains have been found in central and northeastern Brazil. In Pedra Furada, in northeast Brazil, a rock-shelter named Toca do Boqueirão yielded evidence of human presence from as early as 47,000 years ago. The cave, in a region well-known for its prehistoric rock paintings, had previously been explored and was known to have been occupied by hunters about 8000 years ago. However, a team of Brazilians, co-ordinated by Paulista archaeologist Niède Guidón, probed more deeply into the ground and claims to have found evidence of much earlier human presence. Guidón's claims sparked hot debate among other experts, many of whom argued that what she described as ash from fireplaces was in fact the remains of naturally caused forest fires. This claim has led to some accusations of racism by Brazilians who argue that if Guidón were American she would have been taken more seriously. This appears not to be the case for similar controversy that was sparked by the findings of a scion of one of the most famous American families, Anna Roosevelt. She claimed that findings in a cave in Monte Alegre, opposite Santarém on the Rio Solimões, suggested that the Amazon had been peopled since at least 11,000 BC and that it had supported large civilizations, also predating previous estimates. These, and other controversial claims have caused a bitter rift in the world of archaeology and led some experts to raise the theory of original human migration from across the Pacific Ocean and others to accuse the newcomers of undertaking amateurish, unprofessional research. For a full account see Charles Mann's excellent *1491* (Vintage 2006).

Amazon lifestyles

Roosevelt's research, together with that being undertaken by ethno-biologists like Wade Davis, anthropologists like Gerardo Reichel-Dolmatoff and Mesoamerica archaeologists and epigraphers like Linda Schele, began to change radically once widely-accepted ideas of the pre-Colombian Americans. Gone is a notion based on an analysis of their technology and concluding that they were prehistoric, primitive peoples, instead is an analysis based on their rich societal structure, speculative philosophy and the mythology which sustained it. We now see the first Americans as a divergent range of peoples who arrived in the Americas at varying times and probably from various locations. Between them they shared a common philosophical world-map – an idea of being – which was radically different from our own Greco-Roman idea and which was rooted in shamanism (see box, page 688). In philosophical terms this assumes that being is as vital a component of reality as energy and matter; and like those two it is shared. In other words the basic stuff of the Universe is threefold – matter (energy), space and time (position) and the perception of those two (being); on which they both depend for their existence. The essence of being can be directly apprehended behind the mind by seers or shaman (Portuguese pajé). In most first American societies it was shaman – together with powerful civic leaders (Portuguese cacique) who guided tribal societies; be they Mayan or Ticuna.

Little is known of these people largely because of the colonial ideas that were handed down to Western archaeologists by the Spanish and Portuguese, who burned and plundered many of the artefacts and books of the first Americans. The Amazonian peoples were decimated by the Portuguese slave trade long before their knowledge could be shared; and as most of their treasures were made from perishable materials like feather, bark and reed, the products of their labour and their knowledge rotted into the forest floor. What we know is scant and trivial. The earliest people lived mainly on the flood plains of the great rivers and caught fish and manatee using spears thrown from the shore, or from dugout canoes. Besides fishing, these people also cultivated manioc and other plants found on the forest floor. They kept turtles in corrals at the river's edge, for eating and also for making tools and other artefacts from their shells.

Their nomadic lifestyle was carefully planned, and they followed planting and harvesting seasons in accordance with the periodic rising and falling river levels. At first, as hunters and gatherers, they built simple, temporary houses out of tree trunks and palm leaves, and slept in hammocks made from plant fibres. Where clothing was used it was simple; a large, ankle-length tunic called a *kushma* was the main garment worn. Although this may sound impractical wear for people living in a warm, humid climate, the *kushma* provided much-needed protection against biting insects. Compensating for their plain clothing, the people painted their bodies and wore colourful jewellery, such as feather head-dresses; the designs for which were often rich and elaborate and drawn from an extensive mythology. Little has remained of the perishable adornments, but cylindrical and flat ceramic stamps have been found throughout Amazônia, which may have been used to apply ink designs onto the face and other parts of the body, still common today among ethnic groups.

Migration to the coast

Around 7000-4000 BC a climatic change increased the temperature throughout the south of Brazil, drawing people down from the inland *planalto* region to the coasts, and leading to an upsurge in population here. These coastal inhabitants lived on shellfish collected from the water's edge, as evidenced by *sambaquis* (huge shell mounds), discovered on the coast. In rare cases they also fed on whales that had probably been beached, but they did not go far out to sea to fish. Some of the *sambaquis* found measure up to 25 m high; many of them also served as dwellings, with floors and fireplaces, and as burial sites, with graves often underneath the houses. The dead were buried with personal adornments and some domestic artefacts.

Settlement and political structure

By about 100-200 BC, people throughout Brazil were settled in structured, fixed communities by the coasts and rivers, living increasingly by farming instead of nomadic hunting and gathering. The subsequent population growth spread communities further along river courses and into seasonally flooded savannah lands.

Until Anna Roosevelt's research it had been thought that unlike the great empires of the Andes, the lowland peoples did not form political groupings much larger than a few villages. However it is now suggested that much of Brazil was settled by chiefdoms, some of which were substantial and the seat of sophisticated civilizations. The most notable of these was probably Marajó which Roosevelt has called 'one of the outstanding indigenous achievements of the New World.' The Marajó people occupied thousands of square kilometres in the lower portion of the Amazon basin in a civilization which perhaps numbered around 100 000 people and which endured for some 1000 years. They had an advanced tropical rainforest agriculture in which fruit-bearing and utilitarian trees were planted within the forest (as opposed to in cleared areas); in much the same way as the Lacandon Maya today. The Marajó people were either influential on Brazilian indigenous people as a whole or they were part of a widespread practice, for by about 2000 BC peoples throughout the lower Amazon were planting at least 138 species of crop plant; including manioc which remains a staple in Brazilian diet to this day.

Linguistic groups

The most widespread linguistic grouping in Brazil at the time of the European conquest was the Tupi-Guarani. These people originated from the Atlantic coast around AD 500-700. By the 1500s the Tupi-Guarani, who often moved from place to place could be found from north of the Amazon south to Rio de la Plata, and west into Paraguay and Bolivia; they were probably the first Americans the Portuguese encountered

Another large, organized group of people were the Tupinambá. They lived on the coast, from the mouth of the Amazon south to São Paulo state. The Tupinambá lived by cultivating crops, such as manioc, sweet potato, yams, as well as cotton, gourds and tobacco. They lived in villages of four to eight large, rectangular, thatched houses, each containing up to 30 families. They usually built their villages on an elevation to catch the breeze, and moved to new sites every five years or so.

Cannibalism was also an important custom for the Tupinambá, as it had been for many other peoples throughout South America for thousands of years. The practice was a highly ritualized military practise, using prisoners of war. The victims were kept as slaves, often for long periods, being well fed and looked after; in some cases even marrying the owner's daughter or sister, who had their children. But all such slaves were eventually eaten, after an elaborate ceremony with much singing and dancing. An appointed executioner would kill them with a club and they were then cooked and different parts of the body divided up among various participants in the ritual. There have been many theories as to why people practised cannibalism; since they tended to eat victims of war it was thought that it gave them power over the spirits of their dead enemies. It is most commonly argued that human flesh supplemented the diet for large populations who had scarce resources. But this was not the case for the Tupinambá, who had ample food supplies. When the Tupinambá themselves were asked why they ate human meat they simply said they liked the taste of it.

European colonization

Arrival of the Portuguese

Pedro Álvares Cabral is believed to be the first Portuguese explorer to land on the Brazilian coast, having been blown off his course to India and making landfall on

22 April 1500. He claimed the territory for Portugal as a result of agreements with Spain under the papal bull of 1493 and the Treaty of Tordesillas (1494), but it was some years before the Portuguese realized that this was not just another island as the Spanish had found in the Caribbean – in reality they had stumbled across a huge new continent. Further expeditions were sent out in 1501 and 1503-1504 and a few trading stations were set up to export the only commodity they felt was of commercial interest: a species of dyewood known as 'pau do brasil'. Little attention was paid to the new colony, as the Portuguese concentrated on the more lucrative trade with Africa, India and the Far East. Some settlers, often banished criminals as well as merchants, gained acceptance with the local indigenous tribes and intermarried, fathering the first hybrid cultural Brazilians.

Colonization

The coastal trading stations at Salvador da Bahia, Pernambuco, São Vicente and Cabo Frio soon attracted the attention of French and British traders, who seized Portuguese ships and started to trade directly with the indigenous tribes. The French even proclaimed the right to trade in any part of Brazil not occupied by the Portuguese. This forced the Portuguese Crown to set up a colony and in 1530, Martim Afonso de Sousa was sent out with about 400 men. Faced with the impossibly huge task of colonizing the Brazilian coastline, the Crown turned to private enterprise to stake its claim. In 1534 the coast was divided into 15 captaincies, each of which was donated to an individual captain and governor to develop on behalf of the Crown. Although successful settlements were established in Pernambuco in the north and São Vicente in the south, the problems faced in most captaincies, Indian resistance, lack of capital and the difficulty of attracting settlers, led to the reassertion of Crown control in 1549. The *indígena* had been happy to barter brazil wood with the Portuguese and had helped in the logging and transporting of timber, but the introduction of sugar plantations was a different matter and the hunter-gatherers had no experience of such exhausting work. When they refused to co-operate in this profitable enterprise, the Portuguese took the *indígena* as slaves on a massive scale, which destroyed the good relations previously enjoyed and led to attacks on Portuguese settlements.

The Jesuits

Tomé de Sousa was sent out as Governor-General to the vacant captaincy of Bahia in 1549. He established his seat at Salvador, which became the first capital of Brazil. With him travelled six Jesuit priests, the first of what was to become a hugely powerful missionary and educational order in Brazil. Their role was to smooth the path between the indigenous tribes and Europeans, converting and educating them in Christian ways and organizing them into special villages, or *aldeias*. This last move brought them into conflict with the settlers, however, for their control over the labour market, and with the clergy, who regarded the *indígena* as savages who could be enslaved. As a result of disagreements with the first Bishop of Brazil, Fernandes Sardanha, the Jesuits moved in 1554 from Bahia to the captaincy of São Vicente, where they set up an *aldeia* at Piratininga, which later became the city of São Paulo. In 1557 a new governor was appointed, Mem de Sá, who was more sympathetic to the Jesuits and their aims, and the *aldeias* began to spread.

French and Dutch incursions

The Crown still had difficulties in consolidating its hold on Brazil and other European powers continued to encroach on its territory. A Protestant French expedition found an area which had not been settled by the Portuguese and stayed there from the mid-1550s until they were finally ousted in 1567. Their colony was replaced by a new royal captaincy and a town was founded: Rio de Janeiro. São Luís was also occupied by the French in 1612-1615, but it was the Dutch who posed the greatest threat on both sides of the Atlantic. They seized Pernambuco in 1630, Portuguese Angola in 1641 and dominated the Atlantic trading routes until the Portuguese managed to regain Angola in 1648-1649 and Pernambuco in 1654.

Sugar and slaves

Throughout the colonial period Brazil produced raw materials for Portugal. The colonial economy experienced a succession of booms and recessions, the first of these was based on sugar, as during the 17th century the northeastern provinces of Pernambuco, Bahia and Paraíba were the world's main producers of sugar. As European settlement had led to the death of much of the native population (over a third of the *indígena* in coastal areas died in epidemics in 1562-1563 alone) and slavery was unsuccessful, the Portuguese imported African slaves to meet the demand for labour on the sugar plantations (*engenhos*). "The most solid properties in Brazil are slaves", wrote the Governor in 1729, "for there are lands enough, but only he who has slaves can be master of them." As many as 10 million African slaves may have survived the dreadful conditions of the Atlantic crossing before the trade was abolished in 1854.

The gold rush

As the sugar industry declined in the late 17th century in the face of competition from British, French and Dutch Caribbean colonies, gold was discovered inland in 1695 in Minas Gerais, Mato Grosso and other areas. Despite the lack of communications, prospectors rushed in from all over Europe. Shortly afterwards, diamonds were found in the Serra do Frio. The economy was largely driven by gold until the 1760s and a revival of world demand for sugar in the second half of the 18th century. Thereafter, there was diversification into other crops such as cacao, rice, cotton and coffee, all of which were produced for export by large numbers of slaves.

The gold rush shifted the power centre of Brazil from the Northeast to the centre, in recognition of which new captaincies were created in Minas Gerais in 1720, Goiás in 1744 and Mato Grosso in 1748, and the capital was moved from Salvador to Rio de Janeiro in 1763. Legacies of the period can be seen today in the colonial towns of Mariana, Congonhas, São João del Rei, Diamantina and, above all, in the exceptionally beautiful city of Ouro Preto, a national monument full of glorious buildings, paintings and sculpture.

Marquês de Pombal

The decline of gold in the mid-18th century made economic reform necessary and the Marquês de Pombal was the minister responsible for a new programme for Portugal and her empire. Imbalances had arisen particularly in trade with Britain. Portugal imported manufactured goods and wheat but her exports of oil and wine left her in deficit, which for a while was covered by Brazilian gold. Pombal was a despotic ruler from 1750 to 1777, modernizing and reforming society, education, politics and the economy. In order to revive Portugal he concentrated on expanding the economy of Brazil, increasing and diversifying exports to cover the deficit with Britain. Cacao, cotton and rice were introduced by the new monopoly company of Grão Pará e Maranhão in the North and a similar company for Paraíba and Pernambuco revitalized the sugar industry in the Northeast. The monopoly companies led to high prices and were not entirely successful so were closed in 1778-1779, but the effects of Pombal's reforms were felt in the latter part of the 18th century and Portugal's trade with Britain turned into a surplus. From 1776 when the American colonies revolted, Britain was constantly at war and Portugal was able to supply rising British demand.

Rebellion

Pombal's influence on society enabled the Portuguese Empire to last much longer than the Spanish Empire. He deliberately offered posts in the militia and the bureaucracy to Brazilians and was careful not to alienate the Brazilian elites. White Brazilians were on the same standing as the Portuguese and identified strongly with the mother country. Rebellion was therefore rare it still occurred, influenced partly by the turmoil that was going on in Europe with the French Revolution. In 1788-1789 a famous plot was uncovered in Minas Gerais called the *inconfidência mineira* (see page 250), which aimed to establish an independent republic in protest at the decline of the gold industry and high taxes. The rebels, who included many of the local hierarchy, were punished and the most prominent leader, Tiradentes (the teeth-puller), was hanged. Other plots were discovered in Rio de Janeiro in 1794, Pernambuco in 1801 and Bahia in 1807, but they were all repressed.

The Brazilian empire

At the beginning of the 19th century, Napoleon Bonaparte caused a major upheaval in the monarchies of Europe. His expansion into the Iberian peninsula caused panic in both Spain and Portugal. In August 1807 he demanded that Portugal close its ports to British ships but the British sent a fleet to Lisbon and threatened to attack Brazil if that happened. In November of the same year the French invaded and occupied Portugal. The Prince Regent decided to evacuate the court to Brazil and under British escort sailed to Rio de Janeiro, which became the capital of the empire in 1808. The court stayed there even after 1814 when Napoleon was defeated and Portugal was ruled by a Regency Council, but King João VI was forced to return to Portugal in 1820 after a series of liberal revolts in the mother country, leaving his son Dom Pedro as Prince Regent in Brazil.

Independence from Portugal

Dom Pedro oversaw a growing rift between Portugal and Brazil as the liberals in Lisbon tried to return Brazil to its former colonial status, cancelling political equality and the freedom of trade granted when the King left Portugal in the hands of the French. In October 1821 the government in Lisbon recalled the Prince Regent but Brazilians urged him not to go. Encouraged by his chief minister, José Bonifácio de Andrada e Silva, a conservative monarchist, Dom Pedro announced on 9 January 1822 that he would stay in Brazil, thereby asserting his autonomy. After another attempt to recall the Prince Regent, Dom Pedro made the final break with Portugal, proclaiming Brazil's independence on 7 September 1822. He was crowned emperor and Brazil became a constitutional monarchy in its own right. There was resistance in the North and Northeast, particularly from the militia, but by 1824 violence had subsided. In 1825, under pressure from Britain, Portugal recognized the independent state of Brazil.

The first years of independence were unsettled, partly because of the Emperor's perceived favouritism for the Portuguese faction at court and lack of attendance to the needs of the local oligarchy. De Andrada e Silva resigned as opposition grew. In 1823 Dom Pedro dissolved the constituent assembly amidst fears that he had absolutist designs. However, he set up a royal commission to draft a new constitution which lasted from 1824 until the fall of the monarchy in 1889. This gave the emperor the right to appoint and dismiss cabinet ministers, veto legislation and dissolve parliament and call for elections. The parliamentary government consisted of two houses, a senate appointed by the monarch and a legislature indirectly elected by a limited male suffrage. A Council of State advised the monarch and ensured the separation of the executive, the legislature and the judiciary. Catholicism remained the official religion and the monarchy was supported by the Church.

Abdication

Dom Pedro still failed to gain the trust of all his people. A republican rebellion broke out in Pernambuco in 1824, where the elite were suffering from the declining sugar industry, and there was further resentment from all the planter oligarchy as a result of the Anglo-Brazilian Treaty of 1826. This treaty granted British recognition of the independent Brazil in return for certain trading privileges, but, almost more importantly, stipulated that the Atlantic slave trade should come to an end in three years. There was also a territorial dispute in 1825 with the Argentine provinces over the left bank of the Río de la Plata, called the Banda Oriental, which flared up into war and was only settled in 1828 with the creation of Uruguay as a buffer state. The mistrust between the Portuguese and the Brazilians became even more pronounced. Portuguese merchants were blamed for the rising cost of living and in 1831 rioting broke out in Rio de Janeiro. Dom Pedro shuffled and reshuffled his cabinet to appease different factions but nothing worked and on 7 April he abdicated in favour of his five-year-old son, Dom Pedro II, choosing to leave Brazil a week later on a British warship.

Regency and rebellion

During the 10 years of the young prince's boyhood, there were many separatist movements and uprisings by the oppressed lower classes. In 1832-1835 there was the War of the Cabanos, in Pernambuco, a guerrilla war against the slave-owning plantocracy of the Northeast; in 1835 the Cabanagem rebellion of free indigenous tribes and mestizos took place in Pará after a white secessionist revolt and sporadic fighting continued until 1840 (see page 538); in 1837-1838 in Bahia there was a federalist rebellion; in 1835 Rio Grande do Sul proclaimed itself a republic, remaining independent for nearly 10 years, with the movement spreading into Santa Catarina, which also declared itself a republic. By 1840 there was a general consensus that although he had not come of age, it was imperative that the 14 year old, Pedro, should ascend the throne. He was duly crowned. Administration of the country was centralized again, the powers of provincial assemblies were curtailed, a national police force set up and the Council of State restored.

The second empire

It took a couple of years for the balance of power to be worked out between the conservative élites of Rio de Janeiro and the liberal élites of São Paulo and Minas Gerais, but once the interests of different groups had been catered for, the constitutional monarchy worked smoothly for 20 years. Coffee was now the major crop in São Paulo and Minas Gerais and it was important that the wealthy oligarchy who produced it shared in the power structure of the nation in order to prevent secessionist movements.

Abolition of slavery

Despite the Anglo-Brazilian Treaty of 1826, the slave trade continued until the British Royal Navy put pressure on Brazilian ships carrying slaves in 1850 and the trade was halted soon afterwards. As slaves in Brazil did not reproduce at a natural rate because of the appalling conditions in which they lived and worked, it was clear that an alternative source of labour would eventually have to be found. Anti-slavery movements gathered strength and in 1871 the first steps towards abolition were taken. A new law gave freedom to all children born to slaves from that date and compensation was offered to masters who freed their slaves. During the 1870s large numbers of European immigrants, mostly from Italy and Portugal, came to work on the coffee plantations, and as technology and transport improved, so the benefits of slavery declined. During the 1880s the abolition movement became unstoppable and, after attempts to introduce compensation for slave owners failed, a law abolishing slavery immediately was passed on 13 May 1888. Some plantation owners went bankrupt, but the large majority survived by paying immigrant workers and newly freed slaves a pittance. Those freed slaves who left the plantations to find employment in the cities were equally exploited and lived in poverty.

Proclamation of the Republic

The first Republic: 1889-1930

The monarchy did not long survive the end of slavery. The São Paulo coffee producers resented abolition and resented their under-representation in the structures of power nationwide, while being called upon to provide the lion's share of the Treasury's revenues. The republican movement started in the early 1870s in cities all over Brazil, but grew strongest in São Paulo. It gradually attracted the support of the military, who also felt under-represented in government, and on 15 November 1889 a bloodless military coup d'état deposed the monarchy and instituted a federal system. The constitution of the new republic established 20 states with wide powers of self-government, a directly elected president of a national government with a senate and a chamber of deputies. Suffrage was introduced for literate adult males (about 3% of the population) and the Church and state were separated. Although the birth of the Republic was bloodless, there were pockets of resistance in rural areas such as the Northeast, where the sugar estates were in recession. In the 1890s O Conselheiro led tens of thousands of followers against the secular republic at Canudos, nearly all of whom were eventually killed by government troops. In 1911 there was another rebellion in the southern states of Paraná and Santa Catarina, led by a Catholic visionary in defence of the monarchy. The Contestado movement lasted until 1915, when it too was destroyed by the military.

Brazilian politics were now dominated by an alliance known as *café con leite* (coffee with milk), of the coffee growers of São Paulo and the cattle ranchers of Minas Gerais, occasionally challenged by Rio Grande do Sul, with periodic involvement of the military. The first two presidents of the republic were military: Marshal Deodoro da Fonseca (1889-1891) and Marshal Floriano Peixoto (1891-1894). In some ways the military took the place of the Crown in mediating between the states' oligarchies, but its interventions were always unconstitutional and therefore gave rise to political instability. By the 1920s tensions between São Paulo and Minas Gerais had come out into the open with the cattle ranchers resenting the way in which the coffee growers used their position to keep the price of coffee artificially high at a time when there was an oversupply. Other social groups also became restive and unsuccessful coup attempts were launched by junior army officers in 1922, 1924 and 1926.

The end of the First World War saw the rise of the USA as an industrial power and the decline of Britain's traditional supremacy in trade with Latin America. Although Brazil was still exporting its raw materials to Europe at ever lower prices, it now imported its manufactured goods from the USA, leading to difficulties with finance and fluctuating exchange rates. Brazil's terms of trade had therefore deteriorated and the profitability of its export-led economy was declining before the crash of Wall Street in 1929. The cost of stockpiling excess coffee had led to a rise in debt and by 1930 the government was spending a third of its budget on debt servicing. The growth of nationalism was a key feature of this period as well as the emergence of new political factions and parties such as fascists and communists.

Vargas and the Estado Nôvo: 1930-1945

The Wall Street crash led to a sudden decline in demand for coffee and the São Paulo elite saw its hegemony wiped out. The elections of 1930 saw another win for the São Paulo candidate, but the results were disputed by a coalition of opposition forces. After several months of tension and violence, the army intervened, deposed the outgoing president and installed the alternative candidate of Rio Grande do Sul, Getúlio Vargas, a wealthy rancher, as provisional president. Vargas in fact held office until 1954, with only one break in 1945-1950. His main aim, when he took office, was to redress the balance of power away from São Paulo and in favour of his own state.

However, the effects of his reforms were more far-reaching. He governed by decree, replacing all state governors with 'interventors' who reduced the state militias, and reorganized the system of patronage within the states in favour of his own. São Paulo naturally resisted and there was a rebellion in 1932, but it was soon put down by federal troops, effectively wiping out the threat to Vargas' authority. In 1934 a constituent assembly drew up a new constitution that reduced the power of the states and gave more power to the president. The assembly then elected Vargas as president for a four-year term.

With the decline of traditional oligarchic blocs came the rise of political parties. The first to fill the vacuum were the fascists and the communists, who frequently took to street violence against each other. The fascists, called Integralists, were founded by Plínio Salgado in 1932. The Aliança Libertadora Nacional (ALN), a popular front including socialists and radical liberals, was founded by the Brazilian Communist Party in 1935. The ALN attempted to gain power by infiltrating the junior ranks of the army and encouraging rebellions, but Vargas clamped down on the movement, imprisoning its leaders. The fascists aimed to take power in 1938, the year elections were due, at which Vargas was not eligible to stand. However, in October 1937, Vargas declared a state of siege against an alleged communist plot and suspended the constitution which had prevented him being re-elected. Instead, he proclaimed a new constitution and a new state, *Estado Nôvo*. The fascists tried to oust him but failed, leaving Vargas with no effective opposition whatsoever.

The *Estado Nôvo* was also a response to an economic crisis, brought on by a fall in coffee prices, rising imports, a resulting deficit in the balance of payments, a high level of debt and soaring inflation. Vargas assumed dictatorial powers to deal with the economic crisis, censoring the press, banning political parties, emasculating trade unions and allowing the police unfettered powers. There followed a transition from export-led growth to import substitution and industrialization with heavy state intervention. Agricultural resources were channelled into industry and the government became involved in mining, oil, steel, electricity, chemicals, motor vehicles and light aircraft. The military were allowed free rein to develop their own armaments industry. As war approached in Europe, Vargas hedged his bets with both Nazi Germany and the USA, to see who would provide the greatest assistance for Brazil's industrialization. It turned out to be the USA, and in return for allowing US military bases to be built in northern Brazil he secured loans, technical assistance and other investments for a massive steel mill at Volta Redonda and infrastructure projects. Brazil did not declare war on Germany until 1944, but it was the only Latin American country to send troops to join the allies, with a force of 25,000 men going to Italy.

The elections of 1943 had been postponed during the War, but Vargas scheduled a vote for December 1945 in an attempt to dispel his fascist image. He allowed the formation of political parties, which included two formed by himself: the Social Democratic Party (PSD), supported by industrialists and large farmers, and a Labour Party (PTB), supported by pro-Vargas trade unions. There was also the National Democratic Union (UDN), opposed to Vargas, and the newly legalized Communist Party. However, there were growing fears that Vargas would not relinquish power, and when he appointed his brother as chief of police in Rio de Janeiro, the military intervened. Faced with the prospect of being deposed, Vargas chose to resign in October 1945, allowing the elections to take place as planned in the December. They were won by the PSD, led by General Eurico Dutra, a former supporter of the *Estado Nôvo*, who had encouraged Vargas to resign.

The second Republic: 1946-1964

Yet another constitution was drafted by a constituent assembly in 1946, this one based on the liberal principles of the 1891 constitution but including the labour code and the social legislation of the *Estado Nôvo*. Industrialization through state planning was retained, the foreign-owned railways were nationalized, hydroelectric power was developed, but deflation was necessary to bring down spiralling prices. The Communist Party was banned again in 1947. Meanwhile Vargas was elected Senator for Rio Grande do Sul, his home state, and kept active in politics, eventually being elected as candidate for the PSD and PTB alliance in the 1950 presidential elections. Although it was his third presidency, it was only his first by direct elections.

The third Vargas presidency was beset by the problems of fulfilling populist election promises while grappling with debt and inflation. Rapid industrialization required levels of investment which could only be raised abroad, but the nationalists were opposed to foreign investment. He failed to reconcile the demands of the USA and the nationalists, particularly with regards to oil and energy, and he failed to control inflation and stabilize the economy. There were rumours of corruption, and after the president's bodyguard was implicated in a plot to kill a journalist, which went wrong and another man was shot, the army issued him with another ultimatum to resign or be ousted. Instead, on 24 August 1954, Vargas shot himself, leaving a suicide note denouncing traitors at home and capitalists abroad.

The next president was Juscelino Kubitschek, who took office in January 1956 with the aim of achieving economic growth at any cost, regardless of inflation and debt. He is best known for building the new capital of Brazil, Brasília, nearly 1,000 km northwest of Rio de Janeiro in the state of Goiás. This massive modernist project served in the short term to expand the debt and in 1961, the next president, Jânio Quadros, inherited huge economic problems which brought his government down after only seven months and Congress unexpectedly accepted his resignation. Power passed to his vice-president, João Goulart, a populist and former labour minister under Vargas, who was mistrusted by the armed forces and the right wing. His powers were curtailed with the appointment of a prime minister and cabinet who would be jointly answerable to Congress. The 1960s were a turbulent time in Brazil as elsewhere, with the universities a hotbed of revolutionary socialism after the Cuban Revolution, Trotskyist and Communist agitators encouraging land occupations, strikes in industry and a move to secure trade union rights for the armed forces. A nationalist Congress passed legislation cutting foreign companies' annual profit remittances to 10% of profits, which sparked a massive outflow in foreign capital and a halving of US aid. Goulart was forced to print money to keep the economy going, which naturally put further pressure on an already soaring inflation rate. When Goulart clashed with Congress over approval of an economic adjustment programme and tried to strengthen his position by appealing for popular support outside Congress, he alarmed the middle classes, who unexpectedly supported a military coup in March 1964. Goulart took refuge in Uruguay.

Military rule: 1964-1985

The 1964 coup was a turning point in Brazilian political history. This time the armed forces did not return to barracks as they had before. Opposition leaders were arrested, the press censored, labour unions purged of anyone seen as left wing, and the secret police were given wide powers. The political parties were outlawed and replaced by two officially approved parties: the government Aliança Renovadora Nacional (ARENA) and the opposition Movimento Democrático Brasileiro (MDB). Congress, consisting only of members of these two parties, approved a succession of military presidents nominated by the armed forces. A new constitution, introduced in 1967, gave the president broad powers over the states and over Congress. The worst period of repression occurred between 1968 and 1973 with a wave of urban guerrilla warfare. Around this time, the military government's economic adjustment programme paid dividends and the economy began to grow, making life easier for the middle classes and reducing any potential support for guerrilla groups. In 1968-1974 the economy grew at over 10% a year, which became known as the Brazilian 'economic miracle'. This spectacular growth, achieved because of the authoritarian nature of the regime, masked a widening gulf between the rich and poor, with the blacks and mulattos, always at the bottom in Brazilian society, suffering the most. Edwin Williamson (*The Penguin History of Latin America*) quotes statistics showing that in 1960 the richest 10% of the population received 40% of the national income; by 1980 they received 51%, while the poorest 50% received only 13%. In the shanty towns, or *favelas*, which had mushroomed around all the large cities, but especially São Paulo, disease, malnutrition and high mortality rates were prevalent and their citizens battled constantly in appalling housing lacking sewerage, running water and electricity.

By 1973 some military officers and their civilian advisors had become alarmed at the rising level of opposition. Arguing that repression alone would merely lead to further opposition and even to attempted revolution, they pressed for 'decompression': policies to relax the repression while remaining in power. The attempt to carry out this policy by legalizing political parties, permitting freer trade unions and strikes and reducing censorship, gave greater space for the opposition to demand an end to military rule. Attempts to introduce elections to Congress which were less controlled faced the same obstacle: they tended to result in victories for candidates who favoured civilian rule.

One of the main reasons for the military deciding to return to their barracks was the dire state of the economy. The armed forces had taken over in 1964 when the economy had hit rock bottom, their authoritarian regime had allowed rapid expansion and change which brought about the 'economic miracle', yet by 1980 the economy had gone full circle. Inflation was running at 100% a year and was set to go through the roof, foreign debt was the highest in Latin America, estimated at over US$87 billion, and unemployment was soaring. When international interest rates rose sharply in 1982, Brazil was no longer able to service its debt and it suspended interest payments. Unwilling to go through another round of authoritarianism and repression, the military decided to let the civilians have a go. Elections in 1982 produced a majority for the pro-government Social Democratic Party (PDS) in the electoral college which was to elect the next president, but splits in the PDS led to the election in January 1985 of the opposition candidate, (see under São João del Rei, page 257).

The return to democracy

Corruption and impeachment

In 1985 Tancredo Neves was elected as the first civilian president for 21 years. Before he could take office he fell ill and died. His vice-president José Sarney became president at a time of economic crisis, with inflation at 300%. Sarney introduced the Cruzado Plan in 1986, freezing prices and wages, but inflation exploded when the freeze was lifted.

A new constitution brought direct presidential elections in November 1989. After two rounds of voting Fernando Collor de Melo, of the small Partido da Reconstrução Nacional, won 53% of the vote to narrowly defeat his left-wing rival, Luís Inácio da Silva (popularly known as Lula). Collor launched controversial economic reforms, including opening the economy to imports, privatisation and a freeze on savings and bank accounts. The policies failed and by 1991 inflation reached 1,500% and foreign debt payments were suspended.

Just over half way through his term, Collor was suspended from office after Congress voted overwhelmingly to impeach him for corruption. He avoided this by resigning on 29 December 1992. Vice-president Itamar Franco took over, but had scant success in tackling poverty and inflation until the introduction of an anti-inflation package that introduced the *real* as the new currency.

The Plano Real

The architect of the *Real* plan was finance minister Fernando Henrique Cardoso. Three decades earlier he had been a high-profile leftist and opponent of military rule, forced into exile after the 1964 military coup. The success of the *Real* plan led to his election as president in October 1994. After trailing Lula of the Workers Party (PT), Cardoso gained such popularity that he won the election in the first round of voting. However, his alliance of the Brazilian Social Democrat Party (PSDB), the Liberal Front (PFL) and the Labour Party (PTB) failed to gain a majority in either house of Congress. This severely hampered plans to reform the tax and social security systems and the civil service. The government was also criticized for its slowness in addressing social problems. Such problems ranged from the need for land reform and violence associated with landlessness, to the slave-like working conditions in agricultural areas and the human rights of the *indígena* and of street children in large cities.

Towards the end of 1997 the financial crisis in Asia sapped investor confidence throughout the world, and threatened Brazil's currency and economic stability. The failure to cut public spending had swollen the budget deficit and the *real* was exposed to speculation. Cardoso was obliged to take actions to prevent an upsurge in inflation and devaluation of the currency, but at the cost of slowing down economic growth. Crisis was avoided and inflation remained in single figures, in contrast to the hyperinflation of earlier periods.

The government still faced the serious social imbalances that it had failed to redress. However, Cardoso managed to beat Lula again in October 1998 without the need for a second poll. In doing so he became the first Brazilian president to be elected for a second term.

Cardoso's second term

Cardoso and his PSDB party emerged victorious from the 1998 elections with 99 Deputies, but they needed allies both in the 513-seat Chamber of Deputies and in the Senate. Political opponents had also won many powerful state governorships. The PSDB's relations with its major ally, the PFL, came under increasing strain. Unlike the PSDB, the PFL is a conservative group dominated by old-style politicians, typified by its leader Antônio Carlos Magalhães, who increasingly controlled Congress. There were rumours of corruption in Cardoso's government, with not even the president himself above implication. Another financial crisis threatened, which was averted by an IMF loan of US$18 billion at the end of 1998, but the delayed social security reforms had still not been passed. Finally when ex-president Itamar Franco, governor of Minas Gerais, refused to pay his state's debts to the Federal Government in January 1999, foreign investors lost confidence. The pressures on the *real* became too great and the central bank had to let it float freely against the dollar. It lost 50% of its value in the process. Two more stable years followed, but with its economic credibility eroded and shifting alliances in Congress the Cardoso government made little progress with its policies.

The 2002 elections

As in the USA, Brazilian presidents cannot run for a third term. Four front-runners emerged in the 2002 elections. Taking an early commanding lead in the opinion polls was Luiz Inácio Lula da Silva, best known as Lula, who was making his fourth bid for the presidency. With a refurbished image, a new suit, moderated policies and a millionaire running mate, the veteran firebrand, gained support from all classes.

Against a backdrop of global crises, the *real* again lost some 50% of its value in less than a year. Foreign investors were concerned about repeated budget deficits, and the prospect that a more left-wing government might default on debts. In August 2002, the IMF again came to the rescue, this time with a record US$30-billion loan, subject to tough conditions. On 27 October 2002 Lula won a convincing victory against government-backed José Serra. The new president – once shoe-shine boy, ex-leader of the Metal Workers' Union and head of the Workers' Party – set out to lead the first left-wing government in Brazil for 40 years.

For foreigners, what was perhaps most remarkable about Lula's first term of office was how little changed. Whilst Chavez in Venezuela and Ivo Morales in Bolivia forged policies allying their countries with Cuba and Cuban ideology, which included preaching a gospel of hatred and mistrust against the United States, Lula forged a middle way. In one of the first meetings with George Bush, the new president made it clear that Brazil was open for business and that he expected the USA to be open to Brazilian exports, particularly agricultural products that had long been denied access to US markets. Lula also wanted to acknowledge Brazil as a regional power. Nor did Brazil plummet into economic crisis as was predicted by the likes of George Soros. Its economy continued to grow steadily, albeit at a slower rate than its counterparts in Asia. And publicly Lula distanced himself from firebrand left wing Latin Americans like Chavez; preferring to foster closer trade relations with China and India. Lula also attempted to introduce reforms that ran against the grain of Brazilian society and political practice, by filtering money from the elite and the public service establishment to the less privileged. Brazil's public services are among the most cumbersome, financially draining, bureaucratic and corrupt in the world. And none are more so than the pension system. Many public sector professionals collect several pensions and many retire on pensions higher than their final salary. Judges for example receive an average of £1700 per month. Army officers do even better and pass on their pensions to the second generation after their death. In contrast state pensions to the private sector average £80 per month. In 2002 the state pension ran a deficit worth 4.3% of GDP or £12 billion. One of Lula's early achievements was to get the Senate to pass a bill on pensions reform, capping public pensions at £500 per month (still two times higher than the average middle class salary), raising the retirement age and introducing new pension taxes. This resulted in strikes by half of the country's federal workers and the blocking of the bill by judges; a process which can take years to unravel in Brazil's equally bureaucratic courts

2004-2007

In mid-2004 Lula published an impressive proposed bill on Agrarian Reform which promised far more than any Brazilian government ever has: 400,000 families are to be settled via expropriation, 200,000 to be settled on land purchased by a Credito Fundiário small loans bank, designed to sell to small farmers at subsidized interest rates. He also launched a Fome Zero, or 'no hunger' programme, designed to give all poor Brazilians enough to eat.

But the second half of Lula's first term saw his good intentions frustrated by a combination of incompetence and corruption. Municipal governments, principally individual mayors, tried to control the disbursement of funds both for the Credito Fundiário and the Fome Zero programme; raking off public money has long been a way of life in Brazil. As so often in Brazil's history, money dedicated for the poor was ending up in private bank accounts. And in 2005 a corruption scandal called the Mensalão rocked Lula's federal government. Public funds had been used to bribe smaller parties to vote for Lula's government in the two federal chambers. Lula's deputy resigned, together with several senior PT members. Lula denied involvement but was severely compromised and was branded either oblivious and therefore incompetent or corrupt himself. A savage press campaign against him boded ill for the federal elections of 2006. But Lula won again; buoyed by popular support from the poor urban majority. So now it remains to be seen whether his reforms will prove more far-reaching during his second term.

Culture

People

Indigenous peoples

There were probably between three and five million indigenous people in Brazil when the Portuguese arrived. Today there are between 200,000 and 300,000. The effects of European colonization were devastating – whole tribes were wiped out under the Portuguese Amazon slave trade and others set to fight against each other for Portuguese advantage. Present-day tribal groups number about 220; each has a unique dialect, but most languages belong to four main linguistic families, Tupi-Guarani, Gê, Carib and Arawak. A few tribes remain uncontacted, others are exclusively nomadic, others are semi-nomadic hunter-gatherers and farmers, while some are settled groups in close contact with non-indigenous society. There is no agreement on precisely how many tribes are extant, but the Centro Ecumênico da Documentação e Informação (CEDI) of São Paulo said that of the 200 or so groups it documented, 40% have populations of less than 200 people and 77% have populations of less than 1000. Hemming underlines this depressing statistic when he reports that tribes contacted in recent decades have, as have others in previous centuries, suffered catastrophic reductions in numbers as soon as they encounter diseases which are common to non-indigenous people, but to which their bodies have no immunity.

Most of Brazil's indigenous people live in the Amazon region; they are affected by deforestation, encroachment from colonizers, small- and large-scale mining, and the construction of hydroelectric dams. Besides the Yanomami, other groups include the Xavante, Ticuna, Tukano, Kreen Akrore, Kaiapó, Bororo and Arara. The struggle of groups such as the Yanomami to have their land demarcated in order to secure title is well-documented. The goal of the Statute of the Indian (Law 6.001/73), for demarcation of all Indian land by 1978, is largely unmet. It was feared that a new law introduced in January 1996 would slow the process even more. However all is not bleak. The populations of many indigenous groups have grown over the last decade and a number have their land rights, which have been protected under Brazilian Law, by Fernando Henrique Cardoso and by Lula (although the latter is alleged to have reneged on a promise to enshrine an important area territory in Roraima into law at the 11th hour in exchange for support by powerful members of the state elite). On occasion indigenous land rights are enforced. A flight out over the Xingu in northern Mato Grosso shows this starkly, with the indigenous territory as a huge green island in a sea of soya and cattle plantations. Funai, the National Foundation for the Support of the Indian, a part of the Interior Ministry, is charged with representing the Indians' interests, but lacks resources and support. There is no nationwide, representative body for indigenous people, although the Amazon indigenous lobbying group, COIAB, is increasingly powerful and Manoel Moura's FIUPAM (fiupam@yahoo.com.br) is growing daily.

Mestiços

At first the Portuguese colony grew slowly. From 1580 to 1640 the population was only about 50,000 apart from the million or so *indígena*. In 1700 there were some 750,000 non-indigenous people in Brazil. Early in the 19th century Humboldt computed there were about 920,000 whites, 1.96 million Africans, and 1.12 million *indígena* and people of mixed Portuguese and indigenous origin (*mestiços*): after three centuries of occupation a total of only four million, and over twice as many Africans as there were whites.

Racism and Brazil

In 2001 Ivo Meirelles, a samba-funk musician from Rio, sang *Tá Faltando Preto na Televisão* ("there's not enough black people on TV"). Where, he asked, are black people on *Xuxa*'s programmes? Where are they on the top talk show, *Faustão*? And why are they only ever in the kitchen on TV *Globo*'s famous soaps? Meirelles was trying to draw attention to a disparity in Brazil that runs counter to all of the popular myths about racial harmony.

Brazil has an estimated population of 180 million people, of which half are the descendants of African slaves, brought over from the early 1500s up until 1888. Modern Brazil is home to the largest number of black people in any country outside Africa. Yet beyond football and music, African-Brazilians are absent from cultural and political life from the lowest common denominator to the highest: Brazil has only ever had one black 'Miss Brazil' and, until the emergence of *Tais Araújo* in 2004, had no black TV actresses. There are still no black news presenters on Brazil's mainstream channels and precious few black journalists. Pelé became the first black minister in the country's history as recently as 1995, and Barbosa Gomes became Brazil's first black high court judge in 2003.

Yet black Brazilians account for 63% of the poorest section of society. A 2000 census found that 62.7% of Brazil's white population had access to sanitation compared with just 39.6% of its Afro-Brazilians, and the most recent UN report showed that on average black men earn 50% less than their white counterparts. A UNESCO report found that the majority of victims of murder in Brazil are young black men aged between 15 and 24.

Yet things are slowly beginning to change. Gilberto Gil has been tireless in seeding and supporting black culture projects in Brazil's poorest areas. In 2002 university quotas were introduced for black students. And in 2005, in a joint investment with Angola, Brazil's first black television station, TV da Gente, began to broadcast in São Paulo and Fortaleza. "In our day to day lives", said Meirelles in an interview, "TV dictates fashion, the clothes we wear, hairstyle, slang, behaviour – everything...". Many black Brazilians are now hoping that he is right.

The arid wastes of the *sertão* remain largely uncultivated. Its inhabitants are *mestiço*; most live off a primitive but effective method of cultivation known as 'slash and burn'. This involves cutting down and burning the brushwood for a small patch of ground, which is cultivated for a few years and then allowed to grow back.

Afro-Brazilians

Racism is culturally rife in Brazil and often openly expressed in all-white company. Though there is no legal discrimination against black people, the economic and educational disparity – by default rather than intent of the Government – is such that successful Afro-Brazilians are active almost exclusively in the worlds of sport, entertainment and the arts.

Brazilian culture, however would be nothing without its African influences. Those interested in the development of Afro-Brazilian music, dance, religion, arts and cuisine will find the cities of Rio de Janeiro, Bahia and São Luís, which retain the greatest African influences, particularly fascinating. Black Pride movements are particularly strong in Bahia.

After the rigours of transatlantic shipment in tiny rat-infested spaces, the Africans suffered further trauma on arrival at the Brazilian ports. They were often sold in groups that were segregated to avoid slaves from the same family or speaking the same language being together. By breaking all cultural and sentimental ties, the Portuguese hoped to eradicate ethnic pride and rebellions on the estates. As a result African spiritual cults became mixed and syncretistic even before they mixed with Portuguese Catholicism and indigenous spirituality. In what is now modern day Nigeria, for instance, there were different groups of people, each with its own divinity or Orixá (pronounced 'Orisha'). These Orixás were normally the spirit of a distinguished ancestor or a legendary hero and were worshipped only in a particular region. As the slaves went to Brazilian estates in groups made up of people from different African regions, they soon started to worship all the Orixás, instead of just one. As a result uniquely Afro-Brazilian religions were born out of the template of African spirituality, notably Candomblé, Umbanda, and Macumba.

Europeans

Modern immigration did not begin effectively until after 1850. Of the 4.6 million immigrants from Europe between 1884 and 1954, 32% were Italians, 30% Portuguese, 14% Spanish, 4% German, and the rest of various nationalities. Since 1954 immigrants have averaged 50,000 a year. Most of the German immigrants settled in Santa Catarina, Rio Grande do Sul, and Paraná. The Germans (and the Italians, Poles and other Slavs who followed them) did not, in the main, go as wage earners on the big estates, but as cultivators of their own small farms. Here there is a settled agricultural population cultivating the soil intensively.

Asians

There are some one million Japanese-descended Brazilians; they grow a fifth of the coffee, 30% of the cotton, all the tea, and are very active in market gardening. Today the whites and near-whites are about 53% of the population, people of mixed race about 34%, and Afro Brazilians 11%; the rest are either indigenous or Asian. There are large regional variations in the distribution of the races: the whites predominate greatly in the South, which received the largest flood of European immigrants.

Arts and crafts

Woodcarving

Woodworking has two principal origins, the African and the Jesuit. In northeastern Brazil, many woodcarving and sculpting techniques are inherited from the African slaves who were brought across the Atlantic to work the sugar plantations. One of the most prominent examples is the *carranca*, the grotesque figurehead that was placed on a boat's prow to ward off evil spirits. *Carrancas* are an adaptation of the African mask-making tradition and other carved and sculpted masks can be found in the Northeast. The Jesuits passed on skills in the carving and painting of religious figures in wood. Originally they encouraged their indigenous converts in the techniques, but today others practice the art. Woodcarving is widespread in Pernambuco and Bahia in the Northeast. In Rio de Janeiro many contemporary artists work in wood and Embu, near São Paulo (see page 193), is a centre for wooden sculptures and furniture making.

Ceramics

In northeastern Brazil, religious figures are also made in clay, for instance the unglazed, life-sized saints made from red clay in Tracunhaém, near Recife. Another centre for similar work is Goiana, also in Pernambuco. A third place from which the ceramics are even more famous is Alto da Moura, near Caruaru (Pernambuco – see page 442). Here, Mestre Vitalino began modelling scraps of clay into little figures

Amazon spirituality: rainforest shamanism

Shamans of the rainforest

Like most pre-Colombian religions, Amazon spirituality is rooted in shamanism, which originated in Siberia, the point of exodus for most of America's ancestors. In the rainforest, shamanism has evolved into its own, rich form. Above all, it is a way of life; a journey of spiritual evolution in which the shaman is a mentor and guide. The ultimate goal is spiritual enlightenment. However, few people opt for the tortuous, almost monastic path that takes them there. Shamanic practices are more often concerned with the correct ordering of mundane life events and the marking out of ritual and symbolic space.

The material world is attuned to the spiritual through the use of symbols. Everything from a hunt to the positioning of a building has to represent the higher, divine world. Shamans, who teach aspiring religious leaders and oversee all the tribe's spiritual activities, are therefore priests and spiritual professors. Some have attained spiritual realization, whether through intense deprivation and suffering or through the long process of shamanistic education. Others are the holders of tradition that has been passed on to them.

True knowledge

The shamanistic universe comprises two worlds that co-exist: the spiritual and the physical. Spiritual enlightenment involves complete, instinctual understanding of the oneness of both worlds. The 'visible' or material world is the realm of the senses and is governed by the quest for food. Underlying this is a spiritual, 'invisible' world that we share with all objects and beings in the universe. The latter is the realm of pure being, archetype and spirit. It is the ground of our consciousness and is where we perceive and even meet the cosmic and divine powers. Western societies tend to regard only the empirically verifiable and measureable as real. The *indígena*, however, start with the experience of consciousness itself and construct an understanding of reality from here. For example, to the Desano-Tukano people of the upper Amazon, whose philosophy is one of the best documented of Amazon peoples, man is known as *mári ariri kéro dohpá inyarí*, which means 'our existence dream-like appears'. All actions in the visible world must be evaluated in terms of the invisible world, for this is ultimately where they derive their form and meaning. In other words, what we do belongs to the material world; what we are, to the spiritual. When a shaman reaches the point of realization, he is like the enlightened of Buddhism or Hinduism: the scales fall from the eyes, the two realms are perceived as one and 'what- he realizes himself to be' completely informs what he does. Such spiritual realization is accomplished through a journey of direct experience and in rainforest shamanism. It is guided by psychotropic pharmacy and a complex mythical map, as can be seen from the Desano-Tukano understanding of the relationship between the mind and the brain.

The Tukanos equate the invisible world with the left cerebral hemisphere of the brain, and the visible with the right. The left hemisphere is that of the mature, enlightened adult, the 'older brother'. It is the seat of intuition, moral authority, order, intellectual and spiritual endeavours, music, dreams and abstract thought. Its name, *ëmëkori mahsá turí*, means 'sun people dimension'.

The sun is the manifestation of the power of the creator of the universe, the 'sun father'. It is also the home of the *gahi turí* or the other dimension or world, where we apprehend and interact with the archetypes and forms of the invisible world. And it is the instrument for interpreting the *bogári*, which are energy fields and 'transmissions' that emanate from nature. The right hemisphere is called *mahsá turí*, or 'human dimension'. It is subservient and is associated with the younger brother. Here lies practical knowledge and skill, tradition, customary rituals, and everything pertaining to the physical. The corpus callosum – a bundle of nerves that bridges the fissure between the two hemispheres has a very complex symbolism associated with it. Simply speaking, it can be seen as an 'anaconda river', with the dark patterns on the snake's back as stepping stones. The student learns to navigate the river, stepping on the stones to move between the left and right hemispheres. Just in front of the anaconda's head is a rock crystal symbolizing the seat of cosmic (solar) illumination. For Tukanoan *indígena*, the rock crystal is a model of the universe; their hexaganol shape is regarded as a holy shape that infuses the rhythm of daily life.

Mind-altering tonics, such as ayahuasca, are used to help shift perception from the visible (right hemisphere) world to the invisible (left hemisphere). Such remedies collapse the ego and completely silence the mental voice and our tenacious regard for ourselves as separate to the external world. Shamans use these tonics very carefully, and with pharmaceutical precision. All tribal members imbibe at some point, usually to mark key life events.

The cosmos

Shamans are informed not only by intuition but by age-old tradition. If intuition is mystical prayer, then tradition is the text of shamanic life. It comes in the form of the myriad taboos and rituals passed down through generations, and a giant cosmological map in which positions and movements are imbued with religious significance. This map comprises the harmonic movements of the sky above and the forest around. It is used to plot and inform everything, from the timing of different harvesting seasons to the construction of buildings. For the Desano-Tukano, Orion is the single most important stellar constellation.

The constellations along the path announce different harvesting and hunting seasons, ordering the physical world to the cosmic and spiritual. The six stars within Orion and those around the constellation are linked in a series of hexagons, as embodied by the sacred rock crystals. The hexagons in the sky are reconstructed in Tukanoan buildings. Six points mark the positions of the strongest house posts, one at each corner of the hexagon, according to the stars surrounding Orion. Six further posts delimit a central hexagon inside the *maloca*, corresponding to Orion itself. An imaginary line bisects the *maloca* through both hexagons, representing both the Equator and the belt of Orion.

Ritual dances are performed within the inner hexagon, whose movements are also symbolically related to the pattern of Orion. Two groups of dancers, one male and one female, move back and forth dividing the line in triangular formations and tracing the hourglass-shape of Orion. They represent the relationship between feminine and masculine archetypes: light and darkness, sun and moon, fertility and restraint. Thus the human home for the Desano-Tukano becomes a theatre for the play of 'man within the universe', and the dances represent the eternal play that occurs within the soul.

 depicting everyday life (work, festivals, dancing, political events). He died in 1963, but the tradition that he started has continued and is known throughout Brazil.

The pots that are made in the Amazon region come in various styles, some of them quite strange. Bahian and other northeastern pottery shows African influence.

Textiles, clothing and leather

Ceará, in the North, is famous for its lace-making, and beautiful pieces are sold all over Brazil. In other parts of the North, hammocks and other woven items are found. The hammock is, of course, an essential household item and you may well need to buy one if you are travelling up the Amazon on a boat. Other utilitarian articles which have become craft items are the rugs and capes made in the highlands further south, such as Minas Gerais, to keep out the night-time cold.

In the Northeast, traditional costumes have their roots in the rituals of the African religions that came to Brazil with the slave trade. In southern areas where European immigration was heaviest, many traditional costumes can be seen, usually at the festivals and dances that have survived. Another type of clothing from the South is that associated with the *gaúchos*, the Brazilian cowboys of Rio Grande do Sul. As well as the clothes, which normally use hide in their manufacture, you may also buy saddlery, stirrups, silverware and the gourds used for drinking *maté*.

Leatherwork is not confined to the South, but can be found in any region where cattle are raised.

Musical instruments

The most popular instruments that tourists like to buy are those connected with African music, especially the drums, shakers and the *berimbau* (the one-stringed bow that is twanged in accompaniment to Capoeira). Here again, the best place to look is in the Northeast where the African heritage is strongest. You can also purchase guitars and other stringed instruments.

Basketware

In Amazônia, a huge variety of raw materials are available for making baskets, nets, hammocks, slings for carrying babies, masks and body adornments. In the Northeast, too, baskets come in all shapes and sizes, especially in Bahia, Pernambuco and Paraíba. Another northeastern craft, which does not fit into the above categories, is pictures made in bottles with coloured sands (Lençóis, Bahia, and Natal, Rio Grande do Norte, are good places to buy them). In Minas Gerais, two very common things to see and buy are soapstone carvings (for instance birds and animals) and the cooking pots used in *mineira* kitchens.

Gemstones

Even before the discover of rich mineral deposits in the interior of the country, legends told of mountains full of precious stones. Prospectors looked for diamonds and emeralds as well as gold and silver to make them wealthy. The existence of gems was known about almost from the earliest days of the Portuguese colony, from the reports given to the new arrivals by the *indígena* and from scattered discoveries of different stones. But there was nothing to bring riches on the scale of the silver and gold found in the Spanish colonies. Gold was found in Minas Gerais in the 17th century and diamonds in 1725 at Diamantina (Minas Gerais) and thus Brazil's mineral wealth began to appreciate. The search for new deposits has never flagged.

Commercially mined stones include: **diamonds**, found in Minas Gerais, Roraima, Bahia, Tocantins, Mato Grosso and Mato Grosso do Sul. Brazil was the world's largest producer of diamonds until South Africa entered the market in the 19th century. **Emeralds**, not discovered in Brazil until 1963 (many green beryls had been mined before then, but were known not to be true emeralds), are now mined in Bahia, Minas

Gerais and Goiás. **Aquamarine** is a clear blue beryl from Rio Grande do Norte, Paraíba, Bahia, Minas Gerais and Espírito Santo. **Ruby** and **sapphire** are two shades of the same mineral, corundum, the former rich red, the latter a deep blue. Rubies are found in Santa Catarina, sapphires in Minas Gerais. The two most valued forms of *topaz* found are the rare Imperial Topaz from Ouro Preto (Minas Gerais), which comes in a range of colours from honey-coloured through shades of red to pink, and Blue Topaz from Minas Gerais and Rondônia.

Tourmalines are also found and come from Minas Gerais, Ceará and Goiás; they have the widest range of colours of any gemstone, from colourless (white) to red, yellow, greens, blues, lilac and black. They even come in bi- and tricoloured varieties. **Opals**, unique for their rainbow flecks, are mined in Piauí and Rio Grande do Sul. **Amethyst**, a quartz which ranges in colour from pale lilac to deep purple, is mined in Tocantins, Pará, Bahia, Mato Grosso do Sul and Rio Grande do Sul. From the last three states, plus Minas Gerais, comes **citrine**, another quartz which is predominantly yellow. Less well-known, but equally beautiful are **kunzite**, a rare pinkish-violet stone, and **chrysoberyl**, both found in Minas Gerais. Chrysoberyl is found in a variety of forms, a golden-yellow-brown, 'cat's eye' chrysoberyl, which has an luminous thread running through it, and the very rare **alexandrite**, which changes colour according to the light. Its most spectacular form changes from green in daylight to red in artificial light.

Music

Contemporary Brazilian music

Brazil has by far the most interesting and varied musical scene in Latin America, with a range of genres as rich as the USA's or the UK's, or perhaps even richer. As well as international standards like rock, rap and jazz, there are a panoply of uniquely Brazilian styles – samba, choro, frevo, forró, axé, bossa nova, guitarrada, mangue-beat... in fact there is so much choice it is hard to know where to begin.

The music scene in Brazil can perhaps be roughly divided into two categories: music to dance to and music for listening to, though there is a great deal of crossover.

Music to dance to

The most famous of the country's dance rhythms is **samba**; a complex and infectious 2/4 rhythm that came to Rio from Angola via the Brazilian state of Bahia and reached its full fruition in the Rio Carnival of the 1930s. Samba sounds wonderfully happy but is in reality bittersweet, with rhythms filled with joy and optimism and lyrics as sad as a lament. Offshoots of samba include **samba canção** – which is more sedate and highbrow and **pagode** which is the opposite and has been characterized by the founder of Tropicália, Tom Ze, as music Brazilians have on at family beach barbecues.

As popular as samba (and a development of it) is **axé**, which is twice as fast and twice as frenetic and played principally at Brazil's other great and even more hedonistic Carnaval – in Salvador. Axé sounds like salsa sexed-up, fused with rock and roll and overdosing on speed. Less frantic is **forró**, another dance rhythm from the Northeast which was invented at 'For All' barn dances thrown for Brazilian railway workers by their English bosses. 'For all' was rendered 'For Haw' by the northeastern palate which in Brazil is spelt 'Forró'. It is a beach bar dance with yokely lyrics, powered by a pulsating drum and accordion and danced far closer than anything you will find in Hispanic America. Its offspring, **lambada**, which is danced even closer, has all but disappeared in Brazil nowadays. Other dance music styles include **frevo**, a fast 2/4 instrumental style which evolved from the polka, **guitarrada**, electric-guitar driven, from the Amazon and sounding a little like Dick Dale on a cocktail of speed and acid and **samba-rock,** which is known as Rio funk in Europe (and is like 1970s US funk, rendered Brazilian).

Brazilian musical genres at a glance

Axé Frenetic Bahian Carnaval music. Ivete Sangalo is the undisputed queen, Daniela Mercury is the most famous international and Band Beijo's *Ao Vivo* captures the raw energy of live axé.

Bossa electrônica A European and American re-invention of bossa nova for the new millennium club scene. Artists such as Bebel Gilberto and Cibelle found fame abroad and the style reverted to Brazil where it was taken to more sophisticated heights by the likes of Fernanda Porto and Paula Morelenbaum.

Bossa nova Brazil's most famous export, best known through *The Girl from Ipanema*, was born in the 1950s and though it lived on in the USA and Europe with the work of Brazilian ex-pat musicians, it all but died in Brazil by the early 1970s. There are three great bossa nova names to look out for: João Gilberto, Tom Jobim and Vinícius de Moraes.

Brazilian jazz fusion This style emerged in the USA through a meeting of Brazilian session musicians and American jazz players such as Miles Davis and Chic Corea. The most famous of all Brazilian fusion tracks is Eumir Deodato's funked up 1970s *Also Spracht Zarathustra* (the 2001 theme) on his CD *Prelude* and Nana Vasconcelos's groundbreaking *Codona*, recorded with Don Cherry. Airto Moreira's *Identity* is wonderful, as is Flora Purim's *Flight*. Other classics include Egberto Gismonti's *Circense*. For something more off the wall look out for CDs by multi-instrumentalist eccentric Hermeto Pascoal.

Carnaval samba What it says on the tin. Buy a compilation of the best songs from this year's Rio Carnaval.

Club music A fusion of Europe, the USA and Brazil. The big names are hugely influential Drum 'n' Bass DJs Patife and Marky. More interesting is DJ Dolores, a former mangue beat stalwart who fuses traditional Brazilian and international sounds. He who won the BBC World Music Awards in 2004.

Choro Metaphorically Brazilian Dixieland. Choro's most legendary figure is flautist Pixinguinha. His recordings, although re-issued, are as scratchy and ancient as Robert Johnson but show a musician equally as great. For something less gramophone try the James Dean of the choro world, Raphael Rabello – a brilliant violinist who died in the 1980s when still in his 30s. There is plenty of live choro throughout Brazil – see Aprazível page 113, Clan Café, page 120, and Toca do Vinicus, page 121.

Forró Infectious, drum and accordion-driven Northeastern barn dance beach music. The most traditional names and inventors of modern forró are Luiz Gonzaga and Sivuca. Look out for CDs by northeastern bands like Mastruz com Leite or Mel Com Terra. For something a little classier opt for Elba Ramalho.

Frevo Pernambuco carnival and big band music. Many Brazilian singers and bands from Alceu Valença to Zé Ramalho have recorded frevos but Claudionor Germano e Expedito Baracho are two of the few who are specialists in the genre.

Guitarrada Amazon guitar-driven dance. The most famous exponents are Aldo Sena and Mestre Vieira, from Para.

Hip hop Rap fused with repentista poetry, samba and other Brazilian styles. Artists here include Rappin' Hood, Gabriel o Pensador, and Racionais MCs. An excellent introduction would be Rappin Hood's *Sujeito Homen* or Marcelo D2's *Looking for the Perfect Beat*.

Lambada An out-of-fashion version of forró that was popular for a while in southern Bahia. Kaoma and Beto Barbosa are well-known names – though their CDs can be hard to find outside of Bahia.

Mangue-beat Brazil's most exciting and experimental contemporary music is born of this Pernambuco fusion of Brazilian roots and European punk. The key names here are Nação Zumbi, whose groundbreaking CD is *Afrociberdelia*, Mundo Livre, Mestre Ambrosio and the solo albums of the band's former leader, Siba. Also noable is one-time Naçao Zumbi band member, Otto, whose *Sem Gravidade* is a dreamy tour de force of percussion, lyrical singing and samples. Artists borrowing from the mangue-beat heritage are numerous. Among the very best are visionary experimentalist studio wizard, Max de Castro, The Pernambuco Pogues Tiné and Totonho e Os Cabra; whose theatrical, experimental stage sets are a rhythmic and performance showstopper.

Música popular brasileira (MPB) There are a vast panoply of MPB musicians in Brazil. Although founded by Brazil's king of cheese, Roberto Carlos (who remains perhaps the best-selling recording artist in Latin America), a roll call of the greatest names would have to include: Milton Nascimento, the golden voice of Brazil and perhaps the country's greatest ever songwriter, Djavan, Brazil's Stevie Wonder and a master of harmonic complexity, Elis Regina the country's great tragic diva and Chico Buarque, considered by some to be Brazil's greatest living poet and its foremost protest singer. More modern names include silky-voiced Marisa Monte, Bahian Timabalada percussionist and eccentric, Carlinhos Brown and a plethora of bands like Kid Abelha and Paralamas do Succeso. Artists like Grupo Afro-Reggae and Fernanda Abreu have infused life, energy and political purpose into MPB in recent years. Maria Eugenia is one of the best of the new wave of traditional interpreters.

Pagode Samba for the people and the beach barbecue. Look out for CDs by Beth Carvalho or Zeca Pagodinho.

Samba rock and Samba soul Also known as Rio Funk. This style is irresistibly danceable and very popular in Europe. Its godfather, Jorge Ben, wrote one of the country's most famous songs *Mas Que Nada*. He always plays free concerts over New Year on Copacabana. You can find many of his best songs on *Brazilian Hits and Funky Classics*. Almost as important is Tim Maia; a Rio soul singer whose compositions are recorded as standards in Brazil as widely as Holland-Dozier-Holland in the USA. Other famous names include Ed Motta, whose most recently recordings are closer to jazz, Seu Jorge, Ivo Mereilles, Paula Lima, Tutti Bae and Sandra de Sa.

Sertanejo This is easily the most popular style in the country and is characterized by male duos in cowboy hats lamenting lost love. Well-worth exploring for lovers of the kitsch; look out for the film *OS Dos Filhos de Francisco* for a guided tour through the career of the two biggest Sertanejo stars – Zeze de Camargo e Luciano.

Traditional Samba or Samba Canção Sung samba is more reflective and harmonically complex than carnival samba. There are many great names in this genre. Most popular are Martinho da Vila and Bezerra da Silva. More sophisticated are João Bosco and Baden Powell; two of Brazil's very best guitarists, composers and singers. Bosco's classic albums are *Galos De Briga* and *Caça À Raposa*. *Nosso Baden* is a good Powell compilation. Other names to look out for are Nelson Gonçalves and Paulinho da Viola.

Tropicália Brazil's answer to Psychedelia saw western instruments and styles fused with Brazilian rhythms and played by a bunch of stoned middle-class intellectuals in Bahia. The leaders of the movement were Tom Zé, Gilberto Gil, Caetano Veloso, Tom Zé, Maria Bethania and Gal Costa; and after it had spread to São Paulo, Os Mutantes. All have been prolific in their output and continue to be but with the notable exception of Tom Ze's *Estudiando O Pagode*, their best work comes from the 1970s; notably the founder album *Panes e Circenses*, Caetano Veloso's *Bicho* and Gil's *Refazenda*. *Doces Bárbaros* with Caetano, Gil, Gal Costa and Maria Bethânia is an excellent compilation. The movement was as old and outmoded in Brazil as Donovan in the UK; when it finally caught on in Europe in the new millennium.

Music to listen to

The fact that the pedigree of Brazil's serious artists is second to none can be easily seen by a casual look at the guest musicians on their CDs. Names like Herbie Hancock, Joe Henderson, Stan Getz, Stevie Wonder, Wayne Shorter, Billy Cobham and Larry Coryell are commonplace. Serious contemporary music has a long and distinguished pedigree in Brazil. Whilst Scott Joplin was inventing early jazz, Rio musicians were inventing their own kind of ragtime, **choro**, which like jazz was a fusion of Africa and Europe born out of the abolition of the slave trade. Choro never went away and can still be heard in Brazil; it bore children, notably a sit down, more harmonically sophisticated form of guitar samba called **samba canção**. And in the 1950s when this was slowed down and garnished with chord progressions inspired by US jazz, **bossa nova** was born. Bossa will forever be associated with one song in the minds of most non-Brazilians, *The Girl from Ipanema*, which is as integral to Brazilian music as *Norwegian Wood* is to the English and played about as often.

Choro, Samba Canção and Bossa were all acoustically driven. When the Beatles and Hendrix rose to global stardom in the 1960s and even Dylan picked up an electric guitar, there was something of a revolution in Brazil. Conservatives wanted to keep the country's music 'authentic' and unpolluted by foreign influences. Liberals, spearheaded by pop crooner Roberto Carlos and a group of Bahian musicians led by Gilberto Gil and Caetano Veloso and known as the **tropicalistas**, embraced electric instruments and fused Bossa and Jazz to produce a new set of Brazilian sounds collectively known as **música popular brasileira** or **MPB**. What followed was a golden age in Brazil with a fluorescence of talent that ran in parallel with the explosion of new music in the UK and US and encapsulated as wide a diversity of styles. MPB spread like a wave throughout Brazil and spawned all kinds of regional expressions. There were the melancholy, contemplative and richly complex songs of groups of musicians from the inland state of Minas called the **clube da esquina** and headed by Milton Nascimento; the numerous jazzy, poppy records of Gil, Caetano and the other Tropicalistas; the funky catchy Carioca anthems of Jorge Ben; the sophisticated Brazilian soul of Djavan and the pensive anthems of Almir Satir and Zé Ramalho, alongside many more...

Other genres

The most important musical movement in Brazil in the last twenty years has been **Mangue Beat** (or Mangue Bit). This emerged in Recife in the early 1990s and was a conscious attempt by a group of disaffected intellectuals and university students to break with the conservative artistic culture that was strangling the city at that time. Musicians looked beyond samba and classical MPB to traditional African music from the sub-culture in Recife and the backlands of the Pernambuco sertão. And they fused these roots with European punk; fired it with an angry political message and named their movement Mangue Beat – after the swamps that surround Recife and the diversity of life they support. The movement was headed by the charismatic and short-lived **Chico Science**, his band **Naçao Zumbi** and other groups like rocky **Mundo Livre** and rootsier **Mestre Ambrósio**.

Brazilian rap is increasingly popular in Rio and São Paulo. In its crudest favela warehouse-party form it is known as **funk** or **baile funk**, and is characterized by overtly sexual lyrics. Many baile funk singers are women, working as maids by day and funk singers at weekends. More interesting is **rap Brasileiro**, which despite all the MTV posturing on the videos is far from a pale imitation of the US. It is more melodic, funkier and more socially aware and is as strongly influenced by Brazilian musical genres and northeastern **repentista** spontaneous street poetry as it is by Grandmaster Flash and the Furious Five. But like US hip hop, Brazilian hip hop has long been seen as the voice of the voiceless; many of the stars are actually from the favelas. Many were or are gangsters. And like US hip hop, Brazilian hip hop represents a politically motivated alternative to crime and violence. But, unlike it, Brazilian stars really do put their rap into action. Bands like Rappin' Hood and Grupo Afro-Reggae run active social programmes in the very worst Rio *favelas* and many of their ever-rotating teenaged band members have been weaned off guns and drugs.

Concurrent with the rise in popularity of rap has been the rise of all manner of **club music** and **electronica**. The centre of the club scene in Brazil is São Paulo. But world-famous DJs like Marky and Patife, who hail from there, frequently play in Rio (see Bars and clubs page 118) as do São Paulo electronica stars like Fernanda Porto. The most famous international name in Brazilian electronica, Bebel Gilberto is still little-known in Brazil. Her father, João Gilberto, may be the co-inventor of bossa nova, but Bebel lives and was musically created in New York.

Brazilian classical composers

Ever since the Catholic church and its missionaries arrived in all parts of present-day Latin America, appropriate religious music was being composed locally, particularly by the Jesuits, and this led on to Baroque and other classical music. Brazil was no exception and Carlos Gomes' opera *Il Guarany* achieved great popularity after its first performance in 1870. During the present century, Brazilian composers (together with those of Mexico and Argentina) are at the forefront of Latin American classical music and have produced many works based on folk and popular themes. The figure of Heitor Villa-Lobos (1857-1959) towers above all others and achieved world renown well within his lifetime. Largely self-taught, his prodigious output included the celebrated nine *bachianas Brasileiras* and six choros. Given to bold experimentation, he composed two pieces of which the melodic line was based on the skyline of New York and that of the Serra da Piedade mountains near Belo Horizonte, respectively. Other major names among the 'nationalist' composers are Francisco Mignone, Camargo Guarnieri, Radames Gnatalli and Cesar Guerra Peixe (who found inspiration in the regional music of the Northeast).

Festivals

Brazilians love a party and the mixing of different ethnic groups has resulted in some particularly colourful and varied celebrations. The difficulties of daily life are often relieved by the fantasy and release of Carnaval as well as the many other popular festivals held throughout the year. Wherever you go you will find street vendors selling ice-cold beer and the smell of *churrasco* coming from improvised barbecues accompanied by loud vibrant music and dancing in the streets.

Carnaval

Almost all Brazilian towns have some form of Carnaval festivities. Although the most famous is Rio de Janeiro, there are equally spectacular and different traditions in Bahia and Pernambuco, as well as a number of other good locations for those who wish only to party. The colonial mining towns of Diamantina and Ouro Preto in the interior of Minas Gerais are good locations to spend Carnaval in atmospheric surroundings. Florianópolis and Laguna on the coast of Santa Catarina have less traditional but still very popular and lively carnivals.

Out of season carnivals

Street carnivals with *trios eléctricos* in the style of Bahia are held throughout Brazil at various times of the year. Some of the most popular are **Micareta** in Feira de Santana (April), **Fortal** in Fortaleza (July) and **Carnatal** in Natal (December). Although by no means traditional they are nonetheless exuberant and enjoyable.

Other popular festivities

There are several other festivals which are almost as important to Brazilians as Carnaval. Reveillon (New Year's Eve) is a significant event and is generally celebrated on beaches. This can be either a hedonistic party as at Copacabana and Arraial D'Ajuda with the revellers dressed in white for luck, or as a respectful *Candomblé* ceremony in which flowers are launched into the sea at midnight as an offering to Yemanjá.

The **Fiestas Juninhas** (São João) are extremely popular especially in the Northeast and are held around 24 June (St John's day). Fires are built and forró is the music of choice with the festivities lasting for over a week at times. Fireworks and the co-ordinated dancing of groups called *quadrilhas* are also part of the celebrations.

In the North, the African and Indian cultures have mixed to form the Boi-Bumba tradition. In Amazonas, the **Festa do Boi** has become more commercialized but is still very impressive and popular. In Maranhão, where it is known as **Bumba-meu-boi**, the festivities are more traditional but equally as popular.

There are many Catholic saints' days that are sometimes celebrated in conjunction with African deities (especially in Bahia). Every town has a patron saint and his or her day will be an excuse for civic festivities, in addition to those of the foundation day of the town.

Immigrants from Europe to the south of Brazil and elsewhere have brought festivals from their own cultures such as the **Oktoberfest** held in Blumenau, believed to be second only to Munich.

Literature

The colonial period

Some of the major differences between Brazil and Spanish America spring from the history of colonization in the two areas. There were no great empires with large cities like those of the Incas or the Aztecs, and Portuguese exploitation concentrated first on extractive, then on cultivated export products (brazil-wood, then sugar). Although cities like Recife, Bahia and Rio de Janeiro did finally develop, there was, incredible as it may seem, no printing press in Brazil until the flight of the Regent, King João VI to Rio in 1808. This is not to say that there was no colonial literature, though scholars can still quarrel about how 'Brazilian' it was. When the Portuguese set foot in Brazil in 1500, the letter sent back to King Manuel by Pero Vaz de Caminha, already wondering at the tropical magnificence of the country and the nakedness of the inhabitants, set themes that would recur in many later works. The first plays to be put on in Brazil were religious dramas, staged in three languages – Portuguese, Spanish, and Tupi – by the Jesuit **José de Anchieta** (1543-1597). The most notable 17th-century poet is **Gregório de Matos** (1636-1696), famous for his sharp satires on the corrupt life of the city of Salvador, and its tempting black and mulatta women. In the late 18th century, a group of poets from the gold-mining area of Minas, foremost among them **Tomás Antônio Gonzaga** (1744-1810), were at the centre of the early, abortive move for independence, the *Inconfidência* (1789 – see page 250). Although best known as a lyric poet, Gonzaga has been proved to be the author of the anonymous satirical poem *Cartas chilenas*, which gives a vivid portrait of colonial society.

The 19th century

It is helpful to understand Brazilian literature, even long after political independence, as a gradual and, to some extent, contradictory process of emancipation from foreign models. Every European literary movement – Romanticism, Realism, Symbolism, etc – had its Brazilian followers, but in each there was an attempt to adjust the model to local reality. A good example is the first of these, Indianism, which flourished in the mid-19th century, and produced two central figures: the poet **Antônio Gonçalves Dias**

Brazilian cinema

My first encounter with Brazil came through the medium of its cinema when in the early 1980s I saw Hector Babenco's controversial drama *Pixote, a Lei do Mais Fraco*. This left a lasting impression and curiosity that I was never to satisfy until my first visit to São Paulo nearly 15 years later. Hopefully the current resurgence of Oscar-nominated films such as Walter Salles's *Central do Brasil* (Central Station) will inspire more people to explore the country.

No one knows for sure when the first film was made in Brazil but a travelling Italian showman, Vittorio di Maio, was to claim this when he exhibited four films in Petrópolis in 1897. The industry developed steadily at the beginning of the last century with often-repeated adaptations of literary texts such as *O Guaraní* before later specializing in light entertainment musicals known as *chanchadas* during the 1930s and 1940s. A national star, Carmen Miranda, grew out of these before moving to Hollywood where she quickly became America's stereotype of the exotic Latin woman.

During the 1950s more serious films such as Nelson Perreira dos Santos's *Rio 40 Graus* began to appear before Anselmo Duarte's *O Pagador de Promessas* won best film at Cannes. This golden age continued in the 1960s with the birth of *Cinema Novo*. Glauber Rocha's *Deus e o Diabo no Terra do Sol* reinterpreted the popular theme of Lampião and the bandits of the northeast previously used in Lima Barreto's 1953 epic *O Cangaçeiro*. Other films such as *O Barravento* ,also by Glauber Rocha, challenged the passive role of the viewing public.

In the 1970s and 1980s under the military dictatorship the national film industry led by the state-run *Embrafilme* lost its way as *porno-chanchadas* and comedies like *Os Trapalhões* dominated the box office. There were however some films such as Bruno Barreto's *Dona Flor e Seus Dois Maridos* that combined both commercial and critical success and helped to push actress Sonia Braga to international fame.

The return came in the 1990s with Fabio Barreto's *O Quatrilho*, showing the life of Brazil's Italian immigrants and Bruno Barreto's *O Que é Isso Companheiro* based on the 1969 kidnap of the American ambassador. Both were nominated for the Academy Awards best foreign film. Other good recent films include *Anahy de las Missiones* based on the Gaúcho legend of 'Terra Estrangeira', which explores the life of a Brazilian immigrant in Portugal; and *Central do Brasil*, a road movie exploring the relationship between an embittered Carioca man and an idealistic boy from the Northeast. Brazilian cinema came to the fore in 2002 with the smash hit *Cidade de Deus*, which told the story of a photographer in the notorious favela in Rio, and was both grim and powerful. It was preceded and followed by a number of gangster films. The best of these was *O Homem do Ano*, based on a Patricia Melo novel, and a sharp satire on the numb acceptance of violence and political corruption in Brazil.

Concurrent with these have been a series of historical films. *A Selva* is one of the first films to tell the story of the rubber boom, through the eyes of a brutalized Portuguese nobleman who has fallen from grace. *Brava Gente Brasileira* explores the brutal conquest of the *indígena* in the Pantanal. And the charming *Cinema, Aspirinas e Urubus*, which was the hit of 2006, is a road movie set in the sertão of Pernambuco during the 1930s.

(1823-1864), himself partly of indigenous descent, and the novelist **José de Alencar** (1829-1877). It is a form of Romanticism, idealizing the noble savage, and with plots adapted from Walter Scott, and it happily ignored what was happening to real indigenous tribes at the time. However, it does express national aspirations and feelings, if in nothing else, in the nostalgia for a kind of tropical Eden expressed in perhaps the most famous Brazilian poem, Gonçalves Dias *Canção do exílio*: "My land has palm-trees/ where the sabiá sings. /The birds that sing here/ don't sing like those back home." Alencar's novels, not all of them about Indians, are a systematic attempt to portray Brazil in its various settings, including the city. *O guarani* (1857), turned into a famous opera by Carlos Gomes, and *Iracema* (1865), are his most popular. The latter is perhaps the most complete mythical version of the Portuguese conquest, allegorized as a love affair between a native woman and an early colonist, Martim Soares. Iracema, "the virgin with the honeyed lips" dies in childbirth at the end, but the future lies with their mixed-blood son, Moacir.

After his death, Alencar was succeeded as the chief figure in Brazilian letters by **Joaquim Maria Machado de Assis** (1839-1908). Perhaps Brazil's best writer, and certainly the greatest to appear in Latin America until well into the 20th century, he had to fight against formidable obstacles: he was of relatively poor origins, was mulatto, he had a stammer and, in later life, was subject to epileptic fits. He wrote nine novels and more than 200 short stories as well as poetry and journalism. He ended his life as an establishment figure and founder of the Brazilian Academy of Letters. But his novels, especially those written after 1880, when he published *Memórias póstumas de Brás Cubas*, and the best of his stories are surprisingly subversive, covert attacks on slavery and on male power, for instance. He avoided detection by not using his own voice, hiding behind quirky, digressive narrators who are not always trustworthy. All the novels and most of the stories are set in Rio, which he hardly left, and give a remarkably varied account of the city and its different social levels. His most famous novel, *Dom Casmurro* (1900) is one of the best-disguised cases of an unreliable narrator in the history of the novel, and still arouses critical polemics.

Machado's atmosphere is predominantly that of the empire, which fell in 1889, a year after the abolition of slavery. In the Republic, a younger generation, more overtly rebellious in their aims, and affected by new scientific ideas from Europe, came to the fore. If Machado is the most famous Brazilian author, perhaps *Os sertões*, by **Euclides da Cunha** (1866-1909) is the most famous book. It is an account of the Canudos campaign in the interior of the state of Bahia in 1896-1897. The campaign was a horrific failure, victory being won only at a huge cost in casualties, and Euclides, sent to cover it as a journalist, turned this failure into an indictment of a social system, which excluded huge groups of people. Written in a dramatic, somewhat self-indulgent style, with extensive use of scientific words, it has been excellently translated as *Rebellion in the Backlands*.

The other important prose writer of this period, the novelist **Afonso Lima Barreto** (1881-1922), was mulatto like Machado, but there resemblances end. Much more openly rebellious and less of a conscious artist than Machado, his novels, the most notable of which is *Triste fim de Policarpo Quaresma*, are overt attacks on intellectual mediocrity, and the corruption and despotism into which the Republic soon fell. A passing mention ought to be made, too, of one of the 'unclassifiable' books in which Brazilian literature abounds: **Helena Morley**'s *Minha vida de menina* (translated by Elizabeth Bishop as *The Diary of Helena Morley*), and only published in 1942. It is the precocious, funny, and remarkably perceptive teenager's diary, written in Diamantina, Minas Gerais, at the end of the 19th century.

The 20th century

In general, the poetry of the turn of the century was imitative and stuffy. Renewal did not come until the early 1920s, when a group of intellectuals from São Paulo, led by the unrelated **Mário de Andrade** (1893-1945) and **Oswald de Andrade** (1890-1954) began the movement known as modernism. This is conveniently supposed to have begun in 1922, the centenary of political independence, with a Week of Modern Art in São Paulo; in fact it began earlier, and took until the mid-1920s to spread to the provinces. In great part, modernism's ideology was nationalist, and though the word spanned the political spectrum, at its best it simply meant the discovery of a real Brazil behind stereotypes. Mário travelled throughout the country, attempting to understand its variety, which he embodied in his major prose-work, the comic 'rhapsody' *Macunaíma* (1928), which in its plot and language attempts to construct a unity out of a complex racial and regional mix. Also in 1928, Oswald launched the 'anthropophagist', or cannibalist programme, which proclaimed that Brazilian writers should imitate their native predecessors, and fully digest European culture: a new kind of Indianism, perhaps.

The most enduring artistic works to have emerged from modernism, however, are poetic – two of Brazil's major modern poets, **Manuel Bandeira** (1886-1968) and **Carlos Drummond de Andrade** (1902-87) were early enthusiasts of modernism, and corresponded at length with Mário. Bandeira, the older man, made a slow transition to the new, freer style; his poems, often short and based on everyday events or images, nevertheless have a power and rhythmic accuracy that are deceptively simple. Drummond's poetry is more self-conscious, and went through a complex intellectual development, including a period of political enthusiasm during the Second World War, followed by disillusionment with the beginning of the Cold War. His themes, including some remarkable love-poetry addressed by a 50-year old to a younger woman, and a lifelong attachment to Itabira, the small town in Minas Gerais where he was bom, are very varied. Readers without Portuguese can best approach Drummond, widely regarded as Brazil's greatest poet, through an excellent anthology, *Traveling in the Family*.

The 1930s were a crucial decade. With increasing political mobilization, the growth of cities, and of an aspiring middle class, literature began to look to a wider audience; however, at first, it still reflected the dominance of rural life. The realism of this period, which often had a strong regionalist bias, had its raison d'être in a society still divided by huge social and/or geographical differences, and indeed played its part in diminishing those differences. Many of the first group came from the economically and socially backward Northeast. **José Lins do Rego** (1901-1957) is perhaps the most characteristic figure. He was highly influenced by the ideas of **Gilberto Freyre** (1900-1987), whose *Casa grande e sensually* (*The Masters and the Slaves*), published in 1933, was one of the most important and readable of Brazilian books. It is a study of the slave-based, sugar-plantation society, and one of the first works to appreciate the contribution made by Blacks to Brazil's culture. It remains, however, very paternalist, and Lins do Rego's fiction, beginning with the semi-autobiographical *Menino de engenho*, reflects that, commenting on the poverty and filth of the (ex-)slave-quarters as if they were totally natural. His 'sugar-cane cycle' sold in large editions, in part because of its unaffected, simple style.

A greater novelist belonging to the same group is **Graciliano Ramos** (1892-1953). His fiction is much more aggressive, and in later life he became a communist. His masterpiece, turned into an excellent film in the 1960s, is *Vedas secas*, which returns to the impoverished interior of *Os sertões*, but concentrates on an illiterate cowhand and his family, forced from place to place by drought and social injustice; it is a courageous attempt to enter the mental world of such people. *Memórias do cárcere*, published after Ramos's death, is his unflinching account of his imprisonment for a year during the Vargas regime.

The essential novelist to read for anyone visiting the south of Brazil is **Érico Veríssimo** (1905-1975), especially his epic trilogy collectively entitled *O tempo e o vento* (*O continente* [1949], *O retrato* [1951], and *O arquipélago* [1961]) spread over two centuries of the turbulent history of Rio Grande do Sul.

Gradually, in the 1940s and 1950s, a subtler and more adventurous fiction began to be published alongside the regionalist realism that was the major heritage of the 1930s. Three writers stand out: João Guimarães Rosa, Clarice Lispector and João Cabral de Melo Neto. **João Guimarães Rosa** (1908-1967) published his major novel, *Grande sertão: veredas* in 1956. Almost Joycean in its aspirations and linguistic innovations, it is a kind of mixture of a cowboy story and a modern version of Faustian pact with the devil. For those without stamina (and excellent Portuguese), the translation (*The Devil to Pay in the Backlands*) is unfortunately not an adequate alternative. Rosa is best approached through his stories, those of Sagarana (particularly *A hora e vez de Augusto Matraga*) being perhaps the best.

The stories and novels of **Clarice Lispector** (1920-1977) now have a considerable audience outside Brazil, as well as a huge one inside it. Her stories, especially those of *Laços de família* (1960), are in general set in middle-class Rio, and usually have women as their central characters. The turbulence, family hatreds, and near-madness hidden beneath routine lives are conveyed in unforgettable ways, with a language and symbolism that is poetic and adventurous without being exactly difficult (she said she fought with the Portuguese language daily). Some of her novels have over-ambitious metaphysical superstructures, and may not be to some readers' tastes – *A paixão segundo G H*, for instance, concerns a housewife's confrontation with a dead cockroach in her maid's room, and her final decision to eat it, seen as a kind of "communion". When at her best, in some of her journalism, in her late, deliberately semi-pornographic stories, and above all in the posthumous novel, *A hora da estrela*, which approaches the poor in an utterly unsentimental way, Lispector can stimulate and move like no one else.

The greatest poet of this generation is **João Cabral de Melo Neto** (1920-1999), whose best poetry concerns his home state, Pernambuco. The drought-ridden interior, the lush but oppressive landscape of the sugar-plantations, and the city slums are all present in the verse-play *Morte e vida severina* (1956), and his tight, spare poetry often returns to the same places, or analogous ones in the several countries (most importantly, in Spain) in which he has resided as a diplomat.

The 1964 military coup, and the increasing use of torture and censorship in the late 1960s and early 1970s, had profound effects on literature, especially as they were accompanied by vast economic changes (industrialization, a building boom, huge internal migration, the opening up of the Amazon). At first, censorship was haphazard, and the 1960s liberation movements had their – increasingly desperate – Brazilian equivalents. Protest theatre had a brief boom, with *Arena conta Zumbi*, about a 17th-century rebel slave leader, produced by **Augusto Boal** (born 1931), being one of the most important. The best fictional account of those years can be found in two novels by **Antônio Callado** (born 1917), *Quarup* (1967), set in the Northeast and centred on a left-wing priest, and *Bar Don Juan* (1971), whose focus is on the contradictions of a group of middle-class guerrillas; and in **Ivan Ângelo**'s *A festa* (1976), set in Belo Horizonte, a funny and hard-hitting account of a varied set of people, which chronicles the impact of the 'sex and drugs' revolution alongside its political concerns. A remarkable documentary account of the period is ex- guerrilla (subsequently leader of the Green Party) **Fernando Gabeira**'s *O que é isso companheiro?* (1982), which chronicles his involvement in the kidnapping of the American ambassador in 1969. Poetry at this time went through a crisis of self-confidence, and it was widely thought that it had emigrated into the (marvellous) lyrics of such popular composers as **Chico Buarque de Holanda** and **Caetano Veloso**, who were also the foremost standard-bearers of political protest in the 1970s.

It is impossible in the space available to give more than a few suggestions of some of the best work published in recent decades, concentrating on books which have been translated. A brilliant satirical novel by **Paulo Emílio Salles Gomes** (1916-1977) about the São Paulo upper middle class is *Três mulheres e três Pppês*

(1977); **Darcy Ribeiro** (born 1922), an anthropologist and politician, took time off to write *Maíra* (1978), an updating of Indianism, but with real *indígena* and a threatened Amazon environment; **Rubem Fonseca** (born 1925), whose story *Feliz ano novo* (1973) created a scandal because of its brutal treatment of class differences, has dedicated himself to the writing of hard-nosed thrillers like *A grande arte* (1983); **Caio Fernando Abreu** (1948-96) is a short-story writer of considerable talent, dealing with the alienated urban young in such books as *Morangos mofados* and *Os dragões não conhecem o paraíso*; finally, **Milton Hatoum**'s *Relato de um certo oriente* (1989) is a vivid novel set in Manaus, amongst the Lebanese immigrant community. He followed it with the highly acclaimed *The Brothers*. Patricia Melo has devoted her writing to exploring social problems in her native Rio. Several of her books have been filmed; most notably *O Matador* (*O Homen do Ano* or *Man of the Year*), the story of a man who accidentally becomes a ruthless hired gun. The country's leading literary export is without a doubt the popular mystical novelist, Paulo Coelho, most famous for his whimsical novel, *The Alchemist*.

Recommended reading

Essays and books that can be wholeheartedly recommended for those who want more information are: Ray Keenoy, David Treece and Paul Hyland, *The Babel Guide to the Fiction of Portugal, Brazil and Africa in English Translation* (London: Boulevard Books, 1995). Irwin Stern (ed) *Dictionary of Brazilian Literature* (New York: Greenwood Press, 1988). Mike González and David Treece, *The Gathering of Voices* (Verso, 1992) (on 20th-century poetry). Elizabeth Bishop and Emanuel Brasil (eds) *An Anthology of Twentieth-Century Brazilian Poetry* (Wesleyan University Press, 1972); John Gledson, *Brazilian Fiction: Machado de Assis to the Present*, in John King (ed), *Modern Latin American Fiction: A Survey* (Faber, 1987). Many of the essays in Roberto Schwarz, *Misplaced Ideas: Essays on Brazilian Culture* (Verso, 1992), especially those on *Machado de Assis*, and *Culture and Politics in Brazil, 1964-1969* are very stimulating.

See also Books, page 720, for further recommended reading.

Fine art and sculpture

The colonial era: 16th and 17th centuries

No visitor to Brazil should miss visiting a colonial church. During the colonial period in Brazil the Church dominated artistic patronage, with the religious orders vying with each other to produce ever more lavish interiors. In the 17th century the Benedictines included several notable sculptors among their ranks. Much of the magnificent gilded interior of the monastery of São Bento in Rio de Janeiro is by **Frei Domingos da Concelção** (circa 1643-1718), who worked there during the 1660s. His *Crucifixion* of 1688 in the monastery of São Bento in Olinda sets up a deliberately shocking contrast between the sinuous elegance of Christ's body and the terrible lacerations of his flesh. **Frei Agostinho de Piedade** (died 1661) of the Benedictine community in Salvador produced some old-fashioned terracotta reliquary busts during the 1630s and 1640s (Museu de Arte Sacra, Salvador) but the powerful *Penitent Peter* in Salvador's Nossa Senhora do Monte (circa 1636), also attributed to him, prefigures the emotional intensity of subsequent generations.

A distinctive feature of colonial interiors is the incorporation of decorative scenes in blue and white painted tiles, *azulejos*, around the walls. These were imported from Portugal from the earlier 17th century onwards, with subject matter as often secular as religious. Good examples include the Franciscan foundations in Olinda, Salvador and Recife, and the church of Nossa Senhora da Glória in Rio de Janeiro, which has hunting scenes in the sacristy, Old Testament figures in the choir, and in the nave, astonishingly, scenes of pastoral love loosely based on the *Song of Songs*.

The 18th century

Although 17th-century church decoration is often lavish there is little warning of the extraordinary theatricality which characterizes the work of the 18th century. Behind their sober façades churches open out like theatres, with the equivalent of balconies and boxes for the privileged, and a stage for the high altar with a proscenium arch and wings of carved and gilded wood. Cherubs whisper to each other or gesticulate from their perches amongst the architectural scrolls; angels, older and more decorous, recline along a cornice or flutter in two dimensions across an illusionist ceiling. The object of devotion is usually placed high above the altar on a tiered dais, surrounded by a Bernini-esque sunburst of gilded rays. A skilled exponent of this type of design was the Portuguese-born sculptor **Francisco Xavier de Brito** (died 1751), as in Nossa Senhora do Pilar, Ouro Preto and São Francisco de Penitência, Rio.

Xavier de Brito was largely responsible for bringing the Baroque style to Brazil and this style reaches its most ornate and theatrical in the work of Xavier de Brito's pupil, **Aleijadinho**, the 'Little Cripple' (1738-1814) a mulatto artist who worked in the province of Minas Gerais. As by far the most famous artist in the colonial period in the whole of Latin America it is perhaps not surprising to find his name attached to an impossible number of projects, but a consideration even of the securely documented reveals a man of extraordinary passion and energy who worked as a painter, architect and, above all, sculptor. The church at Congonhas do Campo offers the most dramatic example of Aleijadinho's art. Pilgrims paying homage to the miracle-working Bom Jesus do Matozinhos approach the church along a penitential road winding up the hill between six small chapels, each housing scenes from Christ's Passion represented by life-size expressive statues of polychrome wood. The final ascent is up an imposing double staircase under the stony gaze of 12 judgmental prophets who variously lament, threaten or cajole, addressing the heavens, the distant horizon, each other, or the faithful on the stone steps below them. In a building beside the church a fascinating display of drawings and photographs of the many accidents and emergencies from which the Good Jesus has saved people, testifies to the continuing popularity of this shrine.

The painterly equivalent to Aleijadinho's sculptures can be found in the work of his contemporary, **Manuel da Costa Ataíde** (1762-1830) from Mariana, whose vividly colourful narrative scenes decorate numerous churches in Minas Gerais. Ataíde's rococo settings are populated with solidly-built saints and angels whose rolling eyes and exaggerated gestures give them an earthy vigour sometimes at odds with the spirituality of the subject matter, as in the illusionist ceiling of São Francisco de Assis, Ouro Preto, a church whose design is traditionally attributed to Aleijadinho. Both Aleijadinho and Athayde were probably friends of the insurrectionist Tiradentes and criticisms of the Portuguese and the appalling treatment of non-European Brazilians is implicit in their work (for more details see box, page 247)

In Bahia, **José Joaquim da Rocha** (1737-1807), see page 366, was one of the most successful artists of his day and his slightly Italianate ceiling paintings survive in many churches in Salvador. The best sculptor of the late colonial period in Bahia was **Manuel Inácio da Costa** (1763-1857) whose figures, often dramatically gaunt with protruding veins and large eyes, are reminiscent of Aleijadinho's work (see, for example, his *Christ at the Column* in the Museu de Arte Sacra in Salvador). It is in Rio that sculpture first begins to sober up again, as for example in the work of the sculptor Valentim de Fonseca e Silva, known as **Mestre Valentim** (circa 1750-1813), which can be seen in several churches including São Francisco de Paula and Nossa Senhora da Glória. Valentim also designed the first public gardens in Rio: the *Passeio Público* was inaugurated in 1783 and included walks, seats decorated with *azulejos* and pavilions. A unique series of six painted views of Rio and Guanabara Bay by **Leandro Joaquim** (1738-1798), originally made for one of the pavilions, are now in the Museu Histórico Nacional in Rio.

French influence in Imperial Brazil

After the transfer of the Imperial court to Rio in 1808, João VI made a determined effort to renovate Brazilian culture, and in 1816 the French Artistic Mission – a boatload of painters, sculptors, architects, musicians and craftsmen – arrived from France to found what was to become the Imperial Academy. Two artists were particularly influential: **Nicolas-Antoine Taunay** (1755-1830) and **Jean-Baptiste Debret** (1768-1848). Taunay's luminous landscapes of the area around Rio and Debret's lively street scenes helped to open up new areas of secular Brazilian subject matter, and inspired artists throughout the 19th century. The Academy provided scholarships to send promising young artists to Paris, so reinforcing the French influence, and there are echoes of Delacroix in the work of **Vítor Meireles** (1832-1903) as for example, in his *Battle of the Guararapes* of 1879 in the Museu Nacional de Belas Artes, Rio, and of Ingres in *La Carioca* (1882) of **Pedro Américo** (1843-1905) in the same museum. The influence of Courbet can be seen in the so-called belle époque of the first republican years (1889-1922), in particular in the work of Meireles' pupil, **José Ferraz de Almeida Júnior** (1850-1899).

The 20th century, towards a Brazilian vision

Brazil moved from this essentially academic tradition straight into the radicalism of the early 20th century, and movements such as Cubism, Futurism, Fauvism and Constructivism were quickly translated into distinctively Brazilian idioms. **Lasar Segall** (1891-1957), **Anita Malfatti** (1896-1964) and the sculptor **Vitor Brecheret** (1894-1955) were pioneers of modernism, working in relative isolation before the 1922 Semana da Arte Moderna (Modern Art Week) in São Paulo drew together a group of artists and intellectuals whose influence on Brazilian culture can still be felt today. They sought to challenge established bourgeois attitudes, to shake off the traditional cultural subservience to Europe, and to draw attention to the cultural diversity and social inequality of contemporary Brazil. **Emilio di Cavalcanti** (1897-1976) mocked the artificiality of middle-class socialites (examples in the Museu de Arte Contemporânea, São Paulo). **Tarsila do Amaral** (1886-1973) borrowed her loud colours from popular art while her imagery includes ironic reworkings of European myths about the savage cannibalistic *indígena* supposed to inhabit the Brazilian jungle. **Cândido Portinari** (1903-1962) used murals to expose the exploitation and injustice suffered by workers and peasants, while **Osvaldo Goeldi** (1895-1961) explored similar themes in his powerful wood engravings. Portinari, in an interesting revival of the colonial use of *azulejos*, created murals in blue and white painted tiles for modern architecture such as the MES building by Costa and Niemeyer of Rio, begun in 1937, and Niemeyer's church of São Francisco in Pampulha, Belo Horizonte (1943).

The economic strength of the middle years of the century encouraged state patronage of the arts. President Getúlio Vargas recognized that art and architecture could be used to present an image of Brazil as a modern industrialized nation, with Brasília being the culmination of this vision. Museums of Modern Art were founded in São Paulo and Rio, and in 1951 São Paulo hosted its first **Bienal Internacional,** which attracted abstract artists from Europe and the US and confirmed Abstraction – symbol of progress and technological modernization – as the dominant mode in Brazil during the 1950s. Rivalry between the artistic communities of Rio and São Paulo helped to produce some outstanding avant-garde art. In the 1950s **Waldemar Cordeiro** (1925-1973), leader of the São Paulo Grupo Ruptura, painted what at first sight appear to be rather simple geometric patterns in bright, contrasting colours, but on closer attention the flat surface seems to break up, suggesting recession, space and restless movement, in some ways prefiguring the British Op Art movement of the 1960s. The Neo-Concrete group of artists of Rio argued for the integration of art into daily life, and experimented with art that made sensory and emotional demands on the 'spectator' whose participation leads in turn to creation. During the early 1960s, **Lygia Clark** (1920-1988) made *bichos* (*animals*) out of hinged pieces of metal which, as the name implies, are like creatures with a life of their own: they can be rearranged indefinitely but because of their complexity it is impossible to predetermine what shape will result from moving a particular section. Nowadays, unfortunately, they are displayed in museums where touching is not encouraged (as in the Pinacoteca do Estado, São Paulo). **Hélio Oiticica** (1937-1980) took the idea further, working with people (poor and often black) from the samba schools in the Rio *favelas* to create artistic 'happenings' involving dance, music and flamboyant costumes called *parangolés* (capes). The notion that a key function of art should be to shock the bourgeoisie was first voiced in the 1922 Week of Modern Art. Oiticica often succeeded, and he and other artists of the 1960s also realized another of the aims of the first modernists: to create Brazilian modern art that was not the poor relation of developments in Europe or the US. A museum of his work is now open in Rio. Other important figures of this generation include the neo-concretist painter **Ivan Serpa** (1923-1973), **Sérgio Camargo** (1930-1990), who produced textured rhythmic constructions of white on white but because they are made with off-cuts of wood they suggest the tensions between form and material, geometry and nature; and **Amílcar de Castro** (born 1920) whose deceptively simple sculptures are often cut from one large panel of cast iron.

The military coup of 1964 marked the beginning of a period of political repression and of renewed artistic energy, with figurative tendencies re-emerging. In 1970 **Antônio Enrique Amaral** (born 1935) took as his theme the banana, so often used in dismissive references to Latin America, and in an extended series of paintings monumentalized it into an extraordinary symbol of power and productivity. In an ironic neo-colonial altarpiece (circa 1966) installed in the Museu de Arte de São Paulo, **Nelson Leirner** (born 1932) makes the object of devotion the neon-lit head of pop star Robert Carlos. Conceptual art offers different ways of confronting the dominant ideology. Both **Cildo Meireles** (born 1948) and **Jac Lierner** (born 1961) have used, misused or forged banknotes, for example, and both they and **Waltercio Caldas** (born 1946) and **Tunga** (born 1952) have created installations which draw attention, directly and indirectly to environmental issues. The painter **Siron Franco** (born 1947) also often addresses the issue of the destruction of the Amazon rainforest, but his disturbing surreal images explore many other areas – industrial pollution, sexual fantasy, political corruption, national identity – making him one of the most exciting artists in Brazil today.

Architecture

Brazilian colonial style: houses and civic buildings

The earliest Portuguese colonizers to arrive in Brazil in the 16th century faced many problems in building their houses, forts, churches and other necessary structures. First of all there was a lack of building materials, such as bricks, roof tiles and mortar. Second, there were few trained craftsmen, such as carpenters and bricklayers, in the colony. They therefore had to improvise by developing unusual building techniques and trying different materials. In the hinterland, in places like São Paulo, Goiás and Minas Gerais the majority of the houses were built with *taipa de pilão*. This technique consisted in using a wooden form to build thick walls. These forms were filled with a mixture of clay, vegetable fibres, horsehair, ox blood and dung. This paste was then compacted with a pestle and allowed to dry for two to three days before the next layer was added. The roof tiles were often moulded on a female slave's thigh and dried in the sun.

It is quite easy to identify a house in Brazilian colonial style. Their shapes, colours and building techniques remained virtually unchanged for almost three centuries. Firstly, they always had large, visible roofs, made with red clay tiles, finishing in eaves extending beyond the walls. All the buildings were painted in a white wash, with bright colours used only on window and door frames. These were made of wood and had, mostly, elegant arches at the top. In the 19th century, sash windows with squared 10 sq cm pieces of glass were added in many houses, as can be seen in cities like Paraty, Ouro Preto and Salvador.

Urban colonial houses had doors and windows opening directly onto the street. Courtyards were never placed in front of the house, but internally, forming airy patios which protected the privacy of the family. The furniture was extremely simple and rough. Often, the only pieces of furniture in a bedroom would be the bed itself and a leather box to store clothes and personal belongings. In the colonial period, the highest status symbol was to live in a *sobrado* (a house with more than one floor, usually two). The ground floor was normally a commercial business and above it the residence of the owner's family.

Churches, convents and religious buildings: the baroque in Brazil

Houses, public buildings and other colonial civic edifices were generally unelaborate. All the refinement, style and sophistication in art, architecture and decoration was lavished on churches, convents and monasteries. The great religious orders, such as the Jesuits, Franciscans, Carmelites and Benedictines brought to Brazil the latest artistic trends from Europe, mainly the Baroque and Rococo.

Two separate strands in Brazilian religious architecture evolved. In the most important cities, close to the seaboard and more influenced by European culture, the churches and convents were built according to designs brought from Portugal, Italy and Spain. Some were merely copies of Jesuit or Benedictine temples in Europe. Examples of this can be found in Salvador (the main cathedral, the São Francisco church), Rio de Janeiro (the Mosteiro de São Bento, the Convento de Santo Antônio) and Olinda (church and convent of Nossa Senhora das Neves).

Brazilian baroque

At the end of the 17th century gold was found in the region of Minas Gerais. One of the first administrative acts of the Portuguese crown in response to this discovery was to banish the traditional European orders from the mining region. The royal administration wanted to control the mining itself, taxation and traffic in gold and, as the friars were regarded as among the most shameless of smugglers of the metal, the orders in this instance were denied the support they were given elsewhere in the Portuguese colonies. Therefore the majority of the churches in cities like Ouro Preto, Mariana, Congonhas and Sabará were built by local associations, the so-called 'third orders'. These lay orders had the gold and the will to build magnificent temples but, although they wanted their projects to be as European as possible, the original designs were hard to obtain in such out-of-the-way places. So the local artists had to find their own way. Inspired by descriptions and second-hand information, they created their own interpretation of the Baroque, thoroughly infused with regional influences and culture. This is the reason why the 'Barroco Mineiro' is so original.

Curved churches and the decline of the Gold Era

At the beginning of the 18th century, when gold was easily found in Minas Gerais, the main attraction was the inside of the church; richly and heavily decorated in carved wood and gold. Many of the churches built in this period will be a total surprise for the visitor. Their façades and exteriors are so simple and yet the naves and altars are so highly and artistically decorated. As the mines started to decline, the outside of the buildings became more sophisticated, with curves, round towers and sinuous walls, such as the churches of São Francisco de Assis and Rosário, in Ouro Preto. As the gold for covering walls ran out, it was replaced by paintings and murals.

The 19th century and the neoclassic style

The beginning of 19th century brought a major change in the history of Brazilian architecture. When Napoleon invaded Portugal in 1808, the Portuguese royal family and some 15,000 nobles and wealthy families fled to Rio de Janeiro, bringing with them their own view of what was sophisticated in the arts. In 1816 the king, Dom João VI, invited a group of French artists (The French Artistic Mission) to Brazil to introduce the most recent European trends in painting, sculpture, decoration and architecture. This was the beginning of the neoclassic style in Brazil. An Imperial Academy of Fine Arts was created and all the new government buildings were built in neoclassic style. The great name of this period was the French architect Grandjean de Montigny , who planned and built many houses and public buildings throughout the city of Rio de Janeiro.

The rich and famous also wanted their houses in this newly fashionable style, which revolutionized the Brazilian way of building. The large roofs were now hidden by a small wall, the plat band. Windows and doors acquired round arches and walls were painted in ochres and light tones of pink. Public buildings and churches started to look like ancient Greek temples, with triangular pediments and columns. This new style was not best suited Brazil's climate. The earlier, large colonial roofs were much more efficient in dealing with heavy tropical rains and, in consequence, the Neoclassic style never became popular in the countryside.

Even when the coffee planters, in the second half of 19th century, started to become extremely rich and fond of imported fashions, they would build their urban mansions in the neoclassic style, but still keep their farm houses with large roofs, sometimes adding small neoclassic details in windows, doors and internal decoration. Good examples of this 19th-century rural architecture can be found very close to Rio de Janeiro, in cities like Vassouras, Valença, Barra do Piraí and Bananal, where some of the old farm houses are open to visitors.

There are many examples of urban Neoclassic building in Rio de Janeiro, such as the Museu Nacional, the Santa Casa da Misericórdia, the Casa de Rui Barbosa and the Instituto Benjamin Constant. Also very close to Rio, in Petrópolis, the Museu Imperial (formerly the Emperor's summer palace) is also a perfect example of the style. This Neoclassic remained popular in Brazil until the end of the 19th century, being also the 'official' style of the First and the Second Brazilian Empires.

The early 20th century and the eclectic style

After the Republic, in 1889, the neoclassic style lost favour since it had been serving the king and the emperors for such a long time. A new style, or better, a new harmony of different styles started to gain popularity, also under the influence of Paris and the belle époque. There were elements of neoclassic architecture, but also an excess of decoration and adornment on the façades. A broad 'boulevard' was constructed in Rio de Janeiro in 1906, the Avenida Central (today Avenida Rio Branco), with the idea of creating 'a Paris in the Tropics'. There are many examples of buildings in the Eclectic style on this avenue: the Biblioteca Nacional, the Teatro Municipal (Opera House) and the Museu Nacional de Belas Artes, all of them built within the first decade of 20th century. Also in Manaus, during the rubber boom, many buildings adopted this style, such as the Teatro Amazonas (the Opera House). During the first two decades of this century, the Eclectic style remained very popular.

The 'Modern Art Week' of 1922 and national pride

In 1922 a group of artists, painters, poets and architects organized in São Paulo 'A Semana da Arte Moderna' or the Modern Art Week, during which they exhibited their distaste at the influence of foreign standards in Brazilian art. They considered their role to be a quest for a genuine Brazilian form of expression. This resulted in the rejection of all imported standards and, as far as architecture was concerned, two main currents emerged: Neocolonial and Modernism.

The Neocolonial

The first movement sought its true Brazilian style in the past, in the colonial period. Architects like Lúcio Costa, studied the techniques, materials and designs of the 16th, 17th and 18th centuries, soon producing houses with a colonial look, but also combining elements which were only previously found in Baroque churches. These included pediments and decorated door frames. The style was called Neocolonial and remained popular until the 1940s, especially in Rio de Janeiro and São Paulo.

In search of greater authenticity, architects employed original materials brought from demolished old houses. A good example of this can be found in Rio de Janeiro, in the Largo do Boticário (very close to the train station for Corcovado, in Cosme Velho), a small square surrounded by Neocolonial houses painted in fancy, bright colours.

Modernism

The other current generated by the Semana da Arte Moderna looked to the future for its inspiration for Brazilian-ness. Architects such as Oscar Niemeyer, Lúcio Costa, Affonso Eduardo Reidy, the landscape designer Roberto Burle Marx and many others started to design functional and spacious buildings, with large open areas and *pilotis* (pillars carrying a building, leaving the ground floor open). The use of concrete and glass was intense and the masterpiece of the Brazilian architectural Modernism is Brasília, the capital, planned from scratch in the 1950 by Lúcio Costa and Oscar Niemeyer.

Many examples of Modernist building can be found all over Brazil: in Brasília, the Cathedral, the National Congress, the Palácio do Planalto (the presidential palace), in fact the whole city, with its broad freeways and spacious urban blocks, called *quadras*; in Belo Horizonte, the church of São Francisco de Assis, in Pampulha; in São Paulo, the MASP (Museum of Art of São Paulo), the Memorial da América Latina, and many commercial buildings along the Avenida Paulista; in Rio de Janeiro, the Ministério da Educação e Saúde, the Museu de Arte Moderna, the Catedral Metropolitana, the Petrobrás building (Brazilian State Petrol Company), the BNDES building (National Bank of Social and Economic Development), all in the central area of the city.

Brazilian contemporary architecture

The most recent trend is the postmodern. Many business centres, shopping malls and residential buildings are being designed in a style which uses coloured mirror glass, granite and stylized structures reminiscent of classical temples.

Brazilian architects are also famous worldwide for their techniques in designing houses for construction on steeply-inclined hills. In Rio de Janeiro, if you are driving along the coastal road in the neighbourhoods of Barra and São Conrado you can see many of these astonishing projects, which are homes of the very wealthy.

Land and environment

Geography

Brazil is the largest country in South America and the fifth largest in the world. It is almost as large as the USA and over covers 4300 km from north to south and the same from east to west, with land borders of 15,700 km and an Atlantic coastline of 7400 km. It borders all the other South American countries except Chile and Ecuador and occupies almost half the total area of the continent. Its population of 162 million is the fifth largest in the world, and over half that of South America.

Geology

Although Brazil is dominated by the vast river basins of the Amazon and the Paraná which account for about three-fifths of the country, not much of it is 'lowlands'. Ancient rock structures, some of the oldest in the world, underlie much of the area creating resistant plateaux and a rounded hilly landscape. These ancient Pre-Cambrian rocks culminate in the Guiana highlands to the north and the crystalline ranges which run close to the coastline all the way from near the Amazon to the Uruguayan frontier.

It is believed that South America and Africa were joined in the geologic past, and there is a tolerable fit between the easterly bulge of Brazil and the Gulf of Guinea. Persuasive evidence has been found of identical ostracod fossils (freshwater fish) in corresponding Cretaceous rocks in both Brazil and Gabon, overlain by salt deposits that could have been the first appearance of the South Atlantic Ocean. This suggests that the split began some 125 million years ago. What is now accepted is that the South American Plate continues to move westwards with the consequent elevation of the Andes on the other side of the continent where it meets the Pacific Plates.

Amazon basin

The Amazon river is the greatest in the world in area of drainage, about 7,000,000 sq km, and in volume of discharge into the sea averaging 180,000 cu m per second (or 170 billion gallons per hour), 10 times that of the Mississippi, and more than all the rivers of Europe put together. Such is the flow that the salinity of the Atlantic Ocean is affected for 250 km out from the river delta. It is 6,400 km long (marginally shorter than the Nile) from its sources in the Andes of Peru, and still has over 3,000 km to go through Brazil when it leaves Leticia on the Colombia/Brazil border, yet with only a fall of 80 m to sea level. Unlike most major world rivers, the basin is reduced in width near its mouth, indeed hills come down to the river near Monte Alegre only 200 km from the delta. Some 200 km above this at Óbidos, the river is over 75 m deep, that is the bottom is well below sea level. This reflects the more recent geological history of the basin which until the latter part of the Tertiary Period (say 25 million years ago) was connected to the Pacific and drained through what is now Ecuador. With the uplift of the Andes, this route was closed off, and a huge inland sea was formed, helped by a downward folding of the older rocks (some geologists believe there was also significant rifting of the strata) to create a huge geosyncline. Eventually the water broke through the crystalline rocks to the east and made the new connection to the Atlantic. Deep layers of sediment were laid down and have been added to ever since, with today's heavy tropical rains continuing to erode the surrounding mountains. This gives the largest, more or less, level area in Brazil, but it is so heavily forested and the soils so continually leached by the climate, with vast expanses frequently under floodwaters, that the potential for agriculture is strictly limited.

A characteristic of virtually all the tributaries which join the Amazon from the south is that upstream navigation ends where the rivers tumble off the plateaux of central Brazil creating dramatic waterfalls and in many cases now providing hydroelectric power.

Centre West

South of the Amazon basin is a large area of undulating highlands, a dissected plateau mostly between 200 m and 800 m. These are ancient rocks, back as far as Pre-Cambrian crystallines. They produce poor soils but sufficient to provide the grasslands or *cerrado* of the Mato Grosso, Goiás, western Paraná and adjacent areas, widely used for ranching, though now increasingly found suitable for soya bean production, one of Brazil's foremost exports.

From Minas Gerais southwards, the rivers drain into the second largest basin of Brazil, the Paraná, which eventually reaches the Atlantic by way of the River Plate of Argentina/Uruguay. This is another large river system, 4000 km long, of which about

Biological and habitat glossary

Atlantic Coast forest (**Mata Atlântica**) Highly biodiverse with numerous endemic species. Runs in patches from Rio Grande do Norte to Argentina.
Caatinga Shrubland and thorn forest made up of xeric desert-adapted plants and fire-adapted grassland savannahs.
Campo Sujo A type of *cerrado* dominated by small trees, bushes and grassland.
Cerrado Highly threatened dry forest of flowering trees and medicinal plants that once dominated central Brazil. One of the world's biodiversity hotspots.
Igapó Seasonally flooded forest on black-water rivers.
Igarapé Amazonian creek or small stream – often seasonal.
Pantano Wetland/swamp.
Sertão A region that lies in the dry hinterlands of northeastern Brazil, made up princiaplly of *caatinga*.
Terra Firme Amazonian forest on permanently dry ground.
Varzea Seasonally flooded forest on brown-water rivers.
Vereda Buriti palms growing over an underground stream or wet area.

half is in Brazil. A principal tributary of the Paraná is the Rio Paraguai which, in its early stages, flows into a wide depression now filled with many thousands of metres of sediments and known in Brazil as the Pantanal. Further south, the swamps continue into the Chaco of Paraguay and Argentina. To the east of this, again the rivers fall off the old highland strata to form rapids and waterfalls, the largest of which was the former Sete Quedas Falls (Salto de Guaíra) on the Paraná, sadly drowned by the Itaipu Dam lake in 1982. Nearby however are the Iguaçu Falls, the most impressive of South America, created by very resistant layers of basalt.

The coast and escarpment

Highlands follow the coastline, only a short distance inland, for 3,000 km. The ancient crystalline/granite ridges, known as *serras*, stretch from Porto Alegre in the South to near Belém in the North, just short of the Amazon estuary. Long stretches are in the form of a single or stepped escarpment, abrupt in the east and sloping more gently inland to the west. They are not high in South American terms – the highest point, Pico da Bandeira is only 2890 m – but it is no more than 120 km from the ocean near Vitória. The narrowness of the coastal strip has had a profound effect on the history of settlement. Until comparatively recent times, the lack of natural access to the hinterland confined virtually all economic activity to this area, and today most of the major cities of Brazil and 80% of the population are on or near the coast.

Because of varying erosion over many millions of years, there are a number of interesting natural features in these highlands. The many granite 'peaks' in and around Rio de Janeiro are the resistant remnants of very hard rocks providing spectacular viewpoints, Pico da Tijuca (the highest, 1012 m), Corcovado (710 m) and Pão de Açúcar (396 m) the best known. There are others in the neighbouring state of Espírito Santo. Near Curitiba are the eroded sandstones of Vila Velha and the wild scenery through the Serra do Mar towards the coast. In the state of Bahía, there are remarkable caves and waterfalls in the Chapada da Diamantina National Park. In many places, what rivers there are flowing eastwards necessarily have to lose height quickly so that gorges and waterfalls abound. There are also many kilometres of spectacular coastline and fine beaches. South of Porto Alegre, eroded material moved down the coast by the southerly ocean currents added to alluvials brought north from the River Plate by subsidiary currents, have created long sand bars to form several large freshwater lagoons. The longest, Lagoa dos Patos, is over 250 km long.

Rio São Francisco

The escarpment forces most of the rain run-off to flow west into the interior to feed the Amazon and Paraná river systems. However, one major river breaks through the barrier to flow into the Atlantic. The São Francisco rises south of Belo Horizonte – one important tributary starts only 250 km from the sea – but flows, north then east, for 2900 km before it gets there. Almost 500 km of rapids through the escarpment culminate in the 75 m Paulo Afonso falls, before completing the final 240 km to the sea. Where it turns east is one of the driest areas of the country, known as the *sertão*. The river is therefore of great significance particularly as the rains here are so unreliable. Together with the link it provides to so much of the interior and its course wholly within the country (unlike the Amazon and the Paraná), the São Francisco is revered by the Brazilians as the 'river of national unity'. Its value for irrigation, hydroelectric power, fish and navigation above the rapids is inestimable, but because of sand bars at its mouth and close proximity to the fall line, the river has not proved useful for shipping or access generally to the ocean in spite of being the third largest river system on the continent.

Northern Highlands

After sinking below the Amazon estuary, the Brazilian Highlands reappear to the north and sweep round to the west to form the border with the Guianas and Venezuela. The highest tabular uplands are near where Guyana, Venezuela and Brazil meet at Monte Roraima (2810 m) and further west along the border where a national park has been set up focussed on Pico de Neblina, 3014 m, the highest point in Brazil.

Climate

The climate of Brazil is a function of latitude and altitude. The average annual temperature exceeds 26°C along the northeast coast and in the central Amazon with little variation throughout the year. The highlands are cooler and further south there are seasonal variations: Brazil extends to 34° south, which is equivalent to the latitude of North Carolina. High summer temperatures can occur almost anywhere here, yet frosts are not uncommon in July and August as coffee producers know only too well. Rainfall is more complicated. The northeast trade winds bring moist air to the coast north of the Amazon, where there is heavy precipitation all year round. The same winds push saturated air into the Amazon basin where rainfall is progressively greater from east to west throughout the year and virtually on a daily basis. The abrupt rise of the Andes beyond the borders of Brazil increases the precipitation and feeds the many tributaries.

During the period December-May, the northeast trade winds move north and Brazil between Belém and Recife receives less rain-bearing winds. From Salvador, the southeast trade winds bring moisture from the South Atlantic and it is the gap between these two systems, known as the 'doldrums', that explains the dry areas of northeast Brazil. On average there is significant rainfall here, but sometimes it fails to arrive causing prolonged periods of drought. Precipitation in the southern states of Brazil is concentrated in the escarpment thus feeding the Paraná system and is well distributed throughout the year.

Although there are occasional storms causing local damage, for example in the *favelas* (shanty towns) of Rio, Brazil is not subject to hurricanes or indeed to other natural disasters common elsewhere in Latin America such as earthquakes, volcanic eruptions or unexpected widespread and catastrophic floods.

Ecosystems, flora and fauna

The neotropical region is a land of superlatives, it contains the most extensive tropical rainforest in the world, and is drained by the Amazon, which has by far the largest volume of any river system. The fauna and flora are abundant. There are more birds, primates, reptiles, amphibians, freshwater fish and plant species here than in any other region in the world. Ecosystems are to a large extent determined by the influence of the great rivers and mountains: the Amazon river system and the Andes (which, although not part of Brazil, dramatically affect the climate and river drainage) and the far older iron and sandstone hills and depleted soils of the Guiana and Brazilian shields that lie at the heart of the continent in the north along the border with Venezuela and in the heart of Brazil in Goiás, Tocantins and large parts of the Mato Grossos around the world's largest wetland, the Pantanal.

South America's isolation from the rest of the world, until the joining of the continent with North America some four million years ago years ago, has been another crucial contributing factor to its biodiversity. Unique families of birds called the sub-oscine passerines (which are unable to sing in the same way as other songbirds because of a physical peculiarity in their larynx) developed because of this isolation. And prior to the invasion from the north by more aggressive ad competitive mammals (like the coatimundi and the puma) South America was home to large numbers of marsupials; a few of which cling on in the numerous opossum families.

Brazil can be divided into biogeographical zones; two huge river basins comprising the River Amazon and the River Plate, mountains – the Guiana highlands to the north and the Brazilian highlands to the south where the *cerrado* forests lie, and a coastal strip of Atlantic rainforest.

Mata Atlântica (Atlantic rainforest)

The Atlantic rainforest used to cover 2,600,000 sq km in a coastal strip 160 km wide and 4200 km long but now covers less than 5% of that. As the forest ranges from sea level to over 2000 m and has been isolated biologically from the Amazon and Andes, it is one of the most biodiverse regions in the world; so much so; that it is one of Conservation International's designated world biodiversity hotspots: see www.hotspots.com, for further details. There are 21 different primate species found here (compared to, for example Costa Rica's four). Seventeen of these are endemic unique to the Mata Atlântica on, and of these, 13 species, including the golden lion tamarin, are endangered. South America's largest primate, the woolly spider monkey, known locally as *muriqui*, was hunted close to extinction by European colonists who first settled along this coastal zone and subsequently by Brazilian peasant farmers. But the monkey still clings on in private reserves like **Regua** in Rio de Janeiro state (see page 156) and the Parque Nacional Caparaó in Minas Gerais.

Drift net and long line fishing in the 1960s decimated one of the healthiest populations of fish in the tropical Atlantic and the once abundant dolphin fish and tunny are now rarely seen and small fishing villages cannot survive on their catch. This loss in fish stocks has been exacerbated by the destruction of coastal mangroves throughout Brazil. Mangroves provide a breeding ground for numerous species including many that are commercially important and the shallow lagoons near the swamps are important for one of Brazil's two species of manatees. Now extensive areas of mangroves are limited to the Delta da Parnaíba in Piauí and stretches around Boipeba in Bahia and Cananéia in São Paulo. The once abundant *restinga* that lies behind the mangrove forests has also been greatly depleted. *Restinga* consists of shrub forest, coastal sand dunes, ponds and wetlands; there are remnants in areas like Regua (see page 156) and in the Delta do Parnaíba (see page 514). The lush coastal rainforest itself extends to 800 m in elevation and grades into cloud forest between 800 m and 1700 m and although greatly depleted is still abundant in parts of São Paulo state, Paraná and Rio de Janeiro. In the cloud forests (which can be seen in Itatiaia), drenching by mist, fog and rain leads to a profusion of plant growth, trees and shrubs that are covered with a great variety of epiphytes, orchids (including the famous Cattleya which comes from Rio state), mosses, lichens and bromeliads. At the highest elevations, the forest gives way to mountain grasslands or *campos de altitude*. In the southern zone of the Atlantic forest, in Rio Grande do Sul and Santa Catarina, there are large stands of, *araucária*, a relative of the monkey puzzle tree. The best places to see the Mata Atlântica are Itatiaia national park in Rio, the mountains behind Paraty and Ubatuba, and the coastal zone between Cananéia in São Paulo and Paranaguá in Paraná. The forest is immensely rich in bird life, with over 930 bird species, 144 of which are endemic species. The Serra dos Tucanos in Rio is perhaps the best place in Brazil for Mata Atlântica birding – with excellent guiding and facilities, followed closely by Regua (see page 156). Self-guided birding is immensely rewarding – from the hills above Paraty, in the Serra dos Órgãos, in Itatiaia or the forests on the Ilha do Cardoso near Cananéia. The latter island is one of the few places where caiman still bask on coastal beaches. The best places to see the Mata Atlântica itself are Itatiaia national park, in Rio, the mountains behind Paraty and Ubatuba and the coastal zone between Cananéia in São Paulo and Paranaguá in Paraná.

Amazon rivers

The Amazon basin, which is made-up of myriad different rivers; more than four of which are by water volume the largest rivers in the world, contains the greatest area of tropical rainforest in the world, 6,000,000 sq km, 60% of which is located in Brazil. It is home to 20% of the world's plant and bird species; perhaps 10% of mammal species; an inestimable number of insects and perhaps some 2000 species of fish inhabiting the 1000 tributaries of the Amazon. When in flood the great river inundates the forest for a short period in its upper reaches to create a unique habitat called *várzea*; in the lower reaches this flooding may last for four to seven months forming *igapó* swamp forest.

The rivers of the Amazon are either classified as blackwater or whitewater rivers. The former are black-tea coloured due to the brown humic acids derived from the decomposing materials on the forest floor but contain little suspended material. The white waters owe their colour to the suspended soil particles which originate in the run-off from the Andes. Each has its characteristic fish. Within a 30-km radius of Manaus, there are estimated to be over 700 species of fish. Many are biologically curious. The pirarucu or*arapaima,* which can reach over 3 m and weigh in at over 150 kg has a primitive lung that enables it to live in oxygen-depleted water. Its habit of surfacing for air makes it easy prey for fishermen. Despite being served on tables throughout the Amazon it is a threatened species, protected by Ibama; the state environmental body. The Piraiba is one of the world's largest catfish; big and aggressive enough to swallow a human. The candiru is one of the world's smaller catfish. It is parasitic, swimming into the gill spaces of other fish and lodging there to gorge blood. It is said to be attracted to urea and to swim up the urethra of swimmers who pee in the water, with unpleasant or even fatal consequences. The various species of piranha, are much maligned. The largest and most fearsome are the red piranhas and the grey piranhas, but although these fish can be dangerous when trapped in small pools in the dry season Amazonians quite happily swim in oxbow lakes filled with the fish in the wet. The pacu is one of the various species of vegetarian piranha, which feeds on fruit falling from trees in the flooded forest. More dangerous than piranhas are electric eels and sting rays; both of which are relatively common; as are bull sharks. An electrical shock of 650 volts has been recorded from a captive electric eel and Humboldt talks of them being able to knock out a fully grown horse.

Amazon forests

There are various forest types associated with and largely unique to the Amazon rivers. All the Amazonian forests are highly species rich. It has been estimated that 4 sq km of forest can harbour some 1,200 vascular plants, 600 species of tree, and 120 woody plants. Gallery forests are those which are found along the banks of rivers; and which are subject to rapid erosion when the river changes course. These forests tend to grow on nutritionally rich soil and are often high in fruiting plants. *Várzea* is a biodiverse seasonally flooded forest found along the banks of the whitewater rivers; it is very nutritionally rich as a consequence of the huge amount of silt and nutrients washed out of the mountains and trapped by the massive buttress-rooted trees. It can be flooded for as much as six months of the year and is found throughout the Amazon system. One of the most common *várzea* trees, the Pará rubber tree (*Hevea brasiliensis*), is the source of latex. The Brazilian rubber industry foundered in the 19th century when seeds of this tree were smuggled to Asia by the British and grown in vast rubber plantations, which flourished in the absence of Amazonian pest species. Another *varzea* tree is Camu-camu, whose juice has by far the highest vitamin C content of any fruit in the world; despite claims made for various Australian berries. *Varzea* forests are good places to spot waterbirds such as the Amazon's many heron, egret, ibis, duck, cormorant and stork species, at least five kingfisher species, numerous raptors like black-collared hawks and endemic birds like hoatzin. These are generally found along waterways where it feeds on leaves and fruit. The newly hatched chicks of this primitive bird have claws at the tip of each wing which enable them to crawl around in the foliage. *Varzea* is frequently visited by parrots and macaws and by primates, who are all after seasonal fruit and nuts.

Igapó forests are seasonally inundated forests found on blackwater rivers. They grow in sandy soil, which lies as beautiful exposed beaches in the dry. The largest areas of *igapó* are found in the Rio Negro system, which joins the Amazon in Manaus. sandy Despite being flooded for up to seven months of the year to a possible depth of 15 m, palms dominate the *Igapó*, interspersed with large hardwood trees like kapok. During the wet season, these flooded forests are inhabited by turtles and small fish, and the predators that feed upon them – like giant otters and various species of caiman, which can be heard calling to each other at dawn. Bird and primate life is rich with similar families to *varzea*, though with less diversity as *igapó* has fewer fruiting trees.

Flooded meadows are frequently found in the still-flowing reaches of the *várzea*. These vast carpets of floating waterlilies (including the metre-wide *Vitória regia*), water lettuce and water hyacinth are home to the Amazonian manatee, a large herbivorous aquatic mammal, only a little smaller than the manatee associated with Florida and the Caribbean and the dugong of Australia. It is very difficult to see. Two species of dolphin hunt for fish in the *varzea* and *igapó*, as well as in the larger rivers, using sonar to catch their prey. The Amazonian dolphin, or *boto* is unique to the river system, and is bubble-gum pink. There are also enormous numbers of spectacled caiman that populate the forest and feed on the highly productive fish community. The most common species are the spectacled caiman (with a yellow eyelid) and the far larger black caiman.

Varzea and *Igapó*, together with terra firme forest, are the best places to spot wildlife in the wet. In the dry the best locations are the river corridors. Caiman and turtles are commonly seen basking on the riverbanks, and if you are really lucky you may see a jaguar or ocelot draped over a branch or a tapir, the largest South American mammal, taking a bathe or a drink. Birdlife is only a little less rich in the dry than the wet, with fewer migratory species but greater concentrations of water birds hunting for the dwindling supplies of fish. **Giant otters** are found in *varzea* and *igapó* as well as in oxbow lakes and on smaller Amazonian tributaries. They can grow to up to 2 m in length and are active by day when they hunt for food, often in small groups.

In the terra firme forests, which grow on permanently dry soil, the soaring canopy some 45 m overhead is home to the greatest numbers of animals. It is a habitat thick with strangling vines and numerous epiphytic plant species amongst which troupes of squirrel monkeys, in various species, and capuchins forage, alongside **uakari**, **saki** and **titi** monkeys. In the high canopy groups of **spider monkeys** perform their lazy aerial acrobatics, whilst lower down, clinging to epiphyte-clad trunks and branches, groups of tiny **tamarins** and **marmosets** forage for gums, blossom, fruit and the occasional insect prey. Small arboreal cats such as **margay** and large weasels, and racoons like **tayra** and **coatimundi**, prey on them. Families of **howler monkeys** noisily roar out their territorial boundaries at dawn and dusk. Birdlife is very rich, with high numbers of uniquely neotropical species such as turkey-sized **currasows** and **guans**, spectacularly coloured **cotingas**, **trogons** and **motmots**, myriad **tyrant flycatchers** and as many **woodpeckers**, **woodcreepers** and **foliage gleaners**; many associated with particular tree families. Brilliant **tanagers** and **hummingbirds** flit through the canopy flowers and all are watched over by a succession of **raptors**; the largest of which is the elusive metre-tall **harpy eagle**, with ankles as thick as a woman's wrist. These are big and powerful enough to pluck the larger monkeys and the various species of sloth out of the tops of trees. **Antbirds** and **manakins** flutter silently through the forest below; the former in various species each of which follow troupes of specific army ant families through the forest eating the insects they startle as they pass. The best places to see the Amazon wildlife are Cristalino Jungle Lodge (see page 156), Mamirauá Reserve (see page 569), the Anavilhanas Islands (see page 567), preferably on a cruise, and from the best of the jungle lodges around Manaus (see page 574).

The Pantanal

This ecologically diverse zone includes the largest area of wetlands in the world and is the best place in South America for seeing wild animals. Alongside the wetlands are dry savannahs, *cerrado*, chaco scrublands as well as gallery forest. The area is very flat and flooded by the rising rivers leaving isolated islands or cordilheiras between vast lakes *orbaías*, which become saline as the waters evaporate. This mixed ecosystem supports a highly diverse fauna characteristic of the constituent habitat types which includes 200 species of mammal. **Capybara** (a large aquatic rodent that looks like a giant guinea pig), **tapir** and South America bush pigs or **peccaries** are common along the waters edge as are the **web-footed marsh deer**. **Jaguar**, the largest cat in the Americas weighing up to 150 kg, and **puma**, which are only a little smaller are more commonly associated with the forest and savannahs and prey on these herbivores and the cattle and feral pigs which graze here. **Giant anteater**, **armadillos** and **rhea** (South American ostrich(are seen in the grassland areas. Spectacular assemblages of **wading birds** such as egrets, jabiru storks, ibises, spoonbills and herons prey on the abundant invertebrate and fish. **Anacondas** and **Pantanal caiman** (a sub-species of spectacled caiman) are still common, although the large black caiman has been hunted out. The best places to see animals in the Pantanal are the Transpantaneira (see page 662) in Mato Grosso and the *fazendas* around Miranda (see page 650).

The cerrado

The *cerrado* is Brazil's outback and makes up most of the interior of the country between the coast and the Amazon basin, much of Mato Grosso and Mato Grosso do Sul including parts of the Pantanal, almost all of Goiás, Tocantins, Minas Gerais and the far west of the northeastern states are *cerrado*. It is the most extensive woodland-savanna region in South America. Like the Australian outback, the *cerrado* comprises forest, grassland and scrub broken by rivers and underground streams. Also like the outback it grows on ancient, eroded rock and it bursts into bright bloom in the wet. Within the *cerrado*, there is a tapestry of different vegetation types, including tree and scrub savanna, grassland with scattered trees, and occasional patches of a dry, closed canopy forest called the *cerradão*. Gallery forests are found throughout the region, although they are technically not considered part of the typical *cerrado* formations. Unlike the outback the *cerrado* gets plenty of rain (around 1500 m per year), usually between October and April. For the rest of the year the *cerrado* is dry – so much so that many of the plants have adapted to drought conditions – with leathery or waxy leaves and some deciduous tendencies. Much of the vegetation is also adapted to fire. The *cerrado* is Brazil's most critically threatened biome. It is also one of the world's greatest botanical repositories with an estimated 10,000 plant species, of which about 4400 are endemic. Herbaceous species, which include herbs rather than woody plants, are almost entirely endemic. Some of the most remarkable plants in the *cerrado* include the conspicuous *Mauritia flexuosa* palms (known locally as *buritis*) that grow along the swampy headwaters of streams and rivers, and the spectacular *ipê* trumpet flower trees (*Tabebuia*), which are leafless when in bloom and have brilliant purple, pink, yellow or white flowers. There are some 600 bird species, nearly 20 of which are endemic and all of Brazil's spectacular mammals can be seen here. The best places to see the *cerrado* are Chapada dos Veadeiros (see page 619), Jalapão (see page 628), the Parque Estadual São Gonçalo do Rio Preto near Diamantina (see page 267), the Serra da Canastra, the Serra do Cipó and Parque Nacional das Emás (see page 620).

The sertão and caatinga

The sertão is a region which lies in the dry hinterlands of northeastern Brazil; ecologically it is made up principally of *caatinga*. This is South America's least scientifically studied biome and is completely unique to Brazil. The *caatinga* is made up of xeric desert-adapted plants – small, thorny deciduous trees, cacti, succulent plants, and fire-adapted grassland savannas. There are many unique flowering plants that burst into brilliant bloom in the wet. The biome has two seasons: winter (May-November) when it is very hot and dry, and the summer (January-April) when it is very hot and wet. During the dry winter periods trees are bare and their roots begin to protrude through the surface of the stony soil which can reach temperatures of up to 60°C. When the rains begin in January, the bleak, desert-like landscape of the *caatinga* is transformed in an exuberance of green and bright flowers; the rivers start to fill up and birds begin to sing in the trees.

Caatinga makes up some 11% of Brazilian territory, yet only 1% of its habitats are protected – a reflection on the respect given to the sertão by both federal and state governments. And there are no tour operators offering wildlife trips to the region (although companies like **Manary**, see page 25, do operate here). Animal life in the *caatinga* has been adversely affected by hunting and human occupation. Many species have become extinct locally, while others, such as the **three-banded armadillo**, **collared anteater**, **jaguar** and **tufted capuchin**, survive in reduced numbers. Bird species include some of the world's rarest parrots – Lear's and Spix's **macaws** live in tiny numbers on the fringes of Jalapão (see page 628) and near the Serra da Capivara (see page 515) and **cactus parakeets**, **long-billed wrens**, **scarlet-throated tanagers** and **yellow-faced siskins** occur throughout the biome. Beyond hearsay, little is known about the *caatinga* except that it is critically vulnerable. There are no statistics available for flora or fauna species or numbers. The best places to see *caatinga* are anywhere in the sertão, especially the Serra da Capivara and the remote Serra dos Confusões in southern Piauí.

National parks

On paper Brazil has stringent environmental legislation and a large system of very well-protected national parks. However, hunting is rife as none of the parks have rangers. Until recently, unscrupulous and influential businessmen and politicians logged and abused the parks with impunity; a situation which began to change only with the exposure of a logging scandal involving the state governments and **Ibama** (Instituto Brasileiro do Meio Ambiente e dos Recursos Naturais Renováveis – the Brazilian Institute for the Environment and Renewable Natural Resources) in Brazil's southern Amazon and Central West in the new millennium. This still compares favourably with Britain though where agriculture, logging and road construction is permitted within national parks even when they are world heritage sites. **Ibama** has in its care 57 national parks (Parques Nacionais, or PARNA). They are by no means the whole picture, though. They form part of a system of protected areas which go under different titles and which have varying degrees of public access. The network comprises, in addition to the national parks: *estações ecológicas* (ecological stations), *reservas biológicas* (biological reserves), *reservas ecológicas* (ecological reserves), *áreas de relevante interesse ecológico* (areas of relevant ecological interest), *reservas particulares do patrimônio nacional* (private national heritage reserves) and *áreas sob proteção especial* (areas of special protection). In all these entities, the exploitation of natural resources is completely forbidden. They are for research, education and recreation only. Three other types of entity are designed to allow the sustainable use of natural resources, while still preserving their biodiversity: *florestas nacionais* (national forests), *áreas de proteção ambiental* (areas of environmental protection) and *reservas extrativas* (extractive reserves, such as the rubber-tapping zones in Acre state). A new initiative is the **Projeto Corredores Ecológicos** (Ecological Corridors Project), which aims to create avenues of forest between isolated protected areas so that fauna may move over a greater area to breed, thus strengthening the stock of endangered animals, which might otherwise suffer the ills of inbreeding. An example of this is a project to link the Mata Atlântica of Poço das Antas with other pockets of coastal forest to help the survival of the golden lion tamarin.

Ibama was created in 1989 by uniting four separate bodies: the environmental secretariat (SEMA), the Brazilian Institute of Forest Development (IBDF), and the superintendencies for the development of fishing and rubber (SUDEPE and SUDHEVEA). Brazil has a long history of passing laws to protect natural resources, such as that of 1808 that excluded from international trade the export of *pau-brasil* and other woods. At the same time, though, enforcement of such laws has not been easy. Today, the achievement of Ibama's goals is determined by resources, but funds are insufficient to commit either enough money or staff to the job of protecting the areas that have been designated for preservation. Sad though this is, there are still a large number of parks open to visitors that can give a good idea of the variety of Brazil's natural resources and the value that they hold for the country.

This book does not describe all of Brazil's national parks or other conservation entities, but only those which have easy access. Nor does it list all the offices of Ibama or its related departments throughout the country, but those nearest to the parks described are given and it is to these that you should apply to if a permit is needed to visit a specific park.

For more information, contact Ibama at its local addresses, its national headquarters: SAIN, Avenida L-4, bloco B, Térreo, Edifiço Sede do Ibama, CEP 70.800-200, Brasília DF, T061-226 8221/9014, F322 1058, or at its website, www.ibama.gov.br.

Information can also be obtained from the Ministério do Meio Ambiente (MMA – the environment ministry) at Esplanada dos Ministérios, bloco B, 5-9 andar, CEP

70068-900, Brasília DF, or at its website www.mma.gov.br. See also the book *Nacionais Brasil, Guias Philips* (1999), which has a good map, beautiful photographs, sections on history, flora and fauna and tourist services, US$15.

An environmental history of the Amazon

The first white man to cross the Amazon was the conquistador Francisco de Orellana, who ended up here by accident in 1541. The river and its environs were called the 'Land of the Amazons' after accounts by local indigenous people of a tribe of warrior women who dominated the lowland region, documented by the expedition's chronicler, Gaspar de Carvajal. This led to the myth that the Amazon area was a land of great wealth; an idea that has endured to this day and which powers the numerous attempts to exploit the forest.

Since the arrival of the Europeans, successive colonial and Brazilian governments have been hell-bent on developing Amazonia. First it was the gold of the Amazons. Then it was the sugar cane around São Luis and Belém; an industry which saw the introduction of slavery and the genocide of entire indigenous nations, including the magnificent Omagua people – an important pre-Colombian civilization. Then it was rubber, whose harvesting from wild *hevea brasiliensis* trees turned Manaus from a collection of mud huts to being a full-blown belle époque city with an opera house and some of the first street lights and trams in the Americas. Thousands of river people and indigenous tribes lost their liberty and their lives while the rubber barons became rich (see the film *A Selva* for a visual account). But the Amazon forest survived relatively untouched until the building of Brasília. This began to change in 1954 under President Juscelino Kubitschek, who believed in Brazil's destiny as a great country, and whose slogan was 'fifty years in five'. Kubitschek built a new capital in the middle of what was then nowhere, which he called, Brasilia, and he linked it to Belém with the first Amazon road. This marked the beginnings of expansion into the vast Brazilian interior, and the US installed military dictatorship that came to power via a coup in 1964 continued the process.

The military planned massive relocations of the population, mostly the rural poor, to secure what they referred to as empty areas, and to ease the mounting pressure for land reform. The politic rhetoric was one of progress and the protection of Brazil's national security and borders, even from countries as small and impoverished as Guyana, whose entire national population was less than the number of soldiers serving in Brazil's armed forces. Inspired by the slogan 'Integra par no entregar' (integrate to avoid annexation) landless peasants were encouraged to relocate to the new states of Roraima and Rondônia and carve out their own property from the forests. 'The people without land', would be transferred to 'the land without people'. The disputed territories they left behind them could then be incorporated into the vast ranches owned by the powerful political oligarchy of landowners (many of whom were descended from the original Portuguese settlers) who were the political allies of the military, and the Amazon would become a profitable and productive area of export agriculture.

Money for these and other schemes were borrowed from and approved by the World Bank and IMF. A communication network would be crucial. In 1972, the military decided that they should link the Pacific and Atlantic oceans with a trans-Amazon highway, and build a network of filter roads off it, linking the interior with Sao Paulo and Minas Gerais. *Agrovilas*, purpose-built settlements were strung out along these new roads and families were airlifted in from the northeast and south of the country. A network of over a hundred hydroelectric dams was planned to provide energy at places like Presidente Figueiredo and on the Tocantins. They are appallingly inefficient. Another ambitious project, Greater Carajás, followed in 1980, when an

18-billion-ton iron ore mountain was discovered in the eastern Amazon, and in the early 1990s further plans were announced by the military to build 'Calha Norte', a road cutting across the northern Amazon, through the heart of the largest untouched section of virgin rainforest in South America. Its building was thwarted only by the courageous campaigns by the indigenous people of upper Rio Negro.

The 'opening of the Amazon' was a disaster for Brazil's indigenous tribes, as well as the forest and the economic prosperity of the country as a whole. Neither the new settlers in Roraima and Rondônia, nor the government had been aware that the Amazon soils they had planned to farm were so nutrient-poor that they would sustain crops or cattle for only a year or two at most, before turning to desert. Farmers and ranchers ate into the forest near the new roads at a terrifying rate. Soon they had encroached on indigenous territories, inciting conflict in which the *indígena* invariably came off worse, or spreading western disease to which the tribes had no immunity. Not since the days of the Portuguese had the Amazon's *indígena* suffered so badly.

In 1990, after the discovery of gold in Yanomami territories in western Roraima, garmipeiro gold miners from throughout Brazil flooded into the territory of the largest remaining isolated tribe in the Americas, the Yanomami. Many were supplied and supported by local businessmen, who saw them as the vanguard of a new colonization and were eager for a slice of the gold-rich territory. Indigenous 'hunts' were common. In 1990s Boa Vista, it is said that even taxi drivers offered safaris of the *indígena* to visitors: bring a gun and shoot a wild native. Since then, at least 2000 Yanomami have died. Many more have been deprived of their land, either through annexation by gold miners or the pollution of their rivers with mercury and soil. Other tribes fared equally badly. The Parakanâ were deliberately infected with smallpox, influenza, tuberculosis and measles by FUNAI, the government's indigenous peoples' agency, ostensibly set up to protect them. Hundreds died. Then they were forcibly moved to make way for the Transamazon highway, and then again for the Tucuruí dam. The Xavantes lost their territory to the Italian company Liquigas; the Waimiri Atroari saw part of their reserve flooded by the Balbina dam; the Nambiquara were displaced first by a dam and then the Santarém to Cuiabá road, and the uru-Weu-Wau-Wau and the Zorro were in the way of the World Bank funded Polonoroeste road and development project. Ticuna, Guarani and many others were murdered by loggers, gold prospectors or settlers.

The forest's *caboclo* people suffered too. Although the forests were no longer producing rubber in the quantities they once had, rubber tappers still lived and worked in the forests of Acre, Amapá, Rondônia and Roraima, and when the cattle ranchers and their vanguard of displaced (mostly northeastern) peasants began to invade their territories and destroy their livelihood, they set up a resistance movement, organized by unions. A series of empates, or passive stand-offs in the tradition of Gandhi and Martin Luther King, lead by charismatic locals like Francisco 'Chico' Alves Mendes, brought the plight of the rubber tappers to the attention of the world. It did little to assuage the ranchers, who killed and murdered rubber tappers aided and abetted by the local police. As he had predicted, Chico Mendes himself was shot dead in 1988.

Opening up the Amazon did little to help Brazil's economy, although a number of landowners and politicians managed to save enough to bank in the Cayman islands and buy mansions in Miami. The new roads cost billions and many are now impassable. Many of the dams were built in valleys that were insufficiently deep and narrow for the rapid water flow required to produce cheap electricity. The Balbina dam north of Manaus, which was the personal project of President Figueiredo, the last of the military rulers of Brazil, produces electricity four times more expensive than that available on the world market. There are so many rotting logs in its flooded valley that the acidity of the water requires the turbines to be replaced every few years. The

Greater Carajás project, which the then finance minister Delfim Neto claimed would provide enough iron ore to pay off the foreign debt in fact doubled it, and the surrounding forest was cleared for his cattle-ranching friends. Brazil's economy and the Amazon suffered deeply through the 'Integrar para no Entregar' project. Together with the rising cost of oil, opening up the Amazon has made Brazil the Third World's largest foreign debtor.

The massacre of the Yanomami and the murder of Chico Mendes cost Brazil's reputation dear. They were denounced to the United Nations and the Organisation of American States for genocide in the 1990s, and NGOs and campaign groups continued to draw attention to their appalling indigenous rights record and abuses of power. Brazil got frightened and ashamed. When they hosted the 1992 Earth Summit, they showed off a whole infrastructure of specialized agencies for protecting the environment, from a special ministry down to state and municipal secretariats. Constitutional and legislative changes promised indigenous land demarcation and declared explicitly that private land titles on lands traditionally occupied by Indians were null and void. Environmental impact reports would be required before new development or industrial projects could go ahead. The world rejoiced, and Brazil obtained $290 million in grants for forest and indigenous land protection.

But Brazil is a lumbering and corrupt giant, with a tongue that drips honey. The money was gratefully received. But none of it ever reached the *indígena* and the national parks set up by the government were parks just on paper. The powerful and corrupt landowning oligarchy who rule the country, displayed their true colours only four years later, when they forced President Fernando Henrique Cardoso to pass a decree 1775, which revoked the law granting protection of indigenous lands, opening them up to loggers, miners and ranchers. An area the size of Rhode Island was cut from Macuxi indigenous territory in Roraima and handed over to 14 cattle ranchers from the National Institute for Colonisation and Agrarian Reform (INCRA). Further enclaves were created in the heart of the reserve for gold miners. Over the past decade, corrupt officials in the government's own environmental protection agency, Ibama, have been shown to have forged documents on a grand scale to allow the passage of illegally cut mahogany from indigenous reserves and national parks into Europe and the USA and attempts continue in Congress to open up indigenous areas to mining and reduce the size of the Yanomami territories.

Yet some progress was made. Significant areas of land have been marked out as indigenous territories; far more than in the USA or Canada both in real terms and as a percentage of national territory. Whether the indigenous peoples have any real sovereignty is another matter as their rights to the minerals beneath their land is by no means clear under Brazilian law. And in the Amanã Sustainable Development Reserve (SDR) was set up, linking two other reserves to form the world's largest protected rainforest area. The Amanã SDR surrounds Lake Amanã north of Tefé and covers 23,500 sq km. It is sandwiched between the Jaú National Park to the east and the Mamirauá SDR to the west, forming a 640-km long corridor. It is hoped that whole ecosystems will be preserved and that local inhabitants will be able to find sustainable work in the reserve's management.

Since he first came to power, Lula has promised much but has been stringently criticized by the confederation of Amazon Indians for his policy towards them. He failed to demarcate a key indigenous reserve in Roraima, preferring to cut a deal with local politicians for political support. And although down briefly in the late 1990s, deforestation in 2003 was at an all time high thanks to a failure to curb illegal clearance by soya and cattle ranchers. The 2005 murder of the environmentalist and nun Dorothy Stang, by ranch owners in Para, showed that the problem of environmental destruction exists most acutely at a state level. It also brought widespread international condemnation. Once again Brazil was shamed into action.

The environment minister, Marina Silva, said the country could not 'give in to people committing acts of violence' and that the federal government would be 'putting the brakes on the predators.' There has been progress since. Immediately after the murder, large areas of national park were demarcated in Para, by the federal government. In 2005 deforestation in the Amazon slowed down by half – as much because of a fall in soya prices as because of federal policy. And in December 2006 Simão Jatene, the governor of Pará – long a conservative anti-environmentalist – announced the creation of nine new protected areas forming an ecological corridor between Brazil and the Guianas. Yet like all Brazil's national parks, these will exist on paper only – with no rangers and no organized monitoring. And all this good work could be offset by more destruction. On 6 June 2006 – World Environment Day – Lula announced plans to pave the road between Cuiabá and Santarém, in order to make the transport of soya beans cheaper and swifter. He claimed that the government was establishing strict environmental controls, and had created a 'sustainable forestry reserve' of 19 million ha (47 million acres) around the road and that the project 'will show how we can be Brazilian without being predators, as foreigners often say about Brazil'. But roads have always been associated with the arrival of squatters and the birth of towns in the Amazon and the sincerity of his promises remain to be seen.

Books

History and anthropology

Hemming, J, *Red Gold, Amazon Frontier and Die if You Must*, Pan. The little-known history of Brazil's indigenous people is alternatively shocking and inspiring. This wonderful, scholarly and beautifully written account is as readable and exciting as Prescott's *Conquest of Peru* and will in time rank alongside it. A must for anyone with an interest in Brazil.

Reichel-Dolmatoff, G, *Rainforest Shamans*, Themis books. The best introduction to the philosophy of an Amazon people available in English.

Literature

Amado, J, et al, *Gabriela, Clove and Cinnamon*, *Dona Flor and her two Husbands*, Avon Books. Very poor translations of these captivating novels, almost all of which are set in Bahia, and which read like a cross between Poldark and Angelique. Romps through 19th- and 20th-century Bahia. Ripping yarns though not literary masterpieces. Over a long career Amado published many best sellers, many of which are available in English. He is often criticized for producing an overly optimistic, sexily tropical view of the country, and of Bahia, his home state.

Andrade, Mário de, *Macunaíma*. Written in the 1920s, this is a comic statement in picaresque form about Brazilian nationality, by the leader of Modernism.

Ângelo, I, *The Celebration*, Avon Books. Much the best novel about the political, social and economic crisis at the end of the 1960s, the worst period of the military regime.

Buarque, C, *Turbulence*, and *Budapest*, Bloomsbury. The first is a short, pacey allegory of modern Brazil, the second which has been recently translated, is a labyrinthine Borgesian magic realist novel set in Budapest. It was top of the best sellers list in Brazil for many months – something unusual for literary fiction. Buarque is the son of a distinguished social historian and is most famous as a singer and composer.

da Cunha, E, *Rebellion in the Backlands*, University of Chicago Press. The book that inspired Mario Vargas Llosa and which is the country's most famous piece of sustained journalistic writing.

Freyre, Gilberto, *The Masters and the Slaves*, out of print. One of the central figures in the story of Brazil's struggle to define its identity. Controversial and sometimes viewed as implicitly racist, this account traces the psychology of Brazil to its sugar plantation past.

Guimarães Rosa, J, *The Jaguar and Other Stories*, Boulevard Books. Decent translations of Brazil's greatest novelist are hard to come by. There are none at all of his masterpiece, *Grande sertão, veredas: As trilhas de amor e guerra de Riobaldo*. Guimarães Rosa is, in a sense, the first great magic realist author, and is by far the most respected author within Brazil. He is credited with having invented a new kind of poetically colloquial literary Portuguese. This draws its inspiration from the mystical and lyrical language of the interior of Brazil, a region which was gradually cut off from the rest of the country. *The Jaguar* is little more than an introduction to his writing.

Hatoum, M, *The Brothers*. One of the most interesting of Brazilian contemporary writers who focusses on the experience of being Brazilian-Lebanese in the dangerous world of the early 20th-century Amazon. Wonderfully evocative.

Lins do Rego, J, *The Masters and the Slaves*, University of California Press. Highly influenced by Gilberto Freyre, this is an evocative account of childhood on a northeastern sugar plantation.

Lispector, C, *Family Ties*, *The Hour of the Star* and *Soulstorm*, University of Texas Press, Carcanet Press and New Directions. Brazil's other great modernist and the country's most highly revered woman's writer.

Llosa, M V, *The War of the End of the World*, Penguin. An enthralling dramatisation of the Canudos rebellion. Very hard to put down and beautifully structured.

Machado de Assis, J M, The Posthumous Memoirs of Bras Cubas, *Dom Casmurro*, Oxford University Press and *Philosopher or Dog*, Bloomsbury. At last some decent translations of Brazil's most acerbic and witty literary social commentator. With a black mother and white Portuguese-descended father, Machado de Assis was a bridge between the 2 Brazil's: the haves and the have nots.

Morley, H, *The Patriot*, London: Rex Collings. The diary of a girl's life in Diamantina, in Minas Gerais. Translated by the great American poet Elizabeth Bishop who lived in Brazil for many years. A delightfully intimate and frank portrait of small-town life.

Ramos, G, *São Bernardo* (Peter Owen) *Anguish* (Knopf, 1972) and *Barren Lives* (University of Texas Press, 1965). The greatest of the novelists of the 1930s and 1940s: a harsh realist.

Torres, A, *Blues for a Lost Childhood*, (1989) Readers International. An idealistic Brazilian journalist leaves his rural town for Rio only to be crushed by the realities of the city. Sobering and not very cheerful reading.

Ubaldo Ribeiro, J, *The Lost Manuscript*, Bloomsbury. A panoramic historical novel, originally entitled *Long Live the Brazilian People*.

Poetry

Bandeira, M, *This Earth, that Sky: Poems by Manuel Bandeira*, University of California Press. The oldest member of the Modernist movement, and one of Brazil's greatest poets, master of the short, intense lyric.

Drummond de Andrade, C, *Plantation Boy*, New York: Knopf. Perhaps Brazil's greatest poet, with a varied, lyrical, somewhat downbeat style.

Photography

Andujar, Claudia, *A vulnerabilidade do ser*, Cosacnaify, Wonderful evocative and masterful images that capture the poetry of Brazil's landscapes and people; often fused in a double exposure. Her Amazon images are startlingly original.

Bassit, José, *Imagens Fiéis*. A moving account of traditional religious life in the backlands of the northeast. Again, masterfully shot.

Salgado, S, *Migrations*, Aperture. The most recent volume from the world's most highly respected photojournalist renowned for transcendental images of the world's silent majority and their daily lives. Incredible.

Social comment

Bellos, A, *Futebol: The Brazilian Way of Life*, (2003) Bloomsbury. A loving look at the beautiful game, its history, its players, supporters and its legendary feats. Alex Bellos is one of the UK's leading Brazilian experts and was the Guardian correspondent based in Rio.

Castro, R, *Rio de Janeiro*, (2004) Bloomsbury. An anecdotal history and profile of Rio de Janeiro written by a Carioca.

Fausto, B, *A Concise History of Brazil*, Cambridge University Press. Dry as dust but the only readily available, reliable history of the country available in English.

Harvey, **Constable** and **Robinson**, *Liberators*, (2002). A wonderful romp through the

Liberation of South America from Europe with a colourful section on imperial Brazil. How all history should be written.
McGowan, C and **Pessanha, R**, *The Brazilian Sound: Samba, Bossa Nova and the Popular Music of Brazil*, (1998) Temple University Press. An encyclopaedic survey of Brazilian popular music with interviews from many of the key players.
Page, J, *The Brazilians*, (1995) Da Capo Press. One of the few popular books on Brazil which really gets under the country's skin. With excellent chapters on Carnaval, football, Brazilian society and character and plenty of information on Rio.

Travel writing

Davis, W, *One River*. A remarkable travel book: Hunter S Thompson meets George Forrest and Levi Strauss in the heart of the Amazon.
Fawcett, P, *Exploration Fawcett*, (2001) Weidenfeld & Nicholson. The diaries of the intrepid explorer who disappeared in Mato Grosso in the 1920s and whose descriptions of the table-top mountains there inspired Conan Doyle to write *The Lost World*. Some beautiful writing on the Amazon, Rio de Janeiro and the Andes.
Fleming, P, *Brazilian Adventure*, (1998) Pimlico. The sparkling, delightfully humorous account of a 1930s expedition in search of Colonel Percy Fawcett.
Robb, P, *A Death in Brazil*, (2004) Bloomsbury. A poetic odyssey through Brazil's history, culture and landscape.

Wildlife field guides

General

Kricher, J, *A Neotropical Companion*, Princeton University Press. A very clear, intelligent introduction to the ecosystems, biology and botany of the neotropical region.
Pearson, D & **Beletsky, L** *Brazil - Amazon & Pantanal*, Academic Press. By far the best of the introductory wildlife and botanical guides.

Birds

de la Peña, M & **Rumboll, M**, *Birds of Southern South America and Antarctica*, Harper Collins & Princeton University Press. A slim volume, but with comprehensive information on most of Brazil's non-neotropical species.
Dunning, J, *South American Birds: A Photographic Aid to Identification*, Harrowood Books, Pennsylvania, 1987. The best of the current photguides with more than 2700 species, over 1400 colour photographs.
Hilty, S and **Brown, W** *Birds of Colombia*. The best book for the northern Amazon region.
Ridgely, R & **Tudor, G**, *The Birds of South America, Volume 1 & II*, University of Texas Press & Oxford University Press (UK). One of the most important bird books of the century.
Sibley, D, **Alfred, A**, *Sibley's Birding basics*, Knopf, 2002. Very useful aid to bird identification giving clues through appearance, behaviour, flight and song. Invaluable for inexperienced bird wathchers.
Sick, H, *The Birds of Brazil*, Princeton University Press. Currently the only widely available book covering almost all Brazil's species (there are more species added almost monthly).
Souza, D, *All the Birds of Brazil*, Gráfica Santa Helena, 2002. Covering most Brazilian species and include illustrations, albeit rather poor ones. English and Portuguese.
Wheatley, N, *Where to Watch Birds in South America*, Princeton University Press. A little out of date but with an interesting list of places and useful bird inventories.
Zimmer, K & **Whittaker, A**, *Birds of Brazil*, Princeton University Press. The first comprehensive, modern illustrated field guide to the birds of Brazil. Due out in 2008.

Mammals

Eisenberg, J F & **Redford, K**, *Mammals of the Neotropics Vol 3: The Central Neotropics - Ecuador, Peru, Bolivia, Brazil*.
Emmons, L H, *Neotropical Rainforest Mammals: A Field Guide*, University of Chicago Press. Excellent illustrated field guides which between them cover pretty much everything in tropical Brazil.

Plants

Henderson, A, **Galeano, G** & **Bernal, R**, *A Field Guide to the Palms of the Americas*, Princeton University Press. A comprehensive illustrated guide. Well worth having.

Reptiles and amphibians

Bartlett, R D & **Pope Bartlett, P**, *Reptiles and Amphibians of the Amazon: An Ecotourist's Guide*, University of Florida Press. With 250 common species.

Footnotes

Basic Portuguese for travellers

Learning Portuguese is a useful part of the preparation for a trip to Brazil and no volume of dictionaries, phrase books or word lists will provide the same enjoyment as being able to communicate directly with the people of the country you are visiting. It is a good idea to make an effort to grasp the basics before you go. As you travel you will pick up more of the language and the more you know, the more you will benefit from your stay. ▸▸ *See also Language in Essentials, page 27.*

General pronunciation

Within Brazil itself, there are variations in pronunciation, intonation, phraseology and slang. This makes for great richness and for the possibility of great enjoyment in the language. A couple of points which the newcomer to the language will spot immediately are the use of the tilde (~) over 'a' and 'o'. This makes the vowel nasal, as does a word ending in 'm' or 'ns', or a vowel followed by 'm' + consonant, or by 'n' + consonant. Another important point of spelling is that for words ending in 'i' and 'u' the emphasis is on the last syllable, though (unlike Spanish) no accent is used. This is especially relevant in place names like Buriti, Guarapari, Caxambu, Iguaçu. Note also the use of 'ç', which changes the pronunciation of c from hard [k] to soft [s].

Personal pronouns

In conversation, most people refer to 'you' as *você*, although in the south and in Pará *tu* is more common. To be more polite, use *O Senhor/A Senhora*. For 'us', *gente* (people, folks) is very common when it includes you too.

Portuguese words and phrases

Greetings and courtesies

hello	*oi*
good morning	*bom dia*
good afternoon	*boa tarde*
good evening/night	*boa noite*
goodbye	*adeus/tchau*
see you later	*até logo*
please	*por favor/faz favor*
thank you	*obrigado* (if a man is speakinng) /*obrigada* (if a woman is speaking)
thank you very much	*muito obrigado/muito obrigada*
How are you?	*Como vai você tudo bem?/tudo bom?*
I am fine	*vou bem/tudo bem*
pleased to meet you	*um prazer*
no	*não*
yes	*sim*
excuse me	*com licença*
I don't understand	*não entendo*
Please speak slowly	*fale devagar por favor*
What is your name?	*Qual é seu nome?*
my name is...	*O meu nome é...*
Go away!	*Vai embora!*

Basic questions

where is?	*onde está/onde fica?*
why?	*por que?*
how much does it cost?	*quanto custa?*
what for?	*para que?*
how much is it?	*quanto é?*
how do I get to...?	*para chegar a...?*
when?	*quando?*
I want to go to...	*quero ir para...*
when does the bus leave?/arrive?	*a que hor sai/chega o ônibus?*
is this the way to the church?	*aquí é o caminho para a igreja?*

Basics

bathroom/toilet	*banheiro*
police (policeman)	*a polícia (o polícia)*
hotel	*o (a pensão, a hospedaria)*
restaurant	*o restaurante (o lanchonete)*
post office	*o correio*
telephone office	*(central) telefônica*
supermarket	*o supermercado*
market	*o mercado*
bank	*o banco*
bureau de change	*a casa de câmbio*
exchange rate	*a taxa de câmbio*
notes/coins	*notas/moedas*
traveller's cheques	*os travelers/os cheques de viagem*
cash	*dinheiro*
breakfast	*o cafede manh*
lunch	*o almoço*
dinner/supper	*o jantar*
meal	*a refeição*
drink	*a bebida*
mineral water	*a água mineral*
soft fizzy drink	*o refrigerante*
beer	*a cerveja*
without sugar	*sem açúcar*
without meat	*sem carne*

Getting around

on the left/right	*à esquerda/à direita*
straight on	*direto*
to walk	*caminhar*
bus station	*a rodoviária*
bus	*o ônibus*
bus stop	*a parada*
train	*a trem*
airport	*o aeroport*
aeroplane/airplane	*o avião*
flight	*o vôa*
first/second class	*primeira/segunda clase*
train station	*a ferroviária*
combined bus and train station	*a rodoferroviária*
ticket	*o passagem/o bilhete*
ticket office	*a bilheteria*

Accommodation

room	*quarto*
noisy	*barulhento*
single/double room	*(quarto de) solteiro/(quarto para) casal*
room with two beds	*quarto com duas camas*
with private bathroom	*quarto com banheiro*
hot/cold water	*água quente/fria*
to make up/clean	*limpar*
sheet(s)	*o lençol (os lençóis)*
blankets	*as mantas*
pillow	*o travesseiro*
clean/dirty towels	*as toalhas limpas/sujas*
toilet paper	*o papel higiêico*

Health

chemist	*a farmacia*
doctor	*o coutor/a doutora*
(for) pain	*(para) dor*
stomach	*o esômago (a barriga)*
head	*a cabeça*
fever/sweat	*a febre/o suor higiênicas*
diarrhoea	*a diarréia*
blood	*o sangue*
condoms	*as camisinhas/os preservativos*
contraceptive (pill)	*anticonceptional (a pílula)*
period	*a menstruação/a regra*
sanitary towels/tampons	*toalhas absorventes/absorventes internos*
contact lenses	*lentes de contacto*
aspirin	*a aspirina*

Time

at one o'clock (am/pm)	*a uma hota (da manhã/da tarde)*
at half past two/two thirty	*as dois e meia*
at a quarter to three	*quinze para as três*
it's one o'clock	*é uma*
it's seven o'clock	*são sete horas*
it's twenty past six/six twenty	*são seis e vinte*
it's five to nine	*são cinco para as nove*
in ten minutes	*em dez minutos*
five hours	*cinco horas*
does it take long?	*sura muito?*

Days

Monday	*segunda feiro*
Tuesday	*terça feira*
Wednesday	*quarta feira*
Thursday	*quinta feira*
Friday	*sexta feira*
Saturday	*sábado*
Sunday	*domingo*

Months

January	*janeiro*
February	*fevereiro*

March	*março*
April	*abril*
May	*maio*
June	*junho*
July	*julho*
August	*agosto*
September	*setembro*
October	*outubro*
November	*Novembro*
December	*dezembro*

Numbers

one	*um/uma*
two	*dois/duas*
three	*três*
four	*quatro*
five	*cinco*
six	*seis* ('*meia*' half, is frequently used for number 6 ie half-dozen)
seven	*sete*
eight	*oito*
nine	nove
ten	*dez*
eleven	*onze*
twelve	*doze*
thirteen	*treze*
fourteen	*catorze*
fifteen	*quinze*
sixteen	*dezesseis*
seventeen	*dezessete*
eighteen	*dezoito*
nineteen	*dezenove*
twenty	*vinte*
twenty-one	*vente e um*
thirty	*trinta*
forty	*cuarenta*
fifty	*cinqüe*
sixty	*sessenta*
seventy	*setenta*
eighty	*oitenta*
ninety	*noventa*
hundred	*cem, cento*
thousand	*mil*

Useful slang

that's great/cool	*que legal*
bloke/guy/geezer	*cara* (literally 'face')
biker slang for bloke/guy	*mano*
cheesy/tacky	*brega*
posh, spoilt girl/boy with rich parents	*patricinha/mauricinho*
in fashion/cool	*descolado*

Index

D

E

F

Complete title listing

Footprint publishes travel guides to over 150 destinations worldwide. Each guide is packed with practical, concise and colourful information for everybody from first-time travellers to travel aficionados. The list is growing fast and current titles are noted below. Available from all good bookshops and online Www.footprintbooks.com

(P) denotes pocket guide

Latin America & Caribbean

Antigua & Leeward Islands (P)
Argentina
Barbados (P)
Bolivia
Brazil
Caribbean Islands
Chile
Colombia
Costa Rica
Cuba
Cuzco & the Inca heartland
Discover Belize, Guatemala & Southern Mexico
Discover Patagonia
Discover Peru, Bolivia & Ecuador
Dominican Republic (P)
Ecuador & Galápagos
Havana (P)
Jamaica (P)
Mexico & Central America
Nicaragua
Peru
St Lucia (P)

North America

Discover Western Canada
Vancouver (P)

Africa

Cape Town (P)
Kenya
Morocco
Namibia
South Africa
Tanzania

Middle East

Dubai (P)
Egypt
Jordan

Australasia

Australia
Discover East Coast Australia
New Zealand
Sydney (P)

Asia

Borneo
Cambodia
Discover Vietnam, Cambodia & Laos
India
Laos
Malaysia & Singapore
Rajasthan
South India
Sri Lanka
Thailand
Vietnam

Europe

Andalucía
Antwerp & Ghent (P)
Barcelona (P)
Bilbao and the Basque country (P)
Bologna (P)
Cardiff (P)
Copenhagen (P)
Costa de la Luz (P)
Croatia
Dublin (P)
Lisbon (P)
London
London (P)
Madrid (P)
Naples & the Amalfi Coast (P)
Northern Spain
Paris (P)
Reykjavík (P)
Scotland Highlands & Islands
Seville (P)
Siena & the heart of Tuscany (P)
Tallinn (P)
Turin (P)
Valencia (P)
Verona (P)

Lifestyle guides

Body & Soul Guide to the World
Diving the World
European City Breaks
Snowboarding the World
Surfing Britain
Surfing Europe
Surfing the World
Wine Travel Guide to the World

Also available
Traveller's Handbook (WEXAS)
Traveller's Healthbook (WEXAS)
Traveller's Internet Guide (WEXAS)

Map index

Advertisers' index

Credits

Footprint credits
Editor: Nicola Gibbs
Map editor: Sarah Sorensen
Picture editor: Robert Lunn
Proofreaders: Davina Rungasamy and Sarah Sorensen

Publisher: Patrick Dawson
Editorial: Sophie Blacksell, Felicity Laughton, Alan Murphy, Jo Williams
Cartography: Robert Lunn, Kevin Feeney,
Design: Mytton Williams
Sales and marketing: Andy Riddle
Advertising: Debbie Wylde
Finance and administration: Elizabeth Taylor, Vassia Efstathiou

Photography credits
Front cover: Alamy, Jericoacoara
Back cover: Alex Robinson, Carnaval
Inside: Alex Robinson

Print
Manufactured in Italy by LegoPrint
Pulp from sustainable forests

Footprint feedback
We try as hard as we can to make each Footprint guide as up to date as possible but, of course, things always change. If you want to let us know about your experiences – good, bad or ugly – then don't delay, go to www.footprintbooks.com and send in your comments.

Publishing information
Footprint Brazil
5th Edition

February 2007

ISBN: 978 1 904777 71 7
CIP DATA: A catalogue record for this book is available from the British Library

Published by Footprint
6 Riverside Court
Lower Bristol Road
Bath BA2 3DZ, UK
T +44 (0)1225 469141
F +44 (0)1225 469461
discover@footprintbooks.com
www.footprintbooks.com

Distributed in the USA by
Publishers Group West

Neither the black and white nor colour maps are intended to have any political significance.

Every effort has been made to ensure that the facts in this guidebook are accurate. However, travellers should still obtain advice from consulates, airlines etc about travel and visa requirements before travelling. The authors and publishers cannot accept responsibility for any loss, injury or inconvenience however caused.

Acknowledgements

Many thanks to Gardênia and Raphael; Silvana Nascimento and all at Embratur in London and Brasília for their professionalism and warmth; Steven Chew of the Brazilian Beach house company. Also thanks to: Amazonas, Para, Amapá & Roraima – Doutora Oreni Campelo Braga da Silva, James at Ecopark; Gero; Steve; Moreno in Manaus; Ariaú; Othon Jungle Palace; Yeda Maria Bezerra de Oliveira; Carlos Probst from Amazon Clipper for the excellent accommodation in Parintins. Bahia – William Wisden, Roman Pankofer at Vila Santo Antônio. Brasília and Goiás – Rodrigo and Alessandra at Drena, Newton Povoa, Maria Eugenia and Luiz Chaffin, Refúgio Vagafogo, Sasa, Denis and all at Alternativas; Silvia Luz; Newton Póvoa Coelho. Mato Grosso do Sul & Mato Grosso – Simone Rondon; Lilian at Impacto in Campo Grande; Fatima and Marcelo Yndio all at Meia Lua in Miranda; Roberto Coelho at Fazenda San Francisco; Roberto Klabin for an excellent dinner and conversation at Refugio Caiman; Juliana Albuquerque in Campo Grande; Luís Vicente and Marina from Pouso Alegre for the folder; Laercio and Alex in Cuiabá; Braulio Carlos and Juan Mazar for birding advice; Vitória, Zuleika and Jorge in Alta Floresta; Jens and Cathy from Utah for the great birding advice. Minas Gerais – Dr Roberto Fagundes; Bira for great company. Santa Catarina – Ponta dos Ganchos resort. Pernambuco – Francisco Rosário at Empetur, Michelle Lima on Noronha for their warmth and professionalism. Rio de Janeiro – Bromelias Spa in Paraty; Hotel Coxixo, Bealocal.com, Camaecafe.com.br, Carina at Rio Hostel in Santa Teresa, Dani Migueletto, Les Suites hotel; Otto, Totonho e Os Cabra and Os Ipanemas, Rocinha Graffiti Crew; Valerie and Olivier at Le Gite d'Indaiatiba. São Paulo – João Paulo and Angatu; Emanuel in Piçinguaba; Seu Jorge; Tutti Bae; Bill Hinchenberger. Tocantins – Luciano of Korubo, Arienar, Claudia, Dorivã; Gabriela from Ambiental. Thanks to Mick Day for the advice on Rio de Janeiro's surf beaches.

Brazil

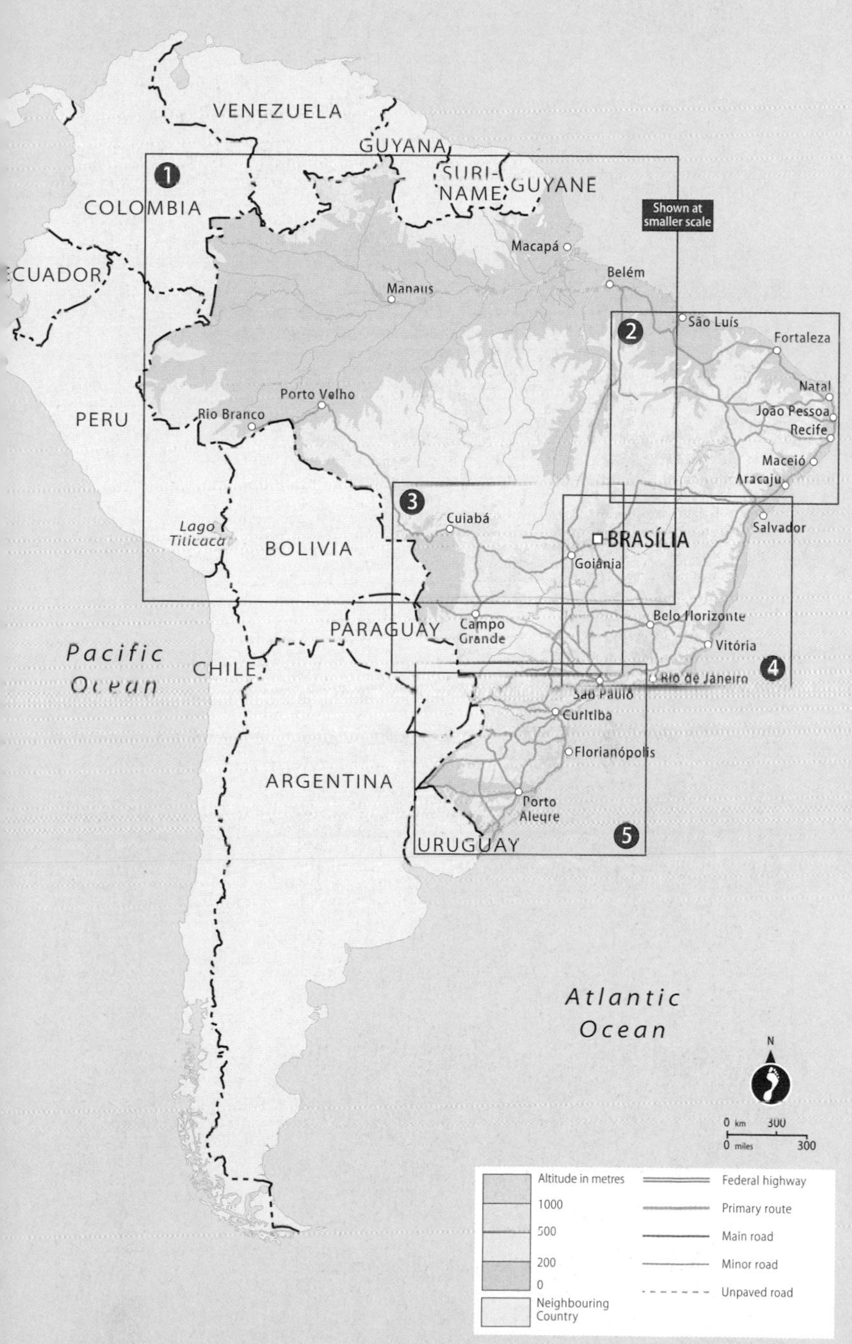

VENEZUELA
GUYANA
SURI-NAME
GUYANE
COLOMBIA
ECUADOR
PERU
BOLIVIA
PARAGUAY
CHILE
ARGENTINA
URUGUAY
Pacific Ocean
Atlantic Ocean
Lago Titicaca
Shown at smaller scale
Macapá
Belém
Manaus
São Luís
Fortaleza
Natal
João Pessoa
Recife
Maceió
Aracaju
Salvador
Porto Velho
Rio Branco
Cuiabá
BRASÍLIA
Goiânia
Campo Grande
Belo Horizonte
Vitória
Rio de Janeiro
São Paulo
Curitiba
Florianópolis
Porto Alegre
1
2
3
4
5
N
0 km 300
0 miles 300
Altitude in metres
1000
500
200
0
Neighbouring Country
Federal highway
Primary route
Main road
Minor road
Unpaved road

Map 1
VENEZUELA
COLOMBIA
PERU
BOLIVIA
Pacific Ocean
Lake Titicaca
A
B
C
1
2
3
Santa Elena de Uairén
Pacaraima
Araça
BR174
Bonfim
Lethem
Alto Alegre
Boa Vista
RORAIMA
Serra Parima
Floresta Nacional de Roraima
Caracaraí
Novo Paraiso
São Luis
Rio Branco
Cucuí
Parque Nacional Pico da Neblima
São Gabriel da Cachoeira
Uaimiri Atroari Reserve
Represa Balbina
Rio Negro
Parque Nacional do Jaú
Presidente Figueiredo
Novo Airão
Arquipélago de Anavilhanas
Manaus
Manacapuru
Careiro da Várzea
Codajás
Careiro
Borba
Foz do Mamaria
Santo Antônio do Iça
Tonantins
Fonte Boa
Rio Içá
Monte Cristo
São Paulo de Olivença
Mamirauá
Tefé
Rio Solimões
Coari
Al Tikuna Evare
Leticia
Tabatinga
Benjamin Constant
Rio Javari
AMAZONAS
Reserva Biológica de Abufari
(Closed)
Rio Madeira
BR319
Manicoré
Lábrea
Humaitá
Maici
Rodovia Transamazônica
Japim
Cruzeiro do Sul
BR364
Feijó
Parque Nacional Serra do Divisor
ACRE
Boco do Acre
Porto Velho
Calama
Represa de Samuel
Tabajara
Abunã
Rio Abunã
Rio Branco
Xapuri
Assis Brasil
Brasiléia
Taquaras
RONDÔNIA
Ariquemes
Aripuanã
Jaru
Ouro Preto d'Oeste
Ji Paraná
Parque Nacional dos Pacaás Novos
Presidente Médici
Cacoal
Pimento Bueno
Rolim de Moura
Guajará Mirim
Costa Marques
Principe da Beira
Reserva Biológica do Guaporé
Vilhena
Colorado do Oeste
Comodoro
Vila Bela da Sma Trindade
Pontes e Lacerda
Bala Grande
San M
Lake O (Provide
N
0 km 100
0 miles 100

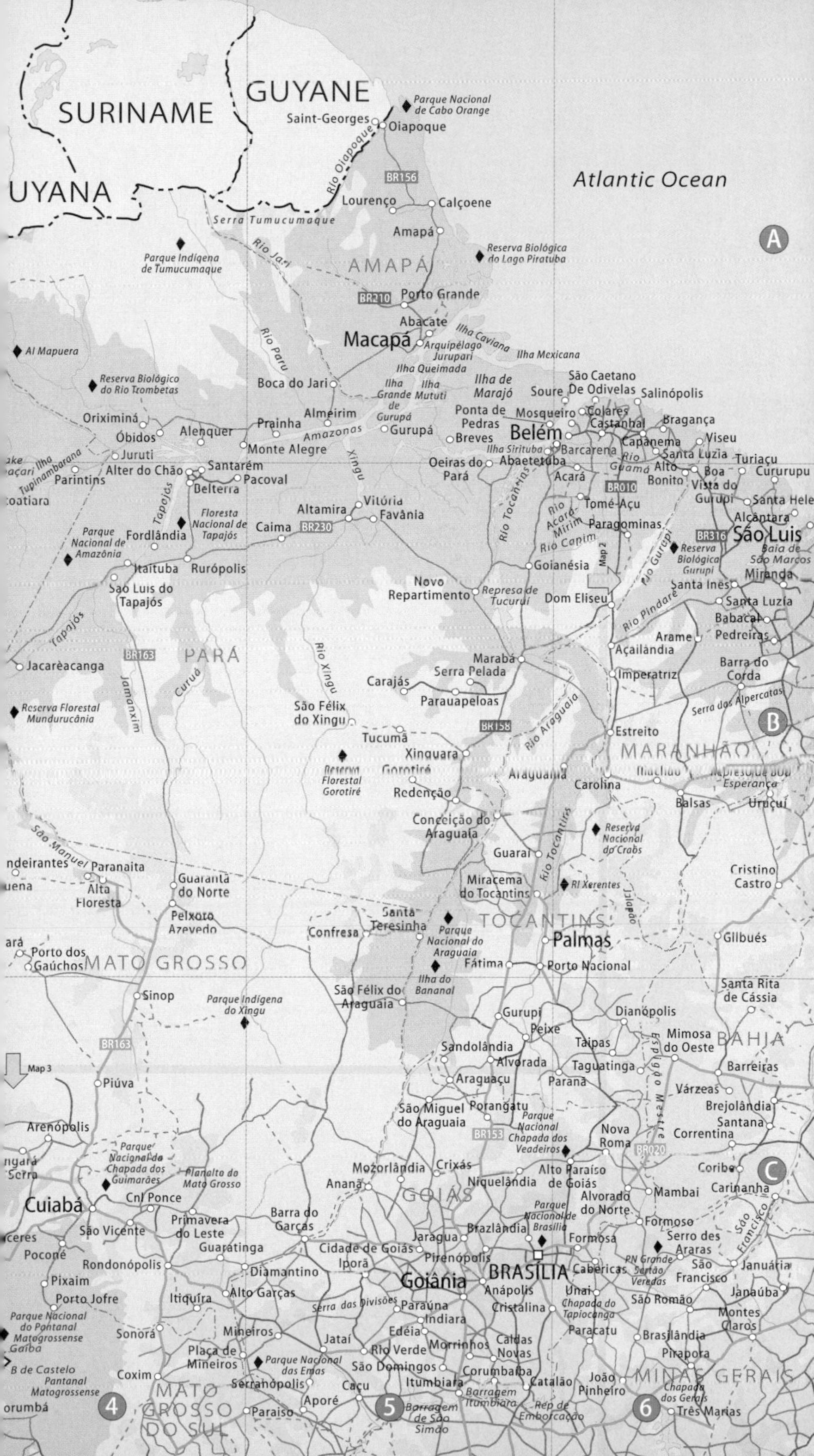
SURINAME
GUYANE
UYANA
Atlantic Ocean
Parque Nacional de Cabo Orange
Saint-Georges
Oiapoque
Rio Oiapoque
BR156
Lourenço
Calçoene
Serra Tumucumaque
Amapá
Reserva Biológica do Lago Piratuba
Parque Indígena de Tumucumaque
Rio Jari
AMAPÁ
BR210
Porto Grande
Abacate
Macapá
Ilha Caviana
Arquipélago Jurupari
Ilha Mexicana
Rio Paru
Ilha Queimada
Al Mapuera
Reserva Biológico do Rio Trombetas
Boca do Jari
Ilha Grande de Gurupá
Ilha Mututi
Ilha de Marajó
Soure
São Caetano De Odivelas
Salinópolis
Oriximiná
Óbidos
Alenquer
Prainha
Almeirim
Gurupá
Ponta de Pedras
Breves
Mosqueiro
Colares
Castanhal
Belém
Bragança
Viseu
Capanema
Amazonas
Monte Alegre
Juruti
Ilha Tupinambarana
Barcarena
Santa Luzia
Turiaçu
Ilha Sirituba
Rio Guamá
Alter do Chão
Santarém
Oeiras do Pará
Abaetetuba
Alto Bonito
Boa Vista do Gurupi
Cururupu
Parintins
Pacoval
Xingu
Acará
BR010
Belterra
Rio Tocantins
Tomé-Açu
Santa Helen
Vitória
Rio Acará-Mirim
Altamira
Favânia
Paragominas
Alcântara
Tapajós
Floresta Nacional de Tapajós
Parque Nacional de Amazônia
Fordlândia
Caima
BR230
Rio Capim
BR316
São Luis
Reserva Biológica Gurupi
Baia de São Marcos
Miranda
Map 2
Rio Gurupi
Itaituba
Rurópolis
Goianésia
São Luis do Tapajós
Novo Repartimento
Represa de Tucuruí
Dom Eliseu
Santa Inês
Santa Luzia
Rio Pindaré
Babacal
Arame
Pedreiras
Açailândia
Tapajós
BR163
PARÁ
Rio Xingu
Jacarèacanga
Marabá
Serra Pelada
Barra do Corda
Imperatriz
Carajás
Parauapeloas
Serra das Alpercatas
Reserva Florestal Mundurucânia
Jamanxim
Curuá
São Félix do Xingu
Rio Araguaia
BR158
Estreito
Tucumã
Xinguara
MARANHÃO
Reserva Florestal Gorotiré
Gorotiré
Araguaina
Carolina
Esperança
Redenção
Balsas
Uruçuí
Conceição do Araguaia
Reserva Nacional do Crabs
Guaraí
Rio Tocantins
São Manuel
ndeirantes
Paranaita
Alta Floresta
Guarantã do Norte
Miracema do Tocantins
RI Xerentes
Cristino Castro
Jalapão
Peixoto Azevedo
Santa Teresinha
Confresa
Parque Nacional do Araguaia
TOCANTINS
Palmas
Gilbués
Porto dos Gaúchos
MATO GROSSO
Fátima
Porto Nacional
Ilha do Bananal
Santa Rita de Cássia
Sinop
Parque Indígena do Xingu
São Félix do Araguaia
Gurupi
Dianópolis
Peixe
BR163
Taipas
Mimosa do Oeste
BAHIA
Sandolândia
Espigão Mestre
Map 3
Alvorada
Taguatinga
Barreiras
Piúva
Araguaçu
Paranã
Várzeas
São Miguel do Araguaia
Porangatu
Parque Nacional Chapada dos Veadeiros
Brejolândia
Santana
Arenópolis
Nova Roma
Correntina
BR153
BR020
Parque Nacional da Chapada dos Guimarães
Planalto do Mato Grosso
Mozorlândia
Crixás
Alto Paraíso de Goiás
Coribe
Serra
Cuiabá
Cnl Ponce
Ananá
Niquelândia
GOIÁS
Mambai
Carinanha
Alvorado do Norte
Primavera do Leste
Barra do Garças
Parque Nacional de Brasília
Formoso
São Francisco
São Vicente
Jaraguá
Brazlândia
Formosa
Serro des Araras
Cáceres
Guarátinga
Cidade de Goiás
Pirenópolis
Poconé
Iporá
BRASÍLIA
Cabeceiras
PN Grande Sertão Veredas
São Francisco
Januária
Rondonópolis
Diamantino
Pixaim
Goiânia
Anápolis
Unaí
Alto Garças
Janaúba
Porto Jofre
Itiquira
Serra das Divisões
Paraúna
Cristalina
Chapada do Tapiocanga
São Romão
Parque Nacional do Pontanal Matogrossense
Indiara
Montes Claros
Gaiba
Sonorá
Mineiros
Edéia
Paracatu
Brasilândia
Jataí
Rio Verde
Morrinhos
Caldas Novas
Placa de Mineiros
Parque Nacional das Emas
Pirapora
São Domingos
Corumbaíba
B de Castelo
Coxim
Itumbiara
Catalão
João Pinheiro
MINAS GERAIS
Pantanal Matogrossense
Serranópolis
Caçu
Barragem Itumbiara
Chapada dos Gerais
Aporé
Rep de Emborcação
MATO GROSSO DO SUL
Corumbá
4
Paraiso
5
Barragem de São Simão
6
Três Marias
A
B
C

Map 2
São Luís
Teresina
MARANHÃO
PIAUÍ
TOCANTINS
BAHIA
Paragominas
Reserva Biológica Gurupi
Rio Gurupi
Pinheiro
Alcântara
Baia de São José
Primeira Cruz
Parque Nacional Lençois Maranhenses
Barreirinhas
São Bento
Baia de São Marcos
Ribamar
Morros
Rosário
Paulino Neves
Tutóia
Ilha do Caju
Parnaíba
Luís Corre
Rio Paraná
Rio Pindaré
Santa Inês
Miranda do Norte
Vargem Grande
Brejo
Rio Paranaíba
Luzilândia
Cocal
Ibugua
Viçosa do Ce
Entroncamento
Santa Luzía
Chapadinha
BR316
BR135
BR222
Babacal
Caxuxa
Coroatá
Timbiras
Porto
Piracuruca
Miguel Alves
Batalha
Parque Nacional Sete Cidades
Peritoró
Pedreiras
Coelho Neto
Barras
Piripiri
Arame
Açailândia
Codó
União
Tocaia
Caxias
Campo Maior
Imperatriz
Presidente Dutra
BR226
Barra do Corda
BR010
Santana
Rio Itapecuru
Alto Longa
Beneditinos
Sa das Alpercatas
Porto Franco
Estreito
Colinas
Barro Duro
Água Branca
São Gonçalo do Piauí
Chapada Grande
BR316
Amarante
Pastos Bons
Valença do Piauí
Pimenteir
San Domingos
Carolina
Riachão
Represo Boa Esperança
Floriano
Nazaré do Piaui
Oeiras
Goiatins
Balsas
Uruçuí
BR343
Picos
CE
Bertolínia
Itaueira
Flores do Paul
Formosa
Itainópolis
Elisau Martins
Canto do Buriti
Simplício Mendes
Parque Nacional Serra da Capivara
São João do Piauí
Paulistana
Cristino Castro
Serra
Afrânio
Alto Parnaíba
Map 1
Bom Jesus
Redenção de Gurguéia
São Raimundo Nonato
Raja
Casa Nova
Gilbués
Remanso
Pilão Arcado
Sento Sé
Barragem de Sobradinho
Corrente
Amaniú
Santa Rita de Cássia
Ibiraba
Xique-Xique
Barra
Carna
Dianopolis
Boqueirão
Espigão Mestre
Juçara
Irecê
Copixaba
Rio Grande
Jacob
Mimosa do Oeste
Taipas
Taguatinga
BR020
Barreiras
Rio São Francisco
Javí
Ibotirama
Brotas
Várzeas
Roda Velha
Brejolândia
Mur
No
BR242
Campos Belos
Map 4
Palmeiras
Lençóis
Parque Nacional da Chapada Diamantina
Bom Jesus
A
B
C
1
2
3

Atlantic Ocean
N
0 km 50
0 miles 50
A
B
C
4
5
6
CEARÁ
RG DO NORTE
PARAÍBA
PERNAMBUCO
ALAGOAS
SERGIPE
Nova
Jericoacoara
Barinha
Jijoca
Cruz
Almofala
Granja
Marco
CE165
Senador Sá
Moraújo
Meruoca
Alcântara
Aprazível
Sobral
Itapipoca
Mundaú
Fleixeiras
Paracuru
Trairi
Tururu
Taíba
Pecém
Cumbuco
Tabuba
PN de Ubajara
Ubajara
São Benedito
Patos
BR222
Icaraí
Fortaleza
Ponta do Mucuripe
Praia Futuro
Porto das Dunas
Barro Preto
Maranguape
Aquiraz
Iguape
Cascavel
Caponga
Varjota
Santa Quitéria
Açude Araras
Ipueiras
Canindé
Pacoti
Guaramiranga
Baturité
CE032
CE021
Beberibe
Morro Branco &
Praia das Fontes
Sucatinga
Nova Russas
BR116
Targinos
Boqueirão do Cesário
BR304
Canoa Quebrada
Aracati
Majorlândia
Itaiçaba
CE044
BR122
CE075
Crateús
Boa Viagem
Quixadá
Ibicutinga
Russas
Jaguaruana
Icapuí
Ibicuitaba
Tibau
Grossos
Independencia
CE021
Limoeiro do Norte
Novo Oriente
São Joaquim do Salgado
Quixeramobim
Morada Nova
Açude Bariabuiu
CE02
Rio Jaguaribe
Tabuleiro do Norte
Mossoró
Areia Branca
Macau
Guamaré
Parazinho
Touros
Mineirolândia
Mombaça
Jaguaretama
Senador Pompeu
RN117
Rio Assu
Pendências
CE020
Piquet Carneiro
BR 405
BR406
Tauá
Novo
Apodi
Caraúbas
Assu
Angicos
Bento Fernandes
João Câmara
Acopiara
Floresta
BR116
Itaú
Paraú
Ceará-Mirim
Muriú
Genipabu
Catarina
Açude Orós
Pereiro
São Rafael
BR304
Redinha
Orós
Pau de Ferros
Patu
Barragem Armando R Gonçalves
Rio Potengi
Riachuelo
Natal
Iguatu
Bom Jesus
Jucás
Antonina do Norte
Cedro
Icó
Alexandria
Brejo da Cruz
Rio Piranhas
Currais Novas
Santa Cruz
Pirangi do Norte
Várzea Alegre
Uiraúna
Brejo dos Santos
Florânia
Búzios
Campos Sales
CE184
Assaré
BR 230
Mangabeira
Caicó
BR427
Tangará
Tibau do Sul
Novo Olinda
Farias Brito
Lavras da Mangabeira
Souza
Acari
Goianinha
Pipa
Aratama
Serra Negra Do Norte
Araripe
Cajazeiras
Pombal
Picuí
Cuité
Canguaretama
Chapada do Araripe
Juazeiro do Norte
São José das Piranhas
Santa Luzia
Araruna
Tacima
Baía Formosa
Santana do Cariri
Crato
Missão Velha
BR104
Belém
Barra de Camaratuba
BR101
Rio Tinto
Mamanguape
BR361
Patos
BR230
Exu
Itaporanga
Teixeira
Alagoa Grande
Campina
Cabedelo
João Pessoa
Jardim
Bela Vista
Campina Grande
Jati
Dodocó
Conceição
São João do Cariri
Sapé
Ouricuri
Ingá
Itabaiana
Cabo Branco
BR122
BR316
BR412
Queimadas
Jacumá
Salgueiro
BR232
Triunfo
Sumé
Boqueirão
Timbaúba
Itambé
Pitimbu
Santa Cruz
Flores
Jabitacá
BR104
Tambaba
Serra Talhada
Caraúbas
Goiana
Pontas de Pedra
Sítio dos Nunes
Sertânia
Taquaritinga do Norte
Surubim
Carpina
Ilha de Itamaracá
Reserva Biológica de Serra Negra
BR110
PE090
Limoeiro
Igarassu
Paulista
Cruzeiro do Nordeste
Fazenda Nova
Olinda
Lagoa Grande
Floresta
Ibo
PE360
Belo Jardim
Caruaru
Gravatá
Jaboatão
Recife
Rio São Francisco
Arcoverde
Pesqueira
Bezerros
Vitória de Santo Antão
Pau Ferro
Barragem de Itaparica
Reserva Biológica da Pedra Talhada
Tupanatinga
PE180
Gaibu
Venturosa
Lajedo
Reserva Biológica de Saltinho
Cabo
Petrolândia
BR424
Porto de Galinhas
Petrolina
Itaíba
Catende
Barra de Sirinhaém
Juazeiro
Garanhuns
Palmares
Águas Belas
Bom Conselho
PE177
Quipapá
Barreiros
Tamandaré
Paulo Afonso
BR423
São José de Laje
São José da Coroa Grande
Delmiro Gouveia
União de Palmares
BR407
Uauá
Santana do Ipanema
Palmeira dos Índios
Maragogi
To Fernando de Noronha
Pão de Açúcar
AL110
Taquarana
BR101
São Luís do Qitunde
Canudos
Campo Alegre
Barra de Santo Antônio
Feira Nova
Arapiraca
Maceió
Jeremoaba
NS da Glória
Marechal Deodoro
Senhor do Bonfim
Traipu
Junqueiro
Praia do Francês
Euclides da Cunha
BR110
Porto Real do Colégio
São Miguel dos Campos
Monte Santo
Carira
Propriá
Coruripe
Cansanção
Ribeirópolis
NS das Dores
Neópolis
Penedo
Heliópolis
Simão Dias
Itabaiana
Japaratuba
EE Foz de São Francisco
Poço Verde
Pacatuba
Piaçabuçu
Tucano
Lagarto
Laranjeiras
Pirambu
Reserva Biológica de Santa Isabel
Capim Grosso
Cipó
NS do Socorro
Aracaju
BR116
Riachão do Dantas
Salgado
São Cristóvão
Vázea de Poço
Tobias Barreto
Mosqueiro
Itapicuru
Itabaianinha
Estância
Serrinha
Cristinápolis
Barra de Estância
Inhambupe
Indiaroba
Mangue Seco
Esplanada
Feira de Santana
BR101
Sítio de Conde
Alagoinhas
BR099
Cachoeira
Imbassaí

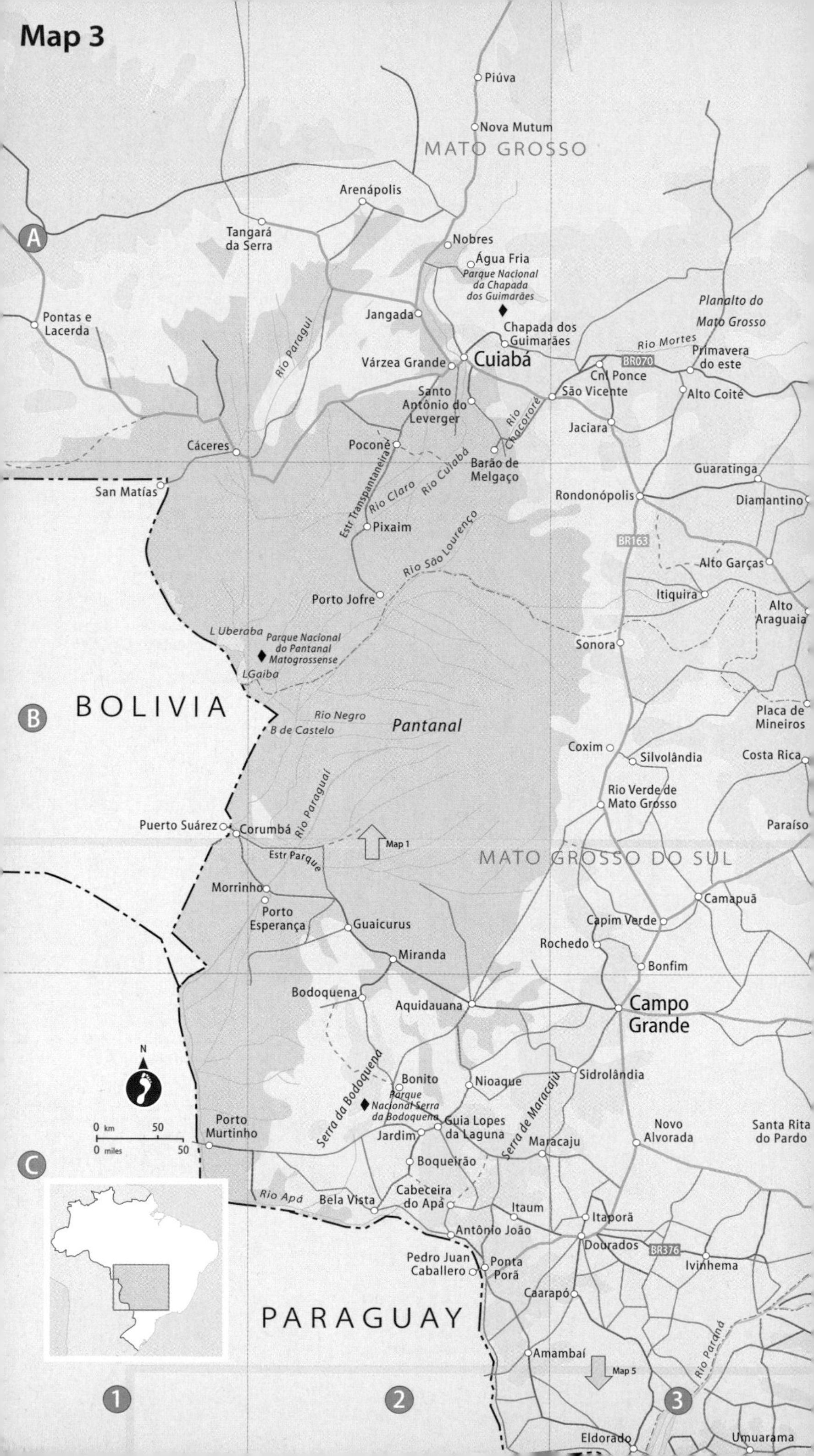

Map 3
Piúva
Nova Mutum
MATO GROSSO
Arenápolis
Tangará da Serra
Nobres
Água Fria
Parque Nacional da Chapada dos Guimarães
Jangada
Chapada dos Guimarães
Pontas e Lacerda
Rio Paraguai
Várzea Grande
Cuiabá
Planalto do Mato Grosso
Rio Mortes
BR070
Primavera do este
Cnl Ponce
São Vicente
Alto Coité
Santo Antônio do Leverger
Rio Chacororé
Jaciara
Cáceres
Poconé
Barão de Melgaço
Rio Cuiabá
Rio Claro
Estr Transpantaneira
Guaratinga
San Matías
Rondonópolis
Diamantino
Pixaim
BR163
Rio São Lourenço
Alto Garças
Porto Jofre
Itiquira
Alto Araguaia
L Uberaba
Parque Nacional do Pantanal Matogrossense
LGaiba
Sonora
BOLIVIA
Placa de Mineiros
Rio Negro
B de Castelo
Pantanal
Coxim
Silvolândia
Costa Rica
Rio Verde de Mato Grosso
Rio Paraguai
Puerto Suárez
Corumbá
Paraíso
Map 1
Estr Parque
MATO GROSSO DO SUL
Morrinho
Camapuã
Porto Esperança
Guaicurus
Capim Verde
Rochedo
Miranda
Bonfim
Bodoquena
Aquidauana
Campo Grande
Serra da Bodoquena
Bonito
Nioaque
Sidrolândia
Parque Nacional Serra da Bodoquena
Serra de Maracaju
Porto Murtinho
Guia Lopes da Laguna
Jardim
Novo Alvorada
Santa Rita do Pardo
Maracaju
0 km 50
0 miles 50
Boqueirão
Rio Apá
Bela Vista
Cabeceira do Apá
Itaum
Itaporã
Antônio João
Dourados
BR376
Pedro Juan Caballero
Ponta Porã
Ivinhema
Caarapó
PARAGUAY
Rio Paraná
Amambaí
Map 5
Eldorado
Umuarama
A
B
C
1
2
3
N

Sandolândia
Alvorada
Araguaçu
São Salvador do Tocantins
Paranã
Palmeirópolis
Arraias
Luis Alves
Bandeirantes
São Miguel do Araguaia
Novo Planalto
Porangatu
RI Pimental Barbosa
Serra Dourada
Mundo Novo
Xixá
Rio Mortes
Rio Cristalinho
Rio Paranã
Água Boa
Mutunópolis
Estrela do Norte
Novo Crixás
Mara Rosa
Parque Nacional de Chapada dos Veadeiros
Teresina de Goiás
Nova Roma
Barragem da Serra da Mesa
Colinas
Cocalinho
Pelxe
Campinorte
São Jorge
Alto Paraíso
A
Areões
Nova Xavantina
Crixás
Map 4
Niquelândia
Mozarlândia
Uruaçu
Pindaíba
Aruanã
Britânia
Araguapaz
Rio Tocantins
Dois Irmãos
Ceres
Goianésia
Serra Bonita
Rio Araguaia
Jacilândia
Parque Nacional de Brasília
Santa Fe
Jaraguá
Brazlândia
Sobradinho
Formosa
Barro do Garças
Jucara
Cidade de Goiás
BRASÍLIA
Planaltina
Buritis
Aragarças
Aparecida do Rio Claro
Bom Jardim de Goiás
Pirenópolis
Taguatinga
Cabeceiras
Gama
Iporã
Abadiânia
Luziânia
Anápolis
Garapuava
Amorinópolis
Trindade
Doverlândia
Leopoldo de Bulhões
Unaí
Goiânia
Palestina
Caiapônia
Bela Vista
Cristalina
Chapada do Tapiocanga
Sa das Divisões
Paraúna
Aparecida de Goiânia
Portelândia
Indiara
Edéia
Piracanjuba
Mineiros
GOIÁS
Pires do Rio
Paracatu
Pontalina
Jataí
Rio Verde
Caldas Novas
BR040
Parque Nacional das Emas
Morrinhos
Rio Quente
B
São Domingos
Chapadão de Céu
Aparecida do Rio Doce
Corumbaíba
João Pinheir
Serranópolis
Catalão
Quirinópolis
Itumbiara
Caçu
Barragem de São Simão
Cachoeira
Coromandel
Barragem de Embarcação
Aporé
Araguari
Patos de Minos
BR365
Uberlândia
Patrocínio
Raimundo
Prata
BR152
Ti
Paranaíba
Rio Grande
Ibiá
Uberaba
Araxá
Aparecida do Taboado
Barragem Agua Vermelha
Igarapava
Estala
Santa Fe do Sul
Jales
Fernandópolis
Agua Clara
Colombia
BR050
Rio Grande
Parque Nacional da Serra da Canastra
Votuporanga
Icém
Ituverava
Nhandeara
Barretos
Franca
Três Lagoas
Castilho
Represa Peixoto
São Roque de Minas
Piu
Andradina
Rio Tietê
José do Rio Preto
Cassia
Mirandópolis
Passos
Bebedouro
Batatais
Panorama
Represa do Furnas
Araçatuba
Cantanduva
Guararapes
Birigui
São Sebastião do Paraíso
Penápolis
Sertãozinho
Ribeirão Preto
Bataguassu
Cajuru
C
Adamantina
Promissão
Represa Promissão
Guaxupé
Lins
Mococa
Osvaldo Cruz
Matão
Icanga
São José do Rio Pardo
Alfenas
Tupã
Ibitinga
Araraquara
Planalto do Sul
Pirajui
Poços de Caldas
Rancheria
Bariri
Presidente Prudente
Marília
Garça
Sao Carlos
Pirassununga
Paraguaçu Paulista
São João da Boa Vista
Gália
Bauru
Leme
Rio Paranapanema
Assis
Jaú
Araras
Santo Inácio
Ubirajara
Rio Claro
Moji-Guaçu
Pouso Alegre
Rep Capivari
Lençóis Paulista
Barra Bonita
Moji-Mirim
Paranavaí
Limeira
Bela Vista do Paraíso
Piracicaba
Americana
Ourinhos
Cornélio Procópio
Botucatu
Sta Bárbara d'Oeste
Sumaré
Camp
Londrina
Jacarezinho
Avaré
Jord
4
5
SÃO PAULO
6
Maringá
Bandeirantes
Piraju
Campinas
Arapongas
Santo Antonio de Platina
Jundiaí
Tatuí
Atibaia
São Jo

Map 4
Porangatu
Mutunópolis
Estrela do Norte
Mara Rosa
Barragem da Serra da Mesa
Campinorte
Crixás
Uruaçu
Niquelândia
Colinas
Rio Paraná
Parque Nacional de Chapada dos Veadeiros
Teresina de Goiás
São Domingos
Nova Roma
Alto Paraíso de Goiás
Posse
Alvorada do Norte
Mambaí
Santana
Correntina
BR349
Santa Maria da Vitória
Coribe
Carinanha
Malhad
Rio São Francisco
Manga
Matias Cardoso
Mocambinha
Jaíba
Januária
Janaúba
A
Rio Tocantins
Dois Irmãos
Ceres
Goianésia
Jaraguá
Brazlândia
Parque Nacional de Brasília
Sobradinho
Formosa
Formoso
Serra Bonita
Parque Nacional Grande Sertão Veredas
Serra das Araras
dade Goiás
Pirenópolis
BRASÍLIA
Planaltina
Taguatinga
Cabeceiras
Buritis
Gama
Abadiânia
Anápolis
Luziânia
Arinos
Garapuava
São Francisco
Rio Urucuia
Trindade
Goiânia
Leopoldo de Bulhões
Unaí
Aparecida de Goiânia
Bela Vista
Cristalina
Chapada do Tapiocanga
São Romão
MINAS GERAIS
Rio São Francisco
Piracanjuba
Pontalina
Pires do Rio
Paracatu
Brasilândia
Montes Claros
Morrinhos
Caldas Novas
Rio Quente
BR040
Pirapora
Domingos
Corumbaíba
Catalão
João Pinheiro
Chapada dos Gerais
BR135
Itumbiara
Barragem Itumbiara
Barragem de Embarcação
BR365
Três Marias
B
Araguari
Coromandel
Patos de Minos
Map 1
Serro do Espinhaço
Uberlândia
Patrocínio
Corinto
Diamantina
Datas
Represa Três Marias
Prata
BR452
Tiros
Curvelo
Serro
Gruta de Maquiné
Pompeu
Martinho Campos
Ibiá
Uberaba
Araxá
Paraopeba
Dordisburgo
Sete Lagoas
Caetanópolis
Parque Nacional da Serra do Cipó
Estalagem
Gruta de Lapinha
Igarapava
BR262
Parque Nacional da Serra da Canastra
Colombia
BR050
Rio Grande
Itabira
Icém
Ituverava
Belo Horizonte
Betim
Sabará
Barretos
Franca
Represa Peixoto
São Roque de Minas
Divinópolis
Caeté
Santa Bárbara
José do Rio Preto
Cassia
Nova Lima
Barão de Cocais
Passos
Piumhi
Formiga
Itabirito
Caraça
Bebedouro
Batatais
Ouro Preto
Mariana
Cantanduva
São Sebastião do Paraíso
Represa do Furnas
Congonhas do Campo
Sertãozinho
Ribeirão Prêto
Campo Belo
Cons Lafaiete
Ponte Nova
Cajuru
Guaxupé
Viçosa
Matão
Mococa
BR381
São João del Rei
Prados
Icanga
Ibitinga
Araraquara
São José do Rio Pardo
Alfenas
Lavras
Tiradentes
Rio Pomba
Ubá
Pirajui
Barirí
Poços de Caldas
Três Corações
Barbacena
São Carlos
Pirassununga
Map 3
São Tomé das Letras
Santos Dumont
Rio Novo
Bauru
Leme
São João da Boa Vista
Ibitipoca
Lima Duarte
C
Jaú
Cambuquirá
Leopoldina
Barra Bonita
Río Claro
Araras
Moji-Guaçu
Pouso Alegre
Lambari
Caxambu
Juiz de Fora
Moji-Mirim
Carmo de Minas
São Lourenço
Parque Nacional do Itatiaia
Matias Barbosa
Lençóis Paulista
Rio Paraíba Do Sul
Limeira
Visande de Mauá
Rio Preto
Piracicaba
Americana
Map 5
Itajubá
Valença
Botucatu
Santa Bárbara d'Oeste
Sumaré
Penedo
Conservatória
Vassouras
Três Rios
Campinas
Campos do Jordão
Resende
Miguel Pereira
Sierra dos Orgãos
Avaré
Res Armando
SÃO PAULO
Jundiaí
Pindamonhangaba
Guaratinguetá
Getulândia
Teresópolis
Novo Friburgo
Itu
Atibaia
Taubaté
Aparecida do Norte
Japeri
Petrópolis
RB do Poço dos Antas
Tatuó
Pirapora de Bom Jesus
São Paulo
Lagoinha
Itauruçá
Neves
Itapetininga
São José dos Campos
Cunha
Mangaratiba
Itaguaí
Niterói
Sorocaba
São Miguel Paulista
PN da Serra da Bocaina
Muriqui
Araruama
Itapeva
Capão Bonito
1
Piedade
Santo Andre
Moji das Cruzes
2
Paraty
Angra dos Reis
Ilha Grande
3
Rio de Janeiro
Saquarema
L de Araruama
São Bernardo
Ubatuba
Bertioga
São Sebastião
Ilhabela
Pedro Barras
Cubatão

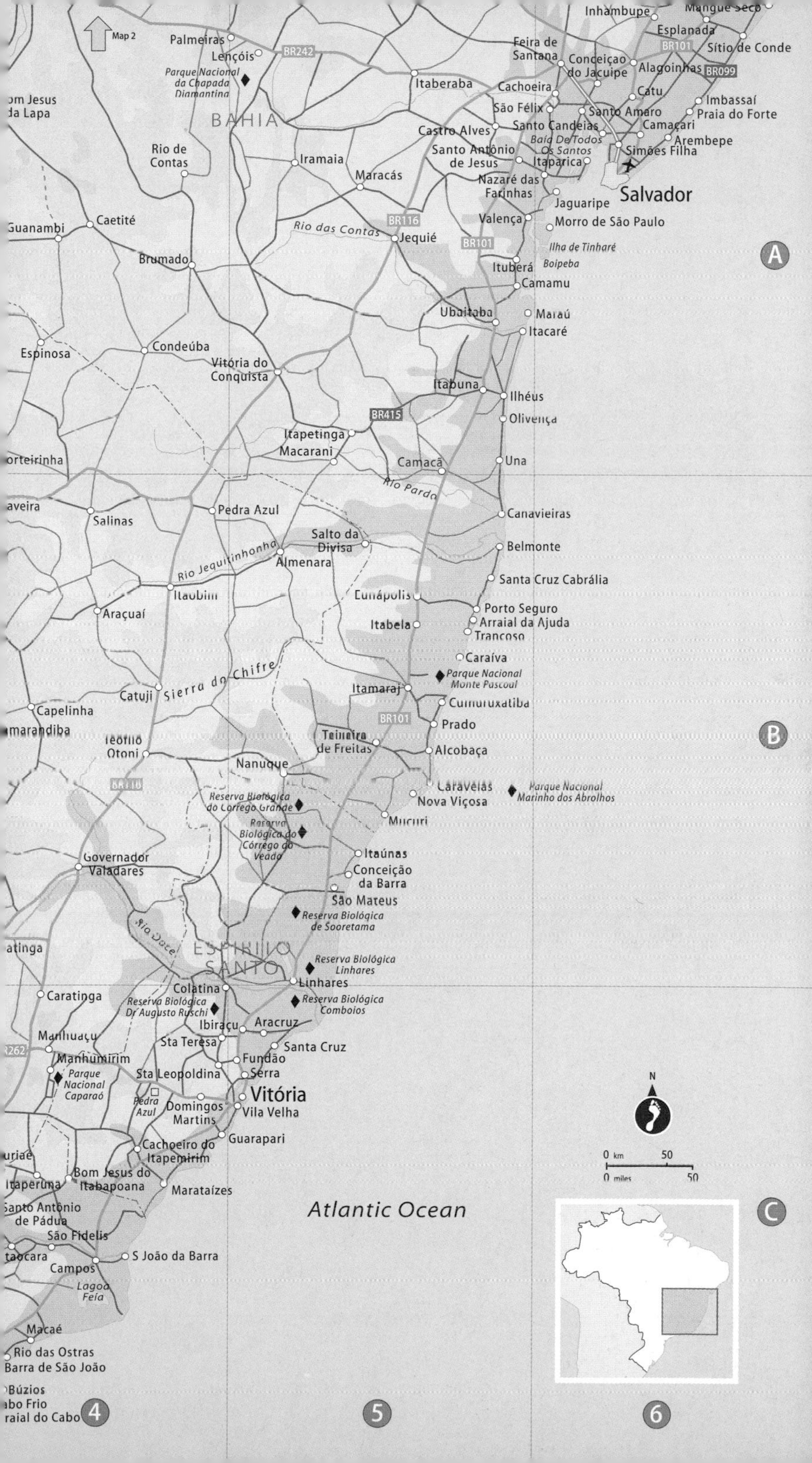

Map 2
Palmeiras
Lençóis
BR242
Parque Nacional da Chapada Diamantina
BAHIA
Inhambupe
Mangue Seco
Esplanada
BR101
Sítio do Conde
Feira de Santana
Conceiçao do Jacuipe
Alagoinhas
BR099
Itaberaba
Cachoeira
Catu
Imbassaí
Praia do Forte
São Félix
Santo Amaro
Camaçari
Arembepe
Castro Alves
Santo Candeias
Baía De Todos Os Santos
Simões Filha
Santo Antônio de Jesus
Itaparica
Salvador
Nazaré das Farinhas
Jaguaripe
Valença
Morro de São Paulo
Ilha de Tinharé
Boipeba
Ituberá
Camamu
Ubaitaba
Maraú
Itacaré
Rio de Contas
Iramaia
Maracás
BR116
Rio das Contas
Jequié
BR101
Guanambi
Caetité
Brumado
Espinosa
Condeúba
Vitória do Conquista
Itabuna
Ilhéus
BR415
Olivença
Itapetinga
Macarani
Camacã
Una
Rio Pardo
Porteirinha
Salinas
Pedra Azul
Canavieiras
Salto da Divisa
Rio Jequitinhonha
Almenara
Belmonte
Santa Cruz Cabrália
Itaobim
Eunápolis
Porto Seguro
Araçuaí
Itabela
Arraial da Ajuda
Trancoso
Caraíva
Parque Nacional Monte Pascoal
Sierra do Chifre
Catuji
Itamaraju
Cumuruxatiba
BR101
Capelinha
Prado
Teixeira de Freitas
Teófilo Otoni
Alcobaça
Nanuque
Caravelas
Parque Nacional Marinho dos Abrolhos
Nova Viçosa
Reserva Biológica do Córrego Grande
Reserva Biológica do Córrego do Veado
Mucuri
Itaúnas
Governador Valadares
Conceição da Barra
São Mateus
Reserva Biológica de Sooretama
Rio Doce
ESPÍRITO SANTO
Reserva Biológica Linhares
Linhares
Colatina
Caratinga
Reserva Biológica Comboios
Reserva Biológica Dr Augusto Ruschi
Ibiraçu
Aracruz
Manhuaçu
Sta Teresa
Santa Cruz
Manhumirim
Fundão
Parque Nacional Caparaó
Sta Leopoldina
Serra
Pedra Azul
Vitória
Domingos Martins
Vila Velha
Guarapari
Cachoeiro do Itapemirim
Itaperuna
Bom Jesus do Itabapoana
Marataízes
Atlantic Ocean
Santo Antônio de Pádua
São Fidelis
Campos
S João da Barra
Lagoa Feia
Macaé
Rio das Ostras
Barra de São João
Búzios
Cabo Frio
Arraial do Cabo
N
0 km 50
0 miles 50
A
B
C
4
5
6

Map 5

PARAGUAY
ARGENTINA
URUGUAY
PARANÁ
RIO GRANDE DO SUL
Map 3
Eldorado
Parque Nacional da Ilha Grande
Umuarama
Cianorte
Maringá
Mundo Novo
Guaíra
Palotina
Campo Mourão
Termas de Jurema
Campina
Iretama
Represa de Itaipu
Toledo
Cascavel
Pitanga
Medeaneira
Catanduvas
Ciudade del Este
Foz do Iguaçu
Parque Nacional Foz do Iguaçu
Iguaçu Falls
Rio Iguaçu
Laranjeiras do Sul
Guarapua
Represa de Salto Santiago
Campo Erê
Pato Branco
São Lourenço d'Oeste
São Miguel d'Oeste
Horizont
Bom Jesus
Xanxeré
Itapiranga
Chapecó
Treze Tília
Salto do Yucumá
Iraí
Concórdia
Joaçaba
Federico Westphalen
Erexim
Campos Nov
Tupitanga
Barragem Passo Fundo
Santa Rosa
Porto Xavier
São Luís Gonzaga
Santo Ângelo
Carazinho
Passo Fundo
Lagoa Vermelha
Santo Tomé
São Borja
São Miguel das Missões
Ijuí
Cruz Alta
BR285
Encruzilhada
Soledade
Itaqui
Santiago
Bento Gonçalves
Farroupilha
Garibaldi
Lajeado
Paso de las Letras
Uruguaiana
Manuel Viana
Alegrete
Santa María
Candelária
Santa Cruz do Sul
Novo Hamburg
Sapucaia do Su
São Leopoldo
Esteio
Canoas
Guaíba
Barra do Quaraí
Bella Unión
Rio Jacuí
Rosário do Sul
São Gabriel
BR290
Porto Alegre
Caçapava do Sul
Barra do Ribeiro
Santana do Livramento
Encruzilhada do Sul
Aguas Brancas
Camaquã
Rivera
Arambaré
Santa Rita
Bagé
Mostard
Tavares
São Lourenço do Sul
Canguçu
Parque Nacional Lagoa do Pe
BR293
Pelotas
Dunas
Aceguá
Estreito
São José do Norte
Rio Grande
Cassino
Jaguarão
Rio Branco
Estação Ecológica do Taim
Lagoa Mirim
Curral Alto
Laguna Mangabeira
Santa Vitória do Palmar
Chuí
A
B
C
1
2
3

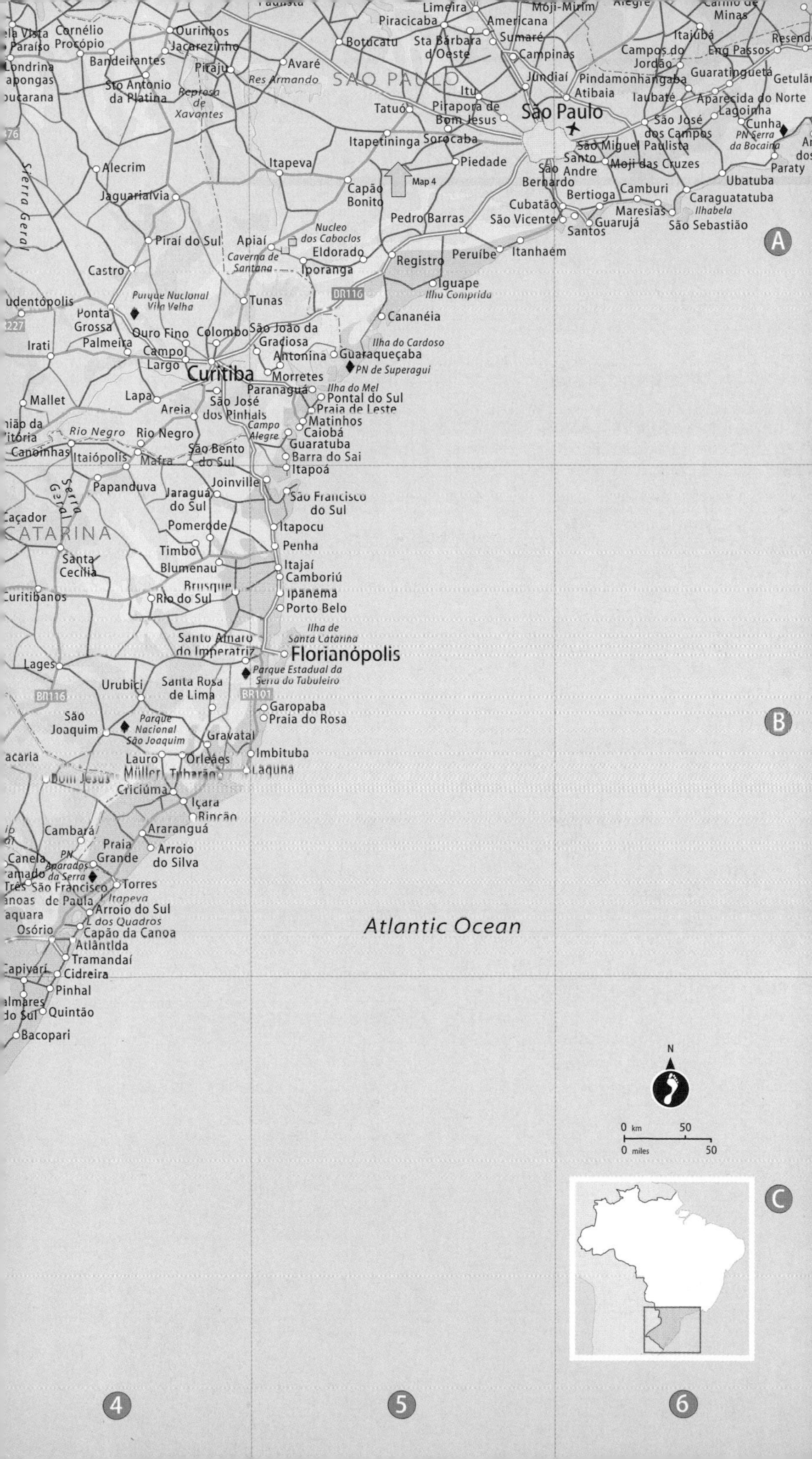

São Paulo
Curitiba
Florianópolis
Atlantic Ocean
Campinas
Sorocaba
Itapetininga
Piedade
Registro
Iguape
Ilha Comprida
Cananéia
Ilha do Cardoso
Guaraqueçaba
PN de Superagui
Paranaguá
Ilha do Mel
Pontal do Sul
Praia de Leste
Matinhos
Caiobá
Guaratuba
Barra do Sai
Itapoá
Joinville
São Francisco do Sul
Itapocu
Penha
Itajaí
Camboriú
Ipanema
Porto Belo
Ilha de Santa Catarina
Santo Amaro do Imperatriz
Parque Estadual da Serra do Tabuleiro
Garopaba
Praia do Rosa
Imbituba
Laguna
Criciúma
Içara
Rincão
Araranguá
Arroio do Silva
Torres
Arroio do Sul
Capão da Canoa
Atlântida
Tramandaí
Cidreira
Pinhal
Quintão
Bacopari
Osório
Ponta Grossa
Castro
Lapa
Mafra
Blumenau
Pomerode
Brusque
Lages
São Joaquim
Parque Nacional São Joaquim
Urubici
Santos
Guarujá
Bertioga
Maresias
São Sebastião
Ilhabela
Caraguatatuba
Ubatuba
Paraty
Peruíbe
Itanhaém
São Vicente
Cubatão
Map 4
SÃO PAULO
CATARINA
BR116
BR101
N
0 km 50
0 miles 50
A
B
C
4
5
6

Map symbols

Administration

- Capital city
- Other city, town
- International border
- Regional border
- Disputed border

Roads and travel

- Main road (National highway)
- Unpaved or *ripio* (gravel) road
- Track
- Footpath
- Railway with station
- Airport
- Bus station
- Metro station
- Cable car
- Funicular
- Ferry

Water features

- River, canal
- Lake, ocean
- Seasonal marshland
- Beach, sandbank
- Waterfall
- Reef

Topographical features

- Contours (approx)
- Mountain, volcano
- Mountain pass
- Escarpment
- Gorge
- Glacier
- Salt flat
- Rocks

Cities and towns

- Main through route
- Main street
- Minor street
- Pedestrianized street
- Tunnel
- One-way street
- Steps
- Bridge
- Fortified wall
- Park, garden, stadium
- Sleeping
- Eating
- Bars & clubs
- Building
- Sight
- Cathedral, church
- Chinese temple
- Hindu temple
- Meru
- Mosque
- Stupa
- Synagogue
- Tourist office
- Museum
- Post office
- Police
- Bank
- Internet
- Telephone
- Market
- Medical services
- Parking
- Petrol
- Golf
- Detail map
- Related map

Other symbols

- Archaeological site
- National park, wildlife reserve
- Viewing point
- Campsite
- Refuge, lodge
- Castle, fort
- Diving
- Deciduous, coniferous, palm trees
- Hide
- Vineyard, winery
- Distillery
- Shipwreck
- Historic battlefield